199902292
C-2
np

SOURCEBOOK ON SUBSTANCE ABUSE

Etiology, Epidemiology, Assessment, and Treatment

Edited by

Peggy J. Ott
University of Pittsburgh School of Medicine

Ralph E. Tarter
University of Pittsburgh School of Medicine

Robert T. Ammerman
MCP—Hahnemann University

ALLYN AND BACON
Boston   London   Toronto   Sydney   Tokyo   Singapore

Vice President and Editor-in-Chief: Sean W. Wakely
Series Editorial Assistant: Susan Hutchinson
Manufacturing Buyer: Suzanne Lareau

Library of Congress Cataloging-in-Publication Data

Sourcebook on substance abuse : etiology, epidemiology, assessment, and treatment /
edited by Peggy J. Ott, Ralph E. Tarter,
    Robert T. Ammerman.
        p. cm.
    Includes bibliographical references and index.
    ISBN 0-205-19802-3
    1. Substance abuse. I. Ott, Peggy J. II. Tarter, Ralph E. III. Ammerman, Robert T.
RC564.S66 1999
616.86—dc21   98-35240
                                                                         CIP

Printed in the United States of America
10 9 8 7 6 5 4 3 2 1   03 02 01 00 99

I dedicate this effort to my mother, Jean Ott, and my daughter, Gwyneth
Peggy J. Ott

To Caroline
Robert T. Ammerman

To Sharon
Ralph E. Tarter

CONTENTS

PREFACE

According to the National Comorbidity Survey conducted in 1991, an estimated 20 million people in the United States have substance abuse disorders. An additional 8 million people have substance abuse disorders that are comorbid with other mental health disorders (Kessler, McGonagle, Zhao, & Nelson, 1994). When measured in terms of health care, work productivity, and crime, the economic cost of substance abuse in the United States is estimated to be $166 billion per year (Rouse, 1995). In addition, public health risk due to the spread of diseases like hepatitis and AIDS is far-reaching. With regard to the association between crime and substance abuse, 40% of all crime in the United States has substance abuse as a contributing factor. Some crimes, like domestic violence and child abuse, involve substance abuse in at least 65% of the cases. The implication of these percentages, measured in terms of deleterious effects on the family and the community in general, is incalculable. Substance abuse, either directly or indirectly, affects everyone in this country.

Given the widespread and multifaceted impact of substance abuse, it is quite disheartening that less than 10% of people with addictive disorders receive any form of treatment. In spite of national antidrug media campaigns and advances in the prevention and treatment of substance abuse, there are still many myths and misunderstandings regarding addiction. Misinformation contributes to the continued stigmatization and scapegoating of individuals with addictive disorders. In part, misinformation emerges from prevention strategies that are not empirically based and thus are misguided, premature, and often ineffective.

People with addictive disorders are a heterogeneous group with individual risk factors as well as individual sources of resilience. Until recently, treatment of substance abuse disorders has tended to be anonymous and generic. The recent transition to managed health care requires an emphasis on cost-effective treatment that can be documented with observable and measurable treatment outcomes. This emphasis forces health care professionals to work in tandem with clinical researchers, thus shifting the focus from mass-produced treatment to personally adapted care based on the individual's strengths and weaknesses. According to treatment outcome research, treatment needs to be individualized in order to be effective.

A sourcebook on substance abuse is important for several reasons. First and foremost, the intention of this book is to provide an up-to-date reference on substance abuse that is empirically based and clinically sound. As such, this comprehensive reference can accomplish three overarching objectives: (1) dispel myths and misinformation that can mislead and obscure our knowledge of substance abuse, thus preventing affected individuals from obtaining appropriate treatment; (2) serve as a reference to health care delivery providers on up-to-date clinical tools such as assessment instruments and treatment techniques, and along these same lines (3) serve as a companion guide to the fourth edition of the *Diagnostic and Statistical Manual of Mental Disorders* (American Psychiatric Association, 1994). In this latter use, the *Sourcebook on Substance Abuse* can provide supplemental information on the prevalence and incidence of addictive disorders, gender differences, developmental risk and protective factors, and appropriate prevention and treatment modalities.

To accomplish these objectives, we asked each of the authors, all recognized in the field of substance abuse, to provide a review of the research in their area of expertise. We also asked all contributors to focus on the most clinically relevant material to make the chapters equally relevant to researchers as well as to individuals facing addictive disorders in their professional lives—physicians, psychologists, counselors, teachers, lawyers, judges, and so on.

Our knowledge of the causes, consequences, behavioral manifestations, and societal impact of substance abuse disorders is increasing rapidly. This growth is generated by increased public awareness, and changes in health care delivery, as well as concomitant changes in public policy regarding addiction. This proliferation of knowledge about substance abuse is supported by the Clinton administration's commitment to reversing the national trends of alcohol and drug abuse. Over the past 5 years, there has been a 32% increase in funds allocated for drug control and treatment and a projected increase in the 1999 federal budget for the prevention and treatment of alcohol abuse.

It is our hope that this *Sourcebook on Substance Abuse* will provide relevant information to health care professionals and policy makers to continue to encourage funding of the prevention and treatment of substance abuse. This book represents a small contribution to this national problem.

REFERENCES

American Psychiatric Association. (1994). *Diagnostic and statistical manual of mental disorders* (4th ed.). Washington, DC: Author.

Kessler, R. C., McGonagle, K. A., Zhao, S., & Nelson, C. B. (1994). Lifetime and 12-month prevalence of DSM-III-R psychiatric disorders in the U.S. *Archives of General Psychiatry, 51,* 8–19.

Rouse, B. A. (Ed.). (1995). *Substance abuse and mental health statistics sourcebook* (DHHS Publication No. SMA 95-3064). U.S. Department of Health and Human Services, Washington, D.C.

P. J. O.
R. E. T.
R. T. A.

ACKNOWLEDGMENTS

We want to express our gratitude to each of the contributors to this sourcebook on addictive disorders. Each primary contributor is a recognized expert in some aspect of the field of addiction. Each author was also held to the standard of providing the most current, empirically based findings on substance abuse. We believe that each chapter surpasses these expectations, and, moreover, makes a substantive contribution to this reference guide to a difficult and diverse area of study.

There are two individuals who deserve special recognition. Patricia Park was steadfast in her dedication to the preparation of this manuscript. Without fail, Ms. Park juggled the myriad details of this project while also providing reflective commentary on the editorial process. Her resourcefulness and even temper were dependable assets to this ambitious project. Likewise, Susan Hutchinson at Allyn and Bacon provided timely and insightful guidance through this laborious process. Both individuals were the mainstays of this endeavor. And finally, a special note of gratitude to Laura Ashley, Erika Newcomer, Tyrone Swink, and Rita Santucci for their assistance with the subject and author indices.

ABOUT THE EDITORS
AND CONTRIBUTORS

ABOUT THE EDITORS

Robert T. Ammerman, Ph.D. (University of Pittsburgh, 1986) is Professor of Psychiatry, MCP-Hahnemann University, and Director, Mental Health Progams in Childhood Disabilities, Department of Psychiatry and Allegheny Neuropsychiatric Institute, Allegheny General Hospital (Pittsburgh, PA). He is a Diplomate in Behavioral Psychology from the American Board of Professional Psychology. He is the recipient of grants from the National Institute on Disabilities and Rehabilitation Research, Vira I. Heinz Foundation, Children's Trust Fund of Pennsylvania, National Institute on Drug Abuse, National Institute on Alcoholism and Alcohol Abuse, and the Staunton Farm Foundation. His research interests are child abuse and neglect, psychopathology in children and youth with disabilities, psychosocial impact of congenital neurological syndromes, and adolescent substance abuse.

Peggy J. Ott, Ph.D., is Director of Education and Training for the Center for Education and Drug Abuse Research. Dr. Ott obtained her doctorate degree in clinical psychology at Duquesne University. She completed an internship in Medical Psychology at Johns Hopkins Hospital. Additional training included completion of a two-year certification program in group psychotherapy sponsored by the American Group Psychotherapy Association. Dr. Ott also has maintained a private practice and has extensive clinical experience in treating substance abuse and affective disorders. She has been in the Department of Psychiatry at the University of Pittsburgh's School of Medicine for the past 10 years as Research Administrator for several major research projects. Dr. Ott's training experience has included supervising a team of clinical psychologists, providing consultation liaison services to the University Medical Center, supervising numerous psychology graduate students for state licensure, initiating and coordinating undergraduate and graduate training opportunities at CEDAR in substance abuse research, developing and implementing research curriculum in substance abuse for psychiatric residents, coordinating the annual CEDAR Conference, and initiating the CEDAR Summer Student Research Program. In addition, Dr. Ott has coauthored articles in the area of behavioral medicine and substance abuse.

Ralph E. Tarter, Ph.D., received his doctorate in biological psychology from the University of Oklahoma. Currently he is professor of psychiatry and neurology at the University of Pittsburgh Medical School. He is Director of the Center for Education and Drug Abuse Research, a consortium between the University of Pittsburgh Medical School and St. Francis Medical Center. He has published over 200 articles in the field of alcohol and drug abuse pertaining to etiology, measurement, and neurobehavioral consequences.

ABOUT THE CONTRIBUTORS

Bryon Adinoff, M.D., is the distinguished professor of alcohol and drug abuse research and associate professor in the Department of Psychiatry at the University of Texas Southwestern Medical Center and the medical director of the Substance Abuse Team at the Dallas Veterans Affairs Medical Center. He obtained his psychiatry training at

Tulane University Affiliated Hospitals and his fellowship training at the National Institute of Alcohol Abuse and Alcoholism intramural program. He has published extensively in the biology and treatment of addiction.

James C. Anthony, Ph.D., is a professor at the Johns Hopkins University, where he holds faculty appointments in the School of Hygiene and Public Health (mental hygiene; epidemiology), and in the School of Medicine (psychiatry and behavioral sciences). A main research focus is epidemiology and prevention of drug-dependence syndromes.

Raymond F. Anton, M.D., professor of psychiatry and behavioral sciences at the Medical University of South Carolina, is the co-scientific director of the Alcohol Research Center and Director of the Clinical Neurobiology Laboratory at the Institute of Psychiatry. Dr. Anton is a past chairman of the Clinical Treatment and Prevention Initial Review Group (IRG) for NIAAA. He has been a principal or co-investigator in numerous pharmacology trials for alcohol withdrawal or relapse prevention. In addition he has authored or coauthored over 100 scientific papers and book chapters in the area of biological psychiatry, psychopharmacology, and alcoholism. He is a member of several prestigious professional societies including the American College of Neuropsychopharmacology. Dr. Anton is presently serving as an associate editor of *Alcoholism: Clinical and Experimental Research* and is on the editorial board of the *Journal of Studies on Alcohol*.

Amelia M. Arria, Ph.D., is assistant scientist at the Johns Hopkins University, where she holds a faculty appointment in the School of Hygiene and Public Health (mental hygiene). She works closely with city and state departments of health to plan and evaluate alcohol and drug service delivery and sustains lines of research on health effects of alcohol consumption, interrelationships between youthful drug-taking and conduct problems (including weapon carrying), and the epidemiology of stimulant drug use, especially methamphetamine.

Jerald G. Bachman, Ph.D., is a program director and senior research scientist at the Institute for Social Research, the University of Michigan. For more than three decades he has directed a program of research on youth and social issues, beginning with the *Youth in Transition* project and continuing with the *Monitoring the Future*

project. Publications include *The All-Volunteer Force*, five volumes in the *Youth in Transition* series, and numerous journal articles. Current research interests focus on drug use and its correlates among youth and young adults as well as a variety of other public policy issues.

Howard T. Blane, Ph.D., senior research scientist at the Research Institute on Addictions, is former director of the Institute and research professor emeritus of psychology, social and preventive medicine and psychiatry at SUNY Buffalo. Dr. Blane is author of *The Personality of the Alcoholic* and coeditor of other works including *Psychological Theories of Drinking and Alcoholism*.

Kathleen T. Brady, M.D., Ph.D., is active in research and teaching as an associate professor of psychiatry in the Department of Psychiatry at the Medical University of South Carolina, where she is the director of the Addiction Psychiatry Fellowship Program. Dr. Brady has over 90 publications in the area of psychiatric disorders and substance abuse. She has a Ph.D. in pharmacology from the Medical College of Virginia where she did basic science work with substances of abuse. She completed medical school, a residency in psychiatry, and a fellowship in substance abuse at the Medical University of South Carolina. Her special areas of interest include the comorbidity of substance use disorders with anxiety, affective, and psychotic disorders and the pharmacotherapy of substance use disorders.

Gena Covell Britt, Ph.D., earned her bachelor of arts from Randolph-Macon Woman's College. She went on to receive a doctoral degree from Virginia Commonwealth University, where she is currently an assistant professor in the Division of Substance Abuse Medicine on the Medical College of Virginia Campus. Her research interests focus on how parental substance use and other risk factors impact infant and child outcome.

Stephanie Brown, Ph.D., is a clinician, theoretician, author, teacher, researcher, and consultant in the field of alcoholism. A psychologist, she founded the Stanford Alcohol Clinic and originated the developmental model of alcoholism. She is the author of *Treating the Alcoholic*, *Treating Adult Children of Alcoholics*, and *Safe Passage*, (all John Wiley), coauthor of *Adult Children of Alcoholics in Treatment* (Health Communications), editor of *Treating Alcoholism* (Jossey-Bass) and coauthor of a forthcoming book on the process of recovery for the alcoholic family. She also has recently produced (through Jaylen Productions) two training videos. She maintains a private practice, codirects the Family Recovery Research Project (through MRI), and directs the Addictions Institute in Menlo Park, CA. She is the director of a postgraduate training institute at Santa Clara University focusing on the integration of mental health, psychotherapy models with addiction theory and treatment.

Duncan B. Clark, Ph.D., M.D., obtained doctorates in psychology from the University of California at Los Angeles and in medicine from Harvard University. Dr. Clark is the clinical director of the Center for Education and Drug Abuse Research, the scientific director of the Pittsburgh Adolescent Alcohol Research Center, and the medical director of the University of Pittsburgh Smoking Research Group. He is an associate professor of psychiatry at the University of Pittsburgh.

R. Lorraine Collins, Ph.D., is senior research scientist, Research Institute on Addictions and adjunct research associate professor of psychology, SUNY Buffalo. Her research interests include cognitive and behavioral approaches to the conceptualization, prevention and treatment of addictive behaviors and commonalities among addictions. Dr. Collins is active in conducting federally funded research and publishing scientific articles.

Marie D. Cornelius, Ph.D. is an assistant professor of psychiatry and epidemiology at the Western Psychiatric Institute and Clinic, University of Pittsburgh School of Medicine. She received her doctorate in epidemiology at the University of Pittsburgh Graduate School of Public Health. Her primary research interests include substance use patterns among adolescents and young adults and the effects of parental tobacco, alcohol, and marijuana exposure on the offspring of teen mothers.

Dennis C. Daley, M.S.W., is director of the Center for Psychiatric and Chemical Dependency Services and an assistant professor of psychiatry at the University of Pittsburgh Medical Center, Department of Psychiatry, at Western Psychiatric Institute and Clinic in Pittsburgh. He is the principal investigator on a federally funded research project aimed at enhancing treatment adherence of dual-diagnosis patients.

Nancy L. Day, Ph.D. is a professor of psychiatry, epidemiology, and pediatrics at the Western Psychiatric Institute and Clinic, University of Pittsburgh School of Medicine. She is the director of the psychiatric epidemiology and alcohol research training programs. She completed her doctorate in epidemiology at the University of California at Berkeley. Her research has been on the long-term effects to the offspring of prenatal exposure to substance use.

Kathleen Dohoney, Psy. D., is a clinical assistant professor of psychiatry, Division of Psychology at the University of Texas Southwestern Medical School in Dallas. She is currently the director of mental health rehabilitation in the Mental Health Service at the Veterans Affairs Medical Center in Dallas. Dr. Dohoney is the Coordinator of the Clinical Substance Abuse Fellowship at the Dallas VA Medical Center and is cochair of the Mental Health Service's Addiction Council. Her clinical and research interests are in the areas of substance disorders, substance disorders with comorbid psychiatric disorders ("dual disorders"), and psychiatric rehabilitation.

Brad Donohue, Ph.D., is assistant professor at the University of Nevada, Las Vegas. He is currently an editorial board member of several scientific journals, including the *Journal of Child and Adolescent Substance Abuse*, *Behavior Modification*, and the *Journal of Developmental and Physical Disabilities*. He has published controlled treatment outcome studies in the area of substance abuse and other related areas, including conduct disorder and child maltreatment. Currently, he is involved with intervention studies targeting session attendance, treatment completion, child maltreatment, and substance abuse. He is also currently developing and evaluating the psychometric properties of several assessment instruments pertinent to substance abuse and child maltreatment.

Peter R. Finn, Ph.D., is an associate professor of psychology at Indiana University at Bloomington. He received his doctorate in psychology from McGill University in Montreal. His research focuses on biobehavioral risk factors in alcoholism and antisocial behavior, and includes studies of psychophysiological response to alcohol and psychophysiological correlates of familial risk and personality risk for alcoholism and antisocial personality.

Lisa A. Fisher, Ph.D., is an assistant professor in the Department of Psychiatry at the University of Texas Southwestern Medical School and a staff psychologist at the Dallas Veterans Affairs Medical Center. She received her doctorate in clinical psychology at Texas Tech University. Her research interests include substance abuse among spinal cord injury populations and the role of personality in substance use disorders.

Marc Galanter, M.D., is professor of psychiatry and director of the Division of Alcoholism and Drug Abuse at NYU Medical Center. He also serves as director of the Division of Substance Abuse at the Nathan Kline Institute World Health Organization Collaborating Center. Dr. Galanter is editor of the journal *Substance Abuse* and the book series *Recent Developments in Alcoholism*, and is recipient of the Gold Award for innovative treatment of the American Psychiatric Association and the McGovern Award for excellence in medical education of the Association for Medical Education and Research in Substance Abuse. He is currently president-elect of the American Society of Addiction Medicine.

Bruce A. Goldberger, Ph.D., is director of toxicology and assistant professor at the University of Florida College of Medicine. He obtained his doctorate in Toxicology from the University of Maryland in Baltimore. His research interests include drug testing in alternate matrices including hair and nail, distribution of therapeutic and illicit drugs in postmortem specimens, and new analytical techniques. Dr. Goldberger has published numerous articles related to forensic toxicology and is coeditor of the *Handbook of Workplace Drug Testing* (AACC Press).

Edith S. Lisansky Gomberg, Ph.D., is currently a professor in the Department of Psychiatry, University of Michigan School of Medicine and an adjunct professor in the University of Michigan School of Social Work. She received her doctorate in experimental/clinical psychology at Yale University, and she has worked at Yale University as a research associate and as an associate professor at the University of Puerto Rico. She has published extensively in alcohol and drug studies, and in substance use and abuse among women, older people, and minorities. Her latest book (coedited with T. P. Beresford) was *Alcohol and Aging*, published in 1995 by Oxford University Press.

Dorothy Hatsukami, Ph.D., is professor of psychiatry, Division of Neurosciences at the University of Minnesota. She is also director of the Tobacco Research Programs. Her research involves characterization and treatment of nicotine dependence. She has examined different populations of tobacco users including smokeless tobacco users, women, adolescents, and recovering alcoholics. She has served on a number of national committees that are relevant to drug abuse and has been on the board of directors of several scientific organizations.

Dwight B. Heath, Ph.D. earned his A.B. at Harvard University and doctorate at Yale. He is a professor of anthropology at Brown University, with diverse research interests including alcohol use and its outcomes cross-culturally and throughout history as well as drugs and related policies. Among numerous publications, his most recent book is *International Handbook on Alcohol and Culture*.

Michel Hersen, Ph.D. (State University of New York at Buffalo, 1966) is professor and Dean, School of Professional Psychology, Pacific University, Forest Grove, Oregon. He is past president of the Association for Advancement of Behavior Therapy. He has coauthored and coedited 111 books, including the *Handbook of Prescriptive Treatments for Adults* and *Single Case Experimental Designs*. He has also published more than 220 scientific journal articles and is coeditor of several psychological journals, including *Behavior Modification*, *Clinical Psychology Review*, *Journal of Anxiety Disorders*, *Journal of Family Violence*, *Journal of Developmental and Physical Disabilities*, *Journal of Clinical Geropsychology*, and *Aggression and Violent Behavior: A Review Journal*. With Alan S. Bellack, he is coeditor of the forthcoming 11-volume work entitled *Comprehensive Clinical Psychology*. Dr. Hersen has been the recipient of numerous grants from the National Institute of Mental Health, the Department of Education, the National Institute of Disabilities and Rehabilitation Research, and the March of Dimes Birth Defects Foundation. He is a Diplomate of the American Board of Professional Psychology, distinguished practitioner and member of the National Academy of Practice in Psychology, and recipient of the Distinguished Career Achievement Award in 1996 from the American Board of Medical Psychotherapists and Psychodiagnosticians.

Michie N. Hesselbrock, Ph.D., is a professor and is director of research at the University of Connecticut School of Social Work. She received her doctorate in social work from Washington University (St. Louis). She has published extensively on a variety of topics, including cross-cultural factors in the development of addictive disorders; typologies of substance abuse; and gender, alcoholism, and comorbidity.

Victor M. Hesselbrock, Ph.D., is a professor and director, Alcohol Research Center, Department of Psychiatry, University of Connecticut School of Medicine. He received his doctorate from Washington University (St. Louis). He has published on the genetic epidemiology of alcoholism, comorbid psychiatric conditions and alcoholism, and psychosocial and cognitive risk factors for alcoholism.

Karen Ingersoll, Ph.D., is assistant professor of psychiatry and internal medicine at the Medical College of Virginia of Virginia Commonwealth University. Her clinical and research interests include health psychology, perinatal addiction, HIV and substance abuse, brief interventions, and health promotion among high-risk populations.

Theodore Jacob, Ph.D., is a research career scientist at the Veterans Affairs Palo Alto Health Care System. He received his doctorate in psychology from the University of Nebraska in 1969, and has held positions at the University of Pittsburgh and the University of Arizona. Dr. Jacob's major interests have focused on family environmental antecedents, correlates, and consequences of alcohol abuse disorders. Dr. Jacob has published extensively on these topics.

Amanda J. Jenkins, Ph.D., obtained her doctorate in toxicology from the University of Maryland in Baltimore. She has worked at the Office of the Chief Medical Examiner, State of Maryland and also at the Intramural Research Program, National Institute on Drug Abuse, where she investigated the pharmacokinetics and pharmacodynamics of smoked drug. She is currently affiliated with the Cuyahoga County Coroner's Office in Cleveland, Ohio. Her research interests include drug testing in alternate matrices, onsite drug-testing devices, and distribution of therapeutic and illicit drugs in postmortem specimens.

Sheri Johnson, Ph.D., obtained her doctorate in clinical psychology from the University of Pittsburgh and completed a postdoctoral fellowship at Brown University. She is an assistant professor of psychology at the University of Miami. Her research focuses on the role of the social environment in the course of mental disorders.

Lloyd D. Johnston, Ph.D., is program director and senior research scientist at the Institute for Social Research, the University of Michigan, where he is principal investigator on the ongoing national research project entitled *Monitoring the Future*. He has written numerous articles, chapters, monographs, and books—largely in the field of substance abuse. He also has played a central role in the development of many other national, foreign, and multinational studies in the substance abuse area.

Ronald M. Kadden, Ph.D., obtained his doctorate from Columbia University in 1971. He is currently professor of psychology in the Department of Psychiatry at the University of Connecticut School of Medicine. His clinical orientation is cognitive-behavioral. His research focuses on treatment effectiveness for chemical dependence, especially patient–treatment matching.

Denise Kandel, Ph.D., is professor of public health in psychiatry at the College of Physicians and Surgeons of Columbia University. She received her doctorate in sociology from Columbia University. Her major interests are in the natural history, risk factors and consequences of drug use, the epidemiology of substance dependence, the intergenerational transmission of drug behavior, and developmental pathways of various risk behaviors in adolescence. She has published numerous articles on these topics in *Science*, the *American Journal of Public Health*, *Drug and Alcohol Dependence*, *Archives of General Psychiatry*, and the *American Sociological Review*.

Edward J. Khantzian, M.D., is clinical professor of psychiatry, Harvard Medical School at the Cambridge Hospital and associate chief of psychiatry at Tewksbury Hospital. Past-president of the American Academy of Addiction Psychiatry, he has also served as a consultant to the NFL Drug Control Program. He is best known for his contributions to the self-medication hypothesis of substance use disorders and modified dynamic group psychotherapy for substance abusers.

Levent Kirisci, Ph.D., is assistant professor of psychiatry, University of Pittsburgh. He has expertise in conducting reliability and validity studies using both classical measurement and item response theory (IRT) methodology. He has published in the areas of IRT-based studies. He has extensive experience in computerized adaptive testing and multivariate statistics.

Danica Kalling Knight, Ph.D., received her doctorate from Texas Christian University in 1992 and is currently an associate research scientist at the Institute of Behavioral Research. Her interests focus on the effects of substance abusing lifestyles on parenting and child development, and she has examined changes in family relations over time and how they are associated with drug abuse treatment process and outcomes.

Harry A. Lando, Ph.D., is a professor in the Division of Epidemiology at the University of Minnesota. He received his doctorate in psychology from Stanford University. His primary work is in smoking cessation and he has published widely in this area. He has consulted with numerous federal, state, and private nonprofit agencies.

Bill Latimer, Ph.D., is research associate within the Institute on Community Integration and the Division of General Pediatrics and Adolescent Health at the University of Minnesota. He received his masters in developmental psychology from Teachers College, Columbia University, and his doctorate in clinical psychology from the University of Rhode Island. His research focuses on the reduction of drug-related morbidity and mortality among adolescents, with a special attention toward comorbid learning disabilities and the development and pilot-testing of a cognitive-behavioral therapy designed to promote abstinence among adolescent substance abusers. Recent publications have appeared in the *American Journal of Drug and Alcohol Abuse* and the *Journal of Studies on Alcohol.*

George De Leon, Ph.D., received his doctorate in psychology from Columbia University. He is director of the Center for Therapeutic Community Research (CTCR) at National Development and Research Institutes, Inc. (NDRI) in New York City. He is also a research professor of psychiatry at New York University. A founding member of the American Psychological Association's Division on

Addictions (Division 50), he served as its 1996–97 president. He received the 1993 National Institute on Drug Abuse Pacesetter Award for Outstanding Leadership in Pioneering Research on the Therapeutic Community Approach to Drug Abuse Treatment. His numerous publications and papers address scientific treatment and policy issues in the areas of substance abuse. He has maintained a private practice for over 20 years.

Kenneth E. Leonard, Ph.D., is a senior research scientist at the Research Institute on Addictions and director, Division of Psychology in Psychiatry, SUNY Buffalo School of Medicine. He received his doctorate in clinical psychology from Kent State University. Dr. Leonard's research has focused on alcohol and marital/family processes. He is coeditor of *Psychological Theories of Drinking and Alcoholism* with Howard Blane (published by Guilford Press).

Michael S. Levy, Ph.D., received his doctorate in professional psychology from the California School of Professional Psychology at Berkeley. He is the Director of Clinical Treatment Services at CAB Health and Recovery Services in Salem, Massachusetts and is a faculty member at the Zinberg Center for Addiction Studies, Harvard Medical School. He has published articles on the understanding and treatment of addictive disorders in journals such as the *Journal of Substance Abuse Treatment*, the *Journal of Psychoactive Drugs*, and *Psychotherapy.*

Stephen A. Maisto, Ph.D., received his doctorate in experimental psychology from the University of Wisconsin-Milwaukee in 1975, and he completed a postdoctoral respecialization in clinical psychology at George Peabody College of Vanderbilt University in 1985. He began doing research in the addictions in the mid-1970s, and since then has authored over 125 articles, chapters, and books on the etiology, assessment, and treatment of the substance use disorders. As an outgrowth of his clinical work Dr. Maisto became interested in the use of brief motivational and other psychotherapies, and now is principal or co-investigator of several clinical trials of the effectiveness of these methods in the prevention and treatment of substance use disorders and HIV risk behaviors.

G. Alan Marlatt, Ph.D., is professor of psychology and director of the Addictive Behaviors Research Center at the

University of Washington. He received his Ph.D. in clinical psychology from Indiana University in 1968. After serving on the faculties of the University of British Columbia (1968-1969) and the University of Wisconsin (1969-1972), he joined the University of Washington faculty in the fall of 1972. His major focus in both research and clinical work is the field of addictive behaviors. In addition to many journal articles and book chapters, he has published several books in the addictions field, including *Relapse Prevention* (1985), *Assessment of Addictive Behaviors* (1988), and *Harm Reduction* (1998). In 1996, Dr. Marlatt was appointed a member of the National Advisory Council on Drug Abuse for the National Institute on Drug Abuse (NIH). His research is supported by a Senior Scientist Award and a MERIT Award from the National Institute on Alcohol Abuse and Alcoholism. In 1990, Dr. Marlatt was awarded the Jellinek Memorial Award for outstanding contributions to knowledge in the field of alcohol studies.

Mary E. McCaul, Ph.D., received her doctorate in psychology from Boston University and completed a postdoctoral Fellowship in behavioral pharmacology research at Johns Hopkins University School of Medicine. She is currently an associate professor in the departments of psychiatry and medicine, The Johns Hopkins University School of Medicine. She is the director of the Johns Hopkins Hospital Comprehensive Women's Center, a specialized intensive outpatient treatment program for drug-dependent women. She is the principal investigator on several federally funded research projects, including a HCFA funded project examining effectiveness of outreach and case management services for pregnant drug-dependent women. She has authored numerous papers and book chapters on substance abuse treatment issues.

Elissa R. Miller is a doctoral student in clinical psychology at Nova Southeastern University. Her primary area of study is forensic psychology including the assessment and treatment of adolescent and adult offenders. For the past 3 years, she has conducted individual and group therapy with adolescent offenders who have been referred for treatment by local police departments in Broward County, Florida. She has facilitated group therapy for batterers and victims of domestic violence, inmates at the Broward County Jail, and families characterized by child maltreatment at the Interpersonal Violence Program of Nova Southeastern University. Her research interests include adolescent delinquent behavior, forensic neuropsychology, and domestic violence issues.

Darlene H. Moak, M.D., is assistant professor of psychiatry and behavioral sciences at the Medical University of South Carolina. Dr. Moak is a graduate of the College of Medicine and Dentistry, New Jersey Medical School. She completed her residency and a fellowship in substance abuse at the Medical University of South Carolina. Dr. Moak is board certified in psychiatry. She also has completed the additional certifications exams in addiction psychiatry given by the American Psychiatric Association and the American Society of Addiction Medicine. Presently Dr. Moak is principal investigator of a NIAAA-sponsored study on depression and alcohol. She is also co-principal investigator of several other studies involving research in alcoholism. She is author or coauthor of several scientific papers and book chapters in the area of biological psychiatry, psychopharmacology, and alcoholism.

Sara Jo Nixon, Ph.D., is director of the Cognitive Studies Laboratory and associate director of the Oklahoma Center for Alcohol and Drug-Related Studies at the University of Oklahoma Health Sciences Center. She has many varied research interests, particularly as they pertain to gender, neurocognition, and dual diagnosis and aging.

Patrick M. O'Malley, Ph.D., is a senior research scientist at the Survey Research Center, Institute for Social Research, the University of Michigan. He received a Ph.D. in psychology from the University of Michigan in 1975. Since 1976, he has been involved in the *Monitoring the Future* Project, which annually surveys national samples of secondary school students in grades 8, 10, and 12, and of young adults through age 35. The project, funded by the National Institute on Drug Abuse, provides the nation with annual reports on trends in the use of tobacco, alcohol, and illicit drugs.

Surita Rao, M.D., is an assistant professor with the Department of Psychiatry and Behavioral Sciences at Emory University School of Medicine. Her clinical interests include treating patients with drug and alcohol dependence in a variety of treatment settings. She is currently working on developing a substance abuse program for the Emory Department of Psychiatry, and is medical director of the Methadone Maintenance Program at Grady Memorial Hospital. Prior to this she was an assistant professor at Yale

University and the Medical Director of the Methadone Maintenance Program there. Her research interests include the use of imaging and behavioral techniques to define the effects of treatment of drug craving and relapse in opioid dependence.

Gale A. Richardson, Ph.D. is an associate professor of psychiatry and epidemiology at the Western Psychiatric Institute and Clinic, University of Pittsburgh School of Medicine. She received her doctorate in developmental psychology from West Virginia University. Her research has been concerned with the effects of cocaine, alcohol, and marijuana use during pregnancy on child development.

Lisa Roberts, M.A., is a doctoral student in clinical psychology at the University of Washington. Her interests include comorbidity and clinical significance. She has written a manual on relapse prevention skills for schizophrenics (Substance Abuse Management Module), coauthored five peer-reviewed empirical papers, including one paper in the *New England Journal of Medicine,* and eight book chapters on schizophrenia and/or addictive behaviors.

Ihsan M. Salloum, M.D., M.P.H., is medical director of the Center for Psychiatric and Chemical Dependency Services and an assistant professor of psychiatry at the University of Pittsburgh School of Medicine, Pittsburgh. He received an NIAAA fellowship in alcohol research. His research interest has focused on psychiatric and alcohol use disorders comorbidity.

Stacy Scannell, M.D., received her medical training at University of Texas Southwestern Medical School, graduating in 1988. She then completed her residency in psychiatry in 1993 at University of Texas Southwestern Medical School. Since that time she has been an assistant professor at UT Southwestern Medical School, Department of Psychiatry and on staff at the Department of Veterans Affairs Medical Center at Dallas. She is the medical education coordinator for substance abuse at the VA and coordinates the psychopathology course for medical students.

Joyce Schmid, Ph.D., received her doctorate from the Pacific Graduate School of Psychology, and her B.A. from Harvard University. She was a staff psychotherapist and the coordinator of psychotherapy groups for ACOAs at the Stanford Alcohol and Drug Treatment Center. Currently

she is an Associate of the Addictions Institute and is in private practice as a LMFCC in Menlo Park, California. Her specialty is psychodynamic psychotherapy with alcoholics, ACOAs and other members of alcoholic families. She teaches classes for psychotherapists on Alcoholism and the alcoholic family through the extension divisions of Santa Clara University and the University of California at Santa Cruz.

Sidney H. Schnoll, M.D., Ph.D., is chairman, division of substance abuse medicine and professor of medicine and psychiatry at the Medical College of Virginia of Virginia Commonwealth University (MCV/VCU), Richmond, Virginia. Dr. Schnoll has published over 100 articles in the field of substance abuse and is currently actively involved with basic and clinical research in addictions with special emphasis on the problems of perinatal addiction and chronic pain. He is also involved in drug policy at the local and national level.

Richard S. Schottenfeld, M.D., professor of psychiatry, Yale University School of Medicine, directs substance abuse treatment, research, and training at the Connecticut Mental Health Center and is CEO of the APT Foundation, Inc. Dr. Schottenfeld's research interests are in the areas of behavioral and pharmacologic treatment and service delivery, with a focus on developing and evaluating innovative strategies to improve access to drug abuse treatment, including integrating services into primary care settings. Dr. Schottenfeld is a member of the Connecticut Alcohol and Drug Policy Council. He has been active on CPDD committees, and he currently chairs the Committee of Training and Education of Addiction Psychiatry of the American Psychiatric Association.

D. Dwayne Simpson, Ph.D., is director of the Institute of Behavioral Research (IBR) and Saul B. Sells professor of psychology at Texas Christian University where he also received his Ph.D. in experimental psychology. He specializes in evaluation research with particular emphasis on drug addiction and treatment effectiveness, and has published over 175 papers on the basis of several large-scale longitudinal evaluations in national and regional multisite projects. His current work focuses primarily on service delivery process and client attributes, and how these factors influence treatment engagement and retention rates, stages of recovery, and long-term outcomes of addicts. Simpson has been an advisor to a variety of international, national, and regional organizations that address drug abuse and related policy issues. He holds memberships in major professional psychological and evaluation societies, is a fellow in the American Psychological Association, and serves on the scientific advisory boards for several national drug abuse assessment and treatment research centers.

Randy Stinchfield, Ph.D., is the associate director of the Center for Adolescent Substance Abuse in the Department of Psychiatry at the University of Minnesota and he maintains a research consulting practice. He received his Ph.D. in clinical psychology from Brigham Young University in 1988. His research interests include the assessment and treatment of addictions, namely alcohol and drug abuse and pathological gambling. Dr. Stinchfield has published numerous articles and book chapters in these areas and serves on the editorial board of the *Journal of Gambling Studies*.

Dace S. Svikis, Ph.D., obtained her doctoral degree in clinical psychology from the University of Minnesota. She is currently an associate professor in the Department of Psychiatry and Behavioral Sciences at the Johns Hopkins University School of Medicine. Dr. Svikis is also program director for the Center for Addiction and Pregnancy (CAP) at Johns Hopkins Bayview Medical Center. Her research interests include behavioral pharmacological drug abuse treatment efficacy (with particular emphasis on women) and the impact of drug abuse/dependence on the developing fetus. She is also involved in twin/family studies of alcoholism and drug dependence and has a variety of publications in both domains.

Paul M. Taylor, M.D. is a professor emeritus of pediatrics, obstetrics and gynecology, and psychiatry at the University of Pittsburgh School of Medicine. He received his doctorate in medicine from Johns Hopkins University and board certifications in pediatrics and neonatal–perinatal medicine. Dr. Taylor's expertise is in clinical neonatology, and his research has been concerned with parent–infant bonding, teratology, prematurity and child abuse, and mother–infant interaction.

Vincent B. Van Hasselt, Ph.D., is professor of psychology and director of the Interpersonal Violence Program at Nova Southeastern University in Fort Lauderdale, Florida. Dr. Van Hasselt received his M.S. and Ph.D. from the University of Pittsburgh and completed an internship in clinical psychology at the Western Psychiatric Institute and Clinic of the University of Pittsburgh School of Medicine. He is editor of the *Journal of Family Violence, Aggression and Violent Behavior: A Review Journal, Journal of Child and Adolescent Substance Abuse, Handbook of Family Violence*, and the soon to be published *Handbook of Psychological Approaches with Violent Offenders: Contemporary Strategies and Issues*. He has published over 150 journal articles, books, and book chapters including several on the assessment and treatment of family violence and substance abuse. Dr. Van Hasselt is also a certified police officer in the state of Florida.

Michael M. Vanyukov, Ph.D., was born in the city of Chelyabinsk, which is now famous for a nuclear reactor explosion on a scale larger than Chernobyl's. He received his master's degree in genetics from the Moscow State University in 1978 and his Ph.D. in genetics from the Institute of Medical Genetics, USSR Academy of Medical Sciences in 1984. Dr. Vanyukov is currently assistant professor of psychiatry at the Western Psychiatric Institute and Clinic, University of Pittsburgh School of Medicine. His main interests are in behavior genetics, and substance abuse is a good model phenotype for studies in that area that delve into "normal" behavioral variation (as compared to, e.g., psychoses) because it is a consequence of voluntary choices. Currently, in his work with the Center for Education and Drug Abuse Research project of the University of Pittsburgh School of Medicine he is involved in the genetic analyses of CEDAR data, molecular genetic association studies of substance abuse, and studies of spousal similarity for the risk for substance abuse.

Kimberly S. Walitzer, Ph.D., is a senior research scientist at the Research Institute on Addictions in Buffalo, New York. She obtained her doctorate in clinical psychology at the University of Missouri—Columbia. Her research interests include alcoholism treatment outcome, spouse-involved alcohol treatment, and risk for alcoholism. One recent research project focuses on examining the effects of spouse support and behavioral marital therapy in the context of a drinking moderation program for nonphysically dependent problem drinkers.

John Wallace, Ph.D., is currently the director of Alcoholism and Substance Abuse Services at St. Vincent's Hospital in Harrison, New York. He has held regular faculty appointments at Stanford University and the University of California. He served as the director of treatment at Edgehill Newport for many years and was also the director of alcoholism rehabilitation for the State of New York.

Ken Winters, Ph.D., is the director of the Center for Adolescent Substance Abuse and an associate professor in the Department of Psychiatry at the University of Minnesota. He received his B.A. from the University of Minnesota and Ph.D. in Psychology (Clinical) from the State University of New York at Stony Brook. His research interests include the assessment and treatment of adolescent drug abuse, ADHD as a risk for drug involvement,

and problem gambling. Dr. Winters has published several assessment tools and numerous articles in the area of adolescent health. He is a consultant to many organizations, including the Hennepin County Community Prevention Coalition, the National Institute on Drug Abuse, and the World Health Organization. Recent publications have appeared in the *Journal of Studies on Alcohol* and *Psychology of Addictive Behaviors*.

Kazuo Yamaguchi, Ph.D., is professor of sociology at the University of Chicago. His principal research interest includes models for event-history data and categorical data, life course, and drug-use history. His recent publications on drug use have appeared in *Journal of the American Statistical Association*, *Journal of Marriage and the Family*, *Social Forces*, *American Journal of Public Health*, and *Evaluation Review*.

CHAPTER 1

EPIDEMIOLOGY OF SUBSTANCE USE DURING PREGNANCY

Marie D. Cornelius
Nancy L. Day
Gale A. Richardson
Paul M. Taylor

The notion that the ingestion of foreign substances during the prenatal period is unwise has been held since antiquity. In the Old Testament (Judges 13:3–4), an angel appears to Samson's mother and foretells her pregnancy, saying: ". . . thou shalt conceive, and bear a son. Now therefore beware, I pray thee, and drink not wine nor strong drink, and eat not any unclean thing." Other early civilizations also demonstrated concern about alcohol use during pregnancy. For example, Carthage and Sparta had laws prohibiting the use of alcohol by newlyweds to prevent conception during intoxication, and Plato recommended the same rule (Warner & Rosett, 1975). Despite the long history of concerns about substance use during pregnancy, only in the past few decades has an attempt been made to assess the extent of this public health problem.

In this chapter we discuss the epidemiology of substance use during pregnancy. In the first section we discuss methodologic problems regarding the measurement of the prevalence of substance use during pregnancy. The next four sections describe the prevalences, correlates, and fetal effects of the four most commonly used licit and illicit substances: alcohol, tobacco, marijuana, and cocaine. The last section of this chapter focuses on the problem of substance use among pregnant teenagers.

MEASURING SUBSTANCE USE DURING PREGNANCY—METHODOLOGIC ISSUES

A number of methodologic issues must be considered to assess accurately the prevalence of substance use in pregnant women. For example, data about substance use during pregnancy can be acquired from a variety of sources, including medical records, laboratory tests, interviews, or self-reports. Each source of information has its advantages and disadvantages. Review of existing medical records can be easier and more efficient, yet data from medical records underestimate the prevalence of substance use. Medical records are often incomplete because time restraints limit the amount of information that the health professional can elicit from the patient interview. Also, women may be less willing to report honestly any behavior that is negatively labeled or illegal.

Laboratory assessments provide a biological and precise measure of some substances. However, these assessments only cover a specific time period, and they also do not provide any information about the pattern of use over time. Furthermore, laboratory results from screenings are often not representative of the entire population. For example, Matera, Warren, Moomjy, Fink, and Fox (1990) compared a group of women who underwent urine screens with a non-screened group and found that the nonscreened women were more likely to be Caucasian, multiparous, and to have had a previous preterm delivery. Therefore, prevalence rates that are derived from toxicology screens should be considered specific for the population screened.

Interviews can provide information on patterns of substance use over different periods of time. They are susceptible, however, to problems of under- or overreporting, recall problems, and poor instrument design. Underreporting may be more common when the interviewer and the subject being interviewed differ on demographic factors, such as gender, race, or age. Overreporting of prepregnancy drug use may occur in order to rationalize current pregnant use (e.g., "My use now isn't so bad since it is much less than before I got pregnant"). Self-reports are more anonymous and may minimize problems with lying. However, problems may arise with subject misinterpretation or illiteracy.

Substance use can be measured in terms of (a) quantity, (b) frequency, and (c) duration of use. The amount of use, or quantity, can be specified in more detail as the usual, maximum, and minimum amount. Questions that focus only on usual quantity may elicit the socially acceptable response and thus underestimate use (Day, Cottreau, & Richardson, 1993). The frequency of use describes how often a particular quantity is used. Asking questions only about quantity of use will not, for example, separate women who use substances heavily on fewer occasions from those who use smaller amounts on many occasions. Thus the quantity and frequency must be considered together to give a sense of the pattern of use. Therefore, it is important to include both components of substance use, and to acquire information on usual as well as maximum and minimum patterns of use, to describe the substance use most accurately.

It is also essential to have an accurate picture of the substance use over the entire prenatal period. The effects of substance exposure vary depending on the time of exposure in pregnancy (Day, 1995). Therefore, multiple assessments during the perinatal period are needed to provide information about changes in the pattern of use. One common problem with measuring substance use during the first trimester of pregnancy is that women often do not report their use from the point of conception. Instead, they tend to report first trimester use from the time of pregnancy recognition or medical confirmation (Day et al., 1993). When this is the case, the substance use between conception and recognition is often underestimated, because women are still using substances at a rate more similar to their rate before pregnancy than to their later first trimester use (Day, Goldschmidt, et al., 1991). Therefore, efforts should be made to get an accurate description of substance use before and during pregnancy. This can be done by measuring use from conception to recognition, from recognition to confirmation, from the time of confirmation to the end of the first trimester (Day & Robles, 1989), and again for the second and third trimesters.

An additional issue is that chronicity of use may affect an individual's response to substances. Studies of adolescents and young adults indicate that early onset of use is a predictor of heavy or problematic use in later years (Donovan, Jessor, & Costa, 1991; Kandel, 1978). The duration of use may potentially affect the biological capacity of the mother. Long-term substance use or heavy levels of use can affect reproductive capacity and the ability to carry the pregnancy to term.

Another potential uncertainty in the assessment of substance use is the concentration of the substance ingredients. The amount of absolute alcohol in a standard glass of beer, mixed drink, or wine is roughly equivalent, and therefore most researchers combine drinks across the categories. Finer estimations of alcohol intake can be made from the contents of alcohol printed on beverage containers. However, people do not always drink standard amounts, and to the extent that they do not, the dose will be estimated incorrectly. Also, merging beverages may obscure the effect of congeners that may be present in some types of alcoholic beverages (Day et al., 1993).

In contrast, the constituents and their concentrations are not specified for illicit drugs as they are for alcohol. There is no "truth in labeling" law on the streets. Marijuana, for example, contains a mixture of compounds in addition to tetrahydrocannabinol, and their presence and concentration may vary from sample to sample. The size of the product (joint versus blunt) and the number of people sharing the substance are important to quantify dose accurately. The same is true of cocaine and crack. There are diluents, adulterants, additives, fakes, look-alikes, and substitutes, each of which may have different teratologic effects (Day et al., 1993).

PREVALENCE OF SUBSTANCE USE DURING PREGNANCY

In recent years, there have been many estimates of the prevalence of prenatal substance exposure. These estimates have resulted from local community or clinical survey studies as scientists and public health personnel have attempted to describe the nature and extent of drug use during pregnancy and its potential impact on the offspring. In order to provide a nationally representative estimate of both the number of pregnant women who reported the use of licit and illicit drugs during their pregnancy and the number of infants who were born to these women, a national survey on the prevalence of drug use among women who gave birth in the United States was conducted. The National Pregnancy and Health Survey (NIDA, 1994) was conducted by the National Institute on Drug Abuse of the National Institutes of Health. The data for this survey were collected from October 1992 through August 1993. Approximately 4 million women were estimated to have given birth in the United States in 1992, the year on which the study estimates were based. The survey estimated that 221,000, or 5.5%, of these women used some illicit drug during pregnancy.

The following sections describe secular trends, correlates, and fetal effects of prenatal alcohol, tobacco, marijuana, and cocaine use.

ALCOHOL USE DURING PREGNANCY

Recent Trends

Alcohol use during pregnancy has decreased dramatically in recent years. Data from the CDC Behavioral Risk Factor Surveillance System showed a decline from 32% in 1985 to 20% in 1988 (Centers for Disease Control and Prevention, 1991) to 14% in 1991 (CDC, 1994) in the overall rate of prenatal alcohol use. This reduction was caused, in part, by the increased awareness of the negative effects of prenatal alcohol use (Serdula, Williamson, Kendrick, Anda, & Byers, 1991). However, among pregnant women who drank alcohol, the median number of drinks per month remained constant between 1985 and 1988 (Serdula et al., 1991). Furthermore, the prevalence of prenatal drinking did not decrease among some subgroups of pregnant women, such as those age 18–24 years, cigarette smokers, and women with a high school education or less. In the Pregnancy Risk Assessment Monitoring Systems (PRAMS) study of Maine, Michigan, Oklahoma, and West Virginia, over 6,000 mothers were surveyed 2–6 months after delivery (Bruce, Adams, & Shulman, 1993). State-specific prevalences of drinking during the third trimester were low: 6.8% to 15.1% of the mothers reported drinking 1–6 drinks per week; 0.06% to 0.30% reported 7–13 drinks per week; and 0.03% to 0.13% reported consuming 14 or more drinks per week. By contrast, prevalences for drinking in the 3 months prior to pregnancy were much higher: 31.9% to 52.8% (1–6 drinks per week); 1.6% to 3.0% (7–13 drinks per week); and .6% to 1.3% (14 or more drinks per week). In the National Pregnancy and Health Survey (NIDA, 1994), 757,000, or 18.8%, of the women drank at some time during pregnancy.

Patterns and Correlates of Drinking During Pregnancy

Drinking usually decreases after a woman realizes that she is pregnant, and continues to decrease through pregnancy. In the mid 1980s, a large prospective study, the Maternal Health Practices and Child Development (MHPCD) study, was initiated in Pittsburgh (Day et al., 1989). Forty-four percent of the women in the sample consumed one or more alcoholic drinks per day before pregnancy. That rate dropped to 37% by the end of the first month of pregnancy and then decreased sharply to 21% and 13.6% in the second and third months of the first trimester, respectively. By the end of pregnancy, only 4.6% of the women were drinking at least one drink per day.

According to the National Pregnancy and Health Survey (NIDA, 1994), rates of alcohol use during pregnancy were highest among Caucasian women, 22.7% (n = 588,600), compared to 15.8% (n = 105,000) among African American women, and 8.7% (n = 53,600) among Hispanic women. Women who were tobacco smokers, unmarried, less educated, older, and had lower incomes were also more likely to drink during pregnancy. In the MHPCD study of adult women (Day et al., 1989), there were differences between women who drank only at the beginning of pregnancy and women who continued to drink throughout pregnancy. The drinkers who quit early in pregnancy were more likely to be Caucasian and single, whereas the women who continued to drink through the third trimester were more likely to be older, African American, to have used more illicit drugs, and to have had more life events (Day et al., 1989).

Effects of Prenatal Alcohol on the Offspring

Alcohol has been well established as a teratogenic agent for the human fetus (National Institute on Alcoholism and Alcohol Abuse, 1994). A definition of fetal alcohol syndrome (FAS) has been arrived at by consensus that mandates effects in three domains: morphological anomalies, specifically facial anomalies; growth retardation; and central nervous system deficits (Sokol & Clarren, 1989). The term *fetal alcohol effects* (FAE) was first proposed (Clarren & Smith, 1978) as a term for use when some, but not all, of the domains were affected. The term *alcohol-related birth defect*s (ARBD) was later suggested for clinical use (Sokol & Clarren, 1989) when prenatal alcohol exposure was suspected to be related to a physical malformation. To separate those with physical anomalies (ARBD) from those offspring with neurodevelopmental problems, the term *alcohol-related neurodevelopmental disorder* (ARND) has been proposed (Institute of Medicine, 1996).

Although FAS only occurs at high levels of exposure and with maternal alcoholism, fetal alcohol effects result from lower levels of prenatal alcohol exposure. Reports from several studies have shown that alcohol use, even at levels of less than a drink per day, can affect the growth and development of the fetus (Day et al., 1994; Jacobson & Jacobson, 1994). Follow-up assessments of children who were prenatally exposed to alcohol also show a slower rate of postnatal growth (Day et al., 1990; Day, Goldschmidt, et al., 1991; Day, Robles, et al., 1991) and more developmental deficits (Streissguth et al., 1989). Prenatal alcohol exposure has been associated with increased rates of hyperactivity and impulsivity (Brown et al., 1991) and decreases in short-term memory (Coles et al., 1991) in a sample of 5-year-olds. In the MHPCD study, first trimester alcohol exposure was associated with a significant increase in impulsivity among exposed 6-year-olds as measured by the SNAP Checklist (Day, unpublished data; Pelham & Bender, 1982).

TOBACCO USE DURING PREGNANCY

Recent Trends

According to the National Natality Survey data, smoking among pregnant women over age 20 decreased from 40% to 25% among Caucasians and from 33% to 23% among African Americans between the years 1967 to 1980 (Kleinman & Kopstein, 1987). In 1985, an estimated 25% of women smoked during pregnancy (Floyd, Zahniser, Gunter, & Kendrick, 1991), whereas in 1988, the National Health Interview Survey measured a period prevalence of smoking among pregnant women of 28.8% (Overpeck & Moss, 1991). National studies that have relied on self-reports have produced estimates of 18.4% and 19.0% for the prevalence

of smoking among pregnant women (U.S. Department of Health and Human Services, 1990; CDC, 1991, respectively). In the CDC study (1991), the self-reported smoking rate was 19% for pregnant women and 30% for nonpregnant women in their reproductive years (18–44).

Fingerhut, Kleinman, and Kendrick (1990) measured prevalence rates from before, during, and after pregnancy, and found that 39% of the smokers reported quitting during pregnancy. The prevalence of smoking after pregnancy (30%), however, was almost the same as it was before pregnancy (32%). This self-reported quit rate is higher than rates measured in clinical trials where cessation can be validated biochemically (Li, Windsor, & Perkins, 1993; Windsor, Low, & Perkins, 1993). Fourteen percent of pregnant women who received an intensive smoking cessation intervention quit smoking, as determined by serial urine cotinine levels, compared to 8% given standard obstetrical care. The national rate of prenatal smoking has declined somewhat in the general population, but is still quite high in populations characterized by other maternal risk factors: for example, higher prevalence rates are found among women of lower socioeconomic status (Day et al., 1992; Kleinman & Kopstein, 1987). In the National Pregnancy and Health Survey (NIDA, 1994), 820,000 women, or 20.4%, smoked cigarettes at some time during pregnancy. Twenty percent is much higher than the national objective projected in the Healthy People 2000 National Health Promotion and Disease Prevention Objectives (USDHHS, 1990), namely, to reduce the prevalence of prenatal smoking to 10% by the year 2000.

Patterns and Correlates of Smoking During Pregnancy

The MHPCD cohort was selected from healthy, lower-socioeconomic-status pregnant women attending an outpatient prenatal clinic; 54% smoked in the first trimester of pregnancy and by the third trimester, 53% were still smoking (Day et al., 1992). Cigarette smoking did not follow the pattern of decrease shown by alcohol use or other substance use during pregnancy. Cigarette use decreased little if at all, whereas use of alcohol and other substances dropped sharply. It is not known whether failure to decrease smoking during pregnancy is accounted for by lack of knowledge about adverse effects of this behavior or by the difficulty the women encounter in decreasing their smoking.

In the National Pregnancy and Health Survey (NIDA, 1994), Caucasians had the highest rates of cigarette use,

24.4% (n = 632,000), compared with 19.8% (n = 131,600) for African Americans and 5.8% (n = 35,600) for Hispanics. Heavier smokers had less education and were younger. In the MHPCD study of lower-social-status women, heavy smoking was also significantly associated with being Caucasian and having less than a high school education. Neither age nor gravidity was significantly correlated with tobacco use (Day et al., 1992).

There was a strong link between cigarette smoking and alcohol use and the use of illicit drugs during pregnancy (NIDA, 1994). Of those who reported no illicit drug use, 6% used alcohol and/or cigarettes during pregnancy, whereas among those who used illicit drugs, 32% smoked cigarettes and drank alcohol. Among the women who reported alcohol or cigarette use, 0.2% used marijuana and 0.1% used cocaine, whereas among those who reported use of both alcohol and cigarettes, 20.4% used marijuana and 9.5% used cocaine. These findings have important public health implications. They highlight the need for health professionals to appreciate the strong link between licit and illicit drug use and to monitor women who use alcohol and cigarettes during pregnancy for the use of other substances.

Effects of Prenatal Tobacco on the Offspring

A recent review article estimated that in 1 year, maternal tobacco use was responsible for up to 4,800 infant deaths, the birth of 61,000 low-birth-weight (LBW) infants, and 26,000 infants who required neonatal intensive care (DiFranza & Lew, 1995). Prenatal tobacco use is commonly associated with growth retardation in the offspring (Day et al., 1992; Harrison, Branson, & Baucher, 1983; Kline, Stein, & Hutzler, 1987). Birth weight decreases in direct proportion to the number of cigarettes smoked (Persson, Grennert, Gennser, & Kullander, 1978; Yerushalmy, 1971), and the offspring of smokers are, on average, 150–250 grams lighter than the offspring of nonsmokers (USDHHS, 1990).

In addition, the offspring of both smoking and nonsmoking mothers can be exposed to tobacco smoke through their passive exposure of the mother to tobacco. Data from the National Health Interview Survey of nonsmoking mothers showed that, after controlling for potentially confounding variables, women with high exposure to passive smoke were 1.6 times more likely to have a LBW infant than those with low or no exposure (Mainous & Hueston, 1994). The causal relationship between passive exposure to tobacco smoke and birth weight was supported by examining the

serum cotinine levels of pregnant nonsmokers (Haddow, Knight, Palomaki, & McCarthy, 1988). This study found that the infants of the passively exposed mothers weighed 107 grams less than the infants of the unexposed women, even after controlling for covariates known to be associated with birth weight. Therefore, when considering the epidemiology of tobacco exposure during pregnancy, both the direct and indirect effects of tobacco exposure should be considered. Women should be asked about personal smoking, as well as amount and frequency of exposure to cigarette smoke in their environment.

MARIJUANA USE DURING PREGNANCY

Recent Trends

The National Pregnancy and Health Survey was the first study to use nationwide representative sampling, thus producing data reflective of the general U.S. population. The prevalence of prenatal marijuana use was estimated at 2.9% (119,000 women) (NIDA, 1994). However, most data on the prevalence of marijuana use among pregnant women have been obtained from research studies on populations that are not representative of the general population. In the MHPCD study (Day, Sambamoorthi, et al., 1991), it was found that 30% of a random sample of 1,360 low-income women from a Pittsburgh outpatient clinic reported marijuana use during pregnancy. Another study, which interviewed women from prenatal clinics at two Denver hospitals, reported a prevalence rate of 34% (Tennes et al., 1985). In a low-income sample in Boston (Zuckerman, Frank, & Hingson, 1989), 23% of the women reported smoking marijuana and 16% of the women had a positive urine screen for marijuana use.

In middle-class samples, the reported rates of prenatal marijuana use have been lower. In one sample recruited from private obstetric practices in Ottawa (Fried, Watkinson, Grant, & Knights, 1980), 13% percent reported first trimester marijuana use. In another study of Utah women who were primarily middle-class Caucasians, urine specimens were analyzed for illicit drug use (Buchi, Varner, & Chase, 1993). At delivery, only 2.9% of the samples were positive for marijuana.

Patterns and Correlates of Marijuana Use during Pregnancy

Women who use marijuana during pregnancy are more likely to be African American, of lower socioeconomic status, less educated, younger, and unmarried. In addition, they are more likely to use other substances, including alcohol, tobacco, and other illicit drugs (Day, Sambamoorthi, et al., 1991; Fried et al., 1980; Tennes et al., 1985). Among heavier users, the women who quit during pregnancy are different from those who continue to use marijuana throughout pregnancy. In the Day, Sambamoorthi, et al. (1991) study, women who were heavy users during the third trimester were slightly younger, more likely to be African American, poorer, less educated, and less likely to be employed than women who used marijuana heavily during only the first trimester. Thus women with a large number of risk factors for poor pregnancy outcome are also the least likely to change their substance use during pregnancy.

Effects of Prenatal Marijuana on the Offspring

A number of studies have investigated the relationship between prenatal marijuana exposure and birth outcome. However, the results of these studies are not consistent (Richardson, Day, & McGaughey, 1993). Gestational age has been reported to be shortened by about 1 week among mothers who use five or more joints per week as compared with nonusing mothers (Fried, Watkinson, & Willan, 1984). A similar finding was reported by Cornelius, Taylor, Geva, and Day (1995) in a population of newborn infants whose teenage mothers smoked marijuana during pregnancy. However, other studies have not found this relationship between prenatal marijuana exposure and shortened gestational age (Day, Sambamoorthi, et al., 1991; Hayes, Lampart, Dreher, & Nugent, 1991; Tennes et al., 1985).

Study findings regarding the relationship between prenatal marijuana exposure and reduced birth weight are also inconsistent. A negative relationship has been found in some studies (Hatch & Bracken, 1986; Zuckerman et al., 1989), although not in others (Day, Sambamoorthi et al., 1991; Fried & O'Connell, 1987).

Some authors have reported effects of exposure on infant behavior (Fried & Makin, 1987), whereas others have not (Hayes, Dreher, Nugent, & Morgan, 1988; Richardson, Day, & Taylor, 1989). Fried and Watkinson (1990) found that 4-year-olds of heavy users had poorer memory skills than children of moderate- or light-using mothers. In a recent analysis (Day et al., 1994), marijuana use during first and second trimesters of pregnancy was

associated with poorer performance on the Stanford–Binet Intelligence Scale composite score, and the short-term memory, verbal, and abstract-visual reasoning subscales among the exposed 3-year-old offspring. Streissguth et al. (1989) reported no association between prenatal marijuana use by women and the IQ scores of their 4-year-olds.

COCAINE/CRACK USE DURING PREGNANCY

Recent Trends

The prevalence of cocaine use by pregnant women has been estimated to range between 1% and 31%. The rates vary by geographic location and method of ascertainment, with rates generally higher in city or tertiary medical settings. According to national prevalence data collected by the National Pregnancy and Health Survey, 45,000 women, or 1.1%, reported use of cocaine (NIDA, 1994). This rate is comparable to those in other studies of large population samples. Urine screen and medical record data collected from over 14,000 women who delivered in Greenville County, South Carolina yielded a prevalence of 1% (Weathers, Crane, & Sauvain, 1993). Over 1,000 urine samples were obtained anonymously from women presenting for delivery in seven hospitals in Jacksonville, Florida. In this sample, the overall prevalence of cocaine exposure was 2.1% (Vaughn, Carzoli, & Sanchez-Ramos, 1993). In 1990, population-based data were collected from 25 Ohio hospitals (Moser, Jones, & Kuthy, 1993). Urine samples were screened for benzoylecgonine (BZE), a metabolite of cocaine. The overall prevalence rate was 2.0%, 7.2% among African American mothers and 0.3% for Caucasian mothers. At delivery, Forman, Klein, and Barks (1994) estimated the prevalence of fetal exposure of cocaine in Toronto between 1990 and 1991 to be 6.3%, using neonatal hair and urine tests for BZE. Eight percent of all women admitted to the labor and delivery unit of a Chicago hospital had urine screens positive for cocaine (Neerhof, MacGregor, Retzky, & Sullivan, 1989). Nine percent of the urine samples obtained from pregnant women over a 1-year period who attended a tertiary obstetric center in California were positive (Gillogley, Evans, Hansen, Samuels, & Batra, 1990). In 1991, McCalla et al. reported that 12% of the urine samples were positive for cocaine from mothers who delivered at a New York City hospital. In a high-risk urban obstetric population of over 3,000 in Detroit, 31% of newborns were positive for cocaine exposure by meconium analysis (Ostrea, Brady, Gause, Raymundo, & Stevens, 1992).

Patterns and Correlates of Prenatal Cocaine Use

The rate of cocaine use usually diminishes as the pregnancy progresses, similar to patterns of alcohol and marijuana use (Richardson, Day, & McGaughey, 1993). Women who use cocaine are significantly more likely to use other drugs such as alcohol, tobacco, and marijuana (Frank et al., 1988; Gillogley et al., 1990; Graham & Koren, 1991; McCalla et al., 1991; Richardson & Day, 1991). They are usually older and have had more pregnancies (Gillogley et al., 1990; McCalla et al., 1991; Neerhof et al., 1989), and investigators have reported that more of the pregnant cocaine users were African American compared with noncocaine users (Frank et al., 1988; Gillogley et al., 1990; McCalla et al., 1991; Oro & Dixon, 1987; Richardson et al., 1993). Ostrea et al. (1992) presented this profile of the pregnant cocaine user: single, multigravida, consumer of public health services, and little or no prenatal care.

Effects of Prenatal Cocaine on the Offspring

The results of research on the effects of prenatal cocaine exposure on the neonate are inconsistent. Cocaine use has been reported to be associated with decreased birth weight, length, and head circumference by some researchers (Bingol, Fuchs, Diaz, Stone, & Gromisch, 1987; Chasnoff, 1988; Coles, Platzman, Smith, James, & Falek, 1992; Eyler, Behnke, Conlon, Woods, & Woble, 1994), whereas others have found no relationship between cocaine use and neonatal growth (Hurt, Brodsky, & Betancourt, 1995; Jacobson, Jacobson, & Sokol, 1994; McCalla et al., 1991; Richardson & Day, 1991). Results are also conflicting for physical malformations. Some authors have reported that cocaine use is associated with morphologic changes (Lipshultz, Frassica, & Orav, 1991; Madden, Payne, & Miller 1986). However, larger prospective studies have not found this relationship (Coles et al., 1992; Richardson & Day, 1991; Zuckerman et al., 1989).

Several authors have reported that prenatal cocaine exposure is associated with changes on the Brazelton Neonatal Behavior Assessment Scale (BNBAS) (Chasnoff,

Griffith, MacGregor, Dirkes, & Burns, 1989; Coles et al., 1992; Eisen, et al., 1991; Hume, O'Donnell, Stanger, Killam, & Gingras, 1989; Mayes, Granger, Frank, Schottenfeld, & Bornstein, 1993), whereas other researchers have found no differences on the BNBAS when appropriate confounding variables were controlled (Neuspiel, Hamel, Huchberg, Greene, & Campbell, 1991; Richardson & Day, 1991; Woods, Eyler, Behnke, & Conlon, 1993).

Reports of development of cocaine-exposed infants beyond the neonatal period have again been inconsistent. Prenatal exposure to cocaine was found to affect infant mental and motor development in studies by Chasnoff, Griffith, Freler, and Murry (1992) and Singer et al. (1994), but not by Graham et al. (1992) or Hurt, Brodsky, and Betancourt (1995). The only published report of follow-up to the preschool period found no effects of prenatal cocaine exposure on 3-year growth or the composite score of the Stanford–Binet, although cocaine use did predict lower scores on the verbal reasoning subscale (Griffith, Azuma, & Chasnoff, 1994).

Recent research does not confirm earlier reports of the devastating effects of prenatal cocaine exposure—the so-called "crack baby." Although there have been numerous reports and high levels of concern about the effects of crack/cocaine use during pregnancy, the data are still inconsistent and await further research. Furthermore, it is critical to control the covariates of prenatal cocaine use such as alcohol, marijuana, tobacco use, and demographic and health characteristics when evaluating the effects of prenatal cocaine exposure on the offspring.

SUBSTANCE USE AND THE PREGNANT TEENAGER

Most of the data on prenatal substance use come from studies on adults. However, more recently, a few studies have described the prevalence, patterns, and correlates of adolescent drug use during pregnancy. The results of these studies are summarized next.

Adolescent pregnancy and adolescent drug use are both public health and clinical problems in the United States. In the past decade, the rate of teenage pregnancy has been rising (National Center for Health Statistics, 1993). Teenagers are at higher risk for perinatal problems and their offspring are at higher risk for neonatal and early childhood problems (Croen & Shaw, 1995; Fraser, Brockert, & Ward, 1995). These problems are exacerbated by the fact that pregnant adolescents are at higher risk for substance use than are adolescents who delay childbearing. Also, adolescents generally take longer to recognize that they are pregnant than adult women (Cornelius, Richardson et al., 1994) and may continue to use substances further into the pregnancy than adults. Moreover, the increased vulnerability of the adolescents' offspring, related to both biological and environmental factors, may lead to an increased expression of teratogenic effects resulting from prenatal substance use (Cornelius et al., 1995; Cornelius, 1997).

Prevalence of Substance Use among Pregnant Teenagers

In 1989, Amaro, Zuckerman, and Cabral studied pregnant teenagers, 19 years of age and younger, who attended the Boston City Hospital for prenatal care (n = 253). Alcohol was used prenatally by 52.2%, marijuana by 31.6%, and cocaine by 13.8%. No information was provided on tobacco use. Pletsch (1988) compared Chicago teens under age 19 who were pregnant (n = 119) to those who were not pregnant (n = 313). No differences were found in the quantity of alcohol and marijuana use between the two groups. However, she found that pregnant teenagers smoked significantly more cigarettes than nonpregnant teenagers. In 1991, Streissguth et al. examined the prevalence of drug use among 14–19-year-old pregnant girls in Seattle (n = 130). Forty percent of the sample used alcohol, 57% smoked cigarettes, 29% used marijuana, and 14% used cocaine. Prevalence data were provided from another sample of Seattle pregnant adolescents (n = 241) (Gilchrist, Gillmore, & Lohr, 1992). In this sample, 33% drank during pregnancy, 50% smoked cigarettes, 10% used marijuana, and 6% used cocaine.

Data from these studies were collected in the mid- to late 1980s. From 1990 to 1995, a prospective study of 415 pregnant teenagers was conducted by Cornelius and colleagues in Pittsburgh. In this study, the pregnant teenagers were, on average, 16.3 years old (range 12–18); 68% were African American and 32% were Caucasian. Ten (2.4%) teenagers were married at the time of delivery.

In the year prior to pregnancy, 74% drank alcohol. In the first, second and third trimesters, 36%, 12%, and 8%, respectively, used alcohol. Thirty-five percent were binge drinkers (5+ drinks per occasion) during the first trimester (Cornelius et al., 1993).

In the year prior to pregnancy, 53% of the teenagers smoked cigarettes. This rate was 3 times higher than among U.S. nonpregnant high school seniors (Johnston, O'Malley, & Bachman, 1994). This rate of 53% dropped to 47% in the first trimester and then rose to 59% by the third trimester (Cornelius, Geva, Day, Cornelius, & Taylor, 1994). In the year prior to pregnancy, 38% of the teenagers used marijuana, a rate that was twice the national average (Johnston et al., 1994). The rate dropped to 16.4% in the first trimester and 4.4% and 3.4% in the second and third trimesters, respectively. Cocaine/crack use was rare in this cohort (1.2%).

Patterns and Correlates of Substance Use

Alcohol use declined precipitously from before pregnancy to the first trimester and even further from the first to second trimesters. Caucasians were more likely than African Americans to be drinkers and to drink heavily. Heavier drinkers were more likely to have had earlier ages of onset of alcohol use, tobacco use, and sexual intercourse than lighter drinkers. Heavier drinkers recognized their pregnancy later and had fewer prenatal visits than nondrinkers (Cornelius et al., 1993). An analysis was performed to determine what association, if any, there was between actual drinking behavior and attitudes about drinking and knowledge about possible harmful fetal effects. It was found that those pregnant teenagers with attitudes that were intolerant of drinking were significantly less likely to be drinkers. Furthermore, among those who did drink during pregnancy, knowledge about the potential harmful fetal effects of alcohol exposure was significantly associated with a reduction in drinking during the pregnancy (Cornelius, Lebow, & Day, 1997).

The use of all substances except tobacco decreased during pregnancy. There was a significant racial difference in smoking rates. Caucasian teenagers were significantly more likely to be smokers and to be heavier smokers than African American teenagers. By the third trimester, 79% of the Caucasians were smokers compared to 49% of the African Americans. Heavier smokers were more likely to drink alcohol, to use marijuana and cocaine, and to have more friends who smoked, drank, and used marijuana than light or nonsmokers (Cornelius, Geva, et al., 1994). Heavier smokers also gained significantly less weight during pregnancy than nonsmokers (Cornelius, Geva, et al., 1994).

Marijuana use, similar to alcohol use, declined during pregnancy. The prevalence of marijuana use was not different between African Americans and Caucasians, although African Americans used marijuana more heavily. Marijuana use was significantly related to earlier age of first sexual intercourse, and earlier age of first alcohol use. Those who used marijuana were less likely to be in school full time, less likely to attend church regularly, and were more depressed (Cornelius, Geva, et al., 1994).

Thus the offspring of adolescents are at significant risk for prenatal substance exposure. The rates of tobacco use among pregnant teenagers were double those reported among nonpregnant teenagers in national surveys. Adolescents are at increased risk of having offspring with low birth weight. That risk is exacerbated when the pregnant teenager smokes. Furthermore, many of the correlates of substance use are potential risk factors for negative pregnancy outcome. For example, heavy drinkers recognized their pregnancies later than nonheavy drinkers, resulting in more exposure and in the later initiation of prenatal care. Both heavy smokers and heavy drinkers tended to gain less weight during pregnancy. The young adolescent is still in a growth spurt, which may interfere with shifting necessary nutrition to the fetus. Thus weight gain is conceivably more critical to the adolescent pregnancy (Scholl, Miller, Salmon, Cofsky, & Shearer, 1987). Also, as with adults, the use of alcohol, tobacco, marijuana, and cocaine are correlated, so many offspring may be exposed to multiple substances.

SUMMARY AND FUTURE RESEARCH DIRECTIONS

The prevalence of alcohol use during pregnancy has been decreasing over the past several decades. However, among those who use alcohol during pregnancy, the level of drinking is about the same as what it had been in earlier years. Caucasian women are more likely to use alcohol during early pregnancy, but they are most likely to quit or decrease use as the pregnancy progresses. Women who continue to drink throughout pregnancy are more likely to be African American, older, cigarette smokers, and less educated.

The prevalence of cigarette smoking among pregnant women in the United States is slightly lower than the prevalence of alcohol use. However, the rate and level of smoking does not show the same rate of decrease during pregnancy that is seen with alcohol and other drugs.

Among less educated, younger, and Caucasian women, the rate of smoking during pregnancy is twice as high as for the general population. Among adolescents who carry their pregnancies to term, the rates of tobacco use are close to 50%. In both adult and adolescent populations, those who drink and use other drugs are also more likely to be smokers.

Women who use marijuana during pregnancy are more often African American, unmarried, and of lower socioeconomic status. Cocaine users tend to be African American, older, unmarried, and also of lower socioeconomic status. Both groups more frequently use other illicit drugs, and, in general, receive later and less prenatal care.

The women most likely to use substances during pregnancy are women who also have other characteristics that are, in themselves, significant risk factors for poor pregnancy outcome. These covariates must be considered in the evaluation of the effects of prenatal substance use and in the development of prevention programs targeted to the highest risk groups.

Pregnant adolescents have higher rates of prepregnancy substance use than adolescents from national samples. However, with the exception of tobacco, rates and levels of use decrease during the pregnancy. Adolescence is a risk factor for poorer fetal outcome even when substance use is not present, and some evidence suggests that prenatal substance use may further increase the problems of offspring of teenagers.

Future research should focus on etiological and epidemiological questions that have specific prevention implications. For example, why are some offspring who are heavily exposed to a particular teratogenic substance not affected while others are? What are the protective factors, if any, that guard a positive fetal outcome? What is the role of the postnatal environment in modifying the effects of prenatal substance exposure? What are the association and temporal ordering of substance use and unprotected sexual activity? How influential are sexual partners in the initiation and maintenance of substance use before, during, and after pregnancy? To what extent does substance use predict which women experience multiple pregnancies? Why are some women able to maintain no or low substance use in spite of use among key members of their social support network? Finally, what are the most efficacious prevention or intervention programs that will reduce prenatal exposure of tobacco, alcohol, marijuana, and cocaine to the offspring?

REFERENCES

Amaro, H., Zuckerman, B., & Cabral, H. (1989). Drug use among adolescent mothers: Profile of risk. *Pediatrics, 84,* 144–151.

Bingol, N., Fuchs, M., Diaz, V., Stone, R., & Gromisch, D. (1987). Teratogenicity of cocaine in humans. *Journal of Pediatrics, 110,* 93–96.

Brown, R., Coles, C., Smith, I., Platzman, K., Silverstein, J., Erickson, S., & Falek, A. (1991). Effects of prenatal alcohol exposure at school age. II. Attention and behavior. *Neurotoxicology & Teratology, 13,* 369–376.

Bruce, F., Adams, M., & Shulman, H. (1993). Alcohol use before and during pregnancy. PRAMS Working Group. *American Journal of Preventive Medicine, 9,* 267–273.

Buchi, K., Varner, M., & Chase, R. (1993). The prevalence of substance abuse among pregnant women in Utah. *Obstetrics & Gynecology, 81,* 239–242.

Centers for Disease Control and Prevention. (1991). Cigarette smoking among reproductive-aged women—Behavioral risk factor surveillance system. *MMWR, 40,* 719–723.

Centers for Disease Control and Prevention. (1994). Frequent alcohol consumption among women of childbearing age—Behavior risk factor surveillance system. *Journal of the American Medical Association, 271,* 1820–1821.

Chasnoff, I. (1988). Cocaine: Effects on pregnancy and the neonate. In I. Chasnoff (Ed.), *Drugs, alcohol, pregnancy and parenting* (pp. 97–103). Boston: Kluwer Academic.

Chasnoff, I., Griffith, D., Freler, C., & Murry, J. (1992). Cocaine/polydrug use in pregnancy: Two-year follow-up. *Pediatrics, 89,* 284–289.

Chasnoff, I., Griffith, D., MacGregor, S., Dirkes, K., & Burns, K. (1989). Temporal patterns of cocaine use in pregnancy. *Journal of the American Medical Association, 261,* 1741–1744.

Clarren, S., & Smith, D. (1978). The fetal alcohol syndrome. *New England Journal of Medicine, 298,* 1063–1067.

Coles, C., Brown, R., Smith, I., Platzman, K., Erickson, S., & Falek, A. (1991). Effects of prenatal alcohol exposure at school age. I. Physical and cognitive development. *Neurotoxicology & Teratology, 13,* 357–367.

Coles, C., Platzman, K., Smith, I., James, M., & Falek, A. (1992). Effects of cocaine and alcohol use in pregnancy on neonatal growth and neurobehavioral status. *Neurotoxicology & Teratology, 14,* 23–33.

Cornelius, M. (in press). Adolescent pregnancy and the complication of prenatal substance use. *Physical and Occupation Therapy in Pediatrics.*

Cornelius, M., Day, N., Cornelius, J., Geva, D., Taylor, P., & Richardson, G. (1993). Drinking patterns and correlates of drinking among pregnant teenagers. *Alcoholism: Clinical & Experimental Research, 17,* 290–294.

Cornelius, M., Geva, D., Day, N., Cornelius, J., & Taylor, P. (1994). Patterns and covariates of tobacco use in a recent sample of pregnant teenagers. *Journal of Adolescent Health, 15,* 528–535.

Cornelius, M., Lebow, H., & Day, N. (1997). Attitudes and knowledge about drinking: Relationships with drinking behavior among pregnant teenagers. *Journal of Drug Education, 27*(3), 231–243.

Cornelius, M., Richardson, G., Day, N., Cornelius, J., Geva, D., & Taylor, P. (1994). A comparison of prenatal drinking in two recent samples of teenagers and adults. *Journal of Studies on Alcohol, 55,* 412–419.

Cornelius, M., Taylor, P., Geva, D., & Day, N. (1995). Prenatal tobacco and marijuana use among adolescents: Effects on offspring gestational age, growth and morphology. *Pediatrics, 95,* 438–443.

Croen, L., & Shaw, G. (1995). Young maternal age and congenital malformations: A population-based study. *American Journal of Public Health, 85,* 710–713.

Day, N. (1995). Research on the effects of prenatal alcohol exposure: A new direction. *American Journal of Public Health, 85,* 1614–1616.

Day, N., Cornelius, M., Goldschmidt, L., Richardson, G., Robles, N., & Taylor, P. (1992). The effects of prenatal tobacco and marijuana use on offspring growth from birth through age 3 years. *Neurotoxicology & Teratology, 14,* 407–414.

Day, N., Cottreau, C., & Richardson, G. (1993). The epidemiology of alcohol, marijuana, and cocaine use among women of childbearing age and pregnant women. *Clinical Obstetrics & Gynecology, 36,* 232–245.

Day, N., Goldschmidt, L., Robles, N., Richardson, G., Cornelius, M., Taylor, P., Geva, D., & Stoffer, D. (1991). Prenatal alcohol exposure and offspring growth at 18 months of age: The predictive validity of two measures of drinking. *Alcoholism: Clinical & Experimental Research, 15,* 914–918.

Day, N., Jasperse, D., Richardson, G., Robles, N., Taylor, P., & Cornelius, M. (1989). Prenatal exposure to alcohol: Effect on infant growth and morphologic characteristics. *Pediatrics, 84,* 536–541.

Day, N., Richardson, G., Goldschmidt, L., Robles, N., Taylor, P., Stoffer, D., Cornelius, M., & Geva, D. (1994). The effect of prenatal marijuana exposure on the cognitive development of offspring at age three. *Neurotoxicology & Teratology, 16,* 169–175.

Day, N., Richardson, G., Robles, N., Sambamoorthi, U., Taylor, P., Scher, M., Stoffer, D., Jasperse, D., & Cornelius, M. (1990). The effect of prenatal alcohol exposure on growth and morphology of the offspring at 8 months of age. *Pediatrics, 85,* 748–752.

Day, N., & Robles, N. (1989). Methodological issues in the measurement of substance use. In D. Hutchings (Ed.), Prenatal abuse of licit and illicit drugs. *Annals of the New York Academy of Science, 562,* 8–13.

Day, N., Robles, N., Richardson, G., Geva, D., Taylor, P., Scher, M., Stoffer, D., Cornelius, M., & Goldschmidt, L. (1991). The effects of prenatal alcohol use on the growth of children at three years of age. *Alcoholism: Clinical & Experimental Research, 15,* 67–71.

Day, N., Sambamoorthi, U., Taylor, P., Richardson, G., Robles, N., Jhon, Y., Scher, M., Stoffer, D., Cornelius, M., & Jasperse, D. (1991). Prenatal marijuana use and neonatal outcome. *Neurotoxicology & Teratology, 13,* 329–334.

DiFranza, J., & Lew, R. (1995). Effect of maternal cigarette smoking on pregnancy complications and sudden infant death syndrome. *Journal of Family Practice, 40,* 385–394.

Donovan, J., Jessor, R., & Costa, F. (1991). Adolescent health behavior and conventionality and unconventionality: An extension of the problem behavior theory. *Health Psychology, 10,* 52–61.

Eisen, L., Field, T., Bandstra, E., Toverts, J., Morrow, C., Larson, S., & Steele, B. (1991). Perinatal cocaine effect on neonatal stress behavior and performance on the Brazelton scale. *Pediatrics, 88,* 477–480.

Eyler, F., Behnke, M., Conlon, M., Woods, N., & Woble, K. (1994). Prenatal cocaine use: A comparison of neonates matched on maternal risk factors. *Neurotoxicology & Teratology, 16,* 81–87.

Fingerhut, L., Kleinman, J., & Kendrick, J. (1990). Smoking before, during and after pregnancy. *American Journal of Public Health, 80,* 541–544.

Floyd, R., Zahniser, S., Gunter, E., & Kendrick, J. (1991). Smoking during pregnancy: Prevalence, effects and intervention strategies. *Birth, 18,* 48–53.

Forman, R., Klein, J., & Barks, J. (1994). Prevalence of fetal exposure to cocaine in Toronto, 1990–1991. *Clinical and Investigative Medicine—Medicine Clinique et Experimentale, 17,* 206–211.

Frank, D., Zuckerman, B., Amaro, H., Bauchner, M., Hingson, R., & Parker, S. (1988). Cocaine use during pregnancy: Prevalence and correlates. *Pediatrics, 82,* 888–895.

Fraser, A., Brockert, J., & Ward, R. (1995). Association of young maternal age with adverse reproductive outcomes. *New England Journal of Medicine, 332,* 113–117.

Fried, P., & Makin, J. (1987). Neonatal behavioural correlates of prenatal exposure to marihuana, cigarettes and alcohol in a low risk population. *Neurotoxicology & Teratology, 9,* 1–7.

Fried, P., & O'Connell, C. (1987). A comparison of the effects of prenatal exposure to tobacco, alcohol, cannabis and caffeine on birth size and subsequent growth. *Neurotoxicology & Teratology, 10,* 305–313.

Fried, P., & Watkinson, B. (1990). 36- and 48-month neurobehavioural follow-up of children prenatally exposed to marijuana, cigarettes and alcohol. *Neurotoxicology & Teratology, 11,* 49–58.

Fried, P., Watkinson, B., Grant, A., & Knights, P. (1980). Changing patterns of soft drug use prior to and during pregnancy: A prospective study. *Drug & Alcohol Dependence, 6,* 323–343.

Fried, P., Watkinson, B., & Willan, A. (1984). Marijuana use during pregnancy and decreased length of gestation. *American Journal of Obstetrics & Gynecology, 150,* 23–27.

Gilchrist, L., Gillmore, M., & Lohr, M. (1992). Drug use among pregnant adolescents. In G. Lawson, & A. Lawson (Eds.), *Adolescent substance abuse* (pp. 351–363). Gaithersburg, MD: Aspen.

Gillogley, K., Evans, A., Hansen, R., Samuels, S., & Batra, K. (1990). The perinatal impact of cocaine, amphetamine, and opiate use detected by universal intrapartum screening. *American Journal of Obstetrics & Gynecology, 163,* 1535–1542.

Graham, K., Feigenbaum, A., Pastuszak, A., Nulman, I., Weksberg, R., Elnarson, T., Goldberg, S., Asby, S., & Koren, G. (1992). Pregnancy outcome and infant development following gestational cocaine use by social cocaine users in Toronto, Canada. *Clinical & Investigative Medicine, 15,* 384–394.

Graham, K., & Koren, G. (1991). Characteristics of pregnant women exposed to cocaine in Toronto between 1985 and 1990. *Canadian Medical Association Journal, 144,* 563–568.

Griffith, D., Azuma, S., & Chasnoff, I. (1994). Three-year outcome of children exposed prenatally to drugs. *Journal of the American Academy of Child & Adolescent Psychiatry, 33,* 20–27.

Haddow, J., Knight, G., Palomaki, G., & McCarthy, J. (1988). Second trimester serum cotinine levels in nonsmokers in relation to birth weight. *American Journal of Obstetrics & Gynecology, 159,* 481–484.

Harrison, G., Branson, R., & Baucher, Y. (1983). Association of maternal smoking with body composition of the newborn. *American Journal of Clinical Nutrition, 38,* 757–762.

Hatch, E., & Bracken, M. (1986). Effect of marijuana use in pregnancy on fetal growth. *American Journal of Epidemiology, 124,* 986–993.

Hayes, J., Dreher, M., Nugent, J., & Morgan, L. (1988). Newborn outcomes with maternal marihuana use in Jamaican women. *Pediatric Nursing, 14,* 107–110.

Hayes, H., Lampart, R., Dreher, M., & Nugent, J. (1991). Five-year follow-up of rural Jamaican children whose mothers used marijuana during pregnancy. *West Indian Medical Journal, 40,* 120–123.

Hume, R., O'Donnell, D., Stanger, C., Killam, A., & Gingras, J. (1989). In utero cocaine exposure: Observations of fetal behavioral state may predict neonatal outcome. *American Journal of Obstetrics & Gynecology, 161,* 685–690.

Hurt, H., Brodsky, N., & Betancourt, L. (1995). Cocaine-exposed children: Follow-up through 30 months. *Journal of Developmental & Behavioral Pediatrics, 16,* 29–35.

Institute of Medicine. (1996). *Fetal alcohol syndrome: Diagnosis, epidemiology, prevention, and treatment.* K. Stratton, C. Howe, & F. Battaglia (Eds). Washington, DC: National Academy Press.

Jacobson, J., & Jacobson, S. (1994). Prenatal alcohol exposure and neurobehavioral development: Where is the threshold? *Alcohol Health and Research World, 18,* 30–36.

Jacobson, J., Jacobson, S., & Sokol, R. (1994). Effects of prenatal exposure to alcohol, smoking and illicit drugs on postpartum somatic growth. *Alcoholism: Clinical & Experimental Research, 18*, 317–323.

Johnston, L., O'Malley, P., & Bachman, J. (1994). *National survey results on drug use from monitoring the future study, 1975–1992* (NIH Publication No. 13-3597). Rockville, MD: NIDA.

Kandel, D. (1978). *Longitudinal research on drug use.* Washington, DC: Hemisphere.

Kleinman, J., & Kopstein, A. (1987). Smoking during pregnancy, 1967–1980. *American Journal of Public Health, 77*, 823–825.

Kline, J., Stein, Z., & Hutzler, M. (1987). Cigarettes, alcohol and marijuana: Varying associations with birthweight. *International Journal of Epidemiology, 16*, 44–51.

Li, C., Windsor, R., & Perkins, I. (1993). The impact on infant birth weight and gestational age of cotinine-validated smoking reduction during pregnancy. *Journal of the American Medical Association, 269*, 1519–1524.

Lipshultz, S., Frassica, J., & Orav, E. (1991). Cardiovascular abnormalities in infants prenatally exposed to cocaine. *Journal of Pediatrics, 118*, 44–51.

Madden, J., Payne, T., & Miller, S. (1986). Maternal cocaine abuse and effect on the newborn. *Pediatrics, 77*, 209–211.

Mainous, A., & Hueston, W. (1994). Passive smoke and low birth weight. *Archives of Family Medicine, 3*, 875–878.

Matera, C., Warren, W., Moomjy, M., Fink, D., & Fox, H. (1990). Prevalence of use of cocaine and other substances in an obstetric population. *American Journal of Obstetrics & Gynecology, 163*, 797–801.

Mayes, L., Granger, R., Frank, M., Schottenfeld, R., & Bornstein, M. (1993). Neurobehavioral profiles of neonates exposed to cocaine prenatally. *Pediatrics, 91*, 778–783.

McCalla, S., Minkoff, H., Feldamn, J., Delke, I., Salwin, M., Valencia, G., & Glass, L. (1991). The biologic and social consequences of perinatal cocaine use in an inner-city population: Results of an anonymous cross-sectional study. *American Journal of Obstetrics & Gynecology, 164*, 625–630.

Moser, J., Jones, V., & Kuthy, M. (1993). Use of cocaine during the immediate prepartum period by childbearing women in Ohio. *American Journal of Preventive Medicine, 9*, 85–91.

National Center for Health Statistics. (1993). Advance report of the final natality statistics, 1991. *Monthly Vital Statistics Report, 42* (Supplement). Hyattsville, MD: Public Health Service.

National Institute on Alcoholism and Alcohol Abuse. (1994). *Alcohol and health: Eighth special report to the U.S. Congress* (NIH Publication No. 94-3699). Alexandria, VA: Author.

National Institute on Drug Abuse. (1994). *National pregnancy and health survey* [Press release]. Rockville, MD: National Clearinghouse for Alcohol and Drug Information.

Neerhof, M., MacGregor, S., Retzky, S., & Sullivan, T. (1989). Cocaine abuse during pregnancy: Peripartum prevalence and perinatal outcome. *American Journal of Obstetrics & Gynecology, 161*, 633–638.

Neuspiel, D., Hamel, S., Huchberg, E., Greene, J., & Campbell, D. (1991). Maternal cocaine use and infant behavior. *Neurotoxicology & Teratology, 13*, 229–233.

Oro, A., & Dixon, S. (1987). Perinatal cocaine use and methamphetamine exposure: Maternal and neonatal correlates. *Journal of Pediatrics, 111*, 571–578.

Ostrea, E., Brady, M., Gause, S., Raymundo, A., & Stevens, M. (1992). Drug screening of newborns by meconium analysis: A large-scale, prospective, epidemiologic study. *Pediatrics, 89*, 107–113.

Overpeck, M., & Moss, A. (1991). *Children's exposure to environmental cigarette smoke before and after birth: Health of our nation's children, United States 1988.* (Advance data from vital and health statistics, No. 202). Hyattsville, MD: National Center for Health Statistics.

Pelham, W. & Bender, M. (1982). Peer relationships in hyperactive children: Descriptions and treatment. In *Advances in learning and behavioral disabilities* (pp. 365–436). City: JAI Press.

Persson, P., Grennert, L., Gennser, G., & Kullander, S. (1978). A study of smoking and pregnancy with special reference to fetal growth. *Acta Obstetricia et Gynecologica Scandinavica, 78*, 33–39.

Pletsch, P. (1988). Substance use and health activities of pregnant adolescents. *Journal of Adolescent Health Care, 9*, 38–45.

Richardson, G., & Day, N. (1991). Maternal and neonatal effects of moderate cocaine use during pregnancy. *Neurotoxicology & Teratology, 13*, 455–460.

Richardson, G., Day, N., & McGaughey, P. (1993). The impact of prenatal marijuana and cocaine use on the infant and child. *Clinical Obstetrics Gynecology, 36*, 302–318.

Richardson, G., Day, N., & Taylor, P. (1989). The effect of prenatal alcohol, marijuana, and tobacco exposure on neonatal behavior. *Infant Behavior & Development, 12*, 199–209.

Scholl, T., Miller, L., Salmon, R., Cofsky, M., & Shearer, J. (1987). Prenatal care adequacy and the outcome of adolescent pregnancy: Effects on weight gain, preterm delivery, and birth weight. *Obstetrics & Gynecology, 69*, 312–316.

Serdula, M., Williamson, D., Kendrick, J., Anda, R., & Byers, T. (1991). Trends in alcohol consumption by pregnant women: 1985–1988. *Journal of the American Medical Association, 265*, 876–879.

Singer, L., Yamashita, T., Hawkins, S., Cairns, D., Baley, J. & Kellegman, R. (1994). Increased incidence of intraventricular hemorrhage and developmental delay in cocaine-exposed, very low birth weight infants. *Journal of Pediatrics, 124*, 765–771.

Sokol, R., & Clarren, S. (1989). Guidelines for use of terminology describing the impact of prenatal alcohol on the offspring. *Alcoholism: Clinical & Experimental Research, 13*, 597–598.

Streissguth, A., Barr, H., Sampson, P., Brown, Z., Martin, J., Mayock, D., Landesman, R., & Leejon, M. (1989). IQ at age

4 in relation to maternal alcohol use and smoking during pregnancy. *Developmental Psychobiology, 25,* 3–11.

Streissguth, A., Grant, T., Barr, H., Brown, Z., Martin, J., Mayock, D., Landesman, R., & Leejon, M. (1991). Cocaine and the use of alcohol and other drugs during pregnancy. *American Journal of Obstetrics & Gynecology, 164,* 1239–1243.

Tennes, K., Avitable, N., Blackard, C., Goyles, C., Hassoun, B., Holmes, L., & Kreya, M. (1985). Marijuana: Prenatal and postnatal exposure in the human. In T. Pinkert (Ed.), *National Institute of Drug Abuse Research Monographs 59,* 48–62.

U.S. Department of Health and Human Services. (1990). *The health consequences of smoking for women* (HHS 396). Rockville, MD: Author.

U.S. Department of Health and Human Services. (1993). Advance report of maternal and infant health data from the birth certificate, 1990. *Monthly vital statistics report, 42,* 1–31. (Publication No. 93-1120). Public Health Service, Centers for Disease Control and Prevention, Atlanta, GA.

U.S. Department of Health and Human Services (1990). *Healthy people 2000. national health promotion and disease prevention objectives* (Publication No. 91-50213). Washington, DC: Author.

Vaughn, A., Carzoli, R., & Sanchez-Ramos, L. (1993). Community-wide estimation of illicit drug use in delivering women: Prevalence, demographics, and associated risk factors. *Obstetrics & Gynecology, 82,* 92–96.

Warner, R., & Rosett, H. (1975). The effects of drinking on offspring: A historical survey of the American and British literature. *Journal of Studies on Alcoholism, 36,* 1395–1420.

Weathers, W., Crane, M., & Sauvain, K. (1993). Cocaine use in women from a defined population: Prevalence at delivery and effects on growth in infants. *Pediatrics, 91,* 350–354.

Windsor, R., Low, J., & Perkins, L. (1993). Health education for pregnant smokers: Its behavioral impact and cost benefit. *American Journal of Public Health, 83,* 201–206.

Woods, N., Eyler, F., Behnke, M., & Conlon, M. (1993). Maternal depressive symptoms and infant neurobehavior over the first month. *Infant Behavior & Development, 16,* 83–98.

Yerushalmy, J. (1971). The relationship of parent's cigarette smoking to outcome of pregnancy complications as to the problem of inferring causation from observed associations. *American Journal of Epidemiology, 93,* 443–456.

Zuckerman, B., Frank, D., & Hingson, R. (1989). Effects of maternal marijuana and cocaine use on fetal growth. *New England Journal of Medicine, 320,* 762–768.

CHAPTER 2

EPIDEMIOLOGY OF SUBSTANCE ABUSE IN ADOLESCENCE

Patrick M. O'Malley
Lloyd D. Johnston
Jerald G. Bachman

Epidemiology was originally the science of epidemics, investigating the source, spread, and control of communicable diseases (Rogers, 1965). The definition has broadened with time to encompass not just communicable diseases, but almost any health-related behavior or condition. One definition is that epidemiology is the study of the incidence, prevalence, causes, and consequences of health problems in human populations. In this chapter, the emphasis will be on the first two of these areas of study: the incidence and prevalence of substance abuse among adolescents.

The definition of drug abuse is a basic issue, and it is one about which there is some difference of perspective, if not of opinion. There is a clinical perspective in which substance abuse is viewed as a disease (a categorical diagnosis) and a more behavioral perspective in which substance abuse is viewed as a continuum—as a behavior that may in some individuals be properly viewed as a disease, but more generally can be characterized along dimensions of frequency, quantity, and duration. The first perspective lead to clinical diagnoses identifying categories or clinical syndromes (a disease), and the second to a quantitative statistical or psychometric approach yielding a dimensional classification (severity). Each perspective has its proponents, and there are others who see value in using both approaches (Skinner, 1995).

Researchers and clinicians commonly distinguish three levels or stages of drug behavior: use, abuse, and dependence (Gerstein & Harwood, 1990). The stage of dependence is most clearly amenable to a diagnostic perspective, whereas use seems characterized by frequency, quantity, and duration. The abuse stage is more ambiguous. Generally speaking, it is much easier to measure drug use. It is more difficult to determine when that use has become abuse, and it is more difficult still to determine whether an individual's use has produced a definable disorder of substance use dependence.

This chapter primarily emphasizes the behavioral perspective rather than the disease or clinical perspective, and use rather than abuse. In part, this is due simply to the available data. Use of substances is (relatively) well measured in the United States, whereas abuse or dependence is far less well measured. Moreover, because abuse and dependence disorders tend to take some time to develop—perhaps a period of some years—many adolescents may not yet exhibit the symptoms of such disorders, though they may be using drugs.

In assessing the epidemiology of drug use and abuse among adolescents, the chapter relies heavily on self-reports of use. Although biological indicators of drug use are often thought to be more valid than self-reports, they are subject to some important limitations. Compared to self-reports, they are considerably more complicated and more expensive to implement, and more restricted in the amount and time frame of use that can be detected, and may provoke less cooperation from potential respondents. Consequently, self-report methods are often more practical and more desirable. It is therefore fortunate that self-report measures have been shown to be generally reliable and valid when gathered under the proper conditions (Johnston & O'Malley, 1985; O'Malley, Bachman, & Johnston, 1983). These conditions include clear and understandable interview procedures and questionnaires, confidence by the respondent that responses will be kept confidential, and some degree of willingness by the respondent to provide accurate information. However, under other conditions, for example when arrestees or pregnant women are being questioned about recent drug use, self-reports are likely to be far less valid. With respect to adolescents in particular, the available evidence suggests that the best method for securing drug use reports from general populations of youth is to use school-based sampling procedures, with anonymous or confidential self-administered questionnaires. These conditions seem to elicit higher levels of reports than individual interviews in a home, or by telephone (Rootman & Smart, 1985).

The primary focus in this chapter is on rates of use of illicit and licit drugs by nationally representative samples of 8th-, 10th-, and 12-grade students, from both public and private schools. The term "licit drugs" includes alcohol and tobacco, which are legally available to adults, although proscribed for adolescents under age 18 (for tobacco, in most states) or age 21 (for alcohol). The term "illicit drugs" includes controlled substances, both those that are essentially proscribed for everyone (marijuana, LSD, heroin, etc.), and those that are available by prescription (for example, tranquilizers). In addition, inhalants are discussed. Although the substances themselves may not be illegal, inhalants are used for the purpose of getting intoxicated (and are a serious problem among adolescents). Finally, anabolic steroids are considered.

The epidemiologic data come primarily from the Monitoring the Future surveys (Johnston, O'Malley, & Bachman, 1996). That series of surveys, which began in 1975, provides the most complete consistent reporting of trends in use of drugs among America's young people.[1] Until 1991, the surveys were of students in grade 12 only; beginning in 1991, students in grades 8 and 10 were added, and this chapter concentrates on the results of the survey in 1995. The core of the study consists of annual surveys of nationally representative samples of 8th-, 10th-, and 12-grade students; in-school questionnaires are administered by professional interviewers to over 45,000 students in approximately 420 public and private schools per year.

PREVALENCE

Table 2.1 shows 1995 prevalence (proportion of students who used a substance in the relevant time period—lifetime, last 12 months, or last 30 days) for the various classes of drugs, by grade level (8th, 10th, 12th).

The table shows that nearly half (48%) of 12th-grade students in the United States have used an illicit drug at least once in their lifetime. Among 10th-graders, the figure is 41%; among 8th graders, it is 29%. These data show clearly that the use of illicit drugs is an important problem, in the sense that use is not at all uncommon.[2] To the extent that willingness to use an illicit drug is an important step on the way to substance abuse, then a great many American adolescents take that step at an early age.

ILLICIT DRUGS

Marijuana

Among the various illicit drugs, the most prevalent is marijuana. As shown in Table 1, in 1995 about two in five (42%) American high school seniors had used marijuana in their lifetime, one in three 10th graders (34%), and two in five 8th graders (20%). About one half of the lifetime users were current users, that is, had used in the past 30 days.

Table 2.1 Lifetime, Annual, and 30-Day Prevalence Rates for 8th, 10th, and 12th Graders, 1995

	Lifetime			Annual			30-Day		
Grade	8th	10th	12th	8th	10th	12th	8th	10th	12th
Any Illicit Drug[a]	28.5	40.9	48.4	21.4	33.3	39.0	12.4	20.2	23.8
Marijuana/Hashish	19.9	34.1	41.7	15.8	28.7	34.7	9.1	17.2	21.2
Inhalants[b]	21.6	19.0	17.4	12.8	9.6	8.0	6.1	3.5	3.2
Hallucinogens	5.2	9.3	12.7	3.6	7.2	9.3	1.7	3.3	4.4
LSD	4.4	8.4	11.7	3.2	6.5	8.4	1.4	3.0	4.0
Cocaine	4.2	5.0	6.0	2.6	3.5	4.0	1.2	1.7	1.8
Crack	2.7	2.8	3.0	1.6	1.8	2.1	0.7	0.9	1.0
Other Cocaine[c]	3.4	4.4	5.1	2.1	3.0	3.4	1.0	1.4	1.3
Heroin	2.3	1.7	1.6	1.4	1.1	1.1	0.6	0.6	0.6
Amphetamines[d]	13.1	17.4	15.3	8.7	11.9	9.3	4.2	5.3	4.0
Tranquilizers[d]	4.5	6.0	7.1	2.7	4.0	4.4	1.2	1.7	1.8
Steroids[e]	2.0	2.0	2.3	1.0	1.2	1.5	0.6	0.6	0.7
Alcohol	54.5	70.5	80.7	45.3	63.5	73.7	24.6	38.8	51.3
Been Drunk[e]	25.3	46.9	63.2	18.4	38.5	52.5	8.3	20.8	33.2
Cigarettes	46.4	57.6	64.2	——	——	——	19.1	27.9	33.5
Smokeless Tobacco[f]	20.0	27.6	30.9	——	——	——	7.1	9.7	12.2

Note: Approximate numbers of cases are 17,500, 17,000, and 15,400, respectively, for grades 8, 10, and 12. Dashes indicate data not available. From the Monitoring the Future Study, University of Michigan.

[a]For 12th graders only: Use of "any illicit drugs" includes any use of marijuana, LSD, other hallucinogens, crack, other cocaine, or heroin, or any use of other opiates, amphetamines, barbiturates, or tranquilizers not under a doctor's orders. For 8th and 10th graders only: The use of other opiates and barbiturates is not included, because these younger respondents appear to overreport use (perhaps because they include the use of nonprescription drugs in their answers).

[b]For 12th graders only: Data based on five of six forms; N is 5/6 of N indicated.

[c]For 12th graders only: Data based on four of six forms; N is 4/6 of N indicated.

[d]Only drug use that was not under a doctor's order is included here.

[e]For 12th graders only: Data based on two of six forms; N is 2/6 of N indicated.

[f]For 8th and 10th graders only: Data based on one of two forms; N is _ of N indicated. For 12th graders only: Data based on one of six forms. N is 1/6 of N indicated.

Inhalants

Although marijuana is the most prevalent illicit substance, inhalants (which are not themselves illicit drugs, but are used for illicit purposes) have a higher lifetime prevalence among 8th graders than marijuana. In fact, lifetime prevalence of inhalants is higher among 8th graders than among 10th graders and 12th graders. This seemingly anomalous phenomenon of lower lifetime prevalences among younger students can occur for any of several reasons. One is that there could be cohort effects such that more recent birth cohorts have higher rates of use than slightly older cohorts.

Another is that there could be denial—deliberate or not—at the higher grade levels of use. A third is that the difference in population coverage, primarily due to dropping out of school but also due to absenteeism, could account for the difference. And of course, there could be a mixture of these factors. In the present situation, the third explanation is probably most important. Specifically, because perhaps 15% of 8th graders will drop out of school before finishing their senior year, and because those who use inhalants at an early age are more likely to drop out, the difference in population covered may be the primary reason for the seemingly anomalous result.

Amphetamines

Amphetamines are used by substantial portions of American secondary school students: 15%, 17%, and 13% of 12th, 10th, and 8th graders, respectively, have tried them at some time. Note that a higher percentage of 10th graders report having tried amphetamines than 12th graders. As with the inhalants, the most likely reason for this is that some 10th graders drop out of school before finishing 12th grade.

Hallucinogens

Hallucinogens, including LSD and other hallucinogens, have been used by 13% of 1995 seniors, 9.3% of 10th graders, and 5.2% of 8th graders. The corresponding figures for LSD specifically are 12%, 8.4%, and 4.4%. Given the potentially devastating effects that strong hallucinogens such as LSD could have on a developing brain, these percentages are unfortunately high.

Cocaine

Use of cocaine has declined from its peak years, but it is still very much a part of the drug scene among students. Percentages having ever used it are 6.0%, 5.0%, and 4.2% for grades 12, 10, and 8 respectively. Most of this use is cocaine in powder form (usually sniffed), rather than in crack form (usually smoked).

Heroin

Heroin use shows an inverse relationship with grade level. Lifetime use is highest among 8th graders (2.3%) and lower in the 10th (1.7%) and 12th (1.6%) grades. The explanation for this is likely due to dropouts, who come disproportionately from heavier users.

Tranquilizers

Nonmedical use of tranquilizers is not uncommon: 7.1% of seniors, 6.0% of 10th graders, and 4.5% of 8th graders report having used a tranquilizer for nonmedical reasons.

Anabolic Steroids

Less than 3% of students report ever having used an anabolic steroid, and less than 2% used a steroid in the past 12 months.

LEGAL DRUGS

Alcohol

Alcohol use is widespread. Within just the past 30 days, about half the seniors (51%), 2 in 5 (39%) of 10th graders, and 1 in 4 (25%) 8th graders have drunk alcohol. A more important measure is use of alcohol to the point of intoxication. Fully a third (33%) of seniors report having been drunk in the past 30 days, 1 in 5 (21%) 10th graders, and 1 in 12 (8.3%) 8th graders. Note that, among those who drank at all in the past 30 days, the proportion who became intoxicated rose with age. A third of the 8th graders who drank became intoxicated, compared to about half of the 10th graders, and two thirds of the 12th graders.

Tobacco

Very substantial minorities of American students were smokers in 1995, more than 30 years after the Surgeon General's declaration that smoking causes lung cancer and other diseases. Among 12th graders, 34% reported having smoked at least one cigarette in the past 30 days; for 10th and 8th graders, the corresponding figures are 28% and 19%. A substantial proportion of students used smokeless tobacco instead of, or in addition to, smoking cigarettes. The 1995 figures for current use among 12th, 10th, and 8th graders were 12%, 10%, and 7%, respectively. However, because there was considerable overlap in users of both forms of tobacco, the combined total tobacco users was only 2% to 5% higher than for smoking only.

MORE FREQUENT USE

Any use of substance by adolescents is problematic, but even more problematic is frequent or heavy use. Table 2.2 provides an indication of the percentages who use at levels that would certainly be considered more serious. About 1 in 22 (4.6%) high school seniors reported that they had used marijuana on 20 or more days in the past 30 days, or essentially on a daily or near-daily basis. This means that the average classroom would have one or two seniors who were using marijuana daily, a serious impediment to learning. The figures are lower for 10th and 8th grades, under 3% and under 1%, respectively.

Alcohol, though used by many students, is rarely used on a daily basis. Indeed, the figures are (slightly) lower than those for daily use of marijuana. Heavy drinking, on

Table 2.2   Prevalence of More Serious Substance Use behaviors 8th, 9th, and 10th Graders, 1995

Grade	8th	10th	12th
Approximate N	17,500	17,000	15,400
Marijuana/Hashish			
Daily use	0.8	2.8	4.6
Alcohol			
Daily use	0.7	1.7	3.5
5+ drinks in last 2 weeks	14.5	24.0	29.8
Cigarettes			
Daily use	9.3	16.3	21.6
½ pack+/day	3.4	8.3	12.4
Smokeless Tobacco [a]			
Daily use	1.2	2.7	3.6

Note: Entries are percentages. From the Monitoring the Future Study, the University of Michigan.

[a]For 8th and 10th graders only: Data based on one of two forms; N is _ of N indicated. For 12th graders only: Data based on one of six forms. N is 1/6 of N indicated.

the other hand, is very prevalent. Nearly a third of seniors (30%) report having had five or more drinks in a row at least once in the past 2 weeks. The rates for 8th and 10th graders are likely exaggerated, based on the proportion who report being drunk at least once in the past 30 days; nevertheless the proportion getting drunk suggests considerable drinking to excess.

Cigarettes are used on a daily basis (one or more cigarettes per day in the past 30 days) by substantial minorities: 9%, 16%, and 22% of 8th, 10th, and 12th graders. Roughly half of the 10th and 12th graders who smoke daily smoke one half a pack or more per day. About one third of 8th-grade daily smokers are at that level. As noted previously, there is some additional tobacco use in the form of smokeless tobacco, with 1% to 4% of students using it on a daily basis.

MULTIPLE DRUG USE

One important aspect of adolescent drug use is the degree to which multiple substances are used. Figure 2.1 documents that many adolescents are using more than one substance. Counting only the following nine substances—marijuana, inhalants, hallucinogens, cocaine, heroin, amphetamines, tranquilizers, alcohol, and cigarettes—the figure shows that even among 8th graders, 16% used two or more substances in just the past 30 days. Among 10th and 12th graders, the corresponding numbers are 27% and 33%. Three or more substances were used by 8%, 13%, and 15%, respectively. These are remarkably high numbers, considering that the behaviors are illegal and in many cases put these adolescents very much at risk for some serious consequences.

With that much multiple drug use occurring, there is very likely to be a high degree of association among the various substances, including the legal and illegal substances. Figure 2.2, 2.3, and 2.4 provide the percentages of 10th graders in 1995 who used selected substances according to whether they used one of the "gateway" substances, cigarettes, alcohol, and marijuana. (In order to make the figure more readable, only 10th graders are charted. Tenth graders were chosen because they include most dropouts and their use rates are higher than those of 8th graders.)

Among 10th graders who smoked one or more cigarettes in the past 30 days, 73% also used alcohol in that period, a rate that is almost 3 times higher than among those who did not smoke any cigarettes (26% of whom had used alcohol). The association of cigarettes with marijuana is even stronger: more than 2 of 5 (43%) cigarette smokers

Figure 2.1   Number of Drugs Used in Past 30 Days

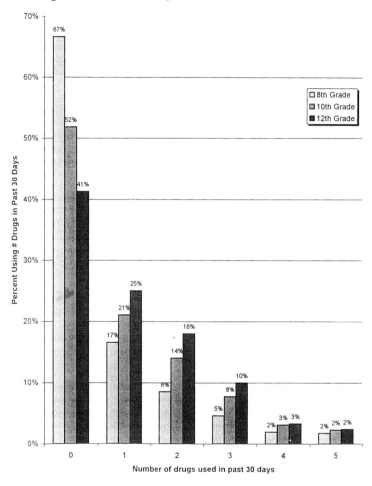

Source: The Monitoring the Future Study, The University of Michigan.

had also used marijuana in the past 30 days, compared to 7% of nonsmokers, a ratio of about 6 to 1. The link is higher still with use of cocaine in the past 12 months: 9.9% versus 1.0%, a ratio of about 10 to 1. The association between cigarette use and inhalant use (past 30 days) is also very strong, with 8.2% of smokers using inhalants compared to 1.7% of nonsmokers (a ratio of almost 5 to 1). Alcohol shows similarly strong relationships with marijuana and cocaine use, as Figure 2.3 demonstrates. Tenth graders who used alcohol in the past 30 days are substantially more likely to have used cigarettes, marijuana, and cocaine, and inhalants. There is a particularly high correspondence between marijuana use and cocaine use among 10th graders: 16% of marijuana users also used cocaine, compared to 0.8% of nonusers of marijuana (ratio of about 20 to 1). The associations among the various substances are strongly evident among 8th and 12th grade students, as well.

Figure 2.2   Percent Cigarette User/Nonuser Who Use Other Drugs

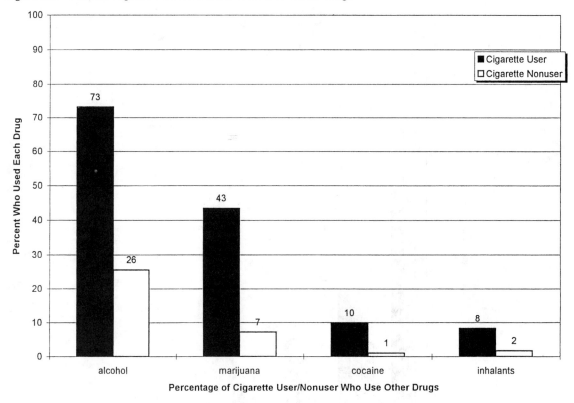

Source: The Monitoring the Future Study, The University of Michigan.

USE AMONG SUBGROUPS

Table 2.3 provides information on the variation of drug use by race and gender subgroups among 10th graders. Tenth-grade students were chosen for presentation here because there is much less use at the 8th grade level, and therefore less variation between subgroups. Twelfth-grade data suffer from the loss of high school dropouts as well as higher rates of absenteeism, and therefore subgroup comparisons are somewhat confounded. In 1993, an estimated 10% of White, non-Hispanic 21–22-year-old Americans had not completed high school, 16% of Black non-Hispanics, and 37% of Hispanics (McMillen, Kaufman, & Whitener,

1994). Because of relatively small numbers of cases in most racial/ethnic subgroups, only Whites, Hispanics, and African Americans are included in the table. (See Bachman et al., 1991, for a description of drug use rates among other racial/ethnic groups.) Figure 2.5 provides a graphic display of monthly prevalence for selected substances.

The various substances show some variation in the patterning of differences. Use of any illicit drug in the past 12 months was about equal between white males and females (30 to 31%), slightly higher among Hispanic students (32% for each gender), and distinctly lower among African American males (22%) and females (17%).[3] Across the individual illicit drugs (marijuana, hallucinogens, cocaine,

---

[3]A question that is sometimes raised regarding racial/ethnic differences in reported rates is whether the differences may be due to

differential validity of reporting; Wallace and Bachman (1993) discuss various potential reasons for the differences and conclude that, most likely, the differences are valid.

Figure 2.3   Percent of Alcohol User/Nonuser Who User Other Drugs

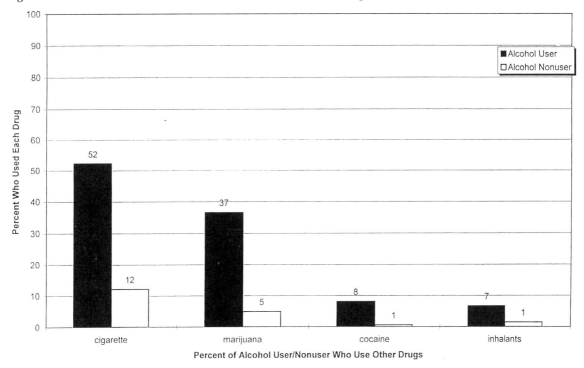

Source: The Monitoring the Future Study, The University of Michigan.

heroin, and steroids), male 10th graders tended to be higher than females in all three race/ethnic groups.

Marijuana use was highest among Hispanic males (27%), followed by White males (24%) and Hispanic and white females (21%); African American males were slightly lower at 18%, and African American females were lowest at 9%.

In contrast, the drugs available by prescription (amphetamines and tranquilizers) were used at higher rates by females in all three race/ethnic groups (except for tranquilizers among African Americans). It is the higher rates of nonmedical use of these prescription drugs that produce the basically equal rates of annual use of illicit drugs by male and female 10th graders.

Alcohol was used in the past 30 days by more males than females within each of the three race/ethnic groups. About half of the White students who were current drinkers (that is, they used alcohol in the past 30 days) had also gotten drunk at least once in that period. Slightly under half of the Hispanic students who were current

drinkers had gotten drunk. Among African American students, however, the proportion of current drinkers who reported getting drunk was distinctly lower: about 40% of males and 30% of females. In other words, African American students not only had a lower than average rate of drinking, but even among those current drinkers, a relatively low proportion drank to the point of intoxication.

Tobacco use shows a very wide variation by gender and racial/ethnic category. Cigarettes were used at least once in the past month by 27% and 28% of White 10th graders of both genders, compared to only 8% of African American females, and 10% of African American males. Hispanic students were in between. Smokeless tobacco (not shown in the table) is primarily a male activity, with use among White males being much higher than either Hispanic or African American males. The pattern of 30-day marijuana use is similar to the 12-month pattern, with Hispanic male students being highest, followed by White male students; African American females are lowest.

Figure 2.4   Percent of Marijuana User/Nonuser Who Use Other Drugs

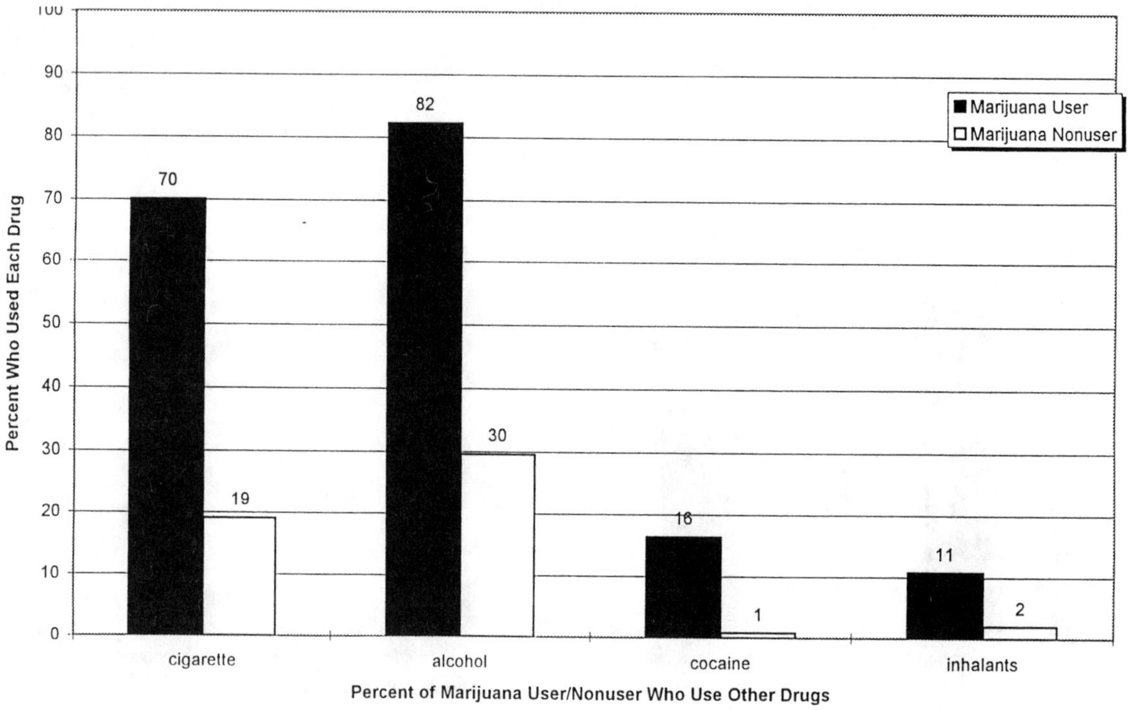

Source: The Monitoring the Future Study, The University of Michigan.

Summary of Race/Ethnic and Gender Differences

A variety of patterns are associated with race and gender groups and substance-use behaviors. Generally, Hispanic and White usage rates are similar, with both being somewhat higher than the rate for African Americans. Use of the major illicit drugs (marijuana, hallucinogens, cocaine) tends to be highest among Hispanic and White males, followed by Hispanic and White females, then African American males, and finally, African American females. Illicit use of psychoactive prescription drugs is higher among Hispanic and white students than among African American students, but in these cases use is equal or higher among females compared to males. Cigarette use is much higher among White students of both genders (and roughly equal for males and females), compared to African-American students; Hispanic students are intermediate. Smokeless tobacco use is concentrated among males, particularly White males. Anabolic steroid use is also concentrated among males.

USE AT EARLIER GRADES

Although 8th graders are the youngest respondents who are included in the Monitoring the Future surveys, an indication of use rates at earlier grade levels is made possible by questions that ask the 8th graders about the grade in which they first used each drug. Table 2.4 provides information on use by 6th, 7th, and 8th grades, based on responses of 8th-grade students in 1995. About 30% of those students initiated alcohol use in 6th grade (when they would be 11–12 years old) or earlier. Almost that many had smoked their first cigarette (29%), and 4% had already begun smoking on a daily basis. Ten percent had at least tried smokeless tobacco. About 1 in 12 (7.8%) had already gotten drunk by 6th grade, and another 9% did so in 7th grade.

Table 2.3 Annual Prevalence of Selected Substances 10th Graders, 1991–1994 Combined, by Race/Ethnicity and Gender

	White		*Hispanic*		*African-American*	
	Male	*Female*	*Male*	*Female*	*Male*	*Female*
Approximate N =	26,170	26,670	3,260	3,470	3,920	4,680
Any Illicit Drug[a]	30.0	30.6	32.2	32.3	22.4	17.1
Marijuana	23.6	20.5	27.2	21.0	17.6	9.4
Inhalants	10.2	8.8	7.8	7.7	2.7	3.7
Hallucinogens	6.7	5.1	5.2	4.6	1.0	0.3
Cocaine	2.6	2.3	5.0	4.1	1.0	0.5
Heroin	1.0	0.6	0.7	0.7	0.7	0.2
Amphetamines[b]	9.1	12.7	6.3	8.9	3.0	3.6
Tranquilizers[b]	3.5	4.3	2.1	4.1	0.9	0.8
Alcohol	69.2	69.5	67.2	68.2	58.5	56.3
Steroids	1.8	0.3	1.9	0.5	1.3	0.3

Note: Entries are percentages. From the Monitoring the Future Study, the University of Michigan.

[a]Use of "any illicit drug" includes any use of marijuana, hallucinogens, cocaine, heroin, or any use of amphetamines or tranquilizers not under a doctor's orders.

[b]Includes only use that is not under a doctor's orders.

Figure 2.5 Thirty-day Prevalence of Selected Behaviors, by Race/Ethnicity and Gender

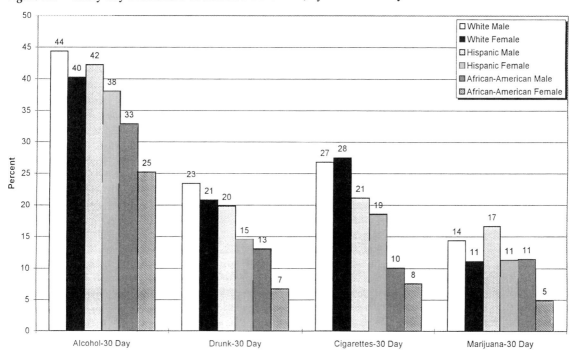

Source: The Monitoring the Future Study, The University of Michigan.

Table 2.4   Grade of First Use for 8th Graders, 1995

	Grade in which drug was first used			*Ever Used*
	6th	7th	8th	
Alcohol	29.6	15.6	9.3	54.5
Got Drunk	7.8	9.1	8.4	25.3
Cigarette (any)	28.5	12.4	5.5	46.4
Cigarette (daily)	3.9	4.3	3.4	11.6
Smokeless Tobacco	10.1	6.5	3.4	20.0
Marijuana	5.3	7.4	7.2	19.9
Inhalants	11.6	6.1	3.9	21.6
Hallucinogens	1.2	1.7	2.3	5.2
LSD	1.0	1.6	1.8	4.4
Cocaine	1.1	1.4	1.7	4.2
Crack Cocaine	0.6	1.0	1.1	2.7
Powder Cocaine	0.8	1.1	1.5	3.4
Heroin	0.6	0.8	0.9	2.3
Amphetamine	3.3	4.7	5.1	13.1
Tranquilizer	1.4	1.8	1.3	4.5
Anabolic Steroids	0.9	0.6	0.5	2.0

Note: Entries are percentages. Percentages are based on approximately 8,750 cases for hallucinogens, LSD, heroin, amphetamines, tranquilizers, and smokeless tobacco, and approximately 17,500 for the remaining drugs. Source: The Monitoring the Future Study, the University of Michigan.

Inhalants are particularly likely to be used at an early age, with 1 in 8 (12%) reporting sniffing inhalants to get high by 6th grade. Five percent had used marijuana at that early age, with another 7% using in each of 7th and 8th grades. Amphetamines were the other substance used by more than 3% by 6th grade.

TRENDS IN USE

The prevalence figures noted in this chapter thus far indicate that the problem of drug use among American secondary school students in 1995 is a severe one. But the problem is not static. The drug problem changes, sometimes dramatically, over time.

Among American high school seniors, the problem, defined in terms of illicit drug use, increased very rapidly in the 1960s and 1970s, reaching a peak in the late 1970s. The decade of the 1980s showed a considerable diminution in illicit drug use, particularly the most popular drug, marijuana. Alcohol use, including heavier use, also declined,

though not as dramatically. Tobacco use was steady overall, though there was a sharp decline in tobacco use among African American seniors.

The decade of the 1990s presents a very different picture: illicit drug use is up substantially among secondary students. Figures 2.6, 2.7, 2.8, and 2.9 show the recent trends for selected substances for 8th-, 10th-, and 12th-grade students. Marijuana use is up substantially, by a factor of 45% among 12th graders, 74% among 10th graders, and 155% among 8th graders (Figure 2.6). Use of inhalants is also up substantially, by factors of 20% to 40% (Figure 2.7). Cigarette use is up sharply, particularly among the younger students, with both 8th and 10th graders showing increases of 34% (Figure 2.8). The prevalence of getting drunk has also begun to increase, but much less sharply (Figure 2.9). All of the behaviors in Figures 2.6, 2.7, 2.8, and 2.9, can reasonably be called "abuse." Sniffing glue or other volatile substances for the purpose of getting high; drinking alcohol to the point of intoxication; smoking cigarettes; and smoking an illegal psychoactive substance by youngsters not yet in high school are all behaviors that can cause significant problems for the developing adolescent. These trends clearly demonstrate that the problem of youthful drug use has not been solved. Indeed, the data indicate a need for increasing the effort to understand the causes of drug use (and drug abuse).

OTHER POPULATIONS

The discussion in this chapter has focused on quantitative measures of use among student populations. There are two variations that can be mentioned: more qualitative or categorical measures of abuse or dependence disorders, and populations other than students.

With respect to the issue of measures of abuse or dependence disorders, there is considerable interest and research activity focused on improvement of clinical assessment procedures for adolescents (Rahdert & Czechowicz, 1995). However, epidemiological data on the extent of adolescent abuse and dependence disorders is lacking (Newcomb, 1995). One recent study did assess the degree of DSM category disorders in a nationally representative sample that included the age range from 15 to 59 (Warner, Kessler, Hughes, Anthony, & Nelson, 1995), but because the study design contained relatively few respondents in the age range from 15 to 18, any statements about the extent of such disorders are subject to large sampling errors. Moreover, the study used standard adult diagnostic interviews for all the respondents, which may not be optimal for the adolescents.

With respect to the issue of nonstudent populations, this too is of considerable interest and concern. Dropouts are thought to be at higher risk for drug use and abuse, and that is almost certainly true. However, the extent to which dropouts are thought to be at greater risk may perhaps be exaggerated. Many individuals who choose to leave school prior to graduation are not more deviant than those who stay. Some leave because they need to help support their family; others because they realize they will not be going on to college, and they wish to get on with their occupational career; others because they have become or are about to become parents. Many of these individuals are at no higher risk of becoming drug abusers than those who stay in school. (See Fagan & Pabon, 1990, for a study comparing dropouts with stay-ins among a sample of inner-city youth; this study shows that the usual assumption that dropouts invariably use drugs more than students

is not always true.) Of course, many dropouts are more deviant than stay-ins; moreover, becoming involved with drugs at an early age tends to lead to poor academic performance, and higher rates of dropping out (Krohn, Thornberry, Collins-Hall, & Lizotte, 1995; Mensch & Kandel, 1988).

Other groups of nonstudent adolescents are almost surely at very high risk: these include runaways and homeless adolescents (Rotheram-Borus, Parra, Cantwell, Gwadz, & Murphy, 1996). There is very little epidemiological data on drug use and abuse among representative samples of such individuals.

CONCLUSION

During the period from the late 1970s to the early 1990s, there was considerable improvement in the rates of substance abuse among American adolescents. Use of illicit drugs in general was down quite sharply from peak levels in the late 1970s (for marijuana) or the mid-1980s (for cocaine). Use of the legally available drugs, alcohol and tobacco, did not change very much after the early 1980s, although the trend for alcohol was down very gradually. The decrease in initiation meant that there were fewer adolescents beginning what could become a progression into serious drug involvement for some of them. Unfortunately, this favorable trend reversed, sharply and dramatically in the early 1990s, and through 1995 the trend lines were headed back up for several drugs, including tobacco, marijuana, inhalants, and some other drugs as well (Johnston et al., 1996). These disturbing trends demonstrate that the problems of adolescent drug abuse are very far from having been solved.

Solutions to the problems will be easier to find and to apply if we have a better understanding of the causes of drug use and abuse. A great deal of progress has been made in recent years in understanding the etiology of drug use (Glantz & Pickens, 1992). Epidemiology has an important role to play in helping to further our understanding. For example, epidemiological research has provided an important source of information regarding the etiology of drug use and the social attitudes and norms pertaining to drug use. Data from the Monitoring the Future study have been used to demonstrate a close link between certain attitudes or beliefs about drugs and use of those drugs. In particular, a measure of perceived risk associated with use of marijuana or cocaine seemed to covary quite closely with actual

Figure 2.6 Trends in Annual Prevalence of Marijuana Use

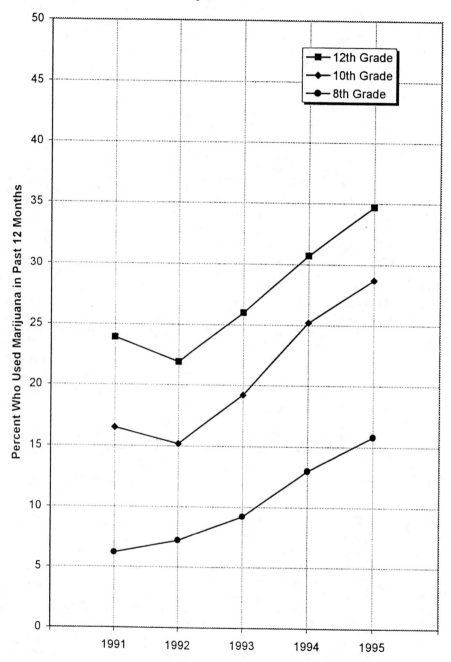

Source: The Monitoring the Future Study, The University of Michigan.

Figure 2.7   Trends in Annual Prevalence of Inhalant Use

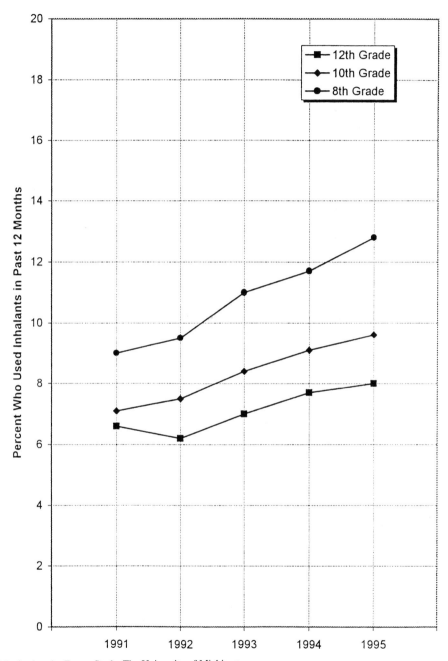

Source: The Monitoring the Future Study, The University of Michigan.

Figure 2.8   Trends in 30-day Prevalence of Cigarette Use

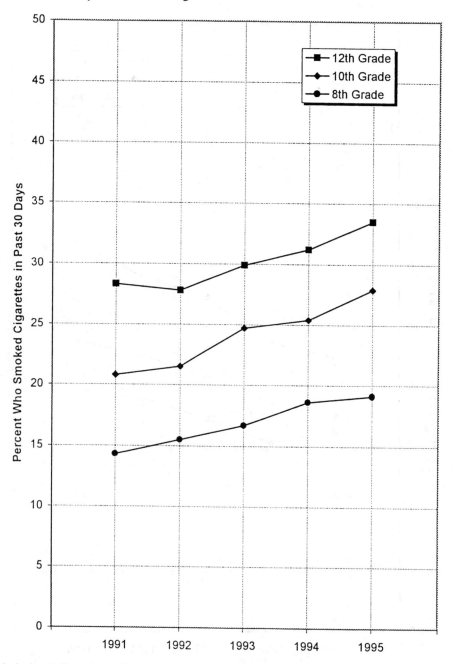

Source: The Monitoring the Future Study, The University of Michigan.

Figure 2.9   Trends in 30-day Prevalence of Getting Drunk

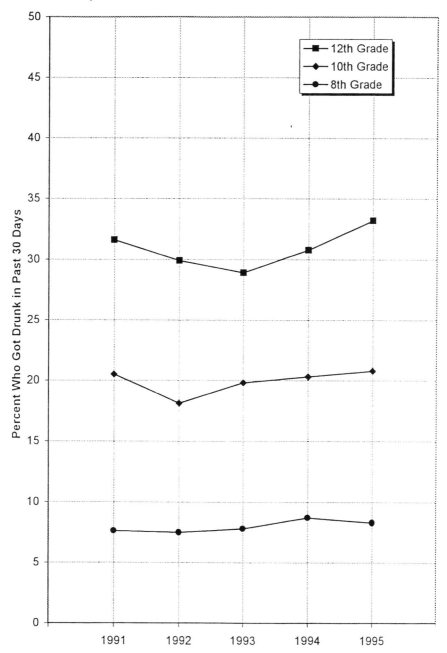

Source: The Monitoring the Future Study, The University of Michigan.

use of the specific drug. At the aggregate level, there is a very close association between perceived harm and use, and an extensive series of analyses of data at the individual level supported a causal interpretation of the belief–behavior link (Bachman, Johnston, & O'Malley, 1990; Bachman, Johnston, O'Malley, & Humphrey, 1988). A better understanding of the ways in which these social norms seem to influence drug use will help to determine ways to reduce drug use and abuse among adolescents. And of course there are many other factors that must be addressed as well.

AUTHOR NOTE

Patrick M. O'Malley, Survey Research Center, Institute for Social Research; Lloyd D. Johnston, Substance Abuse Research Center; Jerald G. Bachman, Substance Abuse Research Center.

This work was supported in part by Research Grant DA01411 from the National Institute on Drug Abuse.

Correspondence concerning this chapter should be addressed to Patrick M. O'Malley, Ph.D., Institute for Social Research, P.O. Box 1248, Ann Arbor, Michigan 48106.

REFERENCES

Bachman, J. G., Johnston, L. D., & O'Malley, P. M. (1990). Explaining the recent decline in cocaine use among young adults: Further evidence that perceived risks and disapproval lead to reduced drug use. *Journal of Health and Social Behavior, 31,* 173–184.

Bachman, J. G., Johnston, L. D., O'Malley, P. M., & Humphrey, R. H. (1988). Explaining the recent decline in marijuana use: Differentiating the effects of perceived risks, disapproval, and general lifestyle factors. *Journal of Health and Social Behavior, 29,* 92–112.

Bachman, J. G., Wallace, J. M., Jr., O'Malley, P. M., Johnston, L. D., Kurth, C. L., & Neighbors, H. W. (1991). Racial/ethnic differences in smoking, drinking, and illicit drug use among American high school seniors, 1976–1989. *American Journal of Public Health, 81,* 372–377.

Fagan, J., & Pabon, E. (1990). Contributions of delinquency and substance use to school dropout among inner-city youths. *Youth and Society, 21,* 336–354.

Gerstein, D. R., & Harwood, H. J. (Eds.). (1990). *Treating drug problems* (Vol. 1). Washington, DC: National Academy of Sciences.

Glantz, M. D., & Pickens, R. W. (Eds.). (1992). *Vulnerability to drug abuse.* Washington, DC: American Psychological Association.

Johnston, L. D., & O'Malley, P. M. (1985). Issues of validity and population coverage in student surveys of drug use. In B. A. Rouse, N. J. Kozel, & L. G. Richards (Eds.), *Self-report methods of estimating drug use: Meeting current challenges to validity* (NIDA Research Monograph 57). Washington, DC: National Institute on Drug Abuse.

Johnston, L. D., O'Malley, P. M., & Bachman, J. G. (1996). *National survey results on drug use from the Monitoring the Future study, 1975–1995: Vol. I. Secondary school students and Vol. II. College students and young adults.* Rockville, MD: National Institute on Drug Abuse.

Kaminer, Y., Bukstein, O., & Tarter, R. E. (1991) The Teen-Addiction Severity Index: Rationale and reliability. *International Journal of the Addictions 26,* 219–226.

Kolbe, L. J., Kann, L., & Collins, J. L. (1993). Overview of the Youth Risk Behavior Surveillance System. *Public Health Reports 108,* (Supplement 1), 2–10.

Krohn, M. D., Thornberry, T. P., Collins-Hall, L., & Lizotte, A. J. (1995). Family relationships, school dropout, and delinquent behavior. In H. B. Kaplan (Ed.), *Drugs, crime, and other deviant adaptations: Longitudinal studies* (pp. 163–183). New York: Plenum Press.

McMillen, M. M., Kaufman, P., & Whitener, S. D. (1994). *Dropout rates in the United States, 1993.* Washington, DC: National Center for Education Statistics.

Mensch, B., & Kandel, D. B. (1988). Dropping out of high school and drug involvement. *Sociology of Education, 61,* 95–113.

Newcomb, M. D. (1995). Identifying high-risk youth: Prevalence and patterns of adolescent drug abuse. In E. Rahdert & D. Czechowicz (Eds.), *Adolescent drug abuse: Clinical assessment and therapeutic interventions* (pp. 7–38 NIDA Research Monograph 156). Rockville, MD: National Institute on Drug Abuse.

O'Malley, P. M., Bachman, J. G., & Johnston, L. D. (1983). Reliability and consistency of self-reports of drug use. *International Journal of the Addictions, 18,* 805–824.

Rahdert, E., & Czechowicz, D. (Eds.). (1995). *Adolescent drug abuse: Clinical assessment and therapeutic interventions* (NIDA Research Monograph 156). Rockville, MD: National Institute on Drug Abuse.

Rogers, F. B. (Ed.). (1965). *Studies in epidemiology*. New York: Putnam Press.

Rootman, I., & Smart, R. G. (1985). A comparison of alcohol, tobacco, and drug use as determined from household and school surveys. *Drug and Alcohol Dependence 16*, 89–94.

Rotheram-Borus, M. J., Parra, M., Cantwell, C., Gwadz, M., & Murphy, D. A. (1996). Runaway and homeless youth. In R. J. DiClemente, W. B. Hansen, & L. E. Ponton (Eds.), *Handbook of adolescent health risk behavior* (pp. 369–392). New York: Plenum Press.

Skinner, H. A. (1995). Critical issues in the diagnosis of substance use disorders. In J. D. Blaine, A. M. Horton, & L. H. Towle (Eds.), *Diagnosis and severity of drug abuse and drug dependence*. (NIH Publication No. 95-3884) Rockville, MD: National Institute on Drug Abuse.

Substance Abuse and Mental Health Services Administration. (1995). *Preliminary estimates from the 1994 National Household Survey on Drug Abuse. Advance report number 10*. Rockville, MD: Substance Abuse and Mental Health Services Administration.

Wallace, J. M., & Bachman, J. G. (1993). Validity of self-reports in student-based studies on minority populations: Issues and concerns. In M. R. DeLaRosa & J. L. R. Adrados (Eds.), *Drug abuse among minority youth: Advances in research and methodology* (pp. 167–200, NIDA Research Monograph 130, NIH Publication No. 93-3479). Rockville, MD: National Institute on Drug Abuse.

Warner, L. A., Kessler, R. C., Hughes, M., Anthony, J. C., & Nelson, C. B. (1995). Prevalence and correlates of drug use and dependence in the United States: Results from the National Comorbidity Survey. *Archives of General Psychiatry 52*, 219–229.

CHAPTER 3

EPIDEMIOLOGY OF SUBSTANCE ABUSE IN ADULTHOOD

James C. Anthony
Amelia M. Arria

Given a concentration of public attention and resources on teenage smoking, underage drinking, and youthful consumption of other psychoactive drugs, it sometimes is easy to forget that the periods of risk for alcohol and drug dependence extend beyond the teen years. In many places, the peak levels of risk are reached after age 18. The best epidemiological estimates in the United States indicate that the risk of acquiring an alcohol or drug dependence syndrome in the young adult years is at a level of about 4% to 6% per year for 18–29 year-old-males and at a level of about 1% to 2% per year for 18–29-year-old females. Hence the force of morbidity associated with these alcohol and drug dependence syndromes carries forward toward the middle years of adulthood, and after that the levels of risk become quite low.

Consistent with these recent epidemiological estimates, the focus of this sourcebook chapter is the epidemiology of dependence on psychoactive drugs in adulthood, taking into account that caffeine, alcohol, and tobacco are the three most widely used psychoactive drugs. In passing, the chapter addresses related topics such as the epidemiology of psychoactive drug *use* and other selected adverse consequences of drug use that fall within the purview of population-based epidemiological studies (e.g., death by overdose).

Considering the full span of human experience from an individual's very first use of a drug, through the suffering associated with drug dependence, and ending with a terminal stage of death, we note a continuing controversy about dividing lines between abusive and nonabusive drug use. We also note some controversy about whether adulthood begins at age 18, at age 21, or later in the life course (e.g., as gauged in relation to adoption of adult social roles). For the purposes of this chapter, we prefer to leave resolution of these controversies to another time and place. We refrain from using the term "drug abuse" in favor of less judgmental terms such as "drug use" and "drug dependence." Moreover, we summarize evidence from epidemiological studies with samples that run a span of ages from the teen years into the late years of life, allowing readers to apply their own concepts of adulthood in relation to this span of ages.

This chapter is a presentation of basic descriptive findings about the epidemiology of psychoactive drug use and dependence, selected to help students, faculty members, and investigators who wish to evaluate the relative magnitude of problems associated with each drug or drug category (e.g., marijuana vs. cocaine vs. prescribed analgesic drugs or inhalant drugs). In another recent chapter (Anthony & Helzer, 1995), we presented material on the worldwide distribution of drug involvement and we summarized estimates from two decades worth of studies, but here we focus on two of the most recent epidemiologic surveys of drug use and drug dependence among adults living in the United States: (a) the 1994 National Household Survey on Drug Abuse, (U.S. Department of Health and Human Services, 1995) conducted as intramural research under the auspices of the Office of Applied Studies within the U.S. Substance Abuse and Mental Health Services Administration (SAMHSA); and (b) the National Comorbidity Survey (Warner, Kessler, Hughes, Anthony, & Nelson, 1995) conducted as extramural research between 1990 and 1992 under the auspices of the National Institute of Mental Health.

In order to reduce duplication of epidemiological evidence being presented in other chapters of this sourcebook and in our own prior review articles, this chapter concentrates on basic descriptive features of the epidemiology of psychoactive drug use and dependence in adulthood. As a result, we give a selective view of the scope of epidemiological evidence and the inferences that can be drawn from epidemiological data. In counterpoint, consider a perspective offered by one of the most prominent epidemiologists of the twentieth century, Wade Hampton Frost, who wrote that epidemiology at any given time is something more than the total of its established facts. It includes the orderly arrangement of facts into chains of inference that extend more or less beyond the bounds of direct observation. Such of those chains as are well and truly laid guide investigation to the facts of the future; those that are ill made fetter progress (Frost, 1936).

Readers who are interested in more than the basic descriptive findings of epidemiology as applied to drug use and drug dependence will want to read the other chapters of this sourcebook, where inferences about vulnerability and causes of drug use and drug dependence are sustained not only by evidence from epidemiological samples, but also by important data from laboratory, clinical, and high-risk research. Section I also points to pertinent and more comprehensive reviews of these topics (e.g., Adams, Gfroerer, & Rouse, 1989; Anthony, 1991; Anthony & Helzer, 1991, 1995; Fillmore, 1987; Kandel, 1991, 1992).

The last section of this chapter introduces some potentially fruitful directions for new research and points to some gaps in knowledge that can be filled with existing research tools. It also seeks to clarify the continuing public health significance of psychoactive drug use and dependence in adulthood during an era when most of the recent etiological and prevention studies have focused on adolescence and earlier stages of life course development.

BASIC DESCRIPTIVE EPIDEMIOLOGY OF PSYCHOACTIVE DRUG USE AND DEPENDENCE IN ADULTHOOD

This section of the chapter is intended to serve as an introduction to the descriptive epidemiology of adult drug use and drug dependence for each of the following drug categories: alcoholic beverages, tobacco, cannabis, cocaine, stimulants other than cocaine, psychedelics, anxiolytics, sedatives and hypnotics, analgesics, inhalants, heroin, and caffeine. In each of the subsections there is a review of the most recently published epidemiologic survey evidence on the age-specific and sex-specific prevalence of drug involvement, based primarily upon the 1994 National Household Survey on Drug Abuse (NHSDA) and the National Comorbidity Survey (NCS) conducted in 1990–1992. These results, from probability sample surveys of the U.S. population's drug experience of the 1990s, may or may not apply to other times and places. For example, this type of data on both drug use and drug dependence is not now readily available in more than a handful of countries.

Our estimates from the NHSDA are based on personal interviews and/or questionnaires administered to 17,809 individuals during the calendar year 1994. The survey participants were sampled from the noninstitutionalized population of the United States with a range of ages starting at 12 years. The age-specific curves in the figures are based upon our own analyses of the public-use data from the NHSDA, kindly made available by the SAMHSA Office of Applied Studies. In order to throw light on the age-specific variation in prevalence of drug use, we have used a regression model with a logistic link function and a scatterplot smoother (Statistical Sciences, 1994). These are weighted estimates that take into account variation in the probability of selection into the sample as well as poststratification adjustment so that the survey estimates for sociodemographic distributions are comparable to those of the most recent U.S. Census values for the U.S. population age 12 years and older. Details on the NHSDA survey methodology are provided in the codebook documentation for the public use data set and elsewhere (e.g., Lillie-Blanton, Anthony, & Schuster, 1994).

Estimates from the National Comorbidity Survey are based on personal interviews conducted between 1990 and 1992. The survey participants were sampled from the population of household residents in the United States with a range of ages from 15 to 54 years. The survey-based estimates are based on our previously reported analyses (e.g., Anthony, Warner, & Kessler, 1994; Warner et al., 1995).

These analyses also involved weighting and poststratification adjustment (e.g., to compensate for variation in household size and other determinants of each subject's probability of selection for the sample). Details on the NCS survey methodology are found in the publications just cited as well as in Kessler et al. (1994). Table 3.1 cites comparisons in survey data.

Incidence of Alcohol and Drug Dependence Syndromes

Before turning to a drug-by-drug review of prevalence estimates in adulthood, it may be helpful to review the only published estimates for the annual incidence of alco-

hol and drug dependence syndromes in adulthood, based on data gathered prospectively from an epidemiological sample in the United States (Eaton et al., 1989). These estimates, mentioned briefly in the introduction to this paper, derive from the NIMH Epidemiologic Catchment Area (ECA) surveys conducted in five metropolitan areas of the United States. In the ECA surveys, drug dependence was one of a number of mental disorders under study. To produce these estimates, more than 10,000 Americans were sampled, recruited, and studied over a 1-year period in the early 1980s. The case definitions for alcohol and drug dependence and related syndromes were based on the DSM-III diagnostic criteria, and the measurements were taken by personal interviews.

Table 3.1 Characteristics of and Prevalence Estimates Derived from Major Epidemiologic Surveys of Alcohol and other Drug Use and Dependence.

Survey Characteristics	National Comorbidity Survey		National Household Survey on Drug Abuse	
Sampling Strategy	National, stratified, multistage area probability same		National household sample	
Age Range	15–54		12+	
Number of respondents	8,098		Varies by year; 1994 = 17,809	

Specific Drugs	Lifetime Dependence	Dependence Among Users	Ever Used	Past Year Use
Alcohol	14.1	15.4	83.6	66.9
Tobacco	24.1	31.9	73.3	31.7
Any Illicit Drug[a]	7.5	14.7	34.4	10.8
Marijuana	4.2	9.1	33.7	8.5
Cocaine	2.7	16.7	11.3	1.7
Stimulants	1.7	11.2	6.0	0.7
Sedatives	1.2[b]	9.2[b]	3.4	0.4
Tranquilizers	[b]	[b]	4.6	1.1
Analgesics	0.7	7.5	6.8	2.0
Inhalants	0.3	3.7	5.3	1.1
Hallucinogens	0.5	4.9	8.7	1.3
Heroin	0.4	23.1	1.1	0.1

[a] Including nonmedical and extramedical use of prescribed drugs.

[b] Sedatives = anxiolytics, sedatives, and hypnotics.

Note: National Comorbidity Survey data from "Lifetime and 12 Month Prevalence of DSM-111R Psychiatric Disorders in the United States Results from the National Comorbidity Survey," by R. C. Kessler, K. A. McGonagle, S. Zhao, C. B. Nelson, M. Hughes, S. Eshleman, N. U. Wittshen, and K. S. Kendler, 1994, *Archives of General Psychiatry, 51,* pp. 8–19. National Household Survey data from Office of Applied Studies, Substance Abuse and Mental Health Services Administration.

Estimated in this fashion via epidemiological research in the United States, the mean probability of becoming a new case of alcohol disorder during 1 year of adulthood is 1.79% per year. For controlled drugs such as marijuana, cocaine, stimulants, or anti-anxiety medicines, the corresponding estimate is 1.09% per year.

Higher values were seen for men than for women in all adult age groups. For adult men, the risk of becoming a case of alcohol disorder during a 1-year period was estimated to be 3.67% per year. As for dependence or other mental disorders involving controlled drugs, risk for adult men was estimated to be 1.66% per year. The corresponding estimates for adult women were 0.61% and 0.66% per year of adulthood (i.e., for adult women, a greater risk to become dependent upon drugs like marijuana, amphetamines, or anti-anxiety drugs than to become dependent upon alcoholic beverages).

For both alcohol and other drugs, the highest risk values were observed among the youngest adults surveyed for the ECA study (i.e., among 18–24-year-olds). At these peaks, the level of risk was 2 to 3 times the mean risk estimates for all adults, all ages combined (Eaton et al., 1989).

Prevalence of Alcohol and Other Drug Involvement

Alcohol

Figure 3.1 depicts age-specific variation in the prevalence of recent beverage alcohol consumption (based on the 1994 NHSDA survey data for both sexes combined), and for males and females separately. Here, and in the other figures, these prevalence values are proportions and can be expressed as percentages. The numerator for each proportion is the estimated number of persons who consumed alcoholic beverages during the year just prior to assessment: this numerator includes persons who started drinking in the past year, as well as persons who started before

Figure 3.1   Age-specific variation in the prevalence of recent alcohol consumption.

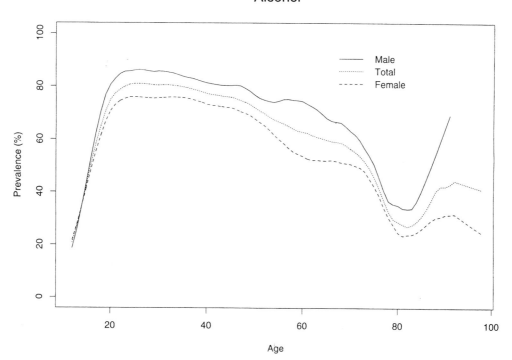

the past year and whose drinking persisted into this recent period. The denominator for each prevalence proportion includes all persons, without respect to their past or recent history of drinking.

Considering all ages and both sexes, an estimated 67% consumed alcoholic beverages during the year prior to survey. For males, the estimate is 72%, whereas for females, it is 62% (data not shown in a table).

Examining Figure 3.1, few readers will be surprised to see that some alcoholic beverage consumption occurs among the underage drinkers 12–17 years old and among the 18–20 year-olds as well. Peak prevalence values are observed in young adulthood and among middle-aged adults. The lower prevalence values in later life are well replicated and can be attributed in part to cessation of drinking or reduced drinking for health reasons (e.g., subjectively felt complaints such as disruption of sleep or gastrointestinal problems secondary to drinking). To be sure, alcohol-related mortality plays some role, but more so in relation to the prevalence of alcohol dependence than in relation to prevalence of drinking per se.

The upturn in the age-specific prevalence values that can be seen past age 80 deserves comment. Because the NHSDA sample includes a relatively small number of 80–100-year-olds (n=72), these estimates are unstable (i.e., statistically imprecise). Until replicated elsewhere, they should be regarded as no more than a possibly important lead to future research. Nonetheless, there is some supportive evidence on late-life drinking including some evidence of increased risk of alcohol dependence in late life, especially among males (e.g., Anthony & Aboraya, 1992; Eaton et al., 1989).

Prevalence estimates for alcohol dependence from the National Comorbidity Survey reflect a similar pattern by age: peak values are observed in the years of young adulthood and middle age. Specifically, an estimated 24% of household residents age 15–54 years are found to qualify as recently active or past cases of DSM-IIIR alcohol dependence. The estimated prevalence value during the adult years is 27%. By comparison, the estimated prevalence value for 15–24-year-olds is 15%. To some extent, the lower value for 15–24-year-olds is due to greater numbers of nondrinkers in this age group. However, it also is due to another phenomenon: namely, older adult drinkers have had more time to accumulate drinking experiences and problems and to have become cases, as compared to the younger drinkers. For example, among 15–24-year-olds who have started to drink alcohol, an estimated 24% have become cases of alcohol dependence. By compari-

son, among 25–34 year olds who have started to drink, an estimated 35% have become cases (Anthony et al., 1994).

The same sort of observation can be made about male–female differences in the occurrence of alcohol dependence. Women are somewhat less likely than men to be recent drinkers, and are more likely to be abstainers. However, among those who have started drinking, men are more likely to have developed alcohol dependence as compared to women: 32% of male drinkers have become cases as compared to 9% of female drinkers.

As new research throws light on these age-specific and sex-specific patterns of drinking and alcohol dependence, we can expect additional evidence on age, aging, and sex as manifestations of biological processes that account for variation in the risk and duration of these conditions. Some of these biological processes will be traced back to inherited characteristics (e.g., sex-linked traits, apoptosis). Some will be expressed or amplified via age-related and sex-related social and psychological processes, including those associated with gender roles and gender-linked performance expectations. As specific inherited or acquired markers of vulnerability are identified, it will become possible to test for the dynamic interplay of vulnerabilities and interpersonal or social contexts under an expectation that context is helping to shape the expression of these vulnerabilities, even when there is a strong genetic liability for alcohol dependence, and even when inherited traits have helped to shape the interpersonal and social contexts. To be sure, the rise and fall of drinking levels over the course of the twentieth century have been shaped as much by experiences such as the temperance movement and Prohibition as by any other single factor. These social and historical forces have conditioned the drinking and alcohol dependence prevalence estimates we observe in the mid-1990s in a variety of ways, but more among the elderly segment of the population, which accumulated personal experience with temperance and Prohibition, than among persons born more recently.

Due to space limitations, we can do little more than mention these vulnerability and risk factors for drinking and alcohol dependence in this chapter. Fortunately, elsewhere in this sourcebook, there is ample coverage of such gaps as we have left. Seriously interested readers will want to review this material for themselves in order to evaluate our judgment that no single discipline such as molecular biology, molecular genetics, psychology, sociology, anthropology, or history has the resolving power to meet the challenges represented in the age- and sex-specific prevalence curves for a complex disturbance such as alcohol dependence or even in a simpler behavior such as the persistence of drinking. Just as there is no simple way to summarize the personality traits or gender roles that promote drinking and the occurrence of alcohol dependence, we are unlikely to find a specific gene or gene product that by itself accounts for drinking behavior and its consequences. The strength of the individual disciplines can be expected to grow, but individually it will be insufficient for these challenges: truly interdisciplinary programs of research will be required.

Finally, before turning from alcohol to the other categories of psychoactive drugs, we will mention our judgment that drinking and alcohol dependence are not unique in their requirements for interdisciplinary approaches. What we have just stated about the alcohol research challenges applies as well to research on the characteristics, conditions, and processes that determine onset and persistence of drug taking and the onset and persistence of psychoactive drug dependence, no matter which drug is under

scrutiny. This conclusion holds but will not be restated in each of the subsequent sections of this chapter.

Tobacco

According to U.S. population estimates from the 1994 NHSDA, an estimated 32% of this population smoked tobacco cigarettes during the year prior to the survey. The corresponding estimate for males of all ages is 35%; for females, it is 29% (data not shown in a table).

The age-specific prevalence for recent tobacco smoking is depicted in Figure 3.2, where the NHSDA evidence on both sexes is combined. As with alcohol, there is considerable underage (illicit) smoking of tobacco; peak values for recent smoking are seen in young adulthood, with subsequent declines. (As observed in relation to alcohol, the estimates past age 80 are statistically imprecise and merit replication before they are regarded as definitive.)

Figure 3.2   Age-specific variation in the prevalence of recent tobacco use.

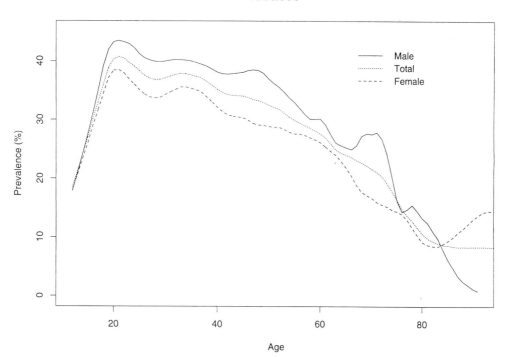

Looking across the sexes in Figure 3.2, it is possible to see evidence that women in some age groups have achieved parity or near parity with men in relation to tobacco smoking. As with alcohol, we must look to research from disciplines such as sociology, social psychology, and history if we are to understand the forces that account for variation in the sex ratio across the span of ages depicted in this figure (i.e., the ratio of male prevalence estimates to female prevalence estimates, which is close to 1.0 in many age categories).

The persistence of tobacco smoking is influenced heavily by the occurrence of tobacco dependence. Table 3.2 clarifies this point, showing that the NCS estimate for the proportion who have become cases of tobacco dependence (24%) is three quarters of the NHSDA estimate for the proportion who are recent smokers (32%). To some extent the age-specific prevalence values for tobacco dependence

echo those for recent tobacco smoking, and the differences are due mainly to nondependent users who smoke occasionally and also to tobacco dependence cases who have stopped smoking successfully.

Tobacco ranks above even cocaine and heroin when we consider the NCS cross-sectional and retrospective results on how many users have become dependent. As shown in Table 3.2, an estimated 32% of persons who started to smoke tobacco were found to have qualified as cases of tobacco dependence. As we show in later sections of this chapter, the corresponding values for cocaine and heroin are 17% and 23%, respectively (Anthony et al., 1994).

The only clear age-specific variation in the estimated probability of tobacco dependence among tobacco smokers is seen in relation to younger smokers. Among smokers age 15–24, an estimated 24% are found to qualify as former or currently active cases of tobacco dependence,

Figure 3.3   Age-specific variation in the prevalence of recent extramedical use of controlled substances and inhalant drugs.

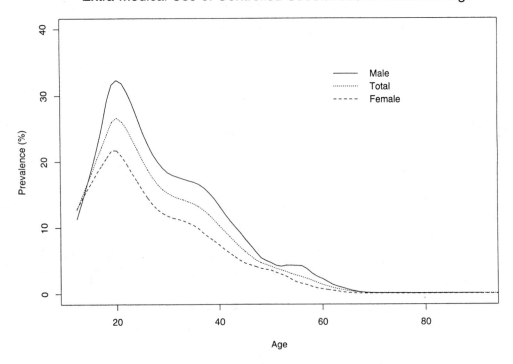

whereas among older smokers, the estimates are in the 33% to 35% range (Anthony et al., 1994).

In contrast with the evidence on alcohol, female smokers seem to be almost as likely as male smokers to progress to the stage of tobacco dependence. Among males who have started smoking, an estimated 33% have become cases of tobacco dependence. The corresponding value for females who have started smoking is 31% (Anthony et al., 1994).

Extramedical Use of Controlled Substances and Inhalant Drugs

In order to provide a summary overview for the extramedical use of controlled substances and inhalant drugs, we have created a combined category. Here, extramedical use is specified in relation to the definition provided elsewhere, and the numerators for the prevalence proportions refer to individuals who have engaged in extramedical use of any one or more of the following categories of psychoactive drugs: marijuana and other cannabis products (e.g., hashish); cocaine (including crack cocaine); amphetamines and other psychostimulants other than cocaine; anxiolytic, sedative, and hypnotic drugs (e.g., diazepam, secobarbital); analgesic drugs (e.g., propoxyphene, meperidine); LSD, PCP, and other psychedelic drugs; heroin; and inhalant drugs (e.g., volatile solvents, glue).

Based on the 1994 NHSDA estimates (Figure 3.3), the prevalence of recent extramedical drug use (i.e., use in the year prior to the survey) rises from about 11% to 12% at age 12–15 toward a peak of about 26% at age 20–22, and with declining values across subsequent age strata. The NHSDA found essentially no cases of extramedical drug use among persons aged 65 years and older, but the estimates were in the 1% to 5% range for persons between age 50 and 59 (Figure 3.3).

Figure 3.4 Age-specific variation in the prevalence of recent cannabis use.

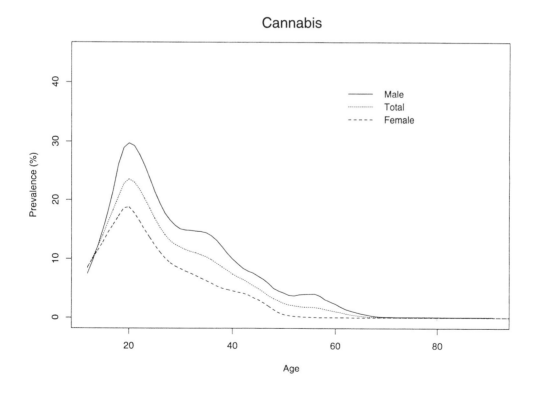

Except among the youngest teens surveyed and after middle age, the prevalence of recent extramedical drug use was estimated to be greater for males than for females. For example, the peak prevalence value for males was an estimate of 32% as compared to 22% for females, both observed at age 20–26 years (Figure 3.3).

The NCS found that approximately 7.5% of individuals met criteria for DSM-IIIR dependence on controlled drugs or inhalants. There is not much variation in this estimate by age in individuals 44 or younger (7.4% for 15–24-year-olds, 9.5% for 25–34-year-olds, and 8.5% for 35–44-year-olds); persons over 45, however, have a much lower prevalence value (2.9%). Dependence upon these drugs was much more common among men than women (9.2% vs. 5.9%); but the difference in the proportion of male and female users who became cases of dependence was not as great (16.4% vs. 12.6%).

Cannabis

Cannabis (marijuana, hashish) ranks as the most frequently used controlled substance in the United States population. In 1994, about 38% of the NHSDA population reported having ever tried marijuana, with 8.5% reporting that they had used it in the past year and 4.2% in the past 30 days. As can be seen in Figure 3.4, the highest prevalence of past year use of marijuana, based on the 1994 NHSDA results, is observed for young adults, with a peak at about 20 years of age for both males and females. Combining all ages and sexes, an estimated 8.5% of the U.S. population used marijuana in the year prior to being surveyed. This estimate was higher among males than females (11.3% vs. 5.9%).

Males were more likely than females to have reported marijuana use in the past year (11% vs. 6%). Continued use of marijuana, defined as use on at least 51 days during the past year, was reported by approximately 2.7% of the U.S. population in 1994. This estimate is down from 1985, when 4.6% of the population reported such use (U.S. Dept. of Health & Human Services, 1995). The age-specific prevalence estimates graphically depicted in Figure 3.4 indicate that the prevalence of past-year marijuana use, with few exceptions, shows a steady decline across the age categories from the early 20s onward.

The National Comorbidity Survey provides information about the proportion of males and females who qualify for a lifetime or current diagnosis of cannabis dependence, summarized in Table 3.1. The highest prevalence of cannabis dependence is observed in the 15–24-

year-olds (5.6%) followed by the 25–34 age group (5.0%). As would be expected, dependence is least common among adults over age 45 (0.8%). For all adults combined, the estimated lifetime prevalence is 4.2%.

Among cannabis users age 15–24 years, 15.3% have become cases of marijuana dependence in comparison to the middle adult age categories where just over 8% of users have become dependent (Anthony et al., 1994). Although it is tempting to speculate that this finding supports an increased vulnerability to problems due to marijuana smoking in the youngest age category, one must keep in mind other potential reasons for the discrepancy including methodological issues such as overreporting of problems by younger individuals and the lag time required to develop cannabis dependence after initial use.

Men are 2 to 3 times more likely to have developed cannabis dependence as compared to women (6.2% vs. 2.3%). Sharpening the focus to just those who are marijuana users, the same type of male excess can be seen: 12.0% of male users and 5.5% of female users have met criteria for dependence.

Cocaine

Based on the 1994 NHSDA survey of noninstitutionalized persons age 12 and older, an estimated 1.7% of the U.S. population engaged in cocaine use in the year prior to the survey. Approximately 60% of current cocaine users were young and middle-age adults in 1994. Figure 3.5 shows age-specific variation in the prevalence of past-year cocaine use, based on the data for both sexes combined and for males and females separately. The preponderance of male users in early and middle adulthood can be seen in the figure. Men have a little over twice the prevalence value as women (2.4% vs. 1.1%). Although it appears that the prevalence values increase slightly for men in their early 60s, this finding is due to a small number of cocaine users at this age and it is a statistically unstable estimate.

The findings from the National Comorbidity Survey on the prevalence of cocaine dependence reveal interesting patterns by age. In contrast to the situation with cannabis, where the highest prevalence values are in the 15–24 age group, the highest rate of cocaine dependence is observed for the 25–34-year-olds (4.2%). For all age groups combined, as shown in Table 3.1, an estimated 2.7% of adults qualify as current cases or as having a history of DSM-IIIR cocaine dependence. After age 45, the prevalence value for cocaine dependence is lower (0.5%).

Figure 3.5   Age-specific variation in the prevalence of recent cocaine use.

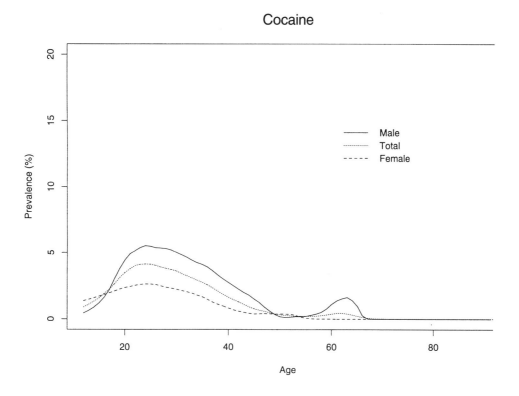

Among cocaine users, the youngest age category of 15–24 year olds was most likely to have become affected by cocaine dependence (24.5%) vs. the 25–34-year-old users (15.5%) and 35–44-year-old users (15.3%) (Anthony et al., 1994). This is the same pattern observed for cannabis, and as in that instance, the same type of concern about overinterpretation is warranted. These issues will be unresolved until methodologic studies are completed to examine whether younger individuals tend to overreport drug-related problems or whether they really do experience more problems related to their use of either marijuana or cocaine.

With regard to sex differences in cocaine dependence, the NCS estimates show a higher prevalence of dependence among males (3.5%) as compared with females (1.9%). In the same direction as this finding, male cocaine users are slightly more likely to become dependent as compared to female cocaine users (18% vs. 15%).

Psychedelic Drugs

According to the 1994 survey of the NHSDA population sample, an estimated 1.3% of the U.S. population reporting using psychedelic compounds in the year prior to survey. Figure 3.6 graphically shows the variation in prevalence estimates by age and sex. Although the scale on this graph is different from the scale on the marijuana graph, the shapes of these curves for psychedelic drugs are similar to those observed for marijuana, with males and females in their early 20s reporting the highest values of past-year use. The overall prevalence estimates are 1.9% for males and 0.7% for females.

The proportion of individuals either using or meeting criteria for dependence on psychedelic compounds is relatively low compared to other illicit drugs. The NCS estimates for all age groups combined is 0.5%, with 0.4% of men and 0.1% of women qualifying as DSM-IIIR cases of

Figure 3.6   Age-specific variation in the prevalence of recent use of psychedelics.

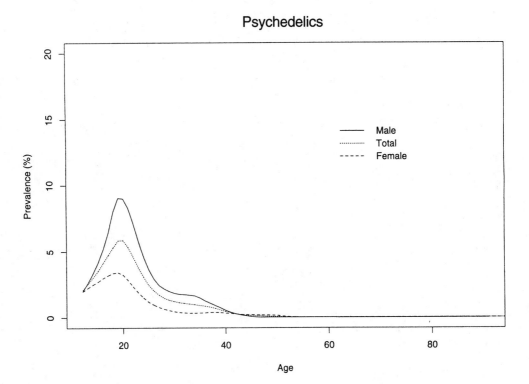

dependence. It is not surprising that the highest prevalence values are found among the younger age categories (0.7%, 0.7%, 0.5%, respectively) versus 0.02% of individuals age 45 and older. It may be important to note that many of the individuals reporting a sufficient number of problems to qualify them for a diagnosis of dependence on psychedelic drugs also qualify for a diagnosis of another type of drug dependence (Anthony et al., 1994).

The prevalence of dependence among male and female psychedelic users is essentially the same for both men and women. For male users, the NCS estimate is 5%; for female users, it is 4.7% (Anthony et al., 1994).

Inhalants

The NHSDA estimates that 1.1% of U.S. household residents age 12+ are current inhalant users. With regard to sex differences, males are twice as likely to be current inhalant users as females (1.4% vs. 0.7%). It is clear from Figure 3.7

that the majority of individuals reporting inhalant use in the year prior to being surveyed in the NHSDA are adolescents and young adults. More specifically, more than three quarters of users are 25 years old or younger.

The NCS data indicate that a very small proportion of adults living in households in the United States meet criteria for inhalant dependence. The overall NCS estimate for adults age 15–54 living in households in the United States is 0.5%, with men having higher rates than women (0.4% vs. 0.1%). The proportion of inhalant users qualifying as cases of dependence also is slightly higher among men (4.1% vs. 2.7% in women) and in the youngest age category (7.9% among 15–24-year-olds as compared to less than 3% in all other age groups surveyed).

Whereas some observers have regarded the use of inhalants to be an inconsequential "transitional" behavior, recent epidemiological evidence suggests otherwise. For example, analyzing cross-sectional survey data from the NHSDA, Schütz, Chilcoat, & Anthony (1994) found

Figure 3.7 Age-specific variation in the prevalence of recent inhalant use.

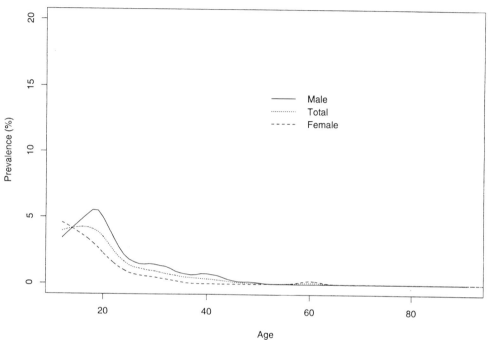

strong associations between inhalant use and later injection drug use. In a later study with a prospective research design, Johnson, Schütz, Anthony, & Ensminger (1995) found that inhalant use before age 17 was strongly associated with later occurrence of heroin use.

Anxiolytics, Sedatives, and Hypnotics

Overall, an estimated 1.3% of Americans age 12 and older living in households report extramedical use of one or more of the medically prescribed compounds we group together under the heading of anxiolytic, sedative, and hypnotic drugs ("ASH"). The age distribution for extramedical use of ASH drugs in the past year, based on the NHSDA data, is shown in Figure 3.8. The curve has several peaks, with the first cluster of users between the ages of 20 and 40 and the second cluster between ages 50 and 65. Although males and females do not differ in their prevalence of current ASH drug use, females

appear to have slightly higher peak prevalence values than males.

The NCS prevalence estimate for dependence on ASH drugs is greater in the over 45+ age category (1.6%) than in the two youngest age categories (0.2% in 15–24-year-olds and 1.1% in 25–34-year-olds). It was only slightly less than the estimate for the 35–44 age group (1.9%). Prevalence of dependence was slightly higher for females than males (1.4% vs. 1.0%). However, the proportion of users qualifying as cases of dependence is almost twice as high among females as males. Among male users, the proportion of users who developed dependence was 6.6%. Among female users, this estimate was 12.3%.

Amphetamines and Controlled Stimulant Drugs

Figure 3.9 illustrates age-specific variation in the prevalence of recent use of controlled stimulants (other than

Figure 3.8   Age-specific variation in the prevalence of recent anxiolytic, sedative, and hypnotic drug use.

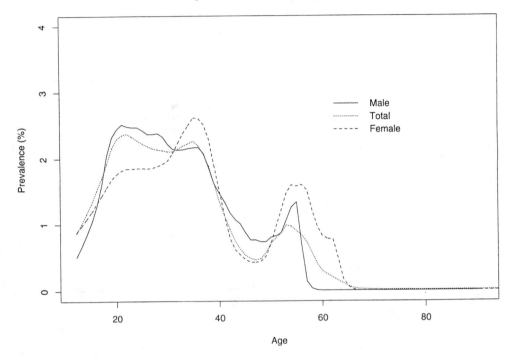

cocaine), based on the 1994 NHSDA survey data for males and females and both sexes combined. Less than one percent (0.7%) of individuals 12 and older reported using these stimulants in the year prior to the survey. Males had a slightly higher prevalence value across the lifespan (0.9% vs. 0.5%). Peak values for men can be seen around age 20 at the 2% level, whereas the peak value for women was lower, and occurred in the teen years. (The peak at age 55 in males appears to be a statistical artifact based on no more than a handful of users at this specific age.)

According to the NCS, an estimated 1.7% of 15–54-year-olds in the U.S. household population had become cases of stimulant dependence. As with cocaine, adults age 45 and over have the lowest prevalence value for stimulant dependence, with only 0.5% meeting criteria. As distinct from cocaine, the prevalence of stimulant dependence was similar for males and females (1.8% vs. 1.6%, respectively). Compared to male stimulant users, a somewhat higher proportion of female users meet criteria for dependence (9.7% vs. 13.3%).

Analgesics

According to the 1994 survey of the NHSDA population, an estimated 2.0% of individuals 12+ years and older are recent extramedical users of analgesic substances. Figure 3.10 shows the age-specific variation in past year use: the curve is fairly flat all along the span of ages, with peak values for males occurring in the early 30s and declining steadily thereafter.

Data from the National Comorbidity Survey reflect a different pattern of association between age and dependence for analgesic drugs than for most other drug categories. Congruent with the NHSDA evidence, the NCS data also show extramedical analgesic use in the years of middle adulthood. The NCS estimate for all 15–54 year olds was 0.7%, but was at the 1% level for adults age 35 years and older and was only 0.2% for 15–24-year-olds

Figure 3.9 Age-specific variation in the prevalence of recent use of controlled stimulants other than cocaine.

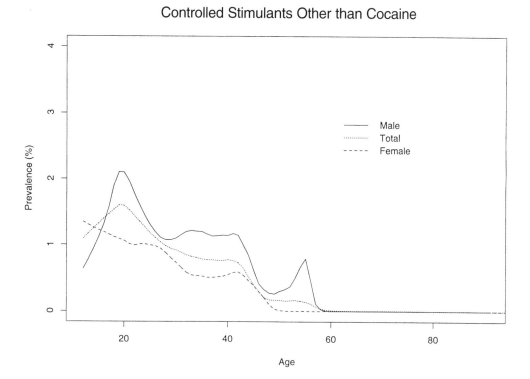

(Anthony et al., 1994). Among extramedical analgesic users, an estimated 1% was found to have become cases of DSM-IIIR dependence upon analgesics. For male users and female users, the corresponding estimates were 6.7% and 8.6%, respectively.

Heroin

The 1994 NHSDA data show a very low prevalence of recent heroin use in the noninstitutionalized population. Specifically, 0.1% of males and females reported using heroin in the past year; in the unweighted sample data, there were 59 recent heroin users, representing an age span from 12 to 60 years, with no cases past age 60. The smoothed estimates in Figure 3.11 reflect this relatively even age distribution of the users, as well as the absence of recent users in the later years of adult life. This rare occurrence of heroin use in late life most likely reflects a reduced survivorship of heroin users, although outside the United States and within some U.S. population subgroups, elderly heroin users are known to exist (e.g., in Southeast Asia and among Southeast Asian refugees in the United States).

Figure 3.11 shows some patterning of use by age in men, with peak values for men observed at age 40 and in the late 50s. The curve for women appears flatter, with women in early to middle adulthood having a prevalence of about 0.2%, and then dropping to almost zero thereafter. Nonetheless, the relatively small number of recent heroin users in this large epidemiological sample argues against firm conclusions about these patterns.

According to NCS estimates, dependence upon heroin is the least prevalent of all drug disorders in the United States population under study (0.4%); however, it ranks second to tobacco in terms of the proportion of dependence among users. Based on the NCS data, 23.1% of heroin users have become cases of heroin dependence.

To be sure, the NHSDA and NCS surveys of noninstitutionalized U.S. residents fail to capture the full

Figure 3.10   Age-specific variation in the prevalence of recent analgesic use.

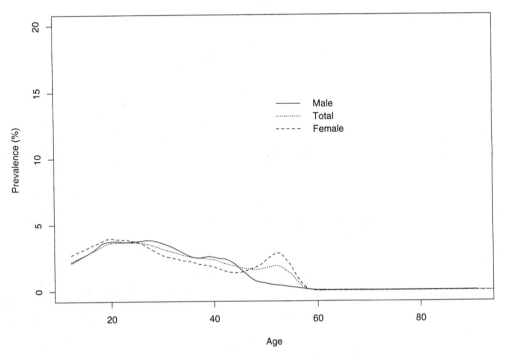

experience of heroin dependence in the population. This perhaps is a much greater problem in relation to heroin than for other drugs.

Caffeine

Epidemiologic data on caffeine use patterns among American adults are more scarce than data on alcohol and illicit drugs. On a per capita basis in the United States, caffeine is usually consumed in the form of coffee and tea with much lower levels of consumption of over-the-counter caffeine products. In 1976, as part of the Health Interview Survey, a representative cross-sectional sample of the noninstitutionalized population of the United States was asked questions about their use of coffee (Dept. of Health, Education, and Welfare, 1976). In this survey, 80% of adults age 20 and older reported having tried coffee, with coffee drinkers consuming an average of 3.2

cups each day. More than half of the people in their early 20s did not drink coffee or drank less than one cup per day. Heavy coffee drinking (five or more cups/day) was related in a curvilinear fashion to age, with heavy coffee drinking more common among middle-aged adults (35–54) than individuals either older or younger. Just over 25% of adults age 35–54 drank five or more cups per day, compared to 16.5% of 25–34-year-olds and 11.6% of 65–74-year-olds. Men were slightly more likely to drink coffee than women (81.4% vs. 78.7%) and to be heavy coffee drinkers (20.3% vs. 15.8%). A number of sociodemographic characteristics appeared to be associated with heavy coffee drinking; Whites reported more heavy coffee drinking than African Americans and individuals of other racial backgrounds (19.6% vs. 4.1% vs. 7.5%, respectively). Persons not in the labor force were less likely to be heavy coffee drinkers than any other occupational group. With respect to marital status, persons living with

Figure 3.11   Age-specific variation in the prevalence of recent heroin use.

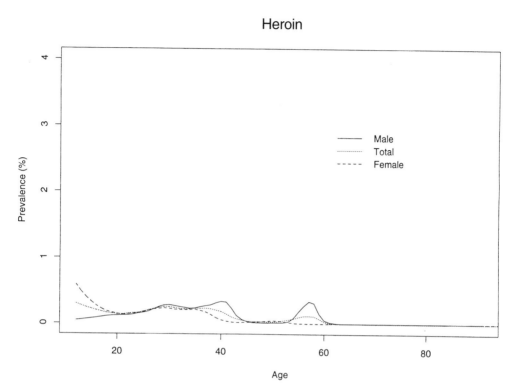

their spouses were the most likely to drink large amounts of coffee, regardless of sex or age.

A very recent review by Barone and Roberts (1996) provides data on the 14-day average daily intake of caffeine by age group and type of caffeine-containing product consumed. The data are taken from the 1975 and 1989 Nationwide Food Consumption Survey (NFCS) conducted for the U.S. Department of Agriculture and the 1989 Market Research Corporation of America (MRCA) database. Using 1989 MRCA estimates, the mean daily caffeine intake from all sources for adults age 25 and older was 2.3 milligrams per kilogram of body weight. The 1987–88 NFCS yielded estimates for a greater number of age categories, with the highest levels reported by 35–49-year-olds (9.9 mg/kg/day). Overall, the authors estimate that the mean daily caffeine intake for all U.S. adults in the general population is approximately 3 mg/kg, and for all adult consumers of caffeine containing products, approxi-

mately 4 mg/kg/day. For an average 70-kg individual, this amount would translate into approximately three cups of coffee per day. To our knowledge, the nature and extent of caffeine-dependence syndromes have not been investigated as part of national population surveys, and this is a limitation of current data that can be remedied quite readily in future research.

FORECAST

We forecast a sustained emphasis upon large-scale nationally representative cross-sectional epidemiological sample surveys in the United States and elsewhere, despite their clear limitations for answering the most challenging research questions that face this field. This prediction is based upon a sense that the drug involvement of youth and adults will continue to be treated as a sensitive political issue, responding more to policy initiatives of the administrations in power than to longer term processes that require attention over long spans of time and a succession of administrations. Given this political situation, there will be a continuing demand for basic descriptive statistics about drug taking, and due to linkages of this demand with decisions about budget appropriations process, epidemiologists will be pressed into duty to respond.

In recent years, the epidemiological research community has become more fortunate, in that now the data sets from some of these large-scale national surveys are made available for secondary analyses that can be used to throw light on more challenging research problems than those faced in the basic survey reports and tasks of basic descriptive epidemiology. There are clear limitations when analyzing data gathered for purposes other than to test specific hypotheses. Nonetheless, the results of these analyses can be used to guide the research plans used for new projects designed specifically to test these hypotheses.

Indeed, the advantages of creating these "public use" data sets are so great that doing so may become common practice. Some investigators regard their projects as a matter of public trust, and are pleased to turn the data set over to other investigators, once the primary hypotheses have been tested, and subject to provisions for protection of confidentiality. This is a trend to be encouraged. It is a practice that is well worth the relatively small amount of additional funding required to create and document a public use version of each study's data set.

As long as nationally representative surveys are required for political purposes, they will continue to require a large fraction of any national budget allocation for epidemiological research as applied to the study of drug involvement. Against this backdrop, there also should be important progress in relation to local area samples. Given renewed interest in the interactions of genes and environment along the causal pathways that lead toward continued drug use and risk of psychoactive drug dependence, some of this research will entail careful sampling and recruitment of twin study samples, informative pedigrees, deliberate samples of affected and unaffected siblings, and high-risk samples of the type already being studied by many epidemiologically oriented research groups. In a current burst of enthusiasm for molecular biology and genetics, it will be important to stress the translational character of this research agenda. That is, barring interventions such as gene replacement therapy, we must find the gene products that can be altered to change the risk of developing a dependence syndrome, and

we must find environmental conditions and processes that modify the inherited vulnerabilities that foster drug taking and the development of psychoactive drug dependence. Whereas hypotheses about these matters might surface in observational studies, the evidence for or against the hypotheses ultimately may rest upon randomized experiments with large population samples.

Given that the period of risk for developing alcohol and drug dependence extends into the years of middle adulthood and possibly into later years, there is ample reason to include adults in the samples for these epidemiological and etiological studies. Indeed, for many experimental intervention studies, it might be unethical to recruit pediatric samples or minors.

Finally, examining our most basic descriptive epidemiological estimates on the prevalence of drug taking, it is possible to see that psychoactive drug involvement persists through adulthood, even when the risk periods for developing alcohol and drug dependence are played out by the middle years of adulthood. Appearing in multiple studies, the apparent upturn in alcohol involvement and alcohol dependence in the retirement years deserves the attention of gerontologists who can help account for this nonlinear tendency of our estimates and indicate what interventions are needed, if any. A similar set of issues confronts epidemiologists concerned with the health of both women and men in the middle years of adulthood, where there is evidence of nonlinearities in the age-specific estimates, also deserving more detailed scrutiny. Whereas there is good reason to concentrate epidemiological research on the young adult years, where risk of serious drug involvement appears to be greatest, the health implications of extramedical drug use and alcohol consumption in these other age groups merits investigation as part of an overall plan for future epidemiological research.

REFERENCES

Adams, E. H., Gfroerer, J. C., & Rouse, B. A. (1989). Epidemiology of substance abuse including alcohol and cigarette smoking. *Annals of the New York Academy of Science, 562*, 14–20.

Anthony, J. C. (1991). The epidemiology of drug addiction. In N. S. Miller (Ed.), *Comprehensive handbook of drug and alcohol addiction* (pp. 55–86). New York: Marcel Dekker.

Anthony, J, C. & Aboraya, A. (1992). The epidemiology of selected mental disorders in later life. In J. E. Birren, R. B. Slane, & G. D. Cohen (Eds.), *Handbook of mental health and aging* (2nd ed., pp. 27–73). Orlando: Academic Press.

Anthony, J. C., & Helzer, J. E. (1991). Syndromes of drug abuse and dependence. In L. N. Robins & D. A. Regier (Eds.), *Psychiatric disorders in America* (pp. 116–154). New York: Free Press.

Anthony, J. C., & Helzer, J. E. (1995). Epidemiology of drug dependence. In M. T. Tsuang, M. Tohen, & G. Zahner (Eds.), Textbook in *Psychiatric epidemiology*. New York: Wiley-Liss.

Anthony, J. C., Warner, L. A., & Kessler, R. C. (1994). Comparative epidemiology of dependence on tobacco, alcohol, controlled substances and inhalants: Basic findings from the National Comorbidity Survey. *Experimental & Clinical Psychopharmacology, 2,* 244–268.

Barone, J. J., & Roberts, H. R. (1996). Caffeine consumption. *Food & Chemical Toxicology, 34,* 119–129.

Department of Health, Education and Welfare. (1976). *Use habits among adults of cigarettes, coffee, aspirin and sleeping pills, United States* (Vital and health statistics—Series 10-131, Publication No. 80-1559). Office of Health Research, Statistics, and Technology, National Center for Health Statistics.

Eaton, W. W., Kramer, M., Anthony, J. C., Dryman, A., Shapiro, S., & Locke, B. (1989). The incidence of specific SIS/DSM-III mental disorders: Data from the NIMH Epidemiologic Catchment Area Program. *Acta Psychiatrica Scandinavica, 79,* 163–178.

Fillmore, K. M. (1987). Prevalence, incidence and chronicity of drinking patterns and problems among men as a function of age: A longitudinal and cohort analysis. *British Journal of Addiction, 82,* 77–83.

Frost, W. H. (Ed.). (1936). *Snow on cholera.* New York: The Commonwealth Fund.

Johnson, E. O., Schütz, C. G., Anthony, J. C., & Ensminger, M. E. (1995). Inhalants to heroin: A prospective analysis from adolescence to adulthood. *Drug & Alcohol Dependence, 40,* 159–164.

Kandel, D. B. (1991). The social demography of drug use. *Milbank Quarterly, 69,* 365–414.

Kandel, D. B. (1992). Epidemiological trends and implications for understanding the nature of addiction. *Research Publications—Association for Research in Nervous & Mental Disease, 70,* 23–40.

Kessler, R. C., McGonagle, K. A., Zhao, S., Nelson, C. B., Hughes, M., Eshleman, S., Wittshen, H. U., & Kendler, K. S. (1994). Lifetime and 12 month prevalence of DSM-IIIR psychiatric disorders in the United States results from the National Comorbidity Survey. *Archives of General Psychiatry, 51,* 8–19.

Lillie-Blanton, M., Anthony, J. C., & Schuster, C. (1994). Probing the meaning of racial ethnic group comparisons in crack cocaine smoking. *Journal of the American Medical Association, 269,* 993–997.

Schütz, C. G., Chilcoat, H. D., & Anthony, J. C. (1994). The association between sniffing inhalants and injecting drugs. *Comprehensive Psychiatry, 35,* 99–105.

Statistical Sciences. (1994). *S-Plus for Windows version 3.2 supplement.* Seattle: Author.

U.S. Department of Health and Human Services (1995). *National household survey of drug abuse: Population estimates 1994* (DHHS Publication No. SMA 95-3063). Washington, DC: U.S. Government Printing Office.

Warner, L. A., Kessler, R. C., Hughes, M., Anthony, J. C., & Nelson, C. B. (1995). Prevalence and correlates of drug use and dependence in the United States: Results from the National Comorbidity Survey. *Archives of General Psychiatry, 52,* 219–229.

CHAPTER 4

DEVELOPMENTAL STAGES OF INVOLVEMENT IN SUBSTANCE USE

Denise B. Kandel

Kazuo Yamaguchi

It is well established that in any population the use of various drugs is interrelated and that users of any class of drug, whether legal or illegal, are much more likely than nonusers to report using other classes as well. Furthermore, not only is the use of drugs interrelated at one point in time, but also sequential patterns of drug involvement have been documented. Drugs that are legal for adults in a society, namely alcohol and tobacco, are an integral and crucial part of the sequence. Their use precedes the use of illicit drugs, irrespective of the age at which initiation to illegal drugs takes place.

In this chapter we (1) present the evidence for the existence of stages in drug use; (2) review the risk factors for progression from one stage to another; (3) raise methodological issues regarding the investigation of developmental stages of drug involvement; and (4) discuss the implications of stages of drug use for policy, research, and theory. Our focus is on onset and progression; we do not discuss potential stages involved in regression and cessation of use.

MULTIPLE DRUG USE: A STAGE-BASED DEVELOPMENTAL PERSPECTIVE

The aggregation of the use of different drug classes is well documented. Users of any type of drugs are much more

likely than nonusers to consume other classes of drugs, during their lifetime or currently. For example, in 1994 in the United States, 93.1% of young adults age 18–25 who had ever used marijuana had also smoked, 99.1% had drunk alcohol and 27.9% had ever used cocaine compared with 51.5%, 77.1%, and 0.7%, respectively, of those who had never used marijuana. [Based on data from the 1994 National Household Survey on Drug Abuse, Substance Abuse and Mental Health Services Administration, (SAMHSA, 1995).]

The developmental stage model has been proposed to account for this aggregation. Based on a lifespan approach to development, this model is based on the premise that involvement in various behaviors is not opportunistic but follows definite pathways, in which specific factors place the individual who has participated in one behavior at risk of initiating another.

STAGES IN DRUG USE

The notion of stages in drug use, first proposed more than 20 years ago (Hamburg, Kraemer, & Jahnke, 1975; Kandel, 1975), represents an influential model to describe the developmental progression of young people's involvement in using drugs. Much of the evidence for this conceptualization derives from work that we carried out over the last two decades, and, in particular, on a longitudinal cohort that we have followed over 19 years from adolescence to the fourth decade of life, the New York State Cohort. We have considered the whole range of mood-changing drugs, including drugs that are legal for adults, such as cigarettes and alcohol, illegal drugs, and mood-changing drugs that are medically prescribed and are used with and without a prescription, such as the minor tranquilizers. Indeed, the mood-changing effects of various drugs are independent of their legal status. Furthermore, access to drugs is partially determined by social factors. Young people are less likely to consult a physician than are adults; males are less likely to do so than females.

The New York State Cohort Studies

The New York State Cohort (NYSC) is representative of adolescents formerly enrolled in grades 10 and 11 in public secondary schools in New York State in 1971–1972. Participants were initially sampled twice in high school and reinterviewed in three follow-ups in 1980, 1984, and 1990, from ages 15–16 to ages 34–35. The target population for the follow-ups was drawn from the enrollment list of half the homerooms in grades 10 and 11, with high-marijuana-using homerooms sampled at twice the rate of the others. Students who had not participated either in the initial 1971 study, and who presumably were chronic absentees, were also selected for inclusion (and sampled at a lower rate) to permit unbiased estimates of the former student population at the time of the adult follow-up. An overall completion rate of 71.5% of the initial high school cohort of former regular students and absentees was obtained at the last interview.

At each survey, information was collected on the histories of use of twelve drugs or drug classes: two legal (cigarettes, alcohol), four illegal (marijuana, psychedelics, cocaine and heroin), and medical and nonmedical use of six classes of psychotropic drugs: methadone, minor and major tranquilizers, sedatives, stimulants, antidepressants, and opiates other than heroin. Time lines with differentiations in years and months allowed for the timing of the use of the different drugs. Although age of onset was ascertained for all users of each drug, the detailed retrospective drug histories, including periods of highest use, were obtained only for drugs used a minimum of 10 times in order to eliminate experimenters.

Periods of Risk for Initiation, Stabilization, and Decline in the Use of Various Drugs

The investigation of developmental stages needs to take place with knowledge of the periods of risk for initiation into different drug classes.

The continuous observations obtained retrospectively on the use of drugs by members of the cohort over a 19-year period made it possible to examine drug behavior as a dynamic process. The rates of initiation into most drugs increase sharply through age 18, when they rapidly begin to decline (Kandel & Chen, 1995; Kandel & Logan, 1984; Raveis & Kandel, 1987). This holds for cigarettes, alcohol, and marijuana. The pattern for cocaine differs from the patterns for legal and other illegal drugs: use of cocaine begins at a later age than either alcohol, cigarettes, or marijuana. Reflecting historical factors, cocaine is the only illicit drug that shows increases in the risk of initiation through age 24, with a flattening throughout the late 20s. Starting with lower rates of initiation than those observed for the nonmedical use of prescription psychotropic drugs, rates for prescribed use are higher than for nonprescribed use beginning at age 22. Initiation drops off sharply at age 24 and shows a slight rebound later. It should be kept in mind that these patterns are based on one cohort and may reflect historical as well as maturational changes.

Short-Term Follow-Up in Adolescence

Having followed adolescents for a short-term 6-month period from the fall to the spring term of a school year, we first examined the sequence in adolescence in the use of three alcoholic beverages (beer, wine, and distilled spirits), cigarettes, and illicit drugs (Kandel, 1975; Kandel & Faust, 1975). By extrapolating from the behavior of adolescents with different drug-using patterns over a 5- to 6-month interval and constructing a synthetic cohort, we made inferences about developmental stages in drug behavior (Figure 4.1).

Four stages were identified: (1) beer or wine, (2) cigarettes and/or hard liquor, (3) marijuana, and (4) other illicit drugs. The first substances used in adolescence are either beer or wine. Tobacco and, especially, hard liquor are next. Adolescents are very unlikely to experiment with marijuana without prior experimentation with an alcoholic beverage or with cigarettes. Very few try illicit drugs other than marijuana without prior use of marijuana. The order between cigarettes and hard liquor could not be

Figure 4.1 Major stages of adolescent involvement in drug use.

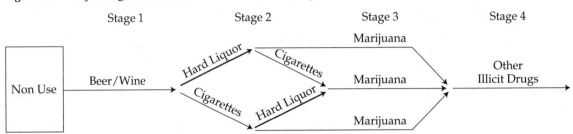

established. These longitudinal analyses confirmed the ordering observed in prior cross-sectional Guttman Scale analyses (Kessler, Paton, & Kandel, 1976; Single, Kandel, & Faust, 1974).

Analytical Strategies: Modified Guttman Scaling

More extensive analyses were subsequently conducted on the same cohort surveyed over a 19-year interval from adolescence to adulthood among men and women separately, past the period of risk for onset into the different classes of drugs (Kandel & Yamaguchi, 1985; Kandel, Yamaguchi, & Chen, 1992; Yamaguchi & Kandel, 1984a, b). Five drug classes were distinguished: alcohol, cigarettes, marijuana, other illicit drugs, and prescribed psychotropic drugs. Analyses of progression were based on the year and month of onset ascertained for each drug ever used 10 or more times. The earliest drug used within a class determined the age of onset for the class.

Major pathways of progression were identified from the ordering of initiation among the five classes of drugs observed in the cohort from ages 15–16 to ages 34–35. Specific cumulative progression models or scale types were hypothesized and estimated through loglinear methods and tested for fit to the data. The proportion of persons classified in the scale type beyond that expected from the marginals was estimated. Statistical procedures, based on maximum likelihood estimations, were applied to identify the efficiency of various cumulative models in fitting the data. For a given model of stages of progression, the observed proportion of individuals who could be classified in the scale type was calculated, although, as in Guttman scaling, not all individuals were required to reach the highest stage in the progression. In testing the fit of each model, it was important to ascertain not only the observed

proportion of individuals who fell in the scale type but also the expected proportion not due to chance. The model assumed that some individuals fell in the scale type as well as in the nonscale type by chance.

Tests of Specific Sequential Models

Except for three pairs (alcohol and cigarettes, cigarettes and marijuana, and other illicit and prescribed psychoactive drugs), each drug in a pair preceded the other in at least 80% of the cases for men and women (Table 4.1). The exceptions were important as they helped specify modifications to the model.

Stages of progression beyond pairwise comparisons of two events were specified and alternate cumulative progression models were tested against a baseline model that assumed independence and no ordering. We tested the fit to the data of *entire trajectories*, and not the transition probabilities from one drug to another; the latter consider only transitions between any two drugs between two time periods.

The baseline model assumed independence and no ordering. A basic model and three variants based on observed deviant patterns of progression (see Table 4.1) were tested against the baseline model. The hypothesized sequences reflected unidirectional pairwise orderings with transitions over 80%. No clear ordering was hypothesized between the use of alcohol and cigarettes, between cigarettes and marijuana, and between illicit drugs other than marijuana and prescribed psychoactive drugs.

The basic model was defined as follows:

1. Alcohol precedes marijuana
2. Alcohol, cigarettes, and marijuana precede other illicit drugs
3. Alcohol, cigarettes, and marijuana precede prescribed psychoactive drugs

Table 4.1   Pairwise Comparisons of Order of Initiation among 5 Classes of Drugs Used 10 Times or More by Age 34–35

Drug Used Earlier	Drug Used Late	Specified Ordering Among Persons Who Used Both	
		Male	Female
Alcohol	Cigarettes	.72	.60
Alcohol	Marijuana	.90	.86
Alcohol	Other illicit drugs	.96	.94
Alcohol	Rx psychoactive	.97	.92
Cigarettes	Marijuana	.66	.72
Cigarettes	Other illicit drugs	.81	.87
Cigarettes	Rx psychoactive	.86	.84
Marijuana	Other illicit drugs	.90	.86
Marijuana	Rx psychoactive	.87	.79
Other illicit drugs	Rx psychoactive	.74	.54

Source: Kandel, Yamaguchi, & Chen, 1992

By ages 34–35, this model fit the data for 75% of men (70% not by chance) and 71% of women (62% not by chance).

To improve the fit of the model, three deviant patterns of progression relatively more frequent than others were taken into account separately and in combination. These variant models were suggested by the results on pairwise ordering. Each involved modifications in the role of a legal drug in drug progression, leading to less restrictive models.

Condition A: The use of cigarettes does not have to precede the use of other illicit drugs.

Condition B: If the use of cigarettes precedes the use of marijuana, the use of alcohol does not have to precede the use of marijuana.

Condition C: The use of alcohol and either cigarettes or marijuana, but not both, can precede the use of prescribed psychoactive drugs.

Tests of comparisons between pairs of hierarchical models that included various combinations of these combinations were carried out.

Slightly different progression models were found for men and women. Among men, a model that incorporated conditions A and C, and which hypothesized that cigarettes did not have to precede the use of illicit drugs, improved the basic model substantially in terms of the chi-square test and the increase in the proportion of persons in the scale type not by chance. For men, the best fitting model represents a pattern of progression in which alcohol precedes marijuana; alcohol and either cigarettes or marijuana precede other illicit drugs; and alcohol, cigarettes, and marijuana precede the use of prescribed psychoactive drugs. By ages 34–35, the model fit 84.5% of men, 79% not by chance. Among women, all three conditions A, B, and C jointly improved significantly the fit of the basic model and most parsimoniously characterized the pattern of drug progression through the middle 30s. For women, the best fitting model represents a pattern of progression in which either alcohol or cigarettes precedes marijuana; alcohol, and marijuana precede other illicit drugs; and alcohol and either cigarettes or marijuana precede prescribed psychoactive drugs. By ages 34–35, the model fit the behavior of 87% of women, 76% not by chance (Kandel et al., 1992).

A graphic representation of the developmental process illustrates the patterns for men (Figure 4.2) and for women (Figure 4.3).

There are clear temporal developmental stages in the use of licit and illicit drugs from adolescence through young adulthood, when the period of risk for initiation into drugs other than the prescribed psychoactives terminates. The general sequence of involvement into drugs progresses from the use of at least one legal drug, alcohol and/or cigarettes, to marijuana; and from marijuana to other illicit drugs and/or to prescribed psychoactive drugs. The use of illicit drugs in adolescence puts individuals at

Figure 4.2 Sequential stages of drug involvement; Men age 34–35. Model QAC.

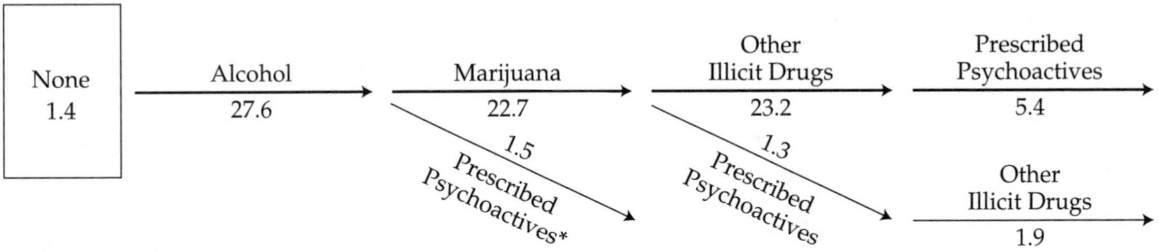

* Preceded by both alcohol and cigarettes

Model accounts for 85.1% of men (80.1% not by chance)

Source: Data from "Stages of Progression in Drug Involvement from Adolescence to Adulthood: Further Evidence for the Gateway Theory" by D. B. Kandel, K. Yamaguchi, and K. Chen, 1992, Journal of Studies on Alcohol, 53, pp. 447–457.

greater risk of using medically prescribed psychotropic drugs in adulthood.

The gender differences in the role of the legal drugs in the progression into drug involvement need to be emphasized. Cigarettes play a more important role in the sequence for women, whereas alcohol plays a more important role for men. Cigarettes can precede the use of marijuana or other illicit drugs in the absence of alcohol consumption among women, whereas alcohol, even in the absence of cigarettes, consistently precedes marijuana and other illicit drugs among men. Furthermore, for a larger proportion of women than of men, prescribed psychoactive drugs can be initiated in the absence of prior experimentation with marijuana if cigarettes have been used, with alcohol consistently a prior stage for both sexes. These are the results through ages 34–35 (Kandel, Yamaguchi et al., 1992). As women age, the extent to which prior involvement in cigarettes is required prior to progression to illicit drugs other than marijuana and to prescribed drugs appears to weaken. Although by age 25, experience with both alcohol and cigarettes (in addition to marijuana) was necessary for women (Yamaguchi & Kandel, 1984a), by ages 34–35 experience with alcohol (in addition to marijuana) was sufficient. By age 25, prescribed psychoactive drugs could be initiated in the absence of prior experimentation with marijuana if cigarettes had been used among women, but not among men; by age 35, this pattern held for both men and women.

The majority of deviations from the scale patterns involved mostly either experimentation with marijuana without prior use of a legal drug or use of an illicit drug other than marijuana without prior use of marijuana. The latter pattern characterized mainly individuals who started using these drugs after their late 20s. Prior to that age, there were relatively few errors of that type.

Analyses on the 1994 National Household Survey of Drug Abuse indicate that in the United States almost one fifth (19.3%) of youths age 18 to 25 had proceeded through all three developmental stages of drug use; 22.5% had reached the marijuana stage; almost half (46.5%) had stopped at the first stage of alcohol and/or cigarettes. Of those who had ever used alcohol or cigarettes, marijuana, and other illicit drugs, 38.8% reported to be still using all three classes of dugs within the last year. These individuals represented 7.4% of the age group in the population. The proportions reported to be smoking cigarettes within the last year decreased from 83.8% of those currently at the stage of other illicit drugs, to 64% of those at the marijuana stage, and 38% of those who were at the alcohol stage and had not used any illicit drug within the last year. A substantial proportion of individuals concurrently retain the behavioral repertoire characteristic of lower stages while also using drugs at the higher stages.

Additional Documentation in Support of Stages of Drug Involvement

Numerous cross-sectional and longitudinal investigations describe regular sequences of progression from legal to illegal drugs among adolescents and young adults of both sexes, irrespective of the age of first initiation into drugs, among different ethnic groups, in different countries, and

Figure 4.3   Sequential stages of drug involvement: Women age 34–35. Model QABC.

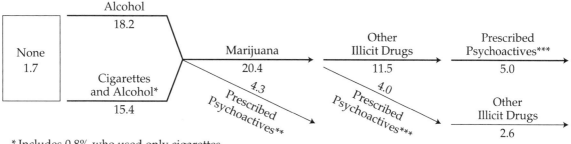

* Includes 0.8% who used only cigarettes
** Preceded by both alcohol and cigarettes
*** Preceded by both alcohol and marijuana

Model accounts for 83.1% of women

Source: Data from "Stages of Progression in Drug Involvement from Adolescence to Adulthood: Further Evidence for the Gateway Theory" by D. B. Kandel, K. Yamaguchi, and K. Chen, 1992, Journal of Studies on Alcohol, 53, pp. 447–457.

at different historical periods spanning a 20-year interval. The basis sequence from alcohol and/or cigarettes, to marijuana, and to illicit drugs other than marijuana is almost universally accepted. The stages are hierarchical and cumulative, and characterize not only lifetime but also current patterns of use.

Although the notion of stages has been very influential, close examination of existing studies reveals that many studies do not meet the criteria necessary to establish the stages. The documentation of stages requires that at least the first two of the following three criteria be met: (1) established order of initiation among the various drugs; (2) significance in the effect of a substance lower in the sequence on a drug higher in the sequence; (3) nonspuriousness of the sequential drug effects. (See also O'Donnell & Clayton, 1982.) Whereas all three criteria are desirable, nonspuriousness is difficult to establish because covariates entered as controls do not exhaust all causal antecedents; it is easier to prove spuriousness. Most studies fail to meet all three criteria. Furthermore, although many studies meet one or two criteria, they are often based on indirect inferences from cross-sectional data rather than direct tests that explicitly take into account a temporal order based on longitudinal data. We discuss the studies that have claimed support for the existence of stages according to the criterion they addressed (implicitly), whether or not they took an order into account, and the methods that they used. Only studies that

take order into account can be considered to have adequately addressed each relevant criterion.

Order of initiation. Criterion 1 (A): Studies have inferred an order, in the absence of timing information, on the basis of traditional Guttman scaling of cross-sectional data (Adler & Kandel, 1981; Blaze-Temple & Lo, 1992; Brook, Hamburg, Balka, & Wynn, 1992; Brook, Whiteman, & Gordon, 1983; Donovan & Jessor, 1983; Kandel, 1975; Mills & Noyes, 1984; Sorenson & Brownfield, 1989; Welte & Barnes, 1985; Yu & Williford, 1992); loglinear models (Miller, 1994); latent class analysis (Sorenson & Brownfield, 1989); and cross-tabulations of use patterns at one point in time (Free, 1993). Historically, Guttman scaling has been the most frequently used method. However, Guttman scaling based on cross-sectional patterns of use reflects a hierarchical and unidimensional order of use, which in the absence of age of onset or longitudinal data does not necessarily reflect an order of initiation.

Criterion 1 (B): A second group of studies document an order by taking timing into account. These include studies based on age of onset into various classes of drugs (Golub & Johnson, 1994; Hamburg et al., 1975; Kandel, Davies, & Davis, 1990; O'Donnell, 1985; Taub & Skinner, 1990; Voss & Clayton, 1987); cross-tabulations of use patterns at different point in time (Elliott, Huizinga, & Menard, 1989); modified loglinear Guttman-scale analysis (Ellickson, Hays, & Bell, 1992; Gould, Berberian, Kasl, Thompson, &

Kleber, 1977; Hays & Ellickson, 1990–91; Kandel & Faust, 1975); latent transition analysis (Collins, 1991; Graham, Collins, Wugalter, Chung, & Hansen, 1994); and parametric event sequence analysis (Yamaguchi & Kandel, 1996). Some investigators have combined an initial Guttman scale analysis of cross-sectional data with an examination of patterns of subsequent transitions (Andrews, Hops, Ary, Lichtenstein, & Tildesley, 1991; Fleming, Leventhal, Glynn, & Ershler, 1989; Kandel & Faust, 1975).

Significance of drug effects, without control for nondrug covariates. Criterion 2 (A): Studies that do not take temporal order into account include path or structural equation models based on cross-sectional data (Hays, Stacy, Widaman, DiMatteo, & Downey, 1986; Huba & Bentler, 1982; Huba, Wingard, & Bentler, 1981; Newcomb & Bentler, 1986; Windle, Barnes, & Welte, 1989); and the latent class model (Sorenson & Brownfield, 1989), which tries to establish the spuriousness rather than the presence of association by testing the hypothesis that drug-use patterns can be explained by latent population heterogeneity and not by a direct association among the drugs.

Criterion 2 (B): Another subgroup of studies take temporal order into account in establishing the associations: path or structural equation models of panel data (e.g., Osgood, Johnston, O'Malley, & Bacman, 1988); event history analysis (Yamaguchi & Kandel, 1984a); extensions of loglinear models (Kandel et al., 1992); parametric event sequence analysis (Yamaguchi & Kandel, 1996); and latent transition analysis (Collins, Graham, Long, & Hansen, 1994; Graham et al., 1991).

Specificity of drug effects, with control for other covariates. Criterion 3: Very few studies meet the third criterion, which is difficult to satisfy adequately through the inclusion of all relevant control variables. (A) Most of the relevant studies meet criteria 2 and 3, but not criterion 1. These studies have taken the stage concept for granted and built it into their analyses by testing sequential paths among various drugs in cross-sectional causal models that include other covariates, but did not take order into account (Free, 1993; Hays et al., 1986; Marcos & Bahr, 1995; Potvin & Lee, 1980; Taub & Skinner, 1990). In these analyses, significant effects of a presumed lower stage drug on higher stage drug(s) do not necessarily reflect an order of initiation but do reflect the potential reciprocal effects of the use of different substances on each other, once onset has taken place.

Criterion 3 (B): The studies in this group have taken order into account and provide the most rigorous test of the stage notion. However, the relevant studies are few and include a limited number of covariates. These studies comprise the event history and parametric event sequence analyses that we conducted (Yamaguchi & Kandel, 1984b, 1996) and structural equation models for panel data (Kaplan, Martin, & Robbins, 1984; Osgood et al., 1988).

The issue of causality in establishing sequences in drug use is discussed further in the section on "Methodological Challenges."

Because studies that meet all three criteria confirm the existence of stages in drug use, one can infer that the documentation of an order by itself, although inadequate, probably reflects a developmental sequence. This sequence occurs in countries other than the United States, such as France, Israel (Adler & Kandel, 1981) and Australia (Blaze-Temple & Lo, 1992). The stage model may be a somewhat better representation of lifetime than of current use (Hays et al., 1986; Hays, Widaman, DiMatteo, & Stacy, 1987), although Gould et al. (1977) reported as good a fit for current as for lifetime use patterns. Much less work has been done to uncover steps in regression than in progression. The fact that current patterns parallel lifetime patterns implies that regression mirrors progression. Indeed, the same steps appear in regression as in progression (Kandel & Faust, 1975). Whereas illicit drugs other than marijuana are usually aggregated in a single group, several investigators have examined the order among specific illicit drugs other than marijuana (Ellickson et al., 1992; Mills & Noyes, 1984; Newcomb & Bentler, 1986; Single, Kandel, & Faust, 1974; Sorenson & Brownfield, 1989; Welte & Barnes, 1985). The greater the number of drugs to be ordered, the poorer the fit. A distinction is usually made among pills (e.g. barbiturates, stimulants), cocaine, hallucinogens, and heroin. The greater the number of drugs to be ordered, the poorer the fit. There is much similarity across studies in this order: marijuana, pills, cocaine, heroin. The position of hallucinogens is the most unstable; it preceded cocaine in the New York State sample studied in 1971 (Single et al., 1974), but followed cocaine in samples of Maryland high school students surveyed in 1978–81 (Mills & Noyes, 1984) or of White males surveyed in 1980 in Seattle (Mills & Noyes, 1984). Sorenson and Brownfield (1989), who conducted systematic analyses based on Guttman scaling and latent structure analyses, found that the most unscalable scale types resulted from an assumed order between cocaine and hallucinogens. (Heroin was not included among the drugs scaled.) Examination of finer transitions is illustrated by Golub and Johnson's (1994) analysis of the stages preceding crack experimentation among crack abusers in inner-city Manhattan in 1988–1989. Alcohol and/or marijuana were as likely to precede the use of cocaine, crack, and heroin. However, the patterns observed among the latter varied for different birth cohorts. Among the youngest cohorts, born between 1968 and 1972, more than a third preceded directly from marijuana to crack cocaine, although snorting cocaine was still the most prevalent intermediary step. Hays et al. (1987) and Windle, Barnes, & Welte (1989) differentiated illicit drugs other than marijuana into enhancers and dampeners but could not successfully identify a sequential order between these two classes. Stenbacka, Allebeck, and Romelsjö (1993) investigated the progression from cannabis to intravenous drug use in Sweden.

Differentiation among illicit drugs would be useful, because slightly different progressions seem to characterize different groups of adolescents, especially different ethnic groups. (See the section, "Ethnic Differences in Patterns of Progression").

Stages of Progression within Individual Drug Classes

The stages of drug involvement highlighted in this chapter involve progressions from one class of drugs to another. Sequences of involvement can also be distinguished *within specific classes of drugs*, involving shifts from initiation, to experimentation, casual use, regular use, abuse, and dependence (Clayton, 1992; Glanz & Pickens, 1992; Werch & Anzalone, 1995). With the exception of early discussions of heroin (Robins, 1979), most of this work has focused on cigarette smoking (e.g., Chassin, Presson, & Sherman, 1984; Flay, 1993; Leventhal & Cleary, 1980; Werch & Anzalone, 1995) and alcohol (Tarter, Moss, & Vanyukov, 1991; Zucker, Fitzgerald, & Moses, 1995). Stages of involvement within a particular drug class may provide important specifications of progressions across classes of drugs. For example, Donovan and Jessor (1983) identified problem drinking as intervening between the use of marijuana and the use of other illicit drugs, and Ellickson et al. (1992) stressed that increasing involvement with alcohol and cigarettes preceded the use of illicit drugs other than marijuana. Although Collins and her colleagues (Collins, 1991; Collins et al., 1994; Graham, Collins, Wugalter, Chung, & Hanse, 1991) emphasized the role of drunken-

ness as a stage between the use of alcohol and tobacco and advanced use, "advanced use" is an ill-defined latent construct that cannot be properly interpreted as representing a specific and higher stage of drug use and cannot be clearly differentiated from the preceding stages. The five manifest indicators of advanced use were alcohol use in the prior month, use in the past week, tobacco use in the prior month, use in the prior week, and lifetime marijuana use.

Finally, some investigators, mostly those who study cigarette smoking, advocate focusing on stages prior to the onset of smoking itself, namely precontemplation, contemplation, and maintenance (Stern, Prochaska, Velicer, & Elder, 1987; Werch & Anzalone, 1995). The latter stage extends beyond simple acquisition.

Ethnic Differences in Patterns of Progression

The overall developmental model of stages in drug use appears to fit various ethnic groups drawn from the general population (Brook et al., 1992; Ellickson et al., 1992; Yamaguchi & Kandel, 1996), although it may fit Whites somewhat better than non-Whites. In the New York State Cohort, for instance, in the 1970s, blacks were more likely than Whites to try heroin before cocaine while in high school (Single et al, 1974). From adolescence to adulthood, the sequence from alcohol to marijuana fit Whites better than minorities, especially Black females. Cigarette use was a strong precursor of marijuana use for white men and women, and a weaker precursor for Black women, whereas cigarette use was not a reliable precursor of marijuana use for Black men (Yamaguchi & Kandel, 1996). Similarly, Collins et al.'s (1994) basic model fitted Whites better than Latinos and Asian-American high school students. In a street and treated sample of minority serious drug abusers and sellers in Manhattan, marijuana was consistently found to be a precursor to other illicit drugs, whereas prior use of a legal drug, alcohol in particular, did not appear to be necessary (Golub & Johnson, 1994). (Cigarette smoking was not ascertained in that study.)

The Role of Cigarettes in the Progression

The order between the onset of smoking and drinking of alcoholic beverages is ambiguous. Investigators who apply Guttman scaling to identify a sequence among drugs are more likely to ask about cigarettes than investigators who use structural equation modeling (SEM) for identifying sequences or for identifying the predictors of the use of different drugs. Out of 15 Guttman Scale studies that we identified, 13 asked respondents specifically about their smoking of cigarettes. Although five of the ten SEM studies did so, three of these studies included cigarettes in latent alcohol and marijuana factors. (See the discussion that follows) Seven studies reported that the use of cigarettes followed alcohol (e.g., Andrews et al. 1991; Collins et al., 1994; Ellickson et al., 1992, but only for White students (Marcos & Bahr, 1995; Newcomb & Bentler 1986; Welte & Barnes, 1985; Yu & Williford, 1992), whereas three others reported the opposite order, with cigarettes preceding alcohol (e.g., Fleming et al., 1989; Voss & Clayton, 1987; Welte & Barnes, 1985, for young adolescent females). Still others were unable to specify an order (e.g., Adler & Kandel, 1981; Blaze-Temple & Lo, 1992; Kandel, 1975; Gould et al., 1977; Mills & Noyes, 1984; O'Donnell, 1985); did not discuss order (Brook, Whiteman, Gordon, & Cohen, 1986; Brook et al., 1992; 1983); or could not discuss an order as tobacco was a manifest indicator for two separate latent constructs (Hays et al., 1987; Huba et al, 1981; Windle et al, 1989). Some of these discrepant results may be due to divergent definitions of alcoholic beverages. The inclusion of beer, wine, and distilled spirits (or hard liquor) in the alcohol category may lead to the finding that alcohol onset precedes tobacco onset. However, irrespective of the resulting order, there seems to be agreement that smoking is more important than alcohol as an initial experience in the progression to drugs higher in the sequence of drug use (e.g., Blaze-Temple & Lo, 1992; Henningfield, Clayton, & Pollin, 1990; Marcos & Bahr, 1995). The evidence is particularly convincing when it is based on longitudinal studies (e.g., Fleming et al., 1989; Newcomb & Bentler, 1986). Collins et al. (1994) reported that although fewer adolescents reported using cigarettes than alcohol, students who started the process of drug involvement with cigarettes progressed faster through the other stages than those who started with alcohol. We found that cigarette smoking was more important for females than for males (Yamaguchi & Kandel, 1984a; Kandel et al., 1992) and more important for Whites than for Blacks (Yamaguchi & Kandel, 1996). Similarly, Ellickson, Hays, and Bell (1992) found that smoking was an important stage only for White adolescent females.

Predictors of Progression

Behavioral Features of Drug Histories Associated with Progression

Two behavioral characteristics of an individual's drug history are strongly associated with progression from a lower to a higher stage of drug use: (a) age of onset into the use of the lower drug class, and (b) extent of use of the lower drug.

Earlier onset of use of any drug is associated with greater involvement in use of all other drugs (Colliver, 1989; Kandel & Yamaguchi, 1985; Robins & Przybeck, 1985; Yu & Williford, 1992). The earlier the experimentation with legal drugs, the greater the probability that the youth will also experiment with illicit drugs and progress to heavier involvement. For example, in the New York State Cohort (NYSC), the proportions of men age 34–35 who had experimented with marijuana ranged from 85% among those who reported to have first tried alcohol or cigarettes at ages 14 or below to 46% among those who had first tried a legal drug at age 18; comparable percentages among women were 78% and 38%, respectively. Similarly, the earlier the experimentation with marijuana, the greater the involvement and the greater the likelihood of progressing to other illicit drugs. Almost all (96%) young men in the NYSC who initiated marijuana at age 14 or younger had tried an illicit drug other than marijuana by age 29. The proportion declined to 66% among those who first tried marijuana at age 18 and to 33% among those who first tried marijuana at age 20; only 6% ever used an illicit drug other than marijuana among those who never experimented with marijuana. The parallel proportions among women were 84%, 46%, 43%, and 9%, respectively.

Furthermore, progression to a higher ranked drug is related to intensity of use of the lower stage drug (Bailey, 1992; Kandel & Faust, 1975; Kandel & Yamaguchi, 1985). For instance, in the NYSC, 82% of men and 60% of women who had ever used marijuana 1,000 or more times by ages 24–25 started to use other illicit drugs within the next 4 years compared with 18% and 17%, respectively, of those who had ever used marijuana only 10–99 times. The differences were even more striking with respect to the proportions who had used illicit drugs other than marijuana more than a few times. The proportions who used these drugs more than 9 times ranged from 1%–2% among those who had never used marijuana to 38% of men and 46% of women who had used it more than 1,000 times.

Cross-sectional data reflect these longitudinal associations. In the United States in 1994, of persons age 18–25 who had ever used marijuana, the proportion having used cocaine or crack increased from 8.2% among those who reported to have ever used marijuana only once or twice in their lives to 18.8% among those who used it 3–11 days, 29.7% among those who used it 12–100 days, 44.6% among those who used it 101–300 days, and 66.2% among those who had used marijuana more than 300 days. [Based on the 1994 NHSDA (SAMHSA, 1995).]

At each stage in the continuum of drug use, age of onset and frequency of use are associated with progression. Whereas behavioral features of drug involvement at each stage of drug use are predictors of progression to the next stage, there are also stage-specific social-psychological predictors of progression.

Social-Psychological Predictors of Stages of Drug Involvement

The identification of stages allows one to define a population at risk and to isolate systematically within that population those individuals who succumb to the risk within a specific time interval. As we discuss in greater detail next ("Research Implications of the Stage Concept"), the role and structure of different causal factors at different stages of involvement can be specified. However, appropriate stage-specific analyses of risk factors have very rarely been implemented. Most often, researchers investigate the correlates of use or more rarely the predictors of the onset of individual drug classes, without taking into account the individual's developmental position in the sequence of drug involvement. Those who have taken order into account by creating hierarchical classifications of drug use based on an assumed sequential order have analyzed cross-sectional samples in which it is not possible to disentangle the determinants from the consequences of being in a particular stage. Furthermore, some investigators treat the hierarchical stage variable as a continuous analytical variable (Brook et al., 1986), precluding the possibility of identifying stage-specific risk factors. Another common strategy for identifying drug-specific predictors of use is the estimation of cross-sectional causal models in which the use of specific drug classes is included as endogenous variables and paths estimated from each drug to another in an assumed hierarchical order. Direct paths are also estimated from each predictor to each specific drug stage

(e.g., Free, 1993; Marcos & Bahr, 1995). The same limitation applies to this approach as to the comparison of mutually exclusive groups based on a hierarchical classification. Antecedents of use cannot be disentangled from consequences. Significant paths reflect stage-specific correlates of substance use but not risk factors.

The work still most relevant has been carried out by our research group, some completed 20 years ago, and by Andrews et al. (1991) and Osgood et al. (1988). In our analyses, we applied several statistical techniques to identify the predictors of progression: regressions based on longitudinal samples decomposed into stages of drug use, regressions based on a longitudinal sample where interaction terms between each covariate and initial stage were included in the models, and event-history analyses. A stage-based decomposed analytical sample is the strategy used in an earlier phase of the research carried out when members of the longitudinal cohort were adolescents (Kandel, 1980; Kandel, Kessler, & Margulies, 1978) and by Andrews et al. (1991). As discussed next in "Research Implications of the Stage Concept," the use of decomposed samples has limitations. In our analyses, the social-psychological characteristics of adolescents at a particular stage of drug use who progressed to the next higher stage over a short interval of 5–6 months were investigated for the three sequential stages of use of hard liquor, marijuana, and other illicit drugs. Four clusters of social-psychological predictor variables were examined: parental influences, peer influences, adolescent involvement in various behaviors, and beliefs and values. Each cluster and single predictors within each cluster assumed differential importance for each stage of drug behavior. The analyses were replicated using interaction terms between drug-use stage and the covariates, as previously described (Kandel, Margulies, & Davies, 1978).

At the earlier level of drug involvement, that of involvement in a legal drug such as alcohol, adolescents who had engaged in a number of minor delinquent or deviant activities, who enjoyed high levels of sociability with their peers, and who were exposed to peers and parents who drank, started to drink. The relationship with parental use of hard liquor suggested that these youths learned drinking patterns from their parents. The use of marijuana was preceded by acceptance of a cluster of beliefs and values favorable to marijuana use and in opposition to many standards upheld by adults, by involvement in a peer environment in which marijuana was used, and by participation in the same minor forms of deviant behaviors that preceded the use of hard liquor. By comparison, use of illicit drugs other than marijuana was preceded by poor relationships with parents; by exposure to parents and peers who themselves used a variety of legal, medical, and illegal drugs; by psychological distress; by heavy involvement in marijuana; and by personal characteristics somewhat more deviant than those characterizing the novice marijuana or hard liquor user.

Peer influences were more important at certain points in the process of involvement. Friends' behaviors were especially important in predicting marijuana use and relatively less important for predicting drinking or the use of illicit drugs other than marijuana. Parental factors were most important for the progression into illicit drugs other than marijuana. Additional stage-specific differences were identified within classes of predictors. As regards interpersonal influences, at different stages there were not only differences in the source of influence but also differences in important aspects of interpersonal influences. In the early stage of drug use, parental behaviors (drinking or use of psychoactive substances) seemed to be critical in predicting which young people would experiment with hard liquor. In later phases of initiation, the quality of the parent–child relationship was important, with closeness to parents shielding adolescents from involvement in the most serious forms of drug use. It is striking that feelings of depression and lack of closeness to parents were two important factors that characterized marijuana users who proceeded to use other illicit drugs. The role of the family was confirmed by Andrews et al. (1991), who examined the quality of family relationships as a predictor of moving from one stage on a Guttman scale to the next stage over a 1-year interval. Perceived family cohesion and conflicts with parents predicted initiation to alcohol and cigarette use for girls and progression to marijuana and other illicit drugs for boys in a self-selected sample of parents and young adolescents.

In subsequent event-history analyses, we included time-varying measures of drug use in dynamic models, together with other time-varying and time-constant covariates, to predict the hazard of experiencing progression to the next higher drug class (Yamaguchi & Kandel, 1984b). There was a unique effect of the use of a prior drug on the use of a subsequent drug in the sequence. Additional specific risk factors for each particular progression were identified. These risk factors were often gender specific. For example, whereas friends' marijuana use increased the rate of initiating marijuana among both men and women, delinquency and the perception that marijuana was harmful affected the rate of marijuana initiation among men but not among women. Similarly, depressive symptoms and maternal use of psychoactive drugs both increased the rate of initiating prescribed psychoactive drugs among women but not among men.

Andrews et al. (1991) found that mothers' self-reported conflict with their daughters predicted the daughters' transition to alcohol use, whereas fathers' self-reported lack of family cohesion predicted daughters' initiation to smoking and sons' transition to marijuana use from cigarettes.

CHALLENGES AND UNRESOLVED ISSUES

The evidence is strong that participation in a drug at a lower stage indicates a greater risk of participating in a higher stage drug, over and above any other risk factors that are common to both stages. However, one must acknowledge the limitations in the nature of the evidence available to date regarding risk factors for progression to various classes of drugs and limitations in the conceptualization of the stages themselves.

The limitations arise from several sources: limitations in the nature of the methods available to describe developmental pathways and stages of progression, limitations in the statistical models and methods to establish causal linkages between stages and specific risk factors for each stage, limitations in data available for analysis, and conceptual limitations.

Methodological Challenges

Methods and Models for the Identification of Stages and Sequences

One methodological challenge is the choice of statistical methods and models to identify behavioral sequences and developmental trajectories. Although several methods have been proposed, each has its own limitations, some more serious than others. Next we discuss methods and models that have been employed to delineate pathways of drug-use progression as well as a new method with much potential.

The simplest approach is to examine the ages of onset into different drug classes and infer an order of initiation. Another descriptive approach is to examine transitions over time between pairs of behaviors within a specific time period. The proportions of individuals who have moved to using one class of drugs can be compared among those who had earlier used another class and those who had not. This simple analysis of transition rates, however, cannot provide an overall description of drug-use progression patterns.

Historically, the most commonly used method is Guttman Scale analysis. Instead of determining a unidimensional order or assessing *scalability* among attitudinal items, the drug researcher determines the order among behaviors, namely the use of specific drug classes. The Guttman Scale was considered to be well suited to analyses of progressions as it assumed both cumulativeness and unidimensionality (Guttman, 1950). As we noted earlier, however, most investigators have relied on cross-sectional data and have not taken order into account. Statistical methods have been developed to assess scalability, that is, to test whether nonsalable response patterns result from random response errors, and to assess the effects of covariates on scalability and positions on the scale (Andrich, 1985; Clogg & Sawyer, 1981; Goodman, 1975; Schwartz, 1986; Yamaguchi, 1989). Except for subjects with nonscalable response patterns, or for random response errors, a person's position on the scale identifies the stage of his/her drug use progression. Sorenson and Brownfield (1989), for example, apply latent-class models to cross-sectional data on five classes of drugs (alcohol, marijuana, barbiturates, cocaine, hallucinogens). A model with three latent classes (persons who use alcohol only, those who use alcohol and marijuana but not other illicit drugs, and those who use some other illicit drugs in addition to alcohol and marijuana) fits the data well.

However, the application of Guttman Scale analysis creates a conceptual problem. Whereas drug-use progression is concerned with patterns of intraindividual changes in behavior, traditional Guttman Scale analysis identifies stages from interindividual differences and does not take personal histories and ages of onset into account. Collins, Cliff, and Dent (1988) proposed an extension of Guttman scale analysis to longitudinal data, the Longitudinal Guttman Simplex model (LGS), which assesses Guttman scalability from cumulative and unidimensional patterns of intraindividual behavioral changes and its consistency across individuals. The model was applied to drug use data by Ellickson and her colleagues, first in a reanalysis of the NYSC data (Hays & Ellickson, 1991), and to a California sample (Ellickson et al., 1992). While LGS represents a significant conceptual advance, drug-use progression patterns do not satisfy the unidimensionality requirement if one attempts to elaborate stages over and beyond the distinction of major stages, such as the four major stages identified among three broad drug classes: no drug use, use of licit drugs, use of marijuana, and use of illicit drugs other than marijuana. The identification of diverging paths as well as major pathways of progression among a larger number of drug classes, such as specific illicit drugs other than marijuana or prescribed drugs, requires other methods.

One such technique is latent transition analysis (van del Pol & Langeheine, 1990), which has been applied to drug-use progression patterns by Collins and her associates (Collins, 1991; Collins et al., 1994; Collins & Wugalter, 1992; Graham et al., 1991). Latent transition analysis combines Markov chains with latent classes. Its application to drug-use progression assumes that the latent stages are stages of drug-use progressions. The advantages of this model are that (1) the analysis uses data on intraindividual changes in behavior, rather than interindividual differences, to identify progression patterns; (2) the goodness-of-fit of each model and of alternative models can be tested so as to identify the best, or the most parsimonious, characterization of stages; and (3) not only do the estimated probabilities of latent stages identify the proportions of persons in each stage at a given time, but also the estimated transition probabilities between stages distinguish major from minor transition patterns. However, the approach has three major limitations, one substantive and two technical. Substantively, one cannot identify the stage of drug use for each person; one can only estimate the probabilities of the person being in the various stages. However, the associations between the latent stages and the manifest drug-use patterns is often not very strong. Graham et al. (1991) reported that among adolescents in the "tobacco only" latent stage, only 64.9% had ever smoked, whereas 21.7% had ever drunk alcohol, 0.2% had ever gotten drunk, and 9.1% had ever participated in "advanced drug use." Separating a particular risk group from groups at different stages of drug-use progression is problematic.

A technical limitation of latent-transition analysis is the assumption of first-order Markov chains. To date, the applications presented by Collins and her colleagues have been based on transitions in drug use across only two time points, from the 7th to the 8th grade of high school. The first-order Markov assumption that a person's stage at a particular time depends only on the stage at the prior time but not on prior stages further in the past may not adequately characterize data with multiple observations at more than two time points and for older subjects. In addition, unlike conventional latent-class models, where latent classes capture unobserved population heterogeneity, latent transition analysis assumes that individuals' heterogeneity characterized by their being in different latent stages is only temporary because everybody is assumed to be subject to the same Markov process. Although some persons in stage 1 at time 1 may progress to stage 3 at time 2, whereas others remain in stage 1 or progress only to stage 2, the model assumes that differences among individuals in experiencing these alternative progression patterns are solely due to chance, and not to heterogeneity in individuals' propensities to progress in their drug use. This assumption is unrealistic and may generate distorted characterizations of drug-use progression patterns.

One group of methods that we have proposed to identify pathways of drug-use progression modify and extend loglinear Guttman Scale models (Goodman, 1975) to analyze cross-classified data of temporally ordered events based on the concept of quasi-independence (Kandel & Yamaguchi, 1993; Kandel, Yamaguchi, & Chen, 1992; Yamaguchi & Kandel, 1984a). This extended loglinear Guttman Scale model assumes that, for persons who do not follow a scale-type pattern, event occurrences are random and alternative orders for the events are equally likely. By specifying an alternative set of scale-type response patterns, the goodness-of-fit of each model can be tested and alternative models can be compared. Unlike the original Guttman Scale analysis, the method does not require unidimensional ordering among the scale types and thereby permits the inclusion of branching in addition to major pathways of drug use progression.

Compared with latent-transition analysis, this method has an additional major advantage, as well as a major limitation. The advantage is that because the method classifies all subjects by their manifest drug-use patterns, the current stage of drug-use progression can be identified for the majority of individuals other than those with nonscale-type response patterns. The limitation is that the method does not have any clear correspondence to an underlying stochastic process model of drug use progression and, therefore, cannot predict transition rates and probabilities. It can only describe the major pathways and diverging branches and the proportions of individuals at each stage.

Both latent-transition and extended loglinear Guttman Scale analyses have an additional limitation in common. Neither includes covariates to assess directly group differ-

ences in patterns of drug-use progression, although each group can be analyzed separately. Such extensions are not logically impossible. We recently developed a parametric event sequence that extends loglinear analysis for the occurrence and association of events. These models parameterize the odds of a particular sequence versus the reverse sequence for each pair of events, and the potential dependence of each sequence on the prior occurrence or sequencing of other events, whereas parameters for the sequencing of all pairs of events are simultaneously taken into account (Yamaguchi & Kandel, 1996). Parametric sequence analysis thus provides a powerful new tool for the simultaneous analysis of multiple ordered events. It is particularly suited to the identification of patterns of drug-use progression from the initiation of different classes of drugs. Furthermore, the method makes it possible to introduce covariates, such as gender and race/ethnicity, to assess their effects on the sequential order between pairs of drugs and the potential dependence of the order on the prior initiation of other drugs. The method can be used to test systematically group differences in patterns of sequencing of drug use.

As previously reviewed, structural equation modeling (Hays et al., 1987; Huba & Bentler, 1982; Huba et al., 1981; Windle et al., 1989) contrasts a simplex model, in which sequential paths from one substance to another represent the stage model, with a nonsimplex model. In the latter, the introduction of additional direct paths from a drug representing an earlier stage to a drug at least two stages beyond the earlier one represents the common influence model. The comparison of the statistical fit of nested models provides a test of the adequacy of the stage model.

Two issues of operationalization in these models are questionable. First, the indicators of the latent constructs are allowed to overlap. For example, cigarette smoking and wine drinking are indicators of both latent "alcohol use" and "cannabis use," hashish use is an indicator of both latent "cannabis use" and "hard drug use," and liquor is an indicator of both "alcohol use" and "hard drug use" in the Huba et al. (1981) study. This creates ambiguity in the conceptual distinction of the stages. Although this ambiguity was stressed by Martin (1982), the same parameterization has been consistently followed in subsequent structural equation models estimated over the next 15 years (e.g., Hays et al., 1986; 1987; Windle et al., 1989). Second, the assumption that only a simplex model is an accurate representation of a true sequential model is incorrect. For a three-stage model, the simplex model assumes no direct association between the first (alcohol) and third (other illicit drugs) stages (i.e., $\rho_{13} = 0$, where ρ_{13} is the population partial correlation of first- and third-stage drugs controlling for ρ_{12} and ρ_{23}). The alternative hypothesis of common rather than sequential pathways is assumed to be supported by the significant path between the first and third stages (i.e., $p_{13} > 0$). However, these criteria to test the sequential stage versus the common factor hypotheses are problematic and favor the common factor hypothesis. Instead, the criterion $\rho_{12} = \rho_{23} = p_{13}$ should have been employed for the common factor hypothesis and $\rho_{12} > \rho_{13}$ and $\rho_{23} > \rho_{13}$ for the sequential stage hypothesis. Indeed, the concept of sequential stages emphasizes, besides the temporal order of stages, the relative importance of causal associations between adjacent-stage drugs compared with nonadjacent-stage drugs rather than the complete absence of association between nonadjacent classes of drugs. A finding that the use of licit drugs generates an additional risk of initiating illicit drugs other than marijuana among marijuana users does not contradict the stage notion. A revaluation of Huba et al. (1981) data with these criteria clearly rejects the common factor hypothesis and supports the sequential stage hypothesis. Similarly, Windle, Barnes, and Welte (1989) confirmed the fit of a four-variable simplex model, in which illicit drugs were separated into enhancers and dampeners, in contradiction to the lack of fit reported by Hays et al. (1987) for a similar classification. Windle, Barnes, and Welte concluded that, in view of statistical features of the Hays et al. (1987) analysis, the simplex model was indeed the most appropriate representation of adolescents' involvement in substance use.

None of these methods and models, however, will be very effective in identifying patterns of drug-use progression if the number of classes of drugs to be distinguished is too large (such as more than 8 or 10 classes), and the major concern shifts from identifying major pathways that characterize the majority of individuals to detecting major regularities among numerous observed sequences of progression. In that case, the nonparametric sequence analysis method advocated by Abbott (1991; Abbott & Hrycak, 1990), especially a recent version based on the use of Gibbs sampling (Abbott & Barman, 1997), will be useful. The method can detect relatively numerous sequences of specified size out of a number of relevant events and can indicate what proportions of the sample fall into these various sequences. For example, the method can identify the five most typical sequences among sequences of three illicit drugs and what proportion of individuals fall into each sequential pattern.

The method, however, serves only a heuristic descriptive purpose and does not provide any significance test of the fit of alternative patterns. Its application to the study of drug-use progression remains to be implemented.

Causal Linkages among Stages and the Estimation of Specific Risk Factors

A second methodological challenge is to establish causal linkages among the different stages of drug use, such that entry into an earlier stage creates an increased risk of entering later stages (see O'Donnell & Clayton, 1982). The documentation of a developmental order representing stages or sequences of drug use does not necessarily establish such linkages. The observed sequences could reflect two processes: (1) some common causes of multiple drug involvement, such as a general tendency to deviance; and (2) the association of each class of drugs with different ages of initiation. It is necessary to assess the extent to which the use of a particular drug actually causes or influences initiation of the use of a drug at a next higher stage.

Based on event-history analyses, we documented that alcohol use and cigarette smoking indicated a significantly higher rate of initiating marijuana, and marijuana use indicated a significantly higher rate of initiating other illicit drugs in high school, after controlling for age and other covariates, including measures of deviance (Yamaguchi & Kandel, 1984b). Furthermore, there was an effect of former use among those who were not currently using a drug on their progression to higher stage drugs. As it is difficult to control completely for the selection bias of using a lower stage drug, the possibility that unobserved common causes generate the spurious effect of one class of drug over another remains. To address this issue, in event-history analysis, the dependent and selection processes are modeled simultaneously to allow correlated errors (e.g., Lillard & Waite, 1993; Lillard, Brian, & Waite, 1995). Whether such methods provide reliable estimates for the effect of one drug on the rate of initiating another drug, controlling for selection bias, is not yet certain because the effectiveness of the method depends in part on the availability of instrumental variables that affect one drug but not the other. However, it is very difficult to identify instrumental variables that will affect only one of the variables being simultaneously estimated, especially when the instrumental variables originate from the same respondents and the same data set as those with which the model is estimated.

Analyses that employ structural equation models have also addressed the issue of specific versus common pathways. Most investigators (e.g., Huba et al., 1981; Windle et al., 1989), however, have used cross-sectional data and have been limited in their assessment of the influence of one class of drug over another because the influence is measured by the association of different classes of drugs among individuals, rather than by the intraindividual association of multiple drugs over time. The approach used by Huba, Wingard, and Bentler (1981) was previously discussed.

Based also on structural equations models with latent variables, the study by Osgood et al. (1988) represented a significant advance in the field. It analyzed panel data and developed models that incorporated behavior-specific components as well as a general component of deviance. Thus, it could test time-lagged cross-behavior effects controlling for the effects of general deviance. Whereas deviant behaviors, including drug use, could be explained by a common general tendency for deviance, marijuana use retained a specific effect on the later use of other illicit drugs, an effect that could not be explained by this common cause. However, there was no effect of alcohol use on marijuana use, when the common tendency for deviance was controlled.

An alternative method for controlling for individuals' unobserved tendencies for using drugs in assessing the effect of one class of drug over an other is the latent-trait model that assumes person-specific constant parameters. We recently used this technique to assess the competing hypotheses of marital influence versus marital homophily on marijuana use using data on the association of the spouses' marijuana use over time (Yamaguchi & Kandel, 1993, 1997). The method can be applied to assess cross-drug influence from data on the association of a person's use of two classes of drugs over time, controlling for unobserved individual traits for drug use.

Drug-Specific Risk Factors

Not everyone who reaches a lower stage drug progresses to the next higher level of use; additional specific causes, either additively or interactively, affect the rate of progression into higher stages. The identification of drug-specific risk factors for progression is technically related to the documentation of causal linkages between stages. The estimation of specific risk factors for the use of a particular drug class, over and beyond common causes, assumes that all the relevant common causes have been measured

and entered as covariates in the models. In analyses of the natural histories of individuals, however, this assumption can always be faulted. In the absence of random assignment to the groups being compared, selection bias into particular states always exist and controls for such bias are difficult to implement.

Irrespective of the specific method used, it is essential to take into account the order of initiation and the person's position on the scale. We will elaborate this point in our discussion of the research implications of the stage concept.

Event-history analysis is a particularly appropriate method for identifying the determinants of each stage of progression separately. Specific predictors can be assessed with control for common causes, including *unobserved common causes*, by a simultaneous modeling of the initiations of two classes of drugs with error terms allowed to be correlated across events (e.g., Montgomery, 1992). However, such assessments lead to an issue similar to that in assessing the causal effect of one class of drug other the other: appropriate drug-specific instrumental variables are required. Such instruments are very difficult to obtain. Work needs to be carried out on statistical methods to solve this problem.

Timing of Longitudinal Data Collection

In addition to these statistical problems, a major impediment to the development of sequential models of drug involvement is the lack of sufficiently detailed longitudinal data on participation in the different drug classes and on the presumed risk factors and consequences. Multiwave longitudinal studies are required that carefully monitor adolescents involvement in the various behaviors over time, and that measure patterns of initiation, progression, stabilization and regression within each class. At each wave, measures need to be taken of the drug behaviors and the other relevant variables. In developmental periods of rapid behavioral change, the intervals need to be closely spaced in order to get reliable and valid data on the variables of interest. The timing between waves needs to be carefully planned, although it is not always clear what intervals would be most appropriate for which events.

Conceptual Challenges
Selection of Drug-Use Behavioral Units

The developmental stages identified to date have been based mostly on experimentation with four broad classes of drugs: alcohol, tobacco, marijuana, and other illicit drugs.

Finer differentiation of the drug-using behavior would provide a better understanding of developmental changes but would also probably reduce the orderliness of the observed patterns. Differentiation among different drug classes would be useful at different periods in the life cycle. At the earliest stages in early adolescence, differentiation among the alcoholic beverages would be appropriate. At later stages of involvement in late adolescence or adulthood, differentiation among illicit drugs other than marijuana, such as pills, cocaine, and heroin, would be helpful.

A major limitation of the stage model, as it has been developed to date, is that it does not differentiate degree of use within a particular class of drug and does not address the progression from use to dependence or intravenous drug use (Clayton & Ritter, 1985). The Stenbacka, Allebeck, and Romelsjö (1993) study is a rare exception, although it is based on cross-sectional data and only addresses the association between marijuana use and intravenous drug use. The developmental stage model describes qualitative changes from consumption of one drug to another rather than quantitative changes within a specific drug class. It is well known that persons who are the heaviest drug users in one stage are those most likely to go on to the next stage. Furthermore, the liability for drug dependence increases with increasing degree of drug use (Chen, Kandel, & Davies, submitted). Whether dependence on a drug at one stage increases the probability of going on to the next stage is not known.

In addition, as we noted, investigators who study smoking stress the importance of considering motivational stages even prior to actual use (Stern, Prochaska, Velicer, & Elder, 1987; Werch & Anzalone, 1995).

Domains of Risk Factors

The domains of risk factors considered to explain progression through the various stages has been limited to social-psychological variables. Efforts must be implemented to include biological variables on the one hand and community factors on the other. Thus, as regards alcoholism, different stages have been postulated to result either from biological maturation under genetic control or from the interaction of the organism with the environment, physical, social, or cultural (Zucker et al., 1995).

Conceptualization of Stages

The notion of stages itself needs clarification. In the literature on cognitive development, much discussion has sur-

rounded the conceptualization, definition and measurement of developmental stages. (See, for example, Flavell, 1982; Gibbs, 1977; Goulet, Hay, & Barclay, 1974; Phillips & Kelly, 1975; Schaie, 1965; Wohlwill, 1973.) The conceptual issues being debated include whether true developmental stages involve quantitative or qualitative changes; an invariant sequential and hierarchical order; progression or also regression; continuity or discontinuity. The common element in any definition of stages appears to be a sequential order. As stated by Kagan, "The idea of a developmental stage refers to a special hierarchical organization of psychological processes that is part of an invariant sequence of theoretically related stages" (1976, p. 116). Loeber and LeBlanc (1990) discuss some of these conceptual issues as they apply to a developmental perspective on delinquent behavior.

IMPLICATIONS OF THE STAGE MODEL FOR POLICY, RESEARCH, AND THEORY

The concept of stages in involvement of drugs has important implications for theory, research, and policy.

Policy Implications

The development of appropriate preventive programs aimed at reducing drug abuse in the general population depends upon understanding two aspects of the phenomenology of drug involvement: (1) the natural history of the use of various drugs, and (2) the factors that predict initiation and movement into the various phases of use for each drug. The first provides guidelines regarding when in the life cycle and for which substances it is most profitable to intervene. The second provides guidelines regarding which preventive strategies would be most effective. Both help identify the populations that should be the target of the interventions.

The concept of developmental stages in drug use has important implications for the development of preventive and educational efforts. The stage notion provides an optimum specification of the period in the life span when intervention efforts should be initiated, the types of drugs to be targeted, and characteristics of population groups at a particular stage who are most at risk for progression to the next stage or stages.

Prevention efforts must be initiated in adolescence. Early onset into a lower stage drug is emerging as a consistently crucial risk factor for progression to higher stage drugs. The earlier the age of onset into a lower stage drug, the higher the risk of progressing to a higher stage and the higher the risk of becoming a heavy user. As noted earlier, the period of highest risk for initiation for the legal drugs, cigarettes and alcohol, and for most illicit drugs, except cocaine, peaks at age 18 and declines sharply thereafter. The risk for initiation terminates by the late teens for alcohol and cigarettes, and by age 20–21 for marijuana; the risk continues at least through the late 20s for cocaine.

Major prevention efforts and educational efforts need to be targeted toward preventing initiation into alcohol drinking and cigarette smoking, drugs that are legal and commonly used for recreational purposes by adults in our society.

For all drugs, prevention efforts will be more effective if they are targeted at reducing the risk of initiating the use of drugs rather than decreasing use among users, as former and not only current drug use at a lower stage increases the risk of progression to a higher stage.

However, the factor of self-selection into drug use needs to be considered. Early initiators self-select themselves into early use and are already different from their peers at the time of initiation. One cannot naively assume that, by postponing initiation into drugs, one will simultaneously change adolescents in such a way that their chances of subsequent involvement in other drugs will be substantially reduced. One may simply shortcut a process in which risk-taking and nonconforming tendencies will express themselves eventually in the use of drugs other than marijuana or in other ways. However, postponement of initiation itself can have beneficial effects, by simply reducing the period in a formative period of the lifespan when the individual experiences the effects of drugs. An analogy with early teenage pregnancy may be illuminating. Simply postponing the timing of the first birth greatly improves the life chances of young women by eliminating the burden created by a child.

The importance of the notion of stages in drug use and of the crucial role played by the legal drugs in drug involvement is underscored in preventive and educational efforts of the National Institute on Drug Abuse and of the Substance Abuse and Mental Health Administration initiated over the last several years. Major efforts are underway to intervene in the process of drug involvement at the earliest stages of involvement, those preceding the use of illegal drugs and involving alcohol and especially cigarettes. However, because most programs target all classes of drugs, marijuana as well as cigarettes and alcohol, it cannot

be determined whether early prevention efforts targeted exclusively toward reducing young people's initiation into the use of cigarettes and/or alcohol reduces the use of marijuana. Unpublished data from Botvin's school-based interventions, with minimal focus on tobacco, alcohol and marijuana, indicate that students exposed to the interventions report lower rates of use of illicit drugs other than marijuana at age 18.9, 4 years after the last booster session (Botvin, personal communication, January 16, 1997).

Research Implications of the Stage Concept

The identification of cumulative stages in drug behaviors has important methodological implications for studying the factors that predict, differentiate, or result from drug use.

The identification of a developmental sequence of drug use improves the ability to identify populations at risk for each of the stages under consideration. If it is indeed the case that adolescents do not progress to a given stage without having experienced all prior stages, the population at risk for any particular stage is one that has reached the preceding stage. However, not everyone in the population follows exactly the sequence of progression identified in any particular model. This sets limits to an analytical approach based on decomposed subsamples, as discussed next.

The notion of stages of progression implies that in order to identify stage-specific risk factors for progression one needs to take into account an individual's position in the sequence. One approach is to decompose the sample into appropriate subsamples of individuals at a particular stage who are at risk for progression to the next stage. However, the use of decomposed subsamples can potentially introduce two kinds of sample selection biases. One source of bias arises from censoring; some of those who will ultimately reach a particular stage, for example, marijuana use, may not have initiated use by the time of the survey. Their exclusion may lead to an inadequate representation of the target at-risk population for progression to the use of other illicit drugs. A second source of sample bias is the elimination for the subsample of individuals whose progression patterns do not follow the modal patterns. These individuals may not be a random subsample of the population. Thus, we have shown that the sequencing tendency from alcohol to marijuana is weaker among Blacks than Whites (Yamaguchi & Kandel, 1996). If alcohol use is defined as the first stage in the analysis; proportionally more Blacks than Whites may be excluded, not because they did not initiate marijuana use but because they started marijuana use without using alcohol. This sample selection bias leads to the identification of risk factors for marijuana initiation only among those who follow the normal progression steps. However, those with deviant patterns of progression, whose proportion in the population would be small, may develop more serious drug problems.

Due to these two issues of sample selection bias, the use of decomposed subsamples is not necessarily the optimum approach. A preferable approach is to include all sampled subjects in the analysis, so as to take into account two implications of the stage notion: control for attainment of the prior stage and interaction terms between stages and covariates. However, as this alternative requires longitudinal data, it may be difficult to implement.

The analysis of a particular progression has to control for the attainment of the previous stages by including them as covariates. This eliminates the indirect effects of other covariates that influence the progression only through attainment of the previous stages. The failure to control for the previous stages may mistakenly give rise to the conclusion that the same factors predict different substances (e.g., Jessor & Jessor, 1977; Robinson et al., 1987), because the indirect effects of risk factors through the attainment of previous stages and the direct effects of other risk factors on the attainment of the stage of interest are confounded. The extent of this bias depends upon the distribution of individuals at different stages in the sample. The bias will be especially strong for the identification of risk factors for later stages, because each subsequent stage contains fewer individuals than the preceding stage in the sequence (Kandel, 1989). Because the onset of the previous stage is time varying, the analysis requires longitudinal data and methods that can handle time-varying covariates.

The notions of stages and stage-specific risk factors also imply that interaction effects between the prior stages and other risk factors will affect only those who reach the preceding stages (Kandel, Margulies, & Davies, 1978). Simple additive-effect models, which do not include interaction effects between the attainment of the previous stages and other covariates, obscure the presence of stage-specific risk factors.

Even when all individuals are included in the analysis, those who have progressed to a particular stage are not randomly selected. The selection bias of having attained the preceding stage generates a problem for deriving *causal implications* for stage-specific risk factors that are *applicable to the total population under the assumption that everyone was exposed to the preceding stages.*

Self-selection can be eliminated in laboratory animal-based experiments in which the drug consumption of animals previously exposed to various drugs by the experimenter can be observed. Cocaine self-administration by rats increases and develops more rapidly following pretreatment with caffeine (Schenk et al., 1994), amphetamine (Horger, Giles, & Schenk, 1992; Valadez & Schenk, 1994), and nicotine (Horger et al., 1992). In contrast to amphetamine, preexposure to nicotine selectively affects the reinforcing but not the locomotor activating effects of cocaine. This body of work was conducted by a single laboratory. We were unable to locate any other relevant experiments that would replicate the stage paradigm in the laboratory and would monitor the consumption of a higher stage drug among animals with different histories of exposure to presumed lower stage substances. Such experiments are needed and would provide a test of the sequential paradigm of involvement in drugs. This example also illustrates the important role of epidemiological research in stimulating biological and laboratory research.

Theoretical Implications of the Stage Model

The stage model comprises several basic assumptions. First, there is a regular ordering in the participation in different behaviors; involvement in using various drug classes is not opportunistic but follows definite pathways. Thus, legal or illegal drugs are not used indifferently solely as a function of availability or opportunity. Second, specific factors explain why some individuals are more likely than others to proceed further along a particular developmental sequence. As previously noted, by identifying populations at risk for progression from one behavioral stage to the next, it becomes possible to identify more accurately the factors that determine these transitions. The concept specifically draws attention to the possibility that different factors account for progression at different stages of the process of involvement in drugs. Third, participants in the different behaviors, such as users of different drugs, will also share certain attributes in common, as they started from the same behavior and shared certain initial characteristics at that point. Finally, controlling for common risk factors, one behavior will retain a causal impact on other behaviors. In the same way that initiation is not a random phenomenon, progression and regression are not random phenomena either. Specific factors will explain why some persons stop using drugs and others do not.

However, the stage notion confronts another theoretical perspective according to which the use of various drugs is part of a complex of problem behaviors and is influenced by a common set of risk factors. Jessor's Problem Behavior Theory, for example, postulates a common syndrome of transition proneness (Jessor & Jessor, 1977). Participation in any one behavior is an opportunistic response to environmental conditions on the part of individuals who share a certain proneness to deviance. Use of a particular drug or participation in any other nonconforming behavior is assumed to be the result of availability and particular environmental circumstances. "Where there is general proneness to problem behavior, what may determine the specific behavior engaged in may be the *specific exposure to* it, the *specific support for* it, or the *specific models for* it . . . risk factors that are represented in the proximal perceived environment may conceivably *channel* a general psychosocial proneness to problem behavior into the specific problem behaviors that are actually engaged in" (Jessor, Chase, & Donovan, 1980, italics added).

Thus, the stage and problem behavior perspectives reflect a fundamental theoretical antithesis concerning the relative importance of common versus specific risk factors to explain the manifestations of different forms of drug use or deviance. The results of empirical investigations suggest that both common and specific risk factors are important.

Conceptual Implications: Developmental Stages across Domains

In the same way that the use of different drugs is interrelated, the evidence is strong that participation in different classes of problem behaviors is interrelated (e.g., Donovan & Jessor, 1985; Dryfoos, 1990; Elliott, 1990; Osgood, 1991). Adolescents who use drugs, especially illegal drugs, are more likely than nonusers to engage in early sexual experimentation (Donovan, Jessor, & Costa, 1988; Elliott & Morse, 1989; Ensminger, 1987; Hundleby, 1987; Kandel, Raveis, & Davies, 1991; Mott & Haurin, 1988; Rosenbaum & Kandel, 1990; Zabin, Hardy, Smith, & Hirsch, 1986), to experience premarital pregnancies (Mensch & Kandel, 1992), to participate in delinquent activities (Akers, 1984; Hundleby, 1987; Jessor & Jessor, 1977; Johnston, O'Malley, & Eveland, 1978; Loeber & Stouthamer-Loeber, 1987), to drop out of school (Kaplan & Liu, 1994; Mensch & Kandel, 1988), to experience eat-

ing problems (Kandel et al., 1991; Killen et al., 1987), and psychological and/or psychiatric problems, including suicidal ideation (Choquet & Menke, 1990; Elliott, Huizinga, & Menard, 1989; Kandel et al., 1991). This covariation occurs also for the most extreme forms of drug involvement that meet criteria for substance-use disorders. Multiple diagnoses involving substance abuse, alcoholism and antisocial personality occur more frequently than expected in the general population (Anthony & Helzer, 1991; Kessler et al., 1996; Regier et al., 1990) and among psychiatric patients (Schubert, Wolf, Patterson, Grande, & Pendleton, in press). There is high comorbidity between substance-use disorders and other psychiatric disorders.

However, little work has been done to date to chart potential developmental sequences across different domains of problem behaviors. In part, this delineation has not been attempted because the appropriate data are not available. Rarely are more than two behaviors considered at a time. Most of the research has centered on the relationship of drug use with delinquency and sexual behavior. Minor delinquency typically precedes drug use (Elliott et al., 1989; Johnston et al., 1978; Kandel, Simcha-Fagan, & Davies, 1986). A unique time order between sexual behavior and drug use is more difficult to establish than between delinquency and drug use. Drug use and delinquency tend to precede the initiation of sexual activity (Elliott & Morse, 1989; Rosenbaum & Kandel, 1990). Elliott et al. (1989) identified a major developmental path from minor delinquency and/or alcohol, to marijuana, index crimes, polydrug use, and mental health problems. There appeared to be numerous deviations, however, and it was difficult to specify precisely these deviations.

CONCLUSION

Many aspects of cognitive and moral functioning (Kohlberg, 1966; Piaget, 1970; Preece & Read, 1995) are characterized by well-defined developmental sequences. The evidence presented in this chapter documents that the notion of stages is relevant to the study of involvement in drugs when choices must be made between successive behavioral alternatives. Individuals' involvement in drugs follows well-defined paths. Alcohol and/or tobacco, drugs that are legal for adults in our society, are used first; the use of marijuana rarely takes place without prior use of liquor or tobacco, or both; the use of illicit drugs other than marijuana rarely takes place in the absence of prior experimentation with marijuana. The notion of stages provides a useful organizing framework around which to develop specific theories of initiation, progression, and regression in drug use, as well as other problem behaviors, and specific intervention strategies to deal with the various stages and phases of participation in these behaviors. By identifying populations at risk for progression from one behavioral stage to the next, it becomes possible to identify more accurately the factors that impact on those transitions. Many theories of risk factors for drug involvement offer some concept of individual pathology as a primary explanation, whereas others stress social factors. Each of these concepts may apply to different stages of the process of involvement in drug behavior, social factors playing a more important role in the early stages and psychological factors in the later ones.

As we stressed previously (Kandel et al., 1992), it should be emphasized that, although a clear developmental sequence in drug involvement has been identified, use of a drug at a particular stage in the sequence does not invariably lead to the use of other drugs higher up in the sequence. Many youths stop at a particular stage and do not progress further. Most youths eventually stop using most of the drugs in adulthood. The notion of stages in drug behavior does not imply that these stages are either obligatory or universal such that all adolescents must progress through each in turn, as has been proposed by Piaget for stages in cognitive development or Kohlberg for stages in moral development. Rather, the phases in drug behavior are facilitative. The use of a drug at a lower stage is necessary but not sufficient for progression to a higher stage indicating involvement with more serious drugs. (See also O'Donnell & Clayton, 1982.) As suggested by Loevinger (1966) for ego development, such stages are hierarchical rather than embryonic.

This review makes clear that five questions, in particular, need to be clarified further and represent neglected areas in the study of stages in drug use. First, what are the quantitative stages or phases, if any, within classes of drugs? Does dependence constitute a stage separate from other patterns of use of particular drug classes? Second, is it possible to disaggregate illicit drugs other than marijuana and differentiate stages of use among illicit drugs other than marijuana? Third, what are the similarities and differences in sequential patterns of use among subgroups of the population, in particular different genders and different ethnic groups, and groups located in different ecological areas? Fourth, what risk factors explain progression from one stage of drug use to another, both across drug classes

and within each specific class, and among different sociodemographic groups? What are the risk factors for dependence compared with risk factors for casual use? Fifth, what methods are most suitable or need to be developed for identifying stages of drug use?

A major effort needs to be expanded to determine the existence of developmental patterns within and among different classes of drugs and different problem behaviors in adolescence. Such an effort requires an integrated approach to the investigation of adolescent development and youths at risk. It will provide an understanding of the relative role of these behaviors with respect to each other and would contribute to the understanding of adolescent development more generally. Developmental sequences have been found also to characterize delinquent participation (Lahey & Loeber, 1994; Loeber & LeBlanc, 1990) and may characterize other problem behaviors as well. Perhaps, certain behaviors are equivalent across sexes or across subgroups, as may be the case for delinquency among men and illicit drug use among women (Kandel et al., 1986) or depression among adolescent girls and delinquency among adolescent boys (Kandel & Davies, 1982). It is necessary to determine whether there tends to be a typical though not necessarily invariant sequence across various domains, or, whether there tends to be a common partial sequence with branching at some point. Drug involvement must be considered within a developmental framework in which it is acknowledged that there may be orderly transitions from one behavior to another. The task is to identify these transitions, the subgroups most at risk of making them, and the intervention strategies to intervene in the process, if it is decided that interventions are warranted.

In considering developmental transitions across a broad variety of problem behaviors, in addition to transitions within a single domain such as drug use, two questions, in particular, need to be addressed: (1) Are alternative behaviors opportunistic and functionally equivalent responses to common risk factors, or are there regular developmental paths underlying participation in the different behaviors, in which certain ones contribute increased and specific risks for others? (2) What is the commonality as well as the specificity of risk factors underlying participation in the different behaviors? Rather than being viewed as two opposed and competing explanations of problem behaviors, the stage and common syndrome perspectives ultimately will need to be reconciled to provide a comprehensive accounting of drug involvement by itself and in conjunction with other problem behaviors in adolescence and early adulthood.

As a final note, we wish to emphasize that recent advances in the biology of addiction also will need to be taken into account to elucidate the risk factors for drug-use progression. Marijuana, cocaine, heroin, alcohol, and nicotine have been found to have similar effects on dopamine release and the reward pathway that reinforces dependence on various drug (Bassareo & Chiara, 1997; de Fonseca, Carrera, Navarro, Koob, & Weisds, 1997; Tanda, Pontierei, & and Chiara, 1997). These biologists speculate that "the demonstration that long-term exposure to a cannabinoid agonist evokes neuroadaptive processes in the limbic system that resemble those associated with other major drugs of abuse may provide a neurobiological basis for the gateway hypothesis. Cannabinoid abuse, by activating CRF [corticotrophin-releasing factor] mechanisms, may lead to a subtle disruption of hedonic systems in the brain that are then 'primed' for further disruption by other drugs of abuse." (de Fonseca et al.)

Challenging conceptual and methodological issues remain to be solved. The limitations that we have discussed provide the outline of an agenda for further research in the field.

AUTHOR NOTE

Work on this research was partially supported by research grants DA00064, DA01097, DA03196, DA04866, DA02867, and DA09110, and a research scientist award KO5 DA00081 from the National Institute on Drug Abuse.

REFERENCES

Abbott, A. (1991). The order of professionalizations. *Work and Occupations, 18,* 355–384.

Abbott, A., & Barman, E. (1997). Sequence comparison via alignment and Gibbs sampling. *Sociological Methodology,*

Abbott, A., & Hrycak, A. (1990). Measuring remembrance in sequence data. *American Journal of Sociology, 96,* 144–185.

Adler, I., & Kandel, D. B. (1981). Cross-cultural perspectives on developmental stages in adolescent drug use. *Journal of Studies on Alcohol, 42,* 701–715.

Akers, R. L. (1984). Delinquent behavior, drugs, and alcohol: What is the relationship? *Today's Delinquent, 3,* 19–47.

Andrews, J. A., Hops, H., Ary, D., Lichtenstein, E., & Tildesley, E. (1991). The construction, validation and use of a Guttman scale of adolescent substance use: An investigation of family relationships. *Journal of Drug Issues, 21,* 557–572.

Andrich, D. (1985). An elaboration of Guttman scaling with Rasch models for measurement. In N. B. Tuma (Ed.), *Sociological Methodology 1985* (pp. 33–80), San Francisco: Jossey Bass.

Anthony, J. C., & Helzer, J. E. (1991). Syndromes of drug abuse and dependence. In L. Robins & D. Regier (Eds.), *Psychiatric disorders in America* (pp. 116–154), New York: The Free Press.

Bailey, S. (1992). Adolescents' multisubstance use patterns: The role of heavy alcohol and cigarette use. *American Journal of Public Health, 82,* 1220–1224.

Bassareo, V., & Di Chiara, G. (1997). Differential influences of associative and nonassociative learning mechanisms on the responsiveness of prefrontal and accumbal dopamine transmission to food stimuli in rats fed ad libitum. *Journal of Neuroscience, 17*(2), 851–861.

Bentler, P. M. (1990). Latent variable structural models for separating specific from general effects. In L. Sechrest, E. Perrin, & J. Bunker (Eds.), *Research methodology: Strengthening causal interpretations of nonexperimental data* (pp. 61–83) Rockville, MD: Agency for Health Care Policy and Research.

Blaze-Temple, D., & Lo, S. K. (1992). Stages of drug use: A community survey of Perth teenagers. *British Journal of Addictions, 87,* 215–225.

Brook, J. S., Hamburg, B. A., Balka, E. B., & Wynn, P. S. (1992). Sequences of drug involvement in African-American and Puerto Rican adolescents. *Psychological Reports, 71,* 179–182.

Brook, J. S., Whiteman, M., & Gordon, A. S. (1983). Stages of drug use in adolescence: Personality, peer, and family correlates. *Developmental Psychology, 19,* 269–277.

Brook, J. S., Whiteman, M., Gordon, A. S., & Cohen, P. (1986). Some models and mechanisms for explaining the impact of maternal and adolescent characteristics on adolescent stage of drug use. *Developmental Psychology, 22,* 460–467.

Chassin, L., Presson, C., & Sherman, S. (1984). Cigarette smoking and adolescent development. *Basic and Applied Social Psychology, 5,* 295–315.

Chen, K., Kandel, D. B., & Davies, M. (1997). "Relationships between frequency and quantity of marijuana use and last year dependence among adolescents and adults in the United States. Submitted for publication.

Choquet, M., & Menke, H. (1990). Suicidal thoughts during early adolescence: Prevalence associated troubles and help-seeking behavior. *Acta Psychiatrica Scandinavica, 81,* 170–177.

Clayton, R. R. (1992). Transitions in drug use: Risk and protective factors. In M. Glantz & R. Pickens (Eds.), *Vulnerability to drug abuse* (pp. 15–51). Washington, DC: American Psychological Association.

Clayton, R. R. & Ritter, C. (1985). The epidemiology of alcohol and drug abuse among adolescents. *Advances in Alcohol and Substance Abuse, 4,* 69–97.

Clogg, C. C., & Sawyer, D. O. (1981). A comparison of alternative models for analyzing scalability of response patterns. In S. Leinhardt (Ed.), *Sociological methodology 1981* (pp. 241–280). San Francisco: Jossey-Bass.

Collins, L. M. (1991). Measurement in longitudinal research. In L. M. Collins & J. L. Horn (Eds.), *Best methods for the analysis of change. Recent advances, unanswered questions, future directions*. Washington, DC: American Psychological Association.

Collins, L. M., Cliff, N., & Dent, C. W. (1988). "The longitudinal Guttman simplex: A new methodology for measurement of dynamic constructs in longitudinal panel studies. *Applied Psychological Measurement, 12,* 217–230.

Collins, L. M., Graham, J. W., Long, J. D., & Hansen, W. B. (1994). Cross-validation of latent class models of early substance use onset. *Multivariate Behav Res, 29,* 165–183.

Collins, L. M., & Wugalter, S. E. (1992). Latent class models for stage-sequential dynamic latent variables. *Multivariate Behavior Research, 27,* 131–157.

Colliver, J. D. (1989). Age at first use as a factor in the progression from cigarettes and alcohol to marijuana/hashish and cocaine among 18–25 year olds: Data from the 1985 National Household Survey on Drug Abuse. (Unpublished manuscript prepared for the Division of Epidemiology and Statistical Analysis, National Institute on Drug Abuse.

de Fonseca, R. F., Carrera, M. R. A., Navarro, M., Koob, G. F., & Weiss, F. (1997). Activation of corticotropin-releasing factor in the limbic system during cannabinoid withdrawal. *Science, 276,* 2050–2054.

Donovan, J. E., & Jessor, R. (1983). Problem drinking and the dimension of involvement with drugs: A Guttman scalogram analysis of adolescent drug use. *American Journal of Public Health, 73,* 543–552.

Donovan, J. E., & Jessor, R. (1985). Structure of problem behavior in adolescence and young adulthood. *Journal of Consulting and Clinical Psychology, 53,* 890–904.

Donovan, J. E., Jessor, R., & Costa, F. M. (1988). The syndrome of problem behavior in adolescence: A replication. *Journal of Consulting and Clinical Psychology, 56,* 762–65.

Dryfoos, J. G. (1990). *Adolescents at Risk*. London: Oxford University Press.

Ellickson, P. L., Hays, R. D., & Bell, R. M. (1992). Stepping through the drug use Sequence: Longitudinal scalogram analysis of initiation and regular use. *Journal of Abnormal Psychology, 101,* 441–451.

Elliott, D. S. (1990). Health enhancing and health compromising lifestyles. Prepared for the Carnegie Corporation Volume on Adolescent Health Promotion.

Elliott, D. S., Huizinga, D., & Menard, S. (1989). *Multiple problem youth*. New York: Springer-Verlag.

Elliott, D. S., & Morse, B. J. (1989). Delinquency and drug use as risk factors in teenage sexual activity. *Youth and Society, 21,* 21–60.

Ensminger, M. (1987). Adolescent sexual behavior as it relates to other transition behaviors in youth. *Reviews of research on the antecedents and consequences of adolescent pregnancy and childbearing: Volume II*, Final report of the Panel on Adolescent Pregnancy and Childbearing. Washington, DC: National Academy Press.

Flavell, J. H. (1982). Structures, stages, and sequences in cognitive development. In W. A. Collins (Ed.), *The Concept of Development* (pp. 1–28). Hillsdale, NJ: Lawrence Erlbaum.

Flay, B. R. (1993). Youth tobacco use: Risks, patterns, and control. In J. Slade & C. T. Orleans (Eds.) *Nicotine addiction: Principles and management* (pp. 365–384). New York: Oxford University Press.

Fleming, R., Leventhal, H., Glynn, K., & Ershler, J. (1989). The role of cigarettes in the initiation and progression of early substance use. *Addictive Behavior, 14,* 261–272.

Free, M. D. (1993). Stages of drug use. A social control perspective. *Youth and Society, 25,* 251–271.

Gibbs, J. C. (1977). Kohlberg's stages of moral judgement: A constructive critique. *Harvard Educational Review, 47,* 43–61.

Glantz, M., & Pickens, R. (Eds.). (1992). *Vulnerability to drug abuse*. Washington, DC: American Psychological Association.

Golub, A., & Johnson, B. (1994). The shifting importance of alcohol and marijuana as gateway substances among serious drug abusers. *Journal of Studies on Alcohol, 55,* 607–614.

Goodman, L. A. (1975). A new model for scaling response patterns: An application of quasi-independence concept. *Journal of the American Statistical Association, 70,* 755–768.

Gould, L. C., Berberian, R. M., Kasl, S. V., Thompson, W. D., & Kleber, H. D. (1977). Sequential patterns of multiple-drug use among high school students. *Archives of General Psychiatry, 34,* 216–226.

Goulet, L. R., Hay, C. M., & Barclay, C. R. (1974). Sequential analysis and developmental research methods. *Psychological Bulletin, 81,* 517–521.

Graham, J. W., Collins, L. M., Wugalter, S. W., Chung, N. K., & Hansen, W. B. (1991). Modeling transitions in latent stage-sequential processes: A substance use prevention example. *Journal of Consulting and Clinical Psychology, 59,* 48–57.

Guttman, L. (1950). The principal components of scale and analysis. In S. A. Stouffer, L. Guttman, E. A. Sichmas, P. F. Lazarsfeld, S. A. Star, & J. A. Clausen (Eds.), *Measurement and Prediction* Vol. IV (pp. 312–361). Princeton, NJ: Princeton University Press.

Hamburg, B. A. Kraemer, H. C., & Jahnke, W. (1975). A hierarchy of drug use in adolescence: Behavioral and attitudinal correlates of substantial drug use. *American Journal of Psychiatry, 132,* 1155–1163.

Hays, R. D., & Ellickson, P. L. (1991). Guttman scale analysis of longitudinal data: A methodology and drug use applications. *The International Journal of the Addictions, 25,* 1341–1352.

Hays, R. D., Stacy, A. W., Widaman, K. F., DiMatteo, M. R., & Downey, R. (1986). Multistage path models of adolescent alcohol and drug use: A reanalysis. *The Journal of Drug Issues, 16,* 357–369.

Hays, R. D., Widaman, K. F., DiMatteo, M. R., & Stacy, A. W. (1987). Structural-equation models of current drug use: Are appropriate models so simple(x)? *Journal of Personality and Social Psychology, 52,* 134–144.

Henningfield, J. R., Clayton, R., & Pollin, W. (1990). Involvement of tobacco in alcoholism and illicit drug use. *British Journal of Addiction, 85,* 279–292.

Horger, B. A., Giles, M. K., & Schenk, S. (1992). Preexposure to amphetamine and nicotine predisposes rats to self-administer a low dose of cocaine. *Psychopharmacology, 107,* 271–276.

Huba, G. J., & Bentler, P. M. (1982). On the usefulness of latent variable causal modeling in testing theories of naturally occurring events. *Journal of Personality and Social Psychology, 43,* 604–611.

Huba, G. J., Wingard, J. A., & Bentler, P. M. (1981). A comparison of two latent cariable causal models for adolescent drug use. *Journal of Personality and Social Psychology, 40,* 180–193.

Hundleby, J. D. (1987). Adolescent drug use in a behavioral matrix: A confirmation and comparison of the sexes. *Addictive Behaviors, 12,* 103–112.

Jessor, R., Chase, J. A., & Donovan, J. E., (1980). Psychosocial correlates of marijuana use and problem drinking in a national sample of adolescents. *American Journal of Public Health, 70,* 604–613.

Jessor, R., & Jessor, S. L. (1977). *Problem behavior and psychosocial development—A longitudinal study of youth.* New York: Academic Press.

Johnston, L. D., O'Malley, P. M., & Eveland, L. K. (1978). Drugs and delinquency: a search for causal connections. In D. B. Kandel (Ed.), *Longitudinal Research on Drug Use.* New York: Wiley.

Kagan, J. (1976). New views on cognitive development. *Journal of Youth and Adolescence, 5,* 113–129.

Kandel, D. B. (1975). Stages in adolescent involvement in drug use. *Science, 190,* 912–914.

Kandel, D. B. (1980). Developmental stages in adolescent drug involvement. In D. Lettieri, M. Sayers, & H.W. Pearson (Eds.), *Theories on drug abuse* (pp. 120–127). Rockville, MD: National Institute on Drug Abuse.

Kandel, D. B. (1989). Issues of sequencing of adolescent drug use and other problem behaviors. *Drugs and Society, 3,* 55–76.

Kandel, D. B., & Chen, K. (1995). The natural history of drug use in a general population sample from adolescence to the midthirties. *American Journal of Public Health, 85,* 41–47.

Kandel, D. B., & Davies, M. (1982). Epidemiology of adolescent depressive mood. *Archives of General Psychiatry, 39,* 1205–1212.

Kandel, D. B., Davies, M., & Davis, B. (1990). New York State youth survey. Epidemiological survey of drug use among New York State junior and senior high school students. Final report, New York State Psychiatric Institute and New York State Office of Mental Health.

Kandel, D. B., & Faust, R. (1975). Sequence and stages in patterns of adolescent drug use. *Archives of General Psychiatry, 32,* 923–932.

Kandel, D. B., Kessler, R. C., & Margulies, R. Z. (1978). Antecedents of adolescent initiation into stages of drug use: A developmental analysis. *Journal of Youth and Adolescence, 7,* 13–40.

Kandel, D. B., & Logan, J. A. (1984). Patterns of drug use from adolescence to young adulthood—I. Periods of risk for initiation, continued use, and discontinuation. *American Journal of Public Health, 74,* 660–666.

Kandel, D. B., Margulies, R. Z., & Davies, M. (1978). Analytical strategies for studying transitions into developmental stages. *Sociology of Education, 51,* 162–176.

Kandel, D. B., Raveis, V. H., & Davies, M., (1991). Suicidal ideation in adolescence: Depression, substance use and other risk factors. *Journal of Youth and Adolescence, 20,* 287– 307.

Kandel, D. B., Simcha-Fagan, O., & Davies, M., (1986). Risk factors for delinquency and illicit drug use from adolescence to young adulthood. *Journal of Drug Issues, 16,* 67–90.

Kandel, D. B., & Yamaguchi, K. (1985). Developmental patterns of the use of legal, illegal and medically prescribed psychotropic drugs from adolescence to young adulthood. In C. L. Jones, & R. Battjes (Eds.), *Etiology of drug abuse: Implications for prevention* (pp. 193– 235, NIDA Research Monograph 56, DHHS Pub. No. ADM 85-1335). Washington, DC: Superintendent of Documents, U.S. Government Printing Office.

Kandel, D. B., & Yamaguchi, K. (1993). From beer to crack: Developmental patterns of involvement in drugs. *American Journal of Public Health, 83,* 851–855.

Kandel, D. B., Yamaguchi, K., & Chen, K. (1992). Stages of progression in drug involvement from adolescence to adulthood: Further evidence for the gateway theory. *Journal of Studies on Alcohol, 53,* 447–457.

Kaplan, H. B., & Liu, X. (1994). A longitudinal analysis of mediating variables in the drug use–dropping out relationship. *Criminology, 32,* 415–439.

Kaplan, H. B., Martin, S. S., & Robbins, C. (1984). Pathways to adolescent drug use: Self-derogation, peer influence, weakening of social controls, and early substance use. *Journal of Health and Social Behavior, 25,* 270–289.

Kessler, R. C., Nelson, C. B., McGonagle, K. A., Edlund, M. J., Frank, R. G., & Leaf, P. J. (1996). The epidemiology of co-occurring addictive and mental disorders: Implications for prevention and service utilization. *American Journal of Orthopsychiatry, 66,* 27–31.

Kessler, R., Paton, S., & Kandel, D. B. (1976). Reconciling unidimensional and multidimensional models of patterns of drug use. *Journal of Studies on Alcohol, 37,* 632–647.

Killen, J. D., Taylor, C. B., Telch, M. J., Robinson, T. N., Maron, D. J., & Saylor, K. E., (1987). Depressive symptoms and substance use among adolescent binge eaters and purgers: A defined population study. *American Journal of Public Health, 77,* 1539–1541.

Kohlberg, L. (1966). Cognitive stages and preschool education. *Human Development, 9,* 5–17.

Lahey, B. B., & Loeber, R. (1994). Framework for a developmental model of oppositional defiant disorder and conduct disorder. In D. K. Routh (ed.), *Disruptive behavior disorders in childhood* (pp. 139–180). New York: Plenum Press.

Leventhal, H., & Cleary, P. (1980). The smoking problem: A review of the research and theory in behavioral risk modification. *Psychological Bulletin, 88,* 370–405.

Lillard, L. A., & Waite, L.J. (1993). A joint model of childbearing and marital disruption. *Demography*, 30, 653–681.

Lillard, L. A., Brien, M., & Waite, L. J. (1995). Pre-marital cohabitation and subsequent marital dissolution.*Demography, 32,* 437–457.

Loeber, R., and LeBlanc, M. (1990). Toward a developmental criminology. In N. Morris, & M. Tonry (Eds.), *Crime and justice: Annual review of research (Vol.12)* (pp.375–473). Chicago: 1990.

Loeber, R. and Stouthamer-Loeber, M. (1987). Prediction. In H. C. Quay (Ed.) *Handbook of juvenile delinquency* (pp.325–382). New York: Wiley.

Loevinger, J. (1966). The meaning and measurement of ego development. *American Psychologist, 21,* 195–206.

Marcos, A. C., & Bahr, S. J. (1995). Drug progression model: A social control test. *The International Journal of the Addictions, 30,* 1383–1405.

Martin, J. A. (1982). Application of structural modeling with latent variables to adolescent drug use: A reply to Huba, Wingard, and Bentler. *Journal of Personality and Social Psychology, 43,* 598–603.

Mensch, B. S., Kandel, D. B. (1988). Dropping out of high school and drug involvement. *Sociology of Education, 61,* 95–113.

Mensch, B. S., & Kandel, D. B. (1992). Drug use as a risk factor for premarital teen pregnancy and pregnancy outcome in a national sample of young women. *Demography, 29,* 409– 429.

Miller, T. Q. (1994). A test of alternative explanations for the stage-like progression of adolescent substance use in four national samples. *Addictive Behaviors, 19,* 287–293.

Mills, C. J., & Noyes, H. L. (1984). Patterns and correlates of initial and subsequent drug use among adolescents. *Journal of Consulting and Clinical Psychology, 52,* 231–243.

Montgomery, M. (1992). Household Formation and Home-Ownership in France. In J. Trussell et al. (Eds.), *Demographic Applications of Event History Analysis* (pp. 94–119), Oxford: Claredon Press.

Mott, F. L., Haurin, R. J. (1988). Linkages between sexual activity and alcohol and drug use among American adolescents. *Family Planning Perspectives, 20,* 128–136.

Newcomb, M. D., Bentler, P. M. (1986). Frequency and sequence of drug use: A longitudinal study from early adolescence to young adulthood. *Journal of Drug Education. 16,* 101–120.

O'Donnell, J. A. (1985). Interpreting progression from one drug to another. In L. N. Robins (Ed.), *Studying Drug Abuse.* New Brunswick, NJ: Rutgers University Press.

O'Donnell, J. A., & Clayton, R. (1982). The stepping-stone hypothesis—Marijuana, heroin and causality. *Chemical Depend, 4,* 229–241.

Osgood, D. W. (1991). Covariation among health compromising behaviors in adolescence. (Background paper for United States Congress Office of Technology Assessment's Adolescent Health Project, Washington, D.C. Prepared under contract to the Carnegie Council on Adolescent Development.)

Osgood, D. W., Johnston, L. D., O'Malley, P. M., & Bachman, J. G. (1988). The generality of deviance in late adolescence and early adulthood. *American Sociological Review, 53,* 81–93.

Phillips, D. C., & Kelly, M. E. (1975). Hierarchical theories of development in education and psychology. *Harvard Educational Review, 45,* 351–375.

Piaget, J. (1970). Piaget's theory. In P. H. Mussen (Ed.), *Carmichael's Manual of Child Psychology* (pp. 703–732), New York: Wiley.

Potvin, R. H., & Lee, C. (1980). Multistage path models of adolescent alcohol and drug use. *Journal of Studies on Alcohol, 41,* 531–542.

Preece, P. F. W., & Read, K. L. Q. (1995). A stage theory model of cognitive development. *British Journal of Mathematical and Statistical Psychology, 48,* 1–7.

Raveis, V. H., & Kandel, D. B. (1987). Changes in drug behavior from middle to late twenties: Initiation, persistence and cessation of use. *American Journal of Public Health, 77,* 607–611.

Regier, D. A., Farmer, M. E., Rae, D.S., et al. (1990). Comorbidity of mental disorders with alcohol and other drug abuse. *Journal of the American Medical Association, 264,* 2511–2518.

Robins, L. N. (1979). Addict careers. In R. Dupont, A. Goldstein and J. O'Donnel (Eds.) *Handbook on drug abuse* (pp. 325-355). Washington, DC: National Institute on Drug Abuse and Office of Drug Abuse Policy.

Robins, L. N., & Przybeck, T. R. (1985). Age of onset of drug use as a factor in drug and other disorders. In C.L. Jones and R.J. Battjes (Eds.) *Etiology of Drug Abuse: Implications for Prevention* (pp. 178–192). Washington, DC: U.S. Government Printing Office.

Robinson, T. N., Killen, J. D., Taylor, B., Telch, M. J., Bryson, S. W., Saylor, K. E. (1987). Perspectives on adolescent substance use. *Journal of the American Medical Association, 258,* 2072–2076.

Rosenbaum, E., & Kandel, D. (1990). Early onset of adolescent sexual behavior and drug involvement. *Journal of Marriage and the Family, 52,* 783–798.

Schaie, K. W. (1965). A general model for the study of developmental problems.*Psychological Bulletin, 64,* 92–107.

Schenk, S., Valadez, A., Horger, B. A., Snow, S., et al. (1994). Interactions between caffeine and cocaine in tests of self-administration. *Behavioral Pharmacology, 5,* 153–158.

Schubert, D. S. P., Wolf, A. Q., Patterson, M. B., Grande, T. P., Pendleton, L. (1988). A statistical evaluation of the literature regarding the associations among alcoholism, drug abuse and antisocial personality disorder. *International Journal of the Addictions, 23*(8), 797–808.

Schwartz, J. E. (1986). A general reliability model for categorical data applied to Guttman scales and current status data. *Sociological Methodology, 16,* 79–119.

Single, E., Kandel, D. B., & Faust, R. (1974). Patterns of multiple drug use in high school. *Journal of Health and Social Behavior, 15,* 344–357.

Sorenson, A. M., & Brownfield, D. (1989). Patterns of adolescent drug use: Inferences from latent structure analysis. *Social Science Research, 18,* 271–290.

Stenbacka, M., Allebeck, P., & Romelsjö, A. (1993). Initiation into drug abuse: The pathway from being offered drugs to trying cannabis and progression to intravenous drug abuse. *Scand J Soc Med* 1993, 21:31–39.

Stern, R. A., Prochaska, J. O., Velicer, W. F., & Elder, J. P. (1987). Stages of adolescent cigarette smoking acquisition: Measurement and sample profiles. *Addictive Behavior, 12,* 319–329.

Substance Abuse and Mental Health Services Administration. (1995). *National household survey on drug abuse: Population estimates 1994.* Rockville, MD: Author.

Tanda, G., Pontieri, F. E., Chiara, G. D. (1997). Cannabinoid and heroin activation of mesolimbic dopamine transmission by a common $_1$ opioid receptor mechanism. *Science, 276,* 2048–2050.

Tarter, R. E., Moss, H. B., & Vanyukov, M. M. (1991). Stepwise developmental model of alcoholism etiology (NIAAA Monograph, November 14–16, 1991).

Taub, D. E., Skinner, W. F. (1990). A social bonding-drug progression model of amphetamine use among young women. *American Journal of Drug and Alcohol Abuse, 16,* 77–95.

Valadez, A., & Schenk, S. (1994). Persistence of the ability of amphetamine preexposure to facilitate acquisition of cocaine self-administration. *Pharmacology, Biochemistry and Behavior, 47,* 203–205.

van del Pol, F., & Langeheine, R. (1990). Mixed Markov latent class models. *Sociological Methodology,* 20, 213–248.

Voss, H.L., & Clayton, R. R. (1987). Stages in involvement with drugs. *Pediatrician, 14,* 25–31.

Welte, J. W., & Barnes, G. M. (1985). Alcohol: The gateway to other drug use among secondary-school students. *Journal of Youth and Adolescence, 14,* 487–498.

Werch, C. E., & Anzalone, D. A. (1995). Stage theory and research on tobacco, alcohol, and other drug use. *Journal of Drug Education, 25,* 81–98.

Windle, M., Barnes, G. M., & Welte, J. (1989). Causal models of adolescent substance use: An examination of gender differences using distribution-free estimators. *Journal of Personality and Social Psychology, 56,* 132–142.

Wohlwill, J. F. (1973). *The study of behavioral development.* New York: Academic.

Yamaguchi, K. (1989). Log-quadratic models for the analysis of Guttman scales and their status correlates. *Quality and Quantity, 23,* 21–38.

Yamaguchi, K., & Kandel, D. B. (1984). Patterns of drug use from adolescence to early adulthood—II. Sequences of progression. *American Journal of Public Health, 74,* 668–672.

Yamaguchi, K., & Kandel, D. B. (1984). Patterns of drug use from adolescence to early adulthood—III. Predictors of progression. *American Journal of Public Health, 74,* 673–681.

Yamaguchi, K., & Kandel, D. B. (1993). Marital homophily on substance use among young adults. *Social Forces, 72*(2):505–528.

Yamaguchi, K., & Kandel, D. B. (1996). Parametric event sequence analysis: An application to an analysis of gender and racial/ethnic differences in patterns of drug-use progression. *Journal of the American Statistical Association, 91,* 1388–1399.

Yamaguchi, K., & Kandel, D. B. (1997). The influences of spouses' behavior and marital dissolution on marijuana use: Causation or selection. *Journal of Marriage and the Family, 59*(1), 22–36.

Yu, J., & Williford, W. (1992). The analysis of drug use progression of young adults in New York State. *The International Journal of the Addictions, 27,* 1313–1323.

Zabin, L. S., Hardy, J. B., Smith, E. A., & Hirsch, M. B. (1986). Substance use and its relation to sexual activity among inner-city adolescents. *Journal of Adolescent Health Care, 7,* 320–331.

Zucker, R. A., Fitzgerald, H. E., & Moses, H. D. (1995). Emergence of alcohol problems and the several alcoholisms: A developmental perspective on etiologic theory and life course trajectory. In D. Cicchetti and D. J. Cohen (Eds.), *Developmental psychopathology volume 2: Risk, disorder, and adaptation* (pp. 677–711). New York: Wiley.

CHAPTER 5

DEVELOPMENTAL CONSEQUENCES OF EARLY EXPOSURE TO ALCOHOL AND DRUGS

Gena Covell Britt
Karen S. Ingersoll
Sidney H. Schnoll

This chapter reviews the effects of early exposure to alcohol and drugs. Primarily, this entails the effects of prenatal exposure. Infants can also be exposed via breast milk; the effects of this are less well studied, however, and such exposure is less potent. In addition, the role played by the environment cannot be ignored, and there are certain characteristics of environments in which substance use occurs that make it difficult to differentiate between outcomes caused by prenatal substance exposure versus those related to the environment. Such environmental effects include lifestyle factors of drug-abusing parents, such as poverty, poor nutrition, and inadequate medical care. Maternal psychopathology is also an environmental factor that plays a role in child development. The effect of psychopathology must be considered both when substances are taken for psychotherapeutic reasons, as well as in cases of abuse, as many substance abusers have other comorbid psychopathology. The importance of these environmental factors cannot be minimized, making it impossible to separate the effects of substance exposure from environmental factors.

A myriad of methodological problems encountered in reviewing the literatures of each of these substances also make it difficult to draw strong conclusions about the specific effects of individual substances. Few studies are suf-ficiently large, prospective, multisite, and double-blind. Even fewer adequately control for confounding variables (including the environmental factors just discussed) such as the mother's sociodemographic characteristics, nutrition during pregnancy, level of prenatal care, and other drug and alcohol use. Indeed, the important variables are not always known. In the case of illicit substances, the dose is seldom known and difficult to quantify, and the time during pregnancy when the drug was taken is often impossible to ascertain. In addition, most studies have small sample sizes (due partially to noncompliance with research activities) that tend to get smaller and more select in longitudinal investigations because of high dropout rates. There is also increasing evidence that genetics plays an important role in the development of addictive behaviors. Therefore, women and their partners who use drugs can pass on a genetic predisposition for drug abuse and other behavioral impairments to their children. This means outcomes that appear related to substance exposure might actually be related to inherited traits. Although the specific methodological problems vary among different substances, the study of any prenatal substance exposure is generally faced with at least some of these. Any discussion of the effects of prenatal exposure needs to be considered in the context of these methodological limitations.

This chapter provides an extensive (although not exhaustive) review of the scientific human studies investigating the effects of prenatal exposure to alcohol and a variety of drugs. An exhaustive review could fill the pages of a book rather than a chapter; however, references are also extensive so interested readers have a wealth of resources to which they can turn. In general, the studies discussed consist of only those utilizing a control group, rather than case studies (although case studies are included for substances such as LSD and inhalants, for which very little empirical work exists). In addition, animal studies are excluded, given their questionable generalizability to humans. The substances to be discussed mirror the DSM-IV (American Psychiatric Association, 1994) categories of substances.

ALCOHOL

It is estimated that 35% of pregnant women drink alcohol regularly (Rosenthal, 1990) despite current knowledge that alcohol intake during pregnancy is teratogenic. Dysmorphic effects, growth retardation, and cognitive/behavioral deficits are all associated with prenatal alcohol exposure, probably in a dose–response relationship that has been partially obscured by the underreporting of drinking during pregnancy. The teratogenicity of high doses of alcohol during pregnancy is well accepted. Numerous studies have found that high-dose consumption can produce Fetal Alcohol Syndrome (FAS), fetal growth retardation, malformations, and childhood cancer, in addition to affecting cognitive and behavioral functioning.

Fetal Alcohol Syndrome

Fetal Alcohol Syndrome is defined by infant problems in three areas: characteristic facial dysmorphia, mental retardation, and growth deficiency. FAS is estimated to be between the first and third leading cause of mental retardation and is one of the few causes that is preventable. FAS occurs in approximately 1.5 cases per 1000 births and is more prevalent among certain ethnic minority groups, including Blacks and Native Americans. FAS among newborns in the United States increased fourfold from 1979 to 1992, either due to increased incidence or better detection (Centers for Disease Control, 1995). FAS-like facial features have been detected clinically and morphometrically by computer in male infants born to mothers who consumed 2 oz of alcohol per day in early pregnancy (Astley,

Clarren, Little, Sampson, & Daling, 1992). The association of lower doses of alcohol with poor pregnancy outcomes is less clear. The recognition of FAS in the early 1970s led to an explosion of research into the effects of prenatal exposure to alcohol.

Growth Parameters

A longitudinal study confirmed that prenatal alcohol exposure reduces fetal growth in length and head circumference, and reduces weight through 8 months, with no catch-up growth found (Geva, Goldschmidt, Stoffer, & Day, 1993). Others have also reported significant effects on growth through the age of 8 months (Streissguth, Barr, Sampson, & Bookstein, 1994). A 6-year prospective follow-up study found a dose–response relationship between first and third trimester alcohol intake and 18-month decreases in weight, height, and head circumference. This well-designed study with random selection of women at 4 months gestation used standardized instruments, multiple measurements of substance-use levels, and sophisticated multivariate techniques; it found that prenatal alcohol exposure predicted offspring size at age 6 after appropriate covariates were considered. Alcohol exposure and weight, height, head circumference, and palpebral fissures were related in a dose-response manner; no catch-up growth occurred after considering the 8-month size of the infant (Day, Richardson, Geva, & Robles, 1994). Alcohol's effects on growth may be lessened, however, if the mother stops drinking before the 3rd trimester (Weiner, Morse, & Garrido, 1989).

Fetal Malformations and Childhood Cancer

Alcohol consumption during pregnancy may also be related to fetal malformations, and there is developing evidence that some forms of cancer may be related to prenatal alcohol exposure. Retrospectively, maternal alcohol consumption during the first trimester of pregnancy has demonstrated a relationship with cardiovascular malformations in children (Tikkanen & Heinonen, 1991), including atrial septal defect (Tikkanen & Heinonen, 1992a) and conal malformations of the heart (Tikkanen & Heinonen, 1992b), brain hemorrhage and white-matter damage (Holzman, Paneth, Little, & Pinto-Martin, 1995), and childhood acute nonlymphocytic leukemia (van Duijn, van Steensel-Moll, Coebergh, & van Zanen, 1994).

Cognitive and Neurobehavioral Functioning

A prospective population-based longitudinal study with emphasis on ranges of alcohol exposure, including moderate-dose drinking such as social drinking, was conducted in a Seattle cohort (Streissguth et al., 1994). This study used standardized interviewing and testing procedures; 500 infants who had experienced prenatal alcohol exposure were selected. The study avoided some of the common pitfalls of response bias, partly due to its inception in the mid-1970s, when alcohol consumption during pregnancy was not known to be harmful. Thus, subjects in all SES groups drank, and there may have been less minimization of drinking reported by pregnant women in the study. Mothers were assessed at 5 months gestation, and children were assessed on days 1 and 2, at months 8 and 18, and years 4, 7, and 14.

Prenatal alcohol exposure was associated with poorer habituation to light or rattle, and low arousal, weaker Moro reflex, and other effects on day 1. On day 2, prenatal alcohol exposure alone decreased infant sucking pressure and increased the latency to first suck. The authors interpreted the day 1 and 2 findings as demonstrating that "subtle central nervous system (CNS) effects of prenatal alcohol are already measurable before the infant has ever encountered a postnatal environment" (Streissguth et al., 1994, p. 93). At 8 months, prenatal alcohol exposure remained significantly related to decrements in motor and mental development after other risk factors were considered. At 4 years, CNS effects of prenatal alcohol exposure included Full Scale IQ decrements of 4 points on the WPPSI, a sixfold increase in incidence of IQs less than 85 when the exposure was three drinks per day in utero, more "time in error" on a stylus maze task, and more attention difficulties. By 7 to 8 years of age, children prenatally exposed to alcohol continued to evidence many neurobehavioral test performance decrements. Visual-spatial tasks were more strongly affected than verbal tasks. Notably, a 7-point decrement in WISC-R Full Scale IQ was associated with 1 oz or more of average alcohol per day in utero. Alcohol effects in the neurobehavioral area did not attenuate with age by 8 years. At age 11, children who were prenatally exposed to alcohol evidenced distractibility, restlessness, lack of persistence, reluctance to meet challenges, poorer arithmetic performance, and poorer "total achievement." At age 14, arithmetic scores remained affected, as did word-attack skills, attention measures, and spatial learning.

Taken together, the results of this longitudinal study indicate that neurobehavioral outcomes of prenatal alcohol exposure remain significantly affected from day 1 to 14 years. "The effects were dose-dependent, generally without a threshold, and in the school age years, more salient for binge-type drinking patterns" (Streissguth et al., 1994, p. 98).

Other studies assessing children's cognitive functioning after prenatal alcohol exposure have found similar evidence of a dose-response relationship. Dose-dependent reductions in infant reaction time were found for babies prenatally exposed to alcohol; exposure explained 4 to 13% of the variance (Jacobson, Jacobson, & Sokol, 1994). In that study, the majority of mothers screened negative for alcohol abuse on the Michigan Alcoholism Screening Test (MAST), possibly indicating that adverse fetal effects can occur in the absence of "problem drinking." Sixty 27-month-old children exposed to alcohol in utero were tested in a prospective follow-up design to assess mental development. Those exposed to alcohol in the second and third trimester had lower scores on the Bayley Mental Development Index (MDI) and lower verbal comprehension scores on the Reynell test compared to those exposed only in the 1st trimester (Autti-Ramo et al., 1992). Korkman, Hilakivi-Clarke, Autti-Ramo, Fellman, and Granstrom (1994) compared the cognitive status of 2-year-olds with varying durations of exposure to alcohol in utero to children surviving preeclampsia or birth asphyxia, and to normal controls. Alcohol exposure throughout pregnancy was associated with impaired language and visual-motor development, and alcohol exposure until the third trimester was associated with attention deficit disorder.

Not all studies, however, have found cognitive problems in children prenatally exposed to alcohol. Greene, Ernhart, Martier, Sokol, and Ager (1990) found no effect of exposure on the language development of toddlers. Instead, aspects of the home environment predicted language development.

Summary

Alcohol exposure during gestation is clearly harmful to a subset of those exposed; there is no known safe level of consumption. Although dysmorphic effects tend to be seen only in those with high levels of consumption, subtler neurobehavioral effects occur and persist throughout childhood even among those with moderate exposure levels. Of interest to current researchers are questions about the vulnerability to addiction or second generation effects of those exposed to alcohol in utero who may then drink during their own pregnancies.

CANNABIS

Among the outcomes that have been investigated for an association with prenatal marijuana exposure are growth during infancy and childhood, birth characteristics, physical abnormalities, and various developmental assessments.

Growth Parameters

Investigations of growth parameters at birth often include measures such as birth weight, length, and head and chest circumference. Studies generally report no relationship between marijuana exposure and growth parameters at birth (Astley et al., 1992; Cornelius, Taylor, Geva, & Day, 1995; Day et al., 1991; Dreher, Nugent, & Hudgins, 1994; Fried, Watkinson, & Willan, 1984). Isolated associations have been found for some of these measures. For instance, Day et al. (1991) reported a relationship between first trimester exposure (particularly heavy exposure) to marijuana and decreased birth length, and between heavy exposure in the third trimester and increased birth weight. Although Cornelius et al. report no relationship between growth parameters and exposure to marijuana, they did find an increased risk for being small for gestational age among a small subsample of those exposed during the second trimester. Gestational age can also be considered along with these measures of newborn growth. Some reports find no relationship between marijuana exposure and gestational age (Astley et al., 1991; Day et al., 1991; Dreher et al., 1994). Both Cornelius et al. and Fried et al. (1984) found a relationship prenatal marijuana exposure and shorter gestation, although in both studies the exposed and unexposed infants had a mean gestational age of greater than 38 weeks.

Some researchers have investigated growth beyond the infancy period among those prenatally exposed to marijuana (Barr, Streissguth, Martin, & Herman, 1984; Day et al., 1992, 1994). Barr et al. (1984) found a significant negative relationship between prenatal exposure and 8-month length, but no relationship for weight and head circumference. However, Day et al. (1992) found the effect on birth length reported above had disappeared by 8 months, whereas current maternal use of marijuana was positively associated with head circumference. They report no significant relationships between growth and either prenatal mar-

ijuana exposure or maternal current use at 18 or 36 months (Day et al., 1992) or 6 years of age (Day et al., 1994).

Newborn Characteristics

The relationship between other newborn characteristics such as Apgar scores and neurobehavioral characteristics have also been investigated. Studies that report findings on the Apgar scale found no effect of marijuana exposure on newborn status (Astley et al., 1992; Dreher et al., 1994). Fried, Watkinson, Dillon, and Dulberg (1987) administered the Prechtl neurological assessment at 9 and 30 days postpartum. No relationship was found between marijuana exposure and the Prechtl syndrome scores of hyperexcitability, apathy, and hemisyndrome (although some individual scores significantly discriminated between exposed and nonexposed at both 9 and 30 days). Newborn behavior has been examined using the Neonatal Behavioral Assessment Scale (NBAS). Dreher et al. (1994) found no differences between exposed and nonexposed infants on any cluster scores or supplementary items when the NBAS was administered at 3 days. At 1 month, exposed infants had significantly more optimal scores on the clusters of autonomic stability and reflexes, and the supplementary item general irritability; heavily exposed infants had significantly more optimal scores on the orientation, autonomic stability, and reflex clusters, and on the supplementary items of quality of alertness, robustness, regulatory capacity, motor tone, general irritability, examiner's persistence, and reinforcement value. The authors suggest the unexpected more optimal scores among the exposed infants may be related to the better social and economic standing of the mothers who used marijuana in their Jamaican sample. Some other important issues related to these findings are the relatively small sample size (fewer than 25 in each group), the large number of mean comparisons, and the fact that many of the statistically significant differences were clinically very small (1 scale point or less). Richardson, Day, and Taylor (1989) conducted NBAS exams at 2 days postpartum on more than 350 infants (146 of whom were exposed during the first trimester) and found no relationship between the number of joints smoked per day during any trimester and any NBAS cluster scores using regression analyses.

Physical Anomalies

There is not strong evidence for a relationship between prenatal marijuana exposure and physical anomalies. Most studies report no such relationship (Astley et al., 1992; Cornelius et al., 1995; Day et al., 1991, 1992, 1994). However, among the White subsample of infants born to adolescent mothers studied by Cornelius et al., there was an increased risk of minor physical abnormalities associated with exposure during the first trimester.

Child Development

Fried and his colleagues have conducted a wide array of follow-up assessments to document the developmental status of children prenatally exposed to marijuana through the age of 6 years. Most of the measures showed no relationship to marijuana exposure; the number of characteristics measured far outweighed the number of relationships that were revealed. At 3 years, children who had experienced moderate levels of marijuana exposure prenatally performed better on the motor scale of the McCarthy Scales of Children's Abilities compared to both those who had experienced light and heavy exposure, although no differences emerged for the other five subscales (Fried & Watkinson, 1990). At 4 years, heavily exposed children scored lower on the McCarthy verbal and memory subscales, and the Peabody Picture Vocabulary Test compared to moderately and lightly exposed children; no differences were found for the other McCarthy subscales or for the Reynell Developmental Language Scales (expressive and comprehensive language), Tactile Form Recognition Task, or the Pegboard test (eye–hand coordination), (Fried & Watkinson, 1990). At both 5 and 6 years, no relationships emerged between prenatal marijuana exposure and any of the McCarthy subscales or the Peabody Picture Vocabulary Test (Fried, O'Connell, & Watkinson, 1992). Also measured at the age of 6 was memory (Sentence Memory Test and Target Test), vigilance and sustained attention (Gordon Diagnostic System), and hyperactivity/impulsivity (Conner's Parent Rating Scale). Among these outcomes, heavily exposed children were found to perform more poorly than lightly/nonexposed on the vigilance task and have higher parent ratings of hyperactivity/impulsivity (Fried, Watkinson & Gray, 1992). O'Connell and Fried (1991) administered 12 assessments resulting in 27 different subscale scores; scales that demonstrated a statistically marginal ability to discriminate between exposed and nonexposed children were considered in further analyses. No relationship was found between any of these outcomes and prenatal marijuana exposure when the children were between the ages of 6 and 9 years. An interaction between

maternal age and exposure was revealed for sequential memory and syntax quotient with exposed children of younger mothers scoring lowest and nonexposed children of younger mothers scoring highest, although mean scores for all groups were higher than published norms.

Summary

Studies investigating the effects of prenatal exposure to marijuana generally report few ill effects in areas including growth, newborn functioning, physical anomalies, or long- term child development.

COCAINE

Cocaine is the primary illicit substance of abuse for a large proportion of women of childbearing age. The recent proliferation of research investigating the effects of prenatal cocaine exposure reflects this trend. A variety of outcomes have been explored including obstetric complications, growth, newborn characteristics, physical anomalies, and later child development.

Obstetric Complications

Many studies report a relationship between prenatal cocaine use and a variety of individual pre- and perinatal complications such as spontaneous abortions, infections during pregnancy, pregnancy-induced hypertension, preeclampsia, abruptio placentae, stillbirth, premature labor and/or delivery, caesarean delivery, meconium staining, fetal monitor abnormality, and fetal distress (Bingol, Fuchs, Diaz, Stone, & Gromisch, 1987; Chasnoff, Burns, & Burns, 1987; Chasnoff, Burns, Schnoll, & Burns, 1985; Chasnoff, Griffith, MacGregor, Dirkes, & Burns, 1989; Chasnoff, Lewis, Griffith, & Willey, 1989; Cohen, Green, & Crombleholme, 1991; Fulroth, Phillips, & Durand, 1989; Hadeed & Siegel, 1989; Little, Snell, Klein, & Gilstrap, 1989; Mastrogiannis, Decavalas, Verma, & Tejani, 1990). It is important to note that each of these studies reports a relationship for some but not all such complications. In addition, the findings of other researchers do not support a relationship between prenatal cocaine use and many of these complications (Chouteau, Namerow, & Leppert, 1988; Mayes, Granger, Frank, Schottenfeld, & Bornstein, 1993). Others who found a relationship for an individual complication found no relationship when the total number of complications was considered (Richardson & Day,

1991). It is hard to draw conclusions from these findings, but important to note that, in some instances, women who used cocaine during the pregnancy under study also had a history of significantly more complications, such as spontaneous abortions and abruptio placentae, during previous pregnancies (Chasnoff et al., 1985; Hadeed & Siegel, 1989). This history of pregnancy complications might increase the risk of complications in the pregnancy under study. It is also important to remember that women who use cocaine during pregnancy often use it along with other drugs, such that some of these effects may be due to other drugs or interactions among substances. In addition, some complications might be confounded with each other. For example, infections like hepatitis B and venereal disease could at the same time be associated with both cocaine use and other pregnancy complications.

Growth Parameters

The majority of research regarding the effects of prenatal cocaine exposure include reports on growth parameters at birth (birth weight, birth length, head circumference), and most studies report a relationship with at least some of these parameters. Because of the quantity of these reports and because they are cited elsewhere in this section they are not listed here, although it is important to note that some studies fail to support such a relationship (Chasnoff et al., 1987; Chasnoff et al., 1985; Richardson & Day, 1991, 1994). Although findings are strongly in support of the effect of prenatal cocaine exposure on prenatal growth, some differences in size are statistically significant but clinically of questionable importance. It may be more meaningful to examine outcomes such as increased incidence of low birth weight or growth retardation. Investigators who have examined growth in this way have found some support for a higher incidence of low birth weight (Chasnoff, Griffith, et al., 1989; Chouteau et al., 1988; Cohen et al., 1991) and growth retardation (Chasnoff, Griffith, et al., 1989; Chasnoff, Lewis, et al., 1989; Cherukuri, Minkoff, Feldman, Parekh, & Glass, 1988; Fulroth et al., 1989; Hadeed & Siegel, 1989; Keith et al., 1989) related to prenatal cocaine exposure. However, there is evidence that maternal cessation of cocaine use early in pregnancy can reduce these effects (Chasnoff, Griffith, et al., 1989). Other studies do not support a relationship between prenatal cocaine exposure and low birth weight (Richardson & Day, 1991) or growth retardation (Little et al., 1989; Richardson & Day, 1991). Follow-up studies report a sig-

nificant contribution of cocaine exposure to head circumference through the age of 12 months (Chasnoff, Griffith, Freier, & Murray, 1992), and significantly lower weight and head circumference through 30 months of age (Hurt et al., 1995), but no cocaine-specific effect on weight, height, or head circumference by the age of 3 years (Azuma & Chasnoff, 1993; Griffith, Azuma, & Chasnoff, 1994; Hurt et al., 1995).

Newborn Characteristics

Newborns can be characterized in a variety of ways. The most common descriptions in the literature on prenatal cocaine exposure include the Apgar scale, the Neonatal Behavioral Assessment Scale (NBAS), and reports of neonatal complications such as withdrawal. Most studies report no relationship between cocaine exposure and Apgar scores (Chasnoff, Griffith, et al., 1989; Chasnoff, Lewis, et al., 1989; Coles, Platzman, Smith, James, & Falek, 1992; Fulroth et al., 1989; Hadeed & Siegel, 1989; Kaye, Elkind, Goldberg, & Tytun, 1989; Richardson & Day, 1991, 1994; Woods, Eyler, Behnke, & Conlon, 1993), although some reports do support such a relationship (Cohen et al., 1991; Keith et al., 1989; Little et al., 1989; Neuspiel, Hamel, Hochberg, Greene, & Campbell, 1991).

Regarding NBAS performance, most studies report at least some significant effects on NBAS scores related to cocaine exposure, although different studies report different effects, such that no pattern emerges (Black, Schuler, & Nair, 1993; Chasnoff et al., 1987; Chasnoff et al., 1985; Chasnoff, Burns, Schnoll, & Burns, 1986; Chasnoff, Griffith, et al., 1989; Chasnoff, Lewis, et al., 1989; Coles et al., 1992; Eisen et al., 1991; Griffith, Chasnoff, Dirkes, & Burns, 1988; Tronick, Frank, Cabral, & Zuckerman, 1994). Five studies found no significant relationship between prenatal cocaine exposure and NBAS behavior (Eyler, Behnke, Conlon, Woods, & Wobie, 1995; Hawley, Brodsky, Giannetta, & Hurt, 1992; Neuspiel et al., 1991; Richardson & Day, 1991; Woods et al., 1993). Although the list of studies supporting the relationship between cocaine exposure and NBAS performance seems impressive, some studies found few differences out of many NBAS items that were compared. Chasnoff et al. (1987) found group differences on only three items; assuming all NBAS items were compared (the description is not clear), this is a very small percentage of the total number of items. Coles et al. (1992) found only two clusters out of seven to differentiate the groups. In addition, some significant differences were clinically very small. Black et al. (1993) found significant differences on three out of six clusters; when comparing the mean cluster scores, however, only one of these differences exceeded 1 scale point (scores within 1 point of each other are considered to be reliable). Chasnoff et al. (1985) and Chasnoff, Burns, Schnoll, and Burns (1986) found two (out of four) significant group differences for clusters; neither of the mean differences on these exceeded 1 scale point. It bears repeating that no consistent pattern of differences emerged among the studies.

Postnatal complications have been investigated by some researchers. When a constellation of withdrawal symptoms from cocaine is investigated, inconsistent findings are reported with some findings supporting neonatal cocaine withdrawal (Fulroth et al., 1989) and others not (Coles et al., 1992). Similarly, when individual neonatal complications (some of which might be related to withdrawal) are investigated, inconsistent findings emerge. Most studies report no relationship between cocaine exposure and complications such as respiratory distress, seizures, hyperresponsiveness, hyperbilirubinemia, hypertonia, jitteriness, poor feeding, tachypnea (Hadeed & Siegel, 1989; Little et al., 1989; Mayes et al., 1993; Parker et al., 1990), whereas others have reported similar symptoms related to cocaine exposure (Chasnoff, Griffith, et al., 1989; Mastrogiannis et al., 1990).

Anomalies

Although early studies suggested a possible relationship between prenatal cocaine exposure and congenital anomalies, those studies usually had a small sample size and did not report statistical significance. While a few studies do report a significant relationship between birth defects and cocaine exposure (Bingol et al., 1987; Little et al., 1989), cocaine is not generally considered to be teratogenic with most studies failing to support such a relationship (Fulroth et al., 1989; Hadeed & Siegel, 1989; Richardson & Day, 1991, 1994; Zuckerman et al., 1989).

Child Development

In general, there is little evidence for a relationship between prenatal cocaine exposure and later developmental outcome. Studies have generally failed to find significant effects of cocaine exposure on the Bayley Scales of Infant Development (Chasnoff et al., 1992; Hurt, Betancourt, Malmud, Brodsky, & Giannetta, 1994), although the find-

ings of Singer et al. (1994) do support a relationship. Performance on the Stanford–Binet Intelligence Scale has also been unable to differentiate cocaine-exposed and nonexposed children, with both groups generally scoring in the normal range (Azuma & Chasnoff, 1993; Griffith et al., 1994). In addition, child problem behavior as measured by the Child Behavior Checklist has not demonstrated a relationship with prenatal cocaine exposure (Azuma & Chasnoff, 1994; Griffith et al., 1994). Hurt et al. (1994) report a cocaine-related difference on only one of five domains on the Battelle Developmental Inventory.

Summary

Although research does suggest an effect of cocaine on measures of growth, there is not strong evidence for the teratogenic nature of cocaine or cocaine's impact on later child development. The support for cocaine's role in obstetric complications and newborn behavior is questionable.

NICOTINE

Between 25% and 40% of pregnant women smoke during the gestational period (Floyd, Zahniser, Gunter, & Kendrick, 1991). Prenatal exposure to cigarette smoke not only appears to influence birth weight and postnatal height negatively, but also has effects including increased incidence of abruptio placentae, placenta previa, prematurity, premature membrane rupture, and small-for-gestational-age infants, as well as Sudden Infant Death Syndrome (SIDS) (Harlap & Shiono, 1980; Naeye, 1980, 1982).

Growth Parameters

Children born to heavy smokers are on average 200 g lower in birth weight (ACOG, 1993). In a large population-based study, smoke exposure levels have been shown to predict decrements in birth weight in a dose-dependent fashion. Infants of nonsmoking mothers exposed passively to smoking weighed 45 g less than infants born to nonsmoking mothers unexposed to passive smoking, while smokers' infants weighed between 78 and 233 g less depending on their level of exposure (Eskenazi, Prehn, & Christianson, 1995). However, another study found that nonsmoking mothers exposed to smoke do not have an increased risk of bearing small-for-gestational-age infants (Chen & Petitti, 1995). Generally, tobacco-affected children evidenced catch-up growth unless they were also affected by prenatal alcohol exposure (Day et al., 1992).

Respiratory Illness

A number of studies have compared the incidence of respiratory problems in infants and children exposed to environmental tobacco smoke due to parents' smoking. These have found consistent relationships between exposure to passive smoke (exposure to exhaled "mainstream" smoke and noninhaled "sidestream" smoke) and respiratory disorders (Colley, Holland, & Corkhill, 1974; Cuijpers, Swaen, Wesseling, Sturmans, & Wouters, 1995; Duff et al., 1993; Eskenazi et al., 1995; Ogston, Florey, & Walker, 1987; Willers, Svenonius, & Skarping, 1991). Children under the age of 2 exposed to passive smoke were nearly 5 times more likely to experience wheezing (Duff et al., 1993). Retrospectively, a significant relationship has been found between childhood asthma and maternal smoking (Willers et al., 1991). In addition, children of smoking mothers evidenced higher incidence of bronchitis and pneumonia in the first year of life, along with continued impairments in pulmonary function (Levy & Koren, 1990). An American Heart Association report on cardiovascular disease in the young summarized these findings: "Considering the substantial morbidity, and even mortality, of acute respiratory illness in childhood, a doubling in risk attributable to passive smoking clearly represents a serious pediatric health problem" (Gidding, Morgan, Perry, Isabel-Jones, & Bricker, 1994, p. 2583).

SIDS

Several population-based studies have implicated prenatal and postnatal smoking in the increased risk of SIDS (Bulterys, 1990; Haglund & Cnattingius, 1990; Malloy, Kleinman, Land, & Schramm, 1988; Schoendorf & Kiely, 1992). SIDS is known to relate to sociodemographic characteristics, and appears related to impairments in infants' cardiorespiratory functioning. A Swedish study found a greater level of nicotine exposure in infants who died of SIDS than would be expected. The authors suggested "that exposure to tobacco smoke may be the factor that can precipitate a potentially fatal event in a number of different circumstances" (Milerad, Rajs, & Gidlund, 1994, p. 61). A retrospective epidemiological study of SIDS in Kentucky using birth certificate data found that maternal smoking of

one pack per day nearly doubled the risk of SIDS (Sanghavi, 1995).

Other Outcomes

Although prenatal smoke exposure has not been implicated in birth defects, occasional reports have found increased risk. In a retrospective study, maternal smoking was associated with a significantly increased risk of craniosynostosis (premature closure of the structural joints of the infant skull) (Alderman, Bradley, Greene, Fernbach, & Baron, 1994), and with a higher risk of childhood cancer, including Acute Lymphoblastic Leukemia (ALL), Hodgkin's disease, and Wilms' tumors in children born to smoking mothers (Stjernfeldt, Berglund, Lindsten, & Ludvigsson, 1986). In addition, independent of birth weight, maternal smoking is associated with higher infant mortality rates (Kleinman, Pierre, Madans, Land, & Schramm, 1988).

Summary

Documentation is extensive and clear that prenatal tobacco smoke exposure is related to decrements in growth parameters and increases in adverse pregnancy outcomes. There is also evidence of a relationship between prenatal and postnatal exposure and a higher incidence of childhood respiratory problems and SIDS. More research is needed to determine if a relationship exists for birth defects and childhood cancer, as well as into the mechanisms of effects and separation of pre- and postnatal exposure effects.

OPIOIDS

The perinatal effects of opioids have been studied for over 20 years; however, much of the information developed from early studies was marred by design flaws (Hans, 1989). More recent studies on the effects of opioids on pregnancy and later development are beginning to take these factors into consideration. However, it is difficult to make precise statements as to the effect of opioids on pregnancy, as well as on newborn and later development, because of the large number of confounding variables and the small populations often involved in the studies.

Growth Parameters

Various studies have reported intrauterine growth deficiencies related to prenatal opioid exposure as evidenced in significantly lower birth weight, length, and/or head circumference in comparison to nonexposed neonates (Chasnoff, Burns, Burns, & Schnoll, 1986; Chasnoff, Burns, & Schnoll, 1984; Kaltenbach & Finnegan, 1987; Kaye et al., 1989; Keith et al., 1989), although other reports found no differences related to opioid exposure in these outcomes (Chasnoff et al., 1985; Chasnoff, Burns, Schnoll, & Burns, 1986; Chasnoff, Schnoll, Burns, & Burns, 1984; Strauss, Lessen-Firestone, Starr, & Ostrea, 1975). Similar inconsistent findings are reported regarding gestational age, with some investigators reporting significantly younger gestational age related to opioid exposure (Kaye et al., 1989; Keith et al., 1989), but most finding no effect (Chasnoff, Burns, Burns, & Schnoll, 1986; Chasnoff, Burns, & Schnoll, 1984; Chasnoff, Schnoll et al., 1984; Kaltenbach & Finnegan, 1987; Ryan, Ehrlich, & Finnegan, 1987). One report of follow-up growth found deficiencies in weight and length through 6 months, and in head circumference through 2 years of age (Chasnoff, Burns, Burns, & Schnoll, 1986). Strauss, Starr, Ostrea, Chavez, & Stryker (1976) found no evidence of growth retardation at 12 months of age. More recent findings suggest that the association between low birth weight and illicit substance use may be related more to the concomitant use of nicotine and alcohol, although reduced head circumference appears to be directly related to the use of opioids during pregnancy (Jacobson, Jacobson, Sokol, Martier, et al., 1994).

It is important to note that placing opioid-dependent women on a long-acting drug like methadone enables them to stabilize their lifestyles. This may result in increased prenatal care with reductions in spontaneous abortions and premature labor, and increases in birth weight. Some reports, however, continued to find lower birth weights compared to women who did not use drugs (Finnegan, 1975; Householder, Hatcher, Burns, & Chasnoff, 1982; Strauss, Andresko, Stryker, Wardell, & Dankell, 1974).

Newborn Characteristics

Research has also explored for an association between prenatal opioid exposure and various newborn characteristics such as Apgar scores, withdrawal, and neonatal behavior. None of the studies reviewed reported differences in Apgar scores related to opioid exposure (Chasnoff, Burns, Burns, & Schnoll, 1986; Chasnoff, Burns, & Schnoll, 1984; Chasnoff et al., 1985; Chasnoff, Burns, Schnoll, & Burns,

1986; Chasnoff, Schnoll, et al., 1984; Fulroth et al., 1989; Jeremy & Hans, 1985; Kaye et al., 1989).

Neonatal withdrawal after prenatal exposure to opioids, on the other hand, has been well documented (Chasnoff, Burns, Burns, & Schnoll, 1986; Chasnoff, Burns, & Schnoll, 1984; Chasnoff, Schnoll, et al., 1984; Desmond & Wilson, 1975; Finnegan, 1986; Fulroth et al., 1989; Kaltenbach & Finnegan, 1986, 1987), with incidence ranging from 21 (Fulroth et al., 1989) to 81% (Kaltenbach & Finnegan, 1986) of opioid-exposed infants experiencing levels of withdrawal symptoms severe enough to require pharmacologic intervention. This neonatal abstinence is characterized by central nervous system irritability with high-pitched crying, increased tone, tremors, respiratory distress, gastrointestinal dysfunction, and poor sucking reflex. The hyperactivity can result in excoriations on the elbows and knees of the newborn. In severe cases, seizures can occur. In mild cases of the neonatal abstinence syndrome, swaddling the newborn can be very effective. However, in more severe cases, pharmacotherapy may be necessary. Finnegan (1986) developed a scoring system to rate the neonatal abstinence syndrome and determine the need for medication. Although death from opioid withdrawal is not a consequence in adults, it can occur in untreated newborns.

Behavioral studies in the immediate postpartum period have utilized the Neonatal Behavioral Assessment Scale (NBAS). Most studies utilizing this scale have found opioid-exposed infants to perform less optimally than nonexposed infants (Chasnoff, Burns, Burns, & Schnoll, 1986; Chasnoff, Burns, & Schnoll, 1984; Chasnoff et al., 1985; Chasnoff, Burns, Schnoll, & Burns, 1986; Chasnoff, Schnoll, Burns, & Burns, 1984; Jeremy & Hans, 1985; Kaplan, Kron, Litt, Finnegan, & Phoenix, 1975; Kaplan, Kron, Phoenix, & Finnegan, 1976; Lesser-Katz, 1982; Strauss et al., 1975, 1976). However, most of these studies, also conducted multiple mean comparisons to explore for group differences, increasing the likelihood of spurious findings. Group differences on NBAS items in these studies range from as few as 2 to as many as 12 individual items. Considering that the NBAS consists of almost 50 items, the clinical significance of the reported differences needs to be considered tentative. In addition, although many of the reported differences were statistically significant, clinically they were small.

Most of these studies were conducted and published before the use of NBAS cluster scores was considered standard. Although the studies by Chasnoff and his colleagues often summarize the differences as reflecting deficits in interactive, motor maturity, and state organization behaviors, they did not have a system for assigning scores to those categories of behaviors, but rather were grouping them based on clinical relevance. Similarly, Jeremy and Hans (1985) discuss significant differences as related to motoric behavior and irritability, although they did not assign scores to these categories. When others assigned scores to groups of items labeled irritability, motor, and alertness, both irritability and alertness differentiated opiate-exposed from nonexposed infants, although only two individual items were found to be significantly different between groups (Kaplan et al., 1975). Although Chasnoff et al. (1985) and Chasnoff, Burns, Schnoll, and Burns (1986) found no item differences, they did find opioid-exposed infants to score worse on an interactive cluster.

Although cluster scores were generally not analyzed in these studies, the item differences do tend to fall into categories resembling behaviors related to interaction, motor performance, alertness, irritability, and state organization. Notably, some of these behaviors have been found to be related to ratings of withdrawal severity (Strauss et al., 1976), suggesting transient effects of opioid exposure. Indeed, Jeremy and Hans (1985), who found differences in NBAS behavior assessed at 2 days of age, report only one significant difference by 3 to 4 weeks of age. These findings are consistent with symptoms of neonatal withdrawal that can persist for up to a week with short acting opioids and for several weeks following the use of methadone. In summary, if true differences exist in newborn behavior due to opioid exposure, they seem to be transient effects related to withdrawal that abate over time.

Methadone has been used in pregnant women for over 20 years, although little is actually known about its metabolism during pregnancy. Pond, Kreek, Tong, Raghunath, and Benowitz (1985) demonstrated that in the third trimester there is more rapid metabolism of methadone resulting in the onset of withdrawal prior to the next daily dose. One of the consequences of high doses of methadone, especially in the third trimester, is an increased chance of neonatal abstinence occurring postpartum (Doberczak, Kandall, & Freedman, 1993; Zelson, Lee, & Casalino, 1973). Literature reviewing this issue presents inconsistent conclusions, with some studies suggesting a lower dose of methadone (20 mg or less) be used to reduce the incidence of the neonatal abstinence syndrome, whereas other studies have shown no difference in the rate of newborn methadone withdrawal related to

maternal methadone dose (Schnoll, 1986). More studies are necessary to determine whether there is a correlation between methadone blood level in the pregnant woman and the development of a neonatal abstinence syndrome.

Despite the incomplete data on methadone and pregnancy, it has been demonstrated that placing a woman on methadone reduces the chaotic lifestyle of the street addict, resulting in less chance for infection, including HIV, which can then be passed on to the fetus (Martin, Payte, & Zweben, 1991).

Child Development

The relationship between opioid exposure and later development has been investigated most often using the Bayley Scales of Infant Development. Several researchers have administered the Bayley scales at various ages from 3 to 24 months (Chasnoff, Burns, Burns, & Schnoll, 1986; Chasnoff, Schnoll, Burns, & Burns, 1984; Hans & Marcus, 1983; Kaltenbach & Finnegan, 1984, 1987; Strauss et al., 1976), generally reporting no differences related to exposure at most ages on either the mental or psychomotor subscales. When group differences were found (Chasnoff, Burns, Burns, & Schnoll, 1986; Strauss et al., 1976), performance was still reported to be within the normal range. It is important to remember that some studies have suggested the significance of the child's environment on developmental status rather than prenatal exposure to drugs (Johnson, Glassman, Fiks, & Rosen, 1987; Lifschitz, Wilson, Smith, & Desmond, 1985).

Studies conducted with children from school age up to mid-adolescence have indicated hyperactivity and other school problems (Rosen & Johnson, 1985; Wilson, 1989). However, these studies have significant methodological flaws in that the use of drugs during pregnancy is often determined retrospectively; therefore there is little information on the timing and the nature of all the drugs used during pregnancy, or on the environment in which these children were raised that could have affected the outcomes found.

Summary

Despite numerous studies of opioid use during pregnancy, few have taken into consideration the enormous number of confounding variables that can affect the outcome. Postnatally, the newborn can go through a neonatal abstinence syndrome that, in its most severe form, should be treated medically. Postnatal development may be affected by the drug use, but more recent data indicate that postnatal development may be more significantly influenced by the environment in which the child is raised, including whether or not the mother continues to use drugs.

AMPHETAMINE

Amphetamine use in the United States is less common than in some countries, such as Sweden, and research on prenatal exposure to amphetamines is scarce. However, a few controlled studies exist. Injected amphetamine use during pregnancy is associated with decreases in growth parameters, including head circumference, as well as with increased risk of fetal death in utero and placental abruption (Little, Snell, & Gilstrap, 1988; Oro & Dixon, 1987).

A prospective follow-up study of 65 children whose mothers used amphetamines during pregnancy revealed that 8-year-old children with more exposure were more aggressive and had poorer psychometric test outcomes for general adjustment (Billing, Eriksson, Jonsson, & Steneroth, 1994). A stepwise forward regression analysis determined that duration of amphetamine use during pregnancy, alcohol use, and attitude toward the pregnancy predicted aggressiveness and general adjustment. Duration of use only emerged at age 8; an earlier study of the cohort at age 4 failed to reveal this relationship, but had not considered aggression as an outcome (Billing, Erikkson, Steneroth, & Zetterstrom, 1988). The most recent report on this study found that socioenvironmental factors predicted the child's long-term growth and health status (at age 10), but amphetamine exposure continued to predict aggressive behavior and other psychological outcomes (Eriksson & Zetterstrom, 1994).

Studies of stimulant-exposed infants (cocaine or amphetamine, sometimes in combination with marijuana, opiates, PCP, or alcohol) have also reported neurobehavioral effects, including lower scores than controls on a test of visual recognition memory, the Fagan Test of Infant Intelligence (FTII; Struthers & Hansen, 1992). Drug exposure accounted for 11% of the variance in FTII scores; these scores are predictive of later performance on tests of discrimination, categorization, retention, and retrieval skills. Infants exposed to stimulant drugs in utero performed more poorly on standard tests of visual recognition memory than did controls; this test has been shown to differentiate between normal infants and those with cognitive deficits (Hansen, Struthers, & Gospe, 1993). This effect is not explained by delayed neurological maturation, but may be due to visual processing or attention problems in the drug-exposed group.

Further research is needed to determine whether amphetamine exposure during pregnancy is related to dysmorphic changes, to further describe the effects on growth parameters and cognitive functioning, and to separate the effects of amphetamine from other stimulants.

CAFFEINE

The majority of studies investigating the effects of prenatal caffeine exposure concentrate on outcomes such as obstetric complications or newborn characteristics such as growth parameters and newborn behavior. The few studies assessing the effects of prenatal caffeine exposure beyond the newborn period generally employ various developmental assessments.

Obstetric Complications

Most studies report weak or no relationships between prenatal caffeine use and various obstetric complications such as early pregnancy loss, spontaneous abortion, hypertensive disorder, predelivery hospitalizations, vaginal bleeding, placental or cord abnormalities, amnionitis, premature rupture of membranes (PROM), and preterm delivery (Armstrong, McDonald, & Sloan, 1992; Barr & Streissguth, 1991; Jacobson, Fein, Jacobson, Schwartz, & Dowler, 1984; McDonald, Armstrong, and Sloan, 1992b; Wilcox, Weinberg & Baird, 1990). Williams et al. (1992), however, found consumption of three or more cups of coffee per day was related to a significantly increased risk of PROM, although they did not find a relationship between caffeine consumption and preterm labor uncomplicated by PROM.

Growth Parameters

Findings regarding the relationship between prenatal caffeine exposure and growth parameters at birth are inconsistent. Most studies do not report effects of prenatal caffeine exposure on growth at birth (Barr & Streissguth, 1991; Jacobson et al., 1984) or at later ages (Barr & Streissguth, 1991; Barr et al., 1984), or on being born prematurely (Fenster, Eskenazi, Windham, & Swan, 1991; Fortier, Marcoux, & Beaulac-Baillargeon, 1993; McDonald et al., 1992b). Findings regarding low birth weight (less than 2500 g) are inconsistent, with some studies reporting no relationship (Fortier et al., 1993), and others (Fenster et al., 1991; McDonald et al., 1992b) reporting a relationship, especially for heavy exposure. Studies have also found a relationship between being small for gestational age and caffeine exposure (Fenster et al., 1991; Fortier et al., 1993; Jacobson et al., 1984; McDonald et al., 1992b). Fenster et al. (1991), however, did not control for prepregnancy weight or pregnancy weight gain, and report the mean birth weight for those who experienced heavy exposure to be 3170 g. The findings of McDonald et al. (1992b) were significant but small, and although prepregnancy weight was controlled, pregnancy weight gain was not. Only 6% of infants studied by Jacobson et al. (1984) were born earlier than 37 weeks gestation. These qualifiers call into question the clinical importance of the statistically significant findings regarding low birth weight and being small for gestational age.

Infant Behavior

A few studies have investigated the relationship between prenatal caffeine exposure and infant behavior. Using the Neonatal Behavioral Assessment Scale (NBAS), Jacobson et al. (1984) found a relationship between only the abnormal reflex cluster and prenatal caffeine exposure; however, they did report a relationship between maternal consumption of caffeine prior to pregnancy and the clusters of orientation, range of state, and general irritability. Barr and Streissguth (1991) found no relationship between prenatal caffeine exposure and NBAS factors or measures of neonatal sucking. Using a measure for neonatal abstinence syndrome, Hadeed and Siegel (1993) compared newborns exposed to more than 500 mg of caffeine per day (four cups of coffee) and those exposed to less than 250 mg per day and found that the more heavily exposed newborns demonstrated greater tachyrhythmia, premature atrial contractions, fine tremors, and tachypnea; these symptoms resolved within the first week.

Physical Anomalies

There is not strong evidence for the teratogenic nature of caffeine. One study found no association between exposure and cleft lip or palate, CNS defects, or defects of the cardiovascular or musculoskeletal systems. Although this study found an elevated incidence of heart defects related to heavy exposure to caffeine, no specific type of defect was overrepresented; given the number of statistical tests

conducted, the authors present this as a weak finding (McDonald, Armstrong, & Sloan, 1992a). Tikkanen and Heinonen (1991) retrospectively investigated risk factors potentially associated with cardiovascular malformations and found no relationship between maternal coffee, tea, or cola consumption during 1st trimester and malformations in infants. No other studies reported a relationship between congenital defects and prenatal caffeine exposure.

Child Development

Few studies have examined the relationship between prenatal caffeine exposure and later developmental status; those that do find few significant effects. No significant relationship was found for 8-month performance on the mental or psychomotor subscales of the Bayley Scales of Infant Development (Streissguth, Barr, Martin, & Herman, 1980). At 4 years of age, Barr, Streissguth, Darby, and Sampson (1990) did find a relationship between prenatal caffeine exposure and performance on fine motor tasks, but no relationship for gross motor performance or a global examiner rating of fine or gross motor performance. Caffeine exposure has failed to demonstrate a relationship with IQ at both 4 and 7 years (Barr & Streissguth, 1991). In addition, a vigilance task showed no relationship with exposure (Barr & Streissguth).

Summary

In general, few effects are found for prenatal caffeine exposure. Although transient effects on newborn behavior may exist, there is little evidence for a relationship with obstetric complications, growth, anomalies, or child development.

HALLUCINOGENS

Very little research has investigated the effects of prenatal hallucinogen exposure on infant development. The research that has been conducted reports on the effects of LSD (lysergic acid diethylamide). One difference that separates LSD from other substances discussed in this chapter is that it has sometimes been suggested to have negative effects via chromosomal damage in the mother and/or the infant. Case studies report various congenital malformations, including deformities of the hands and feet, among infants whose mothers used LSD before and/or during pregnancy (Carakushansky, Neu, & Gardner, 1969; Eller & Morton, 1970; Hecht, Beals, Lees, Jolly, & Roberts,

1968; Hsu, Strauss, & Hirschhorn, 1970; Zellweger, McDonald, & Abbo, 1967). Some of these malformations were accompanied by some level of chromosomal abnormalities (Carakushansky et al., 1969; Hsu et al., 1970; Zellweger et al., 1967), whereas in other cases chromosomal studies were normal (Eller & Morton, 1970), or were unknown in the infant and showed no breakage in the mother (Hecht et al., 1968). However, because these reports consist of case studies, most of which indicate substance exposure in addition to LSD, the outcomes cannot necessarily be attributed to LSD exposure.

The findings of two studies that used control groups suggest a higher rate of chromosomal breakage related to prenatal LSD exposure (Cohen, Hirschhorn, Verbo, Frosch, & Groeschel, 1968; Egozcue, Irwin, & Maruffo, 1968), although this breakage was not necessarily associated with health problems or birth defects (Cohen et al., 1968). One report tentatively suggested a relationship between maternal exposure to LSD prior to conception and a higher incidence of spontaneous abortion, but not premature birth or congenital defects (McGlothlin, Sparks, & Arnold, 1970).

The sparsity of research makes it impossible to draw any conclusions regarding the effects of maternal LSD exposure prior to and during pregnancy. Reviews of the effects of LSD, however, conclude that moderate doses of LSD in humans are not associated with chromosomal damage (Dishotsky, Loughman, Mogar, & Lipscomb, 1971; Houston, 1969) and are not teratogenic (Dishotsky et al., 1971; Werner, 1993).

INHALANTS

The literature on the effects of prenatal inhalant exposure is very scattered. Prenatal exposure to inhalants has generally been studied at two levels: inhalant abuse during pregnancy and occupational exposure to solvents during pregnancy. Although inhalant abuse is often considered to be isolated to adolescent boys, it is a common form of substance abuse among some minority populations (including women of childbearing age) in certain areas of the United States. Investigations of the effects of inhalant abuse have consisted mostly of case reports and small sample sizes with no control groups. Although dramatic effects have been suggested, strong conclusions cannot be made due to the methodology. One investigation that examined pregnancy and delivery complications reported a high percentage of symptoms related to renal tubular acidosis as well

as a high incidence of preterm labor and delivery among a group of toluene-abusing women (Wilkins-Haug & Gabow, 1991). Common outcomes among infants exposed to prenatal inhalant abuse include pre- and/or postnatal growth deficiencies and facial dysmorphia or other (usually minor) physical anomalies (Goodwin, 1988; Hersh, 1989; Hersh, Podruch, Rogers, & Weisskopf, 1985; Hunter, Thompson, & Evans, 1979; Toutant & Lippmann, 1979; Wilkins-Haug & Gabow, 1991). Other reports include occurrences of developmental delay and language or attention deficits (Hersh, 1989; Hersh et al., 1985; Wilkins-Haug & Gabow, 1991). Although these outcomes are common in a number of reports, they overwhelmingly consist of case studies and studies with no control groups. No conclusions can be made until more rigorous research has been conducted.

Investigations of prenatal occupational exposure to inhalants have generally been more rigorous than investigations of inhalant abuse, with larger sample sizes, comparison groups, and statistical controls. Retrospectively, occupational exposure has shown relationships with congenital central nervous system (CNS) defects (Holmberg, 1979; Holmberg & Nurminen, 1980), and oral clefts (Holmberg, Hernberg, Kurppa, Rantala, & Riala, 1982). Weak associations have been reported between exposure and major congenital defects (Tikkanen & Heinonen, 1991) and specifically ventricle septal defects (McDonald, Lavoie, Cote, & McDonald, 1987). The results of other retrospective studies, however, suggest no relationship between occupational exposure and congenital malformations (Taskinen, Anttila, Lindbohm, Sallmen, & Hemminki, 1989), or specifically CNS, skeletal, or cardiovascular defects, or oral clefts (Kurppa, Holmberg, Kuosma, & Saxen, 1983). One retrospective study reported an increased risk of spontaneous abortions related to paternal but not to maternal exposure (Taskinen et al.).

Methodologically stronger are the prospective studies of prenatal occupational exposure to inhalants. One study found a higher incidence of certain pregnancy complications among women who experienced occupational exposure to inhalants during pregnancy, although no relationship was found for most pregnancy complications or for labor and delivery complications (Eskenazi, Bracken, Holford, & Grady, 1988). Some studies have reported an increased incidence of spontaneous abortions related to occupational inhalant exposure (Cohen, Bellville, & Brown, 1971; Strandberg, Sandback, Axelson, & Sundell, 1978), although the findings of others have not supported this relationship

(Eskenazi, Bracken, Holford, & Grady, 1988; Pharoah, Alberman, Doyle, & Chamberlain, 1977). No relationship has been reported between exposure and perinatal death/stillbirth (Meirik, Kallen, Gauffin, & Ericson, 1979; Pharoah et al., 1977). Studies are inconsistent with each other in relation to growth parameters at birth. Pharoah et al. (1977) found the group of exposed infants to have significantly lower birth weight as well as a higher proportion of low-birth-weight infants, although others have not found differences in birth weight, length, head circumference, or gestational age (Eskenazi, Bracken, Holford, & Grady, 1988). Conflicting findings have also been reported regarding congenital malformations and occupational exposure; some studies report no relationship (Cohen et al., 1971; Eskenazi, Bracken, Holford, & Grady, 1988), although other findings do suggest a relationship for some, but not all, malformations investigated (Meirik et al.;, 1979 Pharoah et al.,1977) . Regarding later developmental outcome, two studies that have followed exposed children beyond infancy found no differences related to exposure for age at first sitting, crawling, or talking (Cohen et al., 1971; Eskenazi, Gaylord, Bracken, & Brown, 1988), although the latter (but not the former) of these reports found that exposed infants walked later than unexposed. Eskenazi, Gaylord, Bracken and Brown found no differences related to exposure for growth parameters at 3 years or on measures of cognitive status, personality, or hyperactivity.

Although the prospective studies are methodologically stronger than other studies of prenatal inhalant exposure, only tentative conclusions can be drawn based on their findings. For one, exposure status was generally based on job descriptions rather than a quantified measure of exposure. Although some studies had industrial hygienists classify subjects for levels and types of exposure (Eskenazi, Bracken, Holford, & Grady, 1988; Eskenazi, Gaylord, Bracken, & Brown, 1988), most simply compared those from two job classifications, one of which was likely to have been exposed (such as anesthetists; Cohen et al., 1971; Meirik et al., 1979; Pharoah et al., 1977; Strandberg et al., 1978). In addition, although levels of exposure were not quantified, they were generally considered to be low, and type of exposure varied across studies as well.

PHENCYCLIDINE

Phencyclidine (PCP) is an arylcyclohexylamine originally developed as a general anesthetic; however, because of hallucinations and seizures, the drug was withdrawn from the market for human use. It emerged in the drug scene in the 1960s when it was used as a psychoactive contaminant in many street drugs. It surfaced as a primary drug of abuse during the 1970s and pockets of PCP use have appeared periodically in larger cities around the country. The drug is rarely used alone and is often used in conjunction with marijuana, alcohol, hallucinogens, and opioids. It has often been sold as tetrahydrocannabinol (THC), the active ingredient in marijuana. A congener of PCP, ketamine, has recently become popular on the street drug scene.

There are several reports in the literature regarding the effects of PCP on pregnancy and newborn development; however, all of these studies are plagued by small sample size and poor history regarding other drug use. Therefore, some of the findings attributed to PCP may be the result of drug combinations used by the women. Isolated studies have described dysmorphic teratology in humans (Golden, Sokol, & Rubin, 1980; Strauss, Mondalou, & Bosee, 1981), although others (Golden, Kuhnert, Sokol, Martier, & Williams, 1987) have failed to find any structural abnormalities. In addition, meta-analytic studies have failed to show any dysmorphia (Fico & Nanderwende, 1989). All of the studies show a high incidence of intrauterine growth retardation with rates as high as 35% (Rahbar, Fomufod, White, & Westney, 1993; Tabor, Smith-Wallace, & Yonekura, 1990; Wachsman, Schuetz, Chan, & Wingert, 1989). In addition, Tabor et al. found a high incidence (43%) of precipitate labor in the PCP-exposed group. Newborns exposed to PCP in utero have been reported to show irritability, hypertonicity, jitteriness, diarrhea, and vomiting; abnormal reflexes (Golden et al., 1987); increased state lability, poor consolability (Chasnoff, Burns, Burns, & Schnoll, 1986); high-pitched crying, poor tracking (Rabhar et al., 1993); and deficient attention (Golden et al., 1987; Rabhar et al.,1993). It is not clear, however, whether these findings represent an effect of the drug or a withdrawal phenomenon from PCP or other drugs that have been used by the mother. It is important to note that a specific withdrawal syndrome from PCP has not been described in adults. The jitteriness and hypertonicity described in PCP withdrawal in newborns have been noted to be similar to opioid withdrawal. However, a significant proportion of women (48%) using PCP may have also used opioids and other substances at some point during their pregnancy (Wachsman et al., 1989).

Two studies have attempted to determine the later developmental effects associated with PCP and other substance use (Beckwith et al., 1994; Rodning, Beckwith, &

Howard, 1991). Beckwith et al. found that the play of 24-month-old drug-exposed children was significantly more immature than that of their nonexposed peers from similar environments. Drug effects remained even after statistically controlling for birth weight and developmental quotient. Rodning et al. compared attachment among polydrug-exposed 15-month-old children whose mothers had tested positive for PCP at delivery to a comparison group of nonexposed children reared in similar environments and found significantly higher rates of insecure attachment classifications among the drug-exposed children. Whether the children were living with their biological mothers, extended family, or in foster care did not affect attachment classification. The authors suggested that mothers' intermittent unavailability due to drug use resulted in the high rates of insecure attachment. In both studies, the information on drug use other than PCP was collected retrospectively, therefore it is difficult to determine whether the effects were due to other drugs or were specifically related to PCP.

In summary, although it does not appear that PCP exposure leads to dysmorphia, it may be related to intrauterine growth retardation and a hypertonic agitated syndrome in the newborn. Initial studies also suggested later effects on child development, including immature play and insecure attachment. Research in the area is still maturing, so few conclusions can be drawn. With the emergence of ketamine as a primary drug of abuse, it will be important to perform controlled, prospective studies to enable us to determine the true effects of arylcyclohexylamines on pregnancy, and neonatal and later development.

SEDATIVES, HYPNOTICS, ANXIOLYTICS

This section discusses research investigating the effects of prenatal exposure to two of the most commonly abused drugs from these classes: benzodiazepines and phenobarbital.

Benzodiazepines

In retrospective studies, prenatal benzodiazepine exposure has demonstrated a significant relationship with congenital malformations in general (Bracken & Holford, 1981; Laegreid et al., 1990; Laegreid, Olegard, Walstrom, & Conradi, 1989), and oral clefts in particular (Aarskog, 1975; Safra & Oakley, 1975; Saxen & Saxen, 1975). The findings of other studies, however, failed to support a rela-

tionship with oral clefts (Czeizel, 1976; Rosenberg et al., 1983), anencephalus, or spina bifida (Czeizel, 1976), although one study suggested a possible relationship with inguinal hernia (Rosenberg et al.). Studies without control groups have also failed to support a relationship between congenital anomalies and benzodiazepine exposure (Bergman, Rosa, Baum, Wiholm, & Faich, 1992; Starreveld-Zimmerman, van der Kolk, Meinardi, & Elshove, 1973). Methodologically stronger prospective studies have also failed to support a relationship between congenital malformations in general (Bergman, Boethius, Swartling, Isacson, & Smedby, 1990; Czeizel & Lendvay, 1987; Laegreid, Hagberg, & Lundberg, 1992a), or oral clefts in particular (Shiono & Mills, 1984), although a higher rate of minor facial dysmorphism has been suggested (Laegreid, Hagberg, & Lundberg, 1992b).

Various outcomes in addition to congenital malformations have been investigated for a relationship with prenatal benzodiazepine exposure. Case studies have suggested possible withdrawal from benzodiazepine exposure (Mazzi, 1977; Rementeria & Bhatt, 1977). Prospective studies have reported benzodiazepine-exposed infants to have a higher number (although not a higher proportion) of nonoptimal pre- and perinatal factors compared to a nonexposed group, although there was no difference in the amount of hospital care they needed (Laegreid et al., 1992a). In one study, some measures of growth, such as birth weight for gestational age and birth weight for length, were lower in the benzodiazepine-exposed group compared to a group exposed to other psychotropic drugs but not compared to a nonexposed group; in addition, general measures of growth, such as birth weight and gestational age, were within normal ranges (Laegreid et al., 1992a). Follow-up measures of growth through 18 months of age revealed no further significant differences (Laegreid et al., 1992b). Retrospective studies have reported a relationship between prenatal benzodiazepine exposure and deficient development including diminished growth, hypotonia, feeding problems, and various degrees of mental and motor retardation (Laegreid et al., 1989). Reports also suggested possible differences related to benzodiazepine exposure on measures of neurodevelopment at birth (Laegreid et al., 1992a), and follow-up studies continued to report some deficiencies in neurodevelopment through 18 months of age (Laegreid et al., 1992b), and general development, attention, and activity at some (but not all) ages measured through 18 months (Viggedal, Hagberg, Laegreid, & Aronsson, 1993).

Although not a current use of benzodiazepines, older studies report on the neonatal consequences of benzodiazepine administration for the treatment of labor-related anxiety and preeclampsia/eclampsia. Some studies suggested consequences such as lower Apgar scores, changes in vital signs, and hypotonia. However, experimental studies, that randomly administered benzodiazepines or a placebo to labor patients did not suggest effects on Apgar scores, vital signs, mode of delivery, or neurobehavioral assessments, although they reported conflicting findings regarding the effect on length of labor (Bepko, Lowe, & Waxman, 1965; Decancq, Bosco, & Towsend, 1965; McAuley, O'Neill, Moore, & Dundee, 1982; Niswander, 1969).

In summary, methodologically stronger prospective studies suggest no causal relationship between congenital malformations and benzodiazepine exposure, the most commonly discussed outcome measure. Conclusions regarding other findings need to be considered preliminary and tentative. Not only have the prospective studies not yet been replicated, but they also suffer from small sample sizes, many statistical comparisons, and examiners who are not always blind to exposure status. In addition, the role of maternal psychiatric condition needs to be considered when drawing conclusions related to general child development (Viggedal et al., 1993), as does the role of the other confounding factors that often occur with benzodiazepine use such as hypertension, diabetes, obesity, malnutrition, older parity, as well as other medications and substance abuse (Bergman et al., 1992).

Phenobarbital

For many years, use of barbiturates (such as phenobarbital) during pregnancy has been known to be teratogenic. Phenobarbital and other antiepileptic medications are associated with dysmorphic features including congenital heart defects, cleft lip and palate, and neural tube defects (Lindhout, Meinardi, Meijer, & Nau, 1992). In addition, phenobarbital-exposed children have been shown to have smaller head circumferences at birth (van der Pol, Hadders-Algra, Huisjes, & Touwen, 1991). In the past, it was not known whether individual drugs or their combination led to birth defects, or whether maternal seizure activity was implicated. Recent studies have attempted to resolve the contributions to teratogenic effects of exposure to the various drugs. A prospective study of epileptic pregnant women and their offspring found phenobarbital to be the riskiest drug, resulting in major anomalies or fetal death more often than other antiepileptic drugs, with an incidence of 23.8% (Waters, Belai, Gott, Shen, & DeGiorgio, 1994). In addition, barbiturate-exposed children of epileptic mothers had lower mean head circumferences than those prenatally exposed to other antiepileptic drugs or drug-free children (Gaily, Granstrom, & Hiilesmaa, 1990).

Recent research has examined the neurobehavioral effects of phenobarbital exposure. A prospective follow-up study of the relationship of functional CNS aberrations and prenatal exposure to antiepileptic drugs found that phenobarbital exposure during pregnancy resulted in later teacher-rated poor attention span, along with poor arithmetic and spelling performance. Controlling for maternal seizure activity, phenobarbital exposure alone related to the neurobehavioral findings. The authors stated that ". . . phenobarbital should be regarded as a more potent teratogen than carbamazepine" (van der Pol et al., 1991, p. 126).

There are contrasting reports on the risk of brain cancer in children exposed to barbiturates in utero. Gold, Gordis, Tonascia, and Szklo (1978) found evidence of increased risk after barbiturate exposure, but Goldhaber, Selby, Hiatt, and Quesenberry (1990) found no evidence of increased risk.

In summary, the extant research on barbiturates, primarily phenobarbital, comes from the epilepsy literature rather than the drug abuse literature. It is well-established that dysmorphic effects can result from phenobarbital exposure during pregnancy. Recent research has pointed to lingering cognitive/CNS effects as well. These effects appear to result from the barbiturate exposure rather than maternal seizure activity, although this is still a matter of some debate. Other outcomes remain to be confirmed by future research. Studying substance-abusing mothers who use barbiturates would provide welcome additional information in this literature.

SUMMARY

With a few exceptions, pregnant women are advised to avoid the ingestion of alcohol and drugs during gestation. Although prenatal exposure to some substances (such as alcohol, nicotine, and phenobarbital) clearly has negative effects on infants, exposure to others (such as marijuana and caffeine) appears more benign. Research on the effects of most substances, including cocaine, opioids, LSD, PCP, and stimulants, has demonstrated inconsistent findings across studies such that strong conclusions cannot be drawn. Discrepant findings may result largely from the methodological difficulties prevalent in this area of research: sample sizes tend to be small; drug dosage and timing of exposure are difficult to quantify; many factors that are difficult to control (and not always known) covary with substance use; and most women use more than one substance, making it difficult to isolate the effects of specific substances.

The use of illicit drugs is overwhelmingly discouraged and there is a stigma attached to the use of such substances; however, given the inconsistent findings, the true risks of exposure need to be considered in the context of other existing lifestyle factors—exposure to substances is just one of many risk factors for these infants; other risks often include poverty, poor nutrition and health care, and low maternal education. Identifying the role of various risk factors for infant and child development will enable more appropriate advice and services to be offered to substance-abusing women. Indeed some of the clearest negative effects, both physical and psychological, emerged regarding exposure to the legal substances of nicotine and alcohol, partially due to the lengthier period of study and better quality of research that exists for these substances. Use of drugs needed for the management of physical or psychological problems presents a special dilemma as the risks of substance exposure need to be weighed against the need for pharmacological treatment.

There is a necessity for additional rigorous research investigating the effects of prenatal substance exposure. Efforts should focus on separating the effects of substance exposure from environmental effects. This will enable us to determine the role of substance exposure as a risk factor in the context of other influential factors and determine the needs of these children and their families, such that appropriate intervention can be targeted at enhancing the development of these at-risk children and promoting the well-being of their families.

AUTHOR NOTE

Gena Covell Britt, Division of Substance Abuse Medicine, Department of Internal Medicine; Karen S. Ingersoll, Division of Substance Abuse Medicine, Department of Psychiatry; Sidney H. Schnoll, M.D., Ph.D., Division of Substance Abuse Medicine, Departments of Internal Medicine and Psychiatry.

REFERENCES

Aarskog, D. (1975). Association between maternal intake of diazepam and oral clefts [Letter to the editor]. *Lancet, 2,* 921.

Alderman, B. W., Bradley, C. M., Greene, C., Fernbach, S. K., & Baron, A. E. (1994). Increased risk of craniosynostosis with maternal cigarette smoking during pregnancy. *Teratology, 50,* 13–18.

American College of Obstetricians and Gynecologists (ACOG). (1993, May). Smoking and reproductive health. *ACOG Technical Bulletin 180.* Washington, DC: Author.

American Psychiatric Association. (1994). *Diagnostic and statistical manual of mental disorders* (4th ed.). Washington, DC: Author.

Armstrong, B. G., McDonald, A. D., & Sloan, M. (1992). Cigarette, alcohol, and coffee consumption and spontaneous abortion. *American Journal of Public Health, 82,* 85–87.

Astley, S. J., Clarren, S. K., Little, R. E., Sampson, P. D., & Daling, J. R. (1992). Analysis of facial shape in children gestationally exposed to marijuana, alcohol, and/or cocaine. *Pediatrics, 89,* 67–77.

Autti-Ramo, I., Korkman, M., Hilakivi-Clarke, L., Lehtonen, M., Halmesmaki, E., & Granstrom, M.-L. (1992). Mental development of 2-year-old children exposed to alcohol in utero. *Journal of Pediatrics, 120,* 740–746.

Azuma, S. D., & Chasnoff, I. J. (1993). Outcome of children prenatally exposed to cocaine and other drugs: A path analysis of three-year data. *Pediatrics, 92,* 396–402.

Barr, H. M., & Streissguth, A. P. (1991). Caffeine use during pregnancy and child outcome: A 7-year prospective study. *Neurotoxicology and Teratology, 13,* 441–448.

Barr, H. M., Streissguth, A. P., Darby, B. L., & Sampson, P. D. (1990). Prenatal exposure to alcohol, caffeine, tobacco, and aspirin: Effects on fine and gross motor performance in 4-year-old children. *Developmental Psychology, 26,* 339–348.

Barr, H. M., Streissguth, A. P., Martin, D. C., & Herman, C. S. (1984). Infant size at 8 months of age: Relationship to maternal use of alcohol, nicotine, and caffeine during pregnancy. *Pediatrics, 74,* 336–341.

Beckwith, L., Rodning, C., Norris, D., Phillipsen, L., Khandabi, P., & Howard, J. (1994). Spontaneous play in two-year-olds born to substance-abusing mothers. *Infant Mental Health Journal, 15,* 189–201.

Bepko, F., Lowe, E., & Waxman, B. (1965). Relief of the emotional factor in labor with parenterally administered diazepam. *Obstetrics and Gynecology, 26,* 852–857.

Bergman, U., Boethius, G., Swartling, P. G., Isacson, D., & Smedby, B. (1990). Teratogenic effects of benzodiazepine use during pregnancy [Letter to the editor]. *Journal of Pediatrics, 116,* 490–491.

Bergman, U., Rosa, F. W., Baum, C., Wiholm, B. E., & Faich, G. A. (1992). Effects of exposure to benzodiazepine during fetal life. *Lancet, 340,* 694–696.

Billing, L., Eriksson, M., Jonsson, B., & Steneroth, G. (1994). The influence of environmental factors on behavioral problems in 8-year-old children exposed to amphetamine during fetal life. *Child Abuse and Neglect, 18,* 3–9.

Billing, L., Eriksson, M., Steneroth, G., & Zetterstrom, R. (1988). Predictive indicators for adjustment in 4-year-old children whose mothers used amphetamine during pregnancy. *Child Abuse and Neglect, 12,* 503–507.

Bingol, N., Fuchs, M., Diaz, V., Stone, R. K., & Gromisch, D.S. (1987). Teratogenicity of cocaine in humans. *Journal of Pediatrics, 110,* 93–96.

Black, M., Schuler, M., & Nair, P. (1993). Prenatal drug exposure: Neurodevelopmental outcome and parenting environment. *Journal of Pediatric Psychology, 18,* 605–620.

Bracken, M. B., & Holford, T. R. (1981). Exposure to prescribed drugs in pregnancy and association with congenital malformations. *Obstetrics and Gynecology, 58,* 336–344.

Bulterys, M. (1990). High incidence of sudden infant death syndrome among northern Indians and Alaska natives compared with southwestern Indians: Possible role of smoking. *Journal of Community Health, 15,* 185–194.

Carakushansky, G., Neu, R. L., & Gardner, L. I. (1969). Lysergide and cannabis as possible teratogens in man [Letter to the editor]. *Lancet, 1,* 150–151.

Centers for Disease Control. (1995). Update: Trends in Fetal Alcohol Syndrome—United States, 1979–1993. *Morbidity and Mortality Weekly Report, 44.* 249–251.

Chasnoff, I. J., Burns, K. A., & Burns, W. J. (1987). Cocaine use in pregnancy: Perinatal morbidity and mortality. *Neurotoxicology and Teratology, 9,* 291–293.

Chasnoff, I. J., Burns, K., Burns, W. J., & Schnoll, S. H. (1986). Prenatal drug exposure: Effects on neonatal and infant growth and development. *Neurobehavioral Toxicology and Teratology, 8,* 357–362.

Chasnoff, I. J., Burns, W. J., & Schnoll, S. H. (1984). Perinatal addiction: The effects of maternal narcotic and nonnarcotic substance abuse on the fetus and neonate. *NIDA Research Monograph Series, 49,* 220–226.

Chasnoff, I. J., Burns, W. J., Schnoll, S. H., & Burns, K. A. (1985). Cocaine use in pregnancy. *New England Journal of Medicine, 313,* 666–669.

Chasnoff, I. J., Burns, W. J., Schnoll, S. H., & Burns, K. A. (1986). Effects of cocaine on pregnancy outcome. *National Institute on Drug Abuse: Research Monograph Series, 67,* 335–341.

Chasnoff, I. J., Griffith, D. R., Freier, C., & Murray, J. (1992). Cocaine/polydrug use in pregnancy: Two-year follow-up. *Pediatrics, 89,* 284–289.

Chasnoff, I. J., Griffith, D. R., MacGregor, S., Dirkes, K., & Burns, K. A. (1989). Temporal patterns of cocaine use in pregnancy: Perinatal outcome. *Journal of the American Medical Association, 261,* 1741–1744.

Chasnoff, I. J., Lewis, D. E., Griffith, D. R., & Willey, S. (1989). Cocaine and pregnancy: Clinical and toxicological implications for the neonate. *Clinical Chemistry, 35,* 1276–1278.

Chasnoff, I. J., Schnoll, S. H., Burns, W. J., & Burns, K. (1984). Maternal nonnarcotic substance abuse during pregnancy: Effects on infant development. *Neurobehavioral Toxicology and Teratology, 6,* 277–280.

Chen, L. H. & Petitti, D. B. (1995). Case-control study of passive smoking and the risk of small-for-gestational-age at term. *American Journal of Epidemiology, 142,* 158–165.

Cherukuri, R., Minkoff, H., Feldman, J., Parekh, A., & Glass, L. (1988). A cohort study of alkaloidal cocaine ("crack") in pregnancy. *Obstetrics and Gynecology, 72,* 147–151.

Chouteau, M., Namerow, P.B., & Leppert, P. (1988). The effect of cocaine abuse on birth weight and gestational age. *Obstetrics and Gynecology, 72,* 351–354.

Cohen, E. N., Bellville, J. W., & Brown, B. W. (1971). Anesthesia, pregnancy, and miscarriage: A study of operating room nurses and anesthetists. *Anesthesiology, 35,* 343–347.

Cohen, H. R., Green, J. R., & Crombleholme, W. R. (1991). Peripartum cocaine use: Estimating risk of adverse pregnancy outcome. *International Journal of Obstetrics and Gynecology, 35,* 51–54.

Cohen, M. M., Hirschhorn, K., Verbo, S., Frosch, W. A., & Groeschel, M. M. (1968). The effect of LSD-25 on the chromosomes of children exposed in utero. *Pediatric Research, 2,* 486–492.

Coles, C. D., Platzman, K. A., Smith, I., James, M. E., & Falek, A. (1992). Effects of cocaine and alcohol use in pregnancy on neonatal growth and neurobehavioral status. *Neurotoxicology and Teratology, 14,* 23–33.

Colley, J. R. T., Holland, W. W., & Corkhill, R. T. (1974). Influence of passive smoking and parental phlegm on pneumonia and bronchitis in early childhood. *Lancet, 2,* 1031–1034.

Cornelius, M. D., Taylor, P. M., Geva, D., & Day, N. L. (1995). Prenatal tobacco and marijuana use among adolescents: Effects on offspring gestational age, growth, and morphology. *Pediatrics, 95,* 738–743.

Cuijpers, C. E. J., Swaen, G. M. H., Wesseling, G., Sturmans, F., & Wouters, E. F. M. (1995). Adverse effects of the indoor environment on respiratory health in primary school children. *Environmental Research, 68,* 11–23.

Czeizel, A. (1976). Diazepam, phenytoin, and aetiology of cleft lip and/or cleft palate [Letter to the editor]. *Lancet, 1,* 810.

Czeizel, A., & Lendvay, A. (1987). In-utero exposure to benzodiazepines [Letter to the editor]. *Lancet, 1,* 627–628.

Day, N., Cornelius, M., Goldschmidt, L., Richardson, G., Robles, N., & Taylor, P. (1992). The effects of prenatal tobacco and marijuana use on offspring growth from birth through three years of age. *Neurotoxicology and Teratology, 14,* 407–414.

Day, N. L., Richardson, G. A., Geva, D., & Robles, N. (1994). Alcohol, marijuana, and tobacco: Effects of prenatal exposure on offspring growth and morphology at age six. *Alcoholism: Clinical and Experimental Research, 18,* 786–794.

Day, N., Sambamoorthi, U., Taylor, P., Richardson, G., Robles, N., Jhon, Y., Scher, M., Stoffer, D., Cornelius, M., & Jasperse, D. (1991). Prenatal marijuana use and neonatal outcome. *Neurotoxicology and Teratology, 13,* 329–334.

Decancq, H. G., Jr., Bosco, J. R., & Townsend, E. H., Jr. (1965). Chlordiazepoxide in labor: Its effect on the newborn infant. *Journal of Pediatrics, 67,* 836–840.

Desmond, M.M., & Wilson, G.S. (1975). Neonate abstinence syndrome: Recognition and diagnosis. *Addictive Diseases, 2,* 113–121.

Dishotsky, N. I., Loughman, W. D., Mogar, R. E., & Lipscomb, W. R. (1971). LSD and genetic damage. *Science, 172,* 431–440.

Doberczak, T. M., Kandall, S. R., & Friedmann, P. (1993). Relationship between maternal methadone dosage, maternal-neonatal methadone levels, and neonatal withdrawal. *Obstetrics and Gynecology, 81,* 936–940.

Dreher, M. C., Nugent, K., & Hudgins, R. (1994). Prenatal marijuana exposure and neonatal outcomes in Jamaica: An ethnographic study. *Pediatrics, 93,* 254–260.

Duff, A. L., Pomeranz, E. S., Gelber, L. E., Price, G. W., Farris, H., Hayden, F. G., Platts-Mills, T. A. E., & Heymann, P. W. (1993). Risk factors for acute wheezing in infants and children: Viruses, passive smoke, and IgE antibodies to inhalant allergens. *Pediatrics, 92,* 535–540.

Egozcue, J., Irwin, S., & Maruffo, C. A. (1968). Chromosomal damage in LSD users. *Journal of the American Medical Association, 204,* 122–126.

Eisen, L. N., Field, T. M., Bandstra, E. S., Roberts, J. P., Morrow, C., Larson, S. K., & Steele, B. M. (1991). Perinatal cocaine effects on neonatal stress behavior and performance on the Brazelton scale. *Pediatrics, 88,* 477–480.

Eller, J. L., & Morton, J. M. (1970). Bizarre deformities in offspring of user of lysergic acid diethylamide. *New England Journal of Medicine, 283,* 395–397.

Eriksson, M. & Zetterstrom, R. (1994). Amphetamine addiction during pregnancy: 10-year follow-up. *Acta Paediatrica, 404* (Suppl.), 27–31.

Eskenazi, B., Bracken, M. B., Holford, T. R., & Grady, J. (1988). Exposure to organic solvents and hypertensive disorders of pregnancy. *American Journal of Industrial Medicine, 14,* 177–188.

Eskenazi, B., Gaylord, L., Bracken, M. B., & Brown, D. (1988). *In utero* exposure to organic solvents and human neurodevelopment. *Developmental Medicine and Child Neurology, 30,* 492–501.

Eskenazi, B., Prehn, A. W., & Christianson, R. E. (1995). Passive and active maternal smoking as measured by serum cotinine: The effect on birthweight. *American Journal of Public Health, 85,* 395–398.

Eyler, F. D., Behnke, M., Conlon, M., Woods, N. S., & Wobie, K. (1995, March-April). *A controlled evaluation of neonatal cocaine "withdrawal": Neurobehavioral effects over the first week.* Poster session presented at the biennial meeting of the Society for Research in Child Development, Indianapolis, IN.

Fenster, L., Eskenazi, B., Windham, G. C., & Swan, S. H. (1991). Caffeine consumption during pregnancy and fetal growth. *American Journal of Public Health, 81,* 458–461.

Fico, F. A., & Nanderwende, C. (1989). Phencyclidine during pregnancy: Behavioral and neurochemical effects in the offspring. *Annals of the New York Academy of Sciences, 562,* 319–326.

Finnegan, L. P. (1975). Narcotics dependence in pregnancy. *Journal of Psychedelic Drugs, 7,* 299–311.

Finnegan, L. P. (1986). Neonatal abstinence syndrome: Assessment and pharmacotherapy. In F.F. Rubaltelli & B. Granati (Eds.), *Neonatal therapy: An update* (pp. 122–146). New York: Elsevier Science.

Floyd, R. L., Zahniser, S. C., Gunter, E. P., & Kendrick, J. S. (1991). Smoking during pregnancy: Prevalence, effects, and intervention strategies. *Birth, 18,* 48–53.

Fortier, I., Marcoux, S., & Beaulac-Baillargeon, L. (1993). Relation of caffeine intake during pregnancy to intrauterine growth retardation and preterm birth. *American Journal of Epidemiology, 137,* 931–940.

Fried, P. A., O'Connell, C. M., & Watkinson, B. (1992). 60- and 72-month follow-up of children prenatally exposed to marijuana, cigarettes, and alcohol: Cognitive and language assessment. *Journal of Developmental and Behavioral Pediatrics, 13,* 383–391.

Fried, P. A., & Watkinson, B. (1990). 36- and 48-month neurobehavioral follow-up of children prenatally exposed to marijuana, cigarettes, and alcohol. *Journal of Developmental and Behavioral Pediatrics, 11,* 49–58.

Fried, P. A., Watkinson, B., Dillon, R. F., & Dulberg, C. S. (1987). Neonatal neurological status in a low-risk population after prenatal exposure to cigarettes, marijuana, and alcohol. *Journal of Developmental and Behavioral Pediatrics, 8,* 318–326.

Fried, P. A., Watkinson, B., & Gray, R. (1992). A follow-up study of attentional behavior in 6-year-old children exposed prenatally to marijuana, cigarettes, and alcohol. *Neurotoxicology and Teratology, 14,* 299–311.

Fried, P. A., Watkinson, B., & Willan, A. (1984). Marijuana use during pregnancy and decreased length of gestation. *American Journal of Obstetrics and Gynecology, 150,* 23–27.

Fulroth, R., Phillips, B., & Durand, D. J. (1989). Perinatal outcome of infants exposed to cocaine and/or heroin in utero. *American Journal of Diseases of Children, 143,* 905–910.

Gaily, E. K., Granstrom, M.-L., Hiilesmaa, V. K., & Bardy, A. H. (1990). Head circumference in children of epileptic mothers: Contributions of drug exposure and genetic background. *Epilepsy Research, 5,* 217–222.

Geva, D., Goldschmidt, L., Stoffer, D., & Day, N. L. (1993). A longitudinal analysis of the effect of prenatal alcohol exposure on growth. *Alcoholism: Clinical and Experimental Research, 17,* 1124–1129.

Gidding, S. S., Morgan, W., Perry, C., Isabel-Jones, J., & Bricker, J. T. (1994). Active and passive tobacco exposure: A serious pediatric health problem. *Circulation, 90,* 2581–2590.

Gold, E., Gordis, L., Tonascia, J., & Szklo, M. (1978). Increased risk of brain tumors in children exposed to barbiturates. *Journal of the National Cancer Institute, 61,* 1031–1034.

Golden, N. L., Kuhnert, B. R., Sokol, R. J., Martier, S., & Williams, T. (1987). Neonatal manifestations of maternal phencyclidine exposure. *Journal of Perinatal Medicine, 15,* 185–191.

Golden, N. L., Sokol, R. J., & Rubin, I. L. (1980). Angel dust: Possible effects on the fetus. *Pediatrics, 65,* 18–20.

Goldhaber, M. K., Selby, J. V., Hiatt, R. A., & Quesenberry, C.P. (1990). Exposure to barbiturates in utero and during childhood: Risk of intracranial and spinal cord tumors. *Cancer Research, 50,* 4600–4603.

Goodwin, T. M. (1988). Toluene abuse and renal tubular acidosis in pregnancy. *Obstetrics and Gynecology, 71,* 715–718.

Greene, T., Ernhart, C. B., Martier, S., Sokol, R., & Ager, J. (1990). Prenatal alcohol exposure and language development. *Alcoholism: Clinical and Experimental Research, 14,* 937–945.

Griffith, D. R., Azuma, S. D., Chasnoff, I. J. (1994). Three-year outcome of children exposed prenatally to drugs. *Journal of the American Academy of Child and Adolescent Psychiatry, 33,* 20–27.

Griffith, D., Chasnoff, I., Dirkes, K., & Burns, K. (1988). Neurobehavioral development of cocaine-exposed infants in the first month. *Pediatric Research, 23* (abstract #55).

Hadeed, A. J., & Siegel, S. R. (1989). Maternal cocaine use during pregnancy: Effect on the newborn infant. *Pediatrics, 84,* 205–210.

Hadeed, A., & Siegel, S. (1993). Newborn cardiac arrhythmias associated with maternal caffeine use during pregnancy. *Clinical Pediatrics, 32,* 45–47.

Haglund, B. & Cnattingius, S. (1990). Cigarette smoking as a risk factor for sudden infant death syndrome: A population-based study. *American Journal of Public Health, 80,* 29–32.

Hans, S. L. (1989). Developmental consequences of prenatal exposure to methadone. *Annals of the New York Academy of Sciences, 562,* 195–207.

Hans, S. L., & Marcus, J. (1983). Motor and attentional behavior in infants of methadone maintained women. *NIDA Research Monograph Series, 43,* 249–293.

Hansen, R. L., Struthers, J. M., & Gospe, S. M., Jr. (1993). Visual evoked potentials and visual processing in stimulant drug-exposed infants. *Developmental Medicine and Child Neurology, 35,* 798–805.

Harlap, S., & Shiono, P. H. (1980). Alcohol, smoking, and incidence of spontaneous abortions in the first and second trimester. *Lancet, 2,* 173–176.

Hawley, J., Brodsky, N., Giannetta, J., & Hurt, H. (1992). Comparison of neonatal behavioral assessment scale (NBAS) in cocaine-exposed and controls. *Pediatric Research, 31* (4 part 2; abstract #1483).

Hecht, F., Beals, R. K., Lees, M. H., Jolly, H., & Roberts, P. (1968). Lysergic-acid-diethylamide and cannabis as possible teratogens in man [Letter to the editor]. *Lancet, 2,* 1087.

Hersh, J. H. (1989). Toluene embryopathy: Two new cases. *Journal of Medical Genetics, 26,* 333–337.

Hersh, J. H., Podruch, P. E., Rogers, G., & Weisskopf, B. (1985). Toluene embryopathy. *Journal of Pediatrics, 106,* 922–927

Holmberg, P. C. (1979). Central-nervous-system defects in children born to mothers exposed to organic solvents during pregnancy. *Lancet, 2,* 177–179.

Holmberg, P. C., Hernberg, S., Kurppa, K., Rantala, K., & Riala, R. (1982). Oral clefts and organic solvent exposure during pregnancy. *International Archives of Occupational and Environmental Health, 50,* 371–376.

Holmberg, P. C., & Nurminen, M. (1980). Congenital defects of the central nervous system and occupational factors during pregnancy. A case-referent study. *American Journal of Industrial Medicine, 1,* 167–176.

Holzman, C., Paneth, N., Little, R., Pinto-Martin, J. (1995). Perinatal brain injury in premature infants born to mothers using alcohol in pregnancy. *Pediatrics, 95,* 66–73.

Householder, J., Hatcher, R. P., Burns, W. J., & Chasnoff, I. (1982). Infants born to narcotic-addicted mothers. *Psychological Bulletin, 92,* 453–468.

Houston, B. K. (1969). Review of the evidence and qualifications regarding the effects of hallucinogenic drugs on chromosomes and embryos. *American Journal of Psychiatry, 126,* 251–254.

Hsu, L. Y., Strauss, L., & Hirschhorn. (1970). Chromosome abnormality in offspring of LSD user: D trisomy with D/D translocation. *Journal of the American Medical Association, 211,* 987–990.

Hunter, A. G. W., Thompson, D., & Evans, J.A. (1979). Is there a fetal gasoline syndrome? *Teratology, 20,* 75–80.

Hurt, H., Betancourt, L. M., Malmud, E., Brodsky, N. L., & Giannetta, J. M. (1994). The Battelle Developmental Inventory (BDI): Scores of children with *in utero* cocaine exposure are different from controls. *Pediatric Research, 35,* (118), 22A.

Hurt, H., Brodsky, N. L., Betancourt, L., Braitman, L. E., Malmud, E., & Giannetta, J. (1995). Cocaine-exposed children: Follow-up through 30 months. *Journal of Developmental and Behavioral Pediatrics, 16,* 29–35.

Jacobson, S. W., Fein, G. G., Jacobson, J. L., Schwartz, P. M., & Dowler, J. K. (1984). Neonatal correlates of prenatal exposure to smoking, caffeine, and alcohol. *Infant Behavior and Development, 7,* 253–265.

Jacobson, S. W., Jacobson, J. L., & Sokol, R. J. (1994). Effects of fetal alcohol exposure on infant reaction time. *Alcoholism: Clinical and Experimental Research, 18,* 1125–1132.

Jacobson, J. L., Jacobson, S. W., Sokol, R. J., Martier, S. S., Ager, J. W., & Shankaran, S. (1994). Effects of alcohol use, smoking, and illicit drug use on fetal growth in black infants. *Journal of Pediatrics, 124,* 757–764.

Jeremy, R. J., & Hans, S. L. (1985). Behavior of neonates exposed in utero to methadone as assessed on the Brazelton scale. *Infant Behavior and Development, 8,* 323–336.

Johnson, H. L., Glassman, M. B., Fiks, K. B., and Rosen, T. S. (1987). Path analysis of variables affecting 36-month outcome in a population of multirisk children. *Infant Behavior and Development, 10,* 451–465.

Kaltenbach, K., & Finnegan, L. P. (1984). Developmental outcome of children born to methadone maintained women: A review of longitudinal studies. *Neurobehavioral Toxicology and Teratology, 6,* 271–275.

Kaltenbach, K., & Finnegan, L. P. (1986). Neonatal abstinence syndrome, pharmacotherapy and developmental outcome. *Neurobehavioral Toxicology and Teratology, 8,* 353–355.

Kaltenbach, K., & Finnegan, L. P. (1987). Perinatal and developmental outcome of infants exposed to methadone in-utero. *Neurotoxicology and Teratology, 9,* 311–313.

Kaplan, S. L., Kron, R. E., Litt, M., Finnegan, L. P., & Phoenix, M. D. (1975). Correlations between scores on the Brazelton Neonatal Assessment Scale, measures of newborn sucking behavior, and birthweight in infants born to narcotic addicted mothers. In N. R. Ellis (Ed.), *Aberrant development in infancy: Human and animal studies* (pp. 139–148). Hillsdale, NJ: Lawrence Erlbaum.

Kaplan, S. L., Kron, R. E., Phoenix, M. D., & Finnegan, L. P. (1976). Brazelton neonatal assessment at three and twenty-eight days of age: A study of passively addicted infants, high risk infants, and normal infants. In A. Schecter, H. Alksne, & E. Kaufman (Eds.), *Critical concerns in the field of drug abuse* (pp. 726–730). New York: Marcel Dekker.

Kaye, K., Elkind, L., Goldberg, D., & Tytun, A. (1989). Birth outcomes for infants of drug abusing mothers. *New York State Journal of Medicine, 89,* 256–261.

Keith, L. G., MacGregor, S., Friedell, S., Rosner, M., Chasnoff, I .J., & Sciarra, J. J. (1989). Substance abuse in pregnant women: Recent experience at the Perinatal Center for Chemical Dependence of Northwestern Memorial Hospital. *Obstetrics and Gynecology, 73,* 715–720.

Kleinman, J. C., Pierre, M. B., Jr., Madans, J. H., Land, G. H., & Schramm, W. F. (1988). The effects of maternal smoking on fetal and infant mortality. *American Journal of Epidemiology, 127,* 274–282.

Korkman, M., Hilakivi-Clarke, L. A., Autti-Ramo, I., Fellman, V., & Granstrom, M.-L. (1994). Cognitive impairments at two years of age after prenatal alcohol exposure or perinatal asphyxia. *Neuropediatrics, 25,* 101–105.

Kurppa, K., Holmberg, P. C., Kuosma, E., & Saxen, L. (1983). Coffee consumption during pregnancy and selected congenital malformations: A nationwide case-control study. *American Journal of Public Health, 73,* 1387–1399.

Laegreid, L., Hagberg, G., & Lundberg, A. (1992a). The effect of benzodiazepines on the fetus and the newborn. *Neuropediatrics, 23,* 18–23.

Laegreid, L., Hagberg, G., & Lundberg, A. (1992b). Neurodevelopment in late infancy after prenatal exposure to benzodiazepines—A prospective study. *Neuropediatrics, 23,* 60–67.

Laegreid, L., Olegard, R., Conradi, N., Hagberg, G., Wahlstrom, J., & Abrahamsson, L. (1990). Congenital malformations and maternal consumption of benzodiazepines: A case-control study. *Developmental Medicine and Child Neurology, 32,* 432–441.

Laegreid, L., Olegard, R., Wahlstrom, J., & Conradi, N. (1989). Teratogenic effects of benzodiazepine use during pregnancy. *Journal of Pediatrics, 114,* 126–131.

Lesser-Katz, M. (1982). Some effects of maternal drug addiction on the neonate. *International Journal of the Addictions, 17,* 887–896.

Levy, M., & Koren, G. (1990). Obstetric and neonatal effects of drug abuse. *Emergency Medicine Clinics of North America, 8,* 633–652.

Lifschitz, M. H., Wilson, G. S., Smith, E. O., & Desmond, M. M. (1985). Factors affecting head growth and intellectual function in children of drug addicts. *Pediatrics, 75,* 269–274.

Lindhout, D., Meinardi, H., Meijer, J. W. A., & Nau, H. (1992). Antiepileptic drugs and teratogenesis in two consecutive cohorts: Changes in prescription policy paralleled by changes in pattern of malformations. *Neurology, 42* (Suppl. 5), 94–110.

Little, B. B., Snell, L. M., & Gilstrap, L.C. (1988). Methamphetamine abuse during pregnancy: Outcome and fetal effects. *Obstetrics and Gynecology, 72,* 541–544.

Little, B. B., Snell, L. M., Klein, V. R., & Gilstrap, L. C. (1989). Cocaine abuse during pregnancy: Maternal and fetal implications. *Obstetrics and Gynecology, 73,* 157–160.

Malloy, M. H., Kleinman, J. C., Land, G. H., & Schramm, W. F. (1988). The association of maternal smoking with age and cause of infant death. *American Journal of Epidemiology, 128,* 46–55.

Martin, J., Payte, J. T., & Zweben, J. E. (1991). Methadone maintenance treatment: A primer for physicians. *Journal of Psychoactive Drugs, 23,* 165–176.

Mastrogiannis, D. S., Decavalas, G. O., Verma, U., & Tejani, N. (1990). Perinatal outcome after recent cocaine usage. *Obstetrics and Gynecology, 76,* 8–11.

Mayes, L. C., Granger, R. H., Frank, M. A., Schottenfeld, R., & Bornstein, M. H. (1993). Neurobehavioral profiles of neonates exposed to cocaine prenatally. *Pediatrics, 91,* 778–783.

Mazzi, E. (1977). Possible neonatal diazepam withdrawal: A case report. *American Journal of Obstetrics and Gynecology, 129,* 586–587.

McAuley, D. M., O'Neill, M. P., Moore, J., & Dundee, J. W. (1982). Lorazepam premedication for labour. *British Journal of Obstetrics and Gynaecology, 89,* 149–154.

McDonald, A. D., Armstrong, B. G., & Sloan, M. (1992a). Cigarette, alcohol, and coffee consumption and congenital defects. *American Journal of Public Health, 82,* 91–93.

McDonald, A. D, Armstrong, B. G., & Sloan, M. (1992b). Cigarette, alcohol, and coffee consumption and prematurity. *American Journal of Public Health, 82,* 87–90.

McDonald, J. C., Lavoie, J., Cote, R., & McDonald, A. D. (1987). Chemical exposure at work in early pregnancy and congenital defect: A case-referent study. *British Journal of Industrial Medicine, 44,* 527–533.

McGlothlin, W. H., Sparkes, R. S., & Arnold, D. O. (1970). Effect of LSD on human pregnancy. *Journal of the American Medical Association, 212,* 1483–1487.

Meirik, O., Kallen, B., Gauffin, U., & Ericson, A. (1979). Major malformations in infants born of women who worked in laboratories while pregnant [Letter to the editor]. *Lancet, 2,* 91.

Milerad, J., Rajs, J., & Gidlund, E. (1994). Nicotine and cotinine levels in pericardial fluid in victims of SIDS. *Acta Paediatrica, 83,* 59–62.

Naeye, R. L. (1980). Abruptio placentae and placenta previa: Frequency, perinatal mortality, and cigarette smoking. *Obstetrics and Gynecology, 55,* 701–704.

Naeye, R. L. (1982). Factors that predispose to premature rupture of the fetal membranes. *Obstetrics and Gynecology, 60,* 93–98.

Neuspiel, D. R., Hamel, S. C., Hochberg, E., Greene, J., & Campbell, D. (1991). Maternal cocaine use and infant behavior. *Neurotoxicology and Teratology, 13,* 229–233.

Niswander, K. R. (1969). Effects of diazepam on meperidine requirements of patients during labor. *Obstetrics and Gynecology, 34,* 62–67.

O'Connell, C. M., & Fried, P. A. (1991). Prenatal exposure to cannabis: A preliminary report of postnatal consequences in school-age children. *Neurotoxicology and Teratology, 13,* 631–639.

Ogston, S. A., Florey, C. D., & Walker, C. H. (1987). Association of infant alimentary and respiratory illness with parental smoking and other environmental factors. *Journal of Epidemiology and Community Health, 41,* 21–25.

Oro, A. S., & Dixon, S. D. (1987). Perinatal cocaine and methamphetamine exposure: Maternal and neonatal correlates. *Journal of Pediatrics, 111,* 571–578.

Parker, S., Zuckerman, B., Bauchner, H., Frank, D., Vinci, R., & Cabral, H. (1990). Jitteriness in full-term neonates: Prevalence and correlates. *Pediatrics, 85,* 17–23.

Pharoah, P. O. D., Alberman, E., Doyle, P., & Chamberlain, G. (1977). Outcome of pregnancy among women in anaesthetic practice. *Lancet, 1,* 34–36.

Pond, S. M., Kreek, M. J., Tong, T. G., Raghunath, J., & Benowitz, N. L. (1985). Altered methadone pharmacokinetics in methadone-maintained pregnant women. *Journal of Pharmacology and Experimental Therapeutics, 233,* 1–6.

Rahbar, F., Fomufod, A., White, D., & Westney, L. S. (1993). Impact of intrauterine exposure to phencyclidine (PCP) and cocaine on neonates. *Journal of the National Medical Association, 85,* 349–352.

Rementeria, J. L., & Bhatt, K. (1977). Withdrawal symptoms in neonates from intrauterine exposure to diazepam. *Journal of Pediatrics, 90,* 123–126.

Richardson, G. A, & Day, N. L. (1991). Maternal and neonatal effects of moderate cocaine use during pregnancy. *Neurotoxicology and Teratology, 13,* 455–460.

Richardson, G. A., & Day, N. L. (1994). Detrimental effects of prenatal cocaine exposure: Illusion or reality? *Journal of the American Academy of Child and Adolescent Psychiatry, 33,* 28–34.

Richardson, G. A., Day, N. L., & Taylor, P. M. (1989). The effect of prenatal alcohol, marijuana, and tobacco exposure on neonatal behavior. *Infant Behavior and Development, 12,* 199–209.

Rodning, C., Beckwith, L., & Howard, J. (1991). Quality of attachment and home environments in children prenatally exposed to PCP and cocaine. *Development and Psychopathology, 3,* 351–366.

Rosen, T. S., & Johnson, H. L. (1985). Long-term effects of prenatal methadone maintenance. *NIDA Research Monograph Series, 59,* 73–83.

Rosenberg, L., Mitchell, A. A., Parsells, J. L., Pashayan, H., Louik, C., & Shapiro, S. (1983). Lack of relation of oral clefts to diazepam use during pregnancy. *New England Journal of Medicine, 309,* 1282–1285.

Rosenthal, E. (1990, February 4). When a pregnant woman drinks. *New York Times Magazine,* pp. 30, 49, 61.

Ryan, L., Ehrlich, S., & Finnegan, L. P. (1987). Cocaine abuse in pregnancy: Effects on the fetus and newborn. *Neurotoxicology and Teratology, 9,* 295–299.

Safra, M. J., & Oakley, G. P., Jr. (1975). Association between cleft lip with or without cleft palate and prenatal exposure to diazepam. *Lancet, 2,* 478–481.

Sanghavi, D. M. (1995). Epidemiology of sudden infant death syndrome (SIDS) for Kentucky infants born in 1990: Maternal, prenatal, and perinatal risk factors. *Journal of the Kentucky Medical Association, 93,* 286–290.

Saxen, I., & Saxen, L. (1975). Association between maternal intake of diazepam and oral clefts [Letter to the editor]. *Lancet, 2,* 498.

Schnoll, S. H. (1986). Pharmacologic basis of perinatal addiction. In I.J. Chasnoff (Ed.), *Drug use in pregnancy: Mother and child* (pp.7–16). Norwell, MA: MTP Press.

Schoendorf, K. C. & Kiely, J. L. (1992). Relationship of sudden infant death syndrome to maternal smoking during and after pregnancy. *Pediatrics, 90,* 905–908.

Shiono, P. H., & Mills, J. L. (1984). Oral clefts and diazepam use during pregnancy [Letter to the editor]. *New England Journal of Medicine, 311,* 919–920.

Singer, L. T., Yamashita, T. S., Hawkins, S., Cairns, D., Baley, J., & Kliegman, R. (1994). Increased incidence of intraventricular hemorrhage and developmental delay in cocaine-exposed, very low birth weight infants. *Journal of Pediatrics, 124,* 765–771.

Starreveld-Zimmerman, A. A. E., van der Kolk, W. J., Meinardi, H., & Elshove, J. (1973). Are anticonvulsants teratogenic? [Letter to the editor]. *Lancet, 2,* 48–49.

Stjernfeldt, M., Berglund, K., Lindsten, J., & Ludvigsson, J. (1986). Maternal smoking during pregnancy and risk of childhood cancer. *Lancet, 1,* 1350–1352.

Strandberg, M., Sandback, K., Axelson, O., & Sundell, L. (1978). Spontaneous abortions among women in hospital laboratory [Letter to the editor]. *Lancet, 1,* 384–385.

Strauss, M. E., Andresko, E. M., Stryker, J. C., Wardell, J. N., & Dankell, L. D. (1974). Methadone maintenance during pregnancy: Pregnancy, birth, and neonate characteristics. *American Journal of Obstetrics and Gynecology, 120,* 895–900.

Strauss, M. E., Lessen-Firestone, J. K, Starr, R. H., Jr., & Ostrea, E. M., Jr. (1975). Behavior of narcotics-addicted newborns. *Child Development, 46,* 887–893.

Strauss, A. S., Mondalou, H. D., & Bosee, S. K. (1981). Neonatal manifestations of maternal phencyclidine (PCP) abuse. *Pediatrics, 68,* 550–552.

Strauss, M. E., Starr, R. H., Jr., Ostrea, E. M., Jr., Chavez, C.J., & Stryker, J.C. (1976). Behavioral concomitants of prenatal addiction to narcotics. *Journal of Pediatrics, 89,* 842–846.

Streissguth, A. P., Barr, H. M., Martin, D. C., & Herman, C. S. (1980). Effects of maternal alcohol, nicotine, and caffeine use during pregnancy on infant mental and motor development at eight months. *Alcoholism: Clinical and Experimental Research, 4,* 152–164.

Streissguth, A. P., Barr, H. M., Sampson, P. D., & Bookstein, F. L. (1994). Prenatal alcohol and offspring development: The first fourteen years. *Drug and Alcohol Dependence, 36,* 89–99.

Struthers, J. M., & Hansen, R. L. (1992). Visual recognition memory in drug-exposed infants. *Journal of Developmental & Behavioral Pediatrics, 13,* 108–111.

Tabor, B. L., Smith-Wallace, T., & Yonekura, M. L. (1990). Perinatal outcome associated with PCP versus cocaine use. *American Journal of Drug and Alcohol Abuse, 16,* 337–348.

Taskinen, H., Anttila, A., Lindbohm, M.-L., Sallmen, M., & Hemminki, K. (1989). Spontaneous abortions and congenital malformations among the wives of men occupationally exposed to organic solvents. *Scandinavian Journal of Work, Environment, and Health, 15,* 345–352.

Tikkanen, J., & Heinonen, O. P. (1991). Maternal exposure to chemical and physical factors during pregnancy and cardiovascular malformations in the offspring. *Teratology, 43,* 591–600.

Tikkanen, J. & Heinonen, O. P. (1992a). Risk factors for atrial septal defect. *European Journal of Epidemiology, 8,* 509–515.

Tikkanen, J. & Heinonen, O. P. (1992b). Risk factors for conal malformations of the heart. *European Journal of Epidemiology, 8,* 48–57.

Toutant, C., & Lippmann, S. (1979). Fetal solvents syndrome [Letter to the editor]. *Lancet, 1,* 1356.

Tronick, E. Z., Frank, D.A., Cabral, H., & Zuckerman, B. S. (1994). A dose response effect of in utero cocaine exposure on infant neurobehavioral functioning. *Pediatric Research, 35,* (152), 28A.

van Duijn, C. M., van Steensel-Moll, H.A., Coebergh, J.-W. W., & van Zanen, G. E. (1994). Risk factors for childhood acute non-lymphocytic leukemia: An association with maternal alcohol consumption during pregnancy? *Cancer Epidemiology, Biomarkers, and Prevention, 3,* 457–460.

van der Pol, M. C., Hadders-Algra, M., Huisjes, H. J., & Touwen, B. C. L. (1991). Antiepileptic medication in pregnancy: Late effects on the children's central nervous system development. *American Journal of Obstetrics and Gynecology, 164,* 121–128.

Viggedal, G., Hagberg, B. S., Laegreid, L., & Aronsson, M. (1993). Mental development in late infancy after prenatal exposure to benzodiazepines-A prospective study. *Journal of Child Psychology and Psychiatry and Allied Disciplines, 34,* 295–305.

Wachsman, L., Schuetz, S., Chan, L. S., & Wingert, W. A. (1989). What happens to babies exposed to phencyclidine (PCP) *in utero*? *American Journal of Drug and Alcohol Abuse, 15,* 31–39.

Waters, C. H., Belai, Y., Gott, P. S., Shen, P., & DeGiorgio, C. M. (1994). Outcomes of pregnancy associated with antiepileptic drugs. *Archives of Neurology, 51,* 250–253.

Weiner, L., Morse, B. A., & Garrido, P. (1989). FAS/FAE: Focusing prevention on women at risk. *International Journal of the Addictions, 24,* 385–395.

Werner, M. J. (1993). Hallucinogens. *Pediatrics in Review, 14,* 466–472.

Wilcox, A. J., Weinberg, C. R., & Baird, D. D. (1990). Risk factors for early pregnancy loss. *Epidemiology, 1,* 382–385.

Wilkins-Haug, L., & Gabow, P. A. (1991). Toluene abuse during pregnancy: Obstetric complications and perinatal outcomes. *Obstetrics and Gynecology, 77,* 504–509.

Willers, S., Svenonius, E., & Skarping, G. (1991). Passive smoking and childhood asthma: Urinary cotinine levels in children with asthma and in referents. *Allergy, 46,* 330–334.

Williams, M. A., Mittendorf, R., Stubblefield, P. G., Lieberman, E., Shoenbaum, S. C., & Monson, R. R. (1992). Cigarettes, coffee, and preterm rupture of the membranes. *American Journal of Epidemiology, 135,* 895–903.

Wilson, G. S. (1989). Clinical studies of infants and children exposed prenatally to heroin. *Annals of the New York Academy of Sciences, 562,* 183–194.

Woods, N. S., Eyler, F. D., Behnke, M., & Conlon, M. (1993). Cocaine use during pregnancy: Maternal depressive symptoms and infant neurobehavior over the first month. *Infant Behavior and Development, 16,* 83–98.

Zellweger, H., McDonald, J. S., & Abbo, G. (1967). Is lysergic-acid diethylamide a teratogen? *Lancet, 2,* 1066–1068.

Zelson, C., Lee, S. J., & Casalino, M. (1973). Comparative effects of maternal intake of heroin and methadone. *New England Journal of Medicine, 289,* 1216–1220.

Zuckerman, B., Frank, D.A., Hingson, R., Amaro, H., Levenson, S.M., Kayne, H., Parker, S., Vinci, R., Aboagye, K., Fried, L.E., Cabral, R., Timperi, R., & Bauchner, H. (1989). Effects of maternal marijuana and cocaine use on fetal growth. *New England Journal of Medicine, 320,* 762–768.

CHAPTER 6

ALCOHOLISM IN ADULTHOOD

Michie N. Hesselbrock
Victor M. Hesselbrock

Adulthood is often characterized as the most productive stage of life. The achievement of certain adulthood developmental milestones, along with certain social and psychological expectations, are associated with efforts to build a better life for the next generation. A sense of generativity is achieved through family, work, civic activities, and helping others. A person with alcohol and other drug problems experiences obstacles to achieving all aspects of adult life satisfaction, ranging from one's sense of belonging to work success, intimate relationships, and the rearing of children. However, not all substance-abusing persons are affected in the same manner or with the same consequences. There is a growing body of literature recognizing the heterogeneity among persons addicted to alcohol and other drugs in relation to risk factors, etiology, drug use patterns and pathways to recovery from the addiction. This chapter reviews the literature on adult-onset alcoholism, longitudinal pathways to recovery, and the consequences of continued substance abuse.

Epidemiological surveys of alcohol use and alcohol-related consequences have repeatedly shown that the rates of alcohol misuse, including abuse, are highest among men and women between the ages of 18 and 29 years. The Epidemiological Catchment Area (ECA) data found that

18% of men and 11% of women between 18 and 29 years old met the DSM III criteria for alcohol abuse/dependence, whereas the 1988 NHIS reported that 26% of men and 11% of women in this age group met the DSM III-R criteria for alcohol abuse and dependence. In both studies, the rate of problem drinking declined whereas the rate of abstinence increased as the subjects grew older (National Institute of Health, National Institute of Alcohol Abuse & Alcoholism, 1993). Why do some persons continue to drink, often heavily, without progressing toward problem with drinking while others develop a problem drinking? This question is without a clear answer, although several possibilities exist. Several factors associated with the possible development of alcohol abuse and alcoholism in adulthood are considered next.

FACTORS ASSOCIATED WITH THE DEVELOPMENT OF ALCOHOLISM IN ADULTHOOD

Problems in Childhood

Several longitudinal studies have found that childhood behavior problems, including hyperactivity and conduct problems, are often associated with the development of alcoholism in adulthood. Among child guidance samples, childhood problem behavior characteristics often found to be associated with the later development of alcoholism and other drug abuse include aggression, sadistic behaviors, and conduct problems (McCord & McCord, 1960; Robins, 1966). Similarly, rebelliousness, extroversion, impulsivity, hostility and irritability have been identified as predictors of adult drinking problems in longitudinal studies of community samples. Zucker and Gomberg (1986), in their review of retrospective studies of alcoholism, postulated a longitudinal developmental framework of alcoholism and found that antisocial behavior (including aggression, sadistic behavior, conduct problems, or rebelliousness) as well as difficulty in academic achievement in childhood and adolescence were consistently related to the development of alcoholism in adulthood. Achievement-related variables included poor school performance, low productivity in high school, truancy, and dropping out of high school. DeObaldia, Parsons, and Yohman (1983) also found that hyperactivity and minimal brain dysfunction (MBD) symptoms in childhood were associated with severe symptoms of alcohol dependence and poor cognitive performance. However, not all hyperactive children develop alcohol problems in adulthood. Furthermore, problem behavior in childhood is often an etiologic factor not only for alcoholism but also for a variety of adult psychiatric disorders (cf. Robins & Price, 1991). Although the most consistent finding is an association between childhood conduct disorder and adult antisocial behaviors, not all children who display conduct-disordered behavior become antisocial adults. Zucker and Gomberg (1986) caution that antisocial behaviors and academic maladjustment are also found among the "high-risk" children who do not go on to develop alcoholism later in life. For example, a prospective study of hyperactive children found marked improvement in this category of behaviors among the subjects as they grew older. (August, Stewart, & Holmes, 1983; Mendelson, Johnson, & Stewart, 1971; Weiss, Hechtman, Perlman, Hopkins, & Wender, 1979).

Searches for factors that distinguish those hyperactive children who later develop alcoholism from those children who do not have found possible contributory genetic influences and have identified specific behaviors that may serve as markers for eventual poor outcome. Alterman and Tarter (1983) suggest that some individuals with an alcohol disorder may have an inherited predisposition for hyperactivity. An increased rate of hyperactivity, alcoholism, sociopathy, and aggression among the biological fathers and other relatives of hyperactive children has been reported (Cantwell, 1972; Goodwin, Schulsinger, Hermansen, Guze, & Winokur, 1975; Mendelson et al., 1971; Morrison & Stewart, 1971; Tarter, Hegedus, & Gavaler, 1985). However, a specific mechanism linking hyperactivity to the development of alcoholism has not been identified.

Stewart, deBlois, and Cummings (1980) found that antisocial personality disorder (ASPD) and alcoholism in adulthood were more frequently found in fathers of the aggressive antisocial boys compared to boys without these characteristics. August and Stewart (1983) suggest that conduct problems and aggressiveness may involve genetic factors and may be important etiologic factors for alcoholism. Further, conduct disorder and aggressiveness in childhood may continue through the teen years and be associated with alcohol and substance use. August et al. (1983) found that hyperactive boys who were undersocialized and aggressive continued to be aggressive, noncompliant, antisocial, alcohol-using or -abusing teenagers. Allen and Frances (1986) also found that childhood conduct problems and aggression predict antisocial personality disorder and alcoholism in adulthood. Hesselbrock (1986) found that childhood attention, impulsivity, hyperactivity, and conduct problems were important precursors of adult antisocial personality disorder among both males and females with alcohol dependence.

A Family History of Alcoholism

The familial nature of alcoholism is well documented. Higher lifetime rates of alcoholism have been found among the biological relatives of alcoholic probands compared to the general population. Goodwin (1979) proposed that persons with "familial alcoholism" have severe alcoholism with an early onset of the disorder, enter treatment at an early age, and have absence of other conspicuous psychopathology, including other substance abuse. However, this conceptualization of "familial alcoholism" has not held up under more intensive investigation, particularly the requirement of the absence of other psychopathology (cf. Frances, Timm, & Bucky, 1980; Hesselbrock, Stabenau, Hesselbrock, Meyer, & Babor, 1982; Penick, Read, Crawley, & Powell, 1978). In fact, this type of alcoholism requiring treatment in early adulthood is most often associated with the presence of conduct problems. Alcoholism that occurs in the relative absence of additional psychopathology is more often less severe, with an onset in later adult life.

Studies of both clinical and community samples of alcoholics have found a strong association between antisocial personality disorder and alcoholism. However, these two disorders share a variety of symptoms and it is difficult to distinguish antisocial personality disorder (ASPD) and alcoholism on the basis of phenomenology alone. Persons with alcohol disorders often display a variety of antisocial behaviors, whereas persons with antisocial personality disorder often abuse alcohol. Further, it is also difficult to separate antisocial personality disorder from early onset of alcoholism from ASPD, as alcohol abuse at an early age is a criterion for ASPD. Conversely, alcoholics often exhibit conduct problems, particularly while intoxicated (Gerstley, Alterman, McLellan, & Woody, 1990; Meyer, 1986). There is, however, general agreement that ASPD alcoholics compared to non-ASPD alcoholics have an earlier onset of alcoholism followed by a more chronic and severe course. Consequently, they tend to be much younger when they seek treatment (Hesselbrock et al., 1984; Lewis, Rice, & Helzer, 1983; Penick, Powell, Othmer, Bingham, & Rice, 1984; Stabenau, 1984). Hesselbrock et al. (1984) found that hospitalized ASPD alcoholics took their first drink and began regular drinking and drunkenness much earlier than their non-ASPD counterparts. They also reported more substance abuse. Although ASPD alcoholics were nearly 10 years younger than the non-ASPD alcoholics at the time of hospitalization, they reported having a drinking problem just as long as the older non-ASPD alcoholics. Similarly, Penick et al. (1984) found that ASPD alcoholics had an early onset of alcoholism, poor psychosocial functioning, more alcohol-related hospitalizations, arrests, indicators of alcohol abuse symptoms, and familial psychopathology. The presence of ASPD was also related to other substance-abuse problems and multiple treatments for these problems (Cadoret, Troughton, & Widmer, 1984).

Whereas there is a striking comorbidity of alcoholism with ASPD among both males and females with alcohol disorders, it does appear that alcoholism and ASPD are separately transmitted across generations (Cloninger, Christiansen, Reich, & Gottsman, 1978; Reich, Cloninger, Lewis, & Rice, 1981). Alcoholism in the biological father is clearly associated with an increase in alcoholism among his offspring (Cotton, 1979; Hesselbrock, 1995), and adoption studies have found that paternal criminality and psychopathy are associated with an increased vulnerability for antisocial personality disorder among the progeny (Cadoret, Yates, Troughton, Woodworth, & Stewart, 1995;

Goodwin, Schulsinger, Hermansen, Guze, & Winokur, 1973; Hesselbrock, Meyer, & Keener, 1985).

TYPES OF ALCOHOLISM IN ADULTHOOD

Both clinicians and researchers recognize the heterogeneous nature of alcohol problems and alcoholism in adulthood. Adult alcoholism can be characterized by its differential presentation of demographic characteristics, alcohol use history, comorbid psychiatric disorders, and familial alcoholism, all of which have been identified as affecting the course of the disorder, treatment -seeking behavior, and treatment outcomes (Hesselbrock, 1995). Studies that have attempted to subclassify alcoholism often suggest two major types of alcoholism. A common observation from clinical samples of alcoholism is that those who become addicted to alcohol during late adolescence and early adulthood are quite different from those who begin their abusive use of alcohol at middle to late adulthood in terms of their alcohol use patterns, comordid psychiatric disorders, family history of alcoholism, and natural history of the disorder.

Some investigators have attempted to subclassify persons with alcoholism according to one of its major distinguishing characteristics, the age of onset of alcoholism and its related problems. The onset of alcohol-related problems in early adolescence and adulthood is often associated with an earlier age of entry into a treatment program. The early onset group is, on average, in their early to mid-30s at the time of their first treatment experience, whereas the middle adult onset groups typically first enter treatment in their late 40s (Irwin, Schuckit, & Smith, 1990; Schuckit, 1985).

Alcohol Related Symptoms and Severity

A number of studies have found that persons with a severe adult form of alcoholism often experience a variety of behavior problems during childhood. This subgroup of alcoholics is often characterized by an early onset, severe form of alcoholism, having a family history of alcoholism among their biological relatives, and history of childhood problems that include hyperactivity and MBD symptoms (Tarter, McBride, Buonpane, & Schneider, 1977). Similarly, Hesselbrock et al. (1984) found that alcoholics with antisocial personality disorder began problem drinking at a much younger age, followed by a more chronic and severe course of alcoholism.

Irwin et al. (1990) compared early (before age 25) and late onset (after age 25) alcoholism in 171 primary alcoholic men who were sampled upon entry into treatment. An early onset of alcoholism was associated with a variety of severe clinical characteristics. The men who began having alcohol problems before age 25, as compared to those who began to experience their problems after age 25, were more likely to use marijuana, stimulants, and other drugs; to experience a greater number of drug-related problems; and to report more childhood criminal activities. Schuckit (1985) later compared primary and secondary alcoholism in relation to the age of onset of other psychiatric disorders. The primary alcoholics typically had an onset of alcoholism after age 25 whereas those whose alcoholism was secondary to antisocial personality disorder and/or other substance abuse tended to have alcohol problems before age 25. Primary alcoholism was associated with being older (mean age 47 years), and a later onset of first alcohol-related problems (mean age 32 years for primary substance abuse and 35 years for the antisocial personality disorder). Further, the secondary diagnosis of alcoholism was associated with a greater likelihood of heavier alcohol involvement, drug abuse, and more police and social problems at the 1-year follow-up evaluations. Despite their younger age, the secondary alcoholics reported more frequent and larger amounts of drinking prior to entering a treatment program than the later onset, primary alcoholic group. Similarly, other studies have found that primary alcoholics report frequent work-related problems and previous treatments, but are seldom involved in substance abuse or fighting due to alcohol or substance abuse (Cook, Winokur, Fowler, & Liskow, 1994).

An association between the age of onset of alcohol problems and symptom severity has also been found in a nonclinical sample. Bucholz et al. (in press) used a latent class analysis of 36 alcohol dependence symptoms and treatment variables to identify four classes of drinkers in a sample of biological relatives of alcohol dependent drinkers and a sample of controls. The first latent class ("unaffected") reported the fewest number of alcohol-related problems. These subjects also reported a later age of onset of the first drinking problems than all other groups. The Class 2 (prealcoholic problem) group reported experiencing losing control over drinking and drinking excessively. However, this group experienced fewer adverse social, psychological, and physical consequences than Class 3 and Class 4 subjects. Class 3 subjects reported more adverse psychological and social consequences of drinking, but few indicators of physical dependence. Important gender differences were noted in Class 3 subjects, with men reporting higher rates of more severe problems such as morning drinking, narrowing of the drinking repertoire, recurrent fighting while drinking, tolerance, and hazardous use than the females. However, 98% of female subjects and 100% of male subjects in this class met the criteria for the DSM III-R alcohol dependence. Class 4 subjects reported the highest rates of indicators of physical dependence and achieved several drinking 'milestones' at an earlier age compared to the other three classes of subjects. Both male and female subjects in Class 4 began regular drinking, drank to intoxication, and experienced their first drinking problems much earlier than subjects in classes 1, 2, or 3. All (100%) of the men and women in this class met DSM III-R criteria for alcohol dependence.

Comorbidity, Gender, and the Age of Onset of Alcohol Abuse

Persons who suffer from alcoholism often have other comorbid psychiatric disorders. This finding has been consistent regardless of whether alcohol-dependent samples are drawn from clinical settings or from the general population (Hesselbrock et al., 1985; Kessler et al., 1985; Regier, 1984). The types of comorbid psychiatric disorders and their prevalence differs by gender and by the age of onset of alcohol problems. For example, antisocial personality disorder and substance abuse are more frequently found among men, and are associated with an early onset of alcohol abuse and a younger age at treatment entry. Affective disorder and anxiety disorder occur more commonly among female alcoholics and tend to indicate a later age of onset of alcohol related problems than either ASPD or substance abuse. Cook et al. (1994) studied 224 consecutive admissions for alcoholism and found that 57% were primary alcoholics whereas 22% were secondary to antisocial personality disorder and 21% were secondary to other psychiatric disorders. Patients with comorbid antisocial personality disorder were the youngest, followed by those with organic brain syndrome, affective disorders, schizophrenia, and anxiety disorders. The primary compared to the secondary alcoholics were older. Similarly, primary alcoholism was associated with the lowest rates of panic attacks, delusional symptoms, and affective disorder.

Studies of alcoholic women have found different psychiatric symptom clusters compared to those typically found in men. Cocaine abuse among alcoholic women is associated with an early alcohol symptom onset, whereas the abuse of benzodiazepines is more common among late-onset alcoholic women. Further, symptoms of depression and anxiety were more prevalent among the early-onset group (Glenn & Nixon, 1991). Findings from studies of alcoholism that sample only men or only women without including a comparison to the other gender are difficult to generalize. The importance of including both male and female subjects can be seen in the Bucholz (in press) study. Bucholz found higher rates of other drug dependence and anxiety disorder among both men and women in the class of alcoholism associated with an early onset of alcohol abuse whereas a higher rate of depression was found among Class 4 men but not women. The rate of major depression among females was similar across all four classes (22% to 26%).

Although gender differences were apparent in terms of types of comorbid psychiatric disorders, the course of alcoholism and alcohol-related life experiences also vary by gender. Women typically begin abusive drinking later in life than men, often secondary to depressive disorder or anxiety disorder (Hesselbrock et al., 1985). However, women experience a variety of alcohol-related problems at an earlier age than men. Schuckit, Anthenelli, Bucholz, Hesselbrock, & Tipp (1995) examined the time course of development of alcohol related problems in 317 men and 161 women who met the DSM III criteria for alcohol dependence. Although the order of appearance of 44 alcohol-related problems was similar for men and women, women experienced indicators of more severe alcohol-abuse problems including repeated attempt to cut down, psychological problems, relationship problems, using despite harm to health, help from a professional, and the first abstinence of 3 or more months at an earlier age than men. Similarly the indicators of physical addiction including shakes following abstinence, withdrawal syndrome, delirium tremens, impaired liver, ulcers, pancreatitis, and convulsions following abstinence were also experienced at an earlier age among women compared to men.

FAMILY HISTORY OF ALCOHOLISM

A family history of alcoholism may be one factor that differentiates primary and secondary alcoholism. This finding is consistent with a variety of studies that indicate that the sons of alcoholic fathers tend to develop early onset of alcoholism. Cook et al. (1994) found that the frequency of

a family history of alcoholism was higher among antisocial men with alcohol disorders. Higher rates of both maternal and paternal alcoholism in early-symptom-onset women was also found. Furthermore, fathers of the early-symptom-onset women suffered more adverse consequences of alcoholism as compared to the fathers of the late-symptom-onset group. The relationship between a family history of alcoholism and psychiatric comorbidity was also documented by a study of 568 alcoholic men in treatment. Read et al. (1990) summarized two different studies and found that familial alcoholism was associated with an earlier onset of problem drinking and increased rates of psychopathology among both alcoholic probands and their first-degree relatives. However, Read et al. (1990) conclude that the course and severity of abusive drinking is mostly influenced by the existence of psychiatric comorbidity.

Biological Markers

Although the age of onset of alcoholism seems to be an important factor in distinguishing a clinical course of alcoholism, it is also associated with a typology that combines biological and personality factors considered to be associated with heritability of alcoholism. Cloninger, Bohman, and Sigvardsson (1981) proposed two distinct types of alcohol abuse based on a study of Swedish men who were adopted away to nonrelatives within the first few months of life. The sample included 862 men who were born between 1930 and 1949 to single women in Stockholm. These men were followed up at ages between 23 and 43 years. Cloninger (1987) considered the individual and combined effects of clinical, genetic, and psychopharmacological variables on etiological factors in the development of alcoholism. He suggested that different types of alcohol-seeking behavior involves neurogenetic processes that modulate the activation, maintenance, and inhibition of behavioral responses to the effects of alcohol. An early onset of alcoholism is most closely associated with Cloninger et al. (1981) Type 2 or 'male limited' alcoholism. This type of alcoholism is thought to be highly heritable, independent of environmental influences, and characterized by moderate alcohol abuse in the probands and by criminality and severe alcohol use in their fathers. Type 2 alcoholism is distinguished by an onset prior to age 25 and is associated with the three personality traits of high novelty seeking, low harm avoidance, and reward dependence. Type 2 alcoholics display spontaneous alcohol-seeking behaviors and convey an increased risk of alcoholism to their sons, mostly due to genetic rather than environmental influences. Type 1 or "milieu limited" alcoholism was characterized by mild or severe alcohol abuse in the probands and mild to moderate alcohol abuse without criminality in their biological fathers. Type 1 alcohol abuse typically begins after age 25 and both environment and genetic factors contribute to the risk of developing alcoholism. In the second part of this cross-fostering study, Bohman et al. (1981) analyzed data on 913 adopted women. Among those with alcohol abuse, the pattern of alcohol abuse was homogeneous and similar to Type 1 alcoholism. A replication of the Cloninger typology with a U.S. sample resulted in equivocal results. Gilligan, Reich, and Cloninger (1987) examined the heritability of alcohol abuse in the family members of a hospitalized alcoholic sample. The relatives of 'male-like' alcoholics had characteristics that were similar to Type 2 alcoholics. These alcoholics were characterized by an early age of onset of drinking problems and a high prevalence of antisocial personality disorder. The relatives of 'female type' probands displayed Type 1 features, that is, had onset of drinking problems after age 25, felt guilt about drinking, and suffered more adverse physical consequences as a result of drinking.

The association between Type 1 and Type 2 alcoholism in terms of the age of onset of alcohol-related problems and a history of parental alcoholism was also found in a Swedish study of treated alcoholics. In addition to alcoholism, higher rates of depression were reported among the Type 2 alcoholic subjects, and the dual disorders of depression and alcoholism were found among the parents of Type 2 alcoholics (von Knorring, von Knorring, Smigan, Lindberg, & Edholm, 1987). The association of familial depression among Type 2 alcoholics was not supported by Pandey, Fawcett, Gobbons, Clark, and Davis (1988), who found no significant differences between Type 1 and Type 2 alcoholism in regard to either history of primary major depression or a parental history of alcoholism. However, they did support the finding of high rates of alcoholism among the extended family members of Type 2 alcoholics (Pandey et al., 1988).

Attempts to replicate Type 1 and 2 alcoholism among US samples in relation to the symptom patterns and personality traits proposed by Cloninger et al. (1981) have often found an overlap between two types (Hesselbrock & Hesselbrock, 1992; Penick et al., 1990; Schuckit, Irwin, & Mahler, 1990; von Knorring et al., 1987), although the age of onset of alcohol problems has been the single factor that

has consistently separated these two types of alcoholism (Glen & Nixon, 1991; Irwin, Schuckit, & Smith, 1990; Penick et al., 1990; von Knorring, Bohman, von Knorring, & Oreland, 1985).

Von Knorring et al. (1987) examined the personality traits of Type 1 and Type 2 alcoholism. Personality traits consistent with antisocial personality disorder were higher among Type 2 alcoholics than Type 1 alcoholics. Both types of alcoholics were found to have high scores on somatic anxiety, psychic anxiety, muscular tension, impulsiveness, detachment, psychasthenia, suspicion, guilt, and aggression. However, Type 2 alcoholics had significantly higher scores than Type 1 alcoholics on somatic anxiety and verbal aggression scales, but significantly lower scores on socialization and inhibition of aggression scales. Von Knorring et al. suggest that conduct disorder may be genetically transmitted by alcoholic parents with antisocial personality disorder and that it is related to alcoholism with early onset of abuse and intoxication.

Several investigators have explored several possible biological markers and personality traits that may be associated with Type 1 and Type 2 alcoholism. Low platelet monoamine oxidase activity (MAO) has often been observed in samples of alcoholics when compared with control samples. In a study of the Cloninger subtypes, von Knorring et al. (1985) found that platelet MAO activity was similar in Type 1 alcoholics and healthy controls, but was lower in Type 2 alcoholics. Similar findings were reported by Sullivan, Baenziger, and Wagner (1990) who studied men 20 and 59 years of age with a DSM III-R diagnosis of alcohol dependence at a VA medical center. MAO activity was significantly lower for the Type 2 compared to the Type 1 alcoholics, whereas the alcoholic sample as a whole had lower MAO activity than the nonalcoholic controls. Sullivan et al. (1990) also found personality trait differences among the Type 1 and Type 2 alcoholics. Higher scores on the traits of novelty seeking, boredom susceptibility, thrill and adventure seeking, and disinhibition, as well as total sensation seeking, were observed with Type 2 alcoholics.

Babor et al. (1992), employing an empirical clustering technique from the sample of 321 male and female alcoholics, derived two types of alcoholism. Although the two types were quite similar in terms of alcohol use, several other characteristics replicated the Cloninger et al. typology. Babor et al.'s Type A was similar to Cloninger's Type 1 and was characterized by a later onset of alcohol problems, fewer childhood risk factors, and less psychopathology. The other cluster, Type B alcoholism, resembled Type 2. Type B alcoholism was typified by a number of childhood problem behaviors, an early onset of alcohol problems, familial alcoholism, a more chronic treatment history, and greater variety of other psychiatric problems.

Onset of Alcoholism in Late Adulthood

Whereas epidemiological data suggest the rate of problem drinking is lower among persons aged 65 years or older (Grant et al., 1991), others have found that alcohol use tends to increase with age (NIH, 1993). With the aging of the population in the United States it is expected that the rates of alcohol-related health and social problems will increase. Although high mortality rates are found among long-term chronic heavy drinkers who begin abusing alcohol in early adulthood, some persons do not begin problem drinking until later in life (e.g., after the age of 65). It has been suggested that alcoholism in the elderly may be associated with isolation from sources of social support, loss of family members, or retirement (McNeece & DiNitto, 1994). A retrospective examination of alcohol related problems (including both psychosocial and physical consequences) in the elderly is difficult due to problems in recalling the temporal order of the occurrence of problems Generally, however, the form of alcoholism that begins at age 65 or older tends to be associated with a more favorable socioeconomic status.

The majority of contemporary studies of alcoholic subtypes have used an onset of alcohol problems occurring prior to age 25 to define "early onset alcoholism" and the onset of alcohol problems occurring after the age of 25 years of age as the principal indicator of "late onset alcoholism". This categorization thus combines all alcoholism occurring in both middle and late adulthood. Whereas chronic alcoholism diagnosed in early and middle adulthood is associated with high mortality, little is known about the form of alcoholism that has an onset in late adult life. However, United States researchers have begun to recognize the importance of studying the alcohol problems of older adults. Both longitudinal and cross-sectional studies of alcohol use over the life course show that the heaviest use of alcohol tends to peak around age 30 and, in general, the use of alcohol declines after reaching the age of 65. Some studies have found that women are more likely to increase their alcohol intake after age 65 than men (Stall, 1987). However, those with high level of alcohol-related problems in early and middle adult life tended

to continue their problem drinking over time (Temple & Fillmore, 1985). Stall's (1987) review of cross-sectional studies conducted during the 1970s indicates that the prevalence rate of alcoholism ranges from 8% to 56% depending on the sample, region of the country, and setting (i.e., VA, psychiatric hospitals, San Diego to New York City, etc.). More recent studies reviewed by King, Van Hasselt, Segal, and Hersen (1994) report that approximately 10% of older patients in mental health facilities are affected. However, the diagnosis of alcoholism is often missed by health care professionals caring for the elderly as the physiological effects of alcohol may resemble the aging process. Symptoms of alcohol abuse may be mistaken for the manifestation of dementia and other organic disorders that are common among elderly. King et al. suggest that there may be some difficulty applying the DSM IV diagnostic criteria to older individuals. The criteria, which pertain to social and occupational problems, may not be reported by those who are retired or who have lost a spouse or other family members. King et al. suggest redefining alcohol problems in the elderly based on the existence of family or social relationship problems consequent to alcohol use. The characteristics of those drinkers who first experienced alcohol-related problems in later life versus those whose problems began in early adulthood but continued into later life are clearly different. Early-onset heavy drinkers were less likely to have strong family ties but be unemployed, whereas the late-onset drinkers often enjoyed a higher occupational status throughout their adult lives (Stall, 1987).

Atkinson, Tolson, and Turner (1990) examined individuals with different ages of onset of alcoholism in relation to the demography, alcohol use history, self-reported psychological status, and treatment compliance. They divided the subjects into three onset age groups. Early onset was defined as having the first alcohol problem at or before age 40, "middle onset" as having problems first occurring between the ages of 41 and 59; and "late onset" as having problems begin at age 60 and older. Early-onset subjects comprised 38% of the sample, middle onset 47%, and late onset as 15%. The late onset groups had the oldest age at the first admission, the lowest rates of family members affected with alcoholism, the lowest rates of alcohol-related arrests and jailing, as compared to early- and mid-life-onset groups. The late-onset age group also reported better treatment compliance and treatment completion, but were rarely treated in a residential setting. However, most (90%) were receiving court supervision due to a recent drinking driver offense. It is suggested that late-onset alcoholism tends to be a milder and more circumscribed disorder than early or mid-life-onset alcoholism (Atkinson et al., 1990; Atkinson, Turner, Kofoed, & Tolson, 1985). Brennan and Moos (1991) compared late-onset problem drinkers, early-onset problem drinkers, and nonproblem drinkers in terms of alcohol-use patterns, alcohol-related problems, general functioning, and treatment seeking in a sample of middle- to late-aged adults. Unlike Atkinson et al.'s study (1990), the sample included women. Late-onset problem drinkers reported consuming less alcohol, fewer drinking problems, fewer alcohol-related negative consequences, and fewer symptoms of physical dependence. As expected, later onset problem drinkers, as compared to nonproblem drinkers, consumed more alcohol, functioned more poorly, and experienced more negative life events. The rate of seeking treatment during the previous year was similar between late- and early-onset problem drinkers (25% and 23%). The problem drinkers in both groups who were functioning more poorly, with more life stressors, and fewer social resources, were more likely to seek help.

In summary, the alcoholism that develops in later life is often a mild form that is not associated with either a family history of alcoholism or severe psychopathology. Consequently it typically has a better prognosis. The development of alcoholism in later life could be accounted for by physiological, as well as environmental, factors. Alexander and Duff (1988) suggest that increased biological sensitivity to ethanol, life stress, free time, and social pressure in the retirement community are some of the factors that induce the elderly to drink heavily.

TREATMENT OUTCOMES— SUCCESS AND FAILURE

Longitudinal studies of the course of alcoholism have found that alcoholism is a chronic and unstable condition, with repeated periods of abstinence and relapse following treatment (Polich, Armor, & Braiker, 1980). Follow-up studies of treated alcoholics report variable rates of abstinence and relapse depending on the types of subjects studied and the duration of the follow-up period. Short-term follow-up studies conducted within 1 year posttreatment suggest rates of abstinence ranging from 18% to 68%. Mosher, David, Mulligan, and Iber (1975) found 32% to 35% of subjects abstinent at 3 months and 18% to 23% abstinent at 6 months following treatment, whereas Finney, Moos, and Mewborn (1980) reported a higher

abstinent rate of 68% for alcoholics who received family treatment at the 6-month follow-up interval. Longabaugh and Lewis (1988) indicate that the first relapse following treatment typically occurs within the first 3 months after discharge. Although long-term follow-up studies have also found a variety of drinking outcomes, the rate of continuous abstinence decreases with increasing elapsed time between the initial assessment and the time of the follow-up evaluation (Institute of Medicine, 1990). Wiens and Menstik (1983) followed patients who completed inpatient treatment and found that the frequency of abstinence decreased from 62% at 1 year to 33% at the 3-year follow-up. The cumulative survival curve at long-term posttreatment resulted in only a 9% abstinence rate (Taylor et al. , 1985). However, the literature also suggests that the drinking status of alcoholics appears to fluctuate over time. Whereas clients in remission at any one follow-up evaluation do not necessarily remain in remission at successive evaluations (Polich et al., 1980), those who have relapsed to drinking may become abstinent at a later time. Willems, Letemendia, and Arroyave (1973) evaluated male alcoholics with varying lengths of inpatient treatment at 1-year and 2-year follow-up intervals and found that the percentage of patients who were classified as "recovered" increased from 29% to 39% for a "short" stay and for "long" stay, 44% to 54%. Finney and Moos (1992) reported fluctuations in drinking days, abstinence, physical symptoms, social activities and the number of days worked at 6 months, 2 years and 10 years after treatment. Vaillant (1988) found that rates of abstinence fluctuate, ranging from 5% within 2 years of treatment to 59% at different points during a 12-year follow-up period. Similarly, Taylor et al. (1985), in their long term survival analysis of alcoholics found that the probability of remaining abstinent dropped dramatically at the end of the first year, but stabilized at 10% by the fifth posttreatment year. Cross-sectional results from a 20-year follow-up study have also reported a high abstinence rate among long-term surviving subjects (O'Connor & Daly, 1985).

von Knorring et al. (1985) examined 39 ex-alcoholic men and 30 active alcoholic men by subclassifying them into two groups according to the age of onset of their alcoholism. The ex-alcoholics were verified to have been abstinent for at least 1 year. Although both groups reported a similar duration of alcohol misuse, the rate of active alcoholism was significantly higher among the early onset of alcoholism group. Significantly more ex-alcoholics were in the later age of onset group.

Recovery without Treatment

The possibility of spontaneous recovery from alcoholism has been gaining support in recent years. Although it is difficult to study untreated alcoholics due to their lack of accessibility, evidence for "natural recovery" from alcohol abuse has been in existence since earlier in the twentieth century (Sobell, Sobell, Toneatto, & Leo, 1993; Vaillant, 1983). Vaillant (1983), in a review of longitudinal studies of untreated alcoholics dating back to the early 1950s, found evidence that problem drinkers increasingly achieved abstinence and nonproblematic drinking as they grew older. His prospective study of inner city youths and college students provide support for the notion of the "self-limiting nature of alcoholism as a disease." Nonetheless, Vaillant (1983) suggests that treatment may not be a significant factor in the natural history of some types of alcoholism. However, it is difficult to assess the nature and extent of alcohol dependence in his original sample. The studies of problem drinkers who do not seek treatment may help the broader understandings of the natural history of alcoholism. Sobell et al. (1993) estimate that the ratio of untreated to treated alcohol abusers to be 3:1, and suggest that researchers may have a highly biased view of alcohol abuse by studying only clinical cases. The understanding of recovery without formalized treatment may also contribute to the literature regarding the motivation, cognitive process, and other environmental factors associated with the decision to quit and to maintain abstinence. Tuchfield (1981) interviewed 51 former problem drinkers who achieved at least 1 year of abstinence or occasional drinking ascertained through a newspaper advertisement, and found that the resolution of problem drinking can occur without formal treatment. Those who recovered without benefit of a formal treatment program indicated that they were resistant to being labeled an alcoholic. Many had social pressure as well as support for abstinence from their family and friends, whereas others experienced negative role models or extraordinary events (mostly negative events). Tucker (1995) compared three groups of problem drinkers who had maintained stable abstinence: those with no treatment, those who participated in AA only, or those who received treatment plus AA participation. Although neither demographic variables nor the amount of heavy drinking distinguished the three groups, the best predictor of help-seeking behavior was the experiencing of greater alcohol-related psychosocial problems, (particularly in their interpersonal relationships). Health concerns were also reported by those who sought recovery. Tucker, Vuchinich, and Gladsjo (1994) investigated environmental events related to relapse and recovery, and found that recovered subjects were concerned about health and maintained relatively stable work habits. Subjects also cited problems with family or children, and work-related, financial, legal, and social problems as motivating factors for resolution of their alcohol problems, whereas changes in health, personal willpower, or self control, the role of spouse or other partner, changes in social life, hobbies, leisure activities, and friends were cited as contributing factors for maintaining the resolution. Perceived barriers to treatment entry included potential embarrassment, concerns about stigma, wanting privacy, and negative attitudes toward treatment or hospitals, or the cost of treatment.

Studies on the natural recovery from alcohol problems describe factors associated with the resolution of alcohol problems and maintenance of their resolution. Tuchfield (1981) suggests that the resolution of alcohol problems involves an internal, psychological commitment activated by social phenomena in the external environment, whereas the commitment to the maintenance of the resolution requires reinforcement by socially based maintenance factors. In terms of motivators for the resolution, "hitting rock bottom" and alcohol-related physical problems or adverse reaction to alcohol are often mentioned as the primary reasons for cessation of drinking. Tuchfield (1981) reports that hitting the lowest point of their lives, personal illness, or having an accident were the situations most frequently cited for resolving their drinking problem among a sample of former problem drinkers. Ludwig (1983) interviewed 29 alcoholics who claimed to be in remission without benefit of formal treatment. Only 6 subjects reported to be relative abstainers, whereas 23 claimed to be teetotalers. Magruder-Habib, Aling, Saunders, and Stevens (1989) reported that health problems were the main motivation to stop drinking among medical patients with problem-drinking histories.

Klingemann (1991) suggests that the motivation to change could be attributed to specific negative experiences (e.g., "hitting rock bottom," physical and psychological collapse) or by nonspecific positive motivational factors prompted by quality of life changes or positive experiences. Sobell et al. (1993) studied several groups of subjects who had resolved their drinking problems on their own and analyzed the data by three age cohorts: 20–35, 36–50, and 51 and older. Unlike other reports, their study included a comparison group of nonresolved problem drinkers and the use of collateral informants. Several age-related factors emerged. The one age-related factor that did not involve the resolution process was that the older age cohort had an onset of drinking problems in middle age and shorter problem-drinking histories. The younger aged cohort reported a higher number of factors helping them to maintain recovery as compared to the older age cohort. In the year prior to the resolution of the drinking problem, no significant main effects were found between resolved and nonresolved groups in terms of life events. However, regardless of the resolution status, the younger cohort experienced more events than the older cohorts.

Sobell et al. (1993) suggest that the resolution to abstain or to reduce drinking is related to cognitive evaluations of the pros and cons of drinking rather than to specific life events. However, regardless of the types of triggers to motivate problem-drinking resolution, the existence of consistent support from family and friends was the main factor most often cited for maintaining the resolution. (Klingemann, 1991; Sobell et al., 1993; Tuchfield, 1981). Additional factors frequently associated with maintaining the resolution included reduction in health-related problems, legal events, and other negative events.

Problems are common to studies of the natural recovery from problem drinking. One problem is that most studies seek subjects by self-referral through advertisements. Small sample sizes or case studies are common in these types of studies. Further, the identification of persons with problem drinking often relies on the use of the MAST score, without verifying the presence of physical addiction or the use of a standardized diagnostic assessment. The exception is the study by Sobell et al. (1993), who verified that their subjects met the DSM III-R criteria for alcohol dependence. Consequently, it is difficult to assess the severity of the drinking problem among most subjects.

Because many of the factors that are associated with the resolution of drinking problems are similar to the reasons problem drinkers seek treatment, differentiating those problem drinkers who seek treatment from those who do not seems worth investigating. Many investigators have found the severity of alcohol-related problems to be related to treatment seeking. Finney and Moos (1995) found that people with severe drinking problems, more dependence symptoms, and more adverse consequences were likely to enter treatment. The Sobell et al. study also indicates that most subjects, whether they received treatment or not, met the DSM III-R criteria for alcohol dependence. Those who achieved abstinence through treatment

were higher on the total MAST score, had experienced a greater mean number of consequences, and consumed more drinks per drinking days prior to treatment than those who relapsed. Similarly, the results of their 3-year follow-up study of previously untreated alcoholics found that individuals who sought treatment versus those who remained untreated had more severe drinking problems, poorer psychosocial functioning and more negative life events (Timko, Finney, Moos, & Moos, 1995). It should be noted, however, that Tucker (1995) found that help seeking was associated with greater alcohol-related psychosocial problems but not with heavier drinking practices.

Clearly, further research is needed to study the natural recovery process as well as the motivations and barriers to entering treatment programs. Tucker found that subjects' beliefs about solving their own problem, concern about labeling, privacy, denial of the problem, and cost or inadequate insurance coverage were barriers to entering treatment. Sobell et al. (1993) examined specific reasons for not seeking treatment among alcohol abusers who did not seek treatment. The most common reasons cited for not entering treatment were embarrassment or pride, not perceiving drinking as a problem, unable to share problems, stigma, negative attitudes toward treatment, or wanting to handle the problem on their own. It is also noteworthy that 8.4% of subjects indicated an ignorance about the availability of treatment and 10% expressed concerned about the cost of treatment.

Mortality

Higher mortality rates among alcoholics, as compared to age-similar nonalcoholics, have been reported by several studies (Berglund, 1984(a); DeLint & Levinson, 1975; DeLint & Schmidt, 1976; Edwards, Kyle, Nicholls, & Taylor, 1978; Finney & Moos, 1992; Mackenzie, Allen, & Funderburk, 1986; Smith, Cloninger, & Bradford, 1983; Taylor et al. 1985; Thorarinsson, 1979). Marshall, Edwards, and Taylor (1994) found that the mortality rate of married men with drinking problems of over 20 years duration was nearly 4 times higher than the expected rate. The largest excess in death rates was found among the 45- to 54-year old group. "Natural causes" often precipitated by the patient's deteriorated physical condition due to the continuous use of alcohol (Barr, Antes, Ottenberg, & Rosen, 1984; Edwards et al., 1978; Smith et al., 1983; Thorarinsson, 1979), suicide, and accidents, contribute to the increased mortality rate among alcoholics (Barr et al.,

1984; Beck, Steer, & Trexler, 1989; Berglund, 1984(b); Edwards et al., 1978; Mackenzie et al., 1986; Murphy, Armstrong, Hermele, Fischer, & Clendenin, 1979; Robins, 1981; Smith et al., 1983; Thorarinsson, 1979). Increased mortality has been associated also with the patient's age (Berglund, 1984(a); Smith et al., 1983), the number of hospitalizations (Finney & Moos, 1992; Mackenzie et al., 1986), continuous drinking after treatment (Barr et al. 1984; Berglund, 1984(a); Smith et al., 1983; Smith, Lewis, Kercher, & Spitznagel, 1994), and the diagnosis of antisocial personality disorder (Smith et al., 1983). Whereas the more common causes of death were due to carcinoma of the bronchus and diseases of circulatory system among married men between 45 and 74 years of age, violent death and suicide are often causes of death among younger persons with alcohol problems (Andreasson, Allebeck, & Romelsjo, 1988).

Gender differences have been observed in the rates and causes of mortality. Using survival analysis methods, Lewis, Smith, Kercher, and Spitznagel (1995) showed that men have a significantly shorter time to death than women in a 21-year follow-up study. However, the men were affected by more alcohol-related medical complications when they entered the study. Except for age, though, few gender interactions were found in terms of the correlates of death. Marital disruption tended to be a stronger predictor of mortality for males, whereas binge drinking and delirium tremens were better predictors of mortality for women than for men (Lewis et al., 1995).

The association of alcohol use and suicide attempts and completion is well documented by epidemiological studies. Makela (1996) found the suicide rate of Finnish men in the 15–49 age group was associated with the per capita alcohol consumption among Finnish men. Similarly, suicide rates were positively correlated with spirit sales in the United States from 1970 to 1989. However, beer and wine sales were not associated with suicide rates in the United States (Gruenewald, Ponicki, & Mitchell, 1995). Factors associated with alcohol-related suicides include recent interpersonal loss (Murphy et al. ,1979), divorce (Rossow, 1993), separations and family discord, financial troubles, and unemployment (Heikkinen et al., 1994). Suicide attempters who later suicided often have a history of suicide attempts (Robins, 1981; Roy, 1982; Tefft, Pederson, & Babigian, 1977). Beck et al. (1989) examined a sample of alcohol abusers who had been hospitalized following a suicide attempt and found that the majority of the former patients who eventually suicided did so within 5 years of

the treatment experience. Investigations of the predictors of suicide among alcoholics have found that additional psychopathology, especially affective disorder, increased the risk of suicide (Berglund, 1984; Murphy et al., 1979; Robins, 1981; Thorarinsson, 1979). Similarly, investigations of suicide attempts among alcoholics have found the diagnosis of affective disorder, substance abuse, and feelings of hopelessness to predict suicide attempts (Beck et al., 1989; Hesselbrock, Hesselbrock, Syzmanski, & Weidenman, 1988; Schuckit, 1986; Whitters, Cadoret, & Widmir, 1985; Windle, 1994).

Thus, studies of alcoholics who continue to drink indicate not only high mortality rates from physical causes, but also high rates of suicide and suicide attempts. Further, the risk of mortality is increased by comorbid psychiatric disorders including affective disorders and polysubstance abuse. However, current predictors of mortality, particularly suicide and suicide attempt, are not especially strong, which, limits their usefulness in the development of programs and interventions to prevent premature death among alcoholics.

SUMMARY

This chapter reviewed alcoholism in adulthood from several different perspectives. Although epidemiological data suggest that alcohol misuse among the general population reaches its peak during the third decade of life, life events and personal factors both earlier and later in life may influence the severity and course of adulthood alcohol problems. A family history of alcoholism, for example, increases the risk for developing alcohol problems in adulthood, although the mechanisms associated with this risk are not well understood. Childhood problem behavior, particularly conduct behaviors and hyperactivity, have been associated with early-onset alcoholism and other psychiatric problems. When childhood conduct problems continue as adult antisocial personality disorder that is comordid with alcoholism, these individuals (both male and female) typically develop severe alcohol problems that are very difficult to treat. Other psychiatric disorders (particularly affective and anxiety disorders) are also often found among clinical and nonclinical samples of alcoholics, but their etiologic importance for the development of alcoholism remains to be determined. Such conditions are, however, associated with a greater risk of suicide attempts and suicide completion. Although the rate of problem drinking appears to decrease among older persons, the alcohol use tends to increase. With the aging of the population, alcohol-related health and social problems are likely to increase in the coming years. To date, estimates of the prevalence of late onset alcoholism are not very good, although when present it appears to be less severe than early-onset alcoholism and more responsive to treatment.

Alcoholism in adulthood is a very heterogeneous disorder in terms of etiology and clinical phenomenology. There have been many attempts to identify more homogeneous subtypes of alcoholism in order to improve our understanding of etiologic factors and to improve treatment outcome. Although there are no definitive subtypes of alcoholism that are consistently found across clinical and nonclinical populations, several common factors do emerge in relation to the age of onset of alcohol-related problems. Early-onset alcoholics typically displayed conduct problems in childhood: have social, psychological, and medical problems associated with their alcohol use: and will repeatedly seek treatment. Persons with a later onset of alcohol problems often have a less severe form of alcoholism, have fewer social and psychological problems associated with alcohol abuse and have a better treatment prognosis. Much work remains to identify specific psychological, environmental, and biological factors responsible for the development of alcohol problems in adulthood.

REFERENCES

Alexander, F., & Duff, R. W. (1988). Social interaction and alcohol use in retirement communities. *Gerontologist, 28,* 632–638.

Allen, M. H., & Frances, R. J. (1986). Varieties of psychopathology found in patients with addictive disorders: A review. In R. E. Meyer (Ed.), *Psychopathology and addictive disorders.* New York: Guilford Press.

Alterman, A., & Tarter, R. (1983). The transmission of psychological vulnerability: Implications for alcoholism etiology. *Journal of Nervous Mental Disorders, 171,* 147–154.

Andreasson, S., Allebeck, P., & Romelsjo, A. (1988). Alcohol and mortality among young men: Longitudinal study of Swedish conscripts. *British Medical Journal, 296,* 1021–1025.

Atkinson, R. M., Tolson, R. L., & Turner, J. A. (1990). Late versus early onset problem drinking in older men. *Alcoholism: Clinical and Experimental Research, 14,* 574–579.

Atkinson, R. M., Turner, J. A., Kofoed, L. L., & Tolson, R. L. (1985). Early versus late onset alcoholism in older persons: Preliminary findings. *Alcoholism: Clinical and Experimental Research, 9,* 513–515.

August, G. J., & Stewart, M.A. (1983). Familial subtypes of childhood hyperactivity. *Journal of Nervous Mental Disorders, 171,* 362–368.

August, G. J., Stewart, M. A., & Holmes, C. S. (1983). Four year follow-up of hyperactive boys with and without conduct disorder. *British Journal of Psychiatry, 143,* 192–198.

Babor, T. F., Hofmann, M., DelBoca, F. K., Hesselbrock, V. M., Meyer, R. E., Dolinsky, Z. S., & Rounsaville, B. (1992). Types of alcoholics: II. Evidence for an empirically-derived typology based on indicators of vulnerability and severity. *Archives of General Psychiatry, 49,* 599–608.

Barr, H., Antes, D., Ottenberg, D. J., & Rosen, A. (1984). Mortality of treated alcoholics and drug addicts: The benefits of abstinence. *Journal of Studies on Alcohol, 45,* 440–452.

Beck, A. T., Steer, R. A., & Trexler, L. D. (1989). Alcohol abuse and eventual suicide: A 5 to 10 year prospective study of alcohol-abusing suicide attempters. *Journal of Studies on Alcohol, 50,* 202–209.

Berglund, M. (1984a). Mortality in alcoholics related to clinical state at first admission. *Acta Psychiatrica Scandinavica, 70,* 407–416.

Berglund, M. (1984b). Suicide in alcoholism: A prospective study of 88 suicides. I. The multidimensional diagnosis at first admission. *Archives of General Psychiatry, 41,* 888–891.

Bohman, M., Sigvardsson, S., & Cloninger, C. (1981). Maternal inheritance of alcohol abuse: Cross-fostering analysis of adopted women. *Archives of General Psychiatry, 38,* 965–969.

Brennan, P. L., & Moos, R. H. (1991). Functioning, life context, and help-seeking among late-onset problem drinkers: Comparisons with nonproblem and early-onset problem drinkers. *British Journal of Addiction, 86,* 1139–1150.

Bucholz, K. K. (in press). *Alcoholism: Clinical and Experimental Research.*

Cadoret, R., Troughton, E., & Widmer, R. (1984). Clinical differences between antisocial and primary alcoholics. *Comprehensive Psychiatry, 25,* 1–8.

Cadoret, R., Yates, W., Troughton, E., Woodworth, G., & Stewart, M. (1995). Adoption study demonstrating two genetic pathways to drug abuse. *Archives of General Psychiatry, 52,* 42–52.

Cantwell, D. P. (1972). Psychiatric illness in the families of hyperactive children. *Archives of General Psychiatry, 27,* 414–417.

Cloninger, C. R. (1987). Neurogenetic adaptive mechanisms in alcoholism. *Science, 236,* 410–416.

Cloninger, C. R., Bohman, M., & Sigvardsson, S. (1981). Inheritance of alcohol abuse: Cross-fostering analysis of adopted men. *Archives of General Psychiatry, 38,* 861–868.

Cloninger, C. R., Christiansen, K. O., Reich, T., & Gottsman, I. I. (1978). Implications of sex differences in the prevalences of antisocial personality, alcoholism, and criminality for familial transmission. *Archives of General Psychiatry, 35,* 941–951.

Cook, B. L., Winokur, G., Fowler, R. C., & Liskow, B. I. (1994). Classification of alcoholism with reference to comorbidity. *Comprehensive Psychiatry, 35,* 165–170.

Cotton, N. S. (1979). The familial incidence of alcoholism. *Journal of Studies on Alcohol, 40,* 89–116.

DeLint, J., & Levinson, T. (1975). Mortality among patients treated for alcoholism: A 5 year follow-up. *Canadian Medical Association Journal, 113,* 385–387.

DeLint, J., & Schmidt, W. (1976). Alcoholism and mortality. In B. Kissin & H. Begleiter (Eds.), *The biology of alcoholism. Vol. 4: Social aspects of alcoholism.* New York: Plenum Press.

DeObaldia, R., Parsons, O., & Yohman, R. (1983). Minimal brain dysfunction symptoms claimed by primary and secondary alcoholics: Relation to cognitive functioning. *International Journal of Neuroscience, 20,* 173–182.

Edwards, G., Kyle, E., Nicholls, P., & Taylor, C. (1978). Alcoholism and correlates of mortality: Implications for epidemiology. *Journal of Studies on Alcohol, 39,* 1607–1617.

Finney, J. W., & Moos, R. H. (1992). The long-term course of treated alcoholism: II. Predictors and correlates of 10-year functioning and mortality. *Journal of Studies on Alcohol, 53,* 142–153.

Finney, J. W., & Moos, R. H. (1995). Entering treatment for alcohol abuse: A stress and coping model. *Addiction, 90,* 1223–1240.

Finney, J. W., Moos, R. H., & Mewborn, C. W. (1980). Post-treatment experiences and treatment outcome of alcoholic patients six months and two years after hospitalization. *Journal of Consulting and Clinical Psychology, 48,* 17–29.

Frances, R., Timm, S., & Bucky, S. (1980). Studies of familial and nonfamilial alcoholism. 1. Demographic studies. *Archives of General Psychiatry, 37,* 564–566.

Gerstley, L. J., Alterman, A. I., McLellan, A. T., & Woody, G. E. (1990). Antisocial personality disorder in patients with substance abuse disorders: A problematic diagnosis? *American Journal of Psychiatry, 147,* 173–178.

Gilligan, S. B., Reich, T., & Cloninger, C. R. (1987). Etiologic heterogeneity in alcoholism. *Genetic Epidemiology, 4,* 395–414.

Glenn, S. W., & Nixon, S. J. (1991). Applications of cloninger's subtypes in a female alcoholic sample. *Alcoholism: Clinical and Experimental Research, 15,* 851–857.

Goodwin, D. W. (1979). Alcoholism and heredity: A review and hypothesis. *Archives of General Psychiatry, 36,* 57–61.

Goodwin, D., Schulsinger, F., Hermansen, L., Guze, S., & Winokur, G. (1973). Alcohol problems in adoptees raised apart from alcoholic biological parents. *Archives of General Psychiatry, 28,* 238–243.

Goodwin, D., Schulsinger, F., Hermansen, L., Guze, S., & Winokur, G. (1975). Alcoholism and the hyperactive child syndrome. *Journal of Nervous Mental Disorders, 160,* 349–353.

Grant, B. F., Harford, T. C., Chou, P., Pickering, R., Dawson, D. A., Stinson, F. S., & Noble, J. (1991). Prevalence of DSM-III-R alcohol abuse and dependence. *Alcohol Health & Research World, 15,* 91–96.

Gruenewald, P. J., Ponicki, W. R., & Mitchell, P. R. (1995). Suicide rates and alcohol consumption in the United States, 1970–89. *Addiction, 90,* 1063–1075.

Heikkinen, M. E., Hillevi, M. A., Henriksson, M. M., Isometsa, E. T., Sama, S. J., Kuoppasalmi, K. I., & Lonnqvist, J. K. (1994). Differences in recent life events between alcoholic and depressive nonalcoholic suicides. *Alcoholism: Clinical and Experimental Research, 18,* 1143–1149.

Hesselbrock, M. N. (1986). Childhood behavior problems and adult antisocial personality disorder in alcoholism. In R. E. Meyer (Ed.), *Psychopathology and addictive disorders* (pp. 41–56). New York: Guilford Press.

Hesselbrock, M. N. (1995). Genetic determinants of alcoholic subtypes. In H. Begleiter & B. Kissin (Eds.), *The genetics of alcoholism.* New York: Oxford University Press.

Hesselbrock, M., & Hesselbrock, V. (1992). Relationship of family history, antisocial personality disorder and personality traits in young men at risk for alcoholism. *Journal of Studies on Alcohol, 53,* 619–625.

Hesselbrock, V. M., & Hesselbrock, M. N. (1994). Alcoholism and subtypes of antisocial personality disorder. *Alcohol & Alcoholism, Suppl. 2,* 479–484.

Hesselbrock, M. N., Hesselbrock, V. M., Babor, T., Stabenau, J., Meyer, R., & Weidenman, M. (1984). Antisocial behavior, psychopathology and problem drinking in the natural history of alcoholism. In D. Goodwin, K. Van Dusen, & S. Mednick (Eds.), *Longitudinal research of alcoholism.* Boston: Kluwer-Nijhoff Publishing.

Hesselbrock, M. N., Hesselbrock, V. M., Syzmanski, K., & Weidenman, M. (1988). Suicide attempts and alcoholism. *Journal of Studies on Alcohol, 49,* 436–442.

Hesselbrock, M. N., Meyer, R. E., & Keener, J. J. (1985). Psychopathology in hospitalized alcoholics. *Archives of General Psychiatry, 42,* 1050–1055.

Hesselbrock, V. M., Stabenau, J., Hesselbrock, M. N., Meyer, R., & Babor, T. (1982). The nature of alcoholism in patients with different family histories for alcoholism. *Progress in Neuropsychopharmacology, 6,* 607–614.

Institute of Medicine. (1990). *Broadening the base of treatment for alcohol problems.* Washington, DC: National Academy Press.

Irwin, M., Schuckit, M., & Smith, T. L. (1990). Clinical importance of age at onset in Type 1 and Type 2 primary alcoholics. *Archives of General Psychiatry, 47,* 320–324.

Kessler, L. G., Folsom, R., Royall, R. (1985). Parameter and variance estimation. In W. W. Eaton & L. G. Kessler (Eds.), *Epidemiologic field methods in psychiatry.* Orlando, FL: Academic Press.

King, C.J., Van Hasselt, V. B., Segal, D. L., & Hersen, M. (1994). Diagnosis and assessment of substance abuse in older adults: Current strategies and issues. *Addictive Behaviors, 19 ,* 41–55.

Klingemann, H. K. (1991). The motivation for change from problem alcohol and heroin use. *British Journal of Addiction, 86,* 727–744.

Lewis, C. E., Rice, J., & Helzer, J. (1983). Diagnostic interactions: Alcoholism and antisocial personality. *Journal of Nervous Mental Disorders, 171,* 105–113.

Lewis, C. E., Smith, E., Kercher, C., & Spitznagel, E. (1995). Assessing gender interactions in the prediction of mortality in alcoholic men and women: A 20-year follow-up study. *Alcoholism: Clinical and Experimental Research, 19*, 1162–1172.

Longabaugh, R., & Lewis, D. C. (1988). Key issues in treatment outcome studies. *Alcohol Health & Research World, 12*, 168–175.

Ludwig, A. M. (1983). Cognitive processes associated with "spontaneous" recovery from alcoholism. *Journal of Studies on Alcohol, 46*, 53–58.

Mackenzie, A., Allen, R. P., & Funderburk, F. R. (1986). Mortality and illness in male alcoholics: An 8 year follow-up. *The International Journal of Addictions, 21*, 865–882.

Magruder-Habib, K., Alling, W. C., Saunders, W. B., & Stevens, H. A. (1989, March). *Spontaneous remission from alcoholism.* Presented at the meeting of the North Carolina Alcoholism Research Authority, Raleigh, NC.

Makela, P. (1996). Alcohol and suicide mortality by age among Finnish men 1950–91. *Addiction, 91*, 101–112.

Marshall, E. J., Edwards, G., & Taylor, C. (1994). Mortality in men with drinking problems: A 20-year follow-up. *Addiction, 89*, 1293–1298.

McCord, W. & McCord, J. (1960). *Origins of alcoholism.* Palo Alto, CA: Stanford University Press.

McNeece, C. A., & DiNitto, D. (1994). *Chemical dependency: A systems approach.* Englewood Cliffs, NJ: Prentice Hall.

Mendelson, W., Johnson, N., & Stewart, M. (1971). Hyperactive children as teenagers: A follow-up study. *Journal of Nervous Mental Disorders, 153*, 273–279.

Meyer, R. E. (1986). How to understand the relationship between psychopathology and addictive disorders: Another example of the chicken and the egg. In R. E. Meyer (Ed.), *Psychopathology and addictive disorders.* New York: Guilford Press.

Morrison, J. R., & Stewart, M. A. (1971). A family study of the hyperactive child syndrome. *Biological Psychiatry, 3*, 189–195.

Mosher, V., David, J., Mulligan, D., & Iber, F. L. (1975). Comparison of outcome in a 9-day and 30-day alcoholism treatment program. *Journal of Studies on Alcohol, 36*, 1277–1281.

Murphy, G. E., Armstrong, J. W., Hermele, S. L., Fischer, J. R., & Clendenin, W. W. (1979). Suicide and alcoholism: Interpersonal loss confirmed as a predictor. *Archives of General Psychiatry, 36*, 65–69.

National Institute of Health, National Institute of Alcohol Abuse and Alcoholism. (1993). *Eighth Special Report to the U.S. Congress on Alcohol and Health.* Washington, DC: U.S. Department of Health and Human Services.

O'Connor, A. & Daly, J. (1985). Alcoholics: A 20 year follow-up study. *British Journal of Psychiatry, 146*, 45–64.

Pandey, G. N., Fawcett, J., Gobbons, R., Clark, C. D., & Davis, J. M. (1988). Platelet monoamine oxidase in alcoholism. *Biological Psychiatry, 24*, 15–24.

Penick, E. C., Powell, B. J., Nickel, E. J., Read, M. R., Gabrielli, W. F., & Liskow, B. I. (1990). Examination of Cloninger's Type I and Type II alcoholism with a sample of men alcoholics in treatment. *Alcoholism: Clinical and Experimental Research, 14*, 623–629.

Penick, E. C., Powell, B. J., Othmer, E., Bingham, S., & Rice, A. (1984). Subtyping alcoholics by coexisting psychiatric syndromes: Course, family history and outcome. In D. Goodwin, K. Van Dusen, & S. Mednick (Eds.), *Longitudinal research in alcoholism.* Boston: Kluwer-Nijhoff Publishing.

Penick, E. C., Read, M. R., Crawley, P. A., & Powell, B. J. (1978). Differentiation of alcoholics by family history. *Journal of Studies on Alcohol, 39*, 1944.

Polich, J. M., Armor, D. J., & Braiker, H. B. (1980). *The course of alcoholism: Four years after treatment.* Santa Monica: Rand Corporation.

Read, M. R., Penick, E. C., Powell, B. J., Nickel, E. J., Bingham, S. F., & Campbell, J. (1990). Subtyping male alcoholics by family history of alcohol abuse and co-occurring psychiatric disorder: A bi-dimensional model. *British Journal of Addiction, 85*, 367–378.

Regier, D. A., Myers, J. K., Kramer, M., et al. (1984). The NIMH Epidemiological Catchment Area (ECA) Program: Historical context, major objectives, and study population characteristics. *Archives of General Psychiatry, 41*, 934–41.

Reich, T., Cloninger, C., Lewis, C., & Rice, J. (1981). Some recent findings in the study of genotype-environment interaction in alcoholism. In R. Meyer, T. Babor, J. Stabnau, J. O'Brien, & J. Jaffe (Eds.), *Evaluation of the alcoholic,* (NIAAA Research Monograph 5). Washington, DC: U.S. Government Printing Office.

Robins, E. (1981). *The final months: A study of the lives of 134 persons who committed suicide.* New York: Oxford Press.

Robins, L. N. (1966). *Deviant children grown up: A sociological and psychiatric study of sociopathic personality.* Baltimore: Williams & Wilkins.

Robins, L. N. & Price, R. K. (1991). Adult disorders predicted by childhood conduct problems. *Psychiatry, 54*, 113–132.

Rossow, I. (1993). Suicide, alcohol and divorce. *Addiction, 88*, 1659–1665.

Roy, A. (1982). Risk factors for suicide in psychiatric patients. *Archives of General Psychiatry, 39*, 1089–1095.

Schuckit, M. A. (1985). The clinical implications of primary diagnostic groups among alcoholics. *Archives of General Psychiatry, 42*, 1043–1049.

Schuckit, M. A. (1986). Primary men alcoholics with history of suicide attempts. *Journal of Studies on Alcohol, 47*, 78–81.

Schuckit, M. A., Anthenelli, R. M., Bucholz, K. K., Hesselbrock, V. M., & Tipp, J. (1995). The time course of development of alcohol-related problems in men and women. *Journal of Studies on Alcohol, 56*, 218–225.

Schuckit, M. A., Irwin, M., & Mahler H. (1990). Tridimensional personality questionnaire scores of sons of alcoholic and nonalcoholic fathers. *American Journal of Psychiatry, 147*, 481–487.

Smith, E. M., Cloninger, C. R., & Bradford, S. (1983). Predictors of mortality in alcoholic women: A prospective follow-up study. *Alcoholism: Clinical and Experimental Research, 7*, 237–243.

Smith, E. M., Lewis, C. E., Kercher, C., & Spitznagel, E. (1994). Predictors of mortality in alcoholic women: A 20-year follow-up study. *Alcoholism: Clinical and Experimental Research, 18*, 1177–1186.

Sobell, L. C., Sobell, M. B., Toneatto, T., & Leo, G. I. (1993). What triggers the resolution of alcohol problems without treatment? *Alcoholism: Clinical and Experimental Research, 17*, 217–224.

Stabenau, J. R. (1984). Implications of family history of alcoholism, antisocial personality, and sex differences in alcohol dependence. *American Journal of Psychiatry, 141*, 1178–1182.

Stall, R. (1987). Research issues concerning alcohol consumption among aging populations. *Drug and Alcohol Dependence, 19*, 195–213.

Stewart, M. A., deBlois, G. S., & Cummings, C. (1980). Psychiatric disorder in the parents of hyperactive boys and those with conduct disorder. *Journal of Child Psychology Psychiatry, 21*, 283–292.

Sullivan, J. L., Baenziger, J. C., & Wagner, D. L. (1990). Platelet MAO in subtypes of alcoholism. *Biological Psychiatry, 27*, 911–922.

Tarter, R. E., Hegedus, A. M., & Gavaler, J. S. (1985). Hyperactivity in sons of alcoholics. *Journal of Studies on Alcohol, 46*, 259–261.

Tarter, R. E., McBride, H., Buonpane, N., & Schneider, D. (1977). Differentiation of alcoholics according to childhood history of minimal brain dysfunction, family history, and drinking pattern. *Archives of General Psychiatry, 34*, 761–768.

Taylor, C., Brown, D., Duckitt, A., Edwards, G., Oppenheimer, E., & Sheehan, M. (1985). Patterns of outcome: Drinking histories over ten years among a group of alcoholics. *British Journal of Addictions, 80*, 45–50.

Tefft, B. M., Pederson, A. M., & Babigian, H. M. (1977). Patterns of death among suicide attempters, a psychiatric population, and a general population. *Archives of General Psychiatry, 33*, 1155–1161.

Temple, M. T., & Fillmore, K. M. (1985). The variability of drinking patterns and problems among young men, age 16–31: A longitudinal study. *International Journal of the Addictions, 20*, 1595–1620.

Thorarinsson, A. A. (1979). Mortality among men alcoholics in Iceland: 1951–1974. *Journal of Studies on Alcohol, 40*, 704–718.

Timko, C., Finney, J. W., Moos, R. H., & Moos, B. S. (1995, November). Short-term treatment careers and outcomes of previously untreated alcoholics. *Journal of Studies on Alcohol*, 597–610.

Tuchfield, B. S. (1981). Spontaneous remission in alcoholics. *Journal of Studies on Alcohol, 42*, 626–641.

Tucker, J. A. (1995). Predictors of help-seeking and the temporal relationship of help to recovery among treated and untreated recovered problem drinkers. *Addiction, 90*, 805–809.

Tucker, J. A., Vuchinich, R. E., & Gladsjo, J. A. (1994). Environmental events surrounding natural recovery from alcohol-related problems. *Journal of Studies on Alcohol, 55*, 401–410.

Vaillant, G. E. (1983). *The natural history of alcoholism: Paths to recovery*. Cambridge, MA: Harvard University Press.

Vaillant, G. E. (1988). What can long-term follow-up teach us about relapse and prevention of relapse in addiction? *British Journal of Addictions, 83*, 1147–1157.

von Knorring, A. L., Bohman, M., von Knorring, L. & Oreland, L. (1985). Platelet MAO activity as a biological marker in subgroups of alcoholism. *Acta. Psychiatrica Scandinavica, 72*, 51–58.

von Knorring, L., von Knorring, A. L., Smigan, L., Lindberg, U., & Edholm, M. (1987). Personality traits in subtypes of alcoholics. *Journal of Studies on Alcohol, 48*, 523–527.

Weins, A. N., & Menustik, C. E. (1983). Treatment outcome and patient characteristics in an aversion therapy program for alcoholism. *American Psychologist, 38*, 1089–1096.

Weiss, G., Hechtman, L., Perlman, T., Hopkins, J., & Wender, P. (1979). Hyperactive as young adults: A controlled prospective ten year follow-up of 75 children. *Archives of General Psychiatry, 36*, 675–681.

Whitters, A. C., Cadoret, R. J., & Widmir, R. B. (1985). Factors associated with suicide attempts in alcohol abusers. *Journal of Affective Disorders, 9*, 19–23.

Willems, P., Letemendia, F., & Arroyave, F. (1973). A two year follow-up study comparing short with long stay in-patient treatment of alcoholics. *British Journal of Psychiatry, 122*, 637–648.

Windle, M. (1994, September). Characteristics of alcoholics who attempted suicide: Co-occurring disorders and personality differences with a sample of male Vietnam era veterans. *Journal of Studies on Alcohol*, 571–577.

Zucker, R. A. & Gomberg, E. S. (1986). Etiology of alcoholism reconsidered: The case for a biopsychosocial process. *American Psychology, 41*, 783–793.

CHAPTER 7

SUBSTANCE ABUSE IN THE ELDERLY

Edith S. Lisansky Gomberg

SUBSTANCE ABUSE IN OLDER INDIVIDUALS

When the media refer to "the greying of America," there is substantial statistical support for the description. In 1900, only 4% of the American population was 65 and older; currently, that proportion approaches 13% and the percentage will increase slowly over the next 15 years. It is anticipated that starting with the year 2011, when the current babyboomers begin to reach 65, there will be a sharp rise in the proportion of the American population defined as elderly.

Older people constitute an age cohort but they are not homogeneous. The most obvious differences lie in gender, socioeconomic status, and ethnicity. Among older people there are gender differences in life expectancy, marital status, living conditions, and poverty levels. There are also differences among different social class/income groups of older people as well as differences in income, attitudes, housing, health status, and even life expectancy among different ethnic/racial groups. When we approach the question of alcohol and drug use and abuse among older people, it is important to remember the differences; the heterogeneity also extends to substance use and abuse.

There are a number of biological, social, and psychological issues in studying and dealing with the older population. Issues like health status, the increasing incidence of medical impairment, and shifts in cognitive abilities are relevant. With age the number of medical problems increases and the amount of medication taken rises. Healthy old age, however, requires the same attention to nutrition, exercise, and lifestyle as does healthy young adulthood or healthy middle age. Gerontological study is in its early stages and we are constantly learning new facts about this stage of life, for example, current research indicates that there is less cognitive loss in late life than has been assumed in the past. It is useful to distinguish "successful" aging from "usual" aging (Rowe & Kahn, 1987); "usual" aging involves the heightening of negative aging effects by extrinsic factors like poverty, poor nutrition, depression, age discrimination, and the like. "Successful" aging means that loss and impairment are minimized by factors like nutrition, exercise, continued work and activity, and social involvement.

Among other issues to be considered are socially defined role changes, such as retirement and changes in financial status. Widowhood is obviously more common in this age group than in younger cohorts. The role of social networks, involvement with family, and participation in work or community activities is significant. It should be noted that the older cohort reports a reasonable degree of life satisfaction as much as, if not more than, other age groups.

CHANGES IN THE AGING BODY'S RESPONSE TO DRUGS

Pharmacokinetics is the study of the time course of absorption, tissue distribution, metabolism, and excretion of drugs and their metabolites from the body, and the relationship of drug disposition to the duration and intensity of drug effects. The study of aging effects on pharmacokinetics yields information about the mechanism of altered pharmacodynamics among older people. *Pharmacodynamics* is the physiological and psychological response to drugs, with the greater or lessor response of older people to particular drugs independent of pharmacokinetic effects. Different psychoactive drugs may produce different pharmacodynamic effects among older persons; for example, the response of many older persons to some benzodiazepines is an enhanced response.

Pharmacokinetic Age Changes

Although there do not appear to be significant age changes in drug absorption, there are changes in body composition among older people that influence drug distribution; for example, the decline in fluid relative to body mass means that ingestion of alcoholic beverages produces a higher blood alcohol level and greater central nervous system effects. Age changes in respiratory functioning and in renal function also influence the response to drugs. In consuming alcoholic beverages, older people may find the amount they tolerated well at younger ages now results in more adverse effects (Wartenberg & Nirenberg, 1994).

Pharmacodynamic Age Changes

Pharmacodynamic age changes as well as pharmokinetic changes have been reviewed by Gambert (1992). With aging, there are changes, in sensitivity to some drugs; increased sensitivity to drugs acting on the central nervous system has been observed. The susceptibility among older people to adverse drug reactions seems to be increasing.

Adverse Drug Reactions

Adverse reactions among older people can result from multiple drug therapies, noncompliance such as drug overuse or misuse, the slowing of drug metabolism or elimination, or age-related chronic diseases, alcohol intake, and food/drug incompatibilities. Whatever the cause, adverse drug reactions are more severe among elderly people than among younger patients. Risk factors include living alone, multiple chronic diseases, being female, multiple drug intake, and poor nutritional status (Beresford & Gomberg, 1995).

When the Medical Examiner Data of drug-related deaths for the year 1993 are examined (Annual Medical Examiner Data 1993, 1995) for those 55 and older, deaths linked to selected drug groups are as follows, ranging from the most frequently mentioned on down: alcohol in combination, heroin/morphine, cocaine, codeine, amitriptyline (antidepressant), diphenhydramine, diazepam, acetaminophen, secobarbital/amobarbital, aspirin. With some exceptions the percentage of medical-examiner-reported deaths is reasonably similar for the different age groups. For example, persons in the age group 18–54 report more than twice as many deaths from heroin and cocaine than occur among older people. Alcohol in combination occurs more frequently among the 18–54 group, but deaths occur more frequently among the 55-and-older group related to use of nonnarcotic analgesics (aspirin and acetaminophen), antidepressants, barbiturates, and diphenhydramine. Street drugs are not a problem for older men and women, but there *are* problems with prescribed and over-the-counter psychoactive drugs and self-prescribed medications.

SUBSTANCES OF ABUSE

In studies of older adults, the use and abuse of alcoholic beverages gets the most attention. Scheduled substances are not often bought on the street and abused by the elderly, although the prescribed use of narcotics in medical control of pain may be an issue—more knowledge is needed about appropriate doses. Tobacco has been widely used and figures in several health problems. There is relatively little research or clinical interest in the use or abuse of prescribed or over-the-counter medications although some questions have been raised, for example, the widespread prescription of minor tranquilizers for older women (Gomberg, 1995b), the use of sedative drugs in nursing homes, and the general issue of medication compliance and noncompliance. Finally, there are alcoholic beverages and their recreational uses (Beresford & Gomberg, 1995; Gomberg, 1982, 1990; Hartford & Samorajski, 1984; Maddox, Robins, & Rosenberg, 1984; McKim & Mishara,

1987; Mishara & Kastenbaum, 1980; Wartenberg & Nirenberg, 1994). Each drug category will be reviewed, next followed by a brief discussion of intervention experience and issues.

ILLEGAL DRUGS

Use of marijuana, heroin, and cocaine does occur among some older individuals but the numbers involved are small. There are users of illicit drugs (e.g., heroin) who have used the narcotic drugs for many years but have managed to survive into old age. It was a widely held belief that opiate addicts did not survive to old age: their choice was death or "maturing out." This belief persisted in the face of evidence that there were in some countries (e.g., the United Kingdom or Holland) older addicts who had been using drugs like heroin for many years. A report of older heroin addicts from New York City is of interest (DesJarlais, Joseph, & Courtwright, 1985). These heroin-dependent individuals, 65 and older, were interviewed at the methadone maintenance clinics they attended. Some of the features in the lives of these drug-dependent survivors into old age are that they avoided violence, used clean needles when injecting, and showed some capacity for holding a drug supply in reserve. They also avoided other drugs like alcohol. Ironically, their major health problems were related to a lifetime of smoking. In Michigan (Michigan Department of Public Health, 1994), treatment admissions for heroin-dependent people are 6% for those under 60, and 3% for those 60 and older. The contrast is greater with use of cocaine: treatment admissions for dependence on cocaine or crack are 18% for those under 60 and 2% for those 60 and older. The use of illegal, banned substances is a minor issue with the elderly.

There is a way in which substances of abuse combine and interact. For example, it has been estimated that alcoholism is "a common problem" among those enrolled in methadone programs, involving an estimated half of such patients (Alcohol Alert, 1988). A recent study of methadone treatment clients reports differences between alcohol-dependent clients and nondependent clients (Chatham, Rowan-Szal, Joe, Brown, & Simpson, 1995). These differences include differences in history, personality profile, and response to treatment. Contrary to what was anticipated, methadone clients with alcohol dependency were more likely to remain in treatment longer than the others. The authors suggest that this may be due to prior experience with self-help groups and less denial.

TOBACCO

Men are more likely to be smokers than women although the gender gap has narrowed in recent decades. The National Center for Health Statistics reported that in 1965, 28.5% of older men and 9.6% of older women were smokers. Twenty years later, the percentages had become 19.6% of older men and 13.5% of older women. Among women age 20–64 the percentage of current smokers has been dropping (Berman & Gritz, 1993).

The female cohort that began smoking during and immediately after World War II currently constitute the older population group of women. Smoking was one kind of liberation and women in the workplace often became smokers. The price of the liberation, however, has been high. In the 1960s, female deaths from lung cancer began to increase and by 1985, lung cancer surpassed breast cancer as the chief cause of cancer death among women.

A study of women alcoholic patients, matched with a nonalcoholic comparison group (Gomberg, 1989b) showed fewer smokers among the nonalcoholic women, whereas the alcoholic women more frequently were smokers.

Current Smokers	Nonalcoholic Women (%)	Alcoholic Women (%)
Age 20–29	24	90
Age 30–39	38	82
Age 40–49	38	75

It has long been noted that problem drinkers are more likely to be smokers than abstainers or social drinkers. The age differences are of interest: in the control group, younger women in their 20s are less likely to be smokers than their older peers; among problem-drinking women, the youngest group studied (also the biggest risk takers) were significantly more likely to be smokers than their somewhat older alcoholic peers.

PRESCRIBED PSYCHOACTIVE MEDICATIONS

Because of increased medical problems, the older age cohort uses more medication and incurs greater health care expenditure. Older people currently constitute 12% to 13% of the general population but estimates are that they receive about a third of all prescriptions. The medications most frequently prescribed and used are cardiovascular medication, diuretics, antibiotics, analgesics and psychoactive drugs (e.g., sedative-hypnotics, antidepressants, stimulants). Hospital admissions are estimated to be associated more with adverse drug reactions for elderly people than for younger age peers. In the emergency rooms, overdose reactions are most frequently linked to ". . . misuse of a psychoactive drug" (LaRue, Dessonville, & Jarvik, 1985).

Although treatment facilities that see older patients do report problems with dependence on prescribed psychoactive drugs, the issue has not evoked interest among researchers, clinicians, or legislators. Older persons associate their intake of such medication with insomnia or depression; almost half of those taking such medication say in interview that they could not perform their daily activities without the medication (Prentice, 1979). Kleber (1990) has differentiated primary low-dosage dependency, primary high-dosage dependency, and secondary dependence for benzodiazepine usage. Multiple drug use or secondary dependence most frequently involves alcohol as well as a benzodiazepine. Finlayson (1984) has classified usage as appropriate use, unintentional misuse, and purposeful abuse; among 248 patients in a hospital setting, 86% were alcohol dependent, 8% were dependent on prescription drugs, and 6% were dependent on a combination of alcohol and prescription drugs.

Several related questions arise in connection with elderly use of prescribed psychoactive medication. Questions have been raised about the appropriate prescription and use of such medications in nursing homes. What is the risk of adverse drug reactions with elderly patients and what is the appropriate dosage? There are a number of medications that need to be monitored for ADRs when used by older patients, for example, dioxin, diuretics, aspirin, cytoxins, nonsteroidal anti-inflammatories, and psychoactive drugs.

Noncompliance with prescribed drug regimens is an interesting and understudied phenomenon. Such noncompliance occurs in all age groups and in all conditions (think of the mentally ill persons who forget or refuse to take their medications). Noncompliance has traditionally been attributed to cognitive loss and memory failure among the elderly but we believe it to be a more complex phenomenon possibly linked to limited financial resources, loss of status, issues of autonomy, denial, rebellion against authority, and/or the quality of communication between patient and prescribing physician (Gomberg, in press). Noncompliance includes nonuse, partial use, and incorrect dosage. A survey by a large organization of older persons found 40% of the respondents reporting side effects with a large proportion of those respondents noncompliant. Noncompliance is an issue that needs to be considered in legislation and policy relating to health care in general.

OVER-THE-COUNTER DRUGS

The most commonly used nonprescription drugs are analgesics, nutritional supplements like vitamins, laxatives, and antacids. Nonnarcotic analgesics are the most commonly reported drugs purchased by older persons.

The Food and Drug Administration has suggested that there be special labeling on packages advising about dosage for older persons similar to information on the package about dosage for children. The general response has been that special age-related labeling on over-the-counter drugs is less useful than labeling by specific medical condition.

The question of medicinal herbs and alternative medicine has recently evolved into a major health debate. The National Institute of Health established an Office of Alternative Medicine in 1992 and some controlled, experimental studies of the efficacy of herbal remedies are under way. There is some concern about safety issues although herbal remedies are often perceived as "natural" and therefore harmless. We know very little at this time about the extent to which older patients use alternative medicine therapies.

ALCOHOL

Epidemiologically, moderate drinking—any drinking—declines with passage into the senior years. There are a number of exceptions to this decline. Some epidemiological data suggest a moderate increase in alcohol intake among older men and women (e.g., Eaton et al., 1989; Huffine, Folkman, & Lazarus, 1989). A longitudinal study in a Massachusetts community reports a fairly large increase in alcohol intake among older women (Gordon & Kannel, 1983). A question has been raised about drinking in retirement communities (Alexander & Duff, 1988). What it comes down to is a decline for the older population in percentage of social drinkers and problem drinkers, with exceptions to the decline, depending on age, gender ratio, and geographical site. The young old (60–75) are more likely to drink than the older old. As is the case in all age groups, there are fewer women social drinkers and fewer women problem drinkers than men. Adams and colleagues reported a high correlation between alcohol-related hospitalizations of elderly people and the per capita consumption of alcohol by state in the United States (Adams, Yuan, Barboriak, & Rimm, 1993).

Problem Drinking

Because of their reluctance to seek help with substance-abuse problems and because alcohol-related consequences may be misdiagnosed as senility, it is difficult to estimate the extent of problem drinking among the older population. Are we looking for heavy drinking (however defined), alcohol-associated problems, or clinically diagnosed abuse or dependence? Helzer, Burnam, and McEvoy (1991) noted that a much higher percentage of older respondents in the NIMH Epidemiological Catchment Area studies showed *less severe* alcohol problems than those diagnosable as abuse or dependence.

The patterns of heavy drinking and alcohol-related problems are fairly similar for younger and older problem drinkers (DeHart & Hoffman, 1995). Older alcoholics are less likely to have work-associated problems but more likely to have alcohol-related health problems, accidents, financial concerns, and possibly more binge drinking. Older problem drinkers range from the homeless (Rubington, 1995) to retired corporation executives and they will vary in private versus public drinking, beverages consumed, consequences, and likelihood of seeking treatment.

A recent report comparing older men and women problem drinkers (Gomberg, 1995b) showed the same gender differences that appear throughout the lifespan. Women reported more marital disruption (i.e., widowhood), more recent onset, shorter duration of drinking, more heavy/problem drinking by a spouse or significant other, more drinking at home than in public, and more heavy use of prescribed psychoactive drugs than did the older men problem drinkers.

A comparison of older African American and Caucasian men with alcoholism in treatment showed some significant differences (Gomberg & Nelson, 1995). Although all respondents came from the same clinical and community sources, the African American respondents had significantly less education, occupational status, and income. They drank larger quantities, preferred distilled beverages, and were more likely to drink in public places than the Caucasian patients. African American patients also reported more alcohol-related health problems, more difficulties in the workplace, and more trouble with the police. A regression analysis to predict social/community consequences of heavy drinking indicated that educational achievement, lifetime daily drinking average, drinking in public places, and race were most relevant.

Among all age groups there has been significant research interest in neuropsychological or cognitive loss as a consequence of heavy drinking. Deficits have been studied in relationship to age, gender, and intellectual functions; studies focus on specific cognitive functions like short-term memory or the ability to process new information. A significant clinical issue is the reversibility of cognitive loss. Most clinicians who work with older patients agree that these patients, when given sufficient time, are likely to regain most of their lost functioning. However, reversal of cognitive loss will take longer than it does with younger patients. A few patients with alcohol disorders will exhibit the selective memory disturbance of the Korsakoff syndrome (Kopelman, 1995) involving anterograde and retrograde memory deficit.

Older individuals with chronic alcoholism are, currently, little studied. These chronic offenders have merged into the homeless population (Rubington, 1995). Historically, a disproportionately high percentage of arrests for public intoxication occurred among men 60 years of age and older (Epstein, Mills, & Simon, 1970). Since the Supreme Court ruling in the l960s that arrests for public intoxication violated the 8th Amendment for people who had the "disease of alcoholism," detoxification units have become "the revolving door" through which many of these many homeless problem drinkers pass instead of the local jail.

Etiology and the Age of Onset

Age of onset of problem drinking is a question raised about all age groups (Lee & DiClimente, 1985; Parrella & Filstead, 1988). Age of onset is a key variable in the typology offered by Cloninger (Cloninger, 1987): for Type 1 alcoholism, the usual age of onset is after 25 and for Type 2, it occurs before the age of 25. Among older problem drinkers, there is apparently a distinction between those alcoholics who have managed to survive into old age ("survivors") and those alcoholics for whom the heavy/problematic drinking began more recently. The terms used to describe these two groups has been *early versus late onset* (Atkinson, Turner, Kofoed, & Tolson, 1983). The cutoff age for *late onset* was 40; if the person developed problem drinking at 42 or 48, they were "late-onset drinkers." Estimates, based largely on observations in hospitals and clinics, were that late-onset alcoholics constituted about a third of older patients seen. In our research at the University of Michigan Alcohol Research Center, mandated for the study of alcohol and aging, we have added a term for those who develop problem drinking late in life, "recent onset." Our criteria for *recent onset* involves the development of problem drinking within the last ten years—this is, more realistically, late life development.

Age of onset links to the question of etiology. For those individuals we see during their older years with a lifetime of heavy/problem drinking behind them, there is reason to assume that whatever is known about the etiology of alcoholism would be relevant. If we believe that etiology is fundamentally biopsychosocial (Zucker & Gomberg, 1986), the older patients who began problem drinking in adolescence or young adulthood are presumably characterized by the same etiological factors as those alcoholics who recover or die before becoming elderly. It is the late-onset or recent-onset alcoholic individuals who present some interesting questions about etiology (Atkinson, Tolson, & Turner, 1990).

The role of the stressors of aging such as losses of health, status, or significant others is controversial. Although many investigators have posited that the role of aging stressors lead to late-onset or recent-onset alcohol disorders (Atkinson, 1984; Finlayson, Hurt, Davis, & Morse, 1988; Gomberg, 1982), current evidence does not support a stress etiology (Welte & Mirand, 1993). A comparison of early- and late-onset alcohol abusers (Schonfeld & Dupree, 1991) showed *both* groups experiencing the losses and stresses associated with aging, for example, diminished social support, loneliness, and depression.

SCREENING FOR ALCOHOL-RELATED DISORDERS

The diagnostic manual in current use (DSM IV, American Psychiatric Association, 1994) lists the criteria for substance abuse, substance dependence, and substance-induced disorders (intoxication, withdrawal, delirium, persisting amnestic disorder, mood disorder, anxiety disorder, sexual dysfunction and sleep disorder, all drug-induced). The criteria for diagnosing substance abuse or dependence are in wide clinical use. In clinical terms, the criteria for drug dependence includes tolerance, withdrawal, loss of control, a lifestyle with much time and/or effort to obtain or recover from drug use, and continued use in spite of consequences. The criteria for the diagnosis of drug abuse include persistent use so that major role obligations are failed, and persistent use despite drug-related hazards, and legal, social, or interpersonal problems, consequences of the drug use.

There is a problem in applying the DSM IV criteria to older people. Because this stage in the life course may not include the standard obligations of early adulthood and middle age, such as school, job, child rearing, and community participation, drug-related consequences as they affect role obligations are less obvious. In addition, among older persons, medical problems unrelated to drug ingestion may conceal signs of unwise substance abuse.

The widely used assessment instruments, such as the Michigan Alcoholism Screening Test (Selzer, 1971) or the CAGE questions (Ewing, 1984), need to be evaluated for use among older patients. Jones, Lindsey, Yount, Soltys, and Farant-Enayat (1993) report low sensitivities at the conventional screening cutoffs; Willenbring, Christensen, Spring, and Rasmussen (1987) found the standard MAST screening instrument to have very good sensitivity with the older population. Blow and colleagues (1992) introduced a geriatric version of the MAST. This screening instrument, specific for older patients, needs further development. Finney, Moos, and Brennan (1991) have offered a Drinking Problems Index, a test with 17 items assessing older persons' drinking.

As with all age groups, interview items should attempt to minimize issues of memory loss (Babor, Stephens, and Marlatt, 1987). In addition to asking the client about his or her alcohol and drug use, additional collateral measures might be obtained such as medical and family history, utilization of breathalyzer results, and drug screen indices.

Diagnosis of alcohol and drug abuse or dependence will involve rather different criteria depending on whether the older person is in a hospital or clinic or whether the older person is a respondent in a large survey. For epidemiological surveys, a cutoff criterion (usually in terms of quantity and/or frequency) is used. For clinicians, a few questions about drug and/or alcohol-related problems as well as consumption may be more useful. The question of diagnosing older problem substance users is open. However, one thing is certain—more data are needed to define the parameters of substance abuse in older people. It may well be that among some subgroups of the older population, such as women, abuse of prescribed psychoactive drugs is a larger problem than alcohol abuse.

INTERVENTIONS

Older people are underrepresented in all mental health facilities and this is true of substance-abuse treatment facilities as well (Brennan & Moos, 1991). Older patients are less likely to be screened accurately, partly because of health professionals' lack of sophistication and partly because of their own denial and reticence. Older patients are less likely to be referred to alcohol or drug treatment facilities. Only when an older patient is given a thorough medical workup does the likelihood of spotting the problem alcohol or drug intake, past or present, appear.

What are some of the *barriers* to diagnosis and referral? Such barriers come from at least three sources. First, the *older persons* themselves. That is, there may be denial, shame, a mind-your-own-business attitude, and there may be older persons who are drinking in a self-destructive, suicidal way who resent intervention. Also, for some older individuals there are realistic barriers, such as a lack of money or difficulty in obtaining transportation. Second, there are barriers that stem from *family and friends*, that is, nonconscious blocks to head off intervention due to denial. Sometimes there are embarrassment and shame among family and friends as well as a genuine (if unhelpful) attitude that this older person has earned the right to have "a good time." Finally, there are barriers that are generated by *health care professionals*. That is, due primarily to lack of knowledge and training, the behaviors reported and observed are viewed often as "aging," although falls, blackouts, poor nutrition, and changes in social networks should merit further study of the patient's alcohol and drug history and present use.

In a recent research report, Finney and Moos (1995) list several characteristics of those who are more likely to seek out help: women more than men, experience of more negative life events, social networks with fewer people who approve of drinking, more avoidant coping, and an earlier history of treatment use. On the other hand, a study of hospital physicians' screening and referral patterns (Curtis, Geller, Stokes, Levine, & Moore, 1989) showed *less* likelihood of accurate diagnosis and referral when the patients were white, female, or well educated. Another recent report about 104 male alcoholics in treatment and 67 male alcoholics not in treatment (Gomberg, 1995a) showed that those who were in treatment were characterized by more severe problems and heavier alcohol intake, the urging of family and friends to seek help, presence in the labor market, self-identification as alcohol dependent, and other health-care-seeking behaviors.

Because older individuals who abuse alcohol and/or drugs are underdiagnosed and inadequately referred to treatment, and because many barriers to treatment exist for elderly alcohol and/or drug abusers, a suggestion by Lawson (1989) seems wise. Lawson suggests that older individuals be treated in settings in which they are fre-

quently seen. This would include primary care physicians' practices, hospital outpatient clinics, and senior centers. Another suggestion for casefinding is the standard screening of adults 60 and older who are more likely to have an alcohol problem diagnosed *after* being admitted with a non-alcohol-related diagnosis than adults in any other age group (Stinson, Dufour, & Bertolucci, 1989). This suggests that hospital inpatient services for older adults would be a sensible place to screen for alcohol-related problems.

MODALITIES

There have been a number of reviews of treatment programs for older substance abusers (Atkinson, 1995; Miller, Belkin, & Gold, 1991; Nirenberg, Gomberg, & Celucci, in press; Schonfeld & Dupree, 1995; Wartenberg & Nirenberg, 1994). Most of these modalities deal with alcohol abuse and dependence and include detoxification, chemotherapy, counseling, family and group therapies, self-help groups, such as Alcoholics Anonymous, behavioral-cognitive therapies, and adjunctive services.

Detoxification

There is agreement that withdrawal symptoms are more severe and more prolonged with older patients than with younger patients (Brower, Mudd, Blow, Young, & Hill, 1994; Liskow, Rinck, Campbell, & DeSouza, 1989). Older patients are likely to present symptoms of cognitive impairment, daytime sleepiness, weakness, and elevated blood pressure (Brower et al., 1994). It is a prudent policy to consider the patient's clinical status and have him or her medically monitored including nutritional status (Wartenberg & Nirenberg, 1994; Nirenberg et al., in press). The extent of use of benzodiazepines in withdrawal is not agreed upon. Liskow and colleagues (1989) describe a more severe withdrawal among older patients, ". . . for which they received higher doses of chlordiazepoxide" (p. 414). On the other hand, Miller et al. (1991) recommend lowered doses because of elderly patients' ". . . enhanced sensitivity to drugs, particularly benzodiazepines" (p. 161). The use of short-acting benzodiazepines and an extended time for withdrawal is generally recommended.

Chemotherapy

In the past, antabuse has been the drug of choice in alcohol abuse treatment. It should be noted, however, that little is known about the limits and contraindications for the use of antabuse with older patients. Currently, naltrexone is recommended as the medication that minimizes craving. Again, there is no information on the applicability or limitations of the use of naltrexone with older patients.

Counseling

If one assumes that alcohol problems are based on a biopsychosocial etiology, the study of life circumstances and coping mechanisms of older people is relevant. Brennan & Moos (1995) report that older problem drinkers (drawn from medical facilities) report fewer material resources, less social support, and more family difficulties and interpersonal conflict than older nonalcoholic patients. Coping mechanisms of older problem drinkers are resignation and avoidance.

Counseling may be long-term, psychodynamic (Cox, 1987), or short-term counseling that will involve family, group support, and community service and other "social therapies" (Blake, 1990). There is research in progress studying the efficacy of brief intervention counseling with older alcohol abusers. Schonfeld and Dupree (1995) point out the paucity of information available about the effectiveness of counseling approaches.

Family Therapies

The limitation of family therapies seems obvious. Many older people who are problem drinkers no longer have parents, a spouse, or significant others. It must also be noted that family members, particularly the spouse, may function as enablers (Thomas, Yoshioka, & Ager, 1996). A Canadian group has described a program for older substance abusers based in an acute care hospital (Tabisz, Jacyk, Fuchs, & Grymonpre, 1993) in which a third of the patients had family enablers. It is of interest that many in this group of patients were women. There is little by way of reports of family therapy with older patients but there are questions of interest, such as: Would family therapy with the adult children of an elderly substance abuser be helpful?

Group Treatment

Zimberg (1995) has argued that group intervention is probably the most important aspect of therapy for older problem drinkers. Due to factors like isolation, depression, and loneliness associated with substance abuse in older people,

the recommendation makes good sense. As discussed next, age-specific groups give an opportunity for an exchange of experiences and support from one's age peers. Although there is little quantitative data about efficacy, reports of observers and anecdotal evidence indicate that such therapy groups explore themes about loss and grief, confronting problems of aging, and reminiscence. This modality is used and reported on in the Veterans Administration hospital system (Atkinson, 1995) and in a variety of community-based programs (Zimberg, 1995).

Self-Help Groups

Alcoholics Anonymous is the model for a number of so-called 12-step programs. For older alcoholics, AA can provide the social support and networks to help in rehabilitation (Carle, 1980). In some regions, AA has groups specifically designed for older recovering alcohol abusers. Although empirical outcome data are lacking, there are health care personnel in gerontological substance abuse programs who believe that ". . . with a largely age-homogeneous group the AA experience is positive" (Schiff, 1988).

Behavioral-Cognitive Therapies

These have been among the few treatment modalities in which outcome is studied and evaluated. One Veterans Administration hospital program involved not only medical attention but also alcohol education, counseling, and training in self-management and problem-solving skills (Carstensen, Rychtarik, & Prue, 1985). In a follow-up study, many older patients showed a positive response: for example, 50% of the 65 and older patients had maintained sobriety and another 12% significantly decreased the quantity of alcohol. Behavioral-cognitive therapies emphasize observable behavior patterns, clearly defined operational treatment approaches, specific goals, and outcome measures. Although aversion therapy has been experimented with, it is not considered an advisable technique for older patients (Schonfeld & Dupree, 1995).

To some extent, cognitive-behavioral and self-management techniques have been demonstrated as effective with older patients. The Gerontology Alcohol Project in Florida (Dupree, Broskowski, & Schonfeld, 1984) demonstrated results from such a program based on 48 late-onset problem drinkers, average age 64. The program included intensive assessment (behavior analysis and functional analysis of drinking behavior), a self-management treatment approach, skill acquisition, and reconstruction of social networks. The treatment was provided in a senior center and consisted of modules: analysis of antecedents and consequences of drinking, self-management, alcohol education, problem solving, and so on. One-year follow-up after completion of the program showed a 74% rate of success. This impressive result is limited by the small sample size, the selection sample of late-onset alcohol abusers, and a high rate of dropout. Glantz (1995) has outlined a program for cognitive therapy with older alcohol abusers. The first task consists of screening, patient selection, eliciting the patient's history and patterns of alcohol use, and establishing goals. Subsequent sessions involve problem solving, resolving long-standing issues, skills training, work on social relationships and self-image, and, finally, relapse prevention. To date, cognitive therapy with an individual plan for each patient seems to be a promising approach.

Adjunctive Services

As is true with many groups of alcohol abusers (e.g., chronic drunkenness offenders), more is needed in the rehabilitation process than therapeutic intervention for the substance abuse. Those agencies and therapists who will be working with older patients need to maintain contact with resources in the community such as agencies to work with the older population, senior centers, medical and dental resources, home health services, meals-on-wheels, and the like. Johnson (1989), who studied a small group of recovering elderly alcoholics, made recommendations to health care professionals that include group work, reading materials with large print, and a slow tempo.

ELDER-SPECIFIC TREATMENT

Age-specific treatment for this age cohort means group therapy with other elderly patients. "Mainstreaming," on the other hand, describes mixed-age treatment. There is general agreement among those working with older patients that age-specific treatment is advantageous (Atkinson, 1995; Kofoed, Tolson, Atkinson, Toth, & Turner, 1987; Schonfeld & Dupree, 1995; Zimberg, 1995). Kofed et al. (1987) compared a mixed-age treatment group with an age-specific similar group; the latter had better attendance, and two-thirds of them completed a year in the program. Schonfeld and Dupree (1995) point out that older patients' treatment concerns are more about depression,

loneliness, and social networks than with ". . . job-hunting, dating, or marital problems." Zimberg (1995) offers the observation that many older problem drinkers are more comfortable in senior-oriented programs. In a six-state survey of older problem drinkers' treatments, Hinrichsen (1984) recommended elder-specific groups. Johnson (1989) noted that elder-specific groups were preferred by the patients. Although there is not much empirical evidence, the support of clinicians and researchers lends credence to the idea of elder-specific treatment. There are advantages and disadvantages (e.g., costs) but it is not difficult for any treatment facility, if it has a fair number of older patients, to establish special group meetings for them.

DUAL DIAGNOSIS

Unlike younger alcohol abusers who manifest comorbidity of schizophrenia, multiple substance abuse, and personality disorders, older alcohol abusers are more likely to manifest depression as comorbidity. Among early-onset alcoholics, there may also be an accompanying personality disorder (Speer & Bates, 1992). Blow and his colleagues (1992) found, among older veteran patients, comorbidities like dementia, depression, and impairment in adaptive functioning. There is no indication that older patients would be less responsive than patients in other age groups to a treatment program that sought to deal with both diagnoses.

STRESS AS ETIOLOGY?

In earlier classifications of older problem drinkers, it seemed useful to describe early onset alcoholics as "survivors" and recent-onset alcoholics as "reactive" problem drinkers (Gomberg, 1982). Furthermore, the assumption was made that the stresses which tend to accompany aging, such as loss, health problems, depression, lowered status, and so on, were the basic etiology of late-onset alcohol abuse. However, the evidence has been ambiguous. Jennison (1992) found older subjects who experienced significant losses to be more likely to drink heavily. Welte and Mirand (1993) did not find a relationship between acute stress and heavy drinking in a sample of older subjects. Interestingly enough, there was a stronger relationship between *chronic* stress and alcohol problems. The significance of chronic stressors in the etiology of alcoholism as opposed to the importance of acute, temporary stress situations runs through the entire age spectrum. It has often been found that women with alcohol problems

(Gomberg, 1989a) have *not* experienced more childhood stressors, such as the loss of a parent, than matched control groups—the groups differ in affective reaction and coping with similar stresses.

OUTCOME STUDIES

There is not a good deal to report in this area. There are few outcome studies on many of the recommended treatment modalities. In the absence of such studies, the best course seems to be to try the recommended procedures of those clinicians experienced in working with older patients. Several reports have indicated that cognitive-behavioral treatments are relatively effective with older patients. By and large, success and failure rates with older patients are comparable to results from younger patients: for example, older alcohol abusers whose problems have begun relatively recently, those with shorter duration of problem drinking, are found to have better prognosis than early-onset alcohol abusers. Measures used to determine outcome include compliance with the treatment program, abstinence, improved psychosocial behaviors, and increased social activities. Atkinson (1995) has pointed out that compliance or short-term success are weak predictors of outcome. Outcome is also influenced by treatment of accompanying medical and psychiatric disorders, duration of the problem drinking history, the mechanics of getting to and from a facility, and family participation (Schonfeld & Dupress, 1995).

RECOMMENDATIONS

1. There is a need for more sensitivity among health care professionals to the problems of the older person who abuses substances. Clinicians would do well to examine their attitudes, fears, and perceptions about aging.
2. Age-specific group treatment has been recommended and may be set up within treatment facilities with little extra cost.
3. Confrontation has not been found to be helpful with this age group.
4. Older substance abusers may present with all kinds of psychiatric syndromes but chances are that they will include depression. Coping with losses—surviving and going on constructively—is the task of the older person, particularly the one who has gotten into difficulty with substance abuse.
5. Skills to rebuild social networks are important components of treatment.

6. Anyone working with older patients, whether clinician or researcher, will need to have contacts with all community resources for older people including medical services, both inpatient and outpatient. Contact with nursing homes is useful; there are sick older persons in those facilities who are drinking problematically.
7. For clinicians working with older alcohol abusers, patience and a somewhat slower pace is useful.
8. Above all, the dignity of the older person, who is likely to be considerably older than the clinician, must be respected. That is true for all patients but particularly true for the older person, whose status has diminished and whose role in society is unclear.

AUTHOR NOTE

Edith S. Lisansky Gomberg, University of Michigan Alcohol Research Center and the Department of Psychiatry, University of Michigan Medical Center, and School of Social Work.

This review was supported by a National Institute on alcohol Abuse and Alcoholism on Grant P50 AA 07378.

REFERENCES

Adams, W. L., Yuan, Z., Barboriak, J., & Rimm, A. A. (1993). Alcohol-related hospitalizations of elderly people. Prevalence and geographic variation in the United States. *Journal of the American Medical Association, 270,* 1222–1225.

Alcohol Alert. (1988). Methadone maintenance and patients in alcoholism treatment (No. 1). *National Institute on Alcohol Abuse and Alcoholism* (pp. 1–4).

Alexander, F., & Duff, R. W. (1988). Drinking in retirement communities. *Generations, XII,* 58–62.

American Psychiatric Association. (1994). *Diagnostic and statistical manual of mental disorders* (4th ed.). Washington DC: Author.

Annual Medical Examiner Data 1993. (1995). *Data from the drug abuse warning network* (Series 1, No. 13-B DHHS Publication No. SMA 95-3019). Washington, DC: Government Printing Office.

Atkinson, R. M. (1984). Substance use and abuse in late life. In R. M. Atkinson (Ed.), *Alcohol and drug abuse in old age* (pp. 1–21). Washington, DC: American Psychiatric Press.

Atkinson, R. M. (1995). Treatment program for aging alcoholics. In T. Beresford & E. Gomberg (Eds.), *Alcohol and aging* (pp. 186–210). New York: Oxford University Press.

Atkinson, R. M., Tolson, R. L., & Turner, J. A. (1990). Late versus early onset drinking in older men. *Alcoholism: Clinical and Experimental Research, 9,* 574–579.

Atkinson, R. M., Turner, J. A., Kofoed, L. L., & Tolson, R. L. (1985). Early versus late alcoholism in order persons (preliminary findings). *Alcoholism: Clinical and Experimental Research, 9,* 513–515.

Babor, T. F., Stephens, R. S., & Marlatt, G. A. (1987). Verbal report methods in clinical research on alcoholism. Response bias and its minimization. *Journal of Studies on Alcohol, 48,* 410–424.

Berman, B. A., & Gritz, E. R. (1993). Women and smoking: Toward the year 2000. In E. S. L. Gomberg, & T. D. Nirenberg (Eds.), *Women and substance abuse* (pp. 258–285). Norwood, NJ: Ablex.

Beresford, R., & Gomberg, E. (1995). *Alcohol and aging.* New York: Oxford University Press.

Blake, R. (1990). Mental health counseling and older problem drinkers. *Journal of Mental Health Counseling, 12,* 354–367.

Blow, F. C., Brower, K. J., Chulenberg, J. E., Demo-Dananberg, L. M., Young, K. J., & Beresford, T. P. (1992). The Michigan Alcoholism Screening Test. Geriatric version (MAST-G). A new elderly-specific screening instrument. *Alcoholism: Clinical and Experimental Research, 16,* 372 (Abstract 105).

Brennan, P. L., & Moos, R. H. (1991). Functioning, life context, and help-seeking among late-onset problem drinkers. Comparison with nonproblem drinkers and early-onset problem drinkers. *British Journal of Addiction, 86,* 1139–1150.

Brennan, P. L., & Moos, R. H. (1995). Life context, coping responses, and adaptive outcomes: A stress and coping perspective on late-life problem drinking. In T. Beresford & E. Gomberg (Eds.), *Alcohol and aging* (pp. 230–248). New York: Oxford University Press.

Brower, K. J., Mudd, S., Blow, F. C., Young, J. P., & Hill, E. M. (1994). Severity and treatment of alcohol withdrawal in elderly versus younger patients. *Alcoholism: Clinical and Experimental Research, 18,* 196–201.

Carle, C. E. (1980). *Letters to elderly alcoholics.* Center City, MN: Hazelden Foundation.

Carstensen, L. L., Rycharik, R. G., & Prue, D. M. (1985). Behavioral treatment of the geriatric alcohol abuser: A long term follow-up study. *Addictive Behaviors, 10,* 307–311.

Chatham, L. R. M., Rowan-Szal, G. A., Joe, G. W., Brown, B. S., & Simpson, D. D. (1995). Heavy drinking in a population of methadone-maintained clients. *Journal of Studies on Alcohol, 56,* 417–422.

Cloninger, C. R. (1987). Neurogenetic adaptive mechanisms in alcoholism. *Science, 236,* 410–416.

Cox, W. M. (1987). Personality theory and research. In H. T. Blane & K. T. Leonard (Eds.), *Psychological theories of drinking and alcoholism* (pp. 55–89). New York: Guilford.

Curtis, J. R., Geller, G., Stokes, E. J., Levine, D. M., & Moore, R. D. (1989). Characteristics, diagnosis and treatment of alcoholism in elderly patients. *Journal of the American Geriatrics Society, 37,* 310–316.

DeHart, S. S., & Hoffman, N. G. (1995). Screening and diagnosis of alcohol abuse and dependence in older adults. In A. M. Gurnack (Ed.), Drugs and the elderly: Use and misuse of drugs, medicines, alcohol and tobacco. *The International Journal of the Addictions (Special issue), 30*(13, 14), 1717–1747.

DesJarlais, D. C., Joseph, H., & Courtwright, D. (1985). Old age and addiction: A study of elderly patients in methadone maintenance treatment. In E. Gottheil, K. A. Druley, T. E. Skoloda, & H. M. Waxman (Eds.), *The combined problems of alcoholism, drug addiction and aging* (pp. 201–209). Springfield, MA: C. C. Thomas.

Dupree, L. W., Broskowski, H., & Schonfeld, L. (1984). The Gerontology Alcohol Project: A behavioral treatment program for elderly alcohol abusers. *The Gerontologist, 24,* 510–516.

Eaton, W. W., Kramer, M., Anthony, J. C., Dryman, A., Shapiro, S., & Locke, B. Z. (1989). The incidence of specific DIS/DSM III mental disorders. Data from the NIMH Epidemiology Catchment Area Program. *Acta Psychiatrica Scandinavica, 79,* 163–178.

Epstein, L. L., Mills, C., & Simon, A. (1970). Antisocial behavior of the elderly. *Comprehensive Psychiatry, 11,* 36–42.

Ewing, J. A. (1984). Detecting alcoholism: The CAGE questionnaire. *Journal of the American Medical Association, 252,* 1905–1907.

Finlayson, R. E. (1984). Prescription drug abuse in older persons. In R. M. Atkinson (Ed.), *Alcohol and drug abuse in old age* (pp. 61–70). Washington, DC: American Psychiatric Press.

Finlayson, R. E., Hurt, R. D., Davis, N. J., & Morse, R. M. (1988). Alcoholism in elderly persons. A study of the psychiatric and psychosocial features of 216 inpatients. *Mayo Clinic Proceedings, 63,* 761–768.

Finney, J. W., & Moos, R. H. (1995). Entering treatment for alcohol abuse: A stress and coping perspective. *Addiction, 90,* 1223–1240.

Finney, J. W., Moos, R. H., & Brennan, P. L. (1991). The drinking problems index: A measure to assess alcohol-related problems among older adults. *Journal of Substance Abuse, 3,* 395–404.

Gambert, S. R. (1992). Substance abuse in the elderly. In J. H. Lowinson, P. Ruiz, R. B. Millman (Eds.), *Substance abuse: A comprehensive textbook* (2nd ed.). Baltimore: Williams & Wilkins.

Glantz, M. D. (1995). Cognitive therapy with elderly alcoholics. In T. Beresford & E. Gomberg (Eds.), *Alcohol, and Aging* (pp. 211–229). New York: Oxford University Press.

Gomberg, E. S. L. (1982). Alcohol use and alcohol problems among the elderly. *Alcohol and Health Monograph No. 4* (Special Population Issues, NIAAAA, DHHS Publication No. ADM 82-1193, pp. 263–290).

Gomberg, E. S. L. (1989a). Alcoholic women in treatment: Early histories and early problem behaviors. *Advances in Alcohol Substance Abuse, 8,* 133–147.

Gomberg, E. S. L. (1989b). Alcoholism in women: Use of other drugs. *Alcoholism: Clinical and Experimental Research, 13,* 38 (Abstract 215).

Gomberg, E. S. L. (1990). Drugs, alcohol and aging. In L. T. Kozlowski, H. M. Anbnis, H. D. Cappell, F. B. Glaser, E. M.

Sellers, M. S. Goodstadt, Y. Israel, H. Kalant, & E. R. Vingilis (Eds.), *Research advances in alcohol & drug problems, Vol. 10* (pp. 171–213). New York: Plenum.

Gomberg, E. S. L. (1995a). Older alcoholics: Entry into treatment. In T. Beresford & E. Gomberg (Eds.), *Alcohol and aging* (pp. 169–185). New York: University Press.

Gomberg, E. S. L. (1995b). Older women and alcohol: Use and abuse. In M. Galanter (Ed.), *Recent developments in alcoholism* (Vol. 12, pp. 61–79). New York: Plenum.

Gomberg, E. S. L. (in press). Alcohol and drugs. In J. E. Birren (Ed.), *The encyclopedia of gerontology.* San Diego: Academic Press.

Gomberg, E. S. L., & Nelson, B. W. (1995). Black and white older men: Alcohol use and abuse. In T. Beresford & E. Gomberg (Eds.), *Alcohol and aging* (pp. 307–323). New York: Oxford University Press.

Gordon, T., & Kannel, W. B. (1983). Drinking and its relation to smoking, blood pressure, blood lipids, and uric acid. *Archives of Internal Medicine, 146,* 262–265.

Hartford, J. T., & Samorajski, T. (Eds.) (1984). *Alcoholism in the elderly: Social and biomedical issue* New York: Raven Press.

Helzer, J. E., Burnam, A., & McEvoy, L. T. (1991). Alcohol use and dependence. In L. N. Robins & D. A. Regier (Eds.), *Psychiatric disorders in America: The epidemiologic catchment area study* (pp. 81–115). New York: Macmillan.

Hinrichsen, J. (1984). Toward improving treatment services for alcoholics of advanced age. *Alcohol Health and Research World, 8,* 31–49.

Huffine, C., Folkman, S. & Lazarus, R. S. (1989). Psychoactive drugs, alcohol, and stress and coping processes in older adults. *American Journal of Drug and Alcohol Abuse, 15*(1): 101–13.

Jennison, K. M. (1992). The impact of stressful life events and social support on drinking among older adults: A general population survey. *International Journal of Aging and Human Development, 35,* 99–123.

Johnson, L. K. (1989). How to diagnose and treat chemical dependency in the elderly. *Journal of Gerontological Nursing, 15,* 22–26.

Jones, T. V., Lindsey, B. A., Yount, P., Soltys, R., & Farant-Enayat, B. (1993). Alcoholism screening questionnaires: Are they valid in elderly medical outpatients? *Journal of General Internal Medicine, 8,* 674–678.

Kleber, H. D. (1990). The nosology of abuse and dependence. *Journal of Psychiatric Research 24, (Suppl. 2),* 57–64.

Kofoed, L. O., Tolson, R. L., Atkinson, R. M., Toth, R. L., & Turner, J. A. (1987). Treatment compliance of older alcoholics: An elder-specific approach is superior to "mainstreaming." *Journal of Studies on Alcohol, 48,* 47–51.

Kopelman, M. D. (1995). The Korsakoff syndrome. *British Journal of Psychiatry, 166,* 154–173.

LaRue, A., Dessonville, C., & Jarvik, L. K. (1985). Aging and mental disorders. In J. E. Birren & K. W. Schaie (Eds.),

Handbook of the psychology of aging (pp. 664–702). New York: Van Nostrand Reinhold.

Lawson, A. W. (1989). Substance abuse problems of the elderly: Considerations for treatment and prevention. In G. W. Lawson & A. W. Lawson (Eds.), *Alcoholism and substance abuse in special populations* (pp. 96–113). Gaithersburg, MD: Aspen Publishers.

Lee, G. P., & DiClemente, C. C. (1985). Age of onset versus duration of problem drinking on the Alcohol Use Inventory. *Journal of Studies on Alcohol, 46,* 398–402.

Liskow, B. L., Rinck, C., Campbell, J., & DeSouza, C. (1989). Alcohol withdrawal in the elderly. *Journal of Studies on Alcohol, 50,* 414–421.

Maddox, G., Robins, L. N., & Rosenberg, N. (Eds.). (1984). *Nature and extent of alcohol problems among the elderly.* (Research Monograph 14, NIAAA, DHHS No. ADM 84-1321). Washington, DC: Government Printing Office.

McKim, W. A., & Mishara, B. L. (1987). *Drugs and aging.* Toronto: Butterworths.

Michigan Department of Public Health. (1994). *Substance abuse services for older adults.* (OA 089/10M/9-94/NOG). Lansing, MI: Author.

Miller, N. S., Belkin, B. M., & Gold, M. S. (1991). Alcohol and drug dependence among the elderly: Epidemiology, diagnosis and treatment. *Comprehensive Psychiatry, 32,* 153–165.

Mishara, B. L., & Kastenbaum, R. (1980). *Alcohol and old age.* New York: Grune & Stratton.

Nirenberg, T. D., Gomberg, E. S. L., & Cellucci, A. (in press). Substance abuse disorders. In M. Hersen & V. B. Van Hasselt (Eds.), *Handbook of clinical geropsychology.* New York: Plenum.

Parrella, D. P., & Filstead, W. J. (1988). Definition of onset in the development of onset-based alcoholism typologies. *Journal of Studies on Alcohol, 49,* 85–91.

Prentice, R. (1979). Patterns of psychotherapeutic drug use among the elderly. In *The aging process and psychoactive drug use* (pp. 17–41). National Institute of Drug Abuse, Washington, DC: Government Printing Office.

Rowe, J. W., & Kahn, R. L. (1987). Human aging: Usual and successful. *Science, 237,* 143–149.

Rubington, E. (1955). Elderly homeless alcoholic careers. In T. Beresford & E. Gomberg (Eds.), *Alcohol and aging* (pp. 293–306). New York: Oxford University Press.

Schiff, S. M. (1988). Treatment approaches for older alcoholics. *Generations XII,* 41-45.

Schonfeld, L., & Dupree, L. W. (1991). Antecedents of drinking for early- and late-onset elderly alcohol abusers. *Journal of Studies on Alcohol, 52,* 587–591.

Schonfeld, L., & Dupree, L. W. (1995). Treatment approaches for older problem drinkers. In A. M. Gurnack (Ed.), Drugs and the elderly: Use and misuse of drugs, medicine, alcohol, and tobacco. *The International Journal of the Addictions, 30,* 1819–1842.

Selzer, M. L. (1971). The Michigan Alcoholism Screening Test: The quest for a new diagnostic instrument. *American Journal of Psychiatry, 127,* 1653–1658.

Speer, D. C., & Bates, K. (1992). Comorbid mental and substance disorders among older adults. *Journal of American Geriatrics Society, 40,* 886–890.

Stinson, F. S., DuFour, M. C., & Bertolucci, D. (1989). Alcohol related morbidity in the aging population. *Alcohol Health & Research World, 13,* 80–87.

Tabisz, E. M., Jacyk, W. R., Fuchs, D., & Grymonpere, R. (1993). Chemical dependency in the elderly: The enabling factor. *Canadian Journal on Aging, 12,* 78–88.

Thomas, E. J., Yoshioka, M., & Ager, R. D. (1996). Spouse enabling of alcohol abuse: Conception, assessment, and modification. *Journal of Substance Abuse 8,* 61–80.

Wartenberg, A. A., & Nirenberg, T. D. (1994). Alcohol and other drug abuse in older persons. In W. Reichel (Ed.), *Care of the elderly: Clinical aspects of aging* (4th ed., pp. 133–141). Baltimore: Williams & Wilkins.

Welte, J. W., & Mirand, A. L. (1993). Drinking, problem drinking, and life stressors in the elderly general population. *Journal of Studies on Alcohol, 56,* 67–73.

Willenbring, M. L., Christensen, K. J., Spring, W. D., & Rasmussen, R. (1987). Alcoholism screening in the elderly. *Journal of the American Geriatric Society, 35,* 864–869.

Zimberg, S. (1995). The elderly. In A. M. Washton (Ed.), *Psychotherapy and substance abuse* (pp. 413–427). New York: Guilford.

Zucker, R. A., & Gomberg, E. S. L. (1986). Etiology of alcoholism reconsidered: The case for a biopsychosocial process. *American Psychologist, 41,* 783–793.

CHAPTER 8

GENETICS

Michael M. Vanyukov

It would be difficult to argue against the notion that drug addiction is induced by certain substances. Nevertheless, it would be a leap of logic to assume that substance abuse (SA) and dependence are properties of a drug. Clearly, these conditions develop as an organism's response to drug exposure, which includes the very presence of psychoactive substances in the environment. The developmental process is guided by factors, both internal and external, that lead to the initiation of drug use, its maintenance, and the rise of psychological and/or physical dependence, or to their absence. At all points in the developmental trajectory, there are differences between individuals' responses to drug exposure, which may depend on the relevant individual variation in biochemistry, physiology, personality, intelligence, life events, culture, and so on, and, in the final account, on the differences between individual genotypes and between environmental conditions (Tarter & Vanyukov, 1994). At the individual level, the factors that underlie risk for SA converge into a *phenotype*, a certain value, for a quantitative trait termed *liability* (Falconer, 1965) to SA, just as the factors influencing stature result in a certain individual height phenotype. Behavior genetic (family, twin, and adoption) studies have shown that individual differences in the risk for substance-use disorders in the population likely result from the additive effect of a

number of variable genetic and environmental factors. This puts the liability to SA into the category of complex traits characterized by multifactorial inheritance (which is another way to say that variation in the trait is based on an indeterminate number of genetic and environmental variables). The complexity of this trait is exacerbated by the fact that various liability phenotypes result from a long developmental process. The relative contribution of the genetic and environmental groups of factors into liability variation has been estimated. It is important, however, to learn exactly what genes and environmental influences constitute these groups and how their relative roles change during development. Association and linkage approaches in humans and animal models have been used to test the relationships between genetic variation and SA as well as personality traits related to the risk for SA.

HERITABILITY OF THE LIABILITIES TO SUBSTANCE USE DISORDERS AND ASSOCIATED TRAITS

Behavior genetic studies demonstrate that phenotypic variation in the liability to substance-use disorders is determined by differences in both individual genotypes and environmental conditions. The contribution of genotypic differences into the phenotypic variation is termed *heritability*. It should be emphasized that heritability is determined both by the existence of trait-relevant genetic polymorphisms (when certain genes in the population exist in two or more variants that determine differences in the structure or the rate of metabolism of hormones, receptors, or enzymes that participate in drug-related processes) and by the role the environment plays in the liability variation. The absence of variation in the trait-related gene(s) may be due to the fact that mutations in that gene are not compatible with life (e.g., the function is too critical to allow for any genetic variation). In this case, if any phenotypic differences in the population exist, they will all be due to environmental variation, and heritability will be zero, while the trait is in fact very strictly genetically determined. Trait-related genetic polymorphism(s) may exist, but their influence on phenotypic differences may be masked by a wide range of responses to a relevant environmental characteristic(s), which will also result in a low heritability. In this case, controlling for that environmental factor(s) would allow for detecting the genetic contribution into phenotypic differences. It should be emphasized that heritability as well as its environmental complement in phenotypic variation (sometimes termed *environmentality*) do not have any direct relation to the causes of phenotypes (e.g., etiology of a disorder). By definition, heritability and environmentality refer only to the causes of phenotypic *variation* and covariation. Clearly, if "it is important to avoid such short-hand expressions as 'height is genetic' when really we mean 'individual differences in height are mainly genetic'" (Neale & Cardon, 1992, p. 4), it is even more important when we consider behavioral/psychological traits. For instance, even if heritability of the liability to SA were in fact 100%, it would neither give us information about the causes of a particular individual's drug dependence nor tell us how to treat (or, as some might think, not to treat, because it is "genetic") this person's addiction. Preventing an individual from exposure to drugs would prevent his or her drug use and abuse regardless of heritability. Such a heritability would tell us, however, that in the population where this estimate was obtained, variation in relevant environmental conditions is negligible compared to relevant genotypic variation (this situation could probably be observed, for instance, if everybody was getting the same exposure to a drug as a matter of everyday routine). For many disorders, liability to which is far from being 100% heritable, efficient treatment methods are not encountered within the range of natural environmental conditions (e.g.,

synthetic antibiotics). Conversely, the treatment of a disorder, the liability to which has heritability close to 100%, can be entirely environmental (e.g., phenylketonuria). In addition, a particular heritability estimate refers only to the population and the time point where and when this estimate was obtained. Heritability estimates obtained in one population cannot be automatically assumed to be the same in another population and cannot be used to explain phenotypic differences *between* populations (even if heritability within each population were unity, phenotypic differences between populations could be entirely environmental). Within these constraints, twin and adoption studies are used to estimate heritability.

Twin and Adoption Studies

Substantial contribution of genetic variation has been shown for a diagnosis of the presence/absence of SA (other than alcohol abuse and excluding tobacco abuse). Heritability was estimated in one study at 0.31 in males and 0.22 in females (Pickens et al., 1991). An adoption study in females (Cadoret, Yates, Troughton, Woodworth, & Stewart, 1996) showed a pattern of relationships between biological family background and SA/dependence outcome similar to that in males (Cadoret, Troughton, O'Gorman, & Heywood, 1986), with strong associations between alcohol abuse/dependence and antisociality in biologic parents and drug abuse in offspring. An additive genetic model fit best for the abuse of various classes of drugs, with heritability estimates reaching 0.62 (Goldberg, Lyons, Eisen, True, & Tsuang, 1993). Significant heritability of the liability to drug abuse (0.46) has been shown in a study of monozygotic twins reared apart (Grove et al., 1990). Importantly, a high genetic correlation (0.78) between alcohol abuse and/or dependence and drug abuse was found in this study. It has also been shown that alcohol problems in the biological parents predicted drug abuse in the adopted-out offspring. This indicates that the liabilities to these disorders share a proportion of genes determining their phenotypic variation. Parallel results from twin studies of alcoholism show heritability estimates reaching 0.73 in males (McGue, Pickens, & Svikis, 1992) and 0.61 in females (Kendler, Neale, Heath, Kessler, & Eaves, 1994), varying for different definitions of the threshold phenotype (increasing with an increase in severity). Beginning with the studies of Goodwin, Schulsinger, Hermansen, Guze, and Winokur (1973), and Goodwin et al. (1974), adoption studies of alcoholism have consistently shown that the risk for alcoholism in the offspring of alcoholics is higher than in the children of nonalcoholics even when they are separated from their biological parents early in life (Bohman, Sigvardsson, & Cloninger, 1981; Cloninger, Bohman, & Sigvardsson, 1981).

Elucidating the role of *environment* in SA liability variation, adoption research has pinpointed certain environmental factors such as divorce (marital disharmony) and psychiatric disturbance in the adoptive family to be associated with increased drug abuse in adoptees (Cadoret et al., 1986, 1996). An example of influential environmental factors revealed in adoption studies is substantial sibling environmental effects on adolescent alcohol use (McGue, Sharma, & Benson, 1996). This study also showed that the significant nonbiological sibling correlation for involvement with alcohol was moderated by sibling pair demographic similarity. As a twin-family showed, an environmental factor of parental loss increases risk of alcoholism (Kendler et al., 1996). Familial religiosity is another environmental variable shown to affect variation in the risk for SA (Kendler, Gardner, & Prescott, 1997).

It can be concluded that the twin and adoption studies of SA produce substantial evidence for a genetic influence on individual differences in the risk for the disorder, and provide the grounds for research into particular genes influencing liability variation. At the same time, these genetic studies suggest the importance of the *environmental* causes of liability variation and the need to consider such causes along with genotypic information in candidate gene research.

Genetics of Behavioral Traits Associated with the Liability to Substance Abuse

A significant genetic component has been shown for variability in temperament and personality characteristics including those associated with the liability to SA. Thus, correlations between MZ twins reared apart (which give the direct estimate of genetic contribution into phenotypic variation, broad heritability) range between 0.4 and 0.5 for the personality traits measured by the Multidimensional Personality Questionnaire and California Psychological Inventory (Bouchard et al., 1990). Significant estimates of heritability have also been derived from twin studies for the dimensions of locus of control and for Type A-like behaviors (Pedersen, Gatz, et al., 1989; Pedersen, Lichtenstein, et al., 1989), and from twin and adoption studies for scales measuring temperament (Buss & Plomin, 1984; Plomin et

al., 1988). Liability to personality deviations, such as antisocial personality disorder (ASP), has been shown to have a considerable genetic component in its phenotypic variation (Bohman et al., 1983; Christiansen, 1970; Crowe, 1974), and adopted-away children of antisocial biological parents have an increased frequency of ASP as adults (Cadoret, 1978). Importantly, men with ASP are 5 times as likely to abuse drugs as those without this disorder, whereas the risk of drug abuse for women is 12 times higher in the presence of ASP than without ASP (Robins & Price, 1991).

There are both transgenerational and developmental continuities for antisocial symptoms. Ninety-five percent of males having four or more adult ASP symptoms have had at least one childhood conduct disorder (CD) symptom, whereas 76% have had three or more symptoms (Farrington, 1991). Parents of children with CD have a higher prevalence of both ASP and SA than parents of children without CD (Lahey et al., 1988). CD symptoms in childhood account for approximately 25% of the variation in adulthood ASP symptoms, and there is significant correlation between parental CD and ASP symptom counts and CD counts of their young children (Vanyukov et al., 1993; Vanyukov, Moss, & Tarter, 1994). In turn, CD is associated with an increased risk for alcoholism, drug abuse, and ASP (Robins & Price, 1991).

From the research conducted to date, it can be concluded that there is an association between heritable personality features and the liability to SA. Although there is no single "substance abuse personality," a certain proportion of variation in the liability may be explained by personality phenotypic variation preexisting the outcome of liability phenotype development.

Assortative Mating for the Liability to Substance Abuse and for Associated Personality Traits

Assortative mating is nonrandom pairing of mates with regard to a trait or traits. Spousal/mate correlation, or *homogamy*, may be due not only to phenotypic assortative mating, but also to social homogamy and contagion/effects of cohabitation (convergence). In *social homogamy*, correlations for behavioral traits between mates are caused by primary correlations in their environments that contribute to variation in the trait. *Contagion* refers to the direct influence of one partner's behavior on the other partner's behavioral phenotype. In contrast to the effects of phenotypic assortment, neither social homogamy for the trait (unless there is genotype–environment covariation) nor contagion leads to changes in the genetic structure of the population, because these causes of spousal phenotypic similarity generally do not alter the frequencies of genotypes.

The significant heritability of the liability to SA and temperament/personality characteristics indicate that assortative mating for these traits could considerably influence the relationship between parental phenotypes and the expression of these traits in the offspring (Vanyukov, Neale, Moss, & Tarter, 1996). Assortment may lead to, and maintain, the increase in both genetic and environmental (in the presence of cultural transmission) covariance between parents and their children.

Marital assortment on personality characteristics associated with, and/or contributing to, the variability of the liability to SA may mediate the assortment for this liability, resulting in the increase in offspring's liability even in the absence of the manifest disorder in the parent(s). It has been shown that there is spousal similarity possibly caused by positive assortment on traits measured by the Eysenck Personality Questionnaire Extroversion (Buss & Plomin, 1984; Mascie-Taylor & Vandenberg, 1988), Inconsistency (Lie) (Eaves, Eysenck, & Martin, 1989; Mascie-Taylor & Vandenberg, 1988), and Psychoticism (Eaves et al., 1989). Positive mate correlation was also found for almost all of the California Psychological Inventory scales (Buss, 1984; Swan, Carmelli, & Rosenman, 1986), as well as for sensation-seeking (Farley & Davies, 1977; Farley & Mueller, 1978), which has been shown to be associated with antisocial behavior (Hesselbrock & Hesselbrock, 1992) and correlates with alcohol use (Zuckerman, 1972) and the liability to alcoholism in general (Cloninger, Sigvardsson, von Knorring, & Bohman, 1988).

Homogamy has also been found for various forms of psychopathology, including neuroses, affective disorders, phobia, hysteria, and antisocial personality (Merikangas, 1982). Parental concordance for alcoholism, for instance, has been shown to be associated with an increased risk for conduct disorder in childhood and antisocial personality disorder in adulthood (Merikangas, Leckman, Prusoff, Pauls, & Weissman, 1985; Merikangas, Weissman, Prusoff, Pauls, & Leckman, 1985). High phenotypic resemblance among spouses was found for wives of sociopathic males (spousal correlation, 0.70) and husbands of sociopathic females (0.60) (Cloninger, Reich, & Guze, 1975). Importantly, the hypothesis of behavioral contagion among spouses as the cause of spousal phenotypic resemblance does not seem to

be supported by the data obtained. Spousal differences in personality tend to increase rather than decrease as a function of marriage length (Buss, 1984). Homogamy for antisocial personality was observed in an adoption study (Crowe, 1974). It is noteworthy that five of the six antisocial children of female offenders in this study also had antisocial fathers. A higher prevalence of both antisocial personality and alcohol abuse is found in parents of children with conduct disorder compared to parents of children without conduct disorder (Lahey et al., 1988). The liabilities to personality disorders, including antisocial personality, have been shown to have significant heritabilities (McGuffin & Thapar, 1992). Also, it has been found that both CD and ADHD are associated with the increased risk for SA, and with the risk of psychopathology in general (Merikangas, Weissman, Prusoff, & John, 1988). Hence, it is plausible that assortment for the liability to SA and for these liabilities (insofar as the latter are associated with the former) mutually increase parent–offspring resemblance for these traits (Vanyukov et al., 1996). This, in turn, may lead to further strengthening of the association between the liabilities to SA and other behavior deviations due to an increase in both genetic and environmental correlations between the traits. Therefore, marital phenotypic assortment for personality traits, which might underlie assortment for the liability to SA (that is, when there is secondary assortment for the liability) can be considered by itself an important potential risk factor (Vanyukov et al., 1996).

Spousal similarity (suggesting the possibility of assortment) has been observed for the liability to alcoholism (Hall, Hesselbrock, & Stabenau, 1983a, b; Jacob & Bremer, 1986; Moskalenko, Vanyukov, Solovyova, Rakhmanova, & Vladimirsky, 1992; Penick et al., 1987). Phenotypic similarity of parents on this trait correlates not only with the risk of alcoholism in offspring but also with the risk of antisocial personality/conduct disorder and attention deficit disorder (ADHD) (Moskalenko et al., 1992; Penick et al., 1987). In the latter study, significant differences were found in the frequencies of phenotypic classes: female alcoholic probands married predominantly alcoholics, whereas no male alcoholic proband had an alcoholic wife. Although the baseline rates of alcoholism among males and females necessary for correction in comparison are unknown for that population, the magnitude of the difference suggests that the likelihood of having a mate with a certain liability phenotype depends on the gender of the proband more than on the differences in populational phenotypic distributions in males and females. Moreover, the probability of a female proband marrying an alcoholic depended on her family history of alcoholism: 80% of husbands were alcoholic if at least one of the parents of the proband was affected, compared to 33% of husbands when none of the alcoholic proband's parents was affected.

High phenotypic resemblance between mates was shown for the liability to SA (diagnosis of SA) (Vanyukov et al., 1994, 1996). Interestingly, not only quantitative but also qualitative homogamy was observed. The wife's addiction phenotype was specific for the group of abusers her husband belonged to: whereas spouses of substance-abusing probands abused or were dependent on a variety of drugs only alcohol dependence or abuse were diagnosed among the wives of alcoholics.

Significant correlations between spousal antisocial behavior measured as retrospective conduct disorder and antisocial personality symptom counts were jointly estimated from clinically ascertained and control samples using a minimum chi-squared fit function (Vanyukov, Neale, Moss, & Tarter, submitted). The data suggest that spousal similarity for the liability to SA may be due to direct (primary) homogamy for this trait or secondary to (mediated by) homogamy for antisocial behavior. The results obtained suggest that observed spousal similarity in the presence or absence of SA disorder cannot be accounted for by direct homogamy for antisocial behavior, whereas the opposite can be true.

Resolution of the origins of marital resemblance could have both research and practical implications as well as pose new important questions. Failure to take assortment into account can lead, in twin research, to overestimation of shared environmental influences and underestimation of additive genetic variance when the DZ twin correlation is greater than half the MZ correlation (Allison et al., 1996). Allison and coauthors give an example where taking into account phenotypic assortment as low as 0.13 changes additive genetic and common environment estimates from 70% to 78% and from 10% to 2%, respectively.

With the heritability of 0.5 and correlation between spouses of 0.5, the eventual (at equilibrium) increase in phenotypic variance for a multifactorial trait is estimated to be 21% (Crow & Felsenstein, 1968). For a population with 5% affected individuals (as is, approximately, the case for substance abuse) this would be equivalent to a shift of the threshold to the left from its position on the z-scale of the standard normal distribution at 1.645 to 1.36 and an increase in the frequency of the disorder to 8.7% (Vanyukov et al., 1996). Considering that assortment for

the liability to substance abuse may be higher than 0.5 (0.6–0.9 [Vanyukov et al., submitted]), this increase may be even larger. Therefore, the mechanisms of assortment may partly account for the secular trends observed for substance abuse. Particularly, increase in lifetime prevalences of alcoholism and decrease in its age of onset in younger generations (Reich, Cloninger, Van Eerdewegh, Rice, & Mullaney, 1988) could be partly caused by assortment. This kind of "anticipation," one expression of which is the decreased age of onset, could also lead to increased liability to polysubstance use, deeper involvement with more dangerous substances, more severe drug dependence, and greater affectedness of females. Because of the associations existing between drug use and antisocial behavior, assortment for the liability to substance abuse could cause analogous anticipation in antisociality. This effect would be further exacerbated by phenotype–environment correlation (selection of environment promoting phenotype expression) and increase in antisociality concomitant to drug-use environment. It is, therefore, important to know whether mate similarity for the liability to substance abuse is caused by direct or indirect assortment and sources of possible indirect assortment, as opposed to social homogamy and contagion. Such research has yet to be conducted.

ASSOCIATION AND LINKAGE STUDIES

Familial aggregation of substance-use disorders and significant heritability of the liabilities suggest the existence of genetic polymorphisms contributing to variation in individual liability phenotypes. Consequently, there have been a number of investigations in search of genetic markers, that is simply inherited traits linked to or associated with a liability that could point to a particular part of human genome. These include classic genetic markers, that is, those with easily observable phenotypic expression (e.g., color blindness, blood groups) whose inheritance parallels the inheritance of the alleles of a gene; and DNA markers, for which the notions of the phenotype and the allele coincide.

Classic Markers

The research in the genetic markers of SA has mostly focused on alcoholism. The traits studied included classic genetic markers such as phenylthiocarbamide taste sensitivity (Swinson, 1973) and color blindness (Cruz-Coke & Varela, 1966). Whereas associations with these traits were soon shown to *result from* alcoholism, other classic markers, such as blood groups attracted repeated attention. "Linkage in repulsion between the D gene of the Rh system and alcoholism" was reported (Hill, Goodwin, Cadoret, Osterland, & Doner, 1975), although the data contradicted the linkage hypothesis (Wilson, Elston, Mallott, Tran, & Winokur, 1991) and were not confirmed (Hill et al., 1988). Linkage with the MNS blood groups (Hill, Aston, & Rabin, 1988) was not replicated as well (Tanna, Wilson, Winokur, & Elston, 1988).

Specific to the liability to alcoholism, research in genetic polymorphisms of ethanol-metabolizing enzymes revealed that about half of the individuals of Oriental ancestry have the deficient mitochondrial ALDH2 isozyme of aldehyde dehydrogenase the enzyme catalyzing the second step of alcohol oxidation, whereas this deficiency is not found in the Caucasian and Black populations (Agarwal & Goedde, 1992). Because the presence of the ALDH2*2 allele correlates with acute reaction to ethanol (alcohol-flush reaction), and it is found in only 2% of alcoholics in Japan while being present in 44% of nonalcoholics, it seems to protect from alcoholism (Harada, Agarwal, Goedde, Tagaki, & Ishikawa, 1982). This ALDH2 polymorphism, however, cannot influence variation in the liability to the disorder in the Caucasian and Black populations, where it is absent. A variant of alcohol-flush reaction that is not associated with ALDH2 deficiency does not reduce drinking (Higuchi et al., 1992). Alcohol-flush reaction observed in Caucasians does not result from ALDH2 deficiency (Thomasson, Crabb, Edenberg, & Li, 1993).

Monoamine oxidase (MAO), one of the primary enzymes regulating metabolism of neurotransmitters in the brain, has also been studied as a plausible marker for SA liabilities and in relation to personality traits associated with the increased risk for SA. It is known to exist in two forms, MAO-A and MAO-B. MAO-A differs from MAO-B in its substrate and inhibitor specificity and localization. MAO-A has a higher affinity to endogenous neurotransmitters, whereas MAO-B has a higher affinity to dietary amines, although dopamine, tyramine, and tryptamine are substrates common to both forms (Shih, Grimsby, Chen, & Zhu, 1993). There is no evidence for structural variation in either MAO form; the interindividual differences in activity are caused by the variation in the enzyme concentrations (Fowler, Wiberg, Oreland, Marcusson, & Winblad, 1980). There is suggestive evidence that low platelet MAO activity may be associated with an increased risk for mental disorders, including alcoholism, as well as with sensa-

tion seeking and antisociality (Alm et al., 1994; Fowler et al., 1980; Oreland, von Knorring, von Knorring, & Bohman, 1985). Platelet MAO-B activity has also been reported to be lower in alcoholics who have an earlier onset age and more severe form of the disorder (von Knorring, Hallman, von Knorring, & Oreland, 1991). However, in view of findings that alcohol inhibits MAO-B (Tabakoff, Lee, De Leon-Jones, & Hoffman, 1985), such differences may be secondary to alcohol exposure.

In summary, these and other traditional marker studies (for review see Devor & Cloninger, 1989; Schuckit, Li, Cloninger, & Dietrich, 1985) have mainly been concerned with alcoholism and not with other forms of SA. Despite the fact that the data suggest the existence of nonspecific associations between genetic polymorphisms and the liability, the findings of these studies have been inconclusive.

Association and Linkage with DNA Polymorphisms

Methodological Issues

Both linkage and association studies in humans are fraught with problems when applied to complex behavioral traits such as the liability to SA. The linkage approach generally assumes the presence of a major gene, which, to be detected, needs to contribute to about 10% or more of total variance in a trait even under the favorable circumstances of no recombination, a fully informative marker, and a selected proband sample with the sib-pair analysis (Carey & Williamson, 1991). The power of analysis significantly increases when extremely discordant sib pairs are sampled (Risch & Zhang, 1995). However, because the liability to SA is not indexed in nonaffected individuals (the degree of "normality" regarding substance abuse is not estimated), it is not possible to select extremely low liability phenotypes. The moderate heritability of the liability to SA is accounted for mostly by the additive component, and the system of liability phenotype determination, considering the number of critically important processes involved in the initiation and continuation of substance use and dependence development, is extremely complex. The SA liability phenotype is dynamic, that is, it evolves and fluctuates during lifetime. Hence, it is more likely that any gene involved in the liability variation has a weak effect (accounting for a small proportion of the trait variance), and thus the association approach may be more fruitful or even the only one to allow detecting the loci involved in the liability variation (Carey, 1994; Hodge, 1994). As Risch and Merikangas (1996) show, linkage analysis has limited power to detect genes of modest effect (i.e., for a genotype relative risk below 4, the number of families needed to detect linkage becomes unrealistic), whereas association studies with candidate genes have far greater power, even if one needs to test every gene in the genome. These authors also note that although the effects of such genes are small, their attributable risk may be large because of a high frequency of high-risk-associated alleles in the population. In addition, their combined effect may be substantial. Moreover, the effect of measures of drug-abuse prevention that could be developed based on the knowledge of genetic mechanisms contributing into the SA risk variation in the population may be much greater than the "natural" contribution of such mechanisms. The same can be said about the concrete modifiable environmental characteristics that could be revealed because controlling for genetic associations would make it possible to evaluate their role in the liability phenotypic variation.

It should be noted that the strength of an association may differ in populations, because of differences in both the genetic structure (as is the case, for instance, for the association between the aldehyde dehydrogenase gene and the risk for alcoholism among Orientals but not Caucasians) and environmental conditions. Therefore, a failure to confirm an association finding in a different population does not necessarily invalidate it.

An association between a genetic polymorphism and the liability in the population may be observed when the polymorphism is directly involved in liability variation, or under the conditions of linkage disequilibrium (an association of a disease-associated allele with an allele of another neighboring gene), or when a sample is stratified (derived from more than one population with different frequencies of the disorder and the alleles of a polymorphism) (Kidd, 1993). In *population-based* studies (patient and control samples), the spurious associations of this Type 3 variety may arise. It is not, however, a priori obvious that there is population heterogeneity for a particular polymorphism (Devlin, Krontiris, & Risch, 1993). In the absence of heterogeneity, the population-based design is more economical as it requires less genotypings (and subjects) than family-based designs. The latter, in turn, solve the matching problem. The family-based methods (e.g., haplotype relative risk method [Falk & Rubinstein, 1987] and transmission/disequilibrium test [Spielman, McGinnis, & Ewens, 1993]) use case and control samples of *alleles* or haplotypes (rather than subjects),

which are drawn from the same pool of the parental alleles that are *transmitted* or *not transmitted*, respectively, *to the affected offspring*. On the other hand, it would probably be unproductive to reject the population-based approach completely on the a priori assumption of population heterogeneity. Population-based research is often more feasible because it requires fewer genotypings (and subjects) and allows for studying disorders with relatively late onset, such as SA, where probands' parents are less likely to be available for genotyping. In addition, avoiding such sources of stratification as ethnic/racial heterogeneity may decrease the risk of spurious findings. Heterogeneity for a particular polymorphism within a sample of, for example, European Americans, may be insignificant (e.g., Devlin et al., 1993) and thus exert no influence on the association data. A reproduction of positive results of a population-based study on an independent sample or a subsequent family-based research could serve to validate such data.

Another important problem concerning both linkage and association studies of complex traits is a high likelihood of obtaining false-positive results, and certain high threshold levels of significance have been proposed to ensure against that. However, the loci subjected to association analyses are usually not randomly chosen markers but instead represent candidate genes selected on the basis of thorough theoretical and/or experimental considerations. The likelihood that a functional polymorphism, if present at such a gene, influences liability variation, is much higher than that for a randomly selected gene. In addition, the number of genes with functional polymorphisms may be much less than the number of expressed genes. Potential sources of information necessary for the candidate gene selection for drug-related research include neurobiological findings about the role of particular systems and their components in both reward mechanisms and drug response as well as data on genetic polymorphisms in these systems. The power of the candidate gene approach is supported by recent findings (see the next section). Additional information is obtained in substance-use-related linkage studies in animal models.

Human Studies: Substance-Use Disorders

A restriction fragment length polymorphism (RFLP) in the 3' flanking region of the dopamine D_2 receptor gene (DRD2 A), resulting from the alternative presence (A2 allele) or absence (A1 allele) of a restriction site for *Taq*I endonuclease, has been studied in relation to the risk or severity of alcoholism and other forms of SA. Among the results from a number of studies published to date, some revealed association with substance-use disorders (e.g., Arinami et al., 1993; Blum et al., 1990; Comings et al., 1991; Smith et al., 1992), whereas others failed to demonstrate any association (e.g., Bolos et al., 1990; Gelernter et al., 1991; Turner et al., 1992). A study by Parsian et al. (1991) suggested an association based on the results of a population-based analysis, but failed to demonstrate it in a family-based analysis. In a later work from the same group (Suarez et al., 1994), the authors reached an overall conclusion of noninvolvement of "the DRD2 region in the etiology of alcoholism." One meta-analysis of the DRD2 A polymorphism supports an association "between the A1 allele of DRD2 and alcoholism" while pointing out that it is still unproven and the results should be interpreted cautiously because of considerable interpopulational variation in allelic frequencies (Pato, Macciardi, Paato, Verga, & Kennedy, 1993). Another analysis (Gelernter, Goldman, & Risch, 1993) also notes heterogeneity among reported alcoholics and reported controls, but, in contrast with Pato et al.'s conclusions, finds no association and no significant differences in the frequency of the A1 allele between alcoholics and nonalcoholics, or between severe and not severe alcoholics. The direct contribution of this polymorphism to the liability variation seems less likely than linkage disequilibrium between this polymorphism and a liability-influencing polymorphism, considering the location of the DRD2 *Taq*I A variation at approximately 13 kb from the terminal exon of the DRD2 gene. The *Taq*I A polymorphism was in linkage disequilibrium with another *Taq*I RFLP located 5' from the first coding exon of the DRD2 gene (Hauge et al., 1991). DRD2 B has also been studied in relation to alcoholism/SA and was shown in one study to be associated with the liability to polysubstance abuse in a sample of White subjects (Smith et al., 1992). This association was stronger than that reported for *Taq*I A RFLP, which was expected based on the location of the polymorphisms. Moreover, the association with both RFLPs remained significant when heavy alcohol users were removed from the substance-abuse group. The current data suggest a possibility that the DRD2 gene is nonspecifically associated with various liabilities to addictive, compulsive, and impulsive disorders (e.g., Comings et al., 1996).

There have been several studies investigating other genes encoding dopamine receptors and other components of the dopaminergic system, which seems to be a common pathway for the effect of many drugs of abuse. Virtually all of them stimulate dopaminergic neurons and their reinforcing effects—the basis of addiction development—are associated with dopamine release and mesolimbic dopamine reward system (e.g., Koob & Nestler, 1997). The dopamine D1 receptor together with the D5 dopamine receptor are known to constitute the D1 receptor family, whereas D2, D3, and D4 receptors constitute the D2 dopamine receptor family. Both families of receptors function via coupling with G-proteins and stimulating (the D1 family) or inhibiting (the D2 family) adenylate cyclase (Kebabian & Calne, 1979). Relevant to substance abuse, the two receptor families have been found to differ in their role in cocaine reinforcement. Particularly, in rats, the D2-like receptor agonists increase the drive to seek cocaine reinforcement, whereas the D1-like receptor agonists suppress the initiation of cocaine self-administration (Self, Barnhart, Lehman, & Nestler, 1996). An interaction between the two receptor families may, therefore, be important in the determination of drug response. Data obtained in a population-based study on a non-Hispanic Caucasian sample suggest that a polymorphism at the DRD1 gene and the *Taq*I DRD2 A polymorphism are both associated, in the additive fashion, with certain "addictive behaviors" (drinking, smoking, and gambling including pathological gambling) (Comings et al., 1997). No evidence for an association with the liability to alcohol dependence was found in a German sample for DRD2 A polymorphism or for another DRD1 polymorphism, a *Bsp1286I* RFLP (Sander et al., 1995) located in the 3' UTR, whereas there was an elevated frequency of the A1 allele of an exonic DRD3 polymorphism in individuals with a history of alcoholic delirium. No association with the risk for alcoholism was found in a Finnish sample for a functional polymorphism in the DRD4 gene (Adamson et al., 1995), whereas a significant increase in the frequency of one of the alleles was found by an Israeli group in male subjects diagnosed with opioid dependence compared to controls with no history of SA (Ebstein, Kotler, et al., 1996). No association with the liability to SA was found for two polymorphisms located at the 5' and 3' nontranslated regions of the dopamine transporter gene (DAT1) (Persico, Vandenbergh, Smith, & Uhl, 1993). These polymorphisms were also not in linkage disequilibrium with each other. Therefore, as the authors note, a probability still exists that there is a functional polymorphism at this locus whose association with the liability is not detected with the two studied markers because they are not in linkage disequilibrium with that polymorphism. Whereas the dopamine D5 receptor (DRD5) is not directly involved in the mesolimbic dopaminergic reward pathways usually targeted in substance abuse research, it is expressed in the limbic system, particularly the hippocampus, thus potentially participating in the processes involved in memory, emotion regulation, and response to novel stimuli (e.g., Knight, 1996). *In utero* cocaine exposure has been shown to lead to up-regulation of the DRD5 in the fetus (Choi & Ronnekleiv, 1996). The DRD5 has a 10-fold higher affinity for dopamine than the DRD1 and thus may play an important role in the physiology of the central dopaminergic system (Sunahara et al., 1991). Pilot data indicate that variation at the DRD5 gene may be associated with the liability to drug abuse (Vanyukov et al., in press).

Studies of the monoamine oxidase A gene (MAOA) suggest its association with liability to SA/alcoholism (Hsu et al., 1996; Parsian et al., 1995; Vanyukov, Moss, Yu, Tarter, & Deka, 1995). A microsatellite polymorphism at the cannabinoid CB1 (brain) receptor gene (CNR1) (the length of an $(AAT)_n$ repeat) has been found to be associated with IV drug use (Comings et al., 1997). The genotype for this polymorphism coded according to the dichotomized length of the repeat showed the association with drug-related but not alcohol-related variables separated by factor analysis. Other potential candidate genes that may contribute to or be associated with the liability to SA have yet to be studied.

Human Studies: Personality and Behavioral Traits Associated with the Risk for Substance Abuse

It seems plausible that the genetic correlations observed between liabilities to different forms of SA and between these liabilities and certain personality/behavioral traits could be due to the existence of genetic polymorphisms with nonspecific pleiotropic effects contributing to behavioral variation. Recently, data have been obtained indicating associations between temperament/personality dimensions correlated with the liability to SA and polymorphisms at candidate genes. An association has been observed between a polymorphism at the DAT1 gene and attention deficit disorder in children (Cook et al., 1995). Whereas, as previously noted, this polymorphism was not shown to be associated with the liability to SA itself, that negative finding was obtained on an older sample (i.e., for an older population), in which the role of childhood factors in the liability variation may not be as high as for early-onset SA. For instance, *phenotypic* correlations between childhood antisocial problems (the childhood aspects of antisocial personality disorder symptom count) and adult drug-use problems (symptom count constructed from three diagnostic instruments) were lower than those for adult antisocial symptoms and drug problems (0.48 vs. 0.62) (Grove et al., 1990). Nevertheless, childhood psychological problems may be *genetically* more closely related to adult variation in SA liability than adult problems: a genetic correlation between childhood antisocial problems and adult drug problems was higher than the genetic correlation between adult antisocial problems and drug problems (0.87 vs. 0.53).

Testing a hypothesis about involvement of the dopaminergic system in variation in Novelty Seeking, a temperament domain associated with the risk for SA (Cloninger, Svrakic, & Przybeck, 1993), a polymorphism in exon 3 of the dopamine D4 receptor gene has been studied by two research groups, in Israel and the United States (Benjamin et al., 1996; Ebstein, Novick et al., 1996). This polymorphism in the number of repeats of a 48 bp sequence is related to differences in the receptor's properties (its binding to agonists and antagonists and possibly other functional variation). The subjects were grouped by their having 4,4 versus 4,7 (repeats) genotype (the two most common genotypes), or by binning alleles into short and long. Both approaches resulted in the observation of significantly lower scores being associated with short alleles. Sex, age, and population stratification were not found to have an effect on the observed association.

Supporting genetic commonality between novelty seeking and SA liability, a significant increase in the frequency of the longer, 7 repeats, allele was later found by the Israeli group in male subjects diagnosed with opioid dependence compared to controls with no history of SA (Ebstein, Kotler, et al., 1996). This group has also shown a significant reduction of scores on two other traits reflecting the temperament dimensions of Reward Dependence and Persistence, in individuals having the rarer allele causing a *cys-ser* substitution in the serotonin HT2C receptor (Ebstein et al., 1997). This polymorphism and the *gly-ser* variation in the dopamine D3 receptor, another polymorphism in a coding region, were found to interact with the DRD4 exon 3 polymorphism and account together for 13% of Reward Dependence variance and 30% in Persistence variance.

An association between child and adolescent aggression and an increased risk for substance-use disorders is well documented (e.g., Brook, Whiteman, & Finch, 1992; Kandel, Simcha-Fagan, & Davies, 1986; Kellam, Brown, & Fleming, 1982; McCord, McCord, & Gudeman, 1960; White, Brick, & Hansell, 1993). Adult aggressive behavior while under the influence of alcohol and the presence of criminality among adult substance abusers have also been linked to retrospective histories of childhood and adolescent aggression (Jaffe, Babor, & Fishbein, 1988; Muntaner et al., 1989). A study in one Dutch family reported linkage of a dinucleotide polymorphism at the monoamine oxidase A gene with proneness to characteristic behavioral deviations in males featuring aggressive and impulsive behavior and mild mental retardation associated with MAO-A deficiency (Brunner, Nelen, van Zandvoort et al., 1993). A subsequent report by the same authors showed that this syndrome was directly related to a point mutation in the eighth exon of the MAOA gene causing complete absence of MAO-A activity (Brunner, Nelen, Breakefield, Ropers, & van Oost, 1993). Even though this rare mutation hardly contributes to variation in aggressiveness in the general population, the finding suggests that polymorphisms at the MAOA gene could influence this variation.

In summary, the data obtained indicate that certain genes can be strong candidates for association studies involving liability to SA and personality/behavioral characteristics associated with this trait.

Animal Models and Quantitative Trait Loci (QTL)

Despite difficulties in modeling complex human behavior such as drug use, some of its components have been successfully studied in laboratory mice and rats. The aspects studied included sensitivity to drug effects; neuroadaptation related to tolerance, dependence, and withdrawal; and reward/aversion effects. Differences in alcohol preference were found among standard inbred strains of mice (McClearn & Rodgers, 1959). Later, inbred mouse and rat strains were shown to differ in drug tolerance, severity of withdrawal, and operant responding (self-administration) (reviewed by Crabbe, Belknap, & Buck, 1994). This indicated that the mechanisms of variation in these facets of the drug–organism interaction could be based on genetic polymorphisms. Drug-related phenotypic differences standard between inbred strains may be associated with a particular polymorphism by chance, because of parallel differences at another, functionally significant locus. Genetic differences between strains selectively bred to differ in a particular trait,

however, are likely to be either functionally related to the behavior variation or closely linked to such functional polymorphism. The table in the Crabbe et al. (1994) review lists 22 pairs of strains that have been selectively bred for differences in initial sensitivity to alcohol and other drugs (cocaine, diazepam, pentobarbital, levorphanol, haloperidol), as well as preference for, tolerance to, and dependence on, alcohol. Neurochemical and physiological differences and commonalities between the opposite strains point to the systems involved in variation in a particular drug-related phenomenon, such as withdrawal. Common genetic determination of variation, for instance, in the severity of withdrawal from ethanol, diazepam, phenobarbital, and nitrous oxide has been shown by studying mice selectively bred specifically for differences in alcohol-withdrawal severity. A number of provisional markers and candidate genes are identified in the QTL research as associated with various drug-related behaviors and reactions to psychoactive drugs.

A significant proportion of the murine drug-related QTL have human homologs and, moreover, are known to be involved in the determination of central nervous system functioning and drug reaction. For example, a QTL for acute alcohol withdrawal severity has been established and confirmed at a high level of significance (lod score 4.1) for a marker located on murine chromosome 11, contributing 12% of genetic variance (J. Crabbe, personal communication). The region covered includes the potentially relevant loci of GABA-A receptor subunits alpha-1 (19 cM) and gamma-2 (19 cM). Sex-specific QTL for alcohol preference in mice were found on chromosome 2 for males (a region including the cluster of sodium channel alpha-subunit genes), and on chromosome 11 for females (a region including the serotonin transporter locus) (Melo, Shendure, Pociask, & Silver, 1996). A mutation at the gene encoding cAMP-responsive element-binding protein (CREB, a transcription factor) in mice prevents physical symptoms of morphine withdrawal (Maldonado et al., 1996).

Therefore, murine data implicate involvement of certain neurobiological systems in drug-related behaviors, confirm the results obtained in humans, and can serve as additional support for candidate loci. For instance, male mice lacking MAO-A have been shown to manifest increased aggressiveness with parallel dramatic increases in serotonin brain concentrations in the pups (normal levels in adults) as well as elevations in dopamine and norepinephrine (Cases et al., 1995). The DRD2 knockout mice have a total suppression of rewarding behavior with morphine (whereas they show normal response when food is used as a reward) (Maldonado et al., 1997). The DRD3-deficient mice display increased locomotor activity (Accili et al., 1996), which in humans has been associated with an increased risk for SA.

In conclusion, individual differences in substance-use behavior and risk for SA have been shown to be due to both environmental and genotypic variability. Further genetic research may reveal both concrete genes and environmental factors that underlie this variation, and determine the pattern of their interaction along the developmental trajectory toward a positive or negative outcome. This information will provide the basis for individualized prevention and treatment measures.

REFERENCES

Accili, D., Fishburn, C. S., Drago, J., Steiner, H., Lachowicz, J. E., Park, B.-H., Gauda, E. B., Lee, E. J., Cool, M. H., Sibley, D. R., Gerfen, C. R., Westphal, H., & Fuchs, S. (1996). A targeted mutation of the D3 dopamine receptor gene is associated with hyperactivity in mice. *Proceedings of the National Academy of Sciences, 93*, 1945–1949.

Adamson, M. D., Kennedy, J., Petronis, A., Dean, M., Virkkunen, M., Linnoila, M., & Goldman, D. (1995). DRD4 dopamine receptor genotype and CSF monoamine metabolites in Finnish alcoholics and controls. *American Journal of Medical Genetics (Neuropsychiatric Genetics), 60*, 199–205.

Agarwal, D. P., & Goedde, H. W. (1992). Pharmacogenetics of alcohol metabolism and alcoholism. *Pharmacogenetics, 2*, 48–62.

Allison, D. B., Neale, M.C., Kezis, M. I., Alfonso, V. C., Heshka, S., & Heymsfield, S. B. (1996). Assortative mating for relative weight: Genetic implications. *Behavior Genetics, 26*, 103–111.

Alm, P. O., Alm, M., Humble, K., Leppert, J., Sorensen, S., Lidberg, L., & Oreland, L. (1994). Criminality and platelet monoamine oxidase activity in former juvenile delinquents as adults. *Acta Psychiatrica Scandinavica, 89*, 41–45.

Arinami, T., Otokawa, M., Komiyama, T., Mitsushio, H., Mori, H., Mifune, H., Hamaguchi, H., & Toru, M. (1993). Association between severity of alcoholism and the A1 allele of the dopamine D2 receptor gene TaqI A RFLP (in Japanese). *Biological Psychiatry, 33*, 108–114.

Benjamin, J., Li, L., Patterson, C., Greenberg, B. D., Murphy, D. L., & Hamer, D. (1996). Population and familial association between the D4 dopamine receptor gene and Measures of Novelty Seeking. *Nature Genetics, 12*, 81–84.

Blum, K., Noble, E. P., Sheridan, P. J., Montgomery, A., Ritchie, T., Jagadeeswaran, P., Nogami, H., Briggs, A., & Cohn, J.B. (1990). Allelic association of human dopamine D2 receptor gene in alcoholism. *Journal of the American Medical Association, 263*, 2055–2060.

Bohman, M., Cloninger, C. R., Sigvardsson, S., & von Knorring, A.-L. (1983). Gene-environment interaction in the psychopathology of Swedish adoptees: Studies of the origins of alcoholism and criminality. In S. B. Guze, F. J. Earls, & J. E. Barrett (Eds.), *Childhood psychopathology and development* (pp. 265–278). New York: Raven Press.

Bohman, M., Sigvardsson, S., & Cloninger, C. R. (1981). Maternal inheritance of alcohol abuse. *Archives of General Psychiatry, 38*, 965–968.

Bolos, A. M., Dean, M., Lucas-Derse, S., Ramsburg, M., Brown, G. L., & Goldman, D. (1990). Population and pedigree studies reveal a lack of association between the dopamine D2 receptor gene and alcoholism. *Journal of the American Medical Association, 264*, 3156–3160.

Bouchard, T. J., Lykken, D. T., McGue, M., Segal, N. L., & Tellegen, A. (1990). Sources of human psychological differences: The Minnesota study of twins reared apart. *Science, 250*, 223–228.

Brook, J. S., Whiteman, M. M., & Finch, S. (1992). Childhood aggression, adolescent delinquency and drug use: A longitudinal study. *Journal of Genetic Psychology, 153*, 369–383.

Brunner, H. G., Nelen, M., Breakefield, X. O., Ropers, H. H., & van Oost, B. A. (1993). Abnormal behavior associated with a point mutation in the structural gene for monoamine oxidase A. *Science, 262*, 578–580.

Brunner, H. G., Nelen, M. R., van Zandvoort, P., Abeling, N. G. G. M., van Gennip, A. H., Wolters, E. C., Kuiper, M. A., Ropers, H. H., & van Oost, B. A. (1993). X-Linked borderline mental retardation with prominent behavioral disturbance: Phenotype, genetic localization and evidence for disturbed monoamine metabolism. *American Journal of Human Genetics, 52*, 1032–1039.

Buss, A. H., & Plomin, R. (1984). *Temperament: Early developing personality traits.* Hillsdale, NJ: Erlbaum.

Cadoret, R. J. (1978). Psychopathology in adopted-away offspring of biologic parents with antisocial behavior. *Archives of General Psychiatry, 35*, 176–184.

Cadoret, R. J., Troughton, E., O'Gorman, T. W., & Heywood, E. (1986). An adoption study of genetic and environmental factors in drug abuse. *Archives of General Psychiatry, 43*, 1131–1136.

Cadoret, R. J., Yates, W. R., Troughton, E., Woodworth, G., & Stewart, M. A. (1996). An adoption study of drug abuse/dependency in females. *Comprehensive Psychiatry, 37*, 88–94.

Carey, G. (1994). Genetic association study in psychiatry: Analytical evaluation and a recommendation. *American Journal of Medical Genetics (Neuropsychiatric Genetics), 54*, 311–317.

Carey, G., & Williamson, J. A. (1991). Linkage analysis of quantitative traits: Increased power using selected samples. *American Journal of Human Genetics, 49*, 786–796.

Cases, O., Seif, I., Grimsby, J., Gaspar, P., Chen, K., Pournin, S., Müller, U., Aguet, M., Babinet, C., Shih, J. C., & De Maeyer, E. (1995). Aggressive behavior and altered amounts of brain serotonin and norepinephrine in mice lacking MAOA. *Science, 268,* 1763–1777.

Choi, W. S., & Ronnekleiv, O. K. (1996). Effects of in utero cocaine exposure on the expression of mrnas encoding the dopamine transporter and the d1, d2 and d5 dopamine receptor subtypes in fetal rhesus monkey. *Brain Research/Developmental Brain Research, 96,* 249–260.

Christiansen, K. O. (1970). Crime in a Danish twin population. *Acta Geneticae, Medicae et Gemellologiae, 19,* 323–326.

Cloninger, C. R., Bohman, M., & Sigvardsson, S. (1981). Inheritance of alcohol abuse: Cross-fostering analysis of adopted men. *Archives of General Psychiatry, 38,* 861–868.

Cloninger, C. R., Reich, T., & Guze, S. B. (1975). The multifactorial model of disease transmission: II. Sex differences in the familial transmission of sociopathy (antisocial personality). *British Journal of Psychiatry, 127,* 11–22.

Cloninger, C. R., Sigvardsson, S., von Knorring, A.-L., & Bohman, M. (1988). The Swedish studies of the adopted children of alcoholics: A reply to Littrell. *Journal of Studies on Alcohol, 49,* 500–509.

Cloninger, C. R., Svrakic, D. M., & Przybeck, T. R. (1993). A psychobiological model of temperament and character. *Archives of General Psychiatry, 50,* 975–990.

Comings, D. E., Comings, B. G., Muhleman, D., Dietz, G., Shahbahrami, B., Tast, D., Knell, E., Koscis, P., Baumgarten, R., Kovacs, B. W., Levy, D. L., Smith, M., Borison, R., Evans, D. D., Klein, D., MacMurray, J., Tosk, J. M., Sverd, J., Gysin, R., & Flanagan, S. D. (1991). The dopamine D_2 receptor locus as a modifying gene in neuropsychiatric disorders. *Journal of the American Medical Association, 266,* 1793–1800.

Comings, D. E., Gade, R., Wu, S., Chiu, C., Dietz, G., Muhleman, D., Saucier, G., Ferry, L., Rosenthal, R. J., Lesieur, H. R., Rugle, L. J., & MacMurray, P. (1997). Studies of the potential role of the dopamine D_1 receptor gene in addictive behaviors. *Molecular Psychiatry, 2,* 44–56.

Comings, D. E., Rosenthal, R. J., Lesieur, H. R., Rugle, L. J., Muhleman, D., Chiu C., Dietz, G., & Gade, R. (1996). A study of the dopamine d-2 receptor gene in pathological gambling. *Pharmacogenetics, 6,* 223–234.

Cook, E. H., Stein, M. A., Krasowski, M. D., Cox, N. J., Olkon, D. M., Kieffer, J. E., & Leventhal, B. L. (1995). Association of attention-deficit disorder and the dopamine transporter gene. *American Journal of Human Genetics, 56,* 993–998.

Crabbe, J. C., Belknap, J. K., & Buck, K. J. (1994). Genetic animal models of alcohol and drug abuse. *Science, 264,* 1715–1723.

Crow, J. F., & Felsenstein, J. (1968). The effect of assortative mating on the genetic composition of a population. *Social Biology, 15,* 85–97.

Crowe, R. R. (1974). An adoption study of antisocial personality. *Archives of General Psychiatry, 31,* 785–791.

Cruz-Coke, R., & Varela, A. (1966). Inheritance of alcoholism. Its association with colour-blindness. *Lancet, 2,* 1282–1284.

Devlin, B., Krontiris T., & Risch, N. (1993). Population genetics of the HRAS1 minisatellite locus. *American Journal of Human Genetics, 53,* 1298–1305.

Devor, E. J., & Cloninger, C. R. (1989). Genetics of alcoholism. *Annual Review of Genetics, 23,* 19–36.

Eaves, L. J., Eysenck, H. J., & Martin, N. G. (1989). *Genes, culture and personality: An empirical approach.* San Diego: Academic Press.

Ebstein, R. P., Kotler, M., Cohen, H., Segman, R., Gritsenko, I., Nemanov, L., Lerer, B., Kramer, I., Zer-Zion, M., & Kletz, I. (1996, October–November). *Excess dopamine D4 receptor exon III (D4DR) seven repeat allele in opioid dependency.* Abstract, 6th Annual Meeting of The American Society of Human Genetics (San Francisco, California).

Ebstein, R. P., Novick, O., Umansky, R., Priel, B., Osher, Y., Blaine, D., Bennett, E. R., Nemanov, L., Katz, M., & Belmaker, R. H. (1996). Dopamine D4 receptor (D4DR) exon III polymorphism associated with the human personality trait of Novelty Seeking. *Nature Genetics, 12,* 78–80.

Ebstein, R. P., Segman, R., Benjamin, J., Osher, Y., Nemanov, L., & Belmaker, R. H. (1997). 5-HT2C (HTR2C) serotonin receptor gene polymorphism associated with the human personality trait of Reward Dependence. *American Journal of Medical Genetics (Neuropsychiatric Genetics), 74,* 65–72.

Falconer, D. S. (1965). The inheritance of liability to certain diseases, estimated from the incidence among relatives. *Annals of Human Genetics, 29,* 51–76.

Falk, C. T., & Rubinstein, P. (1987). Haplotype relative risks: An easy reliable way to construct a proper control sample for risk calculation. *Annals of Human Genetics, 51,* 227–233.

Farley, F. H., & Davies, S. A. (1977). Arousal, personality, and assortative mating in marriage. *Journal of Sex and Marital Therapy, 3,* 122–127.

Farley, F. H., & Mueller, C. B. (1978). Arousal, personality, and assortative mating in marriage: Generalizability and cross-cultural factors. *Journal of Sex Marital Therapy, 4,* 50–53.

Farrington, D. P. (1991). Antisocial personality from childhood to adulthood. *The Psychologist, 4,* 389–394.

Fowler C. J., Wiberg, A., Oreland, L., Marcusson, J., & Winblad, B. (1980). The effect of age on the activity and molecular properties of human brain monoamine oxidase. *Journal of Neural Transmission, 49,* 1–20.

Gelernter, J., Goldman, D., & Risch, N. (1993). The A1 allele at the D2 dopamine receptor gene and alcoholism. A reappraisal. *Journal of the American Medical Association, 269,* 1673–1677.

Gelernter, J., O'Malley, S., Risch, N., Kranzler, H. R., Krystal, J., Merikangas, K., Kennedy, J. L., & Kidd, K. K. (1991). No association between an allele at the dopamine receptor gene

(DRD2) and alcoholism. *Journal of the American Medical Association, 266*, 1801–1807.

Goldberg, J., Lyons, M. J., Eisen, S. A., True, W. R., & Tsuang, M. (1993). Genetic influence on drug use: A preliminary analysis of 2,674 Vietnam Era veteran twins. *Behavior Genetics, 23*, 552.

Goodwin, D. W., Schulsinger, F., Hermansen, L., Guze, S. B., & Winokur, G. (1973). Alcohol problems in adoptees raised apart from alcoholic parents. *Archives of General Psychiatry, 28*, 238–243.

Goodwin, D. W., Schulsinger, F., Moller, N., Hermansen, L., Winokur, G., & Guze, S. B. (1974). Drinking problems in adopted and nonadopted sons of alcoholics. *Archives of General Psychiatry, 31*, 164–169.

Grove, W. M., Eckert, E. D., Heston, L., Bouchard, T. J., Segal, N., & Lykken, D. T. (1990). Heritability of substance abuse and antisocial behavior: A study of monozygotic twins reared apart. *Biological Psychiatry, 27*, 1293–1304.

Hall, R. L., Hesselbrock, V. M., & Stabenau, J. R. (1983a). Familial distribution of alcohol use: I. Assortative mating in the parents of alcoholics. *Behavioral Genetics, 13*, 361–372.

Hall, R. L., Hesselbrock, V. M., & Stabenau, J. R. (1983b). Familial distribution of alcohol use. II. Assortative mating of alcoholic probands. *Behavioral Genetics, 13*, 373–382.

Harada, S., Agarwal, D. P., Goedde, H. W., Tagaki, S., & Ishikawa, B. (1982). Possible protective role against alcoholism for aldehyde dehydrogenase isozyme deficiency in Japan. *Lancet, 2*, 827.

Hauge, X. Y., Grandy, D. K., Eubanks, J. H., Evans, G. A., Civelli, O., & Litt, M. (1991). Detection and characterization of additional DNA polymorphisms in the dopamine D2 receptor gene. *Genomics, 10*, 527–530.

Hesselbrock, M. N., & Hesselbrock, V. M. (1992). Relationship of family history, antisocial personality disorder and personality traits in young men at risk for alcoholism. *Journal of Studies on Alcohol, 53*, 619–625.

Higuchi, S., Muramatsu, T., Shigemori, K., Saito, M., Kono, H., Dufour, M. C., & Hartford, T. (1992). The relationship between low K_m aldehyde dehydrogenase phenotype and drinking behavior in Japanese. *Journal of Studies on Alcohol, 53*, 170–175. Hill, S.Y, Aston, C., & Rabin, B. (1988). Suggestive evidence of genetic linkage between alcoholism and the MNS blood group. *Alcoholism: Clinical and Experimental Research, 12*, 811–814.

Hill, S. Y., Goodwin, D. W., Cadoret, R., Osterland, C. K., & Doner, S. M. (1975). Association and linkage between alcoholism and serological markers. *Journal of Studies on Alcohol, 36*, 981–992.

Hodge, S. E. (1994). What association analysis can and cannot tell us about the genetics of complex disease. *American Journal of Medical Genetics (Neuropsychiatric Genetics), 54*, 318–323.

Hsu, Y.-P., Loh, E. W., Chen, W. J., Chen, C. C., Yu, J.-M., & Cheng, A. T. A. (1996). Association of monoamine oxidase A with alcoholism among male Chinese in Taiwan. *American Journal of Psychiatry, 153*, 1209–1211.

Jacob, T., & Bremer, D. A. (1986). Assortative mating among men and women alcoholics. *Journal of Studies on Alcohol, 47*, 219–222.

Jaffe, J. H., Babor, T. F., & Fishbein, D. H. (1988). Alcoholics, aggression and antisocial personality. *Journal of Studies on Alcohol, 49*, 211–218.

Kandel, D. B., Simcha-Fagan, O., & Davies, M. (1986). Risk factors for delinquency and illicit drug use from adolescence to young adulthood. *Journal on Drug Issues, 60*, 67–90.

Kebabian, J. W., & Calne, D. B. (1979). Multiple receptors for dopamine. *Nature, 277*, 93–96.

Kellam, S. G., Brown, C. H. & Fleming, J. P. (1982). Developmental epidemiological studies of substance abuse in Woodlawn: Implications for prevention research strategy. *National Institute on Drug Abuse (NIDA) Research Monograph, 41*, 21–33.

Kendler, K. S., Gardner, C. O., & Prescott, C. A. (1997). Religion, psychopathology, and substance use and abuse; a multimeasure, genetic-epidemiologic study. *American Journal of Psychiatry, 154*, 322–329.

Kendler, K. S., Neale, M. C., Heath, A. C., Kessler, R. C., & Eaves, L. J. (1994). A twin-family study of alcoholism in women. *American Journal of Psychiatry, 151*, 707–715.

Kendler, K. S., Neale, M. C., Prescott, C. A., Kessler, R.C., Heath, A. C., Corey, L. A., & Eaves, L. J. (1996). Childhood parental loss and alcoholism in women: A causal analysis using a twin-family design. *Psychological Medicine, 26*, 79–95.

Kidd, K. K. (1993). Associations of disease with genetic markers: Déjà vu all over again. *American Journal of Medical Genetics (Neuropsychiatric Genetics), 48*, 71–73.

Knight, R. T. (1996). Contribution of human hippocampal region to novelty detection. *Nature, 383*, 256–259.

Koob, G. F., & Nestler, E. J. (1997). The neurobiology of drug addiction. *Journal of Neuropsychiatry and Clinical Neurosciences, 9*, 482–497.

Lahey, B. B., Piacentini, J. C., McBurnett, K., Stone, P., Hartdagen, S., & Hynd, G. (1988). Psychopathology in the parents of children with conduct disorder and hyperactivity. *Journal of the American Academy of Child and Adolescent Psychiatry, 27*, 163–170.

Maldonado, R., Blendy, J. L., Tzavara, E., Gass, P., Roques, B. P., Hanoune, J., & Schütz, G. (1996). Reduction of morphine abstinence in mice with a mutation in the gene encoding CREB. *Science, 273*, 657–659.

Maldonado, R., Salardi, A., Valverde, O., Samad, T. A., Roques, B. P., & Borrelli, E. (1997). Absence of opiate rewarding effects in mice lacking dopamine D2 receptors. *Nature, 388*, 586–589.

Mascie-Taylor, C. G. N., & Vandenberg, S. G. (1988). Assortative mating for IQ and personality due to propinquity and personal preference. *Behavioral Genetics, 18*, 339–345.

McClearn, G. E., & Rodgers, D. A. (1959). Differences in alcohol preference among inbred strains of mice. *Quarterly Journal of Studies on Alcohol, 20*, 691–695.

McCord, W., McCord, J., & Gudeman, J. (1960). *Origins of alcoholism*. Palo Alto, CA: Stanford University Press.

McGue, M., Pickens, R. W., & Svikis, D. S. (1992). Sex and age effects on the inheritance of alcohol problems: A twin study. *Journal of Abnormal Psychology, 101*, 3–17.

McGue, M., Sharma, A., & Benson, P. (1996). Parent and sibling influences on adolescent alcohol use and misuse—Evidence from a US adoption cohort. *Journal of Studies on Alcohol, 57*, 8–18.

McGuffin, P., & Thapar, A. (1992). The genetics of personality disorder. *British Journal of Psychiatry, 160*, 12–23.

Melo, J. A., Shendure, J., Pociask, K., & Silver, L. M. (1996). Identification of sex-specific quantitative trait loci controlling alcohol preference in C57BL/6 mice. *Nature Genetics, 13*, 147–153.

Merikangas, K. (1982). Assortative mating for psychiatric disorders and psychological traits. *Archives of General Psychiatry, 39*, 1173–1180.

Merikangas, K. R., Leckman, J. F., Prusoff, B. A., Pauls, D. L., & Weissman, M. M. (1985). Familial transmission of depression and alcoholism. *Archives of General Psychiatry, 42*, 367–372.

Merikangas, K. R., Weissman, M. M., Prusoff, B. A., & John, K. (1988). Assortative mating and affective disorders: Psychopathology in offspring. *Psychiatry, 51*, 48–57.

Merikangas, K. R., Weissman, M. M., Prusoff, B. A., Pauls, D. L., & Leckman, J. F. (1985). Depressives with secondary alcoholism: Psychiatric disorders in offspring. *Journal of Studies on Alcohol, 46*, 199–204.

Moskalenko, V. D., Vanyukov, M. M., Solovyova, Z. V., Rakhmanova, T. V., & Vladimirsky, M. M. (1992). A genetic study of alcoholism in the Moscow population: Preliminary findings. *Journal of Studies on Alcohol, 53*, 218–224.

Muntaner, D., Nagoshi, C., Jaffe, J. H., Walter, D., Haertzen, C., & Fishbein, D. (1989). Correlates of self-reported early childhood aggression in subjects volunteering for drug studies. *American Journal on Alcohol Abuse, 15*, 383–402.

Neale, M. C. & Cardon, L. R. (1992). *Methodology for genetic studies of twins and families*. Boston: Kluwer Academic.

Oreland, L., von Knorring, L., von Knorring, A.-L., & Bohman, M. (1985). Studies on the connection between alcoholism and low platelet monoamine oxidase activity. *Progress in Alcohol Research, 1*, 83–117.

Parsian, A., Suarez, B. K., Tabakoff, B., Hoffman, P., Ovchinnikova, L., Fisher, L., & Cloninger, C. R. (1995). Monoamine oxidases and alcoholism. I. Studies in unrelated alcoholics and normal controls. *American Journal of Medical Genetics (Neuropsychiatric Genetics), 60*, 409–416.

Parsian, A., Todd, R. D., Devor, E. J., O'Malley, K. L., Suarez, B. K., Reich, T., & Cloninger, C. R. (1991). Alcoholism and alleles of the human D_2 dopamine receptor locus. Studies of association and linkage. *Archives of General Psychiatry, 48*, 655–663.

Pato C. N., Macciardi, F., Pato, M. T., Verga, M., & Kennedy, J. L. (1993). Review of the putative association of dopamine D2 receptor and alcoholism: A meta-analysis. *American Journal of Medical Genetics (Neuropsychiatric Genetics), 48*, 78–82.

Pedersen, N. L., Gatz, M., Plomin, R., Nesselroade, J. R., & McClearn, G. E. (1989). Individual differences in locus of control during the second half of the life span for identical and fraternal twins reared apart and reared together. *Journal of Gerontology, 44*, 100–105.

Pedersen, N. L., Lichtenstein, P., Plomin, R., DeFaire, U., McClearn, G. E., & Matthews, K. A. (1989). Genetic and environmental differences for Type A-like measures and related traits: A study of twins reared apart and reared together. *Psychosomatic Medicine, 51*, 428–440.

Penick, E. C., Powell, B. J., Bingham, S. F., Liskow, B. I., Miller, N. S., & Read, M. R. (1987). A comparative study of familial alcoholism. *Journal of Studies on Alcohol, 48*, 136–146.

Persico, A. M., Vandenbergh, D. A., Smith, S. S., & Uhl, G. R. (1993). Dopamine transporter gene polymorphisms are not associated with polysubstance abuse. *Biological Psychiatry, 34*, 265–267.

Pickens, R. W., Svikis, D. S., McGue, M., Lykken, D. T., Heston, L. L., & Clayton, P. J. (1991). Heterogeneity in the inheritance of alcoholism: A study of male and female twins. *Archives of General Psychiatry, 48*, 19–28.

Plomin, R., Pedersen, N. L., McClearn, G. E., Nesselroade, J. R., & Bergeman, C. S. (1988). EAS temperaments during the last half of the life span: Twins reared apart and twins reared together. *Psychology and Aging, 3*, 43–50.

Reich, T., Cloninger, C. R., Van Eerdewegh, P., Rice J. P., & Mullaney, J. (1988). Secular trends in the familial transmission of alcoholism. *Alcoholism: Clinical and Experimental Research, 12*, 458–64.

Risch, N., & Merikangas, K. (1996). The future of genetic studies of complex human diseases. *Science, 273*, 1516–1517.

Risch, N., & Zhang, H. (1995). Extreme discordant sib pairs for mapping quantitative trait loci in humans. *Science, 268*, 1584–1589.

Robins, L. N., & Price, R. K. (1991). Adult disorders predicted by childhood conduct problems: Results from the NIMH epidemiologic catchment area project. *Psychiatry, 54*, 116–132.

Sander, T., Harms, H., Podschus, J., Finckh, U., Nickel, B., Rolfs, A., Rommelspacher, H. & Schmidt, L. G. (1995). Dopamine D1, D2 and D3 receptor genes in alcohol dependence. *Psychiatric Genetics, 5*, 171–176.

Schuckit, M. A., Li, T.-K., Cloninger, C. R., & Dietrich, R. A. (1985). Genetics of alcoholism. *Alcoholism: Clinical and Experimental Research, 9*, 475–492.

Self, D. W., Barnhart, W. J., Lehman, D. A., & Nestler, E. J. (1996). Opposite modulation of cocaine-seeking behavior by

D_1- and D_2-like dopamine receptor agonists. *Science, 271,* 1586–1589.

Shih, J. C., Grimsby, J., Chen, K., & Zhu, Q. (1993). Structure and promoter organization of the human monoamine oxidase A and B genes. *Journal of Psychiatry and Neuroscience, 18,* 25–32.

Smith, S. S., O'Hara, B. F., Persico, A. M., Gorelick, D. A., Newlin, D. B., Vlahov, D., Solomon, L., Pickens, R., & Uhl, G. R. (1992). Genetic vulnerability to drug abuse. The D_2 dopamine receptor TaqI B1 restriction fragment length polymorphism appears more frequently in polysubstance abusers. *Archives of General Psychiatry, 49,* 723–727.

Spielman, R. S., McGinnis, R. E., & Ewens, W. J. (1993). Transmission test for linkage disequilibrium: The insulin gene region and insulin-dependent diabetes mellitus (IDDM). *American Journal of Human Genetics, 52,* 506–516.

Suarez, B. K., Parsian, A., Hampe, C. L., Todd, R. D., Reich, T., & Cloninger, C. R. (1994). Linkage disequilibria at the D2 dopamine receptor locus (DRD2) in alcoholics and controls. *Genomics, 19,* 12–20.

Sunahara, R. K., Guan, H. C., O'Dowd, B. F., Seeman, P., Laurier, L. G., Ng, G., Georger, S. R., Torchia, J., Van Tol, H. H. M. & Niznik, H. B. (1991). Cloning of the gene for a human dopamine D_5 receptor with higher affinity for dopamine than D_1. *Nature, 350,* 614–619.

Swan, G. E., Carmelli, D., & Rosenman, R. H. (1986). Spouse-pair similarity on the California Psychological Inventory with reference to husband's coronary heart disease. *Psychosomatic Medicine, 48,* 172–186.

Swinson, R. P. (1973). Phenylthiocarbamide taste sensitivity in alcoholism. *British Journal of Addiction: Alcohol and Other Drugs, 68,* 33–36.

Tabakoff, B., Lee, J. M., De Leon-Jones, F., & Hoffman, P. L. (1985). Ethanol inhibits the activity of the B form of monoamine oxidase in human platelet and brain tissue. *Psychopharmacology, 87,* 152–156.

Tanna, V. L., Wilson, A. F., Winokur, G., & Elston, R. C. (1988). Possible linkage between alcoholism and esterase-D. *Journal of Studies on Alcohol, 49,* 472–476.

Tarter, R. E., & Vanyukov, M. M. (1994). Stepwise developmental model of alcoholism etiology. In R. Zucker, G. Boyd, & J. Howard, (Eds.), *The development of alcohol problems: Exploring the biopsychosocial matrix of risk* (pp. 303–330, NIH Publication No. 94-3495). Rockville, MD: NIAAA.

Thomasson, H. R., Crabb, D. W., Edenberg, H. J., & Li, T.-K. (1993). Alcohol and aldehyde dehydrogenase polymorphisms and alcoholism. *Behavior Genetics, 23,* 131–136.

Turner, E., Ewing, J., Shilling, P., Smith, T. L., Irwin, M., Schuckit, M., & Kelsoe, J. R. (1992). Lack of association between an RFLP near the D_2 dopamine receptor gene and severe alcoholism. *Biological Psychiatry, 31,* 285–290.

Vanyukov, M. M., Moss, H. B., Gioio, A. E., Hughes, H. B., Kaplan, B. B, & Tarter, R. E. (1998). An association between a microsatellite polymorphism at the DRD5 gene and the liability to substance abuse. *Behavior Genetics, 28,* pp. 75–86.

Vanyukov, M. M., Moss, H. B., Plail, J. A., Blackson, T., Mezzich, A. C., & Tarter, R. E. (1993). Antisocial symptoms in preadolescent boys and in their parents: Associations with cortisol. *Psychiatric Research, 46,* 9–17.

Vanyukov, M. M., Moss, H. B., & Tarter, R. E. (1994). Assortment for the liability to substance abuse and personality traits. *Annals of the New York Academy of Science, 708,* 102–107.

Vanyukov, M. M., Moss, H. B., Yu, L. M., Tarter, R. E., & Deka, R. (1995). Preliminary evidence for an association of a dinucleotide repeat polymorphism at the MAOA gene with early onset alcoholism/substance abuse. *American Journal of Medical Genetics (Neuropsychiatric Genetics), 60,* 122–126.

Vanyukov, M. M., Neale, M. C., Moss, H. B., & Tarter, R. E. (1996). Mating assortment and the liability to substance abuse. *Drug and Alcohol Dependence, 42,* 1–10.

Vanyukov, M. M., Neale, M. C., Moss, H. B., & Tarter, R. E. (submitted) Homogamy for antisocial behavior and the liability to substance abuse.

von Knorring, A.-L., Hallman, J., von Knorring, L., & Oreland, L. (1991). Platelet monoamine oxidase in Type 1 and Type 2 alcoholism. *Alcohol and Alcoholism, 26,* 409–416.

White, H. R, Brick, J., & Hansell, S. (1993). A longitudinal investigation of alcohol use and aggression in adolescence. *Journal of Studies on Alcohol, Suppl. 11,* 62–77.

Wilson, A. F., Elston, R. C., Mallott, D. B., Tran, L. D., & Winokur, G. (1991). The current status of linkage studies of alcoholism and unipolar depression. *Psychiatric Genetics, 2,* 107–124.

Yates, R. W., Cadoret, R. J., Troughton, E., & Stewart, M. A. (1996). An adoption study of DSM-IIIR alcohol and drug dependence severity. *Drug and Alcohol Dependence, 41,* 9–15.

Zuckerman, M. (1972). Drug usage as one manifestation of a "sensation seeking" trait. In W. Keup (Ed.), *Drug abuse: Current concepts and research* (pp. 54–163). Springfield, IL: Thomas.

CHAPTER 9

PSYCHOPHYSIOLOGY

Peter R. Finn

Psychophysiology is essentially the study of psychological processes using physiologically based measurement methods (Turpin, 1989). Typically, psychophysiologists assess the electrical correlates of central (CNS) and/or autonomic nervous system (ANS) activity (e.g., electrocortical, electrodermal, cardiac, vasomotor, muscular) associated with psychologically relevant manipulations (e.g. stress induction, placebos), states (e.g., sleep, intoxication), and/or traits (e.g., psychological disorders, personality traits). Psychophysiological studies of substance use and abuse represent a diverse literature of studies examining the autonomic, somatic, and electrocortical correlates of abuse/dependence diagnoses, level of drug use, elevated risk status, drug challenge and intoxication, withdrawal, tolerance, relapse, fetal drug exposure, treatment response, predictors of treatment response, and the sequelae of abuse.

This chapter only discusses those studies that are potentially informative about etiological processes in substance abuse (SA) and does not represent an exhaustive review of this literature. The discussion has a heavy focus on high-risk studies that represent the major etiological themes and findings. In addition, the primary emphasis is on alcohol abuse because the bulk of psychophysiological studies focus on alcohol.

The risk factors receiving the most attention in this literature are a positive family history of (FHP) substance abuse and undercontrolled antisocial behavior. Considerable empirical support for these two general risk factors comes from family and adoption studies (e.g., Cadoret, Troughton, O'Gorman, & Heywood, 1986; Cloninger, Bohman, & Sigvardsson, 1981) and longitudinal studies of behavioral/personality predictors of SA (Farrington, 1991; Rydelius, 1983; Shedler & Block, 1990). The primary goal of high-risk research is to identify characteristics that distinguish unaffected (i.e., nonabusing) high-risk individuals from persons at low risk for SA. Such factors are thus predictive of risk and may be related to a predisposition to develop SA.

ELECTROCORTICAL STUDIES

Much of the high-risk research is inspired by the notion that genetic factors play a significant role in the etiology of SA (Cloninger et al., 1981; McGue, Pickens, & Svikis, 1992). Many studies seek to identify genetic markers for a predisposition to SA by first identifying risk-specific psychophysiological characteristics that are, themselves, also genetically transmitted. Studies of genetic markers generally do not aim to elucidate etiological mechanisms per se,

141

but simply assess the predictive relationship between the marker and the risk factor. The majority, and perhaps the most promising, of such studies have focused on measures of electrocortical activity as candidate markers for a genetic predisposition to alcoholism (Begleiter & Porjesz, 1988). These studies include studies of the event-related potential (e.g., Begleiter, Porjesz, Bihari, & Kissin, 1982) and quantitative electroencephalographic (EEG) activity (e.g. Gabrielli et al., 1982). In addition to electrocortical studies of risk markers, there is literature on the effects of alcohol on EEG activity that investigates etiological mechanisms, such as reinforcement and/or individual differences in sensitivity or tolerance to drug challenge.

Event-Related Potentials (ERPs)

Background

The ERP is an EEG waveform that is elicited in response to specific events (stimuli) and is thought to reflect fundamental cognitive processes. The P300 is a large positive moving component of the ERP with a latency of about 300 ms that is generated in tasks where the subject has to attend to, or discriminate between, different stimuli (Polich, 1991). Typically, studies use "oddball" discrimination tasks where the subject has to detect the occurrence of an infrequent target stimulus from a set of stimuli, presented one at a time at a rapid rate, containing mostly nontarget stimuli. The P300 is thought to reflect the brain activity associated with the allocation of attentional resources to a specific stimulus (Polich, Pollock, & Bloom, 1994). The P300 is usually larger for infrequent, task-relevant, important stimuli presented in tasks where discrimination is difficult.

Family History Risk

Because the early studies associating a family history of alcoholism with an attenuated amplitude of the P300 component of the ERP (Begleiter et al., 1982; Elmasion, Neville, Woods, Schuckit, & Bloom, 1982), an extensive literature on risk-related ERP characteristics has accumulated. In fact, the ERP is probably the most widely studied risk-related psychophysiological measure in the SA literature. Although the literature is not entirely consistent, overall the data suggest that males with a positive family history (FHP) of alcoholism have reduced P300s on difficult visual discrimination tasks compared with family his-

tory negative (FHN) subjects (Polich et al., 1994). Many studies report that nonalcoholic subjects (mostly males) with a FHP for alcoholism have smaller P300s to target stimuli, when presented in the standard oddball task, compared with FHN subjects (e.g., Hill & Steinhauer, 1993; O'Connor, Hesselbrock, & Tasman, 1986; Porjesz & Begleiter, 1990; Ramachandran, Porjesz, Begleiter, & Litke, 1996; Whipple, Parker & Noble, 1988). One report linked reductions in P300 amplitude and a positive family history for SA other than alcoholism (Brigham, Herning, & Moss, 1995). However, a substantial number of studies have reported no P300 differences between FHP versus FHN samples (e.g., Hill, Steinhauer, Zubin, & Baughman, 1988; Polich & Bloom, 1987, 1988). To make sense of the discrepancies between studies, Polich et al. (1994) conducted a meta-analysis of P300 studies and examined the influence of moderator variables, such as recruitment sources, task difficulty and modality (auditory/visual), and subject age, on P300 amplitude. Polich et al. (1994) found an overall effect size of 0.33 indicating that across all studies, FHP subjects had smaller P300s than FHN subjects. Furthermore, moderator analyses indicated that attenuated P300s in FHP subjects were more likely to be observed with younger subjects (<17 years) on difficult visual tasks. Polich et al.'s (1994) results suggest that reduced P300s may be related to maturational lags in FHP subjects and may possibly reflect subtle cognitive deficits only apparent on tasks with a high processing demand.

Undercontrolled, Antisocial Behavior

Whereas the research supports a link between a FHP for SA and a reduced P300 amplitude, the relationship between antisocial personality (ASP) and P300 is less clear (Bauer, O'Connor, & Hesselbrock, 1994; Howard, 1989). Some studies associate ASP with enhanced P300s (e.g., Raine & Venables, 1988), but others report smaller P300s in antisocial individuals (Bauer, O'Connor, & Hesselbrock, 1994; Herning, Hickey, Pickworth, & Jaffe, 1989). Potential reasons for these discrepancies are differences across studies in sample composition, task types, P300 measurement criteria (see Howard, 1989), and definitions of antisocial traits, as well as a lack of control for previous head injury, and other psychiatric or neurological disorders (see Bauer et al., 1994). Studies that employ standard oddball tasks and P300 measurement criteria while controlling for head injury and psychiatric/neurological disorder report that ASP is associated with decrements in P300 amplitudes

(Bauer, 1996; Bauer, Hesselbrock, et al., 1994; Bauer, O'Connor, & Hesselbrock, 1994; O'Connor, Bauer, Tasman, & Hesselbrock, 1994). The data also indicate that alcoholics, or abstinent substance abusers, who also have histories of antisocial/violent behavior have the largest decrements in P300 amplitude (Branchey, Buydens-Branchey, & Horvath, 1993; Branchey, Buydens-Branchey, & Lieber, 1988). Interestingly, Bauer (1996) reported that reduced P300s in abstinent cocaine abusers were more strongly correlated with a history of childhood conduct problems than adult ASP symptoms.

Conclusion

Although there does appear to be a relationship between SA risk and a reduced P300, the precise meaning of the reduced P300 and its implication for the etiology of SA are not known. Nevertheless, the amplitude of the P300 is significantly influenced by genetic factors (Polich & Burns, 1987) and, as it is attenuated in both alcoholics and their offspring (Whipple, Berman, & Noble, 1991; Whipple et al., 1988), it has good potential as a genetic marker for alcoholism (Begleiter & Porjesz, 1988), and possibly other SA. Indeed, recent studies suggest that reduced P300s in childhood are predictive of adolescent drug and alcohol abuse (Berman, Whipple, Fitch, & Noble, 1993; Hill, Steinhauer, Lowers, & Locke, 1995). In addition, reduced P300s have been reported to be predictive of relapse in abstinent cocaine abusers (Bauer, 1996).

Quantitative EEG Activity

Background

EEG studies of SA typically focus on differences between abusers and nonabusers, or between high- and low-risk subjects, in EEG activity (energy or power) while sober or after drug challenge. EEG activity is quantified in terms of the power or energy with the standard frequency bands, delta (.7–3.8 Hz), theta (4–7 Hz), slow alpha (8–10 Hz), fast alpha (10–12 Hz), slow beta (13–18 Hz), and fast beta (19–28 Hz). Although there are a number of reports of risk-related differences in EEG activity (sober or postalcohol), the studies often do not discuss at any length the psychological significance of these differences. This is because EEG, in general, is a rather crude measure of CNS activity, and the relationship between EEG activity and psychological process is complex and often dependent on the type of task or sample (Davidson & Ehrlichman, 1980; Ray & Cole, 1985). A relatively simplistic interpretation of EEG activity is that (1) a preponderance of slower wave activity (delta, theta, slow alpha) is associated with cortical underarousal (Raine, Venables, & Williams, 1990); (2) drug-induced increases in slow alpha are associated with euphoria or relaxation (Lukas, Mendelson, Benedikt, & Jones, 1985); (3) suppression of alpha is associated with greater activation (Blackburn, 1978); (4) greater alpha suppression in right versus left hemisphere is associated with negative emotion (Henriques & Davidson, 1990); and (5) higher beta activity is associated with cortical arousal during cognitive, emotional, and stress tasks (Finn, Ramsey, & Earleywine, 1996; Ray & Cole, 1985).

Family History Studies

Although studies indicate that alcoholics tend to have lower levels of EEG alpha activity and higher levels of beta activity (Begleiter & Platz, 1982), the results of research on resting EEG activity in the offspring of alcoholics are mixed. One study reported that nonalcoholic FHP subjects show larger amounts of fast beta activity (Gabrielli et al., 1982) with no differences in alpha. Another reported that only FHP subjects with a history of ASP show excess fast beta (Bauer & Hesselbrock, 1993). Still another study showed that FHP subjects had higher levels of fast alpha (Ehlers & Schuckit, 1991). Finally, many studies have failed to find any FHP/FHN differences in resting EEG activity while sober (Cohen, Porjesz, & Begleiter, 1991, 1993a; Ehlers & Schuckit, 1990; Finn et al., 1996; Kaplan, Hesselbrock, O'Connor, & De Palma, 1988; Pollock et al., 1983).

The inconsistencies across studies may be due to the heterogeneity within FHP risk (Finn et al., 1997) with samples varying in terms of parental psychopathology, offspring psychopathology, or the density of familial alcoholism. It may also be that resting quantitative EEG, which is a linear and static measure of activity, is not sensitive to the type of brain function that characterizes familial risk. Two types of findings suggest that FHPs do differ from FHNs on EEG indices of brain dynamics: studies that involve CNS challenge (e.g., Bauer & Hesselbrock, 1993) and studies that employ dynamical systems approaches to assessing brain activity (Ehlers, Havstad, & Schuckit, 1995).

Studies indicate that when you challenge the CNS with a stressor (Finn et al., 1996), a placebo (Bauer & Hesselbrock, 1993), or a drug (Pollock et al., 1983), FHPs clearly differ from FHNs on EEG measures of responsiveness. Finn et al. (1996) report that under conditions of threat, FHP subjects show significant decreases in frontal EEG alpha and no increases in frontal and central beta, whereas FHN subjects show large increases in frontal and central beta with little change in alpha. Finn et al. (1996) interpret their findings as suggestive of disinhibitory adaptive mechanisms in FHP subjects. Also, Bauer and Hesselbrock (1993) report that FHP subjects show significantly larger increases in EEG fast alpha after placebo, possibly reflecting greater activation, or compensatory responses after placebo challenge (see Earleywine & Finn, 1994). Numerous studies, reviewed next, indicate differential EEG responses to alcohol challenge in FHPs versus FHNs.

In order to capture nonlinear, dynamical aspects of brain activity (e.g., complexity), Ehlers, Havstad, and Schuckit (1995) employed a dynamical systems approach to analyzing EEG, rather than a standard Fourier transform. Ehlers et al. (1995) found that FHP subjects had a lower EEG attractor dimension than did FHN controls, suggesting that the EEG of FHPs is less complex than that of FHN subjects. A less complex EEG may reflect a more immature, less sophisticated or well developed level of CNS functioning. The results of Ehlers et al. (1995) indicates the strong potential that dynamical systems analyses has for assessing CNS activity.

Undercontrolled, Antisocial Behavior

The literature on EEG correlates of antisocial behavior is also inconclusive (Raine, 1995). Whereas some reviews suggest a link between antisocial personality or traits and lower levels of cortical arousal (e.g., Hare, 1970), others indicate major problems with the research (e.g., Raine, 1995) and some studies suggest that ASP is related to high levels of cortical activation (Bauer & Hesselbrock, 1993; Blackburn, 1978). On the one hand, Raine et al. (1990) report that increased EEG slow-wave activity at age 15 years was strongly predictive of criminal activity at age 24 years. But on the other hand, Bauer and Hesselbrock (1993) report that ASP in young adults was associated with faster resting frontal EEG activity (beta). Blackburn (1978) also found that psychopaths had greater alpha suppression during cold pressor challenge compared with controls, which is suggestive of greater cortical activation. Finally, in Finn et al.'s (1996) study of EEG responses to threat, antisocial, aggressive traits were associated with a somewhat paradoxical pattern of increased activation (sup-

pression of frontal alpha), and decreased activation (smaller increase in beta).

Drug Challenge Studies

Most EEG/drug challenge studies set out to assess basic drug reinforcement mechanisms. In general, drug-induced increases in slow alpha activity are thought to reflect positively reinforcing drug effects because of their association with euphoria (Lukas et al., 1985). Conversely, researchers also imply that reductions in faster EEG activity (fast alpha or beta activity) reflect negative reinforcement processes (Pollock et al., 1983), although the psychological/mood correlates of reductions in fast EEG activity are not known.

There is considerable evidence that euphoria experienced after psychoactive drug ingestion (alcohol, marijuana, morphine, cocaine, pentobarbital) is associated with enhanced slow alpha EEG activity (Lukas et al., 1985, 1989). In fact, the primary effect of alcohol on human EEG is to increase slow alpha activity (Begleiter & Platz, 1972; Cohen, Porjesz & Begleiter, 1993b). Interestingly, a recent study of the predictors of ad lib laboratory drinking found that low levels of slow alpha power significantly predict amount of alcohol consumed (Finn, Casey, Ramsey, & Sharkansky, 1994). Although research findings are again somewhat mixed overall, the studies suggest that FHP males are more sensitive to the slow alpha enhancing effects (Cohen et al., 1993a; Pollock et al., 1983) and the fast alpha reducing effects of alcohol (Bauer & Hesselbrock, 1993; Pollock et al., 1983).

Pollock et al. (1983) found that FHP subjects had greater increases in slow alpha and greater decreases in fast alpha after alcohol compared with FHN subjects. Bauer and Hesselbrock (1993) found that FHP subjects had greater decreases in fast alpha after alcohol, but did not differ from FHNs in slow alpha alcohol effects. Kaplan et al. (1988) report similar trends for enhanced slow alpha in FHPs versus FHNs after alcohol. In a recent study of effects of alcohol on rising and descending limbs of the blood-alcohol curve (BAC), Cohen et al. (1993a) found that FHP subjects showed a greater enhancement of slow alpha on the rising BAC limb compared with FHN subjects. Furthermore, FHP subjects showed significantly larger decreases in slow alpha on the descending BAC limb. Cohen et al. (1993a) comment that their results indicate that FHPs show greater acute sensitization to alcohol on the rising BAC limb and greater acute tolerance on the descending limb compared with FHNs. Cohen et al.'s (1993a) findings are consistent with Newlin and Thompson's (1990) differentiator model of FHP alcohol effects, where FHP subjects are more sensitive to alcohol's reinforcing effects at rising BACs and more tolerant when the BAC is descending. Although these studies are interesting, other studies report that FHN subjects show greater decreases in fast alpha after alcohol (Ehlers & Schuckit, 1991) and FHP subjects show greater increases in fast beta after alcohol (Ehlers & Schuckit, 1990).

Conclusion

Research in support of a relationship between resting EEG and risk for SA is weak. There appears to be a stronger relationship between EEG measures and risk when the CNS is challenged or when one employs a dynamical analysis of EEG. Drug challenge studies suggest that a FHP of SA is associated with an increased sensitivity to the positive and negatively reinforcing effects of alcohol, especially on the rising limb of the BAC. Less is known about the specific response to drug challenge in persons with undercontrolled behavior. Newlin and Thompson's (1990) differentiator model is a promising framework to investigate the relationship between SA risk and sensitivity and tolerance to drugs.

AUTONOMIC AND SOMATIC NERVOUS SYSTEM (ANS/SNS) STUDIES

Autonomic Nervous System (ANS) Function in At-Risk Individuals.

Background

Studies of ANS/SNS function in at-risk individuals typically use ANS (e.g., heart rate, skin conductance) or SNS (muscle tension) measures to assess response characteristics (traits) in sober, at-risk individuals that may predispose toward SA. These studies are based on two general models of vulnerability: a disregulated hyperreactive, FHP disposition model (Finn, Zeitouni & Pihl, 1990) and a low-fear, disinhibited, antisocial disposition model (Iacono, Lyyken & McGue, in press). These two types of vulnerability may represent different pathways to drug problems (Finn et al., 1997). A disregulated hyperreactive disposition may lead individuals to abuse drugs or alcohol as a means of self-medication, whereas, in the case of a disinhibited disposition, substance abuse may be one of many examples of the failure to appropriately inhibit behavior in the face of negative consequences.

Family History Studies

There is substantial evidence that FHP males with multi-generational family histories of alcoholism are hyperreactive to stress on cardiovascular measures. In a number of studies, Finn and colleagues found that adult FHP males with a multigenerational family history of alcoholism (but not unigenerational FHP males) were hyperreactive to the threat of aversive stimulation on measures of heart rate (HR) and vasoconstriction (VC) compared with controls (Finn, Earleywine, & Pihl, 1992; Finn & Pihl, 1987; Finn, Zeitouni, & Pihl, 1990; Stewart, Finn, & Pihl, 1992). In addition, Harden and Pihl (1995) reported that FHP boys were hyperreactive to a stressor on HR and VC measures compared with FHN boys. Conrod, Pihl, and Ditto (1995) reported a similar, but nonsignificant, trend for multigenerational FHP adult males to be hyperreactive to stress on measures of heart rate and muscle tension. Hill, Steinhauer, and Zubin (1992) reported that FHP subjects had higher baseline heart rate levels compared with FHN controls, although other studies report no baseline FHP/FHN differences in ANS activity (e.g., Finn et al., 1992; Harden & Pihl, 1995; McCaul, Turkkan, Svikis, & Bigelow, 1990). Finally, O'Malley, Sinha, & Babineau (1993) found that only FHP subjects whose alcoholic parent also had an anxiety disorder were hyperreactive on cardiovascular measures to a stressor. Levenson, Oyama, and Meek (1987) did not report any family history differences in reactivity to a stressor, although it is unclear whether their FHP subjects had multigenerational histories of alcoholism. Some studies also suggest that, in addition to being hyperreactive to aversive stimulation, FHP males (Cohen, Schandler, & McArthur, 1990; Finn, Zeitouni, & Pihl, 1990) and FHP females (Stewart, Finn, Peterson, & Pihl, 1996) are hyperreactive on skin conductance (SC) measures to nonaversive stimuli as well.

Recent studies of SC reactivity by Finn and colleagues suggest a somewhat different pattern of SC reactivity in FHP males. In a classical conditioning study designed to test the low-fear, disinhibited model of vulnerability, FHP males failed to develop a classically conditioned SC response to tones signalling shock and did not show SC response differentiation between signal and nonsignal stimuli (Finn, Kessler, & Hussong, 1994). In addition, a smaller SC response to conditioned stimuli was predictive of an increased level of alcohol problems (Finn, Kessler, & Hussong, 1994). Interestingly, the FHP subjects in Finn, Zeitouni, and Pihl's (1990) study who were hyperreactive on cardiovascular measures also tended to show smaller increases in SC to unavoidable shock compared with FHN subjects, a pattern similar to that reported by Hare, Frazelle, and Cox (1978) in psychopaths. FHPs also did not differentially respond to avoidable versus unavoidable shock, whereas FHNs did show the expected pattern of greater SC reactivity to unavoidable versus avoidable shock (Finn, Zeitouni, & Pihl, 1990). Furthermore, another study showed that FHP males fail to show SC discrimination between target and nontarget stimuli in an operant-type task (Finn, Earleywine, & Ramsey, 1990). The reasons for the differences in FHP reactivity between studies is unclear, but it is possible that somewhat different populations were being sampled in Quebec (Finn, Zeitouni, & Pihl, 1990; Stewart et al., 1992) and in Indiana (Finn, Earlywine, & Ramsey, 1990; Finn, Kessler, & Hussong, 1994). However, a failure to discriminate between important classes of stimuli was apparent in three different contexts (anticipation, operant, and classical conditioning) with three different FHP samples (Finn, Earleywine, & Ramsey, 1990; Finn, Kessler, & Hussong, 1994; Finn, Zeitouni, & Pihl, 1990).

Undercontrolled, Antisocial Behavior

Research suggests that undercontrolled, antisocial behavior is associated with electrodermal underresponsivity to the threat of aversive stimulation (e.g., Lyyken, 1957; Siddle, 1977). Lyyken (1957, 1995) proposed that a fundamental mechanism underlying a propensity toward antisocial, psychopathic behavior was a lack of fear when faced with the prospect of aversive events and a failure to learn to avoid such events. A large body of literature provides strong support that, on SC measures, antisocial individuals are underreactive to conditioned stimuli signaling aversive events (Hare, 1965; Hare & Quinn, 1971; Lyyken, 1957), to conflict (Waid & Orne, 1982), and while anticipating an aversive event (Hare et al., 1978). In addition, the data suggest that antisocial individuals also experience large increases in heart rate, concomitant with smaller SC increases, while awaiting an unavoidable aversive event (Hare et al., 1978). The increased heart rate in psychopaths has been interpreted to reflect behavioral activation or active coping, rather than fear (Fowles, 1983; Hare, 1978). It should be noted that Finn and colleagues observed sim-

ilar increases in heart rate while anticipating an aversive event, but in the absence of reduced overall SC reactivity (Finn, Zeitouni, & Pihl, 1990). Consistent with a low-fear, disinhibitory model of risk for SA, Finn, Kessler, & Hussong (1994) also report that smaller SC responses to conditioned stimuli signaling shock are predictive of alcohol problems in FHP males. Furthermore, other work suggests that smaller SC orienting responses are predictive of antisocial behavior (Raine et al., 1990; Siddle, 1977). A promising avenue of research would be the investigation of the relationship among measures of autonomic reactivity, antisocial tendencies, anxiety/depression, familial psychopathology, and SA problems as a means of testing the disregulated hyperreactive and the disinhibited model of SA vulnerability.

Conclusion

The research indicates a somewhat consistent relationship between risk for SA (FHP and undercontrolled behavior) and electrodermal (SC) underresponsiveness and poor electrodermal differentiation between signal and nonsignal stimuli. Furthermore, both risk factors have been associated with increased cardiovascular reactivity while anticipating an aversive stimulus. In spite of these consistencies, questions remain about the comparability between FHP and ASP risk factors on measures of ANS responsivity and the relationship between comorbid parental psychopathology and FHP proband ANS activity.

Autonomic and Somatic Nervous System Responses to Drug Challenge

Studies of ANS/SNS responses to drug challenge are usually designed to identify potential reinforcing effects of substances of abuse. The majority of ANS studies have focused on negative reinforcement models of alcohol effects, such as tension-reduction (Cappell & Herman, 1972), stress-response dampening (Sher & Levenson, 1982), and appraisal-disruption models (Sayette, 1993). Because activity in the sympathetic branch of the ANS is increased when exposed to stressful or aversive events, the typical experimental paradigm involves the examination of the effects of alcohol on stress-induced sympathetic activation (heart rate, vasoconstriction, and SC). Studies of potential positive reinforcement mechanisms typically interpret drug-induced increases in baseline heart rate as reflecting the stimulating effects of a drug (Peterson, Pihl,

Sequin, Finn, & Stewart, 1993), as heart rate increases have been associated with positive reinforcement mechanisms (Fowles, 1983) and increases in plasma endorphin levels (Peterson et al., 1996).

Negative Reinforcement Mechanisms

The majority of the human studies have investigated the tension-reduction hypothesis by assessing the effects of alcohol on stress-related ANS activity. Reviews of studies testing the tension-reduction hypothesis of alcohol effects often present a mixed picture (see Cappell & Herman, 1972). Some studies reported that alcohol, and expectancies for alcohol, were associated with heart rate increases during a stressor (e.g., Abrams & Wilson, 1979), whereas others reported that alcohol is associated with decreased heart rate reactivity to a stressor (e.g., Wilson, Abrams, & Lipscomb, 1980). Different methodologies and various conceptual problems plagued the early literature, making it difficult to assess whether alcohol actually does reduce stress-related ANS activity. For instance, moderate to high doses of alcohol typically result in large increases in baseline heart rate (e.g., Stewart et al., 1992). Some of the past studies may have incorrectly interpreted alcohol-related heart rate increases as reflecting increased stress (e.g., Keane & Lisman, 1980; Sutker, Allain, Brantley, & Randall, 1982); however, recent research suggests that alcohol-induced baseline heart rate increases are manifestations of positive reinforcement processes, rather than stress related (Peterson et al., 1996).

Another reason for the mixed results of the studies testing the tension-reducing effects of alcohol may be due to the effects of temporal sequence of stressor and alcohol consumption (Sayette & Wilson, 1991). Sayette and Wilson (1991) found that heart rate reactivity is accentuated if drinking occurs after stress induction, whereas it is dampened if the stress is applied after alcohol consumption (Sayette & Wilson, 1991). In other words, alcohol may serve to buffer the autonomic response to an impending stressor, but it could make matters worse if one tries to drink to reduce the ANS arousal due to an already present stressor.

A recent study of alcohol's effect on startle–eyeblink responses suggests that the startle–eyeblink–emotion methodology may provide a unique window on drug effects on general CNS arousal and the processing of emotion (Stritzke, Patrick, & Lang, 1995). Stritzke et al. (1995) report that alcohol does not alter the normal pattern of affective modulation of the startle reflex, although it does appears to dampen the overall magnitude of the startle reflex (i.e., basic CNS arousal mechanisms). Subjects, whether sober or intoxicated, still showed a potentiation of the startle response when exposed to aversive visual stimuli and an attenuation of startle when exposed to pleasant stimuli (Stritzke et al., 1995). However, the overall magnitude of the startle response was reduced in all affective conditions (Stritzke et al., 1995). On the other hand anxiolytic drugs, such as diazepam, block the startle potentiation effect of aversive stimuli, but do not affect the degree of startle reactivity (Patrick, Berthot, & Moore, 1993). These two studies suggest that separate neural processes mediate the processing of emotions related to aversive events and the arousal processes that may influence the overall psychological significance of these emotions. Furthermore, this methodology seems to be a useful tool for the process of separating out the important neuropsychopharmacological actions of drugs. Startle–probe methodology, perhaps combined with traditional ANS/SNS methodologies, is a promising tool for understanding the interaction between drug effects, psychological states, and neural processes.

Negative Reinforcement and Individual Differences

Another factor that contributed to the inconsistencies in the literature on alcohol's tension-reduction effect was that studies failed to account for individual differences in sensitivity to alcohol's tension-reducing effects. A substantial literature has accumulated over the past 15 years that indicates that individuals at risk for alcohol problems are more sensitive to the stress-dampening effects of alcohol. Numerous studies indicate that FHP subjects, especially those with a multigenerational family history of alcoholism, are more sensitive to the stress-response-dampening (SRD) effects of alcohol, compared with FHN controls (Conrod et al., 1995; Finn & Pihl, 1987; Finn, Zeitouni, & Pihl 1990; Finn et al.,1992; Levenson, et al., 1987). The cardiovascular SRD effect of alcohol may serve to normalize the hyperreactivity of some FHP subjects, perhaps increasing the likelihood for abuse. O'Malley et al.'s (1993) findings suggest that only FHP subjects whose alcoholic parent also has an anxiety disorder experience SRD effects, although these results require further replication. Stewart et al. (1992) report that FHP subjects only experience the SRD effects of alcohol at moderate to high doses (0.75 ml/kg and above). Research also suggests that FHP subjects are more sensitive to alcohol's dampening of stress-induced SNS (muscle tension) reactivity (Conrod et al., 1995; Finn, Zeitouni, & Pihl, 1990; Schuckit, Engstrom, Alpert, & Duby, 1981). In addition, alcohol has been reported to dampen SC hyperreactivity to nonaversive stimuli in FHP males and females (Finn, Zeitouni, & Pihl, 1990; Stewart et al., 1996).

Research also indicates that undercontrolled personality traits (Sher & Levenson, 1982; Levenson et al., 1987), trait hostility (Zeichner, Giancola, & Allen, 1995), and Type A personality traits (Zeichner, Edwards, & Cohen, 1985) also are associated with an increased sensitivity to the SRD effects of alcohol.

Positive Reinforcement Mechanisms

Although relatively understudied, as suggested by recent research, alcohol-induced increases in heart rate are ANS manifestations of the positive reinforcement effects of alcohol (and possibly other drugs as well). Numerous studies show that moderate to high doses of alcohol result in a significant increase in heart rate (Levenson, Sher, Grossman, Newman, & Newlin, 1980; Stewart et al., 1992). Furthermore, increases in alcohol-induced heart rate are reported to correspond to periods when reports of intoxication (Sutker et al., 1982) or euphoria (Lukas et al., 1985) are the highest. In addition, the immediate intoxicating effects of marijuana (oral and smoked) are strongly associated with substantial heart rate increases (Chait & Zacny, 1992; Kelly, Foltin, & Fischman, 1993). Fowles (1983) convincingly demonstrates that heart rate increases,associated with consummatory or approach situations,are linked to positive reinforcement. It is interesting to note that in Abrams and Wilson (1979) the largest increases in heart rate are associated with the expectation (approach preparedness) of consuming alcohol.

Recent research has provided more direct support for the association between alcohol-induced heart rate increases, positive reinforcement, and risk for alcoholism. Peterson et al. (1993) report that the degree of alcohol-induced increases in resting heart rate predicts the degree of self-reported alcohol intake. A number of studies report that FHP subjects show larger increases in resting heart rate than FHN subjects (Conrod et al., 1995; Finn, Zeitouni, & Pihl, 1990; Stewart et al., 1992). Furthermore, Peterson et al. (1996) report that alcohol-induced increases in heart rate are strongly correlated with plasma beta-

endorphin levels (r = 0.8). Considerable evidence suggests that alcohol's positive reinforcing effects are mediated via the endorphin system (Froehlich, 1994). Recent research by J. B. Peterson (personal communication, May 1996) indicates that the heart rate increases seen in FHP subjects occur only on the rising BAC limb, suggesting that FHP subjects are more sensitive to the positive reinforcing effects of alcohol but only on the rising BAC limb (see Newlin & Thompson, 1990, for a discussion of BAC limb and alcohol effects).

A cautionary note should be added with respect to the relationship between heart rate increases and drug-related positive reinforcement. First, drug-induced increases in heart rate may also be due to other aspects of drug action completely unrelated to any CNS reinforcement effects (e.g., the action of the drug directly on the cardiovascular system or on adrenal glands secreting adrenaline). Second, the positive reinforcing effects of some drugs of abuse may not be reflected in increased heart rate (e.g., morphine). Finally, the heart rate increase is itself not taken as being reinforcing; it is interpreted as reflecting some other neuropsychological event that is the putative primary reinforcer (e.g., dopamine activation).

Conclusion

There is very strong support for the relationship between risk factors for alcoholism and the cardiovascular stress-reactivity-dampening effect of alcohol. However, it seems to be the case that alcohol may accentuate stress reactions when consumed after a stressor, at least in some persons and in laboratory situations. Studies of the effects of alcohol and diazepam on the affective modulation of startle suggest differential actions between these two drugs (Patrick et al., 1993; Stritzke et al., 1995). Furthermore, the startle methodology appears to be a promising new avenue for psychophysiological investigations of drug action and SA etiology.

SUMMARY

Psychophysiological research has provided a number of valuable clues about the etiology of substance abuse. Research suggests that a predisposition to drug abuse may be associated with certain cognitive brain deficits (P300/ERP), potential brain activity differences (EEG), cardiovascular hyperreactivity to stressors, electrodermal (SC) hyporeactivity to aversive stimuli, and an increased sensitivity to the negative and positive reinforcing effects of drugs, specifically alcohol. Although these studies provide potentially valuable information and promising approaches in research in etiology, there are a number of issues and gaps in the research that must be addressed. First, there is a general lack of research with women, and we still know much less about etiological factors with women.

Second, there are many studies that are essentially atheoretical (especially the electrocortical studies), and do not address the importance of the results for etiology. Studies addressing the relevance of P300 deficits, for example, in the etiology of SA are long overdue. Longitudinal analyses using multiple outcome measures (SA, behavior problems, cognitive functioning) as well as multiple predictive measures (density of family history, other familial psychopathology, personality/behavioral traits, relational/family functioning) could help shed light on the role of electrocortical or autonomic deficits.

Finally, the risk factors noted (FHP and undercontrolled behavior) are heterogeneous, with considerable variation across individuals included in these categories (Finn et al., in press; Lyyken, 1995; Penick et al., 1984). The research has generally failed to account for this heterogeneity by treating a risk factor (e.g., FHP) as if it were homogeneous. It is imperative that studies account for the overlap between family history of SA and family/personal history of antisocial behavior, the overlap between antisocial behavior and other types of dysfunction (negative affect), and patterns of co-occurrence between SA and other psychopathology. This necessitates the use of much larger samples in order to account for the effects of these important sources of variance.

REFERENCES

Abrams, D. B., & Wilson, G. T. (1979). Effects of alcohol on social anxiety in women: Cognitive versus physiological processes. *Journal of Abnormal Psychology, 88,* 161–173.

Bauer, L. O. (1996). *Frontal P300 decrements, childhood conduct disorder, and the prediction of relapse among abstinent cocaine abusers.* Manuscript submitted for publication.

Bauer, L. O., & Hesselbrock, V. M. (1993). EEG, autonomic and subject correlates of the risk for alcoholism. *Journal of Studies on Alcohol, 54,* 577–589.

Bauer, L. O., Hesselbrock, V., O'Connor, S., & Roberts, L. (1994). P300 differences between nonalcoholic young men at average and above average risk for alcoholism: Effects of distraction and task modality. *Progress in Neuropsychopharmacology and Biological Psychiatry, 18,* 263–277.

Bauer, L. O., O'Connor, S., & Hesselbrock, V. M. (1994). Frontal P300 decrements in antisocial personality disorder. *Alcoholism: Clinical and Experimental Research, 18,* 1300–1305.

Begleiter, H., & Platz, A. (1972). The effects of alcohol on the central nervous system in humans. In B. Kissin & H. Begleiter (Eds.), *The biology of alcoholism* (Vol.2, pp. 293–343). New York: Plenum Press.

Begleiter, H., & Platz, A. (1982). The effects of alcohol on the central nervous system in humans. In B. Kissin & H. Begleiter (Eds.), *The biology of alcoholism* (pp. 293–343). New York: Plenum.

Begleiter, H., & Porjesz, B. (1988). Potential biological markers in individuals at high risk for developing alcoholism. *Alcoholism: Clinical and Experimental Research, 12,* 488–493.

Begleiter, H., Porjesz, B., Bihari, B., & Kissin, B. (1982). Event-related brain potentials in boys at risk for alcoholism. *Science, 225,* 1493–1496.

Berman, S. M., Whipple, S. C., Fitch, R. J., & Noble, E. (1993). P3 in young boys as a predictor of adolescent substance use. *Alcohol, 10,* 69–76.

Blackburn, R. (1978). Psychopathy, arousal, and the need for stimulation. In R. D. Hare & D. Schalling (Eds.), *Psychopathic behavior: Approaches to research* (pp. 156–185). New York: Wiley.

Branchey, M. H., Buydens-Branchey, L., & Horvath, T. B. (1993). Event-related potentials in substance-abusing individuals after long-term abstinence. *American Journal on Addictions, 2,* 141–148.

Branchey, M. H., Buydens-Branchey, L., & Leiber, C. S. (1988). P3 in alcoholics with disordered regulation of aggression. *Psychiatry Research, 25,* 49–58.

Brigham, J., Herning, R. J., & Moss, H. B. (1995). Event-related potentials and alpha synchronization in preadolescent boys at risk for psychoactive substance abuse. *Biological Psychiatry, 37,* 834–846.

Cadoret, R. J., Troughton, E., O'Gorman, T. W., & Heywood, E. (1986). An adoption study of genetic and environmental factors in drug abuse. *Archives of General Psychiatry, 43,* 1131–1136.

Cappell, H., & Herman, C. P. (1972). Alcohol and tension reduction; A review. *Quarterly Journal of Studies on Alcohol, 33,* 33–64.

Chait, L. D., & Zacny, J. P. (1992). Reinforcing and subjective effects of oral D-sup-9-THC and smoked marijuana in humans. *Psychopharmacology, 107,* 255–262.

Cloninger, C. R., Bohman, M., & Sigvardsson, S. (1981). Inheritance of alcohol abuse. *Archives of General Psychiatry, 38,* 861–868.

Cohen, H. L., Porjesz, B., & Begleiter, H. (1991). EEG characteristics in males at risk for alcoholism. *Alcoholism: Clinical and Experimental Research, 15,* 858–861.

Cohen, H. L., Porjesz, B., & Begleiter, H. (1993a). The effects of ethanol on EEG activity in males at risk for alcoholism. *Electroencephalography and Clinical Neurophysiology, 86,* 368–376.

Cohen, H. L., Porjesz, B., & Begleiter, H. (1993b). Ethanol induced alterations in EEG activity in adult males. *Neuropsychopharmacology, 8,* 365–370.

Cohen, M. J., Schandler, A. L., & McArthur, D. L. (1990). Orienting behavior in adult children of alcoholics. *Psychophysiology, 27(4A),* S22.

Conrod, P. J., Pihl, R. O., & Ditto, B. (1995). Autonomic reactivity and alcohol-induced dampening in men at risk for alcoholism and men at risk for hypertension. *Alcoholism: Clinical and Experimental Research, 19,* 482–489.

Davidson, R. J., & Ehlrichman, H. (1980). Lateralized cognitive processes and the electroencephalogram. *Science, 207,* 1005–1006.

Earleywine, M., & Finn, P. R. (1994). Compensatory responses to placebo vary with presumed personality "risk" for alcoholism and drinking habits. *International Journal of Addiction, 29,* 583–591.

Ehlers, C. L., Havstad, J. W., & Schuckit, M. A. (1995). EEG dimension in sons of alcoholics. *Alcoholism: Clinical and Experimental Research, 19,* 992–998.

Ehlers, C. L., & Schuckit, M. A. (1990). EEG fast frequency activity in the sons of alcoholics. *Biological Psychiatry, 27,* 631–641.

Ehlers, C. L., & Schuckit, M. A. (1991). Evaluation of EEG alpha activity in sons of alcoholics. *Neuropsychopharmacology, 4,* 199–205.

Elmasion, R., Neville, H., Woods, D., Schuckit, M., & Bloom, F. (1982). Event-related brain potentials are different in individuals at high and low risk for developing alcoholism. *Proceedings of the National Academy of Sciences, 79,* 7900–7903.

Farrington, D. P. (1991). Childhood aggression and adult violence: Early predictors and later outcomes. In D. J. Pepler & K. H. Rubin (Eds.), *The development and treatment of childhood aggression* (pp. 5–29). New York: Plenum.

Finn, P. R., Casey, A., Ramsey, S., & Sharkansky, E. J. (1994). EEG and personality predictors of ad lib alcohol consumption. *Alcoholism: Clinical and Experimental Research, 18,* 430.

Finn, P. R., Earleywine, M., & Pihl, R. O. (1992). Sensation seeking, stress reactivity and alcohol dampening discriminate the density of a family history of alcoholism. *Alcoholism: Clinical and Experimental Research, 16,* 585–590.

Finn, P. R., Earleywine, M., & Ramsey, S. (1990). Orienting to relevant, irrelevant, and novel stimuli: The effects of alcohol and high-risk status. *Psychophysiology, 27(4A),* S30.

Finn, P. R., Kessler, D. N., & Hussong, A. M. (1994). Risk for alcoholism and classical conditioning to signals for punishment: Evidence for a weak behavioral inhibition system? *Journal of Abnormal Psychology, 103,* 293–301.

Finn, P. R., & Pihl, R. O. (1987). Men at high risk for alcoholism: The effect of alcohol on cardiovascular response to unavoidable shock. *Journal of Abnormal Psychology, 96,* 230–236.

Finn, P. R., Ramsey, S. E., & Earleywine, M. (1996). Threat, EEG, alcoholism-risk, and disinhibition. *Alcoholism: Clinical and Experimental Research, 20* (Suppl.), 34A.

Finn, P. R., Sharkansky, E. J., Viken, R., West, T. L., Sandy, J., & Bufferd, G. M. (1997). Heterogeneity in the families of sons of alcoholics: The impact of familial vulnerability type on offspring characteristics. *Journal of Abnormal Psychology,* 106, pp. 26–36.

Finn, P. R., Zeitouni, N., & Pihl, R. O. (1990). Effects of alcohol on psychophysiological hyperreactivity to nonaversive and aversive stimuli in men at high risk for alcoholism. *Journal of Abnormal Psychology, 99,* 79–85.

Fowles, D. C. (1983). Motivational effects of heart-rate and electrodermal activity: Implications for research on personality and psychopathology. *Journal of Research on Personality, 17,* 48–71.

Froelich, J. C., & Li. T. K. (1994). Opioid involvement in alcohol drinking. *Annals of the New York Academy of Science, 31,* 156–167.

Gabrielli, W. F., Mednick, S. A., Volavka, J., Pollock, V. E., Schulsinger, F., & Itil, T. M. (1982). Electroencephalograms in children of alcoholic fathers. *Psychophysiology, 19,* 404–407.

Harden, P. W., & Pihl, R. O. (1995). Cognitive function, cardiovascular reactivity, and behavior in boys at high risk for alcoholism. *Journal of Abnormal Psychology, 104,* 94–103.

Hare, R. D. (1965). Acquisition and generalization of a conditioned fear response in psychopathic and nonpsychopathic criminals. *Journal of Psychology, 59,* 367–370.

Hare, R. D. (1970). *Psychopathy: Theory and practice.* New York: Wiley.

Hare, R. D. (1978). Electrodermal and cardiovascular correlates of psychopathy. In R. D. Hare & D. Schalling (Eds.), *Psychopathic behavior: Approaches to research* (pp. 107–144). New York: Wiley.

Hare, R. D., Frazelle, J., & Cox, D. N. (1978). Psychopathy and physiological responses to threat of an aversive stimulus. *Psychophysiology, 15,* 165–172.

Hare, R. D., & Quinn, M. J. (1971). Psychopathy and autonomic conditioning. *Journal of Abnormal Psychology, 71,* 223–235.

Henriques, J. B., & Davidson, R. J. (1990). Regional brain electrical asymmetries discriminate between previously depressed and healthy control subjects. *Journal of Abnormal Psychology, 99,* 22–31.

Herning, R. I., Hickey, J. E., Pickworth, W. B., & Jaffe, J. H. (1989). Auditory event-related potentials in adolescents at risk-drug abuse. *Biological Psychiatry, 25,* 598–609.

Hill, S. Y., & Steinhauer, S. (1993). Assessment of prepubertal and post-pubertal boys and girls at risk for developing alcoholism with P300 from a visual discrimination task. *Journal of Studies on Alcohol, 54,* 350–358.

Hill, S. Y., Steinhauer. S., Lowers, L., & Locke, J. (1995). Eight-year longitudinal follow-up of P300 and clinical outcome in children from high-risk for alcoholism families. *Biological Psychiatry, 37*, 823–827.

Hill, S. Y., Steinhauer, S., & Zubin, J. (1992). Cardiac responsivity in individuals at high-risk for alcoholism. *Journal of Studies on Alcohol, 53*, 378–388.

Hill, S. Y., Steinhauer, S. R., Zubin, J., & Baughman, T. (1988). Event-related potentials as markers for alcoholism risk in high density families. *Alcoholism: Clinical and Experimental Research, 12*, 545–554.

Howard, R. (1989). Evoked potentials and psychopathy: A commentary on Raine. *International Journal of Psychophysiology, 8*, 23–27.

Iacono, W. G., Lyyken, D. T., & McGue, M. (in press). Psychophysiological prediction of drug abuse. In H. Gordon & M. Glantz (Eds.), *Biobehavioral etiology of drug abuse.* Rockville, MD: National Institute on Drug Abuse.

Kaplan, R. F., Hesselbrock, V. M., O'Connor, S., & De Palma, N. (1988). Behavioral and EEG responses to alcohol in nonalcoholic men with a family history of alcoholism. *Progress in Neuropsychopharmacology and Biological Psychiatry, 12*, 873–885.

Keane, T. M., & Lisman, A. A. (1980). Alcohol and social anxiety in males: Behavioral, cognitive, and physiological effects. *Journal of Abnormal Psychology, 89*, 213–223.

Kelly, T. H., Foltin, R. W., & Fischman, M. W. (1993). Effects of smoked marijuana on heart rate, drug ratings, and task performance. *Behavioral Pharmacology, 4*, 167–178.

Levenson, R. W., Sher, K. J., Grossman, L., Newman, J., & Newlin, D. (1980). Alcohol and stress response dampening: Pharmacological effects, expectancy, and tension reduction. *Journal of Abnormal Psychology, 89*, 528–538.

Levenson, R. W., Oyama, O. N., & Meek, P. S. (1987). Greater reinforcement from alcohol for those at risk: Parental risk, personality risk, and sex. *Journal of Abnormal Psychology, 96*, 242–253.

Lukas, S. E., Mendelson, J. H., Amass, L., & Benedikt, R. A. (1989). Behavioral and EEG studies of acute cocaine administration: Comparisons with morphine, amphetamine, pentobarbital, nicotine, ethanol, and marijuana. *National Institute on Drug Abuse Research Monograph Series, 95*, 146–151.

Lukas, S. E., Mendelson, J. H., Benedikt, R. A., & Jones, B. (1985). EEG alpha activity increases during transient episodes of ethanol-induced euphoria. *Pharmacology, Biochemistry and Behavior, 25*, 889–895.

Lykken, D. T. (1957). A study of anxiety in the sociopathic personality. *Journal of Abnormal and Social Psychology, 55*, 6–10.

Lyyken, D. T. (1995). *The antisocial personalities.* Hillsdale, NJ: Erlbaum.

McCaul, M. E., Turkkan, J. S., Svilkis, D. S., & Bigelow, G. E. (1990). Alcohol and secobarbital effects as a function of familial alcoholism: Acute psychophysiological effects. *Alcoholism: Clinical and Experimental Research, 14*, 704–712.

McGue, M., Pickens, R. W., & Svikis, D. S. (1992). Sex and age effects on the inheritance of alcohol problems: A twin study. *Journal of Abnormal Psychology, 101*, 3–17.

Newlin, D. B., & Thompson, J. B. (1990). Alcohol challenge with sons of alcoholics: A critical review and analysis. *Psychological Bulletin, 108*, 383–342.

O'Connor, S., Bauer, L., Tasman, A., & Hesselbrock, V. (1994). Reduced P3 amplitudes are associated with both a family history of alcoholism and antisocial personality. *Progress in Neuropsychopharmacology and Biological Psychiatry, 18*, 1307–1321.

O'Connor, S., Hesselbrock, V., & Tasman, T. (1986). Correlates of increased risk for alcoholism. *Progress in Neuropsychopharmacology and Biological Psychiatry, 10*, 211–218.

O'Malley, S., Sinha, R., & Babineau, A. J. (1993). Family history of alcoholism and anxiety; stress response dampening effects of alcohol. *Alcoholism: Clinical and Experimental Research, 17*, 467.

Patrick, C. J., Berthot, B., & Moore, J. D. (1993). Effects of diazepam on startle reflex potentiation in human subjects. *Psychophysiology, 30*, S49.

Penick, E. C., Powell, B. J., Othmer, E., Bingham, S. F., Rice, A. S., & Liese, B. S. (1984). Subtyping alcoholics by coexisting psychiatric syndromes: Course, family history, outcome. In D. W. Goodwin, N. T. Van Dusen, & S. A. Mednick (Eds.), *Longitudinal research in alcoholism* (pp 167–196). Boston: Kluwer-Nijhoff.

Peterson, J. B., Pihl, R. O., Gianoulakis, C., Conrod, P., Finn, P. R., Stewart, S. H., LeMarquand, D. G., & Bruce, K. R. (1996). *Ethanol-induced change in cardiac and endogenous opiate function and risk for alcoholism.* Manuscript submitted for publication.

Peterson, J. B., Pihl, R. O., Sequin, J. R., Finn, P. R., & Stewart, S. H. (1993). Heart-rate reactivity and alcohol consumption among sons of male alcoholics and sons of non-alcoholics. *Journal of Psychiatric Neuroscience, 18*, 190–198.

Polich, J. (1991). P300 in clinical applications: Meaning, method, and measurement. *American Journal of EEG Technology, 31*, 201–231.

Polich, J., & Bloom, F. E. (1987). P300 from normals and adult children of alcoholics. *Alcohol, 4*, 301–305.

Polich, J., & Bloom, F. E. (1988). Event-related brain potentials in individuals at high and low risk for developing alcoholism: Failure to replicate. *Alcoholism: Clinical and Experimental Research, 12*, 368–373.

Polich, J., & Burns, T. (1987). P300 from identical twins. *Neuropsychologia, 25*, 299–304.

Polich, J., Pollock, V. E., & Bloom F. E. (1994). Meta-analysis of P300 amplitude from males at risk for alcoholism. *Psychological Bulletin, 115*, 55–73.

Pollock, V. E., Volvaka, J., Goodwin, D. W., Mednick, S. A., Gabrielli, W. F., Knop, J., & Schulsinger, F. (1983). The EEG after alcohol administration in men at risk for alcoholism. *Archives of General Psychiatry, 40*, 857–861.

Porjesz, B., & Beglieter, H. (1990). Event-related potentials in individuals at risk for alcoholism. *Alcohol, 7*, 465–469.

Raine, A. (1995). *The psychopathology of crime.* New York: Academic.

Raine, A., & Venables, P. H. (1988). Enhanced P3 evoked potentials and longer P3 recovery times in psychopaths. *Psychophysiology, 25*, 30–38.

Raine, A., Venables, P. H., & Williams, M. (1990). Relationships between central and autonomic measures of arousal at age 15 years and criminality at age 24 years. *Archives of General Psychiatry, 47*, 1003–1007.

Ramachandran, G., Porjesz, B., Begleiter, H., & Litke, A. (1996). A simple auditory oddball task in young adult males at high risk for alcoholism. *Alcoholism: Clinical and Experimental Research, 20*, 9–15.

Ray, W. J., & Cole, H. W. (1985). EEG alpha activity reflects attentional demands, and beta activity reflects emotional and cognitive processes. *Science, 228*, 750–752.

Rydelius, P. A. (1983). Alcohol abusing teenage boys: Testing a hypothesis on the relationship between alcohol abuse and social background factors, criminality, and personality in teenage boys. *Acta Psychiatrica Scandinavica, 68*, 368–380.

Sayette, M. A. (1993). An appraisal-disruption model of alcohol's effects on stress responses in social drinkers. *Psychological Bulletin, 114*, 459–476.

Sayette, M. A., & Wilson, G. T. (1991). Intoxication and exposure to stress: Effects of temporal patterning. *Journal of Abnormal Psychology, 100*, 56–62.

Schuckit, M. A., Engstrom, D., Alpert, R., & Duby, J. (1981). Differences in muscle tension response to ethanol in young men with and without family histories of alcoholism. *Journal of Studies on Alcohol, 42*, 918–924.

Shedler, J., & Block, J. (1990). Adolescent drug use and psychological health: A longitudinal study. *American Psychologist, 45*, 612–630.

Sher, K. J., & Levenson, R. W. (1982). Risk for alcoholism and individual differences in the stress–response–dampening effect of alcohol. *Journal of Abnormal Psychology, 91*, 350–367.

Siddle. D. A. (1977). Electrodermal activity and psychopathy. In S. A. Mednick & K. O. Christiansen (Eds.), *Biosocial bases of criminal behavior* (pp. 199–211). New York: Gardner.

Stewart, S. H., Finn, P. R., Peterson, J. B., & Pihl, R. O. (1996). *The effects of alcohol on electrodermal orienting in daughters of multigenerational alcoholic males.* Manuscript submitted for publication.

Stewart, S. H., Finn, P. R., & Pihl, R. O. (1992). The effects of alcohol on the cardiovascular stress response in men at high risk for alcoholism: A dose response study. *Journal of Studies on Alcohol, 53*, 499–504.

Stritzke, W. G., Patrick, C. J., & Lang, A. R. (1995). Alcohol and human emotion: A multidimensional analysis incorporating startle-probe methodology. *Journal of Abnormal Psychology, 104*, 114–122.

Sutker, P. B., Allain, A. N., Brantley, P. J., & Randall, C. L. (1982). Acute alcohol intoxication, negative affect, and autonomic arousal in women and men. *Addictive Behaviors, 7*, 17–25.

Turpin, G. (1989). *Handbook of clinical psychophysiology.* New York: Wiley.

Waid, W. M., & Orne, M. T. (1982). Reduced electrodermal orienting response to conflict, failure to inhibit dominant behaviors, and delinquency proneness. *Journal of Personality and Social Psychology, 43*, 769–774.

Whipple, S., Berman, S., & Noble, E. (1991). Event-related potentials in alcoholic fathers and their sons. *Alcohol, 8*, 321–327.

Whipple, S., Parker, E., & Noble, E. (1988). An atypical neurocognitive profile in alcoholic fathers and their sons. *Journal of Studies on Alcohol, 49*, 240–244.

Wilson, G. T., Abrams, D. B., & Lipscomb, T. R. (1980). Effects of intoxication levels and drinking pattern on social anxiety in men. *Journal of Studies on Alcohol, 41*, 250–264.

Zeichner, A., Edwards, P., & Cohen, E. (1985). Acute effects of alcohol on cardiovascular reactivity to stress in college-age Type A (coronary-prone) individuals. *Journal of Psychopathology and Behavioral Assessment, 7*, 75–89.

Zeichner, A., Giancola, P., & Allen, J. D. (1995). Effects of hostility on alcohol stress-response-dampening. *Alcoholism: Clinical and Experimental Research, 19*, 977–983.

CHAPTER 10

PSYCHOLOGICAL THEORIES OF ETIOLOGY

R. Lorraine Collins
Howard T. Blane
Kenneth E. Leonard

Over the past few years, a number of reviews of psychological theories of substance use and abuse have been published. Whether substance specific (Blane & Leonard, 1987; Chaudron & Wilkinson, 1988) or more generic (Marlatt, Baer, Donovan, & Kivlahan, 1988) these books and chapters have provided in-depth coverage of a variety of theories of the etiology of substance abuse. In this chapter, we present an overview of current psychological thinking concerning the etiology of substance abuse. Although substance use involves multiple phases, we will not consider theories concerning initial use or experimentation with substances (Petraitis, Flay, & Miller, 1995) or factors that place adolescents at risk for substance use (Hawkins, Catalano, & Miller, 1992). Some of these topics will be discussed in other chapters.

Although not comprehensive, this overview presents the state of the art of psychological theorizing in two broad interrelated areas: (1) theories with a behavioral emphasis, such as conditioning and social learning; and (2) theories with a cognitive emphasis, such as expectancy. By critically reviewing a variety of psychological theories, we hope to stimulate further thinking about the etiology of substance abuse and to enhance the contributions of psychological theories of etiology to efforts to prevent and treat substance abuse.

THEORIES WITH A BEHAVIORAL EMPHASIS

The behavioral perspective on the etiology of drug use encompasses a variety of approaches that have evolved from both classical and operant theories of learning. Individual researchers have placed different emphases on what aspects of these theories are most germane for explaining different aspects of drug use, ranging from initial use through to relapse following treatment. We hope to highlight models and notions that have made a lasting contribution to the conceptualization of the etiology of drug use.

Classical Conditioning

Models based on classical conditioning have been used to describe the establishment and maintenance of phenomena related to substance use, such as craving/urges, tolerance, and withdrawal. Although we cannot present these models and related literatures in detail (Grabowski & O'Brien, 1981; Ray, 1988; Sherman, Jorenby, & Baker, 1988), we do highlight key theories and findings within this approach.

Classical conditioning models of drug use are based on Pavlov's notion that the administration of a drug is a conditioning trial in which the drug is the unconditioned stimulus (US), the rituals and procedures of drug administration are the conditioned stimulus (CS), and the unconditioned response (UR) and conditioned response (CR) are responses to the US and the CS, respectively. CRs are evident when drug administration rituals are presented without the drug.

Some 20 years after Pavlov, Wikler (1948) described a classical conditioning model of morphine addiction that was followed by research on the role of classical conditioning in a number of areas. These include craving (Ludwig, Wikler, & Stark, 1974), the development of tolerance and withdrawal (Siegel, 1983), and the use of cue exposure and extinction as a means of treating substance abusers (Childress, McLellan, Ehrman, & O'Brien, 1988; Rohsenow, Niaura, Childress, Abrams, & Monti, 1990–1991).

Wikler's work may have developed as a response to psychoanalytic notions concerning the etiology of addiction that were pervasive in the 1940s. In research from the late 1940s to the 1980s, Wikler and colleagues conducted both animal and human research to explore the parameters of a classical conditioning approach to addiction. Basically, Wikler proposed that the drug user has internal "needs" (e.g., anxiety, dysphoria, social affiliation) that were reduced by the pharmacological and social effects of drug use. With repeated self-administration, drug-seeking behavior was operationally conditioned, whereas an acute abstinence syndrome was classically conditioned to drug-related cues (neighborhood, other drug users) when the drug was not available. Thus, both internal and external cues could become conditioned to aspects of the drug use cycle: drug seeking, self-administration, and withdrawal. Regardless of the intricacies of Wikler's notions of the role of conditioning in the use of drugs, one of his observations has had a lasting impact on treatment for drug use. Wikler observed that classical and operant conditioning factors played a role in relapse. Thus, "mere detoxification, with or without conventional psychotherapy and enforced abstention from self-administration of opioids, will not prevent relapse when the former addict returns to his home environment and other environments where the conditioned stimuli are present. . . . What is needed in treatment after detoxication is *active* extinction of both classically conditioned abstinence and operantly conditioned opioid self-administration" (Wikler, 1980; p. 178). These notions have contributed to the development of cue exposure treatment for substance abuse.

Siegel (1978) developed a classical conditioning model of tolerance that complements some of Wikler's notions. His initial research focused on morphine tolerance as being classically conditioned; that is, an association is developed between the rituals and environments that are involved in administration of the drug and the effects of the drug. Tolerance was said to occur because animals exhibit a "compensatory conditioned response," counter to the pharmacological effect of the drug, when exposed to the drug-related cues. For example, morphine produces analgesia: therefore, its compensatory response attenuates its analgesic effects. Over repeated pairings of drug ritual and drug administration, these anticipatory compensatory responses become stronger. When combined with the drug effects they lead to a gradual decrease in the overall effect of the drug, that is, tolerance.

In a series of experiments, Siegel and others have shown that tolerance is an associative process that is consistent with the principles of classical conditioning (Siegel, 1975, 1976, 1983). These include the fact that morphine tolerance can be extinguished, exhibits decrements related to partial reinforcement, and is specific to the conditioning environment. Similar research indicated that tolerance for alcohol and other substances such as cocaine and marijuana follow the same principles (Krasnegor, 1978).

The human implications of Siegel's animal studies were described by Poulos, Hinson, and Siegel (1981), who suggested that once drug use is established, conditioning principles could explain many other phenomena common to drug use. These include withdrawal symptoms, which may be the drug-compensatory CRs elicited by environmental cues that signal drug use when no drug is available. In this context, withdrawal symptoms were said to be better characterized as "preparation symptoms" (Poulos et al., 1981; p. 206), indicative of the fact that the individual is preparing for the drug by exhibiting compensatory responses counter to the drug effect. Craving for the drug also could be related to conditioning. It may result from negative affective states that are part of the compensatory conditioned response (i.e., opposite to the positive states produced by the drug), which increase the incentive value of the drug.

Notions about the role of classical conditioning in drug use have contributed to current thought about the effects of drug-related environmental stimuli in maintaining drug use and the use of cue exposure procedures (involving extinction of CRs) to treat substance abusers (Niaura et al., 1988). As such they have both served to illuminate some aspects of the development of substance abuse and have provided treatment strategies that are effective for some substance abusers (Childress et al., 1988; Rohsenow et al., 1990–1991; Stasiewicz & Maisto, 1993).

Appetitive Models

Appetitive or incentive motivation models also see learning mechanisms as playing an important role in the development and maintenance of drug use. As outlined by Stewart, de Wit, and Eikelboom (1984) stimulant drugs, such as opiates, act on neurochemical systems of the brain, probably via the mesolimbic dopamine pathway, to generate positive desire for the drugs. Thus, stimulant drugs can serve as positive reinforcers in a fashion resembling food and other substances. Through classical conditioning, neutral stimuli (both internal states and external objects) associated with the drug are conditioned to the drug effects, such that they take on the positive reinforcing properties of the drugs and become experiences or objects to which the organism is attracted. If extinction (i.e., exposure to these stimuli without experiencing drug effects) to these stimuli does not occur, they can come to elicit a state similar to that elicited by the drug itself. This principle could explain the return to drug use even after long periods of abstinence.

An important point made by the appetitive motivation approach is that use of a drug is not a function of deprivation or the need to avoid withdrawal but rather is related to its positive incentive properties. Other models of drug use, consistent with the appetitive approach and invoking the role of brain mechanisms, have been proposed (Robinson & Berridge, 1993; Wise & Bozarth, 1987) to account for various aspects of the maintenance of substance use and abuse. Other learning-based approaches to drug use, such as opponent process theory (Solomon & Corbit, 1973, 1974), which have emphasized the role of deprivation or withdrawal, seem to have made a less enduring contribution to our understanding of substance use and abuse.

Behavioral Choice/Behavioral Economics Approaches

The behavioral choice model suggests that use of a substance becomes a preferred behavior in the individual's repertoire when two conditions are present: (1) there are few constraints on access to the substance; and (2) other reinforcers are either not available or have constraints placed on gaining access to them. The model has relevance for the development of use/abuse of a variety of substances including alcohol (Vuchinich, 1995; Vuchinich & Tucker, 1988), nicotine (Epstein, Bulik, Perkins, Caggiula, & Rodefer, 1991; Perkins, Epstein, Grobe, & Fonte, 1994), food (Lappalainen & Epstein, 1990; Smith & Epstein,

1991), and illicit drugs (Bickel, DeGrandpre, & Higgins, 1993; DeGrandpre & Bickel, 1996; Elsmore, Fletcher, Conrad, & Sodetz, 1980). This approach is consistent with operant learning models in that it focuses on the reinforcing properties of various substances. However, the behavioral choice model does not explicitly include consideration of the variables involved in initiating substance use and establishing its reinforcing properties. Initial use may be related to a variety of factors including sociocultural influences, such as peers, media, and family (Vuchinich & Tucker, 1988). Instead, the focus is on the development and maintenance of substance use once the substance has been established as a reinforcer.

Vuchinich and Tucker (1988) find support for the behavioral economic/behavioral choice approach in both animal and human research. Generally this research suggests that (1) preference for substance use varies inversely with *direct* constraints on access to substances, regardless of the nature of the constraints (e.g., cost, availability); and (2) preference for substance use varies inversely with the availability of alternative reinforcers. When the costs (behavioral and otherwise) of access to alternative reinforcers increases, then substance use is more likely to be preferred. Over the years, Vuchinich and colleagues have pursued both laboratory and clinical research within this framework and have produced findings consistent with the model (Vuchinich, 1995). For example, in an early laboratory analog study with social drinkers, young men were provided with a choice between access to alcohol and access to money (Vuchinich & Tucker, 1983). Access to money was further manipulated in terms of amount (2 cents or 10 cents) and delay in receiving payment (no delay, 2 weeks, 8 weeks). Consistent with the behavioral choice model, subjects showed greater preference for alcohol when money was low (2 cents) and when payment was delayed. More recently, the behavioral choice model was applied to understanding relapse among male alcoholics during the first 6 months following inpatient treatment (Vuchinich & Tucker, 1996). The idea was that following treatment, an alcoholic can make a choice between the smaller more immediate rewards available from drinking and the greater, more long-term rewards in life areas (e.g., family relations and vocational functioning) that can be achieved by maintaining abstinence from alcohol. Alcoholics self-monitored daily alcohol consumption, the occurrence of various life events and mood. As predicted, the results indicated that at posttreatment, negative events related to intimate and family relationships as well as to vocational functioning were more likely to lead to drinking. Also of interest, drinking episodes related to negative life events lasted significantly longer, and involved more total drinks and more drinks per day for each episode. Although relapse following treatment can be seen as far removed from notions about "etiology," this analysis does have implications for the development of problems of substance use/abuse. It suggests that alcohol and other drugs may be chosen when rewards related to other life areas are either delayed or nonexistent.

Social Learning Approaches

In his seminal book outlining social learning theory, Bandura (1969) described substance use as a socially mediated activity. Substance use was said to develop via mechanisms such as vicarious learning, modeling, and the positively reinforcing pharmacological properties of the substance. For example, alcohol is a powerful positive reinforcer because its immediate effects are positive and its negative consequences are delayed. Its depressant effects relieve stress and other forms of aversive stimulation. The use of alcohol and other drugs often occurs in a social context, and therefore use is linked to experiencing social reinforcement. In this case, alcohol serves as an instrumental behavior; the individual drinks or uses other drugs to experience or maintain rewards related to its use. Other social learning variables involved in etiology are said to include the general cultural norms that define the social–cultural reinforcement contingencies related to substance use. These contingencies and the related norms may vary in association with variables such as location (urban vs. rural), religion, occupation, social class, and so on. These norms are transmitted through exposure to socializing agents (e.g., family, peers, media) who engage in the substance use behavior and serve as models of its use. Models can teach new behaviors, strengthen or weaken the performance of previously learned behaviors or enhance the value of a particular stimulus or behavior. In the case of substance use, models can provide guidance on how to use, the situations in which use is appropriate (e.g., drink alcohol with meals, smoke marijuana to feel mellow), and the likely outcomes of use. New behaviors and reinforcement contingencies may be learned vicariously, (i.e., by observation) or by actually engaging in the behavior. Thus, observing a behavior that is followed by positive reinforcement (or a lack of negative consequences) is likely to be learned/exhibited whereas a behavior that is followed

by punishment or other negative consequences is likely to be inhibited. Thus, exposure to models who achieve positive outcomes as a function of substance use (e.g., become more sociable, report less stress) is likely to enhance substance use. The pharmacological effects of the drug also are important. For example, alcohol helps to relieve aversive stimulation (e.g., stress, boredom, frustration). This positive effect can lead to alcohol consumption as a generalized response, as is the case for many alcoholics.

Once a substance is established as a generalized response the individual may continue use not only to experience its benefits but also to forestall aversive reactions associated with withdrawal, thereby establishing a secondary mechanism for maintaining use. This notion is consistent with various psychological theories that link excessive substance use to attempts to forestall withdrawal symptoms.

Other researchers have elaborated on Bandura's general description to present more in-depth explanations of the role of various social learning factors in substance use and abuse. For example, Wills and Shiffman's (1985) notions concerning the role of stress and coping on substance use is consistent with Bandura's notions concerning alcohol and other drugs as helping to relieve aversive stimulation. Similarly, cognitive behavioral models such as Marlatt and Gordon's relapse prevention model can be successfully applied to the etiology of substance abuse when we consider the fact that relapse following abstinence is a function of the individual's lack of effective coping responses and the return to his or her generalized response of using substances to cope (Collins & Marlatt, 1983; Marlatt & Gordon, 1985).

COGNITIVE PERSPECTIVES ON THE ETIOLOGY OF SUBSTANCE ABUSE

Social learning approaches often include cognitive aspects of behavior as one component of the etiology of substance abuse. However, some etiological theories place a major emphasis on the role of cognitive processes. The cognitive wave in addiction theories, like the cognitive wave in psychology as a whole, can be traced to the early 1970s. At that time, two general perspectives began to emerge as to the role of "cognitive" factors in the development of alcohol dependence and alcohol problems: one perspective focusing upon alcohol's impact on the "process" of cognition and the other focusing primarily on the acquired "content" of cognitions regarding alcohol use. It is worthy of note that these cognitive perspectives emerged from the study of alcohol and alcoholism as opposed to the study of illicit drugs.

Although the development of the cognitive "content" perspective developed over several years, the key study that served as an impetus for this development was conducted by Marlatt, Demming, & Reid (1973). At the time of this study, a number of key assumptions concerning the etiology of alcoholism were being challenged. Mendelson and Mello conducted several studies (reviewed by Mello, 1972) in which alcoholics were admitted to inpatient wards and allowed access to alcohol. These studies suggested that alcoholics could and did control their drinking in several ways: (1) they earned and saved tokens in order to "buy" a binge in contrast to buying a single drink at a time: (2) they titrated their consumption to achieve a stable (and high) blood alcohol level, and (3) they reduced their consumption in anticipation of discharge, presumably to avoid withdrawal. In addition, two studies had demonstrated that alcoholic cravings were not directly tied to the simple presence or absence of alcohol in the bloodstream of the alcoholic (Engle & Williams, 1972; Merry, 1966). Marlatt et al. (1973) took the next step and attempted to determine whether the pharmacological properties of alcohol would lead to increased drinking among alcoholics, or whether this "loss of control" might be cognitively mediated. In order to test this, these researchers tested alcoholics and social drinkers with the "balanced placebo" design, which included four conditions: alcohol administration, no alcohol administration (tonic), placebo (subjects told alcohol, but given tonic), and the silent administration or antiplacebo condition (told tonic but surreptitiously given alcohol). The subjects were then allowed to drink alcohol as part of a taste-testing study, and the amount of alcohol they consumed in this task was measured. The results were clear, even among the alcoholics: those who were told that they were given alcohol (alcohol administration and placebo) drank more than those who were told they did not (no alcohol and antiplacebo), regardless of whether they had, in fact, received alcohol. The actual administration of alcohol did not lead to more consumption. This series of findings was broadly interpreted to suggest that craving and loss of control in the alcoholic were the result of the alcoholic's "expectancy" that he or she had consumed alcohol and they provided a very compelling justification for a cognitive approach to alcohol abuse and alcoholism. It should be recognized, however, that these findings could also be interpreted

within a classical conditioning framework (Marlatt & Rohsenow, 1980).

The implications of this study, that a specific effect of alcohol that had previously been thought to be pharmacological instead appeared to be psychological, had a very significant impact on subsequent alcohol research. Two different but related directions emerged simultaneously and were informed by each other. First, it raised the possibility that other purportedly psychopharmacological effects of alcohol, including those reinforcing effects that had been attributed etiologic importance, might actually reflect the impact of an individual's beliefs about alcohol. This paved the way for the development of alcohol expectancies as a component in the initiation of alcohol use and development of alcohol abuse and alcoholism. Second, the fact that loss of control, one of the defining aspects of alcoholism, appeared to be due to cognitive factors raised the possibility that other critical aspects of alcoholism (e.g., craving, inability to abstain) might not be physiologically determined but instead cognitively mediated. This recognition paved the way for the development of relapse prevention approaches to alcoholism (Marlatt & Gordon, 1985).

Alcohol Expectancies

Although some experimental research had previously examined the impact of alcohol and sometimes placebo on social behaviors, investigators armed with the balanced placebo began to explore the pharmacological versus psychological impact of alcohol on tension reduction, aggression, sexual arousal, memory, and graffiti writing. Much of this work has been reviewed elsewhere (Hull and Bond, 1986). Critical to the current discussion, however, was the underlying premise that leading the subjects to expect that they had received alcohol would activate "alcohol expectancies" relevant to the behavior under investigation. For example, in studies of tension reduction, it was assumed that leading subjects to believe that they had received alcohol could lead to tension reduction because the subjects believed that alcohol reduced tension. However, throughout much of this literature, the key issues of whether the subjects actually believed that alcohol had such an effect and how these beliefs actuated a behavioral change were largely ignored.

In 1980, the emerging cognitive theme of alcohol expectancies was significantly advanced by identification of a number of different expectancies and the development of instruments to assess these expectancies (Brown, Goldman, Inn, & Anderson, 1980; Southwick, Steele, Marlatt, & Lindell, 1981). Brown et al.'s instrument included six separate scales derived using factor analysis. These scales identified beliefs that alcohol had the following effects: (1) a global positive transformation; (2) social facilitation; (3) enhanced sexual performance and pleasure; (4) power and aggression; (5) social assertiveness; and (6) relaxation and tension reduction. In subsequent studies, Goldman and his colleagues identified similar expectancies among adolescents (Christiansen, Goldman, & Inn, 1982) and demonstrated that these expectancies were related to the level of drinking exhibited by the individual (Christiansen & Goldman, 1983). From an etiologic standpoint, the development of these measures opened the way to studies concerned with whether individual's beliefs about the *reinforcing* aspects of alcohol (global transformation, social facilitation, relaxation, and tension reduction) could be of value in understanding the onset of drinking and the development of alcohol abuse and alcohol dependence.

Despite some controversies related to the measurement of alcohol expectancies (Leigh, 1989), there have been numerous studies that have documented the importance of alcohol expectancies in understanding alcohol use and abuse. It is clear, for example, that alcohol expectancies correlate with adolescent drinking status, and that this correlation remains after controlling for a variety of other influences (Webb, Baer, Francis, & Caid, 1993). More importantly, alcohol expectancies are prospectively predictive of onset of alcohol use among adolescents who had not drank previously and of the onset of problem drinking (Christiansen, Smith, Roehling, & Goldman, 1989). More recently, Smith, Goldman, Greenbaum, & Christiansen (1995) found that among young adolescents, the expectancy that alcohol is socially facilitating predicted changes in drinking in two consecutive 1-year time spans. Moreover, drinking also predicted changes in this alcohol expectancy over the first 1-year period. For at least this brief period, there appeared to be a positive feedback loop in which drinking influenced positive expectancies, which in turn predicted subsequent drinking. Alcohol expectancies also have been related to drinking in adulthood, though most of this literature has involved cross-sectional designs. Stacy, Newcomb, and Bentler (1991), in one of the few longitudinal studies to span adolescence to adulthood, reported that adolescent alcohol motivations (a construct similar to expectancies) predicted adult drug

problems that consisted of problems with alcohol, marijuana, and cocaine.

Despite the importance of the construct of expectancy in the alcohol use and abuse literature, it has not had a similar impact on the substance use and abuse literature. Threads of this general idea are apparent in the substance abuse literature (Zinberg & Harding, 1982). For example, Bunce (1982) suggested that "bad trips" from psychedelic drugs might be the result of social environmental factors rather than a pharmacological effect. Bunce argued that the political climate surrounding the use of psychedelic drugs created both fear and attraction, and that this led to "bad trips." Phrased in expectancy terms, people came to believe that psychedelics were "the most powerful drug, use of which entails the risk of 'terror of the loss of rational control' in order to experience consciousness-expansion . . . and users' expectations at the time must have been structured and positioned accordingly" (Bunce, 1982; p. 122). More recently, several investigators have begun to translate the expectancy construct from alcohol to nicotine (Brandon & Baker, 1992), cocaine (Schafer & Brown, 1991), and marijuana (Stacy, 1995), and the initial findings appear to be supportive of an important role for drug expectancies. For example, Stacy et al. (1991) reported that marijuana motivations (expectancies) predicted adult drug use frequency, quantity, and drug problems. It will be of interest to follow the future progress in this area of research.

In recent years, the "alcohol expectancy" approach has gradually shifted from a focus on the content of cognitions (alcohol beliefs) to a focus that encompasses both the process and content of cognitions. This shift represents a significant departure in the processes that were hypothesized to link alcohol expectancies to alcohol use. Originally, alcohol expectancies were viewed as attitudes or beliefs about the reinforcing qualities of alcohol. Although the processes linking expectancies to alcohol use were not typically described in detail, the descriptions of expectancies tended to connote a rational, behavioral choice framework. People with expectancies that alcohol relieved tension or stress drank in a more or less rational attempt to achieve these purported effects of alcohol. Current theoretical approaches (Goldman, 1994; Goldman, Christiansen, Brown, & Smith, 1991; Stacy, Widaman, & Marlatt, 1990) have linked alcohol expectancies to memory processes in an attempt to understand their predictive value. One suggestion is that positive alcohol expectancies may be encoded in close association with usual drinking situations, and therefore would be more easily retrieved from memory in future drinking situations. In contrast, expectancies concerned with unpleasant effects would be less likely to be encoded in close association with the usual drinking situation, perhaps being encoded in closer association to episodes of very heavy drinking. Consequently, they would be less likely to be activated and play an inhibitory role.

Cognitive Determinants of Relapse and the Relapse Prevention Perspective

Following the demonstration that the drinking of alcoholics was not influenced by the pharmacological effects of alcohol, Marlatt and his colleagues conducted a number of studies that examined the extent to which alcohol consumption in heavy drinkers (not necessarily alcoholics) was influenced by other social/cognitive factors. Among the factors that influenced alcohol consumption among heavy drinkers was the threat of social evaluation (Higgins & Marlatt, 1975; Miller, Hersen, Eisler, & Hilsman, 1974), insult (Marlatt, Kosturn, & Lang, 1975), and exposure to heavy drinking models (Caudill & Marlatt, 1975; Collins & Marlatt, 1981). Interestingly, similar factors were reported by alcoholics as the major causes of their relapse following treatment. These studies led to the hypothesis that the drinking of heavy drinkers and perhaps of alcoholics (i.e., relapse) might be related to the experience of stress, particularly interpersonal stress. More specifically, individuals with certain characteristics might turn to alcohol to deal with high levels of interpersonal and intrapersonal stress. Among the characteristics that have been thought to predispose individuals to use alcohol in this way are coping efficacy (belief that one is able to cope successfully), the presence of maladaptive coping strategies, and expectancies that alcohol has effects that are useful in coping with stress (e.g., tension reduction, relaxation).

Alcohol and Cognitive Processing

Although most of the cognitive theorizing with regard to alcohol has focused on the "content" of cognitions, several different investigators have developed theoretical advances that rely more on cognitive processes. One of these approaches has attempted to explain cravings and urges in terms of automatic processing (Tiffany, 1990). Although urges had been considered to be phenomena arising from physiologic withdrawal or from the desire for positive effects of the substance and as motivating subsequent substance use, Tiffany argued that empirical support for these approaches was not particularly strong. Particularly troublesome for the withdrawal models of urges was the observation that drug urges often appeared well after the withdrawal symptoms had disappeared and that few addicts reported that cravings or urges were responsible for relapses. Tiffany's approach emphasizes that through habitual drug use, the drug use behavior becomes an action mediated by automatic processing of drug use cues. Although the nature of automatic sequences is beyond the scope of this chapter, the essential elements include very quick processing and behavior reactions, behaviors enacted without intention or conscious awareness, difficulty in controlling the behavior once the sequence has been initiated, and the relatively low cognitive demands necessary for the behavior. Common examples of automatic processing sequences are the well-practiced performance of a musical instrument or the negotiation of an automobile from one's home to work. In contrast, nonautomatic processing is an effortful strategic cognitive operation that is consciously controlled by the individual. These nonautomatic processes come into action under two general conditions. The first occurs when the automatic sequences are interrupted, as when an addicted individual is unable to obtain and use the substance, and nonautomatic processes are engaged in an attempt to reinstitute substance use. These nonautomatic processes are experienced as craving and would be expected to be strongly associated with subsequent substance use. The second situation occurs when an individual is attempting to cease the automatic sequences and abstain from drug use. In this situation, the continued use of nonautomatic cognitive processes to interrupt the automatic drug -eeking sequences is also experienced as craving. However, it is primarily the unsuccessful employment of nonautomatic processes that gives rise to relapse, rather than the use of such processes and craving per se. In summary, cravings and urges are viewed in Tiffany's model as arising from the use of these nonautomatic processes rather than being the inevitable result of physiologic withdrawal or a desire for the drug. Consequently, cravings may have importance with respect to the continuation of drug use and relapse from abstinence, but not necessarily because they reflect the individual's motivational state regarding substance use. One of the primary hypotheses that arises from Tiffany's model is that an individual who is experiencing craving and drug urges (i.e., engaging in nonautomatic processing) should be impaired in the performance of other nonautomatic information-processing tasks. In essence, the cognitive resources involved in the craving would reduce the resources available for the other tasks that require nonautomatic processing. In this regard, Sayette et al. (1994) found that alcoholics had a slower reaction to tones in the presence of an alcoholic versus control beverage. Studies by Tiffany (1995) and colleagues have demonstrated similar phenomena with regard to smoking.

The second cognitive approach to emphasize "process" reflects a continued interest in the acute effects of alcohol on the individual's processing of social information (Hull, 1981). The basis for this perspective was established throughout the 1970s with research examining the acute impact of alcohol intoxication on cognitive processes such as attention, learning, and memory. This research suggested that alcohol had little if any impact on simple perception or retrieval of previously learned information. Relatively simple tasks such as auditory or visual vigilance, simple reaction time, and retrieval from long-term memory were not uniformly impaired by alcohol use. However, tasks that required dealing with multiple information sources, comparing, organizing, or understanding information were fairly consistently impaired by alcohol, sometimes by relatively low doses of alcohol. Consequently, alcohol was seen as impairing attentional faculties, organizing or encoding strategies, and appraisal or decision-making abilities.

Although cognitive disruption due to alcohol had been the focus of some explanations of social behavior (Pernanen, 1976; Taylor & Leonard, 1983), the first explication of such a model with relevance to the development of alcoholism was proposed by Hull (1981). Hull's approach argued that alcohol, through its deleterious impact on higher order information encoding, resulted in a state in which internal and external cues were not processed with respect to their implications for one's view of oneself or a state of low self-awareness. Because of the absence of a link between cues and internal standards, behavior would be less conforming to either internal standards or external expectations. More pertinent to the current discussion of etiology was Hull's hypothesis that this low self-awareness would be positively reinforcing in the presence of personal failure experiences. Specifically, failure experiences are likely to engender negative thoughts about oneself and alcohol may disrupt this encoding link. Although this model was intriguing, empirical support for it was variable, with some notable failures to replicate. Furthermore, the generality of this model is limited in that as alcohol does not uniformly reduce self-awareness and indeed, may sometimes increase it.

Two theories have since elaborated on the basic notion espoused by Hull that the cognitive impairment caused by alcohol could be reinforcing. The most popular of these, the "attention allocation model," was described by Steele and Josephs (1988) and built on work in the alcohol and aggression area that emphasized attentional mechanisms. According to this perspective, alcohol intoxication creates a deficit in the ability to simultaneously attend to and process information in the environment. Consequently, the intoxicated individual may devote disproportionately more attentional resources to the most immediate, dominant, or salient cues, an effect referred to as "alcohol myopia." The importance of this model is that it suggests that alcohol consumption may be reinforcing, particularly in the presence of distracting stimuli, because it renders the individual less able to focus and ruminate on anxiety-arousing stimuli. In the absence of distraction, the model suggests that the intoxicated individual might focus excessively on the anxiety-arousing stimuli and feel more anxious. Although this reinforcing effect is quite similar to the effect described by Hull, it is at the same time more generalizable in that it describes a basic effect of alcohol that would invariably occur (alcohol myopia) as well as additional circumstances that determine whether the myopia would be reinforcing or perhaps punishing.

The second theoretical extension, developed by Sayette (1993), focuses on alcohol's impact on central processing of information. This formulation arose from an attempt to understand the variability of empirical research concerning the stress response dampening (SRD) effect of alcohol. The SRD effect of alcohol refers to the empirical observation that some subjects who are administered alcohol and exposed to stress do not show as strong a stress response as subjects not given alcohol. Sayette (1993) reviewed the SRD research literature and found considerable variability in the findings. He identified a set of methodologic parameters that seemed to be associated with consistent SRD effects. Specifically, studies in which the subjects were given alcohol before they had an opportunity to learn about an upcoming stressor showed SRD effects. This led to the hypothesis that alcohol would be reinforcing because it reduced one's response to stress, primarily because it interfered with a full appraisal of the stressor.

In evaluating these three cognitive process theories, it is important to understand that they share similarities and therefore are by no means mutually exclusive. Self-awareness describes a specific cognitive process that may be impaired as a result of intoxication, whereas both attention allocation and appraisal disruption models describe general cognitive processes that are nearly always impaired by intoxication, and that may under certain circumstances lead to reductions in self-awareness. All three theories provide instances in which the intoxication may be reinforcing. Self-awareness theory suggests that alcohol may be reinforcing if one has received negative self information, a specific form of stress, whereas attention allocation suggests that alcohol may be reinforcing in the presence of any stress, but primarily if there are sufficient distractors so that the stress is not the salient information. Appraisal disruption suggests that alcohol may be reinforcing in the presence of any stress, even if there are no distractors.

THEORIES OF HISTORICAL SIGNIFICANCE

In 1987, Blane and Leonard included several recent theoretical models in their edited work on psychological theories of drinking and alcoholism. It is of interest to examine the fate of these models during the past 10 years. As noted earlier in this chapter, theory and empirical work on expectancies and stress response continue to represent flourishing and productive lines of inquiry. In both areas, research has resulted in conceptual refinements and theoretically grounded empirical extensions into topics beyond those originally envisaged. This kind of growth, in part a consequence of syntheses following upon critiques of theory and methods, has not characterized the other recent models covered by Blane and Leonard, that is, self-awareness, self-handicapping, and opponent process.

A search of the literature from 1987 to June 1996 for each model revealed only one research paper in which one of the models served as a primary guide to the conduct of empirical study (Chassin, Mann, & Sher, 1988). This empirical impoverishment is not accompanied by a similar neglect in the relevant theoretical literature. Each of the models, particularly opponent process and self-awareness, are mentioned, if not always integrated, into critical reviews and presentations of theoretical advances (Steele & Josephs, 1990; Stritzke, Lang, & Patrick, 1996; Vuchinich & Tucker, 1988).

The reasons for some models to flourish and others to remain, so to speak, stillborn, are far from clear. One possibility is suggested in a discussion of the vitality of tension reduction theory by Vuchinich & Tucker (1988), wherein they argue that the conceptual strategy of tension reduction theory involves delineation of the conditions that determine the reinforcement value of alcohol. In this view, a number of organismic states have been put forward as providing these conditions, among them, self-awareness and self-handicapping [or, as Vuchinich & Tucker (1988) phrase it, threats to self-esteem]. Thus, unproductive models may be aspects of larger theoretical approaches potentially carrying more generality and greater explanatory power. This may occur even though these smaller models result in elegant laboratory confirmation, whereas the status of the general theoretical model is ambiguous and clouded, as in the case of tension reduction theory. A related aspect is that single factor models often do not fare well, either in the scientific imagination or empirically. Thus, in regard to the models under discussion, the results of the one independent study (Chassin et al., 1988) of self-awareness did not support the model.

These considerations may be important in attempts to understand the paucity of research conducted to test models such as self-awareness and self-handicapping, but they appear less successful with respect to the opponent process model. Opponent process draws upon a rich tradition in learning theory and is rooted in notions about homeostasis. It is an exquisitely conceived model that resulted in a series of elegant confirmatory experiments. What resulted is an excellent conceptually driven description of a drinking episode and the effect of continued drinking episodes. The model appears sufficient unto itself, and thus admits of no refinements or changes. The only scientific recourse is the conduct of replications that duplicate as precisely as possible the conditions specified by the model. The only innovation that appears possible is the choice of the substance chosen for study. In this view, the model is self-sufficient and in a sense stultifies further research. The situation is not dissimilar to that pertaining to problem behavior theory, in which a complex, elegant, and fully realized model can serve to describe a variety of populations in the most precise terms. As productive as problem behavior theory has been, the studies conducted under its aegis have essentially replicated previous research, and few advances in theory have occurred since its original formulations in the late 1960s and early 1970s. It may be that imperfect or incomplete theories offer more opportunities for growth than their more seamless counterparts.

These speculations aside, it is evident that there are part theories, single-factor models, and complete models that have lived long and healthy empirical and theoretical lives. In alcohol research, expectancy theory, discussed earlier in this chapter, is one such instance, and in substance abuse generally, the aforementioned problem behavior theory is another. Obviously, there are other factors that must be invoked to understand the fate of theoretical developments. One needs perhaps to consider intangibles such as the aggressiveness of a theory's progenitor in advancing the model with students, at professional forums, and in publications.

Given the concern of this section with models that have fallen by the wayside, it may be useful to conclude with a brief consideration of an approach that continues to be important in discussions of the etiology of addictive disorders, even though its empirical support is scanty; that is, psychoanalysis and related psychodynamic formulations. The knowledge base for psychoanalytic models of the etiology of addictive disorders was primarily an amalgam of clinical experience informed by principles of psychoanalytic theory. The early formulations of addictions as simultaneous expressions of and defenses against fixation on or regression to an oral stage of psychosexual development, or latent homosexuality, have little currency in current psychodynamic thinking. Rather the emphasis is on the self and malfunctions of the ego, reflecting advances in psychoanalytic theory led most notably by Kohut (1977). With regard to the addictions, psychodynamic approaches are of great practical importance, for they serve to guide a substantial proportion of clinical practice. These approaches range from sophisticated, systematic approaches (Khantzian, 1980; Vannicelli, 1992) to so-called "watered-down" psychoanalysis; that is, the inclusion of psychodynamic terms and tenets loosely integrated into an eclectic treatment program. The continued strength of psychoanalysis and its derivatives is impressive, particularly in the absence of any solid empirical support and in the face of onslaughts by scientists, philosophers, and other social commentators. Certainly, however, psychoanalysis has shown a great capacity to adapt to new conditions and it has captured the popular imagination, including that of the sizable body of the addiction treatment community. As such, it deserves to be acknowledged in any overview of psychological theories of the etiology of addictive behaviors.

Psychological theories have added much to the rich history of scientific approaches to the etiology of substance use and abuse. However, substance use has many complex determinants, not all of which are encompassed by psychological models. As we learn more about the factors related to drug use, it becomes more apparent that interdisciplinary approaches, in which psychological factors

are combined with social and/or biological approaches (Robinson & Berridge, 1993), are likely to offer the most comprehensive framework for future theorizing.

ACKNOWLEDGMENT

The authors wish to thank Paul Stasiewicz for his helpful comments on an earlier draft of this manuscript.

REFERENCES

Bandura, A. (1969). *Principles of behavior modification*. New York: Holt, Rinehart, and Winston.

Bickel, W. K., DeGrandpre, R. J., & Higgins, S. T. (1993). Behavioral economics: A novel experimental approach to the study of drug dependence. *Drug and Alcohol Dependence, 33,* 173–192.

Blane, H. T., & Leonard, K. E. (Eds.). (1987). *Psychological theories of drinking and alcoholism*. New York: Guilford Press.

Brandon, T. H., & Baker, T. B. (1992). The smoking consequences questionnaire: The subjective utility of smoking in college students. *Psychological Assessment, 3,* 484–491.

Brown, S., Goldman, M., Inn, A., & Anderson, L. (1980). Expectations of reinforcement from alcohol: Their domain and relation to drinking patterns. *Journal of Consulting and Clinical Psychology, 48,* 419–426.

Bunce, R. (1982). Social and political sources of drug effects: The case of bad trips on psychedelics. In N. E. Zinberg & W. M. Harding (Eds.), *Control over intoxicant use* (pp. 105–125). New York: Human Sciences Press.

Caudill, B., & Marlatt, G. (1975). Modeling influences in social drinking: An experimental in social drinking: An experimental analogue. *Journal of Consulting and Clinical Psychology, 43,* 405–415.

Chassin, L., Mann, L. M., & Sher, K. J. (1988). Self-awareness theory, family history of alcoholism, and adolescent alcohol involvement. *Journal of Abnormal Psychology, 97*(2), 206–217.

Chaudron, C. D., & Wilkinson, D. A. (Eds.). (1988). *Theories on alcoholism*. Toronto: Addiction Research Foundation.

Childress, A. R., McLellan, A. T., Ehrman, R., & O'Brien, C. P. (1988). Classically conditioned responses in opioid and cocaine dependence: A role in relapse? In B. A. Ray (Ed.), *Learning factors in substance abuse* (NIDA Research Monograph 84, DHHS Publication No. ADM 90-1576, pp. 25–43). Washington, DC: U.S. Government Printing Office.

Christiansen, B. A., & Goldman, M. S. (1983). Alcohol-related expectancies versus demographic/background variables in the prediction of adolescent drinking. *Journal of Consulting and Clinical Psychology, 51,* 249–257.

Christiansen, B. A., Goldman, M. S., & Inn, A. (1982). Development of alcohol-related expectancies in adolescents:

Separating pharmacological from social learning influences. *Journal of Consulting and Clinical Psychology, 50*, 336–344.

Christiansen, B. A., Smith, G. T., Roehling, P. V., & Goldman, M. S. (1989). Using alcohol expectancies to predict adolescent drinking behavior after one year. *Journal of Consulting and Clinical Psychology, 57*, 93–99.

Collins, R. L., & Marlatt, G. A. (1981). Social modeling as a determinant of drinking behavior: Implications for prevention and treatment. *Addictive Behaviors, 6*, 233–239.

Collins, R. L., & Marlatt, G. A. (1983). Psychological correlates and explanations of alcohol use and abuse. In B. Tabakoff, P. B. Sutker, & C. L. Randall (Eds.), *Medical and social aspects of alcohol abuse* (pp. 273–308). New York: Plenum.

DeGrandpre, R. J., & Bickel, W. K. (1996). Drug dependence as consumer demand. In L. Green & J. Kagel (Eds.), *Advances in behavioral economics*. Norwood, NJ: Ablex Press.

Elsmore, T. F., Fletcher, G. V., Conrad, D. G., & Sodetz, F. (1980). Reduction of heroin intake in baboons by an economic constraint. *Pharmacology, Biochemistry, and Behavior, 13*, 729–731.

Engle, K., & Williams, T. (1972). Effect of an ounce of vodka on alcoholics' desire for alcohol. *Quarterly Journal of Studies on Alcohol, 33*, 1109–1105.

Epstein, L., Bulik, C., Perkins, K., Caggiula, A., & Rodefer, J. (1991). Behavioral economic analysis of smoking: Money and food as alternatives. *Pharmacology Biochemistry and Behavior, 38*, 715–721.

Goldman, M. S. (1994). The alcohol expectancy concept: Applications to assessment, prevention, and treatment of alcohol abuse. *Applied and Preventive Psychology, 3*, 131–144.

Goldman, M. S., Christiansen, B. A., Brown, S. A., & Smith, G. T. (1991). Alcoholism and memory: Broadening the scope of alcohol-expectancy research. *Psychological Bulletin, 110*, 137–146.

Grabowski, J., & O'Brien, C. P. (1981). Conditioning factors in opiate use. *Advances in Substance Abuse, 2*, 69–121.

Hawkins, J. D., Catalano, R. F., & Miller, J. Y. (1992). Risk and protective factors for alcohol and other drug problems n adolescence and early adulthood: Implications for substance abuse prevention. *Psychological Bulletin, 112*, 64–105.

Higgins, R., & Marlatt, G. (1975). Fear of interpersonal evaluation as a determinant of alcohol consumption in male social drinkers. *Journal of Abnormal Psychology, 84*, 644–651.

Hull, J. (1981). A self-awareness model of the causes and effects of alcohol consumption. *Journal of Abnormal Psychology, 90*, 586–600.

Hull, J., & Bond, C. (1986). Social and behavioral consequences of alcohol consumption and expectancy: A meta-analysis. *Psychological Bulletin, 99*, 347–360.

Khantzian, E. J. (1980). An ego-self theory of substance dependence. In D. J. Lettieri, M. Sayers, & H. W. Wallenstein (Eds.), *Theories of addiction* (NIDA Research Monograph No. 30, DHHS Publication No. ADM 80-967). Washington, D.C., U.S. Government Printing Office.

Kohut, H. (1977). *The restoration of the self.* New York: International Universities Press.

Krasnegor, N. A. (Ed.). (1978). *Behavioral tolerance: Research and treatment implications.*(NIDA Research Monograph No. 18, DHHS Publication No. ADM 78-551). Washington, DC: U.S. Government Printing Office.

Lappalainen, R., & Epstein, L. H. (1990). A behavioral economics analysis of food choice in humans. *Appetite, 14*, 81–93.

Leigh, B. C. (1989). In search of the seven dwarves: Issues of measurement and meaning in alcohol expectancy research. *Psychological Bulletin, 105*, 361–373.

Ludwig, A. M., Wikler, A., & Stark, L. H. (1974). The first drink: Psychobiological aspects of craving. *Archives of General Psychiatry, 30*, 539–547.

Marlatt, G., Baer, J. S., Donovan, D. M., & Kivlahan, D. R. (1988). Addictive behaviors: Etiology and treatment. *Annual Review of Psychology, 1988, 39*, 223–252.

Marlatt, G., Demming, B., & Reid, J. (1973). Loss of control drinking in alcoholics: An experimental analogue. *Journal of Abnormal Psychology, 81*, 233–241.

Marlatt, G., & Gordon, J. R. (Eds.). (1985). *Relapse prevention.* New York: Guilford Press.

Marlatt, G., Kosturn, C., & Lang, A. (1975). Meditation, self-control and alcohol use. In R. Stuart (Ed.), *Behavioral self-management*. New York: Brunner/Mazel.

Marlatt, G., & Rohsenow, D. (1980). Cognitive processes in alcohol use: Expectancy and the balanced placebo design. In N. Mello (Ed.), *Advances in substance abuse: Behavioral and biological research*. Greenwich: CT: JAI Press.

Mello, N. (1972). Behavioral studies of alcoholism. In B. Kissin & H. Begleiter (Eds.), *The biology of alcoholism* (Vol. 2).

Merry J. (1966). The loss of control myth. *Lancet, 1*, 1257–1268.

Miller, P., Hersen, M., Eisler, R., & Hilsman, M. (1974). Effects of social stress on operant drinking of alcoholics and social drinkers. *Behavioral Research and Therapy, 12*, 67–72.

Niaura, R. S., Rohsenow, D. J., Binkoff, J. A., Monti, P. M., Pedraza, M., & Abrams, D. B. (1988). Relevance of cue reactivity to understanding alcohol and smoking relapse. *Journal of Abnormal Psychology, 97*, 133–152.

Perkins, K., Epstein, L., Grobe, J., & Fonte, C. (1994). Tobacco abstinence, smoking cues, and the reinforcing value of smoking. *Pharmacology Biochemistry and Behavior, 47*, 107–112.

Pernanen, K. (1976). Alcohol and crimes of violence. In B. Kissin & H. Begletier (Eds.), *The biology of alcoholism: Social aspects of alcoholism*, (Vol. 4, pp. 351–444). New York: Plenum Press.

Petraitis, J., Flay, B. R., & Miller, T. Q. (1995). Reviewing theories of adolescent substance use: Organizing pieces of the puzzle. *Psychological Bulletin, 117*, 67–86.

Poulos, C. X., Hinson, R. E., & Siegel, S. (1981). The role of Pavlovian processes in drug tolerance and dependence: Implication for treatment. *Addictive Behaviors, 6*, 205–211.

Ray, B. A. (Ed.). (1988). *Learning factors in substance abuse* (NIDA Research Monograph 84, DHHS Publication No. ADM 90-1576). Washington, DC: U.S. Government Printing Office.

Robinson, T. E., & Berridge, K. C. (1993). The neural basis of drug craving: An incentive-sensitization theory of addiction. *Brain Research Reviews, 18,* 247–291.

Rohsenow, D. J., Niaura, R. S., Childress, A. R., Abrams, D. B., & Monti, P. M. (1990–1991). Cue reactivity in addictive behaviors: Theoretical and treatment implications. *The International Journal of the Addictions, 25,* 957–993.

Sayette, M. A. (1993). An appraisal-disruption model of alcohol's effects on stress responses in social drinkers. *Psychological Bulletin, 114,* 459–476.

Sayette, M. A., Monti, P. M., Rohsenow, D. J., Bird-Gulliver, S., Colby, S., Sirot, A., Niaura, R. S., & Abrams, D. B. (1994). *Journal of Studies on Alcohol, 55,* 629–633.

Schafer, J., & Brown, S. A. (1991). Marijuana and cocaine effect expectancies and drug patterns. *Journal of Consulting and Clinical Psychology, 59,* 558–565.

Sherman, J. E., Jorenby, D. E., & Baker, T. B. (1988). Classical conditioning with alcohol: Acquired preferences and aversions, tolerance, and urges/craving. In C. D. Chaudron & D. A. Wilkinson (Eds.), *Theories on alcoholism* (pp. 173–237). Toronto: Addiction Research Foundation.

Siegel, S. (1975). Evidence from rats that morphine tolerance is a learned response. *Journal of Comparative and Physiological Psychology, 89,* 498–506.

Siegel, S. (1976). Morphine analgesic tolerance: Its situation specificity supports a Pavlovian conditioning model. *Science, 193,* 323–325.

Siegel, S. (1978). A Pavlovian conditioning analysis of morphine tolerance. In N. A. Krasnegor, (Ed.), *Behavioral tolerance: Research and treatment implications* (pp. 27–53). Washington, DC: U.S. Government Printing Office.

Siegel, S. (1983). Classical condition, drug tolerance, and drug dependence. In Y. Israel, F. B. Glaser, H. Kalant, R. E. Dophama, W. Schmidt, and R. G. Smart (Eds.), *Research advances in alcohol and drug problems* (Vol. 7). New York: Plenum.

Smith, G. T., Goldman, M. S., Greenbaum, P. E., & Christiansen, B. A. (1995). Expectancy for social facilitation from drinking: The divergent paths of high-expectancy and low-expectancy adolescents. *Journal of Abnormal Psychology, 104,* 32–40.

Smith, J. A., & Epstein, L. H. (1991). Behavioral economic analysis of food choices in obese children. *Appetite, 17,* 91–95.

Solomon, R. L., & Corbit, J. D. (1973). An opponent-process theory of motivation: II. Cigarette addiction. *Journal of Abnormal Psychology, 81,* 158–171.

Solomon, R. L. & Corbit, J. D. (1974). An opponent-process theory of motivation: I. Temporal dynamics of affect. *Psychological Review, 81,* 119–145.

Southwick, L., Steele, C., Marlatt, A., & Lindell, M. (1981). Alcohol-related expectancies: Defined by phase of intoxica-tion and drinking experience. *Journal of Consulting and Clinical Psychology, 49,* 713–721.

Stacy, A. W. (1995). Memory, association and ambiguous cues in models of alcohol and marijuana use. *Experimental and Clinical Psychopharmacology, 3,* 183–194.

Stacy, A. W., Newcomb, M. D., & Bentler, P. M. (1991). Cognitive motivation and drug use: A 9-year longitudinal study. *Journal of Abnormal Psychology, 100,* 502–515.

Stacy, A. W., Widaman, K. F., & Marlatt, G. A. (1990). Expectancy models of alcohol use. *Journal of Personality and Social Psychology, 58,* 918–928.

Stasiewicz, P. R., & Maisto, S. A. (1993). Two-factor avoidance theory: The role of negative affect in the maintenance of substance use and substance use disorder. *Behavior Therapy, 24,* 337–356.

Steele, C. M., & Josephs, R. A. (1988). Drinking your troubles away II: An attention-allocation model of alcohol's effect on psychological stress. *Journal of Abnormal Psychology, 97,* 196–205.

Steele, C. M., & Josephs, R. A. (1990). Alcohol myopia. *American Psychologist, 45,* 921–933.

Stewart, J., de Wit, H., & Eikelboom, R. (1984). Role of unconditioned and conditioned drug effects in the self-administration of opiates and stimulants. *Psychological Review, 91,* 251–268.

Stritzke, W. G. K., Lang, A. R., & Patrick, C. J. (1996). Beyond stress and arousal: A reconceptualization of alcohol-emotion relations with special reference to psychophysiological methods. *Psychological Bulletin, 120,* 376–395.

Taylor, S. P., & Leonard, K. E. (1983). Alcohol and human physical aggression. In R. G. Geen & E. I. Donnerstein (Eds.), *Aggression: Theoretical and empirical reviews* (pp. 77–101). New York: Academic Press.

Tiffany, S. T. (1990). A cognitive model of drug urges and drug-use behavior: Role of automatic and nonautomatic processes. *Psychological Review, 97,* 147–168.

Tiffany, S. T. (1995). The role of cognitive factors in reactivity to drug cues. In D.C. Drummond, S. T. Tiffany, S. Glautier, and B. Remington (Eds.) *Addictive behaviour: Cue exposure theory and practice.* New York: Wiley.

Vannicelli, M. (1992). *Removing the roadblocks: Group psychotherapy with substance abusers and family members.* New York: Guilford Press.

Vuchinich, R. E. (1995). Alcohol abuse as a molar choice: An update of a 1982 proposal. *Psychology of Addictive Behaviors, 9,* 223–235.

Vuchinich R. E., & Tucker, J. A. (1983). Behavioral theories of choice as a framework for studying drinking behavior. *Journal of Abnormal Psychology, 92,* 408–416.

Vuchinich, R. E., & Tucker, J. A. (1988). Contributions from behavioral theories of choice to an analysis of alcohol abuse. *Journal of Abnormal Psychology, 97,* 181–195.

Vuchinich, R. E., & Tucker, J. A. (1996). Alcoholic relapse, life events, and behavioral theories of choice: A prospective analysis. *Experimental and Clinical Psychopharmacology, 4,* 19–28.

Webb, J. A., Baer, P. E., Francis, D. J., & Caid C. D. (1993). Relationship among social and intrapersonal risk, alcohol expectancies, and alcohol usage among early adolescents. *Addictive Behaviors, 18,* 127–134.

Wikler, A. (1948). Recent progress in research on the neurophysiological basis of morphine addiction. *American Journal of Psychiatry, 105,* 328.

Wikler, A. (1980). A theory of opioid dependence. In D. J. Lettiere, M. Sayers, & H. Wallerstein-Pearson (Eds.), *Theories of drug abuse: Selected contemporary perspectives* (DHHS Publication No. ADM 80-967, pp. 174–178). Washington, DC: Government Printing Office.

Wills, T. A. & Shiffman, S. (1985). Coping and substance use: A conceptual framework. In S. Shiffman & T. A., Wills (Eds.), *Coping and substance use* (pp. 3–24). Orlando, FL: Academic Press.

Wise, R. A., & Bozarth, M. A. (1987). A psychomotor stimulant theory of addiction. *Psychological Review, 94,* 469–492.

Zinberg, N. E., & Harding, W. M. (1982). *Control over intoxicant use.* New York: Human Sciences Press.

CHAPTER 11

FAMILY INFLUENCES ON ALCOHOL AND SUBSTANCE ABUSE

Theodore Jacob
Sheri L. Johnson

The objective of this chapter is to examine the role of family influences in the development of alcohol and substance abuse. The primary rationale for such an inquiry is based on the repeatedly cited relationship between parental and offspring substance abuse, a relationship that can be understood in terms of family genetic effects, family environmental effects, or most probably, some combination of the two. Although this chapter focuses primarily on family environmental effects, we acknowledge the considerable role that genetics plays in the development of some types of alcoholism and substance abuse, and the need to integrate these different types of influence into more complete models of alcoholism and substance abuse etiology (McGue, 1994).

Three considerations will serve to define this presentation. First, we emphasize alcohol abuse and alcoholism in contrast with the more general and heterogenous disorder of substance abuse. There is limited research literature examining family influences on offspring substance abuse due in large part to difficulty in recruiting intact families with drug abusing-parents. Second, we distinguish between two broad classes of family environmental effects, one referred to as alcohol (or drinking) specific and the other as nonalcohol (or nondrinking) specific. As described by Zucker and Noll (1982), the former type of influence is

specifically and directly tied to the development of drinking behavior, and most notably includes the modeling of an alcoholic parent's drinking behavior and the development of alcohol expectancies that arise from living with and learning from an alcoholic parent. In contrast, nonalcohol-specific effects accrue their potency in influencing child outcomes through more general disruptions in the family environment that are not unique to family environments involving parental alcoholism, and that lead to various adverse outcomes in addition to alcoholism. From this perspective, offspring alcohol abuse is closely linked to a generalized deviant behavior syndrome, which in turn, is traceable to a breakdown in child socialization. Third, we emphasize the need to delineate specific alcoholism subtypes to better clarify the role of family on etiology. Although the issue of alcoholism subgroups has received relatively little attention in the family literature compared to the broader alcoholism literature, we suggest that different subtypes are associated with different developmental pathways, with different implications for family models.

DRINKING-SPECIFIC EFFECTS

Epidemiological studies have reported reliable links between the drinking practices of parents and their children (Cotton, 1979; Merikangas, 1990); these findings provide support for the role of modeling effects or observational learning in the development of drinking behavior (Cahalan, Cisin, & Crossley, 1969; Webster, Harburg, Gleiberman, Schork, & DiFranceisco, 1989). Although parent modeling of alcohol use does not provide a full explanation of adolescent drinking outcomes, various reviewers suggest that a multivariate analysis (involving modeling effects as well as other family influences) should be more thoroughly examined (Barnes, 1990; Harburg, DiFranceisco, Webster, Gleiberman, & Schork, 1990). Beyond analyses of large community samples, interest in parent modeling effects has begun to be examined within families containing alcoholic parents. Recent findings by Zucker and colleagues (Zucker, Kincaid, Fitzgerald, & Bingham, 1995) suggest that children's learning about alcohol takes place much earlier than suspected; that is, "the development of internalized schemas about alcohol, as a drug, its effects, and its appropriate context of use—may also vary as a function of parental alcohol use." These findings indicate that much is to be learned about the mechanisms by which parental alcohol use influences the developing child's understanding and adoption of alcohol use patterns. In this regard, future studies could be profitably directed toward samples of young children raised by both alcoholic and social drinkers, and toward the incorporation of cognitive developmental research in examining such issues. Developmental theory, for example, suggests that modeling is likely to occur in a context where there is a warm parent–child relationship and where the parent controls significant power or rewards (Aronfreed, 1969; Bandura, 1969), a context that no doubt characterizes some types of alcoholics much better than others; for example, the late-onset, internalizing, nonantisocial, socially stable alcoholic.

Researchers have also examined alcohol expectancies in the transmission of maladaptive patterns of substance abuse; that is, investigations concerned with parental influences related to the child's development of alcohol expectancies. Review of this literature indicates that individuals who drink heavily have differing cognitive expectations regarding alcohol, and that expectancies predict (prospectively) the timing of drinking onset (Baumann, Fisher, Bryan, & Chenoweth, 1985) as well as problem drinking (Christiansen, Roehling, Smith, & Goldman, 1989). As noted in the previous reference to Noll and Zucker's work, alcohol-relevant attitudes and expectancies may be shaped quite early, suggesting that there may be a critical developmental period for the transmission of these expectations.

The relationship between parental drinking and child expectancies may be more complicated than currently acknowledged. A recent report by Chassin and Barrera (1993) demonstrates that early childhood expectancies may be modified by changes in parental drinking behavior. Among adolescent children of alcoholics, those whose fathers were no longer demonstrating problems with alcohol were more influenced by their own attitudes toward alcohol. For these adolescents, negative beliefs about drinking influenced them toward restraint. In contrast, adolescents whose fathers were still experiencing alcohol-related problems seemed not to restrain their drinking in response to negative beliefs. Furthermore, the work of Kandel and of Brook indicates that the impact of parental drinking on adolescent substance abuse may be indirect and can occur through at least two pathways: adolescents with heavy-drinking parents have best friends who drink more, and adolescents' perceptions of parental drinking predict their own alcohol use (Brook, Brook, Gordon, Whiteman, & Cohen, 1990; Kandel & Andreas, 1987). These findings suggest that early exposure to parental drinking may play an important role in influencing acceptance of peer drug use as well as in determining children's expectations regarding alcohol and drug use.

NONDRINKING SPECIFIC FAMILY INFLUENCES ON THE DEVELOPMENT OF SUBSTANCE ABUSE

Family effects that are not specific to drinking can be viewed as influences that produce cognitions, affect, and behavior that render the child vulnerable to deviancy, including but not limited to alcohol abuse. As described elsewhere (Jacob & Leonard, 1994), these types of family influences can be expressed as dyadic (marital, parent–child, sibling) as well as whole-family effects. The majority of studies relevant to nondrinking specific family effects has, however, focused on the pivotal role of the parent–child relationship, particularly the impact of parent–child interactions on child socialization and the development of aggressive, antisocial behavior. Given this status, only brief mention will be made of the potential impact of marital, sibling, and whole-family effects on child outcome before devoting major attention to parenting influences.

Marital Effects

Adverse child outcomes often develop in the context of a disturbed or dysfunctional relationship between husband

and wife. Whether or not marital discord has a direct effect on child behavior, or is mediated by other family or non-family relationships, is less certain. Emery's (1982) review of marital conflict and its impact on child maladjustment offers various explanations for how such effects could be mediated. Belsky's (1984) model of how parent personality, marital interactions, and extrafamilial stress and support relate to effective parenting provides an excellent guide for future research efforts. As discussed later, the child socialization model suggests that the most likely mediator of marital influences would be disturbance of the parent–child relationship via disrupted parenting. That is, marital conflict along with a host of other secondary influences (e.g., economic deprivation, family stress, social isolation, parental psychopathology) can disrupt primary parenting behaviors involving patterns of support and control of the child. To the extent that such disruption occurs, adverse child outcomes would be expected.

Sibling Effects

Brook et al. (1990) suggest three pathways by which sibling effects can occur: (1) the older sibling influences the younger sibling's personality via identification and modeling, resulting in similar attitudes, values, and behaviors; (2) the similarity between siblings is explained by common genetic dispositions; and (3) positive, nurturant, and conflict-free sibling relationships result in "decreased inner conflict and less psychic distress in the younger brother . . . [which in turn] . . . is related to more conventional attitudes and behavior, more responsibility, and less drug use." A very different approach is taken by Rowe and colleagues (Rowe & Gulley, 1992; Rowe, Woulbroun, & Gulley, 1994) who hypothesize that sibling similarity can be mediated by common peer effects, and as such, what has been interpreted as a sibling effect actually includes "a peer influence of older adolescents—both the older sibling and his/her friends—on a younger child's deviant behavior."

Family Systems Effects

For many family researchers, what is unique to family effects involves the complex system within which members operate and the impact of this system on individual and relationship behavior (Steinglass, 1987). Moos' notion of family environment and Reiss' work on family paradigm issue from this focus on the family system (Moos & Moos, 1976; Reiss & Klein, 1987). Most relevant to the

etiology of alcohol abuse, the oft-cited work of Wolin and Bennett on family rituals can be noted (Bennett & Wolin, 1990; Wolin, Bennett, & Noonan, 1979; Wolin, Bennett, Noonan, & Teitelbaum, 1980). Briefly, these investigators hypothesized and found support for the contention that cross-generational transmission of alcoholism increases in likelihood to the extent that alcoholism "invades" the family system and disrupts the enactment of family rituals—behaviors that give identity and meaning to the family (e.g., celebration of holidays, special events, routine daily activities such as dinnertime). Although these investigators contend that such disruptions occur at the family level and are independent of alcoholism severity, closer examination of these interpretations is necessary. Further, and in reference to the child socialization model, it seems quite possible that such ritual disruptions reflect familywide dysfunction that is funneled through and disrupts critical parenting behavior.

Parent–Child Effects

The impact of the parent–child relationship on the child's social and cognitive development is well established (Maccoby & Martin, 1983; Martin, 1987; Rollins & Thomas, 1979). Distillation of this body of theory and research yields two conclusions of particular relevance to present concerns: (1) All other variables that can impact child outcomes—parental dispositions, marital and sibling influences, and the sociocultural context in which the family operates—are "played-out" within the interactional sequences that come to define the parent–child relationship. As described by Snyder and Huntley (1990), parent–child interaction is the mechanism through which "developmental, contextual, and historical factors influence development . . . [and it is] . . . the proximal transducer by which these distal variables affect child outcome." (2) Two major parenting dimensions, nurturance and control, have been shown repeatedly to impact on parent–child interactions. Disturbance in either or both of these parenting dimensions can have severe and wide-ranging effects on the child's social–emotional and cognitive development. In particular, inadequate parenting—characterized by lack of affection and/or high levels of criticism and hostility, lax or inconsistent discipline and supervision, and general lack of involvement—provides the foundation for the development of an aggressive, antisocial behavior pattern that can be seen as early as the preschool years in the form of non-compliance and evolving over time into a behavior pattern characterized by early peer rejection and poor academic performance, and by continuing expressions of delinquent acts, alcohol and drug abuse, and association with deviant peers. Significantly, it is well known that child conduct disorder and adolescent delinquency predispose to and covary with early-age onset of alcohol abuse (Jessor & Jessor, 1977; Lewis, 1984; Lewis & Bucholz, 1991; Loeber & Dishion, 1983; Widiger & Corbitt, 1993; Zucker, 1989; Zucker & Gomberg, 1986).

The work of Patterson and his colleagues represents the most thorough explication of the parenting effects model (Dishion, 1990; Patterson, 1976, 1982, 1986; Patterson, Reid, & Dishion, 1992; Snyder & Huntley, 1990). As with other child socialization models (e.g., Barnes, 1990; Brook et al., 1990), the investigative focus is on parent–child interaction relevant to adequate and necessary parenting behavior; namely, to parental warmth, support, and nurturance on the one hand, and to parental involvement, control, and supervision on the other hand. Disturbances in either or both of these dimensions disrupt the child's development of self-acceptance and self-control. The Oregon group has emphasized disturbances in the control dimension as most relevant to the development of undercontrolled behavior; that is, "a failure in compliance training begins during the child's early years and becomes the key feature of those families who produce antisocial children—a breakdown which is defined in terms of inadequate discipline, monitoring, modeling, involvement, and positive reinforcement strategies. The major outcome of this process is the development of a coercive interaction style, which slowly but steadily generalizes to relationships outside the home and severely interferes with the child's social and cognitive development" (Snyder & Huntley, 1990).

Brook et al.'s (1990) family model emphasizes child socialization within the context of parent–child interaction, but gives greater weight to the parental support dimension. Briefly, it is hypothesized that a conflict-free, warm, and supportive relationship between parent and child "enables the parents to convey their version of society's values to their offspring through internalization, leading to increased adolescent identification with the parents . . . [and to the] . . . internalization of more conventional attitudes and behavior. Adolescent conventionality, in turn, serves to diminish the influence of peers compared to that of parents, and protects the adolescent from associating with drug using peers" (p. 342).

Empirical support for the hypothesized relationship between inadequate parenting and the development of aggressive, antisocial behavior in childhood and adolescence is drawn from three literatures. First, the voluminous child development literature has repeatedly, consistently, and strongly linked parenting practices with child development, in particular, to the development of childhood aggression (Maccoby & Martin, 1983; Martin, 1987; Peterson & Rollins, 1987; Rollins & Thomas, 1979). Second, SLT-based studies of child psychopathology and its treatment over the past two decades have continued to refine, clarify, and document the fine-grained nature of parent–child interaction that temporally precedes and is associated with the emergence of aggressive, antisocial behavior (Patterson et al., 1992; Snyder & Huntley, 1990; Wahler & Dumas, 1987). Third, the longitudinal literature relevant to the development of both delinquency and antisocial behavior has repeatedly identified "inadequate parenting" in the early child histories of those who subsequently develop adolescent and adult expressions of antisocial behavior including adolescent delinquency and adult criminality. (See Loeber & Dishion, 1983; Loeber & Stouthamer-Loeber, 1986; McCord, 1991; Zucker, 1989; Zucker & Gomberg, 1986.) Fourth, similar patterns of inadequate parenting, characterized by a lack of control and monitoring, have been demonstrated to relate to substance-use initiation and frequency (Block, Block, & Keyes, 1988; Dishion, Patterson, Stoolmiller, & Skinner, 1991). In an important longitudinal study, Baumrind (1991) found that children whose parents displayed less directive and assertive control behavior during interactions at age 4 were more likely to become heavy marijuana users as adolescents.

ALCOHOLISM SUBTYPES

Alcoholism is an etiologically and developmentally heterogeneous disorder. Antisocial alcoholism, a major subtype of this disorder, has received the most attention. As noted, the family model of alcoholism that has emphasized nondrinking-specific effects and the critical role of inadequate parenting in the development of early childhood aggression seems most relevant to understanding the etiology of antisocial alcoholism. Although other variants have been proposed, the family-influences variant may be particularly relevant to the etiology of negative-affect alcoholism. As Zucker (1987) notes: "a burgeoning developmental literature on parent behavior and child rearing practices in depressive homes suggests that a linkage may be discovered between social deprivation occurring in such households, and the greater vulnerability to interpersonal stress and to problem use of alcohol in adulthood."

Hussong and Chassin (1993) report that negative affect mediates the relationship between stress and drinking behavior among adolescent children of alcoholics. Similar findings have emerged in the work of Aneshensel and Huba (1983) and Newcomb and Harlow (1986), indicating that in a high-risk population, the role of negative affect may help predict drinking behavior. Chassin, Curran, Hussong, and Colder (1996) found that parental alcoholism increased environmental stress among adolescent children, which was then related to increased negative-affect. Affective disorder among the parents was also related to increased emotionality and negative affect, suggesting that both alcoholism and affective disorder make unique contributions to the possible development of negative affect alcoholism among offspring. Interestingly, children with higher levels of negative affect were more likely to associate with drug-using peers, and it was this factor that contributed to increased substance use. Further progress in understanding the development of negative affect alcoholism could also be aided by longitudinal studies that begin during adolescence and continue into young adulthood. For example, individuals with a comorbid disorder of alcoholism and depression have a considerably later onset of alcohol problems than do antisocial abusers. Hesselbrock, Hesselbrock, & Workman-Daniels (1986) report an average age of onset for such individuals to be approximately 27–29 years of age. Zucker (1987) suggests that such individuals may experience difficulties with peers and with their marriage, and may drink in an attempt to deal with such difficulties or to improve their interpersonal relationships. If true, we might expect that such individuals will exhibit fewer alcohol-related or antisocial problems throughout childhood and adolescence, but will begin to escalate their drinking in response to early adult events (marriage, career entry), which for others serve to mitigate excessive alcohol use. A careful analysis of those who develop new alcohol problems after marriage, then, might shed light on the processes involved in the development of this form of alcoholism. A longitudinal study that begins during adolescence and continues through the young adult years would be particularly important in identifying the specific influences that may promote these different developments.

Like alcoholism, depression among parents appears to be expressed in specific patterns of family interaction, characterized by increased negativity and decreased positivity (Hinchcliffe, Hooper, & Roberts, 1978; Jacob & Johnson, 1997; Johnson & Jacob, 1997), and decreased hostility from family members after self-demeaning remarks (Biglan, Hops, Sherman, Friedman, Arthur, & Osteen, 1985). For example, parents with depression may be likely to model helplessness when faced with stress (Nolen-Hoeksema, Wolfson, Mumme, & Guskin, 1995). Alternatively, parents may model more negative cognitions regarding themselves, their future, and their world (Hammen, Adrian, & Hirohito, 1988). Children exposed to depressed parents may internalize this affective style. As these more sophisticated models of parental influences on risk for depression become developed and empirically validated, they will be important to integrate into research on this alcohol subtype.

FUTURE RESEARCH DIRECTIONS

Moderators of Risk

Although family history of alcoholism has generally been related to drinking and nondrinking problems among offspring, children of alcoholics (COAs) as a group exhibit a wide range of outcomes and the majority appear indistinguishable from children without parental alcoholism (Jacob & Leonard, 1986; Johnson, Leonard, & Jacob, 1989). The importance of this finding seems clear: we must move beyond COA–non-COA contrasts to systematic analyses of within-group variance in order to better understand the conditions under which family history of alcoholism results in adverse outcomes. Such a research focus is one that has a primary interest in moderators of risk. Briefly, a moderator is a variable that influences the direction or strength of an association between a predictor and an outcome variable (Barron & Kenny, 1986). Specific to the COA literature, a moderator would serve to attenuate or exacerbate the relationship between family history of alcoholism and offspring outcome. To conclude that a variable is a moderator, the research design must include both COAs and non-COAs and the analysis must demonstrate a significant interaction between the moderator and family history over and above outcome variance accounted for independently by family history and the moderator. Inspection of the relevant literature reveals few studies that have satisfied all of these conditions (Sher, 1991), although the empirical and clinical–theoretical literature suggests various factors that may function as moderators of risk.

Beginning with influences characterized by their molarity and distal relationship to offspring behavior, social class has been implicated as a potential moderator of risk by several writers. Most significantly, the adoption studies of Cloninger, Bohman, and Sigvardsson (1981) indicate that for one type of alcoholism (Type 1 or milieu-limited alcoholism), social class interacted with family history in determining the frequency and severity of off-spring alcoholism. Notwithstanding some inconsistencies in this literature (e.g., Nylander & Rydelius, 1982), it can be argued that social class, to the extent that it is related to differences in material and psychological resources and associated stress and disruption, can affect the stability of family relationships in general and child-rearing practices in particular; in turn, child socialization can be compromised, resulting in personality and interpersonal impairments and the increased likelihood that significant disorder will ensue.

Wolin and colleagues have reported that disruption of family rituals (holidays, vacations, etc.) predicts elevated rates of alcoholism among the offspring of alcoholics (Wolin et al., 1979; Wolin et al., 1980). In addition, McCord's (1988) follow-up data on the Cambridge–Somerville study revealed a significant interaction between family history of alcoholism and the wife's esteem for her husband. For families with an alcoholic father (but not for families with a nonalcoholic father), the mother's "high esteem for her alcoholic husband increased risk for alcoholism of the son" (McCord, 1988, p. 357), a finding that might be explained in several ways; for example, high maternal esteem for father could reflect mother's personality/psychopathology, the severity of the father's drinking and the disruptive nature of his behavior, or the dynamics of the mother–father interaction and associated differences in marital satisfaction.

Alcoholic parents who are characterized by hostile/impulsive features have disruptive family relationships that foster greater family instability and stress, compromised marital and parent–child relationships, and more limited modeling opportunities of a positive, adaptive nature (Sher & Trull, 1994; Zucker, 1987). Similarly, to the extent that the nonalcoholic parent evidenced significant levels of psychopathology, family stability would be adversely affected and the impact of parental alcoholism would be exacerbated (Jacob & Leonard, 1986; Johnson & Jacob, 1995).

Finally, drinking patterns moderate the impact of family history of alcoholism on child outcomes. In-home (versus episodic, out-of-home) drinking patterns are related to less externalizing, acting-out behavior on the part of the alcoholic, greater marital satisfaction, and by implication, better child outcomes (Dunn, Jacob, Hummon, & Seilhamer, 1987; Jacob, Dunn, & Leonard, 1983; Jacob & Leonard, 1988).

AUTHOR NOTE

This research was supported by NIAAA Grant No. 2R37AA0307 from the National Institute on Alcohol Abuse and Alcoholism and by a Research Career Scientist Award from the Palo Alto V.A. Health Care System to Theodore Jacob.

REFERENCES

Aneshensel, C. S., & Huba, G. J. (1983). Depression, alcohol use, and smoking over one year: A four-wave longitudinal causal model. *Journal of Abnormal Psychology, 92*, 134–150.

Aronfreed, J. (1969). The concept of internalization. In D. A. Goslin (Ed.), *Handbook of socialization theory and research* (pp. 263–324). Chicago: Rand McNally.

Bandura, A. (1969). Social-learning theory of identificatory processes. In D. A. Goslin (Ed.), *Handbook of socialization theory and research* (pp. 213–262). Chicago: Rand McNally.

Barnes, G. M. (1990). Impact of the family on adolescent drinking patterns. In R. L. Collins, K. E. Leonard, & J. S. Searles (Eds.), *Alcohol and the family: Research and clinical perspectives*. New York: Guilford Press.

Baron, R., & Kenny, P. (1986). The moderator-mediator variable distinction in social psychological research: Conceptual, strategic, and statistical considerations. *Journal of Personality and Social Psychology, 51*, 1173–1182.

Bauman, K. E., Fisher, L. A., Bryan, E. S., & Chenoweth, R. I. (1985). Relationship between subjective expected utility and behavior: A longitudinal study of adolescent drinking behavior. *Journal of Studies on Alcohol, 46*, 32–38.

Baumrind, D. (1991). The influence of parenting style on adolescent competence and substance use. *Journal of Early Adolescence, 11*, 56–95.

Belsky, J. (1984). The determinants of parenting: A process model. *Child Development, 55*, 83–96.

Bennett, L. A., & Wolin, S. J. (1990). Family culture and alcoholism transmission. In R. L. Collins, K. E. Leonard, & J. S. Searles (Eds.), *Alcohol and the family: Research and clinical perspective* (pp. 194–219). New York: Guilford Press.

Biglan, A., Hops, H., Sherman, L., Friedman, L. S., Arthur, J., & Osteen, V. (1985). Problem-solving interactions with depressed women and their husbands. *Behavior Therapy, 16*, 431–451.

Block, J., Block, J. H., & Keyes, S. (1988). Longitudinally fore-telling drug usage in adolescence: Early childhood personality and environmental precursors. *Child Development, 59,* 336–355.

Brook, J. S., Brook, D. W., Gordon, H. S., Whiteman, M., & Cohen, P. (1990). The psychosocial etiology of adolescent drug use: A family interactional approach. *Genetic, Social and General Psychology Monograph, 116,* 111–267.

Cahalan, D., Cisin, I., & Crossley, H. (1969). American drinking practices: A national study of drinking, behavior and attitudes. *Rutgers Center of Alcohol Studies Monograph No. 7,* Rutgers University, New Brunswick, NJ.

Chassin, L., & Barrera, M. (1993). Substance use escalation and substance use restraint among adolescent children of alco-holics. *Psychology of Addictive Behaviors, 7,* 3–20.

Chassin, L., Curran, P. J., Hussong, A. M., & Colder, C. R. (1996). The relation of parent alcoholism to adolescent substance use: A longitudinal follow-up study. *Journal of Abnormal Psychology, 105(1),* 70–80.

Christiansen, B. A., Roehling, P. V., Smith, G. T., & Goldman, M. S. (1989). Using alcohol expectancies to predict adolescent drinking behavior after one year. *Journal of Consulting and Clinical Psychology, 57,* 93–99.

Cloninger, C. R., Bohman, M., & Sigvardsson, S. (1981). Inheritance of alcohol abuse: Cross fostering analysis of adopted men. *Archives of General Psychiatry, 38,* 861–868.

Cotton, N. (1979). The familial incidence of alcoholism: A review. *Journal of Studies on Alcohol, 40,* 89–116.

Dishion, T. (1990). The peer context of troublesome child and adolescent behavior. In P. E. Leone (Ed.), *Understanding trou-bled and troubling youth.* Newbury Park, CA: Sage.

Dishion, T. J., Patterson, G. R., Stoolmiller, M., & Skinner, M. L. (1991). Family, school and behavioral antecedents to early adolescent involvement with antisocial peers. *Developmental Psychology, 27,* 172–180.

Dunn, N. J., Jacob, T., Hummon, N., & Seilhamer, R. A. (1987). Marital stability in alcoholic–spouse relationships as a func-tion of drinking pattern and location. *Journal of Abnormal Psychology, 96,* 99–107.

Emery, R. E. (1982). Interparental conflict and the children of dis-cord and divorce. *Psychological Bulletin, 92,* 310–330.

Hammen, C., Adrian, C., & Hirohito, D. (1988). A longitudinal test of the attributional vulnerability model in children at risk for depression. *British Journal of Clinical Psychology, 27,* 37–46.

Harburg, E., DiFranceisco, W., Webster, S., Gleiberman, L. & Schork, A. (1990). Familial transmission of alcohol use: II. Imitation of and aversion to parent drinking (1960) by adult offspring (1977)—Tecumseh, Michigan. *Journal of Studies on Alcohol, 51,* 245–256.

Hesselbrock, V., Hesselbrock, M., & Workman-Daniels, K. (1986). Effect of major depression and antisocial personality on alcoholism: Course and motivational patterns. *Journal of Studies on Alcohol, 47,* 207–212.

Hinchcliffe, M., Hooper, D., & Roberts, F. J. (1978). *The melan-choly marriage.* New York: Wiley.

Hussong, A. M., & Chassin, L. (1993). The stress-negative affect model of adolescent alcohol use: Disaggregating negative affect. *Journal of Studies on Alcohol, 55,* 707–718.

Jacob, T., Dunn, N., & Leonard, K. (1983). Patterns of alcohol abuse and family stability. *Alcoholism: Clinical and Experimental Research, 7,* 382–385.

Jacob, T., & Johnson, S. (1997). Parent–child interaction among depressed fathers and mothers: Impact on child functioning. Submitted for publication. *Journal of Family Psychology, 11,* 391–409.

Jacob, T., & Leonard, K. (1986). Psychosocial functioning in chil-dren of alcoholic, depressed and normal control fathers. *Journal of Studies on Alcohol, 47,* 373–380.

Jacob, T., & Leonard, K. E. (1988). Alcoholic spouse interaction as a function of alcoholism subtype and alcohol consumption interaction. *Journal of Abnormal Psychology, 97,* 232–237.

Jacob, T., & Leonard, K. (1994). Family and peer influences in the development of adolescent alcohol abuse. In R. Zucker, G. Boyd, & J. Howard (Eds.), *The development of alcohol prob-lems: Exploring the biopsychosocial matrix of risk* (NIAAA Research Monograph No. 26, NIH Publication No. 94-3495, pp. 123–155). Washington, DC: National Institute on Alcohol Abuse and Alcoholism.

Jessor, R., & Jessor, S. L. (1977). *Problem behavior and psy-chosocial development: A longitudinal study of youth.* New York: Academic Press.

Johnson, S., & Jacob, T. (1997). Marital interactions of depressed men and women. *Journal of Consulting and Clinical Psychology, 65,* 15–23.

Johnson, S., & Jacob, T. (1995). Psychosocial functioning in chil-dren of alcoholic fathers. *Psychology of Addictive Behaviors, 9,* 101–113.

Johnson, S., Leonard, K., & Jacob, T. (1989). Drinking, drinking styles, and drug use in children of alcoholics, depressives, and controls. *Journal of Studies on Alcohol, 50,* 427–431.

Kandel, D. B., & Andrews K. (1987). Process of adolescent socialization by parents and peers. *The International Journal of the Addictions, 22,* 319–342.

Lewis, C. E. (1984). Alcoholism, antisocial personality, and nar-cotic addiction: An integrative approach. *Psychiatric Developments, 3,* 223–235.

Lewis, C. E. & Bucholz, K. K. (1991). Alcoholism, antisocial behavior and family history. *British Journal of Addiction, 86,* 177–194.

Loeber, R., & Dishion, T. (1983). Early predictors of male delin-quency: A review. *Psychological Bulletin, 94,* 68–98.

Loeber, R., & Stouthamer-Loeber, M. (1986). Family factors as correlates and predictors of juvenile conduct problems and delinquency. In M. Tonry & N. Morris (Eds.), *Crime and jus-tice: An annual review of research* (Vol. 7, pp. 29–149). Chicago: University of Chicago Press.

Maccoby, E. E., & Martin, J. A. (1983). Socialization in the context of the family: Parent–child interaction. In E. M. Hetherington (Ed.), *Handbook of child psychology: Vol. 4. Socialization, personality and social development* (pp. 1–102). New York: Wiley.

Martin, B. (1987). Developmental perspectives on family theory and psychopathology. In T. Jacob (Ed.), *Family interaction and psychopathology* (pp. 163–202). New York: Plenum Press.

McCord, J. (1988). Identifying developmental paradigms leading to alcoholism. *Journal of Studies on Alcohol, 49,* 357–362.

McCord, J. (1991). Family relationships, juvenile delinquency, and adult criminality. *Criminology, 29,* 397–417.

McGue, M. (1994). Genes, environment and the etiology of alcoholism. In R. Zucker, G. Boyd, & J. Howard (Eds.), *The development of alcohol problems: Exploring the biopsychosocial matrix of risk* (NIAAA Research Monograph No. 26, NIH Publication No. 94-3495, pp. 1–40). Washington, DC: National Institute on Alcohol Abuse and Alcoholism.

Merikangas, K. R. (1990). The genetic epidemiology of alcoholism. *Psychological Medicine, 20,* 11–22.

Moos, R. H., & Moos, B. S. (1976). A typology of family social environments. *Family Process, 15,* 357–371.

Newcomb, M. D., & Harlow, L. L. (1986). Life events and substance use among adolescents: Mediating effects of perceived loss of control and meaninglessness in life. *Journal of Personality and Social Psychology, 51,* 564–577.

Nolen-Hoeksema, S., Wolfson, A., Mumme, D., & Guskin, K. (1995). Helplessness in children of depressed and nondepressed mothers. *Developmental Psychology, 31,* 377–387.

Nye, C. L., Zucker, R. A., & Fitzgerald, H. E. (1995). Early intervention in the path to alcohol problems through conduct problems: Treatment involvement and child behavior change. *Journal of Consulting and Clinical Psychology, 63,* 831–840.

Nylander, I., & Rydelius, P. (1982). A comparison between children of alcoholic fathers from excellent versus poor social conditions. *Acta Psychiatrica Scandinavica, 71,* 809.

Patterson, G. R. (1976). The aggressive child: Victim and architect of a coercive system. In L. A. Hamerlynck, L. C. Handy, & E. J. Mash (Eds.), *Behavior modification and families: Vol. I. Theory and research.* New York: Brunner/Mazel.

Patterson, G. R. (1982). *Coercive family process.* Eugene, Oregon: Castilia.

Patterson, G. R. (1986). Performance models for antisocial boys. *American Psychologist, 41,* 432–444.

Patterson, G. R., Reid, J., & Dishion, T. (1992). *Antisocial boys.* Eugene, Oregon: Castilia.

Peterson, G. & Rollins, B. (1987). Parent–child socialization. In M. Sussman & S. Steinmetz (Eds.), *Handbook of marriage and the family.* New York: Plenum Press.

Reiss, D., & Klein, D. (1987). Paradigm and pathogenesis: A family centered approach to problems of etiology and treatment of psychiatric disorders. In T. Jacob (Ed.), *Family interaction*

and psychopathology (pp. 203–255). New York: Plenum Press.

Rollins, B. C., & Thomas, D. L. (1979). Parental support, power and control techniques in the socialization of children. In W. R. Burr, R. Hill, F. I. Nye, & I. L. Reiss (Eds.), *Contemporary theories about the family: Vol. I. Research based theories* (pp. 317–364). New York: Free Press.

Rowe, D. C., & Gulley, B. L. (1991). Sibling effects on substance use, delinquency, and sexual experience: Decomposing "shared" family influences. Submitted for publication.

Rowe, D. C., Woulbroun, E . J., & Gulley, B. L. (1994). Peers and friends as nonshared environmental influences. In E. M. Hetherington, D. Reiss, & R. Plomin (Eds.), *Nonshared environmental influences in development* (pp. 159–173). New York: Erlbaum.

Sher, K. J. (Ed.). (1991). *Children of alcoholics: A critical appraisal of theory and research.* Chicago: University of Chicago Press.

Sher, K. J., & Trull, T. J. (1994). Personality and disinhibitory psychopathology: Alcoholism and antisocial personality disorder. *Journal of Abnormal Psychology, 103,* 92–102.

Snyder, J., & Huntley, D. (1990). Troubled families and troubled youth: The development of antisocial behavior and depression in children. In P. E. Leone (Ed.), *Understanding troubled and troubling youth.* Newbury Park, CA: Sage.

Steinglass, P. (1987.) A systems view of family interaction and psychopathology. In T. Jacob (Ed.), *Family interaction and psychopathology* (pp. 163–202). New York: Plenum Press.

Wahler, R. G., & Dumas, J. E. (1987). Family factors in childhood psychology. In T. Jacob (Ed.), *Family interaction and psychopathology* (pp. 581–627). New York: Plenum Press.

Webster, D., Harburg, E., Gleiberman, L., Schork, A., & DiFrancesico, W. (1989). Familial transmission of alcohol use: I. Parent and adult offspring use over 17 years—Tecumseh, Michigan. *Journal of Studies on Alcohol, 50,* 557–566.

Widiger, T. A., & Corbitt, E. M. (1993). Antisocial Personality Disorder: Proposals for DSM-IV: Special feature: DSM-IV reviews of the personality disorder: III. *Journal of Personality Disorders, 7,* 63–77.

Wolin, S. J., Bennett, L. A., & Noonan, D. L. (1979). Family rituals and the recurrence of alcoholism over generations. *American Journal of Psychiatry, 136,* 589–593.

Wolin, S. J., Bennett, L. A., Noonan, D. L., & Teitelbaum, M. A. (1980). Disrupted family rituals. *Journal of Studies on Alcohol, 41,* 199–214.

Zucker, R. A. (1987). The four alcoholisms: A developmental account of the etiologic process. In P. C. Rivers (Ed.), *Nebraska symposium on motivation, 1986: Alcohol and addictive behavior* (pp. 27–83). Lincoln: University of Nebraska Press.

Zucker, R. A. (1989). Is risk for alcoholism predictable? A probabilistic approach to a developmental problem. In E. S.

Gomberg (Ed.), *Drugs and society: Current issues in alcohol/drug studies, 3,* 69–92.

Zucker, R. A. (1994). Pathways to alcohol problems and alcoholism: A developmental account of evidence for multiple alcoholisms and for contextual contributions to risk. In R. Zucker, G. Boyd, & J. Howard, (Eds.) *The development of alcohol problems: Exploring the biopsychosocial matrix of risk* (NIAAA Research Monograph No. 26, NIH Publication No. 94-3453, pp. 1–40). U.S. Department of Health and Human Services. Washington, D.C.

Zucker, R. A., & Gomberg, E. S. (1986). Etiology alcoholism reconsidered: The case for a biopsychosocial process. *American Psychologist, 41,* 783–793.

Zucker, R., Kincaid, S., Fitzgerald, H., & Bingham, C. (1995). Alcohol schema acquisition in preschoolers: Differences between children of alcoholics and children of nonalcoholics. *Alcoholism: Clinical and Experimental Research, 19,* 1–7.

Zucker, R. A., & Noll, R. B. (1982). Precursors and developmental influences on drinking and alcoholism: Etiology from a longitudinal perspective. In NIAAA (Ed.), *Alcohol and Health Monographs No. 1: Alcohol Consumption and Related Problems* (DAAS Publication, No. (ADM) 82-1190). Rockville, MD: .

ADDENDUM

A notable exception can be found in the recent work of Zucker and colleagues, who are conducting an early-intervention study of conduct problems in preschool children of alcoholic parents (Nye, Zucker, & Fitzgerald, 1995). In brief, these researchers hypothesized that such interventions may change risk for alcoholism among these children, which in effect will allow the investigators to test a model of risk of alcoholism that is mediated by antisocial behavior.

CHAPTER 12

CULTURE

Dwight B. Heath

CULTURE AND DRUGS

In the most general terms, various authors have found it helpful to refer to the cultural (or sociocultural) model of substance abuse. This model encompasses the widely accepted proposition that different beliefs and attitudes about drugs and their effects, combined with beliefs and attitudes about how, what, where, when, with whom, and for what purposes one should or should not use drugs, together with attitudes toward the meanings of all of those, are directly related to the frequency with which problems are associated with substance use, and to differences in the nature of such problems, when they occur, in various cultures (Heath, 1988).

In one sense, it may seem inappropriate to discuss culture—an inanimate concept, completely devoid of agency—as an etiological factor in relation to substance abuse. But in another sense, it is just as appropriate to speak of culture in that way as it is to speak of genetics, biochemistry, psychophysiology, psychology, family, or sociology—all similarly inanimate and without agency. In each instance, the precision and accuracy of scientific concerns about etiology give way to colloquial convenience and a popular manner of speaking that has come to be understood, even accepted by professionals as well as laypersons—a reliance on metaphor in which we speak *as if* these systems of ideas and bunches of types of influence were in themselves influential.

In the field of substance abuse, some people refer to "systems theory," which emphasizes that drug use, as any human behavior, cannot be understood by biological, psychological, or social approaches alone. The term "system" here implies a web of integral interrelationships, such that the whole is different from the sum of its parts and, by implication, a change in any of the component parts reverberates, affecting many of the other parts of the system and even effecting changes in some. It is difficult to search for single determining factors in a complex world where the individual human being is one biopsychosocial system, and which is part of a society that is an even more encompassing biopsychosocial system. If systems theory is wanting in its ability to make precise predictions about how specific variables will react, its value is more apparent in alerting us to the shortcomings of many other more simplistic theories that purport to be explanatory but that overlook whole categories of variables that are relevant. "Cultural" or "sociocultural" theory is systemic, but it tends to emphasize the cultural and social parts of the mix, if only because most other theories (especially biological and psychological) tend to slight or ignore them.

A literalist could justifiedly say that culture does not cause anything—least of all, substance abuse. But it is equally justifiable to say that cultural factors influence virtually all aspects of human lifestyles, and are dramatically apparent in "causing" different populations to use different drugs, in different ways, resulting in different effects and different kinds and rates of associated problems. One of the most compelling aspects of a cultural perspective on substance use is that a single species, Homo sapiens, often uses a single substance such as marijuana, coca, ethanol, and opium in so many different ways and with such varied attitudes, values, beliefs, and practices about who should use it, when, in what context, for what purposes, with what outcomes, and so forth. For that matter, culture is equally important in designating who should *not* use a substance, or when and where its use is *in*appropriate, as well as what aims and outcomes of use are "excessive," "abusive," or otherwise wrong.

It is all very well to speak in general terms about how cultural factors are manifest in relation to drugs; however for the sake of clarity it is important to flesh out such a proposition with some specific examples. At the simplest level, we can talk about some ways in which the ecological setting appears to set severe limits on drug use, but importantly, human ingenuity has devised cultural adaptations that partly overcome such limits. A vivid example is that of the Koryak of Siberia, (Jochelson, 1905) who live in a frigid environment where very few of the world's many psychoactive plants can grow. The Koryak do, however, have the hallucinogenic mushroom fly-agaric (*Amanita muscaria*), and eat it for an intoxication that they consider enjoyable and transcendentally revealing. The mushroom is in such short supply, however, that there is never enough to go around in the all-male social settings where it is taken. They have a folk belief that much of the psychoactive agent passes through the body virtually unchanged, so it is common for them to enjoy it second-hand, by drinking the urine of a comrade who has eaten a mushroom. In recent years, biochemical analysis has proved that this works. Use of similar hallucinogenic mushrooms is solemnly and sedately integrated in religious and medically diagnostic ceremonies, held largely by women among the Mazatec Indians of Mexico (Wasson, Cowan, Cowan, & Rhodes, 1974).

Closer to home for many may be the varied uses of peyote. To the Huichol Indians of Mexico, peyote is a sacrament to be hunted, praised, and consumed for a deeply personal revelation (Myerhoff, 1974). Similarly revelatory but intimately linked to a strict religious and moral code, peyote is also used by Indians of many tribal and linguistic affiliations in the widespread Native American Church (La Barre, 1970). Both ritual usages contrast markedly with its adoption as a secular recreational drug by hippies and "flower children" of diverse ethnicity during the counterculture of the 1960s.

Alcohol—or, more accurately, ethanol, the only one among many types of alcohol that human beings customarily drink—is viewed by some groups as an important part of the diet and by others as a dangerously harmful poison. To some it is a gift of the gods and a sacred substance facilitating transcendental drunkenness, whereas to others it is considered an anathema and drinkers are sinners. Even in the same society, ethanol can be viewed as a sedative and relaxant or feared as likely to trigger violence or aggression (Heath, 1982).

Marijuana cigarettes were used by Jamaican sugarcane cutters to give them extra energy while working. It surprised researchers to find that the heaviest smokers earned the most, had the best houses, and provided the most schooling for their children (Rubin, 1975). A similarly ambitious study, also involving elaborate collaboration between biomedical and psychosocial investigators, revealed a similar pattern among longshoremen and other manual laborers in Costa Rica (Carter, 1980). Ironically, at the same time, college students in both Costa Rica and United States were using marijuana as a "drop-out drug" that was said to cause "the amotivational syndrome" of overwhelming relaxation and indifference. Tourists in the Netherlands are often surprised at decals in the windows of coffee shops that signal easy availability of marijuana. In sharp contrast, the United States recently banned its sale even for medical purposes, for which it is widely recognized to be beneficial (e.g., relief for glaucoma and from the nausea of chemotherapy). "The killer weed" that was supposed to trigger "reefer madness" among adolescents in the 1930s was virtually emblematic of their pacifist agemates a generation later. That a single substance can have such different uses and meanings in a single society, or in nearby societies, demonstrates that something very different from biochemistry and physiology must be involved.

CULTURE AND THE INDIVIDUAL

In describing these above situations, I have used a convenient shorthand that many construe as meaning "culture A does this and culture B does that." In fact, cultures do not do much of anything, but people do. When most members of a given population do much the same thing, it is tempting to suggest that their culture does it, or at least prescribes it. More to the point, some would even say that their culture "makes" individuals believe and behave in a given manner.

Of course, it would be nonsense to suggest that all members of a population behave identically, or even that the range of variation is so slight around a norm that there is no significant deviance. But it is important to keep in mind that the very idea of "normal behavior" is more often phrased in sociocultural terms than it is in statistical terms, so that the significance of "deviance" is similarly judged by social and not numerical standards. In most populations most of the time, there is substantial regularity within a tolerated range, which we tend to call "patterns" or "norms" for both beliefs and behaviors. The major reason why we find so much consistency among the unique and diverse members of a society is that they have been shaped by a process of social learning, with rewards (affective as well as material) and punishments (similarly psychic as well as physical). The human neonate has a few instincts, but the vast majority of what an older infant, a child, a youth, or an adult does—or says—or thinks—results from a never-ending process of learning, in which social reinforcements, both positive and negative, explicit and implicit, play a dominant role.

Males are taught that they are expected to behave, and even to evaluate, differently from females. As an individual gradually matures, different patterns are acceptable (or expected, or required, or disapproved, or disallowed) at different ages. Myths and heroes convey values just as do proverbs and classroom exercises. Formal schooling must be recognized as only a small part of education and socialization; norms or social consensus usually guide people's everyday behavior far more than do laws. In some respects, it is probably more psychologically efficient when "the formal system" echoes and reinforces "the informal system," but both can have major effects on what an individual will think or do.

One analogy that is often helpful in conceiving of culture is: culture is to behavior as grammar is to speech. One learns many of the rules of grammar without ever being aware of them—or of anything called "grammar" for that matter. Most children are speaking clearly and imaginatively long before they are confronted with grammar, parts of speech, tenses, gender, moods, or voices. In a similar way, most individuals incorporate the world view, ideas about their place in relation to others, gestures, manner of eating, and such customs, mores, or cultural traits, long before they have heard anything about culture.

Then too, we must recognize that there is usually a broad range of flexibility in either system, grammatical or cultural. For all of the rules of grammar, we do not speak alike. In fact, every one of us is constantly combining the limited set of components that is available to produce sentences at a great rate, most of which we have never uttered or heard before, and many of which we will never encounter again. Even within the apparent limitations set by a strict grammatical system, historical uniqueness is so commonplace that we rarely notice it. In much the same way, the rules of culture are not a straitjacket in which we chafe, nor are they like a cookie-cutter or a punch-press from which would emerge identical automatons.

With reference to substances, a culture may "determine" what is readily available. It may also signal what is preferable (Heath, 1990) among what is available at different levels of cost and risk. Culture may "determine" what is highly valued at a given time, what's passé, or whether experimentation with novel drugs is acceptable. Culture even shapes one's expectations of what a given drug will do—and many elaborately controlled clinical experiments have amply demonstrated that expectation plays a major role in shaping the experience one has with drugs. To be specific, for all but extremely heavy doses, a user generally has to learn from others how to feel, what to see, and so forth, when using an unfamiliar drug. Similarly, with reference to alcohol, using double-blind research techniques (in which the dosage was unknown to *both* subject and experimenter), it has been demonstrated repeatedly that subjects respond more to what they *thought* they had ingested than to what in fact they *had* drunk. Those who thought they were getting alcohol (but were not) felt and acted more intoxicated than those who had been drinking (but thought they had not).

DRUGS AND CULTURES AROUND THE WORLD

Populations are irregularly distributed around the world, and so are psychoactive drugs; the diffusion of knowledge is affected by language, natural barriers, social relationships among peoples, and other factors. For all of these reasons, it is not surprising that both cultures and patterns of substance use have spatial and geographic aspects. This is not to imply that the environment "determines" what people will think and do, including how or whether they will use drugs, but it does mean that the communities within which social learning is shared are not distributed in an orderly array across the surface of the earth. Although it is true that increasingly rapid means of mass communication and transportation have, to some degree, resulted in the spread of some phenomena, the degree of local heterogeneity that persists is truly remarkable. Contrary to widespread predictions in the mid-1900s of impending cultural homogenization, it did not occur. In many parts of the world, forces favoring cultural autonomy are stronger than ever. The importance of this for an appreciation of substance use and abuse lies in recognition that comparative study shows the importance of attitudes, values, norms, and expectations—almost as much as pharmacological and biophysiological processes—in shaping how people choose substances, how they use them, and what they get from such use.

For example, hallucinogenic snuffs are commonplace throughout the Amazon Basin of South America, but are virtually unknown elsewhere in the world. Cactus wines and pulque are viewed as gifts of the gods and still enjoy great popularity in Mexico, although they are little used elsewhere. As widespread as rice is as a food crop, its conversion to beers and wines is rare; maize, millet, and barley, by contrast, are often brewed, throughout Europe, the Americas, Asia, and sub-Saharan Africa.

The diffusion of tobacco around the world in less than a century can be traced historically, but local cultures sometimes adopted cigars and sometimes pipes; in some areas tobacco was thought to have magical powers and was not made available to women. Styles of smoking, chewing, and sniffing tobacco vary among different populations.

Coffee, tea, and chocolate were commodities in the emerging mercantilist world economy of recent centuries, but each found distinctive local expressions that now seem to be firmly imbedded in different cultures. The tea ceremonies of Japan and England contrast markedly. Coffee may be equally integral to a person's daily routine in Ankara, Buenos Aires, Rome, or New York, but it doesn't look the same, taste similar, appear in the same ambiance, or serve the same social functions. Chocolate as a breakfast treat in Spain is far removed from the craftsmanship and connoisseurship that are associated with chocolate in neighboring France. Drugs that were identified with prostitutes and jazz musicians in one setting became the focus of literary experimentation by wealthy intellectuals in another. As commonplace as gasoline is throughout the

world today, only in a few parts of Australia and North America does it yet appear to be a substance of choice for abuse (Brady, 1992).

In France, wine is considered a food rather than an alcoholic beverage. Parents teach their children how to drink wine with meals, airline pilots drink it on the job, and any 6-year-old may buy wine at the store. No meal is complete without wine, and it is said both to "cleanse the blood" and to "build a strong body." Italians have a rich corpus of proverbs that similarly praise wine. Germans, as well as others, hail beer as a boon to nursing mothers. There are dozens of medicines in China, each for a specific ailment or organ, and they differ little from what people elsewhere would call herbal liqueurs. Drugs that are strictly controlled and reported, with signed slips at every level of sale in some countries, are available over-the-counter in others. In a single village in India, members of one caste drink marijuana tea, while those of another drink distilled liquor, and each group scorns the other's choice.

As counterintuitive as it may at first appear, it is commonplace that people who have the easiest access to a given substance may not use it in a way that is physically, socially, or psychologically damaging. Opium producers in "the Golden Triangle" of southeastern Asia or in Turkey or Mexico may process and work closely with the potent substance in great quantities for years without experimenting (Westermeyer, 1982). Similarly, in the Andes of South America, Quechua and Aymara Indians have produced coca for market for centuries. Those who bought or bartered for leaves used them as medicines, as offerings to deities and to dead ancestors, for divination, infused as tea, or chewed in a way that relieves cold, hunger, and thirst but that results in no psychic disturbances (Allen, 1988). In recent decades, the coca leaves have been diverted to other uses. With relatively simple technology, they are processed to yield coca paste, which enjoys a more profitable market in different directions. When the paste is subsequently refined to cocaine hydrochloride, it has an international market and is a potent drug to be sniffed, injected, or ingested as "crack." Only one of the new uses—cocaine paste smoked in a tobacco cigarette—has caught on with a few urban Bolivians and Peruvians, and ironically, the inflated prices now paid for coca leaves may result in an end to traditional uses.

Khat, a leaf chewed by groups of men throughout much of the Near East, has been brought to Europe by migrant laborers who are replicating the traditional sociable and conversational pattern in new venues. Kava, a traditional beverage with strong political and hierarchical overtones in its ritual usage in areas of Oceania, has recently been adopted as an adjunct to informal beer drinking in both Australia and New Zealand (Lebot, Merlin, & Lindstrom, 1992). Just as North Americans blamed the Chinese for bringing opium smoking as a costly, enervating, and demoralizing pastime in the mid-19th century, the Chinese blamed the English for bringing it from India to them only a little earlier. Large-scale marijuana growers in Kentucky have turned to the crop as an alternative to unemployment, and usually sell without sampling their harvest (Clayton, 1995).

DRUGS AND CULTURES IN HISTORY

In paying attention to drugs and culture, another variable that is of great importance is time. The same culture can reject a single drug at one time and embrace it at another. Similarly, a culture can take a generally abstemious approach to life during one given period of history, and be quite generally permissive at another. The same psychoactive substance can be popular in many cultures at once, or can be favored by only a few people while being depreciated by most. Recognition of these changing patterns is often lost sight of by those who tend to think of culture as if it were bound by tradition, or even static.

For example, few people are now aware that both chocolate and tea were viewed with suspicion when they were first introduced, with their potential harm characterized in terms very similar to those that are used for "hard drugs" in the latter half of the 20th century. Coffee shops in the Near East were once scorned as places where seditious talk and immoral behavior were commonplace, although they have since become respected as local places of recreation and social clubs for middle-class citizens (Hattox, 1985). King James I of England was so disgusted by tobacco smoking that he would have banned it if his advisors had not dissuaded him, on economic grounds. Tobacco snuff, the height of fashion early in U.S. history, was very much looked down on for a full century, but is enjoying new popularity in some circles. The drinking of all alcoholic beverages climbed steadily in the United States after World War II, until it peaked in the early 1980s, briefly leveled off, and has been declining since then. With a few dramatic exceptions, the same holds throughout Europe. By contrast, homebrews are losing ground in sub-Saharan Africa, whereas imported drinks are rapidly becoming popular (Heath, 1995).

The history of the United States is especially illuminating, not only because so much of the context is familiar to most readers, but also because it contains, in microcosm, an elaborate chronicle of changing cultural tastes in drugs. Beer was a staple beverage among the Pilgrims, and they might have gone on to Virginia if their supply on the Mayflower had not been so depleted that they put ashore in what is now Massachusetts. Rum from the West Indies played an important role in social and political occasions throughout the colonial period, but was replaced by whiskey produced from surplus corn on the western frontier of the newly independent United States. A brief period of religious and moral fervor brought Prohibition to nearly half of the states in the 1850s, but consumption increased rapidly after local repeals. In the 1920s, a peculiar mix of xenophobia, economic liberalism, and religious conservatism culminated in nationwide Prohibition—the first amendment to the Constitution in modern times that dealt with workaday behavior. To be sure, it was repealed 14 years later, and per capita sales of all types of alcoholic beverages—beers, wines, and spirits—went up steadily until their recent fall.

Morphine had been developed during the Civil War to relieve the pain of wounded soldiers and became a popular analgesic and relaxant. Some decades later heroin was developed as a cure for morphine addiction. Opium and coca derivatives were widely available and used in multipurpose patent medicines and tonics, until the Harrison Act of 1914 brought many drugs under strict control. The familiar categorizations of drugs as "hard" or "soft," or as "illegal," "over-the-counter," or "by prescription only" may appear to relate to potential for harm, but are actually cultural constructions with boundaries that shift over time. Within living memory the following took place: Cigarettes became commonplace, largely during World War I. Wine coolers enjoyed a brief but dazzling popularity, and the federal government in 1995 reversed its official stance (in *Dietary Guidelines for Americans*) from warning against drinking to recommending moderate drinking for its health benefits. Also during that period, both popular use and professional medical opinion have changed markedly with respect to marijuana, amphetamines, cocaine, and some other drugs. "Designer drugs," developed in the laboratory rather than derived from plants, have opened a broad new range of possibilities. Clearly, time is a crucial variable in any discussion of culture and drugs.

THEORETICAL LINKAGES

We have already made the point that a cultural approach is more a model or a perspective—a way of identifying and not neglecting important parts of any biopsychosocial system—than it is a tidy theory for explaining how and why such a system exists and functions as it does. Nevertheless, in the context of this volume, it appears important to point out several linkages between the concept of culture and various theories that have been proposed to account for substance abuse.

There are a number of such theories that are intimately linked with a sociocultural perspective, although the names given to them do not normally pinpoint culture as an etiological factor. Among the most popular with respect to the analysis of drugs within any specific society are those that focus on deviance, labeling, reference groups, anomie, time-out, and ambivalence. Along the most important sociocultural theories about drugs in cross-cultural perspective are those that emphasize social learning, symbolic interaction, social organization, conflict over dependency, and power. We briefly look at each in turn.

One of the earliest and best known among such interpretations was that of Bales, (1946), who contrasted Irish and Jewish drinking patterns. Only a small portion of the Irish population drink at all, but they have a reputation for drunkenness, economic and psychological problems, run-ins with the law, and violence and aggression out of all proportion to their numbers. By contrast, nearly all Jews drink with considerable frequency and yet few ever become drunk, and alcohol-related problems have traditionally been rare among them. Bales analyzed historical as well as contemporary ethnographic evidence and attributed the differences to culture. Specifically, he pointed out that drinking served as a habitual escape for poor and sexually repressed Irish men who drank in groups where drunkenness and aggression were both acceptable. Women almost never drank, and men rarely drank with meals, in moderate quantities, or in contexts where drunkenness and aggression were disapproved. By contrast, Jews of both sexes and all ages drank wine at least weekly, in the context of religious rituals, at home among the family. Such drinking was sacramental, and occasional other drinking was made much of in esthetic terms. Moderation was so highly valued that to be drunk was "un-Jewish" behavior. The significant differences between those groups were not in terms of stress, anxiety, tension, or social prejudice, but in terms of attitudes, meanings, and values—that is, of culture. A number of other examples of cultural variation will be cited next, but this "classic" case will serve to introduce the applicability of the culture concept in relation to theories about substance use and its outcomes.

What some would call "deviance theory" has to do with recognition that, beyond the cluster of alternatives that are generally approved within a culture, there is also a range of other choices that are possible but less approved. This can be viewed statistically, with the norm being approximately "average" or "normal," what most people do or think. Ideas and actions are "abnormal" or "deviant" to the degree that they differ from such norms. But such divergence is not viewed or treated in a neutral manner, rather it is disapproved of, devalued, and punished with sanctions, in which case such "deviance" has a strongly negative connotation. We see this in people who drink in "the wrong" places, at "the wrong" times, or who drink "too much" in a given context, just as we see it in people who use certain drugs without official permission. In evaluating deviance, investigators sometimes emphasize an individual's rebellion against dominant norms, and sometimes adhesion to variant norms of a splinter group. It is important to recognize that temperance as well as excessive use can be equally deviant. For example, among members of the Native American Church, the deviant is one who declines to take sacramental peyote in order to follow the sacred path with a knowledgeable guide. Similarly, anyone who declines to participate in the secular ritual of exchanging endless toasts at a Russian party—or to toast a wedding or the New Year in contemporary American culture—may be seen as deviant, just as is the addict who needs heroin, cocaine, or methadone each day.

Deviance is defined in relation to the culture, and when it reaches some point, it results in labeling, the popular designation of a person as deviant in a particular way. Examples of such labels are "dope fiend," "alcoholic," "drunken Indian," and others that focus on a stereotyped form of deviance as exemplifying the faulty character of an individual. In "labeling theory," it is suggested that such stigmatization may reinforce an individual's inclination to behave in that deviant way in protest against popular rejection or, some would say, in acceptance and incorporation of the flawed identity as being valid. That is, if one is expected to misbehave in a given way, why not do it?

"Reference group theory" emphasizes conformity to the norms of a group, which holds the individual's primary allegiance, even if those norms differ from the dominant society's. Thus, for instance, sharing needles may be not just carelessness or economy among intravenous drug users, but it may also have some positive symbolic value as a social leveler, a secular sort of communion among those who frequent the same "shooting gallery." Likewise, sharing cheap wine out of a bottle in a brown paper bag can be a pledge of friendship and mutual aid among members of an urban bottle-gang. Whether one drinks, and how one drinks can be important boundary markers between social and ethnic groups. Among orthodox Jews, anyone who is drunk is, by definition, a member of the out-group. Similarly, any drinker is an outsider to orthodox Muslims, or to members of various ascetic Protestant sects.

"Anomie" is another sociological concept that is often invoked to account for drinking and drug use, especially among culturally marginal populations. Originally, anomie had to do with discrepancy between the norms of an individual and those of the encompassing society. As social scientists came to recognize that variability in norms was commonplace in most societies, anomie was used to refer to a disjunction between the dominant norms of a society and the ability of an individual to achieve those norms (as with the "marginal man" or someone "caught between two worlds"). The supposed stress that results from not being able to assimilate, or "pass" or "blend in", is said to be anomic and to result often in substance abuse, just as does "sociocultural deprivation" resulting from the rejection of one population's values by those of another that is economically and/or politically dominant.

The "time-out hypothesis" is a suggestion, based on a large-scale review of the historical and ethnographic literature about drinking, that emphasizes the role of drunkenness as providing brief periods of relief from the stress of social conformity, during which some of the norms are temporarily suspended. This theory was proposed by MacAndrew and Edgerton (1969) as a direct challenge to the "disinhibition theory" that prevailed at the time, and that saw a chemical action of alcohol as triggering all kinds of inappropriate behavior by automatically overriding those portions of the brain that inhibit asocial and antisocial behavior. It was a triumph for the sociocultural approach when they demonstrated that drunken comportment itself is culturally patterned, and that even it remains "within limits," respecting fundamental taboos and moral imperatives. The analogy is to time-out within a regulated game, or to a psychic "escape valve" (such as the social inversions allowed in comedy, at Carnival, and so forth)—but rejecting the view of alcohol as an agent that interacts with the biological organism to trigger disinhibition automatically.

"Ambivalence" is another concept that is important in understanding meanings and attitudes about drugs. It is not unusual for people to have a simultaneous love–hate relationship with a substance, that is, enjoying what it does for them, but fearing what it might do to them. Americans' attitudes toward alcohol exemplify this in the extreme, with occasional celebratory drinking (e.g., for a wedding, anniversary, special meal) but near paranoia about drunk drivers or images of "down-and-outers" who have lost all to an insidious addiction. Similarly, the casual "chipper" may insist that an occasional snort of cocaine helps keep his or her "edge," while decrying how dealers on the street, muggers, and crack houses blight the community. Drinking gained enormous popularity, especially among young women during Prohibition. Cigars are becoming fashionable in some circles now, even as health warnings, lawsuits, and increasing restrictions make smoking appear to be scorned as hazardous. Culturally patterned behavior is not always logically consistent.

Among theories that are important to the relationship between culture and drugs are some that focus on specific components of culture. Some drugs begin as prerequisites of the rich and powerful, and others among the underclasses. A given drug will often tend to be favored by men or by women, or by a given age group. In recent years, there has been considerable agonizing over poverty, unemployment, and general disillusionment as if they were the causes of alcohol or drug use but, although such actions may be more visible (and more punished) among the poor, they are often part of the most sheltered lives of the most privileged as well.

The "social learning" model can equally be claimed by psychologists who focus on the individual rather than on groups, but it has a clear sociocultural component inasmuch as how people learn and what they learn are both affected by their social milieu. The process of enculturation or socialization takes place, in large part, through social interaction, with peer pressure equally important in terms of conformity to a dominant set of norms as it is (more often cited) in terms of deviance from them in order to conform to an alternate set of norms. One's expectations as well as immediate rewards and punishments are usually learned in a social context, whereby drug use and its consequences are shaped by shared views of the world.

"Symbolic interactionism" is a dramaturgical interpretation of behavior, such that, for example, drinking can be interpreted as a way of avoiding responsibility on the part of someone already labeled a "drunken Indian," or as an excuse for fighting on the part of an already aggressive person.

"Social organization" as a model derives from an empirical study that has little theoretic grounding. When Field (1962) reviewed the ethnographic evidence about drinking in 56 cultures, he found drunkenness far more closely correlated with the absence of corporate kin groups than with most other social or psychological variables that had earlier been hypothesized. Little has been done to elaborate on this finding.

The "conflict over dependency" theory results from an even more broadly cross-cultural comparison of specific traits having to do with drinking, on the one hand, and child-rearing on the other. Using an authoritative compilation of ethnographic texts dealing with 139 cultures around the world, Bacon, Barry, and Child (1965) found significantly high correlations between heavy drinking and drunkenness, with youthful dependence followed by pressures toward assertive independence in adulthood. Major discontinuity in roles and personal expectations may result in excessive drinking and associated problems.

In 1972, McClelland, Davis, Kalin, & Wanner developed the "power" theory on the basis of largely cultural data. Analyzing myths and folklore in relation to drinking, they claimed that the universal sensation of individual power that derived from drinking explained its emergence, survival, and popularity among the world's cultures. Unfortunately, few readers noticed that their generalizations were restricted to men as a social category, and to beer as a beverage.

PRACTICAL IMPLICATIONS

A sociocultural perspective has been gaining currency in the field of alcohol and drugs as recognition of temporal and spatial variation becomes widespread. It is distressing to some and exciting to others to learn that the element of danger or risk often lies less in a substance and its biological, chemical, or pharmacological properties than in the culture's attitudes toward it—attitudes that are themselves subject to change and even reversal in a short time.

Doctors and other treatment providers have found that they cannot comprehend some of their patients' habits or problems without insight into the belief systems of minority populations. Neither could they influence behavior without dealing with other pressures to which their patients were subjected. A dramatic illustration of how cultural views can be more important than biomedical knowledge is the widespread opposition to methadone maintenance on the part of minority clients in the United States who resist it as "trading one addiction for another" or "being dependent on the system." Another is the dramatic success enjoyed by programs of drug maintenance in England and Netherlands, needle exchanges, "ghettoization" as at Zurich's famously permissive but recently closed Needle Park, and a variety of other experiments that are aimed at harm reduction rather than prohibition, interdiction, and judicial punishment.

A social and cultural perspective demands that we consider the biological and psychological aspects of any instance of substance use as partial indicators that have to be further interpreted and evaluated in terms of meanings and values that may be distinctive of a given population. Perhaps most important of all is the need to recognize that not all use is abuse, and that there is a great amount of alcohol and drug use without any consequent problems.

A prevention program designed for a middle-class, overwhelmingly literate population may be meaningless to others. Warnings should be both realistic and phrased in terms that have value to the audience. Expectations about what will happen if certain behaviors occur should be fitting in relation to a group's experience. Treatment based on a sense of shame or guilt or personal responsibility may have no appeal and so be less effective than one that allows the patient to be blameless against a "disease" or helpless in the face of "genetics." Anonymity, valued in some groups, is scorned in others; conversely, the same is true of being designated as "outstanding" or "exceptional." The public confession of unsavory actions that is a fundamental part of many 12-step mutual-help groups may be therapeutic to their devoted members, but would be considered disgusting or shameful by others. One must always try to select among a broad range of alternatives, often adapting them in various ways, in order to accommodate to sociocultural differences in taste and propriety. Even national policies should be revised when they have proven to be culturally incompatible (Heath, 1992).

REFERENCES

Allen, C. J. (1988). *The hold life has: Coca and cultural identity in an Andean community.* Washington DC: Smithsonian Institution Press.

Bacon, M. K., Barry, H., & Child, I. (1965). A cross-cultural study of drinking: II, Relations to other features of culture. *Quarterly Journal of Studies on Alcohol Supplement, 3,* 29–48.

Bales, R. F. (1946). Cultural differences in rates of alcoholism. *Quarterly Journal of Studies on Alcohol, 6,* 480–499.

Brady, M. (1992). *Heavy metal: The social meaning of petrol sniffing in Australia.* Canberra: Aboriginal Studies Press.

Carter, W. E. (1980). *Cannabis in Costa Rica: A study of chronic marihuana use.* Philadelphia: ISHI.

Clayton, R. R. (1995). *Marijuana in the "Third World": Appalachia, U.S.A.* Boulder, CO: Lynne Rienner.

Field, P. B. (1962). A new cross-cultural study of drunkenness. In D. J. Pittman & C. R. Snyder (Eds.), *Society, culture, and drinking patterns* (pp. 48–74). New York: Wiley.

Hattox, R. S. (1985). Coffee and coffeehouses: *The origins of a social beverage in the medieval Near East* (Near Eastern Studies 3). Seattle: University of Washington Press.

Heath, D. B. (1982). In other cultures, they also drink. In E. L. Gomberg, H. R. White, & J. A. Carpenter (Eds.). *Alcohol, science, and society revisited* (pp. 63–79). Ann Arbor, MI: University of Michigan Press.

Heath, D. B. (1988). Emerging anthropological theory and models of alcohol use and alcoholism. In C. D. Chaudron & D. W. Wilkinson (Eds.), *Theories on alcoholism* (pp. 353–410). Toronto: Addiction Research Foundation.

Heath, D. B. (1990). Cultural factors in the choice of drugs. In M. Galanter (Ed.), *Recent developments in alcoholism: Vol. 8.* (pp. 245–254). New York: Plenum.

Heath, D. B. (1992). U.S. drug control policy: A cultural perspective. *Daedalus, 121,* 269–291.

Heath, D. B. (Ed.). (1995). *International handbook on alcohol and culture.* Westport, CT: Greenwood.

Jochelson, W. (1905). *The Koryak* (Memoirs of the American Museum of Natural History 10). New York: American Museum of Natural History.

La Barre, W. (1970). *The peyote cult* (Rev. ed.). New York: Shoe String Press.

Lebot, V., Merlin, M., & Lindstrom, L. (1992). *Kava: The Pacific drug.* New Haven, CT: Yale University Press.

MacAndrew, C., & Edgerton, R. B. (1969). *Drunken comportment: A social explanation.* Chicago: Aldine.

McClelland, D. C., Davis, W., Kalin, R., & Wanner, E. (1972). *The drinking man.* New York: Free Press.

Myerhoff, B. G. (1974). *Peyote hunt: The sacred journey of the Huichol Indians.* Ithaca, NY: Cornell University Press.

Rubin, V. D. (Ed.). (1975). *Ganja in Jamaica.* The Hague: Mouton.

Wasson, R. G., Cowan, G., Cowan, F., & Rhodes, W. (1974). *María Sabina and her Mazatec mushroom Velada.* New York: Harcourt Brace Jovanovich.

Westermeyer, J. (1982). *Poppies, pipes, and people: Opium and its use in Laos.* Berkeley: University of California Press.

CHAPTER 13

DRUG TOXICOLOGY

Bruce A. Goldberger
Amanda J. Jenkins

Substance abuse continues to be a major problem in the United States. According to the 1994 National Household Survey on Drug Abuse conducted by the U.S. Department of Health and Human Services, 77 million people have used illicit drugs. Marijuana continues to be the most frequently used illicit drug, with 18.6 million people reporting use within the past year, and 9 million reporting use within the past month (Substance Abuse and Mental Health Services Administration, 1994). Further, the Drug Abuse Warning Network (DAWN, a national probability survey conducted annually) preliminary estimates for 1995 indicates that drug-related hospital emergency department episodes continued an upward trend that began in 1991 (Substance Abuse and Mental Health Services Administration, 1996). DAWN Medical Examiner data collected during 1993 indicates an 11% increase in drug abuse deaths and drug mentions between 1992 and 1993. During the period 1990–1993, mentions of heroin/morphine increased 27%, and mentions of cocaine increased 10%. The prevalence of other drugs of abuse such as marijuana/hashish and amphetamine also increased (Substance Abuse and Mental Health Services Administration, 1995).

In addition, recent survey data indicates that illicit drug use continues to increase among young people.

According to the National Institute on Drug Abuse (NIDA) 1995 Monitoring the Future Study, the percentage of 8th graders reporting drug use (including alcohol and nicotine) in the 12 months prior to the survey, increased from 11.3% in 1991 to 21.4% in 1995. Marijuana use showed the highest increase among illicit drugs (Monitoring the Future Study, 1996).

The chemical testing of biological specimens is considered the most objective means of assessing drug exposure (Cone, 1993, 1994). The presence of a drug or drug metabolite in a biological specimen is dependent on many factors including the dose and route of administration, single or repeated dosing, physicochemical and biotransformation characteristics, the choice of biological specimen to be tested, and the testing methodologies utilized. Each of these factors makes substance abuse testing and the interpretation of results complex entities.

Substance abuse or drug testing of individuals is performed for many reasons. In physicians offices and hospital emergency departments, the testing is performed for clinical reasons – to explain clinical findings and behavior to aid in the diagnosis and treatment of an individual. In the criminal justice system, drug testing may be performed to ensure compliance with conditions of probation and/or parole. In death investigations, drug testing aids in the determination of cause and manner of death. In the work-place, drug testing is performed as a deterrent to drug use. Because there may be significant penalties if a person tests positive for a drug of abuse, it is critical that individuals are not falsely accused of drug use. Therefore, it is important that drug tests are precise and accurate, utilizing validated methodologies.

The validity of a drug test is defined as the ability of an assay to detect a drug and/or its metabolites in biological fluids following drug administration (Gorodetzky, 1972). This definition encompasses a variety of factors including assay characteristics such as sensitivity and specificity, and metabolic and pharmacological variables such as dose, route of administration, biological fluid pH, and intersubject variability in absorption, metabolism, and excretion (Gorodetsky, 1977). Typical urine drug and drug metabolite detection times are given in Table 13.1.

The aim of this chapter is to describe current methods of analysis for substances of abuse including those most commonly used such as immunoassay and gas chromatography/mass spectrometry. Emphasis has been placed on the analysis of urine as the biological test matrix.

ANALYTICAL METHODS

A wide variety of laboratory procedures are currently available for detecting the presence of substances of abuse and their metabolites in urine. These techniques are based upon immunological or chromatographic techniques. Immunological-based methods utilized to test specimens include radioimmunoassay, enzyme immunoassay, fluorescence polarization immunoassay, and particle immunoassay. The major classes of substances of abuse immunoassays and the commercial source for each are listed in Table 13.2. Chromatographic-based techniques include thin layer chromatography, high performance or "pressure" liquid chromatography; and gas chromatography coupled with either a flame ionization detector, nitrogen-phosphorous detector, or mass spectrometer.

When testing urine specimens for substances of abuse, laboratories usually screen specimens utilizing a nonspecific immunoassay assay. These assays may detect classes of drugs such as the benzodiazepines, rather than specific drugs within a class, such as diazepam. Because the majority of specimens will test negative, this eliminates the need to do more costly additional testing. All specimens that initially screen positive should be confirmed by a more specific analytical technique. The confirmatory technique should be based on a different analytical principle than the screening methodology. In addition, the confirmatory technique, if sufficiently specific, will identify the particular substance present to the exclusion of all other substances (Kapur, 1993; Substance-Abuse Testing Committee, 1988).

The initial testing and confirmatory procedures selected and utilized by a toxicology laboratory are based on a variety of factors including laboratory workload and expected turnaround time, specimen type, number and type of assays, required specificity and sensitivity, expertise of personnel, and available budget and equipment. In

Table 13.1   Typical Urine Drug and Drug Metabolite Detection Times

Drug Class	Detection Times
Amphetamines	1–3 days
Barbiturates	Short-acting, 1 day; intermediate- and long-acting, 1–3 weeks
Benzodiazepines	5–7 days
Cannabinoids	1–3 days; greater (several weeks) with chronic use
Cocaine	1–3 days
LSD	Less than 1 day
Methadone	1–3 days
Methaqualone	1–2 weeks
Opiates	1–3 days
Phencyclidine	Up to 3 days
Propoxyphene	1–2 days

Note. Detection times vary with method of detection, dose, route of administration, frequency of use, and individual factors.
Source: Data from *Disposition of Toxic Drug and Chemicals in Man,* Fourth Edition, by R. C. Baselt and R. H. Cravey, 1995, Chemical Toxicology Institute, Foster City, California; and "Critical Issues in Urinalysis of Abused Substances: Report of the Substance-Abuse Testing Committee," 1988, *Clinical Chemistry 34,* pp. 605–632.

Table 13.2   Commercial Immunoassays for Drugs of Abuse

Immunoassay Technique	*Manufacturer*
Radioimmunoassay (RIA)	Roche Diagnostic Systems
	Diagnostic Products Corporation
	Immunalysis Corporation
Fluorescence polarization immunoassays (FPIA)	Abbott Laboratories
Enzyme Multiplied Immunoassay Technique (Emit)	Behring Diagnostics Incorporated
	(formerly Syva Company)
	Diagnostic Reagents Incorporated
	Solar Technologies Incorporated
Cloned Enzyme Donor Immunoassay (CEDIA)	Boehringer Mannheim Corporation
Kinetic Interaction of Microparticles in Solution (KIMS)	Roche Diagnostic Systems

many cases, the choice of methodology is specified by regulatory federal and state agencies. For example, those laboratories accredited by the National Laboratory Certification Program of the Substance Abuse and Mental Health Services Administration must use immunoassay techniques for initial specimen screening and gas chromatography/mass spectrometry (GC/MS) for confirmation (Mandatory Guidelines, 1988).

The ability of assays to detect low concentrations of substances depends on several factors. The lowest concentration of a substance that can be reliably detected by an assay is known as the limit of detection (LOD) and refers to a qualitative identification of the drug in the biological specimen (i.e., the presence or absence of an analyte). The lowest concentration of a substance that can be reliably determined quantitatively by an assay is known as the limit of quantitation (LOQ) (i.e., drug present at a specific concentration). If the LOD and LOQ are the same concentration, some investigators refer to the combined limit as the limit of sensitivity.

In substance abuse testing, a "cutoff" concentration is commonly utilized. This is an administrative "breakpoint" used to distinguish positive and negative specimens. Cutoff concentrations are determined based on realistic elimination profiles of the drugs of interest. When utilizing assay cutoff concentrations, any specimen that contains a substance at a concentration at or above the cutoff will be reported as positive, and any specimen that is less than the cutoff will be reported as negative. Typically, cutoff concentrations are set significantly above the limit of sensitivity of an assay to minimize the occurrence of true negative specimens giving a false positive result. One advantage of a low cutoff concentration is that a substance can be detected for a longer period of time after administration. However, if the confirmation procedure is not sensitive enough, the result may not be confirmed (Hawks & Chiang, 1986; Montagne, Pugh, & Fink, 1988). Typical immunoassay screening and gas chromatography/mass spectrometry confirmation cutoff concentrations are summarized in Table 13.3.

IMMUNOASSAY TECHNIQUES

Immunoassays are based on the principle of competition between labeled and unlabeled antigen (drug) for binding sites on a specific antibody. The label may be an enzyme (enzyme immunoassay), a radioisotope (radioimmunoassay), a fluorophore (fluorescence polarization immunoassay), or latex particles (particle immunoassay). Immunoassays are characterized by several variables including specificity and sensitivity. Specificity is the ability of an assay to distinguish the target analyte(s) from other compounds including those with and without structural similarity. Specificity data is typically provided by manufacturers of immunoassays in the form of a package insert. Reagent specificity for all available drugs of abuse immunoassay techniques is summarized in Table 13.4.

The specificity requirements and design of a particular assay are critical, and may be dependent on the metabolism of the specific drug. For example, because cocaine is rapidly metabolized, all cocaine immunoassays are formulated to detect the primary cocaine metabolite in urine (benzoylecgonine). Furthermore, assays are often designed to be drug class specific (rather than analyte specific) in order that several analytes within a drug class, such as opiates, may be detected with a single assay.

Table 13.3 Typical Screening and Confirmation Cutoff Concentrations*

Drug Class	Immunoassay Cutoff (ng/ml)		GC/MS Cutoff (ng/ml)	
	Analyte Targeted	Concentration	Analyte Targeted	Concentration
Amphetamines	Amphetamines	1000	Amphetamine	500
			Methamphetamine[1]	500
Barbiturates	Barbiturates	200 or 300	Butalbital	150
			Butabarbital	150
			Amobarbital	150
			Pentobarbital	150
			Phenobarbital	150
			Secobarbital	150
Benzodiazepines	Benzodiazepines	200 or 300	Nordiazepam	150
			Oxazepam	150
		1000	Hydroxyalprazolam	50
Cannabinoids	THC-acid	20, 50, or 100	THC-acid	15
Cocaine	Benzoylecgonine	300	Benzoylecgonine	150
LSD	LSD	0.5	LSD	0.2
Methadone	Methadone	300	Methadone	150
Methaqualone	Methaqualone	300	Methaqualone	150
Opiates	Opiates	300	Morphine	300
		300	Codeine	300
		300	6-Acetylmorphine	10
Phencyclidine	Phencyclidine	25 or 75	Phencyclidine	25
Propoxyphene	Propoxyphene	300	Propoxyphene	300

Source: Data from "Evaluation of Commerical Immunoassay Kits for Effective Workplace Drug Testing" by R. H. Liu; and "Medical Review Officer Interpretation of Urine Drug Test Results" by K. B. Green and D. S. Isenschmid, in Handbook of Workplace Drug Testing, R. A. Liu and B. A. Goldberger, Eds., 1995, AACC Press, Washington, D.C.
[1]The specimen must also contain 200 ng/ml of amphetamine to report positive for methamphetamine.
Abbreviations LSD—Lysergic acid diethylamide
THC-acid—11-nor-s-9-tetrahydrocannabinol-9-carboxylic acid

Radioimmunoassay

The first laboratory assays developed for the detection of substances of abuse and their metabolites in urine were based on the radioimmunoassay technique. Presently, Roche Diagnostic Systems (Nutley, New Jersey), Diagnostic Products Corporation (DPC, Los Angeles, California), and Immunalysis Corporation (Glendale, California) are the major commercial sources of radioimmunoassays.

The Roche Abuscreen® heterogeneous radioimmunoassays are based on the competitive binding of ^{125}I radiolabeled antigen and unlabeled antigen for antibody. Analyte antibody and radiolabeled antigen are added to the specimen and the analyte present in the specimen competes with radiolabeled antigen for antibody sites. After precipitation of the antigen–antibody complex with a sec-

ond antibody reagent, the supernatant is removed and the pellet containing bound antigen is counted using a gamma counter. The amount of radioactivity is inversely related to the concentration of analyte in the specimen (Kricka, 1994; Liu, 1995; Roche Diagnostic Systems, 1996).

The DPC double-antibody procedure, a method similar to the Roche Abuscreen RIA technique, is a liquid-phase competitive heterogeneous radioimmunoassay in which ^{125}I labeled analyte competes with the analyte in the specimen for antibody sites. Following incubation, free antigen is separated from bound antigen using a second antibody. The antibody-bound fraction is precipitated and counted using a gamma counter (Kricka, 1994; Liu, 1995; Diagnostic Products Corporation, 1996).

The DPC coated tube procedure (Coat-a-Count®) is a solid-phase competitive heterogeneous radioimmunoassay

Table 13.4   Specificity of Drugs of Abuse Immunoassays

Assay	Analyte
Amphetamines	Amphetamine, Benzphetamine, Ephedrine, Methamphetamine, Methylenedioxyamphetamine, Methylenedioxymethamphetamine, Phenmetrazine, Phentermine, Phenylpropanolamine, Pseudoephedrine, Propylhexedrine
Barbiturates	Amobarbital, Aprobarbital, Barbital, Butabarbital, Butalbital, Cyclopentobarbital, Pentobarbital, Phenobarbital, Secobarbital, Talbutal, Thiopental
Benzodiazepines	Alprazolam, α-hydroxy-Alprazolam, Bromazepam, Chlordiazepoxide, Clobazam, Clonazepam, Clorazepate, Demoxepam, Diazepam, Estazolam, Flunitrazepam, Flurazepam, Halzepam, Lorazepam, Medezepam, Nitrazepam, Nordiazepam, Oxazepam, Prazepam, Temazepam, Triazolam, α-hydroxy-Triazolam
Cannabinoids	δ-9-Tetrahydrocannabinol, 11-hydroxy—9-Tetrahydrocannabinol, 11-nor—9-Tetrahydrocannabinol-9-carboxylic acid
Cocaine	Benzoylecgonine, Cocaine, Cocaethylene, Ecgonine, Ecgonine ethyl ester, Ecgonine methyl ester, μ-Hydroxybenzoylecgonine, Norcocaine
Lysergic Acid Diethylamide	Lysergic Acid Diethylamide
Methadone	L-Alpha-Acetyl-Methadol, Diphenhydramine, Doxylamine, Methadone
Methaqualone	Methaqualone, hydroxy-Methaqualone
Opiates	Codeine, Diacetylmorphine (Heroin) Dihydrocodeine, Hydrocodone, Hydromorphone, Morphine, Morphine-glucuronide, Nalorphine, Oxycodone, Oxymorphone
Phencyclidine	Phencyclidine, Phencyclidine analogs, Thioridazine
Propoxyphene	Norpropoxyphene, Propoxyphene

Source: Data from "Evaluation of Commercial Immunoassay Kits for Effective Workplace Drug Testing" by R. H. Liu; and "Medical Review Officer Interpretation of Urine Drug Test Results" by K. B. Greene and D. S. Isenschmid, in *Handbook of Workplace Drug Testing,* R. A. Liu and B. A. Goldberger, Eds., 1995, AACC Press, Washington, D.C.

technique in which ^{125}I labeled analyte competes with the analyte in the specimen for antibody sites. The antibody is immobilized on the wall of a polypropylene tube, and decanting of the supernatant terminates the competition and isolates the antibody-bound fraction of the radiolabeled analyte. The advantage of this procedure is that only one reagent needs to be dispensed and centrifugation is not required (Kricka, 1994; Liu, 1995; Diagnostic Products Corporation, 1996).

Radioimmunoassays are very sensitive, generally more so than nonisotopic enzyme immunoassays. Radioimmunoassays have been developed for all common substances of abuse and have been designed to produce qualitative and semiquantitative results. The disadvantages of radioimmunoassays include limited reagent shelf-life due to the short half-life of ^{125}I, and the additional laboratory safety precautions required by radioisotope use.

Enzyme Immunoassay

Enzyme Multiplied Immunoassay Technique

The enzyme multiplied immunoassay technique (Emit®) is presently the most widely utilized enzyme immunoassay. It was initially developed for the detection of drugs of abuse in urine during the early 1970s by Syva Company (now Behring Diagnostics Incorporated, San Jose, California). Similar assays are now also available from SolarCare Technologies Corporation (STC, Bethlehem, Pennsylvania) and Diagnostic Reagents Incorporated (DRI, Mountain View, California). At the time of its introduction, the Emit technology offered several advantages over other available procedures for drug testing. The technique provided moderate sensitivity, eliminated a separation stage, utilized reagents with longer shelf life, could be performed rapidly, and was easily adaptable to manual and automated spectrophotometer-based laboratory instrumentation (Kricka, 1994; Liu, 1995).

The principle of the Emit assay is based upon competition between drug in the specimen and drug labeled with the enzyme glucose-6-phosphate dehydrogenase for antibody binding sites. The enzyme activity decreases following binding to the antibody; therefore, the drug concentration in the specimen can be measured in terms of enzyme activity. In practice, when free analyte is present in the specimen, the displaced free enzyme will convert nicotinamide adenine dinucleotide (NAD) to NADH, resulting in a change in absorbance that is measured spectrophotometrically. The resultant increase in absorbance is proportional to the concentration of the analyte in the specimen (Behring Diagnostics Incorporated, 1996; Kricka, 1994; Liu, 1995).

Cloned Enzyme Donor Immunoassay

In the mid 1990s, Microgenics Corporation (now Boehringer Mannheim Corporation, Indianapolis, Indiana) introduced a new homogeneous assay system for drugs of abuse in urine called cloned enzyme donor immunoassay, or CEDIA®. The CEDIA assay is based on the genetically engineered bacterial enzyme β-galactosidase that consists of two inactive fragments. These fragments spontaneously associate to form an active enzyme that cleaves a substrate, chlorophenol red β-galactopyranoside, producing a color change that is measured spectrophotometrically. In the assay, analyte in the specimen competes with analyte conjugated to one inactive fragment of β-galactosidase for the antibody binding site. If analyte is present in the specimen, it will bind to antibody, leaving the inactive enzyme fragments free to form active enzyme. The amount of active enzyme formed, and resultant increase in absorbance, are proportional to the amount of analyte present in the specimen (Boehringer Mannheim Corporation, 1996; Kricka, 1994; Liu, 1995).

Fluorescence Polarization Immunoassay

Fluorescence polarization immunoassays (FPIA) were initially developed by Abbott Laboratories (North Chicago, Illinois) for use by laboratories performing therapeutic drug monitoring and were subsequently adapted for detection of drugs of abuse in urine specimens. The Abbott FPIA system employs a fluorescein-analyte labeled tracer. The tracer, when excited by linearly polarized light, emits fluorescence with a degree of polarization inversely related to its rate of rotation. The analyte of interest, if present in the specimen, competes for a limited number of antibody binding sites with the labeled tracer. If the tracer molecules become bound to its specific antibody, the rotation of the tracer assumes that of the larger antibody molecule, which is significantly less than the unbound tracer molecule, and the subsequent polarization is high. The remaining unbound tracer becomes randomly oriented and rotates rapidly; the subsequent polarization is low. The degree of fluorescence polarization is inversely related to the concentration of analyte in the specimen (Abbott Laboratories, 1996; Kricka, 1994; Liu, 1995).

The Abbott FPIA abused-substance assays offer laboratories several options that are not available with other systems. All FPIAs utilize a six-point calibration curve, in conjunction with nonlinear regression data manipulation, to estimate unknown specimen drug concentrations. Assay cutoff concentrations can be programmed by the laboratory between the assay sensitivity limit and the highest calibrator concentration. Also, the data printout can be programmed to include either qualitative or semiquantitative results. Presently, FPIA is not widely utilized as the primary screening technique in high volume laboratories because of its limited specimen throughput and cost considerations.

Particle Immunoassay

In the early 1990s, Roche Diagnostic Systems (Branchburg, New Jersey) introduced the Abuscreen ONLINE® immunoassay system (known as the kinetic interaction of microparticles in solution, or KIMS). The assay is based upon the competition of analyte in a specimen for free antibody with analyte-microparticle conjugate. Particle aggregation occurs in the absence of analyte when free antibody binds to the analyte-microparticle conjugate. The formation of an aggregate scatters light, which results in a reduction of light transmission that can be measured spectrophotometrically. The absorbance change is inversely related to the analyte concentration (Kricka, 1994; Liu, 1995; Roche Diagnostic Systems, 1996).

On-Site Drug Testing

A new market of substance-testing devices has grown in recent years due to the desire to decrease turnaround time and cut costs. These on-site drug testing kits are typically used at the specimen collection site and are self-contained devices utilizing immunoassay technology for drug testing. The use of these devices has increased in recent years due to their simplicity, ease of performance, and no requirement for expensive equipment or skilled personnel. Minimal operator training is required, results are typically obtained within 10–15 minutes of specimen application, and the presence or absence of a color is the most common method of reading the results. The cost saving occurs in that only those specimens that test positive by this screening assay will be sent to a laboratory for confirmation by an alternate analytical technique. Depending upon the specific device and the number of substances assayed, the cost per test may range between $3.00 and $25.00 (Wu, 1995).

The kits may be used in emergency rooms, physicians' offices, drug treatment centers, probation services, and by employers for preemployment and random or reasonable cause drug testing to provide preliminary qualitative results. The majority of the devices have built-in validation controls. If the testing is performed for forensic purposes, all positive specimens must be confirmed by an alternate technique. These tests utilize urine as the drug testing matrix and are available to test several drug classes (Wu, 1995).

The following devices are currently available commercially: Triage® (BIOSITE Diagnostics, Inc., San Diego, California); EZ-Screen Profile™ and Verdict® (Editek Inc., Burlington, North Carolina); accuPinch® (Hycor Biomedical Inc., Garden Grove, California); and OnTrak™ and Testcup™ (Roche Diagnostic Systems, Nutley, New Jersey). The efficacy of these tests, as with all assays, depends upon their validity in the detection of substances of abuse. There are several reports of validity assessment studies of these devices (Jenkins et al., 1993; Jenkins, Darwin, Huestis, Cone, & Mitchell, 1995; Wu et al., 1993).

CHROMATOGRAPHIC TECHNIQUES

For purposes of test accuracy, it is highly desirable to subject all presumptive or screening immunoassay positive specimens to confirmatory testing utilizing a technique based on a different chemical principle. The confirmatory test should be more specific and sensitive than the initial test. Clinical toxicology laboratories most often utilize thin layer chromatography, high performance liquid chromatography, and gas chromatography, whereas forensic toxicology laboratories utilize gas chromatography/mass spectrometry (Hawks & Chiang, 1986).

Chromatography is a highly versatile technique, easily adaptable to the analysis of substances of abuse in urine. However, prior to chromatographic analysis, specimens must be subjected to extraction or purification in order to isolate the analytes of interest. The basis for all chromatographic techniques is the separation of a complex mixture into component parts by interaction with a mobile and a stationary phase (Bowers, Ullman, & Burtis, 1994).

Thin Layer Chromatography

Thin layer chromatography is one of the oldest chromatographic techniques, and prior to the development of immunoassays, was often used as an initial, broad spectrum screen for therapeutic and substances of abuse. The sensitivity of thin layer chromatographic assays is generally in the range of 500–1000 ng/ml. In thin layer chromatography, an extract prepared from the specimen is spotted onto a plate of glass or plastic that is covered with an adsorbent such as silica gel. The plate is placed into solvent, and the solvent flows by capillary action facilitating the separation of analytes. The analytes are visualized by reaction with reagents that produce characteristic colors. Analytes are identified based upon distance traveled, color reaction, and metabolic patterns (Bowers et al., 1994).

High Performance Liquid Chromatography

This technique is also known as high pressure, pressure assisted, or high efficiency liquid chromatography. Liquid chromatographic instruments first became available in 1969, but the technique did not gain popularity until the mid 1970s. In this technique separation between compounds is achieved by differential interaction between mobile and stationary phases that are both liquids. Liquid specimen extracts are introduced into the instrument through a sample injector. The extract is pumped through a column under pressure and the components are separated between the phases. Components elute from the column at different times depending upon their relative affinity for the stationary phase. Eluents are connected to a detector such as a multiwavelength ultraviolet spectrophotometer, which enables identification and quantitation of the individual components when compared with authentic standards.

HPLC is a versatile technique permitting various chromatographic separations based upon a wide range of stationary and mobile phases. Compounds that are polar, high molecular weight, or thermally labile may be analyzed with this technique. Barbiturates and benzodiazepines are commonly assayed with this technique with a detection limit of approximately 20–50 ng/ml. In addition, fractions of the eluent may be collected for further analysis so there is no extract or sample loss (Bowers et al., 1994).

Gas Chromatography

Gas chromatography, initially developed in the 1950s, is widely utilized as a confirmation technique. In gas chromatography, extracts are introduced in liquid form via a heated injector, which results in rapid vaporization. The vaporized sample is transferred to a column, and its components are separated by interaction between the gaseous mobile phase and the liquid stationary phase. The column effluent is connected to a detector for identification and quantification of individual components as they elute from the column (Bowers et al., 1994).

The most widely utilized chromatographic detectors are the flame ionization detector, the nitrogen phosphorous detector, and the mass spectrometer. The flame ionization detector is highly versatile, capable of detection of most organic compounds at a detection limit of approximately 100–500 ng/ml. The nitrogen phosphorous detector is highly sensitive, capable of detection of nitrogen and phosphorous-containing organic compounds at a detection limit of approximately 1–50 ng/ml. The mass spectrometer is highly sensitive and specific, capable of providing structural information at a detection limit of approximately 0.1–5 ng/ml (Bowers et al., 1994).

Gas chromatography/mass spectrometry is the technique of choice for the confirmation of drugs of abuse and their metabolites in urine for forensic purposes. Combining the separating power of the gas chromatograph with the specificity of the mass spectrometer, test results are conclusive (Goldberger & Cone, 1994; Hawks & Chiang, 1986; Substance-Abuse Testing Committee, 1988).

SPECIFIC SUBSTANCES

Alcohol

Ethyl alcohol, ethanol, or alcohol is the principle component of alcoholic beverages. Ethanol is a low-molecular-weight organic molecule that is rapidly absorbed following oral ingestion and distributes according to body water content. It is a central nervous system depressant that may cause dete-

rioration of judgment and self-control, incoordination of voluntary muscle activity, as well as impaired vision and hearing. Ethanol is excreted by the body through metabolic processes, principally in the liver, by enzymatic conversion to acetaldehyde and then carbon dioxide and water. In addition, approximately 10% of the ethanol eliminated from the body is excreted in body water such as the breath, urine, sweat, and saliva (Caplan, 1982; Porter & Moyer, 1994).

Enzyme assay techniques are available for the detection of ethanol in urine and other biological specimens. These assays typically measure the conversion of ethanol to acetaldehyde by the enzyme alcohol dehydrogenase. During this reaction, a coenzyme is converted to its reduced form and this is measured colorimetrically or spectrophotometrically. Gas chromatographic methods are widely used for the analysis of ethanol as they may also simultaneously identify other volatile compounds such as isopropanol, methanol, ketones, and aldehydes. Samples may be injected directly or by injection of headspace vapor. Flame ionization and thermal conductivity detectors are the most common detectors used in this analysis. The limit of sensitivity is approximately 10 mg/dL for ethanol (Caplan, 1992; Porter & Moyer, 1994).

Amphetamines

Amphetamines are sympathomimetic phenethylamine derivatives with potent central nervous stimulant activity. Amphetamine and methamphetamine are extensively metabolized and can be detected in urine specimens for up to 3 days. Because methamphetamine is metabolized to amphetamine, amphetamine and methamphetamine are present following methamphetamine ingestion (Baselt & Cravey, 1995; Substance-Abuse Testing Committee, 1988).

Immunoassay techniques are designed to detect amphetamines in urine specimens utilizing amphetamine or methamphetamine as the target analyte. All amphetamine immunoassays are subject to possible false positive test results due to the presence of other structurally related sympathomimetic amines. Many of these agents, including ephedrine, phenylpropanolamine, and phenylephrine, are found in popular nonprescription over-the-counter, cold, allergy, and diet medications. In addition, positive test results are likely following the administration of benzphetamine and selegiline, prescription medications utilized for their anoretic and anti-Parkinsonian effects, respectively, that are metabolized to methamphetamine. Most immunoassays are also subject to significant cross reactivity with the illicit stimulants

3,4-methylenedioxymethamphetamine (MDMA), also known as "Ecstasy," and 3,4-methylenedioxyamphetamine (MDA), also known as the "love pill" (Liu, 1995).

Barbiturates

Barbiturates are central nervous system depressants and are utilized as sedative-hypnotic and anticonvulsant agents. There are many barbiturate derivatives that constitute this class of drugs and are classified as ultra-short-, short-, intermediate-, and long-acting. Detection of a specific barbiturate in urine depends on the type of barbiturate ingested, and ranges from 24 hours (short-acting) to several weeks (long-acting) (Baselt & Cravey, 1995; Substance-Abuse Testing Committee, 1988).

All immunoassay techniques are designed to detect the majority of short-, intermediate-, and long-acting barbiturates in urine specimens using secobarbital as the target analyte. A positive test result indicates the presence of barbiturates in the urine specimen. Additional testing utilizing a chromatographic technique is necessary in order to identify the specific barbiturate(s) present.

Benzodiazepines

Benzodiazepines are central nervous system depressants utilized for their anxiolytic, sedative-hypnotic, anticonvulsant, and muscle relaxant properties. There are many benzodiazepines that constitute this class of drugs, and are classified as ultra-short, short-, and long-acting. Detection of a specific benzodiazepine in urine depends upon the type of benzodiazepine ingested and ranges from 5 to 7 days (Baselt & Cravey, 1995; Substance-Abuse Testing Committee, 1988).

Immunoassay techniques are designed to detect benzodiazepine compounds and their metabolites in urine specimens utilizing oxazepam or nordiazepam as the target analyte. A positive test result requires further testing utilizing a chromatographic technique to identify the specific benzodiazepine compound and/or metabolite(s) present in the specimen. Depending on the immunoassay technique, newer, more potent benzodiazepines such as alprazolam, flunitrazepam, and triazolam may be difficult to detect.

Cannabinoids

Marijuana is a popular, potent hallucinogen used primarily for its euphoric effects. The psychoactive constituent in marijuana is -9-tetrahydrocannabinol (THC). THC-acid may be detected in urine specimens for variable periods of time and potentially for up to several weeks depending upon the frequency of use (Baselt & Cravey, 1995; Substance-Abuse Testing Committee, 1988).

Immunoassay techniques are designed to detect cannabinoids in urine specimens utilizing THC-acid as the target analyte. Other noncannabinoid analytes usually do not cross react with the cannabinoid assays. Marinol®, synthetic THC, used for the treatment of anorexia associated with AIDS, will produce positive test results. The original formulation of the Emit cannabinoid assay was subject to false positive test results in the presence of ibuprofen. The assay was reformulated in 1986, and is no longer affected by ibuprofen.

Cannabinoid immunoassay cutoff concentrations will affect the percentage of nonconfirmable positive screening results, especially in specimens with urinary concentrations of THC-acid between 50 and 100 ng/ml. Further, it is difficult to correlate immunoassay response with gas chromatography/mass spectrometry confirmation results for THC-acid as immunoassay results reflect total cannabinoid metabolite concentration rather than THC-acid concentration only (Liu, 1995).

A problem associated with the interpretation of urine cannabinoid test results is that a positive test may occur from passive inhalation of marijuana smoke. The presence of cannabinoid metabolites in urine specimens due to passive inhalation is a function of environmental conditions, duration and frequency of exposure, and THC content of the smoked marijuana (ElSohly & Jones, 1995a; Huestis & Cone, 1995). Although passive inhalation studies have shown that individuals exposed to marijuana cigarette smoke under typical conditions would not test positive for cannabinoids, in order to avoid interpretive problems the federally mandated THC-acid cutoff concentration was initially set at 100 ng/ml. The cutoff concentration was lowered to 50 ng/ml in 1995.

Cocaine

Cocaine is a potent central nervous system stimulant and local anesthetic. It is rapidly hydrolyzed to benzoylecgonine and ecgonine methyl ester by metabolic and chemical reactions. Benzoylecgonine, the primary cocaine metabolite in urine, is readily detected for 1–3 days. Following chronic use of cocaine, benzoylecgonine may be detected for longer periods of time (Baselt & Cravey, 1995; Substance-Abuse Testing Committee, 1988).

Immunoassay techniques are designed to detect cocaine metabolites in urine specimens utilizing benzoylecgonine as the target analyte. Cross reactivity with other noncocaine compounds is not usually observed. Despite common belief, other local anesthetic agents such as lidocaine, benzocaine, and procaine do not produce false positive test results.

In the mid 1980s, there was interest in an herbal tea in which the contents were listed as "decocainized coca leaves." Siegel et al. (1986) found that this 'Health Inca Tea' contained 4.8 mg cocaine per bag. Regular coca tea (Mate de Coca) is consumed in South America and contains coca leaves. Although it is not legally available in the United States, significant quantities are purchased by visitors to South America. Jenkins, Ilosa, Montoya, and Cone (1996) identified, quantitated, and compared alkaloids in coca tea obtained from two South American countries. Cocaine, benzoylecgonine, ecgonine methyl ester, and trans-cinnamoyl-cocaine were identified in the teabag contents and also in the coca tea prepared from the bag. Further, these authors determined that detectable concentrations (>10 ng/ml) of the cocaine metabolite, benzoylecgonine, were present in urine for 48 h following consumption of one cup of coca tea prepared with one teabag.

Lysergic Acid Diethylamide

Lysergic acid diethylamide (LSD) is a potent mind-altering psychotropic drug. Although LSD was once used as an aid in psychotherapy and in the treatment of alcohol and drug addiction, it presently has no legitimate therapeutic use (Baselt & Cravey, 1995).

The analysis of LSD in biological tissues is difficult as it is extensively distributed and metabolized. In addition, the effective psychomimetic dose of LSD is small due to its potency, and thus, urine concentrations are exceedingly low. Following administration, LSD can be detected in urine specimens by immunoassay for less than 1 day. The assays do not cross react with other structurally related ergot alkaloids.

Methadone

Methadone is a synthetic opioid that has analgesic actions and potency similar to morphine. Although its use is indicated for treatment of severe pain, its primary use is in the detoxification and maintenance of opiate (heroin) addiction. Methadone is readily detected in urine specimens for

up to 72 hours after administration (Baselt & Cravey, 1995; Substance-Abuse Testing Committee, 1988).

Immunoassay techniques are designed to detect methadone in urine specimens using methadone as the target analyte. Although the methadone assays usually do not cross react with compounds structurally unrelated to methadone, the presence of metabolites in urine specimens from individuals administered L-alpha-acetylmethadol (LAAM), a long-acting methadone analog, may produce positive test results.

Methaqualone

Methaqualone is a central nervous system depressant. Although methaqualone was a popular drug during the 1970s and early 1980s, its use has been replaced by other drugs such as marijuana. Following administration, methaqualone can be detected in urine specimens for up to 14 days (Baselt & Cravey, 1995). Immunoassay techniques are designed to detect methaqualone in urine specimens using methaqualone as the target analyte. Cross reactivity with other nonmethaqualone related compounds is not usually observed.

Opiates

Opiates are potent drugs that are routinely utilized as analgesics to treat moderate to severe pain. Legitimate pharmaceutical sources of opiates include morphine and codeine. Heroin, an illicit substance, is most often abused for production of euphoria and avoidance of withdrawal symptoms. Heroin is rapidly metabolized to 6-acetylmorphine, which is further metabolized to morphine. Codeine is also metabolized to morphine. Opiates may be detected in urine specimens for up to 24 hours or for several days, depending on the amount and type of agent administered (Baselt & Cravey, 1995; Substance-Abuse Testing Committee, 1988).

Immunoassay techniques are designed to detect opiates and their metabolites (primarily morphine, codeine, and their glucuronide metabolites) in urine specimens using morphine as the target analyte. Most opiate assays are generally nonspecific and cross react with many opiate compounds.

Morphine and codeine have been identified in urine specimens of individuals who have ingested poppy seeds and/or poppy seed cakes. Opiate immunoassays are sufficiently sensitive to detect morphine and morphine conjugates in these

Table 13.5   List of Common Adulterants

Alcohols
Ammonia
Apple Juice
Ascorbic Acid
Bleach
Blood
Detergent
Drano®
Ethylene Glycol
Golden Seal Root
Hydrogen Peroxide
Lime-A-Way
Peroxide
Salt
Sodium Bicarbonate
Sodium Phosphate
Urin Aid (glutaraldehyde)
Vanish®
Vitamin C
Water

*Cody, 1995
Source: Data from "Adulteration of Urine Specimens" by J. T. Cody, in *Handbook of Workplace Drug Testing*, R. A. Liu and B. A. Goldberger, Eds., 1995, AACC Press, Washington, D.C.

specimens days following ingestion. These results are true positives, even though not indicative of opiate abuse. Therefore, in the case of a positive opiate test result, additional testing may be required to differentiate the heroin user from the poppy seed consumer (ElSohly & Jones, 1995a, 1995b).

Phencyclidine

Phencyclidine, commonly known as PCP, an hallucinogen and dissociative anesthetic, is readily detected in urine specimens for up to several days following administration (Baselt & Cravey, 1995; Substance-Abuse Testing Committee, 1988). Immunoassay techniques are designed to detect phencyclidine in urine specimens utilizing phencyclidine as the target analyte. Cross reactivity with other nonphencyclidine-related compounds is not usually observed.

Propoxyphene

Propoxyphene is a synthetic opioid that has analgesic actions and potency similar to codeine. Its use is indicated

for the treatment of moderate to severe pain. Propoxyphene and its primary metabolite, norpropoxyphene, are present in urine specimens for several days (Baselt & Cravey, 1995). Immunoassay techniques are designed to detect propoxyphene and norpropoxyphene in urine specimens utilizing propoxyphene as the target analyte. Cross reactivity with other nonpropoxyphene related compounds is not usually observed.

REPORTING OF DRUG TEST RESULTS

Results of all drug testing should be reported to an individual who is familiar with substance-abuse disorders and who has the appropriate training to interpret drug test results. In workplace drug testing, the individual is a licensed physician (also known as a medical review officer, or MRO) who has participated in specialized training, and has been board certified in this specialty. In order to rule out legitimate medical use of many of the drugs that are commonly tested, the physician is required to contact the donor regarding all positive results (Green & Isenschmid, 1995; Shults & St. Clair, 1995).

DILUTION, SUBSTITUTION, AND ADULTERATION OF URINE SPECIMENS

In an attempt to alter drug test results, drug users may dilute, substitute, or adulterate the urine specimen. In vivo dilution through the ingestion of large volumes of liquid or administration of a diuretic could lead to a negative drug test result. Because the mechanism of action varies with the assay and the concentration of drug and adulterant present in the specimen, adulterants may have no affect on the test results, or may produce false positive or false negative test results. Adulterants usually affect the urine pH and/or ionic strength of the specimen, inhibit immunoassay antibody binding, and/or interfere with the method of detection (Cody, 1995). A list of common adulterants is presented in Table 13.5.

ALTERNATE TISSUES FOR DRUG TESTING

Although urine drug testing is reliable, economical, and widely utilized by laboratory and medical professionals, interest in the use of alternate biological tissues such as hair, sweat, and saliva has increased. All common substances of abuse including amphetamines, cannabinoids, cocaine and its metabolites, heroin and its metabolites, and

Table 13.6   Detection Times and Apparent Advantages and Disadvantages of Alternate Biological Tissues

Tissue		Detection Time	Advantages	Disadvantages
Hair	Months		Long-term measure of drug use Easily obtainable Ability to obtain similar specimen for re-analysis Low potential for manipulation of specimen to alter test outcome	New technology Recent drug use not readily detected Potential environmental contamination Potential ethnic bias Limited number of laboratories that offer hair testing services
Saliva	12–24 hours		Easily obtainable Parent drug present Saliva concentration correlates to free drug concentration in plasma	New technology Short-term measure of drug use Potential oral drug contamination Collection methods influence specimen pH and saliva:plasma concentration ration
Sweat	1–4 weeks		Monitor drug use for a period of weeks with the sweat patch Cumulative measure of drug use Parent drug present	Potential environmental contamination High intersubject variability New technology

Source: Reprinted in abbreviated form from *Handbook of Workplace Drug Testing*, R. A. Liu and B. A. Goldberger, Eds., 1995, AACC Press, Washington, D.C. Copyright © 1995 by the American Association for Clinical Chemistry, Inc.

phencyclidine have been detected in hair, sweat, and saliva. In addition, many therapeutic drugs have also been detected in these specimens including antidepressants, antipsychotics, barbiturates, benzodiazepines, methylxanthines, nicotine, opioids, and steroids. Detection times and the advantages and disadvantages of alternate tissues are summarized in Table 13.6 (Cone, 1993, 1994; Inoue, Seta, & Goldberger, 1995).

REFERENCES

Abbott Laboratories. (1996). ADx® System Assay Manuals.

About the Monitoring the Future Study. (1996, January/February). *NIDA Notes, 11*, 8–9, 15, U.S. Department of Health and Human Services, National Institute of Health, Washington, D.C.

Baselt, R. C., & Cravey, R. H. (1995). *Disposition of toxic drug and chemicals in man* (4th ed.). Foster City, CA: Chemical Toxicology Institute.

Behring Diagnostics Incorporated. (1996). Emit®II Assay package inserts.

Boehringer Mannheim Corporation. (1996). CEDIA package inserts.

Bowers, L. D., Ullman M. D., & Burtis, C. A. (1994). Chromatography. In C. A. Burtis & E. R. Ashwood (Eds.), *Tietz textbook of clinical chemistry* (2nd ed.). Philadelphia: Saunders.

Caplan, Y. H. (1982). The determination of alcohol in blood and breath. In R. Saferstein, *Forensic science handbook*. Englewood Cliffs, NJ: Prentice Hall.

Cody, J. T. (1995). Adulteration of urine specimens. In R. A. Liu & B. A. Goldberger, (Eds.). *Handbook of workplace drug testing*. Washington, DC: AACC Press.

Cone, E. J. (1993). Saliva testing for drugs of abuse. *Annuals of the New York Academy of Sciences, 694,* 91–127.

Cone, E. J. (1994). New developments in biological measures of drug prevalence. The validity of self-reported drug use: Improving the accuracy of survey estimates. *NIDA Technical Review.*

Diagnostic Products Corporation. (1996). Coat-a-Count® and Double Antibody Radioimmunoassay package inserts.

ElSohly, M. A., & Jones, A. B. (1995a). Drug testing in the workplace: Could a positive test for one of the mandated drugs be for reasons other than illicit use of the drug? *Journal of Analytical Toxicology, 19,* 450–458.

ElSohly, M. A., & Jones, A. B. (1995b). Origin of morphine and codeine in biological specimens. In R. A. Liu & B. A. Goldberger (Eds.), *Handbook of workplace drug testing.* Washington, DC: AACC Press.

Goldberger, B. A., & Cone, E. J. (1994). Confirmatory tests for drugs in the workplace by gas chromatography-mass spectrometry. *Journal of Chromatography A, 674,* 73–86.

Gorodetzky, C. W. (1972). Validity of urine tests in monitoring drug abuse. Report of the Thirty-Fourth Annual Scientific

Meeting Committee on Problems of Drug Dependence. Ann Arbor, MI.

Gorodetzky, C. W. (1977). Detection of drugs of abuse in biological fluids. In G. V. Born, O. Eichler, A. Farah, H. Herken, & A. D. Welch (Eds.), *Handbook of experimental pharmacology*. Berlin, Germany: Springer-Verlag.

Green, K. B., & Isenschmid, D. S. (1995). Medical review officer interpretation of urine drug test results. In R. A. Liu & B. A. Goldberger (Eds.), *Handbook of workplace drug testing*. Washington, DC. AACC Press.

Hawks, R. L., & Chiang, C. N. (Eds.). (1986). *Urine testing for drugs of abuse* (NIDA, Research Monograph Series, Number 73). Washington, DC: U.S. Government Printing Office.

Huestis, M. A., & Cone, E. J. (1995). Drug test findings resulting from unconventional drug exposure. In R. A. Liu & B. A. Goldberger (Eds.), *Handbook of workplace drug testing*. Washington, DC: AACC Press.

Inoue, T., Seta, S., & Goldberger, B. A. (1995). Analysis of drugs in unconventional samples. In R. A. Liu & B. A. Goldberger (Eds.), *Handbook of workplace drug testing*. Washington, DC: AACC Press.

Jenkins, A. J., Mills, L. C., Darwin, W. D., Huestis, M. A., Cone, E. J., & Mitchell, J. M. (1993). Validity testing of the EZ-Screen® cannabinoid test. *Journal of Analytical Toxicology, 17*, 292–298.

Jenkins, A. J., Darwin, W. D., Huestis, M. A., Cone, E. J., & Mitchell, J. M. (1995). Validity testing of the accuPinch™ THC test. *Journal of Analytical Toxicology, 19*, 5–12.

Jenkins, A. J., Ilosa, T., Montoya, I., & Cone, E. J. (1996). Identification and quantitation of alkaloids in coca tea. *Forensic Science International, 77*, 179–189.

Kapur, B. M. (1993). Drug-testing methods and clinical interpretations of test results. *Bulletin on Narcotics, 45*, 115–154.

Kricka, L. J. (1994). Principles of immunochemical techniques. In C. A. Burtis & E. R. Ashwood (Eds.), *Tietz textbook of clinical chemistry* (2nd ed.). Philadelphia, PA: Saunders.

Liu, R. H. (1995). Evaluation of commercial immunoassay kits for effective workplace drug testing. In R. A. Liu & B. A. Goldberger (Eds.), *Handbook of workplace drug testing*. Washington, DC: AACC Press.

Mandatory guidelines for federal workplace drug testing programs: Final guidelines; notice (1988). *Federal Register, 53*, 11970–11989.

Montagne, M., Pugh, C. B., & Fink, J. L. (1988). Testing for drug use, part 1: Analytical methods. *American Journal of Hospital Pharmacy, 45*, 1297–1305.

Porter, W. H., & Moyer, T. P. (1994). Clinical toxicology. In C. A. Burtis & E. R. Ashwood (Eds.), *Tietz textbook of clinical chemistry* (2nd ed.). Philadelphia, PA: Saunders.

Roche Diagnostic Systems (1996). Abuscreen® Radioimmunoassay and ONLINE® Assay package inserts.

Shults, T. F., & St. Clair, S. (1995). *The medical review officer handbook*. Research Triangle Park, NC: Quadrangle Research, LLC.

Siegel, R. K., ElSohly, M. A., Plowman, T., Rury, P. M., & Jones, R. T. (1986). Cocaine in herbal tea. *Journal of the American Medical Association, 255*, 40.

Substance Abuse and Mental Health Services Administration (1994). *National household survey on drug abuse: Population estimates 1993* (DHHS Publication No. SMA 94-3017). Washington, D.C.

Substance Abuse and Mental Health Services Administration (1995). *Annual medical examiner data, 1993* (DHHS Publication No. SMA 95-3019).

Substance Abuse and Mental Health Services Administration (1996). *Preliminary estimates from the drug abuse warning network*. Advance Report Number 14.

Substance-Abuse Testing Committee. (1988). Therapeutic Drug Monitoring and Clinical Toxicology Division, American Association for Clinical Chemistry. Critical issues in urinalysis of abused substances: Report of the substance-abuse testing committee. *Clinical Chemistry 34*, 605–632.

Wu, A. H. B., Wong, S. S., Johnson, K. G., Callies, J., Shu, D. X., Dunn, W. E., & Wong, S. H. Y. (1993). Evaluation of the Triage system for emergency drugs-of-abuse testing in urine. *Journal of Analytical Toxicology, 17*, 241–245.

Wu, A. H. B. (1995). Near-patient and point-of-care testing for alcohol and drugs of abuse. *Therapeutic Drug Monitoring and Toxicology In-Service Training and Continuing Education Program, American Association for Clinical Chemistry, 16*, 227–236.

CHAPTER 14

PSYCHIATRIC ASSESSMENT

Duncan B. Clark

The essential goal of the psychiatric assessment for patients presenting for difficulties associated with substance use is to diagnose substance use disorders and other related psychiatric disorders (Schottenfeld, 1994). As in many settings, the responsibilities of the psychiatrist typically extend to the overall evaluation. The complex nature of substance use disorders and related psychiatric and medical disorders necessitates that the clinical psychiatric assessment be comprehensive, and that it include evaluation of a variety of domains important for planning treatment with a multidisciplinary team.

The methods for determining psychiatric diagnoses and issues related to their application comprise the central focus of this chapter. In addition to the obvious importance of identifying substance use disorder diagnoses in this context, the psychiatric assessment must also include a systematic evaluation of other comorbid psychiatric disorders. Comorbid psychiatric disorders warranting special attention include antisocial personality disorder, affective disorders, anxiety disorders, and psychotic disorders. These disorders may contribute to the initiation of substance abuse, may exacerbate the problems associated with substance abuse, or may be caused by chronic substance abuse and need to be considered in treatment planning.

Operationalized systems for defining psychiatric diagnoses have led to the development of systematic methods for assessing these disorders. The types of structured interviews for determining substance use disorder and comorbid psychiatric diagnoses will be described. Issues in the application of structured interviews, including selection among available methods, interviewer training, and establishing and maintaining reliability will be discussed. For some research questions and in some clinical situations, it may be appropriate to approach psychopathology domains by utilizing measures that provide dimensional as well as categorical assessments. Although this chapter will primarily review categorical methods, a brief review of continuous methods for some areas of psychopathology will be presented. Technical and practical issues relevant to applying psychiatric assessment methods in research as well as in clinical practice will be discussed.

DOMAINS OF PSYCHIATRIC EVALUATION

The domains of psychiatric assessment are to some extent defined by the psychiatrist's role in evaluation and treatment. From the beginning of American psychiatry in the eighteenth century, psychiatrists have been involved in the conceptualization, assessment, and treatment of substance use disorders. In his treatise "An Inquiry Into the Effects of Ardent Spirits Upon the Human Body," Benjamin Rush (1785/1943), a major influence in the early development of American psychiatry, conceptualized alcohol abuse as a discrete disease entity. In addition, Rush was the first to articulate the concept of addiction to a drug and estimate of the extent of alcohol dependence in the population (American Psychiatric Association [APA] 1995a; Levine 1978). Physicians routinely diagnosed and treated substance use disorders in the nineteenth century (APA, 1995a). According to Dorwart et al. (1992), patients with substance use disorders currently make up approximately 10% of psychiatrists' average caseload. One third of all psychiatrists describe substance use disorders as an area of special interest (APA, 1995a).

The evaluation and treatment of patients with substance use disorders typically occurs through a multidisciplinary team, which may include psychiatrists, nonpsychiatric physicians, psychologists, social workers, nurses, credentialed addiction counselors, and others. The psychiatrist often assumes primary medical responsibility for the evaluation and treatment and is therefore obliged to ensure that a comprehensive assessment is completed (APA, 1995a). This involvement of psychiatrists in providing services for substance use disorders continues to evolve, as evidenced by recent task force reports by the American Psychiatric Association on psychiatric services for addicted individuals (APA, 1995a) and practice treatment guidelines for patients with substance use disorders (APA, 1995b). The psychiatric evaluation describes the assessment necessary for the initiation of treatment as well as aspects of evaluation that may be of interest in research. It should be noted that in most clinical circumstances, components of this evaluation may be carried out by members of a multidisciplinary team.

According to the practice guidelines published by the American Psychiatric Association (1995c), the psychiatric evaluation contains the following domains:

1. Reason for evaluation: Among patients with substance use disorders, the presenting problem may be related to the social consequences of substance use rather than symptoms causing subjective distress as with most other psychiatric disorders.
2. History of the present illness: In addition to a review of the consequences of substance use for the purposes of establishing diagnoses, a focus on recent quantity and frequency of substance consumption may be par-

ticularly important for evaluating the potential for complications associated with withdrawal.
3. Past psychiatric history: A systematic review of the lifetime history of substance use disorders as well as chronological and perceived relationships with other psychiatric disorders may be useful for treatment planning. A history of prior response to and attitude toward treatment may also be helpful in predicting the interventions that may be most effective.
4. General medical history: Screening for the medical consequences of abused substances is particularly critical.
5. History of substance use: Screening methods, which have been most thoroughly developed for alcohol use disorders, can be useful in populations for whom substance use disorders are not identified as a primary concern. Validated methods for alcohol use disorders include the four-question CAGE (Mayfield, McLeon, & Hall, 1974), the Michigan Alcoholism Screening Test (Selzer, 1971), and the Luebeck Alcohol Dependence and Abuse Screening Test (Rumpf, Hapke, Hill, & John, 1997).
6. Psychosocial and developmental history: Childhood school difficulties may indicate attention deficit hyperactivity disorder, early conduct disorder, or developmental disabilities. The possibility of a history of childhood physical and sexual abuse should be considered (Clark, Lesnick, & Hegedus, 1997).
7. Social history: Understanding the impact of substance abuse on family relationships is essential in conducting a substance use disorder diagnostic assessment (Clark, Neighbors, Lesnick, Lynch, & Donovan, 1998). The involvement of family and friends in substance abuse may reveal potential problems in maintaining abstinence. Review of the social history may also reveal antisocial behaviors useful in determining the presence of disruptive behavior disorders and antisocial personality disorders.
8. Occupational history: The effects of substance abuse on the occupational history may be particularly relevant to the reason for evaluation as well as necessary to review for diagnostic purposes. An erratic occupational history may also reveal characteristics of antisocial personality disorder.
9. Family history: As genetic factors have been found to contribute to the development of substance use disorders, a review of family history may contribute to an understanding of the patient's diathesis for these dis-

orders. The parents' substance use disorders may also yield insights into the patient's childhood difficulties.

10. Review of systems: Although many symptoms may be related to substance intoxication or withdrawal, the multiple medical problems complicating substance use disorders necessitates a comprehensive review of systems.

11. Physical examination: Although a physical exam is often completed by a nonpsychiatric physician or other health care provider, the psychiatrist is obligated to ensure that the exam has been completed. Particularly relevant in this population are signs of drug intoxication, impending overdose, or withdrawal; evidence of intravenous drug use; signs of sepsis; and evidence of nutritional deficiencies (Scottenfeld, 1994).

12. Mental status examination: A careful mental status exam, including an evaluation of cognitive functioning, is essential in a comprehensive psychiatric evaluation. Observations concerning the presence or absence of mood and affect disturbances, paranoia, suicidal ideas and plans, violent ideation and behavior, and hallucinatory phenomena are especially important (Scottenfeld, 1994). As the mental status exam will change with the state of intoxication and withdrawal, serial mental status examinations are usually necessary. Knowledge of the neuropsychological consequences of specific substance use disorders may further inform the structure of the exam.

13. Functional assessment: The DSM-IV system provides a systematic method of determining current and past level of functioning. This assessment may be useful in determining the cumulative impact of substance use disorders, comorbid psychiatric disorders, and other complications (Clark, Pollock, et al., 1997).

14. Diagnostic tests: In addition to screening laboratory tests, monitoring of breath alcohol and urine or blood screening for illicit substances are usually necessary to confirm or refute patient reports. However, time of detection varies considerably with drug and chronicity of use. For the major urine metabolite of THC, the average time of detection is 4–6 days for acute uses and 20–30 days in chronic uses (Schwartz & Hawks, 1985). The principal metabolite of cocaine can only be detected for 1–3 days (Gawin, Khalsa, & Ellinwood, 1994).

15. Information derived from the interview process: Although it is critical to document behavioral obser-

vations concerning intoxication and withdrawal, these observations may not generalize to the abstinent state. As in other areas of the evaluation, serial examinations and revisiting prior hypotheses are necessary in the comprehensive evaluation of the patient with substance use disorders.

Defining Psychiatric Diagnoses

Nosology, the science of disease classification, is central to the assessment task of the psychiatrist. The purpose of diagnostic classification is to define psychiatric diagnoses for the facilitation of communication regarding these disorders in order to advance clinical practice and research concerning the etiology, course, and treatment of psychiatric disorders. The development of the current conceptualization of psychiatric disorders has been influenced by the descriptive orientation of the work of several eighteenth and nineteenth century physicians, including Pineal, Kraepelin, and Rush (Thompson, 1992).

In the early to mid-twentieth century, a more theoretically driven orientation to diagnoses became predominant, leading to the first DSM (1951) and the similar DSM-II (1968). In contrast to the descriptive approach, this theoretically derived approach was based on psychodynamic and psychosocial concepts. The movement away from descriptive diagnoses is illustrated in the following statement from Menninger (1963; in Wilson, 1993): "Instead of putting so much emphasis on different kinds and clinical pictures of illness, we propose to think of all forms of mental illness as being essentially the same in quality, and differing quantitatively . . . What is behind the symptom?" Attempts to use the ambiguous diagnostic definitions in DSM-I and DSM-II led to significant problems in establishing reliable and valid psychiatric diagnoses. With little better than chance agreement among psychiatrists utilizing these and similar diagnostic systems (e.g., Ash, 1949; Beck, 1962; Spitzer & Fleiss, 1974), the validity of psychiatric diagnoses, and by extension, psychiatric practice itself, came to be questioned by members of the federal government and insurance companies (Wilson, 1993). Thus, a variety of forces, both internal and external to the profession of psychiatry, led to a return to a descriptive diagnostic system.

It has only been in recent decades that criteria for defining psychiatric diagnoses have been operationalized in a manner that allows systematic assessment. Prior to the 1960s, widely accepted operationalized systems for determining psychiatric diagnoses were not available (Reich,

1992). In the 1970s, the Feighner Criteria (Feighner et al., 1972) and the Research Diagnostic Criteria (RDC) (Spitzer, Endicott, & Robins, 1978) were disseminated and were utilized primarily in research. Whereas the first two editions of the Diagnostic and Statistical Manual of Mental Disorders (DSM) did not have explicit criteria, the third (APA, 1980; DSM-III-R: APA, 1987) and fourth (APA, 1994) editions contained criteria similar to the RDC, and have subsequently become widely accepted for both clinical and research uses. These criterion-based diagnostic systems have led to the development of structured and semistructured interviews for assessing psychiatric diagnoses.

The DSM-IV system is a generally atheoretical, descriptive approach to psychiatric diagnoses (Williams, 1994). This method allows clinicians and researchers to establish diagnoses based on the phenomenology of disorders while withholding judgment about etiological factors. Some diagnostic categories have a hierarchical arrangement in which certain disorders are considered predominant and symptoms are attributed to this primary diagnosis. Substance-induced disorders preempt the diagnosis of other disorders with overlapping symptoms. Similar rules are created for disorders due to an identified medical condition and pervasive disorders such as schizophrenia. In addition to typically considered psychiatric diagnoses (Axis I) and Personality Disorders (Axis II), DSM-IV provides for documentation of other relevant factors that may influence diagnoses, including general medical conditions (Axis III), psychosocial and environmental problems (Axis IV), and a Global Assessment of Functioning (Axis V).

Substance-Use Disorders

In the DSM-IV and other criterion-based diagnostic systems, substance use disorders are defined by the consequences of substance use, including social consequences as well as cognitive, behavioral, and physiological symptoms. DSM-IV (APA, 1994) provides distinct definitions for dependence and abuse. These criteria are similarly applied across various classes of substances, although particular criterion items may be less relevant for particular substances.

The criteria for dependence include tolerance, withdrawal, loss of control, unsuccessful attempts to abstain, much time spent in using or obtaining the substance, social or occupational activities diminished by substance use,

and continued use despite physical or psychological problems. To meet criteria for dependence, a patient must have at least three of these seven symptoms. These criteria deemphasize tolerance and dependence as indicators of dependence (Rounsaville & Bryant, 1992). Although conceptualization of substance dependence traditionally includes physiological indicators, a more broad-based definition has the advantage of universal application to a variety of substances in which physiological dependence may have less predictive validity than other symptoms. For example, in patients with cocaine dependence, Rounsaville and Bryant (1992) found that drug salience, defined as the tendency to give up important activities as a result of drug use, was a better predictor of status at 1-year follow-up than were tolerance or withdrawal symptoms.

Abuse requires only one of four consequences, including failure to fulfill major role obligations, physically hazardous use, legal problems, or interpersonal problems. To meet abuse criteria, the consequences must be substance use related and recurrent. Although not explicitly part of the diagnostic system, quantity and frequency measures are also necessary, and may identify patient for whom substance-use-related difficulties do not exceed diagnostic thresholds but are nevertheless problematic. Questions eliciting diagnostic information need to be systematic and nonjudgmental. Even if not conventionally utilized, structured interviews can provide a guide for the clinically appropriate solicitation of this information.

Whether or not the constructs of alcohol abuse and dependence as just defined are valid for adolescents has been a subject of little empirical study. Bukstein and Kaminer (1994) argue that adult substance use disorder diagnostic criteria have not been established as applicable to adolescents. Martin, Kaczynski, Maistro, Bukstein, and Moss (1995) note that, for alcohol use disorders, tolerance, withdrawal and medical problems may present differently in adolescents than in adults. That is, substance abuse may be a more heterogeneous disorder among adolescents than among adults (Bukstein & Kaminer, 1994; Martin et al., 1995).

DSM-IV identifies the following classes of substances: (a) alcohol; (b) sympathomimetics; (c) cannabis; (d) cocaine; (e) hallucinogens; (f) inhalants; (g) opioids; (h) phencyclidine (PCP) and related arylcyclohexylamines; (i) sedatives, hypnotics, and anxiolytics; (j) caffeine; and (k) nicotine. A comprehensive evaluation requires screening for each substance class as many patients have been involved in polysubstance abuse. For example, the Epidemiologic

Catchment Area study reports that, of subjects with drug abuse or dependence, 47.7% also had alcohol abuse or dependence (Anthony & Helzer, 1991). High prevalences of drug abuse and dependence have been noted in adolescence with alcohol use disorders (Martin, Arria, Mezzich, & Bukstein, 1993). Where consumption of multiple substances is acknowledged, the consequences and symptoms must be systematically assessed for each substance. In polysubstance abusers, difficulties in assigning the attribution of consequences to one substance or another can present diagnostic challenges.

Comorbid Psychiatric Disorders

A consensus concerning the importance of comorbid psychiatric disorders in the etiology and treatment of substance use disorders has yet to be fully established. Several theories concerning the etiology of substance use disorders postulate roles for antisocial personality characteristics, depression, and anxiety (Cloninger, 1987; Mezzich et al., 1993). Furthermore, the influence of substance use disorders in exacerbating comorbid psychiatric disorders needs to be considered in both clinical and research settings. Of the over 100 psychiatric disorders described in DSM-IV, the most prevalent and relevant psychiatric disorders in this population include antisocial personality disorder, affective disorders, anxiety disorders, and psychotic disorders. A discussion of these selected psychiatric diagnoses provides the context for the assessment of comorbid psychiatric disorders in individuals with substance use disorders.

Antisocial Personality Disorder

Epidemiological, clinical, and adoption studies have suggested that a major pathway leading to substance use disorders travels through antisocial characteristics. Prospective research reveals that violence and violation of social norms, key features of conduct disorder (CD) and antisocial personality disorder, predict the consumption of illicit substances in late adolescence (Boyle et al., 1992) and adulthood (Cadoret, Yates, Troughton, Woodworth, & Stewart, 1995). Externalizing behavior disorder characteristics have been shown to be evident in children as young as age 3, with parents who have substance use disorders (Zucker & Fitzgerald, 1991), suggesting the importance of very early intervention for substance use disorder prevention. Cadoret et al. (1995) have presented evidence from an adoption study for a pathway that begins with antisocial personality disorder in the biologic parent, proceeds through adoptee conduct disorder and antisocial personality disorder, and results in substance use disorders. Data from the Center for Education and Drug Abuse Research (Clark, Moss, et al., 1997) suggests that the pathway to substance use disorders may be reflected in parental childhood characteristics. In this study of children at high risk for substance use disorders, paternal childhood disruptive behavior disorders were more strongly associated with the son's disruptive behavior disorders than were paternal antisocial personality disorder. Despite the high prevalence of antisocial personality disorder among patients with substance use disorders, studies using DSM-III-R and DSM-IV criteria may underestimate the problem of antisocial behavior in this population. Brooner, Schmidt, Felch, and Bigelow (1992) noted that, although 44% of intravenous drug abusers met DSM-III-R criteria for antisocial personality disorder (ASPD), an additional 24% met adult ASPD criteria but did not meet the DSM-III-R definition early-onset requirement. In patients with substance use disorders, antisocial personality disorder has been found to be associated with higher morbidity (Yates, Petty, & Brown, 1988) and poorer outcome (Rounsaville, Dolinsky, Babor, & Meyer, 1987). Substance use disorder patients with ASPD may be at higher risk for HIV infection due to increased intravenous drug use (Dinwiddie, Reich, & Cloninger, 1992) and sharing of injection equipment (Brooner, Bigelow, Strain, & Schmidt, 1990). Antisocial behavior is an integral aspect of substance use disorders and careful evaluation of the history of childhood disruptive behavior disorders and antisocial personality disorder needs to be included in the comprehensive psychiatric assessment.

Affective Disorders

Although the high prevalence of comorbidity of substance use disorders and affective disorders, particularly major depression, is well documented, the origins and clinical implications of the relationship remains somewhat controversial. In clinical studies, secondary depression, presumed to be substance induced, is substantially more common in patients with substance use disorders than is primary depression (Clark & Neighbors, 1996). Depression or other affective symptoms may decline dramatically over a brief period of abstinence (Brown & Schuckit, 1988). A 1-month period of abstinence is required by the DSM-IV criteria to distinguish substance-induced depression and anxiety symptoms from independent psychiatric disorders. It has been established that substance use disorder patients have increased morbidity associated with mood disorders (Cornelius et al., 1995; Rounsaville et al., 1987). Methods for distinguishing between substance-induced and independent mood and anxiety disorders have been shown to be problematic with regard to reliability and validity (Kadden, Kranzler, & Rounsaville, 1995). Nevertheless, there are important differences in long-term clinical course between patients with substance-induced and independent affective disorders. While some investigators have seen no difference in outcomes comparing those with primary and secondary depression (Bukstein, Glancy, & Kaminer, 1992; Kadden et al., 1995), most studies show substance use disorder patients with independent affective disorder to have more chronic depression symptoms (Brown et al., 1995; Schuckit, 1985). Similarly, Winokur et al. (1995) found that patients with bipolar disorder, which is primary to alcoholism, have more persistent affective symptoms. Gender differences, often inadequately considered, have been found to be an important factor in understanding the etiological relationships between affective disorders and substance use disorders (Clark, Pollock, et al., 1997). For example, Hartka et al. (1991) found that alcohol consumption leads to depression in both men and women, whereas depression leads to alcohol consumption only in women.

Anxiety disorders

Epidemiological and clinical studies patients with anxiety disorders have approximately double the risk of having a substance use disorder compared with controls (Himle & Hill, 1991; Regier et al., 1990). Patients with alcohol use disorders tend to have higher rates of anxiety disorders than individuals who abuse opiates or cocaine (Hesselbrock, Meyer, & Keene, 1985; Weiss & Rosenberg, 1985). These same patients have also been found to have increased prevalence ratios for panic disorder, obsessive compulsive disorder, social phobia, agoraphobia, and posttraumatic stress disorder (Clark & Sayette, 1993; Helzer, Burnam, & McEvoy, 1991; Himle & Hill, 1991; Kushner, Sher, & Beitman, 1990). Although patients often retrospectively report that the anxiety disorder preceded alcohol abuse and that they used alcohol in an attempt to control phobic anxiety (Clark & Neighbors, 1996), controlled studies have not consistently supported the hypothesis that anxiety disorders contribute to alcohol use disorders. Regardless of the proven pharmacodynamic properties of alcohol or other drugs, the belief that they

reduce anxiety and depression symptoms is clearly one motivating factor for substance consumption (Clark & Sayette, 1993). Schuckit and Hesselbrock (1994) concluded that high prevalences of anxiety disorders in some studies reflect a mixture of primary anxiety disorders among patients with alcohol use disorders at a rate slightly higher than that for the general population along with transient substance-induced anxiety syndromes. The assumption that there is a clear primary and secondary disorder in every case may be an oversimplification. In many patients, a vicious cycle may be created in which a drug is used in an attempt to control anxiety symptoms, and chronic drug intoxication and withdrawal lead to worsening of symptoms of anxiety.

Unlike affective disorders, anxiety disorders are not invariably associated with increased morbidity in substance use disorder patients. Clark, Jacob, and Mezzich (1994) compared three groups of adolescents: (a) those with alcohol use disorders, conduct disorder, and anxiety disorders; (b) those with alcohol use disorders and conduct disorder without anxiety; and (c) a normal control group. Whereas both alcohol use disorder groups showed increased morbidity compared with the control group, those with anxiety disorders showed less morbidity than those without anxiety disorders in several areas, including substance use behavior severity, school problems, peer relationships, and overall problem density. When examined more specifically, adolescent posttraumatic stress disorder, on the other hand, has been found to be associated with increased morbidity in several areas, including depression, overall satisfaction with life, health complaints, and social difficulties (Clark & Kirisci, 1996; Clark, Smith, Neighbors, Skerlec, & Randall, 1994).

Psychotic Disorders

As with affective and anxiety disorders, psychotic symptoms may precede and contribute to the development of substance use disorders, may be a consequence of substance abuse, or may be exacerbated by substance abuse (Milin, 1996). Substance-induced psychotic symptoms typically resolve over a brief period with abstinence (Schuckit, 1982). Chronic, frequent use of stimulants and hallucinogens has been associated with an earlier onset of schizophrenia in vulnerable individuals (Milin, 1996). Patients with schizophrenia or schizophreniform disorders have a fourfold increased prevalence of substance use disorders compared with the general population (Regier et al.,

1990), with younger males being most often affected (Mueser, Bellack, & Blanchard, 1992). Patients with comorbid schizophrenia and substance use disorders have been shown to exhibit increased morbidity and poor prognosis due to the exacerbating effects of substance abuse and treatment noncompliance (Milin, 1996).

ASSESSMENT METHODS FOR PSYCHIATRIC DIAGNOSES

Clinical Interview

Whereas the criteria for substance use disorders and other psychiatric diagnoses have been generally agreed upon through the construction of the recent DSM systems, issues regarding the methods to be utilized to arrive at these diagnoses remain more systematically addressed in research than in clinical practice. The typical clinical diagnostic evaluation is relatively unstructured, leaving to the clinician the selection of diagnoses to be covered, the wording of questions, and the interpretation of responses. Whereas an unstructured interview allows the clinician to focus on the most critical aspects of the assessment, differences among clinicians in interviewing content and style lead to diagnostic disagreements. Sources of disagreement among clinicians include criterion variance, which refers to variance in the application of specific criteria used to make diagnoses, and information variance, which occurs when clinicians gather different information from patients (Reich, 1992). Structured interviews significantly reduce both sources of variance.

The structured interview is a systematically inclusive method that often solicits information that is missed by the unstructured clinical interviewer (Reich, 1992). The additional information contributed by the structured interview compared with the unstructured clinical evaluation is illustrated by a study with 43 hospitalized adolescents identified by structured interview as having alcohol use disorders (Clark et al., 1995). Diagnoses identified by structured interviews were compared with those noted in the medical record. By structured interviews, 40% of patients met criteria for anxiety disorders whereas only 9% were identified as having anxiety disorders in the hospital medical record. Hospital records indicated the detection by clinical assessment of 74% of cases with alcohol use disorders, 92% of cases with disruptive behavior disorders, and 60% of cases with affective disorders. Helzer, Clayton, Pambakian, and Woodruff (1978) similarly

reported that structured interviews compared with unstructured clinical evaluations led to the improved detection of psychiatric disorders.

Structured Interviews

Structured interviews together with specific diagnostic criteria are now considered, in a research context, to be the basis for reliable and valid psychiatric diagnoses (Kosten & Rounsaville, 1992). Several interviews are designed to be administered by clinically experienced and extensively trained interviewers. These measures, sometimes described as semistructured interviews, provide phrasing for questions for determining the presence or absence of criterion symptoms; suggestions for probes where the initial responses are ambiguous; and structured methods for determining disorder age of onset, time course, and severity (Reich, 1992). Semistructured interviews are designed in such a way that the interviewer is allowed and expected to make some judgments during the interviewing process regarding the presentation of questions, the appropriateness of probes, whether or not patient responses indicate symptoms that are sufficiently severe to warrant indication that the criterion item is present, and whether or not diagnoses are presence or absent. Structured interviews focus on a select sample of the over 100 psychiatric disorders defined in DSM-IV.

Several interviews are in use for assessing Axis I psychiatric disorders. The Schedule for Affective Disorders and Schizophrenia (SADS), initially designed to assess RDC criteria, is an early example (Endicott & Spitzer, 1978). A version of this interview has been created for children and adolescents (K-SADS: Chambers et al., 1985). Designed for DSM criteria, the Structured Clinical Interview for Diagnosis (SCID) (Spitzer, Williams, Gibbon, & First, 1990; Williams et al., 1992) is currently the most widely utilized of these interviews. For these methods, the recorded response is not necessarily the subject's answer to the posed question. The interviewer is expected to interpret the response and make a clinical judgment as to whether or not the subject's response meets the diagnostic criteria (Reich, 1992).

More highly structured interviews have been developed to be utilized by nonclinician interviewers. In administering these highly structured instruments, the interviewer is expected to read the questions as written, to record the literal response, and to follow other instructions precisely (Reich, 1992). The interviewer is explicitly instructed against exercising judgment in the presentation of questions, is expected not to deviate from script in explaining questions, and must simply record rather than interpret the response. Such interviews are designed to be utilized by interviewers without consideration of the criteria for psychiatric disorders, as the diagnoses are determined strictly by diagnostic algorithms (Leaf, Myers, & McEvoy, 1991). For example, the NIMH Diagnostic Interview Schedule (DIS) (Helzer, Robins, Croughan, & Welner, 1981; Robins, Helzer, Croughan, & Ratcliff, 1981) was designed to assess RDC criteria in a highly structured manner and was utilized in the National Institute of Mental Health Epidemiologic Catchment Area Program (Leaf et al., 1991). Similar instruments have been designed for children and adolescents (Reich, 1992). The advantage of this method is that less experienced and therefore less expensive interviewers can be utilized. The disadvantage is that subjects may misinterpret questions and invalid diagnoses may result. Hypothetically, more experienced interviewers using a more flexible format may provide additional guidance and judgment in collecting and interpreting diagnostic information. When the two methods have been compared, however, good agreement has been shown (DIS vs. SADS) (Hesselbrock, Stabenau, Hesselbrock, Mirkin, & Meyer, 1982).

Similar measures are available for personality disorders (Dowson, 1995). The Structured Clinical Interview for DSM-III-R personality disorders (SCID-II) (Spitzer, Williams, Kass, & Gibbon, 1987) is designed to be a supplement to the Axis I SCID and contains questions concerning DSM Axis II personality disorders. One method of SCID-II administration involves preceding the interview with a self-report questionnaire, and following with interview questions of only positive responses. Other available structured interviews include the Personality Disorders Examination (Loranger, Susman, Oldham, & Russaroff, 1987) and the Diagnostic Interview for Personality Disorders (Zanarini, Frankenburg, Chauncey, & Gunderson, 1987).

Reliability and Validity of Diagnoses and Structured Interviews

Reliability

Reliability is determined by the extent to which a diagnostic system or interview instrument obtains the same result when utilized by different interviewers (interrater reliabil-

ity) or on two different occasions (test–retest reliability). Diagnostic systems based on explicit criteria substantially enhanced the interrater reliability of psychiatric diagnoses (Spitzer, Forman, & Nee, 1979; Williams, 1994). Structured interviews based on operationalized diagnostic criteria typically show acceptable test–retest and interrater reliabilities (Endicott & Spitzer, 1978; Robins et al., 1981). However, it should be noted that demonstration of reliability for the instrument does not necessarily result in reliability in practice. The assessment of reliability can be accomplished through several methods (Williams, 1994): (a) the use of recorded interviews, including the use of written transcriptions, audiotaped interviews, or videotapes interviews; (b) joint interviews, in which two or more interviewers jointly observe the same live interview; and (c) the test–retest method, in which each interviewer independently conducts and interprets the interview.

Disagreements occur from several sources of variance (Williams, 1994). Reliabilities assessed by the test–retest method tend to be lower than methods in which the same live interview is scored by two raters. Independent interviews result in increased information variance, that is, differences in the interviews result in different information being available to each clinician. Although the test–retest method utilizing independent interviews may be ideal, methods for which the patient is interviewed only once are typically utilized to reduce subject burden and interviewer time. Interviewers observing the same patient interview may show disagreement due to observation variance, interpretation variance, and criterion variance. Observation variance occurs when each interviewer attends to different aspects of the interview. Interpretation variance occurs when raters differ in their interpretation of the responses to questions as well as other information on the patient's symptoms and signs, and therefore they differ in their indication as to whether or not the criteria for a rating item are met. Criterion variance results when interviewers use different rules for summarizing their observations into diagnoses, and variance is minimized when interviewers use a standardized diagnostic system. In calculating reliability, the kappa statistic is utilized. Kappa calculates agreement while correcting for chance agreement and is the standard statistical method for describing interrater reliability (Shrout, Spitzer, & Fleiss, 1987). Kappa reliability statistics above .70 are considered good, between .50 and .70 fair, and below .50 poor (Williams, 1994).

Establishing interrater reliability among a specific set of interviewers requires competent and well-trained interviewers and maintaining interrater reliability requires periodic checks to prevent rater drift (Reich, 1992; Sanson-Fisher & Martin, 1981). Rater drift involves gradual, idiosyncratic, and systematic changes in the presentation of the interview and interpretation of responses by an interviewer. Semistructured diagnostic interviews are more subject to rater drift than are highly structured diagnostic interviews. The continuous monitoring of an interviewer through recording of performance of every interview with interviews randomly selected for formal scoring may reduce rater drift. However, as subjects with more deviant histories may object to interview recording and the recording process may change subject reporting, systematic bias in data collection may result.

Validity

The validity of a psychiatric diagnostic system concerns the extent to which the system serves its intended purpose (Williams, 1994). Four types of validity are recognized in this context: face, descriptive, predictive, and construct validity. For diagnoses, face validity is the extent to which the defining criteria of a diagnostic category resemble the accepted features of the psychiatric disorder. For a structured interview, face validity is the extent to which the questions of the interview directly reflect the diagnostic criteria. Descriptive validity is the extent to which the defining features of a diagnosis are unique to that disorder. Predictive validity is the extent to which the diagnosis is useful in predicting the patient's natural course and treatment response. Construct validity is the extent to which the defined diagnosis represents the true natural phenomena it is attempting to describe.

Construct validity of psychiatric diagnoses and related structured interview methods is difficult to establish in the absence of diagnostic "gold standards" (Faraone & Tsuang, 1994). Data on course, outcome, response to treatment, family aggregation, and biological measures, as well as information derived from such data by statistical techniques such as latent structure modeling, all constitute relevant information for evaluating diagnostic construct validity. For some purposes, validity may be defined more narrowly. If evaluations by experienced psychiatrists are considered the "gold standard" against which lay interviewers are measured, structured interviews administered by lay interviewers have been shown to have acceptable validity, as indicated by agreement with the more experienced assessors (Robins, Helzer,

Ratcliff, & Seyfried, 1982). Structured interviews also have high face validity.

Best Estimate Method

Whereas the use of structured interviews to gather information on criterion items for determining diagnoses has received considerable scrutiny, empirical issues in utilizing such data to construct diagnoses have received less attention. Information gathered from multiple informants may be inconsistent, the subject may withhold or provide false information, or additional sources of information, such as medical records or teacher reports, may provide data critical to determining accurate diagnoses. To address these issues, the assessment process must go beyond algorithmic use of data from a single structured interview.

An increasingly utilized method for determining diagnoses from multiple sources of information is the best estimate method (Leckman, Sholomskas, Thompson, Belanger, & Weissman, 1982). Best estimate diagnoses are those made by expert clinicians based on information collected from structured interviews with the patient in addition to information from medical records and reports from family members. The expert clinicians review collected information only and are not involved with the direct interviewing of subjects. In this context, expert clinicians are defined as clinically experienced faculty-level clinical psychologists or psychiatrists. In this procedure, the two expert clinicians review collected data and determine diagnoses independently. Discrepancies are reviewed and resolved through a consensus conference.

The utility of this method has been specifically studied with regard to detecting comorbid psychiatric disorders in a large family study of opiate addiction (Kosten & Rounsaville, 1992). Compared with diagnoses based on the best estimate procedure, Kosten and Rounsaville (1992) diagnoses based on direct interview only produced a high proportion of false negative cases (i.e., the diagnosis was missed) on antisocial personality disorder (41%), and more modest but nevertheless substantial proportions of false negative cases for alcohol use disorders (24%), other substance use disorders (7%), and depressive disorders (21%). There were few false positives, however, including 2% for depressive disorders, 1% for antisocial personality disorder, and none for other categories. Although this procedure increases costs to determine diagnostic information, there is thus evidence that it produces increased detection of psychiatric disorders. Similar methods have been developed for making personality disorder diagnoses (Spitzer, 1983; Zimmerman, 1994).

Diagnoses based only on family informants, compared with direct interview, result in underreporting of cases (Kosten, Anton, & Rounsaville, in press; Thompson, Orvaschel, Prusoff, & Kidd, 1982; Zimmerman, Coryell, Pfohl, & Stangl, 1988). However, the use of information from a family member informant in the best estimate procedure may improve detection of psychiatric diagnoses in adult patients. Family informants are particularly important in the assessment of children and adolescents. In both research and clinical settings, diagnostic assessment of the child or adolescent usually involves direct interviews with the patient and with one parent, typically the mother, about the child or adolescent's characteristics. Mothers and children tend to report systematically different information. With preadolescent children or retrospective assessment of the early development of the adolescent, mothers tend to report more symptoms of attention deficit hyperactivity disorder and oppositional disorder, whereas children report more symptoms of mood and anxiety disorders (Herjanic & Reich, 1982). As behaviors involved in conduct disorder and substance use disorders occur away from the parent and are typically concealed, adolescents typically report these symptoms whereas the parental informant may be unaware of their presence (Herjanic & Reich, 1982).

In situations where missing a diagnosis would be problematic, the best estimate method is particularly recommended. Another advantage of the best estimate method concerns the potential for idiosyncratic application of diagnostic criteria by interviewers. Although empirical data have not been presented to confirm this observation, the consensus process, together with the monitoring of interrater reliabilities, guards against idiosyncrasies in the application of diagnostic criteria. Methods utilized to combine information collected in clinical and research settings are not often described and need to be included in research reports (Zarin & Earls, 1993).

Dimensional Assessment Methods

Whereas diagnostic methods serve important clinical purposes in identifying syndromes that exceed a defined threshold, dimensional methods often are needed for determining incremental differences, such as changes associated with drug abstinence or other treatment interventions. An extensive variety of psychological assessment methods have been developed to provide quantitative

assessment of symptom severity with specific tests designed to evaluate specific dimensions. Self-report questionnaires and interview rating scales are available for most dimensions of interest in this context. Depression may be assessed through the Beck Depression Inventory (Beck, Ward, & Mendelson, 1961) and the Hamilton Depression Rating Scale (Hamilton, 1960). Similarly, global anxiety may be assessed through the Beck Anxiety Inventory (Beck, Epstein, Brown, & Steer, 1988) and the Hamilton Anxiety Rating Scale (Clark & Donovan, 1994; Hamilton, 1959). For social phobia, the Social Phobia and Anxiety Inventory (Clark et al., 1997; Clark, Turner, et al., 1994; Turner, Beidel, Dancu, & Stanley, 1989) is a comprehensive questionnaire measure. Aggressive behavior and hostile affect can be assessed through the Buss–Durkee Hostility Inventory (Buss & Durkee, 1957). Multidimensional instruments to assess psychiatric symptoms, such as the Symptom Checklist-90 (Derogatis, 1977), are available. Personality disorder dimensions may be assessed by questionnaire, although high false positive rates occur when responses are used to determine personality disorder diagnoses (Hunt & Andrews, 1992). Multidimensional instruments specifically developed to assess substance-use-disorder related problem dimensions have been developed (Tarter & Hegedus, 1991). Although a comprehensive review of such measures is beyond the scope of this chapter, the interested reader is referred to reviews (Clarkin & Hurt, 1988) and reference manuals (Thompson, 1989) for additional details.

CLINICAL AND RESEARCH RECOMMENDATIONS

This review of the methods available for completing the psychiatric assessment and related research leads to four recommendations for conducting the psychiatric assessment in clinical and research settings.

1. The psychiatric assessment should utilize a systematic approach, particularly with regard to substance use disorders and comorbid psychiatric diagnoses. The operationalized method for determining psychiatric diagnoses in DSM-IV has been widely adopted in research and clinical practice. Although the structured diagnostic interview has become accepted as the most effective and efficient method for collecting this information in research contexts, there has been limited adoption of structured interviewing assessment meth-

ods in clinical settings. Nearly two decades ago, Helzer et al. (1978) suggested that the structured interview be utilized effectively for clinical assessment. Although possibly cost effective in the long term, the immediate increased costs associated with administering a comprehensive structured diagnostic assessment instrument likely inhibits clinical adoption. Many clinicians are not familiar with these methods, and an investment in training is therefore necessary for their initiation. Nevertheless, given the importance of accurate diagnoses in the clinical setting, the acceptance of the DSM criteria-based system for diagnosis, and the proven utility of the structured interview for determining these criteria-based diagnoses, it is unfortunate that structured interviews have not become more widely utilized. The use of structured interviews can also facilitate training in diagnostic interviewing. In many clinical settings, a cost-effective approach may be the adoption of parts of structured interviews for specific clinical populations.

2. A drug-free abstinence period and serial evaluations are often necessary as part of the psychiatric assessment. The DSM-IV diagnostic system specifies a 4-week period of abstinence before determination of comorbid psychiatric disorders as independent of the effects of abused substances. There is extensive empirical support for this timeframe with regard to alcohol use disorders (Alterman, Gottheil, & Crawford, 1975; Brown, Irwin, & Schuckit, 1991; Butterworth, 1971; Schuckit, Irwin, & Brown, 1990; Stockwell, Smail, Hodgson, & Carter, 1984), although less data are available concerning other substances. Given the variable effects on cognitive, psychomotor, and psychological functioning of acute intoxication, withdrawal, and chronic dependence with different individual substances or combinations of substances, an evaluation at a single point in time may be misleading. When the state of intoxication or withdrawal changes, or adaptation to chronic consumption or abstinence occurs, the psychiatric assessment will need to be repeated for a comprehensive understanding of the patient's characteristics and treatment needs.

3. The utilization of multiple information sources improves the validity of the assessment. Although sole reliance on family informants leads to underdiagnosis, family members may provide critical supplementary information on substance use and consequences. Research utilizing the best estimate method has demonstrated that the inclusion of information from family members and medical records increases the sensitivity of the psychiatric assessment, particularly for antisocial personality disorder.

4. The relationships among substance use disorders and comorbid psychiatric disorders need to be evaluated with a recognition of the potential complexity involved. When comorbid psychiatric disorders are persistent beyond the initial abstinence period, their prognostic significance in the treatment of substance use disorders remains unclear. Cases with alcoholism and anxiety disorders have been presented in the psychiatric literature for whom treatment for anxiety was thought to contribute to relapse prevention (Quitkin, Rifkin, & Kaplan, 1972). If one accepts the premise that anxiety and depressive symptoms contribute to relapse in some cases, treatment for comorbid psychiatric disorders would be expected to result in reduced relapse rates. However, such specialized treatment may not be necessary in many cases where the comorbid symptoms are substance induced. Support for the distinction between substance-induced and independent disorders has been found in some studies (Schuckit, 1985) but not in others (Kadden et al., 1995). An improved understanding of these relationships is critically important in the development of rational treatment-planning strategies.

CONCLUSIONS

The central focus of the psychiatric assessment in clinical and research contexts is psychiatric diagnosis. In the clinical setting, the responsibility of the psychiatrist typically extends beyond psychiatric diagnoses to other clinical domains. In recent decades, a return to descriptive diagnostic systems, particularly DSM-III and subsequent revisions, has led to an acceleration of advances in clinical practice and psychiatric research. Methods for determining psychiatric diagnoses according to these systems have been developed in parallel. The descriptive diagnostic systems of DSM-III and more recent revisions have been readily translated into interview protocols. Structured interviews have been developed to gather information on substance use disorders, other selected Axis I psychiatric diagnoses, and personality disorders. Data gathered with structured interviews can be used to determine diagnoses by simple algorithms or may be combined with information from multiple sources by the best estimate method. Structured interviews for psychiatric diagnoses have utility as training tools. Although primarily used in research applications, structured interviews may be underutilized as potentially cost-effective approaches for determining diagnoses in clinical settings.

AUTHOR NOTE

This work was supported by Grants No. DA 05605 from the National Institute on Drug Abuse and AA08746 from the National Institute on Alcohol Abuse and Alcoholism.

REFERENCES

Alterman, A. I., Gottheil, E., & Crawford H. D. (1975). Mood changes in an alcoholism treatment program based on drinking decisions. *The American Journal of Psychiatry, 132*, 1032–1037.

American Psychiatric Association. (1950). *Diagnostic and statistical manual of mental disorders* (1st ed.). Washington, DC: Author.

American Psychiatric Association. (1968). *Diagnostic and statistical manual of mental disorders* (2nd ed.). Washington, DC: Author.

American Psychiatric Association. (1980). *Diagnostic and statistical manual of mental disorders* (3rd ed.). Washington, DC: Author.

American Psychiatric Association. (1987). *Diagnostic and statistical manual of mental disorders* (3rd ed. rev.). Washington, DC: Author.

American Psychiatric Association. (1994). *Diagnostic and statistical manual of mental disorders* (4th ed.). Washington, DC: Author.

American Psychiatric Association. (1995a). *Psychiatric services for addicted patients: A task force report of the American Psychiatric Association.* Washington, DC: Author.

American Psychiatric Association. (1995b). Practice guideline for the treatment of patients with substance use disorders: Alcohol, cocaine, opioids. *The American Journal of Psychiatry, 152* (Suppl.), 1–59.

American Psychiatric Association. (1995c). Practice guideline for psychiatric evaluation of adults. *The American Journal of Psychiatry, 152* (Suppl.), 63–80.

Anthony, J. C., & Helzer, J. E. (1991). Syndromes of drug abuse and dependence. In L. N. Robins, & D. A. Regier (Eds.), *Psychiatric disorders in America* (pp. 116–154). New York: Free Press.

Ash, P. (1949). The reliability of psychiatric diagnoses. *Journal of Abnormal Social Psychology, 44*, 272–276.

Beck, A. T. (1962). Reliability of psychiatric diagnoses I: A critique of systematic studies. *The American Journal of Psychiatry, 119*, 210–216.

Beck, A. T., Epstein, N., Brown, G., & Steer, R. A. (1988). An inventory for measuring clinical anxiety: Psychometric properties. *Journal of Consulting and Clinical Psychology, 56*, 6.

Beck, A. T., Ward, C. H., & Mendelson, M. (1961). An inventory for measuring depression. *Archives of General Psychiatry, 4*, 461–471.

Boyle, M. H., Offord, D. R., Racine, Y. A., Szatmari, P., Fleming, J. E., & Links, P. (1992). Predicting substance use in late adolescence: Results of the Ontario Child Health Study Followup. *The American Journal of Psychiatry, 149*, 761–767.

Brooner, R. K., Bigelow, G. E., Strain, E., & Schmidt, C. W. (1990). Intravenous drug abusers with antisocial personality disorder: Increased HIV risk behavior. *Drug and Alcohol Dependence, 26*, 39–44.

Brooner, R. K., Schmidt, C. W., Felch, L. J., & Bigelow, G. E. (1992). Antisocial behavior of intravenous drug abusers: Implications for diagnosis of antisocial personality disorder. *The American Journal of Psychiatry, 149*, 482–487.

Brown, S. A., Inaba, R. K., Gillin, J. C., Schuckit, M. A., Stewart, M. A., & Irwin, M.R. (1995). Alcoholism and affective disorder: Clinical course of depressive symptoms. *The American Journal of Psychiatry, 152*, 45–52.

Brown, S. A., Irwin, M., & Schuckit, M. A. (1991). Changes in anxiety among abstinent male alcoholics. *Journal of Studies on Alcohol, 52*, 55–61.

Brown, S. A., & Shuckit, M. A. (1988). Changes in depression among abstinent alcoholics. *Journal of Studies on Alcohol, 49*, 412–417.

Bukstein, O. G., Glancy, L. J., & Kaminer, Y. (1992). Patterns of affective comorbidity in a clinical population of dually diagnosed adolescent substance abusers. *Journal of the American Academy of Child and Adolescent Psychiatry, 31*, 1041–1045.

Bukstein, O. G., & Kaminer, Y. (1994). The nosology of adolescent substance abuse. *American Journal on Addictions, 3*, 1–13.

Buss, A. H., & Durkee, A. (1957). An inventory of assessing different kinds of hostility. *Journal of Consulting Psychology, 21*, 343–349.

Butterworth, A. T. (1971). Depression associated with alcohol withdrawal. *Quarterly Journal of Studies on Alcohol, 32*, 343–348.

Cadoret, R. J., Yates, W. R., Troughton, E., Woodworth, G., & Stewart, M. A. (1995). Adoption study demonstrating two genetic pathways to drug abuse. *Archives of General Psychiatry, 52*, 42–52.

Chambers, W. J., Puig-Antich, J., Hirsch, M., Paez, P., Ambrosini, P. J., Tabrizi, M. A., & Davies, M. (1985). The assessment of affective disorders in children and adolescents by semi-structured interview. Test–retest reliability of the K-SADS-P. *Archives of General Psychiatry, 42*, 696–702.

Clark, D. B., Bukstein, O. G., Smith, M. G., Kaczynski, N. A., Mezzich, A., & Donovan, J. E. (1995). Identifying anxiety disorders in adolescents hospitalized for alcohol abuse or dependence. *Psychiatric Services, 46*, 618–620.

Clark, D. B., & Donovan, J. (1994). Reliability and validity of the Hamilton Anxiety Rating Scale in an adolescent sample. *Journal of the American Academy of Child and Adolescent Psychiatry, 33*, 354–360.

Clark, D. B., Jacob, R. G., & Mezzich, A. (1994). Anxiety and conduct disorders in early onset alcoholism. In T. S. Babor, V. Hesselbrock, P. E. Meyer, & W. Shoemaker (Eds.), Types of alcoholics: Evidence from clinical, experimental, and genetic research. *Annals of the New York Academy of Sciences, 708,* 181–186.

Clark, D. B., & Kirsci, L. (1996). PTSD, depression, alcohol use disorders, and quality of life in adolescents. *Anxiety, 2,* 226–233.

Clark, D. B., Lesnick, L., & Hegedus, A. M. (1997). Trauma and other adverse life events in adolescents with alcohol abuse and dependence. *Journal of the American Academy of Child and Adolescent Psychiatry, 36,* 1744–1751.

Clark, D. B., Masia, C. L., Spaulding, S. A., Mammen, O., Feske, U., Brown, C., & Shear, M. K. (1997). Systematic assessment of social phobia in clinical practice. *Depression & Anxiety, 6,* 47–61.

Clark, D. B., Moss, H., Kirisci, L., Mezzich, A. C., Ott, P., & Miles, R. (1997). Psychiatric disorders in preadolescent sons of substance abusers. *Journal of the American Academy of Child and Adolescent Psychiatry, 36,* 495–502.

Clark, D. B., & Neighbors, B. (1996). Adolescent psychoactive substance abuse and internalizing disorders. *Child and Adolescent Psychiatric Clinics of North America, 5,* 45–57.

Clark, D. B., Neighbors, B. D., Lesnick, L. A., Lynch, K. G., & Donovan, J. (1998). Family functioning in adolescent alcohol use disorders. *Journal of Family Psychology, 12,* 81–92.

Clark, D. B., Pollock, N., Bukstein, O. G., Mezzich, A. C., Bromberger, J. T., & Donovan, J. E. (1997). Gender and comorbid psychopathology in adolescents with alcohol dependence. *Journal of the American Academy of Child and Adolescent Psychiatry, 36,* 1195–1203.

Clark, D. B., & Sayette, M. (1993). Anxiety and the development of alcoholism: Clinical and scientific issues. *American Journal on Addictions, 2,* 59–76.

Clark, D. B., Smith, M., Neighbors, B., Skerlec, L., & Randall, J. (1994). Anxiety disorders in adolescents: Prevalence and characteristics. *Clinical Psychology Review, 14,* 113–137.

Clark, D. B., Turner, S., Beidel, D., Donovan, J., Kirisci, L., & Jacob, R. G. (1994). Reliability and validity of the Social Phobia and Anxiety Inventory for Adolescents. *Psychological Assessment, 6,* 135–140.

Clarkin, J. F., & Hurt, S. W. (1988). Psychological assessment: Tests and rating scales. In J. A. Talbott, R. E. Hales, & S. C. Yudofsy (Eds.), *The American Psychiatric Press textbook of psychiatry.* Washington DC: American Psychiatric Press.

Cloninger, C. R. (1987). Neurogenetic adaptive mechanisms in alcoholism. *Science, 236,* 410–416.

Cornelius, J. R., Salloum, I. M., Mezzich, J., Cornelius, M. D., Fabrega, H., Ehler, J. G., Ulrich, R. F., Thase, M. E., & Mann, J. J. (1995). Disproportionate suicidality in patients with comorbid major depression and alcoholism. *The American Journal of Psychiatry, 152,* 358–364.

Derogatis, L. R. (1977). *The SCL-90R.* Baltimore, MD: Clinical Psychometric Research.

Dinwiddle, S. H., Reich, T., & Cloninger, C. R. (1992). Psychiatric comorbidity and suicidality among intravenous drug users. *Journal of Clinical Psychiatry, 53,* 364–369.

Dorwart, R. A., Chartock, L. R., Dial, T., Fenton, W., Knesper, D., Koran, L., Leaf, P., Pincus, H., Smith, R., Weissman, S., & Winkelmeyer, R. (1992). A national study of psychiatrists' professional activities. *The American Journal of Psychiatry, 149,* 1499–1505.

Dowson, J. H. (1995). Assessment of personality disorders. In J. H. Dowson & A. T. Grounds (Eds.), *Personality disorders: Recognition and clinical management.* Cambridge, England: Cambridge University Press.

Endicott, J., & Spitzer, R. L. (1978). A diagnostic interview: The schedule for affective disorders and schizophrenia. *Archives of General Psychiatry, 137,* 837–844.

Faraone, S. V., & Tsuang, M. T. (1994). Measuring diagnostic accuracy in the absence of a "gold standard." *The American Journal of Psychiatry, 151,* 650–657.

Feighner, J. P., Robins, E., Guze, S. B., Woodruff, R. A., Winokur, G., & Munoz, R. (1972). Diagnostic criteria for use in psychiatric research. *Archives of General Psychiatry, 26,* 57–63.

Gawin, F. H., Khalsa, M. E., & Ellinwood, E. (1994). Stimulants. In M. Galanter, & H. D. Kleber (Eds.), *The American Psychiatric Press textbook of substance abuse treatment.* Washington, DC: American Psychiatric Press.

Hamilton, M. (1959). The assessment of anxiety states by rating. *British Journal of Medical Psychology, 32,* 50–55.

Hamilton, M. (1960). A rating scale for depression. *Journal of Neurology, Neurosurgery, and Psychiatry, 23,* 56–61.

Hartka, E., Johnstone, B., Leino, E. V., Motoyoshi, M., Temple, M. T., & Fillmore, K. (1991). A meta-analysis of depressive symptomatology and alcohol consumption over time. *British Journal of Addiction, 86,* 1283–1298.

Helzer, J. E., Burnam, A., & McEvoy, L. T. (1991). Alcohol abuse and dependence. In L. N. Robins & D. A. Regier (Eds.), *Psychiatric disorders in America* (pp. 81–115). New York: Free Press.

Helzer, J. E., Clayton, P. J., Pambakian, R., & Woodruff, R. (1978). Concurrent diagnostic validity of a structured diagnostic interview. *Archives of General Psychiatry, 35,* 849–853.

Helzer, J. E., Robins, L. N., Croughan, J. L., & Welner, A. (1981). Renard diagnostic interview: Its reliability and procedural validity with physicians and lay interviewers. *Archives of General Psychiatry, 38,* 393–398.

Herjanic, B., & Reich, W. (1982). Development of a structured psychiatric interview for children: Agreement between child and parent on individual symptoms. *Journal of Abnormal Child Psychology, 10,* 307–324.

Hesselbrock, M. N., Meyer, R. E., & Keene, J. J. (1985). Psychopathology in hospitalized alcoholics. *Archives of General Psychiatry, 42,* 1050–1055.

Hesselbrock, V., Stabenau, J., Hesselbrock, M., Mirkin, P., & Meyer, R. (1982). A comparison of two interview schedules: The Schedule for Affective Disorders and Schizophrenia-Lifetime and the National Institute of Mental Health Diagnostic Interview Schedule. *Archives of General Psychiatry, 39,* 674–677.

Himle, J. A., & Hill, E. M. (1991). Alcohol abuse and the anxiety disorders: Evidence from the epidemiologic catchment area survey. *Journal of Anxiety Disorders, 5,* 237–245.

Hunt, C., & Andrews, G. (1992). Measuring personality disorder: The use of self-report questionnaires. *Journal of Personality Disorders, 6,* 125–133.

Kadden, R. M., Kranzler, H. R., & Rounsaville, B. J. (1995). Validity of the distinction between substance-induced and independent depression and anxiety disorders. *American Journal on Addictions, 4,* 107–117.

Kosten, T. A., Anton, S. F., & Rounsaville, B. J. (in press). Ascertaining psychiatric diagnoses with the family history method in a substance abuse population. *Journal of Psychiatric Research.*

Kosten, T. A., & Rounsaville, B. J. (1992). Sensitivity of psychiatric diagnosis based on the best estimate procedure. *The American Journal of Psychiatry, 149,* 1225–1227.

Kushner, M. G., Sher, K. J., & Beitman, B. D. (1990). The relation between alcohol problems and anxiety disorders. *The American Journal of Psychiatry, 147,* 685–695.

Leaf, P. J., Myers, J. K., & McEvoy, L. T. (1991). Procedures used in the Epidemiologic Catchment Area Study. In L. N. Robins, & D. A. Regier (Eds.), *Psychiatric disorders in America* (pp. 11–32). New York: Free Press.

Leckman, J. F., Sholomskas, D., Thompson, W. D., Belanger, A., & Weissman, M. M. (1982). Best estimate of lifetime psychiatric diagnosis: a methodological study. *Archives of General Psychiatry, 39,* 879–883.

Levine, H. G. (1978). The discovery of addiction. *Journal of Studies on Alcohol, 39,* 143–174.

Loranger, A., Susman, V., Oldham, J., & Russaroff, L. M. (1987). The personality disorder examination: A preliminary report. *Journal of Personality Disorders, 1,* 1–13.

Martin, C. S., Arria, A. M., Mezzich, A. C., & Bukstein, O. G. (1993). Patterns of polydrug use in adolescent alcohol abusers. *American Journal of Drug and Alcohol Abuse, 19,* 511–521.

Martin, C. S., Kaczynski, N. A., Maisto, S. A., Bukstein, O. M., & Moss, H. B. (1995). Patterns of DSM-IV alcohol abuse and dependence symptoms in adolescent drinkers. *Journal of Studies on Alcohol, 56,* 672–680.

Mayfield, D. G., McLeon, G., & Hall P. (1974). The CAGE questionnaire: Validation of a new alcoholism screening instrument. *The American Journal of Psychiatry, 131,* 1121–1123.

Mezzich, A., Tarter, R., Kirisci, L., Clark, D. B., Bukstein, O., & Martin, C. (1993). Subtypes of early age onset alcoholism. *Alcoholism: Clinical and Experimental Research, 17,* 767–770.

Milin, R. P. (1996). Comorbidity of substance abuse and psychotic disorders: Focus on adolescents and young adults. *Child and Adolescent Psychiatric Clinics of North America, 5,* 111–121.

Mueser, K. T., Bellack, A. S., & Blanchard, J. (1992). Comorbidity of substance abuse in schizophrenia: Implications for treatment. *Journal of Consulting & Clinical Psychology, 60,* 845–856.

Orvaschel, H., Puig-Antich, J., Chambers, W., Tabrizi, M., & Johnson, R. (1982). Retrospective assessment of prepubertal major depression with the Kiddie-SADS-E. *Journal of the American Academy of Child and Adolescent Psychiatry, 21,* 393–397.

Quitkin, F. M., Rifkin, A., Kaplan, J., & Klein, D. (1972). Phobic anxiety syndrome complicated by drug dependence and addiction. *Archives of General Psychiatry, 27,* 159–162.

Regier, D. A., Farmer, M. E., Rae, D. S., Locke, B., Keith, S., Judd, L., & Goodwin, F. (1990). Comorbidity of mental disorders with alcohol and other drug abuse: Results from the epidemiologic catchment area (ECA) study. *Journal of the American Medical Association, 264,* 2511–2518.

Reich, W. (1992). Structured and semistructured interviews. In G. Hsu, & H. Herwen (Eds), *Research in psychiatry: Issues, strategies, and methods.* New York: Plenum Press.

Reich, W., Shayka, T., & Taibleson, C. (1991). *The Diagnostic Interview for Children and Adolescents—Revised.* St. Louis Washington University Press.

Robins, L. N., Helzer, J. E., Croughan, J., & Ratcliff, K. S. (1981). The NIMH Diagnostic Interview Schedule: Its history, characteristics and validity. *Archives of General Psychiatry, 38,* 381–389.

Robins, L. N., Helzer, J. E., Ratcliff, K. S., & Seyfried, W. (1982). Validity of the Diagnostic Interview Schedule, Version II: DSM-III diagnoses. *Psychological Medicine, 12,* 822–870.

Rounsaville, B. J., & Bryant, K. (1992). Tolerance and withdrawal in the DSM-III-R diagnosis of substance dependence. *American Journal on Addictions 1992, 1.*

Rounsaville, B. J., Dolinsky, Z. S., Babor, T. F., & Meyer, R. (1987). Psychopathology as a predictor of treatment outcome in alcoholics. *Archives of General Psychiatry, 44,* 505–513.

Rumpf, H., Hapke, V., Hill, A., & John, V. (1997). Development of a screening questionnaire for the general hospital and general practices. *Alcoholism: Clinical and Experimental Research, 21,* 894–898.

Rush, B. (1943). An inquiry into the effects of ardent spirits upon the human body and mind, with an account of the means of presenting and of the remedies for curing them. [Reprinted in Keller, M. Classics of the alcohol literature.] *Quarterly Journal of Studies on Alcohol, 4,* 321–341.

Sanson-Fisher, R. W., & Martin, C. J. (1981). Standardized interviews in psychiatry: Issues of reliability. *British Journal of Psychiatry, 139,* 138–143.

Schottenfeld, R. S. (1994). Assessment of the patient. In M. Galanter & H. D. Kleber, (Eds.), *The American Psychiatric Press textbook of substance abuse treatment.* Washington, DC: American Psychiatric Press.

Schuckit, M. A. (1982). The history of psychotic symptoms in alcoholics. *Journal of Clinical Psychiatry, 43,* 53–57.

Schuckit, M. A. (1985). The clinical implications of primary diagnostic groups among alcoholics. *Archives of General Psychiatry, 42,* 1043–1049.

Schuckit, M. A., & Hesselbrock, V. (1994). Alcohol dependence and anxiety disorders: What is the relationship? *The American Journal of Psychiatry, 12,* 1723–1734.

Schuckit, M. A., Irwin, M., & Brown, S. A. (1990). The history of anxiety symptoms among 171 primary alcoholics. *Journal of Studies on Alcohol, 51,* 34–41.

Schwartz, R. H., & Hawks, R. L. (1985). Laboratory detection of marijuana use. *Journal of the American Medical Association, 254,* 788–792.

Selzer, M. L. (1971). The Michigan alcoholism screening test: The quest for a new diagnostic instrument. *The American Journal of Psychiatry, 127,* 1653–1658.

Shrout, P. E., Spitzer, R. L., & Fleiss, J. L. (1987). Quantification of agreement in psychiatry diagnosis revisited. *Archives of General Psychiatry, 44,* 172–177.

Spitzer, R. L. (1983). Psychiatric diagnosis: Are clinicians still necessary? *Comprehensive Psychiatry, 24,* 399–411.

Spitzer, R. L., Endicott, J., & Robins, E. (1978). Research diagnostic criteria. *Archives of General Psychiatry, 35,* 773–782.

Spitzer, R. L., & Fleiss, J. L. (1974). A reanalysis of the reliability of psychiatric diagnoses. *British Journal of Psychiatry, 125,* 341–347.

Spitzer, R. L., Forman, J. B., & Nee, J. (1979). DSM-III field trials, I: Initial interrater diagnostic reliability. *American Journal of Psychiatry, 136,* 815–817.

Spitzer, R., Williams, B., Gibbon, M., & First, M. (1990). *Users guide for the Structured Clinical Interview for DSM-III-R.* Washington, DC: American Psychiatric Press.

Spitzer, R., Williams, J. B. W., Kass, F., & Gibbon, M. (1987). *Structured interview for DSM-III-R personality disorders.* New York: New York State Psychiatric Institute, Biometrics Research Department.

Stockwell, T., Smail, P., Hodgson, R., & Carter, S. (1984). Alcohol dependence and phobic anxiety states: II. A retrospective study. *British Journal of Psychiatry, 144,* 58–63.

Tarter, R., & Hegedus, A. (1991). The Drug Use Screening Inventory—Its application in the evaluation and treatment of alcohol and drug abuse. *Alcohol, Health, and Research World, 15,* 65–75.

Thompson, C. (Ed.). (1989). *The instruments of psychiatric research.* Chichester, England: Wiley.

Thompson, J. W. (1992). Diagnostic issues. In G. Hsu & H. Herwen (Eds.), *Research in psychiatry: Issues, strategies, and methods.* New York: Plenum Press.

Thompson, W. D., Orvaschel, H., Prusoff, B. A., & Kidd, K. K. (1982). An evaluation of the family history method for ascertaining psychiatric disorders. *Archives of General Psychiatry, 39,* 53–58.

Turner, S., Beidel, D. C., Dancu, C. V., & Stanley, M. A. (1989). An empirically derived inventory to measure social fears and anxiety: The Social Phobia and Anxiety Inventory. Psychological Assessment. *Journal of Consulting and Clinical Psychology, 1,* 35–40.

Weiss, K. J., & Rosenberg, D. J. (1985). Prevalence of anxiety disorder among alcoholics. *Journal of Clinical Psychiatry, 46,* 3–5.

Williams, J. B. W. (1994). Psychiatric classification. In R. E. Hales, S. C. Yudofsky, & J. A. Talbott (Eds.), *The American Psychiatric Press textbook of psychiatry.* Washington DC: American Psychiatric Press.

Williams, J. B. W., Gibbon, M., First, M. B., Spitzer, R., Davies, M., Borus, J., Howes, M., Kane J., Harrison, G., Rounsaville, B., & Wittcher, H. (1992). The Structured Clinical Interview for DSM-III-R (SCID) II: Multisite test–retest reliability. *Archives of General Psychiatry, 49,* 630–636.

Wilson, M. (1993). DSM-III and the transformation of American psychiatry: A history. *The American Journal of Psychiatry, 150,* 399–410.

Winokur, G., Coryell, W., Akiskal, H. S., Maserm J. D., Keller, M. B., Endicott, J., & Muellerm, T. (1995). Alcoholism in manic-depressive (bipolar) illness: Familial illness, course of illness, and the primary–secondary distinction. *The American Journal of Psychiatry, 152,* 365–372.

Yates, W. R., Petty, F., & Brown, K. (1988). Alcoholism in males with antisocial personality disorder. *International Journal of Addictions, 23,* 999–1010.

Zanarini, M. C., Frankenburg, F. R., Chauncey, D. L., & Gunderson, J. G. (1987). The diagnostic interview for personality disorders: Interrater and test-retest reliability. *Comprehensive Psychiatry, 28,* 467–480.

Zarin, D. A., & Earls, F. (1993). Diagnostic decision making in psychiatry. *The American Journal of Psychiatry, 150,* 197–206.

Zimmerman, M. (1994). Diagnosing personality disorders. *Archives of General Psychiatry, 51,* 225–245.

Zimmerman, M., Coryell, W., Pfohl, B., & Stangl, D. (1988). The reliability of the family history method for psychiatric diagnosis. *Archives of General Psychiatry, 45,* 320–322.

Zucker, R. A., & Fitzgerald, H. E. (1991). Early developmental factors and risk for alcohol problems. *Alcohol Health and Research World, 15,* 18–24.

CHAPTER 15

PSYCHOLOGICAL EVALUATION OF ALCOHOL AND DRUG ABUSE IN YOUTH AND ADULTS

Ralph E. Tarter
Levent Kirisci

A comprehensive psychological evaluation encompasses the measurement of cognition, emotion, and behavior. Analogous to a laboratory test in medicine, in which a sample is obtained to document biological functioning, psychological tests provide a sample of the individual's psychological functioning. In both psychological and biological assessment, the evaluation procedure and documentation of the results are invariant, thereby providing the framework for accruing accurate and replicable information.

A thorough psychological assessment yields qualitative and quantitative information. The qualitative facet of the evaluation characterizes the stylistic aspects of psychological functioning; that is, how the person interacts with the environment. For example, a problem can be solved using either an *analytic* or a *wholistic* strategy in performing visuospatial tasks. In a block design test, where the task is to assemble a set of blocks to form a design, a wholistic cognitive strategy is reflected by the propensity to arrange the pieces according to a mental image of the *gestalt* or entire picture. Alternatively, assembling each block one at a time according to fractional components of the design reflects an analytic cognitive style. The type of ego defense (e.g., denial, displacement, repression, sublimation) utilized to cope

with anxiety is another example of individual differences in psychological style. In contrast, quantitative information obtained from the psychological evaluation documents a particular characteristic (e.g., aggressivity, social skill, intelligence) in relation to the population at a given point in time. Comparison of the individual with the population norm or mean score documents the magnitude of deviation, disturbance, or impairment. Evaluating conjointly the qualitative and quantitative facets of cognition, emotion, and behavior provides the opportunity to design interventions that are tailored to the person's psychological orientation and severity of manifest disturbance, which, in turn, maximizes prevention and treatment prognosis.

This chapter reviews the psychological and psychiatric assessment measures that have been used for evaluating alcohol and drug abuse. Because substance abuse is routinely manifest in conjunction with disruptions in multiple spheres, we also describe the various instruments that document the spectrum of disturbances that commonly precede, occur concomitantly, or emerge subsequent to habitual consumption of drugs having addictive properties. In addition, in response to the need for an efficient evaluation system, we also present a succinct discussion of a decision-tree assessment protocol that integrates evaluation and treatment of youth and adults who are at risk for, or already exhibit, substance abuse. Prior to reviewing the literature, however, it is important to first briefly describe the criteria for evaluating the usefulness of any assessment instrument.

PSYCHOMETRIC PRINCIPLES

Reliability refers to the replicability or consistency of test scores by the same individuals under the same conditions. Reliability in practice can be described as the degree of relative consistency of individuals' deviations scores (or z-scores) over repeated administration of the same test or alternate forms. In more technical terms reliability is quantified as the ratio of the variance of the true score to the variance of the observed score. An observed score is the composite of a true score and an error score; this can be written as: Observed score = True score + Error score. Reliability is a necessary condition, but not a sufficient condition, to have valid test scores. If the reliability of a test score is low, the validity of the test score is also low.

Reliability coefficients can be grouped in three broad categories: (1) reliability on a single occasion, (2) reliability over different occasions, and (3) scorer reliability.

Reliability on a Single Occasion

Reliability on a single occasion is concerned with the consistency of two or more scores. Examples of this type of reliability are alternate form, split-halves (Spearman–Brown double-length formula), Kuder–Richardson, and Cronbach coefficient alpha.

Alternate Form Reliability

This reliability coefficient is estimated by correlating two scores obtained from two forms of a test that are administered to the same subjects on the same occasion. Pearson product-moment correlation coefficients are typically used to compute alternate form reliability. Measurement error in alternate form reliability consists only of inconsistencies in content of the two forms.

Split-Halves Reliability Coefficients

This procedure computes the correlation between the scores obtained to form two equivalent halves of a scale. This method is analogous to the alternate form reliability in the sense that measurement error consists only of incon-

sistencies in the content of two forms. The Spearman–Brown double-length formula is one of the split-halves procedures. It estimates the correlation between two alternate forms in such a way that the adjusted correlation will be the reliability coefficient for the whole instrument.

Kuder–Richardson and Cronbach Coefficient Alpha

These two formulas estimate reliability scores for a single form of a test. The Kuder–Richardson formula is used for dichotomously scored items whereas the Cronbach coefficient alpha formula is used for continuously scored items.

Reliability across Different Occasions

This type of reliability coefficient is concerned with consistency of scores obtained over a period of time. Measurement error is attributed to the test occasion rather than the content of the instrument.

Test–Retest Reliability

The test–retest reliability coefficient is a correlation coefficient of scores measured at two different times. This reliability coefficient describes the stability of a test score. The length of time interval between the two administrations of the test and expected stability of performance are important factors considered in evaluating the magnitude of the test–retest reliability coefficient.

Alternate Forms Reliability over Different Occasions

This reliability coefficient is used to compute the correlation between two scores of alternate forms on two occasions to control measurement error due to content and different test occasion.

Scorer Reliability

This correlation coefficient reflects the extent to which scores obtained by different raters are consistent. This reliability coefficient controls measurement error due to the raters.

Validity refers to the ability of an instrument to provide information that enables inferences about broader domains of behaviors beyond the test scores. There are three types of validation: (1) content validation, (2) criterion-related validation, and (3) construct validation.

Content Validation

Content validation refers to the adequacy of the test items to represent the construct. Determination of content validation requires a carefully defined construct or a list of objectives, matching items to the construct or to the objectives by a panel of experts, and a summary of the data from the matching process. The level of validity is demonstrated by the percentage of matching between objectives and items, the correlation between the importance weighting of objectives and the number of items measuring the objectives, and the percentage of objectives that are not assessed by the instrument's items.

Criterion-Related Validation

This type of validation refers to the effectiveness of prediction on an individual's performance on particular criterion. There are two types of criterion-related validation procedures: (1) predictive validity and (2) concurrent validity. Predictive validity refers to the extent to which a test score predicts the criterion measurement in the future. Concurrent validity refers to the association between a test score and the criterion obtained at the same time the test is administered. In selecting criterion measures the following factors should be considered: (1) reliability of the criterion, (2) factors that may bias against certain individuals, (3) relevance to a "real-life" criterion, and (4) availability or convenience of the criterion.

Construct Validation

Construct validation is concerned with what the test actually measures. Construct validation requires multiple types of evidence accumulated from different sources:

Correlation Study

A high correlation between a new test and similar tests is evidence for construct validity.

Between-Groups Comparisons

Groups are contrasted to find expected differences on a particular construct. If differences are not observed, the instrument can be concluded to be inadequate for measuring the construct.

Factor Analysis

Factor analysis is used in two ways to document construct validity. First, factor analysis can be conducted using an item intercorrelation matrix to determine whether the items cluster according to their theoretical structure. Second, factor analysis is applied to a set of different measures to determine their factor structure. This procedure clarifies whether the correlations among the measures are attributable to variance on one or more common factors.

Multitrait Multimethod

According to the multitrait multimethod approach, a test should correlate with other similar theoretically related measures but also should not correlate with measures that are not theoretically similar. The multitrait, multimethod approach provides the following information to support construct validity: (a) a reliability coefficient, reflects the correlation between measures of the same construct using the same measurement method; (b) a convergent validity coefficient, which reflects the correlation between measures of the same construct using different measurement methods; and c) the discriminant validity coefficient, which is the correlation between measures of different constructs using the same method.

Sensitivity and Specificity

This important facet of validity informs about the efficacy of a scale for identifying individuals or subgroups of individuals. It is especially important in clinical settings where the evaluation is directed at classifying the individual. For example, categorical classification (e.g., presence of a psychiatric disorder or brain damage) is typically a criterion for qualification of acceptance into treatment. A sound psychological evaluation maximizes accurate classification.

Table 15.1 depicts the four classification permutations: (1) the disorder is absent and the test classifies the person as normal (true negative); (2) the disorder is absent and the test mistakenly classifies the person as disturbed or impaired (false positive); (3) the disorder is present and the test mistakenly classifies the person as normal (false negative); and, (4) the disorder is present and the test classifies the person as impaired (true positive).

Table 15.1   Classification Outcomes

Disorder	Test Result	
	Negative	*Positive*
Absent	[a]True negative	[b]False positive
Present	[c]False negative	[d]True positive

Sensitivity is defined as the proportion of true positive individuals detected by the instrument. Referring to Table 15.1, sensitivity is derived using the formula

$$\frac{d}{c+d}.$$

Specificity, on the other hand, is defined as the proportion of individuals that an instrument correctly identifies who are "rue negatives.It is computed using the formula

$$\frac{a}{a+b}.$$

A dilemma confronting psychometricians concerns determining the score that best reflects classification accuracy. Greater sensitivity is typically obtained when the score is lowered; however, this almost invariably reduces the specificity of the scale.

The *likelihood ratio* (LR) is another technique for classification. Used to supplement sensitivity/specificity indicators, the LR documents the odds that a particular score accurately classifies the person. The LR is defined as

$$\frac{sensitivity}{1-specificity}.$$

As the ratio increasingly exceeds 1.0, the probability that the person manifests the condition increases, whereas when the LR progressively decreases below 1.0, the probability increases for not having the condition.

Response Bias Analysis

The procedure for obtaining the information from the subject is especially important in the field of substance abuse. Not uncommonly, prolonged consumption of psychoactive compounds is associated with dementia or impaired cognition. Also, evasiveness and minimization of drug-related problems can bias the results of assessment, particularly where there may be legal ramifications. An evaluation that relies exclusively on self-report may thus yield invalid results. Complementing self-report with a structured interview provides the opportunity to probe for inconsistencies and obtain information that is not otherwise readily disclosed by the subject. Whereas classical psychometric analyses may not be capable of detecting a response bias affecting reliability and validity, it is noteworthy that recently developed techniques derived from item response theory can inform about the operations of specific items in an inventory or scale.

Response Format

The manner in which the items are scored impacts on the capacity to capture the entire distribution of values describing the particular trait or variable. For example, dichotomous items (e.g., yes/no, true/false) do not measure the full range of a trait. Diagnostic interviews have a significant shortcoming in this regard because it is not possible to quantify severity apart from merely summing the number of symptoms. In contrast, self-report rating scales, by offering a broader range of response options (e.g., low to high), enable a more complete characterization of severity. Generally, the psychometric properties of a scale or interview are enhanced by inclusive measurement of the full range of the variable.

Item Parameters

Items are characterized by two indices: item difficulty and item discrimination. In a dichotomously scored instrument, item difficulty corresponds to the percentage (or proportion) of subjects who endorse the item. Item difficulty ranges between 0 and 1.0. In the process of instrument construction, the item difficulty index plays an important role in choosing items to assess the subject's trait level. Items endorsed by everyone, or items that are not endorsed by anyone, do not provide information about individual differences. Thus, they do not contribute to the reliability or validity of an instrument. For maximum differentiation among individuals encompassing all levels of a latent trait, items should be chosen at the 0.50 endorsement level.

The item discrimination index indicates how effectively an item discriminates between subjects who are relatively high on the criterion of interest (or behavior) and those who are relatively low on the criterion of interest. The criteria can be the total score obtained from the instrument. Positive values of the item discrimination index indicate that the item discriminates in favor of the upper group on the trait, whereas negative values indicate that the item is a reverse discriminator, that is, it favors the lower group.

Reliable instruments consist of items that are highly discriminative. For a dichotomously scored item, the point biserial correlation between item and total score is used to compute the item discrimination index. If a latent variable underlying item performance is normally distributed, the biserial correlation is used to compute the item discrimination index. If the criterion variable and the item are dichotomous, then the *phi* coefficient is appropriate to compute the item discrimination index. If latent variables underlying item performance and the criterion of interest are assumed to be normally distributed, the tetrachoric correlation coefficient is more appropriate to use as the item discrimination index.

EVALUATION OF ALCOHOL AND DRUG ABUSE

Interview Evaluation

Psychiatric Interview Schedules

Several structured and semistructured interviews have been developed for the objective evaluation of current and lifetime substance use disorder. The interview schedules most commonly employed for adults are the Diagnostic Interview Schedule (Malgady, Rogler, & Tryon, 1992), Composite International Diagnostic Interview (Robins et al., 1989), and Structured Clinical Interview for DSM (Spitzer, Williams, & Gibbon, 1992). The Alcohol Use Disorder and Associated Disabilities Interview (Grant & Toule, 1990) has the advantage of documenting family history of disorder as well as documenting the range of items necessary to diagnose the disorder according to the three most recent versions of the *Diagnostic and Statistical Manual of Mental Disorders* (DSM) as well as the tenth edition of the *International Classification of Disease*. The Psychiatric Research Interview for Substance and Mental Disorders (Grant & Toule, 1990), combining features of these latter interview schedules, accrues information about drug use and its consequences in conjunction with comorbid psychiatric manifestations. Finally, the Substance Use Disorders Diagnostic Schedule (Davis, Hoffmann, Morse, & Luehr, 1992) has the advantage of using either an interview format or a computer interactive administration format.

Several interviews have also been developed for adolescents. The Diagnostic Interview for Children and Adolescents (Reich, Welner, Taibleson, & Kram, 1990), and Kiddie Schedule for Affective Disorders and Schizophrenia (Orvaschel, Puig-Antich, Chambers, Fabrizi, & Johnson, 1982) are most commonly used. No evidence has been accrued to indicate the superiority of any particular interview schedule for diagnostic formulation. They are all comprehensive and have administration guidelines which are clear and straightforward. The quality of information obtained is primarily contingent on the training and skill of the interviewer.

Alcohol and Drug Interview Schedules

The Comprehensive Drinker Profile (Miller & Marlett, 1984) was specifically designed for determining treatment modality. Extensive information is obtained regarding alcohol consumption history, behavior, motivation, and self-efficacy. It is one of the few structured interviews designed to evaluate treatment effects. The Addiction Severity Index (ASI) (McLellan et al., 1992) quantifies disturbance in eight areas of psychosocial functioning frequently disrupted by habitual alcohol or drug consumption. The ASI assesses severity of problems in the following domains: medical, employment, drug use, alcohol use, legal, family functioning, social functioning, and psychiatric disturbance. The ASI is an efficient screening method for characterizing severity of consequences of substance involvement and has been frequently employed to measure both the need for and impact of treatment. It is, however, somewhat lengthy (approximately 200 items) and does not lead directly to diagnostic formulation of a substance use disorder or psychiatric disorder. The Teen-ASI (Kaminer, Bukstein, & Tarter, 1991) is an adaptation of the adult version for adolescents. It has been shown in initial analyses to have promising psychometric properties. The Adolescent Drug Abuse Diagnosis (Friedman & Utada, 1989) is an extensively researched interview that is also modeled on the ASI. It documents level of disturbance in nine domains: medical, school, employment, social relations, family relations, psychological functioning, legal status, alcohol use, and drug use. The ranking of scores across the various scales informs about the type and intensity of treatment. Another interview, the *Adolescent Diagnostic Interview* (Winters & Henley, 1993) evaluates interpersonal and school functioning, cognition, and social stress that may be fostering alcohol or drug use. Because it provides the opportunity for diagnostic formulation in a 15-minute evaluation, it is an expeditious method for objectively determining the need for treatment.

Self-Administered Evaluations

The majority of self-report instruments were developed to evaluate alcohol consumption and associated problems.

Assessment of drug use and its consequences has typically involved modifying an instrument that was originally developed to measure alcohol consumption topography and its consequences. The following discussion reviews the most frequently cited self-report instruments in the empirical literature.

Multidimensional Scales

The Personal Experience Inventory (PEI) (Winters & Henley, 1989) is a comprehensive questionnaire used for detection of problems and determination of a treatment plan. In addition to measuring level of involvement within 12 types of drugs, the PEI also identifies potential risk factors that are thought to predispose to or sustain drug use. Quantification of severity of problems in the areas of personal, family, and psychosocial functioning guides the treatment planning process. Another multivariate instrument is the Drug Use Screening Inventory (DUSI) (Tarter, 1990). This self-report has homologous versions for adults and adolescents. It quantifies severity of problems in 10 domains: (1) substance use, (2) psychiatric disorder, (3) health, (4) behavior, (5) family, (6) peers, (7) work, (8) school, (9) social skill, and, (10) leisure and recreation. The main use of the DUSI is to rank severity of problems using a standard metric so that treatment needs can be prioritized according to the severity of manifest disturbances reported during the past year, past month, or past week. The multiple timeframes also enable the DUSI to be used for charting treatment progress and for monitoring treatment gains during follow-up or aftercare.

Substance Use Severity

The most fundamental indicator of involvement with alcohol or drugs is the quantity × frequency index. Although several different methods have been advanced for computing this index (Cahalan & Room, 1974; Midanik, 1994; Polich, Armer, & Braiker, 1981), a summary score for characterizing total consumption level within a defined timeframe is very informative for documenting changing patterns of involvement concomitant to treatment and prevention as well as changes in health and psychosocial adjustment. However, it should be recognized that quantity (dose) of illicit drug use is difficult to describe in standard units. The accuracy in computing the Q × F index for drug use within a particular timeframe is thus potentially questionable. Furthermore, information comprising this index

requires retrospective recall. The timeline follow-back procedure (Sobell & Sobell, 1992) minimizes error; however, biased or faulty reporting cannot be ruled out.

Numerous screening tests have been developed to determine the consequences of severity of habitual alcohol or drug consumption. The Michigan Alcohol Screening Test (Selzer, 1971) is perhaps the best known screening instrument. The short form, consisting of 26 items, documents overall severity of consequences from alcohol consumption (Crews & Sher, 1992). A drug severity version has also been developed (Skinner, 1982). The CAGE (Mayfield, McLeod, & Hall, 1974) is the briefest screening instrument. Composed of four items, it provides a quick indication of whether the person's drinking behavior has produced problems that warrant treatment. The Alcohol Use Disorders Identification Test (AUDIT) (Saunders, Aasland, Babor, de la Fuente, & Grant, 1993), consisting of 10 items, also informs about the need for treatment. Level of alcohol involvement, severity of dependence, and problem consequences from drinking are recorded. The Addiction Admission Scale (Weed, Butcher, McKenna, & Ben Powath, 1992) embedded within the MMPI-2 is composed of 13 items. Its advantage resides in the fact that numerous personality traits as well as psychopathology are assessed simultaneously.

The Alcohol Dependence Scale (Skinner & Horn, 1984) quantifies physical dependence severity using 25 items. An advantage of this brief scale is that a cut-off can be used to determine accurately whether the person qualifies for a DSM diagnosis of alcohol dependence without having to expend the labor to conduct a comprehensive diagnostic interview, thereby providing a facile method of diagnosis. The Severity of Alcohol Dependence Questionnaire (Stockwell, Murphy, & Hodgson, 1983), another self-administered test of alcohol dependence, is composed of five subscales: affective, withdrawal, physical withdrawal, withdrawal relief drinking, alcohol consumption, and rapidity of dependence reinstatement.

The impact of drinking in five areas (physical, interpersonal, impulsive, social, and interpersonal) can be expeditiously assessed using the Drinker Inventory of Consequences Scale (Miller, Tonigan, & Longabaugh, 1995). Problems during the past 3 months and across the lifetime are documented using this 50-item self-report inventory.

The Alcohol Use Inventory (AUI) (Wanberg, Horn, & Foster, 1977) consists of 24 scales and 228 items that multidimensionally characterize drinking behavior and its consequences. The AUI measures pattern or style of drinking, anticipated benefits of drinking, and problems consequent to drinking. The primary scales are aggregated into second-order scales to document severity of physical and psychological problems, and a third-order scale, which indexes overall alcoholism severity.

Although all of the measures discussed up to this juncture provide treatment relevant information, the Chemical Dependency Assessment Profile (Harrell, Honaker, & Davis, 1991) was specifically designed to evaluate the treatment needs of adolescents and adults. Despite its somewhat lengthy format (232 items) the results inform about important facets of substance involvement and the person's potential to benefit from treatment. The scales measure frequency/quantity, physiological symptoms, situation stressors, affective dysfunction, impact of drug use on life functioning, and treatment attitudes.

Several self-administered instruments have been developed for adolescents. The Adolescent Drinking Index (Harrell & Wirtz, 1985), consisting of about two dozen items, has been used to screen adolescents who require treatment. Two subscales respectively measure drinking for self-medicating benefit and drinking associated with externalizing behavior (Mayer & Filstead, 1979). The Drug Use Screening Inventory (Tarter, 1990) has normative data for characterizing problem severity in ten domains of health, behavior, and psychosocial functioning and a cut-off score for determining whether the client qualifies for a diagnosis of substance use disorder.

Specialized Scales

Self Efficacy

The Alcohol Abstinence Self-Efficacy Scale (DiClemente, Carbonari, Montgomery, & Hughes, 1994) measures confidence to resist consumption in 20 drinking situations. Grounded in social learning theory, 20 temptation and 20 self-efficacy items are self-rated to document the likelihood that a drinking event will occur. This scale was designed to specifically evaluate treatment progress and to gauge the potential for relapse. Another instrument is the Drinking Refusal Self-Efficacy Questionnaire (Young, Oei & Crook, 1991). This 31-item scale is composed of three subscales measuring social pressure, emotional relief, and opportunistic drinking. In addition, the Drinking Related Locus of Control Scale (Koski-Jannes, 1994) consists of 25 items for measuring the person's confidence regarding

control over drinking. The conflicting impulse to drink and level of effortful resistance to drink problematically is measured by the 15-item Temptation and Restraint Inventory (Collins & Lapp, 1992). This latter scale is most appropriately utilized for detection of emerging alcohol problems evidenced by the effort expended by the person to resist consumption. The Yale–Brown Obsessive-Compulsive Scale (Modell, Glaser, Mountz, Cyr, & Schmaltz, 1992) consists of 10 items and complements these latter instruments as a quick measure of preoccupation with and motivation for alcohol consumption.

The Impaired Control Scale (Heather, Tebbott, Mattick, & Zamir, 1993), also derived from social learning theory, contains three scales to assess (1) the extent to which the person attempted to control alcohol intake in the past month; (2) level of success in controlling drinking; and, (3) the strength of belief that drinking can be curtailed if an effort was made. A related instrument, The Drinking Restraint Scale (Curry, Southwick, & Steele, 1987) is composed of 23 items. It provides an efficient method for measuring the person's level of preoccupation with and control over drinking. Finally, the Situational Confidence Questionnaire (Annis & Graham, 1988) measures the person's confidence to resist alcohol consumption in eight areas. To date, the predictive validity of these latter scales remains to be demonstrated. Also, at this juncture, the superiority of any particular self-efficacy instrument for use in clinical settings has yet to be demonstrated.

Expectancy of Consumption Consequences

The Alcohol Effects Questionnaire (AEQ) (Rohsenow, 1983), composed of 40 items, measures the anticipated and adverse consequences of alcohol consumption. Eight areas of expected effects are quantified: (1) global positive effect; (2) social and physical pleasure; (3) sexual enhancement; (4) power and aggression; (5) social expressiveness; (6) relaxation and tension reduction; (7) cognitive and physical impairment; and (8) careless unconcern. The Alcohol Expectancy Questionnaire (Brown, Christiansen, & Goldman, 1987) also evaluates the expected reinforcing effects of alcohol consumption. An adolescent version of this questionnaire has also been developed (Christiansen, Goldman, & Inn, 1992). Like the Alcohol Effects Questionnaire, it is applicable to both adolescents and adults and has normative data. The Drinking Expectancy

Questionnaire (Young & Knight, 1989) parallels these latter two scales.

It is well established that beliefs and expectancies about the consequences of alcohol and drug consumption mediate in part the propensity for and pattern of consumption. Research has yet to demonstrate how modification of these various cognitive attributions impacts on treatment outcomes. In this vein, the predictive validity of these expectancy questionnaires also remains to be documented.

Treatment Focused Assessment

The Brown–Peterson Recovery Progress Inventory, consisting of 53 items, documents the extent to which the person's attitudes and behavior have changed concordant with involvement in a 12-step AA (Alcoholics Anonymous) - oriented recovery program (Brown & Peterson, 1991). This self-administered scale is designed to monitor the rate and level of progress within the 12-step recovery program. The Steps Questionnaire (Gilbert, 1991), containing 42 items, measures the amenability of the person to engage in an AA-oriented recovery program.

The Readiness to Change Questionnaire (Heather, Rollnick, & Bell, 1993) classifies the client according to stage of treatment preparation: precontemplation, contemplation, and action. This brief questionnaire, conforming to the Prochaska and DiClemente model of treatment (Prochaska & DiClemente, 1986), is composed of 12 items.

The Recovery Attitude and Treatment Evaluation (RATE) questionnaire is a 94-item self-administered inventory to be used in conjunction with the interview-based Clinical Evaluator to determine the client's treatment needs (Mee-Lee, 1988). Each of the two components of the RATE contains five scales to measure treatment resistance, resistance to sustained or continuing care, severity of psychiatric problems, severity of medical problems, and social support resources. An advantage of RATE is that it assists decision making regarding treatment placement according to the criteria established by the American Society on Addiction Medicine.

Alcohol Withdrawal

The Clinical Institute Withdrawal Assessment (Sullivan, Sykova, Schneiderman, Naranjo, & Sellers, 1989), a 10-item observational rating scale, documents the severity and progress of alcohol withdrawal. It thus provides an objective method for deciding how best to treat the person manifest-ing withdrawal symptoms as well as for determining the patient's readiness to initiate long-term rehabilitation.

Substance Use in the Elderly

One of the few instruments available for assessing alcohol involvement in older adults is the Drinking Problem Index (Finney, Moos, & Brennan, 1991). Consisting of 17 items, this self-rating scale measures severity of symptoms, drinking motivation, and consequences of alcohol consumption.

Substance Use in College Students

Although alcohol consumption is a recognized problem on most college campuses, there has been surprisingly little research conducted on developing instruments specific to this population. The Young Adult Problem Screening Test (Hurlbut & Sher, 1992) consists of 27 items and is directed at evaluating alcohol-related physical and interpersonal consequences.

Context of Consumption

The contextual aspects of drinking are efficiently measured using the Inventory of Drinking Situations (IDS) (Annis, 1982). A total of 100 items are organized into eight scales to evaluate drinking propensity where there is (1) an unpleasant situation, (2) physical discomfort, (3) pleasant emotions, (4) need to test personal control, (5) a subjective urge or temptation, (6) conflict with others, (7) social pressure, and (8) an opportunity for a pleasant time with others. A parallel version for drug use in these eight contexts has also been developed (Annis & Graham, 1992). In conjunction with other measures used to document treatment planning, the IDS informs about the situations that are most likely to precipitate a relapse. Complementing this latter instrument, the Motivational Structure Questionnaire (Cox & Klinger, 1988) profiles the person's concerns or problems within a motivational perspective. Disturbances in motivation that have led to alcohol consumption thus inform about the most optimum treatment modality.

Work-Related Problems Associated with Substance Abuse

Apart from the DUSI, which contains a scale for measuring the severity of the substance use problem in relation to work adjustment, standardized instruments have not been developed to comprehensively evaluate the reciprocal relationship between alcohol or drug use and vocational adjustment. The 15-item screening instrument, Your Workplace (Beattie, Longabaugh, & Fava, 1992), represents currently the only instrument specifically developed to assess alcohol-related work maladjustment.

HIV/AIDS Risk

Substance abusers are at increased risk for HIV/AIDS concomitant to injecting drugs with contaminated needles and unsafe sexual practices. The sexual partners of drug users are also at increased risk of infection. The instruments cited up to this point do not have an HIV/AIDS risk component; however, this facet of an evaluation is clearly important. A protocol for assessing HIV/AIDS risk has been developed consisting of both interview and self-administered sections. The Drug Abuse Treatment for AIDS Risk Reduction (Simpson, 1990) measures diverse aspects of substance involvement pertaining to peers, criminal behavior, decision making, affect, and readiness for treatment.

Evaluation in the Criminal Justice System

The Offender Profile Index (Inciardi, 1993) is an interview designed to help formulate a treatment plan for individuals whose drug abuse has directly or indirectly resulted in imprisonment. The evaluation, taking approximately 30 minutes, emphasizes the importance of conformity to social norms as an indicator of the intensity of treatment required for successful adjustment following release. In addition to demographic, family, work, and psychological factors, this inventory also evaluates HIV risk behavior, criminal history, and sociodemographic factors surrounding criminal offending.

PSYCHOLOGICAL FACTORS CONTRIBUTING TO SUBSTANCE ABUSE

Substance abuse frequently occurs in conjunction with medical and psychiatric disorders as well as psychosocial maladjustment. These disturbances can be manifest prior to first alcohol or drug exposure as well as emerge concomitantly to habitual consumption. It is important, therefore, that the results of a psychological evaluation delineate the temporal pattern of disturbance as well as elucidate the presence and impact of the manifold factors that maintain the pattern of

substance abuse. Toward this end, a functional analysis is required, that is, an evaluation procedure that informs about the actual as well as the client's perceived benefits associated with alcohol or drug consumption. In effect, understanding the person's motivation for substance use, it is possible to tailor the intervention modality to specific causal factors.

Precursors to Alcohol and Drug Abuse

Many investigations have been directed at determining the characteristics of children who subsequently develop a substance use disorder. To date, a comprehensive multivariate assessment protocol documenting level of risk that has predictive validity remains to be developed. The main problem confronting this effort is the extreme heterogeneity of etiological factors. Moreover, the salience and configuration of etiological variables are idiosyncratic consequent to unique genetic and environment factors operating during socialization and thereafter throughout life. It is well established that the factors predisposing to alcohol and drug abuse span and include multiple environmental contexts such as all levels of biobehavioral organization, family, peers, and demography. Hence, the factors contributing to the development of substance abuse are particular to each individual (Tarter & Vanyukov, 1994). It is consensually recognized that a specific personality type presaging alcohol or drug dependence does not exist; however, certain traits are nonetheless overrepresented in the segment of the population who eventually develop a problem with psychoactive substances. In a postdictive study, the Addiction Potential Scale (Weed et al., 1992), composed of 39 items of the MMPI (Minnesota Multiphasic Personality Inventory), was found to classify accurately individuals who subsequently developed a drug dependence disorder.

Whereas research has not yet yielded a validated psychometric instrument for identifying youth who will eventually manifest a substance use disorder, numerous longitudinal studies and investigations of high-risk youth have been informative for describing the characteristics associated with substance abuse vulnerability. These characteristics have yet to be organized into an inventory having predictive validity. The features that most frequently have been implicated to underlie the liability to substance abuse include high sensation seeking, difficult temperament, high aggressivity, negative affect, social deviance, and poor behavioral self-regulation (Tarter & Vanyukov, 1994). These characteristics can be encompassed within the broad rubric of disinhibitory psychopathology (Gorenstein & Newman, 1980). It should be noted, however, that these characteristics have different salience in males and females with female individuals having a greater propensity for internalizing disturbances (e.g., depression) ,whereas males are featured more prominently by externalizing disturbances.

In the absence of a standardized assessment procedure, the precursors (or risk factors) of substance use can be examined only by instruments that have not yet been standardized and have uncertain predictive validity. One instrument currently undergoing psychometric validation is the Dysregulation Inventory (Mezzich, 1995). Otherwise, evaluation of substance abuse risk entails extrapolating information obtained from diagnostic interviews and rating scales. For example, conduct problems have been shown in many studies to predispose to substance abuse. This behavior disposition can be readily documented by documenting symptom counts from a diagnostic interview or by rating scales such as the Child Behavior Checklist (Achenbach & Edelbrock, 1983). The point to be made is that the many behavioral and psychopathological antecedents of substance abuse are routinely assessed in the context of a comprehensive evaluation. Measurement of other traits known to augment the risk of substance use necessitates utilization of specialized instruments. For example, various standardized personality questionnaires as well as other more focal aspects of psychological functioning are measured by the Dimensions of Temperament Survey (Windle, 1992); disinhibition using the Sensation Seeking Scale for adolescents (Donohew, Helm, Lawrence, & Shatzer, 1990) or adults (Zuckerman, 1979), and self-concept employing the Multidimensional Self-Esteem Inventory (Epstein, 1976), document deviation from the population norm on facets of psychological functioning related to alcohol or drug abuse risk. In the absence of established predictive validity, the scores from these types of instruments must be interpreted cautiously and, where possible, in conjunction with results obtained from other instruments. In effect, to maximize the validity of results, the psychological evaluation of a multimethod, multitrait approach is recommended. Because the risk for drug or alcohol abuse involves many traits, the assessment needs to be encompassing rather than restrictive. Also, because of potential error associated with the use of a single instrument, multiple methods (self-report, interview, informant report) should be utilized when possible.

In addition to gender differences previously noted, age is an important factor determining the pattern of substance involvement and associated disturbance. For example, adolescents commonly develop a substance use disorder subsequent to psychological disorder or social maladjustment. In contrast, adult-onset substance use disorder is typically not preceded by characterological disturbances but instead is a reaction to life stress (work, divorce, bereavement, etc.) and thus emerges as an attempt to self-medicate an aversive emotional or affective state (e.g., anxiety, depression, phobia, panic). It is necessary, therefore, that the evaluation clarifies the ordering of emergence of behavioral and psychiatric problems in relation to substance abuse so that the cause–effect relations, once disentangled inform about designing a treatment plan.

Correlates of Alcohol and Drug Abuse

Habitual consumption of drugs having addiction potential induces central nervous system adaptation to the compound. This is overtly expressed as chronic tolerance. The CNS alterations affect psychological functioning, and to significant degree, trigger craving in the absence of the drug. Certain compounds (e.g., alcohol, inhalants) also produce neurological injury due to their neurotoxic properties. Organ-system disease consequent to habitual drug or alcohol use can impair brain functioning. For example, alcohol abuse frequently results in cirrhosis, which in turn produces an hepatic encephalopathy. Neuropsychiatric disorder, a frequent sequela of cerebrovascular disease from prolonged drug use, has substantial impact on the subsequent course of a substance abuse disorder, motivation to persist in treatment, and social adjustment. A neuropsychological evaluation is thus informative for documenting the extent to which manifest neurological pathology is associated with cognitive and psychomotor functioning.

Social adjustment is commonly adversely affected by a lifestyle involving habitual substance abuse. The particular areas of disturbance in social functioning depend on predisposing factors, substance use topography, psychiatric status, health and physical capacity, and demographic context. In view of the complexity and number of factors, it is essential to adopt a flexible approach to psychological evaluation. Specifically, manifold contextual problems—particularly family, peers, neighborhood, school, and job, and their temporal ordering—need to be assessed in relation to substance use initiation, escalation, and sustained involvement. A feedback cycle of reciprocal effects is commonly established whereby alcohol and drug consumption fuels social maladjustment, which in turn increases the propensity for substance abuse.

Numerous questionnaires and inventories have been developed for characterizing social adjustment in 10 domains. The Family Assessment Measure (Skinner, Steinhauer, & Santa-Barbara, 1983) evaluates the overall quality of the family environment as well as the quality of the dyadic relationships among its members. School adjustment can be determined using the teacher version of the Child Behavior Checklist (Achenbach & Edelbrock, 1983). Academic achievement level is readily documented using the Peabody Individual Achievement Test (Markwardt, 1989) or the Wide Range Achievement Test (Jastak & Wilkinson, 1984). The extent to which physical problems impact on social role functioning can be determined by the General Health Rating Scale (Ware, 1976). Tests of social skill have not been standardized; however, the Social Intelligence Test (Moss, Hung, & Onwake, 1990) is a multivariate self-report for youth and adults. Adjustment in the workplace can be documented using the Index of Job Satisfaction (Brayfield & Rothe, 1951). The quality of the neighborhood and integration into the community can be assessed using the Neighborhood Cohesion Scale (Buckner, 1988). The point to be made is that substance abuse must be evaluated in relation to the person's lifespan adjustment in a variety of contexts that are known to have etiologic significance as well as the potential to sustain or exacerbate alcohol or drug involvement. The previously noted instruments do not encompass the full armament of evaluation instrument modalities; however, they illustrate the importance of measuring the processes that influence drug and alcohol topography as well as the consequences of substance abuse.

Finally, psychiatric comorbidity must be evaluated, because a disturbance predisposes to substance abuse as well as is a consequence of alcohol and drug use. The rate of virtually every Axis I psychiatric disorder is overrepresented in the substance-abusing population. The rate of Axis II disorders, particularly externalizing disorders in men, has also been shown to be elevated among substance abusers. Therefore, to fully understand the natural history and clinical presentation of a substance use disorder, it is necessary to conduct a thorough psychiatric evaluation. This can be readily accomplished using a diagnostic interview schedule in conjunction with administration of a personality disorder questionnaire.

A single comprehensive inventory is not currently available for the evaluation of substance abuse and related problems. Consequently, a protocol that is tailored to the characteristics of the client population needs to be administered. For example, an assessment protocol that is informative for treatment in a prison setting is different from a protocol for patients in a primary care medical service. The emphasis of evaluation varies across settings even though there is the common thread of alcohol and/or drug abuse. In effect, the assessment protocol should be designed to elicit information for addressing intervention needs. As discussed next, this can be accomplished using a three-stage assessment strategy.

DECISION-TREE APPROACH TO ASSESSMENT

Assessment of psychological functioning is an ongoing process integrally linked to all phases of prevention or treatment. At the outset, the objective of the psychological evaluation is to match the treatment modality with identified problems. This in turn enables determining intensity (e.g., outpatient, day care, impatient). Once intervention is initiated, sequential evaluations are informative for objectively documenting change, that is, quantifying cumulative treatment impact as evidenced by the reduction or amelioration of problems causal to, or correlated with, drug consumption. Subsequent to the acute phase of intervention, repeated assessments of psychological functioning should be directed at monitoring the client's status, particularly with respect to the characteristics that have been contributory to the client's problems. However, because substance abuse commonly, if not typically, occurs in conjunction with manifold other disturbances pertaining to health and psychiatric disturbance as well as behavioral and social functioning, it is not practical to conduct an intensive evaluation on each client encompassing all potential problem areas. A decision-tree assessment approach, involving three stages, is thus recommended whereby each phase of the evaluation informs about the need for further detailed information for determination of the best intervention strategy. The multistage approach described next maximizes efficient use of resource while minimizing costs. Also, prognosis is maximized by matching the intervention modality to the client's problems that predisposed to or sustained alcohol and/or drug abuse. The decision-tree approach is summarized in Table 15.2.

Stage 1: Screening

The first task is to determine whether there is an identifiable problem that points to a need for intervention. Commonly, there are multiple problems; hence, the

Table 15.2   Decision-Tree Approach to Psychological Evaluation

Stage 1 Screening	Stage 2 In-Depth Assessment	Stage 3 Intervention
Drug Use Screening Inventory	Comprehensive evaluation in indicated domains	Treatment modality and severity determined by assessment information
Substance Use		
Health		
Behavior		
Psychiatric Disorder		
School Adjustment		
Family Adjustment		
Social Competence		
Peer Relations		
Work Adjustment		
Leisure/Recreation		

Source: Tarter, Kirisci, & Mezzich, 1996

screening assessment should yield results that rank the severity of disturbances across the various domains of health, psychiatric status, behavior, and psychosocial functioning. Ranking problem severity provides the rationale for appropriating treatment resources commensurate with the magnitude of disturbance. Two instruments, the Addiction Severity Index (ASI) (McLellan et al., 1992) and the Drug Use Screening Inventory (DUSI) (Tarter, 1990), enable efficient multidimensional evaluation. The ASI is typically administered as an interview and thus is somewhat labor intensive. The DUSI is self-administered ,thereby enabling rapid screening. Another notable feature of the DUSI is that a summary cut-off score can be used to identify with over 90% accuracy whether an individual surpasses the threshold for diagnosis of a substance use disorder. Several studies have documented the psychometric reliability and validity of the DUSI (Kirisci, Hsu, & Tarter, 1994; Kirisci, Mezzich, & Tarter, 1995; Tarter, Kirisci, & Mezzich, 1996). Considering that the DUSI takes about 20 minutes to administer and 5 minutes to score, it is an efficient method to establish whether intervention or further in-depth assessment is needed.

Stage 2: Comprehensive Evaluation

The second phase is directed at obtaining detailed information about the client in the problem areas detected in stage 1. For example, a high score on the DUSI domain measuring severity of psychiatric disturbance points to the need for a comprehensive diagnostic evaluation. Similarly,

school adjustment problems detected in stage 1 screening point to the need for examination of academic achievement and school adjustment. In effect, the domains indicative of disturbance observed in stage 1 need to be examined in depth in stage 2. The main purpose of evaluation at this stage is to determine whether there is a disorder of sufficient severity to warrant intervention, and to elucidate the degree to which the manifest problems are specifically related to substance use. As discussed elsewhere in this chapter, numerous self-administered instruments and inventories are available for thorough documentation of substance abuse and associated problems.

Stage 3: Treatment Matching

The third phase involves formulation of an intervention plan. For maximum effectiveness, a multidisciplinary team should be assembled so as to capitalize on the expertise required to address the manifold factors spanning biological, behavioral, and social processes. For example, psychiatric disorder, family disorder, and leisure and recreation problems require specialized professional expertise. In each identified problem area, the treatment objective must be explicitly documented in conjunction with intermediate goals to be attained along with anticipated timelines. This level of accountability is increasingly required in the present era of managed care where administrative oversight is routine. Therefore, it is essential to link and justify intervention with assessment information obtained in stages 1 and 2.

During the course of active treatment, the DUSI can additionally be used to monitor change in status. Using either the "past week" or "past month" version of the DUSI, severity of problems are quantified, thereby enabling charting the impact of treatment. This information also provides an objective criterion for terminating acute treatment; that is, the problem has decreased to a specified low level of severity. Finally, during the period of aftercare, the DUSI provides an efficient checkup to determine whether there are any prodromal indicators of incipient relapse and to objectively chart sustained treatment gains.

SUMMARY

Numerous self-report and interview inventories are available for multidimensional characterization of individuals who are problematically involved with alcohol and drugs. These instruments provide the opportunity to objectively quantify substance use behavior and severity of consequences. As discussed herein, a comprehensive psychological evaluation should be directed at delineating the manifold predisposing and concurrent factors contributing to the initiation and maintenance of alcohol and/or drug consumption. A three-stage decision-tree approach is described herein that efficiently identifies and ranks severity of problems in the multiple domains of health, behavior, and psychosocial functioning. This information can be used to guide the comprehensive evaluation as well as to monitor change during the course of intervention and aftercare. Psychological assessment, therefore, is an ongoing process of information gathering that begins prior to treatment and continues until complete rehabilitation is achieved.

REFERENCES

Achenbach, T., & Edelbrock, C. (1983). *Manual of the Child Behavior Checklist and Revised Child Behavior Profile.* Burlington, VT: University of Vermont.

Annis, H. (1982). *Inventory of Drinking Situations.* Toronto: Addiction Research Foundation.

Annis, H. & Graham, J. (1988). *Situational Confidence Questionnaire (User's guide).* Toronto: Addiction Research Foundation.

Annis, H. & Graham, J. (1992). *Inventory of Drug Taking Situations (User's guide).* Toronto: Addiction Research Foundation.

Beattie, M., Longabaugh, R., & Fava, J. (1992). Assessment of alcohol-related workplace activities: Development and testing of "Your Workplace." *Journal of Studies on Alcohol, 53,* 469–475.

Brayfield, A., & Rothe, H. (1951). An index of job satisfaction. *Journal of Applied Psychology, 35,* 307–311.

Brown, H., & Peterson, J. (1991). Assessing spirituality in addiction treatment and follow-up: Development of the Brown–Peterson Recovery Progress Inventory (B-PRPI). *Alcoholism Treatment Quarterly, 8,* 21–50.

Brown, S., Christiansen, B., & Goldman, M. (1987). The Alcohol Expectancy Questionnaire: An instrument for the assessment of adolescent and adult alcohol expectancies. *Journal of Studies on Alcohol, 48,* 483–491.

Buckner, J. (1988). The development of an instrument to measure neighborhood cohesion. *American Journal of Community Psychology, 18,* 771–791.

Cahalan, D., & Room, R. (1974). *Problem drinking among American men.* New Brunswick, NJ: Rutgers Center of Alcohol Studies.

Christiansen, R., Goldman, M., & Inn, A. (1992). The development of alcohol-related expectancies in adolescents. Separating pharmacological from social learning influences. *Journal of Consulting and Clinical Psychology, 50,* 536–544.

Collins, R., & Lapp, W. (1992). The Temptation and Restraint Inventory for measuring drinking restraint. *British Journal of Addictions, 87,* 625–633.

Cox, M., & Klinger, E. (1988). A motivational model of alcohol use. *Journal of Abnormal Psychology, 97,* 168–180.

Crews, T., & Sher, K. (1992). Using adapted short MASTs for assessing parental alcoholism: Reliability and validity. *Alcoholism: Clinical and Experimental Research, 16,* 576–584.

Curry, S., Southwick, L., & Steele, C. (1987). Restrained drinking. Risk factor for problems with alcohol. *Addictive Behavior, 12,* 73–77.

Davis, L., Hoffmann, N., Morse, R., & Luehr, J. (1992). Substance Use Disorder Diagnostic Schedule (SUDDS): The equivalence and validation of a computer-administered and an interview-administered format. *Alcoholism: Clinical and Experimental Research, 16,* 250–254.

DiClemente, C., Carbonari, J., Montgomery, R., & Hughes, S. (1994). The Alcohol Abstinence Self-Efficacy Scale. *Journal of Studies on Alcohol, 85,* 141–148.

Donohew, L., Helm, D., Lawrence, P., & Shatzer, M. (1990). Sensation seeking, marijuana use, and response to prevention methods. In R. Watson (Ed.), *Alcohol abuse prevention* (pp. 79–93). Clifton, NJ: Humana Press.

Epstein, S. (1976). Anxiety, arousal and the self-concept. In J. Sarason & C. Spielberger (Eds.), *Stress and anxiety.* Washington, DC: Hemisphere.

Finney, J., Moos, R., & Brennan, P. (1991). The Drinking Problem Index: A measure to assess alcohol-related problems among older adults. *Journal of Substance Abuse, 3,* 395–404.

Friedman, A., & Utada, A. (1989). A method for diagnosing and planning the treatment of adolescent drug abusers (the

Adolescent Drug Abuse Diagnosis instrument). *Journal of Drug Education, 19*, 285–312.

Gilbert, F. (1991). Development of a "Steps Questionnaire." *Journal of Studies on Alcohol, 52*, 553–560.

Gorrenstein, E., & Newman, J. (1980). Disinhibitory psychopathology. A new perspective and model for research. *Psychological Review, 87*, 301–315.

Grant, B., & Toule, L. (1990). Standardized diagnostic interviews for alcohol research. *Alcohol, Health and Research World, 14*, 340–348.

Harwell, A., & Wirtz, P. (1985). *The Adolescent Problem Drinking Index (Manual)*. Odessa, FL: Psychological Assessment Resources.

Harrell, T., Honaker, L., & Davis, E. (1991). Cognitive and behavioral dimensions of dysfunction in alcohol and polydrug abusers. *Journal of Substance Abuse, 3*, 415–426.

Heather, N., Rollnick, S., & Bell, A. (1993). Predictive validity of the Readiness to Change Questionnaire. *Addiction, 88*, 1667–1677.

Heather, N., Tebbott, J., Mattick, R., & Zamir, R. (1993). Development of a scale for measuring impaired control over alcohol consumption: A preliminary report. *Journal of Studies on Alcohol, 54*, 700–709.

Hurlbut, S., & Sher, K. (1992). Assessing alcohol problems in college students. *Journal of American College Health, 41*, 49–58.

Inciardi, J. (Ed.). (1993). *Drug treatment and criminal justice*. Newbury Park, CA: Sage.

Jastak, S., & Wilkins, G. (1984). *Wide Range Achievement Test*. Wilmington, DE: Justak Associates.

Kaminer, Y., Bukstein, O., & Tarter, R. (1991). The Teen Addiction Severity Index: Rationale and reliability. *International Journal of Addiction, 26*, 219–226.

Kirisci, L., Tarter, R., & Hsu, T-C. (1994). Fitting a two parameter logistic item response model to clarifying the psychometric of the Drug Use Screening Inventory for adolescent alcohol and drug users. *Alcoholism: Clinical and Experimental Research, 18*, 1335–1341.

Kirisci, L., Mezzich, A., & Tarter, R. (1995). Norms and sensitivity of the adolescent version of the Drug Use Screening Inventory. *Addictive Behaviors, 20*, 149–157.

Koski-Jannes, A. (1994). Drinking-related locus of control as a predictor drinking after treatment. *Addictive Behavior, 19*, 491–495.

Malgady, R., Rogler, L., & Tryon, W. (1992). Issues of validity in the Diagnostic Interview Schedule. *Journal of Psychiatric Research, 26*, 59–67.

Markwardt, F. (1989). *Peabody Individual Achievement Test—Revised (Manual)*. Circle Pines, MN: American Guidance Service.

Mayer, J., & Filstead, W. (1979). The Adolescent Alcohol Involvement Scale: An instrument for measuring adolescents' use and misuse of alcohol. *Journal of Studies on Alcohol, 40*, 291–300.

Mayfield, D., McLeod, G., & Hall, P. (1974). The CAGE Questionnaire: Validation of a new alcoholism instrument. *American Journal of Psychiatry, 13*, 1121–1123.

McLellan, A. T., Kushner, H., Metzger, D., Peters, R., Smith, I., Grissom, G., Pettinati, H., & Argeriou, M. (1992). The fifth edition of the Addiction Severity Index. *Journal of Substance Abuse Treatment, 9*, 199–213.

Mee-Lee, D. (1988). An instrument for treatment progress and matching. The Recovery Attitude and Treatment Evaluator (RATE). *Journal of Substance Abuse Treatment, 5*, 183–186.

Mezzich, A. (1995). *The Dysregulation Inventory*. Pittsburgh, PA: University of Pittsburgh Medical School.

Midanik, L. (1994). Comparing usual quantity/frequency and graduated frequency scales to assess yearly alcohol consumption: Results from the 1990 United States National Alcohol Survey. *Addiction, 89*, 407–412.

Miller, W., & Marlatt, G. (1984). *Comprehensive Drinker Profile (Manual)*. Odessa, FL: Psychological Assessment Resources.

Miller, W., Tonigan, J., & Longabaugh, R. (1995). *The Drinker Inventory of Consequences. An instrument for assessing adverse consequences of alcohol abuse*. Project MATCH, National Institute on Alcohol Abuse and Alcoholism, Monograph Series 4, Publication No. 95-5911). Washington, DC: U.S. Government Printing Office.

Modell, J., Glaser, F., Mountz, J., Cyr, L., & Schmaltz, S. (1992). Obsessive and compulsive characteristics of alcohol abuse and dependence: Quantification by a newly developed questionnaire. *Alcoholism: Clinical and Experimental Research, 16*, 266–271.

Moss, F., Hung, T., & Onwake, K. (1990). *Social Intelligence Test*. Montreal: Institute of Psychological Research.

Orvaschel, H., Puig-Antich, J., Chambers, W., Fabrizi, M., & Johnson, R. (1982). Retrospective assessment of prepubertal major depression with the Kiddie-SADS-E. *Journal of the American Academy of Child Psychiatry, 21*, 292–397.

Polich, J., Armer, D., & Braiker, H. (1981). *The course of alcoholism: Four years after treatment*. New York: Wiley.

Prochaska, J., & DiClemente, C. (1986). Toward a comprehensive model of change. In W. Miller & N. Heather (Eds.), *Treating addictive behavior: Processes of change* (pp. 3–27). New York: Plenum.

Reich, W., Welner, Z., Taibleson, C., & Kram, L. (1990). *The DICA-R training manual*. St. Louis, MO: Washington University School of Medicine.

Robins, L., Wing, J., Wittchen, H.-U., Helzer, G., Babor, T., Burke, J., Farmer, A., Jablensky, A., Pickens, R., Regier, D., Sartorius, N., & Toule, L. (1989). The Composite International Diagnostic Interview: An epidemiologic instrument suitable for use in conjunction with different diagnostic systems and in different cultures. *Archives of General Psychiatry, 45*, 1069–1077.

Rosenhow, D. (1983). Drinking habits and expectancies about alcohol's effects for self versus others. *Journal of Consulting and Clinical Psychology, 51*, 752–756.

Saunders, J., Aasland, O., Babor, T., de la Fuente, J., & Grant, M. (1993). Development of the Alcohol Use Disorders Screening Test (AUDIT). WHO collaborative project on early detection of persons with harmful alcohol consumption. *Addiction, 88,* 791–804.

Selzer, M. (1971). The Michigan Alcoholism Screening Test. The quest for a new diagnostic instrument. *American Journal of Psychiatry, 127,* 1653–1658.

Simpson, D. (1990). *Drug Abuse Treatment for AIDS Risk Reduction (DATAR).* Fort Worth, TX: Institute for Behavioral Research, Texas Christian University.

Skinner, H. (1982). The Drug Abuse Screening Test. *Addictive Behaviors, 7,* 363–371.

Skinner, H., & Horn, J. (1984). *Alcohol Dependence Scale (user's guide).* Toronto: Addiction Research Foundation.

Skinner, H., Steinhauer, P., & Santa-Barbara, J. (1983). The Family Assessment Measure. *Canadian Journal of Community Mental Health, 2,* 91–105.

Sobell, M., & Sobell, L. (1992). Timeline follow-back: A technique for assessing self-reported alcohol consumption. In R. Litten & J. Allen (Eds.), *Measuring alcohol consumption: Psychosocial and biological methods* (pp. 41-72). Toronto, NJ: Humana Press.

Spitzer, R., Williams, J., & Gibbon, M. (1992). The Structured Clinical Interview for DSM-III-R (SCID) 1: History, rationale and description. *Archives of General Psychiatry, 49,* 624–629.

Stockwell, T., Murphy, D., & Hodgson, R. (1983). The Severity of Alcohol Dependence Questionnaire: Its use, reliability and validity. *British Journal of Addictions, 78,* 145–156.

Sullivan, J., Sykova, K., Schneiderman, J., Naranjo, C., & Sellers, E. (1989). Assessment of alcohol withdrawal: The revised Clinical Institute Withdrawal Assessment for Alcohol Scale (CIWA-AR). *British Journal of Addiction, 84,* 1553–1557.

Tarter, R. (1990). Evaluation and treatment of adolescent substance abuse: A decision tree method. *American Journal of Drug and Alcohol Abuse, 16,* 1–46.

Tarter, R., Kirisci, L., & Mezzich, A. (1996). The Drug Use Screening Inventory: School adjustment correlates of substance abuse. *Measurement and Evaluation in Counseling and Development, 29,* 25–34.

Tarter, R., & Vanyukov, M. (1994). Alcoholism: A developmental disorder. *Journal of Consulting and Clinical Psychology, 62,* 1109–1107.

Wanberg, K., Horn, J., & Foster, F. (1977). A differential assessment model for alcoholism. *Journal of Studies on Alcohol, 38,* 512–543.

Ware, J. (1976). Scales for measuring general health perception. *Health Services Research, 11,* 396–415.

Weed, N., Butcher, S., McKenna, T., & Ben Powath, Y. (1992). New measures for assessing alcohol and drug abuse problems with the MMPI-2: The APS and AAS. *Journal of Personality Assessment, 58,* 389–404.

Windle, M. (1992). Revised Dimensions of Temperament Survey (DOTS-R): Simultaneous group confirmatory factor analysis for adolescent gender groups. *Psychological Assessment, 4,* 228–234.

Winters, K., & Henly, G. (1989). *Personal Experience Inventory (PEI): Test and Manual.* Los Angeles: Western Psychological Services.

Winters, K., & Henly, G. (1993). *Adolescent Diagnostic Interview (Manual).* Los Angeles: Western Psychological Services.

Young, R., & Knight, R. (1989). The Drinking Expectancy Questionnaire: A revised measure of alcohol related beliefs. *Journal of Psychopathology and Behavioral Assessment, 11,* 99–112.

Young, R., Oei, T., & Crook, C. (1991). Development of a drinking self-efficacy scale. *Journal of Psychopathology and Behavioral Assessment, 13,* 1–15.

Zuckerman, M. (1979). *Sensation seeking: Beyond the optimal level of arousal.* Hillsdale, NJ: Erlbaum.

CHAPTER 16

NEUROPSYCHOLOGICAL ASSESSMENT

Sara Jo Nixon

The term neuropsychology was apparently first coined by Osler in 1913 (Bruce, 1985). It was later used by Hebb in a subtitle for his 1949 book. However, it was not widely applied until a collection of Lashley's writings was published in 1960 (Kolb & Whishaw, 1995). Since its conception, the field of neuropsychology has become recognized as both a method of scientific inquiry and a clinical practice. Thus, neuropsychology has much to offer to both clinicians and researchers who are interested in brain/behavior relations.

Neuropsychology has played a major role in our understanding of the effects of chronic substance abuse on cognitive functions. Given the history of abused substances, most of the work to date has focused on the effects of alcohol abuse or dependence. Several review books and chapters have summarized work in the field (e.g., Evert & Oscar-Berman, 1995; Hunt & Nixon, 1993; Knight & Longmore, 1994; Parsons, Butters, & Nathan, 1987). Recent work also has applied the tools of neuropsychology to the study of the effects of other substances such as cocaine on brain/behavior relations (Ardila, Rosselli, & Strumwasser, 1991; Beatty, Katzung, Moreland, & Nixon, 1995).

In this chapter we limit our discussion to matters particularly relevant to the assessment of non-Korsakoff alcoholics. This focus is imposed for two reasons. First,

although Korsakoff patients demonstrate significant neuropsychological impairment, they represent only a small percentage of the alcoholic population. Current estimates indicate that perhaps only 10% of the alcoholic population has Korsakoff's syndrome. Thus, these patients are not readily available for study for many aspiring clinicians or researchers. Second, the basic principles that are used in the study of alcohol's effects can be easily applied to the study of other abused substances.

In this chapter we review some of the (1) underlying assumptions of the neuropsychological approach and (2) major assessment instruments used in the study of substance abuse. In the course of this discussion, we also address basic issues of experimental design, including questions of subject selection and battery construction.

NEUROPSYCHOLOGY

The basic premise of neuropsychology is that there is an association between cognitive behavior and specific brain areas or brain systems. In a strict interpretation, one might infer that specific brain areas are presumed to be responsible for specific cognitive functions. However, this conclusion is not a necessary corollary of the overarching premise. Indeed, neither research nor clinical experience support this level of localization of function (e.g., Kolb & Whishaw, 1995; Lezak, 1995).

Although specific brain areas may be differentially involved in certain cognitive functions, it is overly simplistic to consider specific skills or functions as residing within specific brain locations. The interconnections among cortical and subcortical areas as revealed in neuroimaging and neurophysiological and neuroanatomical studies reveal intricate systems of intra- and interhemispheric communication that serve to underlie neuropsychological function. Thus, the relation between brain areas/systems and cognition is a complicated one.

Despite this complexity, some general statements regarding neuropsychological functions can be made. A simplistic overview of the relations between brain areas/systems and neuropsychological function is presented in Table 16.1. The neuropsychological domains represent the five types of functions/skills often examined in alcohol studies (e.g., Parsons, 1987; Tivis, Beatty,

Nixon, & Parsons, 1995). The precise factor structure varies among studies. In general, however, the domains include perceptual–motor skills, visuospatial functions, visual–spatial learning/memory, verbal learning/memory, and problem-solving/abstracting. It should be noted that identifying a deficit in a specific neuropsychological domain does not necessarily imply direct damage to the associated areas, although it likely reflects damage within the identified system. Finally, Table 16.1 does not address changes in personality or affect that may accompany brain injury irrespective of its etiology.

NEUROPSYCHOLOGICAL ASSESSMENT

In early studies, participants were often administered complete neuropsychological batteries requiring many hours of testing. These batteries were designed to examine performance on all of the neuropsychological domains described in the previous section. Often, personality assessments

Table 16.1   Brief Overview of Neuropsychological Domain/Brain/Behavior Relations

Neuropsychological Domain	Primary Brain Area/System	Cognitive Behavioral Exemplars of Damage
Abstracting/ problem-solving	Frontal lobes	Poor strategy formation and planning: 1) impaired set-shifting, 2) increases in perseveration, 3) impaired judgment; disrupted behavioral control, decreased spontaneity or decreased response inhibition; poor temporal memory, poor memory for sequence, poor recent memory and frequency estimates, poor delayed responses, poor proverb interpretation, poor verbal fluency, poor language comprehension, production (nonfluent) aphasia.
Verbal learning/memory	Left hemisphere temporal lobe and associative areas	Poor recall of semantic information, Impaired learning of paired associates (words), difficulty in word, number, and recurring nonsense syllables recognition, impaired auditory processing (e.g., dichotic tasks), language comprehension deficits.
Nonverbal learning/ memory	Right hemisphere temporal lobe and associative areas	Poor recall of geometric figures; poor recognition of nonsense figures, faces and unfamiliar melodies; poor acquisition of paired-associates (nonsense figures); poor block construction; impaired tactual spatial using unseen block shapes; impaired recognition of unfamiliar melodies and tunes; poor use of voice tone (prosody).
Visuospatial functions	Right hemisphere, parietal lobe, temporal lobe	Poor mental rotation, poor block construction, impaired performance on mazes.
Perceptual–motor skills	Frontal lobes (motor/premotor areas), parietal lobe (somato-sensory strip), basal ganglia, generalized diffuse damage.	Loss of speed/strength, agrammatisation (use of inappropriate grammar), difficulty in fine motor movements (e.g., grooved pegboard task), reduced speed of information processing.

were also administered. These studies required considerable commitment from both participants and examiners. As the study of substance abuse developed and the cost of research increased, alternate strategies have been used. Current research typically uses shorter, restricted batteries.

Subject Variables

In the neuropsychological assessment of chronic alcoholics, the primary objective has been to identify *alcohol-related* impairment. That is, the purpose is to study the effects of chronic alcohol abuse, per se, on neurocognitive functioning. This focus requires that factors that might affect neuropsychological performance, independent from the primary variable of interest (i.e., alcohol) be identified and controlled. In populations of substance abusers, there are a number of such variables. These potential confounds include low educational level, comorbid psychiatric disorders, medical or neurologic disorders, low intelligence, and insufficient detoxification prior to testing. Another pertinent variable is maternal alcoholism.

To address these problems, subject recruitment is often restricted to individuals with a minimum of 21 days of sobriety, who do not have other medical, neurologic, or psychiatric disorders, and whose mother did not drink alcohol during pregnancy. This latter exclusion prevents the potential confounding effects of Fetal Alcohol Syndrome (FAS) or Fetal Alcohol Effects (FAE). Also, participants are frequently required to have a minimum education level (e.g., 10 or 12 years). Often this information can be obtained only through subject self-report. Although there are questions of accuracy under such circumstances, this approach is superior to ignoring these potentially important variables. Furthermore, the inclusion of collateral reports is an effective means of checking the validity of subject reports.

It is also important that the performance of substance abusers be compared to an appropriate control group. Individuals with alcohol-related disorders do not generally demonstrate levels of performance that would place them in the clinically-impaired range (Nixon, 1995; Parsons, 1986). Therefore, the use of normative data may not be particularly revealing, except in unusual cases. In much of the literature, the comparison groups are samples of community-residing control subjects. This community control sample is appropriate in circumstances where, aside from treatment for substance abuse, the alcohol sample is also community-residing, relatively healthy, and largely

employed. Obviously, the same restrictions regarding health, education, and maternal alcoholism would be required for community control subjects.

Another issue concerns the role of a family history (FH) of alcoholism (aside from maternal alcohol use) on neurocognitive performance. There is now a large, but controversial, literature addressing this question (e.g., Bates & Pandina, 1992; Galanter, 1991; Gillen & Hesselbrock, 1992; Porjesz & Begleiter, 1993; Schandler, Cohen, McArthur, Antick, & Brannock, 1991; Schandler, Thomas, & Cohen, 1995). Inconsistencies arise from differences in the way family history is quantified among studies.

It is now clear that defining FH status on the basis of father alone is too simplistic. Alterman (1988) suggested several mechanisms for assessing FH. These procedures included considering family density, lineality, and the generational transmission of alcoholism. Some data suggest the procedures may be differentially sensitive to alcohol effects (Finn, Earleywine, & Pihl, 1992). Overall, however, it should be noted that the role of FH on neurocognitive performance appears to lack the predictive power first presumed (e.g., Eckardt, Stapleton, Rawlings, Davis, & Grodin, 1995; Glenn, Parsons, & Sinha, 1994; Hill, Steinhauer & Locke, 1995; Parsons & Nixon, 1993; Schafer et al., 1991).

Practical Considerations

A number of practical considerations must be considered. The assessment should be scheduled when the subject is unlikely to be fatigued or emotionally liable. Testing immediately after a difficult group therapy session will likely produce less than optimal performance. The test session should also be coordinated with therapeutic activities and family time. If these issues are overlooked, patients' level of cooperation and performance may be negatively affected. Similar concerns apply to the scheduling of control subjects. If these subjects are required to work all day and then complete the testing in the evening, their performance may also be compromised. Although inconvenient for examiners, weekend or holiday sessions may be more convenient for control subjects.

Battery Construction

The number of available instruments prohibits an exhaustive review (Knight & Longmore, 1994; Lezak, 1995; Spreen & Strauss, 1991). Therefore, only those most frequently encountered are outlined in Table 16.2. It should be recognized that these tests often assess skills from more than one neuropsychological domain. For example, the Trails B requires both perceptual–motor skills and set-shifting ability. These skills are associated with different brain areas. Therefore, the use of the Trails B alone would be inadequate to distinguish between deficits in these brain systems. To establish a finer discrimination, tests providing convergent validity would be required. That is, other tests presumed to separately measure each of the brain systems would be required.

It should also be noted that the tests listed in Table 16.2 are often sensitive to subtle cognitive dysfunction. The relevance of this subtle impairment on daily living tasks is not yet clear. In response to this concern, some investigators are using instruments that focus on tasks relevant to real-life situations. Some of these tasks are shown in Table 16.3.

Table 16.2 Tests Assessing Various Aspects of Neuropsychological Domains

	Overall Mental Assessment	
Test	*Comment*	*Specifics*
Halstead–Reitan Battery (HRB; Reitan & Wolfson, 1993)	Seldom administered in its entirety; subtests used to assess specific NP domains.	Subtests address multiple NP domains, including frontal lobe function and right and left hemisphere function. Provides an "impairment index" as the ratio of failed versus normal tests.
Shipley Institute of Living Scale (Zachary, 1986)	Provides "mental age" scores for vocabulary and abstracting skills. Allows estimate of overall conceptual quotient (i.e., a combination of vocabulary and abstracting skills) and WAIS-R IQ. Performance on the vocabulary test rarely is affected in chronic alcohol studies and often is used as a control measure.	40-item vocabulary test combined with a 20-item verbal problem-solving test. Both parts have items of varying difficulty.
Wechsler Adult Intelligence Scale, Revised (WAIS-R) (Wechsler, 1987a)	Seldom administered in its entirety; subscales used to assess specific neuropsychological (NP) domains.	11 subscales; 6 verbal scales and 5 performance scales. Provides measures of verbal IQ, performance IQ, and full-scale IQ.
	Learning and Memory: Verbal and Visualspatial	
Luria Words Test (Verbal) (Luria, 1976)	Ascertains acquisition patterns of information and differential memory. Uses common concrete nouns, thus reducing confounding issues of familiarity with the words or of abstracting ability.	Assesses acquisition and retention of 10 words over three time periods (2, 8, and 30 minutes).
Rey Auditory Verbal Learning Tests (RAVLT) (for information, see Lezak, 1995)	Not commonly used in alcohol-related studies. Lack of a published manual may contribute to this omission.	Measures the acquisition and retention of multiple verbal lists.
Russell's Version WMS (Russell, 1982)	Provides immediate and delayed (30 minutes) assessment, thus providing a means to determine memory function. Use of both subscales allows assessment of both left hemisphere (verbal memory) and right hemisphere (figural memory) function.	Uses two subscales of the WMS: memory for stories and memory for figural representations.

Wechsler Memory Scale (WMS; Wechsler, 1945, 1987b)	Selected subtests generally are used for specific research questions. Recent revisions of the scale may increase its use (for discussion, see Knight & Longmore, 1994).	Seven subtests assessing general knowledge, mental control, short-term memory, verbal learning, and memory for stories and figural representations.

Problem-Solving Abstracting

California Card Sorting Test (Beatty, Katzung, Nixon, & Moreland, 1993; Beatty & Monson, 1990, 1992; Delis et al., 1989)	Task demands and possible DVs are more extensive than in the WCST (discussed below).	Determines the ability to generate, execute, and identify conceptual strategies. Stimuli consist of cards varying in shape, color, size, and verbal labels.
Category Test (Reitan & Wolfson, 1993)	Component of HRB. Measures efficiency in rule acquisition.	For each of seven sets of items, subject must identify relation between the exemplar and four alternatives. Feedback regarding accuracy is provided after each response. Primary DV is the number of errors.
Conceptual Level Analogy Test (CLAT) (Willner, 1970, 1971)	Verbal problem-solving and abstracting test. Several studies using the CLAT have used abbreviated versions, reducing time requirements and providing items for test–retest protocols.	42 items addressing six levels of complexity, ranging from opposites (e.g., hot–cold, black–white) to two-category contrasts (e.g., wolf–dog, hurricane–breeze).
Wisconsin Card Sorting Test (WCST) (Heaton, 1981)	Classic test of the ability to shift problem-solving strategies with minimal feedback. Successful subjects respond with a change in sorting strategy when told that a sort is "incorrect." Computer assistance facilities test administration and scoring.	Subject sorts cards into one of four piles based on color, form, or number. Primary DVs [1] are the number of categories, and number of perseverative errors (i.e., failure to change categories).
Fluency (Newcomb, 1969; Thurstone, 1938)	Classic assessment of verbal production. Production has been studied for both phonetic and semantic tasks. Data from alcoholics are inconsistent. Some studies reveal significant effects; others do not (for review, see Hewett et al., 1991).	Subject produces as many words as possible beginning with a specific letter (phonetic) or belonging to a specific category (semantic) within a certain time.

Perceptual-Motor Skills

Grooved Pegboard Test (Sander, Nixon, & Parsons, 1989)	Time to completion with the nondominant hand is more sensitive to alcohol effects.	Subject places round, grooved pegs in a grooved pegboard. Task is completed first with the dominant hand, then with the nondominant hand. DV is the time to completion.
Trail Making Test, Form A and B (Reitan & Wolfson, 1993)	Subtest of the HRB; overall, form B appears more sensitive to alcohol effects. Also measures set-shifting. Time to completion is the more frequently reported DV.	Form A: Subject connects numbered dots (number 1 to number 25) with a line. Form B: Subject connects alternating numbers and letters (1 to A to 2 to B, etc.) With a line. DVs are time to completion and number of errors.

(Continued)

Table 16.2 *Continued*

WAIS-R Digit Symbol Substitution Test (Wechsler, 1987a)	A subtest of the WAIS frequently used in alcohol studies.	Subject copies the symbols assigned to digits 1 to 9 below each digit. The symbols are always available For reference. DV is the number of symbols correctly substituted in 90 seconds.
Visuospatial, Nonmemory Skills		
Little Men Test (Acker & Acker, 1982)	Computerized administration facilitates time and accuracy measurements.	A mannequin holding a briefcase is shown in one of four positions (i.e., upright, inverted, facing toward the subject, or facing away from the subject). Subject identifies which hand is holding the briefcase. DVs are reaction time and number of errors.
Mazes (Acker & Acker, 1982)	Part of the same test battery as the Little Men Test. Computerized administration facilitates time and accuracy measurement.	Subject identifies matching but rotated mazes. DVs are reaction time and number of errors.
Tactual Performance Test (Reitan & Wolfson, 1993)	Component of the HRB. Uses modification of Seguin–Goddard form board. Subject is prevented from visually inspecting board. Tests many skills including use of tactile spatial relations.	First task is to fit blocks into proper place with dominant hand while blindfolded. Nondominant hand is then used. Both hands are used in a third attempt. Time to complete is the primary DV. A memory component can be included if subjects are required to draw the board, including the placement of the blocks/shapes on the board without visual access.
WAIS-R-Block Design (Wechsler, 1987a)	Part of the WAIS-R test battery. Classic measure of visuospatial/perceptual–motor skills.	Subject reconstructs designs of red and white squares with a set of red and white blocks. DVs are time to completion of individual designs, number of designs completed, and number of completion errors.

Source: Adapted from "Assessing Cognitive Impairment" by S. J. Nixon, 1995, *Alcohol Health & Research World, 19,* pp. 97-103.

The primary factor that should direct the selection of tests is, of course, the underlying question. If the objective is to *describe* the effects of a substance on neuropsychological function, a wide array of tests might be selected—the purpose being to describe the drug's effects on a variety of neuropsychological functions.

If, on the other hand, there is a testable *hypothesis* regarding drug effects on a specific neuropsychological function, the better strategy might be to select a narrower set of tests. However, this set would include several tests that theoretically assess the neuropsychological function(s) of interest. As noted earlier, the inclusion of several related tests is critical in providing convergent validity. It is also important in eliminating confounds related to test administration, equipment failure, invalid or lost data, and so on.

There is another factor that influences battery construction: time. Many of the individual tests are quite short. When compiled into a battery, however, it is surprising how much time must be accounted for. For example, not only must the time for administration be considered, but also the time for set-up, instructions, and rest breaks.

Interpretation

As previously stated, neuropsychological assessments traditionally have been used in an attempt to localize dysfunction within a brain area or system. This approach has proven very useful in describing the nature of alcohol-related impairment and in directing research (Evert & Oscar-Berman, 1995; Oscar-Berman, 1987).

Recently, another approach has been applied. This approach is adopted from work in neurocognitive studies and focuses on the specific processes that underlie cognitive functioning (e.g., Evert & Oscar-Berman, 1995;

Table 16.3   Exemplars of Alternative Assessment Instruments

Test	Comment	Specifics
Plant Test (Erwin & Hunter, 1984; Nixon & Parsons, 1991)	Modeled from traditional cognitive development tasks, the test appeals to most participants. The task requires less than 5 minutes to administer.	Problem-solving task that requires the subject to identify and isolate relevant from irrelevant variables.
Adaptive Skills Battery (ASB) (Jones & Lanyon, 1981; Nixon et al., 1992)	Current data suggest that "typical" responses are more sensitive to alcohol effects. Test may require 30–45 minutes to administer. Standard scoring protocols are available.	Subject has to produce the "typical" response or the "best possible" response to 30 vignettes involving interpersonal relations.
Face–Name Learning (Becker et al., 1983; Schaeffer & Parsons, 1987)	The multitrial presentation format allows measurement of learning curves as well as of final performance levels.	Subject must learn the correct names for individual faces. Stimuli are presented at a constant pace. Multiple sets of tests are performed.
Rivermead Behavioral Memory Test (RBMT) (Wilson, 1987; Wilson et al., 1985)	Has been applied primarily with Wernicke–Korsakoff patients.	11 subtests assess performance on items relevant to successful independent functioning (e.g., remembering a short route, hidden object, or appointment).
California Verbal Learning Test (CVLT) (Delis et al., 1987, 1988)	The wide variety of dependent variables (i.e., measurements used in the test) makes the test appropriate for many alcohol-related questions.	Uses two different "shopping lists" to assess acquisition of verbal information. Dependent variables are rate of learning, use of strategies, accuracy, interference, order errors, persistence in errors, and confusion between lists.

Source: Reprinted from "Assessing cognitive impairment" by S. J. Nixon, 1995, *Alcohol Health & Research World, 19*, pp. 97–103.
[1]DV = Dependent variable, the measurement used in the test.

Nixon, 1993; Smith & Oscar-Berman, 1992). The tasks and performance requirements are not necessarily different from those associated with traditional neuropsychological assessment. The primary difference lies in the variables that are considered. For example, in both approaches subjects may be asked to memorize a story, draw a picture, or associate pairs of items. The traditional neuropsychological approach might contrast performance on verbal versus nonverbal tasks in an effort to identify differential impairment in the left and right hemispheres, respectively. In contrast, the neurocognitive approach might focus on identifying deficits in processes such as perception, attention, encoding or retrieval of information within and/or across verbal and nonverbal tasks. Obviously, the two approaches are not mutually exclusive and both have much to offer in the study of brain/behavior relations. Given the fact that both approaches can be applied to the same tasks, it would appear appropriate that both be used in future studies.

SUMMARY

Neuropsychological techniques have much to offer in clarifying the role of substance abuse/dependence on brain/behavior relations. The relatively well-defined links between specific tests and brain functions/systems provide a mechanism for understanding the effects of chronic substance abuse on both behavior and presumed CNS dysfunction. The sensitivity of the tests makes them useful in detecting even subtle levels of dysfunction. The noninvasive nature of the approach facilitates the cooperation of subjects whereas flexibility of test administration (computer or paper and pencil) enables the collection of data in virtually any setting. Neuropsychological assessment also may serve as a useful cost-effective initial evaluation or as a complementary evaluation in contexts where measurements are being obtained from other sources (e.g., MRI or CT).

The method is not without limitations, the primary one being its inability to localize function to a specific brain area. However, as we increasingly appreciate, the interactive nature of brain systems complicates the localization of function, regardless of method. Thus, the neuropsychological approach as both a clinical practice and method of inquiry continues to be a useful tool in the study of brain/behavior relations.

REFERENCES

Acker, W., & Acker, C. (1982). *Bexley Maudsley Automated Psychological Screening and Bexley Maudsley Category Sorting Test manual*. Berk, England: NFEK-Nelson.

Alterman, A. I. (1988). Patterns of familial alcoholism, alcoholism severity, and psychopathology. *Journal of Nervous and Mental Disease, 176,* 167–175.

Ardila, A., Rosselli, M., & Strumwasser, S. (1991). Neuropsychological deficits in chronic cocaine abusers. *International Journal of Neuroscience, 57,* 73–79.

Bates, M. E., & Pandina, R. J. (1992). Familial alcoholism and premorbid cognitive deficit: A failure to replicate subtype differences. *Journal of Studies on Alcohol, 53,* 320–327.

Beatty, W. W., Katzung, V. M., Moreland, V. J., & Nixon, S. J. (1995). Neuropsychological performance of recently abstinent alcoholics and cocaine-abusers. *Drug and Alcohol Dependence, 37,* 247–253.

Beatty, W. W., Katzung, V. M., Nixon, S. J., & Moreland, V. J. (1993). Problem-solving deficits in alcoholics: Evidence from the California Card Sorting Test. *Journal of Studies on Alcohol, 54,* 687–692.

Beatty, W. W., & Monson, N. (1990). Problem-solving in Parkinson's disease: Comparison of performance on the Wisconsin and California Card Sorting Tests. *Journal of Geriatric Psychiatry and Neurology, 3,* 163–171.

Beatty, W. W., & Monson, N. (1992). Problem-solving by patients with multiple sclerosis: Comparison of performance on the Wisconsin and California Card Sorting Tests. *Journal of Clinical and Experimental Neuropsychology, 14,* 32.

Becker, J. T., Butters, N., Hermann, A., & D'Angelo, N. (1983). Learning to associate names and faces: Impaired acquisition on an ecologically relevant memory task by male alcoholics. *Journal of Nervous and Mental Disease, 17,* 617–623.

Bruce, D. (1985). On the origin of the term "neuropsychology." *Neuropsychologia, 23,* 813–814.

Delis, D. C., Kramer, J. H., Kaplan, E., & Ober, B. A. (1987). *The California Verbal Learning Test.* New York: Psychological Corporation.

Delis, D. C., Freeland, J., Kramer, J. H., & Kaplan, E. (1988). Integrating clinical assessment with cognitive neuroscience: Construct validation of the California Verbal Learning Test. *Journal of Consulting and Clinical Psychology, 56,* 123–130.

Eckardt, M. J., Stapleton, J. M., Rawlings, R. R., Davis, E. Z., & Grodin, D. M. (1995). Neuropsychological functioning in detoxified alcoholics between 18 and 35 years of age. *American Journal of Psychiatry, 152,* 53–59.

Erwin, J. E., & Hunter, J. J. (1984). Prediction of attrition in alcoholic aftercare by scores on the embedded figures test and two Piagetian tasks. *Journal of Consulting and Clinical Psychology, 52,* 354–358.

Evert, D. L., & Oscar-Berman, M. (1995). Alcohol-related cognitive impairments: An overview of how alcoholism may affect the workings of the brain. *Alcohol Health and Research World, 19,* 89–96.

Finn, P. R., Earleywine, M., & Pihl, R. O. (1992). Sensation seeking, stress reactivity, and alcohol dampening discriminate the density of a family history of alcoholism. *Alcoholism: Clinical and Experimental Research, 16,* 585–590.

Galanter, M. (Ed.). (1991). *Recent developments in alcoholism: Children of alcoholics* (Vol. 9). New York: Plenum Press.

Gillen, R., & Hesselbrock, V. (1992). Cognitive functioning, ASP, and family history of alcoholism in young men at risk for alcoholism. *Alcoholism: Clinical and Experimental Research, 16,* 206–214.

Glenn, S. W., Parsons, O. A., & Sinha, R. (1994). Assessment of recovery of electrophysiological and neuropsychological functions in chronic alcoholics. *Biological Psychiatry, 36,* 443–452.

Heaton, R. K. (1981). *Wisconsin Card Sorting test manual.* Odessa, FL: Psychological Assessment Resources.

Hill, S. Y., Steinhauer, S., & Locke, J. (1995). Event-related potentials in alcoholic men, their high-risk male relatives and low-risk male controls. *Alcoholism: Clinical and Experimental Research, 19,* 567–576.

Hunt, W. A., & Nixon, S. J. (Eds.). (1993). *Alcohol-induced brain damage* (Research Monograph 22). Rockville, MD: National Institute on Alcohol Abuse and Alcoholism.

Jones, S. L., & Lanyon, R. I. (1981). Relationship between adaptive skills and outcome of alcoholism treatment. *Journal of Studies on Alcohol, 42,* 522–525.

Knight, R. G., & Longmore, B. E. (1994). *Clinical Neuropsychology of Alcoholism.* East Sussex, England: Erlbaum.

Kolb, B., & Whishaw, I. Q. (1995). *Fundamentals of human neuropsychology* (4th ed.). New York: W.H. Freeman.

Lezak, M. D. (1995). *Neuropsychological assessment* (3rd ed.). New York: Oxford University Press.

Luria, A. R. (1976). *The neuropsychology of memory.* New York: Wiley.

Newcomb, S. (1969). *Missile wounds of the brain.* London: Oxford University Press.

Nixon, S. J. (1993). Application of theoretical models to the study of alcohol-induced brain damage. In W. A. Hunt & S. J. Nixon (Eds.), *Alcohol-induced brain damage* (Research Monograph 22). Rockville, MD: National Institute on Alcohol Abuse and Alcoholism, pp. 213–228.

Nixon, S. J. (1995). Assessing cognitive impairment. *Alcohol Health & Research World, 19*, 97–103.

Nixon, S. J., & Parsons, O. A. (1991). Alcohol-related efficiency deficits using an ecologically valid test. *Alcoholism: Clinical and Experimental Research, 15*, 601–606.

Nixon, S. J., Tivis, R., & Parsons, O. A. (1992). Interpersonal problem-solving in male and female alcoholics. *Alcoholism: Clinical and Experimental Research, 16*, 684–687.

Oscar-Berman, M. (1987). Neuropsychological consequences of alcohol abuse: Questions, hypotheses, and models. In O. A. Parsons, N. Butters, & P. E. Nathan (Eds.), *Neuropsychology of alcoholism: Implications for diagnosis and treatment* (pp. 256–269). New York: Guilford Press.

Parsons, O. A. (1986). Alcoholics' neuropsychological impairment: Current findings and conclusions. *Annals of Behavioral Medicine, 8*, 13–19.

Parsons, O. A., & Nixon, S. J. (1993). Neurobehavioral sequelae of alcoholism. *Neurologic Clinics, 11*, 205–218.

Parsons, O. A., Butters, N., & Nathan, P. E. (Eds.). (1987). *Neuropsychology of alcoholism: Implications for diagnosis and treatment*. New York: Guilford Press.

Porjesz, B., & Begleiter, H. (1993). Neurophysiological factors associated with alcoholism. In W. A. Hunt & S. J. Nixon (Eds.), *Alcohol-induced brain damage* (Research Monograph 22, pp. 89–120). Rockville, MD: National Institute on Alcohol Abuse and Alcoholism.

Reitan, R. M., & Wolfson, D. (1993). *The Halstead–Reitan Neuropsychological Test Battery: Theory and clinical interpretation* (2nd ed.). South Tucson, AZ: Neuropsychology Press.

Russell, E. W. (1982). Factor analysis of the Revised Wechsler Memory Scale tests in a neuropsychological battery. *Perceptual and Motor Skills, 54*, 971–974.

Sander, A. M., Nixon, S. J., & Parsons, O. A. (1989). Pretest expectancies and cognitive impairment in alcoholics. *Journal of Consulting and Clinical Psychology, 57*, 705–709.

Schaeffer, K. W. & Parsons, O. A. (1987). Learning impairment in alcoholics using an ecologically relevant test. *Journal of Nervous and Mental Disease, 175*, 213–218.

Schafer, K., Butters, N., Smith, T., Irwin, M., Brown, S., Hanger, P., Grant, I., & Schuckit, M. (1991). Cognitive performance of alcoholics: A longitudinal evaluation of the role of drinking history, depression, liver function, nutrition, and family history. *Alcoholism: Clinical and Experimental Research, 15*, 653–660.

Schandler, S. L., Cohen, M. J., McArthur, D. L., Antick, J. R., & Brannock, J. C. (1991). Spatial learning deficits in adult children of alcoholic parents. *Journal of Consulting and Clinical Psychology, 59*, 312–317.

Schandler, S. L., Thomas, C. S., & Cohen, M. J. (1995). Spatial learning deficits in preschool children of alcoholics. *Alcoholism: Clinical and Experimental Research, 19*, 1067–1072.

Smith, M. E., & Oscar-Berman, M. (1992). Resource-limited information processing in alcoholism. *Journal of Studies on Alcohol, 53*, 514–518.

Spreen, O., & Strauss, E. (1991). *A compendium of neuropsychological tests: Administration, norms and commentary*. New York: Oxford University Press.

Thurstone, L. (1938). *Primary mental abilities*. Chicago: University of Chicago Press.

Tivis, R. D., Beatty, W. W., Nixon, S. J., & Parsons, O. A. (1995). Patterns of cognitive impairment among alcoholics: Are there subtypes? *Alcoholism: Clinical and Experimental Research, 19*, 496–500.

Wechsler, D. (1945). A standardized memory scale for clinical use. *Journal of Psychology, 19*, 87–95.

Wechsler, D. (1987a). *Wechsler Adult Intelligence Scale—Revised: Manual*. New York: Psychological Corporation.

Wechsler, D. (1987b). *Wechsler Memory Scale—Revised*. New York: Psychological Corporation.

Willner, A. E. (1970). Toward the development of more sensitive clinical tests of abstraction: The analogy test. *Proceedings of the 78th Annual Convention of the American Psychiatric Association*, 553–554.

Willner, A. E. (1971). *Conceptual Level Analogy Test*. New York: Cognitive Testing Service.

Wilson, B. (1987). Identification and remediation of everyday problems in memory-impaired patients. In O. A. Parsons, N. Butters, & P. E. Nathan (Eds.), *Neuropsychology of alcoholism: Implications for diagnosis and treatment* (pp. 322–338). New York: Guilford Press.

Wilson, B., Cockburn, J., & Baddeley, A. D. (1985). *The Rivermead Behavioral Memory Test*. Reading, England: Thames Valley Test Co.

Zachary, R. A. (1986). *Shipley Institute of Living Scale: Revised manual*. Los Angeles: Western Psychological Services.

CHAPTER 17

FAMILY ASSESSMENT

Danica Kalling Knight
D. Dwayne Simpson

A growing body of literature points to the impact of the family on the development of substance abuse and recovery from addiction (see Kaufman, 1991, for a review). Several studies examining the role of family have found that dysfunction is associated with greater problems, including more severe drug use and poorer psychosocial functioning (Bradshaw, 1988; Kaufman, 1989; Knight, Cross, Giles-Sims, & Simpson, 1995). Generally speaking, families of substance abusers are often characterized by poor interpersonal boundaries, poor communication, and lack of family differentiation (Kaufman, 1985; Maddux & Desmond, 1981; Stanton, Todd, & Associates, 1982). The impact of these dysfunctional relationships begins during childhood when much of the process of socialization normally takes place and continues in various forms into adolescence and adulthood.

Prospective studies that focus on the role of family factors in the onset and continuation of drug use usually examine adolescent users who are still living within the original family environment (e.g., Brody & Forehand, 1993; Bush, Weinfurt, & Iannoti, 1994; Kandel & Andrews, 1987). Sometimes these samples are followed into young adulthood, providing documentation of the role of the family in the development of deviant peer relations

and the transition from moderate to heavy drug use (e.g., Brook, Cohen, Whiteman, & Gordon, 1992). Dysfunctional relationships in the childhood families of addicted adult clients appear to have implications for social and psychological adjustment in adulthood as well. Individuals who recall relatively poor support from parents while growing up tend to have lower self-esteem, greater depression, and poorer social functioning upon entering drug treatment (Knight et al., 1995). Poorer psychosocial functioning not only places these individuals at greater risk for drug use (Simpson, Knight, & Ray, 1993; Stein, Newcomb, & Bentler, 1987), but also at greater risk for continuing the cycle of dysfunctional interaction with their family and friends.

Family functioning also has been shown to be important in an individual's recovery from substance abuse. Knight and Simpson (1996) found significant changes in family relationships over the first 3 months of outpatient drug treatment, and the magnitude of positive change was associated with personal progress during treatment. Follow-up studies of the posttreatment family environment of addicts likewise indicate that those who show greater or longer term improvements in substance use report healthier family systems (Billings & Moos, 1983). On the other hand, individuals who relapse following treatment report poorer family cohesion and greater family conflict than those who improve (Moos, Finney, & Chan, 1981; Moos & Moos, 1984; Stewart & Brown, 1993). When traditional follow-up outcome measures include assessments of social functioning, family factors continue to be highly predictive of favorable outcomes. For instance, Friedman, Tomko, and Utada (1991) report that higher scores on family organization, family independence, and parent–child communication were associated with more appropriate family role behavior, better relationships with mothers, and higher ratings of program effectiveness.

Family assessment among substance abusing populations therefore encompasses a wide variety of issues, including childhood relationships with parents, current family environment, and supportive family involvement during recovery stages. Relationships with family members may differ depending on the developmental phase of the individual, so their relevance for epidemiology and treatment outcome research depends in part on the age and stage of the substance abuser. The purpose of this chapter is to identify some major areas represented in the family functioning literature and discuss some prominent methodological issues that must be considered when assessing family factors. In addition, representative assessment tools for measuring various domains are presented.

METHODOLOGICAL ISSUES

Defining "Family"

An individual's psychological and social well being is tied closely to the quality of relationships experienced within the family, so it is useful to examine factors such as history of family interactions during childhood and relationships with family members in adulthood (Cromwell & Peterson, 1983). However, it is important first to identify which measurement domains are relevant to the research objectives. This depends in part on ages and family development stage as well as the addiction, treatment, or recovery phases being studied (Larsen & Olson, 1990). For example, family roles change developmentally from childhood to early adulthood (e.g., leaving home and marriage) to later adulthood (e.g., having children, divorce, widowhood), and relationships with parents, mates, and siblings must be interpreted within a generational context.

Responses to questions therefore can vary, depending on how "family" is defined. For example, family function-

ing might refer to the quality of interaction among family members in the substance user's family of procreation, or might be defined in terms of the extended family (including living parents, grandparents, aunts, uncles, siblings, and so on). This also is important when investigating the impact of drug use on children of substance users. For single parents, "family" may be limited to a mother and her children with little or no contact with extended family. In other instances, a large support network may be available to the single parent. Children may spend a significant amount of time in the care of other relatives, the father, or may be cared for by nonrelatives who function as significant support persons perceived as "family" by the child. Thus, the family must be assessed in a way that will accurately reflect the complexity of the substance user's situation.

If family systems are to be assessed, obtaining multiple perspectives of family functioning by interviewing or observing different members should be considered. Doing so can provide a relatively comprehensive picture of family interaction. For instance, a substance-abusing woman and her mother might describe family interactions very differently. Whereas the mother may view the family as closely knit with a high degree of interpersonal interaction, mutual enjoyment, and shared goals, the daughter may consider the same family unit as overbearing, inflexible, and as discouraging individual autonomy. Each family member's perspective represents a valid interpretation of the interpersonal relationships within that family and should be considered together when possible (Olson, 1977). Different perspectives on family functioning can help in understanding the etiology of substance abuse for a particular person or the process the person must go through for recovery. Discrepancies between family members may shed even further insight into these issues.

Assessment Strategies

Several data collection strategies are available for assessing family functioning. These generally fall into one of two categories, self-report and observational techniques.

Self-Report Measures

Self-reports commonly serve as the basis for assessing family functioning among substance-abusing populations because of the relative ease in administration. Typically, these measures consist of a series of questions requiring the respondent to choose an appropriate answer from a list of precoded responses. Assessments may be self-adminis-tered or conducted in an interview format and can address a wide range of topics including the individual's role in the family, interaction among family members, time spent with family, and degree of support. Self-report measures provide a subjective, "insider's" view into family interac-tion and are most useful in gaining insight into the atti-tudes and perceptions that an individual has about the family unit.

Although some degree of objectivity and accuracy may be sacrificed through the use of such measures (Maccoby & Martin, 1983), there is increasing acceptance among researchers of the importance of assessing participants' perceptions of relationships with others. Subjective reality has been found to be associated with interpersonal behav-ior (Gottman, 1979), and recollections of parent–child relationships during childhood may reflect the individual's success in dealing with adverse situations within the fam-ily (Main, 1991; Sroufe & Fleeson, 1986).

Several factors can influence the utility of self-report measures. First, the use of well-designed and reliable instruments is imperative. Information about the psycho-metric properties of family assessments, often provided with the instrument, should be consulted before making decisions about which instruments to use. Second, careful consideration should be given to the fact that respondents sometimes interpret response scales differently, depending on their personal histories and experience with completing questionnaires. Third, interviewing one family member provides only one person's view of family interactions. As discussed previously, it may be helpful to collect informa-tion from several family members. Information from alter-nate perspectives may be used to create a "family" composite measure by combining scores from members. Procedures for creating couple and family scores are dis-cussed by Larsen and Olson, 1990. Eliciting information from each member allows for a more objective and com-plete assessment of family functioning, but can present complications when one or more members are inaccessi-ble. This is particularly problematic when the family con-sists of children who are too young to read or comprehend questions asked with self-report measures.

Observational Measures

Generally speaking, two types of observational measures are used in family assessment; these include rating scales and coding schemes (for a thorough description of each,

see Grotevant & Carlson, 1989). Both methods are con-ducted by an observer so they represent an objective or "outsider's" perspective on family interaction. Rating scales require that the observer make global judgments about family interaction on several dimensions, depending on the rating scale used. Rating scales are relatively easy to construct and to administer, and because they require that the observer make summary judgments on each dimension rated, they are efficient tools for assessing fam-ily interaction. The challenge to using rating scales is the possibility of poor interrater reliability among observers. Schumm (1990) discusses reliability issues and methods of computation.

Unlike rating scales, coding schemes provide a microan-alytic assessment of family interaction. Observers are trained to identify and record specific behaviors of family members, rendering a detailed account of each group mem-ber's actions. Coding schemes can be laborious to use, but generally they are more reliable (Cairns & Green, 1979) and less biased (Hartmann, 1982) than rating scales. Furthermore, data collected in this manner are effective for identifying patterns of interaction, examining changes dur-ing the course of the interaction, and investigating each member's contribution to family interaction in greater detail.

Observational measures frequently require greater resources than do self-report measures, particularly in terms of the time required to train observers and conduct observations. Ideally, observations should be conducted in a standard location, and each family observed should be given the same task to complete in order to control for con-founding due to differences in the observational environ-ment. Depending on the resources available, however, the observer may or may not have control over all circum-stances under which the family is observed. Therefore, a "natural" environment such as the home is often a pre-ferred alternative. Although caution must be used in com-paring scores across families when assessments are conducted in unstructured settings, these observations can offer a more accurate account of some aspects of family functioning than self-report measures, thereby justifying the additional effort (Larsen & Olson, 1990).

Observational methods of data collection often are pre-ferred over self-report methods for several reasons. First, they are more objective because someone outside the fam-ily unit is trained to make judgments about the course of interactions. Second, there is greater flexibility in defining the unit of measurement. In instances where an entire fam-ily is being observed while interacting, one member or the entire family might be the focus. Third, more options are available in terms of which behaviors to measure. A broad range of verbal and nonverbal actions of each family member can be recorded sequentially, or only specific behaviors that are of interest to the researcher can be assessed (e.g., recording only those behaviors considered aggressive in nature). A fourth strength of observational measures is that scores for the entire family system can be derived from a single observation. In order to get complete and unbiased assessments of the entire family system using self-report measures, each family member must contribute their perspective by completing the forms. Composite scores can then be constructed using data from all family members.

Although there are clear advantages to using observational methods, it is not always possible to conduct these types of assessments with substance-abusing populations. Procedures for collecting observational data are time consuming, costly in terms of data collection and reduction, and require a commitment from each family member being observed. If family members attend sessions with the addicted member, then observations can be conducted within a regularly scheduled session. However, family members are sometimes inaccessible and complete data are therefore unavailable.

A second consideration involves the time it takes to train observers and establish interrater reliability. On the one hand, training counselors to use rating scales requires that each counselor defines the psychological constructs and response scales in a consistent manner. On the other hand, using coding schemes requires that counselors be trained in identifying specific target behaviors while simultaneously recording them onto a coding sheet. To obtain a measure of interrater reliability, pairs of observers must make independent judgments on the behavior they witness during family interaction. To do this, both observers have to be present at the time of the assessment or the interaction should be videotaped for later coding.

MEASURES OF BACKGROUND AND CURRENT FUNCTIONING

Studies on family functioning have focused primarily on parent–child relationships in one's family of origin and on current (or recent) status of family relationships. As described next, specialized assessment procedures developed in this field of research have helped identify some of the major dynamics in dysfunctional families and have

been adapted for clinical use in family counseling. These results also have implications for the development of substance abuse problems and recovery. Thus, research findings and assessments that illustrate prominent functional attributes of family systems were selected for this measurement overview.

Family of Origin

In the early years of human development, family plays a primary role in the socialization process, with parents exerting unparalleled influence on children (Peterson & Rollins, 1987). Findings from studies on the quality of parent–child relationships and the implications for later socioemotional development suggest that poorer quality relationships in infancy and early childhood are related to adjustment problems, including a greater propensity to use and abuse drugs later in life (see Glantz, 1992, for a review). The impact of poorer quality relationships also has been found to extend into adulthood. For instance, among adult heroin addicts, recollections of poor parental support during childhood were associated with lower psychological and social functioning upon entry into drug treatment (Knight, Broom, Cross, & Simpson 1996; Knight et al., 1995).

Whereas dysfunctional parent–child relationships in childhood may adversely effect the development of self-esteem and self-efficacy (Cassidy, 1988), early interactions with parents also serve as the foundation for later friendships and intimate relations (Hazan & Shaver, 1987; Patterson, DeBaryshe, & Ramsey, 1989). Individuals who experience family dysfunction and who choose to associate with deviant peers are at even greater risk for engaging in deviant lifestyles as adolescents and adults (Brook et al., 1992).

Self-Report Instruments

Several instruments are available for assessing an individual's memories and current representation of relationships with parents during childhood.

The Adult Attachment Interview (AAI) (George, Kaplan, & Main, 1996; Main, Kaplan & Cassidy, 1985) is a structured interview designed to assess the quality of childhood attachment relationships from the perspective of the adult. Clients are asked to recall specific aspects of their childhood relationships with parents or primary caregivers and to consider how these early relationships have influenced their personality and relationships in adulthood. Most questions are open-ended and responses are later scored.

Two primary methods are used for scoring the AAI. One is the Adult Attachment Rating and Classifying System (ARC), developed by Main and Goldwyn (in press). Responses are rated according to how well the individual is able to describe and evaluate early relationships in a coherent and thoughtful manner. Ratings are then used to assign the respondent to one of three classifications: secure/autonomous, dismissing, or preoccupied. These classifications parallel Ainsworth, Blehar, Waters, and Wall's (1978) patterns of infant attachment identified through the Strange Situation Procedure.

Another method for scoring the AAI is the Adult Attachment Interview Q-Set (AAQ) developed by Kobak (1988). Responses are scored by sorting 100 statements into nine categories, ranging from least to most characteristic. The statements reflect characteristics of the attachment classifications used in the ARC Coding System described previously. The distribution is then used to classify individuals along two dimensions, security–anxiety and repression–preoccupation, by comparing the actual Q-Set to a prototypical arrangement of statements for each dimension. Correlations between the actual ratings and the prototype are then used to classify the individual as secure/autonomous, dismissing, or preoccupied. Interrater correlations ranged from .58 to .92, with a mean of .74 (Kobak, Cole, Ferenz-Gillies, & Fleming, 1993).

Because of its format, the Adult Attachment Interview and corresponding scoring systems require in-depth training on administration and scoring procedures. Although detailed information about childhood relationships and the ways in which respondents have come to terms with their histories is informative, the training requirements limit the AAI's accessibility.

The Epstein Mother/Father/Peer Scale (Epstein, 1983) is designed to assess memories of relationships during childhood. This instrument is self-administered and requires that respondents answer a series of questions using a 5-point Likert scale ranging from strongly disagree to strongly agree. Relationships with mother and father are assessed separately using identical sets of 23 questions each. An assessment of peer relationships is also included as part of this instrument. Responses provide an assessment of early relationships along two dimensions: acceptance versus rejection, and encouragement of independence versus overprotection. Reliability coefficients range from .82 to .91.

Because female addicts experience frequent physical, sexual, or emotional abuse during childhood and abuse histories are often related to substance use (Miller, Downs, & Testa, 1993; Teets, 1995), it is important to obtain abuse histories. The Childhood Trauma Questionnaire (Bernstein et al., 1994) is a retrospective assessment obtained through a series of 70 questions measuring the degree of physical and emotional abuse, emotional neglect, sexual abuse, and physical neglect experienced during childhood. This instrument is self-administered, has high internal consistency (Cronbach's coefficient alpha ranges from .79 to .94), and has good test–retest reliability over a 2- to 6-month period (intraclass correlation = .88).

Another self-administered instrument, the Conflict Tactics Scales (CTS) (Straus, 1979), also can be used as a retrospective measure of family conflict during childhood (c.f., Miller et al., 1993). The CTS yields scores on three domains: verbal aggression, moderate violence, and severe violence. It is widely used to measure marital conflict and has internal consistency coefficients ranging from .50 to .88. Using the CTS to measure different areas of family functioning can facilitate comparisons between retrospective accounts of conflict during childhood and reports of marital conflict in adulthood.

Current Family Environment

Individuals who experience dysfunctional relationships in the family of origin often recreate them in their family of marriage (Harbin & Maziar, 1975). Therefore, current family interaction is in part a function of the individual's family history, particularly if extended family members (i.e., living parents, etc.) are included. Defining the current family system is complex because it may be limited to the individual's family of procreation (which may be one intact unit, or may consist of two or more family units as a result of divorce or remarriage) or may include extended family members (parents, aunts, uncles, siblings, etc.) in addition to the nuclear family. The instruments discussed next can provide information on each by varying the instructions given to respondents.

Assessing the current family environment is among the most challenging aspects of family measurement, in part because of the difficulty in defining the family unit and also because of the inherent complexity of measuring a dynamic system that is comprised of several members. A variety of assessment and classification approaches have been developed and are discussed in greater detail elsewhere (Grotevant & Carlson, 1989; Jacob & Tennenbaum, 1988; Olson & Tiesel, 1993; Touliatos, Perlmutter, & Straus, 1990). The self-report instruments and observational techniques described next are appropriate for use with substance-abusing populations, and most have undergone extensive psychometric work to establish their reliability and validity.

Self-Report Instruments

The Conflict Tactics Scales (CTS) developed by Straus (1979) measures how frequently various strategies are used to resolve conflicts between family members. For the self-administered version (Form A), respondents indicate how frequently each of 14 actions occur using a 6-point Likert scale ranging from "never" to "once a month." Scores are then computed for each of three scales: reasoning, verbal aggression, and violence. The CTS is widely used in the developmental and family literature to assess various dyadic relationships including husband–wife, father–child, mother–child, and child–child. An interview version (Form N) that consists of 19 items is also available. Internal consistency for the self-administered version was computed using item-total correlations that ranged from .44 to .91. Alpha coefficients were computed for the interview form and ranged from .50 to .88. Some of the items are very direct in assessing interpersonal violence (e.g., "pushed, grabbed, or shoved her"), and for this reason may be subject to social desirability, particularly when the interview version is used.

The Family Environment Scale (FES) developed by Moos and Moos (1981) was one of the first family measurement tools available for assessing a variety of current family characteristics. It consists of 90 true–false items and provides information along three dimensions of family functioning: relationships, personal growth, and system maintenance. The relationship dimension reflects family communication and mutual support and is subdivided into three scales: family cohesion, expressiveness, and conflict. The personal growth dimension reflects the extent to which family members encourage independence and participation in various types of activities, including religious activities. It is subdivided into five scales: independence, achievement orientation, intellectual–cultural orientation, active–recreational orientation, and moral–religious emphasis. The third dimension, system maintenance, reflects the degree to which the family system is structured and rule-bound, and includes two scales: organization and control. Three differ-

ent versions of the FES are available to assess perceptions of actual functioning (Real Form), ideal functioning (Ideal Form), and expected functioning (Expectations Form). The Expectations Form is particularly useful in situations where the family is undergoing change (i.e., foster families, remarriage). The reliability of the scales ranges from .61 to .78. Test–retest reliability ranges from .68 to .86 when measured over a 2-month period.

The Family Adaptability and Cohesion Evaluation Scales (FACES II) (Olson, Portner, & Bell, 1982) is another widely used measure of family functioning. The development of this instrument was theoretically driven by the Circumplex Model (Olsen, 1989; Olsen, Russell, & Sprenkle, 1980; 1983), assessing family interaction along two primary dimensions (cohesion and adaptability) and one secondary dimension (communication). Cohesion reflects the degree of mutual respect, affection, and support among members, whereas adaptability reflects the ease with which the family changes its rules, expectations, and organization in response to stressful situations. The quality of family communication interacts with each of the two primary dimensions, differentially influencing scores on each. Extreme scores on either dimension imply dysfunctional family interactions; the optimal score falls in the center of the two dimensions and is considered "balanced" family interaction. Its ability to capture the curvilinear nature of family classifications is unique to FACES and is useful in clinical settings (Olsen & Tiesel, 1993).

FACES is self-administered and consists of 30 items that require the respondent to indicate the most appropriate response from a 5-point Likert scale. Although two versions of FACES are available (II and III), FACES II is recommended for research purposes because of its higher reliability due in part to a larger number of items (30 versus 20 items). Internal consistency for FACES II ranges from .62 to .87; test–retest reliability ranges from .80 to .83 over a 1-month period. Version IV of the FACES is currently being developed.

The McMaster Family Assessment Device (FAD) developed by Epstein, Baldwin, and Bishop (1983) consists of 60 items designed to assess general family functioning. Client responses are combined into six scales representing affective involvement, behavioral control, family roles, problem solving, communication, and affective responsiveness. Internal consistency for the seven scales ranges from .72 to .92; test–retest reliability ranges from .66 to .74 over a 1-week period. The FAD is particularly useful in distinguishing between healthy and unhealthy families, and is therefore beneficial for use with clinical samples.

The Family Assessment Measure (FAM III) (Skinner, Steinhauer, & Santa-Barbara, 1983; 1994) is another comprehensive assessment of the family environment. It is designed to assess three conceptually separate but interconnected family units. The respondent is instructed to answer questions regarding how the family operates as a whole (General scale, 50 items), how pairs of members interact with each other (Dyadic–Relationships scale, 42 items), and how the individual views his or her own participation in the family (Self-Rating scale, 42 items). Each scale assesses seven components of family functioning, including affective involvement, control, role performance, task accomplishment, communication, affective expression, and values and norms. A unique feature is that it requires that respondents describe interaction of the family as a whole as well as for its parts, thereby providing different perspectives into the individual's view of family functioning. Internal consistency for the three scales ranges from .89 to .95.

The Self-Report Family Inventory (SFI) (Hulgus, Hampson, & Beavers, 1985) is a 36-item self-administered tool for assessing family functioning. Respondents answer questions using a 5-point Likert scale ranging from "fits our family well" to "does not fit our family well." Scores are computed for six scales reflecting family health, conflict, communication, cohesion, directive leadership, and expressiveness. Internal consistency ranges from .84 to .88 for the instrument as a whole, but is not available for the individual subscales. Test–retest reliability was measured over 1-month and 3-month periods and ranged from .30 to .87.

Observational Measures

A wide range of observational methods also are available that are designed to assist observers in recording various aspects of family interaction. The presentation of available rating scales will include only those that have been developed as companions to the self-rating instruments discussed in the previous section. The presentation of coding schemes will highlight three methods that were not developed as companions to the self-rating instruments but provide comprehensive methods for quantifying family interaction. Readers should refer to Grotevant and Carlson (1989) for a more complete review and discussion of available observational methods.

The Clinical Rating Scale for the Circumplex Model of Marital and Family Systems (Olson & Killorin, 1985) is the

counterpart to the Family Adaptability and Cohesion Evaluation Scales (FACES). Observations are conducted in a semistructured interview format. The family is typically asked as a group to describe how they handle certain issues such as discipline, decision making, and conflict. Using either a 6- or 8-point Likert scale (depending on the item), the interviewer rates either the family as a whole or specific dyads on three dimensions: cohesion (e.g., emotional bonding, family involvement, parent–child coalitions), adaptability (e.g., discipline, negotiation, roles), and communication (e.g., respect and regard, freedom of expression, listener's skills). Interrater reliability was calculated using interrater correlations (ranging from .84 to .92) and using percentage agreement (ranging from 89 to 94).

The McMaster Clinical Rating Scale was developed by Epstein et al. (1983) and is theoretically consistent with the McMaster Family Assessment Device (FAD). A family clinical interview or family therapy session is videotaped and later rated along the same dimensions as the FAD. These dimensions include affective involvement, behavioral control, family roles, problem solving, communication, and affective responsiveness. A seventh dimension, overall family functioning, is also rated in the clinical rating scale version. Scores range from 1 to 7 representing severely disturbed to superior functioning. Interrater reliability was computed using interrater correlations and ranged from .68 to .88.

The Family Assessment Measure Clinical Rating Scale (FAM-CRS) (Skinner & Steinhauer, 1986) is the counterpart to the Family Assessment Measure (FAM). Observations occur during a structured clinical interview with all family members, and scores ranging from 1 (major strength) to 5 (major weakness) are assigned. The family as a whole is rated along six of the seven original components of family functioning including affective involvement, control, role performance, task accomplishment, communication, and values and norms. Information on interrater reliability is not available.

The Beavers Interactional Competence Scale (BICS) (Beavers, 1977; Hampson, Hulgus, Beavers, & Beavers, 1988) and the Beavers Interactional Style Scale (BISS) (Kelsey-Smith & Beavers, 1981) are designed to be used together and are both companions to the Self-Report Family Inventory (SFI). Although the specific domains assessed by each differ slightly, all three assessment devices are based on the Beavers Systems Model of Family Functioning (Beavers, Hampson, & Hulgus, 1985). Ratings on both the BICS and the BISS can be based on one 10- to

15-minute observation. Family members are asked to discuss what they would like to change about their family and interaction is videotaped for later coding. The BICS assesses functioning along six dimensions, which include structure of family (i.e., overt power, parental coalition, closeness), mythology, goal-directed negotiation, autonomy (i.e., clarity of expression, responsibility, permeability), family affect (i.e., range of feelings, mood and tone, unresolvable conflict, empathy) and global health/pathology. The first five dimensions are comprised of 12 scales; all scales including global health/pathology are rated on a 5-point Likert scale ranging from 1 (healthiest) to 5 (dysfunctional). Interrater reliability was assessed using interrater correlations and ranged from .72 to .88 with a median of .84; internal consistency for the scale as a whole is .94 (Hampson, Beavers, & Hulgus, 1989).

The BICS is designed to measure family style using eight subscales, each of which is rated on a 5-point Likert scale ranging from 1 (highly centripetal—most satisfaction sought inside the family) to 5 (highly centrifugal—most satisfaction sought outside the family). The aspects of interaction that are rated include dependency needs, style of adult conflict, proximity, social presentation, verbal expression of closeness, aggressive/assertive behaviors, expression of positive/negative feelings, and global centripetal/centrifugal rating. Interrater correlations ranged from .62 to .83, with a median of .70; internal consistency for the scale is .94 (Hampson et al., 1989).

The Family Interaction Coding System (FICS) developed by Patterson, Ray, Shaw, and Cobb (1969) is a useful method for coding family interaction. This system is based on social learning theory and focuses on aggressive and prosocial behaviors exhibited by family members. Observations are conducted during a semistructured activity in the home environment with all family members present. Although all are interacting together, pairs of participants are chosen for the focus of observation for 5-minute intervals and all combinations of family members are targeted during a 70-minute period. Behavioral units are assigned one or more of 29 possible codes including (but not limited to) approval, compliance, cry, disapproval, destructiveness, humiliate, ignore, indulgence, laugh, noncompliance, negativism, talk, tease, touch, whine, work, and yell. Interrater reliability was calculated by Reid (1978) using percentage agreement (ranging from .30 to .96) and using interrater correlations (ranging from .59 to 1.00).

Another coding scheme designed to measure family functioning is the Interaction Process Coding Scheme (IPCS) developed by Bell, Bell, and Cornwell (1982). With this system, families are observed as a unit during a structured task, and the speech of each participant is recorded. First, each family member is instructed to complete the Moos Family Environment Scale (FES) independently. After they have each completed the form, the family is asked to discuss items on which they disagree and come to a consensus. Each individual speech unit uttered during the interaction is coded for one or more of the following: topic (e.g., interruptions, task avoidance), orientation (e.g., questions, compliance demands, assertion of fact or opinion), focus (e.g., feelings, attitudes, behaviors), support (e.g., rating of acceptance of rejection from tone of voice), and acknowledgment (e.g., no response, invalidation, recognition). Interrater reliability was computed using percentage agreement and ranged from .71 to .97. Although individual responses on the FES are not used in this coding scheme, its administration as part of the task requirements makes this coding scheme useful when the research design includes administering the FES.

Since the degree of individuation in the family system has been implicated in the etiology of substance use (Humes & Humphrey, 1994; Stanton, 1978), the Individuation Code developed by Condon, Cooper, and Grotevant (1984) is particularly of interest for use with families of substance abusers. Observations are conducted in the home environment and family members are given 20 minutes to plan a hypothetical trip together. The family as a whole can serve as the unit of observation, or specific dyads can be targeted. The speech of individual family members is recorded and each independent clause is coded for a response to previous conversation and a new contribution on the part of the participant. Specific behaviors coded include (but are not limited to) the following: suggests action directly, indirect suggestion, acknowledgment, compromise, direct disagreement, indirect disagreement, and requests information/validation. Interrater reliability ranges from 52% to 100%.

Constraints Associated with Applied Research

The self-report instruments and observational methods discussed thus far were developed for use primarily as clinical assessment tools. They provide a wealth of information useful for diagnostic and intervention purposes. Although these comprehensive inventories of family relationships have several advantages, constraints on the amount of time available for data collection often preclude the use of such labor- and time-intensive methods when conducting research in applied settings. In order to assess efficiently a wide range of sociodemographic, personality, and social characteristics that might impact treatment effectiveness, assessment methods often must be abbreviated or simplified. It is not always possible to administer long, specialized instruments in such instances.

Several instruments have been developed that assess major components of individual and family functioning using a smaller set of items. One such instrument is the Addiction Severity Index (ASI) developed by McLellan and colleagues (McLellan et al., 1992; McLellan, Luborsky, O'Brien, & Woody, 1980). Respondents are asked a variety of questions that measure medical status, employment, drug/alcohol use, legal status, family/social relations and psychiatric problems. Although items pertaining to family history and current functioning are included in the ASI, they are global in nature and do not assess specific aspects of family functioning such as the degree of interpersonal conflict and support for treatment.

The TCU/DATAR Intake Form (Simpson, 1992) is another comprehensive interview designed for use with substance-abusing populations. It also assesses characteristics of the individual's childhood family environment, but includes a more comprehensive set of items than does the ASI. These include questions pertaining to the number of times parents were divorced, the age(s) at which divorce occurred, the presence or absence of a parent or stepparent, parental drug use and treatment history, and the frequency of family attendance at religious services. This instrument also contains a 24-item assessment of the client's recollection of parent–child relationships and yields composite scores on parental support and parent–child conflict for both mother and father. Reliability coefficients range from .47 to .80, with a median of .70 (Knight et al., 1995).

The TCU/DATAR Intake Form also measures characteristics of the current family environment and includes questions about family size, the degree to which family members use illegal substances, the amount of time spent with family members, and the degree to which the family supports and participates in treatment. An additional nine items assess client's perceptions of cohesion and conflict among family members. Reliability coefficients are .79 for both cohesion and conflict (Joe & Simpson, 1993).

Another instrument that measures current family functionings is the Family, Friends, and Self (FFS) assessment scales (Simpson & McBride, 1992). It was developed specifically for research primarily with Mexican American adolescents but has been used with other race–ethnic samples as well. Family functioning is one of four general areas measured by the FFS; other areas include peer relations, self-esteem, and quality of life. Responses to 25 items are used to assess three dimensions of current family functioning including warmth, control, and conflict. Reliability coefficients range from .74 to .91.

SUMMARY

A wide variety of instruments exist that are specifically designed to assess family functioning. Each assessment tool renders a unique picture of the family system that can be useful for both clinical and research purposes. In choosing which methods to use with a particular substance-abusing population, the evaluator should (a) determine which domains of family functioning are to be the focus of the evaluation, (b) assess the resources available for administration and coding of interviews or observations, (c) decide whether information about family functioning will be restricted to client perceptions or if family members will also be accessible, and (d) choose assessment protocols that can be administered successfully given these limitations and that can provide meaningful information.

Involvement of family members in the treatment process presents several options for assessing family functioning. Observational methods require that the family only be observed at one point in time and do not address directly the degree to which family members participate in treatment with the client. Preliminary studies investigating the effectiveness of family-oriented treatment strategies suggest that when family therapy is included as part of the treatment requirements, client retention and recidivism rates improve (see Kaufman, 1991, for a review). Assessing family participation in treatment may provide useful information about the client's prognosis and about the quality of family support mechanisms available after discharge.

Family participation in treatment can be assessed through several different means. A relatively straightforward method of assessing family involvement involves monitoring attendance at family therapy sessions and treatment-sponsored events. A structured interview that includes questions about family members' involvement can also be administered to the client or to individual members. Questions might include the degree to which family members support the client's treatment efforts, specific issues addressed in family therapy sessions, and opinions about the utility of family sessions.

Family participation also may be assessed through observational methods such as those just described. For example, changes in family interaction can be assessed over time and related to client progress in other areas.

In addition to family participation, greater emphasis within the field of family assessment recently has been placed on examining the quality of parenting that substance users provide to their children and evaluating the nature of parent–child interaction. Unfortunately, many substance users have inadequate parenting skills and fairly poor relationships with their children (see Mayes, 1995, for a review). Although relationships between parent and child can be examined within the context of the family system using the assessment methods described in this chapter, there are numerous assessment tools available that are specifically designed to assess parenting and parent–child interaction. Most have evolved within the developmental psychology literature for use with nonclinical samples, but several have been developed specifically for use with pathological families or families at risk. Some instruments have been used successfully with substance-abusing populations as well. It was beyond the scope of this chapter to describe comprehensive assessments of parenting skills and parent–child relationships, but they are reviewed elsewhere (e.g., Barnard & Kelly, 1990; Grotevant & Carlson, 1989; Holden & Edwards, 1989; Mayes, 1995).

Assessing the degree of family cohesion, support, and conflict experienced by a substance-abusing individual, both during childhood and in the current family environment, can help researchers and clinicians better understand how family factors contribute to the development of substance abuse problems. Furthermore, information about the quality of client's current relationships with family members can be used in planning effective treatment strategies, thus improving the likelihood of successful recovery.

AUTHOR NOTE

Correspondence concerning this chapter should be addressed to: Danica Kalling Knight, Ph.D., Institute of Behavioral Research, Texas Christian University, TCU Box 298740, Fort Worth, TX 76129.

REFERENCES

Ainsworth, M. D. S., Blehar, M. C., Waters, E., & Wall, S. (1978). *Patterns of attachment: A psychological study of the strange situation*. Hillsdale, NJ: Erlbaum.

Barnard, K. E., & Kelly, J. F. (1990). Assessment of parent–child interaction. In S. J. Meisels & J. P. Shonkoff (Eds.), *Handbook of early childhood intervention* (pp. 278–302. New York: Cambridge.

Beavers, W. R. (1977). *Psychotherapy and growth: A family systems perspective*. New York: Brunner/Mazel.

Beavers, W. R., Hampson, R. B., & Hulgus, Y. F. (1985). Commentary: The Beavers Systems approach to family assessment. *Family Process, 24*, 398–405.

Bell, D. C., Bell, L. G., & Cornwell, C. (1982). *Interaction process coding scheme*. Houston: University of Houston at Clear Lake City.

Bernstein, D. P., Fink, L., Handelsman, L., Foote, J., Lovejoy, M., Wenzel, K., Sapareto, E., & Ruggiero, J. (1994). Initial reliability and validity of a new retrospective measure of child abuse and neglect. *American Journal of Psychiatry, 151*, 1132–1136.

Billings, A. G., & Moos, R. H. (1983). Psychosocial processes of recovery among alcoholics and their families: Implications for clinicians and program evaluators. *Addictive Behaviors, 8*, 205–218.

Bradshaw, J. (1988). *Healing the shame than binds you*. Deerfield Beach, FL: Health Communications.

Brody, G. H., & Forehand, R. (1993). Prospective associations among family form, family processes, and adolescents' alcohol and drug use. *Behaviour Research and Therapy, 32*, 587–593.

Brook, J. S., Cohen, P., Whiteman, M., & Gordon, A. S. (1992). Psychosocial risk factors in the transition form moderate to heavy use or abuse of drugs. In M. Glantz & R. Pickens (Eds.), *Vulnerability to drug abuse* (pp. 359–388). Washington, DC: American Psychological Association.

Bush, P. J., Weinfurt, K. P., & Iannotti, R. J. (1994). Families versus peers: Developmental influences on drug use from Grade 4–5 to Grade 7–8. Special issue: Diversity and development of Asian Americans. *Journal of Applied Developmental Psychology, 15*, 437–456.

Cairns, R. B., & Green, J. A. (1979). Appendix A: How to assess personality and social patterns. In R. B. Cairns (Ed.), *The analysis of social interactions: Methods, issues, and illustrations* (pp. 209–255). Hillsdale, NJ: Erlbaum.

Cassidy, J. (1988). Child–mother attachment and the self in six-year-olds. *Child Development, 59*, 121–135.

Condon, S. L., Cooper, C. R., & Grotevant, H. D. (1984). Manual for the analysis of family discourse. *Psychological Documents, 14*, Ms. No. 2616.

Cromwell, R. E., & Peterson, G. W. (1983). Multisystem-multimethod family assessment in clinical contexts. *Family Process, 22*, 147–164.

Epstein, N. B., Baldwin, L., & Bishop, D. (1983). The McMaster family assessment device. *Journal of Marital and Family Therapy, 9*, 213–228.

Epstein, S. (1983). *The Mother–Father–Peer Scale*. Unpublished manuscript. University of Massachusetts, Amherst.

Friedman, A. S., Tomko, L. A., & Utada, A. (1991). Client and family characteristics that predict better family therapy outcome for adolescent drug abusers. *Family Dynamics of Addiction Quarterly, 1,* 77–93.

George, C., Kaplan, N., & Main, M. (1996). *The Adult Attachment Interview* (3rd ed.). Berkeley: University of California, Department of Psychology.

Glantz, M. D. (1992). A developmental psychopathology model of drug abuse vulnerability. In M. Glantz & R. Pickens (Eds.), *Vulnerability to drug abuse* (pp. 389–418).

Gottman, J. M. (1979). *Marital interaction: Experimental investigations.* New York: Academic Press.

Grotevant, H. D., & Carlson, C. I. (1989). *Family Assessment: A guide to methods and measures.* New York: Guilford Press.

Hampson, R. B., Beavers, W. R., & Hulgus, Y. F. (1989). Insiders' and outsiders' views of family: The assessment of family competence and style. *Journal of Family Psychology, 3,* 118–136.

Hampson, R. B., Hulgus, Y. R., Beavers, W. R., & Beavers, J. S. (1988). The assessment of competence in families with a retarded child. *Journal of Family Psychology, 2*(1), 32–53.

Harbin, H. T., & Maziar, H. M. (1975). The families of drug abusers: A literature review. *Family Process, 14,* 411–431.

Hartmann, D. P. (Ed.). (1982). *Using observers to study behavior: New directions for methodology of social and behavior science.* San Francisco: Jossey-Bass.

Hazan C., & Shaver, P. (1987). Romantic love conceptualized as an attachment process. *Journal of Personality and Social Psychology, 52,* 511–524.

Holden, G. W., & Edwards, L. A. (1989). Parental attitudes toward child rearing: Instruments, issues, and implications. *Psychological Bulletin, 106,* 29–58.

Hulgus, Y. F., Hampson, R. B., and Beavers, W. R. (1985). *Self-report family inventory.* Dallas, TX: Southwest Family Institute.

Humes, D. L., & Humphrey, L. L. (1994). A multimethod analysis of families with a polydrug-dependent or normal adolescent daughter. *Journal of Abnormal Psychology, 103,* 676–685.

Jacob, T., & Tennenbaum, D. L. (1988). *Family assessment: Rationale, methods, and future directions.* New York: Plenum.

Joe, G. W., & Simpson, D. D. (1993). *Development of composite variables from DATAR intake interview.* Fort Worth: Texas Christian University, Institute of Behavioral Research.

Kandel, D. B., & Andrews, K. (1987). Processes of adolescent socialization by parents and peers. *The International Journal of the Addictions, 22,* 319–342.

Kaufman, E. (1985). Family systems and family therapy of substance abuse: An overview of two decades of research and clinical experience. *The International Journal of the Addictions, 20,* 897–916.

Kaufman, G. (1989). *The psychology of shame: Theory and treatment of shame-syndromes.* New York: Springer.

Kaufman, E. (1991). The family in drug and alcohol addiction. In N. S. Miller (Ed.), *Comprehensive handbook of drug and alcohol addiction* (pp. 851–876). New York: Marcel Dekker.

Kelsey-Smith, M., & Beavers, W. R. (1981). Family assessment: Centripetal and centrifugal family systems. *American Journal of Family Therapy, 9,* 3–12.

Knight, D. D., Broom, K. M., Cross, D. R., & Simpson, D. D. (1996). Deviance in adulthood: *Potential long-term effects of parental absence, support, and conflict during childhood.* Manuscript submitted for publication.

Knight, D. K., Cross, D. R., Giles-Sims, J., & Simpson, D. D. (1995). Psychosocial functioning among adult drug users: The role of parental absence, support, and conflict. *The International Journal of the Addictions, 30,* 1271–1288.

Knight, D. K., &. Simpson, D. D. (1996). Influences of family and friends on client progress during drug abuse treatment. *Journal of Substance Abuse, 8,* 417–429.

Kobak, R. R. (1988). *The adult attachment interview Q-set.* Newark, DE: University of Delaware.

Kobak, R. R., Cole, H. E., Ferenz-Gillies, R., & Fleming, W. S. (1993). Attachment and emotion regulation during mother–teen problem solving: A control theory analysis. *Child Development, 64,* 231–245.

Larson, A., & Olson, D. H. (1990). Capturing the complexity of family systems: Integrating family theory, family scores, and family analysis. In T. W. Draper and A. C. Marcos (Eds.), *Family variables: Conceptualization, measurement, and use* (pp. 48–66). Newbury Park, CA: Sage.

Maccoby, E., & Martin, J. (1983). Socialization in the context of the family: Parent-child interaction. In P. H. Mussen (Ed.), *Handbook of child psychology* (pp. 1–101). New York: Wiley.

Maddux, J. F., & Desmond, D. P. (1981). *Careers of opioid users.* New York: Praeger.

Main, M. (1991). Metacognitive knowledge, metacognitive monitoring, and singular (coherent) vs. multiple (incoherent) model of attachment: Findings and directions for future research. In C. M. Parkes and J. Stevenson-Hinde (Eds.), *Attachment across the life cycle.* London: Routledge.

Main, M., & Goldwyn, R. (in press). Adult attachment rating and classification systems. In M. Main (Ed.), *Assessing attachment through discourse, drawings and reunion situations.* New York: Cambridge University Press.

Main, M., Kaplan, N., & Cassidy, J. (1985). Security in infancy, childhood, and adulthood: A move to the level of representation. In I. Bretherton & E. Waters (Eds.), *Growing points of attachment theory and research* (Monographs of the Society for Research in Child Development, 50, Serial no. 209, Nos. 1–2, pp. 66–104).

Mayes, L. C. (1995). Substance abuse and parenting. In M. H. Bornstein (Ed.), *Handbook of parenting: Vol. 4. Applied and practical parenting* (pp. 101–125). Hillsdale, NJ: Erlbaum.

McLellan, A. T., Kushner, H., Metzger, D., Peters, R., Smith, I., Grissom, G., Pettinati, H., & Argeriou, M. (1992). The fifth edition of the Addiction Severity Index. *Journal of Substance Abuse Treatment, 9,* 199–213.

McLellan, A. T., Luborsky, L., O'Brien, C. P., & Woody, G. E. (1980). An improved evaluation instrument for substance abuse patients: The Addiction Severity Index. *Journal of Nervous and Mental Diseases, 168,* 26–33.

Miller, B. A., Downs, W. R., & Testa, M. (1993). Interrelationships between victimization experiences and women's alcohol use. *Journal of Studies on Alcohol, Supplement No. 11, Proceedings of the Symposium on Alcohol and Aggression* (pp. 109–117). Center of Alcohol Studies, Rutgers University.

Moos, R. H., Finney, J. W., & Chan, D. A. (1981). The process of recovery from alcoholism: I. Comparing alcoholic patients and matched community controls. *Journal of Studies on Alcohol, 42,* 383–402.

Moos, R., & Moos, B. (1981). *Family environment scale manual.* Palo Alto, CA: Consulting Psychologists Press.

Moos, R. H., & Moos, B. S. (1984). The process of recovery from alcoholism: III. Comparing functioning in families of alcoholics and matched control families. *Journal of Studies on Alcohol, 45,* 111–118.

Olson, D. H. (1977). Insiders' and outsiders' view of relationships: Research strategies. In G. Levinger & H. Raush (Eds.), *Close relationships.* Amherst: University of Massachusetts Press.

Olson, D. H. (1989). Circumplex model of family systems: Vol. VIII. Family assessment and intervention. In D. H. Olson, C. S. Russell, & D. H. Sprenkle (Eds.), *Circumplex model: Systemic assessment and treatment of families* (pp. 3–50). New York: Haworth.

Olson, D. H., & Killorin, E. (1985). *Clinical rating scale for the circumplex model of marital and family systems.* St. Paul, MN: University of Minnesota, Department of Family Social Science.

Olson, D. H., Portner, J., & Bell, R. Q. (1982). *Family adaptability and cohesion evaluation scales.* St. Paul, MN: University of Minnesota, Department of Family Social Science.

Olson, D. H., Russell, C. S., & Sprenkle, D. H. (1980). Circumplex model of marital and family systems: Vol. II. Empirical studies and clinical intervention. In J. Vincent (Ed.), *Advances in family intervention, assessment and theory: Vol. I.* (pp. 129–179). Greenwich, CT: JAI.

Olson, D. H., Russell, C. S., & Sprenkle, D. H. (1983). Circumplex model of marital and family systems: Vol. VI. Theoretical update. *Family Process, 22,* 69–83.

Olson, D. H., & Tiesel, J. W. (1993). Assessment of family functioning. In B. J. Rounsaville, F. M. Tims, A. M. Horton, & B. J. Sowder (Eds.), *Diagnostic source book on drug abuse research and treatment* (NIDA Research Monograph, NIH ADM 93-1957). Rockville, MD: National Institute on Drug Abuse.

Patterson, G. R., DeBaryshe, B. D., & Ramsey, E. (1989). A developmental perspective on antisocial behavior. *American Psychologist, 44,* 329–335.

Patterson, G. R., Ray, R. S., Shaw, D. A., & Cobb, J. A. (1969). Family Interaction Coding System (FICS). In J. B. Reid (Ed.), *A social learning approach to family intervention: Vol. 2. Observation in home settings.* Eugene, OR: Castalia.

Peterson, G. W., & Rollins, B. C. (1987). Parent–child socialization. In M. B. Sussman and S. K. Steinmetz (Eds.), *Handbook of marriage and the family* (pp. 471–507). New York: Plenum.

Reid, J. B. (Ed.). (1978). *A social learning approach to family intervention: Vol. 2 Observation in home settings.* Eugene OR: Castalia.

Schumm, W. R. (1990) Evolution of the family field: Measurement principles and techniques. In J. Touliatos, B. F. Perlmutter, & M. A. Straus (Eds.), *Handbook of Family measurement techniques* (pp. 23–36). Newbury Park, CA: Sage.

Simpson, D. D. (1992). *TCU forms manual: Drug Abuse Treatment for AIDS-Risk reduction (DATAR).* Fort Worth: Texas Christian University, Institute of Behavioral Research.

Simpson, D. D., Knight, K., & Ray, S. (1993). Psychosocial correlates of AIDS—risky drug use and sexual behaviors. *AIDS Education Prevention, 5,* 121–130.

Simpson, D. D., & McBride, A. A. (1992). Family, Friends, and Self (FFS) Assessment Scales for Mexican American youth. *Hispanic Journal of Behavioral Sciences, 14,* 327–340.

Skinner, H. A., & Steinhauer, P. D. (1986). *Family assessment measure clinical rating scale.* Toronto: Addiction Research Foundation.

Skinner, H. A., Steinhauer, P. D., & Santa-Barbara, J. (1983). The family assessment measure. *Canadian Journal of Community Mental Health, 2,* 91–105..

Skinner, H. A., Steinhauer, P. D., & Santa-Barbara, J. (1994). *Family assessment measure.* Toronto: Multi-Health Systems.

Sroufe, L. A., & Fleeson, J. (1986). Attachment and the construction of relationships. In W. W. Hartup & Z. Rubin (Eds.), *Relationships and development* (pp. 51–72). Hillsdale, NJ: Eribaum.

Stanton, M. D. (1978). Heroin addiction as a family phenomena: A new conceptual model. *American Journal of Alcohol and Drug Abuse, 5,* 125–150.

Stanton, M. D., Todd, T. C., & Associates. (1982). *The family therapy of drug abuse and addiction.* New York: Guilford.

Stein, J. A., Newcomb, M. D., & Bentler, P. M. (1987). Personality and drug use: Reciprocal effects across four years. *Personality and Individual Differences, 8,* 419–430.

Stewart, M. A., & Brown, S. A. (1993). Family functioning following adolescent substance abuse treatment. *Journal of Substance Abuse, 5,* 327–339.

Straus, M. A. (1979). Measuring intra family conflict and violence: The Conflict Tactics (CT) Scales. *Journal of Marriage and the Family, 41,* 75–88.

Teets, J. M. (1995). Childhood sexual trauma of chemically dependent women. *Journal of Psychoactive Drugs, 27,* 231–238.

Touliatos, J., Perlmutter, B. F., & Straus, M. A. (Eds.). (1990). *Handbook of family measurement techniques* (p. 797). Newbury Park, CA: Sage.

CHAPTER 18

PSYCHODYNAMIC PSYCHOTHERAPY

Michael S. Levy
Edward J. Khantzian

Although there are different types of individual therapy available for the person who is addicted to alcohol or drugs, this chapter focuses on the use of psychodynamic psychotherapy for the treatment of substance abuse. Psychodynamic psychotherapy is well suited for the treatment of addiction due to the deficits and dysfunctions in ego and self that many addicts experience. According to Khantzian (1986), these concern regulation and control, self-esteem problems, relationship difficulties, and self-care deficits. These psychological vulnerabilities are seen as critically important in the etiology and development of the substance abuse problem and in the substance abuser's eventual reliance on using chemicals as a way to cope.

Individual psychotherapy, however, if not psychodynamic therapy in particular, has often been discouraged as a therapeutic intervention for the treatment of substance abusers. One element to this thinking is that psychotherapy can serve to increase a patient's denial that a problem with alcohol or other drugs exists. Operating from the stance that a substance abuse problem is a symptom of some underlying difficulty that must be addressed before the patient can be expected to stop drug use, the therapist may overlook or not fully address the substance abuse problem, and thus collude with the patient's denial (Galanter, 1986;

Tiebout, 1951; Vaillant, 1981). Another argument is that the therapist would not be able to tolerate the patient's repeated relapses, which would cause considerable countertransferential difficulties for the therapist (Vaillant, 1981). In addition, substance abusers have not been viewed as good psychotherapy candidates. This may be due to the fact that they are often seen when they are intoxicated, demanding, and in some type of crisis. Undoubtedly another factor is that many substance abusers have been treated by therapists not skilled in the treatment of addiction. As a result, people did not obtain the needed treatment which resulted in a poor outcome and the belief that psychotherapy would not be beneficial to them.

However, individual psychotherapy can be quite efficacious for the treatment of substance abuse. A number of studies have demonstrated the value of individual psychotherapy for people with addictive disorders. Rogalski (1984) found that when psychotherapy was added to paraprofessional drug counseling in an inpatient program, patients were more compliant with treatment as evidenced by a decreased number of against-medical-advice discharges, disciplinary discharges, or unauthorized absences. Woody et al. (1983) found that in five of seven studies investigating the efficacy of psychotherapy with methadone-treated patients, patients randomly assigned to psychotherapy as opposed to a different treatment modality (typically drug counseling) demonstrated superior outcome. Woody, McLellan, Luborsky, and O'Brien (1986) have also found that patients with the most disturbed global psychiatric ratings obtained particular benefit from psychotherapy as compared to drug counseling. More recently, Woody, McLellan, Luborsky, and O'Brien (1995) compared opiate-dependent patients during methadone maintenance treatment who had received counseling along with supportive-expressive therapy to patients who received counseling along with supplemental drug counseling. They found that the patients who received counseling along with supportive–expressive psychotherapy maintained the gains they had accomplished 6 months after treatment, whereas those patients who had received counseling along with supplemental drug counseling failed to maintain the gains that they had initially demonstrated.

In addition to empirical studies, there is a considerable body of literature that discusses the use of psychodynamically oriented psychotherapy for the treatment of chemical dependence (Frances, Khantzian, & Tamerin, 1988; Khantzian, 1986; Krystal, 1982; Krystal & Rankin, 1970; Levy, 1987; Wurmser, 1974). The focus of this literature is on both the psychological vulnerabilities associated with addictive disorders and the technical aspects of a psychodynamically oriented approach. With an increasing understanding of the disease of addiction coupled with a better understanding of the suffering and ego deficits that many substance abusers experience, some modifications have been incorporated into a more psychodynamic approach, thus enhancing its efficacy.

Individuals with addictive disorders present for psychotherapy for a variety of reasons, not necessarily for treatment of addiction. Others come for therapy knowing full well that a problem with alcohol or drugs exists. Such individuals may be unaware of the factors that may be playing a role in their inability to achieve abstinence. Other individuals know that they have an alcohol or drug problem and want to seek professional treatment as opposed to help in self-help organizations such as Alcoholics Anonymous (AA) or Narcotics Anonymous (NA). And others may seek therapy as a way to deny the fact that they have an alcohol or drug problem. They would rather see themselves as having some other psychological problems that are responsible for their heavy use of chemicals, and they prefer to work on such difficulties instead of their substance abuse problems. Whatever route into therapy, psychodynamic psychother-

apy can help such individuals with their substance abuse problems and also address their underlying psychological conflicts and concerns.

A PSYCHODYNAMIC UNDERSTANDING OF ADDICTION

Early psychodynamic understandings of addiction are governed by drive theory, emphasizing pleasure-seeking or destructive motives as leading to substance use and eventual dependence. Contemporary psychodynamic thinking, however, has moved away from pleasure-seeking or masochistic motivation toward an understanding of individuals with addictive disorders as having a range of ego deficits and difficulties involving affect regulation and control that render them susceptible to getting addicted to chemicals. A critical function of substance abuse is the management of overwhelming and intolerable feelings. Krystal and Rankin (1970) speak of a "defective stimulus barrier" in many people with addictive disorders, which makes them susceptible to getting overwhelmed and flooded with their feelings. They describe a normal process of affective development in which affects become differentiated, desomatized, and verbalized. In people with addictive disorders, this process does not occur and feelings remain undifferentiated, global, and overwhelming. Krystal (1988) has also discussed how emotions may be experienced as vaguely distressing reactions rather than as felt emotions and how specific emotions can not be named, a condition for which he has adopted the term "alexithymia." The inability to recognize, name, and use emotions as guides for action may result in an overreliance on chemicals for soothing and comfort.

Khantzian, Halliday, and McAuliffe (1990) discuss how people with addictive disorders get overwhelmed by their feelings, or can feel cut off from their feelings and feel too little. Thus, chemicals are used to quell overwhelming feelings, as well as helping people feel their emotions. Substance abuse is often a sequelae of childhood psychological trauma (Peters 1979; Shearer, Peters, Quaztman, & Ogden, 1991). In this context, chemicals may be used to anesthetize individuals overwhelmed by affect or to enable individuals to feel by lessening their defenses against the reexperiencing of affect.

Khantzian's (1985) self-medication hypothesis proposes that certain substances may be preferentially utilized by individuals as a way to ameliorate or augment particular feelings. For example, narcotics may be used to manage

rage or loneliness, alcohol to soften a rigid character structure, and cocaine to alleviate depression, boredom, and
emptiness or to fuel an already heightened sense of
grandeur in a hypomanic state (Khantzian, 1985;
Wurmser, 1974). There have also been reports of individuals, who were eventually diagnosed with an attention
deficit hyperactivity disorder, using cocaine to "slow
themselves down" and to improve concentration
(Khantzian, 1985; Levy, Saemann, & Oepen, 1996).

In addition to deficits in affect regulation and control,
Khantzian (1986) has noted other problems in individuals
with addictive disorders concerning self-esteem, establishing relationships with others, and self-care. With regard to
the latter, Khantzian and Mack (1983) have articulated self-
care functions as a group of ego functions that involve the
anticipation of danger, self-protective skills, and an overall
caring about oneself. As a result, individuals with addictive
disorders can place themselves in dangerous situations that
look self-destructive, but that may represent an inability to
truly care about, think about, and protect themselves.

Others have noted how an individual's extreme connection to their drug of choice may represent a substitute
for a needed or wished-for relationship (Wieder & Kaplan,
1969; Wurmser, 1974). Kohut (1971) has written how "the
drug serves not as a substitute for loved or loving objects
or for a relationship with them, but a replacement for a
defect in the psychological structure" (p. 46).

A lifestyle centered around the use and abuse of chemicals can cause characterological changes and deficits in
ego functioning (Zinberg, 1975). As a way to cover up a
deteriorating sense of self, grandiose and narcissistic
defenses come to be utilized as well as more primitive
defense mechanisms. Furthermore, if chemical use began
in adolescence, normal development including defensive
organization may never take place, as drugs substitute for
the development of coping mechanisms. Common deficits
include frustration intolerance, attempts at manipulation,
rigid black and white thinking, rebelliousness, and use of
projection and denial. Consequently, what is seen among
many people with addictive disorders is either an erosion
of personality functioning or a lack of ego development.

Clearly, addiction is a biopsychosocial phenomenon. It
is well documented that certain individuals are at greater
risk for developing an alcohol dependence problem due to
genetic predisposition (Goodwin, 1979; Vaillant, 1983). A
psychodynamic understanding of addiction appreciates
that certain individuals may be biologically at-risk for
developing a chemical addiction. However, psychody-

namic issues are still critical factors in understanding the
etiology and manifestation as well as the eventual recovery
from the addictive disorder. Whatever the specific constellation of biological, environmental, and psychological factors maintaining the addiction, a psychodynamic
understanding purports that the person's inner experience
should be explored including the person's psychological
reasons for using chemicals.

TECHNICAL CONSIDERATIONS

Individuals who struggle with addiction come for therapy
at different points of their lives and at different phases of
addiction. Some readily acknowledge a substance dependence problem, but cannot seem to stop and prefer to get
involved in therapy rather than attend self-help meetings.
Others are actively using, but do not see it as a problem or
have never considered it to be a particular concern. Yet others enter therapy fully in recovery from their addiction to
chemicals but not from other emotional difficulties.

Establishing Control

Although there are unique considerations when conducting
psychodynamic therapy with individuals who are or who
have been addicted to chemicals, if a person is still using
chemicals the first step is the need to focus on the person's use
of chemicals and to help the person to see the importance of
establishing control over substance use. As a substance abuse
problem can be defined as using chemicals despite harmful
consequences, unless the person stops using, problems will
continue to occur and the person's life will not improve.
Although chemical use may in some sense be a solution to
some intrapsychic difficulties, more often it simultaneously
causes additional problems essentially unrelated to what
seemed to start it. As previously discussed, the continual use
of chemicals can cause ego regression and an erosion of one's
defensive system (Zinberg, 1975). Consequently, it is essential to focus on the substance abuse as a problem in and of
itself because unless the cycle is interrupted, the person will
continue to experience problems related to substance use rendering successful therapy impossible.

Perhaps one of the greatest dangers for clinicians not
experienced in the treatment of addiction is the failure to
specifically address and focus on the person's substance
abuse. Although the person may achieve insight, the
patient continues to misuse chemicals, which will continue
to create additional problems. An addiction to alcohol or

drugs is a life-threatening illness that must be contained. With individuals who have not yet acknowledged the use of chemicals as being a problem, it is paramount to first address the issue of substance abuse.

As patients acknowledge their addiction, the therapist establishes what treatment interventions will be required to enable them to achieve abstinence. Khantzian (1988) has described the role of the clinician as being that of a primary care therapist who directs, coordinates, and monitors the patient to maximize retention and treatment effectiveness. The primary care therapist may play a secondary or brokering role and refer the patient to other primary treatment interventions or instead may be the central agent involved in the patient's treatment. Whatever the role, the clinician must be concerned with the patient's need for control, containment, contact, and comfort. Levy (1987) has noted how during this phase of treatment, the therapist may need to provide direct advice to patients regarding how to attain abstinence. If patients are unwilling to attend AA or NA, the skills learned in self-help meetings can be brought to the one-on-one relationship or to group therapy.

For a variety of reasons, many patients will be unable or unwilling to acknowledge how their use of chemicals hurts them. At this point in therapy, a number of strategies can be helpful to enable patients to see the destructiveness of their substance abuse. Some people refuse to acknowledge the extent of their drug problem due to defensiveness as well as a desire to continue to use alcohol or drugs. Denying the consequences of drug use gives "permission" to continue to use drugs. In such cases, it is important to discover how chemicals help individuals to cope. Attempting to gain insight into what fuels the substance abuse instead of insisting on abstinence can be useful for a number of reasons. By inquiring what they like about chemicals, the therapist places himself or herself on the side of the patient, thus building the therapeutic alliance. Once patients feel understood by their therapists and it is empathically acknowledged how chemical use helps them to cope, patients then are often more willing to admit that substance use hurts them, which is the first step toward abstinence. Ascertaining what the person likes about chemicals also will help the therapist to discover what the person struggles with and what the person cannot do for him or herself. Thus it enables the therapist to get to know the patient's intrapsychic conflicts, establishes the foundation for subsequent therapy.

For some, the idea of living life without chemicals may be terrifying. For individuals with more serious characterological difficulties and psychiatric impairments, the idea of living without chemicals can be overwhelming. Without the use of chemicals, they may have nothing to fall back on (Levy, 1993). As has been noted, alcohol and drugs help people to regulate and control their feelings, to sustain relationships, or to maintain an identity and self-concept.

Others may not acknowledge the seriousness of their substance abuse problem due to self-care deficits. As has been noted, many people with addictive disorders suffer with ego deficits that render them unable to acknowledge the dangerousness of their behavior. With such people, it may be productive for therapists to assume the role of an observing ego and to gently reflect back to them what they see. When done in an empathic, caring way, patients may be able to internalize the therapist's concern in order to expand their own self-observation and self-care abilities.

With severe substance abuse, it is important for the therapist to confront the patient with how important it is for the individual to enter a program of recovery. For such people, continued substance use will preclude successful treatment and engagement in the therapeutic process. With people who use chemicals intermittently, however, therapy may proceed despite continued drug use. Throughout therapy, however, the substance abuse must remain a treatment focus. The therapist should attempt to understand the meaning of the substance abuse in the person's life in addition to what impact the failure to more fully address the problem may have on the individual. Again, the therapist's concern for the patient may help to augment the patient's possible deficit in self-care.

During this phase of treatment, some people may want to try to control their alcohol intake as opposed to attempting abstinence. Although this can often be a manifestation of denial, there are some people who are able to control their alcohol intake (Bailey & Stewart, 1967; Levy 1990; Nordstrom & Berglund, 1987; Vaillant, 1983). If a patient insists on trying to control drinking, a contract can be made in which the patient will drink, at most, three drinks per day and both the therapist and patient can monitor what transpires. The specifics of the controlled drinking contract can be negotiated with patients on an individual basis.

We have found that even with people who cannot control their drinking, initially giving the person control avoids getting into power struggles later, which helps a healthy therapeutic relationship (Khantzian, 1981; Levy, 1987). People often discover that abstinence is the best means of control when they have been given the choice to control their drinking. People often need to discover for themselves whether or not controlled drinking is possible.

The Use of Self-Help and Other Group Approaches

AA and other self-help support programs can be enormously useful and should be recommended. Although the relationship a patient develops with his or her therapist is very different from relationships to other AA members or even to one's sponsor, the combination of AA and psychodynamic psychotherapy generally poses no problems for most people (Khantzian, 1988). Although AA or NA can be extremely useful, some individuals, due to character structure or comorbid conditions, (e.g., social phobia, agoraphobia, panic disorder), may find it difficult to involve themselves in such programs (Levy, 1990, 1992). If people refuse to attend AA meetings their resistance should be explored and understood. Some people may not fully acknowledge their chemical abuse problems which is why they refuse AA; through exploring this, their resistances can be resolved. However, for others, resistance may be justified and should be accepted. For example, some people may not be able to resonate with the concepts of "powerlessness" or a "higher power." A referral to another self-help organization such as Rational Recovery could be made and might be a better match for certain people. Also, some people may be able to achieve abstinence without any self-help program. Furthermore, many individuals who cannot tolerate large group experiences such as AA will accept and benefit significantly from smaller group experiences such as modified dynamic group therapy (MDGT) (Khantzian et al., 1990).

Whereas some people who get involved in AA may need to attend AA meetings for life, others may eventually stop attending with no deleterious consequences. It has been suggested that the need to attend AA meetings may lessen as an individual's ego functions develop (Dodes & Khantzian, 1991). Dodes (1984) has indicated that individuals who are able to internalize a self-care function may stop attending AA, whereas those who cannot internalize this may need to attend forever to ensure continued sobriety. In addition, many individuals continue to attend AA not only to maintain abstinence but also to develop interpersonal relationships and social activities.

Psychotherapy: Moving Beyond Abstinence

Once the substance abuse problem is under control and a recovery program has been established, therapy can proceed in relatively traditional ways. Typical themes are affect management, relationship difficulties, self-esteem, and self-care. The meaning the drug has for the person can be explored in addition to helping the person discover other ways to get needs met without the use of drugs. Certain affect states may be particularly problematic and will need specific attention. Exploring what appeals to people about their drug of choice can be enormously useful and can provide a direct path to unconscious conflicts.

Modifications in traditional technique, however, are indicated. Levy (1987) has pointed out that therapists must always be mindful of the possibility of resumed drug use and should frequently inquire about how abstinence has been going and whether or not remaining abstinent has been a struggle. As we do not want to add to the patient's possible shame and embarrassment if substance abuse has resumed, questioning should be done in a matter-of-fact, nonjudgmental manner. Therapists can also more actively give advice and suggestions concerning how to remain abstinent (Levy, 1987). Khantzian (1995) has suggested that when working with people with addictive disorders, it is important for therapists to fully appreciate developmental problems. For example, therapists can more directly identify vulnerabilities that have historically been demonstrated by particular patients and more actively confront self-defeating defenses and behaviors when observed.

Relapses

Finally, a few words must be said about relapses (Polich, Armor, & Braiker, 1981). In general, a relapse provides the patient and therapist with an opportunity to discover where the problems are in the patient's recovery. A deliberate and careful exploration of the feelings and events preceding the relapse can be illuminating, as a patient's emotional state prior to a resumption of substance abuse often indicates the conflicts or affects the patient struggles with and what is felt to be intolerable without the use of chemicals. Many patients may initially be unaware of what played a role in the relapse, but with careful attention to this process, insight can be achieved. So often, relapses relate to our patients' difficulties with affect regulation and control, maintaining satisfying relationships, and sustaining self-esteem and positive self-concept. Understanding what factors led to the relapse is often the road to patients' self-understanding and will set the stage for what is needed to be worked on in therapy. In the long run, continued substance abuse will only aggravate the situation and will prevent the development of healthier coping strategies.

Helping patients to understand the triggers to relapse will counter hopelessness and frustration.

Relapse may also be patient's lack of knowledge about their own drug problems and what they need to do to remain abstinent. For example, people may continue to interact with friends who drink, because they feel that they can handle this, and eventually they begin to drink as well. In these cases, the therapist should actively provide some direction to help them to develop a more secure recovery program. Finally, relapse may occur as people begin to feel that drugs can be used in a safe and controlled fashion. In these situations, treatment needs to focus on the inability of individuals to accept that they cannot control their alcohol or drug use. Often, in order to combat their own vulnerabilities, substance abusers take on a demeanor of bravado and counterdependence, which can make it difficult for them to acknowledge that they cannot use drugs safely. Whatever the causes of relapse, by carefully exploring the patients' affect and thinking immediately prior to drug use, much will be learned about ways to intervene and to prevent further relapses. In fact, much of therapy involves a persistent awareness and clarification of how one's defenses and character traits are intimately linked to personal vulnerabilities, and how both the vulnerabilities and defenses predispose to, maintain dependence on, and cause relapse to substances of abuse.

In summation, a model of individual psychodynamic psychotherapy for addictive disorders has been presented that is based on a contemporary psychodynamic understanding of vulnerabilities and conflict areas. These difficulties involve ego deficits that cause disturbances in self-regulation, modulation of feelings, relationships with others, self-esteem, and self-care. Psychodynamic psychotherapy helps people to see the relationship between these difficulties and their addiction to chemicals and helps them to learn other ways to manage their conflicts.

REFERENCES

Bailey, M., & Stewart, J. (1967). Normal drinking by persons reporting previous problem drinking. *Quarterly Journal of Studies on Alcohol, 28,* 305–315.

Dodes, L. M. (1984). Abstinence from alcohol in long-term individual psychotherapy with alcoholics. *American Journal of Psychotherapy, 38,* 248–256.

Dodes, L. M., & Khantzian, E. J. (1991). Individual psychodynamic psychotherapy. In R. J. Frances & S. Miller (Eds.), *Clinical textbook of addictive disorders.* New York: Guilford.

Frances, R. J., Khantzian, E. J., & Tamerin, J. S. (1988). Psychodynamic psychotherapy. In T. B. Karasu (Ed.), *Treatment of psychiatric disorders: A task force report of the American Psychiatric Association* (pp. 1103–1110). Washington, DC: American Psychiatric Press.

Galanter, M. (1986). Treating substance abusers: Why therapists fail. *Hospital and Community Psychiatry, 37,* 769.

Goodwin, D. W. (1979). Alcoholism and heredity. *Archives of General Psychiatry, 36,* 57–61.

Khantzian, E. J. (1981). Some treatment implications of the ego and self disturbances in alcoholism. In M. H. Bean & N. E. Zinberg (Eds.), *Dynamic approaches to the understanding and treatment of alcoholism* (pp. 163–188). New York: Free Press.Khantzian, E. J. (1985). The self-medication hypothesis of addictive disorders: Focus on heroin and cocaine dependence. *American Journal of Psychiatry, 142,* 1259–1264.

Khantzian, E. J. (1986). A contemporary psychodynamic approach to drug abuse treatment. *American Journal of Drug and Alcohol Abuse, 12,* 213–222.

Khantzian, E. J. (1988). The primary care therapist and patient needs in substance abuse treatment. *American Journal of Drug and Alcohol Abuse, 14,* 159–167.

Khantzian, E. J. (1995). Self-regulation vulnerabilities in substance abusers: Treatment implications. In S. Dowling (Ed.), *The psychology and treatment of addictive behavior.* Madison, CT: International University Press.

Khantzian, E. J., Halliday, K. S., & McAuliffe, W. E. (1990). *Addiction and the vulnerable self. Modified dynamic group therapy for substance abusers.* New York: Guilford.

Khantzian, E. J., & Mack, J. (1983). Self-preservation and the care of the self. *Psychoanalytic Study of the Child, 38,* 209–232.

Kohut, H. (1971). *The analysis of the self.* Madison, CT: International University Press.

Krystal, H. (1982). Alexithymia and the effectiveness of psychoanalytic treatment. *International Journal of Psychoanalytic Psychotherapy, 9,* 353–378.

Krystal, H. (1988). *Integration & self-healing: Affect, trauma, alexithymia.* Hillsdale, NJ Analytic Press.

Krystal, H., & Rankin, H. (1970). *Drug dependence: Aspects of ego function.* Detroit, MI: Wayne State University Press.

Levy, M. (1987). A change in orientation: Therapeutic strategies for the treatment of alcoholism. *Psychotherapy, 24,* 786–793.

Levy, M. S. (1990). Individualized care for the treatment of alcoholism. *Journal of Substance Abuse Treatment, 7,* 245–254.

Levy, M. (1992). Alcohol and addictions, (Letter to the editor). *American Journal of Psychiatry, 149,* 1117–1118.

Levy, M. (1993). Psychotherapy with dual diagnosis patients: Working with denial. *Journal of Substance Abuse Treatment, 10,* 499–504.

Levy, M., Saemann, R., & Oepen, G. (1996). Neurological comorbidity in treatment-resistant dual diagnosis patients. To be published in *Journal of Psychoactive Drugs, 28.*

Nordstrum, G., & Berglund, M. (1987). A prospective study of successful long-term adjustment in alcohol dependence:

Social drinking versus abstinence. *Journal of Alcohol Studies, 48,* 95–103.

Peters, J. J. (1979). Children who were victims of sexual assault and the psychology of offenders. *American Journal of Psychotherapy, 30,* 398–421.

Polich, J. M., Armor, D. J., & Braiker, H. B. (1981). *The course of alcoholism: Four years after treatment.* New York: Wiley.

Rogalski, C. J. (1984). Professional psychotherapy and its relationships to compliance in treatment. *International Journal of the Addictions, 19,* 521–539.

Shaffer, H. J. (1985). The disease controversy: Of metaphors, maps, and menus. *Journal of Psychoactive Drugs, 17,* 65–76.

Shearer, S. L., Peters, C. P., Quaztman, M. S., & Ogden, R. L. (1991). Frequency and correlates of childhood sexual and physical abuse histories in adult female borderline patients. *American Journal of Psychiatry, 147,* 214–216.

Tiebout, H. M. (1951). The role of psychiatry in the field of alcoholism. With comment of the concept of alcoholism as symptom and as disease. *Quarterly Journal of Studies on Alcohol, 12,* 52–57.

Vaillant, G. E. (1981). Dangers of psychotherapy in the treatment of alcoholism. In M. H. Bean & N. E. Zinberg (Eds.), *Dynamic approaches to the understanding and treatment of alcoholism* (pp. 36–54). New York: Free Press.

Vaillant, G. E. (1983). *A natural history of alcoholism.* Cambridge, MA: Harvard University Press.

Wieder, H., & Kaplan, E. (1969). Drug use in adolescents. *Psycho-analytic Study of the Child, 24,* 399–431.

Woody, G. E., Luborsky, L., McLellan, A. T., O'Brien, C. P., Beck, A. T., Blaine, J., Herman, I., & Hole, A. (1983). Psychotherapy for opiate addicts: Does it help? *Archives of General Psychiatry, 40,* 639–645.

Woody, G. E., McLellan, A. T., Luborsky, L., & O'Brien, C. P. (1986). *Psychiatric Clinics of North America, 9,* 547–562.

Woody, G. E., McLellan, A. T., Luborsky, L., & O'Brien, C. P. (1995). Psychotherapy in community methadone programs: A validation study. *American Journal of Psychiatry, 152,* 1302–1308.

Wurmser, L. (1974). Psychoanalytic considerations of the etiology of compulsive drug use. *Journal of the American Psychoanalytic Association, 22,* 820–843.

Zinberg, N. E. (1975). Addiction and ego function. *The Psychoanalytic Study of the Child, 30,* 567–588.

CHAPTER 19

RELAPSE PREVENTION

Dennis C. Daley
Ihsan Salloum

Outcome studies show that the majority of individuals who receive treatment for substance use disorders relapse. For many, substance use disorders are chronic conditions characterized by episodes of substance use following periods of abstinence. Hence the issue of relapse is of critical importance in the treatment of clients with substance use disorders. In this chapter, we discuss treatment issues and strategies pertinent to relapse prevention and management. We define recovery, lapse, and relapse; review the stages of change paradigm; summarize the empirical research on outcome studies including those specifically addressing relapse prevention (RP), and discuss limitations of outcome studies. The main focus of this chapter is on reviewing practical clinical strategies to reduce the likelihood of a relapse and to manage actual relapse in order to minimize adverse effects in cases in which a client returns to substance use following a period of recovery.

DEFINITIONS

Recovery refers to the process of initiating and maintaining abstinence from substance use. The factors involved in stopping substance use vary from those involved in maintaining abstinence from substances (Marlatt & Gordon,

1985). Recovery is viewed as a process involving personal and lifestyle change. To maintain abstinence, the client may need to make changes in any domain of functioning—physical, psychological, behavioral, interpersonal, family, social, spiritual, occupational, and financial (Daley, 1988). The recovery process for a specific client is mediated by level of motivation, severity of substance use and related problems (medical, psychiatric, psychosocial), personal factors (age, gender, ethnicity), and social support. Some clients are able to achieve and maintain long-term recovery whereas others experience multiple relapses.

Lapse refers to the initial episode of substance use following a period of recovery and may or may not lead to a relapse. Many clients are able to get back on track following a lapse whereas others continue their use and move toward relapse. Relapse refers to a breakdown in the client's attempt to modify substance use behavior (Marlatt & Gordon, 1985). Relapses vary in terms of severity of substance use and adverse effects. Although some clients return to pretreatment levels of use, others interrupt their lapses early and experience less severe patterns of substance use and less biopsychosocial damage. To a large extent, the client's response to the initial lapse plays a major role in whether or not substance use continues.

STAGES OF CHANGE PARADIGM

Several investigators have developed a paradigm that differentiates six possible stages of change for clients with substance use disorders (Prochaska, Norcross, & DiClemente, 1994). According to this model, most successful changers recycle several times and relapse is the rule rather than the exception when it comes to solving most problems, including substance-related problems.

The first stage, *precontemplation*, is characterized by the client's inability to see the problem and resistance to change. The precontemplator uses denial and projects blame on factors such as genetic makeup, family history, or society. In the second stage, *contemplation*, the client acknowledges a problem and thinks seriously about doing something about it. It is not unusual for the contemplator to remain in this stage for months or even years. In the third stage, *preparation*, the client prepares to take action. In this stage the person begins to think about solutions to the problem despite feeling ambivalent about change. Family or significant others are often informed by the client that he or she is about to start some type of treatment or recovery program. The client who cuts short the preparation stage may lower the ultimate chances of success. In the fourth stage, *action*, the person actually begins to modify the substance use behavior (e.g., quitting smoking, alcohol use, or other drug use). In addition to cessation of substance use, this stage requires the greatest commitment of time and energy. Stage five, *maintenance*, involves the client working in an ongoing fashion to prevent lapses and relapses, the origin of RP. The final stage, *termination*, is reached when the former problem no longer presents a temptation or threat and the client is confident about coping with problems without relapsing.

According to this model, any movement from one stage to the next represents progress. For example, if a *precontemplator* who has avoided facing an alcohol problem for years, finally acknowledges the problem and thinks about changing it, movement is being made in the right direction. This model also views action followed by relapse as better than not taking any action at all. Because change seldom is a linear process, a client may move in and out of various stages after experiencing a lapse or relapse. RP can reduce the risk of relapse as well as help clients who lapse or relapse reenter the action stage and get back on the recovery track.

SUBSTANCE ABUSE TREATMENT OUTCOME STUDIES

Substance use disorders are no different than other chronic medical and psychiatric conditions in that recovery seldom is a linear path and relapse is very common. The outcome literature indicates that 40% to 80% of clients with substance use disorders relapse one or more times (Catalano, Howard, Hawkins, & Wells, 1988; Hoffman & Miller, 1992; Miller & Hester 1980). Studies involving more socially stable clinical populations show excellent results with total and continuous abstinence rates around 50% at 2 years posttreatment (Hoffman & Miller, 1992).

Outcome studies have several limitations. First, most do not differentiate between levels of motivation to quit using. Outcomes of clients highly motivated to quit are assessed in the same way as those mandated to participate in treatment. Second, relapse rates are often assessed in a dichotomous fashion, that is, study subjects either count as having relapsed or not having relapsed, which gives the appearance that the problem is worse than it actually is because many relapses are actually lapses. Some relapses are actually therapeutic and serve to raise a client's level of motivation to change. When outcome is measured by cessation or reduction of substance use and subsequent problems, or improvement in psychosocial functioning, then clearly the majority of individuals who participate in treatment evidence positive gains. Third, outcome studies have many deficiencies in their methodology such as lack of standardized measures of relapse or definition of outcome, problems with small sample size or selection of clients, lack of randomization to study conditions, lack of control groups to compare against RP, early client attrition from treatment, and short length of follow-up posttreatment (Daley & Marlatt, 1997).

EMPIRICAL STUDIES OF RELAPSE PREVENTION

Relapse prevention (RP) emerged to help clients who have successfully stopped using substances maintain abstinence over the long run. RP therefore is most appropriate for the maintenance stage of the change process. RP refers to two types of clinical interventions: (1) any psychosocial or pharmacologic approach aimed at helping clients maintain abstinence from substances; (2) specific, coping skills strategies aimed at helping the client identify and manage potential high-risk factors that raise vulnerability to lapse or relapse. All psychosocial treatment approaches such as cognitive-behavioral therapy or 12-step counseling routinely integrate RP as part of the overall therapy (Beck, Wright, Newman, & Liese, 1993; National Institute on Alcohol Abuse and Alcoholism, 1995a, 1995b). In addition, several models of RP have been developed that focus primarily on the major issues of relapse such as identifying and managing warning signs of relapse, anticipating and preparing for high-risk situations, enhancing social support systems, balancing lifestyle, and managing lapses and relapses (Daley, 1988; Daley & Marlatt, 1997; Gorski, 1986; Gorski & Miller, 1988a, 1988b; Marlatt, 1985a, 1985b; Zackon, McAuliffe, & Ch'ien, 1985, 1993).

To date, there is no superior treatment approach for substance use disorders. Many approaches, including RP, have shown positive results (Carroll, Rounsaville, & Gawin, 1991; Miller et al., 1995). The RP treatment model that has received the most empirical scrutiny is the cognitive-behavioral approach of Marlatt and Gordon (1985). This approach has been adapted and operationalized in clinical manuals and has been used with smokers, and alcohol, cocaine, opiate, and marijuana abusers or addicts. A recent review of 24 randomly controlled clinical trials of RP by Carroll (1996) indicates that the strongest evidence for efficacy of the cognitive-behavioral approach is with smokers. Those with alcohol or nontobacco substance use disorders with high levels of psychiatric impairment and addiction severity benefit most from RP compared to those with less severe levels of impairment (Carroll, 1996).

Several studies of married individuals with alcohol addiction conducted by O'Farrell (1993) and O'Farrell, Choquette, Cutter, Brown, & McCourt (1993) reveal that RP, in addition to behavioral marital therapy (BMT), shows promise. These investigators found that compared to those receiving BMT only, males receiving BMT plus RP had more days abstinent from alcohol, fewer days drinking, and improved marriages. Abstinence rates were highest for subjects receiving this combination of treatment who were in marriages assessed to be "high distress."

The major limitation of RP studies is that some studies used RP as the single treatment intervention for cessation of substance use rather than for maintenance of change once abstinence was initiated. Therefore, it appears that the concepts and interventions of RP, although developed for the later maintenance stage of recovery, are also useful earlier in the recovery process. This probably is due to the universality of certain recovery issues experienced throughout various stages of the change process, for example, encountering high-risk interpersonal situations, emotionally distressing situations, or lifestyle problems raising vulnerability to relapse.

OVERVIEW OF RELAPSE PREVENTION (RP)

RP is based on the assumption that many different intrapersonal, interpersonal, and lifestyle factors contribute to a lapse or relapse and it is usually a combination of interacting factors rather than one that eventuates in a client resuming substance use (Catalano et al., 1988; Daley, 1988; Marlatt & Gordon, 1985). Intrapersonal factors include negative mood states, psychiatric symptoms, urges and temptations, negative physical states, impulsivity, and testing personal control. Interpersonal factors include social pressures to use substances, lack of family or peer support, relationship conflicts, and social skill deficits. Lifestyle factors contributing to relapse include negative life events and lack of productive work or school roles.

Although initially developed for substance use disorders, RP strategies are now being used with sexual offenders; impulse control disorders; psychiatric disorders such as depression, schizophrenia, and eating disorders; marital problems; and substance use combined with psychiatric illness (Daley, 1996; Daley & Lis, 1995; Laws, 1989; Wilson, 1992). The broad application of RP speaks to the importance of emphasizing the maintenance phase of the change process so that clients have a repertoire of coping strategies to draw upon as recovery progresses.

Because managed care emphasizes short-term and time-limited interventions, the need for self-management skills to help clients deal with the ongoing challenges and problems of recovery is more important than ever. Teaching RP strategies is an excellent way for clinicians to prepare clients to manage recovery posttreatment.

CLINICAL STRATEGIES FOR RP

RP strategies can be used in individual, family, or group sessions in any type of treatment setting—outpatient, intensive outpatient, partial hospital, and short- or long-term residential. Clinical interventions should be tailored to the client's presenting problems and level of motivation. Brief clinical examples are provided to illustrate several of the RP interventions. A variety of clinical aids are available to help educate clients about these relapse issues and begin to develop their own RP plan (Daley & Marlatt, 1997).

High-Risk Situations

The main thrust of RP is to help the client anticipate and prepare for the possibility of relapse by identifying personal high-risk (HR) factors and developing appropriate coping strategies to manage them. High-risk situations usually are those in which the client drank or ingested drugs prior to treatment or those that currently contribute to a high likelihood of using substances. These HR factors generally fall into one of the three broad categories mentioned earlier: intrapersonal determinants (e.g., negative mood states), interpersonal determinants (e.g., social pressures to use substances), and lifestyle factors (e.g., lack of productive roles).

Assessing the client's coping skills is very important in order to determine whether a client is likely to be able to successfully cope with particular high-risk situations. Inadequate coping skills raise the client's vulnerability to lapse or relapse, whereas positive coping skills lower them.

Relapse Warning Signs

Lapses and relapses usually are preceded by overt and covert warning signs. These warning signs include subtle or obvious changes in attitudes, thoughts, emotional states, and behaviors that may show days, weeks, or even months before substances are actually ingested. Helpful interventions include teaching clients about relapse as both a process and event, identifying common warning signs encountered in recovery, identifying warning signs unique to the client, and developing strategies to manage these warning signs.

Clients with previous lapse and relapse experiences can benefit from closely examining these in order to learn what went wrong in past attempts at recovery. The relapse process can be conceptualized as a "chain" in which the last "link" represents the lapse or the initial use of a substance. Each previous "link" can represent a specific warning sign. When the client evaluates the entire chain of events, it often becomes clear that early indicators were present throughout the relapse process. Clients with multiple lapses or relapses can benefit from determining whether there is any pattern involved in their return to substance use.

Negative Emotional States

Negative emotional states such as anger, anxiety, boredom, depression, and loneliness are the most common precipitants of relapse across a range of addictive behaviors (Marlatt & Gordon, 1985). In addition to raising relapse risk, poor management of emotions contributes to interpersonal problems and unhappiness for many clients. Clinical interventions include helping clients identify their personal high-risk emotional states, assessing their ability to cope, and helping them acquire appropriate cognitive, behavioral, or interpersonal coping skills to manage negative affect. The following is a case example illustrating how one person developed a plan to address his high-risk emotional state of anger:

Case Example 1

Charles, a high-school teacher with a long-standing problem of alcohol dependence, identified boredom and anger as key high-risk relapse factors. His problem with anger involved a pattern of avoiding interpersonal conflicts and letting his anger build up. Over time, Charles would reach a point of total frustration and use his angry thoughts and feelings to justify drinking binges. To reduce his relapse vulnerability, Charles had to recognize this destructive pattern and modify his faulty beliefs about anger so that he no longer perceived it to be a "bad feeling that could only be expressed through drinking." Clinical interventions with Charles included bibliotherapy, that is, maintaining a daily anger log in which he recorded and rated angry feelings along with the context in which they occurred. This reflective process helped Charles discover that while some of his anger was justified, often he became upset and angry because of certain beliefs he held about how others "should" treat him. Awareness of his anger and associated beliefs led to a reduction in feelings of anger. Behavioral rehearsals helped Charles become more comfortable and confident about his ability to deal directly with other people toward whom he felt angry.

Social Pressures

Social pressures to use substances are the second most common relapse precipitant (Marlatt & Gordon, 1985). Direct and indirect social pressure often contributes to an increased desire to engage in substance use. The most practical RP strategy is to help the client identify anticipated social pressures to use (i.e., specific people, social events, and activities), and strategies to refuse offers to use in cases where the situation cannot be avoided. Interpersonal coping strategies (e.g., refusing offers of alcohol or drugs or to attend parties) can be practiced in behavioral rehearsals with the clinician or treatment group. This provides clients with an opportunity to become aware of nuances of interpersonal encounters involving social pressures and to become confident about refusing requests that pose a serious threat to recovery. Videotaping behavioral rehearsals of clients being confronted with social pressures is an excellent way to analyze such pressures. The advantage of videotaping is that both verbal and nonverbal behaviors and interactions can be analyzed.

Moreover, a major problem in recovery is dealing with a primary partner such as a spouse, lover, roommate, or family member who is an active substance abuser, or a social network comprised mainly of other substance abusers, or potential sexual encounters in which alcohol or drug use is likely. Before they can make reasonable decisions about what is best, clients benefit from exploring all aspects of these types of relationships. The loss of significant relationships is difficult for clients, even those representing a serious relapse risk. Clients often need help and support dealing with the grief and depression associated with interpersonal losses, and in developing new relationships with sober people who can support rather than threaten their recovery.

Case Example 2

Nancy, a nurse in a large metropolitan hospital, is recovering from cocaine and marijuana dependence. She identified two major sources of social pressures to use drugs that posed a threat to her ongoing recovery: (1) the man she has been dating for over a year uses drugs regularly, and (2) many of her friends abuse alcohol and drugs. Initially in recovery she tried to maintain a relationship with her boyfriend despite the fact that he continued abusing substances. His drug use and her sobriety became the focus of many arguments. Nancy decided that the only way to cope with ongoing pressures from him to engage in substance use was to end the relationship. When Nancy made a list of social events and interpersonal interactions in which drugs were used, she was amazed to discover that drugs were more common than not in most of her social encounters. Nancy decided to quit attending parties or functions where drugs were used and promptly left any social situation in which drugs were available or heavy drinking occurred. She also had private conversations with several good friends that she wanted to maintain a relationship with, to inform them of her recovery and discuss situations in which she felt she could socialize with them without the threat of being offered drugs.

Family and Social Support Systems

Family and social support systems play a critical role in ongoing recovery and are associated with improved recovery rates (Galanter, 1992; Havassy, Hall, & Wasserman, 1991; McGrady, 1989). Clients whose social networks consist primarily of others with active substance use disorders need to develop new support systems in order to begin establishing relationships with sober and supportive friends. Often, this starts with active involvement in self-help programs such as AA, NA, Rational Recovery, SMART Recovery, and Women for Sobriety.

Clients with stable family and interpersonal relationships can be encouraged to elicit support from these systems. Other helpful clinical interventions include exploring effects of the substance use disorder on significant others, making amends, and involving others in the recovery process when appropriate. Clients with stable social networks can also benefit from participation in self-help programs, recovery clubs, and related organizations.

Interpersonal Problems and Conflicts

One of the biggest challenges for clients in recovery is to address and resolve interpersonal problems that create stress and increase relapse risk. Some of the more common and serious interpersonal problems faced in recovery are chronic interpersonal conflicts, inability to trust, lack of satisfying intimate relationships, inability to establish or maintain reciprocal relationships that meet emotional needs, jumping from one relationship to the next, premature involvement in an intense sexual or emotional relationship before any stability in recovery is established, involvement in excessive or addictive sexual relationships, and involvement in physically or emotionally abusive relationships. Addressing such issues requires awareness, a willingness to change, and in some instances, help in developing certain social skills such as appropriate self-disclosure, assertiveness, setting limits, and so on. The clinician should never underestimate the difficulty that some clients have in applying what they learn in treatment to their own lives. Knowing "how" to behave in a certain way may require behavioral rehearsal and repeated practice until the client feels comfortable and confident.

Substance Use Triggers and Cravings

Many environmental cues associated with prior use trigger thoughts and cravings to use substances. Helpful environmental interventions include removal of substances and paraphernalia (pipes, needles, mirrors, ashtrays); minimizing exposure to people, places, events, and situations associated with substance use (e.g., bars, parties, drinking buddies, drug dealers); and repeated exposure to select cues under controlled conditions (e.g., treatment setting or in the natural environment under supervision) until the intensity of craving decreases and the client feels confident about managing thoughts and feelings triggered by these environmental cues.

Internal cues such as thoughts, feelings, and physical sensations also trigger cravings. Helpful interventions include monitoring the rate and intensity of cravings on a daily basis, challenging euphoric recall about being high, talking oneself through the cravings by anticipating a positive outcome of not using substances, engaging in pleasant activities, distracting oneself from the craving, sharing the desire to use with a supportive person, especially another person in recovery, or sharing at a recovery meeting, repeating AA/NA slogans (e.g., "this too shall pass"), praying to a higher power, or taking medications such as Antabuse or ReVia.

Cognitive Distortions

Cognitive therapists have identified faulty beliefs and errors in thinking that play a role in substance abuse, depression, anxiety, and other problems (Beck et al., 1993; Burns, 1993; Ellis, McInerney, DiGuiseppe, & Yeager, 1988; Padesky & Greenberger, 1995). These cognitive distortions also contribute to lapse or relapse or the inability to intervene early in the relapse process. Self-help programs such as AA and NA refer to "stinking thinking" to illustrate how thoughts and beliefs impact on addiction, recovery, and relapse. Examples of common beliefs that contribute to relapse include the client thinking that he or she is invulnerable to relapse; can't relax, have fun, or socialize without using alcohol or drugs; can learn to control and limit substance use; is cured from the addiction; or can take a few drinks, hits, tokes, or pills without jeopardizing recovery.

Clinical interventions include helping clients learn to identify and challenge cognitive distortions or negative thinking, use positive self-talk, and use the "slogans" of AA or NA (e.g., work on sobriety "one day at a time"; "this too shall pass"). Cognitive interventions are most effective when they relate to a specific belief or negative thought that the client shares in a treatment session. However, clients can also benefit from reviewing lists of common distortions (e.g., making things out to be worse than they really are, focusing only on

the negative, jumping to conclusions, catastrophizing, black and white thinking) so that they can relate to these concepts in a personal fashion. Keeping a daily journal to record situations and feelings along with related thoughts and beliefs is an excellent mechanism to teach clients how to change their thinking. For example, when the client is recording data related to social pressures to use substances, upsetting feelings, cravings to use substances, or interpersonal conflicts or disputes, he or she can include information on thoughts and beliefs associated with these various situations.

Balanced Lifestyle

Many researchers and clinicians have written about the importance of helping clients balance their lifestyle in order to increase satisfaction, reduce stress, and relapse risk (Daley & Marlatt, 1997; Marlatt & Gordon, 1985; Wanigaratne, 1990). A helpful intervention is to assist the client in evaluating daily activities such as sources of stress; health, relaxation, eating, and exercise patterns; leisure activities and hobbies; religious beliefs; and the ratio of "wants" (needs) to "shoulds" (obligations). Based on this assessment, plans for positive changes can then be developed. For example, many clients benefit from positive habits or substitute behaviors to addiction such as meditation, physical exercise, creative hobbies, or interesting and fun activities.

Case Example 3

Michael is a successful businessman with a long history of alcohol abuse. Despite being abstinent for over a year, he felt something was missing and, moreover, that his wife complained about not seeing him enough, which caused him to worry and feel guilty. When Michael closely examined his time, it was crystal clear that he spent entirely too much time working. It was not unusual for him to work late at least 3 days a week, and to work every single weekend, either at the office or at home. In fact, he often took work along on weekend trips and vacations. In order to regain balance in his life, Michael agreed to (1) limit late work days to two per week; (2) work at home only 1 day each weekend during a designated block of time; (3) delegate more work to his employees; (4) take his wife out alone at least twice a month; (5) spend some time every weekend with his two sons; and (6) resume playing tennis and not use being busy with work as an excuse. In order to successfully make these changes, Michael had to become aware of and challenge some of his ingrained beliefs about work and managing a business (e.g., "I have to work all the time to stay ahead of the competition;

Work is the most important thing in my life;" "My employees constantly need my guidance," "I'm indispensable").

Psychiatric Comorbidity

Many studies have documented high rates of psychiatric disorders among clients with substance abuse problems (Daley, Moss, & Campbell, 1993; Robins & Regier, 1991). Clients with psychiatric comorbidity are at increased risk for substance abuse relapse, particularly when they are not compliant with psychosocial and pharmacologic treatment. For more serious manifestations of mental illness, the treatment plan has to be tailored to include strategies to address the psychiatric illness. Often, psychotropic medication is needed as part of the treatment plan due to the severity and persistence of psychiatric symptoms. In a study of comorbidity we found that substance abuse relapse played a significant role in 60% of psychiatric hospital readmissions among clients with schizophrenia or mood disorders (Daley & Salloum, 1993). In many cases, psychiatric symptoms worsened as a result of poor compliance with outpatient sessions and medication.

Case Example 4

Linda had a heroin addiction off and on for almost 8 years. During the past 4 years, she had been in several addiction rehabilitation programs and psychiatric hospitals. Until she finally agreed to be compliant with treatment for her recurrent depression, her longest sobriety had been 4 months. Linda initially believed that because she had kicked heroin several times, she should be able to "pick myself up, out of depression" on her own. As a result, she twice quit taking antidepressants, and she was poorly compliant with outpatient therapy. When her mood worsened, she relapsed to drug use. Linda finally agreed to stay in psychiatric treatment and take antidepressants. In addition to a major improvement in her mood and ability to function, she has not used any drugs in almost 2 years. Although Linda acknowledges that addiction therapy and NA have played a key role in ongoing abstinence, she strongly believes that sticking with her medications and psychiatric treatment has been a major factor in her recovery.

TRANSITION AMONG LEVELS OF TREATMENT

Due to the chronicity and severity of many types of substance use disorders, clients often need various levels of treatment during the course of their recovery. These levels may include inpatient or residential, partial hospital, intensive outpatient, and traditional outpatient or aftercare treatment. Unfortunately, many clients fail to successfully make the transition from one level of care to another, especially clients who attend hospital-based or residential addiction or dual-diagnosis treatment programs. We found, for example, that only 30% to 40% of psychiatric inpatients with comorbid substance abuse disorders complied with their first outpatient appointment following discharge. Clients who attended their first outpatient appointment had fewer substance abuse and psychiatric relapses and subsequent hospitalizations compared to those who failed to show for this appointment. We were able to improve the initial show rates by 50% to 80% and hence decrease relapse rates by providing a single session of adherence counseling prior to clients' discharge from the hospital. This session adapted the model of motivational interviewing (MI) developed by Miller and Rollnick (1991) and appears to hold much promise for dual-diagnosis inpatients. In a related pilot study of cocaine-dependent clients with comorbid major depression of such severity to warrant antidepressant therapy, we provided weekly individual and group sessions that integrated dual-diagnosis interventions and MI. As a result, we were also able to improve completion rates for the first month of outpatient treatment by over 50%. In addition to improved rates of treatment adherence and completion, these clients also showed better rates of abstinence during the first 30 days of outpatient treatment and improvement in mood compared to clients receiving treatment as usual (individual + group + antidepressants) (Daley, Salloum, Zuckoff, & Kirisci, 1997).

Other interventions that help facilitate the transition from inpatient or emergency room care to outpatient treatment and improve abstinence rates include using prompts (letters or phone calls) to remind the client of the initial outpatient session; providing reinforcements for attending treatment sessions or for providing clean urines; giving appointments within 4 days of discharge from the hospital; collaborating with inpatient referral sources, making outreach calls to clients who fail to show for the initial appointment; and offering intensive treatment (two or more sessions weekly) in the first month of outpatient treatment (Daley & Thase, 1995). In our clinical experience, clients who successfully "enter" outpatient treatment evidence better recovery rates and fewer relapses than clients who fail to comply with outpatient care.

PHARMACOLOGIC ADJUNCTS

Medications, provided in conjunction with psychosocial treatments, may lessen cravings for alcohol or other drugs, enhance motivation to stay sober, or increase confidence of the client to remain abstinent. Several recent studies of O'Malley and colleagues (1992) and Volpicelli, Alterman, Hayashida, and O'Brien (1992), for example, show that naltrexone (ReVia) is helpful in reducing severity of relapses among alcoholics. Kranzler and colleagues (1994) found that clients who received buspirone, an anti-anxiety drug, showed greater treatment retention, reduced anxiety, fewer drinking days, and less severe alcohol relapses compared to those receiving placebo. Gottlieb, Horwitz, Kraus, Segal, and Viscoli (1994) found better treatment adherence rates and lower relapse rates among people with alcohol addiction receiving atenolol, a beta-adrenergic blocker, compared to those receiving placebo.

LAPSE AND RELAPSE MANAGEMENT

Because many clients with substance use disorders lapse or relapse, it is important for them to have a plan to interrupt any return to substance use. Early intervention in a lapse may avert a relapse, and early intervention in a relapse may reduce negative consequences and prevent the client from returning to baseline levels of substance use. Because many clients have a catastrophic reaction to a lapse (e.g., "I ruined my recovery, I'm a failure so why even bother trying to stay sober, I'm not capable of change,"), it is helpful to assess their potential reactions and how they may act so that they can learn ways to counteract negative thinking and emotional reactions that could contribute to ongoing substance use.

Helpful interventions include teaching the client to take action quickly when alcohol or drugs are used, discuss and analyze lapses and relapses with others in the support system and members of the treatment team, use self-talk to lessen the chance that a lapse will eventuate in a full-blown relapse, and be prepared to take other steps in the event that physical addiction recurs and the client cannot stop on his or her own. Using an emergency card and developing a relapse contract in which the client outlines ahead of time specific steps to take in the event of a lapse or relapse are excellent recovery strategies (Marlatt & Gordon, 1985).

Relapse is the rule and not the exception with clients who receive treatment for substance use disorders. However, despite the high rates of relapse, the majority of clients participating in treatment benefit in one or more ways: total cessation or reduction of substance use, reduction in medical or psychosocial problems caused or worsened by substance use, and improvement in any area of life functioning. Many relapse prevention strategies have been developed and described in clinical manuals. These strategies can be adapted to any type of substance use disorder, including those involving psychiatric comorbidity, and can be used throughout the continuum of care. Regardless of the context in which a clinician works or the theoretical orientation of the treatment approach, RP strategies are a necessary and important part of treatment.

REFERENCES

Beck, A. T., Wright, F. D., Newman, C. F., & Liese, B. S. (1993). *Cognitive therapy of substance abuse*. New York: Guilford Press.

Burns, D. D. (1993). *Ten days to self-esteem*. New York: Quill William Morrow.

Carroll, K. M. (1996). Relapse prevention as a psychosocial treatment: A review of controlled clinical trials. *Experimental and Clinical Psychopharmacology, 4*, 46–54.

Carroll, K. M., Rounsaville, B. J., & Gawin, F. H. (1991). A comparative trial of psychotherapies for ambulatory cocaine abusers: Relapse prevention and interpersonal psychotherapy. *American Journal of Drug and Alcohol Abuse, 17*, 229–247.

Catalano, R., Howard, M., Hawkins, J., & Wells, E. (1988). Relapse in the addictions: rates, determinants, and promising prevention strategies. In *1988 Surgeon General's report on health consequences of smoking*. Washington, DC: Office of Smoking and Health, Government Printing Office.

Daley, D. (1988). *Surviving addiction: A guide for alcoholics, drug addicts, and their families*. New York: Gardner Press.

Daley, D. (1996). Relapse prevention strategies for dual disorders. *The Counselor,* March/April, 26–29.

Daley, D., & Lis, J. (1995). Relapse prevention: intervention strategies for mental health clients with comorbid addictive disorders. In A. Washton (Ed.), *Psychotherapy and substance abuse: a practitioner's handbook* (pp. 243–263). New York: Guilford Press.

Daley, D., & Marlatt, G. A. (1997a). *Managing your alcohol or drug problem*. San Antonio, TX: Psychological Corporation.

Daley, D., & Marlatt, G. A. (1997b). Relapse prevention: cognitive and behavioral interventions. In J. Lowinson, P. Ruiz, R. Millman & J. Langrod (Eds.), *Substance abuse a comprehensive textbook* (3rd. ed.). Baltimore: Williams and Wilkins.

Daley, D., Moss, H., & Campbell, F. (1993). *Dual disorders: Counseling clients with chemical dependency and mental illness* (2nd ed.). Center City, MN: Hazelden.

Daley, D., & Salloum, I. (1993). Unpublished data.

Daley, D. C., Salloum, I. M., Zuckoff, A., & Kirisci, L. (1997). *Increasing outpatient treatment compliance among patients with comorbid depression and cocaine dependence: results of a pilot study.* Unpublished manuscript.

Daley, D., & Thase, M. E. (1995). *Dual disorders recovery counseling: A biopsychosocial approach to addiction and mental health disorders.* Independence, MO: Herald House/Independence Press.

Ellis, A., McInerney, J., DiGuiseppe, R., & Yeager, R. (1988). *Rational-emotive therapy with alcoholics and substance abusers.* New York: Pergamon.

Galanter, M. (1992). Office management of the substance abuser: the use of learning theory and social networks. In:J. H. Lowinson, P. Ruiz, R. B. Millman, & J. Langrod (Eds.), *Substance abuse a comprehensive textbook* (2nd ed., pp. 543–549). Baltimore, MD: Williams and Wilkins.

Gorski, T. (1986). Relapse prevention planning: A new recovery tool. *Alcohol Health and Research World, 19,* Fall, 6–11.

Gorski, T., & Miller, M. (1988a). *Staying sober a guide for relapse prevention.* Independence, MO: Independence Press.

Gorski, T., & Miller, M. (1988b). *Staying sober workbook.* Independence, MO: Independence Press.

Gottlieb, L. D., Horwitz, R. I., Kraus, M. L., Segal, S. R., & Viscoli, C. M. (1994). Randomized controlled trial in alcohol relapse prevention: Role of atenolol, alcohol cravings, and treatment adherence. *Journal of Substance Abuse Treatment, 11,* 253–258.

Havassy, B. E., Hall, S. M., & Wasserman, D. A. (1991). Social support and relapse: Commonalities among alcoholics, opiate users, and cigarette smokers. *Addictive Behaviors, 16,* 235–246.

Hoffman, N. G., & Miller, N. S. (1992). Treatment outcomes for abstinence-based programs. *Psychiatric Annals, 22,* 402–408.

Kranzler, H. R., Burleson, J. A., Del Boca, F. K., Babor, T. F., Korner, P., Brown, J., & Bohon, M. J. (1994). Buspirone treatment of anxious alcoholics. A placebo-controlled trials. *Archives of General Psychiatry, 51,* 720–731.

Laws, R., (Ed.). (1989). *Relapse prevention with sex offenders.* New York: Guilford Press.

Marlatt, G. A. (1985a). Lifestyle modification. In G. A. Marlatt & J. Gordon (Eds.), *Relapse prevention: A self-control strategy for the maintenance of behavior change* (pp. 280–350). New York: Guilford Press.

Marlatt, G. A. (1985b). Situational determinants of relapse and skill-training interventions. In G. A. Marlatt & J. Gordon (Eds.), *Relapse prevention: A self-control strategy for the maintenance of behavior change* (pp. 71–127). New York: Guilford Press.

Marlatt, G. A., & Gordon, J. (Eds.). (1985). *Relapse prevention: A self-control strategy for the maintenance of behavior change.* New York: Guilford Press.

McGrady, B. (1989). Extending relapse prevention to couples. *Addictive Behaviors, 14,* 69–74.

Miller, W. R., Brown, J. M., Simpson, T. L., Handmaker, N. S., Bien, T. H., Luckie, L. F., Montgomery, H. A., Hester, R. K., & Tonigan, J. S. (1995). What works? A methodological analysis of the alcohol treatment outcome literature. In W. R. Miller & R. K. Hester (Eds.), *Handbook of alcoholism treatment approaches effective alternatives* (2nd ed., pp. 12–44). Boston: Allyn and Bacon.

Miller, W., & Hester, R. (1980). Treating the problem drinker: Modern approaches. In *The addictive behaviors: Treatment of alcoholism, drug abuse, smoking and obesity.* New York: Pregamon Press.

Miller, W. R., & Rollnick, S. (1991). *Motivational interviewing: Preparing people to change addictive behavior.* New York: Guilford Press.

National Institute on Alcohol Abuse and Alcoholism. (1995a). Cognitive-behavioral coping skills therapy manual: A clinical research guide for therapists treating individuals with alcohol abuse and dependence. *Project MATCH Monograph Series, 3* (NIH Publication No. 94-3724). Rockville, MD: Author.

National Institute on Alcohol Abuse and Alcoholism. (1995b). Twelve step facilitation therapy manual: a clinical research guide for therapists treating individuals with alcohol abuse and dependence. *Project MATCH Monograph Series, 1* (NIH Publication No. 94-3722). Rockville, MD: Author.

O'Farrell, T. J. (1993). Couples relapse prevention sessions after a behavioral marital therapy couples group program. In T. J. O'Farrell (Ed.), *Treating alcohol problems: Marital and family interventions* (pp. 305–326). New York: Guilford Press.

O'Farrell, T. J., Choquette, K. A., Cutter, H. S., Brown, E. D., & McCourt, W. F. (1993). Behavioral marital therapy with and without additional couples relapse prevention sessions for alcoholics and their wives. *Journal of Studies on Alcohol, 54,* 652–666.

O'Malley, S. S., Jaffee, A. J., Chang, G., Schottenfeld, R. S., Meyer, R. E., & Rounsaville, B. (1992). Naltrexone and coping skills therapy for alcohol dependence. *Archives of General Psychiatry, 49,* 881–887.

Padesky, C. A., & Greenberger, D. (1995). *Clinician's guide to mind over mood.* New York: Guilford Press.

Prochaska, J. P., Norcross, J. C., & DiClemente, C. C. (1994). *Changing for good.* New York: William Morrow.

Robins, L. N., & Reiger, D. A. (Eds.). (1991). *Psychiatric disorders in America: The epidemiologic catchment area study.* New York: Free Press.

Volpicelli, J. R., Alterman, A. I., Hayashida, M., & O'Brien, C. P. (1992). Naltrexone in the treatment of alcohol dependence. *Archives of General Psychiatry, 49,* 876–880.

Wanigaratne, S. (1990). *Relapse prevention for addictive behaviors.* London: Blackwell Scientific.

Wilson, P. H. (Ed.). (1992). *Principles and practice of relapse prevention.* New York: Guilford Press.

Zackon, F., McAuliffe, W., & Ch'ien, J. (1985). *Addict aftercare: recovery training and self-help.* (DHHS Publication No. ADM 85-1341). Rockville, MD: NIDA.

Zackon, F., McAuliffe, W. E., & Ch'ien, J. (1993). *Recovery training and self-help: Relapse prevention and aftercare for drug addicts.* (NIH Publication No. 93-3521). Rockville, MD: NIDA

CHAPTER 20

NETWORK THERAPY

Marc Galanter

Individual therapists in office practice are often considered to have limited effectiveness in treating alcohol and drug dependence. This chapter describes network therapy, an approach designed to assure greater success in such treatment, employing behavioral and psychodynamic therapy while engaging the patient in a support network composed of family members and peers (Galanter 1993a, 1993b). It was developed over an extended period of time to meet the practical needs of clinical practice, and encompasses modalities that have been applied in recent years by other clinicians and researchers (Galanter 1983, 1984).

Network therapy is comprised of three key elements: social/peer support, coordination of treatment, and a cognitive behavioral treatment approach. First, support from the patient's natural social network is engaged in treatment. Peer support in Alcoholics Anonymous (AA) has long been shown to be an effective vehicle for promoting abstinence. Also, the idea of the therapist's intervening with family and friends in starting treatment was employed as well in one of the early ambulatory techniques specific to addiction (Johnson, 1986). The involvement of spouses (McCrady, Stout, Noel, Abrams, & Fisher-Nelson, 1991) has also been shown to be effective in enhancing the outcome of treatment.

Second, the orchestration of resources to provide community reinforcement suggests a more robust treatment intervention by providing a support for drug-free rehabilitation (Azrin, Sisson, & Meyers, 1982). In this relation the "primary care therapist" is conceived as one who functions in direct coordinating and monitoring roles in order to combine psychotherapeutic and self-help elements (Khantzian, 1988). The overall management of circumstances outside as well as inside the office session is essential to maximizing the effectiveness of the treatment.

Third, a cognitive behavioral approach is emphasized especially in order to promote relapse prevention. This approach has been empirically demonstrated to be valuable in addiction treatment and positive prognosis (Marlatt & Gordon, 1985). In network therapy, the cognitive behavioral approach is used to identify triggers to relapse and to focus on behavioral techniques for avoiding them, in preference to exploring underlying psychodynamic issues.

Conditioned Abstinence

For many clinicians, the problems of *relapse* and *loss of control* epitomize the pitfalls inherent in addiction treatment. Because people who have a substance abuse disorder are typically under pressure to relapse to ingestion of alcohol or drugs, they are seen as poor candidates for stable treatment. Loss of control has been used to describe a substance abuser's inability to reliably limit consumption once an initial dose is taken (Gallant, 1987). Although these phenomena are generally described anecdotally, they can also be explained mechanistically as well by the model of conditioned withdrawal, a model that relates the pharmacology of dependency-producing drugs to the behaviors they produce. Wikler (1973), an early investigator of addiction pharmacology, developed a related model to explain the spontaneous appearance of drug craving and relapse. He pointed out that drugs of dependence typically produce compensatory responses in the central nervous system at the same time that their direct pharmacologic effects are felt, and that these compensatory effects partly counter the drug's direct action. Thus, when an opiate antagonist is administered to someone who is addicted to morphine, latent withdrawal phenomena are unmasked. Similar compensatory effects are observed in alcoholics who are maintained on alcohol. That is, they evidence evoked response patterns characteristic of withdrawal, while still being clinically intoxicated (Begleiter & Porjesz, 1979).

Wikler studied individuals maintained on morphine and then thrown into withdrawal with a narcotic antagonist. After several trials of precipitated withdrawal, Wikler found that a full-blown withdrawal response could be elicited in his subjects when a placebo antagonist was administered. He concluded that the withdrawal had been conditioned, and later elicited by a conditioned cue, in this case the syringe used to administer the antagonist. This hypothesized mechanism was later confirmed by O'Brien, Testa, O'Brien, Brady, & Wells (1977), who elicited conditioned withdrawal using sound tones as conditioned cues. This conceptualization helps to explain addictive behavior outside the laboratory. A potential addict who has begun to drink or use another drug heavily may be repeatedly exposed to an external stimulus (such as the sight of a liquor bottle) or an internal one (such as a certain mood state) while drinking. Subsequent exposure to these cues may thereby produce conditioned withdrawal symptoms, subjectively experienced as craving.

This model helps to explain why relapse is such a frequent and unanticipated aspect of addiction treatment. Exposure to conditioned cues, ones that were repeatedly associated with drug use, can precipitate reflexive drug craving during the course of therapy, and such cue exposure can also initiate a sequence of conditioned behaviors that lead to relapse. Loss of control has long been recognized on a practical level by members of AA. The sensations associated with the ingestion of an addictive drug, like the odor of alcohol or the euphoria produced by opiates, are temporally associated with the pharmacologic elicitation of a compensatory response to that drug, and can later produce drug-seeking behavior. For this reason, the "first drink" can serve as a conditioned cue for further drinking. These phenomena yield patients with very limited capacity to control consumption once a single dose of drug has been taken.

Social Supports

Professionals can draw on a network of cohesive relationships to enhance the outcome of treatment. Enhanced outcome was reported as well when the community reinforcement techniques developed by Hunt and Azrin (1973) were augmented by greater social relatedness in a club-like setting (Mallams, Godley, Hall, & Meyers, 1982). Similarly, we effected higher rates of retention and social recovery by integrating a peer-led format into a professionally directed alcohol treatment program (Galanter, Castaneda, & Salamon, 1987).

Not surprisingly, the cohesiveness and support offered by group and family therapy have been found effective in rehabilitating substance-abusing patients. Yalom, Bloch, Bond, Zimmerman, & Qualls (1978) reported on benefits derived when interactional group therapy was used as an adjunct to recovery techniques. Couples' group therapy, as well, has been shown to benefit alcoholics and to diminish the likelihood of treatment dropout (Gallant, Rich, Bey, & Terranova, 1970; McCrady et al., 1991).

APPLICATION TO NETWORK THERAPY

The conceptions of relapse prevention and engagement of social supports underlie the network therapy approach. Their use will now be described in relation to the implementation of treatment.

Starting a Network

The weight of clinical experience supports the view that abstinence is the most secure goal to propose to most addicted people for their rehabilitation (Helzer et al., 1985; Vaillant, 1996). For abstinence to be expected, however, the therapist should assure the provision of necessary social supports for the patient. We consider now how a long-term support network is initiated for this purpose, beginning with availability of the therapist and significant others.

The patient should be asked to bring his or her spouse or a close friend to the first session. Alcoholic patients often dislike certain things they hear when they first come for treatment and may deny or rationalize even if they have voluntarily sought help. Because of their denial of the problem, a significant other is essential to both history taking and to implementing a viable treatment plan. A close relative or spouse can often cut through the denial in a way that an unfamiliar therapist cannot and can therefore be invaluable in setting a standard of realism in dealing with the addiction.

Some patients make clear that they wish to come to the initial session on their own. This is often associated with their desire to preserve the option of continued substance abuse and is born out of the fear that an alliance will be established independent of them to prevent this. Although a delay may be tolerated for one or two sessions, it should be stated unambiguously at the outset that effective treatment can be undertaken only on the basis of a therapeutic alliance built around the addiction issue that includes the support of significant others and that it is expected that a network of close friends and/or relatives will eventually be included in treatment.

The inclusion of a social network in treatment undercuts one reason for relapse; the patient's sense of being on his or her own if unable to manage the situation. The patient will develop a support network that can handle the majority of problems involved in day-to-day assistance. This generally will leave the therapist to respond only to questions of interpreting the terms of the understanding between therapist, the patient, and support network members. If there is a question about the ability of the patient and network to manage the period between the initial sessions, the first few scheduled sessions may be arranged at intervals of only 1 to 3 days. In any case, frequent appointments should be scheduled at the outset if a pharmacologic detoxification with benzodiazepines is indicated, so that the patient need never manage more than a few days' dependency-producing medication at a time.

It is essential that the network be forged into a working group to provide necessary support for the patient between the initial sessions. Network membership ranges from one to several persons close to the patient. Contacts between network members at this stage may include only telephone calls initiated by the therapist or by the patient. Dinner arrangements and social encounters can be preplanned to a fair extent during the network sessions. These encounters are most often undertaken at the time when alcohol or drug use is likely to occur. In planning together, however, it should be made clear to network members that relatively little unusual effort will be required for the long term, and that after the patient is stabilized, their participation will amount to little more than attendance at infrequent meetings with the patient and therapist. This is reassuring to those network members who are unable to make a major time commitment to the patient as well as to those patients who do not want to be placed in a dependent position.

Network Membership

Once the patient has come for an appointment, establishing a network is a task undertaken with active collaboration of patient and therapist. The therapist and patient, aided by those parties who join the network initially, must search for the right balance of members. The therapist must carefully promote the choice of appropriate network members, because the network will be crucial in determining the balance of the therapy. This process is not without problems, and the therapist must think in a strategic fashion of the interactions that may take place among network members.

Focusing on the Task

As conceived here, the therapist's relationship to the network is like that of a task-oriented team leader rather than that of an insight-oriented family therapist. The network is established to implement a straightforward task, that of aiding the therapist in sustaining the patient's abstinence. It must be directed with the same clarity of purpose by which a task force is directed in any effective organization. Competing and alternative goals must be suppressed, or at least prevented from interfering with the primary task.

Unlike family members involved in traditional family therapy, network members are not led to expect symptom relief for themselves or self-realization. This is to prevent the development of competing goals for the network's meetings. It also assures the members' protection from having their own motives scrutinized and thereby supports their continuing involvement without the threat of an assault on their psychological defenses. Because network members have kindly- volunteered to participate, their motives must not be impugned. Their constructive behavior should be commended. It is useful to acknowledge appreciation for the contribution they are making to the therapy. There is always a counterproductive tendency on their part to minimize the value of their contribution. The network must therefore be structured as an effective working group with high morale. This is not always easy:

> A 45-year-old single woman served as an executive in a large family-held business—except when her alcohol problem led her into protracted binges. Her father, brother, and sister were prepared to banish her from the business but decided first to seek consultation. Because they had initiated the contact, they were included in the initial network and indeed were very helpful in stabilizing the patient. Unfortunately, however, the father was a domineering figure who intruded in all aspects of the business, evoking angry outbursts from his children. The children typically reacted with petulance, provoking him in return. The situation came to a head when both of the patient's siblings angrily petitioned me to exclude the father from the network, two months into the treatment. This presented a problem because the father's control over the business made his involvement important to securing the patient's compliance. The patient's relapse was still a real possibility. This potentially coercive role, however, was an issue that the group could not easily deal with. The therapist decided to support the father's membership in the group, pointing out the constructive role he had played in getting the therapy started. It seemed necessary to support the earnestness of his concern for his daughter, rather than the children's dismay at their father's (very real) obstinacy. It was clear to the therapist that the father could not deal with a situation in which he was not accorded sufficient respect and that there was no real place in this network for addressing the father's character pathology directly. The hubbub did, in fact, quiet down with time. The children became less provocative themselves, as the group responded to my pleas for civil behavior.

Use of self-help modalities is also desirable whenever possible. Some patients are more easily convinced to attend AA meetings. Others may be less compliant. The therapist should mobilize the support network as appropriate, so as to continue pressure for the patient's involvement with AA for a reasonable trial.

Meeting Arrangements

At the outset of therapy it is important to see the patient with the group on a weekly basis, for at least the first month. Unstable circumstances demand more frequent contacts with the network. Sessions can be tapered off to biweekly and then monthly intervals after a few months. Once the patient has stabilized, the meetings tend less to address day-to-day issues.

Sessions begin with the patient's recounting of the drug situation. Reflections on the patient's progress and goals, or sometimes on relations among the network members, may then be discussed. In any case, it is essential that network members contact the therapist if they are concerned about the patient's possible use of alcohol or drugs, and that the therapist contact the network members if he or she becomes concerned over a potential relapse.

Pharmacotherapy

For the alcoholic, disulfiram may be of marginal use in assuring abstinence when used in a traditional counseling context (Fuller et al., 1986) but it becomes much more valuable when carefully integrated into work with the patient and network, particularly when the drug is taken under observation. It is a good idea to use the initial telephone contact to engage the patient's agreement to abstain from alcohol for the day immediately prior to the first session. The therapist then has the option of prescribing or administering disulfiram at that time. For a patient who is earnest about seeking assistance for alcoholism, this is often not difficult, if some time is spent on the phone making plans to avoid a drinking context during that period. If it is not feasible to undertake this on the phone, it may be addressed in the first session. Such planning with the patient almost always involves organizing time with significant others and therefore serves as a basis for developing the patient's support network.

The following complex case illustrates the implementation of a regimen of network supports designed to stabilize the patient and secure the use of pharmacotherapy. This example shows how network supports can be used with flexibility, as well:

> A 24-year-old college dropout, involved in the arts, came for treatment after she had been using heroin intranasally daily, and drinking heavily for 7 days. This was a relapse to her previous long-standing pattern of drug dependence, as she had been hospitalized twice for heroin addiction in the previous 2 years. Her last hospitalization, 6 months before, had been followed by episodic heroin insufflation and bouts of heavy drinking. Her polysubstance abuse as well as her promiscuity and rebellious behavior dated back to her early teens.
>
> One month prior to presenting, while living in a rural area, she had been abducted by a man whom she had befriended at an

AA meeting, and managed to escape after being held captive in a motel for a week. She was now living alternately with a friend in the city where she presented for treatment, and with her parents who lived 200 miles away; she commuted by train. She had not admitted to her parents that she had relapsed to heroin use. As the patient's history unfolded in her first session, it was clear that she had a long history of major problems of social and residential instability, as well as clear evidences of poor judgment since her hospitalization. Nonetheless, she wanted to escape from her self-destructiveness and her pattern of drug use.

The preliminary structure of a network was established in the second session with her and with the friend with whom she was staying some of the time. The patient, however, acknowledged in this session that she was still using heroin intermittently. In the third session, her parents were added, by having them participate via speaker-phone from their residence in a remote city. This arrangement allowed for simultaneous planning along with the parties on whom her current life was rooted. Given her previous exposure to addiction treatment and AA, she was willing to accept a concrete plan for achieving abstinence from both alcohol and heroin as an appropriate course of action. She agreed to undergo detoxification from heroin while staying in her parents' home with the aid of clonidine, and to then continue with naltrexone and disulfiram treatment. The former was for opiate blockade and for reduction of alcohol craving, and the latter was for securing alcohol abstinence. These medications were to be taken under observation, using the format developed within the network therapy regimen described below.

The patient was initially concerned that her parents would be upset if she told them that she had relapsed to heroin use after her last hospitalization. The therapist pointed out that it was important for them to be told so that they could serve as properly informed members of the network. It was agreed in an individual session that this need not be done until the patient's abstinence was stabilized over two weeks of use of the medications. The patient's concern was discussed in light of the judgmental and highly critical attitude of her mother, which had been influential over the course of the patient's adolescence, and had contributed greatly to her rebellious use of drugs. On a few occasions during the initial weeks, the mother became angry when the patient, while staying at home, had not attended AA meetings as planned.

In a subsequent individual session, the patient reported experiencing posttraumatic stress in dreams and anxiety symptoms, secondary to the kidnapping. She also expressed disillusionment with her ability to manage her own life in light of the experiences of the past few years, having failed at school and, as she saw it, at sobriety. Throughout this phase of individual therapy, treatment was oriented toward providing her with a positive view of her opportunities and encouragement to understand that recovery from drug dependence will allow her to work out the issues contributing to her past problems.

It was important for the sake of the network's stability to make clear that the principal role of network members is to participate with the patient and therapist in discussing opportunities for abstinence and stabilization, and not to scrutinize all aspects of the patient's behavior. Problems in compliance with the regimen of medication observation or AA meetings are discussed in network and individual sessions, and not policed by network members. Thus, if the patient misses a pill, the therapist is to be called and the patient not confronted. This removes network members from the role of independent enforcers, although their perspective and assistance may be solicited by mutual agreement with the patient. In this way, it is the implicit social pressure from members of the network for compliance that is most directed at stabilizing the treatment. Two more of the patient's friends were added to the network after the initial month of stabilization. This helped dilute the role of her parents in the network, and added additional practical resources, perspective, and support for recovery. The patient herself continued to take the medications under the observation of either her father or her friend, depending on where she was residing.

This patient's circumstances illustrate the value of drawing supportive figures into the treatment early on, and using this network resource in combination with the observation of ingestion of a blocking agent or an antidipsotropic—both were used in this case. The fact that the patient was taking these two medications on any given day undercut her craving and left her prepared to be compliant with the medication regimen the next day as well as with the overall treatment plan. In practice, patients experience less craving when such medications are integrated into the treatment regimen, because they know that opiates or alcohol, are not available to them for the next few days after ingestion of the medication.

Format for Medication Observation by the Network:

1. Take the medication every morning in front of a network member.
2. Take the pills so that person can observe you swallowing them.
3. Have the observer write down the time of day the pills were taken on a list prepared by the therapist.
4. The observer brings the list in to the therapist's office at each network session.

5. The observer leaves a message on the therapist's answering machine on any day in which the patient had not taken the pills in a way that ingestion was not clearly observed.

Adapting Individual Therapy to the Network Treatment

As noted, network sessions are scheduled on a weekly basis at the outset of treatment. This is likely to compromise the number of individual contacts. Indeed, if sessions are held once a week, initially the patient may not be seen individually for a period of time. The patient may perceive this as a deprivation unless the individual therapy is presented as an opportunity for further growth predicated on achieving stable abstinence assured through work with the network.

When the individual therapy does begin, the traditional objectives of therapy must be arranged so as to accommodate the goals of the substance abuse treatment. For insight-oriented therapy, clarification of unconscious motivations is a primary objective; for supportive therapy, the bolstering of established constructive defenses is primary. In the therapeutic context that is described here, however, the following objectives are given precedence.

Of first importance is the need to address exposure to substances of abuse or exposure to cues that might precipitate alcohol or drug use. Both patient and therapist should be sensitive to this matter and explore these situations as they arise, focusing heavily on cognitively grounded relapse prevention techniques. Second, a stable social context in an appropriate social environment—one conducive to abstinence with minimal disruption of life circumstances—should be supported. Considerations of minor disruptions in place of residence, friends, or job need not be a primary issue for the patient with character disorder or neurosis, but they cannot go untended here. For a considerable period of time the substance abuser is highly vulnerable to exacerbations of the addictive illness and in some respects must be viewed with the considerable caution with which one treats the recently compensated psychotic.

Finally, after these priorities have been attended to, psychological conflicts that the patient must resolve, relative to his or her own growth, are considered. As the therapy continues, these come to assume a more prominent role. In the earlier phases, they are likely to reflect directly issues associated with previous drug use. Later, however, as the issue of addiction becomes less compelling from day to day, the context of the treatment increasingly will come to resemble

the traditional psychotherapeutic context. Given the optimism generated by an initial victory over the addictive process, the patient will be in an excellent position to move forward in therapy with a positive view of his or her future.

RECENT RESEARCH ON THE NETWORK TECHNIQUE

Pilot Study

A retrospective study was conducted on 60 sequential patients who presented for treatment of alcohol and drug dependence in office practice. The findings demonstrated the mode of operation and the outcome of this approach. Fifty-five of the 60 patients were treated with at least one other network member, and the average network had 2.3 members. Of the 55 so treated, 16 had a parent in the network, 13 a sibling, 28 a peer, 34 a spouse or mate, and 4 a child of their own. Using DSM criteria, 46 experienced major or full improvement, and those using disulfiram under observation of a network member showed the best outcome (Galanter, 1993c).

Standardization of the Treatment

A Network Therapy Rating Scale was used to rate network-related therapist behavior on videotape segments of addiction therapy sessions. Half the video segments illustrated the network format, and the remainder were of family systems therapy. The scale was first applied by medical school teaching faculty expert in the network approach, and later by psychiatric residents who had received a seminar course on network therapy. Responses of both faculty and residents distinguished the two therapy techniques to a significantly high degree, with the faculty distinguishing significantly more effectively than that of the residents (Keller, Galanter, & Weinberg, in press). These scores reflected an acceptable level of integrity and differentiability of the network therapy modality, a greater level of expertise among the faculty who would be providing supervision for the trainees, and the ability of both groups to distinguish network therapy techniques from those of nonnetwork approaches.

Study on Training Naive Therapists

A course of training for psychiatric residents naive to addiction and ambulatory treatments was undertaken over a period of 2 academic years. Before treating patients with this modality, the residents were provided with a structured treatment manual for network therapy and participated in a 13-session seminar on application of the network therapy technique. Cocaine-abusing patients were eligible to be treated in this study if they could come for evaluation with a friend or family member who could participate in their treatment. In all, 24 patients were enrolled. Supervisors' evaluation of videotapes of the network sessions employing a standardized instrument indicated good adherence to the manualized treatment, with effective use of network therapy techniques. The outcome of treatment, to be reported by M. Galanter, D. Keller, and H. Dermatis, reflected retention and abstinence rates as good as comparable ambulatory care carried out by therapists experienced in cocaine addiction treatment. The study demonstrated the feasibility of teaching the network technique to therapists naive to addiction treatment.

MANUALIZED SUMMARY OF THE NETWORK TECHNIQUE

The following summary material defines specific procedures embodied in the network technique:

Start a Network as Soon as Possible

1. It is important to see the alcohol or drug abuser promptly, as the window of opportunity for openness to treatment is generally brief. A week's delay can result in a person's reverting back to drinking or losing motivation.
2. If the person is married, engage the spouse early on, preferably at the time of the first phone call. Point out that addiction is a family problem. For most drugs, you can enlist the spouse in assuring that the patient arrives at your office with a day's sobriety.
3. In the initial interview, frame the exchange so that a good case is built for the grave consequences of the patient's addiction, and do this before the patient can introduce his or her system of denial. That way you are not putting the spouse or other network members in the awkward position of having to contradict a close relation.
4. Then make clear that the patient needs to be abstinent, starting now. (A tapered detoxification may be necessary sometimes, as with depressant pills.)
5. When seeing an alcoholic patient for the first time, start him on disulfiram treatment as soon as possible, in the office if you can. Have the patient continue taking disulfiram under observation of a network member.

6. During the first session, start arranging for a network to be assembled, generally involving a number of the patient's family or close friends.
7. From the very first meeting, consider how to ensure sobriety till the next meeting, and plan that with the network. Initially, their immediate company, a plan for daily AA attendance, and planned activities may all be necessary.

Manage the Network with Care

1. Include people who are close to the patient, have a long-standing relationship with him or her, and are trusted. Avoid members with substance problems, as they will let you down when you need their unbiased support. Avoid superiors and subordinates at work, as they have an overriding relationship with the patient independent of friendship.
2. Get a balanced group. Avoid a network composed solely of the parental generation, or of younger people, or of people of the opposite sex. Sometimes a nascent network selects itself for a consultation if the patient is reluctant to address his or her own problem. Such a group will later supportively engage the patient in the network, with your careful guidance.
3. Make sure that the mood of the meetings is trusting and free of recrimination. Avoid letting the patient or the network members be made to feel guilty or angry in meetings. Explain issues of conflict in terms of the problems presented by addiction—do not get into personality conflicts.
4. The tone should be directive. That is to say, give explicit instructions to support and ensure abstinence. A feeling of teamwork should be promoted, with no psychologizing or impugning members' motives.
5. Meet as frequently as necessary to ensure abstinence, perhaps once a week for a month, every other week for the next few months, and every month or two by the end of a year.
6. The network should have no agenda other than to support the patient's abstinence. But as abstinence is stabilized, the network can help the patient plan for a new drug-free adaptation. It is not there to work on family relations or help other members with their problems, although it may do this indirectly.

Keep the Network's Agenda Focused

1. *Maintaining abstinence.* The patient and the network members should report at the outset of each session any exposure of the patient to alcohol and drugs. The

patient and network members should be instructed on the nature of relapse and plan with the therapist how to sustain abstinence. Cues to conditioned drug seeking should be examined.

2. *Supporting the network's integrity.* Everyone has a role in this. The patient is expected to make sure that network members keep their meeting appointments and stay involved with the treatment. The therapist sets meeting times and summons the network for any emergency, such as relapse; the therapist does whatever is necessary to secure stability of the membership if the patient is having trouble doing so. Network members' responsibility is to attend network sessions, although they may be asked to undertake other supportive activity with the patient.

3. *Securing future behavior.* The therapist should combine any and all modalities necessary to ensure the patient's stability, such as a stable, drug-free residence; the avoidance of substance abusing friends; attendance at 12-step meetings; medications like disulfiram or blocking agents; observed urinalysis; and ancillary psychiatric care. Written agreements may be handy, such as a mutually acceptable contingency contract with penalties for violation of understandings.

AUTHOR NOTE

This chapter was adapted in part from articles by the author in the *Journal of Psychiatric Treatment and Evaluation* (1983), *Psychiatric Annals* (1989), and *Network Therapy for Alcohol and Drug Abuse* (1993b).

REFERENCES

Azrin, N. H., Sisson, R. W., & Meyers, R. (1982). Alcoholism treatment by disulfiram and community reinforcement therapy. *Journal of Behavior Therapy and Experimental Psychiatry, 13,* 105–112.

Begleiter, H., & Porjesz, B. (1979). Persistence of a subacute withdrawal syndrome following chronic ethanol intake. *Drug and Alcohol Dependence, 4,* 353–357.

Fuller, R., Branchey, L., Brightwell, D. R., Derman, R. M., Emrick, C. D., Iber, F. L., James, K. E., Lacoursiere, R. B., Lee, K. K., & Lowenstam, I. (1986). Disulfiram treatment of alcoholism. A Veterans Administration cooperative study. *Journal of the American Medical Association, 256,* 1449–1455.

Galanter, M. (1983), Cognitive labelling; psychotherapy for alcohol and drug abuse: An approach based on learning theory. *Journal of Psychiatric Treatment Evaluation, 5,* 551–556.

Galanter, M. (1984). Social networks in the office management of the substance abuser. In M. Galanter & E. M. Pattison (Eds.), *Advances in the psychosocial treatment of alco-*

holism (pp.97–114). Washington, DC: American Psychiatric Press.

Galanter, M. (1993a). Network therapy for addiction: A model for office practice. *American Journal of Psychiatry, 150,* 28–36.

Galanter, M. (1993b). *Network therapy for alcohol and drug abuse: A new approach in practice.* New York: Basic Books.

Galanter, M. (1993c). Network therapy for substance abuse: A clinical trial. *Psychotherapy (American Psychological Association), 30,* 251–258.

Galanter, M., Castaneda, R., & Salamon, I. (1987). Institutional self-help therapy for alcoholism: Clinical outcome. *Alcoholism: Clinical and Experimental Research, 11,* 424–429.

Gallant, D. M. (1987). *Alcoholism: A guide to diagnosis, intervention, and treatment.* New York: W.W. Norton.

Gallant, D. M., Rich, A., Bey, E., & Terranova L. (1970). Group psychotherapy with married couples. *Journal of the Louisiana State Medical Society, 122,* 41–44.

Helzer, J. E., Robins, L. N., Taylor, J. R., Carey, K., Miller, R. H., Combs-Orme, T., & Farmer, A. (1985). The extent of long-term moderate drinking among alcoholics discharged from medical and psychiatric facilities. *New England Journal of Medicine, 312,* 1678–1682.

Hunt, G. M., & Azrin, N. H. (1973). A community reinforcement approach to alcoholism. *Behavior Research and Therapy, 11,* 91–104.

Johnson, V. E. (1986). *Intervention: How to help someone who doesn't want help.* Minneapolis, MN: Johnson Institute.

Keller, D., Galanter, M., & Weinberg, S. (1997). Validation of a scale for network therapy: A technique for systematic use of peer and family support in addiction treatment. *American Journal of Drug and Alcohol Abuse, 23*(1), 115–27.

Khantzian, E. J. (1988). The primary care therapist and patient needs in substance abuse treatment. *American Journal of Drug and Alcohol Abuse, 14,* 159–167.

Mallams, J. H., Godley, M. D., Hall, G. M., & Meyers, R. J. (1982). A social-systems approach to resocializing alcoholics in the community. *Journal of Studies on Alcohol, 43,* 1115–1123.

Marlatt, G. A., & Gordon, J. (1985). *Relapse prevention: Maintenance strategies in the treatment of addictive behaviors.* New York: Guilford Press.

McCrady, B. S., Stout, R., Noel, N., Abrams, D., & Fisher-Nelson, H. (1991). Effectiveness of three types of spouse-involved behavioral alcoholism treatment. *British Journal of Addictions, 86,* 1415–1424.

O'Brien, C. P., Testa, T., O'Brien, T. J., Brady, J. P., & Wells, B. (1977). Conditioned narcotic withdrawal in humans. *Science, 195,* 1000–1002.

Vallant, G. (1996). A long-term follow-up of male alcohol abuse. *Archives of General Psychiatry, 53,* 243–249.

Wikler, A. (1973). Dynamics of drug dependence. *Archives of General Psychiatry, 28,* 611–616.

Yalom, I. D., Bloch S., Bond, G., Zimmerman, E., & Qualls, B. (1978). Alcoholics in interactional group therapy. *Archives of General Psychiatry, 35,* 419–425.

CHAPTER 21

COGNITIVE BEHAVIOR THERAPY

Ronald M. Kadden

Cognitive-behavioral psychology has been adapted to the treatment of a wide range of human problems. As applied to substance abuse, it provides a theoretical framework for understanding the etiology and persistence of this pathological behavior, and suggests a number of clinical treatment approaches. Several of these learning-based clinical interventions are described in this chapter, followed by consideration of their effectiveness.

"BEHAVIORAL" VERSUS "COGNITIVE-BEHAVIORAL"

"Behavioral" approaches focus on observable antecedents and consequences that affect behavior, without reference to mediational states, private events, or cognitions that can be known only through client self-reports or by inference from behavior. "Cognitive-behavioral" approaches, on the other hand, do include cognitions and thoughts, treating them as events that may precipitate or maintain behavior. In cognitive-behavioral treatment, behavioral methods (e.g., repeated practice, reinforcement) may be utilized to modify cognitive processes (Kazdin, 1982). This chapter emphasizes cognitive-behavioral approaches with somewhat less attention paid to the strictly behavioral ones. The

focus is on the assessment and treatment of current problems and the factors maintaining them, rather than on processes or events that may be thought to have been the original basis for them.

COGNITIVE-BEHAVIORAL CONCEPTUALIZATION OF SUBSTANCE ABUSE

The cognitive-behavioral perspective views alcohol and drug dependence as maladaptive ways of coping with problems or meeting certain needs (Mackay, Donovan, & Marlatt, 1991). Alcoholic drinking and drug abuse are considered to be sequences of learned behaviors that are acquired in the same ways as any other learned behaviors (George, 1989): through imitating role models; as a result of experiencing the effects of alcohol or drugs, for example in reducing anxiety, relieving pain, or enhancing sociability; or based on expectations that they will have one or more of these effects (Monti, Abrams, Kadden, & Cooney, 1989). After repeated experiences in which they are found to have desirable effects, drinking and/or drug use may become the preferred way of coping with problems or meeting needs, especially because their effects are felt fairly rapidly and may seem to require relatively less effort on the part of the user than alternative ways of coping. Repeated substance use in these situations, with desired short-term effects, leads to the development of a pattern of substance use in particular situations. This pattern is composed of a sequence of learned behaviors that include initial responses to the cues or "triggers" for use, acquisition of the substance, actual use of it, experiencing its effects, seeking more of the substance to continue the experience, and consequences of the substance use (which may be positive or negative). Just as with any learned behavior pattern, this one too is susceptible to alteration through the application of behavior modification interventions (Miller & Hester, 1989).

Given this perspective, the resulting approach to treatment for substance abuse or dependence focuses on the factors that tend to precipitate episodes of alcohol or drug use and that tend to maintain them once begun. Precipitants are the antecedent events that set an occasion in which substance use is likely or that actually initiate a chain of behaviors that culminates in drinking or drug use (McCrady, Dean, DuBreuil, & Swanson, 1985). A number of different types of antecedents may be involved (Miller & Mastria, 1977), including social (e.g., social pressure, interpersonal conflict), environmental (e.g., alcohol advertisements, settings where use occurred previously), emotional (e.g., frustration, anger, depression), cognitive (e.g., negative self-reference thoughts) and physiological factors (e.g., chronic pain, withdrawal symptoms). An important goal of treatment is to identify, for each client, the most common and most potent antecedents, and train more effective ways to manage them in order to break their connection with substance use.

Other factors may contribute to the maintenance of the behavior patterns that constitute substance dependence. Maintaining factors include various consequences that reinforce drinking and drug use, through either the occurrence of positive events or the elimination or reduction in potency of negative events. Maintenance factors lie in domains similar to the antecedents (Miller & Mastria, 1977), including social (e.g., encouragement from friends), emotional (e.g., enhanced emotional expression, reduced anxiety), cognitive (e.g., increased positive self-reference thoughts) and physiological factors (e.g., decreased pain, reduced withdrawal symptoms). Cognitive-behavioral treatment involves eliminating the positive consequences and identifying alternative ways to reduce or eliminate problems such as anxiety, depression, or chronic pain that are temporarily relieved by substance use. Treatment may also involve arranging for undesirable consequences to occur following incidents of substance use.

Regardless of the accuracy with which the antecedents and consequences of substance use may have been identified, clients may be unable to follow through successfully with a treatment plan because of their behavioral deficits. Clients may have never acquired the necessary coping behaviors in the first place, or having learned them at one time, now find the behaviors unavailable either for lack of recent practice or because of some inhibition (Mackay et al., 1991). Whatever the reason, behavioral deficits are considered to be a major risk factor for relapse because alcohol or drugs are likely to be relied upon in high-risk situations in the absence of more appropriate coping behaviors (Monti et al., 1989). Therefore, skills training is often necessary to teach or refresh deficient behaviors, reduce inhibiting factors that might prevent their use, and provide practice so that the skills will be readily available when needed.

From the cognitive-behavioral perspective, addressing the broad spectrum of precipitating and maintaining factors is more effective than focusing exclusively on the substance use itself. The emphasis in treatment is on modifying these contributing factors and overcoming skills deficits, to increase the client's ability to actively and successfully cope with high-risk situations.

The foregoing rationale follows straightforwardly from general behavioral principles, based on the assumption that normal and abnormal behavior are not qualitatively different (Kazdin, 1982). The applicability of these principles to the specific case of substance abuse behavior has been amply demonstrated (e.g., Abrams & Niaura, 1987). One of the last sections of this chapter reviews empirical support for this approach to substance abuse treatment. In addition to demonstrations of efficacy, there are other considerations that also support the use of learning-based treatment approaches in at least the early stages of recovery. Even after detoxification has been completed, cognitive impairment due to the effects of alcohol or drugs often persists for some time. It has therefore been suggested (e.g., Goldman, 1987) that clients would benefit from a structured treatment approach that breaks learning tasks into small units and provides repeated practice and review of new skills (although not all research supports this recommendation; e.g., Kadden, Cooney, Getter, & Litt, 1989). Another consideration, put forward by some advocates of the psychodynamic viewpoint, is that the uncovering of long-standing psychological problems, conflicts, and emotionally trau-matic events should be avoided early in recovery because the discomfort typically associated with this process is likely to increase the probability of relapse (Zweben, 1986). An intervention that focuses on specific behavior problems and concrete tasks to remedy them, rather than in-depth exploration of emotional material, avoids this problem to a large extent and may therefore be the treat-ment of choice for many clients in early recovery.

COPING SKILLS TRAINING

The coping skills training approach to the treatment of substance abuse is primarily based on social learning the-ory (Abrams & Niaura, 1987). The central focus is to teach or enhance the skills required for achieving absti-nence and for coping with the ongoing problems of daily life that could precipitate a return to drinking or drug use. The initial step in this process is to conduct a functional analysis to determine the nature of the relationship between the client's substance use and the antecedents and consequences that precede or follow that behavior. This helps to clarify the role of substance use in the client's life and its relationship to the factors that main-tain it, thereby providing a focus for behavior modifica-tion efforts. The basic assumption is that the events that precipitate and maintain substance dependence derive their efficacy from a client's learning history and are likely to continue to have an impact unless opportunities are provided to learn new behaviors and develop new associations.

The information necessary for this analysis can be obtained through a clinical interview. However, supple-mental use of structured assessment instruments (Donovan, 1995; Sobell, Toneatto, & Sobell, 1994) is recommended, to assure systematic coverage of all important areas. Although clients can rarely articulate what "causes" them to drink or use drugs, they are often able to identify internal or external events that tend to precede or follow their use of substances, and often can describe their typical pattern of use. Among the most common precipitants of substance use are negative emo-tional states, which have been identified repeatedly in numerous studies. Other common precipitants are social pressure, conflicts with other people, positive emotions, and temptations and urges (Marlatt & Gordon, 1985). In addition to assessing substance use antecedents, behav-iors, and consequences, it is also essential to assess

clients' coping abilities, which will play an important part in their recovery and may need to be a focus of treat-ment (Marlatt, 1985a; Shiffman, 1988).

The process of evaluation, with the review of substance use and other major life events that it entails, helps to focus the client's attention on the frequency and persistence of substance-related behaviors, and their impact on various aspects of their lives. The regularity of these behaviors and their connection to other problems may have previously gone unnoticed. Thus, the assessment process itself often serves a motivational function for the client, in addition to providing necessary information for the treater.

Having conducted a functional analysis to determine the pattern of drinking behavior and the influences that support it, treatment planning can then focus on the skills that need to be trained in order to alter both the chain(s) of events that typically lead to the initiation of drinking or drug use and the consequences that follow it. Monti et al. (1989) have broadly characterized the skills that must be taught as inter-personal or intrapersonal, and they provide a session-by-ses-sion manual for implementing a comprehensive skills training program. A brief description of the skills that fall within each of these two categories, as well as some general considerations regarding skill training methods, follows.

Intrapersonal Skills

The functional analysis of a client's substance use behav-ior may identify various internal experiences that play a role in initiating drinking or drug use. Some of them are likely to be substance related, such as thoughts about or cravings for their drug of choice, and clients must be taught the necessary skills to respond to them effectively. For example, clients are given practice in challenging their thoughts about substance use, and they are assisted in developing a list of activities that could serve to distract their attention until a craving passes. Efforts are also made to disrupt the chain of events that could lead to strong crav-ings as early in the cycle as possible, to catch problems at an incipient stage when they tend to be easiest to manage. For this reason, clients' decision-making patterns and problem-solving skills are examined to determine whether they tend automatically to proceed in directions that would make renewed drinking or drug use more likely. Training in decision-making and problem-solving skills can improve clients' ability to think through problem situations more successfully and anticipate the possible conse-quences of different courses of action.

The negative emotions that most commonly precede substance use are anger, frustration, depression, and loneliness. Therefore, clients are trained to be aware of anger and other forms of negative thinking and are taught skills to manage these emotions when they occur. They are taught to stop their thoughts, calm down, think things through, determine their best interests in this situation, and relabel upset feelings as signals to apply other coping skills (e.g., relaxation, assertive communication) that were previously taught. (See Kadden, Carroll, et al., 1992, regarding additional techniques for coping with depressed mood.) Relaxation training, including slow breathing and deep muscle relaxation, is often provided as a general technique that may be helpful in coping with a number of different intrapersonal states. In addition, methods for stress management may be taught to help clients reduce tension and cope with various forms of stress; these methods may include relaxation training, systematic desensitization, and cognitive strategies (Stockwell & Town, 1989).

Another common problem is the leisure time that suddenly becomes available when drinking and drug use cease. Unless this free time is utilized appropriately it could lead to resumption of high-risk activities that were frequently engaged in previously, thus increasing the chances of substance use. Alternatively, inadequate leisure-time activities may lead to boredom and attendant cravings to get high. Obviously, neither of these is satisfactory. Therefore, it is recommended that clients try out a number of leisure activities to find those that could be enjoyed in their free time, are incompatible with substance use, and that might also be utilized as rewards for specific accomplishments along the road to sobriety.

In these times of decreasing length of treatment, the most that can usually be accomplished during a period of formal treatment is to identify the major problems and introduce clients to the skills they will need to overcome their substance abuse and the factors that maintain it. As they leave formal treatment, they need to develop strategies for coping with persistent problems that have not yet been fully resolved and are likely to present continuing challenges to sobriety. In addition, it is unlikely that even the best functional analysis would identify all possible high-risk situations or other factors relevant to a client's substance use. Therefore clients are assisted in developing a generic set of emergency plans, based on the skills learned in treatment, which could be utilized in response to any of a number of unanticipated situations that may arise after treatment has ended.

Interpersonal Skills

Substance abuse is often tied to problems that clients have in their interactions with their family and/or people they encounter in other situations. Some interpersonal skills that may need to be taught or refreshed are related directly to substance use, such as the ability to resist offers to get high, or related forms of social pressure from coworkers, friends, or even family members. In addition, clients entering treatment for substance use problems may be deficient in some important basic social skills, the absence of which could result in isolation and inadequate social support, which are common antecedents to drinking or drug use. Such clients may benefit from training in basic interpersonal skills such as starting conversations, nonverbal communication (use of body language), giving compliments, assertiveness, and refusing requests, as well as higher order skills such as communicating emotions and improving functioning within an intimate relationship. Clients may also need training to handle criticism more effectively, to reduce the likelihood that either giving or receiving it will arouse strong negative emotions that often precipitate relapse. Finally, it may be necessary to assist clients in the development and nurturance of a social support network, which would enhance the likelihood of maintaining sobriety. McCrady et al. (1985) describe the use of social skills training within the context of a partial hospitalization program.

Skills Training Methods

The cognitive-behavioral approach concerns itself not only with the content of therapy but also with the manner in which it is delivered. Although didactic presentations of new materials are necessary to some degree, they are kept to a minimum. Emphasis is placed instead on modeling new skills and on active practice of them by clients. Practice typically includes a number of in-session role-play scenarios to maximize generalization of skills to a variety of situations, as well as homework assignments to encourage implementation and practice in real-life settings. Frequent reviews of previously taught skills enhance mastery of them and help to counter retention problems due to cognitive impairment, which is fairly common in newly abstinent substance abusers.

Regarding the order in which skills are taught, good pedagogy would suggest that learning proceed from the simplest, most basic skills to the more complex. However, in ambulatory treatment settings where clients live at home and are likely to encounter high-risk situations on a daily basis, it is often necessary to first provide training in some of the fairly complex skills that are essential for abstinence, to prevent both relapse and early drop-out from treatment. Thus, the more complex skills involved in managing thoughts about drinking/drug use, alcohol/drug refusal, or anger management skills, for example, may have to be taught early in treatment, prior to more basic skills such as starting conversations, nonverbal communications, or assertiveness.

Coping skills training can be implemented in either individual or group therapy contexts. Group therapy provides a convenient setting for skills modeling, rehearsal, and feedback, and promotes the sharing of past experiences with respect to the skills being taught. For these reasons, Chaney (1989) recommends group therapy as the treatment format of choice for coping skills training. However, it is also possible to do skills training in the context of individual therapy, with the therapist assuming functions usually assigned to group members.

In addition to being the object of skills training, behavioral techniques can be effectively utilized to maintain client focus and involvement in treatment and to control undesirable behaviors. Organized treatment programs can employ contingency management procedures to reinforce appropriate client behaviors, such as participating in treatment activities, practicing skills, and engaging in discharge planning. Contingency management may be particularly useful with clients who tend to act impulsively, who require structure, or who may be poorly motivated. Kadden and Mauriello (1991) describe the application of contingency management procedures in an inpatient milieu. A clearly written list of program routines and rules should be provided, spelling out consequences both for infractions and for successful completion of program goals. Rewards to reinforce the accomplishment of goals and development of appropriate behaviors can be selected from among options ordinarily available in the program environment, such as freedom to move about the facility unescorted, off-grounds passes, unlimited telephone privileges, gifts of AA literature, and presentation of a certificate on completion of treatment. Negative consequences for infractions of rules may entail a loss of privileges.

RELAPSE PREVENTION

In many ways, relapse prevention has much in common with the coping skills training approach just summarized and employs many of the same interventions. In addition,

it has fostered closer analysis of the relapse process, and has focused clinical attention both on interventions that would interrupt the process and on behaviors to be strengthened to prevent future relapses.

Marlatt (1985b) provided the first detailed analysis of the steps that are typically involved in the relapse process. His conceptualization begins with the types of factors that may lead an individual into a high-risk situation. Once in such a situation, if the person does not have adequate coping responses available to deal with it, for whatever reason, he or she is likely to experience helplessness or passivity, possibly coupled with the expectation that substance use would help in getting through it. Such thoughts are often followed by actual substance use, accompanied by cognitive dissonance pitting the prior perception of oneself as abstinent against the current reality of renewed substance use. This dissonance often leads to feelings of conflict, guilt, or self-blame, and a perception that one has lost control, a syndrome that Marlatt calls the "abstinence violation effect." The occurrence of this syndrome initiates a circular process that increases the likelihood of further substance use and often leads to a full-blown relapse.

Marlatt and Gordon (1985) have proposed a number of interventions to arrest the course of the relapse process. Clients are taught to avoid entering into high-risk situations in the first place through training in decision making, anticipating the consequences of their actions, and making choices that will favor sobriety. Clients are encouraged to give precedence to activities that are incompatible with substance use, and to strike an appropriate balance between the amount of time spent meeting responsibilities and time spent on activities for pleasure or self-fulfillment. Marlatt and Gordon (1989) also point out that in addition to the proximal relapse antecedents just described, there are also more distal family, social, and cultural factors that may affect the likelihood of a relapse occurring. Therefore, another aspect of risk avoidance must be the fostering of lifestyle modifications, which Brownell, Marlatt, Lichtenstein, and Wilson (1986) suggest be undertaken late in treatment, after the skills needed to acquire sobriety have first been taught.

Perhaps the heart of this approach is to make clients more aware of high-risk situations at an early stage, when they are easiest to manage. To accomplish this, they must first identify the main types of situations that would put them at risk. Clients are then taught to monitor their feelings, their thoughts, and the interpersonal and other external situations in which they find themselves, in order to be aware, on an ongoing basis, of potential relapse triggers.

Once they have been identified, successful coping with these potential triggers will likely require a number of the skills previously enumerated. As an aid to clinicians, Dimeff and Marlatt (1995) provide session-by-session instructions for the implementation of the relapse prevention approach in an outpatient setting with both alcoholic and drug-abusing clients.

The chance of relapsing in a high-risk situation may be enhanced by clients' expectancies regarding the positive effects of substance use in that situation. These expectancies can be combated by education about the delayed negative effects of drinking and drug use, and by suggesting that clients carry a reminder card, to be reviewed whenever cravings occur, that lists past negative effects of substance use. If an episode of substance use actually does occur, clients need to combat the negative effect associated with the abstinence violation effect. They are taught to take a constructive approach by viewing the slip as a learning experience and an opportunity to formulate more effective plans for coping with similar high-risk situations in the future. In this way, relapses may be transformed into opportunities to learn how to handle high-risk situations more effectively (Brownell et al., 1986).

Annis and Davis (1989) developed the Inventory of Drinking Situations (IDS) to identify clients' high-risk situations. It offers a systematic way of assessing relapse risk and provides a profile of typical situations that are likely to be problematic, which can be very helpful in treatment planning. Annis and Davis have found that clients with "differentiated profiles," in which some situations are identified as more problematic than others, have better treatment outcomes with relapse-prevention-oriented group therapy than patients with "generalized profiles" that indicate a similar degree of problems across all situations. Annis and Davis also emphasize the importance of assessing clients' strengths and available resources, in addition to high-risk situations, in order to determine the most appropriate starting point for a skills training program.

BEHAVIORAL MARITAL AND FAMILY THERAPY

Although family members would seem to be well positioned to support the recovery process, they may have precious little knowledge and a great deal of misinformation about their loved one's substance dependence, and may have developed troublesome behavior patterns of their own that could sabotage recovery. They generally require education about the substances that their significant other is abusing as well as opportunities to discuss the impact the substances have had on their lives. Coping skills training approaches were developed for alcoholic couples (behavioral marital therapy; O'Farrell & Cutter, 1984), and have been broadened for use with other family members as well (O'Farrell, 1995). Interventions include training in communication skills, conflict resolution, problem solving, breaking the cycle of criticism and recriminations, providing mutual praise for positive changes, and discovering shared leisure activities. Behavior contracts may be drawn up to help structure the newly developing interaction patterns and to clearly specify each partner's role. See O'Farrell (1995) for a more complete description of behavioral marital and family interventions, and McCrady (1985) for a detailed case example.

COMMUNITY REINFORCEMENT APPROACH

This approach combines a number of behavioral procedures into a comprehensive intervention package with special emphasis on utilization of community-based supports (Meyers & Smith, 1995; Sisson & Azrin, 1989). Its development thus far has focused primarily on the problems associated with alcohol dependence. As with the other approaches previously reviewed, it seeks to address not only drinking itself but also a variety of lifestyle factors that would be likely to undermine recovery. The overall goal is to develop a highly reinforcing sober lifestyle that clients will seek to perpetuate. Drinking would be avoided because it would result in a cessation of valued reinforcers. The community reinforcement approach is a form of contingency management, in which desired target behaviors are rewarded and undesirable behaviors are punished by withdrawal of reinforcement.

The community reinforcement approach incorporates a number of interventions. Recognizing the powerful role of social contingencies in the recovery process, it provides social skills training, a "buddy" whose role is to support efforts to maintain sobriety, counseling regarding leisure/recreational activities, and a sober social club that sponsors social activities and provides a safe place to hang out. Clients are also taught strategies for coping with urges to get high and refusing offers to drink. They are encouraged to take disulfiram (Antabuse) as a deterrent to drinking and to identify a significant other who will support them in taking it each day. Behavioral marital counseling is offered as a means of reducing stress at home, improving communications within the family, and enhancing support for sobriety. Finally, those who are unemployed participate in a job counseling program in which they develop a resume, generate job leads, practice filling out applications, rehearse interviews, and learn skills for retaining a job after finding one.

The community reinforcement approach differs from the others described here because of its emphasis on a broad range of social supports and its aggressive efforts to structure daily living activities. Provision of this wide range of services requires that a number of program elements be in place, including individual and marital counseling; groups to provide training in coping, social, and recreational skills; a social club; and a job counseling program. Because a number of these services are already available in many treatment programs, it may be feasible to organize and coordinate them, perhaps with some additions or modifications, into the comprehensive package that constitutes the community reinforcement approach.

BEHAVIORAL SELF-CONTROL TRAINING

This cognitive-behavioral approach focuses on what each client can do to modify his or her own behavior. Treatment may be therapist-directed or self-directed through the use of a self-help manual. In either case, the client is expected to assume responsibility for the content and pace of his or her own treatment. Among the specific elements typically included are goal setting, self-monitoring, recording the details of any drinking or drug use that occur, analysis of situations that tend to trigger cravings or actual use, coping skills training for handling difficult situations, homework exercises to practice new skills, and self-rewards for accomplishing goals (Hester, 1995). Self-control training sometimes has been utilized with a treatment goal of total abstinence, but more often with a goal of "controlled drinking," for clients who have relatively shorter durations of problem drinking, low dependence severity, and few alcohol-related problems. The controlled-drinking approach may be particularly useful with clients who initially refuse to consider a treatment goal of abstinence without first having tried to achieve moderation. In the long run, however, although some clients are successful in moderating their drinking, Hester reports that many eventually shift to abstinence.

AVERSION THERAPY

This behavioral approach seeks to develop a conditioned aversion by repeatedly associating an aversive event with alcohol. Treatment procedures involve either the pairing of stressful or painful stimuli (e.g., nausea or electric shock) with actual alcohol consumption, or the pairing of images of drinking with images of unpleasant scenes or experiences. Results of these procedures have been mixed, a finding that Rimmele, Howard, and Hilfrink (1995) attribute to inconsistencies in implementation. It has been found that their effectiveness can be enhanced by combining them with other cognitive-behavioral strategies. Despite continuing interest in aversion therapies over the years, they have not been widely adopted by treatment providers.

CUE EXPOSURE

Cue exposure therapy is based on conditioning theory, and seeks to diminish responsivity to the antecedent stimuli that precipitate substance use (Cooney, Baker & Pomerleau, 1983). When utilized with alcoholics, it often involves repeated presentations of a client's favorite alcoholic beverage, encouraging the client to observe and smell the drink without actually consuming any of it. For drug abusers, the cues involve drug-related paraphernalia, substances that appear similar to the drug (such as talcum powder for cocaine users), or photographs of high-risk locales and of actual drug use. The arousal generated in these situations may be heightened by at the same time having the client imagine an emotional scene in which drug consumption would be highly likely for the client. In theory, the repeated exposures to these arousing stimuli, without the reinforcement of actual substance ingestion, should eventually extinguish their power to elicit cravings or to signal an occasion to get high. The exposures to these stimuli without accompanying substance use may also provide opportunities to practice coping skills in their presence (Rohsenow, Childress, Monti, Niaura, & Abrams, 1991). The cue exposure approach is still in the experimental stage and cannot yet be recommended for clinical application; support for its clinical efficacy thus far comes mainly from case reports (Institute of Medicine, 1990). Further evidence is needed to demonstrate that conditioned responses to environmental cues are a causal factor in relapse and that cue exposure treatment has distinct advantages over other forms of treatment (Drummond, Cooper, & Glautier, 1990). Rohsenow et al. consider future research needs, which include investigations of dosage and timing, the relative effectiveness of various types of cues, and whether to train concomitant coping behaviors.

MOTIVATIONAL INTERVIEWING

Inadequate motivation for change is an age-old problem, particularly in the addictions field, where lack of treatment compliance due to client ambivalence has been especially troublesome. Over the past 15 years, a systematic approach called "motivational interviewing" has been developed to enhance client motivation to change. It is based on principles of cognitive therapy and the client-centered approach of Carl Rogers (Miller & Rollnick, 1991), with the goal of helping clients to resolve ambivalence and reach a commitment to change.

Motivational interviewing starts with the therapist's recognition and acceptance of client ambivalence. Proceeding through what may be characterized as a gradual shaping process, this approach attempts to move clients toward acknowledging current problems, developing a desire to change them, and identifying strategies that will enable this change. The basic therapist interventions involve getting clients to discuss problems that they have perceived as well as concerns that others have voiced, and responding to these revelations with empathic feedback that communicates understanding and acceptance. These aim at establishing a climate in which clients feels safe enough to identify and explore areas of dissatisfaction with their lives. The process conspicuously avoids labeling, arguing with the client, or confronting resistance head on. The therapist instead assumes a reflective posture that allows exploration of both sides of clients' ambivalence without unduly arousing defensiveness. Throughout the course of the discussion, the therapist provides frequent summaries of what the client has said, to focus his or her attention on the problems that are being uncovered and to highlight whatever motivational statements the client has made along the way.

Through repeated application of this process, that may extend over a few sessions with the therapist, clients are made more aware of problems that they may have avoided recognizing or only barely noticed with great reluctance. As a result of increasing their awareness, clients are brought first to the point of accepting the need for change and then to formulating a strategy for making behavior changes, which may or may not involve professional assistance for doing so. Subsequent check-up visits may be utilized to maintain client motivation and to monitor follow-through with agreed-upon change strategies. Although not strictly a cognitive-behavioral approach, it has been included here because the process of motivational interviewing includes behavioral procedures such as shaping and reinforcement of client verbalizations, and has as a goal the development of strategies for changing specific behaviors.

TREATING DUAL-DIAGNOSIS CLIENTS

One subgroup within the chemically dependent population deserves special mention, those with additional psychiatric diagnoses. In recent years there has been greater awareness of this subgroup with its added burden of problems, particularly as these clients have come to represent an increasing proportion of those who are granted admission to treatment programs. Cognitive-behavioral treatments for this group of clients have focused on relapse prevention and coping skills training (Director, 1995; Nigam, Schottenfeld, & Kosten, 1992). The particular interventions for treating substance use and psychiatric disorders overlap to a considerable degree, so that a number of the skills previously discussed could be employed to deal with both sets of problems. For instance, challenging negative thoughts, problem solving, and increasing pleasant activities are interventions that can be utilized in treating both depression and substance abuse.

As treatment proceeds, linkages between clients' psychiatric symptoms and their use of substances will emerge, helping them to understand how either one may trigger or exacerbate the other. For example, depression or anxiety may lead to a substance use relapse, or renewed substance use may come first and precipitate a recurrence of psychiatric symptoms that had been in remission. As skills are acquired to cope with these problems, the linkages between them can be severed.

In general, treatment of clients with Axis I comorbid disorders should be structured, and supportive rather than confrontational. Rules need to be made very clear but should not be rigidly applied, with greater emphasis on reinforcing behaviors that are likely to enable program completion than on confronting every instance of client "misbehavior" (Kadden & Penta, 1995). Change may be expected to occur at a gradual pace, over a more extended period of time than with other substance abuse clients.

With respect to clients having comorbid Axis II disorders, particularly those with B-cluster (antisocial, borderline, histrionic, or narcissistic) personality disorders, the emphasis needs to be somewhat different (Walker, 1992). A major point of departure is the necessity for strict enforcement of rules to contain these clients' potential for being disruptive and sabotaging the therapy. Nevertheless, the cognitive-behavioral treatments that have been adapted to these special populations (e.g., Linehan, 1993; Mandell, 1981) are generally quite similar to and compatible with those employed to treat substance dependence. As with the Axis I clients, treatment interventions should be kept relatively simple and well structured. Patient–treatment matching research has demonstrated that a coping skills training approach can be effective for alcoholic clients who have strong antisocial features (Cooney, Kadden, Litt, & Getter, 1991; Litt, Babor, DelBoca, Kadden, & Cooney, 1992; Longabaugh et al., 1994).

EFFECTIVENESS

Cognitive-behavioral approaches to alcoholism and drug abuse were developed from broader models that were designed to treat a range of psychosocial disorders. Their specific application to alcohol and drug problems has been guided by the findings of empirical research (George & Marlatt, 1983). This scientifically based origin of cognitive-behavior therapy in general, and the reliance on empirical evidence in developing its application to substance abuse problems, have engendered a tradition of experimental validation of clinical procedures. This may turn out to be an important advantage in the emerging climate of close scrutiny by third-party payers of treatment outcomes and cost effectiveness.

In a review of the cost effectiveness of various treatments for alcoholism (Holder, Longabaugh, Miller, & Rubonis, 1991), those with the best evidence of effectiveness were the cognitive-behavioral and behavioral approaches, including social skills training, self-control training, behavioral marital therapy, the community reinforcement approach, stress management, and motivational interviewing. These were additionally rated as being the most cost effective, falling in a range from minimal to medium-low on a scale of costliness. The aversion therapies were characterized has having either fair evidence of effectiveness (using imagined aversive scenes) or no evidence of effectiveness (using electric shock or nausea).

A comprehensive review of controlled research studies of alcoholism treatment outcomes (Miller & Hester, 1986) identified social skills training, stress management, and the community reinforcement approach as receiving sound support from well-designed studies that have been replicated. The clients who benefited most from these approaches had skill deficits in areas that were specifically

addressed by the treatment they received. Another review of alcoholism treatment effectiveness, by the Institute of Medicine (1990), cited social skills training, marital and family therapy, stress management training, and the community reinforcement approach as showing "promise for promoting and prolonging sobriety" (p. 538). The same report also noted that behavioral self-control training appears effective for clients who are not severely dependent on alcohol and whose related problems are not severe.

Miller et al. (1995) recently conducted a meta-analysis of 211 controlled alcohol treatment outcome studies. They assigned scores to different treatment approaches based on the evidence for their efficacy and the scientific quality of the research. Among the behavioral and cognitive-behavioral approaches studied, social skills training, motivational enhancement, the community reinforcement approach, and behavior contracting ranked among the most effective. Ranking somewhat lower, but still with positive effect, were aversion therapy (using nausea or imagined aversive stimuli), relapse prevention, cognitive therapy, and behavioral marital or family therapy. In this analysis, behavioral or cognitive-behavioral approaches that did not have a positive effect included behavioral self-control training, systematic desensitization, electrical aversion therapy, and relaxation training.

MacKay et al. (1991) have noted that although most of the cognitive-behavioral approaches described in this chapter were initially adapted for use with alcoholics and were evaluated on them, many of these approaches have been successfully utilized with a variety of substance use disorders and with a number of other impulse control disorders as well, such as compulsive gambling, eating disorders, and repeated sexual offenders. It has been suggested that there are certain basic commonalities among various impulse control disorders (Levison, Gerstein, & Maloff, 1983) that make them amenable to generally similar treatment approaches.

Two of the interventions described in earlier sections of this chapter have not been widely utilized as of yet or extensively tested, although promising outcomes have been reported. Studies of motivational interviewing, which is a relatively new technique, have given early indications of effectiveness (e.g., Bien, Miller, & Boroughs, 1993). Cue exposure is still in the experimental stages and is not considered ready for clinical application; as noted previously, support for its efficacy thus far is mainly in the form of case reports.

To date, treatment outcome research has failed to identify any single approach, whether behavioral or any other type, that is superior across a broad spectrum of clients. In the absence of a clear winner in the search for a generally effective treatment, the field is increasingly looking to patient–treatment matching research to identify treatment approaches that may provide the most benefit to subgroups of clients with particular needs.

PATIENT-TREATMENT MATCHING FINDINGS

Although the patient–treatment matching literature is still in its infancy with relatively little empirical support, there nevertheless are some studies which identify clients who could benefit most from cognitive-behavioral treatment approaches. In a series of reports of a matching study that included a cognitive-behavioral intervention, Kadden, Litt, Cooney, and Busher (1992), Kadden et al. (1989), and Cooney et al. (1991) found that clients who had more sociopathic characteristics, more evidence of psychopathology, and greater urge to drink (in a role-play situation) had better outcomes if given coping skills group treatment: they were more likely to remain abstinent and less likely to suffer renewed alcohol-related problems. Clients who were relatively free of these three characteristics fared better if they were assigned to interactional group therapy. One aspect of these results has been replicated by Longabaugh et al. (1994), who also found that clients with antisocial characteristics had better treatment outcomes following coping skills treatment.

Additional findings from other matching studies that employed cognitive-behavioral treatments (see the review by Mattson et al., 1994) indicate that clients with an external locus of control have better outcomes when provided with coping skills counseling; clients who have substantial urges to drink, experience high anxiety, or are less educated, benefit most from communication skills training; clients who can identify specific high-risk situations do better with relapse prevention treatment; single men benefit most from the community reinforcement approach; clients with poor motivation benefit more from motivational interviewing than from skills-based counseling. The emerging literature has thus identified several client characteristics that have potential to serve as the basis for matching clients to behavioral and cognitive-behavioral treatments, but considerably more work is needed to determine which, if any, of these will be practical when applied in clinical settings. A multisite cooperative study is now in progress (Project MATCH Research Group, 1993) that will have sufficient participants (over 1,700) to test a number of matching hypotheses. Clients in that study were assessed for a variety of characteristics and were randomly assigned to one of three different interventions: a cognitive-behavioral coping skills treatment, a 12-step facilitation treatment, and a motivational enhancement treatment. Outcomes will be evaluated on a number of different dimensions. It is anticipated that through this and other ongoing research the matching strategy will enhance the effectiveness of all treatments, including the cognitive-behavioral approaches, by directing their application to the clients who are most likely to benefit from them.

SUMMARY

A cognitive-behavioral conceptualization of addictive behavior has been described in which abusive drinking and drug use are considered to be learned behaviors that can be modified. The coping skills approach to treatment was outlined in some detail, highlighting its attention to both the interpersonal and intrapersonal antecedents and consequences that tend to support substance use. Other cognitive-behavioral and behavioral approaches were also considered, including relapse prevention, behavioral marital therapy, the community reinforcement approach, behavioral self-control training, aversion therapy, cue exposure therapy, and motivational interviewing. A number of these approaches have been found to be both effective and cost effective. However, as no single approach has been shown to be effective for a majority of substance abusers, there has been increased interest in identifying matches between treatments and particular types of clients as a way of further improving treatment effectiveness.

AUTHOR NOTE

The writing of this chapter was supported in part by NIAAA grant R01-AA09648. A condensed version appeared in Alcohol Health and Research World (1994).

Correspondence concerning this chapter should be addressed to Ronald M. Kadden, Ph.D., Department of Psychiatry, University of Connecticut Health Center, Farmington, CT 06030.

REFERENCES

Abrams, D. B., & Niaura, R. S. (1987). Social learning theory. In H. T. Blane & K. E. Leonard (Eds.), *Psychological theories of drinking and alcoholism* (pp. 131–178). New York: Guilford Press.

Annis, H. M., & Davis, C. S. (1989). Relapse prevention. In R.K. Hester & W.R. Miller (Eds.), *Handbook of alcoholism treatment approaches: Effective alternatives* (pp. 170–182). New York: Pergamon Press.

Bien, T. H., Miller, W. R., & Boroughs, J. M. (1993). Motivational interviewing with alcohol outpatients. *Behavioural and Cognitive Psychotherapy, 21,* 347–356.

Brownell, K. D., Marlatt, G. A., Lichtenstein, E., & Wilson, G. T. (1986). Understanding and preventing relapse. *American Psychologist, 41,* 765–782.

Chaney, E. F. (1989). Social skills training. In R.K. Hester, & W.R. Miller (Eds.), *Handbook of alcoholism treatment approaches* (pp. 206–221). New York: Pergamon Press.

Cooney, N. L., Baker, L. H., & Pomerleau, O. F. (1983). Cue exposure for relapse prevention in alcohol treatment. In: K. D. Craig & R. J. McMahon (Eds.), *Advances in clinical behavior therapy* (pp. 194–210). New York: Brunner/Mazel.

Cooney, N. L., Kadden, R. M., Litt, M. D., & Getter, H. (1991). Matching alcoholics to coping skills or interactional therapies: Two-year follow-up results. *Journal of Consulting and Clinical Psychology, 59,* 598–601.

Dimeff, L. A., & Marlatt, G. A. (1995). Relapse prevention. In R. K. Hester & W. R. Miller (Eds.), *Handbook of alcoholism treatment approaches: Effective alternatives* (2nd ed., pp. 176–194). Boston: Allyn and Bacon.

Director, L. (1995). Dual diagnosis: Outpatient treatment of substance abusers with coexisting psychiatric disorders. In A. M. Washton (Ed.), *Psychotherapy and substance abuse: A practitioner's handbook* (pp. 375–393). New York: Guilford Press.

Donovan, D. M. (1995). Assessments to aid in the treatment planning process. In J.P. Allen & M. Columbus (Eds.), *Assessing alcohol problems. A guide for clinicians and researchers* (pp. 75–122). Bethesda, MD: NIAAA.

Drummond, D. C., Cooper, T., & Glautier, S. P. (1990). Conditioned learning in alcohol dependence: Implications for cue exposure treatment. *British Journal of Addiction, 85,* 725–743.

George, W. (1989). Marlatt and Gordon's relapse prevention model: A cognitive-behavioral approach to understanding and preventing relapse. *Journal of Chemical Dependency Treatment, 2,* 125–152.

George, W. H., & Marlatt, G. A. (1983). Alcoholism: The evolution of a behavioral perspective. In M. Galanter (Ed.), *Recent developments in alcoholism: Vol. 1* (pp. 105–138). New York: Plenum Press.

Goldman, M. S. (1987). The role of time and practice in recovery of function in alcoholics. In O.A. Parsons, N. Butters, & P.E. Nathan (Eds.), *Neuropsychology of alcoholism: Implications for diagnosis and treatment* (pp. 291–321). New York: Guilford Press.

Hester, R. K. (1995). Behavioral self-control training. In R. K. Hester & W. R. Miller (Eds.), *Handbook of alcoholism treatment approaches: Effective alternatives* (2nd ed., pp. 148–159). Boston: Allyn and Bacon.

Holder, H., Longabaugh, R., Miller, W. R., & Rubonis, A. V. (1991). The cost effectiveness of treatment for alcoholism: A first approximation. *Journal of Studies on Alcohol, 52,* 517–540.

Institute of Medicine. (1990). *Broadening the base of treatment for alcohol problems.* Washington, DC: National Academy Press.

Kadden, R. M., Carroll, K., Donovan, D., Cooney, N., Monti, P., Abrams, D., Litt, M., & Hester, R. (Eds.). (1992). *Cognitive-behavioral coping skills therapy manual: A clinical research guide for therapists treating individuals with alcohol abuse and dependence.* Rockville, MD: NIAAA.

Kadden, R. M., Cooney, N. L., Getter, H., & Litt, M. D. (1989). Matching alcoholics to coping skills or interactional therapies: Posttreatment results. *Journal of Consulting and Clinical Psychology, 57,* 698–704.

Kadden, R. M., Litt, M. D., Cooney, N. L., & Busher, D. A. (1992). Relationship between role-play measures of coping skills and alcoholism treatment outcome. *Addictive Behaviors, 17,* 425–437.

Kadden, R. M., & Mauriello, I. J. (1991). Enhancing participation in substance abuse treatment using an incentive system. *Journal of Substance Abuse Treatment, 8,* 113–124.

Kadden, R. M., & Penta, C. R. (1995). Structured inpatient treatment: A coping-skills training approach. In A. M. Washton (Ed.), *Psychotherapy and substance abuse: A practitioner's handbook* (pp. 295–313). New York: Guilford Press.

Kazdin, A. E. (1982). History of behavior modification. In A. S. Bellack, M. Hersen, & A. E. Kazdin (Eds.), *International handbook of behavior modification and therapy* (pp. 3–32). New York: Plenum Press.

Levison, P. K., Gerstein, D. R., & Maloff, D. R. (Eds.). (1983). *Commonalities in substance abuse and habitual behavior.* Lexington, MA: Lexington Books.

Linehan, M. (1993). *Skills training manual for treating borderline personality disorder.* New York: Guilford Press.

Litt, M. D., Babor, T. F., DelBoca, F. K., Kadden, R. M., & Cooney, N. L. (1992). Types of alcoholics, II: Application of an empirically derived typology to treatment matching. *Archives of General Psychiatry, 49,* 609–614.

Longabaugh, R., Rubin, A., Malloy, P., Beattie, M., Clifford, P. R., & Noel, N. (1994). Drinking outcomes of alcohol abusers diagnosed as antisocial personality disorder. *Alcoholism: Clinical and Experimental Research, 18,* 778–785.

Mackay, P. W., Donovan, D. M., & Marlatt, G. A. (1991). Cognitive and behavioral approaches to alcohol abuse. In R. J. Frances & S. I. Miller (Eds.), *Clinical textbook of addictive disorders* (pp. 452–481). New York: Guilford Press.

Mandell, W. (1981). Sociopathic alcoholics: Matching treatment and patients. In: E. Gottheil, A.T. McLellan, & K.A. Druley (Eds.), *Matching patient needs and treatment methods in alcoholism and drug abuse* (pp. 325–369). Springfield, IL: Charles C. Thomas.

Marlatt, G. A. (1985a). Situational determinants of relapse and skill-training interventions. In G. A. Marlatt,& J. R. Gordon (Eds.), *Relapse prevention: Maintenance strategies in the treatment of addictive behaviors* (pp. 71–127). New York: Guilford Press.

Marlatt, G. A. (1985b). Relapse prevention: Theoretical rationale and overview of the model. In G. A. Marlatt & J. R. Gordon (Eds.), *Relapse prevention* (pp. 3–70). New York: Guilford Press.

Marlatt, G. A., & Gordon, J. R. (Eds.). (1985). *Relapse prevention.* New York: Guilford Press.

Marlatt, G. A., & Gordon, J. R. (1989). Relapse prevention: Future directions. In M. Gossop (Ed.), *Relapse and addictive behaviour* (pp. 278–292). New York: Tavistock/Routledge.

Mattson, M. E., Allen, J. P., Longabaugh, R., Nickless, C. J., Connors, G. J., & Kadden, R. M. (1994). A chronological review of empirical studies matching alcoholic clients to treatment. In D. M. Donovan & M. E. Mattson (Eds.), Alcoholism treatment matching research: Methodological and clinical approaches. *Journal of Studies on Alcohol Monograph* (Suppl. No. 12), 16–29.

McCrady, B. S, Dean, L., DuBreuil, E., & Swanson, S. (1985). The problem drinkers' project: A programmatic application of social-learning-based treatment. In G.A. Marlatt, & J. R. Gordon (Eds.), *Relapse prevention* (pp. 417–471). New York: Guilford Press.

McCrady, B. S. (1985). Alcoholism. In D.H. Barlow (Ed.), *Clinical handbook of psychological disorders: A step-by-step treatment manual* (pp. 245–298). New York: Guilford Press.

Meyers, R. J., & Smith, J. E. (1995). *Clinical guide to alcohol treatment. The community reinforcement approach.* New York: Guilford Press.

Miller, P. M., & Mastria, M. A. (1977). *Alternatives to alcohol abuse: A social learning model.* Champaign, IL: Research Press.

Miller, W. R., Brown, J. M., Simpson, T. L., Handmaker, N. S., Bien, T. H., Luckie, L. F., Montgomery, H. A., Hester, R. K., & Tonigan, J. S. (1995). What works? A methodological analysis of the alcohol treatment outcome literature. In R. K. Hester & W. R. Miller (Eds.), *Handbook of alcoholism treatment approaches: Effective alternatives* (2nd ed., pp. 12–44). Boston: Allyn and Bacon.

Miller, W. R., & Hester, R. K. (1986). The effectiveness of alcoholism treatment: What research reveals. In W. R. Miller & N. Heather (Eds.), *Treating addictive behaviors: Processes of change* (pp. 121–174). New York: Plenum Press.

Miller, W. R., & Hester, R. K. (1989). Treating alcohol problems: Toward an informed eclecticism. In R. K. Hester, & W. R. Miller (Eds.), *Handbook of alcoholism treatment approaches: Effective alternatives* (pp. 3–13). New York: Pergamon Press.

Miller, W. R., & Rollnick, S. (1991). *Motivational interviewing: Preparing people to change addictive behavior.* New York: Guilford Press.

Monti, P. M., Abrams, D. B., Kadden, R. M., & Cooney, N. L. (1989). *Treating alcohol dependence: A coping skills training guide.* New York: Guilford Press.

Nigam, R., Schottenfield, R., & Kosten, T. R. (1992). Treatment of dual diagnosis patients: A relapse prevention group approach. *Journal of Substance Abuse Treatment, 9,* 305–309.

O'Farrell, T. J. (1995). Marital and family therapy. In R. K. Hester & W. R. Miller (Eds.), *Handbook of alcoholism treatment approaches: Effective alternatives* (2nd ed., pp. 195–220). Boston: Allyn and Bacon.

O'Farrell, T. J., & Cutter, H. S. G. (1984). Behavioral marital therapy couples groups for male alcoholics and their wives. *Journal of Substance Abuse Treatment, 1,* 191–204.

Project Match Research Group. (1993). Project MATCH: Rationale and methods for a multisite clinical trial matching patients to alcoholism treatment. *Alcoholism: Clinical and Experimental Research, 17,* 1130–1145.

Rimmele, C. T., Howard, M. O., & Hilfrink, M. L. (1995). Aversion therapies. In R. K. Hester & W. R. Miller (Eds.), *Handbook of alcoholism treatment approaches: Effective alternatives* (2nd ed., pp. 134–147). Boston: Allyn and Bacon.

Rohsenow, D. J., Childress, A. R., Monti, P. M., Niaura, R. S., & Abrams, D. B. (1991). Cue reactivity in addictive behaviors: Theoretical and treatment implications. *International Journal of the Addictions, 25,* 957–990.

Shiffman, S. (1988). Behavioral assessment. In D. M. Donovan & G. A. Marlatt (Eds.), *Assessment of addictive behaviors* (pp. 139–188). New York: Guilford Press.

Sisson, R. W., & Azrin, N. H. (1989). The community reinforcement approach. In R. K. Hester & W. R. Miller (Eds.), *Handbook of alcoholism treatment approaches: Effective alternatives* (pp. 242–258). New York: Pergamon Press.

Sobell, L. C., Toneatto, T., & Sobell, M. B. (1994). Behavioral assessment and treatment planning for alcohol, tobacco, and other drug problems: Current status with an emphasis on clinical applications. *Behavior Therapy, 25,* 533–580.

Stockwell, T., & Town, C. (1989). Anxiety and stress management. In R. K. Hester & W. R. Miller (Eds.), *Handbook of alcoholism treatment approaches: Effective alternatives* (pp. 222–230). New York: Pergamon Press.

Walker, R. (1992). Substance abuse and B-cluster disorders II: Treatment recommendations. *Journal of Psychoactive Drugs, 24,* 233–241.

Zweben, J. E. (1986). Recovery oriented psychotherapy. *Journal of Substance Abuse Treatment, 3,* 255–262.

CHAPTER 22

SHORT-TERM MOTIVATIONAL THERAPY

Stephen A. Maisto
Wendy Wolfe
Jennifer Jordan

In recent years, conceptions of alcohol and other drug use disorders have changed in significant ways. One of the results of this change has been increasingly wide acceptance of brief interventions for change of patterns of substance use. This chapter concentrates on one type of brief intervention, called motivational therapy. The importance of motivation to the treatment of substance use disorders is underscored by Donovan and Marlatt (1993), who stated that "the focus on the level of the client's motivation and the development of techniques to enhance it represent major advances in the cognitive-behavioral approach to alcohol problems" (p. 402).

DEFINITIONS

It is important to clarify two terms used in the title of this chapter, "short-term" and "motivational." In the substance abuse treatment literature, the definition of short-term treatment is linked to a more commonly used term, "brief intervention." Throughout the rapid growth of the brief intervention literature over the past 10 years, the definition of "brief" has not been clear or consistent. For example, Heather (1989, 1995) has argued that brief interventions are not a specific type of treatment, but rather a collection of interventions that are distinct from but not necessarily incompatible with more traditional treatment approaches. This comparative approach to definition also is seen in the work of Minicucci (1994) and Richmond and Anderson (1994). These authors also define brief as relative to "minimal," "moderate," and "intensive" treatment. In this regard, brief is viewed on a continuum of treatment intensity, lying between minimal and moderate interventions. In an attempt at further definition, Babor (1994) placed numbers on the degrees of treatment intensity. Babor called interventions lasting one (5-minute) session minimal, interventions lasting not more than three 1-hour sessions brief, interventions of five to seven sessions moderate, and interventions of eight or more sessions intensive. Jonson, Hermansson, Ronnberg, Gyllenhammar, and Forsberg (1995) corroborated Babor's definition of "brief" in their review of the literature on brief intervention for alcohol problems.

Donovan and Marlatt's (1993) summary of the brief intervention research includes a list of characteristics that describe brief interventions in substance abuse. These five characteristics are (1) an emphasis on early intervention; (2) a thorough assessment of patterns of substance use, the degree of alcohol dependence, and social and psychological functioning; (3) an educational counseling session in which feedback of assessment results is provided to the individual and, possibly, to his or her family; (4) a manual to guide efforts aimed at self-change; and (5) a follow-up contact with the individual in order to evaluate the status of substance-use patterns, substance use-related health indicators, and movement toward intervention goals.

Definition of Motivational

Historically, the construct of motivation has a prominent role in the behavioral sciences. With regard to psychological treatment, motivation is viewed as an extremely important construct for understanding the initiation and maintenance of behavior change (Bangor & Beutler, 1995). Unfortunately, treatment providers and researchers alike have found adequate definition and measurement of motivation to be elusive. The importance given to the construct of motivation to behavioral change has been pivotal in the treatment of substance abuse as well as in the treatment of other disorders. Addictions researchers and practitioners have given major weight to the construct of *denial*. Denial is a construct that is thought to be common to substance abusers and that is manifested as a failure to acknowledge or to have concern about their patterns of substance use and related problems even though they are obvious to everyone around them. Addictions treatment professionals stress "breaking through" denial as critical to treatment, as it is seen as the primary cause of the substance abuser's failure to initiate or to maintain behavior change.

Miller (1985) has played a primary role in providing a definition of motivation that has proved to be of major theoretical and heuristic value to addictions treatment. Moreover, Miller (1995) has made the argument that motivation is not a trait that is characteristic of substance abusers, but a product of an interaction between therapist and client. In this way, motivation is viewed as a dynamic process of interaction and involves recognition of a problem, a search for a way to change the problem, and the initiation and maintenance of that change. This conceptualization of motivation has been influenced by Prochaska's (1979) transtheoretical model of change. In the field of addiction treatment the most influential aspect of the transtheoretical model is stage of change (Prochaska & DiClemente, 1982; Prochaska, DiClemente, & Norcross, 1992), which is highly relevant to motivation. This model includes *precontemplation*, *contemplation*, *preparation*, *action*, and *maintenance*. According to Prochaska et al. (1992), *precontemplators* have no intention to change, and

probably are most like individuals who professionals have judged to be in denial. *Precontemplators* either are unaware of their problem or show little concern about the severity of their problem. *Contemplators* are conscious that they have a problem and have some desire to change, but are ambivalent about change. In the *preparation* stage, individuals plan to take action in the next month to change a problem, and have tried unsuccessfully in the last year to change. As the name implies, the *action* stage is characterized by the individual taking steps to change that could involve modification of his or her behavior, thought, or environment. Finally, in the *maintenance* stage of change, the individual is making efforts to avoid relapse to the prechange level of problem severity as well as to solidify the changes already made.

An important aspect of this model is that research has shown that each stage is associated with different "processes" of change (Prochaska et al., 1992). That is, processes of change help to "move the individual along" to the *action* stage. For example, Prochaska et al. note that processes that are suited to *precontemplators* are consciousness raising and environmental re-evaluation, whereas self-evaluation is best suited for individuals in the *contemplation* or the *preparation* stages. What is traditionally thought of as methods or procedures that result in behavior change, such as helping relationships and reinforcement management, are best used with individuals in the *action* or *maintenance* stages of change. To be effective, a process of change must be matched to its designated stage(s) (Annis, Schober, & Kelly, 1996).

There are some problems with the stage of change model, in that research suggests that the change process does not meet criteria for a stage model. Also, the stage model does not necessarily describe how all individuals change a problem behavior (Orford, Somers, Daniels, & Kirby, 1992). Nevertheless, the model has been a valuable clinical heuristic. For example, the model is a key to Miller's (1983, 1985) conceptions of an individual's motivation to change whether such change is self-directed or aided by some type of social or psychological intervention. In this regard, motivation to change a problem behavior is viewed as the degree of the individual's readiness to make such a change (Miller & Rollnick, 1991). Moreover, the degree of readiness to change may be influenced by others, including professionals concerned with helping individuals to change problem behaviors. A therapist's influence is heightened if he or she correctly appraises an individual's readiness to change and then tailors interactions accordingly. These models of change advance our understanding of motivation and surpass previous conceptualizations (Donovan & Marlatt, 1993).

CONCEPTUAL BASES OF BRIEF INTERVENTIONS

Traditional Models of Substance Use Disorders

For the past several decades the *dispositional disease model* of addiction (Miller & Hester, 1989, 1995) has been the dominant model guiding substance abuse treatment delivery in the United States. This model has several major features that have implications for treatment. The first premise of this model is that substance use disorders are diseases, analogous to those diseases that have identifiable physical bases. A second premise of this model is that substance abusers have physiological and psychological characteristics that are different from nonsubstance abusers. The primary physical commonality concerns the body's reaction to the ingestion of alcohol or other drugs, and the major psychological trait in common is denial. Finally, substance use disorders are seen as progressive, irreversible diseases that can be arrested but not cured. It should be noted that the *dispositional disease model* may be followed as a single explanation of the etiology and maintenance of substance use disorder patterns, or it may be combined with other single-factor models, such as the belief that substance use disorders are products of a character flaw (Miller & Hester, 1995).

The specific features of the disease model have implications for treatment. First, this model assumes that treatment may be similar across individuals with substance use disorders, because they share a core group of physical and psychological characteristics. Thus, treatment is mass-produced, not custom-made. Second, there is the implicit belief in this model that the individual with a substance abuse disorder is "in denial" and therefore needs to "hit bottom," that is, to suffer extreme substance use-related losses, before he or she may be receptive to behavior change. Third, this model also assumes that substance abuse is irreversible and progressive, and therefore lifetime abstinence from alcohol and illicit drugs is essential to assuring long-term healthy functioning.

The Institute of Medicine report (IOM, 1990) was a major departure from the disease model, first in its view that alcohol problems exist on a continuum from "none" to "severe." In fact, the majority of the adult drinking population who have identified alcohol problems would be judged to have them in the mild–moderate range of severity. Second, the IOM report suggests that treatment intensity should be matched to level of problem severity. In the IOM schema, brief interventions are best suited for individuals whose problems are in the mild-moderate range, as well as for "hazardous" drinkers, who are individuals whose drinking has not yet resulted in identified alcohol-related problems but that places them at risk for that eventuality (Sanchez-Craig, Wilkinson, & Davila, 1995). However, specific alcohol treatment, say intensive inpatient or outpatient care, may be best suited to the minority of individuals with alcohol problems, in that such interventions are a better fit for individuals whose problems are more severe.

Another tenet of the IOM report is that individuals with alcohol problems may be distinguished by factors besides problem severity. For example, moderate, nonproblem drinking may be a reasonable treatment outcome goal for some individuals. Finally, the IOM report suggests that interventions for alcohol problems may be applied effectively at any time, that is, there is no need for individuals to hit bottom before they are receptive to treatment. It follows from this view of timing of intervention that treatment receptivity is not a function of denial, but of a person's readiness to change his or her drinking.

A harm reduction approach to the intervention of substance use disorders was developed in Western Europe and is gaining an increasing number of adherents in the United States (Marlatt, Larimer, Baer, & Quigley, 1993). This approach agrees with the essential tenets of the IOM report in that the primary goal of interventions is to reduce the negative consequences of substance use, whether on the individual or societal level. Therefore, an all or none ("abstinence only will do") approach is not indicated. Rather, any change toward reducing the negative effects of substance use is considered a legitimate intervention goal.

In summary, theoretical models that depart from the dispositional disease model have provided a firm conceptual base for application of brief interventions for substance use disorders in the United States. Research shows that brief interventions are not any less effective in modifying alcohol problems than are traditional, more intensive specialized substance abuse treatments. Concomitantly, considerably reduced health insurance budgets have driven the search for briefer interventions, in comparison to specialized intensive substance abuse treatment, that have empirical evidence for their effectiveness.

BRIEF MOTIVATIONAL INTERVENTIONS

The focus of this chapter is on a type of brief motivational intervention called motivational interviewing (Miller & Rollnick, 1991). Although other brief interventions have been called "motivational enhancement" (Miller et al., 1995), their content varies considerably (Chick, Ritson, Connaughton, Stewart, & Chick, 1988; Mallams, Godley, Hall, & Myers, 1982). However, the fundamental principles of motivational interviewing have been well described and standardized, primarily in the manual written for implementing the motivational enhancement intervention in the ongoing multisite alcohol patient–treatment matching study called Project MATCH (Miller, Zweben, DiClemente, & Rychtarik, 1992).

Description of Motivational Interviewing

Motivational interviewing is based on Miller's (1995) conceptualization of motivation. This conceptualization of motivation was extended in a review of the brief interventions for alcohol problems reported by Bien, Miller, and Tonigan (1993). Part of the integration of the brief intervention literature was to hypothesize six keys to motivation to change that seemed to be common to the descriptions of brief interventions that they reviewed, although none of those interventions contained all six motivational variables. These hypothesized keys are represented by the acronym FRAMES: Feedback, which is a comprehensive assessment given to the individual about his or her current status; Responsibility, emphasizing the individual taking personal responsibility for his or her behavior changes; Advice, which is a clear statement given to the individual to change his or her drinking; Menu, offering the individual different strategies to make behavioral changes; Empathy, stressing the empathic nature of effective therapeutic relationships; and Self-efficacy, reinforcing the idea that individuals are capable of making the changes (Miller & Rollnick, 1991). Thus motivational interviewing is the product of a systematic attempt to combine the FRAMES motivational factors (Miller, 1983, 1995; Miller & Rollnick, 1991; Miller, Sovereign, & Krege, 1988) into one brief intervention.

The fundamental goal of motivational interviewing is to increase awareness of the discrepancy between an individual's current behavior and his or her personal goals (e.g., prolonged excessive alcohol use is not compatible with a goal of a healthy, well-functioning body, or with the desire to achieve academically or professionally). Motivational interviewing stresses five principles. The first, *express empathy*, is a style of therapist–client interaction most identified with the work of Carl Rogers (1961) and that involves the use of "reflective" listening in order to acquire an understanding of the individual's thoughts and feelings without imposing judgment on them. The second principle is *develop discrepancy* between present behavior and personal goals. Third, *avoid argumentation* or confrontation in order to persuade an individual that a problem is evident (to the confronter). The next principle is to *roll with resistance*, which involves the therapist's using the individual's remarks to shift the flow of conversation toward change rather than away from it, and the therapist's making clear that the client makes decisions about change and has the capability of doing so. The last principle is *support self-efficacy*, which refers to the therapist's instilling in the individual hope for change, that is, that the individual can make the behavior changes that are desired (Miller & Rollnick, 1991; Miller et al., 1992).

Procedures Used in Motivational Interviewing

The essentials of motivational interviewing are described in an article by Miller et al. (1988). The process begins with a thorough initial assessment. The Drinker's Check-Up (DCU) is covered in two sessions, the first of which is a 2-hour comprehensive assessment (the "check-up"). The check-up is a multidimensional assessment that includes the Brief Drinker Profile, a blood test to evaluate for signs of alcohol-related health impairment, a battery of eight neuropsychological tests, the Alcohol Use Inventory, and interviews with up to three collaterals, who are individuals able to confirm the client's self-report. As Miller et al. (1988) noted, there is latitude in what measures constitute the check-up. The DCU's second session is held a week later and consists of feedback of the assessment results. There are several key points Miller et al. (1988) describe about the process of the DCU, and thus about motivational interviewing. The DCU is introduced to clients as a nonthreatening, objective evaluation of their status regarding alcohol use and related areas of functioning. The client is encouraged to participated in the DCU to learn about his or her status regarding these factors. Importantly, no labels such as "alcoholic" are used that might elicit a defensive reaction. To prepare for the feedback session the therapist summarizes the assessment data primarily by comparing the client's scores on individual measures to relevant normative ranges. This method of giving assessment feedback makes the findings *personalized*, not global, and therefore more likely to result in behavior change.

The actual feedback session is conducted in the "motivational interviewing style," that is, objective data are presented, but the emphasis is on the client's own interpretations and reactions to the results. When the feedback session is completed and the client is agreeable, different approaches to change are reviewed. In this review, the therapist and the client work together to choose the best approach for the client.

In summary, the essentials of motivational interviewing are comprehensive assessment and personalized feedback. In addition, motivational interviewing is a style of interaction between therapist and client that emphasizes and respects the client's thoughts and feelings, avoids labels, uses reflection and empathy, and encourages hope for change by consideration of use of any of a number of approaches to behavior change that could work for the client. A final point is that motivational interviewing may be used in several different ways. It may be used as a "stand alone" brief intervention or as the initial part of a more intensive intervention (Miller, 1995).

EFFECTIVENESS OF MOTIVATIONAL INTERVIEWING

The research on the effectiveness of motivational interviewing should be viewed in the context of knowledge about the effectiveness of brief interventions in general. This collection of studies has been reviewed by Babor (1994), Bien et al. (1993), and Miller et al. (1995). Overall, the conclusions regarding the effectiveness of brief interventions are favorable. For example, Bien et al. concluded that "the results from this substantial body of clinical trials are remarkably consistent: brief intervention yields outcomes significantly better than no treatment and often comparable to those of more extensive treatment" (1993, p.332). Furthermore, "brief interventions offer a suitable and encouragingly effective option to be implemented as part of routine care" (p. 32). A limitation to this area of research is that the predominant outcome measured is alcohol consumption.

Based on the positive findings about brief interventions for change in alcohol use, it would seem that studies of the effectiveness of motivational interviewing would have a good chance of showing positive outcomes. In the Miller et al. (1995) review, "motivational enhancement" trials are examined separately from those of brief intervention in general. It is important to note that two of the studies (Chick et al., 1988; Mallams et al., 1982) included in Miller et al.'s designated group of seven motivational enhancement trials would not be defined as motivational interviewing as defined in this chapter. Miller et al.'s conclusion about the effectiveness of motivational enhancement interventions is consistent with the conclusion about the effectiveness of brief interventions for alcohol use in general. Indeed, of the seven motivational enhancement studies that Miller et al. included in their review, only two did not show outcomes in favor of the motivational intervention. One of these two studies evaluated an intervention that does not meet the criteria for defining motivational interviewing that is used in this chapter. The motivational enhancement studies included in Miller et al.'s (1995) review primarily concern adults whose alcohol problems were less severe. Furthermore, the participants in these studies often did not present for treatment for alcohol problems, but rather were identified by use of screening procedures (Miller et al., p. 22).

Several clinical trials relevant to the effectiveness of motivational interviewing have been published since the Miller et al. review. These more recent studies are noteworthy in not being limited to adult, alcohol populations (e.g., Baer et al., 1992; Baker, Heather, Wodak, Dixon, & Holt, 1993; Baker, Kochan, Dixon, Heather, & Wodak, 1994; Saunders, Wilkinson, & Phillips, 1995).

More Recent Controlled Trials of Motivational Interviewing

Recently, four controlled clinical trials of motivational interviewing have been published. These studies are summarized in Table 22.1. Three of these studies concern illicit drug users, two of the studies involve methadone maintenance treatment (Baker et al., 1993; Saunders et al., 1995), one of the studies involves subjects injecting drugs and who are not involved in any kind of drug treatment (Baker et al., 1994), and the fourth study involves young adult college students (Baer et al., 1992). In all four studies, participants were randomly assigned to treatment conditions. In addition, at least for the studies focusing on illicit drug users, the outcomes measured went beyond the substance use variables that characterize the rest of the brief intervention literature. Finally, the results summarized in Table 22.1 emphasize treatment condition differences.

Table 22.1 Summary of More Recent Clinical Trials of Motivational Interviewing

Author	Population	N	Interventions Compared	Outcomes Measured	Assessment Times	Results
Baer, Marlatt, Kivlahan, et al. (1992)	College student volunteers	134	6 classroom sessions. Self-help format.[1] One 1-hour motivational interviewing (MI session).	No. of standard drinks in last week. Peak blood alcohol level in last week. No. of drinks consumed in last month.	BL, posttreatment, and 3, 6, 12, and 24 months after program.	Comparisons concerned classroom vs. MI on "short-term" (3 and 6 months), and "long-term" (12 and 24 months) maintenance. *Overall* reduction over time, primarily from BL to posttreatment, in all drinking measures. Changes maintained over 2 years.
Baker, Heather, Wodak, Dixon, & Holt (1993)	Injecting drug users (IDU) enrolled in methadone programs	95	One 60–90 minute MI session. Six 60–90 minute relapse prevention sessions, first of which is MI session. Advice about HIV risk behaviors (Controls).	Opiate Treat-ment Index. Drug use (last date) Scale. HIV Risk-Taking Behavior Scale. HIV antibody test.	BL, and 6 months after BL.	No group differences on needle risk, sex risk, and total HIV risk behaviors, or significant BL—6-mo. changes overall in total risk behaviors. Overall, increase in time since last drug injection. For "highest risk" month in last 6 months, relapse prevention less total risk behavior than MI and controls combined.
Saunders, Wilkinson & Phillips (1995)	Individuals in methadone treatment for opioid dependence α≥3 months.	122	One 1-hour MI session. One 1-hour "educational package" session (Controls). All participants received a 10-minute review at 1-week follow-up.	Opiate related problems. Self-efficacy. Stage of change. Outcome expectancy. Severity of opiate dependence. Intent about opiate use pattern.	BL, and 1 week, 3 month, & 6 month after initial inter-vention.	More MI participants contacted at each follow-up. MI participants fewer opiate problems at 6 months. MI participants more intent of abstinence of reduced drug use at 3 month, but not at 6 months. MI participants improved perception of abstinence or reduced use of opiates. Controls higher self-efficacy at 3 months, but not at 6 months. MI participants stayed in methadone program longer. Controls relapsed to first heroin use sooner.
Baker, Kochan, Dixon, Heather, & Wodak (1994)	IDU not receiving any drug treatment for drug use.	200	One 30-minute MI session. Noninterventon control condition.	Drug use (last 30 days) scale. HIV Risk-Taking Behavior Scale. HIV antibody testing.	BL, and 3 & 6 months after BL assessment.	Injecting risk behavior reduced in total sample, BL follow-up. No group differences on any outcome measure.

[1] The self-help format was not included in the intervention comparisons because of inadequate participant involvement.

As is evident from Table 22.1, two studies show no treatment differences in one or more dependent variables over time (Baer et al., 1992; Baker et al., 1994). In the Baer et al. study, this result was favorable to motivational interviewing in its possible implication that it was as effective as a classroom intervention that lasted six sessions. Conversely, the "no difference" finding in Baker et al. was not supportive of motivational interviewing, as it involves a comparison to a "no treatment" control group. Baker et al. hypothesized that the "personal risk assessment" that participants complete as part of their baseline assessment may itself have served as a brief intervention. In the Baker et al. (1993) study, motivational interviewing was equal in effectiveness to that intervention plus five relapse prevention sessions since last drug injection. However, the more intensive intervention was superior on total risk behavior in the highest risk behavior period in the last 6 months. Among these four recent studies, the strongest, most consistent positive findings for motivational interviewing are reported by Saunders et al. (1995).

It is important to give a few words of caution in interpreting the results of these more recent motivational interviewing studies. First, interpretation of a "no difference" finding, which is common in the brief intervention literature, requires the same degree of reservation needed in explaining any finding of no difference between two or more experimental conditions. That is, two experimental treatment conditions may fail to show a difference for a variety of reasons that may have little to do with their actual effectiveness, such as sampling error (Heather, 1989). Therefore, it is not logical to argue that a finding of no difference between groups "proves" that the groups do not differ. What may be concluded from such findings, however, is that they provide no evidence that the groups in question do differ. Caution also is advised in interpreting the results of these studies because of the high sample attrition rates during follow-up in all except the Baer et al. (1992) study. This difficulty invites caution not only because of the possible poor representativeness of the findings but also because of a loss of statistical power to find group differences.

Directions for Future Research on Motivational Interviewing

As noted earlier, the empirical literature on the effectiveness of brief interventions for alcohol use and related problems has been reviewed by Babor (1994), Bien et al. (1993), Heather (1995), and Miller et al. (1995). These reviews have included a number of recommendations for future research on brief interventions and these same considerations apply to research on motivational interviewing. The issue of client characteristics may be useful in matching aspects of an intervention (e.g., timing of delivery of its components, treatment goals) to the individual. For example, generally it has been concluded that brief interventions are effective with individuals whose alcohol problems are in the mild to moderate range of severity. As important as this issue is, however, it has received little systematic research. This chapter included review of three clinical trials that illustrate that researchers have started to address the issue of client differences in that they have begun to look at modification of the use of drugs other than alcohol.

The question of individual client differences interacting with motivational interviewing relates in part to the generalizability of findings on intervention effectiveness. Also, relevant to generalizability is type of response variables. Review of the literature has shown that the predominant dependent variables in the brief intervention research have been alcohol use and, far less prevalent, alcohol-related problems. However, it is reasonable to ask whether motivational interviewing and other brief interventions have "spill over" effects to other areas of life functioning. This approach to evaluation of treatment effectiveness is standard in research of more intensive alcohol and other drug treatments, and it would seem important to take a similar approach in the evaluation of briefer interventions to achieve a better understanding of the breadth of their effects. In this regard, the three studies reviewed in this chapter concerning illicit drug users did include a range of dependent variables in addition to drug use.

Another area of research that has been neglected in the substance abuse treatment field related to motivational interviewing is therapist variables. In particular, because the style of interaction between therapist and client is considered a core element of motivational interviewing, it is essential to learn whether therapist style does make a difference and, if so, what elements of therapist style seem to be most important. Miller, Benefield, and Tonigan (1993) reported pioneering research on therapist style in delivering personalized feedback to clients, and much more work along this same line needs to be done.

A final priority for future research is investigation of the "active" ingredients of motivational interviewing. The motivational interviewing research, like the brief intervention research in general, has been concerned with whether these interventions are generally effective. However, no systematic research has been done that addresses what underlies the effectiveness of motivational interviewing or of other brief interventions.

AUTHOR NOTE

Preparation of this chapter was supported in part by grant AA 10291 from the National Institute on Alcohol Abuse and Alcoholism. Correspondence should be addressed to Stephen A. Maisto, Department of Psychology, Syracuse University, 430 Huntington Hall, Syracuse, New York 13244.

REFERENCES

Abrams, D. B., & Wilson, G. T. (1986). Habit disorders: Alcohol and tobacco dependence. In A. J. Frances & R. E. Hales (Eds.), *American Psychiatric Association annual review* (Vol. 5, pp. 600–626). Washington, DC: American Psychiatric Press, Inc.

American Psychiatric Association. (1994). *Diagnostic and statistical manual of mental disorders* (4th ed.). Washington, DC: Author.

Annis, H. M., Schober, R., & Kelly, E. (1996). Matching addiction outpatient counseling to client readiness for change: The role of structured relapse prevention counseling. *Experimental and Clinical Psychopharmacology, 4,* 37–45.

Babor, T. F. (1994). Avoiding the horrid and beastly sin of drunkenness: Does dissuasion make a difference? *Journal of Consulting and Clinical Psychology, 62,* 1127–1140.

Baer, J. S., Marlatt, G. A., Kivlahan, D. R., Fromme, K., Larimer, M. E., & Williams, E. (1992). An experimental test of three methods of alcohol risk reduction with young adults. *Journal of Consulting and Clinical Psychology, 60,* 974–979.

Baker, A., Heather, N., Wodak, A., Dixon, J., & Holt, P. (1993). Evaluation of a cognitive-behavioral intervention for HIV prevention among injecting drug users. *AIDS, 7,* 247–256.

Baker, A., Kochan, N., Dixon, J., Heather, N., & Wodak, A. (1994). Controlled evaluation of a brief intervention for HIV prevention among injecting drug users not in treatment. *AIDS Care, 6,* 559–570.

Bien, T. H., Miller, W. R., & Tonigan, J. S. (1993). Brief intervention for alcohol problems: A review. *Addiction, 88,* 315–336.

Bongar, B., & Beutler, L. E. (Eds.). (1995). *Comprehensive textbook of psychotherapy.* New York: Oxford University Press.

Brown, J. M., & Miller, W. R. (1993). Impact of motivational interviewing on participation and outcome in residential alcoholism treatment. *Psychology of Addictive Behaviors, 7,* 211–218.

Chick, J., Ritson, B., Connaughton, J., Stewart, A., & Chick, J. (1988). Advice versus extended treatment for alcoholism: A controlled study. *British Journal of Addiction, 83,* 159–170.

Donovan, D. M., & Marlatt, G. A. (1993). Behavioral treatment. In M. Galanter (Ed.), *Recent developments in alcoholism, Volume 11: Ten years of progress* (pp. 397–411). New York: Plenum Press.

Heather, N. (1989). Psychology and brief intervention. *British Journal of Addiction, 84,* 357–370.

Heather, N. (1995). Brief intervention strategies. In R. K. Hester & W. R. Miller (Eds.), *Handbook of alcoholism treatment approaches* (2nd ed., pp. 105–122). Boston: Allyn and Bacon.

Institute of Medicine. (1990). *Broadening the base of treatment for alcohol problems.* Washington DC: National Academy Press.

Jonson, H., Hermansson, U., Ronnberg, S., Gyllenhammer, C., & Forsberg, L. (1995). Comments on brief intervention of alcohol problems: A review of a review. *Addiction, 90,* 1118–1119.

Mallams, J. H., Godley, M. D., Hall, G. M., & Meyers, R. J. (1982). A social-systems approach to resocializing alcoholics in the community. *Journal of Studies on Alcohol, 43,* 1115–1123.

Marlatt, G. A., Larimer, M. E., Baer, J. S., & Quigley, L. A. (1993). Harm reduction for alcohol problems: Moving beyond the controlled drinking controversy. *Behavior Therapy, 4,* 461–504.

Miller, W. R. (1983). Motivational interviewing with problem drinkers. *Behavioural Psychotherapy, 11,* 147–172.

Miller, W. R. (1985). Motivation for treatment: A review with special emphasis on alcoholism. *Psychological Bulletin, 98,* 84–107.

Miller, W. R. (1995). Increasing motivation for change. In R. K. Hester & W. R. Miller (Eds.), *Handbook of alcoholism treatment approaches* (2nd ed., pp. 89–104). Boston: Allyn and Bacon.

Miller, W. R., Benefield, R. G., & Tonigan, J. S. (1993). Enhancing motivation for change in problem drinking: A controlled comparison of two therapist styles. *Journal of Consulting and Clinical Psychology, 61,* 455–461.

Miller, W. R., Brown, J. M., Simpson, T. L., Handmaker, N. S., Bien, T. H., Luckie, L. F., Montgomery, H. A., Hester, R. K., & Tonigan, J. S. (1995). What works? A methodological analysis of the alcohol treatment outcome literature. In R. K. Hester & W. R. Miller (Eds.), *Handbook of alcoholism treatment approaches* (2nd ed., pp. 12–44). Boston: Allyn and Bacon.

Miller, W. R., & Hester, R. K. (1989). Treating alcohol problems: Toward an informed eclecticism. In R. K. Hester & W. R. Miller (Eds.), *Handbook of alcoholism treatment approaches* (pp. 3–14). Elmsford, NY: Pergamon Press.

Miller, W. R., Hester, R. K. (1995). Treatment for alcohol problems: Toward an informed eclecticism. In R. K. Hester & W. R. Miller (Eds.), *Handbook of alcoholism treatment approaches* (2nd ed., pp. 1–11). Boston: Allyn and Bacon.

Miller, W. R., & Rollnick, S. (1991). *Motivational interviewing*. New York: Guilford Press.

Miller, W. R., & Sanchez, V. C. (1994). Motivating young adults for treatment and lifestyle change. In G. S. Howard & P. E. Nathan (Eds.), *Alcohol use and misuse by young adults* (pp. 55–81). Notre Dame, IN: University of Notre Dame Press.

Miller, W. R., Sovereign, R. G., & Krege, B. (1988). Motivational interviewing with problem drinkers: II. The drinker's check-up. *Behavioural Psychotherapy, 16*, 251–268.

Miller, W. R., Zweben, A., DiClemente, C. C., & Rychtarik, R. G. (1992). *Motivational enhancement therapy manual*. Rockville, MD: U.S. Department of Health and Human Services.

Minicucci, D. S. (1994). The challenge of change: Rethinking alcohol abuse. *Archives of Psychiatric Nursing, VIII*, 373–380.

Orford, J., Somers, M., Daniels, V., & Kirby, B. (1992). Drinking amongst medical patients: Levels of risk and models of change. *British Journal of Addiction, 87*, 1691–1702.

Prochaska, J. O. (1979). *Systems of psychotherapy: A transtheoretical analysis*. Homewood, IL: Dorsey Press.

Prochaska, J. O., & DiClemente, C. C. (1982). Transtheoretical therapy: Toward a more integrative model of change. *Psychotherapy: Theory, Research and Practice, 20*, 161–173.

Prochaska, J. O., DiClemente, C. C., & Norcross, J. C. (1992). In search of how people change. *American Psychologist, 47*, 1102–1114.

Richmond, R. L., & Anderson, P. (1994). Research in general practice for smokers and excessive drinkers in Australia and the U.K. I. Interpretation of results. *Addiction, 89*, 35–40.

Rogers, C. R. (1961). *On becoming a person*. Boston: Houghton Mifflin.

Sanchez-Craig, M., Wilkinson, A., & Davila, R. (1995). Empirically based guidelines for moderate drinking: 1-year results from three studies with problem drinkers. *American Journal of Public Health, 85*, 823–828.

Saunders, B., Wilkinson, C., & Phillips, M. (1995). The impact of a brief motivational intervention with opiate users attending a methadone programme. *Addiction, 90*, 415–44.

Werner, M. J. (1995). Principles of brief intervention for adolescent alcohol, tobacco, and other drug use. *Pediatric Clinics of North America, 42*, 335–349.

CHAPTER 23

THE TWELVE-STEP RECOVERY APPROACH

John Wallace

Without question, the 12-step recovery (TSR) approach to alcoholism and other addictive disorders is pervasive throughout the world and is essential to many treatment programs. That is, the vast majority of people with addictive disorders are in some sort of specific program of recovery, professional or nonprofessional, and are involved with a program based in full or in part on TSR principles. The current world-wide membership of Alcoholics Anonymous (AA) has been estimated at 1,790,528 persons (Alcoholics Anonymous, 1995–96). Moreover, at least this many additional persons are involved in various conjoint programs generated from the mother lode of AA. AlAnon, a TSR program for wives, husbands, parents, adult children, and other adults whose lives are connected to alcoholics, was the first of these offspring from AA. Al-Anon, in turn, gave rise to a program for the teenage children of alcoholics, Alateen. Narcotics Anonymous (NA) and Cocaine Anonymous (CA) are TSR programs developed directly from the steps and concepts of AA. The 12 steps of AA have been generalized to nonchemical addictive disorders such as Gamblers Anonymous (GA) and Overeaters Anonymous (OA). Indeed, the 12 steps of AA have been tried in self-help groups for nonaddictive disorders such as Schizophrenics Anonymous and Neurotics Anonymous.

This chapter examines the concepts, principles, practices, and suggested 12 steps to recovery of this immensely popular approach to treating addictive disorders. Primary sources for interested readers are Alcoholics Anonymous World Services (1935; 1953) and Al-Anon Family Group Headquarters (1981; 1986).

MISCONCEPTIONS

Despite its widespread presence for over 60 years, TSR has often been misunderstood and sometimes misrepresented. It is important to examine these common misconceptions at the outset and explore the reasons for them.

Religiosity Versus Spirituality

TSR approaches have often been confused with formal religions. This confusion is unfortunate because it discourages persons who wish to remain agnostic or atheistic from seeking membership. TSR programs are not religious programs as they do not require belief in a body of dogma or in a particular god or religious figure. In fact, TSR programs such as AA do not require members to believe in or do anything. The only requirement for membership in AA is an honest desire to quit drinking. The 12 steps are suggestions for recovery, not requirements.

TSR programs are, in part, spiritual programs because they do suggest that members rely upon a power greater than themselves for assistance (higher power), but this power greater than self need not be a deistic power. Anything that can serve as a source of guidance, support, comfort, and direction can be employed as a higher power. Although some AA members may embrace conventional religious figures as their higher powers, many do not. Members are free to find a power of their own choosing and are encouraged to do so. For many in TSR programs, the recovery group serves as a power greater than self. For a smaller number of persons, the higher power may consist of abstract principles such as love, justice, knowledge, and truth and these may serve as powerful organizing and directing forces from which meaning and purpose can be derived. Today, TSR programs such as AA include agnostics, atheists, those who have chosen a nonreligious spiritual path of growth, and devout believers in some conventional religious figure.

Multidimensional Concerns Versus Addiction Specific Focus

Some critics believe that TSR programs are limited entirely to a narrow conception of addiction problems and that only drinking and drug use are addressed. In fact, TSR programs are complex, multidimensional, biopsychosocial programs for living that typically address many aspects of the person including wellness activities, emotional and psychological well-being, social relationships, and psychospiritual growth and development. It is important to note, for example, that the first step of AA—"We admitted we were powerless over alcohol and our lives had become unmanageable"—is the only step that mentions alcohol at all. The remaining eleven steps do not mention alcohol or drinking but concern other important aspects of a living program such as values, attitudes, beliefs, actions, and pragmatic practices for achieving satisfaction, serenity, psychological health, and a sense of meaning, purpose, and fulfillment in life. While some AA members, particularly those in the early phases of recovery, do talk at length about their drinking histories, many do not stress their previous experiences with active alcoholism and prefer instead to emphasize how the program has assisted them in coping with what are, in actuality, numerous problems in living once sobriety from alcohol and other drugs has been achieved.

Professional TSR treatment programs are also multidimensional, biopsychosocial endeavors. In such programs, people are not only made familiar with the concepts, principles, and practices of AA, NA, CA, and other TSR programs, they are typically exposed to multimodality treatments. It is not unusual to find some or all of the following treatment modalities presented at modern TSR-oriented professional treatment programs: individual counseling, group therapy, marital couples therapy, family therapy, relaxation and stress management treatment procedures, cognitive-behavioral therapy, recreational therapy, cue exposure therapy, social skills training, gender specific therapies, nutritional therapies, pharmacological therapies, and other specialized treatments. The belief that both professional and nonprofessional TSR approaches address only drinking or substance misuse issues in alcoholics or drug-dependent persons is erroneous.

Professionalism Versus Nonprofessionalism

TSR approaches have been criticized for being antiprofessional. Some of this criticism is deserved and some of it is not. In the early days of AA, people with addictive disorders were often poorly served by professionals in general medicine, psychiatry, psychology, and social work who were unaware of the nature of addictive diseases and how to manage them. Inappropriate, ineffective, and even dangerous interventions and treatments at the hands of poorly informed professionals led to considerable mistrust between recovering persons in TSR programs and professionals in general. Those physicians, for example, who routinely prescribed sedative hypnotics, benzodiazepines, and other addictive chemicals to alcoholics and other addicted persons, thereby creating further secondary addictions, aroused considerable ire and antagonism among persons in TSR programs. Some psychologists who, despite the absence of impressive, strong, and reliable data drawn from replicated experiments, continued to urge the widespread adoption of controlled drinking rather than abstinence for even severely physically dependent alcoholics, did much to widen the gap between members of TSR programs and profession of psychology. And of course, those professionals who persisted in viewing all addicted people as either "sociopaths" or "depressives" did little to encourage trust between the two communities.

Within recent years, mistrust between members of TSR programs and professionals has diminished. This improvement in relationships has come about for two reasons. The first, and perhaps most important reason, is that many members of TSR programs have had expert and caring help from increasingly knowledgeable professionals in medicine, psychology, and social work. Inappropriate and dangerous physician prescribing practices have diminished considerably. Psychologists in increasing numbers have recognized the gross inadequacies of the scientific database as a basis for recommending controlled drinking treatment goals for physically dependent and genetically predisposed alcoholics at any stage of progression of their disease (Wallace, 1993).

Many members of TSR programs need services from professionals in medicine, psychology, psychiatry, and social work. Although the clear majority of primary alcoholics, for example, who are in TSR programs do not suffer from psychiatric disorders (Brown, Irwin, & Schuckit, 1991; Brown & Schuckit, 1988), many do and these persons with dual diagnoses usually require additional pharmacological and psychological therapies. Furthermore, there are many other members of TSR programs who will not suffer from one or more additional psychiatric disorders in recovery but who will still need professional services such as individual psychotherapy, marital and family therapy, stress management, career and vocational counseling, and so forth. It is important, then, that every effort be made to develop open, trusting lines of communication between the TSR community and the various professional communities capable of serving them.

Inevitable Chronic Relapse Versus Continuous Abstinence

Many persons believe that recovery from addictive disorders is not possible, that treatment and TSR programs do not work, and that addicted persons are doomed to lives of chronic relapse. Although it is true that some persons will not recover from addictive illness and will die as a direct or indirect result of continued drinking or other continued substance misuse, many persons do recover and a very large number of persons, particularly those who maintain active involvement in TSR programs, stay alcohol and drug free for entire lifetimes. Because outcome results vary considerably as a result of multiple factors, it is not possible to give a single outcome statistic for all addicted subpopulations. However, there are some generalizations that appear to hold across various studies and observations. Some people recover without

formal treatment through commitment to TSR programs alone. Others appear to need some formal treatment followed by membership in TSR programs. Many of this latter group will not drink or abuse substances again after commencing involvement in a formal treatment program and commitment to AA, NA, or some other TSR program. On the other hand, a large number of persons may relapse one or more times after beginning involvement in either a formal TSR-oriented professional treatment program or nonprofessional program and then stabilize into a pattern of permanent, continuous sobriety. A minority of persons who enter TSR programs may continue to experience periods of abstinence followed by periods of relapse for much of their lives. Such things as differences in social stability, type of addiction, presence or absence of additional psychiatric diagnoses, and many other factors render statements other than these generalities meaningless. Obviously, a great deal of longitudinal research with different subgroups is necessary to clarify the different pathways into recovery that individuals develop and maintain.

Stage of Progression Upon Entry into TSR Groups

Some people, including professionals in psychology, general medicine, and psychiatry, appear to believe that TSR groups are only for older, chronic chemically dependent persons. This misconception probably stems from the early days of AA when the typical member was an older male who was physically dependent on alcohol and who had progressed to a fairly advanced stage of the Illness. "Hitting bottom" at that time meant such things as extreme downward social mobility, job loss, divorce and loss of family, serious alcohol-related diseases, and so forth. Although such personal and social disasters are still in evidence in AA, great changes in AA group populations are also apparent. Today's typical AA group "newcomers" are considerably younger, female as well as male, less or not at all physically dependent on alcohol, employed with good job and social skills, socially stable, and capable of high levels of functioning once the alcohol and drug problem is arrested. "Hitting bottom" is now often a matter of loss of self-respect, dignity, and painful inability to find meaning and purpose in life rather than social and economic considerations alone. Intervention programs in business and industry, schools, colleges, hospitals, as well as greater public access to information about alcoholism and other substance misuse problems have served to "raise bottoms" and bring people to TSR groups considerably earlier in the progression of their illnesses.

Reasons for Misconceptions

Misunderstandings about TSR approaches stem from a number of factors. First, programs like AA and NA are, as they state, anonymous programs. Nonmembers are not welcomed into closed meetings (although they can attend so-called open meetings). This secrecy has discouraged direct, empirical observations of TSR. Second, AA language is a rich, complex language with many concepts, slogans, and phrases that communicate something to members but mislead or fail to communicate anything at all to outsiders. Third, the language of AA is often exaggerated and extreme. Many AA sayings, slogans, and other statements are designed to persuade addicted persons to take action to better their lives and do not constitute carefully crafted, precise statements such as those that scientists use to communicate with each other. As a language of motivation and persuasion rather than a language of analysis, AA language is often characterized by extreme, black and white statements and emotion-filled generalities rather than qualified arguments and caveats. Finally, the formal language of AA as contained in its steps and the informal understandings that members have of these can conflict on important issues. For example, whereas virtually all members of AA insist that their program is a spiritual program and not a religious one, they apparently do not perceive the double message conveyed by referring to a power greater than self as "God" and "Him."

CONCEPTS AND PRINCIPLES

Powerlessness, Inconsistent Control, and the Disease Concept

Although members of AA and other TSR programs often speak of addictive disorders as diseases, it is apparent that most of these persons have not explored the complexities of the issues surrounding a disease concept of alcoholism or other addictive Illnesses. Hence, it is useful to distinguish between a traditional or "naive" disease concept that is held by laypersons and modern, sophisticated biological or biopsychosocial disease concepts hypothesized by professionals (Wallace, 1996). Much of the criticism by psychologists and other social scientists against a disease concept of addictive Illness (e.g., Marlatt, 1983; Peele,

1989) is essentially a quarrel with a concept held by laypersons and not a serious examination of the scholarly literature concerning considerably more complex and intellectually challenging theories and data on the possible biological bases of alcoholism and other addictive illnesses (e.g., Amit & Brown, 1982; Borg, Kvande, Mossberg, Valverius, & Sedvall, 1983; Burov, Zhukov, & Khodoroya, 1986; Daoust et al., 1987; Murphy et al., 1985; Roy, Virkkunen, & Linnoila, 1987; Tabakoff et al., 1988; Linnoila, Eckhardt, Durcan, Lister, & Martin, 1987; Tarter, Alterman, & Edwards, 1987).

Laypersons who are members of TSR programs also are typically unfamiliar with the considerable body of research that has accumulated recently on the neurochemistry, neuropharmacology, and behavioral genetics of addictive illnesses. For most members of TSR programs, the concept of alcoholism and substance dependence as diseases is essentially a way of talking about their increasing powerlessness over the course that their lives had taken while in the grips of active alcoholism and drug addiction, for example, "since I could not control my behavior, I must have a disease since diseases are not controllable." Not only did members of TSR programs experience powerlessness over how much alcohol or drugs they would use, they began to lose choice over when they would drink and/or use, how often they would drink and/or use, with whom they would do this, and the circumstances under which they would carry out their drinking and using. Equally important, the disease concept is a way for them to talk about the growing sense of the unmanageability of their lives. Not only were addicted people increasingly unable to control their use of chemicals as their addiction deepened, they were increasingly unable to control their behavior while using. Attitudes, emotions, beliefs, and actions became more and more disturbing and chaotic in the downward plunge into severe dependence on alcohol and other drugs.

Multidimensionality of Powerlessness and Imperfect Control

Powerlessness and loss of control are actually multidimensional concepts and involve much more than the person's inability to control the quantity of consumption. Hence the first step to recovery in a TSR program is the courageous admission that one's life is out of control—not only with regard to alcohol and drug intake but also with regard to the consequences of that intake. Most of the important factors in the lives of active alcoholics and addicts are disturbed, often to the point of chaos. Finances, marital relationships, parenting, friendships, work, and health are very often seriously impaired as a result of active alcoholism. Without recognition and admission of the truth about their conditions, little progress can be expected. People with addictive disorders who refuse to accept the fact that their lives have been made unmanageable by alcohol and drugs have little reason to attempt recovery and usually do not.

It is important to note that most professional TSR theorists do not regard loss of control as an all-or-none phenomenon. People with addictive disorders may differ considerably in comparisons with each other. Some alcoholics may show considerable control over drinking and their behavior while drinking on some drinking occasions only to lose it altogether on other drinking occasions. Others lose control every time they drink. Stage of progression is an important factor in assessing the degree of control that an alcoholic may possess. In early stages of progression of the disease, considerable control may be present. In later stages, control may be largely or completely absent. Other things such as degree of external control, expectations of approval or disapproval for excessive drinking, level of tolerance and physical dependence, as well as additional factors present in given social situations may influence how much an alcoholic drinks and how she or he behaves. Modern TSR theorists and therapists are more inclined to focus on the inconsistency of control that alcoholics and addicts show as well as their inability to guarantee their drinking behavior and their general comportment across drinking situations rather than upon total loss of control as an all-or-none phenomenon.

Powerlessness, Egocentrism, Will Power, and Higher Powers

The facts of imperfect control and increased unmanageability of their lives provide people with addictive disorders with a dilemma—if they cannot control their lives, then who will? If the illusion of personal control is given up, what will take its place? It is here that the second and third steps of TSR programs come into play. These are clearly the crucial "spiritual steps." The second step is a step that requires a change in belief or cognition. It states, "Came to believe that a power greater than ourselves could restore us to sanity." The third step requires a decision on the part of the person: "Made a decision to turn our will

and our lives over to the care of God as we understood Him." Both of these steps are attempts to stop the people with addictive disease from continued reliance on themselves, their imperfect control system, and the illusory belief in their own will as a way to defeat their addiction. In effect, the person with addictive disorders is being asked to admit to his or her powerlessness, accept the truth of his or her condition, and surrender.

In a sense, members of TSR groups are asked to do what humans everywhere have done for millennia when they find themselves caught up in life-threatening circumstances over which they have no control; appeal to powers outside of themselves. In TSR circles, this appeal to powers outside of self is, in effect, a form of ego-death, of surrendering oneself to something greater than self. It is a frank admission by the person with addictive disorders that he or she is incapable of self-governance and that ultimately that person's destiny is not under personal control. These are, of course, very difficult admissions for people to make and particularly so for those people who have been socialized to believe in the limitless power of disciplined effort, will power, and determination in reaching desired goals. It is very difficult to admit to the fact of one's inability to control one's life, to accept that fact, and then to surrender to the truth of one's situation. In actuality, surrender, is paradoxical as are many TSR concepts. Surrender in TSR circles is not equivalent to defeat. It is, in fact, the means to victory (recovery). By admitting the limits of personal power, the person gains access to even greater sources of power. By admitting that the ability to govern self is impaired and rendered imperfect by alcohol and drugs, the person is released from the ego traps, illusions of personal power, and grandiosity that have kept him or her ensnared in the hopelessness and despair of alcoholism and/or other addictive illnesses. Perhaps the most basic meaning to be taken from steps 2 and 3 is simply that the alcoholic or addict is being asked to stop trying to defeat the addiction in his or her own way and to give another way a chance. By turning to something outside of himself or herself for guidance and direction, the person may be able to stop the ineffective and self-defeating repetitive behaviors that comprise addiction and replace them with effective behaviors. As members of AA put it, "get out of the driver's seat," "let go and let God," or "turn it over." All of these phrases refer to the act of surrendering one's will and life to a power greater than self. And, of course, it is important to remember here that the power greater than self may be the AA group, a conventional religious figure, or a nondeistic ultimate concern such as love, truth, or justice. Any or all of these may serve as an organizing principle for one's life and a source of guidance and direction in the conduct of one's affairs.

Differentiating Helplessness, Hopelessness, and Powerlessness

In understanding how the admission of powerlessness might have beneficial effects in the life of a person with addictive disorders, it is important to distinguish powerlessness from helplessness and hopelessness. Helplessness is a miserable condition in which one has no personal resources and nowhere to turn in order to improve one's condition. It has been associated with depression. Hopelessness means that one's future appears very bleak, that there is no reason to trust in the future or to hold optimistic expectations about altering it. On the other hand, by admitting to powerlessness over alcohol and drugs, the person with addictive disorders is simply acknowledging the truth, that he or she cannot drink or use without negative consequences. And that admission is the necessary first step in seeking and accepting the help outside of self that is available.

Self-Knowledge, Mindfulness, and Self-Correction

As do virtually all forms of psychotherapy and self-improvement, TSR recovery programs encourage continuous self-examination and self-correction. The fourth step of AA suggests that members undertake a "searching and fearless moral inventory of ourselves." This so-called "inventory" step is intended to help the person with addictive disorders to come to further realizations and insights about the self. Because people with addictive disorders during active periods of drinking and using drugs typically employ defenses such as denial, rationalization, and minimization in order to shield themselves from negative consequences while continuing to drink and use, a characteristic "blindness to reality" usually develops. This characteristic blindness must be countered in some manner or another. Repressive defensives are not restricted to matters concerning drinking and drug use but are overlearned and generalized to many other aspects of the person with addictive disorder's life such as marriage, family, interpersonal relationships, work, and so forth. It is therefore necessary to encourage the development of a kind of "mindfulness" with regard to all aspects of recovering persons lives in order to reduce the overlearned "mindlessness" that characterizes active periods of alcohol and drug use.

Whereas step 4 calls for the recovering person to write an initial inventory of self, step ten asks that he or she "continue to take personal inventory and when we were wrong promptly admitted it." In effect, recovering people in TSR programs are encouraged to engage in continuous lifelong self-examination and self-criticism when appropriate.

Changing Undesired Aspects of Self

Once a person has uncovered the exact nature of his or her wrongs and what AA people refer to as "defects of character," the question of how to change these naturally arises. It is here that the spiritual portion of AA's rather unique way of changing undesirable traits is very much in evidence. Step 6 is, "Were entirely ready to have God remove all these defects of character" and step 7 is, "Humbly asked Him to remove our shortcomings." These two steps are often very difficult steps for newcomers to TSR programs. However, if the phrase "power greater than self" or "higher power" is inserted in place of a deity, then important understandings become available. For example, if the power greater than self is construed as the TSR program, then it seems quite reasonable to anticipate that following the program's suggestions, stopping drinking and using, and making a strong commitment to the program's practices and procedures will, in fact, lead to character change.

Steps 4, 6, 7 and 10 are essentially self-knowledge, self-improvement, and self-correction steps. In effect, if sobriety is to be achieved and maintained and relapse avoided, a great deal of self-understanding is invaluable. Insight into one's motives, awareness of one's characteristic patterns of behaving and coping with situations, clear understanding of one's values, and willingness to take responsibility for one's actions including admitting when one is wrong are considered essential for maintaining comfort and serenity in recovery as well as avoiding relapse.

SOCIAL PROCESSES AND TSR PROGRAMS

Although TSR programs generally endorse either a simple or complex disease model, they are essentially psychosocial approaches to changing addictive behavior. Even the most casual observation of these programs reveals that they are saturated with important social processes that include most recent major advances in such areas as social learning, reference group theory, social reinforcement theory, and so forth.

Social Support

The first psychosocial function that TSR programs provide is emotional support for people as they begin the difficult tasks of achieving initial abstinence from alcohol and other drugs and dealing with the many complications that have arisen from their drinking and drug use. It is important to note that many people entering formal treatment or informal TSR recovery programs for alcoholism and drug depen- dence are not only trying to put together a few days, weeks, and months of abstinence from chemicals, they are trying to put lives back together that may have been torn asunder by excessive drinking and drug use. People in initial stages of recovery are usually people in one or more crises that may involve finances, family, employment, legal entanglements, and physical health. In coping with the stress and emotional pain of these crises, many recovering persons have found that nothing works as well as the continuously available peer social support system of community-based TSR pro- grams. AA, NA, and Al-Anon meetings can be found in most towns, even the smallest ones, on a daily basis. In all cities and larger towns, AA meetings can be attended in the mornings, at noon, and in the evenings. In addition to meet- ings, members can call one another, meet for coffee and conversation, or go to each others' houses for help at any time even in the middle of the night if need be. In effect, people who are members of TSR programs and who are in danger of relapse do not have to get through a weekend on their own, wait for offices and clinics to open, hang on until appointments can be made and kept, and so on. Help in the form of peer support is almost continuously available and is just a phone call or a meeting away in many communities.

Identification with Others

Support is only one beneficial social effect of membership in TSR programs. Involvement in a community of other recovering individuals provides people with ready sources of identification. By identifying with peers who have gone through similar experiences with alcohol and drugs, peo- ple in early recovery find it easier to set aside the denial and other defenses that have clouded their judgment and shielded them from the reality of their drinking and drug use. Peer identification also helps them to reduce the shame and guilt associated with past behaviors while intoxicated. Humor is ever present in AA meetings and when a person finds himself or herself in a room full of people laughing at their own past foibles and mistakes while intoxicated, a kind of reciprocal inhibition and desensitization therapy is taking place. It is difficult to be ashamed of one's own actions or critical of the actions of others when everybody is making light of them. Because painful emotions like shame and guilt, if left unresolved, can lead right back to drinking, identification with others is of enormous benefit in TSR groups.

Sharing Secrets with Others

A further way in which shame and guilt are reduced and self-esteem is enhanced is through the fifth step. This step asks the recovering person to not only take a "searching and fearless moral inventory of self" but to make the results of this inventory known by admitting to "God, ourselves, and another human being the exact nature of our wrongs." The fifth step is clearly a tactic for releasing the power of secrets from the past to continue to cause shame and guilt and to damage self-esteem. It is assumed that once a person admits to at least one other person those wrongdoings that occurred while drinking and using drugs, shame, guilt, and remorse will be reduced and self-esteem will be enhanced.

Making Amends

Shame and guilt over past actions are also reduced by steps 8 and 9, the so-called "amends" steps. In step 8, the recov- ering person is asked to "make a list of all persons we had harmed and become willing to make amends to them all" while step 9 asks that members "make direct amends to such people wherever possible except when to do so would injure them or others." These steps are based on the belief that nothing removes the sting of shame and guilt over past actions as does attempting to admit honestly to harm done to others and then making efforts to undo such harm when pos- sible through various means. In practice, amends may involve returning money that was stolen from an employer while drinking, making appropriate apologies and asking forgiveness, paying damages, and so on. Of course, as step 9 states, there is nothing to be gained from indiscriminate amends making. The key to deciding which amends to make is the issue of potential harm to self or others that may result.

Social Reinforcement, Social Models, and Social Learning

TSR programs are also social learning communities in which all of the principles of modern social learning theories can be seen to operate (Wallace, 1983). AA, for example, is in part a "community reinforcement" approach similar to that studied by Azrin, Sisson, Meyers, and Godley (1982). Although AA does not, of course, use reinforcement principles to get people to take disulfiram as did Azrin et al., members do provide each other with continuous positive social reinforcement for staying sober, going to meetings, practicing the steps, going out on 12-step calls to help active alcoholics, and so forth. Such positive reinforcers may be either social (e.g., social recognition and approval, verbal rewards) or symbolic physical rewards (tokens of various kinds coded for increasing weeks, months and years of recovery; birthday cakes, cards, and parties for anniversaries of sobriety).

TSR programs constitute social learning communities for still another reason—the effective use of role models (Bandura, 1977). Sponsors and other "old-timers" not only dispense reinforcers to newcomers in the form of social support, recognition, and affection, they also constitute sober role models who display the kinds of behaviors, attitudes, emotions, tactics, and strategies for staying sober and achieving happiness while sober. AA, in a sense, is a great social learning machine in which members learn effective solution behaviors from each other not only for drinking problems but for many living problems as well.

TSR Groups as Reference Groups

Finally, it is important to note that TSR groups comprise reference groups for members and hence have great capacity to influence and direct members' behaviors. As a great deal of research in sociology and social psychology have shown, when persons perceive themselves as members of a given reference group, influence in terms of the attitudes, values, and sanctioned behaviors of the group is facilitated. Persons in TSR groups perceive themselves as "alcoholics," "addicts," "significant others," "adult children," and so forth. These categorizations provide members with role identifications useful in establishing strong reference group ties. Reference groups such as TSR groups encourage the perception of similarity among members leading to high cohesiveness, low organizational conflict, shared values and expectations, and a robustness capable of leading people with addictive disorders to states of sobriety and sustaining them in such states. Active involvement with other people with addictive disorders in TSR groups serves to reduce guilt and shame over past drunken or drug-involved actions and increases self-esteem and positive self-regard.

PRACTICAL TECHNIQUES IN TSR GROUPS

As we have seen, then, TSR programs are eminently pragmatic programs of behavior change consistent with social learning theories of change. TSR programs change members' cognitions, belief systems, typical behavior patterns, attitudes, emotional reactions to situations, coping skills, and so forth and probably have pronounced effects even on biological events such as physiological reactions to anxiety, stress, and depression. Although it has not been shown, it is may very well be that TSR programs have impact upon neurochemical processes.

SLOGANS AND OTHER COGNITIVE CONTROLS

Whereas much writing on AA and other TSR programs, both positive and negative, has focused upon the ideology and spirituality of these programs, very little has examined the techniques members use to help themselves and others. As Nowinski (1996) has recently pointed out in a discussion of 12-step-oriented treatment, AA is not only a spiritually based program, it is also a pragmatic collection of practical techniques for coping with difficult situations and problems.

The slogans of AA are useful cognitive control devices that remind people of techniques for dealing with stress, fear, anxiety, and other uncomfortable states. AA members constantly remind each other that "Easy does it" is the only way to approach the everyday stresses of life. "Turn it over to God" is another way to get members to stop focusing on anxiety-provoking or stressful thoughts about things that they can do very little about. "Take it 24 hours at a time" or "Day at a time" are reminders that the only reality we have to deal with is the one directly in front of us and trying to deal with life's problems in larger units is nonproductive, as the problems that tomorrow brings are often not the problems we imagined. Also, AA is considered a "day at a time" program because recovering people are told that they do not have to commit to a lifetime of abstinence but have only to try to stay sober a day or "24 hours at a time." "First things first" is a reminder that we should not attempt to solve all of our problems at once but should attempt problem solutions by setting priorities and dealing with manageable units in an orderly fashion. "HALT," which stands for don't get too hungry, angry, lonely, or tired, reminds the recovering alcoholic to pay attention to various stressors and body signals that can serve as warnings about relapse factors.

Some steps of the programs recommend particular methods for achieving peace and serenity. Step 11 asks the recovering person to seek "through prayer and meditation to improve our conscious contact with God as we understood him, praying only for knowledge of His will for us and the power to carry that out." In practice, this step may take the form of established methods of meditation like those found in philosophies and religions of the East. Transcendental meditation, various Buddhist methods of meditation, walking, running, music, self-hypnosis, relaxation methods, prayer, biofeedback, and other methods have been used by members of TSR programs to clear the mind and achieve relaxed states. The so-called "Serenity Prayer," which reminds members to ask God for the serenity to accept those things that cannot be changed, the courage to change the things they can, and the wisdom to know the difference, is a useful device for virtually all recovering people with addictive disorders caught up in troubling circumstances.

Meetings, Friendship Structures, and Alcohol-Free Settings

Although it is rarely considered, the action of attending meetings in and of itself is an important practical technique for altering behavior. Meeting attendance on a daily basis in early sobriety breaks up typical patterns of behavior. When people are sitting in a TSR group meeting in their own communities, they are not out in the familiar circumstances in which they drank, used, or sought drugs. By avoiding stimulus situations in which they drank and used, people with addictive disorders are able to avoid exposure to the cues previously conditioned to drinking and using. Moreover, the availability of meetings gives recovering people somewhere to retreat to when the going gets tough at home, work, or in the community. In addition to formal meeting locations, TSR group informal drop-in-centers, club houses, and coffee houses in many communities provide safe havens for many hours of the day for recovering persons in crisis or in immediate danger of relapse. They also provide alcohol- and drug-free places for lonely persons to go in order to find company and conversation when bars and cocktail lounges can no longer serve that purpose. In some communities, TSR groups hold sober dances, put on jazz-without-booze concerts and other entertainment, sponsor sober vacations such as a week of TSR fellowship fun and recovery activities at a Club Med or on a cruise, and arrange holiday feasts and celebrations. The latter not only serve to combat "holiday blues" and holiday relapses but give recovering people who live alone a place to go to celebrate Christmas, Thanksgiving, New Year's Eve, and other holidays with other sober people.

Within TSR circles, friendships typically develop and these often last a lifetime. In the early period of sobriety, pairs of "buddies" or small groups of men or women often come together to support and motivate each other by driving to meetings together, going out together for dinner or snacks before or after meetings, forming softball and basketball teams, holding and attending sober parties in each others' homes, and so on. These friendships serve to increase members bonding to the larger TSR group, maintain motivation, provide sober partners for recreational purposes, and give members trusted confidants with whom they may share personal information considered too sensitive to be shared in formal group meetings.

12-Step Work: Carrying the Message

A final way in which TSR programs increase and ensure continued commitment is through what is called "12-step work." Essentially, this means "carrying the message" of AA and NA to people who still suffer from addiction. TSR programs generally maintain offices or answering services in their communities where people seeking help for alcohol and other drug problems can call for assistance. When such calls are received, the person calling for assistance is asked if he or she would object to a visit from members of the local TSR program. If the caller agrees, then members of the local TSR program are contacted and they arrange for either a home visit or to pick up the caller and take him or her to a meeting. The purposes a of 12-step call are to explain the program to potential newcomers, expose them to meetings, provide support, and motivate them to join. The 12th and final step of the AA program provides the basis for 12-step work: "Having had a spiritual awakening as a result of these steps, we tried to carry this message to alcoholics, and to practice these principles in all our affairs."

Even when a 12-step call fails, members usually comment that it was worth the effort. Often, members who go on unsuccessful 12-step calls remark that although they weren't able to help the other person, they did help themselves. The experience of looking once again at the lives of those still caught up in active alcoholism or drug addiction further convinced them of the correctness and wisdom of their decision to continue to participate in a sobriety-based TSR program. And, of course, if the 12-step call is successful and the person accepts newcomer status to AA, then the rewards and satisfactions for having helped another person to find a way out of active alcoholism are considered enormous.

SUMMARY

As has been pointed out, TSR approaches are complex, multidimensional, biopsychosocial, and spiritual programs widely available in the United States and some other countries to people with addictive disorders, their family members, and significant others. AA, NA, Al-Anon, Alateen, and other TSR groups as well have flourished for the better part of the twentieth century whereas many other treatment approaches have been tried and abandoned. Although much discussion has centered on their spiritual emphasis, TSR approaches are clearly psychosocial recovery programs in which many important features entirely consistent with behavior modification, recent cognitive therapies, modern social learning theories, social psychology, and sociology are very much in evidence. Although many people are aware that TSR approaches are designed to deal specifically with drinking and drug misuse, it has not been widely recognized that these programs are complex programs for living and address many issues other than alcohol and drug consumption.

REFERENCES

Al-Anon Family Group Headquarters. (1981). *Al-Anon's twelve steps and twelve traditions*. New York: Author.

Al-Anon Family Group Headquarters. (1986). *Ala-Non faces alcoholism*. New York: Author.

Alcoholics Anonymous World Services. (1935). *Alcoholics anonymous*. New York: Author.

Alcoholics Anonymous World Services. (1953). *Twelve steps and twelve traditions*. New York: Author.

Amit, Z., & Brown, Z. W. (1982). Actions of drugs of abuse on brain reward systems: A reconsideration with specific attention to alcohol. *Pharmacology. Biochemistry, and Behavior, 17*, 223–238.

Azrin, N. H., Sisson, R. W., Meyers, R., & Godley, M. (1982). Alcoholism treatment by disulfiram and community reinforcement therapy. *Journal of Behavior Therapy and Experimental Psychiatry, 13*, 105–112.

Bandura, A. (1977). *Social learning theory*. Englewood Cliffs, NJ: Prentice Hall.

Borg, S., Kvande, H., Mossberg, D., Valverius, P., & Sedvall, G. (1983). Central nervous system noradrenaline metabolism and alcohol consumption in man. *Pharmacology, Biochemistry and Behavior, 8* (Suppl. 1), 375–378.

Brown, S. A., Irwin, M., & Schuckit, M. A. (1991). Changes in anxiety among abstinent male alcoholics. *Journal of Studies on Alcohol, 52*, 55–61.

Brown, S. A., & Schuckit, M. A. (1988). Changes in depression among abstinent alcoholics. *Journal of Studies on Alcohol, 49*, 412–417.

Burov, Yu. V., Zhukov, V. N., & Khodoroya, N. A. (1986). Serotonin content in different brain areas and in the periphery: Effect of ethanol in rats predisposed and nonpredisposed to alcohol intake. *Biogenic Amines, 4*, 205–209.

Daoust, M., Lhuintre, J. P., Saligaut, C., Moore, N., Flipo, J. L., & Boismare, F. (1987). Noradrenaline and Gaba brain receptors are co-involved in the voluntary intake of ethanol by rats. *Alcohol and Alcoholism* (Suppl. 1), 319–322.

Linnoila, M., Eckhardt, M. Durcan, M., Lister, R., & Martin, P. (1987). Interactions of serotonin with ethanol: Clinical and animal studies. *Psychopharmacology Bulletin, 23*, 452–457.

Marlatt, G. A. (1983). The controlled drinking controversy. *American Psychologist, 38*, 1097–1110.

Murphy, J. M., Wailer, M. B., Gatto, G. J., McBride, W. J., Lumeng, L., & Li, T. K. (1985). Monoamine uptake inhibitors attenuate ethanol intake in alcohol preferring rats. *Alcohol, 2*, 349–352.

Nowinski, J. (1996). Facilitating 12-step recovery from substance abuse and addiction. In F. Rotgers, D. S. Keller, & J. Morgenstern (Eds.), *Treating substance abuse: Theory and technique* (pp. 37–67). New York: Guilford Press.

Peele, S. (1989). *Diseasing of America*. Lexington, MA: Lexington Books.

Roy, A., Virkkunen, M., & Linnoila, M. (1987). Reduced central serotonin turnover in a subgroup of alcoholics. *Progress in Neuropsychopharmacology and Biological Psychiatry, 11*, 173–177.

Tabakoff, B., Hoffman, P. L., Lee, J. M., Saito, T., Willard, B., & DeLeon-Jones, F. (1988). Differences in platelet enzyme activity between alcoholics and nonalcoholics. *New England Journal of Medicine, 313*, 134–I 39.

Tarter, R. E., Alterman, A. I., & Edwards, K. L. (1987). Neurobehavioral theory of alcoholism etiology. In C. Chaudron & D. Wilkinson (Eds.), *Theories of alcoholism* (pp. 73–102). Toronto: Addiction Research Foundation.

Wallace, J. (1983). Ideology, belief, and behavior: Alcoholics anonymous as a social movement. In E. Gottheil, K. A. Druley, T. F. Skoloda, & H. M. Waxman (Eds.), *Etiologic aspects of alcohol and drug abuse* (pp. 285–306). Springfield, IL: Charles C. Thomas Wallace, J. (1993). Facism and the eye of the beholder: A reply to J. S. Searles on the controlled intoxication issue. *Addictive Behaviors, 18*, 239–251.

Wallace, J. (1996). Theory of 12-step oriented treatment. In F. Rotgers, D. S. Keller, & J. Morgenstern (Eds.), *Treating substance abuse: Theory and technique* (pp. 13–36). New York: Guilford Press.

CHAPTER 24

PHARMACOTHERAPY

Raymond F. Anton
Kathleen T. Brady
Darlene H. Moak

Despite noteworthy advances, a considerable number of individuals do not respond to psychosocial treatment for substance use disorder. New methods of treatment are thus needed to enhance treatment efficacy. Inasmuch as biological factors, especially brain mechanisms associated with reinforcement, are integral to drug dependence (Anton, Kranzler, & Meyer, 1995a; Koob, 1992; Nutt & Glue, 1990), the notion that pharmacological agents that act on brain reward mechanisms may have clinical utility in the treatment of substance dependence has gained increasing interest and support. Although the substitution of an abused drug with a safer controlled medication, such as methadone, for the treatment of opiate addiction has been shown to be effective, recent pharmacotherapy developments in alcohol and cocaine dependence focus more on nonsubstitution treatment (e.g., relapse prevention, reduction of craving) with medications that are not themselves habit forming.

A discussion of pharmacotherapy for treatment of the substance use disorders cannot be undertaken without acknowledging the importance of psychosocial factors. Compliance with a medication regimen is, for example, a requisite for efficacy. In addition, most individuals who are drug dependent experience adverse social, medical, and psychological consequences. Psychosocial approaches are thus conjointly utilized with pharmacotherapy to maximize recovery. Because pharmacotherapy cannot reverse personal and social disruptions experienced by the substance abuser, medication should be viewed as an adjunct to behavioral and supportive (e.g., Alcoholics Anonymous) approaches to treatment.

Furthermore, it should be recognized that no treatment method is universally effective. Hence, an armamentarium of different therapies must be available. For instance, alcohol abusers (those not physically dependent on alcohol) most likely need different treatment than individuals who are physically dependent. In this regard, the particular treatment modality is an important consideration depending on whether the client presents substance abuse or dependence.

Methodology for the evaluation of treatment efficacy has improved considerably in recent years. The most rigorous method for the evaluation of the efficacy of new medications is the randomized double-blind control trial (RCT). In this paradigm, an active medication is tested against a placebo. Neither the individual being treated nor the research team have knowledge about the subject's group assignment. The likelihood of obtaining biased results caused by either the subject or the experimenter knowing the subject's treatment condition (active medication or placebo) is thus eliminated.

Medication compliance and subject retention in the RCT must be considered in evaluating drug efficacy. Differential retention of subjects in the active medication group may indicate a strong therapeutic response to the drug. In contrast, an adverse effect of the pharmacological compound being tested may result in greater attrition in the active medication group.

Moreover, caution must be exercised in interpreting the results of studies in which subjects receiving active medication, commonly measured by the presence of the medication in blood or urine, are compared to the placebo group in whom biological indicators of compliance are unavailable. To circumvent this problem, an inert compound such as riboflavin is administered to both the active medication and placebo groups. Alternatively, pill bottle cap microchips are used to record bottle openings. These latter procedures enable direct comparison of compliance in the active medication and placebo groups.

Finally, medications need to be evaluated with respect to their safety. Documentation of adverse reactions or "side effects" is thus essential and forms the basis of a comprehensive risk/reward assessment. Additional factors included in such an assessment, besides injurious side effects, are whether the medication is abusable, the effects of the medication on vital organ-systems (e.g., liver) compromised by chronic substance abuse, and whether the medication adversely interacts with the abused substance in the event the individual relapses.

ALCOHOL

Neurobiology

The rationale underlying the use of medications for treatment of alcoholism stems from data demonstrating that the core symptoms, craving and loss of control, have a neurochemical substrate. Substantial evidence has been marshaled indicating that alcohol acts on the brain reward system to produce a positive reinforcement experience, which in turn predisposes to a persistent pattern of alcohol consumption (Anton, Kranzler, & Meyer, 1995b; Nutt & Glue, 1990). Hence medications that impact on neural systems subserving reinforcement should in theory mitigate alcohol consumption. However, the neurochemical substrate implicated in the pathophysiology of alcohol dependence, particularly craving, is complex and includes the endogenous opiates

(endorphins and enkephlins), dopamine, and serotonin. Alcohol is generally thought to increase dopamine activity via stimulation of the opioid and serotonin systems, particularly in the nucleus acumbens. Medications that block the release or binding of these neurotransmitters may, therefore, attenuate craving for alcohol and concomitantly consumption. For example, the opiate antagonists naltrexone and nalmefene have been shown to reduce relapse drinking and craving while drugs that affect the serotonin system have been widely studied with mixed outcomes.

Alcohol Withdrawal

Benzodiazepines (e.g., diazepam, chlordiazepoxide, lorazepam, oxazepam) have been shown to be effective for the treatment of alcohol withdrawal. Recently, however, concern has been raised about the side effects of these compounds (cognitive impairment) and abuse liability. These concerns, coupled with an understanding of the course of alcohol withdrawal and its manifestations (e.g. seizures) from repeated episodes (Ballenger & Post, 1978; Brown, Anton, Malcolm, & Ballenger, 1988; Moak & Anton, 1996), have also led to the use of anticonvulsant drugs. One such compound is carbamazepine (Malcolm, Ballenger, Sturgis, & Anton, 1989). Much recent interest has focused on a benzodiazepine-like drug, abecarnil. This compound acts on benzodiazepine receptors in the brain without producing the sedative effects or having the abuse liability associated with other compounds in this class, while sharing promise as an agent for the treatment of alcohol withdrawal (Anton, 1996). Medications such as the beta adrenergic blocker, propranolol, and the alpha adrenergic agonist, clonidine, that predominantly block peripheral autonomic activation have also been used to attenuate the adverse experience of alcohol detoxification (Anton & Becher, 1995).

Relapse Prevention

Opiate antagonists, particularly, naltrexone, have been shown to be effective for treatment of alcoholism. The Food and Drug Administration (FDA) approved naltrexone for treatment of alcohol dependence in 1994 based on two relatively small randomized control trials (O'Malley et al., 1992; Volpicelli, Alterman, Hayashidia, & O'Brien, 1992) and a larger open-label safety study (Croop, Faulkner, & Labriola, in press). In the two RCTs noted, a 50-mg daily dose of naltrexone was given over a 12-week period to severe hospitalized alcoholics (Volpicelli et al.,

1992) and to less impaired alcoholics recruited from the community (O'Malley et al., 1992). In both studies, alcoholics who received naltrexone had a relapse rate that was about 50% lower than alcoholics receiving placebo. This effect was independent of any other adjunctive therapy. However, O'Malley et al., (1992) observed an interaction between type of psychosocial therapy and medication when total abstinence was the outcome measure. Specifically, alcoholics who received naltrexone and attended Alcoholics Anonymous had the longest period of total abstinence. At follow-up, 3 months after discontinuation of naltrexone therapy, it was also found that the combination of cognitive behavior therapy and naltrexone produced the best results as indicated by relapse (O'Malley et al., naltrexone, 1996). Nalmefene, another opiate antagonist, has been shown to diminish alcohol consumption and likelihood of relapse (Mason et al., 1994).

A novel compound, acamprosate (calcium, homotaurinate), has been extensively studied in Europe (Sass, Soyka, Mann, & Zieglgansberger, 1996) . The pharmacological actions of this compound are not definitively known (Littleton, 1995). The available evidence suggests that it enhances the function of NMDA, an amino acid receptor. This compound may improve abstinence outcome and has been theorized to diminish craving.

Medications that regulate serotonin function (SSRIs) or block serotonin receptors have been widely studied. Fluoxetine (Prozac), the most widely used antidepressant agent, has been found to reduce alcohol consumption by about 20% (Naranjo, Kadlec, Sanhueza, Woodley-Remus, & Sellers, 1990). In a trial among alcohol dependent outpatients, fluoxetine was compared to placebo as an adjunct to 12 weeks of cognitive behavior therapy (Kranzler et al., 1995). No difference on any drinking outcome measure between placebo and fluoxetine groups was observed. The most balanced conclusion that can be drawn at this time is that SSRIs have a weak impact, if any, on alcohol consumption among non-psychiatrically disturbed alcoholics.

Several studies have examined the efficacy of selective serotonin receptor antagonists. Ondansetron, a drug that selectively blocks serotonin type 3 receptors, has been observed to reduce alcohol consumption by up to 30% in problem drinkers (Sellers et al., 1994). A large multisite study of ritanserin, a drug that selectively blocks serotonin type 2 receptors, yielded no evidence for efficacy in outpatient dependent alcoholics (Johnson et al., 1996).

Medications that exert their action through modulation of brain dopamine, especially in the brain reward circuit, should theoretically be useful for the treatment of alcoholism. Unfortunately, these drugs have many unwanted pharmacologic effects. For instance, dopamine-blocking drugs used for the treatment of psychosis commonly produce movement disorders. In contrast, drugs that stimulate the dopamine system, such as amphetamine and methylphenidate, have abuse liability and thus should not be administered to substance abusers.

Several trials investigating the efficacy of the dopamine receptor stimulator, bromocriptine, have been conducted (Borg, 1983; Dongier, Vachon, & Schwartz, 1991; Powell et al., 1995). Considering the results of these studies in aggregate, it appears that this medication is ineffective.

The only other medication having direct brain effects that has been tested for efficacy in treating alcoholism is the mood-stabilizing drug lithium carbonate (Lejoyeux & Ades, 1993). To date the results are inconclusive. A large multisite RCT found that lithium was not more effective than placebo in alcoholics either with or without a history of depression (Dorus et al., 1989). One RCT found a weak effect among alcoholics who complied with the medication regimen (Fawcett et al., 1987).

The previous discussion focused on medications that act directly on the brain. Another class of drugs, the aversive or "alcohol-sensitizing" medications, have their mode of action in the liver. These drugs, disulfiram and calcium carbamide, block the catabolism of acetaldehyde dehydrogenase leading to its buildup. In high concentrations, acetaldehyde produces a host of aversive physical effects such as nausea, vomiting, headache, flushing, and cardiovascular instability. These drugs thus enhance the motivation of a recovering alcoholic to not drink as long as the person remains compliant with the medication regimen because of the punishing effects associated with drinking under these conditions.

COCAINE

Neurobiology

Cocaine consumption has been hypothesized to alter the serotonergic, noradrenergic, and dopaminergic neurotransmitter systems (Koe, 1976). Most of cocaine's reinforcing effects are, however, thought to emanate from its effects on dopaminergic pathways. Specifically, cocaine causes an increase in extracellular dopamine concentration in mesolimbic and mesocortical reward pathways as the results of reuptake inhibition. This cocaine-induced increase in dopamine is generally thought to be the primary mechanism underlying cocaine's reinforcing properties.

Chronic cocaine use may lead to dopamine depletion in the brain and associated alteration of postsynaptic dopamine receptor sensitivity. This depletion may be partially responsible for the manifest symptoms following cessation of consumption. Recently, neuroimaging techniques have been used to demonstrate that changes in the dopamine system associated with chronic cocaine use, including decreased dopamine receptors, may last for 3 months or longer (Volkow, Mullani, Gould, Adler, & Krajewski, 1988). Medications that are dopamine agonists (i.e., replace depleted dopamine) have been studied as one treatment for cocaine withdrawal symptoms (Giannini, Baumgartel, & Di Marzio, 1987). As will be discussed later, these studies have had some promising results (Dackis, Gold, Sweeny, Byron, & Clinko, 1987; Tennant & Sagherian, 1987).

Cocaine Withdrawal Syndrome

Gawin and Kleber (1986) delineated several specific stages of cocaine withdrawal. The first stage (the "crash") occurs during the first 24 hours and lasts up to 7 days. It is characterized by depressed mood, irritability, decreased energy, fatigue, anhedonia, hypersomnia, and craving. The second stage (the "withdrawal phase") is characterized by continued depression, sleep disturbance, fatigue, and increased appetite. Two short-term studies of inpatients found that depressed mood, anhedonia, irritability, and sleep disturbance were common but mild during withdrawal and decreased linearly during the first month following cessation of consumption (Satel et al., 1991; Weddington et al., 1990).

Treatment and Relapse Prevention

Kosten (1989) proposed that there are three categories of cocaine-dependent patients who are likely to benefit from pharmacologic treatment. The first category includes individuals who have developed neuroadaptation (chronic tolerance). The second group consists of individuals who have a comorbid psychiatric disorder. The third category consists of individuals at high risk concomitant to their chronic cocaine consumption, such as intravenous drug users and persons with major medical illness.

Two general classes of compounds have been developed for the treatment of cocaine dependence. These are displayed in Table 24.1. Agents that directly or indirectly stimulate the dopamine system have been used to minimize the effects of acute cocaine withdrawal. Agents with delayed action on the dopamine system have been used primarily to potentiate abstinence.

Acute Treatments

Dysphoria and craving during withdrawal from cocaine appear to be caused by a decrease of dopamine in the brain. Dopamine-stimulating medications include amantadine, bromocriptine, L-dopa, methylphenidate, and pergolide. These medications have been shown to be effective in several single-dose crossover trials although the results are not consistent across studies (Dackis et al., 1987; Tennant & Sangherian, 1987). Bromocriptine, the most frequently studied compound, has yielded mixed results (Dackis et al., 1987; Kosten, 1989; Tennant & Sangherian, 1987). Studies of the efficacy of amantadine have also yielded mixed results (Kosten, Silverman, et al., 1992). A recent open-label study of pergolide, a dopamine agonist, demonstrated a decrease in craving in recently abstinent inpatient cocaine-dependent individuals (Malcolm, Hutto, Phillips, & Ballenger, 1991).

Maintenance Treatments

A variety of different types of medications have been tested for their effects on sustaining treatment gains during the first 3–6 months following abstinence. The compounds include tricyclic antidepressants, serotonin reuptake inhibitors, carbamazepine, dopamine-blocking agents, and buprenorphine (Dackis et al., 1987; Meyer, 1992).

The tricyclic antidepressants, especially desipramine, have been most researched. These medications reverse certain cocaine-induced neurochemical changes (Gawin, Kleber et al., 1989) and, specifically, reduce anhedonia and depression. Studies of the efficacy of desipramine have, however, yielded equivocal results (Gawin, Kleber et al., 1989; Weiss & Mirin, 1989).

In addition to the side effects of tricyclic antidepressants (e.g., insomnia, anxiety), the delayed onset of action needs to be recognized. Hence the use of a fast acting agent, such as a dopamine agonist, in combination with a tricyclic antidepressant during the first few weeks may improve treatment outcome.

Serotonergic (5-HT) agents have also been evaluated for treatment of cocaine dependence. Cocaine is a power-

Table 24.1 Pharmacologic Treatment of Cocaine Dependence

	Study Design	Results
	Acute Treatments	
Bromocriptine	Single dose, placebo crossover	Decreased craving
Amantidine	Single dose, placebo crossover RCT	Mixed results
Pergolide	Open label	Improved retention in treatment
	Maintenance Treatments	
Desipramine	RCT	Effective in adequate dosage (2.5 mg/kg/day) for sufficient period (6 weeks)
SSRIs	RCT	Ineffective in decreasing cocaine use
Other antidepressants: buproprion, phenelzine, trazodone	Open label	Decreases in cocaine craving/use
Carbamazepine	3 RCTs	Ineffective in decreasing cocaine/use
Fluphenthixol	Open label	Decreases in cocaine craving/use
Disulfram	RCT	Effective in concurrent alcohol/cocaine
Mazindol	Controlled trials in methadone	Promising in comorbid cocaine/opiate dependence
Bupenorphine	maintained patients	
Naltrexone		

Note: RCT = randomized control trial.

ful serotonin reuptake inhibitor. Chronic cocaine administration leads to enhanced 5-HT autoregulation and subsequently decreased 5-HT transmission. Fluoxetine and sertraline, two selective serotonin reuptake inhibitor antidepressant agents, have been shown in a open-label study of a small sample to be of possible benefit (Batki, Manfredi, Jacob, & Ones, 1993). However, Grabowski and colleagues (1995) have observed that fluoxetine is ineffective for treatment of cocaine dependence. Other antidepressants have shown promise in preliminary open trials (Weiss & Mirin, 1989) but RCTs remain to be conducted before definitive conclusions can be drawn.

Carbamazepine (CBZ), an antiseizure medication, has also been administered to cocaine-dependent individuals. Whereas one open study and one controlled trial have noted decreased cocaine use following CBZ treatment (Halikas, Crosby, Pearson, Braves, & Graves, 1997), several controlled trials have not replicated this finding (Halikas, Kuhn, Crea, Carlson, & Crosby, 1992; Cornish et al., 1995; Montoya, Levin, Fudala, & Gorelick, 1993).

Studies of animal subjects and human participants indicate that dopamine-blocking agents (haloperidol, chlorpromazine) can antagonize some of cocaine's effects.

Gawin, Allen, and Humbelstone (1989) found that the dopamine-blocking drug fluphenthixol decreased cocaine craving and cocaine use. Although these preliminary findings are encouraging, the toxicity and side effects caused by these compounds mitigate their widespread use for treatment of cocaine dependence.

POLYSUBSTANCE USE DISORDER

Disulfiram has been reported to be effective in treating concurrent cocaine and alcohol dependence (Carroll et al., 1993; McCance-Katz et al., 1993). Further research is needed, however, to determine whether disulfiram is an effective pharmacotherapeutic agent for treatment of cocaine dependence without comorbid alcoholism.

Patients in methadone maintenance treatment for opiate dependence commonly abuse cocaine. Medications administered to cocaine-dependent individuals with comorbid opiate dependence include buprenorphine, mazindol, and naltrexone. Buprenorphine, a partial opiate antagonist, may reduce the "speedball" effect, thereby making cocaine use less reinforcing. Buprenorphine has been compared to methadone in patients with comorbid opiate and cocaine dependence. In two large RCTs, Kosten, Kleber, and Morgan (1989) and Oliveto et al. (1994) have shown no efficacy beyond that associated with methadone. Naltrexone has been shown in one preliminary study to diminish the acute effects of cocaine among opiate-dependent patients (Kosten, Silverman, et al., 1992). Mazindol was found to not have a significant effect in a short-term crossover study (Diakogiannisis, Steinberg, & Kosten, 1990).

DUAL DIAGNOSIS

Substance use disorders and psychiatric disorders frequently occur together. This comorbidity can be of critical importance for determining the most appropriate treatment. Unfortunately, there are limited data available concerning the efficacy of pharmacotherapeutic agents for treatment of individuals with comorbid disorders. The specific treatment strategy for comorbid or dually diagnosed patients is based on what is known about the particular pharmacologic treatment of each disorder.

Depression

Depression symptoms are common among individuals with drug and alcohol use disorders. Three double-blind, placebo-controlled studies of imipramine treatment have shown at least moderately favorable results, with respect to attenuation of depressive symptoms (Weiss & Mirin, 1989). Nunes and colleagues (1993) found that 45% of depressed alcoholics treated with imipramine experienced improved mood and a reduction of drinking behavior. McGrath et al. (1996) reported similar results. Dosage and effective blood levels of tricyclic antidepressants remain unclear. Lower imipramine blood levels have been reported in alcoholics compared to nonalcoholics (Ciraulo et al., 1982).

Research investigating the use of selective serotonin reuptake inhibitors (SSRIs) in the treatment of depressed alcoholics has also shown promise. A study of fluoxetine in depressed suicidal alcoholics observed an improvement in depression and reduced alcohol consumption (Cornelius et al., 1997).

Doxepin has been reported to relieve symptoms of depression, anxiety, and drug craving among patients in methadone maintenance (Weiss & Mirin, 1989). It must be noted that methadone maintenance clinics have reported abuse of amitriptyline and other sedating tricyclic antide-

pressants (TCAs) (Weiss & Mirin, 1989). TCA plasma level monitoring is important in methadone-maintained patients because the combination of methadone and desipramine produces plasma desipramine levels that are twice as high as the level prior to methadone administration.

Bipolar Disorder

Tohen, Waternaux, Tsuang, and Hunt 1990) and O'Connell, Mayo, and Flatown (1991) observed that substance abuse is associated with a poor response to lithium treatment in patients with bipolar disorder. Brady, Sonne, Ballenger, and Anton (1995) found that valproic acid is safe, well tolerated, and effective in a pilot study of patients with bipolar disorder. Further investigation is clearly warranted in view of the dearth of research on patients with comorbid substance use disorder and bipolar disorder.

Panic Disorder

TCAs and SSRIs are effective for the treatment of uncomplicated panic disorder (Lydiard & Ballenger, 1987). The efficacy of these agents for patients with a substance use disorder and comorbid panic disorder has not been determined. SSRIs are the psychopharmacologic treatment of choice for comorbid panic disorder and substance use disorder because of their low incidence of side effects and their safety.

One drawback of SSRIs and TCAs is their onset latency. These medications may take 2–6 weeks before attaining maximal effectiveness. In addition, these medications may have an initial activating effect that worsens the panic disorder. Consequently, patients may be unable to tolerate group therapy or otherwise dropout of treatment in order to self-medicate during this initial period. In this situation, a brief trial using beta blockers, which have a shorter onset of action, should be considered. Benzodiazepines, which provide immediate relief of panic, are generally contraindicated in the substance-abusing population because of their abuse potential. Benzodiazepine treatment should only be considered when the anxiety disorder is primary, severe, and despite abstinence, the patient's response to other treatment for the anxiety disorder is poor.

Although monoamine oxidase inhibitors (MAOIs) are effective in the treatment of panic disorder (Lydiard, Brawman-Mintzer, & Ballenger, 1996), administration of these compounds is generally discouraged for alcoholics or substance abusers. Patients who resume drinking or abusing drugs while on MAOIs may not follow dietary restrictions, resulting in a hypertensive crisis. Similarly, the conjoint administration of MAOIs and stimulants is not recommended.

Generalized Anxiety Disorder

Buspirone is the most widely studied pharmacologic agent for the treatment of generalized anxiety disorder in alcoholics. Buspirone is a nonbenzodiazepine anxiolytic. Its advantage is that it has no abuse liability. Two of three studies using buspirone in anxious alcoholics have shown decreased alcohol consumption (Kranzler et al., 1994; Malcolm et al., 1989; Malec, Malec, & Doviger, 1996; Tollefson, Montague-Clouse, & Tollefson, 1992). The most substantial reduction of anxiety symptoms appears to occur in conjunction with conjoint coping skills enhancement or cognitive behavioral therapy (Kranzler et al., 1994).

Attention Deficit Disorder (ADHD)

Psychostimulants (amphetamine, methylphenidate, pemoline) are the first line treatment for uncomplicated ADHD in children and adults. Because of the abuse potential of stimulants, caution is needed in the use of these medications for the treatment of adults with comorbid ADHD and substance use disorder. In several case studies of cocaine-dependent individuals with ADHD, it was reported that symptom resolution occurred without relapse to drug abuse following stimulant medication (Kaminer, 1992). Other pharmacologic treatment options include tricyclic antidepressants, bupropion, and clonidine (Wilens, Biederman, Spencer, & Prince, 1995).

Schizophrenia

Little is known about the optimal pharmacotherapeutic strategy for treatment of the schizophrenic substance abuser. In a recent investigation of the efficacy of clozapine in neuroleptic-resistant schizophrenic patients with conjoint substance use disorder, a similar response to non-substance-using patients was observed (Buckley, Thompson, Way, & Meltzer, 1994). The potential benefits of using clozapine must be weighed against the risk of agranulocytosis.

Siris and coworkers (1991) reported preliminary findings indicating that antidepressant medication in conjunction with neuroleptic medication may be useful for the treatment of dysphoria in substance-abusing schizophrenic patients. Ziedonis, Richardson, Lee, Petrakis, & Kosten (1992) studied the impact of desipramine in a small sample of cocaine-abusing schizophrenics. They found that desipramine improved treatment retention. Also, fewer cocaine-positive urine tests were observed in patients receiving desipramine.

NICOTINE

Neurobiology

Nicotine is an agonist at both peripheral and central nicotinic acetylcholine receptors. However, nicotine appears to be uniquely capable of upregulating these receptors, in contrast to the more typical effect of agonists in causing receptor downregulation (Rosecrans, 1991; Sanderson, Drasdo, McCrea, & Wonnacott, 1993). Research conducted on animals demonstrates that nicotine also affects dopaminergic, serotonergic and noradrenergic neurotransmitter systems (Rosecrans, 1991).

Pharmacotherapy

Pharmacological treatment of nicotine dependence is generally directed at allowing the patient to receive nicotine in a less harmful way than inhalation. This usually takes the form of either gum or a transdermal delivery system. Aversive therapy using silver acetate has been reported to be helpful in some individuals, although this approach has not been widely utilized (Haxby, 1995).

Nicotine Replacement

The transdermal nicotine patch is used to attenuate the severity of acute withdrawal and to prevent relapse. Because relapse occurs most commonly within the first 90 days of abstinence, the patch is recommended to be used during this period and then discontinued. The nicotine patch appears to substantially enhance the prospects for abstinence, although there is wide disparity between studies. Efficiency rate ranges from 18% to 77% (Fiore, Jorenby, Baker, & Kenford, 1992). Adverse effects include cutaneous reactions in up to 50% of users (resulting in discontinuation in perhaps as many as 10%) and sleep disturbance.

Alternative methods of nicotine delivery are gum and nicotine nasal spray. Nicotine gum can be obtained without prescription in the United States. It has the advantage of allowing the user to control the delivery schedule. These preparations may have a high abuse potential and it may be difficult for the user to terminate because the pharmacokinetics closely simulate cigarette smoking. These preparations are, therefore, likely to be highly reinforcing (Henningfield & Keenan, 1993). This caveat notwithstanding, there is evidence that a 4-mg dose is more effective than a 2-mg gum preparation (Tonnesen et al., 1988).

Bupropion

Recently the antidepressant bupropion, marketed as Zyban, received approval from the Food and Drug Administration as an adjunctive treatment for nicotine dependence in non-depressed patients. Two double-blind studies conducted by the manufacturer showed an increased rate of smoking cessation in individuals who received a daily dose of 300 mg (Abramowicz, 1997). Concurrent treatment with bupropion and the nicotine patch did not improve outcome above that of bupropion alone.

Other Modalities

The most widely studied alternative to nicotine replacement has been clonidine, an alpha-2 adrenergic agonist. The available evidence supports its use only in women (Haxby, 1995). Although its impact on nicotine dependence remains undetermined, it may be beneficial for women who have severe dependence and who cannot tolerate nicotine replacement.

Blockade therapy, employing anticholinergic agents, has been explored. Mecamylamine has been reported to be effective in blocking nicotine's effects, but it is associated with unacceptable side effects (Tennant, Tarver, & Rawson, 1984). Other anticholinergic agents, particularly scopolamine, have also been examined in small samples (Bachynsky, 1986). Their therapeutic efficiency remains to be documented in controlled trials.

Nicotine and Depression

The comorbidity of nicotine dependence and depression has suggested a possible role for antidepressant treatment in nicotine dependence. Preliminary support for this approach was found by Pomerleau, Pomerleau, Morrell, and Lowenbergh (1991) who found that persons taking fluoxetine had significantly less weight gain after a smok-

ing reduction treatment program compared to persons who received placebo.

OPIOID DEPENDENCE

Prognosis among heroin addicts is poor. At least 25% of individuals die from homicide, suicide, accidents, and infectious disease within 10–20 years of active use (Mirin, 1995).

Opioid Replacement Therapy

Methadone

Methadone has been employed as a detoxifying agent and as an abstinence maintenance medication. It has not been found to have therapeutic utility for the treatment of detoxification (Ling, Rawson, & Compton, 1994). Its efficacy in maintaining abstinence from heroin is well documented (Rawson & Ling, 1991). Nevertheless, methadone treatment is associated with notable shortcomings.

Its primary drawback is the need for frequent (usually daily) clinic visits. This is due to the fact that methadone has a short period of therapeutic activity. Some patients achieve an acceptable level of stability and can be given take-home medications. Nonetheless, ongoing drug use monitoring is required. Many addicted individuals find it difficult to discontinue methadone due to its addictive potential and long duration of withdrawal syndrome. Consequently, most patients remain on a methadone regimen indefinitely. Some studies have shown a superior outcome in addicts who are maintained on high (70–100 mg) doses compared to lower (20–50 mg) doses (Caplehorn, Bell, Kleinbaum, & Gebski, 1993; Maremmani, Nardini, Zolesi, & Castrogiovanni, 1994). Inasmuch as most methadone treatment programs utilize a "standard" dose of 20–40 mg, it is likely that many individuals receive less than the optimal dosage.

LAAM

LAAM (l-alpha-acetylmethadol or levo-methadyl acetate) is a long-acting opioid agonist. It is metabolized to two active metabolites, normethadyl acetate (half-life 31-48 hours) and dinormethadyl acetate (half life >100 hours). It has, therefore, a much longer duration of action than methadone. Onset of action is about 90 minutes administered orally and 3–6 hours administered parenterally. Doses between 70–100 mg given three times a week suppress withdrawal symptoms in opioid-dependent individuals.

An advantage over methadone is that its sustained duration of action requires less frequent clinic visits by the client. This in turn allows for more independence and self-control in daily living.

Higher than optimal dosages may produce symptoms and signs of an excessive opioid effect. Due to the delayed onset of action, it is thus important to warn patients during the induction phase to not use other sedating substances or medications.

LAAM has, however, been shown to be well-tolerated in clinical trials. Importantly, LAAM should be monitored in individuals who use alcohol or sedatives or who take antidepressant medication, because of the increased risk for overdose.

Buprenorphine

Buprenorphine, a mixed opioid agonist-antagonist, has been extensively studied (Kosten, Schottenfeld, Ziedonis, & Falcioni, 1993; Ling, Wesson, Charuvastra, & Klett, 1996; Nigam, Ray, & Tripathi, 1993; Schottenfeld, Pakes, Oliveto, Ziedonis, & Kosten, 1997). It binds to opioid receptors but appears to have a low level of intrinsic activity. This pharmacodynamic profile has contributed to clinical findings that naloxone does not precipitate withdrawal symptoms in individuals who are pretreated with buprenorphine. Furthermore, buprenorphine appears to cause less severe dependence than other opioid substitution agents (Ling et al., 1994). Also, abrupt discontinuation of a daily dosage of 8 mg results in only mild to moderate withdrawal syndrome.

Clinical studies have evaluated different dosage schedules. In general, a daily dosage of at least 8 mg has been found to be superior to lower doses (Johnson, Jaffe, & Fudala, 1992). On the other hand, dosages of 12–16 mg may be necessary to stabilize some patients. Buprenorphine has the advantage of being well tolerated. Due to its opioid antagonist properties, overdose is unlikely. Notably, there is evidence suggesting also that it reduces cocaine intake (Gastfriend, Mendelson, Mello, Teoh, & Reif, 1993; Kosten, Silverman, 1992). However, larger controlled clinical studies are needed to confirm this finding.

Naltrexone

Naltrexone has not been shown to be effective in double-blind clinical trials (Gold, 1993; Rawson & Ling, 1991). Moreover, acceptance of this medication by heroin users was low. Opioid agonists such as methadone are preferred. Naltrexone was, however, found to be useful for highly motivated patients in structured programs.

SUMMARY

The neurobiologic understanding of addiction is advancing at an accelerating pace leading to new medication developmental trials. Presently, naltrexone and possibly acamprosate have been found to be useful for primary alcoholism whereas the antidepressants may favorably impact depression and alcohol use in depressed alcohol abusers. Replacement therapy (methadone, LAAM, buprenorphine) appears to work best for opiate addiction, but an efficacious agent for the treatment of cocaine dependence remains elusive. Nicotine dependence appears to benefit from both replacement (nicotine patch) and anticraving (clonidine, buproprion) treatments. All pharmacotherapy for the addictions is likely to be enhanced when combined with psychosocial interventions.

REFERENCES

Abramowicz, M. (Ed.) (1997). *The Medical Letter, 39*, 77–78.

Anton, R. F. (1996). New methodologies for pharmacologic treatment trials for alcohol dependence. *Alcoholism: Clinical and Experimental Research, 20*, (Suppl.), 3A–9A.

Anton, R. F., & Becker, H. C. (1995). Pharmacotherapy and pathophysiology of alcohol withdrawal. In H. R. Kranzler (Ed.), *The pharmacology of alcohol abuse*. New York: Springer-Verlag.

Anton, R. F., Kranzler, H. R., & Meyer, R. E. (1995a). Neurobehavioral aspects of the pharmacotherapy of alcohol dependence. *Clinical Neuroscience, 3*, 145–154.

Anton, R. F., Kranzler, H. R., & Meyer, R. E. (1995b). New directions in the pharmacotherapy of alcoholism. *Psychiatric Annals, 25*, 353–362.

Bachynsky, N. (1986). The use of anticholinergic drugs for smoking cessation: A pilot study. *International Journal of the Addictions, 21*, 789–805.

Ballenger, J. C., & Post, R. M. (1978). Kindling as a model for alcohol withdrawal syndromes. *British Journal of Psychiatry, 133*, 1–14.

Batki, S. L., Manfredi, L. B., Jacob, P., & Ones, R. T. (1993). Fluoxetine for cocaine dependence in methadone-maintenance; quantitative plasma and urine cocaine/benzoylecogine concentration. *Journal of Clinical Psychopharmacology, 13*, 243–250.

Borg, V. (1983). Bromocriptine in the prevention of alcohol abuse. *Acta Psychiatrica Scandinavica, 68*, 100–110.

Brady, K. T., Sonne, S. C., Ballenger, J. C., & Anton, R. A. (1995). Valproate in the treatment of acute bipolar bipolar episodes complicated by substance abuse: A pilot study. *Journal of Clinical Psychiatry, 56,*118–122.

Brown, M. E., Anton, R. F., Malcolm, R., & Ballenger, J. C. (1988). Alcohol detoxification and withdrawal seizures: Clinical support for a kindling hypothesis. *Biological Psychiatry, 23,* 507–514.

Buckley, P., Thompson, P., Way, L., & Meltzer, H. Y. (1994). Substance abuse among patients with treatment-resistant schizophrenia: characteristics and implications for clozapine therapy. *American Journal of Psychiatry, 151,* 385–389.

Caplehorn, J. R., Bell, J., Kleinbaum, D. G., & Gebski, V. J. (1993). Methadone dose and heroin use during maintenance treatment. *Addiction, 88,* 119–124.

Carroll, K., Ziedonis, D., O'Malley, S., McCance-Katz, E., Gordon, L., & Rounsaville B. (1993). Pharmacological interventions for abusers of alcohol and cocaine: Disulfiram versus naltrexone. *American Journal of Addictions, 2,* 77–79.

Ciraulo, K. D. A., Alderson, L. M., Chapron, D. J., Jaffe, J. H., Slubbarao, B., & Kramer, P. A. (1982). Imipramine disposition in alcoholics. *Journal of Clinical Psychopharmacology, 2,* 2–7.

Cornelius, J. R., Salloum, I. M., Ehler, J. G., Jarrett, P. J., Cornelius, M. D., Perel, J. M., Thase, M. E., & Black, A. (1997). Fluoxetine in depressed alcoholics. *Archives of General Psychiatry, 54,* 700–705.

Cornish, J. W., Maany, I., Fudala, P. J., Neal, S., Poole, S. A., Volpicelli, P., O'Brien, C. P.(1995). Carbamazepine treatment for cocaine dependence [see comments]. *Drug and Alcohol Dependence, 38,* 221–227.

Croop, R. S., Faulkner, E. B., & Labriola, D. F. (1997). The safety profile of naltrexone in the treatment of alcoholism. Results from a multicenter usage study. *Archives of General Psychiatry, 54, 1130–1135.*

Dackis, C. A., Gold, M. S., Sweeny, D. R., Byron, J. P., & Clinko, R. (1987). Single dose bromocriptine reverses cocaine craving. *Psychiatry Research, 20,* 261–264.

Diakogiannisis, I. A., Steinberg, M., & Kosten, T. R. (1980). Mazindol treatment of cocaine abuse. A double-blind investigation. *NIDA Research Monograph, 105,* 514.

Dongier, M., Vachon, L., & Schwartz, G. (1991). Bromocriptine in the treatment of alcohol dependence. *Alcoholism: Clinical and Experimental Research, 15,* 970–977.

Dorus, W., Ostrow, D. G., Anton, R. F., Cushman, P., Collins, J. F., Schaefer, M., Charles, H. L., Desai, P., Hayashida, M., Malkerneker, U., Willenbring, M., Fiscella, R., & Sather, M. R. (1989). Evaluation of lithium treatment of depressed and nondepressed alcoholics in a double-blind placebo controlled study. *Journal of the American Medical Association, 262,* 1646–1652.

Fawcett, J., Clark, D. C., Aagesen, C. A., Pisani, V. D., Tilkin, J. M., Sellers, D., McGuire, M., & Gibbons, R. D. (1987). A double-blind, placebo-controlled trial of lithium carbonate therapy for alcoholism. *Archives of General Psychiatry, 44,* 248–256.

Fiore, M. C., Jorenby, D. E., Baker, T. B., & Kenford, S. L. (1992). Tobacco dependence and the nicotine patch. *Journal of the American Medical Association, 268,* 2687–2694.

Gastfriend, D. R., Mendelson, J. H., Mello, N. K., Teoh, S. K., & Reif, S. (1993). Buprenorphine pharmacotherapy for concurrent heroin and cocaine dependence. *American Journal on Addictions, 2,* 269–278.

Gawin, F. H., Allen, D., & Humbelstone, B. (1989). Outpatient treatment of crack cocaine smoking with flupenthixol decanoate. *Archives of General Psychiatry, 46,* 322–325.

Gawin, F. H., & Kleber, H. D. (1986). Abstinence symptomatology and psychiatric diagnosis in chronic cocaine abusers. *Archives of General Psychiatry, 43,* 322–325.

Gawin, F. H., Kleber, H. D., Byck, R., Rounsaville, B. J., Kosten, T. R., Jatlow, P. I., & Morgan C. (1989). Desipramine facilitation of initial cocaine abstinence. *Archives of General Psychiatry. 46,* 117–121.

Giannini, A. J., Baumgartel, P., & Di Marzio, L. R. (1987). Bromocriptine therapy in cocaine withdrawal. *Journal of Clinical Pharmacology, 27,* 267–270.

Gold, M. S. (1993). Opiate addiction and the locus coeruleus. *Psychiatric Clinics of North America, 16,* 61–71.

Grabowski, J., Rhodes, H., Elk, R., Schmitz, J., Davis, C., Creson, D., & Kirby, K. (1995). Fluoxetine is ineffective for treatment of cocaine dependence or concurrent opiate and cocaine dependence: Two placebo-controlled double-blind trials. *Journal of Clinical Psychopharmacology, 15,* 163–174.

Halikas, J. A., Crosby, K. R. D., Pearson, V. L., Braves, M. T., & Graves, N. (1997). A randomized double-blind study of carbamazepine in the treatment of cocaine abuse. *Clinical Pharmacology and Therapeutics, 27,* 89–105.

Halikas, J. A., Kuhn, K. C., Crea,F. S., Carlson, G. A., & Crosby, S. (1992). Treatment of crack cocaine use with carbamazepine. *American Journal of Drug and Alcohol Abuse, 18,* 45–56.

Haxby, D. G. (1995). Treatment of nicotine dependence. *American Journal of Health Systems and Pharmacology, 52,* 265–281.

Henningfield, J. E., & Keenan, R. M. (1993). Nicotine delivery kinetics and abuse liability. *Journal of Consulting and Clinical Psychology, 61,* 743–750.

Johnson, B. A., Jasinski, D. R., Galloway, G., Kranzler, H., Weinrieb, R., Anton, R. F., Mason, B. J., Bonn, M. J., Pettinatti, H. M., Rawson, R., Urschel, H. C., Clyde, C., & Grebb, J. A. (1996). Ritanserin in the treatment of alcohol dependence—a multi-center clinical trials.

Johnson, R. E., Jaffe, J. H., & Fudala, P. J. (1992). A controlled trial of buprenorphine treatment for opioid dependence. *Journal of the American Medical Association, 267,* 2750–2755.

Kaminer, Y. (1992). Clinical implications of the relationship between attention-deficit hyperactivity disorder and psychoactive substance use disorders. *American Journal on Addictions, 1,* 257–264.

Koe, B. K. (1976). Moleculargeometry of inhibitors of the uptake of catecholamines and serotonin in synaptosomal preparations of rat brain. *Journal Pharmacology Experimental Therapeutics, 199,* 649–661.

Koob, G. F. (1992). Drugs of abuse: Anatomy, pharmacology and function of reward pathways. *TIPs, 13,* 177–184

Kosten, T. R. (1989) Pharmacotherapeutic interventions for cocaine abuse: Matching patients to treatments. *Journal of Nervous and Mental Disease, 177,* 379–389.

Kosten, T. R., Kleber, H. D., & Morgan, C. H. (1989). Treatment of cocaine abuse using buprenorphine. *Biological Psychiatry, 26,* 637–639.

Kosten, T. R., Schottenfeld, R., Ziedonis, D., & Falcioni, J. (1993). Buprenorphine versus methadone maintenance for opioid dependence. *Journal of Nervous and Mental Disease, 181,* 358–364.

Kosten, T. R., Silverman, D. G., Fleming, J., Kosten, T. A., Gawin, F. H., Compton, M., Jatlow, P., & Byck, R. (1992). Intravenous cocaine challenges during naltrexone maintenance: A preliminary study. *Biological Psychiatry, 32,* 543–548.

Kranzler, H. R., Burleson, J. A., Del Boca, F. K., Barbor, T. F., Korner, P., Brown, J., & Bohn, M. J. (1994). Buspirone treatment of anxious alcoholics. *Archives of General Psychiatry, 51,* 720–731.

Kranzler, H. R., Burleson, J. A., Kroner, P., DelBoca, F. K., Bohn, M. J., Brown, J., & Liebowitz, N. (1995). Placebo-controlled trial of fluoxetine as an adjunct to relapse prevention in alcoholics. *American Journal of Psychiatry, 152,* 391–397.

Lejoyeux, M., & Ades, J. (1993). Evaluation of lithium treatment in alcoholism. *Alcohol and Alcoholism, 28,* 273–279.

Ling, W. L., Rawson, R. A., & Compton, M. A. (1994). Substitution pharmacotherapies for opioid addiction: From methadone to LAAM and buprenorphine. *Journal of Psychoactive Drugs 26,* 119–128.

Ling, W., Wesson, D. R., Charuvastra, C., & Klett, C. J. (1996). A controlled trial comparing buprenorphine and methadone maintenance in opioid dependence. *Archives of General Psychiatry, 53,* 401–407.

Littleton, J. (1995). Acamprosate in alcohol dependence: How does it work? *Addiction, 90,* 1179–1188.

Lydiard, R. B., & Ballenger, J. C. (1987). Antidepressants in panic disorder and agoraphobia. *Journal of Affective Disorders, 13,* 153–168.

Lydiard, R. B., Brawman-Mintzer, O., & Ballenger, J. C. (1996). Recent developments in the psychopharmacology of anxiety disorders. *Journal of Consulting and Clinical Psychology, 64,* 660–668.

Malcolm, R., Hutto, B. R., Phillips, J. D., & Ballenger, J. C. (1991). Pergolide mesylate treatment of cocaine withdrawal. *Journal Clinical Psychiatry, 52,* 39–40.

Malcolm, R. J., Ballenger, J. C., Sturgis, E., & Anton, R. F. (1989). A double-blind controlled trial comparing carbamazepine to oxazepam treatment of alcohol withdrawal. *American Journal of Psychiatry, 146,* 617–621.

Malec, T. S., Malec, E. A., & Doviger, M. (1996). Efficacy of buspirone in alcohol dependence. *Alcoholism: Clinical and Experimental Research, 20,* 853–858.

Maremmani, I., Nardini, K. R., Zolesi, O., & Castrogiovanni, P. (1994). Methadone dosages and therapeutic compliance during a methadone maintenance program. *Drug and Alcohol Dependence, 34,* 163–166.

Mason, B. J., Ritvo, E. C., Morgan, R. O., Salvato, F. R., Goldberg, G., Welch, B., & Mantero-Atienza, E. (1994). A double-blind, placebo-controlled pilot study to evaluate the efficacy and safety of oral nalmefene HC1 for alcohol dependence. *Alcoholism: Clinical and Experimental Research, 18,*1162–1167.

McCance-Katz, E. F., Price, L. H., Kosten, T. R., Hameedi, F., Rosen, M. I., & Jatlow, P. I. (1993). Pharmacology, physiology and behavioral effects of cocaethylene in humans. *ACNP Abstracts,* 237.

McGrath, P. J., Nunes, E. V., Stewart, J. W., Goldman, D., Agosti, V., Ocepek-Welikson, K., & Quitkin, F. (1996). Imipramine treatment of alcoholics with primary depression. *Archives of General Psychiatry, 53,* 232–240.

Meyer, R. E. (1992). New pharmacotherapies for cocaine dependence revisited. *Archives of General Psychiatry, 49,* 900–904.

Mirin, S. M. (Chair). (1995). Practice guidelines for the treatment of patients with substance use disorders: Alcohol, cocaine, opioids. *American Journal of Psychiatry, 152,* 39.

Moak, D. H., & Anton, R. F. (1996). Alcohol-related seizures and the kindling effect of repeated detoxifications: The influence of cocaine. *Alcohol and Alcoholism, 31,* 135–148.

Montoya, I. D., Levin, F. R., Fudala, P. J., & Gorelick, D. A. (1993). Double blind study with carbamazepine for treatment of cocaine dependence. *ACNP Annual Meeting Abstracts, 173.*

Naranjo, C. A., Kadlec, K. E., Sanhueza, P., Woodley-Remus, D., & Sellers, E. M. (1990). Fluoxetine differentially alters alcohol intake and other consummatory behaviors in problem drinkers. *Clinical Pharmacology Therapeutics, 47,* 490–498.

Niggam, A. K., Ray, R., & Tripathi, B. M. (1993). Buprenorphine in opiate withdrawal: A comparison with clonidine. *Journal of Substance Abuse Treatment, 10,* 391–394.

Nunes, E. V., McGrath, P. J., Quitkin, F. M., Stewart, J. P., Harrison, W., Tricamo, E., & Ocepek-Welikson, K. (1993). Imipramine treatment of alcoholism with comorbid depression. *American Journal of Psychiatry, 150,* 963–965.

Nutt,D. J., & Glue, P. (1990). Neuropharmacological and clinical aspects of alcohol withdrawal. *Annals of Medicine, 22,* 275–281.

O'Connell, R. A., Mayo, J. A., & Flatown, L. (1991). Outcome of bipolar disorder on long-term treatment with lithium. *British Journal of Psychiatry, 159,* 123–129.

Oliveto, A. H., Kosten, T. R., Schottenfeld, R., Ziedonis, D., & Falcioni, J. (1994). A comparison of cocaine use in buprenorphine and methadone maintained cocaine abusers. *American Journal of Addictions, 3,* 43–48.

O'Malley, S. S., Jaffe, A. J., Chang, G., Rode, S., Schottenfeld, R., Meyer, R. E., & Rounsaville, B. (1996). Six-month follow-up of naltrexone and psychotherapy for alcohol dependence. *Archives of General Psychiatry, 53,* 217–224.

O'Malley, S. S., Jaffe, A. J., Chang, G., Schottenfeld, R. S., Meyer, R. E., & Rounsaville, B. (1992). Naltrexone and coping skills therapy for alcohol dependence. *Archives of General Psychiatry, 49,* 881–887.

Pomerleau, O. F., Pomerleau, C. S., Morrell, E. M., & Lowenbergh, J, M. (1991). Effects of fluoxetine on weight gain and food intake in smokers who reduce nicotine intake. *Psychoneuroendocrinology, 16,* 433–440.

Powell, B. J., Campbell, J. L., Landon, J. F., Liskow, B. I., Thomas, H. M., Nickel, E. J., Dale, T. N., Penick, E. C., Samuelson, S. D., & Lacoursiere, R. B. (1995). A double-blind, placebo-controlled study of nortriptyline and bromocriptine in male alcoholics subtyped comorbid psychiatric disorders. *Alcoholism: Clinical and Experimental Research, 19,* 462–468.

Rawson, R. A., & Ling, W. L. (1991). Opioid addiction treatment modalities and some guidelines to their optimal use. *Journal of Psychoactive Drugs, 23,* 151–163.

Rosecrans, J. A. (1991). The biobehavioral effects of nicotine: Interactions with brain neurochemical systems. In J. A. Cocores (Ed.), *The clinical management of nicotine dependence* (pp. 53–65). New York: Springer-Verlag.

Sanderson, E. M., Drasdo, A. L., McCrea, K., & Wonnacott, S. (1993). Upregulation of nicotinic receptors following continuous infusion of nicotine is brain-region-specific. *Brain Research, 617,* 349–352.

Sass, H., Soyka, M., Mann, K., & Zieglgansberger, W. (1996). Relapse prevention by acamprosate. Results from a placebo-controlled study on alcohol dependence. *Archives of General Psychiatry, 53,* 673–680.

Satel, S., Price, L., Palumbo, J., McDougle, C. J., Krystal, J. H., Gawin, F., Charney, D. S., Heninger, G. R., & Kleber, H. D. (1991). The clinical phenomenology and neurobiology of cocaine abstinence. *American Journal of Psychiatry, 148,* 1712–1716.

Schottenfeld, R. S., Pakes, J. R., Oliveto, A., Ziedonis, D., & Kosten, T. R. (1997). Buprenorphine vs. methadone maintenance treatment for concurrent opioid dependence and cocaine abuse. *Archives of General Psychiatry, 54,* 713–720.

Sellers, E. M., Toneatto, T., Romach, M. K., Somer, G. R., Sobell, L. C., & Sobell, M. B. (1994). Clinical efficacy of the 5-HT3 antagonist ondansetron in alcohol abuse and dependence. *Alcoholism: Clinical and Experimental Research, 18,* 879–885.

Siris, S. G., Bermanzohn, P. C., Mason, S. E., & Shuwall M. A. (1991). Antidepressant for substance-abusing schizophrenic patients: A mini review. *Progress in Neuropsychopharmacology and Biological Psychiatry, 15,* 1–13.

Tennant, F. S., & Sangherian, A. A. (1987). Double blind comparison of amantadine and bromocriptine for ambulatory withdrawal from cocaine dependence. *Archives of Internal Medicine, 147,* 109–112.

Tennant, F. S., Tarver, A. L., & Rawson, R. A. (1984). Clinical evaluation of mecamylamine for withdrawal from nicotine dependence. In *Problems of drug dependence* (NIDA Research Monograph Series No. 49). Rockville, MD: Department of Health, Education and Welfare.

Tohen, M., Waternaux, D. M., Tsuang, M. T., & Hunt, A. T. (1990). Four-year follow-up of twenty-four first-episode manic patients. *Journal of Affective Disorders 19,* 76–86.

Tollefson, G. D., Montague-Clouse, J., & Tollefson, S. L. (1992). Treatment of comorbid generalized anxiety in a recently detoxified alcoholic population with a selective serotonergic drug (buspirone). *Journal of Clinical Psychopharmacology, 12,* 19–26.

Tonnesen, P., Fryd, V., Hansen, M., Helsted, J., Gunnersen, A. B., Forchammer, H., & Stockner, M. (1988). Two and four mg nicotine chewing gum in combination with group counseling in smoking cessation: An open, randomized, controlled trial with a 22 month follow-up. *Addictive Behavior, 13,* 17–27.

Volkow, N. D., Mullani, N., Gould, K. L., Adler, S., & Krajewski, K. (1988). Cerebral blood flow in chronic cocaine users: a study with positron emission tomography. *British Journal of Psychiatry, 152,* 641–648.

Volpicelli, J. R., Alterman, A. I., Hayashida, M., & O'Brien, C. P. (1992). Naltrexone in the treatment of alcohol dependence. *Archives of General Psychiatry, 48,* 876–880.

Weddington, W. W., Brown, B. S., Haertzen, C. A., Cone, E. J., Dax, E. M., Herning, R. I., & Michaelson, B. S. (1990). Changes in mood, craving and sleep during short term abstinence reported by male cocaine addicts. *Archives of General Psychiatry, 47,* 861–868.

Weiss, R. D., & Mirin, S. M. (1989). Tricyclic antidepressants in the treatment of alcoholism and drug abuse. *Journal of Clinical Psychiatry, 5,* 4–9.

Wilens, T. E., Biederman, J., Spencer, T. J., & Prince, J. (1995). Pharmacotherapy of adult attention deficit/hyperactivity disorder: A review. *Journal of Clinical Psychopharmacology, 15,* 270–279.

Ziedonis, D., Richardson, T., Lee, E., Petrakis, I., & Kosten, T. (1992). Adjunctive desipramine in the treatment of cocaine-abusing schizophrenics. *Psychopharmacology Bulletin, 26,* 309–314.

CHAPTER 25

SOCIAL SKILLS TRAINING

Brad Donohue
Elissa Miller
Vincent B. Van Hasselt
Michel Hersen

This chapter reviews several empirically validated social skills assessment and treatment approaches for substance abusers. In particular, the social skills training approach developed by Azrin and his colleagues at Nova Southeastern University will be emphasized. In this strategy, social skills training is an integral component of a multielement cognitive-behavioral substance abuse treatment program that includes behavioral contracting, urge control, and stimulus control therapies. Social skills training is utilized throughout the intervention, especially when identified skill deficits increase risk of using illicit substance use, and/or interfere with therapy protocol (e.g., arguments with spouse during sessions).

There are numerous extant definitions of social skills in the literature. Yet most explanations include or imply receipt of reinforcement contingent on performance of specified verbal and nonverbal behavior(s) in interpersonal situations. Of course, reinforcement may be positive (e.g., receipt of higher wage after an assertive request) or negative (e.g., anxiety reduction following refusal to purchase a product from a "pushy" salesperson). Viewed in this context, social skill deficits may influence substance use in several ways (e.g., inability to refuse illicit substances, engagement in drug-related social activities, diminished

social anxiety when using substances). Indeed, it is well documented that substance abusers exhibit deficiencies in interpersonal situations (Abrams et al., 1991; Hazel, 1990; Monti, Rosenhow, Colby, & Abrams, 1995; Van Hasselt, Null, Kempton, & Bukstein, 1993). Moreover, without intervention, social dysfunction is likely to persist as intoxicating effects precipitate and intensify arguments, lead to exclusion from social gatherings, and restrict opportunities to practice social skills that are incompatible with substance use.

Initial applications of social skill interventions with this population indicated notable improvements in behaviors associated with substance abuse (Chaney, 1989; Van Hasselt, Hersen, & Milliones, 1978). However, only recently have controlled treatment outcome studies indicated significant reductions in the frequency of substance use following the implementation of social skills training. Moreover, social skills interventions for this population have now expanded to include broad-spectrum treatment strategies that have demonstrated reduction in drug and alcohol use, depression, and antisocial conduct; improved functioning in school and work; and enhanced relationship satisfaction across age, education, sex, and race (Azrin et al., 1996; Azrin,

Donohue, Besalel, Kogan, & Acierno, 1994; Azrin, McMahon, et al., 1994).

ASSESSMENT OF SOCIAL SKILLS

The first step of assessment is to determine whether the substance abuser lacks social skills requisite to effective interpersonal interactions (Monti et al., 1995). Skills deficits may be easily identified during assessment (e.g., looking at floor while speaking, telling therapist she looks "sexy"). However, even if unidentified during formal assessment, specific social skill deficits usually will be evidenced over the course of intervention. For example, poor negotiation skills may interfere with the establishment of a sound behavioral contract between the substance abuser and spouse/parent; lack of assertion may result in failure to complete therapy assignments relevant to obtaining a job; poor conflict resolution skills with family members may lead to continued discord during family therapy.

The most commonly explored social skill assessment procedure is the role-play test. In role-play assessment, the client participates in a simulation of a social situation that is likely to lead to substance use such as a friend offering a "joint" (Turner, Calhoun, & Adams, 1992). These situations may be generated from the abuser (e.g., "Tell me about a situation in which you used drugs after getting into an argument with your mother"), professional experience (e.g., "Many of our clients use drugs when they feel uncomfortable around others, such as at parties. Does this happen to you?"), or standardized role-play instruments (see below). After role-play situations are generated, a scenario is read to the client, who is then instructed to respond as he or she would if the situation were actually occurring. During the role-play interaction, the therapist, or experimental confederate enacts the part of a person in the situation (e.g., drug pusher). The confederate's reactions may be limited to one or more standard prompts (e.g., "Go ahead; take a hit"), or reactions may be less restricted, much as in a casual conversation.

Several standardized role-play tests of social skills in substance abusers have been developed. The major strength of standardized role-play procedures is that specific skills may be assessed objectively. However, it should be noted that substance-abusing clients may display adequate social skills in the clinic setting, yet experience negative thoughts or feelings that interfere with the appropriate use of these skills in vivo due to various situational factors.

The Situational Competency Test (Chaney, O'Leary, & Marlatt, 1978) is a standardized role-play procedure that assesses coping skills in 16 situations associated with relapse (e.g., "Everything has been going so well for you lately that you feel like having a drink or two to celebrate"). After each situation is read, the respondent is asked, "What do you do (say)?" Responses are audiotaped and retrospectively rated for response latency, response duration, compliance versus assertive control, and specificity of problem-solving behavior. As recommended by Chaney (1989), a 5-point scale (no response/not adequate/very skillful) may be utilized to rate performance in each situation. Respondents may also rate their own performance and later compare their scores with their therapist's evaluation.

The Alcohol Specific Role Play Test (Abrams et al., 1991) consists of 10 audiotaped situations relevant to alcohol abuse. At the end of each situation, the respondents are asked what they would do if they were actually in the situation and trying not to drink. Trained judges rate responses according to their perceptions of the clients' probability of solving the problem, including manifestations of anxiety. After each situation, clients use an 11-point scale to rate their urge to drink, anxiety level, and expected difficulty to cope with the situation in real life. Monti et al.,(1995) determine the latency of response for each scene, as drinking quantity and frequency have been shown to be lower for alcohol abusers who have faster response latencies.

The Problem Situation Inventory (Hawkins & Fraser, 1985) is a standardized role-play instrument that was initially developed to assess the social skills of drug abusers. This is an audiotaped role-play test that measures social skills in relapse-inducing situations commonly encountered by adult drug abusers (Hawkins, Catalano, & Wells, 1986). Fifty-one items are scored for the presence of 21 response components (e.g., provides a reason, greets the other person). In addition to scoring the occurrence of components, responses to each situation are assigned a global score (10-point scale) based on the number of components present. Bonus points are given for additional behavioral components, and points are subtracted if the response is passive, aggressive, or poorly executed.

Jenson, Wells, Plotnick, Hawkins, and Catalano (1993) developed an audiotaped role-play assessment measure of social skills associated with adolescent relapse-inducing situations (Adolescent Problem Situation Inventory; APSI). This measure was developed for use with substance-abusing delinquent populations and contains three subscales that are grouped according to situation content (i.e., drug and alcohol avoidance skills, social and problem solving skills, self-control skills). In general, interrater reliability of the APSI is good, and there appears to be a positive correlation between intention to use drugs and these social skills (Jenson et al., 1993). Interestingly, there does not appear to be a relationship between APSI social skill scores and post-treatment drug use, according to the results of their study.

SOCIAL SKILLS TRAINING

Most social skill training programs for substance abusers include some form of assertiveness training, although targeted skills and training methods vary considerably. Assertion skills have been conceptualized as the appropriate expression of feelings and personal rights (Lewis, 1994; Lewis, Dana, & Blevins, 1994), and the ability of an individual to deny unreasonable requests of others (Monti et al., 1995). Assertion skills modified in most substance abuse programs include teaching substance abusers to initiate and maintain conversations; give and receive compliments; exhibit appropriate nonverbal behaviors (e.g., body posture, eye contact, affect); listen to others; establish and maintain intimate relationships with abstinent individuals; enhance social-support networks; be specific, objective, and direct; use nonaccusatory statements; give and receive feedback (particularly about substance use); and refuse substances and unreasonable requests. Refusal skills typically include assertively declining requests to accept substances, suggesting non-substance-associated alternative activities, avoiding debate, terminating any discussion of substances, and avoiding the use of excuses and vague answers that imply that the substance may be accepted at a different time (Monti et al. 1995).

Work-related problems leading to unemployment and failure to obtain future employment are prevalent among substance abusers. Thus job skills training is particularly warranted and has demonstrated efficacy in substance-abusing populations (Azrin, 1976; Azrin et al., 1996; Azrin, Donohue, et al., 1994; Azrin, McMahon, et al., 1994; Azrin, Sisson, Meyers, & Godley, 1982). Job skills training includes teaching the substance abusers to develop a resume, complete job applications, and present themselves favorably during interviews (in-person, on the telephone) (Azrin & Besalel, 1980).

Cue-exposure treatment (CET) is an empirically supported therapy that often involves the use of social skills training (Azrin et al., 1996; Azrin, Donohue, et al., 1994; Azrin, McMahon, et al., 1994; Blakely & Baker, 1980; Monti et al., 1993). Although components vary across programs, most CET therapists attempt to teach substance abusers to identify high-risk situations that result in an increased urge to use substances, and to reduce urges to use substances in high-risk situations, for example, by cognitively rehearsing negative consequences of substances, generating and subsequently performing alternative substance-incompatible behaviors, concentrating on stimuli that are not associated with substance use, and using self-instructions and self-mastery statements (Azrin, McMahon, et al., 1994; Monti et al., 1995).

Interestingly, some investigators consider cognitive restructuring a social skill training component, (e.g., interpersonal cognitive problem-solving, ICPS) (Platt & Husband, 1993). According to Platt and Husband (1993), cognitive processing is crucial to the identification, appraisal, and resolution of interpersonal problems. ICPS training is focused on six skills necessary for effective interpersonal problem-solving based on the earlier work of D'Zurilla and Goldfried (1971). These skills include early identification of the problem, generating possible solutions, evaluating the consequences of these possible solutions, rehearsing the steps necessary to perform selected alternatives, understanding causal relationships in behavior, and assessing the perspective of persons involved in the situation.

Social Skills Training Procedures

Role-plays have been the primary vehicle for training social skills in the clinical setting. In this procedure it is first necessary to elicit social situations or scenarios in which the target skill is relevant to the client. Role-playing social skills in the context of situations that are generated from the substance abuser's own experiences will enhance generalization of target skills to the substance abuser's environment. However, personal experiences are frequently associated with negative emotions and biases that interfere with training. Thus, in teaching each target skill, we recommend that situations should initially be generic (hypothetical), particularly when conducting social skills training in the context of group, family, or couples psychotherapy. Scenarios should become increasingly difficult as the substance abuser's skills improve over time. After sufficient skill mastery is achieved in hypothetical situations, "real-life" scenarios may be generated from the substance abuser and subsequently role-played. The format of role-play administration typically involves (a) providing a brief rationale for the importance and applicability of the target skill, (b) disclosing a hypothetical situation or generating a situation from the substance abuser's recent past, (c) modeling effective and ineffective use of the target behavior in the context of the scenario, (d) eliciting positive feedback about the therapist's performance (e.g., "What did you like about what I just did?"), (e) eliciting negative feedback and suggestions to improve the therapist's performance ("What could I have done to improve my performance?"), (f) instructing the substance abuser to attempt the target skill in the context of the scenario (e.g., "Go ahead and try to refuse my offer to sell you cocaine. I'll pretend to be the dealer"), (g) eliciting positive feedback from the substance abuser about his or her performance, (h) eliciting from the substance abuser suggestions to improve his or her performance, (i) provision of positive feedback from the therapist, and (j) instructing the substance abuser to demonstrate the target skill using the feedback provided.

To maintain enduring treatment effects, we also recommend sequential and cumulative targeting of social skills deficits. Specifically, the most problematic, substance-associated, social skill deficit is treated first. Demonstrated proficiency in this initial target skill results in the training of a new social skill. However, the former skill is reviewed during all subsequent sessions, albeit to a progressively lesser degree (i.e., role-play only one scenario involving the target skill). This process continues until all targeted social skills are improved. Thus, during the final phase of treatment, all previously targeted social skills are reviewed. Other role-play strategies include (a) instructing rather than asking substance abusers to attempt role-play interactions, (b) providing assignments to practice targeted social skills at home or in other relevant settings, (c) eliciting positive feedback prior to eliciting or suggesting alternative behaviors, and (d) using difficult scenarios and prompts in training only after basic skills are established.

Azrin's Social Skills Training Approach

In the substance abuse program developed by Azrin and colleagues (Azrin et al., 1996; Azrin, Donohue, et al., 1994; Azrin, McMahon, et al., 1994), social skills training is implemented during the initial session when communication guidelines are reviewed. These guidelines are primarily employed to prevent disruptive communication patterns between family members during therapy sessions. Guidelines include not talking when another person is talking; never refusing a request outright but rather agree to comply with some part of the request and/or suggest something that can be done that approximates what was requested; not swearing, shouting, or using sarcasm; using objective and specific actions when making requests; not talking for more than one minute without initiating or allowing an opportunity for feedback. After each guideline is presented, the therapist asks the substance abuser and his or her family why the guideline is important. Then the therapist elicits their commitments to comply with the guideline. If it appears that a family member is likely to experience difficulty following a particular guideline, the therapist instructs the person to role-play a situation involving compliance with the guideline (e.g., if a substance abuser speaks tangentially for extended periods of time, he or she may role-play a situation in which he or she talks for less than one minute and then attempts to elicit feedback). When a guideline is violated in therapy, the offending family member is immediately reminded of his or her commitment to comply with the guideline, and is then instructed to continue the interaction in compliance with the guideline.

Social interactions are also targeted in family context via reciprocity awareness during the first intervention session. In this social skills procedure the substance abuser is instructed to offer a statement of appreciation to each family member for something positive that the person has done for him or her. After each statement is made, the therapist encourages and descriptively praises the substance abuser for pleasant affect, eye contact, and verbal content reflecting love, concern, and sincerity. The therapist then instructs each family member to provide a statement of appreciation to the substance abuser for something that he or she has done for the family member. The family is also encouraged to provide each other with feedback regarding positive aspects of their communication. After several statements of appreciation are reviewed, the substance abuser and the family members are given an assignment to exchange several "statements of appreciation" throughout the week. One or two such statements are role-played during each of the next three sessions.

The annoyance prevention procedure is designed to help substance abusers and relevant family members control negative emotions and other impulsive behaviors that are often associated with problematic interpersonal situations. Role-playing is utilized to teach the substance abuser and family to (a) relax on first recognition of upset (i.e., deep breaths, cognitive rehearsal of words and/or phrases associated with relaxation), (b) describe the annoying situation using relevant details that are objective (e.g., "You came home two hours after you promised you would have dinner with me"), (c) offer a statement that blames some extraneous variable for the problem (e.g., "You probably were busy at work and forgot to call me"), and (d) provide a statement of personal responsibility ("I probably should have tried to call you").

After performing the annoyance prevention procedure, the substance abuser and family members are taught to positively request a change in the other person's behavior. In doing so, a list is given to each family member that delineates several components of a positive request (e.g., request a specific action, state benefits to recipient and self, offer to help the recipient perform the action, offer to reciprocate a favor or pleasant action, state how completion of request would be appreciated, suggest an alternative behavior). Family members are then instructed to take turns making requests of one another utilizing this handout. During these interactions, the therapist provides feedback and modeling and attempts to elicit descriptive praise from family members concerning targeted communication skills. In responding to a positive request, the recipient is encouraged to state what is liked about the request prior to accepting the request. If the request is unacceptable, the recipient is taught to offer an alternative behavior that better approximates what is requested. These handouts are utilized throughout intervention to maintain focus when stating requests of one another.

Social skills relevant to substance use situations (e.g., substance refusal) are evaluated and treated in a stimulus control procedure that is implemented during the third session. In this strategy, two lists are constructed that include people, places, and situations in which drug use has (at-risk associations), and has not (safe associations), occurred in the past. A list of substance-incompatible activities (e.g., health spas and gyms, jogging, church functions, trips with abstinent family and friends) is used to prompt additional safe associations. The substance abuser is assigned to record time spent with these stimuli at the end of each day. The day is then reviewed with a significant other, and the next day is planned utilizing a daily planner. The stimulus control list is reviewed every session with the therapist and family members. During these reviews, the substance abuser is descriptively encouraged and praised for performance of substance-incompatible behaviors and

social interactions (e.g., refusing drugs, interviewing for a job). Conversely, behaviors and interactions that influence substance use are problem-solved by (a) instructing the substance abuser to provide reasons that his or her behavior may influence drug use, (b) instructing the substance abuser to offer alternative substance-incompatible behaviors, (c) praising the substance abuser for suggesting behaviors that are likely to lead to abstinence, (d) prompting alternative substance-incompatible behaviors whenever necessary, and (e) role-playing the desired substance-incompatible behaviors. At-risk situations typically include parties or "get-togethers," being alone and bored, specific times of day, and events associated with money (i.e., receiving employment check from boss). Initially, family members have difficulty reacting to substance abusers when time has been spent in "at-risk" situations (e.g., they may become verbally abusive for participating in high-risk situations, be overly demanding, or make accusations that the substance abuser is lying). Thus role-playing is frequently employed to teach significant others how to respond to the substance abuser after he or she has participated in high-risk situations and to encourage substance-incompatible behaviors.

The final social skills component involves an urge control procedure in which the substance abuser is taught to engage in substance-incompatible behaviors when exposed to situations that have been associated with substance use in the past. The urge control procedure is implemented during the fourth treatment session and is reviewed during all subsequent intervention sessions. In the first step, the substance abuser is instructed to imagine a recent at-risk situation (e.g., thinking about getting an employment check while fixing a roof with intentions to buy crack cocaine). As soon as the first thought of drug use occurs, the therapist instructs the substance abuser to forcefully say, "Stop!" and then state several of the substance abuser's most aversive consequences of substance use (e.g., loss of job, arguments with spouse, heart attack). After emitting cue words associated with relaxation ("I'm letting myself become relaxed," "calm," "relax," "I feel comfortable"), the substance abuser is prompted to provide the therapist with a "play by play" narrative of himself or herself leaving the substance-associated situation and subsequently engaging in drug-incompatible behavior with an abstinent friend or relative. Finally, the substance abuser is instructed to use self-praise reinforcement for engagement in specific substance-incompatible behaviors, including statements reflecting the pleasant reactions of family and friends. Several trials are performed during each session and feedback is provided after each trial. The number of trials rehearsed in each session fades with abstinence (usually five trials per session to one trial per session over the course of six or more treatment sessions). Role-playing is employed as needed (e.g., declining to attend a social function with a known drug user).

CONCLUSION

It is well established that social skill deficits are prominent among substance abusers. Whereas earlier social skills training programs demonstrated improvements in skills that were thought to influence substance abuse behavior, efficacy of these approaches in decreasing substance use was not demonstrated in controlled treatment outcome studies. Such interventions have now been incorporated into broad spectrum cognitive-behavioral treatment packages that have proved effective in reducing frequency of substance use and substance-associated behavior problems. Specifically, skills training may be utilized to (a) establish and maintain communication guidelines that enhance client adherence to treatment protocol; (b) improve substance refusal skills; (c) ameliorate aversive communication patterns that may lead to substance abuse; and (d) enhance behaviors associated with establishing and maintaining drug-free activities and friendships.

REFERENCES

Abrams, D. B., Binkoff, J. A., Zwick, W. R., Liepman, M. R., Nirenberg, T. D., Monroe, S. M., & Monti, P. M. (1991). Alcohol abusers' and social drinkers responses to alcohol-relevant and general situations. *Journal of Studies on Alcohol, 52*, 409–415.

Azrin, N. H. (1976). Improvements in the community-reinforcement approach to alcoholism. *Behavior Research and Therapy, 14*, 339–348.

Azrin, N. H., Acierno, R., Kogan, E. S., Donohue, B., Besalel, V. A., & McMahon, P. T. (1996). Follow-up results of supportive versus behavioral therapy for illicit drug use. *Behavior Research and Therapy, 34*, 41–46.

Azrin, N. H., & Besalel, V. A. (1980). *Job club counselor's manual*. Baltimore: University Park Press.

Azrin, N. H., Donohue, B., Besalel, V. A., Kogan, E. S., & Acierno, R. (1994). Youth drug abuse treatment: A controlled outcome study. *Journal of Child and Adolescent Substance Abuse, 3*, 1–16.

Azrin, N. H., McMahon, P. T., Donohue, B., Besalel, V. A., Lapinski, K. J., Kogan, E. S., Acierno, R. E., & Galloway, E. (1994). Behavior therapy for drug abuse: A controlled treat-

ment outcome study. *Behavior Research and Therapy, 32*, 857–866.

Azrin, N. H., Sisson, R. W., Meyers, R., & Godley, M. (1982). Alcoholism treatment by disulfiram and community reinforcement therapy. *Journal of Behavior Therapy and Experimental Psychiatry, 13*, 105–112.

Blakely, R. & Baker, R. (1980). An exposure approach to alcohol abuse. *Behavior Research and Therapy, 18*, 319–325.

Chaney, E. F. (1989). Social skills training. In R. K. Hester & W. R. Miller (Eds.), *Handbook of alcoholism treatment* (pp. 206–221). Elmsford, New York: Pergamon Press.

Chaney, E. F., O'Leary, M. R., & Marlatt, G. A. (1978). Skill training with alcoholics. *Journal of Consulting and Clinical Psychology, 46*, 1092–1104.

D'Zurilla, T. J., & Goldfried, M. R. (1971). Problem solving and behavior modification. *Journal of Abnormal Psychology, 78*, 107–126.

Hawkins, J. D., Catalano, R. F., & Wells, E. A. (1986). Measuring effects of a skills training intervention for drug abusers. *Journal of Consulting and Clinical Psychology, 54*, 661–664.

Hawkins, J. D., & Fraser, M. W. (1985). Social networks of street drug abusers: A comparison of two theories. *Social Work Research and Abstracts, 21*, 3–12.

Hazel, J. S. (1990). Social skills training with adolescents. In E. L. Feindler & G. R. Kalfus (Eds.), *Adolescent behavior therapy handbook* (pp. 191–209). New York: Springer.

Jenson, J. M., Wells, E. A., Plotnick, R. D., Hawkins, J. D., & Catalano, R. F. (1993). The effects of skills and intentions to use drugs on posttreatment drug use in adolescents. *American Journal of Drug and Alcohol Abuse, 19*, 1–18.

Lewis, J. A. (1994). *Addictions: Concepts and strategies for treatment*. Gaithersburg, MD: Aspen.

Lewis, J. A., Dana, R. Q., & Blevins, G. A. (1994). *Substance abuse counseling*. Pacific Grove, CA: Brooks/Cole.

Monti, P. M., Rohsenow, D. J., Colby, S. M., & Abrams, D. B. (1995). Coping and social skills training. In R. K. Hester & W. R. Miller (Eds.), *Handbook of alcoholism treatment approaches* (2nd ed., pp. 221–241). Needham Heights, MA: Allyn and Bacon.

Monti, P. M., Rohsenow, D. J., Rubonis, A. V., Niaura, R. S., Sirota, A. D., Colby, S. M., & Goddard, P. (1993). Cue exposure with coping skills treatment for male alcoholics. *Journal of Clinical and Consulting Psychology, 61*, 1011–1019.

Platt, J. J., & Husband, S. D. (1993). An overview of problem-solving and social skills approaches in substance abuse treatment. *Psychotherapy, 30*, 276–283.

Turner, S. M., Calhoun, K. S., & Adams, H. E. (1992). *Handbook of clinical behavior therapy*. New York: Wiley.

Van Hasselt, V. B., Hersen, M., & Milliones, J. (1978). Social skills training for alcoholics and drug addicts: A review. *Addictive Behaviors, 3*, 221–233.

Van Hasselt, V. B., Null, J. A., Kempton, T., & Bukstein, O. G. (1993). Social skills and depression in adolescent substance abusers. *Addictive Behaviors, 18*, 9–18.

CHAPTER 26

THERAPEUTIC COMMUNITIES

George De Leon

THERAPEUTIC COMMUNITIES: THEORY, RESEARCH, AND APPLICATIONS

Therapeutic communities (TCs) for addictions derive from Synanon, founded in 1958 by Charles Dederich with other recovering alcoholics and drug addicts. Although the immediate antecedents of the addiction TC is Alcoholics Anonymous, ancient prototypes exist in all forms of communal healing and mutual self-help. The contemporary therapeutic community for addictions has matured into a sophisticated human services modality in the past 35 years, evident in the broad range of programs that subscribe to the basic TC perspective and approach, serving an estimated 80,000 admissions yearly in the United States (Therapeutic Communities of America, 1993). These comprise a wide diversity of clients who use an expanded cafeteria of drugs and present complex social-psychological problems in addition to their chemical abuse.

THE THERAPEUTIC COMMUNITY MODALITY

The therapeutic community is a drug-free modality that utilizes a social-psychological, self-help approach to the treatment of drug abuse. The characteristic setting for its

programs is a community-based residence in urban and nonurban locales. However, TC programs have been implemented in a variety of other settings, residential *and* nonresidential (e.g., hospitals, jails, schools, halfway houses, day treatment clinics and ambulatory clinics). TCs offer a wide variety of services including social, psychological, educational, medical, legal, and social/advocacy. However, these services are coordinated in accordance with the TC's basic self-help model.

The Traditional Residential TC

Much of what is known about the therapeutic community approach and its effectiveness is based on the long-term residential model, also termed the "traditional" TC. Traditional TCs are similar in planned duration of stay (15–24 months), structure, staffing pattern, perspective, and rehabilitative regime, although they differ in size (30–600 beds) and client demography. Staff are composed of TC-trained clinicians and other human service professionals. Primary clinical staff are usually former substance abusers who themselves were rehabilitated in TC programs. Other staff consists of professionals providing, medical, mental health, vocational, educational, family counseling, fiscal, administrative and legal services.

TCs accommodate a broad spectrum of drug abusers. Although they originally attracted narcotic addicts, the majority of their client populations are nonopioid abusers. Thus, this modality has responded to the changing trend in drug use patterns; treating clients with substance and psychological disorders, problems of varying severity, different lifestyles, and various social, economic, and ethnic/cultural backgrounds.

The TC views drug abuse as a deviant behavior, reflecting impeded personality development or chronic deficits in social, educational, and economic skills. Its antecedents lie in socioeconomic disadvantage, in poor family effectiveness, and in psychological factors. Thus the principal aim of the therapeutic community is a global change in lifestyle: abstinence from illicit substances, elimination of antisocial activity, development of employability, and prosocial attitudes and values. The rehabilitative approach requires multidimensional influence and training, which for most can only occur in a 24-hour residential setting.

Admission Criteria

Traditional TCs maintain an "open-door" policy with respect to admission to residential treatment. However, there are two major guidelines for excluding clients: suitability and community risk. Suitability refers to the degree to which the client can meet the demands of the TC regime and integrate with others. This includes participation in groups, fulfilling work assignments, and living with minimal privacy in an open community, usually under dormitory conditions. Risk refers to the extent to which clients present a management burden to the staff or pose a threat to the security and/or health of others in the community.

Specific exclusionary criteria most often include histories of arson, suicide attempts, and serious psychiatric disorder. Psychiatric exclusion is usually based on documented history of psychiatric hospitalizations or *prima facie* evidence of psychotic symptoms on interview (e.g., frank delusions, thought disorder, hallucinations, confused orientation, or signs of serious affective disorder). Generally, clients on regular psychotropic regimes will be excluded because use of these usually correlates with chronic or severe psychiatric disorder. Clients requiring medication for medical conditions are acceptable in TCs, as are clients with disabilities or those who require prosthetics, providing they can meet the participatory demands of the program.

A full medical history is obtained during the admission evaluation, which includes questions concerning current medication regimes (e.g., asthma, diabetes, hypertension) and the necessity for prosthetics. As discussed later in this chapter, policy and practices concerning testing for HIV status and management of AIDS (acquired immune deficiency syndrome), or AIDS-related complex (ARC) have recently been implemented by most TCs.

The Residential Client

Suitability for long-term treatment in TCs is based on several indicators that can be summarized across five main areas:

1. *Health and Social Risk Status:* The individual's experience of chronic or acute stress concerning physical, psychological, and social problems associated with drug use. Some indicators are
   - out-of-control behavior with respect to drug use, criminality, or sexuality;
   - suicidal potential threat through overdose; threat of injury or death through other drug-related means;
   - anxiety or fear concerning violence, jail, illness, or death; and extent of personal losses (e.g.,financial, relationships, employment).

2. *Abstinence Potential:* The individual's ability to maintain complete abstinence in a nonresidential treatment setting. Some indicators are
   - previous treatment experiences (number, type, and outcomes);
   - previous self-initiated attempts at abstinence (frequency and longest duration);
   - current active drug use versus current abstinence.

3. *Social and Interpersonal Function:* The individual's current capability to function in a responsible way. Some indicators are
   - involvement in the drug lifestyle (friends, places, activities);
   - impaired ability to maintain employment or school responsibility or to maintain social relations and responsibilities (e.g., parental spouse, filial, friendships).

4. *Antisocial Involvement:* The extent to which the individual' drug use is embedded in an antisocial lifestyle. Some indicators are
   - active and past criminal history in term of type and frequency of illegal activities; frequency and duration of incarceration;
   - existing legal pressures for treatment;
   - long-term pattern of antisocial behavior, including juvenile contact with the criminal justice system and early school problems.

5. *Perceived Suitability for the TC:* Individual motivation, readiness and suitability for TC treatment. Some indicators are

- acceptance of the severity of drug problem;
- acceptance for the need for treatment ("can't do it alone");
- willingness to sever ties with family, friends, and current lifestyle while in treatment;
- willingness to surrender a private life meeting the expectations of a structured community.

Health and Social Risk Status

Most abusers who seek treatment in the TC experience acute stress. They may be in family or legal crisis or at significant risk to harm themselves or others such that a period of residential stay is indicated. However, the clients suitable for long-term residential treatment reveal a more chronic pattern of stress that induces treatment seeking, and when relieved, usually results in premature dropout. They require longer term residential treatment because they are a constant risk threat and they must move beyond relief seeking to initiate a genuine recovery process.

Abstinence Potential

In the TC's view of substance abuse as a disorder of the whole person, abstinence is a prerequisite for recovery. Among chronic users the risk of repeated relapse can subvert any treatment effort regardless of the modality. Thus, the residential TC is needed to interrupt out-of-control drug use and to stabilize an extended period of abstinence in order to facilitate a long-term recovery process.

Social and Interpersonal Function

Inadequate social and interpersonal function not only results from drug use but often reveals a more general picture of immaturity or an impeded developmental history. Thus a setting such as the TC, which focuses upon the broad socialization and/or habilitation of the individual, is needed.

Antisocial Involvement

In the TC view, the term "antisocial" also suggests characteristics that are highly correlated with drug use. These include behaviors such as exploitation, abuse and violence, attitudes of mainstream disaffiliation, and the rejection or absence of prosocial values. Modification of these charac-

teristics requires the intensive resocialization approach of the TC setting.

Perceived Suitability for the TC

A number of those seeking admission to the TC may not be motivated to change, ready for treatment in general, or suitable for the demands of a long-term residential regime. Assessment of these factors at admission provides a basis for treatment planning in the TC or sometimes appropriate referral. Although motivation, readiness, and suitability are not criteria for admission to the TC, the importance of these factors often emerges after entry to treatment; not identifying and addressing them is related to early dropout.

ESSENTIAL ELEMENTS OF THE TC

The TC can be distinguished from other major drug treatment modalities in two fundamental ways. First, the TC offers a systematic treatment approach that is guided by an explicit *perspective* on the drug use disorder, the person, recovery, and right living. Second, the primary "therapist" and teacher in the TC is the *community* itself, which consists of the social environment, peers, and staff who, as role models of successful personal change, serve as guides in the recovery process. Thus the community is both *context* in which change occurs and *method* for facilitating change.

Therapeutic Community Perspective

Although expressed in a social/psychological idiom, this perspective evolved directly from the experience of recovering participants in TCs and is organized in terms of four interrelated views of the substance disorder, the person, recovery, and right living. Table 26.1 outlines each of these views. Substance abuse is a disorder of the whole person. The fundamental problem is the person—not the drug. Recovery is a self-help process of incremental learning toward a stable change in behavior, attitudes, and values of right living that are associated with maintaining abstinence.

Elements of Community as Method

The quintessential element of the TC approach may be termed "community as method" (De Leon, 1995a, 1995b). What distinguishes the TC from other treatment approaches (and other communities) is the *purposive use of the peer community to facilitate social and psychological change in*

Table 26.1   The Therapeutic Community Perspective: Four Interrelated Views

View of the Disorder	Drug abuse is a disorder of the whole person involving some or all the areas of functioning: • Cognitive, behavioral, emotional, medical, social, and spiritual problems • Physical dependency must be seen in the context of the individual psychological status and lifestyle • The problem is the person, not the drug
View of the Person	Rather than drug use patterns, individuals are distinguished along dimensions of psychological dysfunction and social deficits. Some shared characteristics: • Poor tolerance for frustration/discomfort/delay of gratification • Low self-esteem • Problems with authority • Poor impulse control • Unrealistic • Coping with feelings • Dishonesty/manipulation/self-deception • Guilt (self, others, community) • Deficits (reading, writing, attention, communication)
View of Recovery	The goals of treatment are global changes in lifestyle and identity. Some assumptions about recovery: • Recovery is a developmental learning • Self-help and mutual self-help • Motivation • Social learning • Treatment is an episode in the recovery process
View of Right Living	Certain precepts, beliefs, and values as essential to self-help recovery, social learning, personal growth, and healthy living. Some examples: • Truth/honesty • Here and now • Personal responsibility for destiny • Social responsibility ("brother's/sister's keeper") • Moral code concerning right and wrong behavior • Work ethic • Inner person is "good," but behavior can be "bad" • Change is the only certainty • Learning to learn • Economic self-reliance • Community involvement • Good citizenry

Source: "Therapeutic Comunities for Addictions: A Theoretical Framework" by G. DeLeon, 1995, *International Journal of Addictions,* pp. 1603–1645.

individuals. Thus in a therapeutic community all activities are designed to produce therapeutic and educational change in individual participants and all participants are mediators of these therapeutic and educational changes. Table 26.2 summarizes the fundamental elements of community as method.

Components of a Generic TC Program Model

The TC perspective on the disorder, the person, recovery, and right living and its distinctive approach, the use of

community as method, provide the conceptual basis for defining a generic TC program model in terms of its basic components. The following is a list of these components, which are adapted in different ways depending on the setting and the populations served.

Community Separateness

TC-oriented programs have their own names, often innovated by the clients and are housed in a space or locale that is separated from other agency or institutional programs, units, or

Table 26.2 Community as Method: Nine Essential Concepts

Use of Participant Roles	Individuals contribute directly to all activities of the daily life in the TC, which provides learning opportunities through engaging in a variety of social roles (e.g. peer, friend, coordinator, tutor). Thus the individual is an active participant in the process of changing themselves and others rather than spectator.
Use of Membership Feedback	The primary source of instruction and support for individual change is the peer membership. Providing observations and authentic reactions to the individual is the shared responsibility of all participants.
Use of the Membership as Role Models	Each participant strives to be a role model of the change process. Along with their responsibility to provide feedback to others as to what they must change, members must also provide examples of how they can change.
Use of Collective Formats for Guiding Individual Change	The individual engages in the process of change primarily with peers. Education, training, and therapeutic activities occur in groups, meetings, seminars, job functions, and recreation. Thus the learning and healing experiences essential to recovery and personal growth unfold in a social context and through social intercourse.
Use of Shared Norms and Values	Rules, regulations, and social norms protect the physical and psychological safety of the community. However, there are beliefs and values that serve as explicit guidelines for self-help recovery and teaching right living. These are expressed in the vernacular and the culture of each TC and are mutually reinforced by the membership.
Use of Structure and Systems	The organization of work, (e.g., the varied job functions, chores and management roles) needed to maintain the daily operations of the facility is a main vehicle for teaching self-development. Learning occurs not only through specific skills training, but in adhering to the orderliness of procedures and systems, in accepting and respecting supervision, and in behaving as a responsible member of the community on whom others are dependent.
Use of Open Communication	The public nature of shared experiences in the community is used for therapeutic purposes. The private inner life of the individual, feelings and thoughts, are matters of importance to the recovery and change process, not only for the individual but for other members. Thus all personal disclosure is eventually publicly shared.
Use of Relationships	Friendships with particular individuals, peers and staff, are essential to encourage the individual to engage and remain in the change process. And relationships developed in treatment are the basis for the social network needed to sustain recovery beyond treatment.
Use of Language	The argot, is the special vocabulary used by residents to reflect elements of its sub culture, particularly, its recovery and right living teachings. As with any special language. TC argot represents individual integration into the peer community. However, it also mirrors the individual's clinical progress. The gradual shift in attitudes, behaviors and values consonant with recovery and right living is reflected how well residents learn, understand and use the terms of the glossary and the argot in general. Thus, resident use of the argot of the TC is an explicit measure of their affiliation and socialization in the TC community.

generally from the drug-related environment. In the residential settings, clients remain away from outside influences 24 hours a day for several months before earning short-term day-out privileges. In the nonresidential "day treatment" settings, the individual is in the TC environment for 4–8 hours and then monitored by peers and family. Even in the least restrictive outpatient settings, TC-oriented programs and components are in place. Members gradually detach from old networks and relate to the drug-free peers in the program.

A Community Environment

The inner environment of a TC facility contains communal space to promote a sense of commonality and collective activities such as groups and meetings. The walls display signs that state in simple terms the philosophy of the program, the messages of right living and recovery. Corkboards and blackboards identify all participants by name, seniority level, and job function in the program and daily schedules are posted. These visuals display an organizational picture of the program that the individual can relate to and comprehend, factors that promote affiliation.

Community Activities

To be effectively utilized, treatment or educational services must be provided within a context of the peer community. Thus, with the exception of individual counseling, all activities are programmed in collective formats. These include at least one daily meal prepared, served, and shared by all members; a daily schedule of groups, meetings, and seminars; team job functions; and organized recreational/leisure time, ceremony, and rituals (e.g., birthdays, phase/progress graduations, and so on).

Staff Roles and Functions

The staff are a mix of self-help recovered professionals and other traditional professionals (e.g., medical, legal, mental health, and educational) who must be integrated through cross-training that is grounded in the basic concepts of the TC perspective and community approach. Professional skills define the function of staff (e.g., nurse, physician, lawyer, teacher, administrator, case worker, clinical counselor). Regardless of professional discipline or function, however, the generic role of all staff is that of community member who are rational authorities, facilitators and guides in the self help community method, rather than providers and treaters.

Peers as Role Models

Members who demonstrate the expected behaviors and reflect the values and teachings of the community are viewed as role models. Indeed, the strength of the community as a context for social learning relates to the number and quality of its role models. All members of the community are expected to be role models—roommates; older and younger residents; junior, senior, and directorial staff. TCs require these multiple role models to maintain the integrity of the community and assure the spread of social learning effects.

A Structured Day

The structure of the program relates to the TC perspective, particularly the view of the client and recovery. Ordered, rou-

tine activities counter the characteristically disordered lives of these clients and distract from negative thinking and boredom, which are factors that predispose drug use. Also, structured activities of the community facilitate learning self-structure for the individual in time management, planning, setting and meeting goals, and in general accountability. Thus, regardless of its length, the day has a formal schedule of varied therapeutic and educational activities with prescribed formats, fixed times, and routine procedures.

Work as Therapy and Education

Consistent with the TC's self-help approach, all clients are responsible for the daily management of the facility (e.g., cleaning, activities, meal preparation and service, maintenance, purchasing, security, coordinating schedules, preparatory chores for groups, meetings, seminars activities, and so on). In the TC, the various work roles mediate essential educational and therapeutic effects. Job functions strengthen affiliation with the program through participation, provide opportunities for skill development, and foster self examination and personal growth through performance challenge and program responsibility. The scope and depth of client work functions depend on the program setting (e.g., institutional vs. free-standing facilities) and client resources (levels of psychological function, social and life skills).

Phase Format

The treatment protocol, or plan of therapeutic and educational activities, is organized into phases that reflect a developmental view of the change process. Emphasis is on incremental learning at each phase, which moves the individual to the next stage of recovery.

TC Concepts

There is a formal and informal curriculum focused on teaching the TC perspective, particularly its self-help recovery concepts and view of right living. The concepts, messages, and lessons of the curriculum are repeated in the various groups, meetings, seminars, and peer conversations, as well as in readings, signs, and personal writings.

Peer Encounter Groups

The main community or therapeutic group is the encounter, although other forms of therapeutic, educational and support groups are utilized as needed. The minimal objective of the peer encounter is similar in TC-oriented programs—to heighten individual awareness of specific attitudes or behavioral patterns that should be modified. However, the encounter process may differ in degree of staff direction and intensity, depending on the client subgroups (e.g., adolescents, prison inmates, the dually disordered).

Awareness Training

All therapeutic and educational interventions involve raising the individuals' consciousness of the impact of their conduct and attitudes on themselves and the social environment; and conversely the impact of the behaviors and attitudes of others on themselves and the social environment.

Emotional Growth Training

Achieving the goals of personal growth and socialization involves teaching individuals how to identify feelings, express feelings appropriately, and manage feelings constructively through the interpersonal and social demands of communal life.

Planned Duration of Treatment

The optimal length of time for full program involvement must be consistent with TC goals of recovery and its developmental view of the change process. How long the individual must be program-involved depends on their phase of recovery, although a minimum period of intensive involvement is required to assure internalization of the TC teachings.

Continuity of Care

Completion of primary treatment is a stage in the recovery process. Aftercare services are an essential component in the TC model. Whether implemented within the boundaries of the main program or separately as in residential or nonresidential halfway houses or ambulatory settings, the perspective and approach guiding aftercare programming must be *continuous* with that of primary treatment in the TC. Thus the views of right living and self-help recovery and the use of a peer network are essential to enhance the appropriate use of vocational, educational, mental health, social and other typical aftercare or reentry services (De Leon, 1995a).

THE TC TREATMENT PROCESS

Understanding the process of change in the TC reflects its perspective and approach. A disorder of the whole person means that change is *multidimensional*. Thus change must be viewed along several dimensions of behavior, perceptions, and experiences. The main approach for facilitating change is the use of the community as method which consists of *multiple interventions*. Recovery unfolds as developmental learning which can be described in terms of characteristic *stages of change*. Details of these process elements are provided elsewhere (e.g., De Leon, 1995a, 1995b; De Leon, in press).

Interventions

In the TC *all* of the activities are designed to produce therapeutic or educational effects. These activities, singly and in various combinations, constitute *interventions* that directly and indirectly impact the individual in the change process. Indeed, it is this element of using every activity for teaching or healing that illustrates the meaning of community as method. The diverse activities of community that are basic to the TC model can be organized into three main classes of interventions: therapeutic/educative (e.g., individual counseling, groups, seminars), community enhancement (e.g., various communitywide meetings, ceremonies, rituals), community and clinical management (e.g., privileges, disciplinary sanctions).

Dimensions

Partitioning the "whole" individual into separate dimensions is a somewhat artificial device analogous to attempting to classify the TC milieu into separate interventions. Thus a complete description of change in the whole person includes both the *objective* behavioral dimensions as well as *subjective* changes reflected in self perceptions and experiences. These are separately discussed for purposes of clarity.

Behavioral change is described along four broad dimensions that reflect the TC perspective. The dimensions of *community/member and socialization* refer to the social development of the individual specifically as a member in the TC community and generally as a prosocial participant in the larger society. The developmental and *psychological* dimensions refer to the evolution of the individual as a unique person in terms of his or her basic psychological function, personal growth, and identity. Each dimension pictures the same individual from different aspects in terms of observable behavioral indicators.

Subjective dimensions of change consist of essential client perceptions and experiences. How clients perceive their problems, their progress, peers, staff, the program environment, treatment demands, and the pushes and pulls from outside of the program compel contemplation and redecision to continue in the process, almost on a daily basis. These perceptions may be grouped under five domains: *circumstances, motivation, readiness, suitability,* and *critical perceptions* of self-change.

As with perceptions, a limited array of experiences are underscored that appear as necessary to the change process within the TC. These can be conceptualized under two dimensions: *healing* and *learning.* Healing refers to the various emotional experiences related to the others, such as nurturance–sustenance, physical and psychological safety, and social relatedness. Subjective learning *experiences* refer to subjective outcomes on the theme of self-efficacy and self-esteem that may occur.

Both healing and subjective learning experiences are interrelated in the process of individual change. Healing experiences are essential for engaging, affiliating and sustaining the individual in the peer community. Subjective outcomes are the basis of achieving *internalized learning,* that is, behavior change that is maintained by fewer external consequences and is more under self-control.

Stages of Change

Stages and phases are definable points in the process. These can be described from two different but interrelated perspectives of change—program stages and treatment stages. *Program stages* refer to change in the four behavioral dimensions described earlier, which picture the individual's movement according to specific goals of the program. Three main program stages and several phases within each stage have been delineated for the traditional long-term process of TC: stage 1, induction/orientation; stage 2, primary treatment, 2–12 months; and stage 3, reentry, 13–24 months. For TCs with shorter planned duration of treatments, the length of each stage is correspondingly shorter but the goals remain the same.

The *treatment stages* perspective more closely captures the evolving relationship between the individual and community. This evolution can be characterized in terms of levels of *internalization*—how much or completely the individual accepts, practices, and applies the behaviors, attitudes, values of the TC's teachings.

The mark of each stage of internalization is the *transfer* of the influences on new learning from the external (objective) consequences to the internal (subjective) outcome experiences of the individual. Internalized learning can be characterized as more stable and self-initiated ("inner directed") than as peer influenced ("outer directed") learning. Thus, as residents move through the program stages, four stages of internalization can be delineated: *compliance, conformity, commitment,* and *integration.* Each stage reflects the gradual transfer from outer- to more inner-directed influences.

For TCs the importance of internalization is especially salient because the power of its community method can readily modify observable behaviors and attitudes in the program setting. However, these changes may not endure once the individual separates from the omnipresent influence of the peer community. Practically all residents in TCs display drug-free behavior during their residential stay. That relapse occurs among a number of the dropouts and some of the graduates, however, underscores the relevance of internalization in the change process.

THERAPEUTIC COMMUNITY RESEARCH

A considerable research literature on the TC has evolved since its inception some 30 years ago. Most studies have focused on description of the social and psychological profiles of TC admissions and evaluations of treatment effectiveness, through assessment of posttreatment outcomes. A smaller number of studies have been concerned with treatment retention and treatment process. This section briefly summarizes the key findings and conclusions in each of these research areas.

Social Profiles

Clients in programs are usually male (70%–75%) but female admissions are increasing in recent years. Most community-based TCs are integrated across gender, race/ethnicity and age, although the demographic proportions differ by geographic regions and in certain programs. In general, Hispanics, native Americans, and clients under 21 of age represent smaller proportions of admissions to TCs.

The majority of entries have histories of multiple drug use including marijuana, opiates, alcohol, and pills, although in recent years most report cocaine or crack as their primary drug of abuse. Most have poor work histories and have engaged in criminal activities at some time in their lives. Less than a third have had full-time jobs for more than 5 months and more than two thirds have been arrested (e.g., De Leon 1984; Hubbard, Valley-Rachal, Craddock, & Cavanaugh, 1984; Simpson & Sells 1982).

About a third of TC admissions are adolescents, although some programs serve adolescents exclusively. Over 70% have dropped out of school and more than 70% have been arrested at least once or involved with the criminal justice system. Compared to adults, more adolescents have histories of family deviance; more have had treatment for psychological problems; and more are legally referred to TC treatment (De Leon & Deitch 1985; Holland & Griffen, 1984; Jainchill, Battacharya, & Yagelka, 1995; Pompi, 1994). These social profiles of admissions to traditional TC programs are similar regardless of drug preference. They do not differ significantly from client profiles in special TC facilities implemented exclusively for certain populations such adolescents, females, ethnic minorities, and criminal justice referrals.

Psychological Profiles

Clients differ in demography, socioeconomic background, and drug-use patterns but psychological profiles obtained with standard instruments appear remarkably uniform, as evident in a number of TC studies (e.g., Barr & Antes, 1981; Biase, Sullivan, & Wheeler, 1986; Brook & Whitehead, 1980; De Leon, 1989; De Leon, Skodol, & Rosenthal, 1973; Holland, 1986; Jainchill, 1994; Kennard & Wilson, 1979; Zuckerman, Sola, Masterson, & Angelone, 1975).

The psychological profiles reveal drug abuse as the prominent element in a picture that mirrors features of both psychiatric and criminal populations. For example, the character disorder characteristics and poor self-concept of delinquent and repeated offenders are present, along with the dysphoria, depression, anxiety, and confused thinking of emotionally unstable or psychiatric populations.

Psychiatric Diagnoses

There are a few recently completed diagnostic studies of admissions to the therapeutic community utilizing the diagnostic interview schedule (DIS). In these, over 70% of the admission sample revealed a lifetime nondrug psychiatric disorder in addition to substance abuse or dependence. A third had a current or continuing history of mental disorder in addition to their drug abuse. The most frequent non-drug diagnoses were phobias, generalized anxiety, psychosexual dysfunction, and antisocial personality. There were only a few cases of schizophrenia but lifetime affective disorders occurred in over a third of those studied (De Leon, 1989; Jainchill, 1994; Jainchill, De Leon, & Pinkham 1986). Studies utilizing a structured diagnostic interview schedule for children (DICA) reveal comparable percentages of dual disorder among adolescent admissions to TCs (Jainchill et al., 1995).

The psychological profiles vary little across age, sex, race, primary drug, or admission year and are not significantly different from drug abusers in other treatment modalities. Thus, in addition to their substance abuse and social deviance, the drug abusers who enter TCs reveal a considerable degree of psychological disability a conclusion confirmed in the diagnostic studies. Despite the TC's policy concerning psychiatric exclusion, the large majority of adult and adolescent admissions meet the criteria for coexisting substance abuse and other psychiatric disorders.

Treatment Effectiveness

A substantial evaluation literature documents the effectiveness of the TC approach in rehabilitating drug abusers (e.g., Anglin & Hser, 1991; Condelli & Hubbard, 1994; De Leon, 1984, 1985; Hubbard et al., 1984; Institute of Medicine Report, 1990; McCusker et al., 1995; Simpson & Sells, 1982, 1990; Tims, De Leon, & Jainchill, 1994; Tims & Ludford, 1984). The main findings on short- and long-term posttreatment follow0up status from single-program and multiprogram studies are reviewed.

Significant improvements occur on separate outcome variables (drug use, criminality, and employment) and on composite indices for measuring individual success. Maximum to moderately favorable outcomes (based on opioid, nonopioid and alcohol use; arrest rates; retreatment; and employment) occur for more than half of the sample of completed clients and drop-outs (De Leon, 1984; Hubbard et al., 1989; Simpson & Sells, 1982).

There is a consistent positive relationship between time spent in residential treatment and posttreatment outcome status. For example, in long-term TCs, success rates (on composite indices of no drug use and no criminality) at 2-years posttreatment approximate 90%, 50%, and 25%, respectively, for graduates/completers and dropouts who remain more than and less than one year in residential treatment, and improvement rates over pretreatment status approximate 100%, 70% and 40% respectively (De Leon, Jainchill, & Wexler, 1982).

In a few studies that investigated psychological outcomes, results uniformly showed significant improvement at follow-up (e.g., Biase et al., 1986; De Leon, 1984; Holland, 1983). A direct relationship has been demonstrated between posttreatment behavioral success and psychological adjustment (De Leon, 1984; De Leon & Jainchill, 1981-1982).

The outcome studies reported were completed on an earlier generation of chemical abusers, primarily opioid addicts. Since the early 1980s, however, most admissions to residential TCs have been multiple drug abusers, primarily involving cocaine, crack, and alcohol, with relatively few primary heroin users (e.g., De Leon, 1989). New studies are needed to evaluate the effectiveness of the TC for this recent generation of abusers. In this regard two large-scale evaluation efforts funded by the National Institute on Drug Abuse are underway: the Drug Abuse Treatment Outcome Study (DATOS) and the multisite program of research carried out in a recently established Center for Therapeutic Community Research (CTCR).

Retention

Drop-out is the rule for all drug treatment modalities. For therapeutic communities, retention is of particular importance because research has established a firm relationship between time spent in treatment and successful outcome. However, most admissions to therapeutic community programs leave residency, many before treatment influences are presumed to be effectively rendered.

Research on retention in TCs has been increasing in recent years. Reviews of the TC retention research are contained in the literature (e.g., De Leon, 1985, 1991; Lewis & Ross, 1994). Studies focus on several questions, retention rates, client predictors of dropout, and attempts to enhance retention in treatment.

Retention Rates

Dropout is highest (30% to 40%) in the first 30 days of admission, but declines sharply thereafter (De Leon, 1985). This temporal pattern of dropout is uniform across TC programs (and other modalities). In long-term residential TCs, completion rates average 10% to 20% of all admissions. One-year retention rates range from 15% to

30%, although more recent trends suggest gradual increases in annual retention compared to the period before 1980 (De Leon, 1991).

Predictors of Dropout

There are no reliable client characteristics that predict retention, with the exception of severe criminality and/or severe psychopathology, which are correlated with earlier dropout. Recent studies point to the importance of dynamic factors in predicting retention in treatment, such as perceived legal pressure, motivation and readiness for treatment (e.g., Condelli & De Leon, 1993; De Leon, 1988; De Leon, Melnick, Kressel, & Jainchill, 1994; Hubbard, Collins, Valley-Rachal, & Cavanaugh, 1988).

Enhancing Retention in TCs

Some experimental attempts to enhance retention in TCs have utilized supportive individual counseling, improved orientation to treatment by experienced staff ("Senior Professors") and family alliance strategies to reduce early dropout (e.g., De Leon, 1988, 1991). Other efforts provide special facilities and programming for mothers and children (Hughes et al., 1992; Stevens, Arbiter, & Glider, 1989; Stevens & Glider, 1994) and curriculum-based relapse prevention methods (Lewis, McCusker, Hindin, Frost, & Garfield, 1993) to sustain retention throughout residential treatment. Though results are promising, these efforts require replication in multiple sites.

Although it is a legitimate concern, retention should not be confused with treatment effectiveness. Therapeutic communities are effective for those who remain long enough for treatment influences to occur. Obviously, however, a critical issue for TCs is maximizing holding power to benefit more clients.

Treatment Process

The area of TC treatment process is still relatively underinvestigated. Research in progress grounded in the above theoretical framework conceptualizes process as the interaction between TC elements and client factors to produce change in treatment. Studies to date have focused on two areas: empirical specification of the essential elements of the TC and assessment of client motivational and readiness factors. The main findings from these studies are briefly summarized.

Essential Elements

The extent to which the current diversity of programs actually incorporates the essential elements of the TC model and method is not completely known. However, the Center for Therapeutic Community Research (CTCR) in collaboration with Therapeutic Communities of America (TCA) have recently assessed this important question with a national survey of member programs in TCA. Information was obtained with the Survey of Essential Elements Questionnaire (SEEQ) an instrument based on the previously described theoretical framework. Approximately 60 program directors representing 80% of the member programs rated the "essentiality" of TC elements. Results show extremely high consensus rates on all elements providing impressive empirical validation for the theoretical framework (CTCR Newsletter, 1996; Melnick & De Leon, 1992). Clarification of the diversity of TCs has broad implications for treatment, policy, and research such as in the areas of staff training, client matching, quality assurance, and managed care, as well as in evaluating the comparative effectiveness and cost benefits of TC-oriented programs.

Motivation and Readiness

Unlike fixed client characteristics such as social background or demography, dynamic variables such as client perceptions continually interact with the treatment and nontreatment influences in the change process. Studies to date have been based upon an instrument measuring client perceptions in terms of four dimensions: circumstances (external pressures), motivation (intrinsic pressures), readiness for treatment, and suitability for TC approach (CMRS). Results show that CMRS scores are the most consistent predictors of early dropout in both adults and adolescents admissions to TCs (e.g., De Leon et al., 1994; Melnick, De Leon, Hawke, Jainchill, & Kressel, 1996).

MODIFICATIONS AND ADAPTATIONS OF THE TC MODEL AND APPROACH

Currently an increasing diversity of programs view themselves as TCs. Today the TC modality consists of a wide range of programs serving a diversity of clients who use a variety of drugs and present complex social-psychological problems in addition to their chemical abuse. Client differences, as well as clinical requirements and funding realities, have encouraged the development of modified residential

TCs with shorter planned duration of stay (3, 6, and 12 months) as well as TC-oriented day treatment and outpatient ambulatory models. Correctional, medical, and mental hospitals, community residence and shelter settings, overwhelmed with alcohol and illicit drug abuse problems, have implemented TC programs within their institutional boundaries. The following sections summarize the main modifications of the TC approach and applications to special populations.

Current Modifications of the TC Model

Most community-based traditional TCs have expanded their social services or incorporated new interventions to address the needs of diverse admissions. In some cases these additions enhance but do not alter the basic TC regime; in others they significantly modify the TC model itself.

Family Services Approaches

The participation of families or significant others has been a notable development in TCs for both adolescents and adults. Some TCs offer programs in individual and multiple family therapy as components of their adolescent programs, nonresidential, and (more recently) short-term residential modalities. However, most traditional TCs do not provide a regular family therapy service because the client in residence is viewed as the primary target of treatment rather than the family unit.

Experience has shown that beneficial effects can occur with forms of significant-other participation other than family therapy. Seminars, support groups, open house, and other special events focus on how significant others can affect the client's stay in treatment; they teach the TC perspective on recovery and provide a setting for sharing common concerns and strategies for coping with the client's future re-entry into the larger community. Thus family participation activities enhance the TC's rehabilitative process for the residential client by establishing an alliance between significant others and the program.

Primary Health Care and Medical Services

Although funding for health care services remains insufficient for TCs, these agencies have expanded services for the growing number of residential clients with sexually transmitted and immune-compromising conditions including HIV seropositivity, AIDS, syphilis, hepatitis B, and recently tuberculosis. Screening, treatment, and increased health education have been sophisticated, both on site and through linkages with community primary health care agencies.

Aftercare Services

Currently, most long-term TCs have linkages with other service providers and 12-step groups for their graduates. However, TCs with shorter term residential components have instituted well-defined aftercare programs both within their systems and through linkages with other non-TC agencies. There are limits and issues concerning these aftercare efforts concerning discontinuities between the perspectives of the TC and other service agencies. These are outlined in the last section of this chapter and are discussed in other writings (De Leon, 1990–1991).

Relapse Prevention Training (RPT)

Based on its approach to recovery, the traditional TC has always focused on the key issues of relapse prevention. The 24-hour TC communal life fosters a process of learning how to resist drug taking and negative behavior. In its social learning setting the individual engages many of the social, emotional, and circumstantial cues for, and influences on, drug use that exist in the larger macrosociety. This broad context of social learning essentially provides a continual relapse-prevention training (De Leon, 1991).

Currently, however, a number of TCs include special workshops on relapse prevention training (RPT) utilizing the curriculum, expert trainers and formats developed outside the TC area (e.g., Marlatt & Gordon, 1985). These workshops are offered as formal additions to the existing TC protocol, usually in the re-entry stage of treatment. However, some programs incorporate RPT workshops in earlier treatment stages, and in a few others RPT is central to the primary treatment protocol (e.g., Lewis et al., 1993). Clinical impressions supported by preliminary data of the efficacy of RPT within the TC setting are favorable, although rigorous evaluation studies are still in progress (Lewis et al., 1993; McCuskor et al., 1995).

12-Step Components

Historically TC graduates were not easily integrated into AA meetings for a variety reasons (De Leon, 1990–1991). In recent years, however, there has been a gradual integration of AA/NA/CA meetings during and following TC treatment, given the wide diversity of users socially and demographically and the prominence of alcohol use regardless of the primary drug. The common genealogical roots found in TCs and the 12-step groups are evident to most participants of these, and the similarities in the self-help view of recovery far outweigh the differences in specific orientation. Today, 12-step groups may be introduced at any stage in residential TCs, but are considered mandatory in the re-entry stages of treatment: in the aftercare or continuance stages of recovery after leaving residential setting.

Mental Health Services

Among those seeking admission to TCs, increasing numbers reveal documented psychiatric histories (e.g., Jainchill, 1994; Jainchill et al., 1986; Jainchill, De Leon, & Yagelka, unpublished manuscript). Certain subgroups of these clients are treated within the traditional TC model and regime, which requires some modification in services and staffing. For example, psychopharmacological adjuncts and individual psychotherapy are utilized for selected clients at appropriate stages in treatment. Nevertheless, the traditional community-based TC models still cannot accommodate the substance abuser with serious psychiatric disorder. As described later in the section on mentally ill chemical abusers, the primary psychiatric substance abuser requires specially adapted forms of the TC model.

The Multimodal TC and Client–Treatment Matching

Traditional TCs are highly effective for a certain segment of the drug abuse population. However, those who seek assistance in TC settings represent a broad spectrum of clients, many of whom may not be suitable for long-term residential stay. Improved diagnostic capability and assessment of individual differences has clarified the need for options other than long-term residential treatment.

Many TC agencies are multimodality treatment centers that offer services in their residential and nonresidential programs, depending on the clinical status and situation needs of the individual. Modalities include short (under 90 days), medium (6–12 months), and long-term (1–2 years) residential components, drug-free outpatient services (6–12 months). Some operate drug-free day treatment and methadone maintenance programs. Admission assessment attempts to match the client to the appropriate modality within the agency. For example, the spread of drug abuse in the workplace, particularly in cocaine use, has prompted the TC to develop short-term residential and ambulatory models for employed, more socialized clients.

As yet, the effectiveness of TC-oriented multimodality programs has not been systematically evaluated, although several relevant studies are currently under way. Of particular interest is the comparative effectiveness and cost benefits of long- and short-term residential treatment. To date however, there is no convincing evidence supporting the effectiveness of short-term treatment in any modality, residential or ambulatory.

Given what is known about the complexity of the recovery process in addiction and the importance of length of stay in treatment, there is little likelihood that shorter term residential treatment alone will be sufficient to yield stable positive outcomes. In the multimodal TCs, combinations of residential and outpatient services are needed to provide a long-term treatment involvement and impact.

Current Applications of Residential TCs for Special Populations

The evolution of the TC is most evident in its application to special populations and special settings. It is much beyond the purview of this chapter to detail the modifications of these adapted TC models. In the main examples of these, the mutual self-help focus is retained along with basic elements of the community approach, meetings, groups, work structure, and perspective on recovery and right living. This section highlights some of the key applications of the TC treatment approach for different client populations in different settings.

TCs for Adolescents

The prominence of youth drug abuse and the unique needs of the adolescent has led to adaptations of the traditional TC approach that appear more appropriate for these clients. These include age-segregated facilities with considerable emphasis on management and supervision, educational needs, family involvement, and individual counseling. More extensive accounts of the treatment of adolescents in TCs and effectiveness are contained in other writings (e.g., De Leon & Deitch, 1985; Jainchill et al., 1995; Pompi, 1994).

Addicted Mothers and Children

Several TCs have adapted the model for chemically dependent mothers with their children. The profile of the addicted mother in residence is generally not different from other abusers, although it reflects more social disadvantage, poor socialization, and a predominance of crack/cocaine abuse. Most evident is that these women need a lifestyle change and an opportunity for personal maturation. Thus, within the context of the basic TC regime, additional services and modifications are provided that address their specific needs and those of their recovery. These include family unit housing for mothers and children, medical and psychological care, parental training, and child care. Further accounts of clinical issues in TC programs for females in general and addicted mothers in particular are contained in other writings (e.g., Jainchill & De Leon, 1992; Hughes et al., 1992; Stevens et al., 1989; Stevens & Glider, 1994).

TCs for Incarcerated Substance Abusers

In recent years TC models have been adapted for incarcerated substance abusers in prison settings. This development has been fostered by overcrowded prisons, the influx of drug offenders, and the documented success of an early TC prison model in reducing recidivism to crime and relapse to drug use (Lockwood & Inciardi, 1993; Wexler & Williams, 1986). Modifications of the TC model are shaped by the unique features of the correctional institution, for example, its focus on security, its goal of early release, its limited physical and social space, and the prison culture itself.

Nevertheless, a peer-managed community for social learning is established for the inmates who volunteer for the program. A prominent feature of the modified prison model is the mutual involvement of correctional officers and prison administrators and mental health and TC treatment paraprofessionals. For inmates who leave these prison TCs, models for continuance of recovery have recently been established outside the walls in TC-oriented halfway houses.

TCs for Mentally Ill Chemical Abusers

Special TC-adapted models have been developed to exclusively treat the more seriously disturbed mentally ill chemical abusers (i.e., MICA clients). Several of these have been developed by community-based TC agencies as special programs in separate facilities; others have been implemented as innovative research demonstration projects in mental hospitals (e.g., Galanter, Franco, Kim, Jamner-Metzger, & De Leon, 1993), and in community residence settings for the homeless mentally ill chemical abuser (e.g., De Leon, 1993; Rahav et al., 1994; Sacks, De Leon, Bernhardt & Sacks, in press).

In these models for the dually disordered the basic peer orientation and elements of the daily regime are retained, although there is more focus on individual differences that is evident in a greater flexibility in planned duration of stay, the structure, and phase format. Specific modifications include the standard psychotropic medication regime, moderated intensity of groups, a less demanding work structure, significant use of individual psychotherapy, case management, and skills training.

TCs and HIV

Therapeutic communities have evolved a sophisticated response to the HIV/AIDS epidemic since its identification in the early and mid 1980s. Special AIDS/HIV-oriented programs are now the rule in most well-managed TCs. These integrate AIDS and HIV seropositive clients into the regular daily regime; they address the special issues of HIV, including education, pretest and posttest counseling for HIV testing, confidentiality concerning disclosure, and support through medical crises. These special programs are directed to the target residential client as well as significant others. Programs include individual and group formats for counseling on sexual practices and on drug and alcohol use behavior and for contact notification. Some TCs have innovated special residential models serving AIDS clients exclusively.

The effectiveness of the TC for special populations has not yet been sufficiently evaluated. Currently, however, multisite studies of adolescents are under way in various adaptations of the community-based TC (Etheridge, 1994; Jainchill et al., 1995); inmates in prison TCs (Knight, Simpson, Chatham, & Camacho, unpublished manuscript; Lockwood & Inciardi, 1993; Wexler & Graham, 1994); mentally ill chemical abusers (Rahav et al, 1994; Sacks et al., in press); addicted mothers with their children (Stevens & Arbiter, 1995; Hughes et al., 1992); and though not described, methadone clients in a day treatment TC model (De Leon et al., 1994).

The modifications of the traditional residential model and its adaptation for special populations and settings are redefining the TC modality within mainstream human and mental health services. However, changes in clients, services and staffing along with conservative funding policies have also uncovered complex issues for TCs that relate to the TC's drug-free philosophy and its self help perspective. These issues represent ongoing challenges to the integrity of the TC approach itself. However, the advances in program adaptation, theory, research and training demonstrate the flexibility and maturity of the TC in meeting these challenges.

REFERENCES

Anglin, D. M., & Hser, Y. (1991). Treatment of drug abuse. In M. Tonry & N. Morris (Eds.), *Drugs and crime: Crime and justice: A review of research*. Chicago: The University of Chicago Press.

Barr, H. & Antes, D. (1981). *Factors related to recovery and relapse in follow-up*. Final report of project activities (Grant No. 1-H81-DA-01864). Rockville, MD: National Institute on Drug Abuse.

Biase, V., Sullivan, A., & Wheeler, B. (1986). Daytop miniversity—phase 2—college training in a therapeutic community: Development of self concept among drug free addict/abusers. In G. De Leon & J. T. Ziegenfuss (Eds.), *Therapeutic communities for addictions: Readings in theory, research and practice* (pp. 121–130). Springfield, IL: Charles C. Thomas.

Brook, R. C., & Whitehead, I. C. (1980). *Drug free therapeutic community*. New York: Human Science Press.

Center for Therapeutic Community Research Communications. (1996). *Newsletter, 1*.

Condelli, W. S., & De Leon, G. (1993). Fixed and dynamic predictors of client retention in therapeutic communities. *Journal of Substance Abuse Treatment, 10*, 11–16.

Condelli, W., & Hubbard, R. (1994). Client outcomes from therapeutic communities. In F. M. Tims, G. De Leon, & N. Jainchill (Eds.), *Therapeutic community: Advances in research and application* (NIDA Research Monograph Number 144, NIH Publication No. 94-3633, pp. 80–98. Rockville, MD: National Institute on Drug Abuse.

De Leon, G. (1984). *The therapeutic community: Study of effectiveness* (NIDA Treatment Research Monograph, DHHS Publication No. ADM 84-1286).Washington, DC: Superintendent of Documents, U.S. Government Printing Office.

De Leon, G. (1985). The therapeutic community: Status and evolution. *International Journal of the Addictions, 20*, 823–844.

De Leon, G. (1988). Legal pressure in therapeutic communities. In C. G. Leukfeld & F. M. Tims (Eds.), *Compulsory treatment of drug abuse: Research and clinical practice* (NIDA Research Monograph No. 86, DHHS Publication No. ADM 88-1578, pp. 160–177. Rockville, MD: National Institute on Drug Abuse.

De Leon, G. (1989). Psychopathology and substance abuse: What we are learning from research in therapeutic communities. *Journal of Psychoactive Drugs, 21*, 177–188.

De Leon, G. (1990–1991). Aftercare in therapeutic communities. *International Journal of the Addictions, 25*, 1229–1241.

De Leon, G. (1991). Retention in drug free therapeutic communities. In R. W. Pickens, C. G. Leukefeld, & C. R. Schuster

(Eds.), *Improving drug abuse treatment* (pp. 218–244, National Institute on Drug Abuse Research Monograph, No. 106). Rockville, MD: National Institute on Drug Abuse.

De Leon, G. (1993). Modified therapeutic communities for dual disorder. In J. Solomon, S. Zimberg, & E. Shollar (Eds.), *Dual diagnosis: Evaluation, treatment, training, and program development* (pp. 147–170). New York: Plenum Press.

De Leon, G. (1995a). Therapeutic communities for addictions: A theoretical framework. *International Journal of the Addictions, 30,* 1603–1645.

De Leon, G. (1995b). Residential therapeutic communities in the mainstream: Diversity and issues. *Journal of Psychoactive Drugs, 27,* 3–15.

De Leon, G. (Ed.) (1997). *Community as method: Therapeutic communities for special populations in special settings.* Westport, CT: Greenwood.

De Leon, G., & Deitch, D. (1985). Treatment of the adolescent substance abuser in a therapeutic community. In A. Friedman & G. Beschner, (Eds.), *Treatment services for adolescent substance abusers* (DHHS Publication No. ADM 85-1342). Rockville MD: National Institute of Drug Abuse.

De Leon, G., & Jainchill, N. (1981–1982). Male and female drug abusers: Social and psychological status 2 years after treatment in a therapeutic community. *American Journal of Drug and Alcohol Abuse, 9,* 465–497.

De Leon, G., Jainchill, N., & Wexler, H. (1982). Success and improvement rates 5 years after treatment in a therapeutic community. *International Journal of the Addictions, 17,* 703–747.

De Leon, G., Melnick, G., Kressel, D., & Jainchill, N. (1994). Circumstances, motivation, readiness and suitability (the CMRS Scales): Predicting retention in therapeutic community treatment. *American Journal of Drug and Alcohol Abuse, 20,* 495–515.

De Leon, G., Skodol, A., & Rosenthal, M. S. (1973). The Phoenix Therapeutic Community for Drug Addicts: Changes in psychopathological signs. *Archives of General Psychiatry, 28,* 131–135.

Etheridge, R. (1994, August). *Drug abuse treatment outcome study: Adolescent.* Paper presented at symposium on evaluation of substance abuse treatment through a system of multisite studies conducted at Annual Conference of the American Psychological Association, Los Angeles, CA.

Galanter, M., Franco, H., Kim, A., Jamner Metzger, E., & De Leon, G. (1993). Inpatient treatment for the dually diagnosed: A peer-led model. In J. Solomon, S. Zimberg, & E. Shollar (Eds.), *Dual diagnosis: Evaluation, treatment, training, and program development* (pp. 171–192). New York: Plenum Press.

Holland, S. (1983). Evaluating community based treatment programs: A model for strengthening inferences about effectiveness. *International Journal of Therapeutic Communities, 4,* 285–306.

Holland, S. (1986). Mental health and the TC. In A. Acampora & E. Nebelkopf (Eds.), *Bridging services* (pp. 122–131). Proceedings of the 9th World Conference of Therapeutic Communities. San Francisco: Walden House.

Holland, S., & Griffen, A. (1984). Adolescent and adult drug treatment clients: Patterns and consequences of use. *Journal of Psychoactive Drugs, 16,* 79–90.

Hubbard, R. L., Collins, J. J., Valley-Rachal, J., & Cavanaugh, E. R. (1988). The criminal justice client in drug abuse treatment. In C. G. Leukefeld & F. M. Tims (Eds.), *Compulsory treatment of drug abuse: Research and clinical practice* (NIDA Research Monograph No. 86, DHHS Publication No. ADM 88-1578, pp. 57–80). Rockville, MD: National Institute on Drug Abuse.

Hubbard, R. L., Marsden, M., Valley-Rachal, J., Harwood, H., Cavanaugh, E., & Ginzburg, H. (1989). *Drug abuse treatment: A national study of effectiveness.* Chapel Hill, NC: University of North Carolina Press.

Hubbard, R. L., Valley-Rachal, J., Craddock, S., & Cavanaugh, E. (1984). Treatment outcome prospective study (TOPS): Client characteristics and behaviors before, during, and after treatment. In F. M. Tims & J. P. Ludford (Eds.), *Drug abuse treatment evaluation: Strategies, progress, and prospects* (NIDA Research Monograph No. 51, Research Analysis and Utilization System Review Report, DHHS Publication No. ADM 84-1329, pp. 42–68. Rockville, MD: National Institute on Drug Abuse.

Hughes, P., Starr, C., Urmann, C., Williams, K., Coletti, S., Neri, R., Landress, H., & Sicilian, D. (1992, September). *Evaluating a therapeutic community for cocaine abusing women and their children.* In P. A. Vamos & P. J. Corriveau (Eds.), *Drugs and society to the year 2000* (pp. 935–38). Proceedings of the XIV World Conference of Therapeutic Communities, Montreal, Canada. Montreal: Portage Program for Drug Dependencies, Inc.

Institute of Medicine. (1990). Treating drug problems: A study of the evolution, effectiveness, and financing of public and private drug treatment systems. *Report by the Institute of Medicine Committee for the Substance Abuse Coverage Study, Division of Health Care Services.* Washington, DC: National Academy Press.

Jainchill, N. (1994). Co-morbidity and therapeutic community treatment. In F.M. Tims, G. De Leon, & N. Jainchill (Eds.), *Therapeutic community: Advances in research and application* (NIDA Research Monograph No. 144, NIH Publication No. 94-3633, pp. 209–231. Rockville, MD: National Institute on Drug Abuse.

Jainchill, N., Bhattacharya, G., & Yagelka, J. (1995). Therapeutic communities for adolescents. In E. Rahdert & D. Czechowicz (Eds.), *Adolescent drug abuse: Clinical assessment and therapeutic interventions* (NIDA Research Monograph, NIH Publication No. 95-3908, pp. 190–217. Rockville, MD: National Institute on Drug Abuse.

Jainchill, N., & De Leon, G. (1992). Therapeutic community research: Recent studies of psychopathology and retention. In G. Buhringer & J. J. Platt (Eds.), *Drug abuse treatment research: German and American perspectives* (pp. 367–388). Malabor, FL: Krieger.

Jainchill, N., De Leon, G., & Pinkham, L. (1986). Psychiatric diagnoses among substance abusers in the therapeutic community. *Journal of Psychoactive Drugs, 8,* 209–213.

Jainchill, N., De Leon, G., & Yagelka, J. *Ethnic difference in psychiatric disorders among adolescent substance abusers in treatment* (Unpublished manuscript).

Kennard, D., & Wilson, S. (1979). The modification of personality disorders in a therapeutic community for drug abusers. *British Journal of Medical Psychology, 53,* 215–221.

Knight, K., Simpson, D. D., Chatham, L. R., & Camacho, L. M. *An assessment of prison-based drug treatment. Texas' in-prison therapeutic community program* (Unpublished manuscript).

Lewis, B.F., McCusker, J., Hindin, R., Frost, R., & Garfield, F. (1993). Four residential drug treatment programs: Project IMPACT. In J. A. Inciardi, F. M. Tims, & B. W. Fletcher (Eds.), *Innovative approaches in the treatment of drug abuse: Program models and strategies* (pp. 45–60). Westport, CT: Greenwood Press.

Lewis, B.F. & Ross, R. (1994). Retention in therapeutic communities: Challenges for the nineties. In F. M. Tims, G. De Leon, & J. Jainchill (Eds), *Therapeutic community: Advances in research and application* (NIDA Research Monograph No. 144, NIH Publication No. 94-3633, pp. 99–116. Rockville, MD: National Institute on Drug Abuse.

Lockwood, D., & Inciardi, J. (1993). CREST outreach center: A work release iteration of the TC model. In J. A. Inciardi, F. M. Tims, & B. W. Fletcher (Eds.), *Innovative approaches in the treatment of drug abuse: Program models and strategies* (pp. 61–69). Newport, CT: Greenwood Press.

Marlatt, G.A., & Gordon, J. (Eds.). (1985). *Relapse prevention.* New York: Guilford Press.

McCusker, J., Vickers-Lahti, M., Stoddard, A., Hindin, R., Bigelow, C., Zorn, M., Garfield, F., Frost, R., Love, C., & Lewis, B. (1995). The effectiveness of alternative planned durations of residential drug abuse treatment. *American Journal of Public Health, 85,* 1426–1429.

Melnick, G., & De Leon, G. (1992). *Therapeutic Community Scale of Essential Elements Questionnaire (SEEQ).* Developed for the Center for Therapeutic Community Research at National Development and Research Institutes, Inc. New York, NY. Supported by NIDA Grant (No. P50 DA03700).

Melnick, G., De Leon, G., Hawke, J., Jainchill, N., & Kressel, D. (1997). Motivation and readiness for therapeutic community treatment among adolescents and adult substance abusers. *American Journal of Drug and Alcohol Abuse, 23,* 485–506.

Pompi, K. F. (1994). Adolescents in therapeutic communities: Retention and posttreatment outcome. In F. M. Tims, G. De Leon, & N. Jainchill (Eds.), *Therapeutic community: Advances in research and application* (NIDA Research Monograph No. 144, NIH Publication No. 94-3633, pp. 128–161. Rockville, MD: National Institute on Drug Abuse.

Rahav, M., Rivera, J., Collins, J., Ng-Mak, D., Sturz, E., Struening, E., Pepper, B., Link, B., & Gross, B. (1994). Bringing experimental research designs into existing treatment programs: The case of community-based treatment of the dually diagnosed. In B. W. Fletcher, J. A. Inciardi, & A. M. Horton (Eds.), *Drug abuse treatment: The implementation of innovative approaches* (pp. 79–93). Westport, CT: Greenwood Press.

Sacks, S., De Leon, G., Bernhardt, A., & Sacks, J. (1997). A modified therapeutic community for homeless mentally ill chemical abusers. In G. De Leon (Ed.), *Community as method: Therapeutic communities for special populations in special settings.* (pp. 19–37). Westport, CT: Greenwood Publishing.

Simpson, D. D., & Sells, S. (1982). Effectiveness of treatment for drug abuse: An overview of the DARP research program. *Advances in Alcohol and Substance Abuse, 2,* 7–29.

Simpson D. D. & Sells, S. B. (1990). *Opioid addiction and treatment: A 12-year follow-up.* Malabar, FL: Krieger.

Stevens, S. J., & Arbiter, N. (1995). A therapeutic community for substance abusing pregnant women and women with children: Process and outcome. *Journal of Psychoactive Drugs, 27,* 49–56.

Stevens, S., Arbiter, N., & Glider, P. (1989). Women residents: Expanding their role to increase treatment effectiveness in substance abuse programs. *International Journal of Addictions, 24,* 425–434.

Stevens, S., & Glider, P. (1994). Therapeutic communities: Substance abuse treatment for women. In F. M. Tims, G. De Leon, & N. Jainchill (Eds.), *Therapeutic community: Advances in research and application* (NIDA Research Monograph No. 144, NIH Publication No. 94-3633, pp. 162–180. Rockville, MD: National Institute on Drug Abuse.

Tims, F. M., De Leon, G., & Jainchill, N. (Eds.) (1994). *NIDA technical review on therapeutic community: Advances in research and application* (NIDA Monograph No. 144, NIH Publication No. 94-3633). Washington, DC: Superintendent of Documents, U.S. Government Printing Office.

Tims, F. M. & Ludford, J. (Eds.) (1984). *Drug abuse treatment evaluation: strategies, progress and prospects* (NIDA Research Monograph No. 51, DHHS Publication No. ADM 84-1329). Rockville, MD: National Institute on Drug Abuse.

Wexler, H. K., & Graham, W. (1994, August). *Prison-based therapeutic communities for substance abusers: Retention, rearrest, and re-incarceration.* Paper presented at American Psychological Association convention, Los Angeles, CA.

Wexler, H. K., and Williams, R. (1986). The stay'n out therapeutic community: Prison treatment for substance abusers. *Journal of Psychoactive Drugs, 18,* 221–230.

Zuckerman, M., Sola, S., Masterson, J., & Angelone, J. (1975). MMPI patterns in drug abusers before and after treatment in therapeutic communities. *Journal of Consulting and Clinical Psychology, 43,* 286–296.

CHAPTER 27

FAMILY THERAPY

Kimberly S. Walitzer

Involving the family in treatment has been a therapeutic strategy examined in several clinical domains, including depression (e.g., Jacobson, Dobson, Fruzzetti, Schmaling, & Salusky, 1991), obesity (e.g., Barbarin & Tirado, 1984), and smoking cessation (e.g., Ginsberg, Hall, & Rosinski, 1991). Family-involved interventions have been adapted as well for alcohol-dependent (c.f., McCrady, 1989a, 1989b; O'Farrell, 1986; Steinglass, 1979) and drug-abusing (Stanton, Todd, et. al., 1982; Szapocznik, Kurtines, Santisteban, & Rio, 1990) populations. The majority of this work has focused on the role that a spouse or significant family member can play in the client's treatment and maintenance of change.

This chapter focuses on two approaches to addictions therapy that include other family members: behavioral marital therapy and family systems therapy. These two forms of therapy were selected from other schools of marital and family therapy based on the availability of empirical research supporting their effectiveness with alcohol-abusing and/or drug-abusing clients. The theory and basic therapeutic strategies of each approach will be described. Although these relatively brief descriptions are not sufficient for a therapist novice in these approaches to apply them effectively, references to detailed descriptions

of the clinical procedures are provided for the interested reader. Following descriptions of the therapies, representative research is presented examining the effectiveness of these approaches.

BEHAVIORAL MARITAL THERAPY

Behavioral marital therapy (BMT) has two main treatment goals—increasing marital reinforcement and improving communication skills. The rationale behind using BMT with couples with substance abuse issues is that improved marital functioning will maximize the likelihood of significant treatment gains. Specifically, increases in positive behavioral exchanges and increased positive affect within the marriage are expected to increase both partners' motivation for the client's abstinence. Improvements in communication skills are expected to have a direct impact on the client's ability to communicate his or her needs and desires to the spouse and on the spouse's ability to provide appropriate support for the client's behavior change efforts.

When a client has recently completed inpatient or outpatient substance abuse treatment, BMT skills are often presented in conjunction with weekly brief monitoring of urges for alcohol or drugs, upcoming high-risk situations, and other drug-related issues. For a client who has not completed substance abuse treatment, however, BMT can be combined with a full outpatient program of substance abuse therapy (see Noel & McCrady, 1993, for an example of conjoint alcohol abuse and BMT treatment). As substance abuse treatment strategies are detailed elsewhere in this volume, they will not be repeated here. However, it should be noted that BMT is most often used as a treatment component adjunctive to more general substance abuse treatment.

Treatment Strategies

The hallmark components of BMT are treatment strategies designed to (a) increase commitment and goodwill within the marriage, and (b) enhance skills for communicating, negotiating, and resolving areas of disagreement. BMT relies heavily on therapist modeling (a male and female cotherapist team often conducts the treatment), client in-session role plays, and client homework assignments throughout treatment. These three techniques—modeling, role-plays, and homework assignments—are incorporated into virtually every skill presented during treatment. BMT for couples with an alcoholic member has been described by McCrady (e.g., McCrady, 1982; Noel & McCrady, 1993) and O'Farrell (e.g., O'Farrell, 1986, 1993a; O'Farrell & Cowles, 1989; O'Farrell & Cutter, 1984), two clinical researchers in the forefront of efforts to apply BMT to alcoholics and their spouses. The interested reader is referred to these sources for additional details on conducting BMT as an adjunctive treatment strategy for individuals with alcohol problems.

Enhancing Commitment and Goodwill

Three exercises frequently are utilized to increase positive exchanges and mutual reinforcement within the relationship: "Catch Your Spouse," "Caring Days," and "Shared Rewarding Activities." As described by O'Farrell (1993a), the exercise "Catch Your Spouse Doing Something Nice" is designed to encourage noticing and acknowledging positive and caring behaviors on the part of each member of the couple. Caring behaviors are behaviors that show caring or consideration on the part of the spouse. These include small, daily caring behaviors (e.g., household tasks, earning money, listening) as well as special events (e.g., flowers, special night out). In the first week of this exercise,

each spouse is asked to notice at least one caring behavior from the partner each day and to record the caring behavior on a homework sheet. These records are reviewed as part of the following week's treatment session.

In the next session, the exercise is expanded to "Catch Your Spouse Doing Something Nice *and* Tell Him/Her." The couple is instructed to notice at least one caring behavior each day and acknowledge the caring behavior to their partner. In order to teach this basic communication skill, the cotherapists model several simple, concise acknowledgements of positive or caring behaviors (e.g., "I liked it when you . . . , it made me feel . . ."). The couple is then asked to each pick their favorite caring behavior from their list from the previous week and to acknowledge it as part of a role-play exercise. Therapists provide positive and constructive feedback for each speaker with regard to eye contact, voice volume and tone, facial expression, conciseness, and other nonverbal and verbal characteristics. When necessary, the speaker does an "instant replay," taking into account constructive feedback from the therapists. The homework for the exercise is to notice, record, and acknowledge to the partner at least one caring behavior each day.

The goal of the "Caring Day," or "Love Day," is to encourage the initiation of caring and pleasing behaviors toward the spouse. The intent of the Caring Day is to greatly increase the frequency of caring behaviors for one day. Typically, each spouse is asked to select one day during the week to "shower" the partner with caring behaviors. In the following therapy session, each spouse is asked to guess which day the partner selected to be his or her caring day.

A third strategy for enhancing goodwill and mutual reinforcement is "Shared Rewarding Activities" (Noel & McCrady, 1993; O'Farrell, 1993a). Frequently, couples and families have decreased the frequency of joint leisure activities as a result of conflict or dysfunction associated with chronic alcohol or drug abuse. In the first stage of this exercise, each spouse is asked to list as many enjoyable activities with the partner as possible, both with and without their children and both within and outside of the home. At the next therapy session, the couple shares their lists, and the therapists as warranted point out areas of similarity and agreement between the two lists. Next, the cotherapists role-play the process of deciding on and planning a shared rewarding activity. Important points to model include beginning with an activity that is mutually agreeable, discussing the positive (i.e., what you want to do) rather than the negative (i.e., what you don't want to do), and foreseeing and problem-solving solutions to potential problems (e.g., who is responsible for any necessary preparation [such as reservations, checking the movie guide, and childcare issues). The couple is then asked to plan a shared rewarding activity from their lists for the upcoming week. The therapists intervene and provide feedback as necessary to assist the couple in preparing concrete plans for a couple or family activity during the week. In subsequent weeks, the couple is asked to continue planning and carrying out joint enjoyable activities.

Enhancing Communication Skills

Increased goodwill and commitment within the relationship provides the groundwork and motivation for enhancing communication and negotiation skills. Communication training is described by Gottman, Notarius, Gonso, and Markman (1976) and has been applied specifically to couples with an alcohol-dependent member by O'Farrell (1986, 1993a) and Noel and McCrady (1993).

The first emphasis in communication training is listening and understanding skills. Spouses often feel that their partner does not listen to or understand them; the technique of *reflective listening* enhances accurate understanding. Reflective listening emphasizes that listening is an active, as opposed to passive, process. The listener reflects back the message spoken by the speaker with the phrase "What I hear you saying is . . . , is that right?" The speaker then either acknowledges that the listener has understood the message correctly, or corrects the listener's understanding of the message (after which the listener again would use a reflective listening statement to check the accuracy of the message). After the speaker has acknowledged that the message has been understood correctly by the listener, the listener becomes the speaker and responds to the message. Reflective listening is first practiced with neutral or positive topics, such as with "Catch Your Spouse and Tell." Once the couple has mastered reflective listening on nonconflicted material and begins to discuss areas of disagreement, the use of reflective listening is critical.

"Communication sessions" are often assigned to the couple as homework in order to increase the frequency of formal communication between the couple and to encourage the practice of communication skills such as reflective listening at home. A communication session is a 5–15 minute planned conversation. Communication sessions take place in a private area free of external distractions.

During the communication session the couple sits face to face, begins by acknowledging a caring behavior, and uses reflective listening. Couples are encouraged to focus early communication sessions on neutral or positive topics and move toward more difficult topics only as they become competent with the communication techniques.

Following the introduction of communication sessions and reflective listening skills, couples are encouraged to communicate positive and negative emotions and feelings by "Expressing Feelings Directly" (O'Farrell, 1993a). This skill emphasizes that the speaker takes full responsibility for his or her emotions and does not blame the other person. The goal of expressing feelings directly is to allow the speaker to communicate feelings, especially negative emotions, while minimizing defensiveness on the part of the listener. The speaker is encouraged to use "I" statements and to avoid accusing, blaming, and hurtful attacks. The listener is encouraged to use reflective listening—again, regardless of whether the listener agrees with the message—to help understanding and to control the pace of communication. Couples are encouraged to use the skills of expressing feelings directly with reflective listening in their communication sessions at home.

Enhancing Negotiation Skills

When a foundation of effective communication has been reached, the couple can begin practicing techniques designed to improve negotiation skills (Noel & McCrady, 1993; O'Farrell, 1993a). The first step in negotiation is identifying "Positive Specific Requests" for expressing needs and desires and for changing aspects of the relationship. Positive specific requests are (a) "positive" and state what is wanted rather than what is not wanted so that the message does not become a complaint; (b) "specific," in terms of what, when, how frequently, and so on, so that the request can be objectively fulfilled and there is less room for misunderstanding; and (c) a "request," indicating that compromise and negotiation is possible. For example, "Help me out around the house more" is not specific; "I would like you to clear the table, do the dishes, and put them away three evenings each week" is more specific. "Quit bringing up the past when we are having a discussion" is negative; "I would like you to try to remain focused on the present during our communication sessions" is positive and more specific. "Spend more time as a family" is not specific; "I would like you and I to spend at least three hours this Saturday afternoon with the kids at the park" is more specific.

The couple is assigned the task of identifying at least five to ten positive specific requests that each would like to discuss with the partner in future therapy sessions. Possible topics include household chores, finances, children, intimacy, family resources, social activities, religion, family and relatives, employment, personal habits, and leisure activities. These positive specific requests form the basis for negotiating "Good-Faith Agreements" between the spouses (O'Farrell, 1993a). A good-faith agreement is an agreement in which each partner agrees to voluntarily make a behavior change either to improve the relationship or to meet a need or desire of their spouse. First, the therapists model a communication session in which a request is selected, described, and "heard" via reflective listening. Then the specifics of the request (e.g., exactly what, when, how, and how frequently) are negotiated and translated into a double agreement to be fulfilled in the upcoming week. During modeling, the therapists demonstrate goodwill and willingness to negotiate.

The couple then negotiates a good-faith agreement with feedback and assistance from the therapists. In order to emphasize the voluntary nature of the agreement, each spouse picks an item of their partner's positive specific request list that her or she would like to fulfill either completely or in part. The couple describes the request, "hears" the request with reflective listening, negotiates the specifics of the request, and documents the double-sided good-faith agreement to be completed in the upcoming week on a homework sheet. The good-faith agreement reflects the attitude that each spouse is willing to follow through with the commitment to improve the relationship, regardless of the actions of the partner. Typically, in addition to completing the good-faith agreement, the couple is asked to use at least one of their weekly communication sessions to develop another good-faith agreement from their positive specific request lists.

Empirical Evidence for Behavioral Marital Therapy

BMT is a well-researched and effective technique for alleviating marital distress (e.g., Hahlweg & Markman, 1988). Further, BMT has been examined empirically as an adjunctive treatment strategy in the treatment of alcohol dependent patients and appears to be a promising strategy (e.g., Collins, 1990; McCrady, 1990).

One study conducted by O'Farrell and colleagues (O'Farrell, Cutter, Choquette, Floyd, & Bayog, 1992; O'Farrell, Cutter, & Floyd, 1985) randomly assigned 34 alcohol-dependent men and their wives to one of three experimental conditions: (a) a 10-session BMT couples group (in addition to BMT, alcoholics also took antabuse as part of an Antabuse Contract with their spouses); (b) a 10-session interactional couples group (four couples per group; treatment emphasized support, expression of emotions, problem solving, and insight into relationship issues); or (c) a control group of standard alcoholism outpatient individual counseling (for the alcoholic only). Alcoholics were recruited during their first month of treatment in a Veterans Administration alcoholism outpatient clinic; most clients had begun outpatient treatment following a 28-day inpatient alcoholism rehabilitation program or a 7-day alcohol detoxification hospitalization. Follow-up data collected on these couples provide mixed results for the superiority of BMT over standard individual alcoholism outpatient therapy and couples interactive marital therapy. Immediately following 10 weeks of treatment (O'Farrell et al., 1985), couples in the BMT condition reported more positive overall marital adjustment than couples in the other two conditions, and reported more marital stability and demonstrated more positive communication behaviors than couples in the control condition. There were no significant differences between treatment conditions in terms of abstinence, although all three treatment conditions exhibited significant increases in percentage of abstinent days from pre- to posttreatment. During follow-up (O'Farrell et al., 1992), wives in the BMT condition reported more positive marital adjustment than wives in the control condition (but not the interactional couples group) 2 months after treatment, but this difference diminished further into the 2-year follow-up. Also, couples in the BMT and the interactional couples group conditions reported fewer days separated than control couples during the majority of the 2-year follow-up. Alcohol dependent men in all three treatment conditions reported more abstinent days during the 2 years following treatment relative to pretreatment levels, although the frequency of drinking increased progressively over the follow-up period.

A second study by O'Farrell and colleagues (O'Farrell, 1993b; O'Farrell, Choquette, Cutter, Brown, & McCourt, 1993) evaluated the effects of relapse prevention sessions during the year following ten BMT sessions. In this study, 59 couples with an alcohol-dependent husband were randomly assigned to receive BMT alone or BMT followed by 15 additional relapse prevention sessions over the course of the following year. The goals of the relapse prevention sessions were to help the couple maintain marital and drinking gains, continue to use their new skills with unresolved marital issues, and rehearse a drinking relapse prevention plan. Data gathered during the year immediately following BMT (i.e., during the year when 30 couples were receiving the additional relapse prevention sessions) indicated that alcohol-dependent men in the relapse prevention condition reported more continued use of the Antabuse Contract as well as more abstinent days at 6 months and 12 months following BMT (97% and 94% days abstinent, respectively) than their counterparts not receiving relapse prevention sessions (88% and 82% days abstinent, respectively). There was some evidence for improved marital adjustment for the couples receiving relapse prevention sessions relative to couples not receiving these sessions. Couples in both conditions used the marital enhancement strategies less frequently during follow-up, although continued use of the marital techniques predicted marital adjustment and the percentage of days abstinent.

McCrady and colleagues (McCrady et al., 1986; McCrady, Stout, Noel, Abrams, & Nelson, 1991) reported the results of a study examining treatment outcome of 33 men and 12 women with alcohol dependence and their spouses who were randomly assigned to participate in either minimal spouse involvement, alcohol-focused spouse involvement, or alcohol BMT. All three treatment conditions included the spouse in fifteen 90-minute therapy sessions. In the minimal spouse involvement condition, all interventions were directed toward the alcoholic; no spouse or marital interventions were included. In the alcohol-focused spouse involvement condition, treatment also included spouse interventions such as reinforcing abstinence, avoiding behaviors that cued drinking, decreasing enabling behaviors, relaxation skills, and assertion skills to express feelings about drinking. In the alcohol BMT condition, all skills in the two other conditions were included as well as basic BMT marital enhancement techniques. Couples in the minimal spouse involvement condition were more likely to drop out of treatment (33%) compared to couples in the alcohol-focused spouse involvement and the alcohol BMT condition (7.8% and 0%, respectively). Six months following treatment (McCrady et al., 1986), there were few differences in drinking behavior, alcohol problems, and marital satisfaction between experimental treatment conditions. Eighteen months after treatment (McCrady et al., 1991), clients in the alcohol BMT condition reported increases in abstinent days whereas clients in the minimal spouse involvement and the alcohol-focused spouse involvement condition reported decreased abstinent days. Further, couples in the alcohol BMT condition reported improvements in global marital satisfaction measures whereas couples in the other two conditions did not.

Bowers and Al-Redha (1990) report 1-year follow-up for 16 alcoholics and their spouses randomly assigned to either couples' group therapy or standard individual outpatient therapy. Couples therapy, although not the complete BMT package as described, included communication training, role plays, and problem solving during approximately 19 hours of therapy. The standard therapy condition focused on the interpersonal relationship between the client and therapist during approximately 11 hours of therapy. Results indicated that clients in the couples' group therapy reported a greater reduction in alcohol use during follow-up. All couples reported marital enhancement following treatment; there were no reliable differences between the conditions.

Summary

Research examining the effectiveness of BMT as an adjunctive treatment for alcoholism reveals moderate support for short-term BMT for married alcoholics. Although the studies reviewed here vary in the advantages reported as a result of BMT (e.g., improved marital functioning for O'Farrell et al., 1992; improved marital functioning and alcohol outcome 18 months following treatment for McCrady et al., 1991; improved alcohol outcome for Bowers and Al-Redha, 1990), BMT typically afforded some improvement in either marital or alcohol outcome, if not both, relative to treatment that excluded the spouse. At this time there is no research examining treatment matching hypotheses to guide predictions of which couples may especially benefit from BMT. It can be speculated, however, that couples possessing at least a minimal level of commitment to the relationship (i.e., separation or divorce is not imminent) but are experiencing deficiencies in positive exchanges, mutual reinforcement, and/or communication may be good candidates.

Unfortunately, BMT has not been studied with other populations of substance abusers. It is more difficult to surmise whether BMT would benefit couples with a primary issue of illegal drug use. Basic differences between alcoholism versus illegal substance abuse and potential differences in client and marital characteristics between these groups suggest some caution in generalizing these results to substance abusers in the absence of controlled outcome research. However, the basic tenets of BMT for alcohol dependence—that improved marital commitment and enhanced communication will enhance treatment gains—would seem to be equally applicable for couples for whom one member has a substance abuse problem.

FAMILY SYSTEMS THERAPY

Family systems therapy takes a very different approach to substance abuse treatment than does BMT. Although still acknowledging that marital and family issues are important—and often critical—in addictive behavior, family systems therapy differentiates itself from BMT in several ways. First, as the name implies, family systems therapy usually includes immediate family members in addition to the marital dyad. Second, the therapy within the family systems model relies heavily on theoretical case conceptualization relative to the more structured approach of BMT. Third, the focus of therapy is typically much broader than that of BMT. In the ideal case, the goal of therapy is to guide the family as it reorganizes many facets of family life and relationships in the absence of alcohol or drugs. As might be expected, family systems therapy for substance abuse is typically longer and more extensive than the typical 10 or 12 session course of BMT. Finally, family systems therapy has been adapted for substance-abusing clients as well as alcohol-dependent clients.

Family Systems Therapy and Alcohol Dependence

Family systems theory as applied to alcohol dependence is richly detailed by Steinglass, Bennett, Wolin, and Reiss (1987). Steinglass and colleagues make an important distinction between the "alcoholic family" and a "family with an alcoholic member." This distinction is critical, as it is the characteristics of the alcoholic family that make the family a good candidate for alcoholism-focused family systems therapy. As described by Steinglass, alcohol has become the "central organizing principle" within the alcoholic family. Two characteristics set apart the alcoholic family from a family with an alcoholic member: (a) problem drinking has altered and been accommodated by the daily routines, rituals, and identity of the family; and (b) alcohol and intoxication facilitate the behaviors necessary for short-term problem solving. For example, a family may alter meal-times, leisure activities, household activities, and other aspects of daily routines, as well as holiday and vacation activities, on the basis of the alcoholic's drinking patterns and intoxication cycles. Further, the presence of alcohol may allow, and may even be necessary for, the family to express emotions or communicate important messages. Indeed, family members may tend toward isolation and distance in the absence of alcohol. These characteristics suggest that this is an alcoholic family as described by Steinglass and colleagues, and as such a candidate for family systems therapy. In contrast, a family whose rituals, routines, and communications patterns endure despite alcoholic drinking may be viewed more accurately as a family that includes an alcoholic member and may be more effectively treated with another modality of treatment (i.e., individual treatment or another form of family or marital therapy).

Another important concept of alcoholism-oriented family systems therapy is that of family homeostasis. Steinglass et al. (1987) define homeostasis as the family's need to maintain the family behavior and environment within an acceptable range. Homeostatic mechanisms are those processes that move the family back within range when the family has strayed out of range. According to Steinglass and colleagues, alcoholic families are characterized by rigid, narrow ranges of acceptable behavior and are particularly sensitive to destabilization. Even slight changes in family functioning and environment trigger homeostatic mechanisms and the family moves back toward their stable and predictable functioning. In the alcoholic family, these homeostatic mechanisms typically require the presence of alcohol to allow short-term problem-solving behaviors to occur. For example, short-term problem-solving behaviors such as assertion, expression of negative affect, intimacy, or isolation may occur within the family only when the alcoholic is intoxicated.

Stages of Therapy

As outlined by Steinglass et al. (1987), family systems therapy as applied to alcoholic families has four general stages. They note that not all families will complete all four stages and that the time spent in each stage can differ dramatically from family to family. The sequence is constant, however, and therapy can be structured along these stages.

The first stage, *diagnosing alcoholism and labeling it a family problem*, is conducted by the therapist during an evaluation with the family. A primary goal of this stage is to determine whether the family fits the description of an alcoholic family or a family with an alcoholic member. Assessment surrounding the presence and role of alcohol in daily family routines and rituals and the extent to which drinking behavior has been accommodated by these family behaviors provide important indications as to whether the family could potentially benefit from alcohol-oriented family systems therapy. The assessment phase includes the perspectives of all family members and all present are encouraged to describe the family and its problems from their own unique viewpoints. Also, families may present with problems other than alcohol abuse. When this is the case and the family assessment suggests that alcoholism is present, the therapist also must make a determination on whether alcoholism or the family's presenting problem is the appropriate treatment priority.

The therapist indirectly and directly can encourage the family's acceptance of alcoholism as a family problem rather than an individual family member's problem. Indirectly, the therapist can suggest a family orientation through word choice ("the problem issue in this family is alcohol," or "alcoholism is the underlying problem in this family"). More directly, as a result of the earlier assessment the therapist can describe the multiple impacts of alcohol abuse on the family. Once the alcoholism has been labeled a family issue, the family may be willing to negotiate a treatment contract with the therapist.

Removing alcohol from the family system is described by Steinglass and colleagues as the second stage of treatment. Steinglass states that this stage must be addressed in the same session in which alcoholism has been labeled a family problem. Once the family and therapist have identified alcoholism as a family treatment priority, the therapist must begin immediate work with the family in planning and contracting how the alcoholic will stop drinking and what the other members will do to support the goal of abstinence. For the alcoholic, this may include arrangements for inpatient detoxification or, in the case of minimal physical dependence on alcohol, drinking cessation in the home environment. The family members, in conjunction with the alcoholic, identify what they can do to support the cessation of drinking (e.g., removing alcohol from the house, whether or not alcohol will be consumed by others in the home). Subsequent sessions may be spent reviewing the successes and setbacks of these agreements and refining, where necessary, the tasks necessary for the alcoholic to achieve abstinence.

Many possible outcomes may result following initial attempts of the family to support drinking cessation and the alcoholic's new sobriety. Treatment may proceed smoothly; the alcoholic may stop drinking and family members may follow through with appropriate supportive behaviors. However, it is not unusual for drinking slips or relapses to occur. Family members may challenge the alcoholic's efforts toward sobriety and directly or subtly encourage drinking. Early treatment sessions may focus on refining the abstinence contract, identifying weaknesses in the agreements, and strengthening the contract. Steinglass suggests that the therapist interpret resistance within the family as anxiety about change in the family system. In an alcoholic family, alcohol has served as the central organizing principle, and loss of alcohol (and the behaviors and communications facilitated by alcohol consumption) may profoundly shake the family system.

The third stage of treatment is described as the *emotional desert*. During its "wet" (i.e., actively drinking) period, the routines, rituals, communication patterns, and general life of the alcoholic family were heavily influenced by the presence of alcohol. In its newly "dry" period, the patterns of the alcoholic family are significantly disrupted. Daily life suddenly is now unstable and less predictable. Steinglass notes that two consequences of drinking cessation are common in this stage. First, all family members, including the alcoholic, may feel depressed, detached, and empty. This "emotional desert" may be especially distressing when the family anticipated that alcohol cessation would provide happiness and a solution to remaining family issues and problems. Second, the entire family may feel an intense pull back toward the old "wet" solutions, methods of communication, and routines. The therapist must guide the family through this period and work toward settling the family in a "dry" state.

During the fourth stage of treatment the family enters a resolution phase, toward either *family restabilization or family reorganization*. Although a restabilized family is "dry," it remains centered on drinking and alcoholism issues. Steinglass (1987) notes that although this outcome is considered successful, alcoholism remains "a core feature of family life" and "the basic relationship patterns within the family have remained by and large unchanged" (pp. 344–345). In addition to the sobriety of the alcoholic, one other major change in the family is that alcohol and intoxication are no longer necessary to facilitate the family's communication and short-term problem solving.

The reorganized family, in comparison, has undergone a fundamental change in family organization and functioning, such that the family is no longer centered on alcoholism issues. Steinglass and colleagues describe this type of family as having experienced a family crisis as a result of the first three stages of therapy, resulting in family disorganization followed by a new, organization. Issues and problems surrounding alcohol, intoxication, and alcoholism now affect the family significantly less as these issues are no longer related to the family functioning.

The first two stages of therapy may require only a matter of weeks—Steinglass indicates that 6 weeks or less is typical. The final two stages of therapy are likely to take several months and require a variety of structural and strategic family therapy techniques as the family moves toward resolution. Family systems therapy is typically viewed as lasting several months as opposed to years.

Empirical Evidence for Family Systems Therapy with Alcoholics

Steinglass (1979) has reported on the 6-month outcome of a pilot study of ten couples treated with the family systems therapy framework. Treatment consisted of a 2-week outpatient phase, a 10-day joint hospitalization phase, and a 30-week outpatient phase (see Steinglass, Davis, & Berenson, 1977, for details and case studies). During each of the outpatient phases, couples participated in six small couples group sessions. During the joint hospitalization phase, alcohol was freely available for the first 7 days and couples participated in daily group therapy sessions. The goals of the hospitalization were to examine intoxicated versus sober behaviors of the couple, identify the functions of intoxication within the couple, and to alter communication patterns so that alcohol would be unnecessary for communication and problem solving. Ten couples completed the program; eight couples (which included nine alcoholics) completed the 6-month follow-up. Outcome data (Steinglass, 1979) yielded mixed results for the efficacy of this program. Six months following treatment, three alcoholics were abstinent, five reported varying degrees of drinking reduction relative to pretreatment drinking, and one reported increased drinking. Although treatment had a positive effect on marital communication, improvements in communication nevertheless were associated with reports of increased behavioral difficulties and decreased marital satisfaction. Finally, the assessments completed by the alcoholics and spouses suggested a great deal of intramarital similarity. Steinglass (1979) interprets this spousal similarity as evidence for the applicability of the family systems model.

Zweben, Pearlman, and Li (1988) conducted a large-scale study examining the relative effectiveness of eight sessions of family (client and spouse only) systems therapy ($n = 139$) with one 90-minute conjoint session of "advice" ($n = 79$). The advice provided to alcoholics and their spouses was consistent with family systems theory, and included a positive expectation for change from the single session, recommendations for improving the alcohol problem and other problems, and relapse prevention. Only 70 couples from the systems therapy and 46 from the advice counseling completed treatment and all follow-up assessments. Among these remaining cases, no differences were found at 18 months after the initial appointment on a variety of measures including drinking outcome and marital adjustment. Of the 116 clients in both conditions, 59% were classified as "greatly improved" on the basis of drinking. The only significant difference between the two randomly assigned conditions was that couples in the systems therapy condition reported greater satisfaction and viewed the treatment as more helpful relative to those couples in the advice counseling condition.

The authors note several possible interpretations for the lack of between group differences. First, the sample was primarily comprised of nondistressed, socially stable couples with only moderate levels of alcohol-related problems. Thus, this relatively higher functioning sample of alcoholics may have had a better prognosis regardless of the type and intensity of intervention. Second, both treatment conditions emphasized a systems approach and the importance of the spouse and the relationship in the resolution of the drinking problem. Although the intensity of the two treatment conditions differed (i.e., eight sessions versus one), the primary approach to treatment did not. Third, the conjoint systems therapy was limited to only eight sessions. A greater number of sessions may be necessary in order to reap fully benefits of the systems approach for alcohol abusers, as described by Steinglass (1987). Finally, attrition was high (47%), but comparable, from both treatment conditions. This level of attrition raises concern about the generalizability of the results. In sum, the findings reported by Zweben et al. (1988) suggest that a single systems-based conjoint session of "advice" may be as effective as eight sessions of conjoint systems therapy with higher functioning alcohol clients and their spouses.

Summary

There are relatively few data to date that test the efficacy of the family systems model in the context of alcoholism treatment. As the findings of Steinglass (1979) and Zweben et al. (1988) are modest at best, additional research is needed to examine more fully the use of this approach with alcoholic families. Several characteristics of family systems therapy make such outcome research unusually difficult. Given the inherently unstructured nature of family systems therapy, standardizing treatment to the extent necessary for controlled outcome research may not be possible. For example, attempting to standardize therapy into a preset number of sessions in a given time frame, using only certain techniques and strategies, may reduce the effectiveness of the approach as originally described by Steinglass et al. (1987). Furthermore, family systems therapy for alcoholism is designed to be effective for alcoholic families. Families for whom alcohol does not serve as the central organizing principle may have less or no response to this treatment approach. In sum, family systems therapy for alcoholism should be considered for families meeting the definition of an alcoholic family. Research that balances the research need for structured and standardized treatment protocol with the clinical needs of this less structured treatment approach is needed.

Family Systems Therapy and Drug Addiction

Family systems therapy also has been applied to adolescent/young adult drug abuse by Stanton et al. (1982). In this model, the adolescent's drug abuse draws attention away from marital conflict and unites the parents in coping with the adolescent. The adolescent stops taking drugs and begins to exhibit competence and independence in the presence of extra structure and attention from the parents. The parents then shift their attention from the adolescent back toward their unresolved marital conflicts. As their focus returns to the marital problems, conflict becomes more apparent and the adolescent relapses to drug abuse to draw attention away from the marital conflict. This cycle may repeat many times with marital and drug issues escalating to threats of separation and divorce and to drug overdose.

Stanton and colleagues emphasize the importance of the parents' role toward the drug-abusing adolescent during treatment. In brief, therapy begins with the therapist placing the parents "in charge" of the youth's problem rather than siding with the adolescent. Rules are set and guidelines are established with regard to abstinence, school, employment, friends, and activities, as necessary. The clear expectation is that the adolescent will become abstinent,

self-sufficient, and independent. As the adolescent begins to improve, Stanton postulates that the marriage and family will become unstable. If unchecked, this stress will trigger a relapse in the adolescent in order to restabilize the family around drug issues. Instead, because the therapist has sided with the parents, the couple will turn to the therapist for assistance in resolving their conflicts, rather than relying on the adolescent's drug relapse to serve that function. As in Steinglass's model of family therapy with alcoholic clients, therapy is conducted with a wide array of structural and strategic family therapy techniques.

Empirical Evidence for Family Systems Therapy with Drug Abusers

Stanton et al. (1982) report an evaluation of their model of family therapy with young (mean age = 25 years) male opiate addicts and their families. Clients were randomly assigned to one of three conditions; random assignment did not occur for the control condition. In the two family therapy conditions, the family received ten therapy sessions (over 4.5–5 months) as outlined by Stanton et al. (1982). In the "Paid Family Therapy" condition ($n = 21$ families), every family member was paid $5.00 for attending each session, with an additional possibility of monetary bonus if the identified patient had abstained from drug use. In the "Unpaid Family Therapy" condition ($n = 25$), the families received the same treatment as the Paid Family Therapy condition but without monetary incentive for attendance. Two control conditions were also included: in the "Paid Family Movie" condition ($n = 19$), families attended once a week for 10 weeks to view noncontroversial anthropological movies. Family members were paid at the same schedule as in the Paid Family Therapy condition. The fourth study condition, the "Nonfamily Treatment" condition ($n = 53$), served as a second control group and consisted of methadone and individual counseling. Subjects for this condition were not told about the family treatment, but were selected if they met eligibility criteria for the study and completed at least 30 days of methadone treatment.

Follow-up results 1 year after treatment (available for 91% of the sample) indicated that clients in the family therapy conditions had improved outcome on drug use measures relative to those in the two control conditions. In terms of illegal opiate use, legal opiate use (primarily methadone), nonopiate illegal drugs, and marijuana, more clients in the two family therapy conditions were classified as "good" outcomes at 1 year (61%, 51%, 79%, and 49%, respectively) relative to those in the control groups (35%, 27%, 52%, and 27%, respectively). There were no differences between conditions on measures of alcohol use, school, or work activities. Although this study provides strong evidence for the effectiveness of family systems therapy with drug abusers, one weakness of the study is the lack of random assignment into all four study conditions. While random assignment did occur for the three family conditions, clients were not randomly assigned into the control condition.

A study conducted in the Netherlands (Romijn, Platt, & Schippers, 1990; Romijn, Platt, Schippers, & Schaap, 1992) sought to replicate the findings of Stanton et al. (1982). Seventy-seven families (including 81 drug abusers) presented to one of two Dutch family therapy programs and agreed to participate in follow-up interviews. Thirty-eight clients who applied for methadone treatment and individual counseling were selected for a control group. This control group was similar to the experimental group in terms of frequency of family contact, demographics, and drug use. The mean age of the sample was 24 years, two thirds were using methadone at intake, most clients were heroin abusers only, and one third were polydrug abusers. Family therapy sessions, using the techniques described in Stanton et al. (1982), apparently occurred infrequently, with an average of 15 sessions over the course of 12–15 months (Romijn et al., 1992).

At 18 months after the *beginning* of treatment (thus, only several months following the end of therapy for some families), information was available from 50 clients (in 48 families) in the family therapy group and from 24 clients in the control group. An additional 22 families in the family therapy group and 6 families in the control group provided information regarding clients who could not be contacted. Although no significant differences were found in drug use between the family therapy group and the control group, more clients in the family therapy group were classified as "good" outcome (i.e., abstaining or "nearly so") versus "poor" outcome (using drugs weekly to daily). More clients who received family therapy were classified as "good" outcome—64% for illegal opiates, 75% for illegal nonopiates, 64% for legal opiates, and 47% for all drugs, compared to 46%, 62%, 54%, and 33%, respectively, for the control group. The only category where the control group appeared more improved than the family therapy group was for alcohol use; 96% of the control group was classified as "good" outcome relative to 82% of

the family therapy group (Romijn et al., 1990). However, as clients were not randomly assigned to the family therapy or the control condition, interpretations of these nonsignificant findings must be considered speculative.

A secondary analysis on a subset of 18 families who received family therapy was conducted in order to identify how changes in family communication may be related to treatment outcome (Romijn et al., 1992). Families were videotaped during a problem-solving discussion at the beginning of treatment and 1 year later. At the 1-year assessment, families were classified as "successful" ($n = 7$) or "unsuccessful" ($n = 11$) based on the clients' drug use and social functioning. Successful treatment appeared to be associated with negative parental communication at the beginning of treatment and improvement toward more positive parental communication during treatment.

Szapocznik and colleagues have examined the effectiveness of an unusual form of family systems therapy—"one-person family therapy." This program of research examined the efficacy of family systems techniques when only one family member (the drug-abusing adolescent) is present in treatment. As described by Szapocznik et al. (1990), the principle of complementarity underlies the effectiveness of one-person family therapy. Complementarity is the interdependence and interaction between members of a family system, such that change in one member will trigger behavior changes in other members of the family. The goals of this therapy are to promote change not only in the drug-abusing adolescent, but also in family functioning (see Szapocznik, Kurtines, Foote, Perez-Vidal, & Hervis, 1983; Szapocznik et al., 1990). Two studies have been conducted to compare the effectiveness of one-person family therapy with adapted structural and strategic family techniques (Szapocznik et al., 1983; Szapocznik, Kurtines, Foote, Perez-Vidal, & Hervis, 1986). A total of 37 families with a drug-abusing adolescent were randomly assigned to receive a maximum 12 (Szapocznik et al., 1983) or 15 (Szapocznik et al., 1986) sessions of either family systems therapy or one-person family therapy. Families improved both in terms of the drug use of the adolescent and in family functioning, regardless of treatment condition, immediately following treatment and for the 61% of the families available at the 6-month follow-up. Although interpretation of these data is hampered by the absence of a no-therapy control group and a no-systems-therapy control group, this research tentatively suggests that systems techniques may be adapted to working with only a single member of a family system.

Summary

Family systems therapy has been applied successfully to families of adolescent and young adult drug abusers. Although this small body of research has some methodical weaknesses that need to be rectified, these findings support the use of family systems interventions directed at the parents and families of young drug abusers. Families in which marital communication and conflict are problematic may be especially responsive to the family systems approach.

Finally, the family systems techniques and research findings of Szapocznik and colleagues deserve special note. As family therapists are well aware, it is not always possible to engage a family in therapy. The adaptation of family systems therapy to "one-person family therapy" is intriguing and deserves further investigation. Although the interpretation of this research is hampered by the absence of appropriate control groups, one-person family therapy may serve as a viable alternative when family participation is not possible.

CONCLUSIONS

Including one or more family members in substance abuse therapy has sufficient empirical support to merit its consideration when planning a course of treatment. Behavioral marital therapy has been examined as an adjunctive treatment strategy in treating alcoholics and their spouses. In general, the relevant research has indicated that improving the marital relationship affords improvements in marital and alcohol outcome relative to treatment that does not include the spouse. Family systems therapy has been evaluated in the contexts of both substance abuse and alcoholism, with both adolescent and adult clients. Although there is modest empirical support in general for family systems therapy with addicted clients, firmer statements regarding its efficacy are precluded by methodological shortcomings in this body of research. Nevertheless, family systems therapy for the addictions has a strong theoretical rationale and may be particularly effective when conducted with appropriate families. Finally, the strategy of "one-person family therapy" for addicted adolescents is intriguing and represents a possible treatment alternative when family systems therapy is deemed appropriate but other family members are unable or unwilling to participate in treatment.

Family systems therapy is more often utilized when the client is an adolescent or young adult substance abuser. In this case, family systems therapy includes the parents and possibly other siblings and family members. When the client is an adult, behavioral marital therapy and family systems therapy both have been shown to have a positive impact. The choice between behavioral marital therapy and family systems therapy may be guided by the assessment of the marriage and family functioning. When the marriage could benefit from increased positive affect and communication and negotiation skills, behavioral marital therapy may be the treatment of choice. When alcoholism or substance abuse appears to serve as the "central organizing principle" for the family (i.e., the family has adjusted to and accommodated substance use and intoxication facilitates family communications), family systems therapy may be the more effective treatment strategy.

At a minimum, the present review of family and marital addiction therapies strongly indicates the critical role family functioning can have in both subtly maintaining an addiction and in creating an environment conducive to abstinence. When marital or family therapy is not the treatment of choice or is not available to the client, assessment of and attention to family functioning should remain an element of treatment. Awareness of a spouse's and other family members' views and opinions of the client's addiction, the effects of substance abuse on the family, and the role that substance abuse and intoxication may serve in family functioning may be crucial to conceptualizing the client's addiction, treatment course, and risks to abstinence. Including the spouse or other family members in one or more therapy sessions during a course of individual treatment may provide useful insights into the conduct of treatment.

Family influences in addictions should not be interpreted as indicating that family members somehow directly *cause* addictive behavior or that family members are responsible for the client's use of alcohol or illicit drugs. The equating of family influences and "blame" or responsibility is a common misconception of family members and occasionally therapists as well. A spouse or family may need to be reassured that their involvement in treatment does not suggest or imply that they are to "blame" for the client's substance abuse. However, the marriage and family can be central in the client's support network and highly influential during treatment, and spouses and family members should be encouraged that they can be instrumental during treatment and recovery.

Continuing research is needed to evaluate these treatment approaches and identify couples and families with which they are most appropriate. Specifically, the efficacy of behavioral marital therapy as an adjunctive treatment strategy with addictions other than alcohol has not yet been examined. Additional research is needed to examine the effects of family systems therapy with alcohol and other substance abusers. Such efforts will need to balance the needs of research methodology with the relatively unstructured family systems techniques. Further, not yet addressed in this literature is the adaptation of marital and family therapy techniques with couples for whom addiction is present in both spouses. When both spouses are addicted, conflicting rationales can be made arguing for individual or for conjoint treatment. Theoretical and empirical guidance will be helpful in outlining the most appropriate course of treatment.

AUTHOR NOTE

The preparation of this chapter was supported in part by a grant (AA09882) from the National Institute on Alcohol Abuse and Alcoholism. Appreciation is due to Gerard J. Connors and Charles Pierson for helpful comments on a previous draft of this chapter and to Dawn Mach for secretarial support.

Correspondence concerning this chapter should be addressed to the author at Research Institute on Addictions, 1021 Main Street, Buffalo, New York, 14203. E-mail may be sent to WALITZER@RIA.ORG.

REFERENCES

Barbarin, O. A., & Tirado, M. C. (1984). Family involvement and successful treatment of obesity: A review. *Family Systems Medicine, 2,* 37–44.

Bowers, T. G., & Al-Redha, M. R. (1990). A comparison of outcome with group/marital and standard/individual therapies with alcoholics. *Journal of Studies on Alcohol, 51,* 301–309.

Collins, R. L. (1990). Family treatment of alcohol abuse: Behavioral and systems perspectives. In R. L. Collins, K. E. Leonard, & J. S. Searles (Eds.), *Alcohol and the family: Research and clinical perspectives* (pp. 285–308). New York: Guilford Press.

Ginsberg, D., Hall, S. M., & Rosinski, M. (1991). Partner interaction and smoking cessation: A pilot study. *Addictive Behavior, 16,* 195–202.

Gottman, J., Notarius, C., Gonso, J., & Markman, H. (1976). *A couple's guide to communication.* Champaign, IL: Research Press.

Hahlweg, K., & Markman, H. J. (1988). Effectiveness of behavioral marital therapy: Empirical status of behavioral techniques in preventing and alleviating marital distress. *Journal of Consulting and Clinical Psychology, 56,* 440–447.

Jacobson, N. S., Dobson, D., Fruzzetti, A. E., Schmaling, K. B., & Salusky, S. (1991). Marital therapy as a treatment for depression. *Journal of Consulting and Clinical Psychology, 59,* 547–557.

McCrady, B. S. (1982). Conjoint behavioral treatment of an alcoholic and his spouse: The case of Mr. and Mrs. D. In W. M. Hays & P. E. Nathan (Eds.), *Clinical case studies in the behavioral treatment of alcoholism* (pp. 127–156). NY: Plenum Press.

McCrady, B. S. (1989a). Extending relapse prevention models to couples. *Addictive Behaviors, 14,* 69–74.

McCrady, B. S. (1989b). Outcomes of family-involved alcoholism treatment. In M. Galanter (Ed.) *Recent developments in alcoholism: Vol. 7, Treatment research.* NY: Plenum Press.

McCrady, B. S. (1990). The marital relationship and alcoholism treatment. In R. L. Collins, K. E. Leonard, & J. S. Searles (Eds.), *Alcohol and the family: Research and clinical perspectives* (pp. 338–355). New York: Guilford Press.

McCrady, B. S., Noel, N. E., Abrams, D. B., Stout, R. L., Nelson, H. F., & Hay, W. M. (1986). Comparative effectiveness of three types of spouse involvement in outpatient behavioral alcoholism treatment. *Journal of Studies on Alcohol, 47,* 459–467.

McCrady, B. S., Stout, R., Noel, N., Abrams, D., & Nelson, H. F. (1991). Effectiveness of three types of spouse-involved behavioral alcoholism treatment. *British Journal of Addiction, 86,* 1415–1424.

Noel, N. E., & McCrady, B. S. (1993). Alcohol-focused spouse involvement with behavioral marital therapy. In T. J. O'Farrell (Ed.), *Treating alcohol problems: Marital and family interventions* (pp. 210–235). New York: Guilford Press.

O'Farrell, T. J. (1986). Marital therapy in the treatment of alcoholism. In N. S. Jacobson & A. S. Gurman (Eds.), *Clinical handbook of marital therapy* (pp. 513–535). New York: Guilford Press.

O'Farrell, T. J. (1993a). A behavioral marital therapy couples group program for alcoholics and their spouses. In T. J. O'Farrell (Ed.), *Treating alcohol problems: Marital and family interventions* (pp. 170–209). New York: Guilford Press.

O'Farrell, T. J. (1993b). Couples relapse prevention sessions after a behavioral marital therapy couples group program. In T. J. O'Farrell (Ed.), *Treating alcohol problems: Marital and family interventions* (pp. 305–326). New York: Guilford Press.

O'Farrell, T. J., Choquette, K. A., Cutter, H. S. G., Brown, E. D., & McCourt, W. F. (1993). Behavioral marital therapy with and without additional couples relapse prevention sessions for alcoholics and their wives. *Journal of Studies on Alcohol, 54,* 652–666.

O'Farrell, T. J., & Cowles, K. S. (1989). Marital and family therapy. In R. K. Hester & W. R. Miller (Eds.), *Handbook of alcoholism treatment approaches: Effective alternatives* (pp. 183–205). New York: Pergamon Press.

O'Farrell, T. J., & Cutter, H. S. (1984). Behavioral marital therapy for male alcoholics: Clinical procedures from a treatment outcome study in progress. *American Journal of Family Therapy, 12*, 33–46.

O'Farrell, T. J., Cutter, H. S. G., Choquette, K. A., Floyd, F. J., & Bayog, R. D. (1992). Behavioral marital therapy for male alcoholics: Marital and drinking adjustment during the two years after treatment. *Behavior Therapy, 23*, 529–549.

O'Farrell, T. J., Cutter, H. S. G., & Floyd, F. J. (1985). Evaluating behavioral marital therapy for male alcoholics: Effects on marital adjustment and communication from before to after treatment. *Behavior Therapy, 16*, 147–167.

Romijn, C. M., Platt, J. J., & Schippers, G. M. (1990). Family therapy for Dutch drug abusers: Replication of an American study. *International Journal of the Addictions, 25*, 1127–1149.

Romijn, C. M., Platt, J. J., Schippers, G. M., & Schaap, C. P. (1992). Family therapy for Dutch drug users: The relationship between family functioning and success. *International Journal of the Addictions, 27*, 1–14.

Stanton, M. D., Todd, T. C., & Associates. (1982). *The family therapy of drug abuse and addiction*. NY: Guilford Press.

Steinglass, P. (1979). An experimental treatment program for alcoholic couples. *Journal of Studies on Alcohol, 40*, 159–182.

Steinglass, P., Bennett, L. A., Wolin, S. J., & Reiss, D. (1987). *The alcoholic family*. New York: Basic Books.

Steinglass, P., Davis, D. I., & Berenson, D. (1977). Observations of conjointly hospitalized "alcoholic couples" during sobriety and intoxication: Implications for theory and therapy. *Family Process, 16*, 1–16.

Szapocznik, J., Kurtines, W. M., Foote, F. H., Perez-Vidal, A., & Hervis, O. (1983). Conjoint versus one-person family therapy: Some evidence for the effectiveness of conducting family therapy through one person. *Journal of Consulting and Clinical Psychology, 51*, 889–899.

Szapocznik, J., Kurtines, W. M., Foote, F. H., Perez-Vidal, A., & Hervis, O. (1986). Conjoint versus one-person family therapy: Further evidence for the effectiveness of conducting family therapy through one person with drug-abusing adolescents. *Journal of Consulting and Clinical Psychology, 54*, 395–397.

Szapocznik, J., Kurtines, W., Santisteban, D. A., & Rio, A. T. (1990). Interplay of advances between theory, research, and application in treatment interventions aimed at behavior problem children and adolescents. *Journal of Consulting and Clinical Psychology, 58*, 696–703.

Zweben, A., Pearlman, S., & Li, S. (1988). A comparison of brief advice and conjoint therapy in the treatment of alcohol abuse: The results of the marital systems study. *British Journal of Addiction, 83*, 899–916.

CHAPTER 28

ADOLESCENT TREATMENT

Ken C. Winters
William L. Latimer
Randy D. Stinchfield

The extent of substance use among adolescents has been well documented (e.g., O'Malley, Johnston & Bachman, 1995), as has its short- and long-term physiologic, behavioral, and social consequences (e.g., Newcomb & Bentler, 1988). In stark contrast to the adult alcoholism and substance abuse treatment field, inadequate attention has been paid to the specific clinical needs of adolescents. Traditional substance abuse treatment may not be sufficient to meet the needs of substance-abusing youths, yet many adolescent treatment programs have been organized around an adult view of rehabilitation. For example, success in treatment programs for adults has been traditionally defined as the patient's maintenance of abstinence. Such a limited definition of success may be inappropriate to the broader range of problems and deficits encountered in the young substance abuser. Furthermore, the multiple personal and environmental problems facing the adolescents require a full range of comprehensive, integrated, and systematic services while tailoring treatment to the needs of each young person.

To compound matters, there is a paucity of research and clinical evaluation of the treatment approaches and settings best suited for adolescents with varying demographic characteristics. The body of adolescent literature is predominately descriptive and nonempirical in nature, focusing on various treatment modalities and strategies. Indeed, the field is a long way from firmly establishing answers to what are viewed as benchmark treatment outcome questions: Do adolescents improve after treatment? What types of treatments in what settings work best? For which types of young patients?

In the context of large scientific knowledge gaps are several political forces that impinge on the adolescent treatment field. As society becomes desensitized to the stigma attached to substance abuse problems, adolescents and their parents may more readily accept a diagnosis of substance use disorder than attribute problems to mental illness or delinquency, or acknowledge that the problem lies within the chaotic family (Winters & Henly, 1988). For some, substance abuse treatment may be the service option of first choice. Unfortunately, this trend may promote the labeling of a youth as "chemically dependent" when, in fact, such a label may be inappropriate. Moreover, from a public health standpoint, there is increasing pressure to identify teenagers who are either at risk to develop a substance abuse problem or have already done so (Tarter, 1990). This identification may require skills from a wide array of therapists and counselors with varying degrees of clinical training in assessment and treatment (Leccese & Waldron, 1994; Winters, 1990). Such diversity of clinical expertise and training raises the concern that diagnostic and treatment referral standards may vary greatly (Owen & Nyberg, 1983). Additional concerns are being raised by the trend of third-party payers who are restricting reimbursement to less intensive treatment and requiring service providers to treat more and more complex youth problems with greater efficiency. Some professionals say this growing tension between health coverage limitations and greater clinical demands is compromising the effectiveness of care (Ross, 1994).

This chapter describes four primary theoretical approaches practiced in the United States for treating adolescent substance abusers: the Minnesota model, therapeutic communities, family-based approaches, and cognitive-behavioral therapy. We provide an overview of the core assumptions and common therapeutic techniques of each approach.

TREATMENT APPROACHES

The Minnesota Model

In the words of Ehrlich (1987), rehabilitation is for "understanding recovery as a process of new knowledge construction including the progressive development and integration of behavior, cognition and affect" (p. 313). No treatment better epitomizes this view of rehabilitation than the Minnesota model, widely recognized as the most commonly practiced form of adolescent substance abuse treatment in the United States (Bukstein, 1994). Historically considered a long-term residential model, current Minnesota model approaches take on many forms of intensity and are no longer exclusively practiced in just residential settings.

Core Assumptions

This model, which combines the traditions of Alcoholics Anonymous (AA) and the principles of psychotherapy, is an intensive 12-step program specialized to meet the adolescent's developmental needs. This model views "chemical dependency" as a disease in its own right, not caused by another disease, with abstinence as the therapy goal. Its impact is considered so powerful that the chemical dependency must be treated before other coexisting mental or behavioral problems are addressed (although a life-threatening eating disorder, for example, would be an excep-

tion). The counselor, often a recovering alcoholic, is the primary therapist who utilizes intensive group processes and self-help group participation as the pivotal therapeutic interventions (Hoffmann, Sonis & Halikas, 1987). Central to the Minnesota model is the expectation that the client will help others through mutual sharing in the peer and self-help group settings.

"Step-work" serves as the primary therapeutic content around which the groups are organized. The first three steps of AA help substance-abusing adolescents become more honest, decide to stop using substances, and embark on a changed lifestyle. AA steps 4 through 9 are action steps designed to help recovering teenagers continue to be more honest, develop and implement a plan of action to change, and rectify past mistakes when possible and appropriate. Steps 10 through 12 are growth steps designed to encourage the adolescents to continue to work a program of recovery as they grow in sobriety. In essence, the AA approach strives to convince the young client to develop a new life course, a transformation of sorts (see Tiebout, 1953), that incorporates changes in behavior patterns, choices, and values.

Common Techniques

Traditionally, most Minnesota model programs focus on the first five steps of AA, with the expectation that the remaining seven steps will be addressed during aftercare and continued involvement in AA groups. Provided next are steps 1 through 5 and how they are translated into understandable concepts for adolescents (Winters & Schiks, 1989).

Step 1: We admit we are powerless over alcohol and other drugs—that our lives had become unmanageable. With adolescents, the primary goal of this step is to assist them in recognizing their problem by reviewing their substance use history and to have them associate it with harmful consequences. This is done by tracing the times they have unsuccessfully tried to stop or cut down use, and reviewing instances when it may not have occurred to them to stop using in spite of harmful consequences.

Step 2: We come to believe that a higher Power, as we understand it, can restore us to sanity. At a practical level, this step can be simplified to: "*there is hope if you let yourself be helped by a trusted adult, older teenager, or the therapy group.*" A powerful way to convey this message involves having new clients interact with those who are progressing well through the program or participating in the graduation ceremony for successful clients.

Step 3: We decide to turn our will and our lives over to the care of a higher Power. The focus of this step is to instill hope by emphasizing that the adolescent try to make decisions in a different way and allow others to provide help. While in treatment, the adolescent receives suggestions from counselors and older clients and group members. A key challenge for aftercare planning is to convince the young clients to seek out trusted individuals in their posttreatment environment.

Step 4: We conduct a complete and fearless moral inventory of ourselves.

Step 5: We admit to the higher Power, to ourselves, and to another human being the exact nature of our wrongs. Steps 4 and 5 encourage the adolescents to take a "personal inventory" of their regrettable past behaviors and self-defeating patterns, and to open-up to another person so they can experience acceptance by another person in spite of one's past wrongdoing. Thus, the primary aim of these steps is to enable clients to put some of their past unpleasant experiences behind them and to refocus energy toward developing a recovery lifestyle.

A key adjunct to step-work is family week, during which time parents engage in adult group therapy to gain an understanding of the nature of adolescent substance abuse, of their personal relationship with substance abuse, and how they can facilitate their child's recovery. Also common to the Minnesota model are in-treatment schooling, recreation and leisure counseling, self-help group orientation, and special topics groups (e.g., sexuality, victimization of abuse).

A therapeutic extension of the Minnesota model growing in popularity is the multidisciplinary professional model. This approach grew from concerns that the 12-step model may not adequately address comorbid psychiatric disorders so often seen with adolescent substance abuse (Kaminer, 1994). The multidisciplinary professional approach employs a diverse team of service providers experienced and trained in the evaluation and treatment of adolescent substance abuse. The team is usually led by a physician and operates according to a case-management philosophy (Hoffmann et al., 1987). The multiple problems of the adolescent, which may include psychiatric, family, legal, medical, peer, and school or work, are addressed by one or more team members with specialized training in their respective domain. However, major treatment decisions are made by the entire team. Interventions often employed by this model include individual, family, and various group therapies, self-help groups, behavioral

contracting, relapse-prevention techniques, social-skills training, and psychotropic medications (Kaminer & Frances, 1991).

Therapeutic Community

It is the tradition of most therapeutic communities (TCs) for substance abuse to provide services for adolescents. Whereas a number of residential TC programs have developed adolescent-only facilities, much of what is written about the TC approach for the adolescent client is based on experiences from the more long-standing adult TCs (De Leon & Deitch, 1985). Although the optimal stay in TC is traditionally residential-based and at least 15 months of care, some TCs have incorporated shorter periods of stay (e.g., 6–12 months) based on client progress (De Leon, 1985). But still common to TCs are their highly structured nature, which is quite suitable for treating many adolescent substance abusers. The typical TC day is very organized, beginning with a 7 a.m. wake-up and ending at 11 p.m. in the evening. This 16-hour day consists of morning and evening house meetings, job functions, classroom attendance, therapeutic groups, special seminars, and individual counseling as needed.

Core Assumptions

A detailed presentation of the TC model and underlying assumptions for substance abuse treatment can be found in De Leon and Deitch (1985). These authors note that central to the TC philosophy is that substance abuse is a deviant behavior stemming from an interruption of normal personality development and deficits in interpersonal and goal-attainment skills. This view conceptualizes substance abuse as a disorder of the entire person, with the signs of addiction being symptoms of the disorder rather than its core essence. Thus the goal of treatment is to globally change the individual through an integration of behavior, affect, values, and life choices associated with a drug-free lifestyle.

Foremost, substance abuse recovery from the TC perspective is the responsibility of the individual, facilitated by the client's progress through sequenced stages of learning to change. These stages of self-help change occur within the treatment milieu's social organization, which serves as a family surrogate for the client. The major aim of the stages is to provide the learning environment for the social maturation of the individual.

Common Techniques

This social maturation begins with participation by the client in a stratified structure of peer groups and their component membership status. The collection of peer subgroup constitutes the community, or family, in the residential setting. This peer-to-community bond strengthens the individual's identification with a perceived and ordered network of social members.

The management of the community itself is the full responsibility of the residents with minimal staff supervision. Job functions are arranged in a hierarchy, according to seniority, individual progress, and productivity. The new client enters a setting of upward mobility, beginning with the most menial tasks (e.g., mopping the floor), leading upward to levels of management or coordination. The rehabilitative approach is manifested by this social organization of self-help, responsible performance, and earned successes. This social milieu provides an orderly environment, reduces boredom, and offers the opportunity to achieve satisfaction from a busy schedule and the completion of daily chores. These characteristics of the regimen are viewed as stark contrast to the chaotic and disruptive settings that often accompany substance abuse.

An example of a position of increased responsibility that can be achieved by an adolescent's mobility in TC is being promoted to the role of expediter. An expediter is the "eyes and ears of the community" (De Leon & Deitch, 1985). This individual reports to the head counselor or director of the facility regarding a wide variety of daily activities. Successful performance in this role produces additional privileges in the program and social recognition and admiration by staff and peers. The underlying principle of the promotion system is that the rewards of substance abuse will be minimal in comparison to the social rewards obtained by satisfactory achievement in school, work, and other social interactions.

Another central therapeutic mechanism of the TC approach is the peer encounter group. The TC attempts to utilize the positive components of peer group cohesiveness and, at the same time, deflect the possible negative consequences. To prevent the peer group from becoming rigid or segregated from the larger community, it is common to rotate the group participants. Peer groups can be either age integrated or age segregated. Age integrated groups provide younger members with a vivid retrospective or prospective view of their behavior and attitudes. The age-segregated groups offer clinical advantages in that problem recogni-

tion, insight, and understanding probably occur more readily through identification of same-age youth.

In addition to peer encounter groups, other essential TC elements include one-to-one counseling, tutorial learning sessions, remedial and formal educational classes, residential job functions, and occupational training. Another special treatment element for adolescents includes participation by a family member. Although most TCs do not have resources needed to significantly change family dysfunctional behaviors, clinical experience indicates that family participation in low-intensity education sessions has positive impacts (De Leon & Deitch, 1985). Some TCs base acceptance of the adolescent into treatment contingent upon an agreement (not necessarily mandatory) to participate by a family member. Other specialized groups common to TCs deal with guilt, sexuality, and use of leisure time. Primary staff at TCs are paraprofessionals, most often ex-offenders or ex-clients successfully rehabilitated in TC programs.

Family Therapy

A steady increase in the use of family therapy to treat adolescent substance abuse has coincided with the rapid increase in applying systems approaches to treat a wide array of behavioral disorders during the past 15 years (Heath & Stanton, 1991; Szapocznik, Kurtines, Santisteban, & Rio, 1990). Indeed, a growing base of research has begun to suggest the critical role familial factors play in the development and maintenance of adolescent substance abuse (Hawkins, Catalano & Miller, 1992; Stanton & Todd, 1982).

Core Assumptions

From the family therapy perspective, substance abuse is viewed as a symptom of maladaptive familial relationships, expectancies, and interactions. A fundamental assumption underlying this view is that personality development and psychopathology are shaped largely by observable family relationships and interactions (Nichols & Schwartz, 1991). Because this view places etiological significance on current, day-to-day communication patterns between family members, inclusion of all family members within family therapy sessions is critical. A second prominent family therapy principle concerns a view of the family as being comprised of subsystems having various roles within a family structure (Minuchin, 1974). In addition, subsystems are evaluated according to boundaries or the extent to which members are engaged with one another in meaning-ful ways. Typical family subsystems include the parents, whose primary role is to nurture and set limits for their chil-dren; the siblings, whose key role during adolescence is to develop a clearer sense of self separate from the parents, and a range of child–parent relationships that serve a vari-ety of functions. Boundaries within and between subsys-tems ideally are permeable enough such that an adolescent, for example, feels comfortable approaching a parent for advice on important issues, yet firm enough such that ado-lescent and parental roles remain distinct.

A third family therapy principle is that problem behav-iors between individuals often feed into one another in pat-terns that make change difficult. Such patterns identified within families with substance-abusing adolescents often involve the parental subsystem losing its ability to set appropriate limits, thus giving too much autonomy and authority to the target adolescent. Therapy goals might include re-establishing parental authority and developing a relationship between parent and child (Santisteban & Szapocznik, 1994).

Other fundamental family therapy principles incorpo-rate developmental and generational theory within a family treatment context. Developmentally, families are viewed as evolving over time with each stage of development being characterized by a unique set of tasks and challenges. Thus a pattern of excessive overprotection by a parent of a child may not produce significant distress until certain develop-mental milestones are attempted, such as the adolescent leaving home for school. Although the reason for the par-ents being overly protective may be completely justified, the subsequent outcome may be the inability to achieve healthy independence during adolescence and young adult-hood. Also, current family interactions associated with pre-senting problems may have evolved over several generations. Thus the examination of multigenerational patterns with a family diagram or genogram (McGoldrick & Gerson, 1985) can provide a historical context to the pre-sent condition. For example, the target adolescent may be compared within the family to the "black sheep" aunt or uncle who had a history of alcohol abuse. The genogram can help highlight that the adolescent is indeed a different person who has his or her own unique features.

Common Techniques

The initial engagement process known as joining has been identified as critical to the success of therapy, particularly

as a majority of families presenting with an adolescent sub-stance abuser tend not to make it past the intake process. Resistance to change occurs throughout therapy and thus requires continual monitoring and the use of a range of intervention strategies along the way (Szapocznik et al., 1988). Liddle (1995) provides a useful summary of under-lying principles and associated strategies for engaging fam-ilies early in treatment. These strategies include emphasizing the presenting problem, mobilizing commu-nity resources such as school staff and probation personnel, evaluating stressors that contribute to problems and target-ing those that are most amenable to change, and assuming that crises occur in therapy and preparing for them.

Another common family therapy technique is organized around the goal of changing interaction patterns. Family therapists acquire critical information by encouraging fam-ily members to speak to each other directly. For example, the inability of a mother and son to carry on a conversation, or a father's harsh criticism of his daughter resulting in the adolescent's silence and emotional withdrawal, often reflect longstanding interaction patterns that contribute to presenting problems involving substance abuse. Therapy techniques used to clarify boundaries also serve to change interaction patterns. For example, several sessions may be held with a substance-abusing son and his disengaged father without additional family members in order to pro-vide opportunities for building their relationship. Once such a relationship begins to develop, additional family members might be reintroduced to the therapy to help fur-ther solidify the new father–son relationship.

A third family therapy technique involves reframing or relabeling problems. This occurs when the therapist attempts to make sense of a problem in a new way. For example, the substance abuse of an adolescent may ini-tially be presented by parents as proof that their son or daughter is simply a "bad" and "willful" child. Following assessment of interaction patterns and family structure, the therapist might suggest that the adolescent's substance abuse appears to have more to do with a lack of closeness within the family. Subsequent sessions might then work toward developing relationships between family members who are not well connected.

Cognitive-Behavioral Therapy

The use of treatment approaches that focus on a range of cognitive processes and behavioral coping skills represent a recent trend in adolescent substance abuse treatment and have labeled behavior therapy, cognitive therapy, and cognitive-behavioral therapy (CBT). CBT offers a logical strategy for treating adolescent substance abuse given that the high-risk literature has identified a range of maladaptive thoughts and behaviors that place adolescents at risk for substance abuse (e.g., Hawkins et al., 1992) as well as relapse from treatment (Berdiansky, 1991; Myers & Brown, 1990).

Core Assumptions

CBT strategies are informed by the multiperspectival view that substance abuse is a learned behavior disorder that develops within a cultural context comprised of family, peers, and social institutions that define drug-related beliefs and behaviors (Bandura, 1977; Marlatt & Gordon, 1980). Fundamental CBT principles share assumptions that cognitive processes affect behavior, cognitive mediational processes may be monitored and altered, and changes in cognitive mediational processes lead to behavioral change (Dobson & Block, 1988). Thus the goal of CBT is to diminish factors contributing to substance abuse (e.g., maladaptive beliefs) and promote factors that protect against relapse (e.g., coping skills, drug-free social network, academic achievement).

Common Techniques

In the area of maladaptive beliefs and attitudes, rational-emotive therapy (RET) (Ellis, 1962) and Beck's cognitive therapy (Wright, Beck, Newman, & Liese, 1993) have been applied to the treatment of adolescent substance abuse. The primary principles of RET are that a person's thoughts and beliefs about activating events and experiences underlie emotional and behavioral consequences. Disordered behavior stems primarily from irrational beliefs. Therefore, RET seeks to identify activating, or precursor, events for substance use, define and examine beliefs mediating between these activating events and substance use, analyze the evidence for identified irrational beliefs, and develop alternative beliefs the validity of which are subsequently tested during homework assignments.

Another core CBT approach focuses on developing coping skills for substance-abusing adolescents (e.g., Hawkins, Catalano, Gillmore, & Wells, 1989). Specifically, skills taught across studies have included resisting peer pressure to use substances, stress management, anger management, communication, problem solving, assertive behavior, self-monitoring and self-control strategies, and social network development. An important feature of skill-building approaches is the initial application of skills in low-risk situations (e.g., during session role-plays) followed by application in progressively more difficult and real-life situations (e.g., while attending a party). Such shaping allows the adolescent to experience success early in treatment, which enhances his or her self-efficacy, followed by practice in real-life situations, which increases the likelihood that new skill will generalize to the posttreatment environment.

Thus the ideal application of CBT would begin with an examination and modification of the thoughts and beliefs held by the teenager that contribute to substance use. Next, a functional analysis of coping skill strengths and weaknesses and an identification of stressors that typically precipitate use would occur. Explicit training would follow on selected skill areas (e.g., stress management) and irrational beliefs (e.g., substance abuse's temporary rewards give way to chronic problems) in order to develop competencies within the adolescent to both attain and maintain abstinence. Typical CBT learning techniques would include multiple strategies, including direct instruction, modeling, reciprocal peer instruction, guided and self-guided instruction, vignette analysis, and homework assignments.

A more recent variant of CBT, based on the comorbidity of adolescent substance abuse and learning problems (e.g., Latimer, Winters & Stinchfield, in press), is particularly relevant to promoting school achievement among adolescent substance abusers. Treatments fostering academic achievement among substance-abusing youth have reduced substance-abuse-related problems and substance abuse relapse following treatment (e.g., Eggert, Thompson, Herting, & Nicholas, 1994). The primary principle underlying this approach starts with the understanding that for a given learning situation, knowledge acquisition is promoted by the person's awareness and subsequent analysis of key learning processes, including the text to be learned, the task to be completed, and the strategies to be applied (Armbruster, Echols, & Brown, 1982). School achievement would be enhanced by providing explicit instruction on cognitive strategies to improve reading comprehension and memory, organizational skill, and writing and test-taking ability (e.g., Paris, Wasik, & Van-der-Westhuizen, 1988). Strategies are also taught that develop the adolescents' ability to monitor their school performance and make subsequent modifications in their learning approach.

Developmental Considerations

As noted at the beginning of the chapter, adolescent substance abuse treatment approaches have largely represented adaptations of adult models. This phenomenon is apparent, for example, in the wide use of 12-step programs within adolescent treatment settings. It is essential that developmental issues be considered when working with adolescents. Issues that arise when adolescent substance abuse treatment is placed within a developmental framework include the extent to which normative patterns of adolescent substance use can impact diagnostic and treatment referral decisions, the extent to which treatment strategies primarily developed for use with adults can be applied to adolescents, which treatment strategies are uniquely suited for use with adolescents, and the common developmental issues and themes that need to be addressed to enhance treatment efficacy. Thus the efficacy of adolescent substance abuse treatments will likely be enhanced by the incorporation of developmental theory and the promotion of self-efficacy in relation to stage-appropriate accomplishments (Erikson, 1963; Pandina, Labouvie, Johnson, & White, 1990). In addition, treatment strategies are likely to have optimal effects when targeted to individual strengths of recovering adolescents (Latimer, et al., in press), and by approaches that focus on a gradual development of competence in relation to real-life problems and settings (Brown, Stetson, & Beatty, 1989).

Furthermore, group therapies that incorporate peer-facilitated change strategies are consistent with developmental considerations because they capitalize on the considerable influence of peers (Bangert-Drowns, 1988). Peer influences, which have been shown to be the most powerful predictor of substance abuse among adolescent treatment samples (Winters, Latimer, & Stinchfield, 1997), are likewise vital to the development of a prosocial identity (Erikson, 1963) and to establishing normative expectations regarding recovery and abstinence (Brown, 1993).

TREATMENT OUTCOME

Empirical Evidence of Treatment Effectiveness

As noted earlier in the chapter, there is little rigorous empirical evaluation of adolescent substance abuse treatment. Although there has been some progress in addressing the question of whether adolescents improve after sub-

stance abuse treatment, as well as the question of treatment being superior to waiting-list controls (Grenier, 1985; Winters, Stinchfield, Opland & Weller, 1996), we know very little about matching adolescents to optimal treatment approaches. Even inpatient versus outpatient comparisons have revealed no significant differences (e.g., Amini, Zilberg, & Burke, 1982). This position that positive outcomes for adolescents are observable yet no approach has been shown to be more effective than another is fairly consistent throughout the adolescent literature (Beschner, 1985; Catalano, Hawkins, Wells, Miller, & Brewer, 1991; Harrison & Hoffmann, 1989; Hubbard, Cavanaugh, Craddock, & Rachal, 1985; Keskinen, 1986; Sells & Simpson, 1979; Stinchfield, Niforopulos, & Feder, 1994).

In the late 1960s and early 1970s the Drug Abuse Reporting Program (DARP) reported outcome results from numerous substance abuse treatment programs (Sells & Simpson, 1979). DARP included an adolescent sample of approximately 5,400, with 4–6-year follow-up results reported on 400. High relapse rates were reported for both alcohol and marijuana use, although use of other substances had decreased. Another major national study, the Treatment Outcome Prospective Study (TOPS), provided 1-year outcome data for 132 adolescents treated between 1979 and 1981 (Hubbard et al., 1985). Abstinence was exhibited in 60% of the follow-up sample. Because the DARP and TOPS studies are somewhat dated and based on findings from only subsamples of eligible clients, their generalizability to current treatment systems is limited.

The Minnesota model has received considerable treatment outcome attention over the years, perhaps owing to its popularity in the adolescent service sector. In the mid-1980s, Hazelden's Youth and Family Center conducted a treatment outcome study of 480 clients who completed treatment. 53% of the sample was contacted 1-year after treatment, with almost half (46%) reporting no use of alcohol and over two thirds (68%) indicating no use of other substances during the follow-up period (Keskinen, 1986). Another Minnesota model-based study was reported by Harrison and Hoffmann (1989) and revealed that based on data from 924 adolescents (49% of the eligible follow-up sample), that 42% reported total abstinence during the follow-up period and another 23% had used alcohol and other substances less than monthly.

Recent evaluations of the Minnesota model provide convergent data that 1-year follow-up data produce abstinence rates typically in the range of about 50% to 60%, with an additional 20% or so of subjects reporting greatly reduced substance use levels during the posttreatment period (Alford, Koehler, and Leonard, 1991; Brown, Vik, & Creamer, 1989; Stinchfield et al., 1994; Winters et al., 1996).

As part of a national, multisite evaluation of TC for adolescent substance abusers (N = 358), Jainchill (1996) reported significant reductions at 6-months posttreatment for several substances (inhalants, hallucinogens, and methamphetamines), and more than two thirds of the sample indicated that their alcohol use was either greatly reduced or at the abstinent level. Other outcome measures also showed significant improvements in criminal activity and educational achievement.

The empirical support for family-based treatment of adolescent substance abuse can be traced to the late 1980s when several randomized clinical trials demonstrated their effectiveness (e.g., Henggeler et al., 1991; Joanning, Quinn, Thomas, & Mullen, 1992; Liddle & Dakof, 1992; Szapocznik, Kurtines, Foote, Perez-Vidal, & Hervis, 1986). These studies consistently show the effectiveness of family-based approaches in decreasing client disengagement from treatment and in reducing substance use. For example, drop-out rates are impressively low; Henggeler et al. (1991) reported a 11% drop-out rate whereas the high end usually has been reported to be about only 30% (e.g., Liddle & Dakof, 1992). In terms of substance use outcome, abstinence rates for family-based approaches are impressive, generally between 40% and 80% (see Liddle & Dakof, 1995). These results compare favorably with other studies of non-family-based interventions (Catalano et al., 1991). What is particularly impressive about family-based treatments is that despite the practical difficulties of conducting substance abuse intervention research, this approach has been shown to be superior to peer group therapy (Joanning et al., 1992; Liddle & Dakof, 1992), parent education (Joanning et al., 1992; Lewis, Piercy, Sprenkle, & Trepper, 1990), multifamily intervention (Liddle & Dakof, 1992) and individual counseling (Henggler et al., 1991). Although this group of studies is not without methodological weaknesses (e.g., subjects not always representative of general clinical samples; minimal substance use severity), family-based therapies provide the most scientific rigor in documenting the effectiveness of treatment approaches for substance-abusing adolescents.

Treatment Tenure

Drop-out rates ranging as high as 50% (Friedman & Glickman, 1986) to around 20% (Kaminer, Tarter,

Bukstein, & Kabane, 1992; Winters et al., 1996) have been reported in adolescent studies. Given this problem of early departure from treatment, as well as the fact that a large proportion of families do not return for treatment after intake (Szapocznik et al., 1988), it stands to reason that promoting treatment engagement is a key ingredient to successful treatment. Undoubtedly, there are both patient and treatment factors that contribute to treatment disengagement. As noted, there is growing evidence that family-based approaches can yield dramatically higher retention rates compared to a control group receiving nonfamily therapy (e.g., Liddle & Dakof, 1992). Because the major approaches to adolescent substance abuse treatment have not been directly compared, we do not know if any approaches are superior in terms of treatment retention. There is some evidence that adolescents who engage in treatment yet do not complete the full course have higher rates of conduct disorders whereas treatment completers are more likely to present with a mood or adjustment disorder (Kaminer et al., 1992). Interestingly, studies that have followed treatment noncompleters indicate that such clients can significantly reduce their substance use (Alford et al., 1991; Winters et al., 1996) although reductions are typically to a lesser degree compared to treatment completers.

Studies of Relapse

Brown and her colleagues (Brown, 1993; Brown, et al., 1989; Myers & Brown, 1990; Richter, Brown, & Mott, 1991) engage in the systematic empirical study of relapse events following adolescent substance abuse treatment. Their studies are ongoing and focus on clinical samples from two West Coast inpatient adolescent chemical dependency treatment programs. Individuals with comorbid psychiatric diagnoses were screened out of the study, although subjects did present with considerable behavioral and social problems. Based on Marlatt and Gordon's (1985) cognitive behavioral model of relapse, treatment outcome at 6- and 12-month posttreatment distinguished among abstainers, "minor" relapsers, and "major" relapsers.

Results of these studies reveal that first, the major portion of situations that subjects defined as "high risk" for relapse involved social pressure to drink or use substances. This finding contrasts with the adult data, which suggest that situations involving negative affect are the most common relapse occasions. For adolescents, such situations seem to be a minor proportion of high-risk situations. Another finding is that more severe relapses tended to occur early in the follow-up period, and that more than one earlier severe relapse predicted continued poor functioning later in the follow-up period. Findings also suggest that coping style and social resources are related to outcomes. In this regard, greater behavioral coping skills, in contrast to the emotional or cognitive coping that is effective for adults (Littman, 1986), were associated with better outcomes. This finding is consistent with the importance of social pressure as a relapse precipitant. Relatedly, individuals with a greater number of social supports who did not use drugs tended to have better outcomes. Brown and colleagues concluded from their data that posttreatment social and environmental factors are critical in maintaining an abstinent lifestyle in adolescents following completion of treatment for substance abuse.

SUMMARY AND FUTURE DIRECTIONS

Although further research is needed to help identify the kinds of treatments that work best with adolescents given unique developmental concerns, the most promising treatments seem to be integrative models that address a range of substance abuse determinants, including cognitive, emotional, behavioral, familial, and social-systemic factors (Liddle, 1994). It appears that the four models summarized here (Minnesota model, therapeutic communities, family-based approaches, and cognitive-behavioral treatment) attempt to address many or all of these factors to a varying degree. Unfortunately, current health care realities pose a threat to continued development of comprehensive and integrative treatments. Downsizing in the form of tighter criteria for eligibility for treatment, fewer treatment days allowable by insurance policies, and greater emphasis on less expensive outpatient settings has become commonplace in the 1990s. Unfortunately, this trend appears to be associated with decreasing utilization of substance abuse treatment services (Hubbard, 1996). Adolescent treatments of the 1990s face the challenge of striking a balance between maintaining service comprehensiveness and responsiveness and surviving in the marketplace that is shifting its priorities toward constraint, efficiency, and expediency.

Documenting treatment effectiveness becomes even more critical in this vigilant health care industry. Such results can provide a competitive edge to programs and to treatment approaches, and serve to assist health care planners as they develop treatment benchmarks. However, future outcome studies need to advance beyond descriptive studies. Whereas family-based approaches are the most

promising examples of clinical controlled trials, the other major approaches, including the highly popular Minnesota model, have not been subjected to similar scientific rigor. Thus we still have little basis at this time for claiming with certainty that all forms of adolescent substance abuse treatment work above and beyond no treatment or when compared to a minimal treatment condition.

Furthermore, there is the issue of how to address the relatively high relapse rates found in the adolescent literature. If on the one hand we consider substance abuse a chronic condition, a 50% or so relapse rate is not all that discouraging. Perhaps we need to celebrate the fact that about half of treated adolescents improve and simply acknowledge that many others will not benefit from rehabilitation at this time. Then there are a number of experts who have called for a greater emphasis on the development and provision of posttreatment recovery maintenance services (Marlatt & Gordon, 1985; Saxe, Dougherty, Esty, & Fine, 1983), including more concentrated use of motivational interviewing techniques (Miller & Rollnick, 1991). Marlatt (1985) has stated that relapse prevention is a very difficult task and thus greater effort should be focused on maintaining recovery.

REFERENCES

Alford, G. S., Koehler, R. A., & Leonard, J. (1991). Alcoholics Anonymous–Narcotics Anonymous model inpatient treatment of chemically dependent adolescents: A 2-year outcome study. *Journal of Studies on Alcohol, 52*, 118–126.

Amini, F., Zilberg, N. J., & Burke, E. L. (1982). A controlled study of inpatient vs. outpatient treatment of delinquent drug abusing adolescents. *Comprehensive Psychiatry, 23*, 436–444.

Armbruster, B. B., Echols, C. H., & Brown, A. L. (1982). The role of metacognition in reading to learn: A developmental perspective. *Volta Review, 84*, 45–56.

Bandura, A. (1977). Self efficacy: Towards a unifying theory of behavior change. *Psychological Review, 84*, 191–215.

Bangert-Drowns, R. L. (1988). The effects of school-based substance abuse education: A meta-analysis. *Journal of Drug Education, 18*, 243–264.

Berdiansky, H. (1991). Beliefs about drugs and use among early adolescents. *Journal of Alcohol and Drug Education, 36*, 26–35.

Beschner, G. (1985). The problem of adolescent drug abuse: An introduction to intervention strategies. In A. Friedman & G. Beschner (Eds.), *Treatment services for adolescent substance abusers* (pp. 1–12). Rockville, MD: National Institute on Drug Abuse.

Brown, S. A. (1993). Recovery patterns in adolescent substance abuse. In J. S. Baer, G. A. Marlatt, & R. J. McMahon (Eds.),

Addictive behaviors across the life span (pp. 161–183). London: Sage.

Brown, S. A., Stetson, B. A., & Beatty, P. A. (1989). Cognitive and behavioral features of adolescent coping in high risk drinking situation. *Addictive Behaviors, 14*, 43–52.

Brown, S. A., Vik, P. W., & Creamer, V. A. (1989). Characteristics of relapse following adolescent substance abuse treatment. *Addictive Behaviors, 14*, 291–300.

Bukstein, O. G. (1994). Treatment of adolescent alcohol abuse and dependence. *Alcohol Health and Research World, 18*, 296–301.

Catalano, R. F., Hawkins, J. D., Wells, E. A., Miller, J. M., & Brewer, D. (1991). Evaluation of the effectiveness of adolescent drug abuse treatment, assessment of risks for relapse, and promising approaches for relapse prevention. *International Journal of the Addictions, 25*, 1085–1140.

De Leon, G. (1985). The therapeutic community: Status and evolution. *International Journal of the Addictions, 20*, 823–844.

De Leon, G., & Deitch, D. (1985). Treatment of the adolescent substance abuser in a therapeutic community. In A. S. Friedman & G. M. Beschner (Eds.), *Treatment services for adolescent substance abusers* (DHHS Pub. No. ADM 85-1342, pp. 216–230). Rockville, MD: National Institute on Drug Abuse.

Dobson, K. S., & Block, L. (1988). Historical and philosophical bases of the cognitive-behavioral therapies. In K. S. Dobson (Eds.), *Handbook of cognitive-behavioral therapies* (pp. 3–38). New York: Guilford Press.

Eggert, L. L., Thompson, E. A., Herting, J. R., & Nicholas, L. J. (1994). Preventing adolescent drug abuse and high school dropout through an intensive school-based social network development program. *American Journal of Health Promotion, 8*, 202–215.

Ehrlich, P. (1987). 12 step principles and adolescent chemical dependence treatment. *Journal of Psychoactive Drugs, 19*, 311–317.

Ellis, A. (1962). *Reason and emotion in psychotherapy.* Secaucus, NJ: Citadel Press.

Erikson, E. H. (1963). *Childhood and society.* New York: Norton.

Friedman, A. S., & Glickman, N. W. (1986). Program characteristics for successful treatment of adolescent drug abuse. *Journal of Nervous Mental Disease, 174*, 669–679.

Grenier, C. (1985). Treatment effectiveness in an adolescent chemical dependency treatment program: A quasi-experimental design. *International Journal of the Addictions, 20*, 381–391.

Harrison, P. A., & Hoffmann, N. (1989). *CATOR report: Adolescent treatment completers one year later.* St. Paul, MN: CATOR.

Hawkins, J. D., Catalano, R. F., & Miller, J. (1992). Risk and protective factors for alcohol and other drug problems in adolescence and early adulthood: Implications for substance abuse prevention. *Psychological Bulletin, 112*, 64–105.

Hawkins, J. D., Catalano, R. F., Gillmore, M. R., & Wells, E. A. (1989). Skills training for drug abusers: Generalization, maintenance, and effects on drug use. *Journal of Consulting and Clinical Psychology, 57*, 559–563.

Heath, A. W., & Stanton, M. D. (1991). Family therapy. In R. J. Frances & S. I. Miller (Eds.), *Clinical textbook of addictive disorders* (pp. 406–430). New York: Guilford Press.

Henggler, S. W., Bourdin, C. M., Melton, G. B., Mann, B. J., Smith, L. A., Hall, J. A., Cone, L., & Fucci, B. R. (1991). Effects of multisystemic therapy on drug use and abuse in serious juvenile offenders: A progress report from two outcome studies. *Family Dynamics Addiction Quarterly, 1*, 40–51.

Hoffmann, N. G., Sonis, W. A., & Halikas, J. A. (1987). Issues in the evaluation of chemical dependency treatment programs for adolescents. *Pediatric Clinics of North America, 34*, 449–459.

Hubbard, R. L. (1996, February). Findings from DATOS show clients receiving less drug abuse services. *Connection.* Washington, DC: Association for Health Services Research.

Hubbard, R. L., Cavanaugh, E. R., Craddock, S. G., & Rachal, J. V. (1985). Characteristics, behaviors and outcomes for youth in the TOPS. In A. S. Friedman & G. M. Beschner (Eds.), *Treatment services for adolescent substance abusers* (pp. 49–65). Rockville, MD: National Institute on Drug Abuse.

Jainchill, N. (1996). *Adolescents in TCs: Client profiles and treatment outcomes.* Paper presented at the National Institute on Drug Abuse, Rockville, Maryland (April 26, 1997).

Joanning, H., Quinn, W., Thomas, F., & Mullen, R. (1992). Treating adolescent drug abuse: A comparison of family systems therapy, group therapy, and family drug education. *Journal of Marital and Family Therapy, 18*, 345–356.

Kaminer, Y. (1994). *Adolescent substance abuse: A comprehensive guide to theory and practice.* New York: Plenum.

Kaminer, Y., & Frances, R. J. (1991). Inpatient treatment of adolescents with psychiatric and substance abuse disorders. *Hospital and Community Psychiatry, 42*, 894–896.

Kaminer, Y., Tarter, R. E., Bukstein, O. G., & Kabene, M. (1992). Comparison between treatment completers and noncompleters among dually-diagnosed substance-abusing adolescents. *Journal of the American Academy of Child and Adolescent Psychiatry, 31*, 1046–1049.

Keskinen, S. (1986). *Hazelden Pioneer House, 1984 profile, six-month and twelve-month outcomes.* Center City, MN: Hazelden.

Latimer, W. W., Winters, K. C., & Stinchfield, R. D. (in press). Use of the POSIT in identifying learning disabilities among drug using adolescents at risk for school failure. *International Journal of the Addictions.*

Leccese, M., & Waldron, H. B. (1994). Assessing adolescent substance use: A critique of current measurement instruments. *Journal of Substance Abuse Treatment, 11*, 553–563.

Lewis, R. A., Piercy, F. P., Sprenkle, D. H., & Trepper, T. S. (1990). Family-based interventions for helping drug-abusing adolescents. *Journal of Adolescent Research, 50*, 82-95.

Liddle, H. A. (1994). The anatomy of emotions in family therapy with adolescents. *Journal of Adolescent Research*, *9*, 120–157.

Liddle, H. A. (1995). Conceptual and clinical dimensions of a multidimensional, multisystems engagement strategy in family-based adolescent treatment. *Psychotherapy*, *32*, 39–58.

Liddle, H. A., & Dakof, G. A. (1992, June). *Family-based intervention for adolescent drug abuse*. Paper presented at the meeting of the Society for Psychotherapy Research, Pittsburgh, Pennsylvania.

Liddle, H.A., & Dakof, G.A. (1995). Family-based treatment for adolescent drug abuse: State of the science. In E. Rahdert and D. Czechowicz (Eds.), *Adolescent drug abuse: Clinical assessment and therapeutic interventions* (NIDA Research Monograph No. 156, DHHS Publication No. 95-3908). Rockville, MD: National Institutes of Health.

Littman, G. K. (1986). Alcoholism survival: The prevention of relapse. In W. R. Miller & N. Heather (Eds.), *Treating addictive behaviors* (pp. 391–405). New York: Plenum Press.

Marlatt, G. A. (1985). Relapse prevention: Theoretical rationale and overview of the model. In G. A. Marlatt & J. R. Gordon (Eds.), *Relapse prevention: Maintenance strategies in the treatment of addictive behaviors*. New York: Guilford Press.

Marlatt, G. A., & Gordon, J. R. (1980). Determinants of relapse: Implications for the maintenance of behavior change. In P. 0. Davidson & S. M. Davidson (Eds.), *Behavioral medicine: Changing health lifestyles* (pp. 410–452). New York: Brunner/Mazel.

McGoldrick, M., & Gerson, R. (1985). *Genograms in family assessment*. New York: Norton.

Miller, W. R., & Rollnick, S. (1991). *Motivational interviewing: Preparing people to change addictive behavior*. New York: Guilford Press.

Minuchin, S. (1974). *Families and family therapy*. Cambridge, MA: Harvard University Press.

Myers, M. G., & Brown, S. A. (1990). Coping responses and relapse among adolescent substance abusers. *Journal of Substance Abuse*, *2*, 177–189.

Newcomb, M. D., & Bentler, P. M. (1988). *Consequences of adolescent drug use: Impact on the lives of young adults*. Newbury Park, CA: Sage.

Nichols, M. P., & Schwartz, R. C. (1991). *Family therapy: Concepts and methods*. Needham Heights, MA: Allyn and Bacon.

O'Malley, P. M., Johnston, L.D., & Bachman, J.G. (1995). Adolescent substance use: Epidemiology and implications for public policy. *Pediatric Clinics of North America*, *42*, 241–260.

Owen, P. L., & Nyberg, L. R. (1983). Assessing alcohol and drug problems among adolescents: Current practice. *Journal of Drug Education*, *13*, 249–254.

Pandina, R. J., Labouvie, E. W., Johnson, V., & White, H. R. (1990). The relationship between alcohol and marijuana use and competence in adolescence. *Journal of Health and Social Policy*, *1*, 89–108.

Paris, S. G., Wasik, B. A., & Van-der-Westhuizen, G. (1988). Meta-metacognition: A review of research on metacognition and reading. *National Reading Conference Yearbook*, *37*, 143–166.

Richter, S. S., Brown, S. A., & Mott, M. A. (1991). The impact of social support and self-esteem on adolescent substance abuse treatment outcome. *Journal of Substance Abuse*, *3*, 371–385.

Ross, G. R. (1994). *Treating adolescent substance abuse*. Needham Heights, MA: Allyn and Bacon.

Santisteban, D. A., & Szapocznik, J. (1994). Bridging theory research and practice to more successfully engage substance abusing youth and their families into therapy. *Journal of Child and Adolescent Substance Abuse*, *3*, 9–24.

Saxe, L., Dougherty, D., Esty, J., & Fine, M. (1983). *The effectiveness and costs of alcoholism treatment* (Congressional Office of Technology Assessment Case Study, Publication No. 052-003-00902-1). Washington, DC: U.S. Government Printing Office.

Sells, S. B. & Simpson, D. D. (1979). Evaluation of treatment outcome for youths in drug abuse reporting program (DARP): A follow-up study. In G. M. Beschner & A. S. Friedman (Eds.), *Youth drug abuse: Problems, issues and treatment* (pp. 571–628). Lexington, MA: Lexington.

Stanton, M. D., Todd, T. C., & Associates. (1982). *The family therapy of drug abuse and addiction*. New York: Guilford Press.

Stinchfield, R., Niforopulos, L., & Feder, S. (1994). Follow-up contact bias in adolescent substance abuse treatment outcome research. *Journal of Studies on Alcohol*, *55*, 285–289.

Szapocznik, J., Kurtines, W. M., Foote, F. H., Perez-Vidal, A., & Hervis, O. (1986). Conjoint versus one-person family therapy: Further evidence for the effectiveness of conducting family therapy through one person with drug-abusing adolescents. *Journal of Consulting and Clinical Psychology*, *54*, 395–397.

Szapocznik, J., Kurtines, W. M., Santisteban, D. A., & Rio, A. T. (1990). The interplay of advances among theory, research and application in treatment interventions aimed at behavior problem children and adolescents. *Journal of Consulting and Clinical Psychology*, *58*, 696–703.

Szapocznik, J., Perez-Vidal, A., Brickman, A. L., Foote, F. H., Santisteban, D., & Hervis, 0. (1988). Engaging adolescent drug abusers and their families in treatment: A strategic structural systems approach. *Journal of Consulting and Clinical Psychology*, *56*, 552–557.

Tarter, R. E. (1990). Evaluation and treatment of adolescent substance abuse: A decision tree method. *American Journal of Drug and Alcohol Abuse*, *16*, 1–46.

Tiebout, H. M. (1953). Surrender versus compliance in therapy with special reference to alcoholism. *Quarterly Journal of Studies on Alcohol*, *14*, 58–68.

Winters, K. C. (1990). Need for improved assessment of adolescent substance involvement. *Journal of Drug Issues, 20,* 487–502.

Winters, K. C. & Henly, G. A. (1988). Assessing adolescents who misuse chemicals: The Chemical Dependency Adolescent Assessment Project. In E. R. Rahdert & J. Grabowski (Eds.), *Adolescent drug abuse: Analyses of treatment research* (NIDA research monograph series no. 77, pp. 4–18). Rockville, MD: National Institute on Drug Abuse.

Winters, K. C., Latimer, W. W., & Stinchfield, R. (1997). Psychosocial determinants of drug abuse severity among drug clinic youths. Submitted for publication.

Winters, K. C., & Schiks, M. (1989). Assessment and treatment of adolescent chemical dependency. In P. Keller (Ed.), *Innovations in clinical practice: A source book* (Vol. 8, pp. 213–228). Sarasota, FL: Professional Resource Exchange.

Winters, K. C., Stinchfield, R., Opland, E. O., & Weller, C. (1996). Comparison of outcome between outpatient and inpatient AA-based adolescent drug abuse treatment. Submitted for publication.

Wright, F. D., Beck, A. T., Newman, C. F., & Liese, B. S. (1993). Cognitive therapy of substance abuse: theoretical rationale. *National Institute on Drug Abuse Research Monograph Series, Behavioral Treatments for Drug Abuse and Dependence, 137,* 123–146.

CHAPTER 29

METHADONE MAINTENANCE

Surita Rao
Richard Schottenfeld

Methadone, a long-acting synthetic opiate, has been widely used as a maintenance medication for the successful treatment and rehabilitation of people with opioid dependence. The efficacy of methadone as a maintenance treatment for opioid dependence has been established through carefully controlled clinical trials and more than 30 years of widespread clinical use (Ball & Ross, 1991). Optimal methadone dose, duration of treatment, and level of psychosocial services are critical components of successful outcomes.

WHY DOES METHADONE MAINTENANCE WORK?

The success of methadone as a maintenance medication for opioid dependence is in large part due to three important clinical effects: (a) prevention of opioid withdrawal symptoms for a minimum of 24 hours, (b) elimination or reduction of cravings for heroin and other opioids, whether precipitated by early, mild withdrawal symptoms or by environmental cues (Dole,1980; Dole, 1988; Dole, Nyswander, & Kreek, 1966), and (c) production of narcotic cross tolerance leading to blockade of the effects of heroin and other short-acting opioids (Dole et al., 1966;

Kreek, 1986). In addition, because methadone is administered orally, it reduces the reinforcement associated with intravenous drug use (Schottenfeld & Kleber, 1995). As a result of all of these effects, methadone maintenance enables the patient to stop using illicit opioids and engage in psychosocial treatments. The complex array of positive and negative reinforcements and program structure built into a methadone program also encourages the patient to replace addictive behaviors, such as using illicit drugs and engaging in criminal activities, with healthier behaviors, including finding gainful employment, repairing relationships with family and friends, and developing recreational interests and hobbies.

THE HISTORY OF METHADONE MAINTENANCE

Methadone was developed in Germany at the end of World War II as an analgesic, and was first tested as a maintenance treatment for heroin dependence by Dole and Nyswander in 1963 in the treatment of six heroin-dependent patients at the Rockefeller Institute Hospital. The first pilot program using methadone as a maintenance medication for people addicted to heroin was started at Manhattan

362

General Hospital with 120 patients (Lowinson, Marion, Joseph, & Dole, 1992). In contrast to the generally poor outcomes for other heroin treatment programs, follow-up studies found 107 of the original patients doing well in treatment 10 years later, with 71% steadily employed and/or attending school (Dole et al., 1966). The program was independently evaluated over a 10-year period by the Columbia University School of Public Health. Based on the consistently positive treatment outcomes, expansion was recommended (Gearing & Schweitzer, 1974). Subsequently, methadone maintenance programs were developed in urban areas all over the country and annual methadone conferences were held at Rockefeller University. The Food and Drug Administration (FDA) and the Bureau of Narcotics and Dangerous Drugs (BNDD) jointly approved the use of methadone for "experimental" maintenance programs in 1970. The FDA approved methadone hydrochloride for the treatment of narcotic addiction in 1972 (Federal Register, 1972). Methadone maintenance continues to be the most widely used treatment modality for heroin-dependent people in the world.

Extensive scientific research conducted over three continents has repeatedly demonstrated the efficacy of methadone maintenance in the rehabilitation and treatment of opioid-dependent individuals. Despite its effectiveness, its use continues to evoke controversy among many substance abuse treatment providers, physicians, politicians, public officials, and the community in general (Cooper, 1988).

PHARMACOKINETICS

The pharmacokinetic properties of methadone make it an excellent maintenance medication (Isbell, 1948; Isbel & Vogel, 1949). Following oral administration, methadone is rapidly absorbed into the gastrointestinal tract, reaching peak plasma levels in about 2 hours. It has a half-life of approximately 24 hours (15–55 hours), therefore reaching steady state concentrations between 4 and 10 days (Baselt, 1982). Up to 90% of orally ingested methadone is absorbed following ingestion. Methadone, being highly lipid soluble, easily crosses the blood-brain barrier to enter the central nervous system. Methadone accumulates in tissue and is reversibly bound to tissue and plasma proteins. Unbound methadone undergoes N-demethylation followed by cyclization in the liver. The metabolites are then excreted in the urine and bile. Whereas patients maintained on a stable, daily dose of methadone usually expe-

rience little or no effects of peak or trough methadone levels, peak levels of methadone are more than twice the trough levels when measured over a 24-hour period in patients on a maintenance dose of methadone. Changing to a split-dose schedule may at times be useful for patients who experience withdrawal symptoms late in the day (Inturrisi & Vereby, 1972).

SIDE EFFECTS

Methadone has few side effects and virtually no toxicity when administered to patients on a long-term basis (Goldstein,1971; Jaffe, 1970; Kreek, 1973, 1978). Side effects of methadone are generally encountered early in treatment and most commonly include sedation, constipation, and sweating. Patients usually develop tolerance to the sedating effect of methadone within 4–6 weeks, whereas constipation and sweating may last longer. Less frequent side effects of methadone include weight gain, water retention, and transient skin rashes.

Methadone maintenance does not compromise cognitive and intellectual functioning (Appel & Gordon, 1976; Blumberg & Prueser, 1972; Gordon, 1976; Gordon & Lipset, 1976; Moskowitz & Sharma, 1979). Driving records of patients on methadone maintenance are not significantly different from those of the general population (Babst, Newman, Gordon, & Warner, 1973). (Once stabilized on a maintenance dose, patients can drive cars and trucks, operate heavy machinery and perform complex tasks, even at high daily doses of methadone.) Compared to volunteers and college students with no history of substance abuse, methadone-maintained patients do not exhibit impaired functioning on psychomotor performance tests, measures of intelligence, attention span, driving ability, reaction time, and other abilities. Scores on tests of intelligence measured by the Wechsler Adult Intelligence Scale (WAIS) were found to be slightly higher after 10 years in treatment than at admission (Lowinson et al., 1992).

INTERACTIONS WITH OTHER MEDICATIONS

Methadone does not have any life-threatening interactions with other medications (Lowinson et al., 1992). Some medications, including rifampin, phenytoin, and carbamazepine significantly increase the metabolism of methadone and lead to opioid withdrawal symptoms (Kreek, 1976; Tong, Pond, Kreek, Jaffery, & Benowitz, 1981). Medications such as cimetidine that interfere with the metabolism of methadone by competitive inhibition at the cytochrome p-450 system in the liver can lead to higher and more sustained methadone levels. Opioid antagonists, mixed agonist-antagonists, and partial opioid agonists can also precipitate opioid withdrawal symptoms when administered to methadone-maintained patients (Kreek, 1978).

FACTORS DETERMINING POSITIVE OUTCOMES IN METHADONE MAINTENANCE TREATMENT

Dose

The daily dose of methadone plays an important role in determining efficacy of methadone treatment. In general, higher methadone doses (greater than 50–60 mg daily) are associated with improved retention and decreased illicit opioid use. In some studies, daily doses of 80 mg or more (Caplehorn & Bell, 1991) are associated with the lowest rates of recent use of heroin (Ball & Ross, 1991). The United States General Accounts Office (1990) reviewed 24 programs and concluded that 60 mg of methadone is a minimum effective dose and that lower doses (20–40 mg) are generally inadequate. Within the past several years, three double-blind, randomized clinical trials have demonstrated the dose-dependent efficacy of methadone and confirmed the importance of using higher methadone doses to achieve greatest retention and reduction in illicit opioid use. Plasma levels of methadone may be useful on occasion to assess the adequacy of a methadone dose.

A starting dose of 20–30 mg can be safely administered to the patient with active opioid dependence (Martin, Payte, & Zweben, 1991). In the interest of safety, the initial dose of methadone should never exceed 40 mg (Lowinson et al., 1992). The dose should then be gradually increased by 10 mg every 2–3 days until a stable maintenance dose of methadone has been reached. The maintenance dose of methadone should be determined by an experienced physician taking into account objective findings, patient report, and response to treatment (Payte & Khuri,1993).

Length of Time in Treatment

For methadone maintenance, maximum improvement often occurs gradually over time, pointing to the importance of delivering rehabilitative services for the patient. Early in treatment patients generally need the most inten-

sive level of services, including medical and psychiatric evaluations and treatment, and help with housing, legal, financial, and domestic difficulties. Once stabilized in treatment, many patients cease illicit drug use, maintain full time employment, and require only minimal services. Even with reduced contact, many patients continue to feel a strong sense of connection with their methadone program and are reassured by the knowledge that they can seek help and increase contact if necessary.

An important question for patients in the late phase of treatment is whether detoxification should be a treatment goal, and if it is, when it should be attempted. The high rate of relapse to illicit opioid use following discontinuation of methadone maintenance treatment and the morbidity and mortality associated with relapse provide a compelling rationale for many patients to remain in long-term, open-ended maintenance treatment. Follow-up studies on patients who have been successful in methadone maintenance treatment demonstrate relapse rates between 20% to 50% during the first 3 years following discharge. Overall, 70% to 80% of patients relapse following discharge, with the numbers being higher among patients who were discharged for failing to comply with the program regulations (Schottenfeld & Kleber, 1995). Multiple factors contribute to the high rate of relapse following discharge from methadone maintenance treatment, including re-experiencing of opioid cravings and the physical and psychological symptoms associated with the protracted abstinence syndrome (Dole, 1988; Kreek, 1973, 1986; Martin & Jasinski, 1969).

Discontinuation of methadone for patients who are benefiting from maintenance treatment should be evaluated on an individual basis. Patients who decide to discontinue methadone maintenance should be advised about the potential risks and offered postmethadone treatment, including possibly treatment with an opiate blocker (e.g., naltrexone) and support services to facilitate the transition and reduce the risk of relapse.

BEHAVIORAL REINFORCEMENTS: AN INTEGRAL PART OF METHADONE MAINTENANCE TREATMENT

Successful treatment of patients on methadone maintenance includes an organized program structure and utilization of positive and aversive contingencies available. Positive reinforcements include being promoted through progressive levels of program standing or status, earning take-home-bottle privileges, reducing the number of mandatory counseling hours that the patient has to attend, allowing patients greater flexibility in their lives and the ability to travel, and the eligibility to serve on patient advocacy committees (Schmitz, Rhoades, & Grabowski, 1994). Aversive contingencies can also be used to motivate change and shape patient behavior (Kidorf, Brooner, & King, 1996; Saxon, Calsyn, Kivlahan, & Roszell, 1993). Aversive contingencies commonly include being placed on "program probation" or on "bad standing," revoking of take-home-bottle privileges, having to meet with staff "appeal committees," and the threat of detoxification.

Most programs implicitly utilize a variety of these positive reinforcements and aversive contingencies to motivate patients to refrain from illicit drug use, participate in counseling, medical care, and vocational programs, and find employment. As with all behavioral interventions, however, maximum benefits are achieved when the most salient contingencies are applied consistently and immediately in response to specified behaviors.

Recently, the addition of a voucher-based contingency contracting program to standard methadone maintenance treatment has been demonstrated to lead to substantial reductions in illicit drug use (Silverman et al., 1996). In these voucher programs, patients can earn vouchers worth specific amounts of money for producing clean urine, or in some programs, for participation in counselling (Iguchi, Lamb, Belding, Husgand, & Platt, 1996; Meek et al., 1996; Tusel et al.,1996). Typically the value of the voucher is increased for each consecutive drug-free urine, thus providing an incentive for patients to achieve more prolonged periods of sustained abstinence. Additional research is needed to evaluate the optimal schedule of reinforcement and to evaluate the effectiveness to this approach in more widespread clinical use.

It is important to enforce behavioral reinforcements in an empathic, respectful, nonjudgmental, clear, consistent, and supportive way. Patients need to understand that entering methadone maintenance and following program regulations is a choice on their part and that they have to take responsibility for their choices both within the methadone program and in other aspects of their lives. A strong and positive therapeutic alliance between the patient and his or her treatment team is crucial to successful methadone treatment. The methadone counselor plays a key role in engaging and keeping the patient in treatment. Despite initial resistance, patients often come to internalize the psychological, behavioral, and spiritual principles learned in substance abuse counseling and become self-motivated to lead productive, drug-free lives.

COMORBID SUBSTANCE ABUSE AND METHADONE MAINTENANCE

Polysubstance abuse is a common phenomenon among patents entering methadone maintenance programs. The most commonly abused substances among methadone patients are alcohol, benzodiazepines, and cocaine.

Alcohol and Benzodiazepines

Abuse or dependence on alcohol, benzodiazepines, or other sedatives is a common problem among opioid dependent patients that often complicates methadone treatment. In a study of 385 treatment seeking opioid dependent patients, Rounsaville et al. found lifetime and current rates of alcoholism to be 36.9% and 16.4% respectively (Rounsaville, Wiessman, Wilber, & Kleber, 1983). Alcoholism often continues after the patient enters a methadone maintenance program, with 17% to 30% of patients on methadone maintenance actively abusing alcohol. The pattern of alcohol abuse in this population is often cyclical, with periods of abstinence alternating with periods of heavy drinking (Bickel & Rizzuto, 1991). Alcohol abuse is a common cause of administrative termination from methadone maintenance and is a leading cause of death among patients in methadone maintenance programs.

Treatment of comorbid alcohol or benzodiazepine dependence among patients on methadone maintenance may require pharmacological and psychosocial approaches. Positive and aversive contingencies can be used to motivate the patient to stop using these illicit substances. Physiologically dependent patients need a medically supervised detoxification. Maintenance on disulfiram, taken by the patient under supervision by a methadone nurse at the clinic, may also be indicated (Bickel et al., 1988–1989). Regular monitoring with breathalyzer tests and urine toxicology screening ensures early detection of the problem and ongoing assessment of the patient's condition. Increasing the frequency of individual and group therapy and encouraging the patient to get involved in a 12-step program can help the patient to feel supported and encourage him or her to stop using alcohol or benzodiazepines (Bickel, Marion, & Lowinson, 1987; Schottenfeld & Kleber, 1995).

Cocaine

Comorbid cocaine abuse and dependence among methadone-maintained patients has reached alarming proportions, with rates of up to 60% in some urban, inner-city methadone clinics (Chambers, Taylor, & Moffett, 1972; Kosten, Rounsaville, & Kleber, 1987; Kosten, Rounsaville, & Kleber, 1988). Several patterns of cocaine use exist among opioid dependent patients, including the use of heroin after using cocaine to minimize some of the unpleasant effects of the cocaine high such as paranoia and anxiety, the use of cocaine after using heroin to counteract the sedating effects of heroin, and the intravenous use of cocaine and heroin together. Addicts will inject themselves with a mixture of cocaine and heroin ("speedballing, tango and cash, boy and girl") (Jaffe, 1992; Jainiski & Preston, 1986). Thus far, no pharmacological agent has demonstrated clear efficacy in the treatment of cocaine abuse and dependence (Rao, Ziedonis, & Kosten, 1995). Treatment of the cocaine-abusing methadone-maintained patient should therefore be more focused on psychosocial therapies, with pharmacological agents being utilized adjunctively as needed. In the meantime, the search for effective pharmacological and psychosocial treatments to treat cocaine abuse among methadone-maintained patients continues.

Nicotine

Large numbers of methadone-maintained patients have comorbid nicotine dependence that often remains unaddressed by their treatment team. With the widespread awareness of mortality and morbidity associated with cigarette smoking and a growing awareness among substance abuse treatment centers of nicotine as an addictive, harmful drug, there is a clear need to include pharmacological and psychosocial treatments for smoking as part of the interventions offered in a methadone program (Campbell, Wander, Stark, & Hobert, 1995).

SPECIAL PATIENT POPULATIONS WITHIN METHADONE MAINTENANCE PROGRAMS

Psychiatric Illness among Patients on Methadone Maintenance

The most common psychiatric disorders found among opioid-dependent patients are depression, anxiety disorders, and antisocial personality disorder (Darke, Swift, & Hall, 1994; Rounsaville, Wiessman, Kleber, & Wilber, 1982). Depressive disorders among opioid dependent patients have been shown to have a correlation with the severity of opioid dependence, and their coexistence is strongly associated with relapse into drug use (Rounsaville, Kosten, Wiessman, & Kleber, 1986). Lifetime prevalence of major depression, anxiety disorders and antisocial personality disorder is reported as 53.9 %, 5.4 % and 26.5%, respectively, among patients on methadone maintenance (Rounsaville et al.,1982).

Proper screening, diagnosis, and treatment of comorbid psychiatric disorders among substance-dependent patients can improve the prognosis of both illnesses (Ziedonis, Rao, & Preisig, 1994). Diagnosing and treating psychiatric illnesses in the context of substance dependence is a complex task in any clinical setting. However, methadone maintenance offers certain unique advantages. Patients early in treatment generally come to the methadone clinic every day, and they can be stabilized and evaluated for both psychiatric symptoms as well as any ongoing substance use far more closely than in most other outpatient settings. Methadone maintenance also allows the dually diagnosed person's psychiatric symptoms to be followed over a period of months or years while they are free of illicit drugs. Finally there are some reports suggesting that methadone has some efficacy for the treatment of psychosis (Brizer, Hartman, Sweeney, & Millman, 1985; Millman, 1982) .

Management of methadone-maintained patients with comorbid psychiatric illnesses may include both psychotherapy and pharmacologic treatment. In general, potentially addictive medications such as benzodiazepines should be avoided because of their significant abuse liability in this population. Nonaddictive alternatives such as antidepressants or buspirone are generally preferred to treat anxiety disorders. Integration of psychiatric and substance abuse treatment is vital to the successful treatment of the dually diagnosed patient, with either psychiatric treatment within the methadone program itself, or with ongoing communication between the patient's psychiatric and methadone treatment teams.

It is important to educate substance abuse counselors in methadone programs about psychiatric illnesses so that they can properly screen their patients, make referrals to local mental health centers, and work on an ongoing basis with the psychiatric treatment community. Staff in the methadone program should be educated about the mechanism of action and the nonaddictive nature of commonly used psychotropic medications, (e.g., antidepressants) as the counselor's attitudes toward psychiatric illness and treatment can be an important factor in patient compliance.

HIV/AIDS Issues among Patients on Methadone Maintenance

The Role of Methadone Maintenance in HIV Education and Prevention

Methadone maintenance plays an important role in prevention of HIV infection by reducing continued intravenous drug use among opiate-dependent patients (Hartel, Selwyn, Schoenbaums, Klein, & Friedland, 1988). The use of infected (dirty or shared) needles by the intravenous using population is a major mechanism for the transmission of HIV, in the United States and other parts of the world (Center for Disease Control, 1989a, 1989b; Des Jarlais, Friedman, & Stone, 1988; Downs et al., 1990; Hahn, Onorato, Jones, & Dougherty, 1989; Haverkos & Edelman, 1988; Moss et al., 1988; New York City Dept. of Health, 1990; Pan American Health Organization, 1988; Sato, Chin, & Mann, 1989; Selik, Haverkos, & Curran, 1984; World Health Organization, 1990). Methadone maintenance helps to decrease rates of injection drug use as well as other high-risk behaviors such as prostitution, thus contributing to controlling the spread of HIV and AIDS (Bellis, 1993; Caplehorn & Ross, 1995; Longshore, Hsieh, & Anglin, 1994; Moss et al., 1994). One study of 152 in-treatment, and 103 out-of-treatment opiate-dependent intravenous drug users found that the methadone maintained group had a seroconversion rate of 3.5% as compared to a rate of 22% among individuals who were not in treatment (Metzer et al., 1993). Research has also indicated that even those patients who used drugs while in methadone treatment had a reduced incidence of needle sharing (Longshore, Hsieh, Danila, & Anglin, 1993). Methadone treatment also provides an important opportunity to counsel patients about behaviors that are also significant contributing factors to the transmission of HIV, such as engaging in unsafe sexual practices, exchanging sex for drugs, or turning to prostitution as a way to earn the large amounts of money needed to support drug use.

The HIV-Infected Patient on Methadone Maintenance

Methadone maintenance can also facilitate engagement of the HIV-infected opiate-dependent patient into regular medical treatment at a primary care center or infectious disease clinic. Patient participation in HIV treatment generally improves once the patient has stopped using illicit drugs and has a stable place to live. Eliminating intravenous drug use also helps reduce the risk of contracting hepatitis B, C, or staphylococcal infections. Nutritional status is also often improved during substance abuse treatment. Compliance with HIV treatment can be made an integral part of the treatment plan with reinforcements for keeping medical appointments.

Several methadone clinics have developed specialized programs within the larger program, employing staff specially trained in HIV issues. Examples of such programs are the Holistic Maintenance Service in the APT/Yale University Methadone Maintenance Program and at St. Clare's Hospital in New York City (Lowinson, 1992). Recent research has indicated that methadone may increase the serum levels of AZT (Schwartz et al., 1992). Further research is needed to explore the interaction between antiretrovirals and methadone and to study other clinical issues affecting the HIV-positive methadone-maintained patient.

METHADONE MAINTENANCE FOR PREGNANT WOMEN

Heroin addiction by pregnant women is associated with numerous obstetrical complications, including spontaneous abortion, amnionitis, chorioamnionitis, intrauterine growth retardation, placental insufficiency, postpartum hemorrhage, preeclampsia, premature labor, premature rupture of membranes, eclampsia, toxemia, septic thrombophlebitis, abruptio placentae, and intrauterine death (Finnegan, 1978). Many of the complications seen in infants born to heroin-dependent mothers are a result of low birth weight and prematurity. Inadequate or absent prenatal care is another major factor determining mortality rates among infants born to drug-dependent mothers (Finnegan, Reeser, & Connaughton, 1977). In general, rates of morbidity and mortality are significantly reduced among heroin-dependent pregnant woman treated with methadone maintenance compared to those for heroin-dependent women not in treatment (Blinick, Inturrise, Jerez, & Wallach, 1973; Connaughton, Reeser, Schut, & Finnegan, 1977; Jarvis & Schnoll, 1994; Kandall et al., 1977). Maintenance treatment helps the pregnant woman to get regular prenatal care, stop using illicit substances, lead a more stable life, improve her nutritional status, and receive parenting education during her pregnancy. Maintenance on methadone also prevents the pregnant woman from repeated experience of medically unsupervised withdrawal, which may contribute to the risk for spontaneous trimester abortions.

Infants born to methadone-maintained mothers need to be monitored and treated for symptoms of opioid withdrawal. Opioid withdrawal in the newborn infant may be delayed in onset and last for several weeks, because methadone is stored in the infant's liver, lung, spleen and kidney, thus slowing down its elimination from the body (Jaffe & Martin, 1985). Signs of withdrawal include a high-pitched cry, decreased sleep and appetite, yawning, sweating, skin excoriation, tremor, increased muscle tone, mottling and potentially life-threatening convulsions. One study of infants born to mothers on methadone maintenance (mean daily dose of 45 mg) found signs and symptoms of opiate withdrawal in 80% of the infants, less than one third of whom needed therapy (Davis, Chappel, Mejia-Zelaya, & Madden, 1975). Because onset of withdrawal may be delayed for more than 1 week following discharge, the mother should be educated about the need to monitor the baby for signs of opioid withdrawal and instructed to bring the baby back to the hospital if any such symptoms occur. Initial opioid withdrawal symptoms in the neonate can be managed with nonpharmacological interventions such as demand feeding, swaddling, infrequent handling, and monitoring the infant's fluid electrolyte balance. The neonatal abstinence scoring system developed by Finnegan is a useful tool in monitoring and treating opiate withdrawal in the neonate (Finnegan, 1986; Finnegan, Emich, & Connaughton, 1973). When pharmacotherapy is indicated, opioid withdrawal in the newborn can be treated with phenobarbital or paregoric (Finnegan, 1990; Kandal, Doberczak, Mauer, Strashun, & Korts, 1983).

Various investigators have studied the correlation between maternal methadone dose and severity of opioid withdrawal in the neonate (Harper, Solish, Feingold, Gersten-Woolf, & Sokal, 1977; Madden et al., 1977). During pregnancy the increased volume of distribution may result in a need for higher methadone doses or split-dose administration, especially during the third trimester. Dose determination for the pregnant woman on methadone maintenance should be clinically determined, weighing the risks of continued maternal heroin abuse against that of increased severity of opiate withdrawal in the infant.

Treatment of the pregnant woman on methadone maintenance who continues to use illicit drugs is a clinically challenging task. Psychosocial therapies should be utilized to help the patient to remain clean from illicit drugs and engage in substance abuse treatment and prenatal care. In some instances, hospitalization may be required for women who continue to use illicit drugs during pregnancy.

12-STEP PROGRAMS AND METHADONE MAINTENANCE

Involvement in 12-step programs (Alcoholics Anonymous, Narcotics Anonymous) can be an integral part of substance abuse treatment. Engaging the methadone patient in a 12-step program, however, presents special challenges that are not encountered in other types of substance abuse programs. Not all 12-step meetings are accepting of the heroin-dependent person who has chosen treatment with methadone. Peers in NA or AA meetings may have stereotyped views of methadone as an addictive, mind-altering drug and may be critical of patients on methadone maintenance and not consider them to be truly in recovery. It is important to send the patient to meetings that are known to have a friendly attitude toward people on methadone maintenance. The treatment team can educate the patient and help him or her overcome any guilt and shame about being on a replacement opiate. Several methadone clinics hold NA meetings within the clinic premises. Attending NA meetings at the clinic can be an important initial step as well as a bridge that involves the patients in the larger 12-step organization in the community. The meetings can be a conduit for education about methadone maintenance to be passed along to 12-step groups and help dispel negative stereotypes and myths. People entering treatment can be teamed up with a "buddy" within the methadone program who is doing well in treatment and is involved in a 12-step program, and who can take the patient to a meeting and help him or her to make connections within the local 12-step community. Involvement in a 12-step program is especially crucial for patients who are planning to discontinue methadone in order to provide them with treatment and support outside the clinic.

TAKE-HOME MEDICATION

Take-home medication remains an integral part of methadone maintenance. Bottle privileges may provide positive reinforcement for the patient to stop using illicit drugs, engage in counseling, and find employment (Kidorf, Stitzer, Brooner, & Goldberg, 1994; Kidorf, Stitzer, & Griffiths, 1995; Saxon, Calsyn, Wells, & Stanton, 1996; Stitzer, Iguchi, & Felch, 1992). Take-home bottles also allow patients the freedom to travel or work away from the program. As patients progress in their treatment, bottle privileges also allow patients to wean themselves from daily contact with the clinic or other patients. Finally, providing bottles to patients helps to contain costs within methadone clinics, because the patients do not have to be medicated by a nurse on a daily basis.

Methadone programs need to take special precautions, however, to prevent illegal selling of take-home methadone. Regulations limit the provisions of bottles to patients who have discontinued illicit drug use. Some programs have initiated additional precautions such as "bottle recall." In some programs, patients who obtain "bottle privileges" call the methadone program each night after clinic hours and listen to a recorder message reading off serial numbers. If the patient's number is listed, all methadone bottles for the remainder of the week, both full and empty, must be returned to the clinic the next day. The bottles are examined by a nurse, and bottles may be sent to the laboratory for testing of contents to ensure that they contain the patient's full daily dose of methadone.

PAIN MANAGEMENT AND METHADONE MAINTENANCE

Individuals who require opiate analgesia should continue to receive their usual daily maintenance dose of methadone in addition to opiates for analgesia. Partial agonists such as buprenorphine, butorphanol tartrate, and nalbuphine should not be administered as they can precipitate opiate withdrawal in the person on methadone. Due to tolerance, patients may require larger doses of opioid analgesics or more frequent administration.

Undermedication of pain for methadone-maintained people, is unfortunately, all too common because physicians may hold erroneous beliefs that methadone maintenance provides analgesic effects or that prescribing opiate analgesics for acute pain conditions will cause the patient to relapse into drug use (Portenoy & Payne, 1992). Undermedicating can make the person anxious, fearful, and angry and induce him or her to leave the hospital against medical advice (Zwebe & Payte, 1990). Relapse into active heroin use is unlikely to occur if the prescribing physician is aware of the person's history of addiction and switches to nonnarcotic analgesics as soon as clinically feasible (Kantor, Cantor, & Tom, 1980; Payte & Khuri, 1993). Management of chronic pain in methadone-maintained individuals poses additional challenges. Adequate pain relief in terminally ill patients with severe pain may require chronic administration of long-acting morphine,(e.g., MS Contin) or additional doses of methadone throughout the day. The use of opiates for analgesia in nonterminal patients with chronic pain is controversial and should usually be avoided for patients in methadone programs.

CONCLUSION

Methadone maintenance is a well-established and effective treatment modality for opioid-dependent people that has been successfully used in the United States and other parts of the world. Successful treatment requires utilization of adequate methadone doses, sufficient time to allow recovery, and provision of medical, psychiatric, and vocational treatment. Methadone maintenance programs play a vital role in fighting the AIDS epidemic by reducing intravenous drug use and high-risk sexual behaviors associated with heroin dependence. Long-term, high-dose methadone maintenance is medically safe and does not affect an individual's cognitive or intellectual functioning. Education about the benefits of methadone maintenance among the general population, substance abuse clinicians working in other settings, and public officials can go a long way in dispelling negative myths and stereotypes, thus helping to save more lives by expanding the availability of methadone programs to opioid-dependent individuals.

REFERENCES

Appel, P. W., & Gordon, N. B. (1976). Digit-symbol performance in methadone treated ex-heroin addicts. *American Journal of Psychiatry, 133,* 1337–1340.

Babst, D. V., Newman, S., Gordon, N. B., & Warner, A. (1973). *Driving records of methadone maintained patients in New York State.* New York State Narcotic Control Commission. Albany, NY.

Ball, J. C., & Ross, A. (1991). The effectiveness of methadone maintenance treatment. New York: Springer-Verlag.

Baselt, R. C. (1982). *Disposition of toxic drugs and chemicals in man.* Davis, CA: Biomedical.

Bellis, D. J. (1993). Reduction of AIDS risk among 41 heroin addicted female street prostitutes: Effects of free methadone maintenance. *Journal of Addictive Diseases, 12,* 7–23.

Bickel, W. K., Marion, I., & Lowinson, J. (1987). The treatment of alcoholic methadone patients: A review. *Journal of Substance Abuse Treatment, 4,* 15–19.

Bickel, W. K., & Rizzuto, P. (1991). The naturalistic oscillating pattern of alcohol consumption in alcoholic methadone patients. *Journal of Studies on Alcohol, 52,* 454.

Bickel, W. K., Rizzuto, P., Zielony, R. D., Klobas, J., Pangiosonlis, P., Mernit, R., & Knight, W. F. (1988–1989). Combined behavioral and pharmalogical treatment of alcoholic methadone patients. *Journal of Substance Abuse Treatment,* 161–171.

Blinick, G., Inturrisi, C. E., Jerez, E., & Wallach, R. C. (1973). Methadone maintenance, pregnancy and progeny. *Journal of the American Medical Association, 225,* 477.

Blumberg, R. D., & Pruesser, D. F. (1972). *Drug abuse and driving performance.* (Final Report Control DOT-HS-009-1-184). Washington, DC: U.S. Department of Transportation.

Brizer, D. A., Hartman, N., Sweeney, J., & Millman, R. B. (1985). Effects of methadone plus neuroleptics in treatment-resistant chronic paranoid schizophrenia. *American Journal of Psychiatry, 142,* 1106–1107.

Campbell, B. K., Wander, N., Stark, M. J., & Hobert, T. (1995). Treating cigarette smoking in drug-abusing clients. *Journal of Substance Abuse Treatment, 12,* 89–94.

Capelhorn, J. R., & Bell, J. (1991). Methadone dosage and retention of patients in maintenance treatment. *Medical Journal of Australia, 154,* 195–199.

Caplehorn, J. R., & Ross, M. V. (1995). Methadone maintenance and the likelihood of risky needle-sharing. *International Journal of the Addictions, 30,* 685–698.

Centers for Disease Control. (1989a). Update: Acquired immunodeficiency syndrome—United States, 1981–1988. *MMWR, 38,* 229–236.

Centers for Disease Control. (1989b). First 100,000 cases of acquired immunodeficiency syndrome—United States. *MMWR, 38,* 561–563.

Chambers, C. D., Taylor, W. J., & Moffett, A. D. (1972). The incidence of cocaine abuse among methadone maintenance patients. *International Journal of the Addictions, 7,* 427–441.

Connaughton, J. F., Reeser, D., Schut, J., & Finnegan, L. P. (1977). Perinatal addiction: outcome and management. *American Journal of Obstetrics and Gynecology, 129,* 679.

Cooper, J. B. (1988). Methadone treatment in the United States. In A. Awni & J. Westmermeyer (Eds.), *Methadone in the management of opioid dependence: Programs and policies around the world.* Geneva, Switzerland: World Health Organizations.

Darke, S., Swift, W., & Hall, W. (1994). Prevalence, severity and correlates of psychological morbidity among methadone maintenance clients. *Addiction, 89,* 211–217.

Davis, R. C., Chappel, J. N., Mejia-Zelaya, A., & Madden, J. (1975). Clinical observations on methadone-maintained pregnancies. In R. D. Harbison (Ed.), *Perinatal addiction* (pp. 101–112). New York: Spectrum.

Des Jarlais, D. C., Friedman, S. R., & Stone, R. L. (1988). HIV infection and intravenous drug use: Critical issues in transmission dynamics, infection outcomes, and prevention. *Reviews of Infectious Diseases, 10,* 151–158.

Dole, V. P. (1980). Addictive behavior. *Scientific American, 234,* 138–154.

Dole, V. P. (1988). Implications of methadone maintenance for theories of narcotic addiction. *Journal of the American Medical Association, 260,* 3025–3029.

Dole, V. P., Nyswander, M. E., & Kreek, M. J. (1966). Narcotic blockade. *Archives of Internal Medicine, 118,* 304–309.

Downs, A. M., Ancelle-Park, R. A., Costagliola, D. C., Rigaut, J. P., & Brunet, J. B. (1990, June). *Monitoring and short-term forecasting of AIDS in Europe* (Abstract F.C.220) VI International Conference on AIDS, San Francisco, CA.

Federal Register. December 15, 1972, 37.16790.

Finnegan, L. P. (Ed.). (1978). *Drug dependence in pregnancy: Clinical management of mother and child.* A manual for medical professionals and paraprofessionals prepared for the National Institute on Drug Abuse, Services Research Branch, Rockville, MD. Washington, DC: U.S. Government Printing Office.

Finnegan, L. P. (1986). Neonatal abstinence syndrome: Assessment and pharmacotherapy. In F. F. Rualtelli & B. Granati (Eds.), *Neonatal therapy: An update.* New York: Elsiever Science.

Finnegan, L. P., & Ehlrich, S. M. (1990). Maternal drug use during pregnancy: Evaluation and pharmacotherapy for neonatal abstinence. *Modern Methods of Pharmacological Testing and Evaluations of Drugs and Abuse, 6,* 255.

Finnegan, L. P., Emich, J. P., & Connaughton, J. F. (1973). Abstinent score in the treatment of the infants of drug dependent mothers. *Pediatric Research, 7,* 319.

Finnegan, L. P., Reeser, D. S., & Connaughton, J. F. (1977). The effects of maternal drug dependence on neonatal mortality. *Drug and Alcohol Dependence, 2,* 131.

Gearing, F. R., & Schweitzer, M. D. (1974). An epidemiological evaluation of long-term methadone maintenance treatment for heroin addiction. *American Journal of Epidemiology, 100,* 101–112.

Goldstein, A. (1971). Blind dosage comparisons and other studies in a large methadone program. *Journal of Psychedelic Drugs, 4,* 177–181.

Gordon, N. B. (1976). Influence of narcotic drugs on highway safety. *Accident Analysis and Prevention, 8,* 3–7.

Gordon, N. B., & Lipset, J. S. (1976, September). *Intellectual and functional status of methadone patients after nearly ten years of treatment.* Internal report, the Rockefeller University and New York State Officer of Drug Abuse Services. Presented at the 85th annual convention of the American Psychological Association, Washington, DC.

Hahn, R. A., Onorato, I. M., Jones, T. S., & Dougherty, J. (1989). Prevalence of HIV infection among intravenous drug users in the United States. *Journal of the American Medical Association, 261,* 2677–2684.

Harper, R. G., Solish, G., Feingold, E., Gersten-Woolf, N. A., & Sokal, M. M. (1977). Maternal ingested methadone, body fluid methadone and the neonatal withdrawal syndrome. *American Journal of Obstetrics and Gynecology, 129,* 417.

Hartel, D., Selwyn, P. A., Schoenbaums, E. E., Klein, R. S., & Friedland, G. H. (1988). *Methadone maintenance treatment and reduced risk of AIDS and AIDS-specific mortality in intravenous drug users* (Abstract 8526). 4th International Conference on AIDS, Stockholm, Sweden.

Haverkos, H. W., & Edelman, R. (1988). The epidemiology of acquired immunodeficiency syndrome among heterosexuals.

Journal of the American Medical Association, 260, 1922–1929.

Iguchi, M. Y., Lamb, R. J., Belding, M. A., Husband, S. D., & Platt, J. J. (1996). An evaluation of three contingency management protocols in a methadone maintenance program. In L. S. Harris (Ed.), *Problems of Drug Dependence 1995: Proceedings of the 57th Annual Scientific Meeting, The College on Problems of Drug Dependence* (NIDA Research Monograph 162).

Inturrisi, C. E., & Vereby, K. (1972). The levels of methadone in the plasma in methadone maintenance. *Clinical Pharmacology and Therapeutics, 13,* 633–637.

Isbell, H. (1948). Methods and results of studying experimental human addiction to the newer synthetic analgesics. *Annals of the New York Academy of Sciences, 51,* 108.

Isbell, H., & Vogel, V. (1949). The addiction liability of methadone (Amidone, Dolophine, 10820) and its use in the treatment of the morphine abstinence syndrome. *American Journal of Psychiatry, 105,* 909.

Jaffe, J. H. (1970). Further experience with methadone in the treatment of narcotic users. *International Journal of the Addictions, 5,* 375–389.

Jaffe, J. H. (1992). Opiates: Clinical aspects. In J. H. Lowinson, P. Ruiz, & R. B. Millman (Eds.), *Substance abuse. A comprehensive textbook* (2nd ed.). Baltimore: Williams and Wilkins.

Jaffe, J. H., & Martin, W. R. (1985). Opioid analgesics and antagonists. In A. G. Gilman, L. S. Goodman, T. W. Rall, & F. Murad (Eds.), *Goodman and Gilman's. The pharmacological basis of therapeutics* (7th ed., p. 518). New York: Macmillan.

Jainiski, D. R., & Preston, K. (1986). Evaluation of mixtures of morphine and D-amphetamine for subjective and physiological effects. *Drug and Alcohol Dependence, 17,* 1–13.

Jarvis, M. A., & Schnoll, S. H. (1994). Methadone treatment during pregnancy. *Journal of Psychoactive Drugs. 26,* 155–161.

Kandall, S. R., Albin, S., Gartner, L. M., Lee, K., Eidelman, A. I., & Lowinson, J. (1977). The narcotic dependent mother: Fetal and neonatal consequences. *Early Human Development, 1,* 159.

Kandall, S. R., Doberczak, T. M., Mauer, K. R., Strashun, R. H., & Korts, D. C. (1983). Opiates v CNS depressant therapy in neonatal drug abstinence syndrome. *American Journal of Diseases of Children, 137,* 378.

Kantor, T. G., Cantor, R., & Tom, E. (1980). A study of hospitalized surgical patients on methadone maintenance. *Drug and Alcohol Dependence. 6,* 163–173.

Kidorf, M. S., Brooner, R. K., & King, V. L. (1996). Behavioral contingent pharmacotherapy for opioid abusers: An outpatient randomized clinical trial. In L. S. Harris (Ed.), *Problems of Drug Dependence 1995: Proceedings of the 57th Annual Scientific Meeting, The College on Problems of Drug Dependence.* (NIDA Research Monograph 162).

Kidorf, M., Stitzer, M. L., Brooner, R. K., & Goldberg, J. (1994). Contingent methadone take-home doses reinforce adjunct therapy attendance of methadone maintenance patients. *Drug and Alcohol Dependence, 36,* 221–226.

Kidorf, M., Stitzer, M. L., & Griffiths, R. R. (1995). Evaluating the reinforcement value of clinic-based privileges through a multiple choice procedure. *Drug and Alcohol Dependence, 39,* 167–172.

Kosten, T. R., Rounsaville, B. J., & Kleber, H. D. (1987). A 2.5 year follow-up of cocaine use among treated opioid addicts. Have our treatments helped? *Archives of General Psychiatry, 44* 281–284.

Kosten, T. R., Rounsaville, B. J., & Kleber, H.D. (1988). Antecedents and consequences of cocaine abuse among opioid addicts: A 2.5 year follow-up. *Journal of Nervous and Mental Disorders, 176,* 176–181.

Kreek, M. J. (1973). Medical safety and side effects of methadone in tolerant individuals. *Journal of the American Medical Association, 223,* 665–668.

Kreek, M. J. (1976). Drug interactions with methadone. *Annals of the New York Academy of Sciences, 281,* 350–371.

Kreek, M. J. (1978). Medical complications in methadone patients. *Annals of the New York Academy of Sciences, 311,* 110–134.

Kreek, M. J. (1986). Tolerance and dependence: Implications for the pharmacological treatment of addiction. In L. S. Harris (Ed.), *Problems of drug dependence* (NIDA Research Monograph 76). Rockville, MD: National Institute on Drug Abuse.

Longshore, D., Hsieh, S. C., & Anglin, M. D. (1994). Reducing HIV risk behavior among injection drug users: Effect of methadone maintenance treatment on number of sex partners. *International Journal of the Addictions, 29,* 741–757.

Longshore, D., Hsieh, S. C., Danila, V., & Anglin, M. D. (1993). Methadone maintenance and needle/syringe sharing. *International Journal of the Addictions, 28,* 983–96.

Lowinson, J. H., Marion, I. J., Joseph, H., & Dole, V. P. (1992). Methadone Maintenance. In J. H. Lowinson, P. Ruiz, & R. B. Millman (Eds.), *Substance abuse. A comprehensive textbook.* (2nd ed.). Baltimore: Williams and Wilkins.

Madden, J. D., Chappel, J. N., Suzpan, F., Gumpel, J., Meijia, A., & Davis, R. (1977). Observation and treatment of neonatal narcotic withdrawal. *American Journal of Obstetrics and Gynecology, 127,* 199.

Martin, J., Payte, J. T., & Zweben, J. E. (1991). Methadone maintenance treatment: A primer for physicians. *Journal of Psychoactive Drugs, 23,* 165–176.

Martin, W. R., & Jasinski, D. R. (1969). Physiological parameters of morphine dependence in man-tolerance, early abstinence, protracted abstinence. *Psychiatry Research, 7,* 9–17.

Meek, P. S., Piotrowski, N. A., Tusel, D. J., Henke, C. J., Hartz, D. T., Delucchi, K., Sees, K. L., & Hall, S. M. (1996). Cost-effectiveness of contingency contracting with opioid addicts in methadone treatment. In L. S. Harris (Ed.), *Problems of Drug Dependence 1995: Proceedings of the 57th Annual Scientific Meeting, The College on Problems of Drug Dependence, Inc* (NIDA Research Monograph 162, p. 161).

Metzger, D. S., Woody, G. E., McLellan, A. T., O'Brien, C. P., Druley, P., Navaline, H., DePhilippis, D., Stolley, P., & Abrutyn, E. (1993). Human immunodeficiency virus seroconversion among intravenous drug users in- and out-of-treatment: An 18-month prospective follow-up. *Journal of Acquired Immune Deficiency Syndrome, 6*, 1049–1056.

Millman, R. B. (1982). The provision of opioid therapy to the mentally ill: Conceptual and practical considerations. In K. Vereby (Ed.), *Opioids in mental illness: Theories, clinical observations and treatment possibilities* (pp. 178–185). New York: New York Academy of Sciences.

Moskowitz, H., & Sharma, S. (1979). *Skills performance in methadone patients and ex-addicts.* Presentation at the annual meeting of the American Psychological Association, New York City.

Moss, A. R. (1988). Epidemiology of AIDS in developed countries. *British Medical Bulletin, 44*, 56–67.

Moss, A. R., Vranzian, K., Gorter, R., Baccetti, P., Walters, J., & Osmond, D. (1994). HIV seroconversion in intravenous drug users in San Francisco, 1985–1990. *AIDS, 8*, 223–231.

New York City Department of Health. (1990, October 31). *AIDS surveillance update.*

Pan American Health Organization. (1988). AIDS situation in the Americas 1988. *Epidemiological Bulletin, 9*, 1–11.

Payte, J. T., & Khuri, E. T. (1993). Principles of methadone dose determination. In M. W. Parrino (Chair), *State methadone treatment guidelines. Treatment improvement protocol (TIP) series* (pp. 47–58). U.S. Department of Health and Human Services, Public Health Service, Substance Abuse and Mental Health Services Administration, Center for Substance Abuse Treatment.

Portenoy, R. K., & Payne, R. (1992). Acute and chronic pain. In J. H. Lowinson, P. Ruiz, & R. B. Millman (Eds.), *Substance abuse. A comprehensive textbook* (2nd ed.). Baltimore: Williams and Wilkins.

Rao, S., Ziedonis, D. M., & Kosten, T. R. (1995). The pharmacotherapy of cocaine dependence. *Psychiatric Annals, 25*, 5.

Rounsaville, B. J., Kosten, T. R., Wiessman, M. M., & Kleber, H. D. (1986). Prognostic significance of psychopathology in treated opiate addicts. *Archives of General Psychiatry, 43*, 739–745.

Rounsaville, B. J., Wiessman, M. M., Kleber, H. K., & Wilber, C. (1982). Heterogeneity of psychiatric diagnosis in treated opiate addicts. *Archives of General Psychiatry, 39.*

Rounsaville, B. J., Wiessman, M. M., Wilber, C., & Kleber, H. D. (1983). Identifying alcoholism in treated opiate addicts. *American Journal of Psychiatry, 140*, 764–766.

Sato, P. A., Chin, J., & Mann, J. M. (1989). Review of AIDS and HIV infection: Global epidemiology and statistics. *AIDS, 3* (Suppl. 1), S301–S307.

Saxon, A. J., Calsyn, D. A., Kivlahan, D. R., & Roszell, D. K. (1993). Outcome of contingency contracting for illicit drug use in a methadone maintenance program. *Drug and Alcohol Dependence, 31*, 205–214.

Saxon, A. J., Calsyn, D. A., Wells, A., & Stanton, V. (1996). Take-home doses as reinforcers of abstinence for methadone main-

tenance patients. In L. S. Harris (Ed.), *Problems of Drug Dependence 1995: Proceedings of the 57th Annual Scientific Meeting, The College on Problems of Drug Dependence.* (NIDA Research Monograph 162).

Schmitz, J. M., Rhoades, H., & Grabowski, J. (1994). A menu of potential reinforcers in a methadone maintenance program. *Journal of Substance Abuse Treatment, 11*, 425–431.

Schottenfeld, R . S., & Kleber, H. D. (1995). Methadone maintenance. In H. I. Kaplan, & B. J. Sadock (Eds.), *Comprehensive textbook of psychiatry. VI, Vol 2.* Baltimore: Williams and Wilkins.

Schwartz, E. L., Brechbuhl, A. B., Kahl, P., Miller, M. A., Selwyn, P. A., & Friedland, G. H. (1992). Pharmacokinetic interactions of zidovudine and methadone in intravenous drug-using patients with HIV infection. *Journal of Acquired Immune Deficiency Syndromes, 5*, 619–626.

Selik, R. M., Haverkos, H. W., & Curran, J. W. (1984). Acquired immune deficiency syndrome (AIDS) trends in the United States, 1978–1982. *American Journal of Medicine, 76*, 493–500.

Silverman, K., Higgins, S. T., Brooner, R. K., Montoya, I. D., Cone, E. J., Schuster, C. R., & Preston, K. L. (1996). Sustained cocaine abstinence in methadone maintenance patients through voucher-based reinforcement policy. *Archives of General Psychiatry, 53*, 409–415.

Stitzer, M. L., Iguchi, M. Y., & Felch, L. J. (1992). Contingent take-home incentive: Effects on drug use of methadone maintenance patients. *Journal of Consulting and Clinical Psychology, 60*, 927–934.

Tong, T. G., Pond, S. M., Kreek, M. J., Jaffery, N. F., & Benowitz, N. L. (1981). Phenytoin-induced methadone withdrawal. *Annals of Internal Medicine, 94*, 349–351.

Tusel, D. J., Piotrowski, N. A., Sees, K., Reilly, P. M., Banys, P., Meek, P., & Hall, S. M. (1996). Contingency contracting for illicit drug use with opioid addicts in methadone treatment. In L. S. Harris (Ed.), *Problems of Drug Dependence 1995: Proceedings of the 57th Annual Scientific Meeting, The College on Problems of Drug Dependence* (NIDA Research Monograph 162, p. 162).

United States General Accounting Office. (1990). *Methadone maintenance: Some treatment programs are not effective. Greater Federal oversight needed.* (Publication No. GAO/HRDE-90-104). Washington, DC: U.S. Government Printing Office.

World Health Organization Collaborating Centre on AIDS. (1990). AIDS surveillance in Europe. *Quarterly Report No. 26*, Paris.

Ziedonis, D. M., Rao, S., & Preisig, M. (1994). Comorbidity blues. *Employee Assistant Journal*, 7–34.

Zweben, J. E., & Payte, J. T. (1990). Methadone maintenance in the treatment of opioid dependence. A current perspective. *Western Journal of Medicine, 152*, 588–599.

CHAPTER 30

INPATIENT TREATMENT

Bryon H. Adinoff
Stacy Scannell
Lisa A. Carter
Kathleen Dohoney

The setting for alcohol and drug abuse treatment has been dramatically altered over the past two decades. In the 1980s, the traditional treatment setting typically consisted of a 28-day inpatient hospitalization. Presently, most substance abuse programs only provide inpatient treatment for 3–14 days, followed by some form of outpatient treatment. Inpatient treatment is now generally reserved only for those conditions that cannot be treated in a "lower level of care," such as a significant withdrawal syndrome or substance abuse complicated by coexisting psychiatric or medical disorders. Interestingly, both the traditional 28-day inpatient hospitalization and the newly popularized outpatient approaches have been dictated more by financial incentives than by empirically based research. Subsequently, the consequences of such a marked change in treatment approach is still in question and a topic for passionate debate (Annis, 1986; Nace, 1990).

In this review the pros and cons of this debate are discussed from both a clinical and economic perspective. We begin with a brief history of the development and changes that have occurred in inpatient substance abuse treatment, followed by a review of the empirical literature that explores the specific advantages and relevant indications for inpatient treatment. The clinical indications and finan-

cial considerations for inpatient and residential care will then be discussed. Three case vignettes will provide a bridge to discussing the rationale and potential pitfalls in obtaining third party payments for inpatient treatment.

It should be noted that the authors share a somewhat limited perspective, having all spent the majority of their careers working in public sector substance abuse treatment programs, particularly VA Medical Centers. Although many VA Medical Centers had until recently remained one of the last bastions of the 28-day inpatient program, this, too, has changed. Thus,the authors write with an eye toward the complications and costs of treating substance abuse patients with multiple social, psychiatric, and medical needs within the confines of limited treatment options.

HISTORICAL PERSPECTIVE

The grassroots founding of Alcoholics Anonymous in 1935 provided perhaps the first effective intervention for alcoholism. In doing so, AA also offered a socially sanctioned method for an alcoholic to obtain outside help. This assistance frequently consisted of a "sober house," where a recovering alcoholic would take another alcoholic into his or her home. The removal of an alcoholic from their drinking environment into a safe, alcohol-free setting was viewed as critical in the initial phase of recovery. In the late 1940s, the Minnesota model was developed from programs initiated at the Pioneer House (1948), Hazelden (1949), and Willmar State Hospital (1950) (Anderson, 1981). Treatment programs at these sites took place in hospital-based or residential settings and appear to have been the origin of the 28-day stay for substance abuse treatment. The Minnesota model consisted of several components, including group therapy, lectures, "recovering" addicts and alcoholics as counselors, multiprofessional staff, a therapeutic milieu, family counseling, and a 12-step program (Cook, 1988). "Therapeutic communities" appeared to develop independently from the Minnesota model, although the two share many philosophical elements (Breecher, 1972; Kennard 1983). Therapeutic communities were residential settings that promoted recovery by having alcoholics or addicts live together in a highly structured, alcohol- and drug-free environment. Therapeutic approaches included 12-step participation, confrontive group encounter sessions, and a modeling of responsibility and recovery-oriented behaviors.

Many addicts, however, were unable or unwilling to leave their families and other commitments for an extended period of time in order to live in hospital-based or residential settings. The creation of methadone maintenance clinics in the 1960s were subsequently welcomed by some as a viable treatment for heroin addiction that did not require an extended inpatient stay. However, this treatment choice was not without controversy. Whereas proponents asserted that a rather "benign dependence on methadone" allowed patients to experience a more productive lifestyle (Dole & Nyswander, 1965; Fields, 1992; Musto, 1992), others would contend that treatment should be aimed at stopping drug use instead of "catering" to it (Musto, 1992). As a result of these incompatible treatment approaches, participation in a methadone maintenance program precluded taking part in a therapeutic community. Thus the choice for an opiate-addicted patient was generally either a long-term, intensive stay in a therapeutic community or an outpatient methadone treatment program with limited concomitant therapy. This compartmentalization between strategies utilizing either pharmacologic support or requiring strict adherence to a "drug-free" lifestyle extended to the treatment of patients with coexisting psychiatric problems ("dual diagnosis" patients).

In the 1970s, the treatment of alcohol and drug abuse was incorporated into mainstream health care (Hubbard,

1992; Reader & Sullivan, 1992). The philosophies and character of the sober houses, therapeutic communities, and Minnesota model programs were transformed into a time-limited, inpatient treatment approach acceptable to both the lay public and the professional therapist. Although dissimilar in both philosophy and structure from treatment approaches used for other medical and psychiatric disorders, the "28-day substance abuse program" quickly emerged as the treatment of choice for alcohol dependence. With the onset of the cocaine and crack epidemics of the 1980s, this model was applied to the treatment of drug abuse as well. These programs typically utilized a Minnesota model format, coupled with relapse prevention, occupational and/or recreational therapy, group and/or individual psychotherapy, and vocational counseling or work therapy (Craig, Olson, & Shalton, 1990; Geller, 1992).

The rising popularity of the 28-day program can be attributed to its early financial success. As public awareness of alcoholism and drug abuse increased and private insurers and company programs provided economic incentives, the demand for these treatment programs peaked in the early 1980s. During this period of generous and largely uncontested third-party coverage of substance abuse programs, inpatient hospitalization was freely reimbursed by insurance companies, but approval for less expensive outpatient care was frequently denied. Hospital days for substance abuse treatment subsequently increased and free-standing programs proliferated. Between 1983 and 1988, total costs for inpatient substance abuse treatment increased almost 25%. In addition to generous reimbursement by insurance companies, a number of Employee Assistance Programs often insisted that employees participate in order to keep their jobs. The utilization of such private programs, however, dropped dramatically in the late 1980s as market forces changed. The realities of managed care provided an impetus to find more cost-effective methods of treating substance abuse. For example, the original rationale for the 28-day program as the optimal length of stay could not be justified on an empirical basis (Reader & Sullivan, 1992). Additionally, addiction therapists, insurance providers, and substance abuse researchers began to recognize that the same treatment protocol may not work for all addicted patients. Thus attempts were made to design the level of care and treatment approach to fit the particular needs of the patient. The heroin-addicted patient, for example, may benefit from both inpatient hospitalization and methadone maintenance. Or a patient requiring an intensive, confrontive approach may nevertheless best be served by remaining in the home environment while in outpatient treatment.

In order to provide different levels of care, alternatives to inpatient treatment developed. In the day treatment or partial hospitalization program, patients participate in rehabilitation programming during the day and return home each evening. Participation may vary from a few hours to several hours a day. Alternatively, patients may attend a treatment program only in the evenings and on weekends, allowing them to continue with both work and family responsibilities. A clear benefit of this mode of treatment is the cost saved by not requiring overnight hospitalization (Schneider & Googins, 1989). There has also been a growth of intensive outpatient treatment programs where patients may come for treatment 1–5 days a week for a limited number of hours a day. Length of participation may range anywhere from two to several weeks. An advantage of outpatient programs is that they tend to be more flexible and patients can continue to meet job and family commitments while participating in treatment.

Clearly, having alternatives available for patients who are appropriate for a lower level of care is a positive change in the recent history of substance abuse treatment. However, inpatient treatment continues to be a necessary and essential treatment modality for many substance abusers. Which substance abusers benefit from inpatient treatment, how long the treatment should be, and what kind of treatment they require remain critical questions.

OUTCOME STUDIES OF INPATIENT TREATMENT

The use of inpatient hospitalization for the treatment of substance use disorders has been the subject of much debate (Annis, 1986; Nace, 1990). This controversy has been fueled by differences in treatment philosophies, economic perspectives, and interpretations of the literature. Although a number of investigators have explored the efficacy of inpatient treatment, the resultant studies have not produced a definitive, generally accepted conclusion regarding the appropriateness and/or utility of inpatient treatment. This is due, at least in part, to the large number of critical factors that may influence or mitigate outcome findings, such as patient characteristics, programmatic characteristics of inpatient treatment and comparison treatment, length of treatment, patient experiences outside of or after treatment, time of evaluation in relation to treatment,

definition and measurement of outcome variables, and analysis and interpretation of data. Variables such as investigator orientation, funding sources, and demand characteristics must also be considered. In the following section we will review some of the most frequently cited studies of inpatient substance abuse treatment. In doing so, the strengths and flaws of these studies will be discussed.

Patient Characteristics

The weight of evidence from well-controlled clinical trials strongly suggests that outpatient treatment of heterogeneous groups of alcohol dependent patients produces an essentially equivalent outcome to inpatient treatment at substantially lower cost (Miller and Hester, 1986). A critical confounding factor, however, is that the use of heterogeneous samples can mask treatment effects for selected groups within the sample (Nace, 1990). This issue is generally referred to as "treatment matching," and has been reviewed elsewhere (Finney & Moos, 1986; Miller, 1989).

The importance of treatment matching was demonstrated by a frequently referenced study by Edwards et al. (1977), in which brief counseling was compared to intensive treatment. The study sample consisted of 100 men (all of whom were married or in a continuing cohabitation) referred to an outpatient alcoholism clinic. These men were referred from a wide range of sources, such as their general practitioner, Alcoholics Anonymous, or probation officer. Following admission to the clinic, the patients were randomly assigned to either an "advice" group or a "treatment" group. All patients were told they were suffering from alcoholism and total abstinence was recommended by the physician. The advice group patients were told in a supportive and constructive manner that they were personally responsible for attaining the treatment goal of abstinence rather than it being a problem that could be addressed by others. It was explained that no further appointments would be offered but that a staff member would contact them each month for news of progress. The treatment group patients were offered extensive outpatient therapy, including 12-step orientation, pharmacotherapy for detoxification and to maintain abstinence, and personal and conjoint counseling. If outpatient therapy was unsuccessful, the treatment group was offered inpatient treatment on a specialized alcohol treatment unit for approximately 6 weeks. At the end of 12 months, there were no significant differences between groups in drinking behavior or social adjustment. The conclusion drawn from these results was that a reasonably intensive and conventional treatment regimen conferred no additional benefit over a simple, inexpensive, and unobtrusive approach.

Orford, Oppenheimer, and Edwards (1976) reassessed this data of Edwards et al. (1977) with particular attention given to the severity of patients' alcoholism. In this reanalysis, patients were dichotomized into two distinct groups as a function of their addiction severity: (1) patients exhibiting loss of control and physical dependence ("gamma alcoholics") (Jellenik, 1960), suggesting a more severe level of alcohol dependence; and (2) patients with "psychological" dependence only ("nongamma alcoholics," primarily "alpha") (Jellenik, 1960), suggesting a lesser degree of alcohol dependence. The resultant analysis demonstrated that the nongamma alcoholics appeared to benefit from advice only, rather than intensive treatment, as reflected by rates of both abstinence and controlled drinking at the 2-year follow-up. On the other hand, the gamma alcoholics responded significantly better to intensive treatment than to just advice. This study thus demonstrates the complexity of influencing variables when using a heterogeneous sample. The more severely ill, gamma alcoholics tended to do well and nongamma alcoholics tended to do poorly with intensive, aggressive treatment. Advice only, however, was beneficial only to the less severely dependent, nongamma alcoholic patients. These results suggest that not only can specific treatments be more effective when matched to an identified patient population, but that a high-cost, time-intensive treatment may be less beneficial than an inexpensive, unobtrusive approach. Because the number of patients in the treatment group who required inpatient treatment was not discussed, it is not possible to ascribe differences in outcome specifically to inpatient hospitalization.

The role of psychiatric severity in a retrospective assessment of treatment matching was reported in 742 alcohol and drug addicted patients participating in one of six VAMC substance abuse programs (McLellan, Luborsky, Woody, O'Brien, & Druley, 1983). Two of the programs were outpatient and four were inpatient. Patients were divided into three distinct groups based on level of psychiatric severity as determined by the Addiction Severity Index (ASI) (McLellan, Luborsky, O'Brien, & Woody, 1980). Patients with low psychiatric severity generally demonstrated improvement regardless of the program type attended. On the other hand, patients with high psychiatric severity (pronounced, recurring symptoms) did poorly wherever they were treated. The results for patients with midrange psychiatric severity (significant symptoms

without recurrent history) were more equivocal. Whereas many midrange patients responded well to outpatient treatment, those with significant family, social, or legal problems tended to do better in an inpatient program.

In order to assess the clinical utility of these findings, McLellan, Woody, Luborsky, O'Brien, & Druley (1983) prospectively assigned patients to outpatient or inpatient treatment programs based on psychiatric severity. All patients were detoxified (presumably on an inpatient unit) prior to assessment. Patients with low psychiatric severity were assigned to outpatient treatment, unless they also experienced significant family and/or employment problems. Midrange patients were assigned to an outpatient or inpatient program based on their concurrent severity of drug abuse and legal, employment, family, and medical problems. Patients with high psychiatric severity were never recommended for either treatment. Patients in each program were considered as either "matched" or "mismatched" to treatment, as many patients did not go to the programs assigned. At the 6-month follow-up, patients who had been properly matched to inpatient treatment had significantly better outcomes—as measured by lower alcohol and drug use severity, fewer family problems, and less psychiatric impairment—than those who had been mismatched.

The importance of a "commonsense" approach to treatment matching must also be considered. Utilizing the Cleveland Admission, Discharge, and Transfer Criteria (Institute of Medicine, 1990), patients were retrospectively matched to inpatient or day treatment (McKay, McLellan, & Alterman, 1992). The Cleveland Criteria recommends inpatient hospitalization for patients with either significant psychiatric complications, life area impairments (violent when intoxicated, legal or EAP mandate to attend inpatient care), treatment resistance, loss of control/relapse crisis (evidenced by fewer than 5 days for alcohol or 10 days for cocaine abstinence in the preceding 30 days), or a nonsupportive recovery environment (as evidenced by seriously impaired social, family, or occupational environment). Outcome was assessed at 4 and 7 months with the ASI. The results did not reveal significant differences in patients who were "matched" to treatment according to the Cleveland Criteria. However, it does not appear intuitively obvious to the present authors why violence while intoxicated, legal or EAP mandate to attend inpatient care, treatment resistance (commonly considered to be an integral aspect of substance use disorders as opposed to an outcome predictor), or loss of control (as previously defined) would require inpatient treatment. On the other hand, variables such as psychiatric complications and nonsupportive recovery environment would seem to lend themselves to inpatient treatment. In fact, McKay et al. noted that patients who qualified for inpatient treatment based on these latter two variables, yet were treated in day treatment, did more poorly on follow-up. The relative importance of psychiatric comorbidity and recovery environment support the findings of McLellan, Woody, et al. (1983) previously discussed.

The absence of a beneficial effect of inpatient hospitalization in relatively healthy addicted patients was also suggested by the work of Longabaugh et al. (1983). In this study, partial hospitalization was compared to inpatient treatment on a general psychiatry unit. From the description offered, study patients appeared to be relatively healthy. Patients who required inpatient hospitalization for other psychiatric reasons were excluded from the study population, and all patients appeared to have third-party coverage—suggesting family and/or occupational stability. Patients were also described as having a stable living environment, spouses, and the ability to commute to and from treatment on a daily basis. Follow-up data on these patients did not demonstrate a benefit from inpatient hospitalization.

Wanberg, Horn, and Fairchild (1974) compared inpatient treatment compared to community treatment. At 3-months follow-up, the inpatient treatment group was significantly improved compared to the community treated group. Patients in the hospital sample reported better relationships with others, a changed circle of friends, fewer fears and worries, and better general health. Most interesting, however, was the bimodal distribution in the community treatment group: a noteworthy proportion (24%) in this group obtained high outcome scores whereas a relatively large proportion (50%) obtained low outcome score. Thus it would seem that community treatment is highly effective for a subgroup of patients seeking entry into an alcoholism treatment center. Unfortunately, Wanberg et al. were unable to isolate any clinical variables that characterized the good outcome community sample.

Treatment Characteristics

Not all inpatient treatment is the same. Medical and psychiatric intensive care units, free-standing substance abuse programs, and residential treatment centers are all referred to as "inpatient treatment." Similarly, outpatient treatment can vary from the "advice" offered in the work of Edward et al. (1977) to the intensive day treatment provided by McLellan, Luborsky, et al. (1983). Large disparities

between the treatment provided in inpatient and outpatient settings can make a meaningful comparison between the two treatment offerings problematic. Although many studies clearly describe significant differences between the program offerings of the inpatient and outpatient approach, subsequent referrals to this literature may neglect all but the inpatient versus outpatient dichotomy.

The work of McLellan, Woody, et al. (1983) previously cited offers perhaps the best comparison between inpatient and outpatient programs. Although important confounding factors were present in the form of various inpatient treatment programs, the outpatient program consisted of intensive, daily programming. Thus it is reasonable to conclude that the major difference between the inpatient and outpatient programs in this study was the level of care provided, not the programmatic elements of substance abuse treatment.

On the other hand, the 1991 study by Walsh et al. compared the efficacy of three forms of treatment to 227 alcohol dependent workers referred by to Employee Assistance Program (EAP): (1) community treatment (required attendance at AA), (2) inpatient hospitalization, and (3) patient's choice of treatment, including no treatment. Supplemental inpatient treatment was available to subjects in all three treatment groups who did not succeed in their randomly assigned treatment group. Additional inpatient treatment was required significantly more often by the AA group (63%) and the choice group (38%) than by subjects assigned to initial treatment in the hospital (23%). The estimated costs of inpatient treatment for the AA and choice groups averaged only 10% less than the costs for the hospital group because of their higher rates of additional treatment. This study is often referenced to support the efficacy of inpatient treatment over outpatient treatment. A more rigorous interpretation of the results might suggest that this study demonstrates the efficacy of a supervised, intensive, multimodal treatment approach (as provided by the inpatient setting) compared to an unsupervised, single-modality community support system (as provided in AA). Similarly, Edwards et al. (1977) (previously discussed) compared brief counseling to an intensive outpatient and inpatient program. Although suggesting potential benefits from the intensive treatment of alcoholism, neither study allows any definitive conclusions to be drawn with respect to the specific advantages or disadvantages of inpatient treatment.

The style and intensity of inpatient treatment must also be taken into account. A general psychiatry unit was used by Longabaugh et al. (1983) (previously discussed) to treat alcohol-dependent patients. This setting would not be expected to offer the advantages typically associated with the supportive, recovery-oriented environment of an inpatient program specializing in the treatment of substance abuse patients. Furthermore, as the study patients did not demonstrate significant psychiatric comorbidity, the milieu of a psychiatric unit may have been quite stressful. Thus the inpatient milieu not only may have neglected to provide the advantages of a substance abuse unit, but its potentially stressful setting also may have counteracted any benefit of a substance-free environment.

The amount of therapy attended may also be an important confounding variable. To again refer to the work of Longabaugh et al. (1983), both inpatients and outpatients attended the same substance abuse program. However, inpatients only attended an average of 10.5 days of the treatment programming compared to an average of 14.6 days for the outpatients. The conclusion of Longabaugh et al., that both the inpatient and outpatient setting conferred equal therapeutic benefit, may be complicated by the difference in program attendance.

Length of inpatient treatment has been the critical variable in a number of studies. These studies are of particular interest given the previous standard model of the 28-day treatment program. As discussed in a previous section, the origin of this time period does not appear to be based on objective data. The literature to date has done little to shed light on a more optimal time period that is appropriate or necessary for inpatient substance abuse treatment. For example, Mosher, Davis, Mulligan, and Iber (1975) revealed no differences in abstinence rates, drug use, anxiety, or work records between patients who completed a 9-day inpatient alcoholism treatment program and those who participated in a 21-day treatment program. Stein, Newton, and Bowman (1975) also revealed no outcome differences at 13 months between alcohol-dependent patients treated with 9.31 ± 1.85 (mean $\pm$ SD) days of detoxification or detoxification plus 25 days of inpatient treatment (30.45 ± 2.86 days total). Longabaugh et al. (1986) demonstrated no difference between patients treated with an 8-day detoxification followed by either 14-day inpatient treatment or 14-day partial hospitalization.

An ambitious study by Willems, Letemendia and Arroyave (1973b) compared treatment outcome in alcohol-dependent patients participating in a "short" (14–30 days) inpatient program vs. a "long" (50–144 days) inpatient program. Most patients were described as "gamma" alco-

holics, and no patients were refused entrance into the study because of poor prognosis. At 1 and 2 years postdischarge, patients were categorized as either recovered, improved, or unchanged on the basis of drinking behavior and psychosocial adjustment. For the purposes of statistical analysis, the recovered and improved subjects were collapsed into a single group. At the 2-year follow-up, two thirds of the surviving population of both short- and long-stay subjects were either recovered or improved. The authors concluded that "inpatient" treatment of alcoholism for more than 1 month was not indicated for the treatment of alcohol-dependent subjects.

Sheehan, Wieman, and Bechtel (1981) hypothesized that even the average of 80 treatment days received by the long-stay subjects (Willems et al., 1973b) might not provide sufficiently extensive periods of involvement in psychosocial rehabilitation programs. Sixty-one alcohol dependent subjects were therefore assessed by Sheehan et al. following participation in a one year "broad spectrum" rehabilitation program (Costello, 1975). The group of patients studied may best be described as chronic in terms of length and severity of alcohol dependence. Ninety-five percent were unemployed and receiving public welfare, social security, and/or unemployment benefits on admission. Eight-four percent had previously attended an inpatient rehabilitation program. The program included intensive insight-oriented group psychotherapy conducted by highly trained professionals, comprehensive medical care, occupational recreational and music therapies, family therapy, social casework counseling, Alcoholics Anonymous, and disulfiram maintenance when indicated. At a 3-year follow-up, 75% of these patients were determined to be "successfully adjusted" and demonstrated low rates of rehospitalization (8.3%). Sheehan et al. concluded that long-term treatment may offer substantial benefit to alcohol-addicted individuals. However, this study does little to help discern the critical components of the program's apparent success. Was it the long-term, substance-free environment, the professionally trained staff, the 12-step attendance, or the insight-oriented therapy?

Comparisons between hospital-based and community-based residential treatment units have been undertaken to explore the potential benefits or disadvantages of these relatively similar levels of care. Utilizing a nationwide database for the Department of Veteran Affairs, Moos, King, and Patterson (1996) assessed readmission rates for substance use disorder patients admitted to either a hospital-based (n=2190) or community-based (n=4490) residential unit. Surprisingly, patients treated in the community-based residential program had the lower 1- and 2-year readmission rates. However, all patients were treated in an acute inpatient substance abuse program prior to transferring to the residential program. Thus these findings may only be relevant for patients who initially attend a structured, intensive, inpatient or residential substance abuse treatment program.

An extensive survey recently conducted by the California Drug and Alcohol Treatment Assessment (CALDATA) (Gerstein et al., 1994) strongly supports the cost effectiveness of residential treatment programs. Participants in this study were selected at random from discharge lists from 97 different publicly supported substance abuse treatment programs. Three thousand subjects were assessed to represent the nearly 150,000 patients in treatment. Four different treatment programs were studied: (1) residential (heavily structured and controlled environments), (2) residential "social model" (stressing peer support and communal sober living), (3) outpatient, and (4) outpatient methadone. Subjects were studied prior to, during, and following treatment using telephone and face-to-face interviews, contacting with relatives or institutional connections, and by accessing public records. All four programs were found to produce societal benefits in excess of their costs. Costs to society consisted of criminal justice system costs, victim losses, cost of health care utilization, and loss of legitimate earnings. Residential programs produced a cost:benefit ratio (cost to society compared to cost of treatment) of 2.4 to 1. Outpatient programs produced a cost:benefit ratio of 2.9 to 1, and methadone maintenance of 4.7 to 1. Analysis of length of stay suggests that a 2–3 month stay in a residential program was more cost-effective than a stay of 4 or more months. Although this study demonstrates that residential care is a cost-effective approach to substance abuse, outpatient programs were even more cost effective. Because patient characteristics are not discussed, it is not possible to discern if the patients treated in residential settings were similar to those of the outpatients and subsequently could have been treated in this less restrictive, more inexpensive setting.

Summary of Literature

Due to the wide variation in both patient and treatment characteristics and the myriad measures of treatment outcome, the literature provides little definitive information to guide recommendations for inpatient treatment.

Particularly disturbing is that, despite our best attempts to be current in our review, most of the referenced studies are at least ten years old. There have, however, been several more recent reviews of this literature. These reviews typically reference the same literature, yet the authors often come to different conclusions with respect to the utility of inpatient treatment. These differences may arise from a number of different factors, including possibly an author's individual orientation and experience as opposed to a clear direction offered by the empirical literature.

The literature also offers limited insight into the differential role of inpatient or residential care in the treatment of different substances of abuse. Much of the literature focuses on alcohol dependent patients, which may not be relevant for other substances of abuse. Particularly problematic is the absence of literature on crack cocaine-addicted patients. Although crack addiction does not result in a withdrawal syndrome requiring medical intervention, many clinicians believe that the intensity of craving during the first several days or weeks of drug cessation requires a monitored, drug-free environment to prevent relapse. To our knowledge, the potential benefits of inpatient versus outpatient treatment in this patient population have not been explored.

Future research would be of assistance in identifying the specific clinical and psychosocial variables that might predict which patients require a more intensive, inpatient approach. However, it is unlikely this research will take place. As discussed later, third-party payments have all but ceased for hospital-based substance abuse treatment unless indicated for acute psychiatric or medical conditions. Upcoming studies will most likely be limited to exploring the role of residential settings for substance use disorder patients with severe psychosocial dysfunction.

CRITERIA FOR PLACEMENT

Recognition that patients with substance use disorders require different levels of care and that these levels will change for any given patient during the process of recovery and relapse have forced the therapist to become knowledgeable about the wide variety of treatment options. In order to identify the appropriate level of care, the treatment goal must first be identified. Typical goals include detoxification, the reduction or cessation of substance use, the reduction in the frequency and severity of relapse, and the improvement of a patient's psychological and social functioning. To achieve these goals, one can generally choose along a continuum of interventions, which vary in the intensity of treatment and the site of care. The range of interventions include no formal treatment, brief intervention, self-help groups, outpatient treatment, intensive outpatient treatment, partial hospitalization (nonresidential day or night treatment), community care facility, residential treatment, inpatient rehabilitation, and inpatient hospitalization. In spite of the wide variety of treatment approaches and modalities offered, general guidelines have been established to help practitioners make the important decision regarding which level of care a person might need at a particular time in the course of his or her illness.

The American Psychiatric Association (APA) has developed Practice Guidelines for the treatment of patients with substance use disorders (1995). The APA advises that decisions about placement in treatment be based on a patient's capacity to willingly cooperate and participate in treatment and his or her ability to care for himself or herself. The degree of structure, supervision, and support required to maintain safety are important factors to consider, as well as the need for specific treatments to address any comorbid medical or psychiatric conditions. The patient's preference for a particular treatment setting must also be taken into account. An overall guideline recommended is that patients be treated in "the least restrictive setting that is likely to prove safe and effective," and that they be moved from one level of care to another based on a continuous reassessment. These decisions should be determined following a comprehensive psychiatric assessment which includes a detailed history of the patient's past and present substance use, its effects on his or her cognitive, behavioral, psychological, and physiologic functioning, and the history of prior treatments and outcomes. Social history, family psychiatric and substance abuse history, medical history and exam, and laboratory and screening tests are also critical in the decision-making process.

The American Society of Addiction Medicine (ASAM) (1991) has formulated a more comprehensive set of Placement Criteria to assist the practitioner in prescribing the most appropriate level of care. The ASAM guidelines define four specific levels of care:

Level I: outpatient treatment

Level II: intensive outpatient/partial hospitalization treatment

Level III: medically monitored intensive inpatient treatment

Level IV: medically managed intensive inpatient treatment

The differences between Level III and Level IV require further explanation. Both utilize 24-hour observation and monitoring and the treatment is specific to substance use disorders. However, Level III patients do not require the intense medical or psychiatric care available on Level IV. For example, patients in delirium tremens would typically require inpatient hospitalization in an acute medical care setting (Level IV) and patients who evidence psychotic disorganization during cocaine intoxication would require inpatient hospitalization in an acute psychiatric setting (Level IV). Subacute problems such as moderate alcohol withdrawal or mild suicidality associated with withdrawal from cocaine could be treated in a Level III facility.

Placement in a specific level of care should be based on the careful assessment of a patient along six dimensions. These dimensions reflect pertinent biopsychosocial aspects of addiction and the "medical necessity" for treatment:

1. the presence of acute intoxication and/or the potential for developing withdrawal,
2. any biomedical conditions and complications,
3. emotional and behavioral conditions/complications, which include psychiatric or neuropsychiatric problems,
4. the level of patient's treatment acceptance or resistance,
5. the seriousness of the patient's relapse potential,
6. the type and degree of support available in a patient's "recovery environment."

The ASAM guidelines emphasize the need for continual reassessment in each of the six problem areas to determine when it is appropriate to move a patient from one level of care to another.

Based on these guidelines, one can make some reasonable decisions regarding assignment of patients to particular levels of care. For example, inpatient hospitalization would be most appropriate for those patients whose conditions require a medically monitored environment. These patients would include those with drug overdoses or those at risk for developing a severe or complicated withdrawal syndrome; patients with acute or chronic general medical conditions that would make an outpatient detoxification unsafe; patients with marked comorbid psychiatric disorders, which would put themselves or others in danger if not treated acutely (e.g., acute suicidality, homicidality, or psychotic disorganization); and patients who have a history of not engaging in, or benefiting from, a less intensive treatment setting. In general, the length of stay in an inpatient treatment setting should be dictated by the current need of the patient for this most restrictive setting, as well as his or her ability to safely participate in, and benefit from, a less restrictive treatment setting.

The APA (1995) suggests that residential care is most indicated for those patients who do not meet criteria for a need for a medically monitored intensive inpatient treatment (Level III), but nevertheless require a structured, supervised setting during the early phase of recovery. Although a physician is generally available off-site for consultation, this setting does not provide on-site nursing or medical monitoring. Patients treated in a residential unit typically lack sufficient support in their environment, or the internal motivation needed, to remain substance-free in an ambulatory setting. In addition to providing a drug-free environment, these programs usually provide psychosocial, occupational, and family assessments, and referral to appropriate rehabilitative services and self-help groups in the community. Many also provide their own individual and group counseling, but rely on other programs and staff to provide needed psychopharmacologic treatments and/or psychosocial treatment components. (A variation on residential treatment is the "therapeutic community" [previously described], which typically provides long-term residential care for those with opioid or polysubstance use disorders. These programs, however, use high levels of interpersonal and group confrontation in their approach to treatment, and for that reason, may not be suitable for patients with comorbid psychiatric disorders.) Unfortunately, the residential treatment setting is not discussed in the ASAM guidelines.

FINANCIAL CONSIDERATIONS

The heavy hand of managed care has been felt throughout the practice of medicine, and the field of substance abuse has not been spared. The rapid and dramatic changes required by managed care in the substance abuse arena have been due, at least in part, to the field's common practice of utilizing treatment paradigms dictated by tradition and anecdotal experience rather than empirical evidence. In order to contain costs, third-party payments now encourage the least expensive method of care unless more expensive treatments have been proven more efficacious. Information documenting the efficacy of rehabilitation has been particularly scarce in the area of inpatient substance abuse treatment.

As discussed earlier in this chapter, the 28-day inpatient program is thought to have been derived from the "sober houses" of AA, the milieu of therapeutic communities, and the Minnesota model; the origins for the 28-day time frame are more obscure. Regardless, the intrusion of managed care into the practice of substance abuse subsequently revealed the absence of sound rationale or empirical data to support either the need for inpatient hospitalization during the initial phase of rehabilitation or the 28-day length of stay. Without the presence of empirical evidence to support this traditional treatment paradigm, managed care withdrew its support. The resultant demise of these programs was sudden and severe.

Interestingly, the charges for inpatient treatment seemed to have little relation to the treatment offered or even the costs incurred by the treatment provider (Reader & Sullivan, 1992). In an informal survey, Reader and Sullivan (1992) reported that most rehabilitative programs merely charged what they assumed was the "average rate" of a chemical addiction stay, regardless of their own costs. The costs of a rehabilitative program offered on a psychiatry inpatient unit were up to 35% more than the same treatment in a free-standing rehab unit (Reader & Sullivan, 1992). Zwanziger, Davis, Bamezai, and Hosek (1991) analyzed CHAMPUS inpatient claims for a 1-year period (July 1986 through June 1987) and found that only 4.2% of the costs of inpatient hospitalization could be related to diagnosis (as reported by DRGs). Their findings indicated that (1) there was enormous variability in the services received for the same diagnosis, and (2) substantial variation in lengths of stay and charges were systematically related to the type of hospital providing the service, rather than the services provided. Furthermore, they noted that patients with the same diagnosis could be treated quite differently, with far more outliers than observed with other DRGs. Zanziger et al. concluded that the wide variability in charges and lengths of stay, coupled with the absence of correlation with diagnosis, reflected an absence of treatment consensus in the provider community.

The change in treatment patterns as a result of changing reimbursement patterns was reflected in a study of substance abuse patients attending programs at all Veterans Administration Medical Centers (VAMCs). Between 1981 and 1984 (during which payment schedules to VAMCs did not change) the average length of stay for substance use disorders remained unchanged. Then in 1985 DRGs were instituted. The average length of stay for substance use disorders subsequently decreased approximately 25% between 1984 to 1988. The effect of this substantial decrease in inpatient hospitalization upon treatment was not determined.

The changes in reimbursement patterns has clearly altered treatment patterns. It is not known, however, how these changes have effected treatment outcome. On the one hand, market forces have forced the practitioners to become aware of the necessity of utilizing resources only as necessary and to match treatment setting to patient needs. In addition, the field has become aware of the critical need to assess how treatment outcome is effected by initial presenting problems and treatment approach. On the other hand, the efficacy of substance abuse treatment has been well documented (McLellan et al., 1996). Whether the widespread changes in treatment settings will effect treatment outcome in a positive or negative direction must await future studies. As Rosenheck, Massari, and Astrachan (1990) note, "Cost efficiency, the expense of delivering a unit care, must never be confused with cost effectiveness, the cost of producing an improvement in the health care status of patients."

Chung and Filstead (1995) offer some preliminary findings suggesting that fewer days of inpatient/residential care for substance abuse treatment are not associated with a less positive outcome. This study compared two managed care methods provided by the same managed health care organization. The treatment provider offered a full range of substance abuse services at various levels of care in a vertically integrated system. One managed care approach was "intensive case management" by the approving health care organization, in which treatment plans were targeted to specific clinical issues, there was frequent contact with treatment providers, and case-by-case authorization of care plans was provided without a preset formula for length of stay. In the other approach, little if any case management was furnished by the approving care organization. The findings demonstrated that patients provided intensive case management by the managed care company received 32% of their total services on an inpatient/residential basis versus 46% for the second group. Outcome measures, such as substance use and health, employment, and interpersonal relationships, did not differ between the two groups. This study may therefore suggest that fewer inpatient days do not produce a detrimental treatment outcome when provided in tandem with a close monitoring by the managed care company. Alternately, the investigators' inability to locate two thirds of the study population for a follow-up assessment, and the refusal of another 10% to be interviewed, may suggest that both groups were seriously undertreated.

Treatment Providers versus Third-Party Payers

Most insurance plans, whether fee-for-service, PPO, or HMO, presently provide similar support for substance abuse treatment. Both acute detoxification and rehabilative services are usually offered. Limits on the number of admissions and hospital days allowed may exist, but may not be noted on the plan. In general, plans follow the American Society of Addiction Medicine (ASAM) (1991) guidelines for inpatient care (detailed previously). Residential treatment care is generally considered a type of inpatient care. Specific coverage may also be dictated by state law.

Plans typically state that all necessary services for detoxification and rehabilitation are provided. The term "necessary," which is purposefully vague, denotes the provision of all care that is likely to have some beneficial effect, is medically necessary, and/or has some likelihood of achieving some defined goal. Thus, if further or repeated treatment (i.e., extended or repeated inpatient care) is not thought likely to yield additional benefit, it will be disallowed.

As elsewhere in medicine, payment plans will pay only for the lowest level of care deemed appropriate for a specific condition. Inpatient hospitalization with 24-hour nursing care is provided for patients with significant or complicated withdrawal syndromes and/or coexisting symptoms of other psychiatric disorders. In general, if the medical and/or psychiatric symptoms would require hospitalization on a medical or general psychiatric unit, hospitalization will be allowed until the patient is stable. Inpatient detoxification will be approved only if the withdrawal is of sufficient severity to require 24-hour nursing care.

Perhaps more problematic is payment for residential treatment services. Studies assessing the efficacy of inpatient treatment (previously reviewed) typically compare "inpatient" to "outpatient" treatment. Not clearly discussed in these studies is whether these programs consisted of 24-hour nursing care ("medically monitored intensive inpatient treatment") or residential care. However, as the description of these programs does not mentionrequiring extensive nursing care, it could be assumed that the treatment procedures described could be conducted on a residential treatment unit. These studies suggest that patients with more severe levels of psychiatric distress and/or significant family and employment problems were more successful at 6-months abstinence when treated in an inpatient setting compared to an outpatient setting. Yet anecdotal experience would suggest that many patients meeting these criteria are not approved for inpatient rehabilitation care.

There may be several possible reasons for these apparent difficulties. First, many of the studies noted have been conducted on patients treated in a VA Medical Center. The relevance of these findings to the private pay population may be appropriately questioned. Second, the requested inpatient care is often on a medically monitored intensive inpatient unit rather than on a residential treatment unit. The former will usually be denied for rehabilitative care uncomplicated by coexisting medical or psychiatric disturbances. Third, many of these studies utilize well-validated and reliable measures of psychiatric, occupational, and family disturbance (such as the Addiction Severity Index) (McLellan et al., 1980). These measures provide both the clinician and insurance "care manager" or "physician adviser" clear guidelines on which to base a decision. The absence of such objective measures in many programs, however, provides the insurance reviewers great latitude in interpreting the patient's problems from the chart or therapist's description. Fourth, some insurance providers will deny inpatient stays based on studies that either contain significant methodologic flaws or do not support what the insurance care manager believes they do. Malcolm (1990), for example, notes how a care manager defended her refusal of inpatient rehabilitation based on a study demonstrating the efficacy of outpatient detoxification. And fifth, some insurance companies will refuse to pay for inpatient or residential care even when it is clearly indicated. Some states have levied heavy fines on insurance companies for their arbitrary restrictions on substance abuse treatment (Honberg, 1996).

The ongoing conflict between the practicing therapist or physician, striving to provide optimal care for his or her patient, and the insurance company's reviewer, attempting to provide optimal care for the least cost, can be viewed from the published musings of two highly regarded psychiatrists practicing in an academic setting. Malcolm (1990) discusses his often futile attempts to obtain approval from the utilization review nurse for inpatient rehabilitation for severely addicted patients. One, he notes, is a heroin- and cocaine-addicted patient who "clearly needs in-house rehabilitation for 3 to 4 weeks." Malcolm notes the inappropriate references that the reviewer uses to refuse his request, and the absence of reviewer-recommended day treatment facilities. On the other hand, in Confessions of a

Concurrent Reviewer (1996), Mohl took to task those physicians who routinely prescribe 28-day inpatient programs for substance abuse patients. Mohl requests that the attending clinician describe a patient's clinical portrait that justifies both the specific need for in-house rehabilitative services, 24-hour nursing care, and the time frame requested. Specific "tips" for obtaining appropriate third-party payment is further provided by Sabin (1990): (1) explain how the treatment offered will directly impact on the consequences of the illness; (2) demonstrate how the patient (and family, if appropriate) is highly motivated in the treatment program; (3) make the treatment "modular," explaining how long each treatment segment (i.e., inpatient treatment) will be, what are the expectations for each phase of treatment, and how progress will be assessed; and (4) provide clear reasons for this particular treatment program, as opposed to another local treatment setting.

Unfortunately, the trend away from inpatient care encouraged by managed care providers has not resulted in a higher utilization of outpatient services. Finch, Lurie, Christianson and Moscovice (1992) reviewed inpatient and outpatient care in patients enrolled in both fee-for-service (FFS) and prepayment programs. Although inpatient utilization was significantly lower under the prepayment plan than the FFS coverage, outpatient utilization for substance abuse services was also reduced in patients enrolled in the prepayment plan. In another study (Ellis, 1992), the establishment of a large employer-based PPO led to a 40% decrease in inpatient episodes for substance abuse treatment. This decrease was accompanied by only a 20% increase in outpatient treatment.

CASE EXAMPLES

The guidelines provided by ASAM (1991) and the APA (1995) are relatively vague, and allow for a great deal of interpretation both by the clinician and the insurance reviewer. In general, the clinician should be prepared to justify why a particular treatment cannot be accomplished in a less restrictive and less expensive level of care in a more efficient and effective manner. Next we present three hypothetical cases, followed by a discussion describing the rationale for a chosen level of care.

Case Example 1

Mr. Johnson, a 35-year-old male, presented to the local Emergency Room stating, "I want to speak to a psychiatrist." He was intoxicated with a BAL of 380 mg%. Mr. Johnson claimed that he had put a gun to his wife's head a few days ago while she was sleeping; this followed an argument between them about his continued drinking. Mr. Johnson's wife left him the next day. He admitted that he has been physically abusive toward his wife in the past when drunk, "but I haven't hit her in a long time." Following his wife's departure, Mr. Johnson's drinking escalated, and he lost the job he started that week due to his drinking. He stated that he thought about hurting himself "the other day," but denied active suicidal ideation. He drinks 12–24 beers daily, experiences morning tremors, and reports severe nausea and vomiting during withdrawal. Two years ago, Mr. Johnson experienced a withdrawal seizure when he tried to stop drinking on his own. Mr. Johnson denied using any other substances, and denied ever receiving any substance abuse treatment. He was hospitalized 4 years previously for ruptured esophageal varices. He refused recommended treatment for his alcohol dependence at that time. He reported no prior periods of abstinence.

There are several factors pointing toward an inpatient hospitalization for Mr. Johnson. First, it would probably be unsafe for the patient to leave the hospital due to his high degree of intoxication (Dimension 1). Mr. Johnson's high tolerance to alcohol, as evidenced by his relatively clear mental status yet high BAL, coupled with his morning shakes, suggests that significant withdrawal symptoms will occur as his BAL decreases (Dimension 1). Furthermore, vomiting during withdrawal could rupture his esophageal varices, producing life-threatening complications (Dimension 2). Although the withdrawal syndrome could potentially be treated as outpatient, the absence of any support systems makes outpatient detoxification problematic (Dimension 6). He appears to present a potential harm to his wife, particularly in his intoxicated state (Dimension 3). Given these circumstances, the safest level of care would be inpatient treatment on a substance abuse unit (Level III). In this environment, he would be safely contained and observed while intoxicated and during withdrawal. If his esophageal varices were to rupture, transfer to an acute medical care unit could be easily accomplished. If he began to express an overt plan to harm his wife, transfer to an acute psychiatric unit could be considered.

Three days following admission, Mr. Johnson claimed that he felt much better. His withdrawal syndrome was aggressively treated with a symptom-triggered detoxification protocol, requiring 20 mg of diazepam. Mr. Johnson had called his boss and had been offered another chance at his job if he returned to work within the next few days. His wife refused to return home at this time, but agreed to participate in conjoint counseling. Mr. Johnson was highly motivated to begin rehabilitative treatment, but wanted to return home and begin work. A substance abuse counselor met with the patient to discuss treatment options and conducted an Addiction Severity Index (ASI) interview. Mr. Johnson's ASI demonstrated considerable problems in the areas of alcohol and family/social; moderate problems in the area of employment; slight problems in the medical area (suggesting medical evaluation was a low priority); and no real problems in the areas of drugs, legal, and psychiatric.

The only dimensions that remained problematic for Mr. Johnson at this time were Dimension 5 (relapse potential) and possibly Dimension 6 (recovery environment), as the patient would be living alone. However, the patient had a stable living situation, desired to return home, appeared highly motivated for further treatment, needed to begin work as soon as possible, and had not previously failed treatment at a lower level of care. Thus, the patient and counselor agreed that the patient would begin intensive outpatient treatment (Level II) in the evenings after work. Furthermore, the patient would discuss naltrexone pharmacotherapy with his physician. Mr. Johnson was discharged from the hospital the following day.

The physician involved in the care of Mr. Johnson was relieved that she was successful in obtaining third payment for the 4-day hospitalization. Although she felt there was a serious potential for a complicated withdrawal syndrome and prudence pointed toward hospitalization, most alcohol detoxification can be safely conducted on an outpatient basis (Hayashida et al., 1989). Despite a number of reviews suggesting that a prior history of withdrawal seizures or delirium tremens requires subsequent inpatient treatment for detoxification, aggressive outpatient management of detoxification should prevent such complications from reoccurring.

Case Example 2

Mrs. Martin, a 37-year-old married female, presented to the local emergency room stating that she had relapsed 8 months ago, first by using cocaine, and then drinking on weekends. She stated that she currently drinks two 40-oz. beers and smokes $20 of cocaine daily. She had not used any substances since the previous day, but was not experiencing any withdrawal symptoms. Mrs. Martin participated in a 28-day intensive inpatient program for substance dependence 10 months prior. During this program, a long-standing depressive disorder was diagnosed and Mrs. Martin was started on an antidepressant. She was given an appointment with both an outpatient group and a psychiatrist, and attended both sporadically for the 2 months prior to her relapse. She also went to a few AA meetings following discharge, but stopped after a few weeks. She claims her depression progressively worsened after discharge and she discontinued her medication and therapy sessions after she relapsed. She now expressed moderate symptoms of depression with sporadic suicidality (Beck Depression Inventory was 21). Mrs. Smith had not worked for several years, and lived with her husband of 20 years. Her husband abused both alcohol and other drugs throughout their marriage, and had not been supportive in helping her maintain abstinence. He did, however, have a steady job with good insurance. She was not sure if she wanted to continue with her marriage. Mrs. Martin had no close friends and tended to keep to herself. Most of her daytime hours involved substance use and/or sleeping. An ASI performed during the initial assessment revealed considerable problems in the areas of alcohol, drugs, and psychiatric, and moderate problems in the family/social area.

Residential treatment was considered to be the most appropriate level of care for Mrs. Martin. She did not exhibit any medical or detoxification problems that would require medically monitored hospitalization. However, she exhibited significant problems with depression (Dimension 3) and her recovery environment (Dimension 6). In particular, Mrs. Martin lived an isolated existence essentially focused on substance use. Due to her depression, her motivation (Dimension 4) and likelihood of relapse (Dimension 5) were also problematic. Thus Mrs. Martin required a structured, supportive environment to maintain both abstinence and adequate level of psychiatric functioning.

Mrs. Martin was admitted to a local residential substance abuse program. She was immediately restarted on an antidepressant. Her mood improved within 2 weeks (Beck Depression Inventory 12), and she began

to consider both other living arrangements (away from her husband) and seeking employment. Her therapist and psychiatrist both believed that continued residential care for several weeks would be beneficial. However, the insurance care manager noted Mrs. Martin's improved psychiatric status and suggested that the patient could continue treatment from home. The psychiatrist appealed to the insurance company's physician adviser, noting the patient's need for new housing and employment as well as her imminent risk of relapse. The physician advisor replied that the treating psychiatrist was unable to define any specific treatment goal (i.e., housing, technical training, or employment) that could be accomplished within a specified period of time if residential treatment was continued. The advisor also noted that all substance abuse patients are at high risk of relapse in the early months of abstinence, and there are no useful clinical variables that successfully predict relapse. He suggested that if the patient continued to require a structured environment, she be transferred to a community women's house.

As there was not an appropriate alternative living arrangement in the surrounding area, the patient returned home and began attending a partial hospitalization program. She also continued to see a psychiatrist to monitor her antidepressant therapy.

As noted in a previous section, the physician may have had better success obtaining coverage for additional residential care if he had proposed the treatment plan in "modular" terms (Sabin, 1995); that is, the physician should have requested a specific amount of additional time, identified what specific treatment elements would be included during that time period, what would be the expected patient response to the proposed treatment, and how the patient's progress would be measured. In addition, the physician should have been prepared to identify to the reviewer why the proposed residential care program was appropriate for this particular patient. Specifically, he should have noted that a women's community housing facility was not available in the local area.

The third case involves a patient requesting treatment at a VA hospital. The Veterans Health Administration is the largest provider of health care in the United States. VA Medical Centers have had a long-standing commitment to the treatment of substance abuse disorders, and have committed substantial resources to developing a wide continuum of substance abuse services. The experience in the VA system is relevant to this discussion because the patients treated in this setting (as well as patients treated in other public programs) demonstrate significantly more problems with housing, employment, education, psychiatric and medical comorbidities, and legal issues. Thus a more extensive network of psychosocial supports is required for a population with few, if any, resources.

Case Example 3

Mr. Walker, a 47-year-old divorced male, presented to the nearest VAMC at 2 A.M. The patient had an over 25-year history of substance dependence, including active alcohol, cocaine, and marijuana use. He had one formal rehabilitation experience 10 years previously, but relapsed soon after discharge. The patient was a Vietnam veteran who was diagnosed with PTSD during his previous treatment. He did not follow-up with treatment for substance abuse or PTSD after his last treatment, and relapsed soon after discharge. The precipitant for admission at this time was in response to an exacerbation of PTSD symptoms. Following being robbed and beaten 2 weeks prior to presentation, Mr. Walker had experienced a renewal of flashbacks and nightmares. A BAL was 150 mg%, but there was no evidence of significant intoxication. The patient reported feeling as if "I will probably kill myself" if he did not get admitted at that time. He did not, however, have a prior history of suicide attempts and expressed no clear plan of intent. He was homeless, and had been working day labor off and on for several months. He was estranged from his family, and had no stable relationships. Due to complaints of nausea and abdominal pains, routine laboratory studies and amylase levels were obtained. Except for moderately elevated liver enzymes, however, there was no evidence of an acute medical disorder.

The patient demonstrated elevations in all ASAM Dimensions except for Dimension 2 (biomedical conditions). However, the on-call psychiatry resident did not believe there was a need for emergent hospitalization. Despite an elevated BAL, the patient did not display evidence of acute intoxication such as motor incoordination, slurred speech, or impaired judgment. Mr. Walker did not express depressive symptoms consistent with his suicidal thoughts, nor did he present either a suicide plan or a lethal means to conduct a suicide attempt. There was also no evidence of a withdrawal syndrome. The patient was therefore asked to return to the hospital the next morning to be assessed by the substance abuse program staff.

Mr. Walker to returned to the hospital the next morning and was seen by a substance abuse counselor. At that time, the patient was demonstrating mild symptoms of alcohol withdrawal. He was therefore also assessed by physician's assistant (PA). The PA and counselor determined that the patient could be stabilized and further assessed as an outpatient, while staying at a local shelter. The patient was started on a carbamazepine detoxification protocol (Malcolm, Ballenger, & Sturgis, 1989) and asked to return daily. Three days after initial presentation, an ASI was obtained by the counselor, demonstrating considerable problems in the areas of alcohol and drug use, family/social, employment, and psychiatric.

Due to Mr. Walker's unstable living environment and high psychiatric distress, the patient was admitted to an residential rehabilitation unit. In VA nomenclature, these units are called Substance Abuse Residential Rehabilitation Units. During the patient's 3 weeks on the unit, his PTSD symptoms were aggressively treated. Although his rehabilitation experience was uneventful, the patient's lack of psychosocial supports and poor work skills indicated the need for a more extensive rehabilitative experience. The patient was subsequently transferred to a VA Domiciliary program, which was both oriented toward both maintaining abstinence and improving and solidifying work skills. This rehabilitative program would also help Mr. Walker in obtaining meaningful employment and stable housing in the community.

This last case demonstrates an example of a patient that does not require acute hospitalization for detoxification or psychiatric reasons. However, the consequences of long-standing substance abuse are of such severity as to require intensive and long-term intervention in a structured, supportive environment.

CONCLUSIONS

The use of inpatient substance abuse treatment has rapidly become a time-limited approach utilized for patients exhibiting a somewhat narrow range of substance-related problems. Acute hospitalization is generally reserved for substance abuse patients with dangerous levels of intoxication, severe withdrawal syndromes, or coexisting medical or psychiatric disturbances. Patients with very poor psychosocial support systems or marked psychiatric impairment appear to benefit from inpatient rehabilitation and/or extended residential care.

The cost–benefit savings of this paradigm shift in substance abuse treatment remain in question. Several factors complicate the field's ability to make optimal treatment recommendations: (1) The most effective treatment for any particular patient with a substance use disorder remains an area of significant controversy. To determine whether an identified treatment should take place in a specific setting only adds an additional level of complexity. (2) The question of what treatment setting is the most beneficial must be balanced with what treatment setting may be potentially harmful. As previously noted, healthier patients may tend to do better in outpatient settings than in inpatient environments. (3) Last, the benefit to the patient must be balanced with the cost to society. Although an expensive inpatient treatment may be slightly more effective to an individual patient, the much higher cost to society must be balanced with the more modest individual gains. Alternatively, society may significantly benefit when patients with severe dysfunction and a high risk for subsequent relapse are treated with a more expensive inpatient treatment regimen.

REFERENCES

Anderson, D. J. (1981). *Perspectives on treatment*. Center City, MN: Hazelden.

American Society of Addiction Medicine. (1991). *Adult psychoactive substance use disorders patient placement criteria* (pp. 10–59). Washington, DC: Author.

Annis, H. N. (1986). Is inpatient rehabilitation of the alcoholic cost effective? Con position. *Advances in Alcohol and Substance Use, 5*, 175–190.

Breecher, E. M. (1972). *Licit and illicit drugs* (pp. 52–55). Boston: Little, Brown.

Cook, C. C. (1988). The Minnesota Model in the management of drug and alcohol dependency: Miracle, method or myth? Part I. The philosophy and the programme. *British Journal of Addiction, 83*, 625–634.

Costello, R. M. (1975). Alcoholism treatment and evaluation: In search of methods. II. Collation of two year follow-up studies. *International Journal of the Addictions, 10*, 857–867.

Craig, R. J. (1985). Multimodal treatment package for substance abuse. *Professional Psychology: Research and Practice, 16*, 271–285.

Craig, R. J., Olson, R., & Shalton, G. (1990). Improvement in psychological functioning among drug abusers: Inpatient treatment compared to outpatient methadone maintenance. *Journal of Substance Abuse Treatment, 1*, 11–19.

Dole, V. P., & Nyswander, M. E. (1965). A medical treatment of diacetylmorphine (heroin) addiction. *Journal of American Medical Association, 193*, 646–650.

Edwards, G., Orford, J., Egert, S., Guthrie, S., Hawker, A., Hensman, C., Mitcheson, M., Oppenheimer, E., & Taylor, C. (1977). Alcoholism: A controlled trial of "treatment" and "advice." *Journal of Studies on Alcohol, 38*, 1004–1031.

Ellis, R. (1992). Employers tackle treatment costs. *Substance Abuse Issues, 3*: 1–3.

Federal Bureau of Narcotics. (1955). *Narcotic clinics in the United States*. Washington, DC: U.S. Government Printing Office.

Fields, R. (1992). *Drugs and alcohol in perspective*. Washington, DC: W. C. Brown.

Finch, M., Lurie, N., Christianson, J., & Moscovice, I. (1992). The treatment of alcohol and drug abuse among mentally ill Medicaid enrollees: The utilization of services in prepaid versus fee-for-service care. In R. Frank & W. Manning (Eds.), *Economics and Mental Health* (pp. 292–306). Baltimore: John Hopkins University Press.

Finney, J. W., & Moos, R. H. (1986). Matching patients with treatment: Conceptual and methodological issue. *Journal of Studies on Alcohol, 47*, 122–134.

Geller, A. (1992). Rehabilitation programs and halfway houses. In J. Lowinson, P. Ruiz, R. B. Millman, & J. G. Longrod (Eds.), *Substance abuse and comprehensive textbook* (pp. 596–611). Baltimore: Williams and Wilkins.

Gerstein, D. R., Johnson, R. A., Harwood, H. J., Fountain, D., Suter, N., & Malloy, K. (1994). *Evaluating recovery services: The California Drug and Alcohol Treatment Assessment (CALDATA)*. University of Chicago and Fairfax, VA: National Opinion Research Center.

Hayashida, M., Alterman, A., McLellan, A. T., O'Brien, C. P., Purtill, J. J., Volpicelli, J. R., Raphaelson, A. H., & Hall, C. P. (1989). Comparative effectiveness and costs of inpatient and outpatient detoxification of patients with mild-to-moderate alcohol withdrawal syndrome. *New England Journal of Medicine, 320*, 358–365.

Honberg, R. (1996). RI investigation yields sanctions against managed care company. *NAMI Advocate, 17*, 7.

Hubbard, R. L. (1992). Evaluation and outcome. In J. Lowinson, P. Ruiz, R. B. Millman, & J. G. Longrod (Eds.), *Substance abuse and comprehensive textbook* (pp. 458–466). Baltimore: Williams and Wilkins.

Institute of Medicine. (1990). *Broadening the base of treatment for alcohol problems*. Washington, DC: National Academy Press.

Jellinek, E. M. (1960). *The disease concept of alcoholism*. New Haven, CT: College and University Press.

Kennard, D. (1983). *An introduction to therapeutic communities*. London: Routledge and Kegan Paul.

Kurtz, E. (1979). *Not God: A history of Alcoholics Anonymous*. Center City, MN: Hazeldon Press.

Longabaugh, R. (1986, August). *The matching hypothesis: Theoretical and empirical status*. Paper presented at the American Psychological Association Symposium on the Matching Hypothesis in Alcoholism Treatment, Washington, DC.

Longabaugh, R., McCrady, B., Fink, E., Stout, R., McAuley, T., Doyle, C., & McNeill, D. (1983). Cost effectiveness of alcoholism treatment in partial vs. inpatient settings. *Journal of Studies on Alcohol, 44*, 1049–1071.

Malcolm, R. (1990). A piece of my mind: Little battles. *Journal of the American Medical Association, 263*, 90.

Malcolm, R., Ballenger, J. C., & Sturgis, E. T. (1989). Double-blind controlled trial comparing carbamazepine to oxazepam treatment of alcohol withdrawal. *American Journal of Psychiatry, 146*, 617–621.

McKay, J. R., McLellan, A. T., & Alterman, A. (1992). An evaluation of the Cleveland Criteria for inpatient treatment of substance abuse. *American Journal of Psychiatry, 149*, 1212–1218.

McLellan, A. T., Luborsky, L., O'Brien, C. P., & Woody G. E. (1980). An improved evaluation instrument for substance abuse patients: The Addiction Severity Index. *Journal of Nervous and Mental Disease, 168*, 26–33.

McLellan, A. T., Luborsky, L., O'Brien, C. P., Woody, G. E., & Druley, K. A. (1982). Is treatment for substance abuse effective? *Journal of the American Medical Association, 247*, 1423–1428.

McLellan, A. T., Luborsky, L., Woody, G. E., O'Brien, C. P., & Druley, K. A. (1983a). Predicting response to alcohol and drug abuse treatments: Role of psychiatric severity. *Archives of General Psychiatry, 40*, 620–625.

McLellan, A. T., Woody, G. E., Luborsky, L., O'Brien, C. P., & Druley, K. A. (1983b), Increased effectiveness of substance abuse treatment: A prospective study of patient-treatment "matching." *Journal of Nervous and Mental Disease, 171*, 597–605.

McLellan, A. T., Woody, G. E., Metzger, D., McKay, J., Durell, J., Alterman, A., & O'Brien, C. P. (1996). Evaluating the effectiveness of addiction treatments: Reasonable expectations, appropriate comparisons. *Millbank Quarterly, 74*, 51–85.

Miller, W. R. (1989). Matching individuals with interventions. In R. K. Hester & W. R. Miller (Eds.), *Handbook of alcoholism treatment approaches* (pp. 261–271). New York: Pergamon.

Miller, W. R., & Hester, R. K. (1986). Inpatient alcoholism treatment: Who benefits? *American Psychologist, 41*, 794–805.

Mohl, P. C. (1996). Confessions of a concurrent reviewer. *Psychiatric Services, 47*, 35–40.

Moos, R. H., King, M. J., & Patterson, M. A. (1996). Outcomes of residential treatment of substance abuse in hospital- and community-based programs. *Psychiatric Services, 47*, 68–74.

Mosher, V., Davis, J., Mulligan, D., & Iber, F. (1975). Comparison of outcome in a 9 day and 30 day alcoholism treatment program. *Journal of Studies on Alcohol, 36*, 1277–1281.

Musto, D. (1992). Historical perspectives on alcohol and drug abuse. In J. Lowinson, P. Ruiz, R. B. Millman, & J. G.

Longrod (Eds.), *Substance abuse and comprehensive textbook* (pp. 2–14). Baltimore: Williams and Wilkins.

Nace, E. P. (1990). Inpatient treatment of alcoholism: A necessary part of the therapeutic armamentarium. *Psychiatric Hospital, 21*, 9–31.

Orford, J., Oppenheimer, E., & Edwards, G. (1976). Abstinence or control: The outcome for excessive drinkers two years after consultation. *Behavior Research and Therapy 14*, 409–418.

Polich, J. M., Armor, D. J., & Braiker, H. B. (1981). *The course of alcoholism: Four years after treatment* (ADM 281-76-0006). Santa Monica, CA: Rand.

Reader, J. W., & Sullivan, K. A. (1992). Private and public insurance. In J. Lowinson, P. Ruiz, R. B. Millman, & J. G. Longrod, (Eds.), *Substance abuse and comprehensive textbook* (pp. 1007–1081). Baltimore: Williams and Wilkins.

Rosenheck, R., Massari, L., & Astrachan, B. M. (1990). The impact of DRG-based budgeting on inpatient psychiatric care in veterans administration medical centers. *Medical Care, 28*, 124–134.

Schneider, R., & Googins, B. (1989). Alcoholism day treatment: Rationale, research, and resistance. *Journal of Drug Abuse, 19*, 437–449.

Sheehan, J. J., Wieman, R. J., & Bechtel, J. E. (1981). Follow-up of a twelve month treatment program for chronic alcoholics. *International Journal of the Addictions, 16*, 233–241.

Stein, L., Newton, J. R., & Bowman, R. F. (1975). Duration of hospitalization for alcoholism. *Archives of General Psychiatry, 32*, 247–252.

Walsh, D. C., Hingson, R. W., Merrigan, D. M., Levenson, S. M., Cupples, L. A., Heeren, T., Coffman, G. A., Becker, C. A., Barker, T. A., Hamilton, S. K., McGuire, T. G., & Kelly, C. A. (1991). A randomized trial of treatment options for alcohol-abusing workers. *New England Journal of Medicine, 325*, 775–782.

Wanberg, K. W., Horn, J. L., & Fairchild, D. (1974). Hospital versus community treatment of alcoholism problems. *International Journal of Mental Health, 3*, 160–176.

Willems, P. J., Letemendia, F. J., & Arroyave, F. (1973a). A two year follow-up study comparing short and long stay inpatient treatment of alcoholics. *British Journal of Psychiatry, 122*, 637–640.

Willems, P. J., Letemendia, F. J., & Arroyave, F. (1973b). A categorization for the assessment of prognosis and outcome in the treatment of alcoholism. *British Journal of Psychiatry, 122*, 649–654.

Wright, G. E., & Buck, J. A. (1991). Medicaid support of alcohol, drug abuse, and mental health services. *Health Care Financing Review, 13*, 117–128.

Zwanziger, J., Davis, L., Bamezai, A., & Hosek, S. D. (1991). Using DRGs to pay for inpatient substance abuse services: An assessment of the CHAMPUS reimbursement system. *Medical Care, 29*, 561–577.

CHAPTER 31

HARM REDUCTION

Lisa J. Roberts
G. Alan Marlatt

In this chapter the history of harm reduction, central tenets of harm reduction, and common criticisms of harm reduction are described. Applications of harm reduction techniques across a wide range of addictive behaviors are also presented.

DEFINITIONS AND OVERVIEW

The terms *harm reduction* and *harm minimization* are often used interchangeably. Both terms refer to policies and programs designed to reduce or minimize the harm associated with ongoing or active addictive behaviors. Interest in this approach began in Europe (particularly in the United Kingdom and the Netherlands) in response to the rapidly rising rate of HIV infection among injecting drug users and growing evidence that the criminal justice approach to controlling drug use was exacerbating the problem rather than reducing or eliminating it (Engelsman, 1989; Heather, Wodak, Nadelmann, & O' Hare, 1993; Marks, 1991; O'Hare, Newcombe, Matthews, Buning, & Drucker, 1992).

Harm reduction methods are based on the assumption that habits can be placed along a continuum of harmful consequences. The goal of harm reduction is to move the individual along this continuum, or take steps in the right direction to reduce harmful consequences (Marlatt, Baer, & Larimer, 1995). Figure 31.1 depicts a continuum of risk for harm ranging from excess (maximum harm risk) to abstinence (lowest harm risk) (Marlatt, Larimer, Baer, & Quigley, 1993; Marlatt, Somers, & Tapert, 1993) .

In describing methods and procedures of harm reduction, three basic approaches arise: working with the individual or group, modifying the environment, and implementing public policy changes. At the level of the individual, harm reduction methods include:(a) changing the route of drug administration, (b) providing "alternative," safer substances, and (c) reducing the frequency or intensity (quantity and dose level) or both, of ongoing addictive behaviors (Marlatt, Somers, & Tapert, 1993, p. 153). In behavioral psychology, harm reduction is similar to the process known as shaping, defined as "the progressive modification and subsequent shifting of the boundaries of a response class within which responses are reinforced, outside of which they are extinguished. Used when the operant level of a response is very low or when the final response is *too complex initially*"(Powers & Osborne, 1976, p. 400). This step-down approach has been described by Allan Parry (1989, p. 13), a leader of harm

Figure 31.1   Continuum of Excess, Moderation, and Abstinence

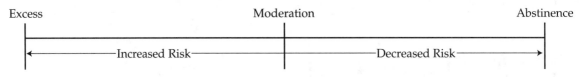

Excess   Moderation   Abstinence

←————————Increased Risk————————|————————Decreased Risk————————→

"Any steps toward decreased risk are steps in the right direction."

Source: "Etiology and Secondary Prevention of Alcohol Problems with Young Adults" by J. S. Baer, 1993, in *Addictive Behaviors Across the Lifespan* by J. S. Baer, G. A. Marlatt, and R. J. McMahon, Eds. Copyright © 1993 by Sage Publications.

reduction approaches to drug addiction and AIDS prevention in Liverpool, England:

> Harm reduction takes small steps to reduce, even to a small degree, the harm caused by the use of drugs. If a person is injecting street heroin of unknown potency, harm reduction would consider it an advance if the addict were prescribed safe, legal heroin. A further advantage if he stopped sharing needles. A further advantage if he enrolled in a needle-exchange scheme. A much further advance if he moved on to oral drugs or to smoked drugs. A further advance in harm reduction if he started using condoms and practicing safe sex practices. A further advance if he took advantage of the general health services available to addicts. A wonderful victory if he kicked drugs, although total victory is not a requirement as it is in the United States.

Harm reduction provides a conceptual umbrella that covers a variety of previously unrelated programs and techniques, including needle-exchange programs for injecting drug users (IDUs), methadone maintenance treatment for opiate users, nicotine replacement therapy for smokers, and moderation oriented drinking programs for problem drinkers (Somers, Tapert, & Marlatt, 1992, p. 222).

HISTORY OF HARM REDUCTION

U.K. Model

The United Kingdom pioneered the "medicalization" approach in which drug abusers can be prescribed drugs such as heroin and cocaine on a maintenance basis. The prescribing of drugs dates back to the Rolleston Committee of the 1920s in which a group of prominent British physicians recommended that in certain cases addicts be prescribed narcotics in order to reduce the harm of their drug use and to help them lead useful lives and to stabilize their lifestyle as a first step in providing addi-

tional treatment services and options (Rolleston, 1926). Although the prescribing drugs for addicts fell into disfavor over the ensuing years, this policy was widely practiced in Meyerside, England, serving the population around the city of Liverpool (Marks, 1991).

In the Meyerside harm reduction model, addicts are offered a wide range of services including needle exchange, prescription of drugs such as heroin and cocaine, outreach education and counseling, employment and housing services. Pharmacists fill prescriptions for smokeable drugs prepared as "reefers," in which drugs such as heroin and methadone are injected into cigarettes. In addition to smokeable reefers, pharmacists dispense drugs in ampules, liquid, and aerosol form (Riley, 1994). As described by Marks (1991), all addicts who register with the Drug Dependency Service in the Meyerside area are initially offered treatment for their addiction, including inpatient detoxification. Only about 10% are interested in treatment geared toward cessation of drug use (Marks, 1991, pp. 307–310). Decisions about each addict's treatment or drug maintenance goals are decided on by members of an interdisciplinary team, including physicians, social workers, nurses, and other therapists. As such the medicalization program is not directed only by the physician who writes prescriptions.

Netherlands (Dutch Model)

Holland, a country with just over 15 million inhabitants, began to make radical changes in national drug policy in the 1970s in response to the drug problem in the late 1960s. Prior to drug policy reform, stiff sentences were meted out to those caught possessing illicit drugs, including prison terms of 1 year or more for possession of marijuana (van de Wijngaart, 1991). In 1972, the Narcotics Working Party published a document concluding that the basic premises of drug policy should be congruent with the extent of the risks involved in drug use (Narcotics Working Party, 1972). This policy change led to the adoption of a revised Dutch Opium Act in 1976, when a distinction was made in the law between drugs of "unacceptable risk" (heroin, cocaine, amphetamines, and LSD) and drugs with lower risk such as marijuana and hashish (van de Wijngaart, 1991). Another goal of this policy change was to separate the markets in which hard drugs and soft drugs circulate.

The Dutch endorse a "normalization policy" in dealing with their addict population. Instead of criminalizing drug use and labeling and stigmatizing drug abusers, the Dutch policy attempts to eliminate the sensational and emotional overtones of the addict lifestyle. Under a normalization policy, "drug takers or even addicts should neither be seen as criminals, nor as dependent patients, but as 'normal' citizens of whom we make 'normal' demands and to whom we offer 'normal' opportunities. Addicts should not be treated as a special category" (Engelsman, 1989, p.215). The normalization policy is summed up by Engelsman, "The Dutch policy of normalization seems to have produced a context where the addict more resembles an unemployed Dutch citizen than a monster endangering society" (Engelsman, 1989, pp. 216–217).

The Dutch harm reduction policy was stimulated in large part by direct input from drug users and addicts themselves. In 1980 the "Junkiebond," a trade union of Dutch drug users and addicts, was established in Rotterdam. These addicts advocated for drug policy changes that would permit the legal exchange of needles to reduce the risk of HIV infection, which led to the development of the first needle exchange program in 1984 (Buning, 1991).

CENTRAL ASSUMPTIONS AND PRINCIPLES

The philosophy of harm reduction is based on two central tenets. First, harm reduction provides a public health alternative to the moral/criminal and disease models of drug use and addiction. Second, harm reduction recognizes abstinence as an ideal distal goal, but accepts other proximal subgoals as acceptable, to the extent that harmful consequences are reduced.

A Public Health Alternative to the Moral/Criminal and Disease Models of Drug Use and Addiction

American views of drug use and addiction have been based on two competing and often conflicting models: the moral model and the disease model. In terms of the moral model, American drug control policy has determined that illegal drug use and/or distribution of such drugs is a crime deserving punishment. As an extension of the moral model (assumption: illicit drug use is morally wrong), the criminal justice system has collaborated with national drug policy makers in pursuing the "War on Drugs," the ultimate aim of which is to foster the development of a drug-free society. The majority of federal funding for drug controls has been based on a supply-reduction approach (Goldstein, 1994; Jarvik, 1990). Federal enforcement agencies (i.e., the U.S. Drug Enforcement Agency) are funded primarily to promote interdiction programs designed to reduce the supply of drugs coming into this country (e.g., to destroy the supply of coca plants used to produce cocaine in Columbia and other Latin countries). National, state and city police are funded to arrest drug dealers and users alike in an attempt to further reduce the supply of drugs. This has resulted in overcrowding of American courts and prisons with inmates convicted of drug offenses.

The second approach is to define addiction (e.g., alcoholism or heroin addiction) as a biological/genetic disease that requires treatment and rehabilitation. Here the emphasis is on prevention and treatment programs that focus on remediation of the individual's desire or demand for drugs, a demand reduction approach (Goldstein, 1994; Jarvik, 1990). Despite the apparent contradiction between viewing drug users as either a criminal deserving of punishment or a sick person in need of treatment, both the supply reduction and demand reduction models are in agreement that the ultimate aim of both approaches is to eliminate the prevalence of drug use by focusing primarily on the drug user ("use reduction").

Harm reduction, with its philosophical roots in pragmatism and its compatibility with a public health approach, offers a practical and humane alternative to either the moral or the disease models. Unlike proponents of the moral model, who view drug use as bad or illegal and who advocate supply reduction (via prohibition and punishment), harm reduction shifts the focus away from drug use itself to the consequences or effects of addictive behavior. Such effects are evaluated primarily in terms of whether they are harmful or helpful to the drug user and to the larger society, and not on the basis of whether the behavior itself is considered morally right or wrong. Unlike supporters of the disease model, who view addiction as a biological/genetic pathology and promote demand reduction as the primary goal of prevention and abstinence as the only acceptable goal of treatment, harm reduction offers a wide range of policies and procedures designed to reduce the harmful consequences of addictive behavior. Advocates of harm reduction accept the practical fact that many people use drugs and engage in other high-risk behaviors and that idealistic visions of a drug-free society are unlikely to become a reality (Des Jarlais, 1995; Goldstein, 1994, p. 269).

Recognizes Abstinence as an Ideal Outcome but Accepts Alternatives That Reduce Harm: Harm Reduction Is NOT Anti-Abstinence

> According to Greek mythology there was a man named Procrustes "who lived beside the road and had two beds in his house, one small the other large. Offering a night's lodging to travelers, he would lay the short men on the large bed, and rack them out to fit it; but the tall men on the small bed, sawing off as much of their legs as projected beyond it. Some say, however, that he used only one bed, and lengthened or shortened his lodgers according to its measure (Graves, 1994, p. 330).

Any reader would perceive Procrustes' behavior as cruel and unnecessary. However, given the current "one-size fits all" mode of addiction treatment, are we not in essence trying to make our patients "fit" into the same treatment bed, irrespective of their individual differences? By trying to make all of our patients fit into one approach to treatment are we not guilty of the same behavior as Procrustes? The moral model and the disease model share one strong common value: the insistence upon total abstinence as the only acceptable goal of either incarceration or treatment. Despite the harsh reality of high recidivism rates for released prisoners and the correspondingly high rate of relapse for treated addicts, there has been no relaxation of this absolute insistence upon abstinence. Contemporary American drug policy is based on the ultimate criterion of "zero tolerance"—a policy that states that any illegal drug use, including the occasional smoking of marijuana, is as intolerable as a daily pattern of intravenous heroin injection. Similarly, the only acceptable goal of almost all American alcohol and drug treatment programs is lifelong abstinence along with continued attendance at 12-step recovery groups. In fact, abstinence is almost always required as a precondition for treatment, as most chemical dependency treatment programs refuse to admit patients who are still using drugs. One must first abstain in order to receive treatment designed to maintain abstinence. According to this perspective, addiction is viewed as a progressive disease that cannot be cured, but only "arrested" by a commitment to abstinence. Any subsequent drug use is defined as a relapse back to the disease condition, an inevitable outcome determined by biological factors beyond the individual's control (craving and "loss of control" triggered by biological effects). The unwillingness of the American alcoholism treatment community to accept moderate alcohol consumption as an alternative to abstinence is clearly evident in the intensity of feelings evoked by the controlled drinking controversy (Marlatt, 1983; Marlatt, Larimer, Baer, & Quigley, 1993).

HARM REDUCTION METHODS AND AREAS OF APPLICATION

In the next section, three different techniques are described that may promote movement along the continuum. The application of these strategies is illustrated using three different types of populations: (1) low threshold delivery of services for intravenous drug users; (2) motivational interviewing with college binge drinkers, and (3) relapse prevention with cocaine-dependent schizophrenics.

Low Threshold Services

An important factor in attempting to facilitate treatment seeking in general is to present services to potential clients (information, referral, prevention, and treatment) as being low threshold: having easy access, being nonthreatening, and having little or no stigma attached. Such programs attempt to address the health and social well-being of drug users without making these services contingent on a total commitment to abstinence on the part of the user. Low threshold programs make every possible attempt to include the needs of drug users within the broader context of health care and social services. This is opposed to high threshold services that require abstinence both as a condition of admission and as a criterion for continued access to treatment (Marlatt, Tucker, Donovan, & Vuchinich, in press). Strang (1994) compares low threshold services to the marketing strategy of providing "loss-leaders" to potential consumers (offering below-cost or even free items to engage the interest of a wider purchasing group). One measure of the value of loss leaders is the extent to which they encourage recruitment and subsequent flow on to the next level of treatment (Strang, 1990, p. 145). Carvell and Hart (1990) suggest that low threshold outreach programs that have open-access policies can attract clients who are not in contact with traditional treatment agencies, and promote a harm reduction focus that can serve successfully as a gateway to other services (Marlatt et al., in press).

Application of Low Threshold Services and Needle Exchange

As described previously in the section on history of harm reduction in the Netherlands, input from the addicts associated with the Junkiebond led to the development of the first needle exchange program in 1984 (Buning, 1991). The Municipal Health Service first delivered disposable needles and syringes in large quantities once a week to the Junkiebond for distribution and collection of used needles. As AIDS and the risk for HIV infection through shared needles increased in the mid-1980s, the number of exchanged needles and syringes rose from 100,000 in 1985 to 720,000 in 1988 (van Brussel & Buning, 1988). One of the most significant results of this easy-access, low-threshold treatment philosophy is that the Dutch claim to be in contact with a majority of the addict population. "In Amsterdam about 60–80% are being reached by any kind of assistance. This percentage is certainly higher in less urbanized regions" (Engelsman, 1989, p. 217). Such a high rate of contact facilitates client access to other AIDS prevention and public health programs.

The first needle exchange program in the United States was founded in 1988, and as of 1994, there were over 40 such programs operating in at least 23 states (Lloyd, O'Shea, & the Injection Drug Use Study Group, 1994). These programs use a variety of techniques to ensure access to services including mobile vans and setting up tables near homeless shelters, food distribution centers, and parks.

Cities with needle exchange programs have shown decreasing incidence rates of HIV; that is, a decrease in the number of new cases each year (Buning, 1991; Hart et al., 1989; Stimson, Donoghoe, Alldritt, & Dolan, 1988). The New Haven needle exchange was evaluated for effectiveness by members of the Yale School of Medicine (Kaplan, O'Keefe, & Heimer, 1991). Estimates of HIV prevalence were made from tests on returned syringes. Using a mathematical model of HIV transmission, the New Haven needle exchange program is estimated to have reduced new infections of HIV among clients by 33%. This finding has encouraged public health officials in other cities to reconsider prohibitive policies.

The most successful needle exchanges are user friendly and administer services in locations, times, and manners appropriate for the clientele. For example, one needle exchange in Boulder, Colorado is located near a gymnasium to target steroid injectors (Keller, 1992). Low threshold harm reduction programs attempt to "meet people where they are" both geographically and with respect to their readiness to change their addictive behaviors (Marlatt & Tapert, 1993).

Motivational Interviewing

Motivational interviewing (Miller & Rollnick, 1991) is a technique designed to cultivate and strengthen an individual's level of commitment to change (Marlatt, Somers, & Tapert, 1993). Consistent with Prochaska and DiClemente's (1982) model of the stages of behavior change, the motivational interviewer's task is to help an individual advance from considering change to attempting change, in a non-confrontational manner (Marlatt, Somers, & Tapert, 1993). The stages of behavior change (also referred to as the transtheoretical model of behavior change) postulate five distinct, well-defined stages that reflect an individual's readiness (motivation) to change the target. These stages and their definitions are precontemplation, in which there is no intention to change behavior; contemplation, in which the person is aware that a problem exists and is seriously thinking about changing, but has not made a commitment to take action; preparation, in which the person is prepared to take action but has not yet done so; action, in which the person has successfully altered behavior from 1 day to 6 months; and maintenance, in which the person is able to remain free of the addictive behaviors for more than 6 months (Prochaska, DiClemente, & Norcross, 1992).

Consistent with harm reduction, motivational interviewing may be used to encourage action to reduce the risk of harm, even among individuals not committed to quitting their addictive behavior. For instance, motivational interviewing could be used to help an individual reduce the frequency or intensity of the addictive behavior, thus moving along the continuum of harm in the direction of reduced risk (Marlatt & Tapert, 1993).

Application of Motivational Interviewing with College Heavy Drinkers

Among college students surveyed, approximately half (44%) were classified as heavy drinkers (Wechsler,

Dowdall, Davenport, & Castillo, 1995) and many studies have identified college students as a population at elevated risk for immediate alcohol-related problems based on high levels of alcohol consumption (Berkowitz & Perkins, 1986; Brennan, Walfish, & AuBuchon, 1986; Engs & Hanson, 1988; Institute of Medicine, 1990; Saltz & Elandt, 1986).

The Lifestyles '94 Project at the University of Washington is based on social learning theory and cognitive-behavioral principles (Marlatt & George, 1984). The goal of the alcohol skills training program is to reduce and moderate the pattern of alcohol consumption among college drinkers (Kivlahan, Marlatt, Fromme, Coppel, & Williams, 1990). All students entering their freshman year during 1990 were screened to participate in the Lifestyles Project, a 4-year longitudinal study. From the screening pool, two groups were selected: a high-risk sample and a control sample.

Students assigned to the high-risk treatment group participated in a motivational intervention provided in the winter of their first year of college. This intervention was based on previous work with brief interventions for college students (Baer et al., 1992; Marlatt, Baer, & Larimer, 1995) and general motivation interviewing techniques (Miller & Rollnick, 1991). In the feedback interview, a professional staff member met individually with the students and gave them concrete feedback about their drinking patterns, risks, and beliefs about alcohol effects. The style of the interview was based on techniques of motivational interviewing. Confrontational communications, such as "you have a problem and you are in denial" are thought to create a defensive response in the client and were specifically avoided. Instead, students were presented data about their drinking patterns and were allowed to evaluate their situation and begin to contemplate the possibility of change. "What do you make of this?", and "Are you suprised?" were common questions raised to students in an effort to facilitate conversations about risk and the possibility of behavior change (Marlatt, Baer, & Larimer, 1995).

From a motivational interviewing perspective (Miller & Rollnick, 1991), students are assumed to be in a natural state of ambivalence, and must come to their own conclusion regarding the need to change behavior and reduce risks. Thus the goals of subsequent behavior changes were left to the student and not outlined or demanded by the interviewer. This style leaves responsibility with the client and hence treats all clients as thoughtful adults. Each stu-

dent left the interview with a "personalized feedback sheet" that compared his or her responses with college norms and listed reported problems, and a "tips" page that described biphasic responses to alcohol, placebo effects, and provided suggestions for reducing the risks of drinking (Marlatt, Baer, & Larimer, 1995).

Early results of this brief intervention with college freshman have been reported previously (Baer, 1993; Baer, Kivlahan, & Marlatt, 1992). Multivariate analyses completed on the 1- and 2-year postbaseline follow-up points revealed that, although all students on average reported reduced drinking over time, significantly greater reductions were continually reported by those given the brief motivational intervention. This intervention seems effective for all students, regardless of risk status. However, several trends suggest that all students are not equally at risk, and therefore, treatment may be more important for certain individuals. Specifically, men living in fraternities who also have a history of conduct problems showed the most severe pattern of drinking problems over time and the least decline. These individuals may benefit most from this type of preventive programming (Marlatt, Baer, & Larimer, 1995).

Relapse Prevention

Relapse prevention (RP) is defined as a cognitive-behavioral self-management program (Craighead, Craighead, Kazdin, & Mahoney, 1994) that combines behavioral skills training procedures with cognitive techniques to help individuals maintain their desired behavioral change (Marlatt & Gordon, 1985). With behavioral skills training as the cornerstone of the RP approach, RP teaches clients how to anticipate, identify, and manage high-risk situations, while also striving for broader lifestyle balance through more global behavior modification.

From a harm reduction perspective, RP programs are designed for relapse management: to reduce the frequency and intensity of relapse episodes, to keep the client involved in the treatment process, and to motivate renewed efforts toward behavior change (Marlatt & Tapert, 1993). The objective of relapse prevention is to reduce the magnitude of relapse. One of the first steps is to explore with the client his or her own subjective associations with the word relapse. Responses often convey a sense of failure to attain a desired goal. This may be particularly true of clients who ascribe to the disease model or 12-step perspective. Viewed in this light, relapse or the recurrence of a disease state is diametrically opposed with doing well or abstaining. Relapse is reframed as a process, which provides an opportunity for additional learning. An individual who is attempting to change an addictive behavior may sometimes find that a lapse provides important information about the factors that led up to the event and how to make corrections in the future. From this perspective, it may be more appropriate to reframe a lapse or relapse as a "prolapse," as the overall beneficial outcome moves the individual along the continuum of behavior change (Marlatt & Gordon, 1985). The client's cognitive-affective response to a slip can further increase the probability of a full-blown relapse. Clients who view relapse in dichotomous terms, in particular, may believe that there is no going back once the line has been crossed: Once committed, the deed is done. To account for this transgression, the abstinence violation effect or AVE (Collins, 1993; Curry, Marlatt, & Gordon, 1987; Marlatt & Gordon, 1985) was postulated. Management of ongoing drug use, coping with lapses or mistakes made while trying to change an addictive behavior, and the responses to these events are the basis of relapse prevention (Dimeff & Marlatt, 1995).

Application of Relapse Prevention with Cocaine-Dependent Schizophrenics

Drug abuse among chronic psychiatric patients is widely recognized as a significant clinical and social problem that presents enormous challenges for patients, clinicians, social service agencies and health care systems (Cooper, Anglin, & Brown, 1989; Drake & Wallach, 1989; Gorman, 1987; Ridgely, Goldman, & Talbott, 1986;). Epidemiological studies have reported a high rate of the co-occurrence of substance abuse and mental illness (Regier et al., 1990). Mentally ill substance abusers tend to relapse more often and require more time to achieve abstinence than non-mentally-ill substance abusers (Carey, 1989). Many dual diagnosis patients either cannot tolerate standard substance abuse interventions or do not benefit from them (Hellerstein & Meehan, 1987; Kofoed, Kania, Walsh, & Atkinson, 1986; Minkoff, 1989; Mueser, Bellack, & Blanchard, 1992).

Typical of this dual diagnosis population are individuals with schizophrenia who are also addicted to drugs and alcohol (Mueser, Bellack, & Blanchard, 1992). Mental health programs responsible for treating this population are rapidly adopting relapse prevention strategies based on harm reduction (Carey, 1996). This adoption of harm

reduction approaches has been driven by the following two observations.

First, very few patients can achieve abstinence immediately and once abstinence is achieved, relapse is common (Carey, 1989). If mental health programs required abstinence as a condition of treatment, then most addicted schizophrenics would not have access to essential mental health interventions such as education, antipsychotic medication, skills training, and case management.

Second, mental health programs cannot simply ignore substance abuse. It interferes with the treatment of schizophrenia (Carey, 1996). For example, substance abuse leads to poor attendance at mental health clinics (Carey & Carey, 1990). So if the program does nothing about the addiction, the result is the same as when abstinence is required—untreated schizophrenia. In this population requiring abstinence is equivalent to ignoring addiction.

At the West Los Angeles Veterans Administration (VA) Medical Center, a specialized Dual Diagnosis Treatment Program (DDTP) was developed for the acute treatment and long-term rehabilitation of stimulant-abusing schizophrenics. Using a multidisciplinary treatment team, patient care is approached using a combination of pharmacological, psychoeducational, behavioral, and case management techniques. The approach is based on comprehensive techniques of psychosocial treatment and rehabilitation adapted to meet the needs of stimulant-abusing schizophrenics. The overriding goal of the program is to help patients achieve and maintain tenure within the community (Roberts, Shaner, Eckman, Tucker, & Vaccaro, 1992). Obviously, successful community tenure is dependent on successful management of both schizophrenia and substance abuse. Thus the rehabilitation goals emphasize overall functioning as opposed to just focusing on whether someone has "relapsed."

To impart relapse prevention skills, patients participate in structured behavioral skills training. This skills training is based on a highly structured and empirically developed learning model that is structured to accommodate the information-processing deficits of schizophrenia (Liberman et al., 1993). Based on the model of relapse prevention described by Marlatt and Gordon (1985), the Substance Abuse Management Module (SAMM) teaches schizophrenics how to avoid drugs and how to replace drug use behaviors with healthy behaviors. In order to avoid using drugs, skills training is directed toward identifying and avoiding common situations that precede drug use. For instance, receipt of disability funds is associated with increased drug use, psychosis, and hospitalization (Shaner et al., 1995). This information has been incorporated into the Substance Abuse Management Module (SAMM), as a high-risk situation so that patients, clinicians, and families can work together to anticipate and effectively manage this high-risk situation. Patient are taught how to refuse drugs offered by friends and by dealers and they practice these skills in group classroom settings. However, most of the skills training focuses on minimizing harm caused by continued substance abuse and increasing behaviors that are incompatible with continued drug use. For example, patients learn that abstinence is the ideal goal, but that if they slip and use, it is important to stop early before further damage to their health, relationships, and finances. They rehearse how to leave a drug-using situation even after having used some drug and how to report the slip to a mental health professional. In other words, not only are they encouraged to return to treatment immediately after using drugs, they are also taught exactly how to do it.

Patients often report that they use drugs to reduce psychiatric symptoms and medication side effects (Dixon, Haas, Weiden, Sweeney, & Frances, 1991; Freed, 1975; Mueser, Bellack & Blanchard, 1992). Consequently, the module teaches them how to discuss these symptoms and side effects with a psychiatrist. The module even teaches patients how to ask another person to join them in activities they consider fun, that are healthy, and do not involve drugs. Patients are encouraged to attend these psychoeducational and skills training groups despite active substance abuse (provided that the group process is not disrupted). Efforts to evaluate the efficacy of this module are under way. [1]

SUMMARY AND CONCLUSIONS

Harm reduction is a humane and pragmatic philosophy that refers to techniques that may be used with individuals or the environment or to shape public policies. Thus harm reduction is a public health alternative to the traditional models of addiction (moral/criminal and disease). The overriding goal of harm reduction is to reduce or minimize the harm with ongoing or active addictive behaviors. Although abstinence may be the ideal or ultimate risk-reduction goal, harm reduction accepts as improvement any movement toward decreased risk.

Historically, harm reduction began with the medicalization approach used by the United Kingdom and the normalization approach used in the Netherlands. However, in recent years, harm reduction techniques have also been used in the United States.

Harm reduction is often described as a conceptual umbrella that covers a variety of unrelated programs and techniques. Examples of harm reduction techniques—such as low threshold delivery of services for injecting drug users, motivational interviewing for heavy drinking college students, and relapse prevention with cocaine dependent schizophrenics—illustrate the emerging theme that harm reduction is broad based and inclusive. In other words, a harm reduction philosophy encourages taking a wide view of the risks associated with addictive behaviors and attempting to take steps to reduce any harm, to promote movement along the continuum of excess risk to zero risk.

NOTE

Support for the development and evaluation of the Substance Abuse Management Module (SAMM) was provided by the National Institute on Drug Abuse (NIDA) to Andrew Shaner, M.D. (principal investigator), grant # RO1 DA09436.

REFERENCES

Baer, J. S. (1993). Etiology and secondary prevention of alcohol problems with young adults. In J. S. Baer, G. A. Marlatt, & R. J. McMahon (Eds.), *Addictive behaviors across the lifespan* (pp. 111–137). Newbury Park, CA: Sage.

Baer, J. S., Marlatt, G. A., Kivlahan, D. R., Fromme, K., Larimer, M., & Williams, E. (1992). An experimental test of three methods of alcohol risk reduction with young adults. *Journal of Consulting and Clinical Psychology, 60*, 974–979.

Berkowitz, A. D., & Perkins, H. W. (1986). Problem drinking among college students: A review of recent research. *Journal of American College Health, 35*, 21–28.

Brennan, A. F., Walfish, S., & AuBuchon, P. (1986). Alcohol use and abuse in college students: 2. Social environmental correlates, methodological issues, and implications for intervention. *International Journal of the Addictions, 21*, 475–493.

Buning, E. C. (1991). Effects of Amsterdam needle and syringe exchange. *International Journal of the Addictions, 26*, 1303–1311.

Carey, K. B. (1989). Treatment of the mentally ill chemical abuser: Description of the Hutchings day treatment program. *Psychiatric Quarterly, 60*, 303–316.

Carey, K. B. (1996). Substance use reduction in the context of outpatient psychiatric treatment: A collaborative, motivational, harm reduction approach. *Community Mental Health Journal, 32*, 291–306.

Carey, K. B., & Carey, M. P. (1990). Enhancing the treatment attendance of mentally ill chemical abusers. *Journal of Behavior Therapy and Experimental Psychiatry, 21*, 205–209.

Carvell, A. M., & Hart, G. J. (1990). Help-seeking and referrals in a needle exchange: A comprehensive service to injecting drug users. *British Journal of Addiction, 85*, 235–240.

Collins, R. L. (1993). Drinking, restraint and risk for alcohol abuse. *Experimental and Clinical Psychopharmacology, 1*, 44–54.

Cooper, L., Anglin, D., & Brown, V. (1989). *Multiple diagnosis: Aspects and issues in substance abuse treatment.* Unpublished white paper for the State of California Department of Alcohol and Drug Programs.

Craighead, L. W., Craighead, W. E., Kazdin, A. E., & Mahoney, M. J. (1994). *Cognitive and behavioral interventions: An empirical approach to mental health problems.* Boston: Allyn and Bacon.

Curry, S. J., Marlatt, G. A., & Gordon, J. R. (1987). Abstinence violation effect: Validation of an attributional construct with smoking cessation. *Journal of Consulting and Clinical Psychology, 55*, 145–149.

Des Jarlais, D. C. (1995). Harm reduction: A framework for incorporating science into drug policy. *American Journal of Public Health, 85*, 10–12.

Dixon, L., Haas, G., Weiden, P. J., Sweeney, J., & Francis, A. J. (1991). Drug abuse in schizophrenic patients: Clinical correlates and reasons for use. *American Journal of Psychiatry, 148*, 224–230.

Dimeff, L. A., & Marlatt, G. A. (1995). Relapse prevention. In R. K. Hester and W. R. Miller (Eds.), *Handbook of alcoholism treatment approaches* (2nd ed., pp. 176–194). Boston: Allyn and Bacon.

Drake, R. E., & Wallach, M. A. (1989). Substance abuse among the chronically mentally ill. *Hospital and Community Psychiatry, 40*, 1041–1046.

Engelsman, E. L. (1989). Dutch policy on the management of drug-related problems. *British Journal of Addiction, 84*, 211–218.

Engs, R. C., & Hanson, D. J. (1988). University students' drinking patterns and problems: Examining the effects of raising the purchase age. *Public Health Reports, 103*, 667–673.

Freed, E. X. (1975). Alcoholism and schizophrenia: The search for perspectives. *Journal of Studies on Alcohol, 36*, 853–881.

Goldstein, A. (1994). *Addiction: From biology to drug policy.* New York: Freeman.

Gorman, C. (1987). Bad trips for the doubly troubled. *Time, 130*(5), 58.

Graves, R. (1994). *The Greek myths* (p. 330, sec. 96.k.6). Wakefield: Moyer Bell.

Hart, G. J., Carvell, A. L. M., Woodward, N., Johnson, A. M., Williams, P., & Parry, J. V. (1989). Evaluation of needle exchange in central London: Behavior change and anti-HIV status over one year. *AIDS, 3*, 261–265.

Heather, N., Wodak, A., Nadelmann, E., & O'Hare, P. (Eds.). (1993). *Psychoactive drugs and harm reduction: From faith to science.* London: Whurr.

Hellerstein, D., & Meehan, B. (1987). Outpatient group therapy for schizophrenic substance abusers. *American Journal of Psychiatry, 144*, 1337–1339.

Institute of Medicine (1990). *Broadening the base of treatment for alcohol problems.* Washington, DC: National Academy Press.

Jarvik, M. E. (1990). The drug dilemma: Manipulating the demand. *Science, 250*, 387–392.

Kaplan, E. H., O'Keefe, E., & Heimer, R. (1991). *Evaluating the New Haven needle exchange program.* Paper presented at the meeting of the International Conference on AIDS, Florence, Italy.

Keller, I. E. (1992, February). Needle exchange: HIV prevention takes on the law. *Exchange of the National Lawyers Guild AIDS Network.*

Kivlahan, D. R., Marlatt, G. A., Fromme, K., Coppel, D. B., & Williams, E. (1990). Secondary prevention with college drinkers: Evaluation of an alcohol skills training program. *Journal of Consulting and Clinical Psychology, 58*, 805–810.

Kofoed, L., Kania, J., Walsh, T., & Atkinson, R. M. (1986). Outpatient treatment of patients with substance abuse and other co-existing psychiatric disorders. *American Journal of Psychiatry, 143*, 867–872.

Liberman, R. P., Wallace, C. J., Blackwell, G., Eckman, T. A., Vaccaro, J. V., & Kuehnel, T. G. (1993). Innovations in skills training for the seriously mentally ill: The UCLA social and independent living skills modules. *Innovations and Research, 2*, 43–60.

Lloyd, I. S., O'Shea, D. J., & the Injection Drug Use Study Group. (1994). *Injection drug use in San Diego County: A needs assessment.* San Diego, CA: Alliance Healthcare Foundation.

Marks, J. (1991). The practice of controlled availability of illicit drugs. In N. Heather, W. R. Miller, & J. Greeley (Eds.), *Self-control and the addictive behaviors* (pp. 304–316). Botany Bay, Australia: Maxwell Macmillan.

Marlatt, G. A. (1983). The controlled drinking controversy: A commentary. *American Psychologist, 38*, 1097–1110.

Marlatt, G. A., Baer, J. S., & Larimer, M. E. (1995). Preventing alcohol abuse in college students: A harm-reduction approach. In G. M. Boyd, J. Howard, & R. A. Zucker (Eds.), *Alcohol problems among adolescents: Current directions in prevention research* (pp. 147–172). Northvale, NJ: Lawrence Erlbaum.

Marlatt, G. A., & George, W. (1984). Relapse prevention: Introduction and overview of the model. *British Journal of Addiction, 79*, 261–273.

Marlatt, G. A., & Gordon, J. R. (1985). *Relapse prevention: Maintenance strategies in the treatment of addictive behaviors.* New York: Guilford.

Marlatt, G. A., Larimer, M. E., Baer, J. S., & Quigley, L. A. (1993). Harm reduction for alcohol problems: Moving beyond the controlled drinking controversy. *Behavior Therapy, 24*, 461–504.

Marlatt, G. A., Somers, J. M., & Tapert, S. F. (1993). Harm reduction: Applications to alcohol abuse problems. In L. S. Onken,

J. D. Blaine, & J. J. Boren (Eds.), *Behavioral treatments for drug abuse and dependence*. Bethesda, MD: National Institute on Drug Abuse.

Marlatt, G. A., & Tapert, S. F. (1993). Harm reduction: Reducing the risks of addictive behaviors. In J. S. Baer, G. A. Marlatt, & R. McMahon (Eds.), *Addictive behaviors across the lifespan* (pp. 243–273). Newbury Park, CA: Sage.

Marlatt, G. A., Tucker, J. A., Donovan, D. M., & Vuchinich, R. E. (in press). To appear in L. S. Onken, J. D. Blaine, & J. J. Boren (Eds.), *Beyond the therapeutic alliance: Keeping the drug dependent individual in treatment*. (NIDA Research Monograph). Rockville, MD: National Institute on Drug Abuse.

Miller, W. R., & Rollnick, S. (1991). *Motivational interviewing: Preparing people to change addictive behavior*. New York: Guilford.

Minkoff, K. (1989). An integrated treatment model for dual diagnosis of psychosis and addiction. *Hospital and Community Psychiatry, 40*, 1031–1036.

Mueser, K. T., Bellack, A. S., & Blanchard, J. J. (1992). Comorbidity of schizophrenia and substance abuse: Implications for treatment. *Journal of Consulting and Clinical Psychology, 60*, 845–856.

Narcotics Working Party. (1972). *Backgrounds and risks of drug use*. The Hague, Netherlands: Government Publishing Office.

O'Hare, P. A., Newcombe, R., Matthews, A., Buning, E. C., & Drucker, E. (Eds.). (1992). *The reduction of drug-related harm*. London: Routledge.

Parry, A. (1989). Harm reduction. *The drug policy letter, 1*(4), 13. Washington DC: Drug Policy Foundation.

Powers, R. B. & Osborne, J. G. (1976). *Fundamentals of behavior* (p. 400). New York: West.

Prochaska, J. O., & Diclemente, C. C. (1982). Toward a comprehensive model of change: In W. R. Miller, and N. Heather. (Eds.), *Treating addictive behaviors* (pp. 3–27). New York: Plenum Press.

Prochaska, J. O., DiClemente, C. C., & Norcross, J. C. (1992). In search of how people change: Applications to addictive behaviors. *American Psychologist, 47*, 1102–1114.

Regier, D. A., Farmer, M. E., Rae, D. S., Locke, B. Z., Keith, S. J., Judd, L. L., & Goodwin, F. K. (1990). Comorbidity of mental disorders with alcohol and other drug abuse: results from the Epidemiological Catchment Area (ECA) study. *Journal of the American Medical Association, 264*, 2511–2518.

Ridgely, M. S., Goldman, H. H., & Talbott, J. A. (1986). *Chronic mentally ill young adults with substance abuse problems: A review of relevant literature and creation of a research agenda*. Mental Health Policy Studies. Baltimore: University of Maryland School of Medicine.

Riley, D. (1994). *The harm reduction model: Pragmatic approaches to drug use from the area between intolerance and neglect*. Ottawa, Canada: Canadian Centre on Substance Abuse.

Roberts, L. J., Shaner, A., Eckman, T. A., Tucker, D. E., & Vaccaro, J. V. (1992). Effectively treating stimulant-abusing schizophrenics: Mission impossible? *New Directions for Mental Health Services, 53*, 55–65.

Rolleston, H. (1926). *Report of the departmental committee on morphine and heroin addiction*. London: HMSO.

Saltz, R., & Elandt, D. (1986, Spring). College student drinking studies 1976–1985. *Contemporary Drug Problems*, 117–159.

Shaner, A., Eckman, T. A., Roberts, L. J., Wilkins, J. N., Tucker, D. E., Tsuang, J. W., & Mintz, J. (1995). Disability income, cocaine use, and repeated hospitalization among schizophrenic cocaine abusers: A government-sponsored revolving door? *New England Journal of Medicine, 333*, 777–783.

Somers, J. M., Tapert, S. F., & Marlatt (1992). Harm reduction: Principles, applications, and possibilities. In A. S. Trebach & K. B. Zeese, *Strategies for change: New directions in drug policy* (pp. 221–226). Washington, DC: Drug Policy Foundation Press.

Strang, J., & Gossop, M. (Eds.). (1994). *Heroin addiction and drug policy: The British system*. New York: Oxford University Press.

Stimson, G. V., Donoghoe, M., Alldritt, L., & Dolan, K. (1988). HIV transmission risk behaviour of clients attending syringe-exchange schemes in England and Scotland. *British Journal of Addiction, 83*, 1449–1455.

van Brussel, G., & Bunning, E. C. (1988). Public health management of AIDS and drugs in Amsterdam. In L.S . Harris (Ed.),,*Problems of drug dependence* (NIDA Research Monograph 90, pp. 295–301). Rockville, MD: National Institute on Drug Abuse.

van de Wijngaart, G. F. (1991). *Competing perspectives on drug use: The Dutch experience*. Amsterdam: Swets and Zeitlinger.

Wechsler, H., Dowdall, G. W., Davenport, A., & Castillo, S. (1995). Correlates of college student binge drinking. *American Journal of Public Health, 85*, 921–926.

CHAPTER 32

SMOKING CESSATION

Dorothy K. Hatsukami
Harry Lando

Great strides have been made in the past 30–40 years in the development of effective behavioral and pharmacological treatments for smoking cessation. The need for effective treatments is evident by the magnitude of economic costs and health consequences associated with cigarette smoking. In the United States alone, 420,000 people die prematurely each year as a result of cigarette smoking-related illnesses. Worldwide, cigarette smoking is estimated to kill approximately 3 million per year and projected to prematurely kill 10 million smokers per year by 2020. Although 17 million smokers in the United States attempt to quit smoking on their own each year, only 10% succeed. Although prevention is the key to limiting this important public health problem, intervention for a significant number of smokers will always be necessary because of the availability and easy access to tobacco products, the glamorization of its use and its affordability, and the highly addictive properties of nicotine. Each day, on the average 3,000 adolescents become regular smokers and significant numbers find themselves addicted to nicotine and experience difficulty quitting. This chapter will describes the types of treatments that have been developed for smoking cessation, the effectiveness of these treatments, and future directions for this area.

BEHAVIORAL TREATMENTS

Behavioral smoking cessation techniques can be used in numerous contexts from self-help manuals to intensive face-to-face clinic methods. A number of intervention approaches have achieved positive results. In general there is a strong relationship between the intensity of treatment and abstinence outcome. However, simple behavioral components can improve outcome across a range of methods. Multisession clinic methods have produced some of the strongest abstinence outcomes, but such methods tend to appeal to only a minority of smokers. These multisession clinic programs also are more costly than self-help approaches, although virtually any effective approach to smoking cessation is likely to have a high level of cost effectiveness (Cummings, Rubins, & Oster, 1989).

There has been considerable evolution of behavioral smoking cessation programs over the past 40 years. Smoking and other tobacco use was seen for many years as essentially a learned activity. More recently, smoking has been recognized as a physical addiction (USDHHS, 1988). Behavioral aspects of smoking are still seen as critical, however. One of the earliest programs, the "Five-Day Plan to Stop Smoking," was initiated by the Seventh Day

Adventist Church in the late 1950s. This program focused primarily on didactic information including health effects of smoking, changes in diet and physical activity, a buddy system, and a public pledge to quit. More formal behavior modification techniques came into favor in the 1960s. These techniques often emphasized conditioning and especially use of aversion. The focus was more on initial quitting than on long-term abstinence.

In the 1970s there was greater emphasis on cognitive in addition to behavioral or conditioning components in treatment. Programs became more complex and multifactorial and increasing attention was paid to issues of long-term maintenance. Abstinence outcomes began to improve. The trend toward multifactorial interventions continued in the 1980s. Two other major developments in the 1980s included relapse prevention strategies (Marlatt & Gordon, 1985) and introduction of the stages-of-change approach (Prochaska & DiClemente, 1983). Marlatt and Gordon viewed total abstinence as an overly limiting goal and argued that viewing any slip as relapse could become a self-fulfilling prophecy. They emphasized anticipation and rehearsal of difficult situations. If a slip did occur, it was critical that the individual not become demoralized but rather learn from the situation and very quickly resume abstinence.

The stages-of-change approach had a dramatic impact on the field that continues to the present. Prochaska and his colleagues maintained that existing smoking cessation programs were overly limiting because they were directed almost exclusively toward smokers who were ready to quit (Prochaska & DiClemente, 1983; Prochaska et al., 1994). In fact, most smokers are not at this point. Prochaska and his colleagues identified a series of stages of readiness, which they defined somewhat arbitrarily. These stages included precontemplation (not thinking about quitting within the next 6 months), contemplation (seriously thinking about quitting within the next 6 months), preparation (added to the original model; smokers who have tried to quit in the past year seriously thinking about quitting within 30 days), action (having quit 1 day to 6 months previously), and maintenance (more than 6 months of abstinence).

These authors provided outcome targets in addition to abstinence. They argued that to move a precontemplator to contemplation is a significant accomplishment (and in fact contemplators are considerably more likely to quit than are precontemplators). Interventions should be tailored to the individual's stage of readiness. Action-oriented treatments would tend not to work well with contemplators or precontemplators, whereas stage-appropriate methods could be effective in moving them through the change process. There is considerable evidence that stage of readiness is a strong predictor of future abstinence.

Literally thousands of studies have been published of smoking cessation interventions (see Lando, 1993; Schwartz, 1987). It is noteworthy that, in developing the Agency for Health Care Policy Research (AHCPR) guidelines on smoking cessation (AHCPR, 1996), approximately 3,000 articles published between 1975 and 1994 were reviewed. However, of these 3,000 articles, fewer than 400 met inclusion criteria for review (e.g., randomized controlled trial, minimum of 5-month follow-up after the quit date, published in peer-reviewed journal).

Provider Advice

The AHCPR guidelines strongly recommend that all patients should be screened for tobacco use. This screening could include expanding the vital signs to include smoking status (Fiore et al., 1995) or the use of such indicators as smoking status chart stickers. It is very clear that when screening systems are in place, the likelihood of smokers receiving smoking cessation advice in outpatient settings is greatly enhanced. The evidence that smoking status identification systems directly improve cessation outcome was not as strong, primarily due to the limited number of studies that addressed this issue. Nonetheless, the AHCPR guidelines concluded that all physicians and all clinicians should strongly advise every patient who smokes to quit.

There also is evidence that smoking cessation interventions delivered by a variety of clinicians and health care personnel increase cessation rates. Repeated advice by multiple types of health care providers is especially effective in producing favorable cessation outcomes (Kottke, Brekke, Solberg, & Hughes, 1988). Smoking cessation interventions using a counseling session lasting more than 10 minutes markedly increase cessation rates relative to no-contact interventions. Even brief counseling (a session lasting 3–10 minutes) increases cessation rates over no-contact interventions.

Self-Help

Self-help interventions for smoking cessation can consist of anything from pure self-help to rather intense but still self-administered methods (Curry, 1993). The exact definition of self-help can be somewhat ambiguous. Self-help interventions most often consist of written materials. A major emphasis of these materials is usually on coping strategies, especially in high-risk situations. Self-help materials also are available in other formats including audio and video tapes. Some promising results have been obtained with computerized programs that attempt to tailor cessation messages to the individual smoker (Prochaska, DiClemente, Velicer, & Rossi 1993).

The AHCPR guidelines conclude that in general, smoking cessation delivered by means of self-help materials may increase cessation rates relative to no intervention. However, their impact is smaller and less certain than that of individual or group counseling. Written self-help materials (pamphlets/booklets/manuals), video and audio tapes, and provision of lists of community programs when used alone do not increase cessation rates relative to no self-help materials. On the other hand, hotlines/helplines do increase smoking cessation rates when used alone.

Formal Programs

The most successful results have been obtained with more intensive formal behavioral treatment programs (Lando, 1993). Several specific components of formal programs have been found to increase abstinence. These components include aversive smoking, intratreatment social support, and problem solving/skills training. It should be recognized, however, that smoking cessation treatments seldom use these components in isolation. In addition, certain types of content tend to be correlated with other treatment characteristics, (e.g., some types of intervention were more likely to be delivered in treatment settings using a greater number of sessions across longer time periods).

Aversion

Despite the favorable conclusions of the AHCPR report, aversive techniques have largely lost favor. These techniques have involved pairing smoking with unpleasant types of stimuli. These unpleasant stimuli are often, but not always, intrinsically related to smoking. Popular types of intrinsically related aversion include rapid smoking, rapid puffing (i.e., not actually inhaling), satiation, and other smoking exposure (e.g., smoke blown directly into the face by means of a portable fan). Rapid smoking has required smokers to take frequent puffs (typically every 6 seconds) for as long as they can tolerate the procedure

(Lichtenstein, Harris, Birchler, Wahl, & Schmahl, 1973). In satiation, smokers are instructed to dramatically increase their cigarette consumption, perhaps to double or even triple their usual intake, prior to attempting abstinence (Lando, 1975).

Concerns pertaining to health risks of these procedures led to use of several types of reduced aversion techniques. These techniques included rapid puffing (unlike rapid smoking, smokers do not actually inhale), "focused smoking" in which the smoker inhales at a regulated but slower rate, and smoke holding in which smokers retain cigarette smoke in the mouth and throat while breathing through the nose.

Contingency Contracting and Relaxation Techniques

Contingency contracting has been used to bolster commitment to abstinence. Several studies have required participants to submit monetary deposits that are refunded contingent on maintained abstinence (Elliott & Tighe, 1968; Lando, 1976). Progressive relaxation and deep breathing strategies have been employed for smoking cessation although rarely in isolation. A major rationale for the use of these procedures is that smoking relapses are very likely to occur during negative emotional states (Brandon, Tiffany, & Baker, 1986; Shiffman, 1982). Relaxation training allows an alternative response for coping with negative emotions or stressful situations and with the stress of quitting smoking and nicotine withdrawal effects. There is little evidence to support the efficacy of relaxation training as a stand-alone technique.

Stimulus Control and Cue Extinction

Stimulus control and cue extinction procedures also have tended to produce weak results. These procedures have been used in an effort to reduce the huge number of environmental cues that have been associated with smoking (Abrams, 1986). In theory, if some of the cues governing smoking can be weakened or extinguished, quitting should be facilitated. One strategy has been to gradually reduce smoking consumption by progressively restricting the types of situations in which smoking is permitted. Another type of stimulus control strategy permits smoking only at set times (e.g., every hour on the half hour) regardless of the individual's desire to smoke (Shapiro, Tursky, Schwartz, & Shnidman, 1971).

Coping Skills

More successful results have been obtained with training in specific coping skills. These coping skills include problem solving and methods for managing stress and preventing relapse. Supportive intervention during direct contact with a clinician or in a group (intratreatment social support) increases smoking cessation rates. However, efforts to improve cessation outcomes by enhancing outside social support have been largely unsuccessful (Lichtenstein, Glasgow, & Abrams, 1986). This is true despite correlational data indicating positive associations between naturally occurring environmental social support and success in quitting.

Reduced Smoking and Nicotine Fading

Nicotine fading and gradual reduction in numbers of cigarettes have been used as nonaversive preparation techniques for smoking cessation. Gradual reduction strategies generally have not worked very well. Smokers typically appear to reach a "stuck point," often 10–12 cigarettes per day (Flaxman, 1978). For the typical smoker of slightly more than a pack per day, compensatory changes in puffing patterns might compensate for reduced numbers of cigarettes above this level. An alternative is to switch brands over several weeks or to use commercially available nicotine reduction filters to progressively lower rated tar and nicotine levels (Foxx & Brown, 1979; McGovern & Lando, 1991). These procedures have not proven successful in improving smoking cessation outcomes.

Multicomponent Treatment Strategies

The most successful behavioral programs have incorporated multiple treatment components. Emphasis has been placed both on initial preparation for quitting and long-term maintenance. Twelve-month abstinence rates for these multicomponent programs have approached 50% (Hall, Rugg, Tunstall, & Jones, 1984; Tiffany, Martin, & Baker, 1986), although more recent outcomes have tended to be less favorable (Lando, Sipfle, & McGovern, 1995).

A focus of many comprehensive behavioral programs is on relapse prevention following the quit date (Marlatt & Gordon, 1985). Rather than an "absolute abstinence" approach, Marlatt and Gordon have suggested preparing the quitter to recover from slips, should they occur. Slips are viewed as a natural part of the learning process in quitting rather than as necessary precursors to renewed addiction. Unfortunately, however, slips do tend to be highly predictive of full-blown relapse.

Surprisingly, far less research has been done on "recycling" of smokers who relapse. Further intervention may be especially indicated for the increasingly hardcore smokers who enter intensive treatment programs. Lando and his colleagues (Lando, Pirie, Roski, McGovern, & Schmid, in press) used telephone support both to sustain abstinence and to encourage renewed quit attempts in smokers who had completed an intensive smoking cessation clinic. Subjects (N = 1,082) attended a multisession clinic. They were then assigned randomly to receive telephone support (intervention calls 3, 9, and 21 months following the targeted cessation clinic quit date) or no further intervention. Subjects who relapsed were significantly more likely to resume abstinence (to recycle) in the intervention condition than in the comparison condition at 24-month follow-up (3 months after the termination of telephone support). These effects did not persist at a 34-month follow-up, nor were there overall treatment effects or effects in preventing relapse.

Hypnosis and Acupuncture

There are numerous approaches to smoking cessation that are not primarily behavioral or pharmacologic. Two commonly advertised methods include hypnosis and acupuncture. Unfortunately, there are few good studies of these methods and overall results tend to be disappointing. Telling, perhaps, was the fact that only three acceptable studies that examined hypnosis were found in preparation of the AHCPR guidelines, despite the widespread use of this technique. Because the studies were of poor quality and their results were inconsistent, the evidence was insufficient to assess the effectiveness of hypnosis. Studies that have compared acupuncture at theoretically correct sites versus "incorrect" or sham sites have found no differences in outcome.

Commercial Programs and Products

A number of commercial programs are available, usually concentrated in larger metropolitan areas. Most programs tend not to be highly profitable and therefore do not remain active. In evaluating commercial methods, it again appears that the most successful are those that include multicomponent cognitive-behavioral techniques. New products are continually being introduced as aids to smoking cessation. Currently, none of these products (excluding nicotine replacement which is discussed elsewhere in this chapter) are recognized as effective.

Evaluation Standards

It is increasingly important that professionals be well informed about smoking cessation services and products. They should be skeptical in evaluating claims of effectiveness. Commercial methods in particular sometimes claim extremely high rates of success. Program and product evaluations should be based on a minimum of 6-month and preferably 12-month follow-up. Programs may present end-of-treatment success based on outcomes only a few days or weeks after a target quit date. End-of-treatment figures of 60% abstinence can easily translate into 1-year outcomes of 5% to 10%.

Participant attrition also must be considered (Glasgow & Lichtenstein, 1987). Programs can dramatically manipulate their outcomes by failing to count nonrespondents to follow-up. Assume, for example, that a program attracts 100 individuals of whom 50 complete treatment, 30 respond to the follow-up, and 20 report abstinence. Claimed abstinence based on these results could be as high as 67%, whereas 20% abstinence would be a more valid outcome figure.

Resources for additional information on behavioral treatments are available both locally and nationally. Local resources include the American Cancer Society, the American Lung Association, and state health departments. The National Cancer Institute provides a toll-free information line (1-800-4CANCER). Information and materials also are available through the U.S. Office on Smoking and Health (1-770-488-5705), the American Medical Association (1-312-464-5000), and the American Society of Addiction Medicine (1-301-656-3920).

PHARMACOLOGICAL TREATMENTS

The smoking cessation area has benefited greatly with the introduction of medications developed specifically for the treatment of nicotine addiction. The primary pharmacological treatments available for cigarette smokers are agonist treatments or nicotine replacements. Other medications that are currently being developed for smoking cessation include combining nicotine replacements with other medications

including nicotine antagonists; and opioid antagonists, the use of nonspecific medications such as clonidine, which has been observed to reduce tobacco withdrawal symptoms; and medications that are targeted toward certain symptoms that are associated with the initiation and/or continued use of nicotine (e.g., depression) or that result from smoking cessation (weight gain). Examples of these medications are antidepressants, anxiolytics, and weight loss agents.

Nicotine Replacement

Nicotine replacement treatments include nicotine polacrilex, transdermal nicotine system, nicotine nasal spray, and the nicotine inhaler/vaporizer. The mechanisms underlying their efficacy include the reduction of withdrawal symptoms from tobacco cessation (Jarvik & Henningfield, 1988), which then facilitates the use of coping skills to assist in smoking cessation efforts (Cinciripini, Cinciripini, Wallfisch, Haque, & VanVunakis, 1996) as well as to augment treatment attendance (Hjalmarson, Franzon, Westin, & Wiklund, 1994; Sutherland, Stapleton, & Russell, 1992). Furthermore, nicotine replacements involve a method of delivering nicotine that is less likely to be abused and gradually weans the individual from nicotine, and are safer or less toxic than cigarettes, because only nicotine is being delivered to the individual. Each nicotine product is associated with a different route of administration, pharmacokinetic profile, and amount of nicotine absorbed per unit dose. These differences result in different patterns of use, side effects, contraindications, and abuse liability. In spite of these differences and although no comparative studies have been conducted, the degree of treatment efficacy across these products tends to be similar.

Nicotine Gum

Nicotine gum was developed in the 1970s, first as a 2-mg dose and then as a 4-mg dose. The product was initially a prescription drug and then because of its safety profile, became an over-the-counter product. Nicotine gum is slowly absorbed via the buccal mucosa by having the individual chew and then park the gum between his or her cheek and gum. The absorption of nicotine is pH dependent with absorption occurring maximally in a base environment. As a result, users of nicotine gum are encouraged not to chew gum while drinking or eating acidic products (Henningfield, Radqius, Cooper, & Clayton, 1990). The amount of nicotine absorbed per unit dose is 1.0 for 2-mg gum and 2.0 for the

4-mg nicotine gum. The peak nicotine plasma levels are achieved at 20–30 minutes; therefore, individuals are asked to chew the gum for about 30 minutes. The blood nicotine levels attained from 2-mg nicotine gum are one quarter to one third of those attained from cigarettes, and from the 4-mg nicotine gum are one half to two third. Although the instructions in the 1996 Physicians Desk Reference indicate that the gum should be chewed ad libitum, some data support the use of nicotine gum on a fixed interval basis (Killen, Fortmann, Newman, & Varady, 1990). By using a fixed interval (one piece every 1–2 hours), the number of pieces of gum chewed tends to be higher, resulting in higher plasma levels of nicotine. More recently, the over-the-counter formulation recommends a fixed schedule for chewing nicotine gum. The recommended duration of nicotine gum use is 3 months, with users gradually weaning themselves from nicotine gum during this time. Retrospective studies show that those who had successfully quit with nicotine gum had used the gum for a longer period of time. Evidence from a prospective study shows that longer duration of use may result in greater treatment success (Hatsukami, Huber, Callies, & Skoog, 1993), although another study shows no difference in success rates based on duration of use (Fagerstrom & Melin, 1985).

Nicotine gum has been shown to significantly reduce withdrawal symptoms (Fagerstrom, 1988). Although some controversy exists as to whether nicotine gum effectively reduces craving and weight gain associated with smoking cessation, recent studies show that with sufficient dosing, these symptoms are positively affected (Glover, 1992; Gross, Stitzer, & Maldonado, 1989). One study found reduced weight from use of nicotine gum only in women and not men (Leischow, Sachs, Bostrom, & Hansen, 1992). No dose–response relationship has been observed with 2-mg and 4-mg nicotine gum in reducing other withdrawal symptoms (Hughes, Gust, Keenan, & Fenwick, 1990), particularly in men (Hatsukami, Skoog, Allen, & Bliss, 1995). Gender differences have been observed in which women experience less relief from the 2-mg nicotine gum compared to men (Hatsukami et al., 1995; Killen et al., 1990), but no differences were observed between the genders from the 4-mg nicotine gum (Hatsukami et al., 1995). This finding would indicate that women may need a higher dose of nicotine to obtain a maximal suppression of withdrawal symptoms.

Four meta-analyses have been conducted with the nicotine gum (Cepeda-Benito, 1993; Lam, Sze, Sacks, & Chalmers, 1987; Silagy, Mant, Fowler, & Lodge, 1994;

Tang, Law, & Wald, 1994). Nicotine gum shows consistently higher rates of success at 12 months than placebo gum across the studies overall (16.9% to 18.2% nicotine gum versus 10.6% to 12.5% placebo gum; OR=1.4–1.6), with higher rates of success obtained when nicotine gum is combined with behavioral treatment versus brief intervention (AHCPR, 1996). Furthermore, among those who are highly dependent on nicotine, those individuals who received 4-mg gum were more successful than those individuals who received 2-mg nicotine gum (e.g., Herrera et al., 1995; Kornitzer, Kittel, Dramaix, & Pourdoux, 1987; Tonnesen et al., 1988).

The persistent use of nicotine gum beyond the recommended duration of time has not been high, but yet is not negligible. The prevalence of continued use of 2-mg nicotine gum among all users of the nicotine gum has been 10% (e.g., Hatsukami et al., 1993) and among those who have been successfully abstinent with nicotine gum it has been about 20% (Hughes et al., 1991). No differences in these percentages seem to exist even when the individual was assigned to chew the nicotine gum for a longer period of time (Hatsukami et al., 1993).

The most prevalent side effects from the nicotine gum tend to be associated with the mechanics of chewing nicotine gum or resulting from chewing too fast. These effects include jaw ache, sore mouth, hiccups, and gastrointestinal distress.

Transdermal Nicotine Systems

Currently, four different pharmaceutical brands of transdermal nicotine systems exist and are listed in Table 32.1. A single patch is placed on a nonhairy, dry area for a period of either 24 hours or 16 hours, depending on the brand of patch, and is worn for a period of 6–16 weeks. The highest dose patch is typically worn from 4 to 8 weeks, the lowest dose patches are worn from 2 to 4 weeks. The unit dose of the highest dose patch varies from 15 to 22 mg depending on whether the patch is a 16-hour patch (15 mg) or a 24-hour patch (21–22 mg). The nicotine is slowly absorbed through the skin. The peak plasma nicotine levels are attained between 4 and 9 hours and the maximum amount observed is 13–23 ng/ml for the highest dose patch with average plasma concentrations ranging from 9 to 17 ng/ml. The plasma concentrations attained across each of the patch doses tend to be linear (Gorseline, Gupta, Dye, & Rolf, 1993). Two studies compared the effects of nicotine patch worn for 24 hours and the same brand of patch worn for 16 hours. No significant differences were observed in treatment outcome (Daughton et al., 1991; Fagerstrom, Lunell, & Molander, 1991). As of yet, no studies have prospectively examined the optimal duration of patch use, although one meta-analysis demonstrated that treatment efficacy was similar between studies using patches for greater than 8 weeks and studies using patches for less than 8 weeks (Fiore, Smith, Jorenby, & Baker, 1994). Furthermore, an analysis of the studies using down-titration as opposed to no down-titration showed no significant differences in treatment outcome across these two approaches, a finding that was confirmed by a prospective study (Stapleton et al., 1995).

The nicotine patch effectively reduces most symptoms of withdrawal (e.g., anxiety, irritability, impatience, difficulty concentrating) including craving. However, increased weight on cessation has not typically been shown to be affected by the nicotine patch, although two studies have found significantly less weight gain among those using 21-mg nicotine patch compared to placebo patch (Allen, Hatsukami, & Gorsline, 1994; Jorenby et al., in press). Dose-related responses in the reduction of withdrawal symptoms have not been observed across patch doses ranging from 7 mg to 21 mg, although craving was significantly less with the 21-mg patch compared to lower doses of the patch during the initial period of cessation (Transdermal Nicotine Study Group, 1991). When doses of the patch higher than 22 mg were examined, one study found no differences in degree of relief from withdrawal symptoms between the 22 mg and 44-mg nicotine patch, although desire to smoke was reduced to a greater extent with the 44 mg patch (Jorenby et al., 1995). Another study showed a positive relationship between the amount of nicotine replacement and the degree of withdrawal relief (Dale et al., 1995).

Five meta-analyses have been conducted with the nicotine patch (Fiore et al., 1994; Gourlay, 1994; Po, 1993; Silagy et al., 1994; Tang et al., 1994). Studies on the nicotine patch have shown remarkable consistency in demonstrating a higher rate of abstinence with the active nicotine patch than with the placebo patch. At 6–12 months follow-up, the odds ratio of treatment success of nicotine patch over placebo patch ranged from 2.1 to 2.6 (approximately 20% success rate with active patch vs. 10% success rate with placebo) across a wide variety of treatment settings. The odds ratio persisted whether the study was undertaken with brief counseling or more intensive counseling. On the other hand, the meta-analyses have shown a slight increase in treatment success when the nicotine patch is combined with behavioral treatment. However, one prospective study did not show a difference in long-term success rates across intensity of behavioral treatments (Jorenby et al., 1995).

Although a dose–response curve is observed in treatment success with the nicotine patch up to the 22-mg dose (TNS study group), two studies do not support an improvement in long-term success rates with higher dose patches (35 mg or 44 mg) compared to the 21–22 mg patches (Dale et al., 1995; Jorenby et al., 1995). On the other hand, the short-term success was enhanced in both studies by the higher dose patch and higher percentage of nicotine replacement. Some limited evidence exists indicating that if one examines the extent of individualized dose replacement, then the success rates can be enhanced over assignment of standardized dose of the patch (David Sachs, personal communication). The abuse and use of nicotine patches beyond the recommended period is nonexistent.

The primary side effect from nicotine patch is skin reactions, with up to 50% of nicotine patch users experiencing some skin reaction. Other side effects include abnormal dreams and sleep disturbance, which may be a result of wearing the skin patch for a period of 24 hours as well as in part a result of tobacco cessation.

Table 32.1 Transdermal Nicotine Systems

	Absorbed Dose	Cmax (ng/ml)	Cavtg (ng/ml)	Cmin (ng/ml)	Tmax
Nicoderm	21 mg	23 ± 5	17 ± 4	11 ± 3	4 ± 3
Habitrol	21 mg	17 ± 2	13 ± 2	9 ± 2	6 ± 3
Prostep	22 mg	16 ± 6	11 ± 3	5 ± 1	9 ± 5
Nicotrol	15 mg	13 ± 3	09 ± 2	3 ± 1	8 ± 3

Source: Data from (Stapleton et al., 1995)

Nicotine Nasal Spray

Other replacement products include the nicotine nasal spray. Nicotine nasal spray has a more rapid delivery that nicotine gum, with the rapid absorption of nicotine occurring within the first 2.5 minutes and levels of nicotine peaking at 5 minutes (Sutherland, Russell, Stapelton, Feyerabend, & Ferno, 1992). The amount delivered with each dose is 1 mg (0.5 mg in each nostril) and use of the spray is recommended for a 3-month period of time. Because of this rapid delivery, this product is considered to be most beneficial to the more highly dependent smoker and presumably may provide more immediate relief of cravings for cigarettes. With the nicotine nasal spray, plasma nicotine concentrations of between one half and three quarters of baseline are achieved (Sutherland, Russell, et al., 1992). Studies have shown that nicotine nasal spray effectively reduces tobacco withdrawal symptoms, craving for cigarettes, and weight gain during the first few days of cessation (Sutherland, Stapleton, et al., 1992; Schneider et al., 1995). However, another study found that withdrawal symptoms were not reduced significantly by active spray compared to placebo spray, although craving for cigarettes was less at the 1-week assessment time, and the time to relieve the urge to smoke was faster (Hjalmarson et al., 1994).

Three clinical trials have been conducted to date with consistent results across the studies. In two of the clinical trials, when combined with supportive group treatment, the rate of success of active nicotine nasal spray was 26% to 27% versus 10% to 15% with the placebo spray at the 12-month follow-up, a statistically significant difference (Sutherland, Stapleton, et al., 1992; Hjalmarson et al., 1994). In both these studies, the greatest effect of nicotine nasal spray on the relapse rates was observed during and shortly after group treatment. In the most recently published study, the results confirm the findings from the previous two studies (Schneider et al., 1995). In this treatment protocol, minimal behavioral intervention accompanied the use of the nicotine nasal spray versus placebo rather than group behavioral treatment and nicotine nasal spray was only made available for 6 months rather than 1 year. At 1-year follow-up, 18% of the active group (N=128 subjects) and 8% of the placebo (N=127 subjects) were continuously abstinent since the onset of treatment. When criteria for treatment success that were similar to previous studies were used, the rate of abstinence was nearly identical. The use of nicotine nasal spray appears to be particularly helpful among heavy smokers as determined by precessation nicotine levels and scores on the Fagerstrom Tolerance Questionnaire (Hjalmarson et al., 1994; Sutherland, Stapleton, et al., 1992).

The findings from these studies suggest a potential for greater dependence on these products compared to nicotine gum or patch (Schneider et al., 1995; Sutherland, Stapleton et al., 1992). Significantly more individuals reported feeling "high" from the active nicotine nasal spray compared to the placebo spray. In two of the studies, approximately, 29% to 43% of the abstainers (or 10% to 11% of those assigned to active spray) had continued to use the active spray at 12 months of using nicotine nasal spray (Hjarmarlson et al., 1994; Sutherland, Stapleton, et al., 1992). In the other study, continued use of the spray occurred in 32% and 13% among active and placebo subjects who remained in the study at 6 months, respectively, and 13% and 3% among the intent-to-treat sample (Schneider et al., 1995). However, these rates of continued use are observed in a situation in which the spray is freely available and therefore is likely to be lower when cost is associated with its use. Futhermore, the rates from two of these studies are only slightly higher than that observed with the use of nicotine gum.

With the nicotine nasal spray, side effects include running nose, eyes watering, coughing, sneezing, and irritation of the nasal passage and throat. Tolerance to these effects develops within the first several days.

Nicotine Inhalers or Vaporizer

The nicotine inhaler or vaporizer is an oral puffing device in the shape of a cigarette that contains a porous plug that is saturated with 10 mg of nicotine. This device is considered to not only provide nicotine, but also to deal with the sensory and oral aspects associated with cigarette smoking. With inhalation on this device, gaseous nicotine is released and is absorbed primarily through the buccal mucosa rather than through the lungs (Russell, Jarvis, Sutherland, & Feyerabend, 1987). Each puff of 50 ml delivers about 0.1 Mmol of nicotine. Subjects can be instructed to puff on this device either by inhaling it in a way similar to smoking a cigarette or by frequent, intensive puffing similar to smoking a pipe. The majority of smokers in one study that compared the two puffing techniques preferred the buccal mode of inhalation over the pulmonary mode (Lunell, Molander, Leischow, & Fagerstrom, 1995). Both puffing techniques lead to similar plasma nicotine levels (Lunell et al., 1995). The level of nicotine achieved by this device with ad libitum use is about 30% of that obtained by smoking (Lunell et al., 1995) with ranges from 24% to 43% (Tonnesen, Norregaard, Mikkelsen, Jorgensen, & Nilsson, 1993). Peak plasma nicotine concentrations occur at 10–15 minutes after the end of puffing (Schneider, 1992). The use of the nicotine inhaler significantly reduced nicotine withdrawal symptoms (impatience, irritability, and dizziness) and craving compared to placebo, with no effect on difficulty with concentration (Lunell et al., 1995). No significant reduction of weight gain on cessation was observed with the use of the inhaler (Tonnesen et al., 1993). Only one randomized, double-blind, placebo-controlled study on the nicotine inhaler has been published. In this study, significantly greater continuous abstinence rates were reported at 1 year for the active nicotine inhaler(N=145) as opposed to the placebo inhaler (N=141) group (15% versus 5%) when given in the context of minimal levels of advice and support given by physicians. Furthermore, by the 6-month visit, only three out of the active and one out of the placebo inhaler group were using the inhaler. The main adverse side effects are irritation in the mouth and throat and coughing.

Nicotine Replacement Combinations

Nicotine Replacements

The combination of the nicotine patch with other nicotine replacements may be beneficial for several reasons. For example, the use of nicotine gum with the patch will increase the levels of nicotine during the day, particularly when urges to smoke are experienced. Furthermore, the use of nicotine gum would address the rituals associated with cigarette smoking. With the increased levels of nicotine, a greater decrease in tobacco withdrawal symptoms is observed with the combination treatment approach compared to the single treatment approach (Fagerstrom, 1994; Fagerstrom, Schneider, & Lunell, 1993). Two studies have been conducted examining the use of patch plus nicotine gum for smoking cessation. In one study conducted in the workplace (Kornitzer, Boutsen, Dramaix, Thijs, & Gustavsson, 1995), abstinence rates were significantly different for active nicotine patch plus active nicotine gum (N=149) versus active nicotine patch plus placebo gum (N=150) at 12 weeks (34.2% versus 22.7%, respectively), 24 weeks (27.5% versus 15.3%) but not at 52 weeks

(18.1% versus 12.7%, respectively) postquit. Moreover, the use of the combination of active treatments delayed relapse to cigarettes to a greater extent than the use of active patch plus placebo gum. The combination of nicotine replacements was also well tolerated. When the active patch plus placebo gum was compared to a placebo patch plus placebo gum (N=75) treatment condition, oddly no significant differences were observed for treatment cessation rates. The researchers attributed this lack of significant differences to the different expectations of the subjects using a placebo gum product compared to those in other transdermal nicotine replacement studies that did not use any gum. Another study compared smoking cessation among those smokers assigned active gum plus active patch (N=150) versus active gum plus placebo patch (N=150) in a general practice setting (Puska, Vartiainen, & Korhonen, 1994). At 12-weeks postquit, the active gum plus active patch produced significantly higher sustained abstinence compared to the active gum plus placebo patch conditions (39% versus 28%, respectively), but no differences were observed at 26 weeks. In summary, the results show that combining nicotine patch and nicotine gum may lead to greater reduction in withdrawal symptomatology and increase smoking cessation success.

Nicotine Patch with Mecamylamine

Several studies have examined the use of nicotine patch with mecamylamine. Mecamylamine is a central-acting nicotinic antagonist. This medication has led to an increase in smoking, which indicates that smokers are compensating for the blocking effects of this medication (Nemeth-Coslett, Henningfield, O'Keefee, & Griffiths, 1986; Pomerleau, Pomerleau, & Majchrzak, 1987; Stolerman, Goldfarb, Fink, & Jarvik, 1973), and shows an increase in levels of nicotine preference (Rose, Sampson, Levin, & Henningfield, 1989) and attenuation of the many effects from nicotine (Clarke, 1991; Stolerman, 1986). Although one study has suggested that mecamylamine alone may be effective in the treatment of smoking cessation, side effects from this medication at therapeutic doses may preclude its wide use (Tennant, Tarver, & Rawson, 1984). Rose and associates proposed combining nicotine patch and mecamylamine. The theory behind the effectiveness of this combination of medications has been that more of the nicotinic receptors are occupied with using this combination of drugs such that smokers will experience a greater reduction in the rewarding effects of nicotine (Rose &

Levin, 1991). Therefore, nicotine replacement would suf-ficiently relieve withdrawal symptoms by maintaining some nicotinic receptor activation, and mecamylamine would limit the activation that could be achieved through cigarette smoking. Using this theoretical model, these investigators have proposed using the combination of these drugs so the smoking behavior is more likely to be extin-guished prior to the time of smoking cessation. Furthermore, when mecamylamine is combined with nico-tine patch, lower doses of mecamylamine can be used. In a preclinical trial, Rose and associates (1994a) examined the effects of mecamylamine versus placebo with and without nicotine preloading prior to smoking a test ciga-rette. Both mecamylamine and nicotine preloading reduced smoking satisfaction and liking of the test ciga-rette, and mecamylamine did not block this effect from the nicotine preloading. On the other hand, mecamylamine blocked the increased heart rate and blood pressure effects from nicotine and nicotine compensated for the perfor-mance decrement effects observed from mecamylamine. These results show that the combination of these medica-tions can work in concert with each other and may have beneficial treatment effects. Thus far, one clinical trial has been conducted (Rose et al., 1994b). In this clinical trial, smokers who were treated with both nicotine patch (6–8 weeks) and mecamylamine (5 weeks of 2.5–5 mg twice a day) experience higher rates of continuous abstinence than with nicotine patch alone at the end of treatment (50% vs. 16%, respectively) and at the follow-up (e.g., 38% vs. 4% at 12-months follow-up, respectively). Mecamylamine in combination with nicotine significantly reduced with-drawal symptoms such as craving, negative affect, and appetite. Mecamylamine has also been observed to signif-icantly reduce the respiratory tract sensations from ciga-rettes (Rose et al., 1994a, 1994b). These sensations have been associated with some of the reinforcing effects from smoking. Additionally, side effects were well tolerated, with the most prevalent symptom being mild constipation, and blood pressure effects were negligible.

Nicotine Patch with Naltrexone

Cigarette smoking has been observed to increase plasma B-endorphin levels (Pomerleau, Fertig, Seyler, & Jaffe, 1983) and this increase is related to plasma nicotine lev-els, resulting in the hypothesis that endogenous opioids play a role in the reinforcing effects from nicotine (Pomerleau & Pomerleau, 1984). The effects of opioid

blockers on smoking behavior have been examined and the results have been equivocal. Some investigators showed a decrease in smoking (Gorelick, Rose, & Jarvik, 1989; Karras & Kane, 1980) and other studies showed no effect (Nemeth-Coslett & Griffiths, 1986; Sutherland, Stapleton, Russell, & Feyerabend, 1995). Furthermore, naltrexone does not seem to affect the satisfaction or enjoyment from smoking a cigarette. A more recent approach has been to examine the effects of combining naltrexone and nicotine patch. The rationale for this approach is unclear, however, trials are being conducted to determine the efficacy of this combination.

Nonspecific Medications

Clonidine

Clonidine is an alpha-agonist, antihypertensive medication. In the past several years, studies have shown clonidine to alleviate withdrawal symptoms from opiates, alcohol, and even cigarettes (Glassman, Jackson, Walsh, Roose, & Rosenfeld, 1984). Because of the observed reductions of nicotine withdrawal symptoms, several clinical trials have been undertaken to determine the efficacy of clonidine in the treatment of cigarette smokers. A meta-analysis was conducted on nine existing double-blind, placebo-con-trolled trials using clonidine for smoking cessation (Covey & Glassman, 1991). These studies were published either as abstracts or articles and ranged in the settings in which the trials were conducted (specialized smoking clinics and gen-eral practice settings), the method of clonidine delivery (oral and transdermal), the dosages (0.1–0.45 mg/day), and duration of treatment (2–12 weeks with most studies involving 3–6 weeks of treatment). The results from these analyses showed that clonidine showed a higher end-of-treatment success rate than placebo in all the studies, with odds ratios ranging from 1.26 to 9.33. However, only four of the nine studies showed significant differences between clonidine and placebo. When the results of the nine trials were combined, the success of clonidine was significantly higher than that of placebo (39% vs. 21%) and the odds ratio was 2.36 indicating that a smoker is twice as likely to stop smoking with clonidine compared to placebo. Furthermore, the use of behavioral or individual therapy enhanced the success rate of clonidine (OR=4.20 vs. 1.74, respectively). No differences were found based on dose of clonidine or duration of treatment. A slight advantage in treatment outcome was observed for the patch compared to the oral dosage form. The results did not look as promising for long-term treatment outcomes. Only two of the five studies examining long-term outcome continued to find a significant positive treatment effect for clonidine (Glassman et al., 1988) with one of the studies finding positive clonidine effects for females but not males (Villagra, Rosenberger, & Girolame, 1989). Three of the positive studies that examined sex differences observed a strong effect of clonidine among females but not among men. However, one study that had enrolled 94% males found a positive effect for clonidine at the end of treatment, though this effect was not evident at follow-up. A more recent study examined the effects of gender, history of major depression, and degree of nicotine dependence on the efficacy of clonidine in smoking cessation (Glassman et al., 1993). This 10-week double-blind trial showed no end-of-treatment effect of clonidine (0.005 mg/kg) among men, and a barely significant effect in women (OR=2.01), but a strong effect among women who tend to be heavily dependent and/or experienced recurrent episodes of depression (OR=8.5). Another recent study showed that the clinical usefulness of clonidine is doubtful because of the frequency of reported adverse effects at the doses that are found to be most effective in reducing craving (Gourlay, Forbes, Marriner, Kutin, & McNeil, 1994). In a double-blind, four-way crossover design, cigarette smokers were given placebo or 300, 200, or 100 Mg clonidine per day during a 4-day period of abstinence. A statistically significant dose–response effect was observed for the craving score, but no effect was observed for the summed tobacco withdrawal scores. The lack of an effect on tobacco withdrawal symptoms is consistent with some studies (Franks, Harp, & Bell, 1989; Murray, Cappello, & Baez, 1989) and inconsistent with others (Glassman et al., 1988; Hao, Young, & Hao, 1988). The primary side effects that were reported in this study as well as others include drowsiness, severe fatigue, light-headedness, strange or spacey feeling, dry mouth, skin rash, nausea, and vomiting.

In summary, the use of clonidine is not likely to be the first line in treatment. The AHCPR guidelines stated that there is little evidence to suggest the use of clonidine in smoking cessation primarily because few studies have examined long-term cessation rates, a selection bias may be operating in studies that have shown success using clonidine among the female population with most studies finding gender differences in post hoc analyses of the data, and the high side effect profile from clonidine. However, clonidine perhaps can be used among those individuals, particularly women, who are highly dependent on cigarettes and who have had previous treatment failures and/or recurrent episodes of depression.

Symptom-Targeted Medications

Most of the other medications that have been used in the treatment of smoking cessation have targeted either symptoms of depression or anxiety or the weight gain associated with smoking cessation. Antidepressant and anti-anxiety agents have been considered for smoking cessation treatment for several reasons including (1) the manifestation of depressed and anxious mood during tobacco withdrawal (American Psychiatric Association, 1994); (2) the strong and positive association between major depressive disorder and cigarette smoking (Anda et al., 1990; Bresleau, Kilbey, & Andreski, 1991; Dalack, Glassman, Rivelli, Covey, & Stetner, 1995; Glassman et al., 1988, 1990; Kendler et al., 1993) and between anxiety disorders and cigarette smoking (Breslau et al., 1991); (3) the increased rate of relapse among those with a history of major depressive disorder (Anda et al., 1990; Covey, Glassman, & Stetner, 1990; Glassman et al., 1988, 1990; Hall, Munoz, Reus, & Sees, 1993); and (4) the positive association between depressed mood experienced during tobacco withdrawal and relapse to smoking (West, Hajek, & Belcher, 1989) with greater severity of dysphoria and negative moods observed among those with a history of major depressive disorder (Covey et al., 1990; Ginsberg, Hall, Reus, & Munoz, 1995; Glassman 1993). Furthermore, nicotine releases many different neurotransmitters that are targeted by these antidepressant and anxiolytic agents. The results from studies examining antidepressant agents in a general population of smokers have shown some promise (Edwards, Murphy, Downs, Ackerman, & Rosenthal, 1989; Ferry, Robbins, Scariate, & Peters, 1992; Hall et al., 1996), although some trials have found no beneficial effects from antidepressants (Jacobs, Spilken, Norman, Wohlberg, & Knapp, 1971). Interestingly, smokers in general rather than those who have a history of MDD have been examined. One study found that nortriptyline produces significantly better long-term treatment outcome results than placebo with no differential effects among those with and without a positive history for major depressive disorder (Hall et al., 1996). Few studies have also been conducted with anxiolytics. Two studies found a significantly higher rate of short-term end-of-treatment abstinence rates or reduced smoking with buspirone (a 5-HT1A partial agonist) compared to placebo (Gawin, Compton, & Byck, 1989; West, Hajek, & McNeill, 1991). However, other studies have found no significant effects of anxiolytics on smoking cessation (Hao et al., 1988; Schwartz & Dubitsky, 1968). Because of the limited number of well-controlled, randomized published studies, the AHCPR panel made no conclusions about the use of antidepressants and anxiolytics for the treatment of smoking.

Weight reduction as a result of smoking and the subsequent weight gain associated with quitting smoking has been a significant issue in the maintenance of smoking and the desire to resume smoking among women in particular. Investigators have speculated that if this weight gain is minimized, then a higher rate of smoking cessation success may ensue. However, the results have shown that although weight has been significantly reduced with the use of medications such as fluoxetine, fenfluramine, and phenylpropanolamine, the treatment success rates are similar between those assigned the active medication and those assigned to placebo (Hughes, 1994). Interestingly, behavioral intervention targeted at reducing weight gain has also not been successful in improving treatment outcome (Hall, Turnstall, Vila, & Duffy, 1992; Pirie et al., 1992). Therefore, targeting this area with medications does not look promising at this time.

Other Smoking Cessation Products

Silver acetate, which upon contact with smoking produces an aversive and metallic taste, has not shown beneficial effects (Hughes, 1994; AHCPR, 1996). Lobeline, a nicotinic receptor agonist, has also shown little promise (Hughes, 1994). However, a promising nonpharmacological product simulates the sensory aspects of smoking (e.g., produces the irritant effects on the respiratory tract) via a citric acid inhaler in the shape of a cigarette. This product appears to be a potentially effective agent for reducing craving (Behm, Levin, Lee, & Rose, 1990; Behm, Schur, Levin, Tashkin, & Rose, 1993; Rose & Behm, 1994; Rose & Hickman, 1987; Westman, Behm, & Rose, 1995), reducing smoking behavior (Rose & Behm, 1987; Rose, Behm, & Levin, 1993), and enhancing short-term abstinence (Behm et al., 1993; Levin, Behm, & Rose, 1990; Westman et al., 1995). These studies demonstrate the importance of targeting the sensory aspects of smoking or stimuli that have become conditioned with smoking or have assumed secondary reinforcing properties during smoking cessation treatment.

Conclusion

The literature on the pharmacological treatment of smoking clearly demonstrates that nicotine replacement agents have been successful in the treatment of smoking. The nicotine replacement products vary in the pharmacokinetic and pharmacological profiles that they produce, with some products delivering nicotine with a quick rate of onset and others with a slower rate of onset. These differences may be important in determining the product that is most suitable for a particular smoker, although no patient and product matching studies have been conducted to date. Furthermore, the results show that a continued improvement needs to be made in smoking cessation success rates, even with the available products, because on average 75% of the smokers have relapsed to cigarettes at the 6-month follow-up. Combining nicotine replacements has been considered as well as combining nicotine replacements with other medications. The combination of nicotine patch with mecamylamine seems particularly promising.

With the availability of a number of different medications, not only is a better strategy necessary for determining the types of medication to be used with a smoker, but also greater refinement in how to use currently available medications. For example, little is known about the optimal duration of nicotine replacement use, whether tapering of medications (particularly nicotine replacements) is necessary, the optimal dose of nicotine, and the characteristics of the smoker that will help us make these determinations. In addition, further research needs to be undertaken to determine the mechanisms by which these medications are effective, for example, reducing craving for cigarettes in high-risk situations, reducing particular withdrawal symptoms, enhancing the use of behavioral tools for smoking cessation, and so on.

CONCLUSIONS AND RECOMMENDATIONS

Smoking cessation treatments has evolved in a number of ways and have greatly advanced in the past several years. Initially they were more intensive individual or group treatment that focused on teaching behavioral and cognitive skills. Although the initial years showed a dramatic improvement in cessation rates with the use of these behavioral treatments, this increase has asymptoted in the past 20 years (Shiffman, 1993). Behavioral treatments have been enhanced with the availability and use of nicotine replacement treatments. Similarly, the use of behavioral treatments can enhance the success of nicotine replacement. A further advancement in the smoking cessation area has been the greater public health focus with the goal of making treatments more widely available and acceptable to smokers who are trying to quit. This effort has been made in the office of health care providers; in the workplace; by pharmaceutical companies that have packaged their nicotine replacement products with an accompanying self-treatment manuals, tailored treatment protocols, and the availability of telephone consulting; and finally, the community. Another significant advancement was the recognition that individuals go through various stages of change and that programs should be tailored to the particular stage in which the individual is experiencing. With the availability of these various approaches, the challenge in the future is the identification of factors that will allow the provider or individual who is trying to quit smoking to choose the most effective treatment for that smoker and exploration of methods to facilitate recycling of relapsers. Furthermore, the challenge is also to understand the mechanism of effectiveness for a particular behavioral or pharmacological treatment and how each of these treatments can augment the effects of the other. Finally, there is a need to continue to understand the fundamental basis for the addiction to nicotine so that more effective treatments can continue to develop.

REFERENCES

Abrams, D. B. (1986). Roles of psychosocial stress, smoking cues and coping in smoking-relapse prevention. *Health Psychology, 5*, 91–92.

Agency for Health Care Policy and Research (AHCPR). (1996). *Smoking cessation* (U.S. Department of Health and Human Services, Publication No. 96-0692). Washington DC: U.S. Government Printing Office.

Allen, S. S., Hatsukami, D. K., & Gorsline, J. (1994). The transdermal nicotine study group. Cholesterol changes in smoking cessation using the transdermal nicotine system. *Preventative Medicine, 23*, 190–196.

American Psychiatric Association. (1994). *Diagnostic and statistical manual of mental disorders* (4th ed.). Washington, DC: Author.

Anda, R. F., Williamson, D. F., Escobed, L. G., Mast, E. E., Giovino, G. A., & Remington, P. L. (1990). Depression and the dynamics of smoking. *Journal of the American Medical Association, 264*, 1541–1545.

Behm, F. M., Levin, E. D., Lee, Y. K., & Rose, J. E. (1990). Low-nicotine regenerated smoke aerosol reduces desire for cigarettes. *Journal of Substance Abuse, 2*, 237–247.

Behm, F. M., Schur, C., Levin, E. D., Tashkin, D. P., & Rose, J. E. (1993). Clinical evaluation of a citric acid inhaler for smoking cessation. *Drug and Alcohol Dependence, 31*, 131–138.

Brandon, T. H., Tiffany, S. T., & Baker, T. B. (1986). The process of smoking relapse. In F. M. Tims & C. G. Leukefeld (Eds.), *Relapse and recovery in drug abuse* (NIDA Research Monograph 72, DHHS Publication No. ADM 86-1473). Washington, DC: National Institute on Drug Abuse.

Breslau, N., Kilbey, M. M., & Andreski, P. (1991). Nicotine dependence, major depression, and anxiety in young adults. *Archives of General Psychiatry, 48*, 1069–1074.

Cepeda-Benito, A. (1993). A meta-analytic review of the efficacy of nicotine chewing gum. *Journal of Consulting and Clinical Psychology, 61*, 822–830.

Cinciripini, P. M., Cinciripini, L. G., Wallfisch, A., Haque, W., & VanVunakis, H. (1996). Behavior therapy and the transdermal nicotine patch: Effects on cessation outcome, affect and coping. *Journal of Consulting and Clinical Psychology, 64*, 314–323.

Clarke, P. B. (1991). Nicotinic receptor blockade therapy and smoking cessation. *British Journal of Addiction, 86*, 501–505.

Covey, L. S., & Glassman, A. H. (1991). A meta-analysis of double-blind placebo-controlled trials of clonidine for smoking cessation. *British Journal of Addiction, 86*, 991–998.

Covey, L. S., Glassman, A. H., & Stetner, F. (1990). Depression and depressive symptoms in smoking cessation. *Comprehensive Psychiatry, 31*, 350–354.

Cummings, S. R., Rubin, S. M., & Oster, G. (1989). The cost-effectiveness of counseling smokers to quit. *Journal of the American Medical Association, 261*, 75–79.

Curry, S. J. (1993). Self-help interventions for smoking cessation. *Journal of Consulting and Clinical Psychology, 61*, 790–803.

Dalack, G. W., Glassman, A. H., Rivelli, S., Covey, L., & Stetner, F. (1995). Mood, major depression and fluoxetine response in cigarette smokers. *American Journal of Psychiatry, 152*, 398–403.

Dale, L. C., Hurt, R. D., Offord, K. P., Lawson, G. M., Croghan, I. T., & Schroeder, D. R. (1995). High-dose nicotine patch therapy: Percentage of replacement and smoking cessation. *Journal of the American Medical Association, 274*, 1353–1357.

Daughton, D. M., Heatly, S. A., Prenderhast, J. J., Causey, D., Knowles, M., Rolf, C. N., Cheney, R. A., Hattelid, K., Thompson, A. B., & Rennard, S. I. (1991). Effect of transdermal nicotine delivery as an adjunct to low intervention smoking cessation therapy: A randomized placebo-controlled, double-blind study. *Archives of Internal Medicine, 151*, 749–752.

Edwards, N. B., Murphy, J. K., Downs, A. D., Ackerman, B. J., & Rosenthal, T. L. (1989). Doxepin as an adjunct to smoking cessation: A double-blind pilot study. *American Journal of Psychiatry, 146*, 373–376.

Elliott, R., & Tighe, T. (1968). Breaking the cigarette habit: Effects of a technique involving threatened loss of money. *Psychological Record, 18*, 503–513.

Fagerstrom, K. O. (1988). Efficacy of nicotine chewing gum. In O. F. Pomerleau & C. S. Pomerleau (Eds.), *Nicotine replacement: A critical review* (pp. 109–128). New York: Alan R. Liss,.

Fagerstrom, K. O. (1994). Combined use of nicotine replacement products. *Health Values, 18*, 15–20.

Fagerstrom, K. O., Lunell, E., & Molander, L. (1991). Continuous and intermittent transdermal delivery of nicotine: Blockade of withdrawal symptoms and side-effects. *Journal of Smoking-Related Diseases, 2*, 173–180.

Fagerstrom, K. O., & Melin, B. (1985). Nicotine chewing gum in smoking cessation: efficacy, nicotine dependence, therapy duration, and clinical recommendations. *Pharmacological adjuncts in smoking cessation* (pp. 102–109). Washington DC: National Institute on Drug Abuse.

Fagerstrom, K. O., Schneider, N. G., & Lunell, E. (1993). Effectiveness of nicotine patch and nicotine gum as individual versus combined treatments for tobacco withdrawal symptoms. *Psychopharmacology, 111*, 271–277.

Ferry, L. H., Robbins, A. S., Scariate, P. D., & Peters, A. (1992, September). *Depression, craving and heavy smoking: A pilot trial using bupropion.* Abstract presented at the 5th National Conference on Nicotine Dependence, Seattle, WA.

Fiore, M. C., Jorenby, D. E., Schensky, A. E., Smith, S. S., Bauer, R. R., & Baker, T. B. (1995). Smoking status as the new vital sign: Effect on assessment and intervention in patients who smoke. *Mayo Clinic Proceedings, 70*, 209–213.

Fiore, M. C., Smith, S. S., Jorenby, D. E., & Baker, T. B. (1994). The effectiveness of the nicotine patch for smoking cessation: A meta-analysis. *Journal of the American Medical Association, 271*, 1940–1947.

Flaxman, J. (1978). Quitting smoking now or later: Gradual, abrupt, immediate, and delayed quitting. *Behavior Research and Therapy, 9*, 260–270.

Foxx, R. M., & Brown, R. A. (1979). A nicotine fading and self-monitoring program to produce cigarette abstinence or controlled smoking. *Journal of Applied Behavior Analysis, 12*, 111–125.

Franks, P., Harp, J., & Bell B. (1989). Randomised, controlled trial of clonidine for smoking cessation in a primary care setting. *Journal of the American Medical Association, 21*, 3011–3013.

Gawin, F., Compton, M., & Byck, R. (1989). Buspirone reduces smoking. *Archives of General Psychiatry, 46*, 288–289.

Ginsberg, D., Hall, S. M., Reus, V. I., & Munoz, R. F. (1995). Mood and depression diagnosis in smoking cessation. *Experimental and Clinical Psychopharmacology, 3*, 389–395.

Glasgow, R. E., & Lichtenstein, E. (1987). Long-term effects of behavioral smoking cessation interventions. *Behavior Research and Therapy, 18*, 297–324.

Glassman, A. H. (1993). Cigarette smoking: Implications for psychiatric illness. *American Journal of Psychiatry, 150*, 546–553.

Glassman, A. H., Covey, L. S., Dalack, G. W., Stetner, F., Rivelli, S. K., Fleiss, J., & Cooper, T. B. (1993). Clinical trials and therapeutics: Smoking cessation, clonidine, and vulnerability to nicotine among dependent smokers. *Clinical Pharmacology and Therapeutics, 54*, 670–679.

Glassman, A. H., Helzer, J. E., Covey, L. S., Cottler, L. B., Stetner, F., Tipp, J. E., Johnson, J. (1990). Smoking, smoking cessation and major depression. *Journal of the American Medical Association, 264*, 1546–1549.

Glassman, A. H., Jackson, W. K., Walsh, B. T., Roose, S. P., & Rosenfeld, B. (1984). Cigarette craving, smoking withdrawal and clonidine. *Science, 226*, 864–866.

Glassman, A. H., Stetner, F., Walsh, B. T., Raizman, P. S., Fleiss, J. L., Cooper, T. B., & Covey, L. S. (1988). Heavy smokers, smoking cessation, and clonidine: Results of a double-blind, randomized trial. *Journal of the American Medical Association, 259*, 2863–2866.

Glover, E. D. (1992). *Safety and efficacy of nicorette gum 4 mg as a smoking cessation aid for highly dependent smokers.* Paper presented at the Eighth World Conference on Tobacco and Health, Buenos Aires, Argentina.

Gorelick, D. A., Rose, J. E., & Jarvik, M. E. (1989). Effect of naloxone on cigarette smoking. *Journal of Substance Abuse, 1*, 153–159.

Gorsline, J., Gupta, S. K., Dye, D., & Rolf, C. N. (1993). Steady-state pharmacokinetics and dose relationship of nicotine delivered from Nicoderm® (nicotine transdermal system). *Journal of Clinical Pharmacology, 33*, 161–168.

Gourlay, S. (1994). The pros and cons of transermal nicotine therapy. *Medical Journal of Australia, 160*, 152–159.

Gourlay, S., Forbes, A., Marriner, T., Kutin, J., & McNeil, J. (1994). Clinical trials and therapeutics: A placebo-controlled study of three clonidine doses for smoking cessation. *Clinical Pharmacology and Therapeutics, 55*, 64–69.

Gross, J., Stitzer, M. L., & Maldonado, J. (1989). Nicotine replacement: Effects of postcessation weight gain. *Journal of Consulting and Clinical Psychology, 57*, 87–92.

Group for Study of Transdermal Nicotine. (1994). Nicotine replacement for patients with coronary artery disease. *Archives of Internal Medicine, 154*, 989–995.

Hall, S. M., Munoz, R. F., Reus, V. I., & Sees, K. L. (1993). Nicotine or tar titration in cigarette smoking behavior? *Psychopharmacology, 112*, 253–258.

Hall, S. M., Reus, V. I., Munoz, R. F., Sees, K. L., Humfleet, G., & Frederick, S. (1996). *Nortriptyline and cognitive-behavioral treatment of cigarette smoking.* Presented at the scientific meeting of the College on Problems of Drug Dependence, San Juan.

Hall, S. M., Rugg, D., Tunstall, C., & Jones, R. T. (1984). Preventing relapse to cigarette smoking by behavioral skill training. *Journal of Consulting and Clinical Psychology, 52*, 372–382.

Hall, S. M., Turnstall, C. D., Vila, K. L., & Duffy, J. (1992). Weight gain prevention and smoking cessation: Cautionary findings. *American Journal of Public Health, 82*, 799–803.

Hao, W., Young, D., & Hao, W. (1988). Effect of clonidine on cigarette cessation and in the alleviation of withdrawal symptoms. *British Journal of Addiction, 83*, 1221–1226.

Hatsukami, D., Huber, M., Callies, A., & Skoog, K. (1993). Physical dependence on nicotine gum: Effect of duration on use. *Psychopharmacology, 111*, 449–456.

Hatsukami, D., Skoog, K., Allen, S., & Bliss, R. (1995). Gender and the effects of different doses of nicotine gum on tobacco withdrawal symptoms. *Experimental and Clinical Pharmacology, 3*, 163–173.

Henningfield, J. E., Radzius, A., Cooper, T. M., & Clayton, R. R. (1990). Drinking coffee and carbonated beverages blocks absorption of cicotine from nicotine polacrilex gum. *Journal of the American Medical Association, 264*, 1560–1564.

Herrera, N., Franco, R., Herrera, L., Partidas, A., Rolando, R., & Fagerstrom, K. O. (1995). Nicotine gum, 2 and 4 mg for nicotine dependence: A double-blind placebo-controlled trial within a behavior modification support program. *Chest, 106*, 447–451.

Hjalmarson, A., Franzon, M., Westin, A., & Wiklund, O. (1994). Effect of nicotine nasal spray on smoking cessation. *Archives of Internal Medicine, 154*, 2567–2572.

Hughes, J. R. (1994). Non-nicotine pharmacotherapies for smoking cessation. *Jounrla of Drug Development, 6*, 197–203.

Hughes, J. R., Gust, S. W., Keenan, R. M., & Fenwick, J. W. (1990). Effects of dose on nicotine's reinforcing, withdrawal-suppression and self-reported effects. *Journal of Pharmacology and Experimental Therapeutics, 252*, 1175–1183.

Hughes, J. R., Gust, S. W., Keenan, R. M., Fenwick, J. W., Skoog, K., & Higgins, S. T. (1991). Long-term use of nicotine vs. placebo gum. *Archives of General Medicine, 151*, 1993–1998.

Jacobs, M. A., Spilken, A. Z., Norman, M. M., Wohlberg, G. W., & Knapp, P. H. (1971). Interaction of personality and treatment conditions associated with success in a smoking control program. *Psychosomatic Medicine, 33*, 545–556.

Jarvik, M. E., & Henningfield, J. E. (1988). Pharmacological treatment of tobacco dependence. *Pharmacology, Biochemistry, and Behavior, 30*, 279–294.

Jorenby, D. E., Hatsukami, D. K., Smith, S. S., Fiore, M. C., Allen, S., Jensen, J., & Baker, T. B. (in press). Transdermal nicotine replacement reduces tobacco withdrawal symptoms. *Psychopharmacology*.

Jorenby, D. E., Smith, S. S., Fiore, M. C., Hurt, R. D., Offord, K. P., Croghan, I. T., Hays, J. T., Lewis, S. F., & Baker, T. B. (1995). Varying nicotine patch dose and type of smoking cessation counseling. *Journal of the American Medical Association, 274*, 1347–1352.

Karras, A., & Kane, J. (1980). Naloxone reduces cigarette smoking. *Life Sciences, 27*, 1541–1545.

Kendler, K. S., Neale, M. C., MacLean, C. J., Heath, A. C., Eaves, L. J., & Kessler, R. C. (1993). Smoking and major depression. *Archives of General Psychiatry, 50*, 36–43.

Killen, J. D., Fortmann, S. P., Newman, B., & Varady, A. (1990). Evaluation of a treatment approach combining nicotine gum with self-guided behavioral treatments for smoking relapse prevention. *Journal of Consulting and Clinical Psychology, 58*, 85–92.

Kornitzer, M., Boutsen, M., Dramaix, M., Thijs, J., & Gustavsson, G. (1995). Combined use of nicotine patch and gum in smoking cessation: A placebo-controlled clinical trial. *Preventative Medicine, 24*, 41–47.

Kornitzer, M., Kittel, F., Dramaix, M., & Pourdoux, P. (1987). A double-blind study of 2 mg versus 4 mg nicotine-gum in an industrial setting. *Journal of Psychosomatic Research, 31*, 171–176.

Kottke, T. E., Brekke, M. L., Solberg, L. I., & Hughes, J. R. (1988). A randomized trial to increase smoking intervention by physicians. *Journal of the American Medical Association, 259*, 2883–2889.

Lam, W., Sze, P. C., Sacks, H. S., & Chalmers, T. C. (1987). Meta-analysis of randomized controlled trials of nicotine gum. *Lancet, 2*, 27–30.

Lando, H. A. (1975). A comparison of excessive and rapid smoking in the modification of chronic smoking behavior. *Journal of Consulting and Clinical Psychology, 43*, 350–355.

Lando, H. A. (1976). Aversive conditioning and contingency management in the treatment of smoking. *Journal of Consulting and Clinical Psychology, 44*, 312.

Lando, H. A. (1993). Formal quit smoking treatments. In C. T. Orleans & J. Slade (Eds.). *Nicotine addiction: Principles and management*. New York: Oxford University Press.

Lando, H. A., Pirie, P. L., Roski, J., McGovern, P. G., & Schmid, L. A. (in press). Recycling of chronic smokers to sustained abstinence. *American Journal of Public Health*.

Lando, H. A., Sipfle, C. L., & McGovern, P. G. (1995). A statewide public service smoking cessation clinic. *American Journal of Health Promotion 10*, 9–11.

Leischow, S. J., Sachs, D. P., Bostrom, A. G., & Hansen, M. D. (1992). Effects of differing nicotine-replacement doses on weight gain after smoking cessation. *Archives of Family Medicine, 1*, 233–237.

Levin, E. D., Behm, F. M., & Rose, J. E. (1990). The use of flavor in cigarette substitutes. *Drug and Alcohol Dependence, 25*, 273.

Lichtenstein, E., Glasgow, R. E., & Abrams, D. B. (1986). Social support in smoking cessation: In search of effective interventions. *Behavior Research and Therapy, 17*, 607–619.

Lichtenstein, E., Harris, D. E., Birchler, G. R., Wahl, J. M., & Schmahl, D. P. (1973). Comparison of rapid smoking, warm, smoky air, and attention placebo in the modification of smoking behavior. *Journal of Consulting and Clinical Psychology, 40*, 92–98.

Lunell, E., Molander, L., Leischow, S. J., & Fagerstrom, K. O. (1995). Effect of nicotine vapour inhalation on the relief of tobacco withdrawal symptoms. *European Journal of Clinical Pharmacology, 48*, 235–240.

Marlatt, G. A., & Gordon, J. R. (Eds.). (1985). *Relapse prevention. Maintenance strategies in the treatment of addictive behaviors*. New York: Guilford Press.

McGovern, P., & Lando, H. (1991). Reduced nicotine exposure and abstinence outcome in two nicotine fading methods. *Addictive Behaviors, 16,* 11–20.

Murray, K. M., Cappello, C., & Baez, S. A. (1989). Lack of efficacy of transdermal clonidine in smoking cessation class. *American Review of Respiratory Diseases, 189,* A338.

Nemeth-Coslett, R., & Griffiths, R. R. (1986). Naloxone does not affect cigarette smoking. *Psychopharmacology, 89,* 261–264.

Nemeth-Coslett, R., Henningfield, J. E., O'Keeffee, M. K., & Griffiths, R. R. (1986). Effects of mecamylamine on human cigarette smoking and subjective ratings. *Psychopharmacology, 88,* 420–425.

Pirie, P. L., McBride, C. M., Hellerstedt, W., Jeffery, R. W., Hatsukami, D., Allen, S., & Lando, H. (1992). Smoking cessation in women concerned about weight. *American Journal of Public Health, 82,* 1238–1243.

Po, A. L. (1993). Transdermal nicotine in smoking cessation: A meta-analysis. *European Journal of Clinical Pharmacology, 45,* 519–528.

Pomerleau, C. S., Pomerleau, O. F., & Majchrzak, M. J. (1987). Mecamylamine pretreatment increases subsequent nicotine self-administration as indicated by changes in plasma nicotine level. *Psychopharmacology, 91,* 391–393.

Pomerleau, O. F., Fertig, J. B., Seyler, L. E., & Jaffe, J. (1983). Neuroendocrine reactivity to nicotine in smokers. *Psychopharmacology, 81,* 61–67.

Pomerleau, O. F., & Pomerleau, C. S. (1984). Neuroregulators and the reinforcement of smoking: Towards a biobehaviorial explanation. *Neuroscience and Biobehaviorial Reviews, 8,* 503–513.

Prochaska, J. O., & DiClemente, C. C. (1983). Stages and processes of self-change of smoking: Toward an integrative model of change. *Journal of Consulting and Clinical Psychology, 51,* 390–395.

Prochaska, J. O., DiClemente, C. C., Velicer, W. F., & Rossi, J. S. (1993). Standardized, individualized, interactive, and personalized self-help programs for smoking cessation. *Health Psychology, 12,* 399–405.

Prochaska, J. O., Velicer, W. F., Rossi, J. S., Goldstein, M., Marcus, B., Rakowski, W., Fiore, C., Harlow, L., Redding, C., & Rosenbloom, D. (1994). Stages of change and decisional balance for 12 problem behaviors. *Health Psychology, 13,* 39–46.

Puska, P., Vartiainen, E., & Korhonen, H. (1994). *Combining patch and gum in nicotine replacement therapy: Results of a double-blind study in North Karelia.* International Congress on Smoking Cessation, Glasgow, Scotland.

Rose, J. E., & Behm, F. M. (1994). Inhalation of vapor from black pepper extract reduces smoking withdrawal symptoms. *Drug and Alcohol Dependence, 34,* 225–229.

Rose, J. E., & Behm, F. M. (1987). Refined cigarette smoke as a method for reducing nicotine intake. *Pharmacology, Biochemistry, and Behavior, 28,* 305–310.

Rose, J. E., Behm, F. M., & Levin, E. D. (1993). Role of nicotine dose and sensory cues in the regulation of smoke intake. *Pharmacology, Biochemistry, and Behavior, 44,* 891–900.

Rose, J. E., Behm, F. M., Westman, E. C., Levin, E. D., Stein, R. M., Lane, J. D., & Ripka, G. V. (1994a). Combined effects of nicotine and mecamylamine in attenuating smoking satisfaction. *Experimental and Clinical Psychopharmacology, 2,* 328–344.

Rose, J. E., Behm, F. M., Westerman, E. C., Levin, E. D., Stein, R. M., & Ripka, G. V. (1994b). Mecamylamine combined with nicotine skin patch facilitates smoking cessation beyond nicotine patch treatment alone. *Clinical Pharmacology and Therapeutics, 56,* 86–99.

Rose, J. E., & Hickman, C. S. (1987). Citric acid aerosol as a potential smoking cessation aid. *Chest, 92,* 1005–1008.

Rose, J. E., & Levin, E. D. (1991). Concurrent agonist-antagonist administration for the analysis and treatment of drug dependence. *Pharmacology Biochemistry and Behavior, 41,* 219–226.

Rose, J. E., Sampson, A., Levin, E. D., & Henningfield, J. E. (1989). Mecamylamine increases nicotine preference and attenuates nicotine discrimination. *Pharmacology Biochemistry and Behavior, 32,* 933–938.

Russell, M. A., Jarvis, M. J., Sutherland, G., & Feyerabend, C. (1987). Nicotine replacement in smoking cessation: Absorption of nicotine vapor from smoke-free cigarettes. *Journal of the American Medical Association, 257,* 3262–3265.

Schneider, N. G. (1992). Nicotine therapy in smoking cessation. Pharmacokinetic considerations. *Clinical Pharmacokinetics, 23,* 169–172.

Schneider, N. G., Olmstead, R., Mody, F. V., Doan, K., Franzon, M., Jarvik, M. E., & Steinberg, C. (1995). Efficacy of a nicotine nasal spray in smoking cessation: A placebo-controlled, double-blind trial. *Addiction, 90,* 1671–1682.

Schwartz, J. L. (1987). Review and evaluation of smoking cessation methods: The United States and Canada 1978–1985 (NIH Publication No. 87-2940). Washington DC: U.S. Department of Health and Human Services.

Schwartz, J. L., & Dubitsky, M. (1968). One-year follow-up results of a smoking cessation program. *Canadian Journal of Public Health, 59,* 161–165.

Shapiro, D., Tursky, B., Schwartz, G. E., & Shnidman, S. R. (1971). Smoking on cue: A behavioral approach to smoking reduction. *Journal of Health and Social Behavior, 12,* 108–113.

Shiffman, S. (1982). Relapse following smoking cessation: A situational analysis. *Journal of Consulting and Clinical Psychology, 50,* 71–86.

Shiffman, S. M. (1993). Smoking cessation treatment: Any progress? *Journal of Consulting and Clinical Psychology, 61,* 718–722.

Silagy, C., Mant, D., Fowler, G., & Lodge, M. (1994). Meta-analysis on efficacy of nicotine replacement therapies in smoking cessation. *Lancet, 343,* 139–142.

Smoking Cessation Guideline Panel. (1996). *The AHCPR smoking cessation clinical practice guideline* (AHCPR Publication No. 96-0692). Washington DC: Centers for Disease Control and Prevention.

Stapleton, J. A., Russell, M. A., Feyerabend, C., Wiseman, S. M., Gustavsson, G., & Sawe, U. (1995). Dose effects and predictors of outcome in a randomized trial of transdermal nicotine patches in general practice. *Addiction, 90,* 31–42.

Stolerman, I. P. (1986). Could nicotine antagonists be used in smoking cessation? *British Journal of Addiction, 81,* 47–53.

Stolerman, I. P., Goldfarb, T., Fink, R., & Jarvik, M. E. (1973). Influencing cigarette smoking with nicotine antagonists. *Psychopharmacology (Berlin), 28,* 247–259.

Sutherland, G., Stapleton, J. A., & Russell, M. A. (1992). Randomised controlled trial of nasal nicotine spray in smoking cessation. *Lancet, 340,* 324–329.

Sutherland, G., Russell, M. A., Stapelton, J., Feyerabend, C., & Ferno, O. (1992). Nasal nicotine spray: A rapid nicotine delivery system. *Psychopharmacology, 108,* 512–518.

Sutherland, G., Stapleton, J. A., Russell, M. A., & Feyerabend, C. (1995). Naltrexone, smoking behavior and cigarette withdrawal. *Psychopharmacology, 120,* 418–425.

Tang, J. L., Law, M., & Wald, N. (1994). How effective is nicotine replacement therapy in helping people to stop smoking? *British Medical Journal, 308,* 21–26.

Tennant, F. S., Tarver, A. L., & Rawson, R. A. (1984). *Clinical evaluation of mecamylamine for withdrawal from nicotine dependence* (NIDA Research Monograph, pp. 239–246). Washington, DC: U.S. Government Printing Office.

Tiffany, S. T., Martin, E. M., & Baker, T. B. (1986). Treatments for cigarette smoking: An evaluation of the contributions of aversion and counseling procedures. *Behavior Research and Therapy, 24,* 437–452.

Tonnesen, P., Fryd, V., Hansen, M., Helsted, J., Gunnersen, A. B., Forchammer, H., & Stockner, M. (1988). Effect of nicotine chewing gum in combination with group counseling on the cessation of smoking. *New England Journal of Medicine, 318,* 15–18.

Tonnesen, P., Norregaard, J., Mikkelsen, K., Jorgensen, S., & Nilsson, F. (1993). A double-blind trial of a nicotine inhaler for smoking cessation. *Journal of the American Medical Association, 269,* 1268–1271.

Transdermal Nicotine Study Group. (1991). Transdermal nicotine for smoking cessation. *New England Journal of Medicine, 266,* 3133–3138.

U.S. Department of Health and Human Services (USDHHS). (1988). *The health consequences of smoking: nicotine addiction. A Report of the Surgeon General, 1988* (DHHS Publication No. CDC 88-8406).   : Centers for Disease Control, Center for Health Promotion and Education, Office on Smoking and Health, Washington, DC.

Villagra, V. G., Rosenberger, J. L., & Girolame, S. (1989). Transdermal clonidine for smoking cessation: A randomized, double blind, placebo controlled trial. *Circulation, 80,* 11–58.

West, R. J., Hajek, P., & Belcher, M. (1989). Severity of withdrawal symptoms as a predictor of outcome of an attempt to quit smoking. *Psychological Medicine, 19,* 981–985.

West, R. J., Hajek, P., & McNeill, A. (1991). Effect of buspirone on cigarette withdrawal symptoms and short-term abstinence rates in a smokers clinic. *Psychopharmacology, 104,* 91–96.

Westman, E. C., Behm, F. M., & Rose, J. E. (1995). Airway sensory replacement combined with nicotine replacement for smoking cessation: A randomized, placebo-controlled trial using a citric acid inhaler. *Chest, 107,* 1358–1364.

CHAPTER 33

ADULT CHILDREN OF ALCOHOLICS

Stephanie Brown
Joyce Schmid

In this chapter we review the historical development of the concept adult children of alcoholics (ACOA) and review early clinical research and more recent empirical studies with attention to the controversies surrounding this idea and its application to treatment. We suggest that the popular and clinical descriptions, plus the label ACOA, originated outside of accepted theory and practice within chemical dependence and mental health, and thus required an expansion in existing diagnostic and treatment frames (Brown, 1991a, 1991b).

The phrase "children of alcoholics" was born in the 1940s (Roe & Burks, 1945) and developed in the 1950s and 1960s with a concomitant empirical research focus on genetic transmission and psychopathology in children (Fox, 1962, 1963; Nylander, 1960, 1963; Schuckit, Goodwin, & Winokur, 1972; Winoker & Clayton, 1968; Winokur, Reich, Rimmer, & Pitts, 1970). The impact of alcoholism on others was further recognized in the self-help arena with the birth of Al-Anon in the 1950s, followed by the introduction of Alateen (the 12-step program for children of alcoholics) shortly thereafter. Then, in the mid-1970s, children of alcoholics were recognized as a treatment population, an awareness and legitimacy forced on the professional domains of chemical dependence and

mental health by the rapid, global public acceptance of the new idea—"adult children of alcoholics"—and the popular social movement it launched.

Prior to this point in time, treatment focused solely on the individual separate from the realities of family life. The label ACOA required an intergenerational, interpersonal perspective in addition to the individual focus that had predominated.

HISTORICAL DEVELOPMENT: FOCUS ON THE INDIVIDUAL

Historically, the field of addiction focused only on the drinking alcoholic. Counselors saw drinking and other drug use as the central issue, or even the only issue for the alcoholic. Family members were acknowledged solely to enlist their support for treatment and recovery. Within the addiction field, the alcoholic/addict has always been the primary patient.

This narrow focus on the individual has also characterized the mental health field, with various schools—behavioral, cognitive, psychodynamic—competing for primacy in explaining etiology and treatment. In contrast to the addiction field, however, mental health viewed alcoholism as secondary—a bad habit, or the consequence or symptom of some other problem rather than the cause. Treatment often focused on the "other" problem, with a limited emphasis on behavior modification or psychodynamic exploration oriented toward cure of the symptom—too much drinking.

Until Jackson (1954) identified an "adjustment" to alcoholism that occurs within the family, the effects of alcohol on family members were not considered. Until recently (Vaillant, 1983), there was no recognition that alcoholism itself was primary and the cause of psychopathology for the drinker and for those close to the drinker. Vaillant's reversal of cause and effect followed the acceptance of the disease model (Jellinek, 1960) which defined alcoholism as a primary disease caused by multiple factors outside of the individual's willful control and affecting the individual on multiple levels. Signs of expansion emerged in the late 1940s and 1950s as practitioners began to explore families and family processes (Ackerman, 1958; Bateson, Jackson, Haley, & Weakland, 1956; Jackson, 1954; Joanning, 1992). Psychoanalytic thinking expanded from a predominant emphasis on instinct to include a separate emphasis on the developmental significance of internalized interactions with other people (Fairbairn, 1952; Winnicott, 1953, 1960). It was within this expanding context that clinicians and researchers began to explore the impact of parental alcoholism on children (Hawkins, 1950; Roe & Burks, 1945). Cork's *Forgotten Children* (1969) drew attention to the plight of children of alcoholics just as systems-oriented family therapy (Bowen, 1971; Minuchin, 1974; Watzlawick, Weakland, & Fisch, 1974) and object relations theories (Kohut, 1971; Mahler, 1975; Masterson, 1976) flowered. As the individual was increasingly seen in an interpersonal context, and as alcoholism was accepted as a multifaceted, primary disease that was the *cause* of other problems, the effect of alcoholism on the family could be recognized.

But there was still a missing piece. We suggest that the inclusion of post traumatic stress disorder (PTSD) into DSM III in 1980 set in motion a more radical change in thinking about psychopathology by linking the development of intrapsychic and interpersonal problems to a real event or chronic external stressors. Although a traumatic neurosis had been defined in relation to war (Kardiner, 1941), it had not been linked to intrapsychic, interpersonal, or developmental psychopathology. This bridge between trauma and psychopathology has now been made by trauma theorists (Eth & Pynoos, 1985; Herman, 1992; Terr,

1990; van der Kolk, 1987a), parallel to the rapid acceptance and development of the idea that living with parental alcoholism could be the cause of psychopathology.

REVIEW OF RESEARCH

In the 1980s, clinicians and clinical researchers described the experiences of living with parental alcoholism, loosely following the format of the Alcoholics Anonymous (AA) "story" or narrative in which the alcoholic remembers "what it was like, what happened, and what it is like now" (Alcoholics Anonymous, 1955). The "what it was like" part of this description of the realities of alcoholism became the foundation for what we will outline later in this chapter as the "environmental/trauma" track.

Responding to the label ACOA, individuals began to "make real" the past, that is, to tell the truth about what it had been like to grow up in a family with one or two alcoholic parents. The National Association for Children of Alcoholics (NACOA) was founded to legitimize and represent children of alcoholics within the educational–cultural context, and the popular press spread the idea rapidly at a social, grass-roots level, all of which caused an immediate backlash within professional communities.

Early researchers, largely based in clinical settings, linked description to developmental theory and treatment (Beletis & Brown, 1981; Brown, 1974, 1988, 1992a, 1992b; Brown & Beletis, 1986; Brown, Beletis, & Cermak, 1989; Cermak, 1986, 1990, 1991; Seixas & Youcha, 1985), and defined characteristics of ACOAs (Woititz, 1983), and role typologies (Black, 1981; Wegsheider, 1981), which also became popularized. Empirical researchers challenged this descriptive base, and, in doing so, set the research agenda for the first half of the 1990s.

BASIC QUESTIONS

1. Information about ACOA characteristics had been based on nonstatistical, descriptive studies. Would the clinical findings on ACOAs be confirmed in rigorously designed empirical studies?
2. ACOAs had been studied without reference to control groups. Are the characteristics and difficulties identified in ACOAs unique to that group, or simply a part of human experience?
3. Much of the clinical research was based on ACOAs who had sought psychotherapeutic treatment. Are nonpatient ACOAs also affected?

4. Large numbers of people were being labeled and were self-identifying as ACOAs. Is the ACOA label helpful or harmful?

5. Some ACOAs were deeply troubled, whereas others seemed to be unaffected. Why are some ACOAs more seriously affected than others? What are the criteria for assessment? What is the difference between coping and defense? Between adjustment and pathology?

BASIC FINDINGS

1. In a comprehensive review of 75 articles and books, Giglio and Kaufman (1990) summarize themes in the literature before 1990 on children of alcoholics (COAs) and adult children of alcoholics (ACOAs). Children (COAs) are found to have difficulties such as anxious and dysphoric feelings, low self-esteem, all-or-none behavior, problems with trust, intimacy and control, antisocial behavior, and school problems. Adults (ACOAs) are more likely to become alcoholics themselves than are adult children of nonalcoholics (ACONAs). ACOAs are found to have psychiatric symptoms such as low self-esteem, anxiety, affective disorders, compulsivity, passive-dependent traits, antisocial traits, and posttraumatic stress disorder, and tend to overuse denial as a defense mechanism. In relationships, ACOAs experience a high level of divorce and separation. The literature describes ACOAs as having difficulty in developing close relationships, poor communication skills, difficulty identifying and expressing their feelings and needs, problems with trust, inappropriate loyalty, and a tendency to take rigid roles. They suffer from a sense of abandonment, discomfort with taking risks, fear of authority figures, and all-or-none thinking.

2. Addressing the question of whether parental alcoholism gives rise to unique problems in ACOAs, Giunta and Compas (1994); Hall, Bolen, and Webster (1994), and Neff (1994) compare ACOAs with other adults raised in emotionally traumatic but not alcoholic circumstances and with adults raised in "normal" circumstances. ("Normal" is defined as having neither alcoholism nor other identifiable trauma.) They find no definable differences between the problems of ACOAs and those of adults raised with other problems, but find that both of these groups experience more disturbance than adults raised in "normal" homes. Similar results are found by Fisher, Jenkins, Harrison, and Jesch,

(1993); and Hardwick, Hansen, and Bairnsfather, (1995). These studies support the view held by Brown (1991a) and Schuckit (1995), that the term ACOA refers neither to an individual diagnosis nor to a specific individual syndrome. In these studies, the comparison adults from troubled backgrounds have parents with mental illness, or in childhood have suffered death of a family member or friend, parental divorce, and/or physical violence. Comparability with this reference group and differences of both groups from those from "normal" backgrounds validate conclusions that growing up in an alcoholic home is, at the least, problematic, and very likely traumatic.

3. Because much of the pre-1990 work on ACOAs is based on clinical samples, studies after that time address the question of whether COAs and ACOAs who are not in treatment are more likely to have psychological problems than ACONAs. Many researchers find that nonclinical adults and/or children with alcoholic parents are indeed more likely to experience symptoms of anxiety and/or depression, antisocial traits, relationship difficulties, behavioral problems, and/or alcohol abuse (Belliveau & Stoppard, 1995; Coleman & Frick, 1994; Connolly, Casswell, Steward, Silva, & O'Brien 1933; Domenico & Windle, 1993; Kashubeck, 1994; Mathew, Wilson, Blazer, & George, 1993; Nordberg, Rydelius, & Zetterstrom, 1994). Others find no differences in personality adjustment (Cartwright, McKay, & Stader, 1990; Harman, Armsworth, Hwang, & Vincent, 1995; Wright & Heppner, 1991) or find the majority of the ACOAs they test to be problem-free (D'Andrea, Fisher, & Harrison, 1994). Although not every investigator finds identifiable psychiatric symptomatology in nonclinical ACOAs, the studies with positive findings tend to be larger, more recent, and in a few cases, prospective (Connolly et al., 1993; Nordberg et al., 1994), lending weight to the conclusion that many ACOAs who are not in treatment do have difficulty with anxiety, mood, behavior, relationships, and/or alcohol.

4. The ACOA or COA label provides information not only about the individual, but also about the formative interpersonal environment. The label indicates that the child and adult child are to be understood in relation to the parents and to the central significance of parental alcoholism within the family (Brown, 1991b). For an ACOA, the label itself helps to prevent intergenerational transmission of alcoholism. As Steinglass,

Bennett, Wolin, and Reiss (1987) demonstrate, prevention requires a conscious choice by the newly forming family to reject the alcoholic traditions of the family of origin ("deliberateness"). Such a conscious choice is predicated on the awareness of parental alcoholism and its negative consequences in one's family.

For troubled ACOAs, the label is a vital cognitive link between their suffering and the source of the suffering, a link that is often denied in the alcoholic family, and that has long been unseen or denied by society and treatment providers as well (Brown, 1991a). It is only in the context of this link that feelings and behaviors of ACOAs make sense. The label grants permission to break denial, reconstruct the realities of alcoholism within the family, and to understand one's adult self in relation to the past.

Recently, concerns have been raised about possible iatrogenic effects of the label. Gallant (1990) cites negative bias toward people bearing COA and ACOA labels, which was found in a study by Burk and Sher (cited in Gallant, 1990). In a similar vein, Wolin and Wolin (1995) assert that focusing on ACOA problems by treatment personnel engenders hopelessness and negativity—a "Damage Model." They recommend that more attention be paid to the strengths of ACOAs—a "challenge model."

The importance of public education to eradicate the stigma of alcoholism, and of recognition of the strengths in ACOAs, cannot be overstated. However, it is equally important to consider that defensive, adaptive behaviors and attitudes that are required for survival in an alcoholic family, and that are often effective in the outside world as well, can also be restrictive and pathological. Failure to recognize the defensive aspects of these behaviors and attitudes may limit recognition of emotional problems as well as opportunities for treatment. ACOAs who are labeled "invulnerable" or "resilient" can be overlooked by treatment personnel like they were in their families (Brown, 1991b; 1995). Strengthening of the ACOA's denial by intentionally avoiding the ACOA label risks iatrogenically exacerbating the emotional symptoms that result from denial.

The field of developmental psychopathology (Rolf, Masten, Cicchetti, Nuechterlein, & Weintraub, 1990) shifts the emphasis from dichotomous positive or negative outcomes to a continuum, recognizing that defensive adaptations have both adaptive and maladaptive consequences. Radke-Yarrow's and Sherman's (1990)

concept of "hard growing" illustrates this continuum with attention paid to both risk and protective factors.

5. Kashubek (1994) raises the question of why some people from alcoholic families have more serious difficulties than others. Johnson, Rolf, Tiegel, and McDuff (1995) summarize the literature on assessment of COAs, with a goal of determining risk factors. Brown and Sunshine (1982) suggest that factors related to emotional outcome include the child's age at onset of parental alcoholism, the relationship with the alcoholic parent independent of drinking behavior, the child's resources outside the family, the availability of and interaction with the nonalcoholic parent (if there is one), as well as the child's innate endowment. Giglio and Kaufman (1990) point to the following variables: birth order, gender of child, type of family system, which parent was alcoholic, and temporal locus of parental drinking (past, present, or both). In addition, Cermak (1990) includes the following: temperament of the child, genetic predisposition to alcoholism, presence of traumatic events, level of stress in childhood, absence of normative experiences, necessity for denying the truth, and presence of other psychiatric conditions in the child. Gunning, Pattiselanno, van der Stelt and Wiers (1994) are currently conducting a longitudinal study to uncover biochemical, psychophysiological, and psychological predictors for later psychological and addiction problems in COAs. To the extent that the focus is on the individual ACOA, only part of the answer to variability will be visible. It is in the environment and interpersonal dynamics that further clues are to be found (Brown, 1991b).

SUMMARY

Evidence from clinical and empirical research supports the recognition of ACOAs as a legitimate clinical population, though there remains much disagreement and considerable variability. In addition, traditional assessment and treatment models are no longer adequate. We must recognize the limitations of a single-dimension focus on the individual. The ACOA concept requires an understanding of three "assessment" or "diagnostic" tracks—the environment, the family system, and the individual, all in response to the organizing dominance of alcoholism.

Also, the concept of ACOA legitimizes the central significance of external reality and thereby expands, or even changes, the locus of pathology from the person to the family or from a strictly intrapsychic frame to the interpersonal.

Within the context of chronic trauma, a pathological system, and unhealthy attachments, "normal" individual development becomes an adaptation to pathology.

ASSESSMENT TRACKS

The Alcoholic Environment

As noted, the "environment" refers to "what it was like": the realities of daily life in a family organized by a parent's alcoholism. It includes the "context": the foreground and background, the atmosphere, mood, the sights and sounds. Many ACOAs can relate a story of daily life based on the memory of drinking within the family. Descriptions of the environment quickly elicit memories of the sensory experience, which, for children, was largely absorbed unconsciously and without language. When denial of reality prevails, the experience cannot be given words, so the affective and cognitive elements remain suppressed or expressed nonverbally. The environment exists all around us, separate from words. Many ACOAs cannot remember the details of family life, but they carry feelings "taken in" from the context and their interactions with others. This sensory experience is brought to awareness through language, including the label "ACOA." Once the alcoholism is named, adults who have grown up literally "absorbing" drunkenness and all its ramifications can give voice to their internal memories and experiences.

The alcoholic family environment is characterized by chaos, uncertainty, and a changing reality (Black, 1981; Brown, 1988; Cermak, 1986, 1988). Inconsistent discipline, emotional and physical neglect, arguments, marital instability, disorganization, violence and/or physical and sexual abuse (Giglio & Kaufman, 1990) are common. The COA must endure the emptiness, loneliness, and terror of repeated abandonment or the witnessing of violence or abuse to others. The atmosphere is characterized by tension, fear, and shame, feelings that become fused with the child's sense of self. At least one person in the family has lost control of drinking and its consequences, which throws the whole family out of control; the hallmark of the environment is a basic lack of safety—physical and emotional. A striking illustration of this is provided by Lillian, who told her ACOA group: "When I went to school in the morning, I would notice blood on the front of Dad's car. I'd try not to think about what—or who—he'd hit."

Marilyn told of the times her drunken father had lined up all the kids against the wall, threatening them with a loaded gun. Steve recalled the times there had been no food in the house, and he'd served ketchup to his younger siblings for dinner. Some describe the sound of ice cracking, waking up to violent arguing in the middle of the night, turkeys sliding off the dining room table at Thanksgiving, or food and dishes routinely thrown across the room. Many ACOAs tell of finding parents passed out on the floor, apparently dead, or passed out on a chair with a lighted cigarette; of brutal beatings and sexual violations. These examples underscore the validity of Cermak's comparison of the ACOA to a military veteran (1988). That is, the degree of environmental trauma in an alcoholic family varies with the stage of alcoholism in the family member, the number of alcoholics, the nature of violence and neglect, and the extent to which basic family functions and rituals are invaded and organized by the alcoholism (Steinglass et al., 1987).

The Trauma of Alcoholism

As the realities of living with parental alcoholism have become known over the past 15 years, a separate trauma field has developed simultaneously. Trauma theory provides a vital theoretical frame to understand the impact of parental alcoholism developmentally and psychodynamically and it offers a bridge between the separate mental health and addiction fields (Brown, 1994).

Krystal (1978) distinguished two types of trauma, acute and chronic. Acute trauma is one or more discrete events that threaten the integrity of the self or family, and is so overwhelming that it cannot be integrated into one's sense of self. Psychological consequences include dissociation, numbing, depersonalization, derealization, confusion, and a "foggy" mental state. Chronic trauma is the normalization of repeated unpredictable, inconsistent, dangerous circumstances or events and relationship patterns. Krugman (1987) elaborated the consequences of this chronic state, describing the development of a traumatic character. Chronic trauma often leads to depression and anxiety. Individual development becomes dominated by defenses, including splitting, disavowal, and blocking (Herman, 1992).

As described by van der Kolk (1987a), trauma can lead either to hyperarousal and intrusion or to numbing and constriction. Intrusive reactions can include explosive outbursts, startle responses, nightmares, and a poor tolerance for psychological or physiological arousal, leading to motoric discharge. The numbing response can include emotional constriction, isolation, anhedonia, a sense of estrangement, and avoidance of intimate relationships. Children who have been traumatized by primary caregivers can demonstrate overreactivity, poor tolerance of anxiety, frozen watchfulness, and an unusual sensitivity to parents' needs (van der Kolk, 1987c.) Traumatized people tend to respond to stress in an all-or-nothing way (van der Kolk & Greenberg, 1987). Animals who are subjected to inescapable shock exhibit deficits in learning to escape new adverse situations, decreased motivation for learning, and chronic subjective distress (van der Kolk & Greenberg, 1987). Fish-Murray, Koby, and van der Kolk (1987) found that abused children were markedly inflexible. These symptoms match those described for the ACOA. Understanding the childhood environment of the ACOA is as essential as taking a complete history in a medical examination.

The Alcoholic Family System

Family systems theory refers to interactional patterns of relationship and behavior that maintain a family's sense of balance or homeostasis (Bowen, 1974; Satir, 1964; Watzlavick et al., 1974). It refers to how the family "works," including the mechanisms or structure and roles that maintain equilibrium.

The alcoholic family system is an adaptation to the ongoing trauma created by drinking and a chief source of maintaining the trauma at the same time (Brown, 1985). The family is dominated by the alcoholic, whose changing moods, out-of-control behavior, and failure to fulfill major roles must be compensated for if the family is to survive. Many families may function in providing food, shelter, and basic necessities, but most will be characterized by rigidity and distortion, if not outright chaos. Family members are connected to one another by the "story"—the explanations and core beliefs that allow drinking behavior to be maintained, denied, and explained at the same time.

Like other families organized around trauma (Krugman, 1987), alcoholic families experience disorders of rules, hierarchies, and boundaries. Rules are often arbitrary and inconsistent. They dictate how the alcoholism will be denied and also explained in a way that allows it to be maintained. Such rules set irrational thinking, based on skewed or reversed cause and effect, as a cornerstone of family membership. Often families will have two different sets of rules: one that applies when the alcoholic is dry and another that applies when the alcoholic is drinking

(Steinglass et al., 1987). The confusion, distortion, and defensive thinking create an unstable foundation for the development of healthy cognitive processes and the range of affects that accompany them (Guidano & Liotti, 1983).

Disorders of hierarchies include parentification and triangulation of children (Krugman, 1987). For example, a child might fill the role vacated by the alcoholic parent, cleaning the house, caring for younger children, or serving as a confidante or even a sexual partner to a parent. June, a 35-year-old ACOA, said, matter of factly:

> One night my father ran into my room and woke me up. He couldn't wake my mother—she was passed out. He was hysterical because he thought he was having a heart attack. He made me drive him to the emergency room. They said his heart was fine—he was just drunk. I was fourteen. It was the first time I ever drove a car.

Children who must respond to developmentally inappropriate demands or fill adult roles are deprived of the opportunity to attend to their own development (Beletsis & Brown, 1981). They automatically shift focus off of their own needs onto the needs of others (Krugman, 1987).

In alcoholic families, boundaries are often disordered in ways that fall into two categories: overly rigid and closed, or almost nonexistent (Krugman, 1987; Steinglass et al., 1987). In the closed system, the outside world is seen as a dangerous place and children are told that the chaotic, dangerous home is the only place of safety. The secret of the alcoholism is closely guarded - children are punished for talking to people outside the home. In such a closed system, the growth of any individual is seen as a threat; the system is so rigid that any potential for change is frightening. The pressure build-up and paranoia of the closed system add to the stress and thus to the potential for danger from within.

At the other extreme is the boundariless system (Krugman, 1987; Steinglass et al., 1987), which people enter and leave with little gatekeeping. Friends of parents are allowed unsupervised access to the children, and in some instances, molest them. Children's whereabouts are often unknown. Parents may disappear, leaving the children unsupervised. As one mother in a disengaged system said, "I never know where Richard and Frank go after dinner. You just can't control kids these days!" (Richard and Frank were nine and seven). The lack of organization, interaction, and supervision in a boundariless family exposes children to danger from the outside world as well as from within.

INDIVIDUAL DEVELOPMENT

Children have little or no choice but to adapt to the environment and the system of the family in which they are raised. In the alcoholic family, adaptation to the traumatic environment and distorted system interferes with healthy individual development and can produce pathology. The child who must be vigilant to potential danger or who focuses on filling the family's needs is distracted from the normal academic, social, and psychological tasks of childhood. The necessity for constant defense in a traumatic environment creates a personality based on defense rather than on self-development (Miller, 1994). In addition, the abusive and neglectful behavior of adults in alcoholic systems can lead to serious damage to the child's capacity for emotional attachment.

Development of the Defensive Self

Krugman (1987) suggests that traumatic experience leads to the dominance of defense to avoid the recurrence of traumatic memory or experience. When trauma is chronic, it becomes normalized and predictable; defense becomes automatic. In conditions of chronic trauma, the need for defense overrides healthy development; more and more of the self is organized to ward off vulnerability. The COA develops a defensive self in response to the trauma of the environment, and the alcoholic family system. Individual development is sacrificed to preserve the pathological system (Brown, 1995; Brown & Lewis, 1995) as family cohesiveness and sometimes even survival are increasingly threatened by the progression of alcoholism.

In addition, defensive behavior is modeled for and even overtly demanded of the children by parents pushed to desperation. In alcoholic families, children and adults alike are driven to defenses such as denial, perceptual and cognitive distortion, a need for control, all-or-none thinking, self-erasure, and an overriding assumption of responsibility for others (Brown, 1988, 1992a). Ultimately, the child shuts out, distorts, and reinterprets reality—makes a "loving sacrifice" (Searles, 1965) of his or her own sanity or reality to support the insanity or distorted reality of the parents.

The child's preoccupation with defense leads to chronic distrust of others, inhibition of curiosity, a distrust of one's own senses, and a feeling that everything is unreal. This constellation of defensive maneuvers becomes identical with a sense of self, and persists into adulthood. A 55-year-old man illustrates: "You think you are seeing me. You're not. This man that you see is a cardboard image of a smiling, successful accountant. I am a little boy hiding behind it, holding it up."

Defensive tactics—adopted to minimize anxiety, fear, the threats of humiliation and annihilation, and to preserve the self—result in isolating, imprisoning, and stunting the flexibility and healthy development of the self.

Attachment

Attachment is now recognized as a cornerstone of human development. It is defined by Bowlby (1969–1980) as a system of behaviors that regulate the child's seeking of closeness with a primary caretaker in order to feel secure. Interactions with early caretakers establish "internal working models" of the self and the attachment figures. Based on these early interactions, the child develops an attachment style (Ainsworth, Blehar, Waters, & Wall, 1978) which is stable from age 1 to at least the 10th year (Berman & Sperling, 1994).

The implications of attachment theory for ACOAs are profound. Parental impairment through alcohol limits parents' ability to provide the healthy, appropriate attachment needed by any child. Whipple, Fitzgerald, and Zucker (1995) observed structured home interactions between preschoolers and their parents in alcoholic and nonalcoholic families. Their findings strongly differentiate these groups:

> Non-alcoholic parents were better able to keep their children on task, and had greater dyadic synchrony. They appeared better connected and better able to read and respond to each others' cues . . . Non-alcoholic parents displayed more instances of facilitating self-regulation; . . . they were better able to provide supportive directions that increased their child's chance of success . . . . Alcoholic parents . . . made more demands for self-reliant behavior (p. 157–148).

In an adult clinical sample, El-Guebaly, West, Maticka-Tyndale, and Pool (1993) found that unhealthy attachment styles were present in female ACOAs, and were suggested in male ACOAs, compared to controls. Difficulties with attachment are likely to be part of the source of the behavioral, relational, and mood difficulties observed for ACOAs. Even farther reaching, unhealthy attachment can impair the adult's capacities for attachment and nurturing, leading to a repetition of pathology with one's own children.

Attachment between the COA and the parent is built around compliance with the parent's need to deny both the alcoholism and the negative consequences of the drinking. For the COA, "attachment . . . is based on denial of perception which results in denial of affect which together result in developmental arrests or difficulties" (Brown, 1988, p. 90). The fact that it is attachment itself—one of the most fundamental and powerful of human functions—that supports continued distortion and denial of experience, makes such distortion and denial extremely resistant to change.

TREATMENT

Because the history of the concept ACOA has been characterized by continuing controversy, it is not surprising that definitions about what constitutes "treatment" or "recovery" are also controversial. A brief 15-year history of "treatment" reflects the growth of the idea and its continuing movement toward legitimacy within mental health as well as chemical dependence.

In the beginning stage of the social movement, "treatment" often meant brief, intense workshops or participation in large conferences designed for both laypeople and professionals. Description predominated as people identified with the narratives of "what it was like," and tried on the label ACOA. Short-term, educational group therapies were offered within the same "consciousness-raising" climate and individuals identified their particular family roles and personality characteristics.

At the same time, clinicians (Brown et al., 1989; Cermak, 1986, 1988; Wood 1987; Vanicelli, 1989) began offering specialized ACOA-labeled traditional psychotherapy, beginning the theoretical and clinical crossing of disciplines between mental health and chemical dependence. These professionals moved beyond description to the dynamics of the pathological alcoholic system and the impact and treatment implications of both the environment and the family system on individual development.

The elucidation of trauma theory provided a key integrative bridge between mental health and chemical dependence, but not without modifications in theory and practice. No single theory or "school" of treatment—behavioral, cognitive, psychodynamic or systems—adequately addresses the three domains that simultaneously affect child development.

Therapists must be knowledgeable and fluent in all of these varied "schools" in order to adapt treatment to the multiple needs of the patient, rather than vice versa. To do so, the therapist must be flexible in professional identity and practice. Often functioning as a coach in early stages of treatment (Brown, 1992b), the professional offers educa-

tion and referral to additional sources of help, such as Al-Anon, in conjunction with psychotherapy. The coaching model allows the therapist to combine active, direct guidance and intervention with nondirective, transference-focused psychodynamic approaches. As treatment proceeds, the balance tends to shift to greater use of psychodynamic methods, with return to coaching as needed.

The Process of Treatment

The reality of alcoholism as an organizing principle in the individual's development forms the core of individual or group therapies for ACOAs. Individuals remember what happened in childhood and tell the "story" of growing up with alcoholic parents, thereby breaking the fundamental rules of denial and adaptation to pathology that governed the alcoholic family. Treatment then unfolds as a process of growing separation from the pathology that constituted "normal" development. This process of separation, or "detachment" (Brown, 1988, 1992a) including a "reconstruction" of the past and a new construction of the self, follows a developmental model similar to the stages of recovery identified for the alcoholic (Brown, 1985).

Although much controversy exists today about what constitutes a "reasonable" length of treatment, we, as developmental theorists and clinicians, believe strongly in the necessity of a long-term, psychodynamic framework to achieve the depth of change that is required to alter core identifications, self-perceptions, and attachment patterns. This intensive reconstruction process cannot be undertaken or achieved within a brief treatment structure. Short-term therapies can, however, be helpful by naming the reality of alcoholism and providing crisis intervention and practical education.

THE DOMAINS

Because the pathology of the ACOA has its origins in three domains—the environment, the family system, and individual development—treatment must address each of these areas. And underlying every aspect of recovery—which we define as separation from the external and internal pathology of alcoholism and growth of a healthier self (Brown, 1988, 1991b, 1992a)—are attachment issues. As the ACOA works to extricate himself or herself from a destructive environment and family system and embark on a course of healthier development, the individual experiences not only guilt and grief and a sense of being utterly alone but also a terrifying loss of identity. Therapeutic work in each domain activates profound distress by challenging the attachment structure, which itself maintains pathology.

Environment

The Present: Establishing Safety

The first requirement of treatment for the ACOA, like other victims of trauma (Herman, 1992), is the establishment of safety. Because trauma survivors often gravitate to further trauma (van der Kolk & Greenberg, 1987), ACOAs may live in situations paralleling those of childhood. Current external dangers may require crisis intervention to provide physical safety, such as a referral to a battered women's shelter, notification of police, or a report to protective agencies. The severity of internal dangers must also be assessed: suicidal, psychotic, or badly fragmented patients may need a structured residential or hospital setting. The alcoholic or other drug-dependent ACOA will also need primary attention to the addiction. For many, identification with and attachment to alcoholic parents complicates the path to abstinence and must be included in the treatment focus (Brown, 1988).

Although most ACOAs no longer live in the alcoholic family, the alcoholic family now lives in the ACOA. To provide safety from the internalized family, the therapist must take care not to recreate it in the office. Confidentiality, a nonjudgmental and noncontrolling stance, clarity of professional boundaries, consistency, and predictability are essential treatment cornerstones.

The Al-Anon program (1984) is also an important source of safety. Structured to allow its members to speak without fear of criticism, shaming, or control from others, Al-Anon provides support and validation of the realities of alcoholism.

The Past: Telling the Story of the Trauma

People who have experienced trauma have an overwhelming need to tell the story of what happened. Van der Kolk (1987a) stressed the importance of the patient's remembering and having feelings about the traumatic events and the necessity for validation of the individual's traumatic experiences (Brown, 1994.) Putting the story into words and telling it to others are important in at least three ways. First, trauma survivors often try to protect themselves from

overwhelming pain by compartmentalizing, denying, or repressing the traumatic events. In an alcoholic family, this normal way of dealing with trauma is often reinforced by parental directive: "There is no alcoholism here, and don't talk about it" (Beletsis & Brown, 1981). Identifying the trauma makes sense of the feelings that arise from the trauma itself—anxiety, rage, and grief—which otherwise must be denied or explained as something else. Second, verbalizing the story helps to prevent unconscious reenactment (van der Kolk & Kadish, 1987) and allows reinterpretation. Old logical connections can be questioned; new ones can be made. Facts that were overlooked or misinterpreted can be noticed and can change the entire meaning of the story (White & Epstein, 1990).

Naming the trauma and telling the story often exact a terrible cost (Brown & Beletsis, 1986). Because attachments have been based on denial of alcoholism, or at least keeping it secret, acknowledging it to oneself and the world threatens that primary bond and begins a process of emotional separation from the family that feels, and may indeed be, cataclysmic. The ACOA needs to tell his or her story to people who understand the dynamics of alcoholism, people who are willing to hear and believe the trauma of an alcoholic home and who understand the impact on development.

And finally, once an ACOA has entered a safe environment and has begun to know and tell the "story," he or she can begin to make changes in his participation in the alcoholic family system.

The System

The alcoholic family system, organized around denying and protecting the drinking, must shift or collapse in order for systemic change to begin (Brown & Lewis, 1995). In many alcoholic families, this never happens. Thus, when the ACOA presents for treatment, it is usually only the ACOA's participation in the system that can be changed. The ACOA can begin to challenge rules and to establish boundaries and limits with the original family.

The alcoholic system operates on denial and distortion of reality and a mandate for silence. The ACOA challenges these rules by naming the alcoholism and seeking help. Early in treatment, the ACOA may move back and forth between seeing and not seeing the alcoholism and the trauma it created, between giving information and taking it back. This process provides a clear window to the rationalizations that maintained the system: Dad wasn't an

CHAPTER 33: ADULT CHILDREN OF ALCOHOLICS

alcoholic; he just worked hard all day and needed to relax when he came home; Mom just liked her brandy; nobody was abused because no bones were broken.

The family system comes alive in therapy as the breaking of rules elicits the same correction from the internalized family as it did from the family of origin. The therapist helps the patient infer the rules and the punishments for breaking them, and to state these clearly, so that their irrational and contradictory nature can be seen. The therapist challenges the rationalizations that support the rules and educates about alcoholism, so that the ACOA can start to liberate himself or herself from the rules of the alcoholic family.

In group therapy, the ACOA establishes a "family transference" (Brown & Beletsis, 1986), which facilitates a reenactment and subsequent challenge to early beliefs and defenses. Interpersonal behavior accenting caretaking and assumption of responsibility for others are critical issues.

When the family of origin does not change, the ACOA can learn to resist the "pull" back into that family system and its pathology, and can generalize these new behaviors and beliefs to other present life situations and relationships.

Individual Development

Trauma Recovery

The COA, or any child exposed to chronic trauma within the family, faces a tragic dilemma: the people who are the source of the trauma are the primary attachment figures, the very people who are supposed to provide comfort and sustenance. This makes trauma recovery even more complicated for the ACOA than it is for the person who suffers an acute trauma or ongoing trauma in adult life, outside the realm of close interpersonal bonds. For the ACOA, recovery threatens primary attachments.

Herman (1992) defines the stages of trauma recovery as establishment of safety remembrance and mourning, and reconnection with ordinary life. Establishment of safety in treatment of ACOAs has been addressed previously. Attachment challenges in the stage of remembrance and mourning are less obvious. Herman (1992) points out that during this process, the trauma survivor "often comes into conflict with important people in his/her life. There is a rupture in his/her sense of belonging within a shared system of belief" (p. 178). This is especially true for the ACOA. Talking about what happened, and reinterpreting it as trauma, breaks fundamental attachment bonds between the ACOA and the parents and family, leaving the ACOA alone and orphaned (Brown, 1988). Parents and ACOAs alike participate in the disaffiliation. ACOAs tell of parents who refuse to speak to them, are angry, or simply seem not to hear when the alcoholism and the trauma are named. For the ACOA, parental denial and rejection of the newly identified reality can be disappointing or enraging. Even if contact with parents is maintained, the relationship is altered. There is tremendous pressure on the ACOA to recant and rejoin the fold. Along with external pressure from the family to return to old ways of thinking and behaving, there is similar pressure from within to escape the loneliness, confusion, and loss of identity that come with naming the realities and beginning the construction of a narrative.

Survivors of acute trauma suffer from serious losses that must be mourned. ACOAs must mourn also for what they never had. As Herman (1992) indicates, "Survivors of chronic childhood trauma face the task of grieving not only for what was lost but also for what was never theirs to lose. . . . They confront the existential despair that they could not face in childhood" (p. 193). The realization that the beloved and needed parents loved alcohol more than the child, that in real ways they failed the child, is devastating. As Herman quotes Shengold: "Without the inner picture of caring parents, how can one survive?"

Herman (1992) calls the final stage of trauma recovery "reconnection" with self and other. For many ACOAs, there is no one to reconnect with who is not connected to the trauma. The ACOA in treatment discovers a self never known: he or she may learn to say "no" and "I"; to distinguish and acquire words for his or her own emotions which he or she can now know and express; and to pay attention to his or her own likes and dislikes, faults and virtues, goals and desires. Side-by-side with the emergence of a new self and disconnection from disturbed bonds is the establishment of new attachments with healthier models (Brown, 1994.)

The Defensive Self

Children living with trauma develop a sense of self that is equated with defending oneself. These defenses are designed to keep the enemy out, to minimize anxiety, fear, and the threat of humiliation (Brown, 1995). The "defensive self" or "false self" (Sullivan, 1953; Winnicott, 1953) creates a deep sense of inauthenticity and a barrier to connectedness with others that exacerbates isolation and loneliness. The defensive mantle tends to be brittle, inflexible, and self-reinforcing, with the potential to break down under stress. Individual therapy within a psychodynamic frame and/or intensive therapy group, with its safety and opportunity for feedback, are particularly helpful over time in challenging the deep, internal structure of the defensive self.

SUMMARY OF TREATMENT

In treating the ACOA, safety is the primary concern, both externally and in the treatment setting. Only in an emotionally and physically safe environment can the ACOA finally tell the truth about the environment of childhood. Once the trauma is recognized and acknowledged, feelings that naturally accompany the trauma can emerge. In the systems arena, the ACOA in treatment is encouraged to disengage from the pathology of alcoholism, although not necessarily from the family members themselves. The ACOA learns to live by different rules, engage in different roles, and erect different boundaries from those learned in childhood. In the domain of individual development, the ACOA relinquishes old attachments tied to the maintenance of a defensive self and slowly learns new beliefs and behaviors in the context of new attachments.

The ACOA faces a constant paradox throughout treatment: the very defenses or character traits that protected the child growing up and became fused with a sense of self become the pathology of adulthood. It is a long arduous task for patient and therapist to dismantle the bricks and mortar of self constructed as an adaptation to pathology, and to reconstruct a new, healthier self that is freer of defense.

CONCLUSION

We have traced the development of the idea "ACOA" from its roots in popular culture to legitimization in professional research and treatment, summarizing the early research questions and recent findings. We suggested that the concept ACOA revealed serious limitations in traditional research and treatment, which had focused on the individual, separate from environmental and systems influence. We also stressed the limitation of the narrow focus on the alcoholic, with no attention paid to the consequences of alcoholism to the family. We advocated an expanded theoretical frame, including three separate "tracks" of assessment, and summarized the tasks for long-term treatment within this broader framework.

REFERENCES

Ackerman, N. W. (1958). *The psychodynamics of family life*. New York
New York: Basic Books.

Ainsworth, M. D. S., Blehar, M. C., Waters, E., & Wall, S. (1978). *Patterns of attachment: A psychological study of the Strange Situation*. Hillsdale, NJ: Erlbaum.

Al-Anon faces alcoholism (1984). New York: Al-Anon Family Groups.

Alcoholics Anonymous (1955). New York: AA World Services.

Bateson, G., Jackson, D. D., Haley, J., & Weakland, J. H. (1956) Towards a theory of schizophrenia. *Behavioral Science, 1*, 251–264.

Beletsis, S. & Brown, S. (1981). A developmental framework for understanding adult children of alcoholics. *Journal of Addictions and Health, Focus on Women, 2*, 187–203.

Belliveau, J. M. & Stoppard, J. M. (1995). Parental alcohol abuse and gender as predictors of psychopathology in adult children of alcoholics. *Addictive Behaviors, 20*, 619–625.

Berman, W. H. & Sperling, M. B. (1994). The structure and function of adult attachment. In M. B. Sperling & W. H. Berman (Eds.), *Attachment in adults* (pp. 3–28). New York: Guilford Press.

Black, C. (1981). *It will never happen to me*. Denver, CO: M.A.C.

Bowen, M. (1971). Family therapy and family group therapy. In H. Kaplan & B. Sadock (Eds.), *Comprehensive group psychotherapy*. New York: Williams and Wilkins.

Bowen, M. (1974). Alcoholism as viewed through family systems theory and psychotherapy. *Annals of the New York Academy of Science, 233*, 115–122.

Bowlby, J. (1969–1980). *Attachment and loss: Vol 1. Attachment, Vol. 2. Separation, Vol 3. Loss: Sadness and depression*. New York: Basic Books.

Brown, K. A., & Sunshine, J. (1982). Group treatment of children from alcoholic families. In *Social work with groups*. New York: Haworth Press.

Brown, S. (1974). *Personality characteristics of the teen-age daughters of male alcoholics*. Unpublished master's thesis, California State University, San Jose, California.

Brown, S. (1985). *Treating the alcoholic: A developmental model of recovery*. New York: Wiley.

Brown, S. (1988). *Treating adult children of alcoholics: A developmental perspective*. New York: Wiley.

Brown, S. (1991a). Adult children of alcoholics: The history of a social movement and its impact on clinical theory and practice. In M. Galanter, H. Begleiter, R. Deitrich, D. M. Gallant, D. Goodwin, E. Gottheil, A. Paredes, M. Rothschild, D. H. Van Thiel, & D. Cancellare (Eds.), *Recent developments in alcoholism: Vol. 9. Children of alcoholics* (pp. 267–285). New York: Plenum Press.

Brown, S. (1991b). Adult children of alcoholics: A theoretical crossroads. In T. M. Rivinus (Ed.), *Children of chemically dependent parents: Multiperspectives from the cutting edge* (pp. 74–102). New York: Brunner/Mazel.

Brown, S. (1992a). *Safe passage: Recovery for adult children of alcoholics.* New York: Wiley.

Brown, S. (1992b, April). *The collaborative treatment of the addict: Combining 12-step programs and psychotherapy.* Unpublished conference manuscript. San Francisco Psychotherapy Research Group and Department of Psychiatry, Mount Zion Hospital, University of California-San Francisco.

Brown, S. (1994). Alcoholism and trauma: A theoretical comparison and overview. *Journal of Psychoactive Drugs, 26,* 345–355.

Brown, S. (1995). Adult children of alcoholics: An expanded framework for assessment and diagnosis. In *Children of alcoholics: Selected readings* (pp. 41–72). Rockville, MD: National Association of Children of Alcoholics.

Brown, S., & Beletsis, S. (1986). The development of family transference in groups for the adult children of alcoholics. *International Journal of Group Psychotherapy, 36,* 97–114.

Brown, S., Beletsis, S., & Cermak, T. (1989). *Adult children of alcoholics in treatment.* Orlando, FL: Health Communications.

Brown, S., & Lewis, V. (1995). The alcoholic family: A developmental model of recovery. In S. Brown (Ed.), *Treating alcoholism* (pp. 279–315). San Francisco: Jossey-Bass.

Cartright, J. L., McKay, B. B., & Stader, S. A. (1990). A cluster analysis of MMPI and CPI profiles of adult children of alcoholics and nonalcoholics. *Alcoholism Treatment Quarterly, 7,* 57–79.

Cermak, T. (1986). *Diagnosing and treating co-dependence.* Minneapolis, MN: Johnson Institute Books.

Cermak, T. (1988). *A time to heal: The road to recovery for adult children of alcoholics.* New York: Avon Books.

Cermak, T. (1990, 1991). *Evaluating and treating adult children of alcoholics: Vol. 1. Evaluation, Vol. 2. Treatment.* Minneapolis, MN: Johnson Institute.

Coleman, F. L., & Frick, P. J. (1994). MMPI-2 profiles of adult children of alcoholics. *Journal of Clinical Psychology, 50,* 446–454.

Connolly, G. M., Casswell, S., Stewart, J., Silva, P., & O'Brien, M. K. (1993). The effect of parents' alcohol problems on children's behavior as reported by parents and by teachers. *Addiction, 88,* 1383–1390.

Cork, M. (1969). *The forgotten children.* Toronto: Addictions Research Foundation.

D'Andrea, L. M., Fisher, G. L., & Harrison, T. C. (1994). Cluster analysis of adult children of alcoholics. *International Journal of the Addictions, 29,* 565–582.

Domenico, D., & Windle, M. (1993). Intrapersonal and interpersonal functioning among middle-aged female adult children of alcoholics. *Journal of Consulting and Clinical Psychology, 61,* 659–656.

El-Guebaly, N., West, M., Maticka-Tyndale, E., & Pool, M. (1993). Attachment among adult children of alcoholics. *Addictions, 88,* 1405–1411.

Eth S., & Pynoos, R. (1985). *Post-traumatic stress disorder in children.* Washington DC: American Psychiatric Association.

Fairbairn, W. R. D. (1952). *Psychoanalytic studies of the personality.* London: Tavistock.

Fish-Murray, C. C., Koby, E. V., & van der Kolk, B. A. (1987). Evolving ideas: The effect of abuse on children's thought. In B. A. van der Kolk (Ed.), *Psychological trauma* (pp. 89–110). Washington, DC: American Psychiatric Press.

Fisher, G. L., Jenkins, S. J., Harrison, T. C., & Jesch, K. (1993). Personality characteristics of adult children of alcoholics, other adults from dysfunctional families, and adults from nondysfunctional families. *International Journal of the Addictions, 28,* 477–485.

Fox, R. (1962). Children in an alcoholic family. In W. C. Bier (Ed.), *Problems in addiction: Alcoholism and narcotics.* New York: Fordham University Press.

Fox, R. (1963). The effect of alcoholism on children. In The proceedings of the 5th international congress of psychotherapy held at Vienna, Austria, August, 1961, (part 5, p. 57). Basel, Switzerland: S. Karger.

Gallant, D. M. (1990). Problems in alcoholism treatment: Labeling and negative stereotyping. *Alcoholism: Clinical and Experimental Research, 14,* 630–631.

Giglio, J. J., & Kaufman, E. (1990). The relationship between child and adult psychopathology in children of alcoholics. *International Journal of the Addictions, 25,* 263–290.

Guidano, V. F., and Liotti, G. (1983). *Cognitive processes and emotional disorders.* New York: Guilford Press.

Giunta, C. T., & Compas, B. E. (1994). Adult daughters of alcoholics: Are they unique? *Journal of Studies on Alcohol, 55,* 600–606.

Gunning, W. B., Pattiselanno, S. E., van der Steit, O., & Wiers, R. W. (1994). Children of alcoholics. Predictors for psychopathology and addiction. *Acta Paediatrica* (Suppl,) *404,* 7–8.

Hall, C. W., Bolen, L. M., & Webster, R. E. (1994). Adjustment issues with adult children of alcoholics. *Journal of Clinical Psychology, 50,* 786–792.

Hardwick, C. J., Hansen, N. D., & Bairnsfather, L. (1995). Are adult children of alcoholics unique? A study of object relations and reality testing. *International Journal of the Addictions, 30,* 525–539.

Harman, M. J., Armsworth, M. W., Hwang, C., and Vincent, K. R. (1995). Personality adjustment in college students with a parent perceived as alcoholic or nonalcoholic. *Journal of Counseling and Development, 73,* 459–462.

Hawkins, H. N. (1950). *Some effects of alcoholism of the parents on children in the home.* St. Louis, MO: Salvation Army Midland Division.

Herman, J. (1992). *Trauma and recovery.* New York: Basic Books.

Jackson, J. K. (1954). The adjustment of the family to the crisis of alcoholism. *Quarterly Journal of Studies on Alcohol, 15,* 562–586.

Jellinek, E. M. (1960). *The disease concept of alcoholism.* New Haven: College and Universities Press.

Joanning, H. (1992). Integrating cybernetics and constructivism into structural-strategic family therapy for drug abusers. In E. Kaufman & P. Kaufman (Eds.), *Family therapy of drug and alcohol abuse* (2nd ed., pp. 94–104). Boston: Allyn and Bacon.

Johnson, J., Rolf, J., Tiegel, S., & McDuff, D. (1995) Developmental assessment of children of alcoholics. In *Children of alcoholics: Selected readings* (pp. 99–136). Rockville, MD: National Association of Children of Alcoholics.

Kardiner, A. (1941). *The traumatic neuroses of war.* New York: Hoeber.

Kashubeck, S. (1994). Adult children of alcoholics and psychological distress. *Journal of Counseling and Development, 72,* 538–543.

Kohut, H. (1971). *The analysis of the self.* New York: International Universities Press.

Krugman, S. (1987). Trauma in the family: Perspectives on the intergenerational transmission of violence. In B. A. van der Kolk (Ed.), *Psychological trauma* (pp. 127–151). Washington, DC: American Psychiatric Press.

Krystal, H. (1978). Trauma and affects. *Psychoanalytic Study of the Child, 33,* 81–116.

Mahler, M. (1975). *The psychological birth of the human infant.* New York: Basic Books.

Masterson, J. (1976) *Psychotherapy of the borderline adult: Adevelopmental approach.* New York: Brunner/Mazel.

Mathew, R. J., Wilson, W. H., Blazer, D. G., & George, L. K. (1993). Psychiatric disorders in adult children of alcoholics: Data from the epidemiologic catchment area project. *American Journal of Psychiatry, 150,* 793–800.

Miller, A. (1994). *The drama of the gifted child.* San Francisco: Harper Collins.

Minuchin, S. (1974). *Families and family therapy.* Cambridge, MA: Harvard University Press.

Neff, J. A. (1994). Adult children of alcoholic or mentally ill parents: Alcohol consumption and psychological distress in a tri-ethnic community study. *Addictive Behaviors, 19,* 185–197.

Nordberg, L., Rydelius, P., & Zetterstrom, R. (1994). Parental alcoholism and early child development. *Acta Paediatrica* (Suppl.) *404,* 14–18.

Nylander, I. (1960). Children of alcoholic fathers. *Acta Paediatrica, 49,* 9–127.

Nylander, I. (1963). Children of alcoholic fathers. *Quarterly Journal of Studies on Alcoholism, 24,* 170–172.

Radke-Yarrow, M. & Sherman, T. (1990). Hard growing: Children who survive. In J. Rolf, A. Masten, D. Cicchetti, K.

Nuechterlein, & S. Weintraub,(Eds.), *Risk and protective factors in the development of psychopathology.* Cambridge, England: Cambridge University Press.

Roe, A., & Burks, B. (1945). Adult adjustment of foster children of alcoholic and psychotic parentage and the influence of the foster home. In *Memoirs of the section on alcoholism studies, 3.* New Haven, CT: Yale University Press.

Rolf, J., Masten, A. Cicchetti, D., Nuechterlein, K., & Weintraub, S. (1990), (Eds.) *Risk and protective factors in the development of psychopathology.* Cambridge, England: Cambridge University Press.

Satir, V. (1964). *Conjoint family therapy.* Palo Alto, CA: Science and Behavior Books.

Schuckit, M. A. (1995). Adult children of alcoholics: Is this an appropriate diagnostic label? *Drug Abuse and Alcoholism Newsletter, 24.* San Diego, CA: Vista Hill Foundation.

Schuckit, M. A., Goodwin, D. W. & Winokur, G. (1972). A study of alcoholism in half-siblings. *American Journal of Psychiatry, 128,* 1132–1136.

Searles, H. F. (1965). *Collected papers on schizophrenia and related subjects.* New York: International Universities Press.

Seixas, J., & Youcha, G. (1985). *Children of alcoholism: A survivor's manual.* New York: Crown.

Steinglass, P., Bennett, L. A., Wolin, S. J., & Reiss, D. (1987). *The alcoholic family.* New York: Basic Books.

Sullivan, H. S. (1953). *The interpersonal theory of psychiatry.* New York: Norton.

Terr, L. (1990). *Too scared to cry.* New York: Harper and Row.

Vaillant, G. E. (1983). *The natural history of alcoholism: Causes, patterns and paths to recovery.* Cambridge, MA: Harvard University Press.

van der Kolk, B.A. (1987a). The psychological consequences of overwhelming life experiences. In B.A. van der Kolk (Ed.), *Psychological trauma,* Washington, DC: American Psychiatric Press.

van der Kolk, B.A. (1987b). The role of the group in the origin and resolution of the trauma response. In B.A. van der Kolk (Ed.), *Psychological trauma,* Washington, DC: American Psychiatric Press.

van der Kolk, B. A. (1987c). The seraration cry and the trauma response: Hyperarousal, constriction, and addiction to traumatic re-exposure. In B. A. van der Kolk (Ed.), *Psychological trauma.* Washington, DC: American Psychiatric Press.

van der Kolk, B. A., & Greenberg, M. S. (1987). The psychobiology of the trauma response: Hyperarousal, constriction, and addiction to traumatic reexposure. In B. A. Van der Kolk (Ed.). *Psychological trauma* (pp. 63–87). Washington, DC: American Psychiatric Press.

van der Kolk, B. A. and Kadish, W. (1987). Amnesia, dissociation, and the return of the repressed. In B. A. van der Kolk (Ed.), *Psychological trauma.* Washington, DC: American Psychiatric Press.

Vanicelli, M. (1989). *Group psychotherapy with ACOAs.* New York, Guilford Press.

Watzlawick, P. l., Weakland, J. H., & Fisch, R. (1974). *Change: Principles of problem formulation and problem resolution* New York: Norton.

Wegsheider, S. (1981). *Another chance: Hope and health for the alcoholic family.* Palo Alto: Science and Behavior Books.

Whipple, E. E., Fitzgerald, H. E. & Zucker, R. A. (1955). Parent-child interactions in alcoholic and nonalcoholic families. *American Journal of Orthopsychiatry, 65.* 153–159.

White, M., & Epstein, D. (1990). *Narrative means to therapeutic ends.* New York: Norton.

Winnicott, D. W. (1953). Transitional objects and transitional phenomena. *International Journal of Psychoanalysis, 34,* 89–97.

Winnicott, D. W. (1960). The theory of the parent–infant relationship. *International Journal of Psychoanalysis, 41,* 585–595.

Winokur, G., & Clayton, P. (1968). Family history studies: IV, Comparison of male and female alcoholics. *Quarterly Journal of Studies on Alcoholism, 29,* 885–891.

Winoker, G., Reich, T., Rimmer, J., & Pitts, F. (1970). Alcoholism: III. Diagnosis of familial psychiatric illness in 259 alcoholic probands. *Archives of General Psychiatry, 23,* 104–111.

Woititz, J. G. (1983). *Adult children of alcoholics.* Pompano Beach, FL: Health Communications.

Wolin, S., & Wolin, S. (1995). Resilience among youth growing up in substance-abusing families. *Pediatric Clinics of North America, 42,* 415–429.

Wood, B. (1987). *Children of alcoholism: The struggle for self and intimacy in adult life.* New York: New York University Press.

Wright, D. M., & Heppner, P. P. (1991). Coping among nonclinical college-age children of alcoholics. *Journal of Counseling Psychology, 38,* 465–472.

CHAPTER 34

INTERVENTION ISSUES FOR WOMEN

Mary E. McCaul
Dace S. Svikis

Historically, addiction treatment programs have predominantly served men. Even in the most recent survey of substance abuse treatment programs in the United States, approximately three quarters of treatment admissions were men (NIDA/NIAAA, 1993). As a result, it is not surprising that therapeutic services have been male-oriented in content and delivery format. Yet it is increasingly clear that alcohol and drug-dependent women experience a variety of medical, psychiatric, and psychosocial problems that may create different treatment needs compared to men. In recent years, specialized programs have been designed to address these gender-specific treatment needs. This chapter reviews the research that characterizes the special needs of addicted women and summarizes the research on substance abuse treatment effectiveness for women.

SPECIAL NEEDS OF SUBSTANCE-ABUSING WOMEN

Medical Issues

Substance-abusing women experience increased medical problems as compared to nonabusing women and substance-abusing men. Common complaints include infec-

tions, anemia, sexually transmitted diseases (particularly gonorrhea, trichomonas, and chlamydia), hepatitis, urinary tract infections, and gynecological problems (Mondanaro, 1990). Further, substance abusing women are at increased risk for a variety of reproductive dysfunctions compared to other women. Some of the disorders that are more prevalent among substance-abusing women include amenorrhea, anovulation, luteal phase dysfunction, ovarian atrophy, spontaneous abortion, and early menopause (Lex, 1991).

Women with alcohol addiction also report a higher frequency of uterine curettage, hysterectomy, oophorectomy, and abortion as compared to age-matched controls (Becker, Tonnesen, Kaas-Claesson, & Gluud, 1989). Women who have chronic alcohol problems are at increased risk of early-onset liver and brain damage (Mann, Batra, Gunthner, & Schroth, 1992) relative to men with alcohol addiction.

It is clear that there are increased maternal and fetal risks associated with pregnancy for substance-abusing women. Across studies, rates of cocaine use during pregnancy are around 10% to 11%, with considerably variability associated with the site of the prenatal clinic and the detection methods used by the clinic. At the Yale New Haven Hospital, 32% of pregnant women reported lifetime use of cocaine and 15% reported continued use during pregnancy (Grossman & Schottenfeld, 1992). Cocaine use during pregnancy causes uterine vasoconstriction, which results in oxygen and nutrient deprivation to the fetus and is associated with intrauterine growth retardation. In addition to the direct effects of cocaine exposure, birth outcomes for substance-abusing women are effected by a variety of environmental and psychosocial risk factors, including poor maternal health, inadequate housing, single-parent households, and poverty. Pregnant substance abusers enter prenatal care later and have higher rates of unregistered deliveries, more emergency room visits, and more missed appointments than do drug-free comparisons (Grossman & Schottenfeld, 1992).

Drug use is the most significant risk factor for HIV infection among women. Approximately 50% of AIDS cases have resulted from IV drug use by the woman herself and an additional 20% from IV use by her sexual partner(s) (Centers for Disease Control, 1994). One recent study of pregnant, cocaine or opiate-dependent women examined AIDS-related knowledge and engagement in high-risk behaviors (Elk et al., in press). Generally, participants demonstrated a high rate of knowledge of HIV high-risk behaviors related to drug use and sexual behavior. Knowledge of medical consequences of HIV infection was somewhat lower, with relatively poor knowledge of AIDS symptomatology. In contrast, recent engagement in high-risk behaviors was relatively common, with 28% reporting multiple sexual partners, 35% reporting sex with an intravenous drug user, 37% reporting that they had exchanged sex for money or drugs, and only 7% of those who had sex in the last month reporting condom use. Similar findings of high rates of HIV sexual-risk behaviors have been reported among pregnant substance abusers entering treatment (Haller, Knisely, Dawson, & Schnoll, 1993). Specifically, 97% of these women failed to use condoms, 45% reported more than five sexual partners in the last 2 years, and 33% had an active STD at the time of program enrollment. These results highlight the importance of providing motivational and behavioral skills training in addition to HIV education for substance-abusing women.

Psychological Issues

As compared with general population women, women with substance use disorders are at elevated risk for a variety of psychological problems, particularly affective disorders (Helzer & Pryzbeck, 1988) and a history of suicide attempts (Gomberg, 1989). In one recent study, psychological characteristics of perinatal substance abusers were determined at the time of admission to specialized women's substance abuse treatment. Approximately half of the patients had not completed high school and cognitive testing revealed low average intellectual functioning (Haller et al., 1993). Rates of depressive (28%) and anxiety (31%) disorders were elevated relative to the general population, with a strikingly high prevalence of personality disorders (75%), particularly antisocial personality disorder (62%).

In a recent study of personality characteristics in a sample of HIV plus pregnant drug-dependent women, Svikis and colleagues (Svikis, Gorenstein, Paluzzi, & Fingerhood, submitted) also found evidence of psychopathology. Using the Minnesota Multiphasic Personality Inventory—Revised (MMPI-2) (Butcher, Dahlstrom, Graham, Tellegen, & Kaemmer, 1989), the mean clinical scale profile was a 6 (Pa)—8 (Sc), with 19% of patients obtaining this two point code-type. This scale elevation pattern is characterized by suspiciousness, guardedness, and paranoia, as well as by unusual thought processes and peculiar life experiences. Similar findings of significant psychopathology have been reported for pregnant women referred by child protective services for outpatient substance abuse treatment (Beckwith, Espinosa, & Howard, 1994). On the Millon Clinical Multiaxial Inventory, women consistently evidenced symptoms of significant psychopathology, including paranoid ideation, thought disorder, depression, and anxiety. Of importance, there was a positive association between years of drug use and severity of psychiatric problems.

There is recent evidence that greater emotional distress and more severe character pathology may be associated with an increased likelihood of successful treatment enrollment among pregnant women seeking substance abuse services in comprehensive day treatment services (Haller, Dawson, & Ingersoll, submitted). Specifically, treatment acceptors as compared with rejecters had higher ASI composite scores for psychiatric severity, were more likely to have elevated clinical scale scores as well as personality disorder scale scores (i.e., antisocial, paranoid, and dependent personality) on the Minnesota Multiphasic Personality Inventory—2, and scored higher on two of the three global severity indices and on six subscales of the Symptom Checklist-90 Revised (Derogatis, 1983). These findings highlight the need for psychiatric services as part of a comprehensive system of care for substance abusing women.

Family and Social Issues

Substance-abusing women report high rates of alcohol and/or drug dependence in their family of origin (Beckwith et al., 1994; Haller et al., 1993; Wallen, 1992). In one recent study, 53% of female substance abusers reported paternal substance abuse and 32% reported maternal substance abuse (Haller et al., 1993). Among patients enrolled in methadone maintenance treatment, 70% of women reported a history of illicit drug use by at least one sibling (Pivnick, Jacobson, Eric, Doll, & Drucker, 1994).

Alcohol- and drug-dependent women also report exceptionally high rates of childhood sexual abuse. In a national survey, women who reported alcohol-related problems were more than twice as likely to report childhood sexual abuse as compared with women without alcohol problems (23% vs. 10%) (Wilsnack, Wilsnack, & Klassen, 1984). When women enrolled in alcohol treatment programs were studied, 66% reported childhood sexual abuse as compared with 35% in a random household sample of women. Even more striking differences were observed in the more extreme forms of childhood abuse and violence, with 47% of women with alcohol problems reporting sexual penetration by the abuser compared with 9% of the household sample (Miller, Downs, & Gondoli, 1989). A number of investigators have described a negative cycle between childhood victimization and substance abuse, with the long-term consequences of victimization such as depression, low self-esteem, and poor interpersonal relationships, increasing the risk for substance use which in turns exacerbates the consequences (Russell & Wilsnack, 1991). Interestingly, in a retrospective study examining predictors of inpatient program outcomes, women reporting a history of childhood sexual abuse were more likely to complete treatment, suggesting that negative feelings about childhood experiences may be related to involvement in the therapeutic process (Wallen, 1992).

For many women, these patterns of childhood exposure to substance-abusing family members and physical/sexual abuse continue into adulthood. One third to one half of substance-abusing women live with a substance-abusing man (Griffin, Weiss, Mirin, & Lange, 1989; Hesselbrock, Meyers, & Keener, 1985; Kosten, Rounsaville, & Kleber, 1985). An even larger proportion of IV-drug-using women report sexual activity with IV-drug-using men. For example, 83% of female methadone patients in one clinic reported having had sex with an active IV drug user (Schilling, El-Bassel, Schinke, Gordon, & Nichols, 1991). These findings

have important implications for women's risk of partner violence. In a national household survey (Kaufman-Kantor & Straus, 1989), women who experienced severe violence were twice as likely to report that their partners had been drunk and six times as likely to report that their partners had been high on drugs at some point during the past year. In one study of pregnant women referred for substance abuse treatment, 70% of women reported histories of physical and/or sexual abuse, and 78% reported having been beaten and/or raped (Beckwith et al., 1994).

Substance use by the woman herself also increases her risk for becoming a victim of violence. Kaufman-Kantor and colleagues (1989) demonstrated a threefold increased likelihood of violence when the woman had been drunk and a sixfold increased risk when she had been high on drugs during the last year. Clearly, women are at elevated risk for assault when they and/or their sexual partners are intoxicated (Downs, Miller, & Panek, 1993; Miller, Downs, & Testa, 1993; O'Campo, Gielen, Faden, & Kass, 1994), with risk particularly increased during pregnancy (Amaro, Fried, Cabral, & Zuckerman, 1990; Campbell, Poland, Waller, & Ager, 1992). In general, female substance abusers tend to be more socially isolated than male substance abusers, have fewer friends, fewer romantic relationships, and report feeling more lonely and have more difficulty socializing (Wallen, 1992).

Finally, substance-abusing women are more likely than substance abusing men to be living with at least one of their children. A qualitative study of family and social networks of women enrolled in methadone maintenance treatment found that slightly more than half lived with at least one of their children (Pivnick et al., 1994). Women averaged 2.4 children under the age of 18, with approximately half living with their mother at the time of the survey. Among those children still residing with their mothers, two thirds lived with a mother who reported regular use of illicit drugs and over 85% lived in a household where at least one adult was a drug user. Clearly, substance-abusing women have very complex and often dysfunctional family relationships that may be expected to negatively impact their opportunities for treatment entry and retention.

Vocational and Legal Issues

Most studies of substance-abusing women report low levels of vocational training and job skills and high rates of unemployment (Allen, 1995; Stevens & Arbiter, 1995; Strantz & Welch, 1995), making employment readiness and placement important treatment goals for many patients. In one recent study, pregnant or recently postpartum women were assessed for their occupational interests and academic skills (Silverman, Chutuape, Svikis, Bigelow, & Stitzer, 1995). Most women scored at or below the 7th grade level in reading, spelling, and arithmetic based on the Wide Range Achievement Test (Jastak & Wilkinson, 1984) and one quarter scored at or below the 4th grade level in these areas. Despite that, eight of the ten jobs that were rated by subjects as highest in occupational interest were office jobs that required well-established skills in reading, spelling, and arithmetic. Generally, there was considerable incongruity between the types of occupations that the women rated as most interesting and their current skills levels, suggesting the need for extensive basic academic training prior to specific vocational preparation.

Although rates of legal involvement are somewhat lower among substance abusing women than men, the majority of women have had at least one legal conviction (Stevens & Arbiter, 1995). In one therapeutic community, half of the women were court-referred and a third were involved with child protective services at time of treatment admission (Stevens & Arbiter, 1995). Interestingly, there is increasing evidence that legal involvement can improve enrollment and retention of women in substance abuse services (Haller et al., submitted; Knisely, Christmas, Dinsmoore, Spear, & Schnoll, 1993).

BARRIERS TO TREATMENT ENTRY AND RETENTION

Although recent efforts to increase the number of women in drug treatment have had modest success, women are still underrepresented in traditional alcohol and drug treatment programs (Finnegan, Davenny, & Hartel, 1993; Mondanaro, 1990). Indeed, it is estimated that women enrolled in treatment represent only about 30% of the 1.5 million women who have a clear or probable need for treatment (Institute of Medicine, 1989). This underrepresentation of women in formal drug treatment programs may be even more severe for minority women in need of substance abuse services. In a survey of women abusing drugs recruited from methadone detoxification programs and from street settings in low-income neighborhoods, African American women were significantly less likely either to be currently enrolled in treatment or to have been in treatment during the previous 5 years as compared with White women (Lewis & Watters, 1989). In this study, only

approximately one third of the African American women interviewed had made contact with a treatment agency during the 5 years preceding the interview.

At present, there is a significant overall shortage of drug treatment slots in our country, and, as a consequence, many substance abusers are not able to enter treatment promptly when the decision to seek help has been made. Women suffer not only from this general lack of resources but also from a variety of gender-specific barriers that are believed to decrease their ability to receive treatment. Such barriers include lack of outreach targeted at women who are not highly motivated to enter treatment, gender and cultural insensitivity in program content, threat of legal sanction such as loss of custody of children, lack of child care, lack of transportation, ineligibility of women for treatment medications if pregnant or not using a reliable form of birth control, lack of heath insurance coverage, the caretaker role that women generally assume within the family such that no one else is available to care for dependent family members, and the societal intolerance and stigmatization of female drug abusers (Chasnoff, 1991; National Institute on Drug Abuse, Fall1990). Indeed, one study found that women are more likely than men to encounter opposition to treatment entry from their families and friends (Beckman & Amaro, 1986). Results also indicated decreased rates of identification and referral for women by traditional providers such as physicians and social workers.

One recent study of African American substance-abusing women examined three potential types of treatment barriers: treatment program characteristics, personal thoughts and beliefs, and socioenvironmental issues (Allen, 1995). Barriers were conceptualized as either external (e.g., lack of insurance coverage, unavailability of child care, lack of treatment slots, lack of transportation) or internal (e.g., failure to recognize the problem, fear of their children being taken away, fear of other's reactions, fear of treatment itself). The most frequently reported barriers for substance abuse treatment entry were responsibilities at home as a mother, wife or partner; inability to pay, lack of insurance; needing alcohol and/or drugs to deal with stresses of daily life in the community; fear that admission of the drug problem would be used by someone to take away their children; shame as a result of their drug problem; being unable to stay alcohol- or drug-free after previous treatment episodes; and having to wait for an opening because the program is full. Findings highlight the importance of both internal and external barriers in deterring greater access to treatment for African American substance-dependent women.

Such barriers to care may be further complicated for pregnant drug-abusing women. Although improved in recent years, many drug treatment programs have prohibited pregnant drug-abusing women from access to care due to perceived liability risks associated with their care. For many of these women, the medical needs associated with pregnancy are viewed as less urgent than the day-to-day survival needs associated with poverty and drug use (Wofsy, 1987).

In a recent comparison of women attending a women's substance abuse treatment program versus mixed-gender treatment services, women attending gender-sensitive programming were significantly more likely to have dependent children, to be lesbian, to have a maternal history of drug or alcohol problems, and to have suffered sexual abuse in childhood (Copeland & Hall, 1992). These findings suggest that women's treatment programs may be recruiting women who have traditionally been underrepresented in mixed-gender programs. Clearly, we must develop strategies for enhancing access to and the effectiveness of drug treatment and medical services if we are to impact on the complex personal and interpersonal needs of substance-abusing women.

SPECIALIZED TREATMENT INTERVENTIONS FOR WOMEN

Historically, men have represented approximately 75% to 80% of substance abuse treatment program patients. Given this fact, it is not surprising that most treatment programs have been male-oriented in content (Vannicelli, 1984). Yet the range of physiological, psychological, and social differences between male and female substance abusers highlights the need for development of specialized women's treatment services. To date, few well-controlled research studies have examined the relative effectiveness of traditional vs specialized treatment services for women (Institute of Medicine, 1990). This lack of information is of concern as approximately one fourth of alcoholism treatment admissions are women (NIDA/NIAAA, 1993).

It has been suggested that women fare poorly in mixed-gender settings where they constitute the minority of program patients. For example, in an examination of women's treatment outcomes in a traditional therapeutic community program, women's retention was significantly poorer than men's, with successful discharge rates for women being only half those of men (Coletti et al., 1992). Further, recent treatment outcome findings from a large, publicly-funded, mixed-gender outpatient substance abuse program also provide evidence that gender is an important predictor of treatment program retention (McCaul, Svikis, Moore, Gupman, & Gopalan, 1994). Specifically, female patients were found to remain in mixed-gender treatment for a significantly shorter period of time and to participate in significantly fewer treatment sessions than male patients. These decreased levels of attendance were particularly striking for African American female patients. Several factors may contribute to these poorer retention rates for women, including the imbalance of male and female patients in the program; the perceived irrelevance of much of the traditional, male-oriented program content; and the lack of opportunity to address male relationship issues, including frequent histories of physical and sexual abuse.

Comprehensive models for women's drug treatment services have been proposed (Finnegan, 1988; Finnegan et al., 1993). Program components include medical services for women and their children, substance abuse education and relapse prevention therapy, psychiatric assessment, social skills training and life management skills development, and early child development and parenting skills courses. Additionally, outreach mechanisms, including indigenous workers, liaison with community-based organizations, and transportation, are needed to enhance women's access to care.

In a recent descriptive study, women enrolled in specialized treatment for female substance abusers were interviewed to determine utilization and perceived helpfulness of services in specialized and nonspecialized drug treatment programs (Nelson-Zlupko, Dore, Kauffman, & Kaltenbach, 1996). Women consistently reported that their needs differed from men, and that these needs were either silenced or minimized in coeducational treatment groups. Indeed, over a quarter of respondents rated coed groups as unhelpful or very unhelpful in their recovery. Reproductive health and sexuality education, parenting education, help obtaining child care, and on-site child care were seen as the least available services; however, when child care services were accessible, they were rated among the most helpful services for improving attendance at drug treatment. Relatedly, parenting skills training was the most frequently identified need by study participants. Other services rated as helpful included transportation assistance; help obtaining such basic needs as food, clothing, and housing; recreational activities; on-site health care; and 12-step meetings.

Several clinical trials have examined interventions intended to improve treatment enrollment, retention, and outcome for women by providing programs or services that more specifically address their needs. One study has explicitly compared specialized women's treatment versus traditional mixed-gender treatment for women in the early stages of alcohol dependence (Dahlgren & Willander, 1989). Services were relatively comparable across the two treatment sites and included individual and group counseling, occupational therapy, and medical care. However, one treatment site was exclusively for female patients and the other served both male and female patients. Women in specialized treatment services remained in treatment longer and had higher rates of program completion than women in the mixed-gender setting. Also, at 2-year posttreatment follow-up, women's program patients reported improved outcomes on a variety of alcohol use, psychosocial, and morbidity measures as compared with mixed-gender program patients. Of particular interest, the children of women in specialized treatment were five times less likely to be placed in foster care during the follow-up period than were the children of women treated in the mixed-gender program.

A recent clinical trial randomized cocaine-abusing women to a standard therapeutic community (TC) program or an enhanced TC program that allowed one or two children to reside with their mothers (Hughes et al., 1995).

Mean length of stay was significantly longer for women in the enhanced TC program (mean = 300.4 days) than for women in standard care (mean = 101.9 days). After 3 months, 77% of women in the enhanced program remained in treatment versus 45% of standard care women, and, after 6 months, retention was 65% versus18% of enhanced as compared with standard program participants. These findings suggest that allowing women to live with their children during residential drug treatment enhances their retention in care, potentially improving mother–child relationship and postdischarge treatment outcomes.

Research also has begun to focus on targeted interventions introduced into mixed-gender programs to address special needs of female clients. For example, Schilling and colleagues conducted a prospective, randomized study of a skills-building intervention to reduce HIV sexual risk behaviors versus an information-only comparison condition in methadone-maintained women (Schilling et al., 1991). During the active intervention, skills-building participants had high rates of group attendance and treatment retention, suggesting that such interventions are well accepted by methadone patients. Results also suggested

that skills-building subjects as compared with information-only controls were more likely to initiate discussion of sexual issues, felt more comfortable talking about safe sex with their partners, and reported obtaining, carrying, and using condoms more frequently. Women who received the skills-building intervention also were more likely to perceive themselves as able to reduce their exposure to AIDS, more interested in learning about AIDS, and more likely to believe that AIDS can be prevented. Importantly, follow-up results indicated that most of the gains demonstrated immediately following the intervention were still apparent 15 months later (El-Bassel & Schilling, 1992).

Finally, preliminary findings has been reported for a psychosocial treatment intervention with versus without a partner as an adjunct to long-term methadone detoxification treatment (Kim, Sees, & Delucchi, 1994). Male and female patients in treatment with their partners had fewer positive urinalysis results and reported decreased withdrawal symptoms and cravings. Overall, treatment attrition did not differ for patients with versus without partners; however, there was a trend for female patients in treatment with their partners to stay longer than female patients without partners. This area of research should be a priority for future study because women who abuse substances frequently select men who abuse substances as their sexual partners (Griffin et al., 1989; Hesselbrock et al., 1985; Kosten et al., 1985).

TREATMENT INTERVENTIONS FOR PREGNANT WOMEN

As described previously, comprehensive and coordinated service delivery systems have been recommended for the provision of women's substance abuse treatment services. To date, the majority of such model, one-stop programs have focused on pregnant women who abuse drugs. Examples of such models include the integration of drug treatment services into obstetric clinics and, conversely, the integration of obstetric services into drug treatment settings. It is expected that, by combining services, the number of women who receive the needed interventions can be maximized, and maternal and infant outcomes can be improved.

One recent study has examined the integration of drug treatment services into the prenatal care clinic of a large, inner-city hospital (McCaul, Svikis, & Feng, 1991; Svikis, McCaul, Feng, Johnson, & Stokes, 1992). Using the traditional hospital consultation model for substance abuse intervention, fewer than 5% of substance-abusing pregnant women kept their initial intake appointment at the substance abuse treatment program to which they were referred. In response to this poor outcome, a number of changes were introduced to improve the integration of drug treatment services into the OB clinic: first, weekly substance abuse support groups were conducted on-site in the clinic; second, substance abusing women were assigned to a special high-risk clinic session, which was coordinated with the support group meeting; and third, lunch was provided for support group attenders to ease the burden of the additional time spent in the clinic. Under this integrated model, approximately 40% of referrals attended two or more support group sessions. When pregnancy outcomes were compared for women who had and had not attended the support group, attenders were found to have significantly higher mean maternal weight gain; their infants had significantly higher mean birth weight, including a reduced incidence of low birth weight, and higher mean 1-minute Apgar scores (Svikis et al., 1992). These improved clinical outcomes for group attenders were paralleled by a significant reduction in short-term health care costs for both the mother and infant. If these preliminary findings are confirmed, this would highlight the positive impact of integrating drug treatment with other health care services, and the potentially robust impact of minimal interventions that are cost effective and easily implemented (Elvy, Wells, & Baird, 1988).

A second model for improved continuity of care for pregnant women who abuse substances is the integration of obstetric services into mixed-gender substance abuse treatment programs. For example, in one outpatient methadone maintenance program, pregnant women received an enriched schedule of obstetric services, including an initial evaluation, biweekly visits until the middle of the third trimester, and then weekly visits until delivery by the clinic obstetrician (Shipley, Gazaway, Brooner, & Felch, 1993). Preliminary findings indicated excellent compliance with prenatal care; specifically, participants kept 96% of scheduled prenatal care appointments. Further, few intrapartum or antepartum complications have been observed; for example, outcomes include 14% caesarean deliveries, 15% meconium staining, and good Apgar scores (i.e., 8—9) for all infants. The most prevalent antepartum complication has been intrauterine growth retardation, with a mean birth weight of 2690 gms. These initial findings support the position that the provision of obstetric services on-site at the drug treatment program

can improve treatment participation and retention in both drug treatment and prenatal care for pregnant, opiate-dependent women, and can improve birth outcomes for mothers and neonates.

The final step in the integration of care is the development of specialized, comprehensive, interdisciplinary programs established explicitly for the care of pregnant, drug-abusing women and their children. One such program, The Center for Addiction and Pregnancy (CAP), combines the disciplines of pediatrics, substance abuse treatment, obstetrics/gynecology, and family planning in an effort to reduce the barriers to care often presenting in this population. Additional resources include a developmental play program created so that children under age 5 can accompany their mothers to the program, and van transportation to and from the program. For the first 100 CAP births, 82% were delivered vaginally, with a mean gestational age of 38 weeks. The Neonatal Intensive Care Unit admission rate was 10%, and the Bayley Scales of Infant Development performed at 6 and 12 months revealed mean developmental indices within the normal range (Jansson et al., in press). Although such programs may initially appear costly to establish and maintain, improvements in maternal and infant outcomes associated with such enriched drug treatment resources are likely to be cost effective through reductions in both short-term and long-term medical and social services costs for both mothers and children. In a recent cost-effectiveness study of CAP, investment of financial resources in drug treatment produced a net cost savings in infant neonatal intensive care unit (NICU) costs alone of nearly $5,000 per infant (Svikis et al., submitted).

Finally, one recent clinical trial has examined the important issue of predictors of treatment retention for cocaine-dependent, postpartum women in specialized intensive day treatment versus traditional outpatient services (Strantz & Welch, 1995). Overall, the completion rate was significantly higher in the intensive day program (45%) as compared to the outpatient program (21%), although there was no significant difference in average length of stay between the two programs (19.9 vs. 17.7 weeks in intensive day and OP, respectively). Retaining custody of the infant (as opposed to having the infant removed to the custody of a relative or foster home) was a strong predictor of treatment success in intensive day treatment services. Interestingly, the number of children with the mother in her household was a strong positive predictor of outpatient program retention, but a negative predictor of intensive day treatment retention, where daily participation was required. Finally, medical and psychiatric severity scores on the Addiction Severity Index were negatively related to length of stay in the intensive day treatment program. The most frequently cited treatment barriers were related to personal feelings ("did not feel like going at times," "program required too much time") and problem denial ("felt I could manage on my own," "felt I was doing fine"). In contrast, such practical barriers as obtaining child care or transportation were not predictors of treatment drop-out. This study highlights the importance of matching treatment intensity to the family, medical, and psychiatric needs of postpartum substance-abusing women in order to increase program retention and successful discharge.

CONCLUSIONS

Increasingly, research is identifying important medical, psychiatric, and social differences between male and female substance abusers. Many of these differences have implications for the content and delivery of therapeutic services for substance-abusing women. Recent studies generally have suggested that women experience improved retention and discharge status in specialized treatment programs tailored to meet their gender-specific needs. The importance of comprehensive and coordinated services is particularly highlighted for pregnant and postpartum women, given the additional health needs and the opportunity for impact on both maternal and fetal outcomes.

Many questions remain to be answered concerning the optimal content and delivery of services to women and, particularly, the matching of services to women's treatment needs based on medical, psychiatric, and family status. It is essential that research in this area continue given the long-term implications for the health of women and their families.

REFERENCES

Allen, K. (1995). Barriers to treatment for addicted African-American women. *Journal of the National Medical Association, 87*, 751–756.

Amaro, H., Fried, L., Cabral, H., & Zuckerman, B. (1990). Violence during pregnancy and substance use. *American Journal of Public Health, 80*, 575–579.

Becker, U., Tonnesen, H., Kaas-Claesson, N., & Gluud, C. (1989). Menstrual disturbances and fertility in chronic alcoholic women. *Drug and Alcohol Dependence, 24*, 75–82.

Beckman, L., & Amaro, H. (1986). Personal and social difficulties faced by females and males entering alcoholism treatment. *Journal of Studies on Alcohol, 45*, 135–145.

Beckwith, L., Espinosa, M., & Howard, J. (1994). Psychological profile of pregnant women who abuse cocaine, alcohol, and other drugs. In L. S. Harris (Ed.), *Problems of drug dependence, 1993: Proceedings of the 55th annual scientific meeting of the College on Problems of Drug Dependence, Inc.* (Research Monograph No.141, pp. 116). Rockville, MD: National Institute on Drug Abuse.

Butcher, J. N., Dahlstrom, W. G., Graham, J. R., Tellegen, A., & Kaemmer, B. (1989). *Minnesota Multiphasic Personality Inventory—2 (MMPI-2): Manual for administration and scoring.* Minneapolis, MN: University of Minnesota Press.

Campbell, J. C., Poland, M. L., Waller, J. B., & Ager, J. (1992). Correlates of battering during pregnancy. *Research on Nursing & Health, 15*, 219–226.

Centers for Disease Control. (1994). *HIV/AIDS Surveillance Report 6.* Atlanta, GA: CDC.

Chasnoff, I. J. (1991). Drugs, alcohol, pregnancy and the neonate: Pay now or pay later. *Journal of the American Medical Association, 266*, 1567–1568.

Coletti, S. D., Hughes, P. H., Landress, H. J., Neri, R. L., Sicilian, D. M., Williams, K. M., Urmann, C. F., & Anthony, J. C. (1992). PAR village. Specialized intervention for cocaine abusing women and their children. *Journal of the Florida Medical Association, 79*, 701–705.

Copeland, J., & Hall, W. (1992). A comparison of women seeking drug and alcohol treatment in a specialist women's and two traditional mixed-sex treatment services. *British Journal of Addiction, 87*, 1293–1302.

Dahlgren, L., & Willander, A. (1989). Are special treatment facilities for female alcoholics needed? A control 2-year follow-up study from a specialized female unit (EWA) versus a mixed male/female treatment facility. *Alcoholism: Clinical and Experimental Research, 13*, 499–504.

Derogatis, L. (1983). *SCL-90-R administration, scoring and procedures manual-II.* Towson, MD: Clinical Psychometric Research.

Downs, W. R., Miller, B. A., & Panek, D. D. (1993). Differential patterns of partner-to-woman violence: A comparison of samples of community, alcohol-abusing and battered women. *Journal of Family Violence, 8*, 113–135.

El-Bassel, N., & Schilling, R. F. (1992). 15-month follow up of women methadone patients taught skills to reduce heterosexual HIV transmission. *Public Health Reports, 107*, 500–504.

Elk, R., Andres, R., Helfgott, A., Rhoades, H., Mangus, L., Mirza, I., Burroughs, R., & Grabowski, J. (in press). AIDS-related knowledge and high-risk behaviors of pregnant women dependent on cocaine or opiates. *American Journal on Addictions.*

Elvy, G. A., Wells, J. E., & Baird, K. A. (1988). Attempted referral as intervention for problem drinking in the general hospital. *British Journal of Addiction, 83*, 83–89.

Finnegan, L., Davenny, K., & Hartel, D. (1993). Drug use in HIV-infected women. In F. Johnstone & M. Johnson (Eds.), *HIV* infection in women (pp. 133–155). Edinburgh: Churchill Livingstone.

Finnegan, L. P. (1988). Management of maternal and neonatal substance abuse problems. In L. S. Harris (Ed.), *Problems of drug dependence* (Vol. 90, pp. 177–182). Rockville, MD: U.S. Government Printing Office.

Gomberg, E. (1989). Suicide risk among women with alcohol problems. *American Journal of Public Health, 79,* 1363–1365.

Griffin, M. L., Weiss, R. D., Mirin, S. M., & Lange, U. (1989). A comparison of male and female cocaine abusers. *Archives of General Psychiatry, 46,* 122–126.

Grossman, J., & Schottenfeld, R. (1992). Pregnancy and Women's Issues. In T. R. Kosten & H. D. Kleber (Eds.), *Clinician's guide to cocaine addiction: Theory, research, and treatment* (pp. 374–388). New York: Guilford Press.

Haller, D. L., Dawson, K. S., & Ingersoll, K. S. Treatment acceptors vs. rejecters: Psychological characteristics of female substance abusers. Submitted for publication.

Haller, D. L., Knisely, J. S., Dawson, K. S., & Schnoll, S. H. (1993). Perinatal substance abusers. Psychological and social characteristics. *Journal of Nervous and Mental Disease, 181,* 509–513.

Helzer, J., & Pryzbeck, T. (1988). The co-occurrence of alcoholism with other psychiatric disorders in the general population and its impact on treatment. *Journal of Studies on Alcohol, 49,* 219–224.

Hesselbrock, M. N., Meyers, R. E., & Keener, J. J. (1985). Psychopathology in hospitalized alcoholics. *Archives of General Psychiatry, 42,* 1050–1055.

Hughes, P. H., Coletti, S. D., Neri, R. L., Urmann, C. F., Stahl, S., Sicilian, D. M., & Anthony, J. C. (1995). Retaining cocaine-abusing women in a therapeutic community: The effect of a child live-in program. *American Journal of Public Health, 85,* 1149–1152.

Institute of Medicine. (1989). *Prevention and treatment of alcohol problems: research opportunities.* Washington DC: National Academy Press.

Institute of Medicine. (1990). *Broadening the base of treatment for alcohol problems.* Washington, DC: National Academy of Sciences.

Jansson, L. M., Svikis, D. S., Lee, J., Paluzzi, P., Rutigliano, P., & Hackerman, F. (in press). Pregnancy and addiction: A comprehensive care model. *Journal of Substance Abuse Treatment.*

Jastak, S. & Wilkinson, G. S. (1984). *Wide Range Achievement Test—Revised.* Wilmington, DE: Jastak Associates.

Kaufman-Kantor, G., & Straus, M. A. (1989). Substance abuse as a precipitant of wife abuse victimizations. *American Journal of Drug and Alcohol Abuse, 15,* 173–189.

Kim, R. I., Sees, K. L., & Delucchi, K. L. (1994). Couples in substance abuse treatment. In L. S. Harris (Ed.), *Problems of drug dependence, 1993: Proceedings of the 55th annual scientific*

meeting of the College on Problems of Drug Dependence, Inc. (Vol. Research Monograph No.141, pp. 357). Rockville, MD: National Institute on Drug Abuse.

Knisely, J. S., Christmas, J. T., Dinsmoore, M., Spear, E., & Schnoll, S. H. (Eds.). (1993). *The impact of intensive prenatal and substance abuse care on pregnancy outcome* (Vol. 132). Rockville, MD: National Institute on Drug Abuse.

Kosten, R. R., Rounsaville, B. J., & Kleber, H. D. (1985). Ethnic and gender differences among opiate addicts. *International Journal of the Addictions, 20,* 1143–1162.

Lewis, D., & Watters, J. (1989). Human immunodeficiency virus seroprevalence in female intravenous drug users: The puzzle of black women's risk. *Social Science Medicine, 29,* 1071–1076.

Lex, B. (1991). Some gender differences in alcohol and polysubstance users. *Health Psychology, 10,* 121–132.

Mann, K., Batra, A., Gunthner, A., & Schroth, G. (1992). Do women develop alcoholic brain damage more readily than men? *Alcoholism: Clinical and Experimental Research, 16,* 1052–1056.

McCaul, M., Svikis, D., Moore, R., Gupman, A., & Gopalan, R. (1994). Does drug use predict poor treatment retention? *Alcoholism: Clinical and Experimental Research, 18,* 494.

McCaul, M. E., Svikis, D. S., & Feng, T. (1991). Pregnancy and addiction: Outcomes and interventions. *Maryland Medical Journal, 40,* 995–1001.

Miller, B., Downs, W., & Gondoli, D. (1989). Spousal violence among alcoholic women as compared to a random household sample of women. *Journal of Studies on Alcohol, 50,* 533–540.

Miller, B., Downs, W., & Testa, M. (1993). Interrelationships between victimization experiences and women's alcohol use. *Journal of Studies on Alcohol,* (Suppl. 11(, 109–117.

Mondanaro, J. (1990). Community-based AIDS prevention interventions: Special issues of women intravenous drug users. In C. G. Leukefeld, R. J. Battjes, & Z. Amsel (Eds.), *AIDS and intravenous drug use: Future directions for community-based prevention research* (Vol. 93, pp. 68–82). Rockville, MD: National Institute on Drug Abuse.

National Institute on Drug Abuse. (Fall,1990). Pregnant drug abusers face obstacles to receiving treatment. *NIDA Notes,* 11–12.

Nelson-Zlupko, L., Dore, M. M., Kauffman, E., & Kaltenbach, K. (1996). Women in recovery: Their perception of treatment effectiveness. *Journal of Substance Abuse Treatment, 13,* 51–59.

NIDA/NIAAA. (1993). *National drug and alcoholism treatment unit survey (NDATUS): 1991 main findings report.* Rockville, MD: U.S. Government Printing Office.

O'Campo, P., Gielen, A. C., Faden, R. R., & Kass, N. (1994). Verbal abuse and physical violence among a cohort of low-income pregnant women. *Women's Health Issues, 4,* 29–37.

Pivnick, A., Jacobson, A., Eric, K., Doll, L., & Drucker, E. (1994). AIDS, HIV infection, and illicit drug use within inner-city families and social networks. *American Journal of Public Health, 84,* 271–274.

Russell, S. A., & Wilsnack, S. (1991). Adult survivors of childhood sexual abuse: Substance abuse and other consequences. In P. Roth (Ed.), *Alcohol and drugs are women's issues. Vol. 1: A review of the issues* (pp. 61–70). Metuchen, NJ: Women's Action Alliance.

Schilling, R., El-Bassel, N., Schinke, S., Gordon, K., & Nichols, S. (1991). Building skills of recovering women drug users to reduce heterosexual AIDS transmission. *Public Health Reports, 106,* 297–303.

Shipley, B. A., Gazaway, P. M., Brooner, R. K., & Felch, L. J. (1993). Prenatal care delivered in a drug abuse setting: Birth outcome compared to ACOG standards. In L. S. Harris (Ed.), *Problems of drug dependence 1992: Proceedings of the 54th annual meeting of the College on Problems of Drug Dependence* (Vol. 132, pp. 301). Washington, DC: U.S. Government Printing Office.

Silverman, K., Chutuape, M. A., Svikis, D. S., Bigelow, G. E., & Stitzer, M. L. (1995). Incongruity between occupational interests and academic skills in drug abusing women. *Drug and Alcohol Dependence, 40,* 115–123.

Stevens, S. J., & Arbiter, N. (1995). A therapeutic community for substance-abusing pregnant women and women with children: Process and outcome. *Journal of Psychoactive Drugs, 27,* 49–56.

Strantz, I. H., & Welch, S. P. (1995). Postpartum women in outpatient drug abuse treatment: Correlates of retention/completion. *Journal of Psychoactive Drugs, 27,* 357–373.

Svikis, D. S., Golden, A. S., Huggins, G. R., Pickens, R. W., McCaul, M. E., Velez, M. L., Rosendale, C. R., Brooner, R. K., Gazaway, P. M., & Ball, C. Cost-effectiveness of treatment for drug-abusing pregnant women. Submitted for publication.

Svikis, D. S., Gorenstein, M. A., Paluzzi, P., & Fingerhood, M. Personality characteristics of treatment-seeking HIV+ pregnant drug dependent women. Submitted for publication.

Svikis, D. S., McCaul, M. E., Feng, T., Johnson, T. B. R., & Stokes, E. J. (1992). Can a weekly support group for pregnant addicts improve maternal and fetal outcome? In L. Harris (Ed.), *Problems of drug dependence, 1991: Proceedings of the 53rd annual scientific meeting of the College on Problems of Drug Dependence* (Vol. 119, pp. 271). Rockville, MD: National Institute on Drug Abuse.

Vannicelli, M. (1984). Treatment outcome of alcoholic women: The state of the art in relation to sex bias and expectancy effects. In S. C. Wilsnack & L. J. Beckman (Eds.), *Alcohol problems in women: Antecedents, consequences, and intervention* (pp. 369–412). New York: Guilford.

Wallen, J. (1992). A comparison of male and female clients in substance abuse treatment. *Journal of Substance Abuse Treatment, 9,* 243–248.

Wilsnack, R. W., Wilsnack, S. C., & Klassen, A. D. (1984). Women's drinking and drinking problems: Patterns from a 1981 national survey. *American Journal of Public Health, 74,* 1231–1238.

Wofsy, C. B. (1987). Human immunodeficiency virus infection in women. *Journal of the American Medical Association, 257,* 2074–2076.

AUTHOR INDEX

SUBJECT INDEX